D0483144

Dedicated to
Theo, Lee, and Ann

May no line separate
your faith and knowledge

Baker Book House   Grand Rapids, Michigan 49506

A
HISTORY
OF
CHRISTIANITY

Readings
in the History
of the Church

VOLUME 2

The Church
from the Reformation
to the Present

Edited by

CLYDE L. MANSCHRECK

Preface

The documents, writings, and illustrations in this volume
are presented as an introduction to the main trends in the
development of Christianity from the Reformation to the
present. Emphasis is placed on the historical selections in order
to help the reader see something of Christianity in its basic
expression and make his own interpretations. Many other items
could have been selected with equal justification. Limitations
of space made necessary the omission of many items; for
example, *Pilgrim's Progress, Apologia Pro Vita Sua, The Thirty-
nine Articles,* and *Holy Living and Holy Dying.* Fortunately,
these are widely available and can be read as supplementary
works. Other major philosophical-theological works that
should be pursued independently are Kant's *Religion Within
the Limits of Reason Alone,* Hegel's *Philosophy of History,*
Schleiermacher's *Christian Faith,* Ritschl's *The Christian
Doctrine of Justification and Reconciliation,* and others. In
making selections, I have sought to avoid short excerpts that
do not faithfully reflect the total meaning of a work. In addition
to these factors, my criteria for including selections were
fourfold: general relevance to the unfolding of Christianity
in Western culture; intrinsic worth; availability; and interest.
To preserve space for the selections, the introductory sections
are brief; even footnotes acknowledging common sources are
eliminated. No special treatment of religion in America is
given, except as the religious developments in America affected
the course of world Christianity. This was done not because
the American developments are not important but because

they deserve special treatment and have recently received such attention in several good works. Recent theological works have also been omitted, again not because they are not important but because of their current nature and availability.

Introductory commentaries are not intended to detail the period but to set the documents and writings in the context of the general story of Christianity, the culture in which Christianity unfolded and which it helped to mold. Little attempt is made to explain or interpret the source materials; the documents are left to speak for themselves. Many of the ideas presented herein are now commonplace, but they were unusual and dynamic in their own time and should be read and discussed in this perspective. The suggested readings provide an opportunity for the student to deepen his understanding of the various periods.

Special thanks are due to the projects committee of the National Council of Religion in Higher Education which, under the direction of Richard C. Gilman, now Dean of the College at Carleton College, perceived the need for such a presentation of church history and initiated the undertaking.

Many libraries have been helpful in making their resources available: The Library of Congress; Folger Shakespeare Library; Duke University Library; Ohio Wesleyan University Library; Library of Pontifical College Josephinum; Universitäts Bibliothek Heidelberg; Bretten's Melanchthon Haus; Library of the Methodist Theological School in Ohio; and Ohio State University Library. The John Simon Guggenheim Memorial Foundation and the Committee on International Exchange of Persons, Conference Board of Associated Research Councils for Grants under the Fulbright and Smith-Mundt Acts, made possible a year of study in Europe during which many of these materials were gathered.

Members of the editorial staff at Prentice-Hall, Inc., Richard J. Trudgen, Mrs. Maurine Lewis, Miss Diana Powers, Clark Inglis, and Marvin Warshaw have been generous in their imaginative assistance and encouragement. Grateful appreciation is also extended to my wife who assisted at every stage of the project. Finally, a word of thanks to the Trustees of the British Museum, to B. Arthaud in Grenoble, France, to the publishers, individuals, and art galleries who gave permission for reprints, and to the scholars whose prior works made this presentation possible.

CLYDE L. MANSCHRECK

Contents

I

THE LUTHERAN REFORMATION   1

II

THE REFORMATION EXTENDED   57

III

IV

V

THE AGE OF REASON   217

VI

THE RISE OF EVANGELICAL PIETISM   263

VII

MODERNISM AND NEW FORMS   315

VIII

IX

X

Conference, 1920. 9. Consideration of the Lambeth Appeal.
10. Baptist View of Organic Union. 11. Resolution of
the International Missionary Council. 12. Faith and
Order. 13. "A Step Forward in Church Relations."
14. The World Council of Churches. 15. The World
Council of Churches, Amsterdam, 1948. 16. World
Council of Churches, New Delhi, 1961. 17. Statement
of Beliefs, the World Evangelical Fellowship, 1951.
18. Pope Pius XI, 1928. 19. Instruction to Local
Ordinaries on the Ecumenical Movement.

IX

THEOLOGICAL TRENDS AND TOTALITARIANISM 509

1. Harry Emerson Fosdick, 1926. 2. J. Gresham Machen.
3. 10 Elements of the Unitarian Religion. 4. "The
Humanist Manifesto." 5. A Goebbels Propaganda
Pamphlet, 1930. 6. Nürnberg Law for the Protection
of German Blood and German Honor, September 15,
1935. 7. The Platform of the German Christians, 1932.
8. The Barmen Declaration, May, 1934. 9. Stuttgart
Declaration of Guilt, October, 1945. 10. "Gazing into
the Pit." 11. Church and State in Czechoslovakia.
12. Universal Declaration of Human Rights. 13. Religious
Liberty in Spain. 14. Baptist World Alliance on
Religious Liberty, 1960. 15. A Letter to Presbyterians.

Illustration opposite page 1: **Melancholia.** *At the edge of destiny, mankind broods, his knowledge of no avail. Engraving by Albrecht Dürer, 1514.*

I

The Lutheran Reformation

The Reformation is the great dividing point
between medieval and modern church history. It was
deeply rooted in the past, which shaped much of its social outlook, but
it was also reaching toward new ideas which had within them power
to begin a new rootage that would nourish the future.
Some historians see the Reformation as the religious phase of the
momentous economic changes that fundamentally affected all
European life of the sixteenth century, for it was an age
of discovery and change. Columbus' discovery of the New World
was hardly noticed in 1492, although it was destined to produce
profound effects. Vasco da Gama reached Calicut, India, in 1498;
Magellan died in the Philippines in 1521, but his crew completed a
circumnavigation of the globe; gold from Mexico and South America
began to reach Europe; Venice, Milan, and Genoa gradually
declined as the world's chief cities; serfdom was giving way to a rising
middle class of craftsmen; and new nations would soon challenge
the supremacy of Spain and Italy and find the strength of their
superiority not in the Mediterranean and Rome, but in America.
Others see the Reformation as a religiously oriented phase

of the humanism of the Renaissance. Following the fall of Constantinople in 1453, refugees brought Greek thought once more into Western Europe, and there was a rebirth of interest in the arts, literature, science, and theology. Everywhere the cry was "back to the sources, to the fountains of our civilization." The printing press, perfected about 1455 by Johann Gensfleisch of Gutenberg and others, was ready to disseminate the new knowledge and ideas. The Renaissance was the age of Raphael and Michelangelo, an age of learning and magnificence, but it was not a new birth of morality.

The Renaissance was pagan to the core. The Renaissance, Rudolph Sohm observes in his *Outlines of Church History*, filled Italy with "violent, remorseless, haughty tyrants, who thirsted for power and glory, and whose geniality was only attained by contempt for all laws of morality." It was brilliant with creative power, but also immoral and corrupt. "This was the age which produced a Caesare Borgia, at once its image, its ideal, and its terror." It was the age in which Machiavelli (1469-1527) glorified selfishness in his *Discourses* and *The Prince*. It gave to the papacy men like Innocent VIII, Alexander VI, Julius II, and Leo X, who brought murder, licentiousness, aggrandizement, and luxurious living to the papal throne.

But the Renaissance also inspired men everywhere to reassess man and his destiny. Luther, Melanchthon, Zwingli, and many others at first considered themselves part of the humanistic movement which was also a revolt against the confinement of scholastic philosophy and ecclesiastical authority. Ximenes in Spain, Colet and More in England, Erasmus in Holland, and Johann Reuchlin in Germany were all figures in this revolt and advocates of new forms of learning, which they hoped would bring reform to culture. They protested the excesses and corruptions of society, especially in the clergy. In his biting satires, *Familiar Colloquies*, and in his *In Praise of Folly*, 1509, Erasmus (1466?-1536) ridiculed pilgrimages, the veneration of images, the hypocrisy of indulgences, and the sanctity of filth. He put Folly on a pedestal as the muse of self-interest, the true spirit promoting the activities of man (*1*).* In a dialogue between St. Peter and the ghost of Pope Julius II, he spotlighted papal crimes. Erasmus' Greek New Testament in 1516 was an attempt to get back to the sources, to the true words of Scripture. At times it seemed as though Erasmus, the prince of humanists, condoned the activities and views of Luther, but they parted company in 1524 and 1525 in a bitter debate over free will. When Erasmus died in 1536, he was still a loyal son of the Roman Catholic Church; he knew what was wrong with it and he criticized, but he did not have the elemental force of creative reform.

The same could be said of Johann Reuchlin (1455-1522), humanist, jurist, and scholar of Hebrew, who in 1506 published the first Hebrew grammar ever to appear in Germany. His efforts to promote learning led to a clash with the Dominicans and their Jewish convert, Pfefferkorn. Pfefferkorn had friends at court, and in 1509 he received a mandate from Emperor Maximilian to destroy any Jewish literature that opposed Christianity. Pfefferkorn could not read Hebrew, but he went

* Italicized numbers in parentheses refer to the documents that follow.

I-1. Portrait of Savonarola. *From a medal struck in his honor.*

2

I-2. The Execution of
Savonarola in the Public
Square in Florence.
An old print.

from town to town fiendishly ordering Jews to surrender their books for burning. When Reuchlin was asked for his opinion, he answered that it would be better to establish chairs of Hebrew in the universities so that the literature could be properly studied and purged. As Pfefferkorn was already beginning to receive large bribes from Jews who wished to keep their books, he and the Dominican monks turned on Reuchlin with savage literary vilification. As evidence of his good character, Reuchlin published a collection of letters which he had received from famous people. Then, in 1515, a collection of letters from obscure men appeared, *Epistolae Obscurorum Virorum*, probably written by Crotius Rubianus and Ulrich von Hutten, both humanists. They were letters from obscure monks addressed to their spiritual leader, Ortuinus Gratius, which laid bare the greed, hypocrisy, and ignorance of the uneducated Dominicans (2). The Dominicans brought legal action against Reuchlin, and the case dragged on in the ecclesiastical courts for a decade, until Reuchlin was broken and ruined. But Reuchlin had no thought of breaking with the Roman faith, even though

he was the great-uncle of Melanchthon, Luther's cohort at Wittenberg. He died loyal to the Roman Church, estranged from his nephew.

In Italy, Savonarola (1452-1498), fiery Dominican friar, tried to reform religion in Florence. In 1496, he burned the vanities of Florence, which he persuaded Lenten celebrators to collect—masks, frivolous books, secular songs, ornaments, mirrors, pictures of nudes, and the like—and crowds responded to his eloquent preaching. That same year he was forbidden to preach; in 1497 he was excommunicated for not obeying; and on May 23, 1498, he was publicly hanged and burned. He had risked calling for a council to reform the church, had disregarded his excommunication, and had caused civil discord. Medals were struck in his honor, relics of drops of his blood and pieces of his hair circulated widely in Europe, and his heroism caught the imagination of many. Luther published comments on the psalms which Savonarola wrote while in prison and hailed him as an evangelical. But he was not that; his death was the result of political involvement as much as anything else. In 1513, Machia-

3

velli finished his little guide for despots, *The Prince*, in which he boldly depicted enlightened self-interest as the realistic guide for all rulers. His book reflected the secular spirit of the time.

The humanists were very much a part of the new age, in possession of much knowledge, inspired by future expectations, but hesitant on the threshold of new spiritual realms. Albrecht Dürer (1471-1528), Germany's great artist of the early Reformation, seems to have caught the feeling of the time in his engraving, *Melancholia*. A winged woman, perhaps symbolizing the intellectual insights of the Renaissance, sits brooding in the midst of the tools of man, unable to enter the future with its rainbow of promises because she senses that destiny is not in her hands, and she seems not to know whether destiny is in evil forces, in fate, or in God. The reformers themselves had no such questions; they were convinced of God's providence and direct activity in their history. D'Aubigne, writing in the nineteenth century, used this as a key to interpret the sixteenth century, for history is the work of a "Supreme Disposer," he said, and "I believe the Reformation to be the work of God." Martin Luther would have agreed.

But others have vehemently dissented. Roman Catholic writers commonly picture the period not as a reformation but as a revolution, promoted by avaricious civil rulers who were bent on enhancing their own power by crippling the church and confiscating her properties, supported by ignorant lower classes who wanted to overthrow authority, and justified by clever heretics who had their axes to grind. In the end this revolution destroyed religious unity and fomented political strife. From Thomas Murner in 1520 and Johann Dobneck in 1549, to Grisar and Denifle in the twentieth century, Roman Catholic writers have continued to picture Luther as a revolutionary radical, an abnormal criminal, a desperate beast, a heretic sick with religious neuroses, and a misguided monk driven by sex. Philip Melanchthon replied by hailing Luther as an Elijah, a Paul, a restorer of pure doctrine; Goethe considered him a genius. Nietzsche saw him as a vulgar peasant who brought to nothing the Renaissance, which with Caesare Borgia as Pope might have abolished Christianity.

Many forces converged to make the Reformation possible, but without a Martin Luther the stirrings of this period might well have ended like all the previous individual and corporate attempts to reform the church —in failure. Luther was the impelling force, and the force which impelled him was his discovery of a mighty fortress, a God who cared for him and who justified him in faith.

Born at Eisleben to parents whose improving finances would soon raise them from peasants to burghers, Luther (1483-1546) received a moderately good education and was scheduled for a career in law when, during a thunderstorm in 1505, he vowed to become a monk if St. Ann would save him. He entered the Augustinian order at Erfurt, and after a probation of two years was ordained a priest. Fear of death had driven him to the monastery, and for many years he was deeply troubled, feeling that if he died he would be cast into hell. He wanted to earn salvation, but he was unable through the sacraments, asceticism, meritorious works, or mysticism, to find forgiveness for his sins. He prayed incessantly day and night, fasted, chastized his body, kept vigils, wept at the altar, confessed his sins, repeated psalms and recited *Ave Marias,* but found no comfort. In 1510 and 1511 he journeyed to the Eternal City of Rome, only to comment later that he went there with onions and came back with garlic. In 1511 he went to Wittenberg to teach, and the next year he was made a doctor of theology. But he later wrote that he had not yet seen the light. In his fear and unexpressed hate of God, his good works were but love of self, for he was trying to compel God to be gracious. Then, in studying the writings of Paul and the Psalms, he suddenly saw that salvation does not come by forcing God to forgive sins on account of good works, but by accepting God's forgiveness in faith. Luther felt released, filled with joy, illumined with a new spirit. Justification by faith alone, a basic trust in the goodness of God, became the fundamental principle informing his entire life. Man does good works not to earn righteousness, for this simply means that man loves himself and breaks the command to love God, but because in his joy and gratitude for what God has already done for him he wants to praise Him and show the same kind of love to others.

The ramifications of this doctrine of justification by faith marked the development of the Reformation. In 1517, Luther realized that indulgences were a mockery of faith and a rejection of the mercy of God in Christ. When Johann Tetzel, a Dominican, came to the borders of Saxony selling indulgences and making wild claims about their full efficacy, even in purgatory, Luther felt bound to debate the entire issue. On October 31, 1517, he nailed his *Ninety-five Theses* to the door of the Wittenberg Castle Church (3). It was the church in which the electors of Saxony had collected almost 18,000 relics, ranging from a twig from Moses' burning bush to a tear that Jesus shed when he wept over Jerusalem. Money from this traffic in relics provided the endowment for the University of Wittenberg. Pilgrims came from miles around, for by making the proper prayers and offerings, one could earn indulgences which would cancel out 1,902,202 years in purgatory. Luther's immediate concern, however, was to debate the excessive claims being made by Tetzel. Luther did not know it, but Albert of Brandenburg, a Hohen-

zollern prince, who already had the sees of Magdeburg and Halberstadt, wanted to be confirmed as Archbishop of Mainz, even though a plurality of bishoprics was illegal and he was too young to be a bishop. Nevertheless, he borrowed money from the Fugger bankers to pay the Pope for the confirmation, and used the Pope's promised indulgence as security. The Fuggers sent their agent around with Tetzel to see that they were repaid. Buyers were told that the money was to help rebuild St. Peter's Church in Rome. In the *Ninety-five Theses,* Luther maintained that the indulgences were unlawful, unscriptural, and harmful. Tetzel's sales suffered immediate decrease, causing him to post two sets of counter-theses which reflect the papal claims of the time (4).

In debating with Johann Eck at Leipzig in 1519, Luther was driven to assert scriptural over papal and conciliar authority, for, he said, popes and councils can and have erred, inasmuch as they are human. Eck openly called him a heretic and schismatic. The controversy attracted widespread attention. Cardinals, papal legates, and lesser officials were sent to Germany to quiet the "wild boar in the vineyard of the Lord." But the Elector Frederick shrewdly protected his prize professor. Even excommunication proved ineffective. On June 15, 1520, in a bull which began *Exsurge Domine,* "Arise, Lord, and defend thine own vineyard against the wild beast

I-3. True and False Forgiveness of Sins. *Note the contrition of the penitents on the left and the indulgence traffic on the right. Woodcut by Hans Holbein, the younger.*

that is devouring it," Pope Leo X gave Luther sixty days to recant or be condemned as a stiff-necked, notorious, damned heretic. In front of the Church of the Holy Cross, outside the walls of Wittenberg on December 10, Luther publicly burned the bull along with other papal documents.

In the meantime, Luther's three 1520 essays appeared: *Appeal to the German Nobility*, *The Babylonian Captivity*, and *The Freedom of the Christian Man*. In the first essay, Luther appealed to the patriotic feelings of the Germans and developed his doctrines of vocation and the priesthood of all believers (5). In the *Babylonian Captivity*, he described withdrawal of the cup from the laity and the doctrine of transubstantiation as the imprisonment of the Lord's Supper. He maintained that Christ instituted two sacraments, the Lord's Supper and Baptism, and that all the others were marks of bondage which he categorically rejected as nonscriptural, although he was uncertain about penance. In the essay on Christian liberty, he discussed faith and the expressions of love that flow from it (6). All three essays have become bulwarks of Protestant thought.

In 1521, Luther was summoned by the Emperor to present himself for judgment at the Diet of Worms (7). At Worms, Luther dramatically appealed to Scripture and right reason as his authorities, justification by faith alone undergirding both (8, 21). Condemned by the Diet of Worms (9), Luther was hidden in the old castle at Wartburg for eleven months, but he returned to Wittenberg in March of 1522 to quiet the disturbances that had arisen in the name of faith and Christian liberty (10).

The years that followed were years of building and consolidation, for Luther realized that the break with Rome would be permanent. The first systematic Protestant theology appeared in 1521, the *Loci Communes*, written by Philip Melanchthon (1497-1560), who joined the Wittenberg faculty in 1518. The New Testament, translated into German, was published in 1522, and Luther sought to bring church forms into harmony with justification by faith. In 1523 he wrote his *Order of Worship*, and in 1526 the *German Mass*. In 1524, Johann Walther issued the first evangelical hymnal, containing four hymns by Luther, a step which marked the increased participation of the congregation in the divine service (19). Later Johann Sebastian Bach (1685-1750) used many of the Lutheran hymns as the bases for his cantatas and passionales.

Four events threatened to shatter the evangelical fold in 1524 and 1525. The first was the eruption of the controversy between Erasmus and Luther over free will, a clash between the critic with his dependence on knowledge and the reformer with his dependence on faith. Erasmus published *De Libero Arbitrio* (*Free Will*), in September, 1524, setting forth a semi-Pelagian view of man's moral ability; Luther replied with *De Servo Arbitrio* (*Bound Will*) in December, 1525, vehemently combating Erasmus' implication that sin does not affect man's freedom to work out his own salvation. Erasmus answered with *Hyperaspistes*, a vindictive attack on Lutheran doctrines, apparently because Luther was unwilling to let the whole exchange be simply an academic exercise. The controversy caused many humanists to withdraw from the reform movement, feeling that man's rational powers were not being given due credit, and also that the reformers were traveling the road to social barbarism.

The second threatening event was the Peasants' Revolt, the climax of centuries of minor revolts by peasants against their hard lot. Their Twelve Articles were not excessive, but the violence and destruction that developed under the inflammatory preaching of Thomas Münzer and others raised fears of anarchy and pillage throughout Germany (11, 12). Luther, who had consistently disavowed violence, at first tried to arbitrate between the peasants and lords, but when rebellion flared he appealed to the princes to restore order with whatever means possible (13, 14). When fifty thousand peasants were wretchedly defeated and butchered at Frankenhausen, May 15, 1525, the peasants believed that they had been betrayed by Luther, and the Reformation lost much of its hold over the poorer classes.

The third event which momentarily disrupted the Reformation was the death of Elector Frederick, the Wise, in May of 1525, for he had been a staunch protector and a wily political maneuverer. However, he was succeeded by John, the Steadfast, who stood even more firmly and openly for the evangelical movement.

The fourth event, which set tongues wagging and seemed inopportune in view of the social distresses, was Luther's sudden marriage to Catharine von Bora on June 13, 1525. She and several other nuns had left the Nimbschen Cistercian Cloister two months previously, and were being cared for in Wittenberg until suitable matches could be arranged. Catharine waited for Luther. Despite malicious gossip, Luther's homelife became a model for the German pastorate (20, 21).

Political events favored the evangelicals in 1526, for Emperor Charles V wanted peace in Germany while he dealt with the Turks, the French, and the machinations of the papacy. The evangelicals secured what appeared to be toleration, for the recess of Speier in 1526 granted a suspension of the Edict of Worms and declared that every ruler should supervise religion so as to be ready to answer for it before God and his Imperial Majesty. The evangelicals felt free to organize and consolidate along scriptural lines. Elector John of Saxony surveyed the schools and churches in his territory and enacted into law Philip Melanchthon's *Visitation Articles* in 1528, thus establishing a Protestant public school system, the first since the days of ancient Rome. Ability to read the Bible was regarded as necessary to an understanding of God's Word to man and the fulfillment of one's vocation. However, the second Diet of Speier in 1529 rescinded its former statement (15), causing the evangelicals to enter their protest on the grounds that religion should be a matter of free conscience (16).

Fearing that Emperor Charles would resort to war, the evangelicals sought to establish political unity among themselves. This prompted the meeting between Luther and Ulrich Zwingli at Marburg in 1529. They agreed on practically everything except the presence of Christ in the elements of the

I-4. Frederick the Wise, Elector of Saxony. *Woodcut by Albrecht Dürer, 1524.*

Lord's Supper. Zwingli stressed a memorial view of the presence, and Luther would not budge from "This is my body." The evangelicals were disheartened and divided when Emperor Charles came to Augsburg in 1530 with the avowed purpose of settling all religious disputes; the Turks had just been repulsed at Vienna, and the Emperor appeared free at last to deal with the evangelicals. The Elector of Saxony resolved to present his confession, and commissioned Melanchthon to draw up the final document which was based heavily on the Marburg Articles and the Schwabach Articles previously drawn up for other purposes. Luther stayed behind at Coburg as he was still under an imperial ban. As the day of reckoning approached, the Protestant princes and representatives of several cities in Germany drew closer together. On June 25, 1530, all of them boldly stood while the Augsburg Confession was read before the imperial Diet (17). This is the one creed acknowledged by Lutherans everywhere, and it is the creed on which the major creeds of Protestantism are based. The basic doctrine is justification by faith. Many things are omitted and other things carefully stated so as not to give offense, for Melanchthon was trying to avoid open conflict, but the document throbs with the power of the evangelical spirit. Zwingli sent his confession, four cities in Southern Germany presented the *Tetrapolitana,* and the Roman Catholic theologians led by Eck read their confutations of the "innovations." But nothing was settled. After much fruitless negotiation, the Diet adjourned and the Protestants were given until April 15 to reconsider and join the Catholics. War, which Melanchthon feared as he composed the confession, seemed imminent.

In the next two years, however, the Turks again threatened the Empire and Charles needed the help of the evangelicals. In 1532, Charles granted the Lutherans the Peace of Nürnberg in recognition of their aid against the infidels. During the truce period that ensued, almost fifteen years, the Lutherans consolidated their political and religious gains. In 1531, Melanchthon wrote his *Apology of the Augsburg Confession,* a masterful reply to the Roman Catholic confutation. The *Apology* is accepted as a Lutheran symbol, as well as one of the best theological treatises to come out of the Reformation. In 1534, the complete German Bible was published, a vigorous translation which was to mold the German language for centuries to come. In 1536, the Swiss under Bucer and the Lutherans were able to settle their differences in the *Wittenberg Concord,* and in 1537 Luther wrote the sharpened statement of evangelical belief to which Melanchthon appended the essay on the power and primacy of the papacy.

From time to time further negotiations were attempted between the Lutherans and Catholics, but they all proved fruitless. In 1542, the Catholics reconstituted the Holy Inquisition to combat Protestantism, and in 1545 they convoked the Council of Trent in an effort to counter the gains of the Reformation. Open warfare did not actually come, however, until the year after Luther's death on February 18, 1546. Because of the treachery of one of their own leaders, the Lutheran princes suffered defeat in battle with the imperial forces at Mühlberg on April 24, 1547. The *Augsburg* and *Leipzig Interims,* in 1548 and 1549, heavily favoring Roman Catholic ceremonies, prevailed for several years in Saxony, causing many to think that Protestantism was being eradicated. But in 1552, the very ones who had earlier betrayed Protestantism turned against the Emperor and secured the temporary Peace of Passau, which led to the Peace of Augsburg of 1555 (18). The latter established the principle of *cuius regio, eius religio* (whose region, his religion), a pact of toleration between the Catholics and Lutherans which lasted until the outbreak of the Thirty Years' War in 1618. The documents which follow were selected to illustrate some of these aspects of the Reformation.

1. *Desiderius Erasmus, 1509*

Among those whom Desiderius Erasmus satirized as followers of Folly were priests, theologians, and monks. The following excerpts are typical of his ridicule (New York: The Truth Seeker Company, 1922).

PRIESTS

The next to be placed among the regiment of fools are such as make a trade of telling or enquiring after incredible stories of miracles and prodigies: never doubting that a lie will choke them, they will muster up a thousand several strange relations of spirits, ghosts, apparitions, raising of the devil, and such like bugbears of superstition, which the farther they are from being probably true, the more greedily they are swallowed, and the more devoutly believed. And these absurdities do not only bring an empty pleasure, and cheap divertisement, but they procure a comfortable income to such priests and friars as by this craft get their gain. To these again are nearly related such others as attribute strange virtues to the shrines and images of saints and martyrs, and so would make their credulous proselytes believe, that if they pay their devotion to St. Christopher in the morning, they shall be guarded and secured the day following from all dangers and misfortunes; if soldiers, when they first take arms, shall come and mumble over such a set prayer before the picture of St. Barbara, they shall return safe from all engagements: or if any pray to Erasmus on such particular holidays, with the ceremony of wax candles, and other fopperies, he shall in a short time be rewarded with a plentiful increase of wealth and riches. The Christians have now their gigantic St. George, as well as the Pagans had their Hercules; they paint the saint on horseback, and picture the horse in splendid trappings, very gloriously accoutred; they scarce refrain in a literal sense from worshiping the very beast.

What shall I say of such as cry up and maintain the cheat of pardons and indulgences? that by these compute the time of each soul's residence in purgatory, and assign them a longer or shorter continuance, according as they purchase more or fewer of these paltry pardons, and saleable exemptions? Or what can be said bad enough of others, who pretend that by the force of such magical charms, or by the fumbling over their beads in the rehearsal of such and such petitions (which some religious impostors invented, either for diversion, or what is more likely, for advantage), they shall procure riches, honor, pleasure, health, long life, a lusty old age, nay, after death a sitting at the right hand of our Saviour in His kingdom; though as to this last part of their happiness, they care not how long it be deferred, having scarce any appetite toward a tasting the joys of heaven, till they are surfeited, glutted with, and can no longer relish their enjoyments on earth.

By this easy way of purchasing pardons, any notorious highwayman, any plundering soldier, or any bribe-taking judge, shall disburse some part of their unjust gains, and so think all their grossest impieties sufficiently atoned for; so many perjuries, lusts, drunkenness, quarrels, bloodsheds, cheats, treacheries, and all sorts of debaucheries, shall all be, as it were, struck a bargain for, and such a contract made, as if they had paid off all arrears, and might now begin upon a new score.

And what can be more ridiculous, than for some others to be confident of going to heaven by repeating daily those seven verses out of the Psalms, which the devil taught St. Bernard, thinking thereby to have put a trick upon him, but that he was over-reached in his cunning. . . .

.   .   .   .   .

There are some more Catholic saints petitioned to upon all occasions, as more especially the Virgin Mary, whose blind devotees think it manners now to place the mother before the son.

And of all the prayers and intercessions that are made to these respective saints, the substance of them is no more than downright Folly.

THE DIVINES

The divines present themselves next; but it may perhaps be most safe to pass them by, and not to touch upon so harsh a string as this subject would afford. Besides, the undertaking may be very hazardous, for they are

I-5. Desiderius Erasmus. *Albrecht Dürer, 1526.*

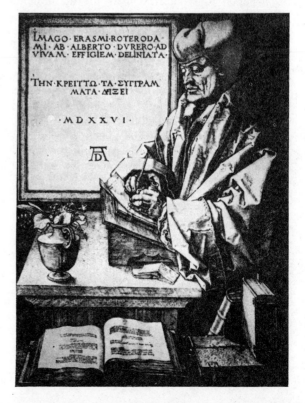

The Devotion to Folly.

They will cut asunder the toughest argument with as much ease as Alexander did the Gordian knot; they will thunder out so many rattling terms as shall affright an adversary into conviction. They are exquisitely dexterous in unfolding the most intricate mysteries; they will tell you to a tittle all the successive proceedings of Omnipotence in the creation of the universe; they will explain the precise manner of original sin being derived from our first parents; they will satisfy you in what manner, by what degrees, and in how long a time, our Savior was conceived in the Virgin's womb, and demonstrate in the consecrated wafer how accidents may subsist without a subject. Nay, these are accounted trivial, easy questions; they have yet far greater difficulties behind, which, notwithstanding, they solve with as much expedition as the former; as namely, whether supernatural generation requires any instant of time for its acting? whether Christ, as a son, bears a double and specifically distinct relation to God the Father, and his virgin mother? whether this proposition is possible to be true, that the first person of the Trinity

a sort of men generally very hot and passionate; and should I provoke them, I doubt not that they would set upon me with a full cry, and force me with shame to recant, which if I stubbornly refused to do, they would presently brand me for a heretic, and thunder out an excommunication, which is their spiritual weapon to wound such as lift up a hand against them.

It is true, no men own a less dependence on Folly, yet have they reason to confess themselves indebted for no small obligations. For it is by one of my properties, self-love, that they fancy themselves, with their elder brother Paul, caught up into the third heaven, from whence, like shepherds indeed, they look down upon their flocks (the laity), grazing as it were, in the vales of the world below. They fence themselves in with so many surrounders of magisterial definitions, conclusions, corollaries, propositions explicit and implicit, that there is no falling in with them; or if they do chance to be urged to a seeming non-plus, yet they find out so many evasions, that all the art of man can never bind them so fast, but that an easy distinction shall give them a starting-hole to escape the scandal of being baffled.

I-6. (*Below and above, left*) Illustrations for Erasmus' *In Praise of Folly. Hans Holbein.*

All Concerns Arranged with Money.

10

hated the second? whether God who took our nature upon him in the form of a man could as well have become a woman, a devil, a beast, an herb, or a stone? and if it were possible that if the Godhead had appeared in any shape of an inanimate substance, how he should then have preached his gospel? or how have been nailed to the cross? whether if St. Peter had celebrated the eucharist at the same time our Savior was hanging on the cross, the consecrated bread would have been transubstantiated into the same body that remained on the tree? whether in Christ's corporal presence in the sacramental wafer, his humanity be not abstracted from his Godhead? whether after the resurrection we shall carnally eat and drink as we do in this life?

There are a thousand other more sublimated and refined niceties of notions, relations, quantities, formalities, quiddities, haecceities, and such like abstrusities, as one would think no one could pry into except he had not only such cat's eyes as to see best in the dark, but even such a piercing faculty as to see through an inch-board, and spy out what really never existed.

Add to these some of their tenets and beliefs, which are so absurd and extravagant, that the wildest fancies of the Stoics, which they so much disdain and decry as paradoxes, seem in comparison just and rational; as their maintaining, that it is a less aggravating fault to kill a hundred men than for a poor cobbler to set a stitch on the sabbath-day; or, that it is more justifiable to do the greatest injury imaginable to others, than to tell the least lie ourselves.

And these subtleties are alchemized to a more refined sublimate by the abstracting brains of their several schoolmen; the Realists, the Nominalists, the Thomists, the Albertists, the Occamists, the Scotists; and these are not all, but the rehearsal of a few only, as specimen of their divided sects; in each of which there is so much of deep learning, so much of unfathomable difficulty, that I believe the apostles themselves would stand in need of a new illuminating spirit, if they were to engage in any controversy with these new divines. . . .

The next to these are another sort of brainless fools, who style themselves monks, or members of religious orders, though they assume both titles very unjustly: for as to the last, they have very little religion in them; and as to the former, the etymology of the word monk implies a solitariness, or being alone; whereas they are so thick abroad that we cannot pass any street or alley without meeting them: and I cannot imagine which degree of men would be more hopelessly wretched if I did not stand their friend, and buoy them up in that lake of misery, which by the engagements of a religious vow they have voluntarily immerged themselves into.

But when these sort of men are so unwelcome to others, as that the very sight of them is thought ominous, I yet make them highly in love with themselves, and fond admirers of their own happiness. The first step whereunto they esteem a profound ignorance, thinking carnal knowledge a great enemy to their spiritual welfare, and seem confident of becoming greater proficients in divine mysteries, the less they are influenced with any human learning.

.   .   .   .   .

It is amusing to observe how they regulate all their actions, as it were by weight and measure, to so exact a proportion, as if the whole loss of their religion depended upon the omission of the least punctilio.

Thus they must be very critical in the precise number of knots requisite for tying on their sandals; what distinct colors their respective habits should be, and of what material made; how broad and long their girdles; how big, and in what fashion, their hoods; whether their bald crowns be to a hair's breadth of the right cut; how many hours they must sleep, at what minute rise to prayers, etc.

.   .   .   .   .

Some are so obstinately superstitious that they will wear their upper garment of some coarse dog's hair stuff, and that next their skin as soft as silk: but others on the contrary, will have linen frocks outermost, and

11

their shirts of wool, or hair. Some again will not touch a piece of money, though they make no scruple of the sin of drunkenness, and the lust of the flesh.

. . . . .

Most of them place their greatest stress for salvation on a strict conformity to their foppish ceremonies, and a belief of their legendary traditions; wherein they fancy to have acquitted themselves with so much of supererogation, that one heaven can never be a condign reward for their meritorious life; little thinking that the Judge of all the earth at the last day shall put them off, with a who hath required these things at your hands, and call them to account for only the stewardship of his legacy which was the precept of love and charity. . . .

2. Johann Reuchlin

Because Johann Reuchlin objec..ed to Pfefferkorn's rash destruction of Jewish literature, the Dominicans, who had converted Pfefferkorn from Judaism, attacked Reuchlin and brought suit against him in court. An exchange of bitter pamphlets ensued, and the case dragged on from 1509 to 1520. In 1515, *Epistolae Obscurorum Virorum*, letters ridiculing the Dominicans, appeared. The probable authors were Crotius Rubianus and Ulrich von Hutten, humanist friends of Reuchlin. Trans. F. G. Stokes (New Haven: Yale University Press, 1925).

XXIII. MAGISTER BERTHOLD HACKERLING TO MAGISTER ORTWIN GRATIUS

Brotherly love, by way of salutation.

Honoured Sir, having in remembrance the promise I made you on parting, that I would tell you all the news, and how I fared, I would have you know that I have now been two months at Rome, but as yet have found no patron. An assessor of the Rota would fain have bespoken me, and I was well pleased, and said, "I am nothing loth, Sir; but I pray your magnificence to apprize me what my charge will be." He replied, that my lodgment would be in the stable, to minister unto a mule, serve it with victuals and drink, curry-comb it, and keep it clean; and that I must have a care that he was ready to carry his master, with bridle and saddle and so forth. And then it would be my office to run by his side to the court, and home again.

Thereupon I made answer that it was not meet for me, who am a Master of Arts of *Cologne*, to drudge thus. Quoth he, "If not, the loss is yours." I am resolved therefore, to return to the fatherland. I, to curry-comb a mule and mundify a stable! The Devil run away with the stable and the mule! I verily believe it would be flying in the face of the Statutes of the University! For a Magister must needs comport himself as a Magister. It would be a scandalous thing for a Master of Arts of *Cologne* to do such drudgery. Nay, for the honour of the University I will return to the fatherland.

Rome moreover pleaseth me not in other ways. You would not believe how arrogant are the Clerks and Curialists.

So be well assured, I shall hie me back to *Germany;* for there Magisters are paramount; and rightly. I can prove it by the Gospel: Christ called himself Magister, and not Doctor, saying, "Ye call me Master and Lord, and ye say well, for so I am."

But I can now write no more, for paper faileth me, and it is a great way to the *Campo dei Fiori.* Farewell. (From the Court of Rome)

XXVI. HEINRICH SCHAFMAUL TO MAGISTER ORTUINUS GRATIUS, MANY GREETINGS

Inasmuch as before I journeyed to Court you charged me to write you oft, and propose from time to time knotty points in Theology, which you would straightway resolve better than the Courticians at *Rome:* therefore, I now write to ask your reverence what opinion you hold concerning one who on a Friday, that is on the sixth day of the week— or on any other fast-day—should eat an egg with a chicken in it?

For you must know that we were lately sitting in an inn in the *Campo dei Fiori,* having our supper, and were eating eggs, when on opening one I saw that there was a young chicken within.

This I showed to a comrade; whereupon quoth he to me, "Eat it up speedily, before the taverner sees it, for if he mark it, you will have to pay a Carline or a Julius for a fowl. For it is the rule of the house that once the landlord has put anything on the table you must pay for it—he won't take it back. And if he sees that there is a young fowl in that egg, he will say 'Pay me for that fowl! Little or big, 'tis all one.'"

In a trice I gulped down the egg, chicken and all.

And then I remembered that it was Friday!

Whereupon I said to my crony, "You have made me commit a mortal sin, in eating flesh on the sixth day of the week!"

But he averred that it was not a mortal sin —nor even a venial one, seeing that such a chickling is accounted merely as an egg, until it is born.

He told me, too, that it is just the same in the case of cheese, in which there are sometimes grubs, as there are in cherries, peas, and new beans: yet all these may be eaten on Fridays, and even on Apostolic Vigils. But taverners are such rascals that they call them flesh, to get the more money.

Then I departed, and thought the matter over.

And by the Lord, Master *Ortwin*, I am in a mighty quandary, and know not what to do.

I would willingly seek counsel of one of the Courticians, but they are not devout men.

It seemeth to me that these young fowls in eggs are flesh, because their substance is formed and fashioned into the limbs and body of an animal, and possesseth a vital principle.

It is different in the case of grubs in cheese, and such-like because grubs are accounted fish, as I learnt from a physician who is also skilled in Natural Philosophy.

Most earnestly do I entreat you to resolve the question that I have propounded. For if you hold that the sin is mortal, then, I would fain get shrift here, ere I return to *Germany*.

You must know, too, that Doctor *Jakob von Hochstraten* hath received a thousand florins through the bankers, and I trow he will gain the day, and that the devil will overthrow *Johann Reuchlin* and the rest of the Poets and Jurists, because they would fain withstand the Church of God—that is, the Theologians, on whom the Church is founded, according to Christ's words—"Thou art *Peter*, and upon this rock I will build my Church."

And so I commend you to the Lord. Farewell. (Rome)

XLVIII. JOHANN KALB TO MAGISTER ORTWIN GRATIUS

Amicable greeting.

Honourable and Reverend Herr Magister, I would have you know that I marvel greatly how it cometh that you importune me in continually bidding me to send you "some news." You are endlessly craving for news, notwithstanding that I have other business to attend to, and therefore cannot occupy myself with gossip; for I must needs run hither and thither in canvassing, lest I miscarry in my candidature, and come not at the benefice.

Nevertheless, I will write to you this once, to satisfy you, so that, after, you may leave me in peace with your "news"!

You have doubtless heard that the Pope had a huge great beast called *Elephant*, and held it in great honour, and mightily loved it. And now I would have you know that this beast is dead. When it was ill the Pope fell into great grief, and he summoned a host of physicians, and said, "If it be possible, cure *Elephant* for me." Thereupon they bestirred themselves, and cast its water, and gave it a cathartic that cost five hundred golden crowns—yet were not the bowels of *Elephant* moved thereby, and so it died. Sorely doth the Pope grieve for *Elephant*, for whom, they say, he'd give a thousand ducats.

In sooth it was a marvellous brute, and it had a great abundance of long snout; and when it saw the Pope it would kneel to him, and cry in a terrible voice, "Bar, bar, bar!" There is, I trow, not the like beast in the whole world.

The rumor goes that the King of *France* and King *Charles* have made a treaty of peace for many years, and have exchanged oaths. But some think this peace is but politic, and will not long endure. I know not if this be so—nor do I greatly care. For when I come home to *Germany*, then I shall betake me to my parsonage, and spend happy days. There shall I keep flocks of geese and hens and ducks, and I shall have in my byre five or six cows to yield me milk for the making of cheese and butter. And I shall keep a cook who can turn her hand to such work. She must be of ripe years, for if she were young she might sorely tempt me, and I might fall into sin. She will spin for me, and I will buy the flax for her. I shall keep two or three pigs, and fatten them to furnish me with good bacon. Before all things I shall keep in my house great store of victuals. Once a year I shall kill an ox and sell half to the country-folk, and cure the rest in the reek. And behind the house there is a garden where I shall sow garlic, and onions and parsley—with pot-herbs, turnips, and the like. Then in the winter I shall sit in my chamber and study how to hold forth to my flock, out of the Paratus, or the Simple Sermons, or even out of the Bible, so that I may become practiced in preaching. But in the summer I shall go a-fishing, or dig in my garden; and I shall take no heed of wars, for I shall live my own life, and preach sermons and read mass, heeding not those worldly concerns that bring damnation to the soul. Farewell. (The Court of Rome)

3. *The Ninety-five Theses of Martin Luther*

Kritische Gesamtausgabe der Werke Luthers, I (Weimar, 1804). Composite translation.

WITTENBERG, OCTOBER 31, 1517

Out of an earnest desire to elucidate the truth, the following theses will be argued at Wittenberg, under the direction of the Rev. Father Martin Luther, Master of Arts and Sacred Theology, and Professor Ordinary of the same. He requests that those who cannot be present to discuss in person do so in writing. In the name of our Lord Jesus Christ. Amen.

1. When our Lord and Master, Jesus Christ, says "Repent ye," etc., he means that the entire life of the faithful should be a repentance.

2. This statement cannot be understood of the sacrament of penance, i.e., of confession and satisfaction, which is administered by the priesthood.

3. However, he does not mean inward repentance only, for inward repentance that does not result in various external mortifications of the flesh is empty.

4. Divine punishment, therefore, remains as long as one loathes himself (i.e., as long as there is inward repentance), namely, until entrance into the kingdom of heaven.

5. The pope does not wish, nor has he the power, to remit any punishments, except those which he, of his own will or according to the canons, has imposed.

6. The pope cannot forgive any sin; he can only declare and confirm God's forgiveness. He can remit cases reserved to himself, but, if they be despised, the sin remains.

7. God forgives no one's sins without at the same time subjecting him in every respect in humility to his vicar, the priest.

8. The canons pertaining to penance are imposed only upon the living, and according to the canons themselves should not be imposed upon the dying.

9. Hence, the Holy Ghost in the pope does well for us by always making an exception in his decrees in case of death and extreme necessity.

10. Those priests who, in the case of the dying, reserve canonical penances for purgatory act ignorantly and wickedly.

11. These tares, namely, canonical punishments changed into the pains of purgatory, were sown apparently while the bishops were asleep.

12. In former times canonical punishments were imposed not after, but before, absolution, in order to test the sincerity of the repentance.

13. The dying by their death become free of all laws; they are dead to the laws of canons, released from their dominion.

14. Since there is imperfect holiness or love in the dying, this necessarily brings with it great fear, and the less there is of holiness and love the greater the fear.

15. This fear and terror is enough in itself (to say nothing of other things) to produce purgatorial punishment, for it comes close to the anguish of despair.

16. Hell, purgatory, and heaven appear to differ as despair, almost despair, and confidence differ.

17. It appears that for souls in purgatory terror decreases as love increases.

18. Also it appears not to be proved either by reason or by Scripture that such souls are beyond the possibility of merit or of increase of love.

19. It does not appear to be proved that they, or at least not all of them, are sure and confident about their salvation, although we may have no doubt about it.

20. The pope, therefore, with his "plenary remission of all punishments," does not mean absolutely all, but only those imposed by himself.

21. Therefore, the preachers of indulgences err when they say that through the papal indulgences a man is freed and saved from all punishment.

22. Rather he [the pope] remits to souls in purgatory not a single penalty which they, according to the canons, were supposed to have paid in this life.

23. If complete remission of punishment can be granted to anyone, then surely it can be given only to the most perfect, i.e., to the very few.

24. It follows, therefore, that the major part of the people is deceived by this indiscriminate and grandiose promise that they are to be exempt from punishment.

25. The same general power which the pope has over purgatory every bishop and pastor has over his own particular diocese and parish.

26. The pope does well in giving remission to souls not by the power of the keys (for he has no such power) but by intercession.

27. They preach human folly who pretend that as soon as money in the coffer rings a soul from purgatory springs.

28. It is true that greed and avarice increase when money in the coffer rings, but the intercession of the church has effect only because of God's will.

29. Who knows if all the souls in purgatory want to be redeemed? After all, we do have the story about Saints Severinus and Paschal.

30. No one is sure of the sincerity of his contrition, much less of obtaining entire remission.

31. Those who have truly purchased in-

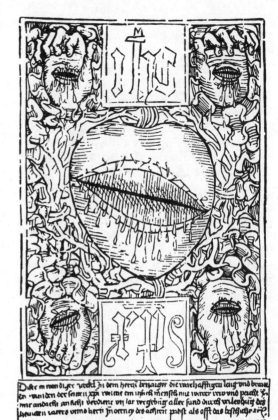

1-7. The Five Wounds of Christ. *Illustration for a letter of indulgence by Pope Innocent VIII, 1485.*

dulgence are as rare as true penitents, which is to say, very rare.

32. Those who suppose that on account of their letters of indulgence they are sure of salvation will be eternally damned along with their teachers.

33. We must especially be wary of those who say that the pope's pardon is that inestimable gift of God by which man is reconciled to God.

34. For these gifts of pardon pertain only to the punishments of sacramental satisfaction imposed by men.

35. Those who teach that contrition is not needed in order to obtain redemption or indulgence are preaching unchristian doctrine.

36. Every Christian who truly repents has

plenary forgiveness both of punishment and guilt bestowed on him, even without letters of indulgence.

37. Every true Christian, whether living or dead, has a share in all the benefits of Christ and the Church, for God has granted him these, even without letters of indulgence.

38. Nevertheless the pope's remission and dispensation is in no way to be despised, because, as I have said, it is a declaration of divine forgiveness.

39. It is very difficult, even for the most learned theologians, to extol publicly at one and the same time both the rich fullness of indulgence and the need for sincere contrition.

40. Sincere contrition desires and loves punishments. But the rich fullness of the indulgence takes away punishments and arouses hatred of them.

41. Apostolic pardons must be preached with great care so that the people will not falsely think they are preferable to the other good works of love.

42. Christians should be taught that it is not the meaning of the pope that the purchase of an indulgence is in any way to be compared with works of mercy.

43. Christians should be taught that one who gives to the poor or lends to the needy does better than one who buys an indulgence.

44. Through a work of love, love increases and man improves, but he does not improve through an indulgence; he is only released from punishment.

45. Christians should be taught that whoever sees a person in need and, instead of helping him, uses his money for an indulgence, obtains not an indulgence of the pope but the displeasure of God.

46. Christians should be taught that, unless they have a superfluity of wealth, they must keep what is necessary for their own household and by no means squander it in the purchase of indulgences.

47. Christians should be taught that the purchase of indulgences is a matter of free choice, not something commanded.

48. Christians should be taught that in granting indulgences the pope needs and has more desire for devout prayer on his behalf than for their money.

49. Christians should be taught that the pope's indulgences are useful, if they do not put their trust in them, but very harmful if through them they lose their fear of God.

50. Christians should be taught that if the pope knew the extortion of the preachers of indulgences, he would rather let St. Peter's Cathedral be burned to ashes than have it built of the skin, flesh, and bones of his flock.

51. Christians should be taught that the pope ought and would give his own substance to the poor from whom certain preachers of indulgences extract money, even if he had to sell St. Peter's Cathedral to do it.

52. It is vain to trust in letters of indulgence for salvation even though the commissioner of indulgences or the pope himself should pledge his soul as a guarantee.

53. They are enemies of Christ and the pope, who, in order to preach indulgences, command the word of God to be kept silent in other churches.

54. The Word of God is wronged when a priest devotes as much time, or more, to the indulgence as to the Gospel in a sermon.

55. The intention of the pope must be this: If the indulgence, an affair of little importance, is celebrated with a single bell and simple pomp and ceremony, then the Gospel, which is of the greatest importance, should be proclaimed with a hundred bells, and a hundred-fold of pomp and ceremony.

56. The treasures of the Church, out of which the pope distributes indulgences, are neither sufficiently mentioned nor known among Christ's people.

57. It is clear that they are not temporal goods, because many of the preachers readily prefer to accumulate these rather than bestow them.

58. Nor are they the merits of Christ and the saints, because at all times, without the aid of the pope, these work the grace in the inner man, and the cross, death, and hell in the outer man.

59. St. Lawrence said the poor were the treasures of the Church, but he was using the language of his own day.

60. With good reason we say the keys of the Church, which are granted through the merits of Christ, are this treasure.

61. For it is clear that for the forgiveness of punishments and reserved cases the power of the pope alone suffices.

62. The true treasure of the Church is the most holy Gospel of God's glory and grace.

63. But this is justly very obnoxious, for it causes the first to be last.

64. On the other hand the treasure of indulgences is truly very agreeable, for it causes the last to be first.

65. Thus, the treasures of the Gospel are nets, with which they formerly fished for men of riches.

66. The treasures of indulgences are nets, with which they now fish for the riches of men.

67. Indulgences, which the preachers loudly proclaim as the "greatest graces," are indeed to be regarded as such because they do produce much money.

68. But when compared with God's grace and the piety of the cross, they are the least of graces.

69. Bishops and pastors are bound to receive the commissioners of the apostolic pardons with all reverence.

70. But they are bound to take even more care to observe with their own eyes and to listen with their own ears to see that these preachers do not proclaim their own dreams instead of the papal warrant.

71. Whoever speaks against the truth of the apostolic pardons, let him be anathema and accursed.

72. But whoever guards against the wanton and shameless words of the preachers of indulgences, let him be blessed.

73. As the pope justly inveighs against those who in any way work to the disadvantage of the matter of pardons,

74. So much the more does he intend to inveigh against those who, under the pretext of the pardons, prejudice the work of holy love and truth.

75. To deem the papal pardon so great that it can absolve a man even if (to assume an impossible thing) he had violated the mother of God is sheer madness.

76. On the contrary, we say that the papal pardons cannot take away the most trivial sin, as regards guilt.

77. To say that even if St. Peter were pope now, he could not bestow greater indulgences, is a blasphemy against St. Peter and the pope.

78. We say, on the contrary, that both this and every other pope has greater graces; namely, the Gospel and its powers, such as the gifts of healing, etc., as in I Cor. 12.

79. It is blasphemy to say that an indulgence cross which is adorned with the papal arms and erected in a church has the same value as the cross of Christ.

80. The bishops, pastors, and theologians who allow such teaching to be disseminated among the people will have to give an accounting for it.

81. This shameless preaching of pardons makes it hard even for learned men to defend the pope's honor against calumny or to answer the indubitably shrewd questions of the laity.

82. For example: Why does not the pope empty purgatory for the sake of holy love and the extreme need of the souls, which is a most righteous reason for doing so, for after all, he does release countless souls for the sake of sordid money contributed for the building of a cathedral, which is a very trifling reason?

83. Why do the requiems and festivals of the departed continue, and why does he not restore the benefices offered on their behalf, since it is now wrong to pray for the redeemed?

84. What kind of a holiness of God and the pope is this, that for the sake of money they allow the godless and the hostile to ransom a pious soul, beloved of God, when for the sake of the need of this same pious and beloved soul they do not ransom it out of love gratuitously?

85. Why are the penitential canons, which long ago were repealed and abandoned, considered dead through lack of use, now once more accepted for money, as though they were still thoroughly alive?

86. Why does not the pope build the Cathedral of St. Peter with his own money

rather than with that of poor believers, because his wealth now exceeds that of the richest Croesus?

87. What does the pope remit or impart to those who through perfect contrition have a right to plenary remission and participation?

88. What greater good could happen to the Church than if the pope were to do a hundred times a day what he now does once a day—namely, bestow these remissions and impartations upon every believer.

89. Since the pope by means of pardons seeks the salvation of souls rather than the money, why does he suspend the letters and pardons formerly granted, since they are equally efficacious?

90. To suppress these very telling arguments of the laity by force instead of answering them with adequate reasons would be to expose the Church and the pope to the ridicule of their enemies and to render Christians unhappy.

91. Now if pardons were preached according to the spirit and intention of the pope, all these questions would easily be answered, nay they would not arise.

92. Away, then, with all those prophets who say to the people of Christ, "Peace, peace," when there is no peace.

93. And farewell to those prophets who say to the people of Christ: "Cross, cross," when there is no cross.

94. We should admonish Christians to strive to follow Christ, their Head, through punishment, death, and hell.

95. And so let them set their trust on entering heaven through many tribulations rather than through some false security and peace.

4. Tetzel's Counter Theses

Stung by the effect of Luther's bold theses, Tetzel, with the aid of his Dominican friends, published two series of theses. The fifty theses in the second series were written in 1517 and publicly debated on January 21, 1518. They uphold papal supremacy and infallibility, although the dogma of infallibility came as late as 1870. *Translations and Reprints,* trans. Henry C. Vedder (Philadelphia: University of Pennsylvania Press, 1905).

1. Christians should be taught that, since the power of the Pope is supreme in the Church and was instituted by God alone, it can be restrained or increased by no mere man, nor by the whole world together, but by God only.

3. Christians should be taught that the Pope, by authority of his jurisdiction, is superior to the entire Catholic Church and its councils, and that they should humbly obey his statutes.

I-8. Tetzel Selling Indulgences. *From a painting by Trenkwald.*

5. Christians should be taught that the judgment of the Pope, in those matters that are of faith and necessary to man's salvation, cannot err in the least.

10. Christians should be taught that those who expose the Pope to jeers and slanders are marked with the stain of heresy and shut out from hope of the kingdom of heaven.

15. Christians should be taught that catholic truth is called universal truth, and that it ought to be believed by Christ's faithful ones, and that it contains nothing either of falsehood or of iniquity.

18. Christians should be taught that all observances regarding matters of faith, defined by the decision of the Apostolic See, are to be reckoned among catholic truths, although not found to be contained in the canon of Holy Scripture.

22. Christians should be taught that those who cherish deliberate doubts concerning the faith should be most clearly condemned as heretics.

... For a beast that has touched the mountain shall be stoned.

5. Appeal to the German Nobility

First Principles of the Reformation of Dr. Martin Luther, trans. Henry Wace and C. A. Buchheim (London: John Murray, 1883). Cf. *Kritische Gesamtausgabe der Werke Luthers,* VI, 404 ff. The bracketed portions are summaries, and the entire essay of some seventy-five pages has been greatly condensed.

[Luther compliments the young Emperor Charles, and appeals to the nobility to reform the grievances of the German nation. He then goes on to explain why the laity has not acted and the basis on which the laity can act—]

The Romanists have, with great adroitness, drawn three walls round themselves, with which they have hitherto protected themselves, so that no one could reform them, and all Christendom has suffered. The first wall is that if pressed by the temporal power, they have affirmed and maintained that the temporal power has no jurisdiction over them, but on the contrary that the spiritual power is above the temporal. Secondly, if it were proposed to admonish them with the Scriptures, they objected that no one may interpret the Scriptures but the Pope.

Thirdly, if they are threatened with a council, they pretend that no one may call a council but the Pope. ... Now may God help us, and give us one of those trumpets, that overthrew the walls of Jericho, so that we may blow down these walls of straw and paper. ...

The first wall is the device whereby the Pope, bishops, priests, and monks are called the spiritual estate; princes, lords, artificers and peasants, are called the temporal estate .... But all Christians are truly of the spiritual estate, and there is no difference among them, save of office alone. As St. Paul says (I Cor. 12), we are all one body, though each member does its own work, to serve the others. This is because we have one baptism, one gospel, one faith, and are all Christians alike; for baptism, gospel and faith, these alone make spiritual and Christian people. We are all consecrated as priests by baptism, a higher consecration in us than Pope or bishop can give. The bishop's consecration is just as if in the name of the whole congregation he took one person out of the community, each member of which has equal power, and commanded him to say mass, preach, and absolve for the rest. ... Since we are all priests, no man may put himself forward or take upon himself, without our consent and election, to do that which we have all alike power to do. For, if a thing is common to all, no man may take it to himself without the wish and command of the community. And if it should happen that a man were appointed to one of these offices and deposed for abuses, he would be just what he was before. Therefore a priest should be nothing in Christendom but a functionary; as long as he holds his office, he has precedence of others; if he is deprived of it, he is a peasant and a citizen like the rest. The only real difference between laymen and priests is one of office and function, and not of estate; they are all priests, though their functions are not the same. Those whom we call spiritual, the priests, are concerned with the word of God, and the sacraments—that being their work and office—in the same way the temporal authorities hold the sword and the rod in their hands to punish the wicked and to protect the good. A cobbler, a smith, a peasant, every man has the office and function of his calling, and yet all alike are consecrated priests and bishops, and every man in his office must be useful and beneficial to the rest, that so many kinds of work may all be united into one community: just as the members of the body all serve one another.

Therefore I say: as the temporal power has been ordained by God for the punishment of the bad, and the protection of the good, therefore we must let it do its duty throughout the whole Christian body, without respect of persons: whether it strike popes, bishops, priests, monks, or nuns: whoever is guilty let him suffer.

The second wall is even more tottering and weak, the claim, namely, that they alone are masters of the Scriptures; although they learn nothing from them during their entire life, they assume authority, and juggle before us impudent words, saying that the Pope cannot err in matters of faith, whether he be evil or good. That is why the canon law contains so many heretical and unchristian, nay, unnatural laws. They cannot quote a single letter to confirm that it is for the Pope alone to interpret the Scriptures or to confirm the interpretation of them; they have assumed the authority of their own selves.... It behooves every Christian to aid the faith by understanding and defending it, and by condemning all errors....

The third wall falls of itself, as soon as the first two have fallen; for if the Pope acts contrary to the Scriptures, we are bound to stand by the Scriptures, to punish and to constrain him.... They can show nothing in the Scriptures giving the Pope sole power to call and confirm councils.... Moreover, the most celebrated Nicene Council was neither called nor confirmed by the Bishop of Rome, but by the Emperor Constantine; and after him many other Emperors have done the same .... Therefore when need requires and the Pope is a cause of offense to Christendom, whoever can best do so, as a faithful member of the whole body, must do what he can to procure a true free council. This no one can do so well as the temporal authorities, and they should exercise the office that they have received from God without hindrance, when-

ever it is necessary and useful that it should be exercised.... No one in Christendom has any authority to do harm, or to forbid others to prevent harm being done....

Let us now consider the matters which should be treated in the councils, and with which popes, cardinals, bishops, and all learned men should occupy themselves day and night, if they loved Christ and His Church. But if they do not do so, the people at large and the temporal powers must do so, without considering the thunders of their excommunications....

1. It is a distressing and terrible thing to see that the head of Christendom, who boasts of being the Vicar of Christ and the successor of St. Peter, lives in a worldly pomp that no king or emperor can equal: so that in him that calls himself most holy and most spiritual, there is more worldliness than in the world itself. [The Pope should be forced to live more simply.]

2. What is the use in Christendom of the people called "Cardinals"? I will tell you. In Italy and Germany there are many rich convents, endowments, fiefs and benefices, and as the best way of getting these into the hands of Rome, they created cardinals, and gave them the sees, convents, and prelacies. That is why Italy is almost a desert. And now that Italy is sucked dry, they come to Germany.... I advise that there be fewer cardinals, or that the Pope support them out of his own purse. It would be sufficient, if there were twelve, and if each had an annual income of one thousand guilders....

3. If we took away ninety-nine parts of the Pope's court, it would still be large enough to answer questions on matters of belief. [Germany pays more to the Pope than it formerly paid the Emperors. It is a wonder that the Germans have anything left to eat. Annates, the taking of one half of the first year's income from every benefice, should be abolished, inasmuch as such money is no longer used to fight the Turks but to feed ravenous wolves in sheep's clothing who profess to be shepherds and rulers. The practice of appointing old men to benefices so that they will become vacant more frequently should be halted. None should be allowed to hold multiple appointments and draw

salaries from all of them. A benefice should not be taken from a priest simply because another priest is willing to let the Pope have a larger share of the salary, if he be appointed, nor can this be justified by mental reservation in the first appointment. And the Datarius should be purged of its prostitution.]

If you bring money to this house, you can arrive at all that I have mentioned; and more than this, any sort of usury is made legitimate for money; property got by theft or robbery is here made legal. Here vows are annulled; here a monk obtains leave to quit his order; here priests can enter married life for money; here bastards can become legitimate; and dishonor and shame may arrive at high honors; all evil repute and disgrace is knighted and ennobled; here a marriage is suffered that is forbidden in a decree, or has some other defect. Oh, what a trafficking and plundering is there! one would think that the canon laws were only so many ropes of gold, from which he must free himself who would become a Christian man. Nay, here the Devil becomes a saint, and a God besides. . . . Let no one think that I say too much. . . . I speak only of well-known public matters, and yet my words do not suffice.

Since this devilish state of things is not only an open robbery, deceit and tyranny of the gates of hell, but also destroys Christianity, body and soul, we are bound to use all our diligence to prevent this misery and destruction of Christendom. If we wish to fight the Turks, let us begin here, where they are the worst. If we justly hang thieves and behead robbers, why do we leave the greed of Rome so unpunished? . . .

Now though I am too lowly to submit articles that could serve for the reformation of these fearful evils, I will yet sing out my fool's song, and will show, as well as my wit will allow, what might and should be done by the temporal authorities or by a general council.

[1. Princes, nobles and cities should promptly forbid all annates.

2. Foreigners from Rome should not be allowed to take benefices in Germany.

3. Ecclesiastical appointments should be confirmed by neighboring bishops, or the archbishop, as set forth in the Nicene Council; appointments should not have to be confirmed in Rome.

4. Temporal matters should not be submitted to Rome; they should be left to the jurisdiction of temporal authorities.

5. There should be no more papal reservations and no more appropriations of benefices by Rome.

6. Special cases that can be tried only in Rome should be abolished.

7. The multitude of papal offices should be reduced, and the Pope's servants supported out of the Pope's own pocket.

8. Bishops should not have to swear allegiance to the Pope, and thus be bound like servants. Civil magistrates should invest bishops as in France.

9. The Pope should have no power over the Emperor, except to anoint and crown him at the altar, as a bishop crowns a king. It is absurd for the Pope to boast that he is the rightful heir to the Empire, if the throne be vacant. The Donation of Constantine is a lie.

10. The Pope should cease being the temporal ruler in Naples and Sicily.

11. Kissing the Pope's feet and other silly customs must cease.

12. Pilgrimages to Rome should be abolished, unless authorized by one's priest or magistrate.

13. No more mendicant monasteries should be built; begging friars are a curse.

14. Priests should be free to marry or not as they choose.

15. Abbots, abbesses and prelates should not insist on confession of secret sins and then say that some secret sins cannot be absolved. That is for God to say.

16. Festivals, processions, masses for the dead and vigils should be abolished or drastically curtailed.

17. Practices under the canon law such as interdict, excommunication, suspension, etc., since they are sinfully abused, should be done away.

18. All saints' days should be abolished, inasmuch as with our drinking, gambling, idling and other sins, we vex God more on holy days than on others.

19. Distant relatives should be allowed to marry without payment to the Pope.

20. Shrines in open fields should be taken down; pilgrimages to them do more harm than good.

21. Begging should be prohibited; communities should take care of their poor.

22. The multiplying of endowed masses should be curbed, especially those set up to supply livings for the children of nobility. They mock true religion.

23. Special fraternities for indulgences, dispensations, masses, etc., should be abolished.

24. John Huss and Jerome of Prague should be restored to places of respect, for they were violently wronged. The Pope should not tyrannize the Bohemians.

25. The universities need a good reform; much of Aristotle should be abolished; the schools of medicine should reform themselves; the Bible should take precedence over secondary theological works; and cities should have schools in which the gospel is read.

26. It should not be taught that the Pope gave Germany to the Emperor and hence has superiority over the Emperor.

27. Exorbitant interests should not be charged by bankers; Christians should not be allowed to maintain brothels; credit buying should be curbed; etc., as all these cause untold harm.]

6. Luther's Treatise on Christian Liberty, 1520

Works of Martin Luther, II, trans. W. A. Lambert (Philadelphia: Muhlenberg Press, 1943).

LUTHER'S LETTER TO POPE LEO X

To Leo the Tenth, Pope at Rome: Martin Luther wishes thee salvation in Christ Jesus our Lord. Amen.

In the midst of the monsters of this age with whom I am now for the third year waging war, I am compelled at times to look up also to thee, Leo, most blessed Father, and to think of thee; nay, since thou art now and again regarded as the sole cause of my warfare, I cannot but think of thee always. . . . It is true, I have made bold almost to despise and to triumph over those who have tried to frighten me with the majesty of thy name

and authority. But there is one thing which I cannot despise, and that is my excuse for writing once more to thy Blessedness. I understand that I am accused of great rashness, and that this rashness is said to be my great fault, in which, they say, I have not spared even thy person.

For my part, I will openly confess that I know I have only spoken good and honorable things of thee whenever I have made mention of thy name. . . . I have indeed sharply inveighed against ungodly teachings in general, and I have not been slow to bite my adversaries, not because of their immorality, but because of their ungodliness. And of this I repent so little that I have determined to persevere in that fervent zeal, and to despise the judgment of men, following the example of Christ, Who in His zeal called His adversaries a generation of vipers, blind, hypocrites, children of the devil. . . . Nowadays, it is true, our ears are made so delicate by the mad crowds of flatterers that as soon as we meet with a disapproving voice we cry out that we are bitten, and when we cannot ward off the truth with any other pretext we put it to flight by ascribing it to a fierce temper, impatience and shamelessness. What is the good of salt if it does not bite? Or of the edge of the sword if it does not kill? Cursed be he that doeth the work of the Lord deceitfully. . . .

. . . . .

But thy See, which is called the Roman Curia, and of which neither thou nor any man can deny that it is more corrupt than any Babylon or Sodom ever was, and which is, as far as I can see, characterized by a totally depraved, hopeless and notorious wickedness —that See I have truly despised, and I have been incensed to think that in thy name and under the guise of the Roman Church the people of Christ are mocked. And so I have resisted and will resist that See, as long as the spirit of faith shall live in me. Not that I shall strive after the impossible in that most disordered Babylon, where the rage of so many sycophants is turned against me; but I acknowledge myself a debtor to my brethren, whom it is my duty to warn, that fewer of them may be destroyed by the plagues of Rome, or at least that their destruction may be less cruel.

For, as thou well knowest, these many years there has flowed forth from Rome, like a flood covering the world, nothing but a laying waste of men's bodies and souls and possessions, and the worst possible examples of the worst possible things. For all this is clearer than the day to all men, and the Roman Church, once the most holy of all, has become the most licentious den of thieves, the most shameless of all brothels, the kingdom of sin, death and hell; so that even Antichrist himself, should he come, could think of nothing to add to its wickedness.

Meanwhile thou, Leo, sittest as a lamb in the midst of wolves, like Daniel in the midst of lions, and, with Ezekiel, thou dwellest among scorpions. What canst thou do single-handed, against these monsters? Join to thyself three or four thoroughly learned and thoroughly good cardinals: what are even these among so many? You would all be poisoned before you could undertake to make a single decree to help matters. . . . The Roman Curia has not deserved to have thee or men like thee, but rather Satan himself; and in truth it is he more than thou who rules in that Babylon.

.   .   .   .   .

To go yet farther, I never intended to inveigh against the Roman Curia, or to raise any controversy concerning it. For when I saw that all efforts to save it were hopeless, I despised it and gave it a bill of divorcement and said to it, "He that is filthy, let him be filthy still, and he that is unclean, let him be unclean still." Then I gave myself to the quiet and peaceful study of holy Scripture, that I might thus be of benefit to my brethren about me. When I had made some progress in these studies, Satan opened his eyes and filled his servant John Eck, a notable enemy of Christ, with an insatiable lust for glory, and thereby stirred him up to drag me at unawares into a disputation, laying hold on me by one little word about the primacy of the Roman Church which I had inci-

dentally let fall. Then that boasting braggart, frothing and gnashing his teeth, declared that he would venture all for the glory of God and the honor of the holy Apostolic See, and, puffed up with the hope of misusing thy power, he looked forward with perfect confidence to a victory over me. He sought not so much to establish the primacy of Peter as his own leadership among the theologians of our time; and to that end he thought it no small help if he should triumph over Luther. When that debate ended unhappily for the sophist, an incredible madness overcame the man: for he feels that he alone must bear the blame of all that I have brought forth to the shame of Rome.

But permit me, I pray thee, most excellent Leo, this once to plead my cause and to make charges against thy real enemies. Thou knowest, I believe, what dealings thy legate, Cardinal of St. Sixtus [Cajetan], an unwise and unfortunate, or rather, unfaithful man, had with me. When, because of reverence for thy name, I at that time promised to keep silent and to end the controversy, if my opponents were ordered to do the same. But as he was a man who sought glory, and was not content with that agreement, he began to justify my opponents, to give them full freedom and to order me to recant, a thing not included in his instructions. . . .

Next came Carl Miltitz. . . . Again I yielded to your name, I was prepared to keep silent, and even accepted as arbiter either the archbishop of Treves or the bishop of Naumburg. So matters were arranged. But while this plan was being followed with good prospects of success, lo, that other and greater enemy of thine, Eck, broke in with the Leipzig Disputation [June 27-July 15, 1519] which he had undertaken against Dr. Carlstadt. When a new question concerning the primacy of the pope was raised, he suddenly turned his weapons against me and quite overthrew that counsel of peace. Meanwhile Carl Miltitz waited: a disputation was held, judges were selected; but here also no decision was reached, and no wonder: through the lies, the tricks, the wiles of Eck everything was stirred up, aggravated and confounded worse than ever, so that whatever decision might have been reached, a greater conflagration would have resulted. For he sought glory, not the truth. . . .

Since we gained nothing by this disputation except that we brought great confusion to the cause of Rome, Carl Miltitz made a third attempt; he came to the fathers of the Augustinian Order assembled in their chapter, and asked counsel in settling the controversy which had now grown most confused and dangerous. Since, by the favor of God, they had no hope of being able to proceed against me with violence, some of the most famous of their number were sent to me, and asked me at least to show honor to the person of thy Blessedness, and in a humble letter to plead as my excuse thy innocence and mine; they said that the affair was not yet in the most desperate state if of his innate goodness Leo the Tenth would take a hand in it. . . .

So I come, most blessed Father, and, prostrate before thee, I pray, if it be possible do thou interpose and hold in check those flatterers, who are the enemies of peace while they pretend to keep peace. But that I will recant, most blessed Father, let no one imagine, unless he prefer to involve the whole question in greater turmoil. Furthermore, I will accept no rules for the interpretation of the Word of God, since the Word of God, which teaches the liberty of all things else, dare not be bound. Grant me these two points, and there is nothing that I could not or would not most gladly do or endure. I hate disputations; I will draw out no one; but then I do not wish others to draw me out; if they do, as Christ is my Teacher, I will not be speechless. For, when once this controversy has been cited before thee and settled, thy Blessedness will be able with a small and easy word to silence both parties and command them to keep the peace, and that is what I have always wished to hear.

Do not listen, therefore, my dear Leo, to those sirens who make thee out to be no mere man but a demigod, so that thou mayest command and require what thou wilt.

.   .   .   .   .   .

Finally, that I may not approach thee empty-handed, blessed Father, I bring with me this little treatise published under thy name as an omen of peace and of good hope. From this book thou mayest judge with what studies I would prefer to be more profitably engaged, as I could be if your godless flatterers would permit me, and had hitherto permitted me. May the Lord Jesus preserve thee forever. Amen. (*Wittenberg, September 6, 1520.*)

A TREATISE ON CHRISTIAN LIBERTY

A Christian man is a perfectly free lord of all, subject to none.

A Christian man is a perfectly dutiful servant of all, subject to all.

Although these two theses seem to contradict each other, yet, if they should be found to fit together they would serve our purpose beautifully. For they are both Paul's own, who says, in I Cor. 9, "Whereas I was free, I made myself the servant of all," and, Rom. 13, "Owe no man anything, but to love one another." Now love by its very nature is ready to serve and to be subject to him who is loved. So, Christ, although Lord of all, was made of a woman, made under the law, and hence was at the same time free and a servant, at the same time in the form of God and in the form of a servant.

Let us start, however, with something more obvious. Man has a twofold nature, a spiritual and a bodily, [and these two] contradict each other, since the flesh lusteth against the spirit and the spirit against the flesh (Gal. 5).

First, let us contemplate the inward man, to see how a righteous, free and truly Christian man, that is, a new, spiritual, inward man, comes into being. It is evident that no external thing, whatsoever it be, has any influence whatever in producing Christian righteousness or liberty, nor in producing unrighteousness or bondage. A simple argument will furnish the proof. What can it profit the soul if the body fare well, be free and active, eat, drink and do as it pleases? For in these things even the most godless slaves of all the vices fare well. On the other hand, how will ill health or imprisonment or hunger or thirst or any other external misfortune

24

hurt the soul? With these things even the most godly men are afflicted, and those who because of a clear conscience are most free. None of these things touch either the liberty or the bondage of the soul. The soul receives no benefit if the body is adorned with the sacred robes of the priesthood, or dwells in sacred places, or is occupied with sacred duties, or prays, fasts, abstains from certain kinds of food or does any work whatsoever that can be done by the body and in the body.... On the other hand, it will not hurt the soul if the body is clothed in secular dress, dwells in unconsecrated places, eats and drinks as others do, does not pray aloud, and neglects to do all the things mentioned above, which hypocrites can do.

One thing and one only is necessary for Christian life, righteousness and liberty. That one thing is the most holy Word of God, the Gospel of Christ.... You ask, "What then is this Word of God, and how shall it be used, since there are so many words of God?" I answer, The Apostle explains that in Romans 1. The Word is the Gospel of God concerning his Son, Who was made flesh, suffered, rose from the dead, and was glorified through the Spirit Who sanctifies. For to preach Christ means to feed the soul, to make it righteous, to set it free and to save it, if it believe the preaching. For faith alone is the saving and efficacious use of the Word of God, Romans 10, "If thou confess with thy mouth that Jesus is Lord, and believe with thy heart that God hath raised Him up from the dead, thou shalt be saved"; and again, "The end of the law is Christ, unto righteousness to every one that believeth"; and, Romans 1, "The just shall live by his faith." The Word of God cannot be received and cherished by any works whatever, but only by faith. Hence it is clear that, as the soul needs only the Word for its life and righteousness, so it is justified by faith alone and not by any works; for if it could be justified by anything else, it would not need the Word, and therefore it would not need faith. But this faith cannot at all exist in connection with works, that is to say, if you at the same time claim to be justified by works, whatever their character; for that would be to halt between two sides, to wor-

ship Baal and to kiss the hand, which, as Job says, is a very great iniquity.... When you have learned this, you will know that you need Christ, Who suffered and rose again for you, that, believing in Him, you may through this faith become a new man, in that all your sins are forgiven, and you are justified by the merits of another, namely, of Christ alone.

Since, therefore, this faith can rule only in the inward man, as Romans 10 says, "With the heart we believe unto righteousness"; and since faith alone justifies, it is clear that the inward man cannot be justified, made free and be saved by any outward work or dealing whatsoever, and that works, whatever their character, have nothing to do with this inward man.... Wherefore it ought to be the first concern of every Christian to lay aside all trust in works, and more and more to strengthen faith alone, and through faith to grow in the knowledge, not of works, but of Christ Jesus.

Should you ask, how it comes that faith alone justifies and without works offers us such a treasury of great benefits, when so many works, ceremonies and laws are prescribed in the Scriptures, I answer: First of all, remember what has been said: faith alone, without works, justifies, makes free and saves, as we shall later make still more clear. Here we must point out that all the Scriptures of God are divided into two parts —commands and promises. The commands indeed teach things that are good, but the things taught are not done as soon as taught; for the commands show us what we ought to do, but do not give us the power to do it; they are intended to teach a man to know himself, that through them he may recognize his inability to do good and may despair of his powers. That is why they are called and are the Old Testament....

But when a man through the commands has learned to know his weakness, and has become troubled as to how he may satisfy the law, since the law must be fulfilled so that not a jot or tittle shall perish, otherwise man will be condemned without hope; then, being truly humbled and reduced to nothing in his own eyes, he finds in himself no means of justification and salvation. Here the second part of the Scriptures stands ready—the promises of God, which declare the glory of God and say, "If you wish to fulfil the law, and not to covet, as the law demands, come, believe in Christ, in Whom grace, righteousness, peace, liberty and all things are promised you; if you believe you shall have all, if you believe not you shall lack all." For what is impossible for you in all the works of the law, many as they are, but all useless, you will accomplish in a short and easy way through faith. For God our Father has made all things depend on faith, so that whoever has faith, shall have all, and whoever has it not, shall have nothing. "For He has concluded all under unbelief, that He might have mercy on all," Romans 11. Thus the promises of God give what the commands of God ask, and fulfil what the law prescribes, that all things may be of God alone, both the commands and the fulfilling of the commands. He alone commands, He also alone fulfils. Therefore the promises of God belong to the New Testament, nay, they are the New Testament. . . .

No work can cling to the Word of God nor be in the soul; in the soul faith alone and the Word have sway. As the Word is, so it makes the soul, as heated iron glows like fire because of the union of fire with it. It is clear then that a Christian man has in his faith all that he needs, and needs no works to justify him. And if he has no need of works, neither does he need the law; and if he has no need of the law, surely he is free from the law, and it is true, "The law is not made for a righteous man." And this is that Christian liberty, even our faith, which does not indeed cause us to live in idleness or in wickedness, but makes the law and works unnecessary for any man's righteousness and salvation.

This is the first power of faith. Let us now examine the second also. For it is a further function of faith, that whom it trusts it also honors with the most reverent and high regard, since it considers him truthful and trustworthy. . . . So when the soul firmly trusts God's promises, it regards Him as truthful and righteous, than which nothing more excellent can be ascribed to God. This is the very highest worship of God. . . . Then

the soul consents to all His will, then it hallows His name and suffers itself to be dealt with according to God's good pleasure, because, clinging to God's promises, it does not doubt that He, Who is true, just and wise, will do, dispose and provide all things well. And is not such a soul, by this faith, in all things most obedient to God? . . .

The third incomparable benefit of faith is this, that it unites the soul with Christ as a bride is united with her bridegroom. And by this mystery, as the Apostle teaches, Christ and the soul become one flesh. . . .

Who can fully appreciate what this royal marriage means? Who can understand the riches of the glory of this grace? Here this rich and godly Bridegroom Christ marries this poor, wicked harlot, redeems her from all her evil and adorns her with all His good. It is now impossible that her sins should destroy her, since they are laid upon Christ and swallowed up in Him, and she has that righteousness in Christ her husband of which she may boast as of her own, and which she can confidently set against all her sins in the face of death and hell. . . .

Just as Christ by his birthright obtained these two prerogatives (priesthood and kingship), so He imparts them to and shares them with every one who believes on Him according to the law of the aforesaid marriage, by which the wife owns whatever belongs to the husband. Hence we are all priests and kings in Christ, as many as believe on Christ, as I Pet. 2 says, "Ye are a chosen generation, a peculiar people, a royal priesthood and priestly kingdom, that ye should show forth the virtues of Him Who hath called you out of darkness into His marvelous light. . . ."

Not only are we the freest of kings, we are also priests forever, which is far more excellent than being kings, because as priests we are worthy to appear before God to pray for others and to teach one another the things of God. For these are the functions of priests, and cannot be granted to any unbeliever. Thus Christ has obtained for us, if we believe on Him, that we are not only His brethren, co-heirs and fellow-kings with Him, but also fellow-priests with Him, who may boldly come into the presence of God in the spirit of faith. . . .

A Christian man is free from all things and over all things, so that he needs no works to make him righteous and to save him, since faith alone confers all these abundantly. But should he grow so foolish as to presume to become righteous by means of some good work, he would on the instant lose faith and all its benefits: a foolishness aptly illustrated in the fable of the dog who runs along a stream with a piece of meat in his mouth, and, deceived by the reflection of the meat in the water, opens his mouth to snap at it, and so loses both the meat and the reflection.

You will ask, "If all who are in the Church are priests, how do those whom we now call priests differ from laymen?" I answer: "Injustice is done those words, 'priest,' 'cleric,' 'spiritual,' 'ecclesiastic,' when they are transferred from all other Christians to those few who are now by a mischievous usage called 'ecclesiastics.' For Holy Scripture makes no distinction between them, except that it gives the name 'ministers,' 'servants,' 'stewards,' to those who are now proudly called popes, bishops, and lords and who should by the ministry of the Word serve others and teach them the faith of Christ and the liberty of believers. For although we are all equally priests, yet we cannot all publicly minister and teach, nor ought we if we could."

But that stewardship has now been developed into so great a pomp of power and so terrible a tyranny, that no heathen empire or earthly power can be compared with it, just as if laymen were not also Christians. Through this perversion the knowledge of Christian grace, faith, liberty and of Christ Himself has altogether perished, and its place has been taken by an unbearable bondage of human words and laws....

Now let us turn to the second part, to the outward man. Here we shall answer all those who, misled by the word "faith" and by all that has been said, now say: "If faith does all things and is alone sufficient unto righteousness, why then are good works commanded? We will take our ease and do no works, and be content with faith." I answer, Not so, ye wicked men, not so. That would indeed be proper, if we were wholly inward and perfectly spiritual men; but such we shall be only at the last day, the day of the resurrection of the dead. As long as we live in the flesh we only begin and make some progress in that which shall be perfected in the future life....

Although, as I have said, a man is abundantly justified by faith inwardly, in his spirit, and so has all that he ought to have, except in so far as this faith and riches must grow from day to day even unto the future life: yet he remains in this mortal life on earth, and in this life he must needs govern his own body and have dealings with men. Here the works begin; here a man cannot take his ease; here he must, indeed, take care to discipline his body by fastings, watchings, labors and other reasonable discipline, and to make it subject to the spirit so that it will obey and conform to the inward man and to faith, and not revolt against faith and hinder the inward man, as it is the body's nature to do if it be not held in check. For the inward man, who by faith is created in the likeness of God, is both joyful and happy because of Christ in Whom so many benefits are conferred upon him, and therefore it is his one occupation to serve God joyfully and for naught, in love that is not constrained.

In doing these works, however, we must not think that a man is justified before God by them: for that erroneous opinion faith, which alone is righteousness before God, cannot endure; but we must think that these works reduce the body to subjection and purify it of its evil lusts, and our whole purpose is to be directed only toward the driving out of lusts. For since by faith the soul is cleansed and made a lover of God, it desires that all things, and especially its own body, shall be as pure as itself, so that all things may join with it in loving and praising God. Hence a man cannot be idle, because the need of his body drives him and he is compelled to do many good works to reduce it to subjection. Nevertheless the works themselves do not justify him before God, but he does the works out of spontaneous love in obedience to God, and considers nothing except the approval of God, Whom he would in all things most scrupulously obey.

In this way every one will easily be able to learn for himself the limit and discretion, as they say, of his bodily castigations: for he will fast, watch and labor as much as he finds sufficient to repress the lasciviousness and lust of his body. But they who presume to be justified by works do not regard the mortifying of the lusts, but only the works themselves, and think that if only they have done as many and as great works as are possible, they have done well, and have become righteousness; at times they even addle their brains and destroy, or at least render useless, their natural strength with their works. This is the height of folly, and utter ignorance of Christian life and faith, that a man should seek to be justified and saved by works and without faith.

.   .   .   .   :

But none of these things does a man need for his righteousness and salvation. Therefore, in all his works he should be guided by this thought and look to this one thing alone, that he may serve and benefit others in all that he does, having regard to nothing except the need and the advantage of his neighbor. Thus, the Apostle commands us to work with our hands that we may give to him who is in need, although he might have said that we should work to support ourselves. And this is what makes it a Christian work to care for the body, that through its health and comfort we may be able to work, to acquire and to lay by funds with which to aid those who are in need, that in this way the strong member may serve the weaker, and we may be sons of God, each caring for and working for the other, bearing one another's burdens, and so fulfilling the law of Christ. Lo, this is a truly Christian life, here faith is truly effectual through love; that is, it issues in works of the freest service cheerfully and lovingly done, with which a man willingly serves another without hope of reward, and for himself is satisfied with the fullness and wealth of his faith. . . .

Although the Christian is thus free from all works, he ought in this liberty to empty himself, to take upon himself the form of a servant, to be made in the likeness of men, to be found in fashion as a man, and to serve, help and in every way deal with his neighbor as he sees that God through Christ has dealt and still deals with himself. And this he should do freely, having regard to nothing except the divine approval. He ought to think: "Though I am an unworthy and condemned man, my God has given me in Christ all the riches of righteousness and salvation without any merit on my part, out of pure, free mercy, so that henceforth I need nothing whatever except faith which believes that this is true. Why should I not therefore freely, joyfully, with all my heart, and with an eager will, do all things which I know are pleasing and acceptable to such a Father, Who has overwhelmed with His inestimable riches? I will therefore give myself as a Christ to my neighbor, just as Christ offered Himself to me; I will do nothing in this life except what I see is necessary, profitable and salutary to my neighbor, since through faith I have an abundance of all good things in Christ."

Lo, thus from faith flow forth love and joy in the Lord, and from love a joyful, willing and free mind that serves one's neighbor willingly and takes no account of gratitude or ingratitude, of praise or blame, of gain or loss. For a man does not serve that he may put men under obligations, he does not distinguish between friends and enemies, nor does he anticipate their thankfulness or unthankfulness; but most freely and most willingly he spends himself and all that he has, whether he waste all on the thankless or whether he gain a reward. For as his Father does, distributing all things to all men richly and freely, causing His sun to rise upon the good and upon the evil, so also the son does all things and suffers all things with that freely bestowing joy which is his delight when through Christ he sees it in God, the dispenser of such great benefits.

Therefore, if we recognize the great and precious things which are given us, as Paul says, there will be shed abroad in our hearts by the Holy Ghost the love which makes us free, joyful, almighty workers and conquerors over all tribulations, servants of our neighbors and yet lords of all. But for those who do not recognize the gifts bestowed upon them through Christ, Christ has been born in vain; they go their way with their works, and shall never come to taste or to feel those things. Just as our neighbor is in need and lacks that in which we abound, so we also have been in need before God and have lacked His mercy. Hence, as our heavenly Father has in Christ freely come to our help, we also ought freely to help our neighbor through our body and its works, and each should become as it were a Christ to the other, that we may be Christs to one another and Christ may be the same in all; that is, that we may be truly Christians.

. . . . .

We conclude, therefore, that a Christian man lives not in himself, but in Christ and in his neighbor. Otherwise he is not a Christian. He lives in Christ through faith, in his neighbor through love; by faith he is caught up beyond himself into God, by love he sinks down beneath himself into his neighbor; yet he always remains in God and in His love.

Liberty is spiritual, and makes our hearts free from all sins, laws and mandates. This liberty may Christ grant us both to understand and to preserve.   Amen.

I-9. Woodcut of Martin Luther, 1520.

7. *Luther's Journey to Worms*

In 1521, the newly elected Holy Roman Emperor, Charles V, summoned Luther to give an account of his position before the Diet of Worms. Although he had letters of safe-conduct from the Emperor and from various princes, Luther did not feel safe. His journey to Worms was, in fact, akin to the triumphal procession of a national hero, but fear and tension were also present, as he indicates in his own account of the journey. M. Michelet, *The Life of Luther Written by Himself,* trans. W. Hazlitt (London, 1898).

The herald summoned me on the Tuesday in Holy Week, and brought me safeconducts from the Emperor, and from several princes. On the very next day, Wednesday, those safe-conducts were, in effect, violated at Worms, where they condemned and burned my writings. News of this reached me when I was at Wittenberg. In fact, the condemnation had already been published in every town, so that the herald himself asked me whether I still intended to go to Worms. Though, in truth I was physically afraid and trembling, I replied to him: "I will repair thither, though I should find there as many devils as there are tiles on the house tops." When I arrived at Oppenheim, near Worms, Master Bucer came to see me, and tried to discourage me from entering the city. He told me that Glapion, the Emperor's confessor, had been to see him, and had begged him to warn me not to go to Worms, for, if I did, I should be burned. [The trip required fifteen days, April 2-16.]

8. *At the Diet of Worms*

On April 17, 1521, Luther appeared before Emperor Charles and the Diet of Worms. Johann Eck, an official of Trier, asked him if he would acknowledge the books on a nearby table and whether or not he would recant. Inasmuch as some of his writings concerned Scripture, Luther asked for time to consider his answer. The next day he again appeared before the august body, and gave his famous "Here I Stand" speech. *The Life and Letters of Martin Luther,* trans. Preserved Smith (New York: Houghton Mifflin Company, 1911). Reprinted by permission of Priscilla Robertson. Cf. *Kritische Gesamtausgabe der Werke Luthers,* VII, 832 ff.

ECK: His Imperial Majesty has assigned this time to you, Martin Luther, to answer for the books which you yesterday openly acknowledged to be yours. You asked time to deliberate on the question whether you would take back part of what you had said or would stand by all of it. You did not deserve this respite, which has now come to an end, for you knew long before why you were summoned. And every one—especially a professor of theology—ought to be so certain of his faith that whenever questioned about it he can give a sure and positive answer. Now at last reply to the demand of his Majesty, whose clemency you have experienced in obtaining time to deliberate. Do you wish to defend all of your books or to retract part of them?

LUTHER (As he later recalled the words which he spoke first in German and then in Latin): Most Serene Emperor, Most Illustrious Princes, Most Clement Lords! At the time fixed yesterday I obediently appear, begging for the mercy of God, that your Most Serene Majesty and your Illustrious Lordships may deign to hear this cause, which I hope may be called the cause of justice and truth, with clemency; and if, by my inexperience, I should fail to give any one the titles due him, or should sin against the etiquette of the court, please forgive me, as a man who has lived not in courts but in monastic nooks, one who can say nothing for himself but that he has hitherto tried to teach and to write with a sincere mind and single eye to the glory of God and the edification of Christians.

Most Serene Emperor, Most Illustrious Princes! Two questions were asked me yesterday. To the first, whether I would recognize that the books published under my name were mine, I gave a plain answer, to which I hold and will hold forever, namely, that the books are mine, as I published them, unless perchance it may have happened that the guile or meddlesome wisdom of my opponents has changed something in them. For I only recognize what has been written by myself alone, and not the interpretation added by another.

In reply to the second question I beg your Most Sacred Majesty and your Lordships to be pleased to consider that all my books are not of the same kind.

In some I have treated piety, faith, and morals so simply and evangelically that my adversaries themselves are forced to confess that these books are useful, innocent, and worthy to be read by Christians. Even the bull, though fierce and cruel, states that some things in my books are harmless, although it condemns them by a judgment simply monstrous. If, therefore, I should undertake to recant these, would it not happen that I alone of all men should damn the truth which all, friends and enemies alike, confess?

The second class of my works inveighs against the papacy as against that which both by precept and example has laid waste all Christendom, body and soul. No one can deny or dissemble this fact, since general complaints witness that the consciences of all believers are snared, harassed, and tormented by the laws of the Pope and the doctrines of men, and especially that the goods of this famous German nation have been and are devoured in numerous and ignoble ways. Yet the Canon Law provides (e.g., distinctions IX and XXV, questions 1 and 2) that the laws and doctrines of the Pope contrary to the Gospel and the Fathers are to be held erroneous and rejected. If, therefore, I should withdraw these books, I would add strength to tyranny and open windows and doors to their impiety, which would then flourish and burgeon more freely than it ever dared before. It would come to pass that their wickedness would go unpunished, and therefore would become more licentious on account of my recantation, and their government of the people, thus confirmed and established, would become intolerable, especially if they could boast that I had recanted with the full authority of your Sacred and Most Serene Majesty and of the whole Roman Empire. Good God! In that case I would be the tool of iniquity and tyranny.

In a third sort of books I have written against some private individuals who tried to defend the Roman tyranny and tear down my pious doctrine. In these I confess I was more bitter than is becoming to a minister of religion. For I do not pose as a saint, nor do I discuss my life but the doctrine of Christ. Yet neither is it right for me to recant what I have said in these, for then tyranny and impiety would rage and reign against the people of God more violently than ever by reason of my acquiescence.

As I am a man and not God, I wish to claim no other defense for my doctrine than that which the Lord Jesus put forward when he was questioned before Annas and smitten by a servant: he then said: If I have spoken evil, bear witness of the evil. If the Lord himself, who knew that he could not err, did not scorn to hear testimony against his doctrine from a miserable servant, how much more should I, the dregs of men, who can do nothing but err, seek and hope that some one should bear witness against my doctrine. I therefore beg by God's mercy that if your Majesty or your illustrious Lordships, from the highest to the lowest, can do it, you should bear witness and convict me of error and conquer me by proofs drawn from the gospels or the prophets, for I am most ready to be instructed and when convinced will be the first to throw my books into the fire.

From this I think it is sufficiently clear that I have carefully considered and weighed the discords, perils, emulation, and dissension excited by my teaching, concerning which I was gravely and urgently admonished yesterday. To me the happiest side of the whole affair is that the Word of God is made the object of emulation and dissent. For this is the course, the fate, and the result of the Word of God, as Christ says: "I am come not to send peace but a sword, to set a man against his father and a daughter against her mother." We must consider that our God is wonderful and terrible in his counsels. If we should begin to heal our dissensions by damning the Word of God, we should only turn loose an intolerable deluge of woes. Let us take care that the rule of this excellent youth, Prince Charles (in whom, next to God, there is much hope), does not begin inauspiciously. For I could show by many examples drawn from Scripture that when Pharaoh and the king of Babylon and the kings of Israel thought to pacify and strengthen their kingdoms by their own wisdom, they really only ruined themselves. For he taketh the wise in their own craftiness

and removeth mountains and they know it not. We must fear God. I do not say this as though your Lordships needed either my teaching or my admonition, but because I could not shirk the duty I owed Germany. With these words I commend myself to your Majesty and your Lordships, humbly begging that you will not let my enemies make me hateful to you without cause. I have spoken.

ECK (with threatening mien): Luther, you have not answered to the point. You ought not to call in question what has been decided and condemned by councils. Therefore I beg you to give a simple, unsophisticated answer without horns (non cornutum). Will you recant or not?

LUTHER: Since your Majesty and your Lordships ask for a plain answer, I will give you one without either horns or teeth. Unless I am convicted by Scripture or by right reason (for I trust neither in popes nor in councils, since they have often erred and contradicted themselves)—unless I am thus convinced, I am bound by the texts of the Bible, my conscience is captive to the Word of God, I neither can nor will recant anything, since it is neither right nor safe to act against conscience. God help me. Amen.

9. *Charles' Reaction at Worms*

Emperor Charles was shocked by Luther's boldness and drew up a statement in which he declared that he would stake his life and dominions to preserve Catholicism from such heretics. On April 26, in the midst of the general excitement and political maneuvering, Luther left Worms, and on May 4 was "captured" by bandits and taken to the Wartburg. Then, after the Elector of Saxony and other supporters of Luther had left Worms, Charles drafted an edict, dated May 8 but actually signed May 26, in which he condemned Luther's doctrine as a cesspool of heresies. J. H. Robinson, *Readings in European History*, II (Boston: Ginn & Company, 1906). Translated also in *Crozer Historical Leaflets*, No. 3, with changes (St. Louis: Concordia Publishing House, 1881-1910). German version in Walch, *Luthers Werke*, Vol. XV, cols. 2264 ff.

CHARLES V'S SPEECH

My predecessors, the most Christian Emperors of the German race, the Austrian archdukes, and dukes of Burgundy, were truest sons of the Catholic Church until they died, defending and extending their belief to the glory of God, the propagation of the

Sieben Köpffe Martini Luthers
Vom Hochwirdigen Sacrament des Altars / Durch
Doctor Jo. Cocleus.

I-10. Woodcut Cartoon Showing Martin Luther with Seven Heads. *Sixteenth century leaflet.*

faith, and the salvation of their souls. Behind them they have left the holy Catholic rites so that I should live and die in them. Until now I have lived with the help of God as a Christian Emperor. It is my privilege to maintain what my forefathers established at Constance and other councils.

A single monk, led astray by private judgment, has set himself against the faith held by all Christians for more than a thousand years. He believes that all Christians up to now have erred. Therefore, I have resolved to stake upon this cause all my dominions, my friends, my body and blood, my life and soul.

We are sprung from the holy German nation and appointed by peculiar privilege to be defenders of the faith. It would be disgraceful, as well as an eternal stain upon us graceful, as well as an eternal stain upon us

and our posterity, if in this day and age not only heresy but also the very suspicion of it were to result from our neglect.

After Luther's stiff-necked reply in my presence yesterday, I am now sorry that I have so long delayed moving against him and his false doctrines. I have made up my mind never again, under any circumstances, to listen to him. Under protection of his safe-conduct he shall be escorted to his home. But he is forbidden to preach and to seduce men with his evil beliefs and incite them to rebellion. I warn you to give witness to your beliefs as good Christians and in consonance with your vows.

EDICT OF THE DIET OF WORMS, MAY, 1521

1. [List of titles of Charles V.]

2. Most reverend, honorable, and illustrious friends and relatives, devoted and loyal: As it pertains to our office of Roman emperor, not only to enlarge the bounds of the Holy Roman Empire, which our fathers of the German nation founded for the defense of the Holy Roman and Catholic Church, subduing unbelievers by the sword, through the divine grace, with much shedding of blood, but also, adhering to the rule hitherto observed by the Holy Roman Church, to take care that no stain or suspicion of heresy should contaminate our holy faith within the Roman Empire, or, if heresy had already begun, to extirpate it with all necessary diligence, prudence, and discretion, as the case might demand; ...

4. Whereas, certain heresies have sprung up in the German nation within the last three years, which were formerly condemned by the holy councils and papal decrees, with the consent of the whole Church, and are now drawn anew from hell, should we permit them to become more deeply rooted, or, by our negligence, tolerate and bear with them, our conscience would be greatly burdened, and the future glory of our name would be covered by a dark cloud in the auspicious beginnings of our reign.

5. Since now without doubt it is plain to you all how far these errors and heresies depart from the Christian way, which a certain Martin Luther, of the Augustinian order,

has sought violently and virulently to introduce and disseminate within the Christian religion and its established order, especially in the German nation, which is renowned as a perpetual destroyer of all unbelief and heresy; so that, unless it is speedily prevented, the whole German nation, and later all other nations, will be infected by this same disorder, and mighty dissolution and pitiable downfall of good morals, and of the peace and the Christian faith, will result.

14. But all the other innumerable wickednesses of Luther must, for brevity's sake, remain unreckoned. This fellow appears to be not so much a man as the wicked demon in the form of a man and under a monk's cowl. He has collected many heresies of the worst heretics, long since condemned and forgotten, together with some newly invented ones, in one stinking pool, under pretext of preaching faith, which he extols with so great industry in order that he may ruin the true and genuine faith, and under the name and appearance of evangelical doctrine overturn and destroy all evangelical peace and love, as well as all righteous order and the most excellent hierarchy of the Church. . . .

25. Accordingly, in view of all these considerations and the fact that Martin Luther still persists obstinately and perversely in maintaining his heretical opinions, and consequently all pious and God-fearing persons abominate and abhor him as one mad or possessed by a demon, . . . we have declared and made known that the said Martin Luther shall hereafter be held and esteemed by each and all of us as a limb cut off from the Church of God, an obstinate schismatic and manifest heretic.

27. And we publicly attest by these letters that we order and command each and all of you, as you owe fidelity to us and the Holy Empire, and would escape the penalties of the crime of treason, and the ban and over-ban of the Empire, and the forfeiture of all regalia, fiefs, privileges, and immunities, which up to this time you have in any way obtained from our predecessors, ourself, and the Holy Empire; commanding, we say, in the name of the Roman and imperial majesty, we strictly order that immediately after the expiration of the appointed twenty days, terminating on the fourteenth day of May, you shall refuse to give the aforesaid Martin Luther hospitality, lodging, food, or drink; neither shall any one, by word or deed, secretly or openly, succor or assist him by counsel or help; but in whatever place you meet him, you shall proceed against him; if you have sufficient force, you shall take him prisoner and keep him in close custody; you shall deliver him, or cause him to be delivered, to us or at least let us know where he may be captured. In the meanwhile you shall keep him closely imprisoned until you receive notice from us what further to do, according to the direction of the laws. And for such holy and pious work we will indemnify you for your trouble and expense.

28. In like manner you shall proceed against his friends, adherents, patrons, maintainers, abettors, sympathizers, emulators, and followers. And the property of these, whether personal or real, you shall, in virtue of the sacred ordinances and of our imperial ban and over-ban, treat in this way; namely, you shall attack and overthrow its possessors and wrest their property from them and transfer it to your own custody and uses; and no one shall hinder or impede these measures, unless the owner shall abandon his unrighteous way and secure papal absolution.

29. Consequently we command you, each and all, under the penalties already prescribed, that henceforth no one shall dare to buy, sell, read, preserve, copy, print, or cause to be copied or printed, any books of the aforesaid Martin Luther, condemned by our holy father the pope as aforesaid, or any other writings in German or Latin hitherto composed by him, since they are foul, harmful, suspected, and published by a notorious and stiff-necked heretic. Neither shall any dare to approve his opinions, nor to proclaim, defend, or assert them, in any other way that human ingenuity can invent, notwithstanding he may have put some good in them to deceive the simple man. . . .

10. The Eight Wittenberg Sermons

The occasion of the eight Wittenberg sermons was the general disorder that had come to Wittenberg while Luther was at the Wartburg during the latter part of 1521 and the early part of 1522. In the name of Christian liberty, Carlstadt, Zwilling, and the Zwickau prophets had stirred the people to rioting, image-breaking, and picture-burning. At the risk of his life, Luther left his hiding place, and three days after arriving at Wittenberg on Thursday, March 6, 1522, preached the first of eight sermons on successive days in the parish church. His theme: Faith alone is essential to Christian living, and faith produces works of love and order. The rioting ceased. Portions of the second sermon are given below. *Works of Martin Luther*, II.

THE SECOND SERMON

Dear Friends: You heard yesterday the characteristics of a Christian man, how his whole life is faith and love. Faith is directed toward God, love toward man and one's neighbor, and consists in such love and service for him as we have received from God without our work and merit. Thus there are two things: the one, which is the most needful, and which must be done in one way and no other; the other, which is a matter of choice and not of necessity, which may be kept or not, without endangering faith or incurring hell. In both, love must deal with our neighbor in the same manner as God has dealt with us; it must walk the straight road, straying neither to the left nor to the right. In the things which are "musts" and are matters of necessity, such as believing in Christ, love nevertheless never uses force or undue constraint. Thus the mass is an evil thing, and God is displeased with it, because it is performed as a sacrifice and work of merit. Therefore it must be abolished. Here there is no room for question, just as little as if you should ask whether you should pray to God. Here we are entirely agreed: the private mass must be abolished, as I have said in my writings. And I heartily wish it would be abolished everywhere and only the evangelical mass for all the people retained. Yet Christian love should not employ harshness here nor force the matter. It should be preached and taught with tongue and pen, that to hold mass in such a manner is a sin, but no one should be dragged away from it by force. The matter should be left to God; His word should do the work alone, without our work. Why? Because it is not in my power to fashion the hearts of men as the potter moulds the clay, and to do with them as I please. I can get no farther than to men's ears; their hearts I cannot reach. And since I cannot pour faith into their hearts, I cannot, nor should I, force any one to have faith. That is God's work alone, who causes faith to live in the heart. Therefore we should give free course to the Word, and not add our works to it. We have the *jus verbi* [right to speak], but not the *executio* [power to do]; we should preach the Word, but the consequences must be left to God's own good pleasure.

Now if I should rush in and abolish the mass by force, there are many who would be compelled to consent to it and yet not know their own minds, but say: I do not know if it is right or wrong, I do not know where I stand, I was compelled by force to submit to the majority. And this forcing and commanding results in a mere mockery, an external show, a fool's play, man-made ordinances, sham-saints and hypocrites. For where the heart is not good, I care nothing at all for the work. We must first win the hearts of the people. And that is done when I teach only the Word of God, preach the Gospel and say: "Dear lords or pastors, desist from holding the mass, it is not right, you are sinning when you do it; I cannot refrain from telling you this." But I would not make it an ordinance for them, nor urge a general law; he who would follow me could do so, and he who refused would remain without. In the latter case the Word would sink into the heart and perform its work. Thus he would become convinced and acknowledge his error, and fall away from the mass; to-morrow another would do the same, and thus God would accomplish more with His Word than if you and I would forge into one all power and authority. For if you have won the heart, you have won the whole man—and the mass must finally fall of its own weight and come to an end. And if the hearts and minds of all men are united in the purpose—abolish the mass; but if all are not heart and soul for its abolishment—leave it in God's hands, I beseech you, otherwise the result will not be good. Not, indeed, that I would again set up the mass; I let it lie in God's name. Faith

34

must not be chained and imprisoned, nor bound by an ordinance to any work. This is the principle by which you must be governed. For I am sure you will not be able to carry out your plans, and if you should carry them out with such general laws, then I will recant all the things that I have written and preached, and I will not support you, and therefore I ask you plainly: What harm can the mass do to you? You have your faith, pure and strong, toward God, and the mass cannot hurt you.

Love, therefore, demands that you have compassion on the weak, as all the apostles had. Once, when Paul came to Athens, a mighty city, he found in the temple many altars, and he went from one to the other and looked at them all, but did not touch any one of them even with his foot. But he stood in the midst of the market-place and said they were all idolatrous works, and begged the people to forsake them; yet he did not destroy one of them by force. When the word took hold of their hearts, they forsook their idols of their own accord, and in consequence idolatry fell of itself. Now, if I had seen that they held mass, I would have preached and admonished them concerning it. Had they heeded my admonition, they would have been won; if not, I would nevertheless not have torn them from it by the hair or employed any force, but simply allowed the Word to act, while I prayed for them. For the Word created heaven and earth and all things; the Word must do this thing, and not we poor sinners.

In conclusion: I will preach it, teach it, write it, but I will constrain no man by force, for faith must come freely without compulsion. Take myself as an example. I have opposed the indulgences and all the papists, but never by force. I simply taught, preached, and wrote God's Word; otherwise I did nothing. And then while I slept, or drank Wittenberg beer with my Philip [Melanchthon] and with Amsdorf, the Word so greatly weakened the papacy, that never a prince or emperor inflicted such damage upon it. I did nothing; the Word did it all. Had I desired to foment trouble, I could have brought great bloodshed upon Germany. Yea, I could have

started such a little game at Worms that even the emperor would not have been safe. But what would it have been? A fool's play. I did nothing; I left it to the Word. What do you suppose is Satan's thought, when an effort is made to do things by violence? He sits back in hell and thinks: How fine a game these fools will make for me! But it brings him distress when we only spread the Word, and let it alone do the work. For it is almighty and takes captive the hearts, and if the hearts are captured the evil work will fall of itself. . . .

.   .   .   .   .

11. The Twelve Articles of the Peasants, March, 1525

For full translations see B. J. Kidd, *Documents Illustrative of the Continental Reformation*, No. 83 (Oxford: Clarendon Press, 1911), and *Translations and Reprints from the Original Sources of European History*, Vol. II, No. 6 (Philadelphia: University of Pennsylvania Press, 1905).

[The peasants appealed to Scripture to justify their revolt, and vowed that they

I-11. Sign of the Fish. *A prophecy of the Peasants' War. Woodcut published in Nürnberg, 1523.*

would withdraw their demands if they were proved to be contrary to the word of God. They demanded:

1. The right to choose and depose their own pastors.

2. That the grain tithe be used for the remuneration of the pastor and relief of the poor, inasmuch as it is commanded in Scripture, and that the tithe on cattle, an invention of man, be withdrawn.

3. Release from serfdom, inasmuch as men are free as Christians.

4. The privilege of hunting and fishing on those lands that do not rightfully belong to overlords.

5. Communal ownership of forests so that poor people may gather firewood and have access to lumber.

6. Relief from the excessive services demanded of peasants.

7. Payment for services not previously agreed upon by the lords and peasants.

8. Redress of excessive rents so that peasants may reap a return from their labors.

9. Judgment according to the old laws, not according to laws recently imposed.

10. The return of communal meadows and fields to the community, with reimbursement to those who may have purchased such lands.

11. The abolition of the Todfall or death tax (heriot) which places an unwarranted burden on widows and orphans.

12. The right in the future to present or withdraw demands in accordance with the Scriptures.]

12. Luther Replies to the Peasants

Before the peasants rose in arms, Luther in large measure sided with them. He called attention to faults on both sides and advised arbitration. The portion of his essay concerning the twelve articles is translated in T. M. Lindsay, *The Reformation* (Edinburgh: T. & T. Clark, 1882). Cf. *Dr. Martin Luthers Sämmtliche Werke* (Erlangen, 1826).

To the princes and proprietors: I might now make common cause with the peasants against you, who impute this insurrection to the Gospel and to my teaching; whereas I have never ceased to enjoin obedience to authority, even to authority so tyrannical and intolerable as yours. But I will not envenom the wound; therefore, my lords, whether friendly or hostile to me, do not despise either the advice of a poor man, or this sedition; not that you ought to fear the insurgents, but fear God the Lord, who is incensed against you. He may punish you and turn every stone into a peasant, and then neither your cuirasses nor your strength would save you. Put then bounds to your exactions, pause in your hard tyranny, consider them as intoxicated, and treat them with kindness, that God may not kindle a fire throughout Germany which none will be able to extinguish. What you may perhaps lose will be made good to you a hundredfold by peace.

Some of the twelve articles of the peasants are so equitable that they dishonor you before God and the world; they cover the princes with shame, as the 109th Psalm says. I should have yet graver things to tell you respecting the government of Germany, and I have addressed you in this cause in my book to the German nobility. But you have considered my words as wind, and therefore all these demands come now upon you. You must not refuse their demand as to choosing pastors who may preach to them the Gospel; the government has only to see that insurrection and rebellion be not preached; but there must be perfect liberty to preach the true Gospel as well as the false. The remaining articles, which regard the social state of the peasant are equally just. Government is not established for its own interest, nor to make the people subservient to caprice and evil passions, but for the interest of the people. Your exactions are intolerable; you take away from the peasant the fruit of his labor, in order to spend his money upon your finery and luxury. So much for you.

Now, as regards you, my dear friends, the peasants: You want the free preaching of the Gospel to be secured to you. God will assist your just cause if you follow up your work with conscience and justice. In that case you are sure to triumph in the end. Those of you who may fall in the struggle will be saved. But if you act otherwise you are lost, soul and body, even if you have success, and defeat the princes and lords. Do not believe the false prophets who have come among you, even if they invoke the holy name of the Gospel. They will call me a hypocrite, but I do not mind that. I wish to save the pious and honest men among you. I fear God and none else. Do you fear Him also, and use not His name in vain, that He may not punish you. Does not the Word of God say: "He who takes the sword, shall perish by the sword"; and, "Let every soul be subject to the higher powers"? You must not take justice into your own hands; that is also the prescription of the natural law. Do you not see that you put yourself in the wrong by rebellion? The government takes away part of what is yours, but you take away all in destroying fixed principles. Fix your eye on Christ in Gethsemane rebuking St. Peter for using the sword although in the defence of his Master; and on Christ on the cross praying for His persecutors. And has not His kingdom triumphed? Why have Pope and Emperor not been able to put me down? Why has the Gospel spread the more, the greater the effort they made to hinder and destroy it? Because I have never had recourse to force, but preached obedience even towards those who persecuted me, depending exclusively on God. But whatever you do, do not try to cover your enterprise by the cloak of the Gospel and the name of Christ. If war there must be, it will be a war of pagans, for Christians use other weapons: their General suffered the cross, and their triumph is humility: that is their chivalry. Pray, my dear friends, stop and consider before you proceed further. Your quotations from the Bible do not prove your case. . . .

You see you are both in the wrong, and are drawing the divine punishments upon you and upon your common country, Germany. My advice would be that arbitrators should be chosen, some from the nobility, and some from the towns. You both have to give up something: let the matter be settled equitably by human law.

13. Stab, Smite, Slay

Luther believed that the peasants' complaints were partially justified, but he would not identify their demands with the Gospel and he turned from tumult as if it were a mark of Antichrist. Luther became acutely aware of the widespread insurrection and potential violence when the revolt reached Thuringia and Saxony in April of 1525. On April 16, Weinsberg was stormed and its inhabitants massacred. Cloisters and castles became smoking embers. At Mühlhausen, Münzer called for slaughter in the name of God. Luther then called on the princes to restore order, even if they had to stab, smite, and slay as if they were among mad dogs. He wrote the following letter from Seeburg. in Mansfeld, after a journey which revealed the horrors of the uprising. Smith, *Life and Letters of Martin Luther.*

TO JOHN RÜHEL, COUNCILLOR OF THE COUNT OF MANSFELD, SEEBURG, MAY 4, 1525

Grace and peace in Christ. Honored and dear doctor and friend! I have been intending to answer your last tidings, recently shown me, here on my journey. First of all I beg you not to make our gracious lord, Count Albert, weak in this matter, but let him go on as he has begun, though it will only make the devil still angrier, so that he will rage more than ever through those limbs of Satan he has possessed. We have God's Word, which lies not but says, "He beareth not the sword in vain, etc.," so there is no doubt that his lordship has been ordained and commanded of God. His Grace will need the sword to punish the wicked as long as there are such sores in the body politic as now exist. Should the sword be struck out of his Grace's hand by force, we must suffer it, and give it back to God, who first gave it and can take it back how and when he will.

May his Grace also have a good conscience in case he should have to die for God's Word, for God has so ordered it, if he permits it; no one should leave off the good work until he is prevented by force, just as in battle no one should forego an advantage or leave off fighting until he is overcome.

If there were thousands more peasants than there are they would all be robbers and murderers, who take the sword with criminal intent to drive out lords, princes, and all else, and make a new order in the world for which they have from God neither command, right, power, nor injunction, as the lords now have to suppress them. They are faithless and perjured, and still worse they bring the Divine Word and Gospel to shame and dishonor, a most horrible sin. If God in his wrath really lets them accomplish their purpose, for which he has given them no command nor right, we must suffer it as we do other wickedness, but not acquiesce in it as if they did right. . . .

· · · · ·

[Luther's well-known pamphlet followed very shortly. But by May 15, the peasants were defeated at Frankenhausen. Münzer had led them to expect divine help, and instead they were wretchedly butchered. Münzer himself was taken and cruelly put to death. Luther's pamphlet abetted the carnage.]

In my former book (Exhortation to Peace) I dared not judge the peasants, since they asked to be instructed, and Christ says, "Judge not." But before I could look around they forget their request and betake themselves to violence—rob, rage, and act like mad dogs, whereby one may see what they had in their false minds, and that their pretence to speak in the name of the gospel in the Twelve Articles was a simple lie. They do mere devil's work, especially that Satan of Mühlhausen does nothing but rob, murder, and pour out blood.

[The peasants have deserved death for three reasons, Luther asserts: (1) because they have broken their oath of fealty; (2) for rioting and plundering; and (3) for having covered their terrible sins with the name of the gospel.]

Wherefore, my lords, free, save, help, and pity the poor people; stab, smite, and slay, all ye that can. If you die in battle you could never have a more blessed end, for you die obedient to God's Word in Romans 13, and in the service of love to free your neighbor from the hands of hell and the devil. I implore every one who can to avoid the peasants as he would the devil himself. I pray God will enlighten them and turn their hearts. But if they do not turn, I wish them no happiness forever more. . . . Let none think this too hard who considers how intolerable is rebellion.

LUTHER TO RÜHEL AT MANSFELD, MAY 23, 1525

It is pitiful that we have to be so cruel to the poor people, but what can we do? It is necessary and God wills it that fear may be brought on the people. Otherwise Satan brings forth mischief. God said: Who hath taken the sword shall perish by the sword. It is gratifying that their spirit be at last so plainly revealed, so that henceforth the peasants will know how wrong they were and perhaps leave off rioting, or at least do it less. Do not be troubled about the severity of their suppression, for it will profit many souls. . . .

14. Peasants' Revolt, 1525, An Eyewitness Account

Documents of German History, ed. Louis L. Snyder (New Jersey: Rutgers University Press, 1958). Originally from F. L. Baumann, *Quellen zur Geschichte des Bauernkriegs aus Rothenburg ob der Tauber* (Stuttgart, 1878), Chap. 139.

On Tuesday, March 21st, some thirty or forty peasants gathered together in a mob in Rothenburg, bought a kettledrum, and marched as many as four hundred.

The working classes in the town now begin to revolt. They refuse to obey the authorities and organize a committee of thirty-six to manage affairs.

March 24th: This evening between five and six o'clock someone knocked off the head of Christ's image on a crucifix and broke off the arms.

March 26th: Chrischainz, the baker, struck the missal from the priest's hand in the chapel of our Lady and chased the priest from mass.

The following Monday, while the priest was chanting "Adjuva nos, deus salutaris noster" at the service, Ernfried Kumpf spoke harshly to him, saying that if he wished to save himself he had best leave the altar. Kumpf then knocked the missal to the floor and drove the scholars from the choir.

On Tuesday night eight hundred peasants gathered together. Those who refused to come along were forced to do so.

On Friday there were as many as two thousand, camped near Neusitz. Messengers were sent into the town to present their demands. Meanwhile, representatives of the Emperor and the Swabian League arrived with the hope of making peace, but they rode away without accomplishing anything.

On this day Kueplein, during the sermon, threw the lighted oil lamps about the church. Some of the peasants came into Rothenburg and the nearby towns, plundering cupboards and cellars everywhere.

On Saturday the blind monk, Hans Rotfuchs, spoke contemptuously of the Holy Sacrament, saying that it was idolatry and heresy.

April 18th: There is a struggle between Kueplein and his followers, on the one hand, who seek to destroy a picture of the Virgin, and the pious old Christians, on the other, who want to protect it. Some of the antagonists draw knives.

April 19th: The peasants take three casks of wine from the priest at Scheckenpach and drink the wine.

April 20th: The women run up and down Hafengasse with forks and sticks, loudly declaring that they will plunder the priests' homes, but they are prevented.

April 26th: Lorenz Knobloch is cut to pieces by the peasants at Ostheim. Then they throw pieces of his body at one another. They accuse him of having been a traitor and say that he wanted to mislead them. He had said that he would not die until he had killed three priests, but, thank God, not one fell into his hands.

April 30th: The monasteries of Anhausen and Dinkelsbühl are plundered and burned in the night.

May 6th: Early in the morning the great bell rang three times, summoning the people to hear a message from Margrave Casimir. All were invited to take refuge in Rothenburg. The greater part refused. Some were noted by the Margrave's representative, and afterward lost their heads.

May 12th: The clergy is forced to take up arms like all the rest. All monks are compelled to lay aside their cowls and the nuns their veils.

May 21st: Certain Hohenlohe peasants burn their lord's castle.

On the next Monday Margrave Casimir subdues the peasants and begins to punish them.

I-12. Peasants Attacking Monks and Knights in 1525. *An old woodcut.*

Hans Krelein the older, priest at Wernitz, is beheaded with four peasants.

Seven have their fingers cut off.

At Kitzingen fifty-eight have their eyes put out and are forbidden to enter the town again.

On Friday before Whitsuntide the forces of the Swabian League slay four thousand peasants at Königshofen.

On Monday after Whitsuntide eight thousand peasants are killed by the troops of the League. In all these battles the League lost not over one hundred and fifty men.

June 17th: Vespers, complines, and matins are once more sung.

June 30th: The citizens of Rothenburg are summoned to the market place by a herald and surrounded by pikesmen. They are accused of deserting the Empire and joining the peasants. The names of a number of citizens are read off. They are beheaded on the spot. Their bodies are left on the market place all day.

July 1st: Fifteen more are beheaded, including the blind monk. All these died without confession or even the Last Sacrament. They did not even ask for it.

15. The Diet of Speier, 1529

The previous Diet of Speier, 1526, proved favorable for the Lutheran evangelicals. Threatened with a war with the French, troubles with the pope, and new advances of the Turks, the Emperor desired peace in Germany. He agreed to a recess decree in 1526, which recognized the need for a general council to settle religious differences, and also to a decree leaving each prince free to conduct religious matters as he saw fit, until a general council could be held. This meant the setting aside of the Edict of Worms, against Luther and his followers. At the second Diet of Speier, 1529, those agreements were summarily abrogated, bringing forth the evangelical protest. The Emperor's throne speech and the resolution of the majority prompted the evangelical protest from which the name "Protestant" is derived. Kidd, *Documents Illustrative of the Continental Reformation.* Cf. I. Ney, *Geschichte des Reichstages zu Speier* (Halle a.d.S.: Verein für Reformationsgeschichte, 1890).,

SPEECH FROM THE THRONE, MARCH 15, 1529

1.   Next, your aforesaid Imperial Majesty has no small grief and trouble that in the German nation, during your reign, such evil, grave, perilous, and pernicious doctrines and errors have arisen in our holy faith, and are now daily increasing more and more. Thereby not only (though this is the most important part of the matter) are the Christian and laudable laws, customs, and usages of the Church held in contempt and disgrace, to the reproach and dishonor of God our Maker; but also to that of your Imperial Majesty and the Empire. In particular, the German nation, its estates, subjects, and allies are thereby roused and inflamed to grievous and pitiful revolts, tumults, war, misery, and bloodshed; while your Majesty's edicts and mandates, together with the recesses of the Empire, are so little regarded, or rather in so many ways treated with such gross opposition and contempt, as that your Majesty is seriously displeased and in no mind (as indeed becomes the Head of Christendom) any further to tolerate or permit the same.

7.   And whereas in the Recess of the Diet of Speier, made in the . . . year 1526, an article was comprised saying that "the Electors, Princes, and Estates of the Empire, and the ambassadors of the same unanimously agreed and resolved, while waiting for the Council, with our subjects, in matters which the edict published by his Imperial Majesty at the Diet holden at Worms may concern, each one so to live, govern, and carry himself as he hopes and trusts to answer it to God and his Imperial Majesty, etc."; and whereas, from the same article, as hitherto understood, expounded, and explained at their pleasure by several of the Estates of the Holy Empire, marvellous great trouble and misunderstanding has arisen against our holy Christian faith, as also against the Magistrates through the disobedience of their subjects, and much other disadvantage, your Imperial Majesty conceives no small astonishment thereat: and to the end that, for the future, the said article may be no further taken and expounded at every man's pleasure, and that the consequences, which hitherto have proved so disastrous to our holy faith, may be averted, your Imperial Majesty hereby repeals, revokes, and annuls the above-mentioned article contained in the aforesaid Recess, now as then, and then as now, all out of your own Imperial absolute power. . . .

THE RESOLUTION OF THE
MAJORITY, APRIL 7, 1529

5.   Whereas, moreover, the said article has since been by many drawn and expounded, under an entire misapprehension, to the excusing of all sorts of new doctrines and sects; therefore, to cut off such occasion and to avert further falling away . . . the Electors, Princes, and other Estates have resolved that those who have hitherto held to the aforesaid Imperial Edict (sc. of Worms) should continue to abide by the same till the coming Council, and hold their subjects thereto.

6.   That by the other Estates, with whom the other doctrine originated and with whom, to some degree, it cannot be abandoned without considerable tumult, trouble, and danger, all further innovation shall nevertheless be prevented till the coming Council, so far as is humanly possible.

7.   That, in particular, such doctrines and sects as deny the most worthy sacrament of

our Lord Jesus Christ's Body and Blood shall in no wise be tolerated by the holy Empire of the German Nation, nor be henceforth suffered . . . to preach in public: nor shall the celebration of the holy Mass be done away: nor shall any one, in places where the new doctrine has got the upper hand, be forbidden to celebrate or to hear Mass, nor be hindered or forced therefrom.

.　　.　　.　　.　　.

16. The Protest at Speier, 1529

Stunned by the imperial speech and the resolution of the majority to revoke the agreements made at the Diet of Speier, 1526, and sensing that their religious faith and political future were jeopardized, the evangelicals entered their famous protest, from which the name "Protestant" is derived. Vedder, *The Reformation in Germany*, appendix; also Walch, *Luthers Werke*, XVI, 266 ff.

Most illustrious King, most venerable, right honorable, noble, esteemed, gracious Lords, uncles, cousins, friends, and especially esteemed ones!

As we ourselves urged upon His Roman imperial Majesty, our most gracious Lord, and wrote in a friendly manner to your royal Highness, in most submissive obedience to his imperial Majesty and in friendly and humble obedience to your royal Highness, as well as for the good of general Christendom and the holy Empire, we have come hither to this Diet, and have now heard read the instructions, together with the authoritative letter in his imperial Majesty's name. Moreover, as we have also examined with diligence the Summons of this Diet in (the name of) his imperial Majesty, and we find that the affair has been settled by an embarrassing device, that the article in the decree of the previously held Diet concerning our holy Christian faith has been annulled, and another very troublesome article is to be set forth instead;

And whereas your royal Highness, and your other colleagues (having authority as his imperial Majesty), governors and commissioners, with the estates of the Empire, at the Diet formerly held at Speier unanimously agreed that pending a general Council or national assembly, each one should live, rule

and act regarding the clauses of the Edict of Worms as every one hopes and trusts to give account for his conduct before God and his imperial Majesty.

.　　.　　.　　.

Therefore, in consideration of this previously settled, written and sealed decree, as well as for the following well-founded reasons (which in part were sent in writing to your royal Highness and the esteemed ones on the 12th day of this April), we cannot and may not consent to the annulment of the aforesaid article, to which we unanimously agreed and which we are pledged to uphold, nor even to the supposed or intended moderation of the same, which yet is nothing of the sort.

.　　.　　.　　.

And if this third announcement of our evident grievances shall not be allowed by your imperial Highness, princes and others, then we herewith *protest* and testify openly before God, our sole Creator, Preserver, Redeemer and Saviour (who, as we mentioned before, alone searches and knows all hearts, and therefore will judge justly) likewise before all men and creatures, that we for ourselves, our subjects and in behalf of all, each and every one, consider null and void the entire transaction and the intended decree, which in the aforementioned or in other cases, is undertaken, agreed and passed, against God, his holy Word, all our soul's salvation and good conscience, likewise against the formerly announced decree of the Diet of Speier—(and we protest) not secretly, nor willingly, but for reasons above stated and others good and well-founded. This protest we are compelled to issue and to make a more thorough and true report to his imperial Majesty, our gracious Lord.

Done at Speier on the twentieth day of April, and in the 1529th year after the birth of Christ, our dear Lord and Saviour.

(*Signed*) John, Duke of Saxony, Elector
George, Margrave of Brandenburg
Ernest, Duke of Lüneberg
Philip, Landgrave of Hesse
Wolf, Prince of Anhalt

17. Augsburg Confession, 1530

Henry E. Jacobs, *Book of Concord* (Philadelphia: United Lutheran Publication House, 1882), 37 ff. Preface omitted.

I. CHIEF ARTICLES OF FAITH

Article I. Our Churches, with common consent, do teach, that the decree of the Council of Nicaea concerning the Unity of the Divine Essence and concerning the Three Persons, is true and to be believed without any doubting; that is to say, there is one Divine Essence which is called and which is God: eternal, without body, without parts, of infinite power, wisdom and goodness, the Maker and Preserver of all things, visible and invisible; and yet that there are three Persons, of the same essence and power, who also are co-eternal, the Father, the Son and the Holy Ghost, And the term "person" they use as the Fathers have used it, to signify, not a part or quality in another, but that which subsists of itself.

They condemn all heresies which have sprung up against this article, as the Manichaeans who assumed two principles (gods), one Good, and the other Evil; also the Valentinians, Arians, Eunomians, Mohammedans, and all such. They condemn also the Samosatenes, old and new, who contending that there is but one Person, sophistically and impiously argue that the Word and the Holy Ghost are not distinct Persons, but that "Word" signifies a spoken word, and "Spirit" (Ghost) signifies motion created in things.

Article II. Also they teach, that since the Fall of Adam, all men begotten according to nature, are born with sin, that is, without the

I-13. Martin Luther. *Portrait by Lukas Cranach.*

42

fear of God, without trust in God, and with concupiscence; and that this disease, or vice of origin, is truly sin, even now condemning and bringing eternal death upon those not born again through baptism and the Holy Ghost.

They condemn the Pelagians and others, who deny that the vice of origin is sin, and who, to obscure the glory of Christ's merit and benefits, argue that man can be justified before God by his own strength and reason.

Article III. Also they teach, that the Word, that is, the Son of God, did take man's nature in the womb of the blessed Virgin Mary, so that there are Two Natures, the divine and the human, inseparably conjoined in one Person, one Christ, true God and true man, who was born of the Virgin Mary, truly suffered, was crucified, dead and buried, not only for original guilt, but for all actual sins of men. He also descended into hell, and truly rose again the third day; afterward he ascended into Heaven, that he might sit on the right hand of the Father, and forever reign, and have dominion over all creatures, and sanctify them that believe in Him, by sending the Holy Ghost into their hearts, to rule, comfort and quicken them, and to defend them against the devil and the power of sin. The same Christ shall openly come again to judge the quick and the dead, etc., according to the Apostles' Creed.

Article IV. Also they teach, that men cannot be justified before God by their own strength, merits or works, but are freely justified for Christ's sake through faith, when they believe that they are received into favor and that their sins are forgiven for Christ's sake, who, by His death, hath made satisfaction for our sins. This faith God imputes for righteousness in his sight (Rom. 3 and 4).

Article V. That we may obtain this faith, the Office of Teaching the Gospel and Administering the Sacraments was instituted. For through the Word and Sacraments as through instruments, the Holy Ghost is given, who worketh faith where and when it pleaseth God in them that hear the Gospel, to wit, that God, not for our own merits, but for Christ's sake, justified those who believe that they are received into favor for Christ's sake.

1526

VIVENTIS·POTVIT·DVRERIVS·ORA·PHILIPPI
MENTEM·NON·POTVIT·PINGERE·DOCTA
MANVS

I-14. Portrait of Philip Melanchthon. *Albrecht Dürer, 1526.*

They condemn the Anabaptists and others, who think that the Holy Ghost cometh to men without the external Word, through their own preparations and works.

Article VI. Also they teach, that this Faith is bound to bring forth Good Fruits, and that it is necessary to do good works commanded by God, because of God's will, but not that we should rely on those works to merit justification before God. For remission of sins and justification are apprehended by faith, as also the voice of Christ attests: "When ye shall have done all these things, say: We are unprofitable servants" (Luke 17:10). The same is also taught by the Fathers. For Ambrose says: "It is ordained of God that he who believes in Christ, is saved; freely receiving remission of sins, without works, by faith alone."

Article VII. Also they teach, that One holy Church is to continue for ever. The Church is the congregation of saints, in which the Gospel is rightly taught and the

Sacraments rightly administered. And to the true unity of the Church, it is enough to agree concerning the doctrine of the Gospel and the administration of the Sacraments. Nor is it necessary that human traditions, rites, or ceremonies, instituted by men, should be everywhere alike. As Paul says: "One faith, one baptism, one God and Father of all," etc. (Eph. 4:5,6).

Article VIII. Although the Church properly is the Congregation of Saints and true believers, nevertheless, since, in this life, many hypocrites and evil persons are mingled therewith, it is lawful to use the Sacraments, which are administered by evil men; according to the saying of Christ: "The Scribes and the Pharisees sit in Moses' seat," etc. (Matt. 23:2). Both the Sacraments and Word are effectual by reason of the institution and commandment of Christ, not withstanding they be administered by evil men.

They condemn the Donatists, and such like, who denied it to be lawful to use the ministry of evil men in the Church, and who thought the ministry of evil men to be unprofitable and of none effect.

Article IX. Of Baptism, they teach, that it is necessary to salvation, and that through Baptism is offered the grace of God; and that children are to be baptized, who, being offered to God through Baptism, are received into His grace.

They condemn the Anabaptists, who allow not the Baptism of children, and say that children are saved without Baptism.

Article X. Of the Supper of the Lord, they teach, that the Body and Blood of Christ are truly present, and are distributed to those who eat in the Supper of the Lord; and they disapprove of those that teach otherwise.

Article XI. Of Confession, they teach, that Private Absolution ought to be retained in the churches, although in confession an enumeration of all sins is not necessary. For it is impossible, according to the Psalm: "Who can understand his errors?" (Ps. 19:12).

Article XII. Of Repentance, they teach, that for those that have fallen after Baptism, there is remission of sins whenever they are converted; and that the Church ought to impart absolution to those thus returning to repentance.

Now repentance consists properly of these two parts: One is contrition, that is, terrors smiting the conscience through the knowledge of sin; the other is faith, which, born of the Gospel, or of absolution, believes that, for Christ's sake, sins are forgiven, comforts the conscience, and delivers it from terrors. Then good works are bound to follow, which are the fruits of repentance.

They condemn the Anabaptists, who deny that those once justified can lose the Holy Ghost. Also those who contend that some may attain to such perfection in this life that they cannot sin. The Novatians also are condemned, who would not absolve such as had fallen after Baptism, though they returned to repentance. They also are rejected who do not teach that remission of sins cometh through faith, but command us to merit grace through satisfactions of our own.

Article XIII. Of the Use of the Sacraments, they teach, that the Sacraments were ordained, not only to be marks of profession among men, but rather to be signs and testimonies of the will of God toward us, instituted to awaken and confirm faith in those who use them. Wherefore we must so use the Sacraments that faith be added to believe the promises which are offered and set forth through the Sacraments.

They therefore condemn those who teach that the Sacraments justify by the outward act, and do not teach that, in the use of the Sacraments, faith which believes that sins are forgiven, is required.

Article XIV. Of Ecclesiastical Order, they teach, that no one should publicly teach in the Church or administer the Sacraments, unless he be regularly called.

Article XV. Of Rites and Usages in the Church, they teach, that those ought to be observed which may be observed without sin, and which are profitable unto tranquillity and good order in the Church, as particular holydays, festivals, and the like.

Nevertheless, concerning such things, let men be admonished that consciences are not to be burdened, as though such observance was necessary to salvation. They are admonished also that human traditions instituted to propitiate God, to merit grace and to make satisfaction for sins, are opposed to the Gospel and the doctrine of faith. Wherefore vows and traditions concerning meats and days, etc., instituted to merit grace and to make satisfaction for sins, are useless and contrary to the Gospel.

Article XVI. Of Civil Affairs, they teach, that lawful civil ordinances are good works of God, and that it is right for Christians to bear civil office, to sit as judges, to determine matters by the Imperial and other existing laws, to award just punishments, to engage in just wars, to serve as soldiers, to make legal contracts, to hold property, to make oath when required by the magistrates, to marry, to be given in marriage.

They condemn the Anabaptists who forbid these civil offices to Christians. They condemn also those who do not place the perfection of the Gospel in the fear of God and in faith, but in forsaking civil offices; for the Gospel teaches an eternal righteousness of the heart. Meanwhile, it does not destroy the State or the family, but especially requires their preservation as ordinances of God, and in such ordinances the exercise of charity. Therefore, Christians are necessarily bound to obey their own magistrates and laws, save only when commanded to sin, for then they ought to obey God rather than men (Acts 5:29).

Article XVII. Also they teach, that at the Consummation of the World, Christ shall appear for judgment, and shall raise up all the dead; he shall give to the godly and elect eternal life and everlasting joys, but ungodly men and the devils he shall condemn to be tormented without end.

They condemn the Anabaptists who think that there will be an end to the punishments of condemned men and devils. They condemn also others, who are now spreading certain Jewish opinions that, before the resurrection of the dead, the godly shall take possession of the kingdom of the world, the ungodly being everywhere suppressed (exterminated).

Article XVIII. Of the Freedom of the Will, they teach, that man's will has some liberty for the attainment of civil righteousness, and for the choice of things subject to reason. Nevertheless, it has no power, without the Holy Ghost, to work the righteousness of God, that is, spiritual righteousness; since the natural man receiveth not the things of the Spirit of God (I Cor. 2:14); but this righteousness is wrought in the heart when the Holy Ghost is received through the Word....

.   .   .   .   .

They condemn the Pelagians and others who teach that, without the Holy Ghost, by the power of nature alone, we are able to love God above all things; also to do the commandments of God as touching "the substance of the act."

For, although nature is able in some sort to do the outward work (for it is able to keep the hands from theft and murder), yet it cannot work the inward motions, such as the fear of God, trust in God, chastity, patience, etc.

Article XIX. Of the Cause of Sin, they teach, that although God doth create and preserve nature, yet the cause of sin is the will of the wicked, that is, of the devil and ungodly men; which will, unaided of God, turns itself from God, as Christ says (John 8:44): "When he speaketh a lie, he speaketh of his own."

Article XX. Our teachers are falsely accused of forbidding Good Works. For their published writings on the Ten Commandments, and others of like import, bear witness that they have taught to good purpose concerning all estates and duties of life, as to what estates of life and what works in every calling be pleasing to God. Concerning these things preachers heretofore taught but little, and urged only childish and needless works, as particular holydays, particular fasts, brotherhoods, pilgrimages, services in honor of saints, the use of rosaries, monasticism, and such like. Since our adversaries have been admonished of these things they are now unlearning them, and do not preach these unprofitable works as heretofore. Besides they begin to mention faith, of which there was heretofore marvellous silence.

They teach that we are justified not by works only, but they conjoin faith and works, and say that we are justified by faith and works. This doctrine is more tolerable than the former one, and can afford more consolation than their old doctrine.

Forasmuch, therefore, as the doctrine concerning faith, which ought to be the chief one in the church, has lain so long unknown, as all must needs grant that there was the deepest silence in their sermons concerning the righteousness of faith, while only the doctrine of works was treated in the churches, our teachers have instructed the churches concerning faith as follows:

First, that our works cannot reconcile God or merit forgiveness of sins, grace and justification, but that we obtain this only by faith, when we believe that we are received into favor for Christ's sake, who alone has been set forth the Mediator and Propitiation (I Tim. 2:5), in order that the Father may be reconciled through Him. Whoever, therefore, trusts that by works he merits grace, despises the merit and grace of Christ, and seeks a way to God without Christ, by human strength, although Christ has said of himself: "I am the Way, the Truth and the Life" (John 14:6).

This doctrine concerning faith is everywhere treated by Paul (Eph. 2:8) "By grace are ye saved through faith; and that not of yourselves; it is the gift of God, not of works," etc.

And lest anyone should craftily say that a new interpretation of Paul has been devised by us, this entire matter is supported by the testimonies of the Fathers....

.   .   .   .   .

Heretofore consciences were plagued with the doctrine of works, nor did they hear any consolation from the Gospel. Some persons were driven by conscience into the desert, into monasteries, hoping there to merit grace by a monastic life. Some also devised other works whereby to merit grace and make satisfaction for sins. There was very great need to treat of and renew this doctrine of faith in Christ, to the end that anxious consciences should not be without consolation, but that they might know that grace and forgiveness of sins and justification are apprehended by faith in Christ.

Men are also admonished that here the term "faith" doth not signify merely the knowledge of the history, such as is in the ungodly and in the devil, but signifieth a faith which believes, not merely the history, but also the effect of the history—namely, this article of the forgiveness of sins, to wit, that we have grace, righteousness, and forgiveness of sins, through Christ.

Now he that knoweth that he has a Father reconciled to him through Christ, since he truly knows God, knows also that God careth for him, and calls upon God; in a word, he is not without God, as the heathen. For devils and the ungodly are not able to believe this article of the forgiveness of sins. Hence, they hate God as an enemy; call not upon Him; and expect no good from Him. Augustine also admonishes his readers concerning the word "faith," and teaches that the term "faith" is accepted in the Scriptures, not for knowledge such as is in the ungodly, but for confidence which consoles and encourages the terrified mind.

Furthermore, it is taught on our part, that it is necessary to do good works, not that we should trust to merit grace by them, but because it is the will of God. It is only by faith that forgiveness of sins and grace are apprehended. And because through faith the Holy Ghost is received, hearts are renewed and endowed with new affections, so as to be able to bring forth good works. For Ambrose says: "Faith is the mother of a good will and right doing." For man's powers without the Holy Ghost are full of ungodly affections, and are too weak to do good works which are good in God's sight. Besides, they are in the power of the devil, who impels men to divers sins, to ungodly opinions, to open crimes. This we may see in the philosophers, who, although they endeavored to live an honest life, could not succeed, but were defiled with many open crimes. Such is the feebleness of man, when he is without faith and without the Holy Ghost, and governs himself only by human strength.

Hence it may be readily seen that this

doctrine is not to be charged with prohibiting good works, but rather the more to be commended, because it shows how we are enabled to do good works. For without faith, human nature can in no wise do the works of the First or of the Second Commandment. Without faith, it does not call upon God, nor expect anything from Him, nor bear the cross; but seeks and trusts in man's help. And thus, when there is no faith and trust in God, all manner of lusts and human devices rule in the heart. Wherefore Christ said (John 15:5): "Without me ye can do nothing," and the Church sings:

> Without Thy power divine
> In man there nothing is,
> Naught but what is harmful.

Article XXI. Of the Worship of Saints, they teach, that the memory of saints may be set before us, that we may follow their faith and good works, according to our callings, as the Emperor may follow the example of David in making war to drive away the Turk from his country. For both are kings. But the Scripture teaches not the invocation of saints, or to ask help of saints, since it sets before us Christ, as the only Mediator, Propitiation, High-Priest and Intercessor. He is to be prayed to, and hath promised that He will hear our prayer; and this worship He approves above all, to wit, that in all afflictions He be called upon (I John 2:1): "If any man sin, we have an Advocate with the Father," etc.

This is about the Sum of our Doctrine, in which, as can be seen, there is nothing that varies from the Scriptures, or from the Church Catholic, or from the Church of Rome as known from its writers. This being the case, they judge harshly who insist that our teachers be regarded as heretics. The disagreement, however, is on certain Abuses, which have crept into the Church without rightful authority. And even in these, if there were some difference, there should be proper lenity on the part of bishops to bear with us by reason of the Confession which we have now drawn up; because even the Canons are not so severe as to demand the same rites everywhere, neither, at any time, have the rites of all churches been the same; although, among us, in large part, the ancient rites are diligently observed. For it is a false and malicious charge that all the ceremonies, all the things instituted of old, are abolished in our churches. But it has been a common complaint that some Abuses were connected with the ordinary rites. These inasmuch as they could not be approved with a good conscience, have been to some extent corrected.

II. ARTICLES, IN WHICH ARE REVIEWED THE ABUSES WHICH HAVE BEEN CORRECTED

Inasmuch then as our churches dissent in no article of the Faith from the Church Catholic, but omit some Abuses which are new, and which have been erroneously accepted by fault of the times, contrary to the intent of the Canons, we pray that Your Imperial Majesty would graciously hear both what has been changed, and also what were the reasons, in order that the people be not compelled to observe those Abuses against their conscience. Nor should Your Imperial Majesty believe those, who, in order to excite the hatred of men against our part, disseminate strange slanders among our people. Having thus excited the minds of good men, they have first given occasion to this controversy, and now endeavor, by the same arts, to increase the discord. For Your Imperial Majesty will undoubtedly find that the form of doctrine and of ceremonies with us, is not so intolerable as these ungodly and malicious men represent. Furthermore, the truth cannot be gathered from common rumors, or the revilings of our enemies. But it can readily be judged that nothing would serve better to maintain the dignity of worship, and to nourish reverence and pious devotion among the people than that the ceremonies be rightly observed in the churches.

Article XXII. To the laity are given Both Kinds in the Sacrament of the Lord's Supper, because this usage has the commandment of the Lord (in Matt. 26:27): "Drink ye all of it"; where Christ has manifestly commanded concerning the cup that all should drink; and lest any man should craftily say that this refers only to priests,

Paul (in Cor. 11:27) recites an example from which it appears that the whole congregation did use both kinds. And this usage has long remained in the Church, nor is it known when, or by whose authority it was changed. . . .

Article XXIII. There has been common complaint concerning the Examples of Priests, who were not chaste. For that reason also, Pope Pius is reported to have said that there were certain reasons why marriage was taken away from priests, but that there were far weightier ones why it ought to be given back; for so Platina writes. Since, therefore, our priests were desirous to avoid these open scandals they married wives, and taught that it was lawful for them to contract matrimony. First, because Paul says (I Cor. 7:2): "To avoid fornication, let every man have his own wife." Also (9): "It is better to marry than

I-15. Title Page of the First Edition of Luther's Complete Bible, 1534.

to burn." Secondly, Christ says (Matt. 19:11); "All men cannot receive this saying," where he teaches that not all men are fit to lead a single life; for God created man for procreation (Gen. 1:28). Nor is it in man's power without a singular gift and work of God, to alter this creation. Therefore those that are not fit to lead a single life ought to contract matrimony. For no man's law, no vow, can annul the commandment and ordinance of God. For these reasons the priests teach that it is lawful for them to marry wives. It is also evident that in the ancient Church priests were married men. . . .

Article XXV. Confession in our churches is not abolished; for it is not usual to give the Body of the Lord, except to them that have been previously examined and absolved. And the people are most carefully taught concerning the faith and assurance of absolution, about which, before this time, there was profound silence. Our people are taught that they should highly prize the absolution, as being the voice of God, and pronounced by His command. The power of the Keys is commended, and we show what great consolation it brings to anxious consciences; that God requires faith to believe such absolution as a voice sounding from Heaven, and that such faith in Christ truly obtains and receives the forgiveness of sins.

Aforetime, satisfactions were immoderately extolled; of faith and the merit of Christ, and the righteousness of faith no mention was made; wherefore, on this point, our churches are by no means to be blamed. For this even our adversaries must needs concede to us, that the doctrine concerning repentance has been most diligently treated and laid open by our teachers.

But of Confession, they teach, that an enumeration of sins is not necessary, and that consciences be not burdened with anxiety to enumerate all sins, for it is impossible to recount all sins, as the Psalm testifies (19:13): "Who can understand his errors?" But if no sins were forgiven, except those that are recounted, consciences could never find peace; for very many sins they neither see, nor can remember. . . .

Article XXVI. It has been the general

persuasion, not of the people alone, but also of such as teach in the churches, that making Distinctions of Meats, and like traditions of men, are works profitable to merit grace, and able to make satisfactions for sins. And that the world so thought, appears from this, that new ceremonies, new orders, new holydays, and new fastings were daily instituted, and the teachers in the churches did exact these works as a service necessary to merit grace, and did greatly terrify men's consciences, if they should omit any of these things. From this persuasion concerning traditions, much detriment has resulted in the Church. . . .

Thus, therefore, they have taught, that by the observance of human traditions we cannot merit grace, or be justified; and hence we must not think such observances necessary acts of worship.

Moreover, they teach, that every Christian ought to exercise and subdue himself with bodily restraints and labors, that neither plenty nor slothfulness tempt him to sin, but not that we may merit grace or make satisfaction for sins by such exercises. And such external discipline ought to be urged at all times, not only on a few and set days. So Christ commands (Luke 21:34): "Take heed, lest your hearts be overcharged with surfeiting"; also (Matt. 17:21): "This kind goeth not out but by prayer and fasting." Paul also says (I Cor. 9:27): "I keep under my body and bring it into subjection." Here he clearly shows that he was keeping under his body, not to merit forgiveness of sins by that discipline, but to have his body in subjection and fitted for spiritual things, and for the discharge of duty according to his calling. Therefore, we do not condemn fasting, but the traditions which prescribe certain days and certain meats, with peril of conscience, as though works of such kinds were a necessary service.

Nevertheless, very many traditions are kept on our part, which conduce to good order in the Church, as the Order of Lessons in the Mass, and the chief holydays. But, at the same time, men are warned that such observances do not justify before God, and that, in such things, it should not be made sin, if they be omitted without scandal. . . .

18. Religious Peace of Augsburg, 1555

After years of turmoil and uncertainty, the Lutherans and the Roman Catholics agreed to a treaty of peace that should bind them until a final settlement of religion took place. Ferdinand, the brother of Charles V, negotiated with the Lutherans and finally worked out the Peace of Augsburg. The main provisions are given below. From *De Pace Religionis acta publica et originalia* (Frankfurt, 1707). Translated in *Crozer Historical Leaflets*, No. 5, ed. Henry C. Vedder. Robinson, *Readings in European History*.

Constitution of the Peace between their Imperial and Royal Majesties, on the one hand, and the Electors and Estates of the realm, on the other:

Whereas, at all the diets held during the last thirty years and more, and at several special sessions besides, there have often been negotiations and consultations to establish between the estates of the Holy Empire a general, continuous, and enduring peace in regard to the contending religions; and whereas several times terms of peace were drawn up, which, however, were never sufficient for the maintenance of peace . . .

To secure again peace and confidence, in the minds of the estates and subjects toward each other, and to save the German nation, our beloved Fatherland, from final dissolution and ruin; we, on the one hand, have united and agreed with the Electors and Estates, that from henceforth no one of whatsoever honor, rank or character, for any cause, or upon any pretense whatsoever, shall engage in feuds, or make war upon, rob, seize, invest, or besiege another. And no one shall descend upon any castle, town, manor, fortification, villages, estates, hamlets, or against the will of that other seize them wickedly with violence, or damage them by fire or in other ways.

And in order that such peace may be the better established and made secure and enduring between his Roman Imperial Majesty and us, on the one hand, and the electors, princes, and estates of the Holy Empire of the German nation on the other, we agree that no one shall make war upon any estate of the empire on account of the Augsburg Confession and the doctrine, religion, and faith of the same, nor injure nor do violence to those estates that hold it, nor force them, against their conscience, knowledge, and will, to abandon the religion, faith, church usages, ordinances, and ceremonies of the Augsburg Confession, where these have been established, or may hereafter be established, in their principalities, lands, and dominions. Nor shall we, through mandate or in any other way, trouble or disparage them, but shall let them quietly and peacefully enjoy their religion, faith, church usages, ordinances, and ceremonies, as well as their possessions, real and personal property, lands, people, dominions, governments, honors, and rights. . . .

On the other hand, the estates that have accepted the Augsburg Confession shall suffer his Imperial Majesty, princes and estates of the Holy Empire, who adhere to the old religion, to abide in like manner by their religion, faith, church usages, ordinances, and ceremonies. They shall also leave undisturbed their possessions, real and personal property, lands, people, dominions, government, honors, and rights, rents, interest, and tithes. . . .

But all others who are not adherents of either of the above-mentioned religions are not included in this peace, but shall be altogether excluded.

And since there has been disagreement as to what should be done with archbishoprics, bishoprics, prelacies, and benefices when a Catholic priest holding same abandons the old religion, we have established and do hereby make known, that where an archbishop, bishop, prelate, or other spiritual incumbent shall depart from our old religion, he shall immediately abandon, without any opposition or delay, his archbishopric, bishopric, prelacy, and other benefices, with the fruits and incomes that he may have had from it. Then the chapters and such as are entitled to do so according to common law or the custom of the place shall elect a person espousing the old religion, who shall then enjoy the rights and income of the place.

But since certain estates or their predecessors have confiscated certain foundations, monasteries, and other spiritual possessions, and have applied the income to churches, schools, charitable institutions, and other purposes, it is herewith ordained that such estates as their original owners had not possessed at the time of the treaty of Passau [1552] shall be considered as confiscated, and shall be regulated by the rules governing each estate in dealing with confiscated properties. . . .

No estate shall urge another estate, or the subjects of the same, to embrace its religion.

But when our subjects and those of the electors, princes, and estates, adhering to the old religion or to the Augsburg Confession, wish, for the sake of their religion, to go with wife and children to another place in the lands, principalities, and cities of the electors, princes, and estates of the Holy Empire, and settle there, such going and coming, and the sale of property and goods, in return for reasonable compensation for serfdom and arrears of taxes . . . shall be everywhere unhindered, permitted, and granted. . . .

But since in many free and imperial cities both religions, namely, our old religion and that of the Augsburg Confession, have already come into existence and practice, the same shall remain hereafter and be held in the same cities; and citizens and inhabitants of the said free and imperial cities, whether spiritual or secular in rank, shall peacefully and quietly dwell with one another; and no party shall venture to abolish the religion, church customs, or ceremonies of the other, or persecute them therefor. . . .

Also herewith, and by the authority of this our imperial edict, we command and order the judges of the imperial courts, and their colleagues, to hold and conduct themselves in conformity with this treaty of peace, as well as to give fitting and necessary relief of the law to the appealing suitors themselves, no matter to which of the aforesaid religions they belong, and against all such to recognize and decree no citation, mandate, or process.

Proclaimed at Augsburg, September 25, 1555.

19. Hymns of Luther

The best known of Luther's hymns is *Ein' Feste Burg*, "A Mighty Fortress," but many others are still sung by Christians throughout the world. Luther is credited with reviving congregational singing as a form of worship, and his musical genius enriched and enlivened the evangelical movement. The first hymn, trans. Catherine Winkworth, 1885 (cf. Luther, *Erfurt Enchiridion*, 1524. *Common Service Book of the Lutheran Church*, 1917. The second hymn, trans. Catherine Winkworth, 1863 (cf. Joseph Klug, *Geistliche Lieder*, 1543).

KOMM, HEILIGER GEIST, HERRE GOTT, 1524

Come, Holy Spirit, God and Lord!
Be all Thy graces now outpoured
On the believer's mind and soul,
To strengthen, save, and make us whole.
Lord, by the brightness of Thy light,
Thou in the faith dost men unite
Of every land and every tongue:
This to Thy praise, O Lord, be sung.
　　　　Alleluia! Alleluia!

Thou strong Defence, Thou Holy Light,
Teach us to know our God aright,
And call Him Father from the heart;
The Word of life and truth impart,
That we may love not doctrines strange,
Nor e'er to other teachers range,
But Jesus for our Master own,
And put our trust in Him alone.
　　　　Alleluia! Alleluia!

Thou sacred Ardor, Comfort sweet,
Help us to wait with ready feet
And willing heart at Thy command,
Nor trial fright us from Thy band.
Lord, make us ready with Thy powers:
Strengthen the flesh in weaker hours,
That as good warriors we may force
Through life and death to Thee our course!
　　　　Alleluia! Alleluia!

ERHALT UNS, HERR, BEI DEINEM WORT, 1541

Lord, keep us steadfast in Thy Word;
Curb those who fain by craft or sword
Would wrest the kingdom from Thy Son,
And set at naught all He hath done.

Lord Jesus Christ, Thy power make known,
For Thou art Lord of lords alone;
Defend Thy Christendom, that we
May evermore sing praise to Thee.

O Comforter, of priceless worth
Send peace and unity on earth;
Support us in our final strife,
And lead us out of death to life.

20. *Luther at Home*

Martin Luther and Catharine von Bora were married on June 13, 1525. To them were born six children, of whom three sons and one daughter survived them. When Hans, the eldest, born on June 7, 1526, was four years old, his father wrote him a letter that has become a children's classic. It is given below, as well as a servant's description of the death of Magdalene, who died on September 20, 1542, at the age of fourteen. These selections typify the tenderness of the reformer's life at home. From *The Life and Letters of Martin Luther*, trans. Smith.

TO HANS LUTHER AT WITTENBERG,
FESTE COBURG, JUNE 19?, 1530

Grace and peace in Christ, dear little son. I am glad to hear that you are studying and saying your prayers. Continue to do so, my son, and when I come home I will bring you a pretty present.

I know a lovely, pleasant garden where many children are; they wear golden jackets and gather nice apples under the trees and pears and cherries and purple plums and yellow plums, and sing and run and jump and are happy and have pretty little ponies with golden reins and silver saddles. I asked the man who owned the garden whose children they were. He said: "They are the children who say their prayers and study and are good." Then said I: "Dear man, I also have a son whose name is Hans Luther; may he come into the garden and eat the sweet apples and pears and ride a fine pony and play with these children?" Then the man said: "If he says his prayers and is good, he can come into the garden and Phil and Justy [Philip Melanchthon and Justus Jonas, juniors, both born 1525], too, and when they all come they shall have whistles and drums and fifes and dance and shoot little cross-bows." Then he showed me a fine large lawn in the garden for dancing, where hang real golden whistles and fine silver cross-bows. But it was yet early and the children had not finished eating and I could not wait to see them dance, so I said to the man: "My dear sir, I must go away and write at once to my dear little Hans about all this, so that he will say his prayers and study and be good, so that he may come into the garden, and he has an Auntie Lena whom he must bring with him." Then the man said: "All right, go and tell him about it." So, dear little Hans, study and say your prayers and tell Phil and Justy to say their prayers and study too, so you may all come into the garden together. God bless you. Give Auntie Lena my love and a kiss from me.

Your loving father, Martin Luther.

ON THE DEATH OF MAGDALENE

As his daughter lay very ill, Dr. Luther said: "I love her very much, but dear God, if it be thy will to take her, I submit to thee." Then he said to her as she lay in bed: "Magdalene, my dear little daughter, would you like to stay here with your father, or would you willingly go to your Father yonder?" She answered: "Darling father, as God wills." Then said he: "Dearest child, the spirit is willing but the flesh is weak." Then he turned away and said: "I love her very much; if my flesh is so strong, what can my spirit do? God has given no bishop so great a gift in a thousand years as he has given me in her. I am angry with myself that I cannot rejoice in heart and be thankful as I ought."

Now as Magdalene lay in the agony of death, her father fell down before the bed on his knees and wept bitterly and prayed that God might free her. Then she departed and fell asleep in her father's arms. . . .

As they laid her in the coffin he said: "Darling Lena, you will rise and shine like a star, yea, like the sun. . . . I am happy in spirit, but the flesh is sorrowful and will not be content, the parting grieves me beyond measure. . . . I have sent a saint to heaven."

21. Luther's Prayers

Luther's many prayers not only reflect his deep trust in God's providence but also his earnestness and warmth. The following are typical. *Prayers of the Reformers*, by Clyde Manschreck (Philadelphia: Muhlenberg Press, 1958). Cf. Charles E. Kistler, *Luther's Prayers, Betbüchlein* (Reading, Pa.: Pilger, 1917). Prayer at Worms in *Golden Book of Prayers*, ed. Donald B. Aldrich (New York: Dodd, Mead & Co., 1941). Cf. Enders, *Luthers Briefwechsel*, III.

TABLE GRACES

Before eating: The eyes of all wait upon thee, O Lord: and thou givest them their meat in due season. Thou openest thine hand, and satisfiest the desire of every living thing. (Then shall be said the Lord's Prayer and after that this prayer:) O Lord God, heavenly Father, bless unto us these thy gifts, which of thy tender kindness thou hast bestowed upon us, through Jesus Christ, our Lord. Amen.

After eating: O give thanks unto the Lord, for he is good: for his mercy endureth forever. He giveth food to all flesh: He giveth to the beast his food, and to the young ravens which cry. He delighteth not in the strength of the horse; he taketh not pleasure in the legs of a man. The Lord taketh pleasure in them that fear him, in those that hope in his mercy.

We give thanks to thee, O God our Father, for all thy benefits, through Jesus Christ our Lord, who with thee liveth and reigneth, forever and ever. Amen.

FOR GREATER SPIRITUALITY

Behold, Lord, an empty vessel that needs to be filled. My Lord, fill it. I am weak in the faith; strengthen thou me. I am cold in love; warm me and make me fervent that my love may go out to my neighbor. I do not have a strong and firm faith; at times I doubt and am unable to trust thee altogether. O Lord, help me. Strengthen my faith and trust in thee. In thee I have sealed the treasures of all I have. I am poor; thou art rich and didst come to be merciful to the poor. I am a sinner; thou art upright. With me there is an abundance of sin; in thee is the fulness of righteousness. Therefore, I will remain with thee of whom I can receive but to whom I may not give. Amen.

LUTHER'S PRAYER AT WORMS, APRIL 18, 1521

O almighty and everlasting God! How terrible is this world! Behold it openeth its mouth to swallow me up, and I have so little trust in thee! How weak is the flesh and how powerful is Satan! If it is in the strength of this world only that I must put my trust, all is over! My last hour is come, my condemnation has been pronounced. O God! O God! O God! Do thou help me against all the wisdom of the world! Do this; thou shouldst do this; thou alone, for this is not my work but thine! I have nothing to do here, nothing to contend for with these great ones of the world! I should desire to see my days flow on peaceful and happy. But the cause is thine, and it is a righteous and eternal cause, O Lord! Help me! Faithful and unchangeable God! In no man do I place my trust. It would be vain—all that is of man is uncertain, all that cometh of man fails. O God! My God, hearest thou me not? My God, art thou dead? No! No, thou canst not die! Thou hidest thyself only! Thou hast chosen me for this work. I know it well! Act then, O God, stand at my side, for the sake of thy well-beloved Son, Jesus Christ, who is my defense, my shield, and my strong tower.

Lord, where stayest thou? O my God, where art thou? Come, come! I am ready to lay down my life for thy truth, patient as a lamb. For it is the cause of justice—it is thine! O I will never separate myself from thee, neither now nor through eternity! And though the world may be filled with devils, though my body, which is still the work of thy hands, should be slain, be stretched upon the pavement, be cut in pieces, reduced to ashes—my soul is thine! Yes, I have the assurance of thy word. My soul belongs to thee! It shall abide forever with thee. Amen. O God! Help me! Amen.

Bainton, Roland H., *Here I Stand: A Life of Martin Luther*. Nashville: Abingdon Press, 1950.

——, *The Reformation in the Sixteenth Century*. Boston: Beacon Press, 1952.

Boehmer, Heinrich, *Road to Reformation*. Philadelphia: Muhlenberg Press, 1946.

Erasmus-Luther, *Discourse on Free Will*, trans. E. F. Winter. New York: Frederick Ungar, 1961.

Grimm, Harold J., *The Reformation Era, 1500-1650*. New York: Macmillan Co., 1954.

Grisar, Hartmann, *Martin Luther, His Life and Work*. Westminster, Md.: Newman Press, 1960.

Huizinga, J., *Erasmus*. New York: Phaidon Publishers, Inc., 1952.

Kristeller, Paul O., *Studies in Renaissance Thought*. Rome: Edizioni di Storia e Letteratura, 1956.

Lindsay, T. M., *A History of the Reformation*. New York: Charles Scribner's Sons, 1950.

Manschreck, Clyde L., *Melanchthon: The Quiet Reformer*. Nashville: Abingdon Press, 1958.

Melanchthon, Philip, *Loci Communes*, trans. C. L. Hill. Boston: Forum Publishing Co., 1944.

Pauck, Wilhelm, *The Heritage of the Reformation*. Glencoe, Ill.: The Free Press, 1950.

Pelikan, Jaroslav and H. T. Lehmann, eds. *Luther's Works*. St. Louis and Philadelphia: Concordia Publishing House and Muhlenberg Press, 1955.

Reu, M., *The Augsburg Confession*. Minneapolis: Augsburg Publishing House, 1930.

Rupp, E. G., *The Righteousness of God*. New York: Philosophical Library, Inc., 1954.

Schwiebert, E. G., *Luther and His Times*. St. Louis: Concordia Publishing House, 1950.

Smith, Preserved, *Age of the Reformation*. New York: Holt, Rinehart & Winston, Inc., 1920.

Smith, Preserved and C. M. Jacobs, *Luther's Correspondence and Other Contemporary Letters*. Philadelphia: Lutheran Publication Society, 1913.

Spinka, Matthew, *Advocates of Reform: Wyclif to Erasmus*. Philadelphia: The Westminster Press, 1953.

Tappert, Theodore G., ed., *Book of Concord: Confessions of Evangelical Lutheran Church*. Philadelphia: Muhlenberg Press, 1959.

Villari, Pasquale, *Life and Times of Savonarola*. New York: Charles Scribner's Sons, 1888.

Watson, Philip S., *Let God Be God*. Philadelphia: Muhlenberg Press, 1947.

Whitney, James P., *History of the Reformation*. London: SPCK, 1958.

Works of Martin Luther, 6 vols. Philadelphia: Muhlenberg Press, 1943.

CHRONOLOGY

Illustration opposite page 57: **John Calvin.** *Copper engraving by René Boivin (1530–1598).*

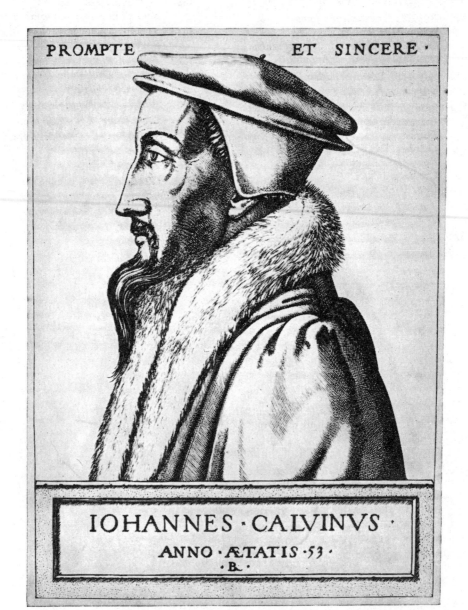

PROMPTE ET SINCERE ·

IOHANNES · CALVINVS ·
ANNO · ÆTATIS · 53 ·
· B ·

II

The Reformation Extended

Religious upheaval and reform were by
no means confined to Germany. Ulrich Zwingli, John Calvin,
and the Anabaptists led reforms which were to prove dynamic not
only in Switzerland but in lands far beyond. The early reform
movement in Switzerland centered around Zwingli, whose influence
was also strong in Southern Germany. Calvinism, a product
of French Protestantism, superseded Zwinglianism, however,
and became the international protest against Catholicism
in the sixteenth century. Luther's ideas also spread throughout
Europe, but Lutheranism, relatively speaking, remained
largely Germanic. The Anabaptists emerged in the throes of the
reform movement in Switzerland, but their ideas spread far
and wide as they were scattered by persecution. Their main thrusts
were aimed at separation of church and state and maintenance of
individual rights. Their name derived from their insistence that
adults be baptized on profession of faith, even though previously
baptized as infants. Hated by both Catholics and
Protestants, they nevertheless bore witness to tenets which
have since proved to be bulwarks of freedom and Protestantism.

Ulrich (Huldreich) Zwingli (1484-1531) came of peasant stock, one of eight sons, born at Wildhaus, Switzerland. He received an education through the offices of his uncle, a parish priest. At the University of Vienna he felt the influence of Wyttenbach, a humanist, became an admirer of Erasmus, and was imbued with a zeal for the sixteenth century's "new learning" which was to continue through his life. His keen intellect enabled him to see the abuses so rampant in religious institutions at the time, and his boldness impelled him to make practical reforms. In 1506, he became the parish priest at Glarus, a large, wealthy church, where he remained for ten years. He excelled as a preacher and became known for his opposition to Swiss mercenary service for anyone except the Pope, which, of course, endeared him to the papacy. He went to the humanist stronghold of Einsiedeln in 1516, where his study of the New Testament was deepened and his outlook on Catholicism began to change. He spoke against penitents undertaking pilgrimages to the Virgin Mary shrine, for he said that their sins could not thus be forgiven, and he thwarted the sale of indulgences by Bernard Samson, a well-known hawker of theological wares. He even went so far as to declare that current papal authority could not be justified in Scripture. Nevertheless, in 1518 the Pope honored him with an appointment as Acolyte Chaplain to the Pope, and this led in the same year to his election as People's Priest of the Great Minster Church in Zurich, where his ability as a preacher enabled him to realize his ecclesiastical and political ambitions.

Zwingli's moral integrity was hardly that of Luther's. At the time of his appointment to the Zurich pulpit, he was investigated for heresy and the seduction of a young girl. He denied the seduction but admitted frequent incontinence and even argued that the vow of celibacy did not mean a vow of chastity. The City Council found him free of moral abuse and heresy, and Zwingli then called on the Council to support him in his ministry. In 1520, with political sagacity he resigned his pension so that as a canon he could have the privileges of a citizen of Zurich and could ask for direct support from the City Council, which he realized was the governing unit. By 1522, his position was such, politically and theologically, that he felt free, along with ten other Swiss priests, to appeal to the Bishop of Constance for permission to marry, inasmuch as Scripture permitted it and as it would but legalize the cohabitation that was already being practiced. The petition was not answered, but it does reflect the times (1). Zwingli was already living with a wealthy widow, Anna Reinhard, whom he publicly married April 2, 1524.

In 1522, Zwingli vigorously preached against Lenten fasts, his followers openly ate meat, and he moved farther from Roman Catholicism. The Bishop of Constance tried to repress the innovation, but Zwingli supported himself and the rebels with citations from the New Testament (2). The cantonal government of Zurich ruled that the New Testament imposed no fasts during Lent, but agreed that they should be observed for the sake of good order. In August, however, the ruling civil authorities passed an edict that henceforth all customs would be based solely on the pure Word of God. This virtually eliminated the rule of the bishop, and was a victory for Zwingli, who believed that the civil authorities should rule in accordance with the Word and that only what the Bible authorized should be binding. This also opened the way for the great Zurich debates which entrenched Zwinglianism in Zurich and extended it to other cantons, for Zwingli was adept at showing that his way was scriptural and also in handling the Council.

In January 1523, the civil authorities ordered a public discussion in which the Bible should be the only touchstone. Zwingli prepared his *Sixty-seven Articles*, which he ably defended (3). He asserted the authority of the Bible over the church, salvation by faith, and the right of priests and nuns to marry. He denied that good works have merit, that the mass is a sacrifice, that saints should be invoked, that monastic vows are binding, and that there is a purgatory. Civil regulations were altered to embrace the new ideas. Many

II-1. Christ, the True Light, with Plato, Aristotle, the Pope, Hooded Monks, and Priests Falling into an Abyss of Darkness. *Woodcut by Hans Holbein, the younger.*

priests and nuns married, and the magistrates declared that ministers should preach only what could be proved from Scripture. Later that year, Zwingli attacked images and the mass, and the Council issued a mandate abolishing both. Immediately after this ornaments were removed from the churches— tapestries, frescoes, relics, crucifixes, candles, and pictures. Clerical robes were banned, as well as the ringing of bells and the playing of the organ. By 1525, a Love Feast had replaced the mass, many monastic properties had been confiscated, and schools had been established or reorganized in line with the reforms. The great organ in Zurich was dismantled in 1527. Zwinglian preachers were sent to other cantons. Zwingli's friend, Johann Oecolampadius (1482-1531), won Basel for the evangelical cause, and Martin Bucer (1491-1551) completed the swing of Strassburg to Zwinglianism. In Berne, the Zwinglian reform prevailed largely as a result of the 1528 debate of the *Ten Theses* by Zwingli and others (4). St. Gallen, Schaffhausen, and Mülhausen soon followed. The sway of Zwingli might have been even greater, but he met death in battle at Kappel in 1531, while leading troops against the Roman Catholic cantons.

The Bible was Zwingli's declared rule of faith and practice; he used it as a legal code, and gave authority to it over against Catholicism, mysticism, custom, and superstition. He subscribed to many common evangelical views: justification by faith, unconditioned election, and infant baptism. But Zwingli experienced trouble with other Protestants over the sacraments.

In 1529 at Marburg, Zwingli and Oecolampadius held a conference with Luther and Melanchthon, hoping to come to an agreement so that a political union might be effected in the face of growing Roman Catholic political strength, but they could not agree on the nature of the presence of Christ in the Lord's Supper. Zwingli believed that physical things could not be vehicles of spiritual grace and interpreted "This is my body" to mean "This signifies" or "represents," so that the Supper was merely a memorial. Luther chalked *"Hoc est corpus Meum"* on the table at Marburg and would not budge from his view of the physical presence (often called consubstantiation). The result was no union, and Zwingli presented a separate confession at Augsburg in 1530 (5).

Zwingli clashed with his co-workers over the question of infant baptism, and precipitated the Anabaptist movement (6-10). Associated with Zwingli in Zurich were Conrad Grebel (1498-1526) and Felix Manz (1498-1527), both well-educated members of prominent Swiss families. Grebel became a convert to earnest Christian living under the preaching of Zwingli in 1522, and he hoped for a quick reform of the entire religious situation in Zurich. After the fall debate in 1523, he felt that Zwingli should have moved rapidly to abolish the mass and other papal ceremonies. Actually, Grebel desired a new

59

church in full conformity with the New Testament. When Zwingli would not cooperate in establishing such a church, Grebel, Manz, and a few others began holding night meetings in the home of Manz' mother, chiefly to study the Bible in Hebrew and Greek.

Questions about baptism soon arose. Since Zwingli had already convinced them that baptism was a symbol, they could not believe in baptismal regeneration of infants. By 1524 they were insisting that the only scriptural baptism was of adults who had first been converted through the gospel. Preceding them in their conclusions was a preacher from Waldshut, Balthasar Hubmaier (1480-1528), once a friend of Luther, who in 1524 ably defended eighteen reform theses at Waldshut (11), which he had to leave because of Catholic opposition. He joined Zwingli in Zurich. As early as May, 1523, he had doubts about infant baptism, for which he could find no scriptural warrant, and declared that Zwingli shared his views. By 1524, his criticisms and those of Grebel and Manz began to irritate Zwingli, who felt that abolition of infant baptism would alienate the Council through which he wished to establish the reformation.

In December of 1524 and early in January of 1525, Zwingli held preliminary discussions with his critics, and then on January 17, 1525, he met them in open debate before the Council. Opposing Zwingli were Grebel, Manz, and Wilhelm Reublin, a pastor near Zurich. The Council favored Zwingli, and on January 18 issued its famous edict for parents to baptize their infants within eight days or be banished (6). Three days later, the Council ordered Grebel and Manz to cease their Bible meetings. Reublin and several other pastors were banished.

According to the *Oldest Chronicle of the Hutterian Brethren,* Grebel and a few of the others met secretly on the night of January 21, 1525, to consider their plight when suddenly the Spirit moved in their hearts (10). Overwhelmed, George Blaurock knelt in prayer and asked Grebel to baptize him, which he did, and they then commissioned one another to preach the Gospel. The form of baptism was, at the beginning, not a question, although they soon advocated immersion. Grebel launched a successful preaching mission in various parts of Switzerland, but was soon jailed in Zurich, along with Manz and Blaurock. At his trial in March, 1526, he received a sentence of life imprisonment, but broke out of jail and resumed preaching, only to fall victim to the plague. He was twenty-eight.

Felix Manz became the first martyr in Zurich. In March, 1525, he was arrested and confined with thirteen men and seven women in the Tower in Zurich (8). Upon denying that he rejected all civil government and that he believed in a communism of goods, he was released, only to continue his evangelizing and be arrested again, a process that was repeated several times. Then, on January 5, 1527, under a 1526 law decreeing death for rebaptizing, the Zurich authorities sentenced him to die by drowning, specifically decreeing that he be bound with his hands between his knees, in a doubled-up position, and pushed from a boat into the deep water of the Limmat River in Zurich.

George Blaurock, so called because of the blue coat which he wore, had been a Catholic priest. He was a man of unusual energy and vigorously preached repentance and baptism. On the day Manz was drowned, Blaurock was whipped out of town, but he resumed preaching and took the place of a Tirolese preacher whom the Catholic authorities had burned at the stake. On August 14, 1529, the Catholic authorities arrested him, and after severe torture, he was burned at the stake on September 6. He was charged with leaving the priesthood, refusing to invoke Mary, repudiating the Mass, and discrediting infant baptism.

Balthasar Hubmaier was also flung into a Zurich prison in 1525, but was unable to bear torture and "recanted" (7). Released from prison, he fled to Moravia where he resumed preaching. At Nikolsburg, he publicly opposed the views of Hans Hut, who represented a violent fringe that was developing among the Anabaptists, later to reach its climax at Münster. Hut preached a doctrine of free love, and said that Christ would soon inaugurate his worldly kingdom, at which time Christ would give swords to the elect for the slaying of priests and nobles. He was killed escaping from prison in 1527, and his corpse was burned where his execution was to have taken place. Hubmaier enjoyed success in Moravia until early in 1528, when he was arrested by Archduke Ferdinand. He was taken to Vienna and tortured, but he would not recant. March 10, 1528, he was bound to a cart and wheeled through the streets of Vienna, his flesh at intervals being torn with hot pincers. He begged the crowd to forgive him, but he would not recant as he had done earlier. Stripped and bound, he was laid on a pile, gunpowder was rubbed into his beard, and he was burned at the stake. He died crying, "O Jesus, Jesus!" Three days later his wife, who was at the stake to encourage him, was drowned in the Danube River. Hubmaier's *Concerning Heretics And Those Who Burn Them,* 1524, was the first plea for religious tolerance in this period (*12*).

Michael Sattler, another acknowledged leader of the Anabaptists, was banished from Zurich on November 18, 1525. He resumed evangelizing in Württemberg, and on February 24, 1527, presided over the meeting at Schleitheim which drew up the first Anabaptist confession of faith (*13*). Zwingli in 1527 and Calvin in 1544 wrote treatises against these articles. Sattler was apprehended, tried at Rothenburg on the Neckar in Roman Catholic territory, and sentenced to have his tongue cut out, and his body torn by pincers and burned. He died May 21, 1527, and his wife was drowned a few days later (*14*).

Such was the fate of the leaders of the Anabaptists. But others also suffered, for from 1525 to 1530 literally hundreds were put to death. Duke Wilhelm of Bavaria mercifully ordered that all who recanted be beheaded instead of burned.

The Anabaptists were a plague to both Protestants and Roman Catholics, and the question inevitably arises: Why? The theological and political ties between the church and state offer a clue. In rebaptizing, in setting up congregations, and in questioning honored doctrines, the Anabaptists were believed to be undercutting the legally established churches, and the governments were so closely linked to the churches that this seemed to be seditious heresy (*9*). And treason was, of course, punishable by death. Luther at first drew back from the death penalty, but by 1529 he had justified the violent treatment of the Anabaptists, and he later sanctioned the death penalty, as did Melanchthon.

Later events seemed to justify the early treatment of the Anabaptists, for persecution often led to religious mania. Some Anabaptists tried to become as little children, to preach from the housetops, and to forsake family—because Scripture enjoined it. Some wandered about with no clothes, accepting literally the injunction to take no thought for the morrow, of what ye shall wear, and so on. Melchior Hofmann was noted for his addition of apocalypticism and the parousia which he predicted would come in 1534. His followers in Holland were called Melchiorites. He died in prison in Strassburg in 1543, after lying in prison for ten years thinking that Strassburg would be the New Jerusalem and that his imprisonment was the prelude to the parousia and the reign of the saints. One of his converts was Jan Matthis, who became a leader of the violent Anabaptists at Münster. Matthis was slain trying to liberate Münster from the bishop's siege, and Jan Brockelson of Leiden succeeded him. Brockelson introduced polygamy, crowned himself King David, enforced communism, and received daily revelations. When Münster fell to the bishop's army in June of 1535, Brockelson and two of his henchmen were captured and tortured, and executed a year and a half later; their corpses were placed in cages on the tower of St. Lambert Church, where the cages are still hanging. After the debacle of Münster, Menno Simons (1492-1559), who was converted indirectly by Hofmann, purged the movement of its radical elements and founded the present-day Mennonites. This peaceful trend among the Anabaptists is reflected in that remarkable apology of Jacob Huter, written in 1535 to offset the cruel edict of Ferdinand (*15*).

The real problem in back of the Anabaptist turmoil was the question of church and state; the Catholics leaned toward control by the church, the Protestants tended to lean toward control by the state, and the Anabaptists wanted a safeguard against both. Today the Anabaptists are freely acknowledged as the sixteenth century bearers of the right of conscience in religion and the advocates of separation of church and state, their legacies to the centuries that followed.

Meanwhile, a fresh form of Protestant authoritarianism was emerging in the person of John Calvin (1509-1564), a Frenchman, the son of a secretary to the Bishop of Noyon. He received an excellent education at Orléans, Bourges, and Paris, his intention being to enter law as his father desired. But Calvin became more interested in humanistic studies, which he pursued so intently that he was nicknamed, "The Accusative Case." His first book on Seneca's *Mercy* in 1532 did not touch on religion, but in that same year he experienced a sudden conversion; like Isaiah of old, he suddenly beheld the holiness of God and the sinfulness of man.

Calvin then became active in an evangelical group that was already established in France. As early as 1512, Renaissance humanism had found vigorous expression in Jacques Lefèvre d'Etaples (1455-1536), whose Latin translation and commentary on Paul's letters raised doubts about transubstantiation as well as the merit of human works apart from the grace of God, though Lefèvre never intended any fundamental departure from Roman Catholicism, apparently believing that more knowledge, a closer study of the Bible, and better administration would bring a reform of morals. A group gathered around him at Meaux, among whom was Guillaume Farel (1489-1565), destined later to draw Calvin into the reform efforts at Geneva. In 1533, when Nicolas Cop was inaugurated as rector of the University of Paris, Calvin probably wrote his speech, calling for a return to the pure Gospel. The speech was burned, and Calvin and Cop both fled from the Roman Catholic authorities. Calvin, disguised as a vinedresser, escaped from Paris in a basket. Shortly thereafter, the persecution of 1534 and 1535 occurred, in which some two dozen Protestants were burned alive. It was this persecution that prompted Calvin to write his *Institutes,* hoping thereby to show the King of France that his loyal subjects were being unjustly punished (*16*).

Calvin completed the *Institutes* in 1536, and was immediately hailed as the leader of French Protestantism. In the same year, Farel called Calvin to join him in an effort to make Geneva an ecclesiastical model (*17*). When opposition developed in 1538, both Farel and Calvin were forced to leave. Calvin worked for three years among the refugees in Strassburg, and was recalled to Geneva in 1541 as the only one strong enough to stave off a trend back to Catholicism.

For twenty-three years Calvin labored in Geneva. He was never ordained; his salary was a modest $600 yearly plus twelve measures of wheat, enough broadcloth for a new coat each year, two tubs of wine, and a house and garden. In 1540 he married a widow with three children; his only son died in infancy. He refused all raises in salary, and in keeping with his modesty asked that no monument be erected for him. He was not without opponents, but he ruled Geneva with an iron hand, like a tyrant in the eyes of those who did not like him, like an emissary from God to the elect for those who did.

Through a consistory of six clergymen and twelve laymen, Calvin enforced piety and rules of conduct more in the spirit of the Old than the New Testament. His over-all rule was "to glorify God and praise him forever," and the practical means of achieving this was strict discipline. He could not tolerate anything that seemed to dishonor God or the elect, and he punished drunkenness, profanity and divergent views with severity (*18*). Fines were assessed for not attending church, adulterers were sentenced to death, dancing was punishable by imprisonment, a child was beheaded for striking his parents, and a critic was beheaded for placing a defaming placard on Calvin's pulpit.

The most noted instance of iron rule was the burning of Michael Servetus on October 27, 1553 (*21-23*). Servetus, a native of Spain, distinguished himself as a physician and is credited with having discovered the circulation of the blood; he was less fortunate in theology. Early in life he became disgusted with corrupt ecclesiastical pomp and turned to the Bible for truth. In 1531, while only twenty years of age, he published *On Errors of the Trinity*, a radical attack on the various doctrines and contentions among Protestants and Catholics concerning the Trinity. Servetus did not think that the Trinity was biblical, nor did he think three beings in one Godhead could be justified. A storm of protest arose, causing Servetus to live for twenty-two years under an assumed name. But he continued corresponding with and writing bitter criticisms of Calvin. When Servetus published his *Restoration of Christianity* in 1553, he was arrested by the French Inquisition, escaped, and was apprehended in Geneva while on his way to Naples. There is some question about Calvin's active prosecution of Servetus, but there is no question about his wishes; seven years before he had told Farel that if Servetus ever came to Geneva he would never leave it alive (22). Servetus was tried and convicted, under the ancient Codex of Justinian, of denying the Trinity and repeating baptism, both punishable by death. Theologians far and wide approved, even Melanchthon. On the day following the sentencing he was chained to a stake, his book fastened to his arm and straw and sulphur placed on his head, and burned. Death came after half an hour of agony; torn by pain he cried, "O Jesus, Son of the Eternal God, have pity on me!"

Critical reaction came quickly, and Calvin published his *Defense of the Orthodox Trinity Against the Errors of Michael Servetus* in 1554. When Sebastian Castellio's anonymous book, *Concerning Heretics*, appeared in the same year, questioning whether the sword should be used against heretics (23), Theodore Beza wrote in Calvin's defense. Later, Calvinists erected a monument of penance to Servetus.

Nevertheless, for all its harshness and unbending discipline, Calvin's system aided the democratic processes which were beginning to develop in the wake of medievalism; Geneva became a model for other evangelical efforts, particularly in Holland, France, Scotland, England, and parts of Germany, Poland, Hungary, and America. Calvin's theological insights have influenced Christian life for four centuries.

Basic to all of Calvin's actions was his belief in the absolute sovereignty of God, to whom he believed all honor and glory were due (19-20). On this belief were based predestination and election, God's inscrutable plan or will for the world. All men are sinners and justly condemned by God, who in his mercy nevertheless elects to save a few through the merits and grace of his Son. Those who are elected are activated by a Spirit that brings forth good fruit in disciplined morality. But election may remain unknown, and this tended to encourage good works on the part of those trying to convince themselves that they were elected. All the reformers stressed justification by faith and the Bible as an infallible guide, but Luther stressed an inward element that one misses in the systematic, legalistic outlook of Calvin. All of them stressed vocations in much the same way, but Calvin's emphasis on vocation as a means of transforming the world and glorifying God motivated Calvinists to penetrate and control society. For Calvin everything pointed finally to the Kingdom and Glory of God, and the Old Testament provided the basis for his theocratic union of church and state with compulsory enforcement of pure doctrine. Luther tended to stress the individual's relationship to God. Yet a comparison of Luther and Calvin will reveal that they are enough alike to justify the statement that Calvinism was the daughter of Lutheranism.

The Calvinists were severely persecuted throughout France; hundreds of them suffered martyrdom, especially in the last half of the sixteenth century. But they did succeed in establishing a church, which in 1559 boldly declared its faith, "The Gallican Confession." It provides a good summary of Calvinism (24). In the Roman Catholic Counter Reformation the Protestants of France received heavy blows, causing them to develop theories of resistance to authority, which at best could only be implied in Calvin's views. This is documented later. Calvin did not leave a successor of his own stature, for Theodore Beza (1519-1605) was by no means his equal; but he left behind a host of strong men who believed in the glory of God and the Scriptures as His Word to man.

1. Priests' Petition to Marry, July 2, 1522

This petition of Zwingli and others reflects attitudes and conditions among the Swiss priests in 1522. Trans. Henry Preble, *Selected Works of Huldreich Zwingli*, ed. S. M. Jackson (Philadelphia: University of Pennsylvania Press, 1901).

Petition of certain preachers of Switzerland to the most Reverent Lord Hugo, Bishop of Constance, that he will not suffer himself to be persuaded to make any proclamation to the injury of the Gospel, nor endure longer the scandal of harlotry, but allow the presbyters to marry wives or at least would wink at their marriages.

To the Most Reverent Father and Lord in Christ, Hugo of Hohenlandenberg, Bishop of Constance, the undersigned offer obedient greeting.... [After an introductory apology, the petition continues:]

For among the things that threaten most to harm the budding teachings of Christ are grounds of offense. For how, by the everlasting God, will the simple-minded commons believe in him who even while he preaches the Gospel is thought by them to be licentious and a shameless dog? Can anything happen more disastrous to our sacred calling? We beg you, therefore, to show yourself as indulgent towards the second part of our petition as we believe you to be. We think that your most Reverent Fatherhood is not unaware how unsuccessfully and scantily the prescriptions in regard to chastity that have come down to us from our predecessors have been kept by the general run of priests, and oh, that they could have vouchsafed us strength to keep their commands as easily as they gave them! Yet God willed not that this be granted to man, that this gift of gods and angels might not be put down to the credit of man, but of God only. For this is plainly shown by the words of Christ (Matt. 19:10-12) when, after much discussion had taken place between himself and the Phari-

sees with regard to marriage, and his disciples said that, if the case were such as the discussion showed, it were better not to marry, he answered that not all men were capable of chastity, but only those to whom it had been given, wishing to show that it was a gift of God, that was given to some men in such wise that they might recognize that the divine goodness and not their own strength was of avail in this thing. And this is evidently indicated by what follows a little later, when, having made particular mention of eunuchs, he leaves it free to every man to keep or not to keep the law of chastity, saying, "He that is able to receive it, let him receive it." He meant, no doubt, that they to whom it was granted from above were bound to keep the law. For otherwise none could hold out under it. We, then, having tried with little enough success alas! to obey the law (for the disease must be boldly disclosed to the physician), have discovered that the gift has been denied unto us, and we have meditated long within ourselves how we might remedy our ill-starred attempts at chastity. And turning the matter over on all sides, we found nothing encouraging or propitious until we began to chew the cuds, it were, like the cattle, over those words of Christ just quoted. For then a sort of loathing of ourselves began to creep over us from the odour of it until we began to be disgusted that through careless thinking we had made a law unto ourselves of that which Christ had left free, as if the maintenance of chastity depended upon our own strength. Then presently a blush of shame overspread our faces, just as Adam, when he was going to be like the gods, found first nothing but his own nakedness, then an angry God, and shortly after a whole cart-load of ills. For who would not repent when he had looked upon the pitiable result of his own carelessness? For what else is it, by the everlasting God, than absolute folly, nay even shamelessness, to arrogate to one's self what belongs to God alone? To think one's self able to do that than which there is nothing one is less able to do? But after that loathing of ourselves, through which we recognized at once our rashness and our weakness, the hope of a remedy began to show itself, though from afar. For weighing more carefully Christ's words and the custom of our predecessors in this matter, we found that the whole question was far easier than we had thought. For when he says, "All men cannot receive this saying," and again, "He that is able to receive it, let him receive it," he prescribes no punishment for them that cannot receive it. Nay, either because of the vastness of the thing which he did not wish enjoined upon each and all, or on account of our weakness, which he knows better than we ourselves, he did not want this thing laid up against us, and so left it free. Therefore our souls which had been nigh unto despair were mightily refreshed when we learned those who were unable to receive the saying were threatened with no punishment by him who can send both body and soul into hell. But the fathers seemed to have cast an anxious eye in this direction too, when they showed themselves unwilling to enjoin chastity upon all without exception or to require a vow of chastity from others—the priests, at least, and even shielded human weakness with clever words, as was proper, in this way: When the sponsor was asked, "Are they righteous, these whom you present?" he was wont to answer: "They are righteous." ... When, however, they came to chastity—"Are they chaste?" he answered, "As far as human frailty allows." Thus it appears that neither our predecessors nor the fathers in our own day wanted that bound hard and fast which Christ had suffered to be free, lest they might smear the sweet yoke of the Lord with bitter wormwood. Having ... [determined] ... that we are held to the maintenance of chastity by neither divine nor human law, we considered nevertheless that though chastity go free, yet animal passion ought not to roam promiscuously, but to be bounded by rule and constancy, and forced into reasonable limits, like the rest of the course of our life, which though free becomes wildness and confusion, unless it be restrained by moderation, that we sink not to the level of swine. And this we see the Maker of all things willed from the beginning of creation, when he fashioned for Adam from his rib one woman only as a help-

meet and not a group or crowd of women, and joined her presently by so firm a bond that a man leaves father and mother sooner than his wife, for the two unite to form one flesh. Furthermore, if we run through the whole of the New Testament we find nowhere anything that favors free concubinage, but everything in approval of marriage. Therefore it appears to us most true and most right that for a Christian no third possibility besides chastity or marriage is left, and that he should live chastely if that is given unto him from above, or marry a wife if he be on fire with passion, and this we shall show more clearly in a little while from the truly sacred writings. Hence we beseech your mercy, wisdom and learning, illustrious Leader, to show yourself the first to lay hold upon the glory of taking the lead over all the bishops of Germany in right thinking upon Christianity ... and while others continue to thrust illfeigned chastity upon the unfortunate general body of our fellow bishops, do you suffer those who are consumed with passion to marry wives, since this, as has been shown, will be lawful according to Christ and according to the laws of men. From the whole vast crowd we are the first to venture to come forward, relying upon your gentleness, and to implore that you grant us this thing, not, as we think, without due consideration. ...

2. Zwingli and the Reformation at Zurich

In January, 1523, Zwingli and the vicar of the bishop of Constance held a conference to discuss the alleged heresy of some of Zwingli's teachings. The discussion revealed differences between the Catholic and Protestant points of view. The extracts given here are taken from the report of Hegenwald, a schoolmaster of Zurich and a friend of Zwingli. J. H. Robinson, *Readings in European History*, Vol. II (Boston: Ginn & Co., 1906). Cf. *Huldrici Zwingli opera*, I, ed. Schuler and Schulthess, trans. Lawrence A. McLouth in *Selected Works of Huldreich Zwingli*.

Then Master Ulrich Zwingli spoke as follows: "Pious brothers in Christ, you know that now in our time, as also for many years heretofore, the pure, clear, and bright light, the word of God, has been so dimmed and confused and darkened with human ambitions and teachings that the majority who call themselves Christians know but little of the divine will. But by their own invented service of God, by their own holiness, by external acts founded upon customs and law, they have gone astray; and the simple-minded have been so influenced by those whom people consider learned guides that they think that such invented external worship is spiritual, although all our true happiness, consolation, and good consist, not in our merits, nor in such external works, but rather alone in Jesus Christ our Saviour. His will and true service we can learn and discover only from his true word in the Holy Scriptures and in the trustworthy writings of his twelve apostles, otherwise from no human laws and statutes.

"And although I know that for the past five years I have preached in this city of Zurich nothing but the true, pure, and clear word of God, the holy gospel—the joyous message of Christ—still I am maligned by many as a heretic, a liar, a deceiver, and one disobedient to the Christian Church. Wherefore I offer here to justify myself to all who think that my sermons or teachings are unchristian or heretical, and to answer kindly and without anger. Now let them speak, in the name of God. Here I am."

At these remarks of Master Ulrich, the vicar from Constance arose, and answered as follows: "My good fellow-brother, Master Ulrich, asserts that he has always preached the holy gospel here publicly in Zurich, of which I have no doubt, for who would not truly and faithfully preach the holy gospel and St. Paul, providing God had ordained him as a preacher? For I am also a preacher, or priest, though perhaps unworthy, but nevertheless I have taught those intrusted to me for instruction in the word of God. . . .

"But if there is a desire to dispute and oppose good old customs, the ways and usages of the past, then in such case I say that I shall not undertake to dispute anything here at Zurich. For, as I think, such matters are to be settled by a general Christian assembly of all nations, or by a council of bishops and other scholars such as are found at universities. . . ."

Then Master Ulrich Zwingli spoke as follows: "Pious brothers in Christ, the worthy lord vicar seeks many evasions and subterfuges, for he claims that he does not desire to discuss the good old customs; but I say that we should not ask here how long this or that custom or habit has prevailed. Our aim is to find out whether a man is bound by divine ordinance to keep that which on account of long usage has been set up as law by men. For we of course think (as also the pope's own decree says) that custom should yield to truth. As to claiming that such matters should be settled by a Christian assembly of all nations, or by a council of bishops, etc., I say that here in this room there is without doubt a Christian assembly. For I hope that the majority of us here desire, by the divine will and love, to hear and know the truth, which Almighty God will not deny us if we desire it to his honor, with right belief and right hearts. For the Lord says, 'Where two or three are gathered together in my name, there am I in the midst of them'. . . . There is then, in spite of what the vicar says, no reason why we should not discuss these matters, why we should not speak and decide as to the truth.

"To the objection that the other nations would not consent, I answer that this brings up just the complaint that is made every day against the 'bigwigs'—the bishops and priests —namely, that they undertake to keep the pure and clear gospel, the Holy Scriptures, from the common people. For they say that it is not proper for any but themselves to expound the Scriptures, just as though other pious men were not Christians and had nothing to do with the spirit of God, and must be without knowledge of God's word. And there are also some of them who might say that it is improper to publish the secrets of the Divine Scriptures. Would you rob these thirsty souls of the truth, let them remain in doubt, frighten them by human ordinances, and leave them to live and die in uncertainty as to the truth? Really, my pious brethren, this is no small thing. God will not demand of us what pope, bishop, and council have established and commanded, nor how long this or that has been a laudable and ancient usage; but he will find out how his divine will, word, and commandments have been kept."...

3. The Sixty-seven Articles of Zwingli, 1523

The disputation of these articles firmly established Zwingli in Zurich. Trans. Lawrence A. McLouth, *Selected Works of Huldreich Zwingli.*

The articles and opinions below I, Ulrich Zwingli, confess to having preached in the worthy city of Zurich as based upon the Scriptures which are called inspired by God, and I offer to protect and conquer with the said articles, and where I have not now correctly understood said Scriptures I shall allow myself to be taught better, but only from said Scriptures.

1. All who say that the Gospel is invalid without the confirmation of the Church err and slander God.

2. The sum and substance of the Gospel is that our Lord Jesus Christ, the true Son of God, has made known to us the will of his heavenly Father, and has with his innocence released us from death and reconciled God.

3. Hence Christ is the only way to salvation for all who ever were, are and shall be.

4. Who seeks or points out another door errs, yea, he is a murderer of souls and a thief.

5. Hence all who consider other teachings equal to or higher than the Gospel err, and do not know what the Gospel is.

6. For Jesus Christ is the guide and leader, promised by God to all human beings, which promise was fulfilled.

7. For he is an eternal salvation and head of all believers who are his body, but which is dead and can do nothing without him.

8. From this follows first that all who dwell in the head are members and children of God, and that is the church or communion of the saints, the bride of Christ, *Ecclesia catholica.*

9. Furthermore, that as the members of the body can do nothing without the control of the head, so no one in the body of Christ can do the least without his head, Christ.

10. As that man is mad whose limbs (try to) do something without his head, tearing, wounding, injuring himself; thus when the members of Christ undertake something without their head, Christ, they are mad, and injure and burden themselves with unwise ordinances.

11. Hence we see in the clerical (so-called) ordinances, concerning their splendor, riches, classes, titles, laws, a cause of all foolishness, for they do not also agree with the head.

12. Thus they still rage, not on account of the head (for that one is eager to bring forth in these times from the grace of God), but because one will not let them rage, but tries to compel them to listen to the head.

13. Where this (the head) is hearkened to one learns clearly and plainly the will of God, and man is attracted by his spirit to him and changed into him.

14. Therefore all Christian people shall use their best diligence that the Gospel of Christ be preached alike everywhere.

15. For in the faith rests our salvation, and in unbelief our damnation; for all truth is clear in him.

16. In the Gospel one learns that human doctrines and decrees do not aid in salvation.

17. That Christ is the only eternal high priest, wherefrom it follows that those who have called themselves high priests have opposed the honor and power of Christ, yea, cast it out.

18. That Christ, having sacrificed himself once, is to eternity a certain and valid sacrifice for the sins of all the faithful, wherefrom it follows that the mass is not a sacrifice, but is a remembrance of the sacrifice and assurance of the salvation which Christ has given us.

19. That Christ is the only mediator between God and us.

20. That God desires to give us all things in his name, whence it follows that outside of his life we need no mediator except himself.

21. That when we pray for each other on earth, we do so in such fashion that we

II-2. Worshippers at a Shrine of Mary. *Woodcut by Michael Oftendorfer* (c. 1519–1559).

believe that all things are given to us through Christ alone.

22. That Christ is our justice, from which follows that our works in so far as they are good, so far they are of Christ, but in so far as they are ours, they are neither right nor good.

23. That Christ scorns the property and pomp of this world, whence from it follows that those who attract wealth to themselves in his name slander him terribly when they make him a pretext for their avarice and wilfullness.

24. That no Christian is bound to do those things which God has not decreed, therefore one may eat at all times all food, wherefrom one learns that the decree about cheese and butter is a Roman swindle.

25. That time and place is under the jurisdiction of Christian people, and man with them, wherefrom is learnt that those who fix time and place deprive the Christians of their liberty.

26. That God is displeased with nothing so much as with hypocrisy; whence is learnt that all is gross hypocrisy and profligacy which is mere show before men. Under this condemnation fall hoods, insignia, plates, etc.

27. That all Christian men are brethren of Christ and brethren of one another, and shall create no father (for themselves) on earth. Under this condemnation fall orders, sects, brotherhoods, etc.

28. That all which God has allowed or not forbidden is righteous, hence marriage is permitted to all human beings.

29. That all who are called clericals sin when they do not protect themselves by mar-

riage after they have become conscious that God has not enabled them to remain chaste.

30. That those who promise chastity (outside of matrimony) take foolishly or childishly too much upon themselves, whence is learnt that those who make such vows do wrong to the pious being.

31. That no special person can impose the ban upon any one, but the Church, that is the congregation of those among whom the one to be banned dwells, together with their watchman, i.e., the pastor.

32. That one may ban only him who gives public offence.

33. That property unrighteously acquired shall not be given to temples, monasteries, cathedrals, clergy or nuns, but to the needy, if it cannot be returned to the legal owner.

34. The spiritual (so-called) power has no justification for its pomp in the teaching of Christ.

35. But the lay has power and confirmation from the deed and doctrine of Christ.

36. All that the spiritual so-called state claims to have of power and protection belongs to the lay, if they wish to be Christians.

37. To them, furthermore, all Christians owe obedience without exception.

38. In so far as they do not command that which is contrary to God.

39. Therefore all their laws shall be in harmony with the divine will, so that they protect the oppressed, even if he does not complain.

40. They alone may put to death justly, also, only those who give public offense (if God is not offended let another thing be commanded).

41. If they give good advice and help to those for whom they must account to God, then these owe to them bodily assistance.

42. But if they are unfaithful and transgress the laws of Christ they may be deposed in the name of God.

43. In short, the realm of him is best and most stable who rules in the name of God alone, and his is worst and most unstable who rules in accordance with his own will.

44. Real petitioners call to God in spirit and truly, without great ado before men.

45. Hypocrites do their work so that they may be seen by men, also receive their reward in this life.

46. Hence it must always follow that church-song and out-cry without devoutness, and only for reward, is seeking either fame before the men or gain.

47. Bodily death a man should suffer before he offend or scandalize a Christian.

48. Who through stupidness or ignorance is offended without cause, he should not be left sick or weak, but he should be made strong, that he may not consider as a sin which is not a sin.

49. Greater offense I know not than that one does not allow priests to have wives, but permits them to hire prostitutes. Out upon the shame!

50. God alone remits sin through Jesus Christ, his Son, and alone our Lord.

51. Who assigns this to creatures detracts from the honor of God and gives it to him who is not God; this is real idolatry.

52. Hence the confession which is made to the priest or neighbor shall not be declared to be a remittance of sin, but only a seeking for advice.

53. Works of penance coming from the counsel of human beings (except the ban) do not cancel sin; they are imposed as a menace to others.

54. Christ has borne all our pains and labor. Hence whoever assigns to works of penance what belongs to Christ errs and slanders God.

55. Whoever pretends to remit to a penitent being any sin would not be a vicar of God or St. Peter, but of the devil.

56. Whoever remits any sin only for the sake of money is the companion of Simon and Balaam, and the real messenger of the devil personified.

57. The true divine Scriptures know naught about purgatory after this life.

58. The sentence of the dead is known to God only.

59. And the less God has let us know concerning it, the less we should undertake to know about it.

60. That man earnestly calls to God to

show mercy to the dead I do not condemn, but to determine a period of time therefor (seven years for a mortal sin), and to lie for the sake of gain, is not human, but devilish.

61. About the consecration which the priests have received in late times the Scriptures know nothing.

62. Furthermore, they know no priests except those who proclaim the word of God.

63. They command honor should be shown, i.e., to furnish them with food for the body.

64. All those who recognize their errors shall not be allowed to suffer, but to die in peace, and thereafter arrange in a Christian manner their bequests to the Church.

65. Those who do not wish to confess, God will probably take care of. Hence no force shall be used against their body, unless it be that they behave so criminally that one cannot do without that.

66. All the clerical superiors shall at once settle down, and with unanimity set up the cross of Christ, not the money-chests, or they will perish, for I tell thee the ax is raised against the tree.

67. If any one wishes conversation with me concerning interests, tithes, unbaptized children or confirmation, I am willing to answer.

Let no one undertake here to argue with sophistry or human foolishness, but come to the Scriptures to accept them as the judge (for as cares! the Scriptures breathe the Spirit of God), so that the truth either may be found, or if found, as I hope, retained. Amen.

Thus may God rule.

4. The Ten Berne Theses, 1528

These Ten Berne Theses were originally drawn up by Berthold Haller and Francis Kolb, ministers at Berne. They were revised and published by Zwingli, and from January 6 to January 26, 1528, they were defended by him and others in public discussion at Berne. The Protestant victory was complete, and Zwinglianism was officially extended through the three most important German cantons—Berne, Zurich, and Basel. *Huldreich Zwingli*, by S. M. Jackson (New York: G. P. Putnam's Sons, 1901); *Creeds of Christendom*, by Philip Schaff (New York: Harper & Row, Publishers, 1877).

1. The Holy Christian Church, whose only Head is Christ, is born of the Word of God, abides in the same, and listens not to the voice of a stranger.

2. The Church of Christ does not add to the laws and ordinances of the Word of God: consequently, human traditions are not binding upon us except so far as they are grounded on and ordained by the Word of God.

3. Christ is the only wisdom, righteousness, redemption, and satisfaction for the sins of the whole world. To acknowledge any other salvation or satisfaction is to deny Christ.

4. That the body and blood of Christ are substantially and corporally received in the bread of the Eucharist cannot be proved from the Bible.

5. Current use of the mass in which Christ is offered to God, the Father, for the sins of the living and the dead is contrary to Scripture, a blasphemy against the immortal sacrifice, passion and death of Christ, and in its abuse an abomination before God.

6. As Christ alone died for us, so he is also to be adored as the only Mediator and advocate between God the Father and believers. Therefore, it is contrary to the Word of God to propose and invoke other mediators.

7. There is nothing in Scripture about a purgatory after this life. Consequently, all services for the dead, such as vigils, requiems, soul-graces, sevens, spiritual consolations, anniversaries, ampullae, candles, etc. are vain.

8. Making pictures for worship is contrary to the Word of God in the New and Old Testaments. Hence, if appointed to be worshipped, they should be abolished.

9. Holy marriage is in the Scripture forbidden to no class, but harlotry and unchastity all are commanded to avoid.

10. As an openly immoral woman is under a heavy ban according to Scripture, it follows that harlotry and unchastity for this reason are in no class more shameful than in the priesthood.

5. Reckoning of the Faith of Ulrich Zwingli to Emperor Charles V, Augsburg, 1530

Coming only one year before the death of Zwingli, this confession represents his mature faith. Distinctive sections are reproduced here. *Book of Concord*, by Henry E. Jacobs (Philadelphia: G. W. Frederick, 1883).

1. [Zwingli confesses belief in God, the Trinity, the Incarnation, and the human-divine nature of Christ.]

2. Sovereignty: I know that this supreme divinity which is my God freely regulates all things, so that His purpose to determine anything does not depend upon the occasion of any creature, preceding reasoning or example; for this is peculiar to defective human wisdom. God, however, who from eternity to eternity regards all things with a single, simple view, has no need of any reasoning or expectation of events; but being equally wise, prudent, good, etc., He freely determines and disposes of all things, for whatever is, is His. Hence it is that, although knowing and foreseeing, He in the beginning formed man who should fall, and nevertheless determined to clothe in human nature His Son, who should restore Him when fallen. For by this means His goodness in every way was manifested. For since He contains in Himself mercy and justice, He exercised His justice when He expelled the transgressor from his happy home in Paradise, when He bound him in the mill of human misery and with the fetters of diseases, when He shackled him with the law, which, although it was holy, he was never to fulfil. For here, twice miserable, he learned not only that the flesh had fallen into trouble, but that the mind also was tortured from dread of the transgressed law. For although, according to the Spirit, he saw that the law is holy and just and a declaration of the divine mind, so that it enjoined nothing but what equity taught, yet when at the same time he saw that by the deeds of the law the mind does not satisfy itself, condemned by his own judgment, with the hope of attaining happiness removed, departing in despair from God's sight, he thought of enduring nothing but the pain of eternal punishment. Thus far was manifested God's justice.

Moreover, when the time came to publish His goodness, which He had determined from eternity to display no less than His justice, God sent His Son to assume our nature in every part, whereby to outweigh the penalty of sin, in order that, being made our brother and equal, He could be a Mediator to make a sacrifice for us to divine justice, which ought to remain holy and inviolate, no less than His goodness, whereby the world might be sure both of the appeased justice and the present kindness of God. For since He has given His Son to us and for us, how will He not with Him and because of Him give us all things?

3. Atonement: I know that there is no other victim for expiating crimes than Christ; for not even was Paul crucified for us; that there is no other name under the sun in which we must be saved than that of Jesus Christ. Here, therefore, not only the justification and satisfaction of our works are denied, but also the expiation or intercession of all saints, whether in earth or heaven, with reference to the goodness or mercy of God. For this is the one, sole Mediator between God and men, the God and man Christ Jesus. Moreover, God's election is manifest and remains firm; for whom He has elected before the foundation of the world, he has so elected, as, through His Son, to receive Him to Himself; for as He is kind and merciful, so also is He holy and just.

4. Original sin: I know that that remote ancestor, our first parent, was induced by self-love, at the pernicious advice suggested to him by the malice of the devil, to desire to become equal to God.

... Hence, I think of original sin as follows: It is truly called sin when it is committed against law; for where there is no law there is no transgression, and where there is no transgression there is no sin in the proper sense, inasmuch as sin is clearly enormity, crime, outrage, or guilt. I confess, therefore, that our father committed what is truly a sin—viz. an enormity, a crime, an execrable deed. But those begotten of him have not sinned in this manner, for who of us destroyed with his teeth the forbidden fruit in Paradise? Therefore, willing or unwilling, we are forced to admit that original sin, as it is in the children of Adam, is not properly sin, as has been explained: for it is no outrage upon any law. It is therefore, properly, a disease and condition—a disease, because just as he fell from self-love, so also do we; a condition, because just as he became a slave and subject to death, so also are we born slaves and children of wrath and subject to death. . . . Therefore, the cause of human calamity is crime, and not nativity; it pertains to nativity not otherwise than as that which proceeds from a source and cause. . . . The children have no crime, but the punishment and penalty of the crime—namely, the condition, servitude, and workhouse.

5-6. [Zwingli speaks of restoration in Christ and the nature of the church.]

7-8. Sacraments: I believe, yea, I know, that all the sacraments are so far from conferring grace that they do not even convey or distribute it. For as grace is produced or given by the Divine Spirit, so this gift pertains to the Spirit alone.

Moreover, a channel or vehicle is not necessary to the Spirit, for He Himself is the virtue and energy whereby all things are borne, and has no need of being borne; neither do we read in the Holy Scriptures that perceptible things, as are the sacraments, bear certainly with them the Spirit, but if perceptible things have ever been borne with the Spirit, it has been the Spirit, and not perceptible things, that has borne them. . . . The sacraments are given as a public testimony of that grace which is previously present to every individual. This baptism is administered in the presence of the Church to one who before receiving it either confessed the religion of Christ, or has the word of promise whereby he is known to belong to the Church. Hence it is that when we baptise an adult we ask him whether he believes. If he answer, Yea, then at length he receives baptism. Faith, therefore, has been present before he receives baptism. Faith, then, is not given in baptism. But when an infant is offered the question is asked whether its parents offer it for baptism. When they reply through witnesses that they wish it baptised, the infant is bap-

tised. Here also God's promise precedes, that He regards our infants as belonging to the Church no less than those of the Hebrews. For when they who are of the Church offer it, the infant is baptised under the law that since it has been born of Christians it is regarded by the divine promise among the members of the Church. By baptism, therefore, the Church publicly receives one who had previously been received through grace. Baptism, therefore, does not bring grace, but testifies to the Church that grace has been given for him to whom it is administered.

I believe, therefore, O Emperor, that a sacrament is a sign of a sacred thing—i.e., of grace that has been given. I believe that it is a visible figure or form of invisible grace—viz., which has been provided and given by God's bounty; i.e., a visible example which presents an analogy to something done by the Spirit. I believe that it is a public testimony. . . .

I believe that in the holy Eucharist—i.e., the supper of thanksgiving—the true body of Christ is present by the contemplation of faith; i.e., that they who thank the Lord for the kindness conferred on us in His Son acknowledge that He assumed true flesh, in it truly suffered, truly washed away our sins in His own blood; and thus everything done by Christ becomes present to them by the contemplation of faith. But that the body of Christ in essence and really—i.e., the natural body itself—is either present in the supper or masticated with our mouth or teeth, as the Papists and some who long for the flesh-pots of Egypt assert, we not only deny, but firmly maintain is an error opposed to God's Word.

9-12. [Zwingli considers ceremonies, preaching, obedience to magistrates, and purgatory.]

Conclusion: The above I firmly believe, teach, and maintain, not from my own oracles, but from those of the Divine Word; and, God willing, I promise to do this as long as life controls these members, unless someone from the declarations of Holy Scripture, properly understood, explain and establish the reverse as clearly and plainly as we have established the above. For it is no less grateful and delightful than fair and just for us to submit our judgments to the Holy Scriptures, and the Church deciding according to them by the Spirit. . . .

6. Order to Baptize Infants, January 18, 1525

The following four documents are from Jackson, Huldreich Zwingli.

Whereas an error has arisen respecting baptism, as if young children should not be baptised until they come to years of discretion, and know what the faith is; and whereas some have accordingly neglected to have their children baptised, our burgomaster, Council, and Great Council—so the Two Hundred of the city of Zurich are called—have held a disputation upon this matter to learn what Holy Scripture has to say about it, and having learned from it that notwithstanding this error the children should be baptised as soon as they are born; so must all those who have hitherto allowed their children to be unbaptised have them baptised inside the next week. Whoever will not do this must with wife and child, goods and chattels leave our city, jurisdiction, and domain, or await what will be done to him. Each one will accordingly know how to conduct himself. Done Wednesday before Sebastian's Day, MDXXV.

7. Zwingli's Letter to Capito, January 1, 1526, Concerning Balthasar of Waldshut

Balthasar of Waldshut has fallen into prison here—a man not merely irreverent and unlearned, but even empty. Learn the sum of the matter. When he came to Zurich our Council fearing lest he should cause a commotion ordered him to be taken into custody. Since, however, he had once in freakishness of disposition and fatuity, blurted out in Waldshut against our Council, of which place he, by the gods, was a guardian (i.e., he was pastor there), until the stupid fellow disunited and destroyed everything, it was determined that I should discuss with him in a friendly manner the baptising of infants and Catabaptists, as he earnestly begged first

from prison and afterwards from custody. I met the fellow and rendered him mute as a fish. The next day he recited a recantation in the presence of certain Councillors appointed for the purpose [and wrote it down]. Later he denied that he had changed his opinion, although he had done so before a Swiss tribunal, which with us is a capital offence, affirming that his signature had been extorted from him by terror, which was most untrue.

The Council was so unwilling that force should be used on him that when the Emperor or Ferdinand twice asked that the fellow be given to him it refused the request. Indeed he was not taken prisoner that he might suffer the penalty of his boldness in the baptismal matter, but to prevent his causing in secret some confusion, a thing he delighted to do. Then he angered the Council; for there were present most upright Councillors who had witnessed his most explicit and unconstrained withdrawal, and had refused to hand him over to the cruelty of the Emperor, helping themselves with my aid. The next day he was thrust back into prison and tortured. It is clear that the man had become a sport for demons, so he recanted not frankly as he had promised, nay he said that he entertained no other opinions than those taught by me, execrated the error and obstinacy of the Catabaptists, repeated this three times when stretched on the rack, and bewailed his misery and the wrath of God which in this affair was so unkind. Behold what wantonness! Than these men there is nothing more foolhardy, deceptive, infamous—for I cannot tell you what they devise in Abtzell—and shameless. To-morrow or next day the case will come up.

8. Zwingli's Letter to Vadian, March 7, 1526

It has been decreed this day by the Council of Two Hundred that the leaders of the Catabaptists shall be cast into the Tower, in which they formerly lay, and be allured by a bread and water diet until they either give up the ghost or surrender. It is also added that they who after this are immersed shall be submerged permanently: this decision is now published. Your father-in-law [Jacob Grebel, father of Conrad], the Senator, in vain implored mercy [for Conrad, who was one of the prisoners]. The incorrigible audacity of these men at first greatly grieved me, now it as greatly displeases me. I would rather that the newly rising Christianity should not be ushered in with a racket of this sort, but I am not God whom it thus pleases to make provision against evils that are to come, as He did when in olden time He slew with a sudden and fearful death Ananias who lied to Peter, so that He might cast out from us all daring to deceive, though there is nothing of which we are naturally such masters.

9. Alleged Errors of Anabaptists

EDICT OF ZURICH, BERNE, AND ST. GALL, SEPTEMBER 9, 1527

They seduce men from the congregations of the orthodox teachers and assail the public preachers with abuse; they babble in corners, woods, and fields; contract spiritual marriages, thereby giving occasion for adulteries; even command crime in the name of the Lord, e.g., the parricide at St. Gall; glory in divine revelations and miracles; teach that the Devil will be saved, and that in their church one could indulge lust without crime; had other signs of the covenant aside from catabaptism; would not carry swords; pronounced usury and the lot wicked; would have all external goods common and deposited in the midst of them, so that no one could use them as his own peculiar right; forbade Christians to accept the magistracy or to say an oath was proper. In order that this growth, dangerous to Christianity, wicked, harmful, turbulent, seditious, may be eradicated, we have thus decreed: if any one is suspected of catabaptism he is to be warned by the magistracy to leave off, under penalty of the designated punishment. Individuals as the civil contract obliges should inform upon those favourable to catabaptism. Whoever shall not fit his conduct to this dissuasion is liable to punishment according to the sentence of the magistracy and as special business; teachers, baptising preachers, itinerants and leaders of conventicles, or those previously released from prison and who have sworn to desist from such things, are to be drowned. Foreigners, their faith being pledged, are to be driven out, if they return are to be drowned. No one is allowed to secede from the Church and absent himself from the Holy Supper. Men led into the error by fraud may receive a mitigation of their punishment in proportion to their property and standing. Whoever flees from one jurisdiction to another shall be banished or given up on demand.

10. The Beginnings of the Anabaptist Reformation, Reminiscences of George Blaurock

An excerpt from the Hutterite *Chronicle*, 1525. From Vol. XXV, *LCC, Spiritual and Anabaptist Writers*, ed. George H. Williams and Angel M. Mergal (Philadelphia: The Westminster Press, 1957). Used by permission.

... Luther, with his following, teaches and holds that the body of the Lord Jesus Christ is essentially in the bread of the Supper [which] therewith is also a [means] of forgiving sins. Zwingli and his, however, taught and held that it [the Supper] is a recollection and a commemoration of the salvation and grace of Christ and not a sacrifice for sin, since Christ accomplished that on the cross. But both of them were pedobaptists and let go of the true baptism of Christ, who most certainly brings the cross with him, followed instead the pope with infant baptism, retained of him also the old leaven, the ferment, and cause of all evil, in fact the access and portal into a false Christianity, however much they otherwise eliminated him. But the pope did not derive infant baptism from Holy Scripture any more than purgatory, the Mass, prayer to the saints, letters of indulgence, and all the rest.

Luther and Zwingli defended with the sword this false teaching [pedobaptism] which [readiness] they really learned from the father and head of Antichrist, well knowing that the weapons of the Christian knight are not carnal but are nevertheless mighty before God in withstanding all human blows. Faith is not like that, a matter of coercion, but rather a gift of God. And Christ speaks to his disciples (Matt. 16:24): If anyone will follow me—notice, if anyone wishes or has a desire—let him deny himself and take his cross upon him. He does not say the sword, for this has no place beside the cross. They stand together like Christ and Pilate; they are to be compared to each other as a wolf and a sheep in the same fold.

But because God wished to have his own people, separated from all peoples, he willed for this purpose to bring in the right true morning star of his truth to shine in fullness in the final age of this world, especially in the German nation and lands, the same to strike home with his Word and to reveal the ground of divine truth. In order that his holy work might be made known and revealed before every man, there developed first in Switzerland an extraordinary awakening and preparation by God as follows:

It came to pass that Ulrich Zwingli and Conrad Grebel, one of the aristocracy, and Felix Mantz—all three much experienced and men learned in the German, Latin, Greek, and also the Hebrew, languages— came together and began to talk through matters of belief among themselves and recognized that infant baptism is unnecessary and recognized further that it is in fact no baptism. Two, however, Conrad and Felix, recognized in the Lord and believed [further] that one must and should be correctly baptized according to the Christian ordinance and institution of the Lord, since Christ himself says that whoever *believes* and is baptized will be saved. Ulrich Zwingli, who shuddered before Christ's cross, shame, and persecution, did not wish this and asserted that an uprising would break out. The other two, however, Conrad and Felix, declared that God's clear commandment and institution could not for that reason be allowed to lapse.

At this point it came to pass that a person from Chur came to them, namely, a cleric named George of the House of Jacob, commonly called "Bluecoat" [*Blaurock*] because one time when they were having a discussion of matters of belief in a meeting this George Cajacob presented his view also. Then someone asked who it was who had just spoken. Thereupon someone answered: The person in the blue coat spoke. Thus thereafter he got the name of Blaurock.... This George came, moreover, with the unusual zeal which he had, a straightforward, simple parson. As such he was held by everyone. But in matters of faith and in divine zeal, which had been given him out of God's grace, he acted wonderfully and valiantly in the cause of truth. He first came to Zwingli and discussed matters of belief with him at length, but accomplished nothing. Then he was told that there were other men more zealous than Zwingli. These men he inquired for diligently and found them, namely, Conrad Grebel and Felix Mantz. With them he spoke and talked through matters of faith. They came to one mind in these things, and in the pure fear of God they recognized that a person must learn from the divine Word and preaching a true faith which manifests itself in love, and receive the true Christian baptism on the basis of the recognized and confessed faith, in the union with God of a good conscience, [prepared] henceforth to serve God in a holy Christian life with all godliness, also to be steadfast to the end in tribulation. And it came to pass that they were together until fear [*angst*] began to come over them, yea, they were pressed [*gedrungen*] in their hearts. Thereupon they began to bow their knees to the Most High God in heaven and called upon him as the Knower of hearts, implored him to enable them to do his divine will and to manifest his mercy toward them. For flesh and blood and human forwardness did not drive them, since they well knew what they would have to bear and suffer on account of it. After the prayer, George Cajacob arose and asked Conrad to baptize him, for the sake of God, with the true Christian baptism upon his faith and knowledge. And when he knelt down with that request and desire, Conrad baptized him, since at that time there was no ordained deacon [*diener*] to perform such work. After that was done the others similarly desired George to baptize them, which he also did upon their request. Thus they together gave themselves to the name of the Lord in the high fear of God. Each confirmed [bestätet] the other in the service of the gospel, and they began to teach and keep the faith. Therewith began the separation from the world and its evil works.

Soon thereafter several others made their way to them, for example, Balthasar Hubmaier of Friedberg, Louis Haetzer, and still others, men well instructed in the German, Latin, Greek, and Hebrew languages, very well versed in Scripture, some preachers and other persons, who were soon to have testified with their blood.

The above-mentioned Felix Mantz they drowned at Zurich because of this true belief and true baptism, who thus witnessed steadfastly with his body and life to this truth.

Afterward Wolfgang Ullmann, whom they burned with fire and put to death in Waltzra, also in Switzerland, himself the eleventh, his brethren and associates witnessing in a valorous and knightly manner with their bodies and their lives unto death that their faith and baptism was grounded in the divine truth. . . .

Thus did it [the movement] spread through persecution and much tribulation. The church [gmain] increased daily, and the Lord's people grew in numbers. This the enemy of the divine truth could not endure. He used Zwingli as an instrument, who thereupon began to write diligently and to preach from the pulpit that the baptism of believers and adults was not right and should not be tolerated—contrary to his own confession which he had previously written and taught, namely, that infant baptism cannot be demonstrated or proved with a single clear word from God. But now, since he wished rather to please men than God, he contended against the true Christian baptism. He also stirred up the magistracy to act on imperial authorization and behead as Anabaptists those who had properly given themselves to God, and with a good understanding had made covenant of a good conscience with God.

Finally it reached the point that over twenty men, widows, pregnant wives, and maidens were cast miserably into dark towers, sentenced never again to see either sun or moon as long as they lived, to end their days on bread and water, and thus in the dark towers to remain together, the living and the dead, until none remained alive— there to die, to stink, and to rot. Some among them did not eat a mouthful of bread in three days, just so that others might have to eat.

Soon also there was issued a stern mandate at the instigation of Zwingli that if any more people in the canton of Zurich should be rebaptized, they should immediately, without further trial, hearing, or sentence, be cast into the water and drowned. Herein one sees which spirit's child Zwingli was, and those of his party still are.

However, since the work fostered by God cannot be changed and God's counsel lies in the power of no man, the aforementioned men went forth, through divine prompting, to proclaim and preach the evangelical word and the ground of truth. George Cajacob or Blaurock went into the county of Tyrol. In the meantime Balthasar Hubmaier came to Nicolsburg in Moravia, began to teach and preach. The people, however, accepted the teaching and many people were baptized in a short time.

11. Balthasar's Eighteen Propositions

Balthazar's Eighteen Propositions, relating to the nature of a Christian life, were disputed at Waldshut in 1524. *Crozer Historical Leaflets*, No. 5, trans. Henry C. Vedder (St. Louis: Concordia Publishing House, 1901). Original may be found in Loserth's *Doktor Balthasar Hubmaier und die Anfaenge der Wiedertaufe in Maehren* (Brünn, 1893).

1. Faith alone makes us just before God.
2. This faith is the knowledge of the mercy of God, which he manifested to us through the giving of his only-begotten Son. Thereby are overthrown all sham Christians, who have only "a historical faith" in God.
3. This faith cannot remain dead, but must manifest itself toward God in thanksgiving, toward our fellow men in works of brotherly love. Thereby are all ceremonies destroyed, tapers, psalms, holy-water.

4. Only those works are good that God has commanded, and those only are evil that he has forbidden. Thereby fall fish, flesh, cowls, plates.

5. The mass is no sacrifice, but a memorial of the death of Christ. Hence it may be offered as a sacrifice neither for the dead nor for the living. Thereby fall masses for souls and the like.

6. When this memorial is celebrated, the death of our Lord should be preached in their mother tongue to believers. Thereby fall private masses.

7. Images are good for nothing; wherefore such expense should no longer be wasted on images of wood and stone, but bestowed upon the living, needy images of God.

8. Just as every Christian should believe and be baptized for himself, so it is his privilege to judge from the holy Scripture, if the bread and wine are rightly given him by his pastor.

9. As Christ alone died for our sins and we are baptized in his name alone, so should we call upon him only as our mediator and intercessor. Thereby fall all pilgrimages.

10. It is better to explain a single verse of a psalm in the vernacular of the people, than to sing five whole Psalms in a foreign language not understood by the people. Thereby vanish matins, prime, tierce, sext, nones, vespers, complins and vigils.

11. All doctrines not planted by God himself are profitless, condemned, and must be rooted up. Here fall to the ground Aristotle, the Scholastics, as Thomas, Scotus, Bonaventura and Occam, and all teachers who in their origin are not from God.

12. The hour is coming and is already here, in which no one will be considered a priest but he who preaches the word of God. Thereby fall the sayers of early mass, suffragists, requiemists, sayers of intercessory masses.

13. It is the duty of church members, to whom the pure word of God is clearly preached, to provide food and clothing for the ministers. Thereby go to the ground the courtesans, pensioners, incorporators, absentees, liars and dream-babblers.

14. Whoso seeks purgatory, the trust of

II-3. Balthasar Hubmaier. *The only known portrait, an old woodcut.*

those whose god is their belly, seeks the grave of Moses—it will never be found.

15. To forbid priests to marry and wink at their carnal lewdness is to release Barabbas and put Christ to death.

16. To promise chastity in the strength of man is nothing else than to fly over the sea without wings.

17. Whoso for worldly advantage denies or remains silent concerning the word of God, sells the blessing of God, as Esau sold his birthright, and will also be denied by Christ.

18. Whoso does not earn his bread by the sweat of his brow is in condemnation, is not worthy of the food that he eats. Herewith are all idlers condemned, whoever they may be.

12. Concerning Heretics and Those Who Burn Them, 1524

While being held in custody in Schaffhausen, Switzerland, Hubmaier wrote letters to the city council asking permission to remain in the city. The Roman Catholics of Austria were belligerently demanding that he be turned over to them. Part of one letter is quoted below, followed by Hubmaier's tract on heretics, the earliest plea in the sixteenth century for complete religious toleration. *Balthasar Hubmaier,* by Henry C. Vedder (New York: G. P. Putnam's Sons, 1905).

Why have I made so long a preface? Because I am called a disturber of the people, a stirrer-up of strife, a Lutheran, a heretic, and so forth, and the pious, honourable city of Waldshut because of my teaching is slandered high and low, which truly pains my heart. No one could ever be more ready and willing than I am to give all men an account of my doctrine, as I have preached it these two years past. If I have taught only truth, why abuse me? If error, any man may set me in the right way with the spiritual word. As man I may very well err, but will be no heretic. I am conscious that in the whole two years past I have not preached a single letter that is not grounded in God's word. I herewith further pledge myself, where the necessity of this my defence presses me, here at Schaffhausen, I will before the court give and receive justice. Only one should not offer violence, either to me or to the pious city of Waldshut. Moreover, I beg you to permit neither me nor other Christian teachers to be urged and compelled, but hear me in the face of my opponents, who accuse me so shamefully. But should this prayer of mine find no hearing, which once I would not have expected of Turks, and I should be tortured by prison, rack, sword, fire, or water, or God otherwise withdraw from me his grace, so that I speak otherwise than now, then do I herewith protest and testify that I will suffer and die as a Christian.

THE TRACT ON BURNING HERETICS

1. Heretics are those who wickedly oppose the Holy Scriptures, the first of whom was the devil, when he said to Eve, "Ye shall not surely die" (Gen. 3:4), together with his followers. 2. Those also are heretics who cast a veil over the Scriptures and interpret them otherwise than the Holy Spirit demands; as those who everywhere proclaim a concubine as a benefice, pasturing and ruling the church at Rome, and compelling us to believe this talk. 3. Those who are such one should overcome with holy knowledge, not angrily but softly, although the Holy Scriptures contain wrath. 4. But this wrath of the Scriptures is truly a spiritual fire and zeal of love, not burning without

the word of God. 5. If they will not be taught by strong proofs or evangelic reasons, then let them be, and leave them to rage and be mad (Tit. 3:2,3), that those who are filthy may become more filthy still (Rev. 22:11). 6. The law that condemns heretics to the fire builds up both Zion in blood and Jerusalem in wickedness. 7. Therefore will they be taken away in sighs, for the judgments of God (whose right it is to judge) either convert or harden them, that the blind lead the blind and both the seduced and the seducer go from bad to worse. 8. This is the will of Christ who said, "Let both grow together till the harvest, lest while ye gather up the tares ye root up also the wheat with them" (Matt. 13:29). "For there must also be heresies among you, that they that are approved may be made manifest among you" (I Cor. 11:19). 9. Though they indeed experience this, yet they are not put away until Christ shall say to the reapers, "Gather first the tares and bind them in bundles to burn them" (Matt. 13:30). 10. This word does not teach us idleness but a strife; for we should unceasingly contend, not with men but with their godless doctrine. 11. The unwatchful bishops are the cause of the heresies. "When men slept, the enemy came" (Matt. 13:25). 12. Again, "Blessed is the man who is a watcher at the door of the bridegroom's chamber" (Prov. 8), and neither sleeps nor "sits in the seat of the scornful" (Ps. 1:1). 13. Hence it follows that the inquisitors are the greatest heretics of all, since, against the doctrine and example of Christ, they condemn heretics to fire, and before the time of harvest root up the wheat with the tares. 14. For Christ did not come to butcher, destroy and burn, but that those that live might live more abundantly (John 10:10). 15. We should pray and hope for repentance, as long as man lives in this misery. 16. A Turk or a heretic is not convinced by our act, either with the sword or with fire, but only with patience and prayer; and so we should await with patience the judgment of God. 17. If we do otherwise, God will treat our sword as stubble, and burning fire as mockery (Job 41). 18. So unholy and far off from evangelical doctrine is the whole order of preaching friars (of which variegated birds our Antony is one), that hitherto out of them alone the inquisitors have come. 19. If these only knew of what spirit they ought to be, they would not so shamelessly pervert God's word, nor so often cry, "To the fire, to the fire!" (Luke 9:54-56). 20. It is no excuse (as they chatter) that they give over the wicked to the secular power, for he who thus gives over sins more deeply (John 19:11). 21. For each Christian has a sword against the wicked, which is the word of God (Eph. 6:17), but not a sword against the malignant. 22. The secular power rightly and properly puts to death the criminals who injure the bodies of the defenseless (Rom. 13:3,4). But he who is God's cannot injure any one, unless he first deserts the gospel. 23. Christ has shown us this clearly, saying, "Fear not them that kill the body" (Matt. 10:28). 24. The (secular) power judges criminals, but not the godless who cannot injure either body or soul, but rather are a benefit; therefore God can in wisdom draw good from evil. 25. Faith which flows from the gospel fountain, lives only in contests, and the rougher they become so much the greater becomes faith. 26. That every one has not been taught the gospel truth, is due to the bishops no less than to the common people—these that they have not cared for a better shepherd, the former that they have not performed their office properly. 27. If the blind lead the blind, according to the just judgment of God, they both fall together into the ditch (Matt. 15:14). 28. Hence to burn heretics is in appearance to profess Christ (Tit. 1:10,11), but in reality to deny him, and to be more monstrous than Jehoiakim, the King of Judah (Jer. 37:23). 29. If it is blasphemy to destroy a heretic, how much more is it to burn to ashes a faithful herald of the word of God, unconvicted, not arraigned by the truth. 30. The greatest deception of the people is a zeal for God that is unscripturally expended, the salvation of the soul, honour of the church, love of truth, good intention, use or custom, episcopal decrees, the teaching of the reason that comes by the natural light. For they are deadly arrows where they are not led and directed by the Scriptures. 31. We should not presume, led away by the deception of our own purpose, to do better or more securely than God has spoken by his own mouth. 32. Those who rely on their good intention and think to do better, are like Uzziah and Peter. The latter was called Satan by Christ (Matt. 16:23), but the former came to a wretched end (I Chron. 13:10). 33. Elnathan, Delaiah and Gemariah acted wisely in withstanding Jehoiakim, the King of Judah, when he cast the book of Jehovah into the fire (Jer. 36:25). 34. But in that, after one book was burnt, Baruch by the express direction of Jeremiah, wrote another much better (Jer. 36:27-32), we see the just punishment of God on the unrighteous burning. For so it shall be that on those who fear the frost, a cold snow falls (Job. 6:16?). 35. But we do not hold that it was unchristian to burn their numerous books of incantations, as the fact in the Acts of the Apostles shows (Acts 19:19). It is a small thing to burn innocent paper, but to point out an error and to disprove it by Scripture, that is art. 36. Now it is clear to every one, even the blind, that a law to burn heretics is an invention of the devil. "Truth is immortal."

13. The Schleitheim Confession of Faith, February 24, 1527

This confession is often called the first Baptist confession of faith. The articles were written chiefly by Michael Sattler, and were adopted by a Swiss Brethren Conference meeting at Schleitheim. Trans. John C. Wenger, *Glimpses of Mennonite History and Doctrine* (Scottdale, Pa.: Herald Press, 1947).

The articles which we discussed and on which we were of one mind are these: 1. Baptism; 2. The Ban (Excommunication); 3. Breaking of Bread; 4. Separation from the Abomination; 5. Pastors in the Church; 6. The Swords; and 7. The Oath.

First. Observe concerning baptism: Baptism shall be given to all those who have learned repentance and amendment of life, and who believe truly that their sins are

II-4. Anabaptists in Chains
Before the Bishop of Münster.

taken away by Christ, and to all those who walk in the resurrection of Jesus Christ, and wish to be buried with Him in death, so that they may be resurrected with Him, and to all those who with this significance request it [baptism] of us and demand it for themselves. This excludes all infant baptism, the highest and chief abomination of the pope. In this you have the foundation and testimony of the apostles. Matt. 28, Mark 16, Acts 2, 8, 16, 19. This we wish to hold simply, yet firmly and with assurance.

Second. We are agreed as follows on the ban: The ban shall be employed with all those who have given themselves to the Lord, to walk in His commandments, and with all those who are baptized into the one Body of Christ and who are called brethren or sisters, and yet who slip sometimes and fall into error and sin, being inadvertently overtaken. The same shall be admonished twice in secret and the third time openly disciplined or banned according to the command of Christ (Matt. 18). But this shall be done according to the regulation of the Spirit (Matt. 5) before the breaking of bread, so that we may break and eat one bread, with one mind and in one love, and may drink of one cup.

Third. In the breaking of bread we are of one mind and are agreed [as follows]: All those who wish to break one bread in remembrance of the broken body of Christ, and all who wish to drink of one drink as a remembrance of the shed blood of Christ, shall be united beforehand by baptism in one body of Christ which is the church of God and whose Head is Christ. For all Paul points out we cannot at the same time be partakers of the Lord's table and the table of devils; we cannot, at the same time drink the cup of the Lord and the cup of the devil. That is, all those who have fellowship with the dead works of darkness have no part in the light. Therefore all who follow the devil and the world have no part with those who are called unto God out of the world. All who lie in evil have no part in the good.

Therefore it is and must be [thus]: Whoever has not been called by one God to faith, to one baptism, to one Spirit, to one body, with all the children of God's church, cannot be made [into] one bread with them, as indeed must be done if one is truly to break bread according to the command of Christ.

Fourth. We are agreed [as follows] on separation: A separation shall be made from the evil and from the wickedness which the devil planted in the world; in this manner, simply that we shall not have fellowship with them [the wicked] and not run with them in the multitude of their abominations. This is the way it is: Since all who do not walk in the obedience of faith, and have not united themselves with God so that they wish to do His will, are a great abomination before God, it is not possible for anything to grow or issue from them except abominable things. For truly all creatures are in but two classes, good and bad, believing and unbelieving, darkness and light, the world and those who [have come] out of the world, God's temple and idols, Christ and Belial; and none can have part with the other.

To us then the command of the Lord is clear when He calls upon us to be separate from the evil and thus He will be our God and we shall be His sons and daughters.

He further admonishes us to withdraw from Babylon and the earthly Egypt that we may not be partakers of the pain and suffering which the Lord will bring upon them.

From this we should learn that everything which is not united with our God and Christ cannot be other than an abomination which we should shun and flee from. By this is meant all popish and antipopish works and church services, meetings and church attendance, drinking houses, civic affairs, the commitments [made in] unbelief and other things of that kind, which are highly regarded by the world and yet are carried on in flat contradiction to the command of God, in accordance with all the unrighteousness which is in the world. From all these things we shall be separated and have no part with them for they are nothing but an abomination, and they are the cause of our being hated before our Christ Jesus, Who has set us free from the slavery of the flesh and fitted us for the service of God through the Spirit Whom He has given us.

Therefore there will also unquestionably fall from us the unchristian devilish weapons of force—such as sword, armor and the like, and all their use [either] for friends or against one's enemies—by virtue of the word of Christ, Resist not [him that is] evil.

Fifth. We are agreed as follows on pastors in the church of God: The pastor in the church of God shall, as Paul has prescribed, be one who out-and-out has a good report of those who are outside the faith. This office shall be to read, to admonish and teach, to warn, to discipline, to ban in the church, to lead out in prayer for the advancement of all the brethren and sisters, to lift up the bread when it is to be broken, and in all things to see to the care of the body of Christ, in order that it may be built up and developed, and the mouth of the slanderer be stopped.

This one moreover shall be supported of the church which has chosen him, wherein he may be in need, so that he who serves the Gospel may live of the Gospel as the Lord has ordained. But if a pastor should do something requiring discipline, he shall not be dealt with except [on the testimony of] two or three witnesses. And when they sin they shall be disciplined before all in order that the others may fear.

But should it happen that through the cross this pastor should be banished or led to the Lord [through martyrdom] another shall be ordained in his place in the same hour so that God's little flock and people may not be destroyed.

Sixth. We are agreed as follows concerning the sword: The sword is ordained of God outside the perfection of Christ. It punishes and puts to death the wicked, and guards and protects the good. In the Law the sword was ordained for the punishment of the wicked and for their death, and the same [sword] is [now] ordained to be used by the worldly magistrates.

In the perfection of Christ, however, only the ban is used for a warning and for the excommunication of the one who has sinned, without putting the flesh to death—simply the warning and the command to sin no more.

Now it will be asked by many who do not recognize [this as] the will of Christ for us, whether a Christian may or should employ the sword against the wicked for the defence and protection of the good, or for the sake of love.

Our reply is unanimously as follows: Christ teaches and commands us to learn of

Him, for He is meek and lowly in heart and so shall we find rest to our souls. Also Christ says to the heathenish woman who was taken in adultery, not that one should stone her according to the law of His Father (and yet He says, As the Father has commanded me, thus I do), but in mercy and forgiveness and warning, to sin no more. Such [an attitude] we also ought to take completely according to the rule of the ban.

Secondly, it will be asked concerning the sword, whether a Christian shall pass sentence in worldly disputes and strife such as unbelievers have with one another. This is our united answer: Christ did not wish to decide or pass judgment between brother and brother in the case of the inheritance, but refused to do so. Therefore we should do likewise.

Thirdly, it will be asked concerning the sword, Shall one be a magistrate if one should be chosen as such? The answer is as follows: They wished to make Christ king, but He fled and did not view it as the arrangement of His Father. Thus shall we do as He did, and follow Him, and so shall we not walk in darkness. For He Himself says, He who wishes to come after me, let him deny himself and take up his cross and follow me. Also, He Himself forbids the [employment of] the force of the sword saying, The worldly princes lord it over them, etc., but not so shall it be with you. Further, Paul says, Whom God did foreknow He also did predestinate to be conformed by the image of His Son, etc. Also Peter says, Christ has suffered (not ruled) and left us an example, that ye should follow His steps.

Finally, it will be observed that it is not appropriate for a Christian to serve as a magistrate because of these points: The government magistracy is according to the flesh, but the Christians' is according to the Spirit; their houses and dwelling remain in this world, but the Christians' are in heaven; their citizenship is in this world, but the Christians' citizenship is in heaven; the weapons of their conflict and war are carnal and against the flesh only, but the Christians' weapons are spiritual, against the fortification of the devil. The worldlings are armed with

steel and iron, but the Christians are armed with the armor of God, with truth, righteousness, peace, faith, salvation and the word of God. In brief, as is the mind of Christ toward us, so shall the mind of the members of the body of Christ be through Him in all things, that there may be no schism in the body through which it would be destroyed. For every kingdom divided against itself will be destroyed. Now since Christ is as it is written of Him, His members must also be the same, that His body may remain complete and united to its own advancement and upbuilding.

Seventh. We are agreed as follows concerning the oath: the oath is a confirmation among those who are quarreling or making promises. In the Law it is commanded to be performed in God's Name, but only in truth, not falsely. Christ, who teaches the perfection of the Law, prohibits all swearing to His followers, whether true or false—neither by heaven nor by the earth, nor by Jerusalem, nor by our head—and that for the reason which He shortly thereafter gives, for you are not able to make one hair white or black. So you see it is for this reason that all swearing is forbidden: we cannot fulfill that which we promise when we swear, for we cannot change [even] the very least thing on us. . . .

14. The Trial and Martyrdom of Michael Sattler, 1527

Michael Sattler, author of the Schleitheim confession, was brought to trial by the Roman Catholics of Austria on May 17, and executed on May 21. The account below is from the *Martyr's Mirror* of Tilman J. van Braght (1660). Translated in Williams and Mergal, *Spiritual and Anabaptist Writers*. Used by permission.

After many legal transactions on the day of his departure from this world, the articles against him being many, Michael Sattler requested that they might once more be read to him and that he might again be heard upon them. This the bailiff, as the attorney [for the defense] of his lord [the emperor], opposed and would not consent to it. Michael Sattler then requested a ruling. After a consultation, the judges returned as their answer that, if his opponents would allow it, they, the judges, would consent. Thereupon the town clerk of Ensisheim, as the spokesman of the said attorney, spoke thus: "Prudent, honorable, and wise lords, he has boasted of the Holy Ghost. Now if his boast is true, it seems to me, it is unnecessary to grant him this; for, if he has the Holy Ghost, as he boasts, the same will tell him what has been done here." To this Michael Sattler replied: "You servants of God, I hope my request will not be denied, for the said articles are as yet unclear to me [because of their number]." The town clerk responded: "Prudent, honorable, and wise lords, though we are not bound to do this, yet in order to give satisfaction, we will grant him his request that it may not be thought that injustice is being done him in his heresy or that we desire to abridge him of his rights. Hence let the articles be read to him again." [The nine charges, seven against all fourteen defendants, two specifically against Sattler, are here omitted, as they are answered seriatim by Sattler.]

Thereupon Michael Sattler requested permission to confer with his brethren and sisters, which was granted him. Having conferred with them for a little while, he began and undauntedly answered as follows: "In regard to the articles relating to me and my brethren and sisters, hear this brief answer:

"First, that we have acted contrary to the imperial mandate, we do not admit. For the same says that the Lutheran doctrine and delusion is not to be adhered to, but only the gospel and the Word of God. This we have kept. For I am not aware that we have acted contrary to the gospel and the Word of God. I appeal to the words of Christ.

"Secondly, that the real body of Christ the Lord is not present in the sacrament, we admit. For the Scripture says: Christ ascended into heaven and sitteth on the right hand of his Heavenly Father, whence he shall come to judge the quick and the dead, from which it follows that, if he is in heaven and not in the bread, he may not be eaten bodily.

"Thirdly, as to baptism we say infant baptism is of no avail to salvation. For it is written [Rom. 1:17] that we live by faith alone. Again [Mark 16:16]: He that believeth and is baptized shall be saved. Peter says the same [I Pet. 3:21]: Which doth also now save you in baptism (which is signified by that [ark of Noah]), not the putting away of the filth of the flesh but rather the covenant of a good conscience with God by the resurrection of Jesus Christ.

"Fourthly, we have not rejected the oil [of extreme unction]. For it is a creature of God, and what God has made is good and not to be refused, but that the pope, bishops, monks and priests can make it better we do not believe; for the pope never made anything good. That of which the Epistle of James [Jas. 5:14] speaks is not the pope's oil.

"Fifthly, we have not insulted the mother of God and the saints. For the mother of Christ is to be blessed among all women because unto her was accorded the favor of giving birth to the Saviour of the whole world. But that she is a mediatrix and advocatess—of this the Scriptures know nothing, for she must with us await the judgment. Paul said to Timothy [I Tim. 2:5]: Christ is our mediator and advocate with God. As regards the saints, we say that we who live and believe are the saints, which I prove by the epistles of Paul to the Romans [Rom. 1:7], the Corinthians [I Cor. 1:2], the Ephesians [Eph. 1:1], and other places where he always writes 'to the beloved saints.' Hence, we who believe are the saints, but those who have died in the faith we regard as the blessed.

"Sixthly, we hold that we are not to swear before the authorities, for the Lord says [Matt. 5:34]: Swear not, but let your communication be, Yea, yea; nay, nay.

"Seventhly, when God called me to testify of his Word and I had read Paul and also considered the unchristian and perilous state in which I was, beholding the pomp, pride, usury, and great whoredom of the monks and priests, I went and took unto me a wife, according to the command of God; for Paul well prophesies concerning this to Timothy [I Tim. 4:3]: In the latter time it shall come to pass that men shall forbid to marry and command to abstain from meats which God hath created to be received with thanksgiving.

"Eighthly, if the Turks should come, we

ought not to resist them. For it is written [Matt. 5:21]: Thou shalt not kill. We must not defend ourselves against the Turks and others of our persecutors, but are to beseech God with earnest prayer to repel and resist them. But that I said that, if warring *were* right, I would rather take the field against so-called Christians who persecute, capture, and kill pious Christians than against the Turks was for the following reason. The Turk is a true Turk, knows nothing of the Christian faith, and is a Turk after the flesh. But you who would be Christians and who make your boast of Christ persecute the pious witnesses of Christ and are Turks after the spirit!

"In conclusion, ministers of God, I admonish you to consider the end for which God has appointed you, to punish the evil and to defend and protect the pious. Whereas, then, we have not acted contrary to God and the gospel, you will find that neither I nor my brethren and sisters have offended in word or deed against any authority. Therefore, ministers of God, if you have neither heard nor read the Word of God, send for the most learned men and for the sacred books of the Bible in whatsoever language they may be and let them confer with us in the Word of God. If they prove to us with the Holy Scriptures that we err and are in the wrong, we will gladly desist and recant and also willingly suffer the sentence and punishment for that of which we have been accused; but if no error is proven to us, I hope to God that you will be converted and receive instruction."

Upon this speech the judges laughed and put their heads together, and the town clerk of Ensisheim said: "Yes, you infamous, desperate rascal of a monk, should we dispute with you? The hangman will dispute with you, I assure you!"

Michael said: "God's will be done."

The town clerk said: "It were well if you had never been born."

Michael replied: "God knows what is good."

The town clerk: "You archheretic, you have seduced pious people. If they would only now forsake their error and commit themselves to grace!"

Michael: "Grace is with God alone."

One of the prisoners also said: "We must not depart from the truth."

The town clerk: "Yes, you desperate villain, you archheretic, I say, if there were no hangmen here, I would hang you myself and be doing God a good service thereby."

Michael: "God will judge aright." Thereupon the town clerk said a few words to him in Latin, what, we do not know. Michael Sattler answered him, *Judica.*

The town clerk then admonished the judges and said: "He will not cease from this chatter anyway. Therefore, my Lord Judge, you may proceed with the sentence. I call for a decision of the court."

The judge asked Michael Sattler whether he too committed it to the court. He replied: "Ministers of God, I am not sent to judge the Word of God. We are sent to testify and hence cannot consent to any adjudication, since we have no command from God concerning it. But we are not for that reason removed from being judged and we are ready to suffer and to await what God is planning to do with us. We will continue in our faith in Christ so long as we have breath in us, unless we be dissuaded from it by the Scriptures."

The town clerk said: "The hangman will instruct you, he will dispute with you, archheretic."

Michael: "I appeal to the Scriptures."

Then the judges arose and went into another room where they remained for an hour and a half and determined on the sentence. In the meantime some [of the soldiers] in the room treated Michael Sattler most unmercifully, heaping reproach upon him. One of them said: "What have you in prospect for yourself and the others that you have so seduced them?" With this he also drew a sword which lay upon the table, saying: "See, with this they will dispute with you." But Michael did not answer upon a single word concerning himself but willingly endured it all. One of the prisoners said: "We must not cast pearls before swine." Being also asked why he had not remained a lord in the convent, Michael answered: "According to the flesh I was a lord, but it is better as it is." He did not say more than what is recorded here, and this he spoke fearlessly.

The judges having returned to the room, the sentence was read. It was as follows: "In the case of the attorney of His Imperial Majesty vs. Michael Sattler, judgment is passed that Michael Sattler shall be delivered to the executioner, who shall lead him to the place of execution and cut out his tongue, then forge him fast to a wagon and thereon with red-hot tongs twice tear pieces from his body; and after he has been brought outside the gate, he shall be plied five times more in the same manner...."

After this had been done in the manner prescribed, he was burned to ashes as a heretic. His fellow brethren were executed with the sword, and the sisters drowned. His wife, also after being subjected to many entreaties, admonitions, and threats, under which she remained steadfast, was drowned a few days afterward. Done the 21st day of May, A.D. 1527.

15. Huter's Apology for Moravian Anabaptists

The royal edict of Ferdinand in the spring of 1535 banished the Anabaptists from Moravia in the belief that heretics in the land would have to go if the land was to be defended against outside enemies, the Turks. Fierce persecutions developed, and the Anabaptists suffered horribly. Jacob Huter met martyrdom at Innsbruck, February 24, 1536. His apology was written for the entire brotherhood and was addressed to Johann von Lipa, Marshall of Moravia. Vedder, *Balthasar Hubmaier*.

We brethren, who love God and his word, the true witness of our Lord Jesus Christ, banished from many countries for the name of God and for the cause of divine truth, and have come hither to the land of Moravia, having assembled together and abode under your jurisdiction, through the favour and protection of the Most High God, to whom alone be praise and honour and laud for ever: we beg you to know, honoured ruler of Moravia, that your officers have come to us and have delivered your message and command, as indeed is well known to you. Already we have given a verbal answer, and now we reply in writing: viz., that we have

forsaken the world, an unholy life, and all iniquity. We believe in Almighty God, and in his Son our Lord Jesus Christ, who will protect us henceforth and forever in every peril, and to whom we have devoted our entire selves, our life, and all that we possess, to keep his commandments, and to forsake all unrighteousness and sin. Therefore we are persecuted and despised by the whole world, and robbed of all our property, as was done aforetime to the holy prophets, and even to Christ himself. By King Ferdinand, the prince of darkness, that cruel tyrant and enemy of divine truth and righteousness, many of our brethren have been slaughtered and put to death without mercy, our property seized, our fields and home laid waste, ourselves driven into exile, and most fearfully persecuted.

After these things we came into Moravia, and for some time have dwelt here in quietness and tranquillity, under your protection. We have injured no one, we have occupied ourselves in heavy toil, which all men can testify. Notwithstanding, with your permission, we are driven by force from our possessions and our homes. We are now in the desert, in woods, and under the open canopy of heaven; but this we patiently endure, and praise God that we are counted worthy to suffer for his name. Yet for your sakes we grieve that you should thus so wickedly deal with the children of God. The righteous are called to suffer; but alas! woe, woe to all those who without reason persecute us for the cause of divine truth, and inflict upon us so many and so great injuries, and drive us from them as dogs and brute beasts! Their destruction, punishment, and condemnation draw near, and will come upon them in terror and dismay, both in this life and in that which is to come. For God will require at their hands the innocent blood which they have shed, and will terribly vindicate his saints according to the words of the prophets.

And now that you have with violence bidden us forthwith to depart into exile, let this be our answer: We know not any place where we may securely live; nor can we longer dare remain here for hunger and fear. If we turn to the territories of this or that sovereign, everywhere we find an enemy. If we go forward, we fall into the jaws of tyrants and robbers, like sheep before the ravening wolf and the raging lion. With us are many widows, and babes in their cradle, whose parents that most cruel tyrant and enemy of divine righteousness, Ferdinand, gave to the slaughter, and whose property he seized. These widows and orphans and sick children, committed to our charge by God, and whom the Almighty has commanded us to feed, to clothe, to cherish, and to supply all their need, who cannot journey with us nor, unless otherwise provided for, can long live—these we dare not abandon. We may not overthrow God's law to observe man's law, although it cost gold, and body and life. On their account we cannot depart; but rather than they should suffer injury we will endure any extremity, even to the shedding of our blood.

Besides, here we have houses and farms, the property that we have gained by the sweat of our brow, which in the sight of God and men are our just possession: to sell them we need time and delay. Of this property we have urgent need in order to support our wives, widows, orphans and children, of whom we have a great number, lest they die of hunger. Now we lie in the broad forest, and if God will, without hurt. Let but our own be restored to us, and we will live as we have hitherto done, in peace and tranquillity. We desire to molest no one; not to prejudice our foes, not even King Ferdinand. Our manner of life, our customs and conversation, are known everywhere to all. Rather than wrong any man of a single penny, we would suffer the loss of a hundred gulden; and sooner than strike our enemy with the hand, much less with the spear, or sword, or halbert, as the world does, we would die and surrender life. We carry no weapon, neither spear nor gun, as is clear as the open day; and they who say that we have gone forth by thousands to fight, they lie and impiously traduce us to our rulers. We complain of this injury before God and man, and grieve greatly that the number of the virtuous is so small. We would that all the world were as we are, and that we could bring and convert all men to the same belief; then should all war and unrighteousness have an end.

We answer further: that if driven from this land there remains no refuge for us, unless God shall show us some special place whither to flee. We cannot go. This land, and all that is therein, belongs to the God of heaven; and if we were to give a promise to depart, perhaps we should not be able to keep it; for we are in the hand of God, who does with us what he wills. By him we were brought hither, and peradventure he would have us dwell here and not elsewhere, to try our faith and our constancy by persecutions and adversity. But if it should appear to be his will that we depart hence, since we are persecuted and driven away, then, even without your command, not tardily but with alacrity, we will go whither God shall send us. Day and night we pray unto him that he will guide our steps to the place where he would have us dwell. We cannot and dare not withstand his holy will; nor is it possible for you, however much you may strive. Grant us but a brief space: peradventure our heavenly Father will make known to us his will, whether we are to remain here, or whither we must go. If this be done, you shall see that no difficulty, however great it may be, shall deter us from the path.

Woe, woe unto you, O ye Moravian rulers, who have sworn to that cruel tyrant and enemy of God's truth, Ferdinand, to drive away his pious and faithful servants! Woe, we say to you! who fear more that frail and mortal man than the living, omnipotent and eternal God, and chase from you, suddenly and inhumanely, the children of God, the afflicted widow, the desolate orphan, and scatter them abroad. Not with impunity will you do this; your oaths will not excuse you, or afford you any subterfuge. The same punishment and torments that Pilate endured will overtake you: who, unwilling to crucify the Lord, yet from fear of Caesar adjudged him to death. God, by the mouth of the prophet, proclaims that he will fearfully and terribly avenge the shedding of innocent blood, and will not pass by such as fear not to pollute and contaminate their hands therewith. Therefore great slaughter, much misery and anguish, sorrow, and adversity, yea, everlasting groaning, pain and torment, are daily appointed you. The Most High will lift his hand against you, now and eternally. This we announce to you in the name of our Lord Jesus Christ, for verily it will not tarry, and shortly you shall see that we have told you nothing but the truth of God, in the name of our Lord Jesus Christ, and are witnesses against you, and against all who set at nought his commandments. We beseech you to forsake iniquity, and to turn to the living God with weeping and lamentation, that you may escape all these woes.

We earnestly entreat you, submissively and with prayers, that you take in good part all these our words. For we testify and speak what we know, and have learned to be true in the sight of God, and from that true Christian affection which we follow after before God and men. Farewell.

16. Calvin's Institutes of the Christian Religion

Calvin revised and enlarged his systematic theology, first published in a small volume in 1536, until by 1559 the *Institutes of the Christian Religion* had become a tome of 1,500 pages. Despite the enlargement, the basic ideas did not change, and this work mirrors a lifetime of thought. The following excerpts point to a few historic doctrines, but they only suggest the dynamic vigor of Calvin. The Preface was translated by Henry Beveridge, 1879; the selections by John Allen, in his translation of the 1559 edition of the *Institutes,* were published in 1841 and many times since.

PREFACE, ADDRESSED TO FRANCIS I,
SOVEREIGN OF FRANCE

Sire—When I first engaged in this work, nothing was farther from my thoughts than to write what should afterwards be presented to your Majesty. My intention was only to furnish a kind of rudiments, by which those who feel some interest in religion might be trained to true godliness.... But when I perceived that the fury of certain bad men had risen to such a height in your realm, that there was no place in it for sound doctrine, I resolved to lay before your Majesty a Confession, from which you may learn what the doctrine is that so inflames the rage of those madmen who are this day, with fire and sword, troubling your kingdom.... The cause which I plead is the common cause of all the godly, and therefore the very cause of Christ—a cause which, throughout your realm, now lies, as it were, in despair, torn and trampled upon in all kinds of ways, and that more through the tyranny of certain Pharisees than any sanction from yourself.... Let not a contemptuous idea of our insignificance dissuade you from the investigation of this cause. We, indeed, are perfectly conscious how poor and abject we are: in the presence of God we are miserable sinners, and in the sight of men most despised—we are the mere dregs and off-scourings of the world.... But our doctrine must stand sublime above all the glory of the world, and invincible by all its power, because it is not ours, but that of the living God and his Anointed. Our adversaries clamorously maintain that our appeal to the word of God is a mere pretext—that we are, in fact, its worst corrupters. How far this is not only malicious calumny, but also shameless effrontery, you will be able to decide, of your own knowledge by reading our Confession.

Our adversaries cease not to assail our doctrine, and to accuse and defame it in what terms they may, in order to render it either hated or suspected. They call it new; they carp at it as doubtful and uncertain; they bid us tell by what miracles it has been confirmed; they ask if it be fair to receive it against the consent of so many holy Fathers and the most ancient custom; they urge us to confess either that it is schismatical in giving battle to the Church, or that the Church must have been without life during the many centuries in which nothing of the kind was heard. Lastly, they say there is little need of argument, for its quality may be known by its fruits, namely, the large number of sects, the many seditious disturbances, and the great licentiousness which it has produced. To them, indeed, I very little doubt our doctrine is new, as Christ is new, and the Gospel new; but those who are acquainted with the old saying of Paul, that Christ Jesus "died for our sins, and rose again for our justification" (Rom. 4:25), will not detect any novelty in us....

Knowledge of God: [The human mind is naturally endued with some sense of Deity, and some knowledge of God is conspicuous in the formation and continual government of the world, says Calvin, but another assist is needed.] Though the light which presents itself to all eyes, both in heaven and in earth, is more than sufficient to deprive the ingratitude of men of every excuse, since God, in order to involve all mankind in the same guilt, sets before them all, without exception, an exhibition of his majesty, delineated in the creatures—yet we need another and better assistance, properly to direct us to the Creator of the world. Therefore he hath not unnecessarily added the light of his word, to make himself known unto salvation, and hath honoured with this privilege those whom he intended to unite in a more close and familiar connection with himself.... For, as persons who are old, or whose eyes are by any means become dim, if you show them the most beautiful book, though they perceive something written, but can scarcely read two words together, yet, by the assistance of spectacles, will begin to read distinctly—so the Scripture, collecting in our minds the otherwise confused notions of Deity, dispels the darkness, and gives us a clear view of the true God.... (Bk. I, Ch. 6)

The testimony of the Spirit is superior to all reason. For as God alone is a sufficient witness of himself in his own word, so also the word will never gain credit in the hearts of men, till it be confirmed by the internal testimony of the Spirit. It is necessary, therefore, that the same Spirit, who spake by the mouths of the prophets, should penetrate into our hearts to convince us that they faithfully delivered the oracles which were divinely intrusted to them. And this connection is very suitably expressed in these words: "My Spirit that is upon thee, and my word which I have put in thy mouth, shall not depart out of thy mouth, nor out of the mouth of thy seed, nor out of the mouth of thy seed's seed, forever." Some good men are troubled that they are not always prepared with clear proof to oppose the impious, when they murmur with impunity against the divine word; as though the Spirit were not therefore denominated a "seal," and "an earnest," for the confirmation of the faith of the pious; because, till he illuminate their minds, they are perpetually fluctuating amidst a multitude of doubts.

Let it be considered, then, as an undeniable truth, that they who have been inwardly taught by the Spirit, feel an entire acquiescence in the Scripture, and that it is self-authenticated, carrying with it its own evidence, and ought not to be made the subject of demonstration and arguments from reason; but it obtains the credit which it deserves with us by the testimony of the Spirit. For though it conciliate our reverence by its internal majesty, it never seriously affects us till it is confirmed by the Spirit in our hearts. Therefore, being illuminated by him, we now believe the divine original of the Scripture, not from our own judgment or that of others, but we esteem the certainty, that we have received it from God's own mouth by the ministry of men, to be superior to that of any human judgment, and equal to that of an intuitive perception of God himself in it. We seek not arguments or probabilities to support our judgment, but submit our judgments and understandings as to a thing concerning which it is impossible for us to judge; and that not like some persons, who are in the habit of hastily embracing what they do not understand, which displeases them as soon as they examine it, but because we feel the firmest conviction that we hold an invincible truth.... It is such a persuasion, therefore, as requires no reasons; such a knowledge as is supported by the highest reason, in which, indeed, the mind rests with greater security and constancy than in any reasons; it is, finally, such a sentiment as cannot be produced but by a revelation from heaven. I speak of nothing but what every believer experiences in his heart, except that my language falls far short of a just explication of the subject. Only let it be known here that that alone is true faith which the Spirit of God seals in our hearts.... (Bk. I, Ch. 7)

Persons who, abandoning the Scripture, imagine to themselves some other way of approaching to God, must be considered as not so much misled by error as actuated by frenzy. For there have lately arisen some unsteady men, who, haughtily pretending to be taught by the Spirit, reject all reading themselves, and deride the simplicity of those who still attend to (what they style) the dead and killing letter.... [The Spirit that seals belief in believers' hearts is the same Spirit that inspired the Scriptures, and this Spirit does not contradict itself.] The Lord hath established a kind of mutual connection between the certainty of his word and of his Spirit; so that our minds are filled with a solid reverence for the word, when by the light of the Spirit we are enabled therein to behold the Divine countenance; and, on the other hand, without the least fear of mistake, we gladly receive the Spirit, when we recognize him in his image, that is, in the word. God did not publish the word to mankind for the sake of momentary ostentation, with a design to destroy or annul it immediately on the advent of the Spirit; but he afterwards sent the same Spirit, by whose agency he had dispensed his word, to complete his work by an efficacious confirmation of that word.... What answer can be given to these things, by those proud fanatics, who think themselves possessed of the only valuable illumination, when, securely neglecting and forsaking the Divine word, they, with equal confidence and temerity, greedily embrace every reverie which their distempered imaginations may have conceived? (Bk. I, Ch. 9)

God's Preservation and Providence: And, indeed, God asserts his possession of omnipotence, and claims our acknowledgment of this attribute, which is not, as imagined by sophists, vain, idle, and almost asleep, but vigilant, efficacious, operative, and engaged in continual action; not a mere general principle of confused motion, as if he should command a river to flow through the channels once made for it, but a power constantly exerted on every distinct and particular movement. For he is accounted omnipotent, not because he is able to act, yet sits down in idleness, or continues by a general instinct the order of nature originally appointed by him; but because he governs heaven and earth by his providence, and regulates all things in such a manner that nothing happens but according to his counsel. For when it is said in the Psalms, that he does whatsoever he pleases, it denotes his certain and deliberate will. For it would be quite insipid to expound the words of the Prophet in the philosophical manner, that God is the prime agent, because his is the principle and cause of all motion; whereas the faithful should rather encourage themselves in adversity with this consolation, that they suffer no affliction, but by the ordination and command of God, because they are under his hand. But if the government of God be thus extended to all his works, it is a puerile cavil to limit it to the influence and course of nature. And they not only defraud God of his glory, but themselves of a very useful doctrine, who confine the Divine providence within such narrow bounds, as though he permitted all things to proceed in an uncontrolled course, according to a perpetual law of nature.... First, then, let the readers know that what is called providence describes God, not as idly beholding from heaven the transactions which happen in the world, but as holding the helm of the universe, and regulating all events.... (Bk. I, Ch. 16)

Predestination: Predestination, by which God adopts some to the hope of life, and adjudges others to eternal death, no one, desirous of the credit of piety, dares absolutely to deny. But it is involved in many cavils, especially by those who make foreknowledge the cause of it. We maintain, that both belong to God; but it is preposterous to represent one as dependent on the other. When we attribute foreknowledge to God, we mean that all things have ever been, and perpetually remain, before his eyes, so that to his knowledge nothing is future or past, but all things are present; and present in such a manner, that he does not merely conceive of them from ideas formed in his mind, as things remembered by us appear present to our minds, but really beholds and sees them as if actually placed before him. And this foreknowledge extends to the whole world, and to all the creatures. Predestination we call the eternal decree of God, by which he has determined in himself, what he would have to become of every individual of mankind. For they are not all created with a similar destiny; but eternal life is foreordained for some, and eternal damnation for others. Every man, therefore, being created for one or the other of these ends, we say, he is predestinated either to life or to death. . . .

In conformity, therefore, to the clear doctrine of the Scripture, we assert, that by an eternal and immutable counsel, God has once for all determined, both whom he would admit to salvation, and whom he would condemn to destruction. We affirm that this counsel, as far as concerns the elect, is founded on his gratuitous mercy, totally irrespective of human merit; but that to those whom he devotes to condemnation, the gate of life is closed by a just and irreprehensible, but incomprehensible judgment. In the elect, we consider calling as an evidence of election, and justification as another token of its manifestation, till they arrive in glory, which constitutes its completion. As God seals his elect by vocation and justification, so by excluding the reprobate from the knowledge of his name and the sanctification of his Spirit, he affords an indication of the judgment that awaits them. (Bk. III, Ch. 21)

Original sin: Infidelity, therefore, was the root of that [Adam's] defection. But hence sprang ambition, pride, and ingratitude, since Adam, by coveting more than was granted, offered an indignity to the Divine goodness, which had so greatly enriched him. Now it was monstrous impiety, that a son of the earth should not be satisfied with being made after the similitude of God, unless he could also be equal to him. . . . As the spiritual life of Adam consisted in a union to his Maker, so an alienation from him was the death of his soul. When the Divine image in him was obliterated, and he was punished with the loss of wisdom, strength, sanctity, truth, and righteousness, with which he had been adorned, but which were succeeded by the dreadful pests of ignorance, impotence, impurity, vanity, and iniquity, he suffered not alone, but involved all his posterity with him, and plunged them into the same miseries. This is that hereditary corruption which the fathers called *original sin:* meaning by

sin, the depravation of a nature previously good and pure. . . . From a putrefied root, therefore, have sprung putrid branches, which have transmitted their putrescence to remoter ramifications. For the children were so vitiated in their parents that they became contagious to their descendants: there was in Adam such a spring of corruption, that it is transfused from parents to children in a perpetual stream. . . . To remove all uncertainty and misunderstanding on this subject, let us define original sin. Original sin, therefore, appears to be an hereditary pravity and corruption of our nature, diffused through all the parts of the soul, rendering us obnoxious to the Divine wrath, and producing in us those works which the Scripture calls "works of the flesh." And this is indeed what Paul frequently denominates *sin.* The works which proceed thence, such as adulteries, fornications, thefts, hatreds, murders, revellings, he calls in the same manner "fruits of sin"; although they are also called "sins" in many passages of Scripture, even by himself. These two things therefore should be distinctly observed: first, that our nature being so totally vitiated and depraved, we are, on account of this very corruption, considered as convicted and justly condemned in the sight of God, to whom nothing is acceptable but righteousness, innocence, and purity. And this liableness to punishment arises not from the delinquency of another; for when it is said that the sin of Adam renders us obnoxious to the Divine judgment, it is not to be understood as if we, though innocent, were undeservedly loaded with the guilt of his sin; but, because we are all subject to a curse, in consequence of his transgression, he is therefore said to have involved us in guilt. Nevertheless we derive from him, not only the punishment, but also the pollution to which the punishment is justly due. (Bk. II, Ch. 1)

17. The Genevan Confession, 1536

On November 10, 1536, Calvin and Farel presented this formula for the church to the magistracy of Geneva. Calvin is traditionally regarded as the main author, and the twenty-one articles in this influential confession serve as an outline of Calvinistic doctrine in the year in which the *Institutes* was published. Vol. XXII, *LCC, Calvin: Theological Treatises,* trans. Rev. J. K. S.

Reid (Philadelphia: The Westminster Press, 1954). Used by permission.

1. *The Word of God.* First we affirm that we desire to follow Scripture alone as rule of faith and religion, without mixing with it any other thing which might be devised by the opinion of men apart from the Word of God, and without wishing to accept for our spiritual government any other doctrine than what is conveyed to us by the same Word without addition or diminution, according to the command of our Lord.

2. *One Only God.* Following, then, the lines laid down in the Holy Scriptures, we acknowledge that there is one only God, whom we are both to worship and serve, and in whom we are to put all our confidence and hope: having this assurance, that in him alone is contained all wisdom, power, justice, goodness and pity. And since he is spirit, he is to be served in spirit and in truth. Therefore we think it an abomination to put our confidence or hope in any created thing, to worship anything else than him, whether angels or any other creatures, and to recognize any other Saviour of our souls than him alone, whether saints or men living upon earth; and likewise to offer the service, which ought to be rendered to him, in external ceremonies or carnal observances, as if he took pleasure in such things, or to make an image to represent his divinity or any other image for adoration.

3. *The Law of God Alike for All.* Because there is one only Lord and Master who has dominion over our consciences, and because his will is the only principle of all justice, we confess all our life ought to be ruled in accordance with the commandments of his holy law in which is contained all perfection of justice, and that we ought to have no other rule of good and just living.... [than that contained in the decalogue in Exodus 20.]

4. *Natural Man.* We acknowledge man by nature to be blind, darkened in understanding, and full of corruption and perversity of heart, so that of himself he has no power to be able to comprehend the true knowledge of God as is proper, nor to apply himself to good works.... Hence he has need to be illumined by God, so that he may come to the right knowledge of his salvation, and thus be redirected in his affections and reformed to the obedience of the righteousness of God.

5-8. [Because man is lost and destitute, Jesus Christ is given by God for man's salvation, righteousness and regeneration, "in order that in him we should recover all of which in ourselves we are deficient."]

9. *Remission of Sins Always Necessary for the Faithful.* Finally, we acknowledge that this regeneration is so effected in us that, until we slough off this mortal body, there remains always in us much imperfection and infirmity, so that we always remain poor and wretched sinners in the presence of God. And, however much we ought day by day to increase and grow in God's righteousness, there will never be plenitude or perfection while we live here. Thus we always have need of the mercy of God to obtain the remission of our faults and offences. And so we ought always to look for our righteousness in Jesus Christ and not at all in ourselves, and in him be confident and assured, putting no faith in our works.

10. *All Our Good in the Grace of God.* In order that all glory and praise be rendered to God (as is his due)... we understand and confess that we receive all benefits from God, by his clemency and pity, without any consideration of our worthiness or the merit of our works, [yet in Christ our works are agreeable and pleasing because] he acknowledges in them nothing but what proceeds from his Spirit.

11. *Faith.* We confess that the entrance which we have to the great treasures and riches of the goodness of God that is vouchsafed to us is by faith; inasmuch as, in certain confidence and assurance of heart, we believe in the promises of the Gospel, and receive Jesus Christ as he is offered to us by the Father and described to us by the Word of God.

12. *Invocation of God Only and Intercession of Christ.* As we have declared that we have confidence and hope for salvation and all good only in God through Jesus Christ,

so we confess that we ought to invoke him in all necessities in the name of Jesus Christ, who is our Mediator and Advocate with him and has access to him. Likewise we ought to acknowledge that all good things come from him alone, and to give thanks to him for them. On the other hand, we reject the intercession of the saints as a superstition invented by men contrary to Scripture, for the reason that it proceeds from mistrust of the sufficiency of the intercession of Jesus Christ.

13. [Prayer is to be intelligible and the Lord's Prayer shows what we ought to ask.]

14. [The two sacraments of Baptism and the Lord's Supper "are to be regarded as exercises of faith for us, both for fortifying and confirming it in the promises of God and for witnessing before men." Papal doctrines concerning the seven sacraments, "we condemn as fable and lie."]

15. *Baptism.* Baptism is an external sign by which our Lord testifies that he desires to receive us for his children, as members of his Son Jesus. Hence in it there is represented to us the cleansing from sin which we have in the blood of Jesus Christ, the mortification of our flesh which we have by his death that we may live in him by his Spirit. Now since our children belong to such an alliance with our Lord, we are certain that the external sign is rightly applied to them.

16. *The Holy Supper.* The Supper of our Lord is a sign by which under bread and wine he represents the true spiritual communion which we have in his body and blood. And we acknowledge that according to his ordinance it ought to be distributed in the company of the faithful, in order that all those who wish to have Jesus for their life be partakers of it. Inasmuch as the mass of the pope was a reprobate and diabolical ordinance subverting the mystery of the Holy Supper, we declare that it is execrable to us, an idolatry condemned by God; for so much is it itself regarded as a sacrifice for the redemption of souls that the bread is in it taken and adored as God. . . .

17. *Human Traditions.* [Laws for good order we accept,] but all laws and regulations made binding on conscience which oblige the faithful to things not commanded

by God, or establish another service of God than that which he demands, thus tending to destroy Christian liberty, we condemn as perverse doctrines of Satan. . . . It is in this estimation that we hold pilgrimages, monasteries, distinctions of foods, prohibition of marriage, confessions and other like things.

18. *The Church.* While there is one only Church of Jesus Christ, we always acknowledge that necessity requires companies of the faithful to be distributed in different places. Of these assemblies each one is called Church. But as all companies do not assemble in the name of our Lord, but rather to blaspheme and pollute him by their sacrilegious deeds, we believe that the proper mark by which rightly to discern the Church of Jesus Christ is that his holy gospel be purely and faithfully preached, proclaimed, heard, and kept, that his sacraments be properly administered, even if there be some imperfections and faults, as there always will be among men. On the other hand, where the Gospel is not declared, heard, and received, there we do not acknowledge the form of the Church. Hence the churches governed by the ordinances of the pope are rather synagogues of the devil than Christian churches.

19. *Excommunication.* Because there are always some who hold God and his Word in contempt . . . we hold the discipline of excommunication to be a thing holy and salutary among the faithful. . . . We believe that all manifest idolators, blasphemers, murderers, thieves, lewd persons, false witnesses, sedition-mongers, quarrellers, those guilty of defamation or assault, drunkards, dissolute livers, when they have been duly admonished and if they do not make amendment, [should] be separated from the communion of the faithful until their repentance is known.

20. *Ministers of the Word.* We recognize no other pastors in the Church than faithful pastors of the Word of God, feeding the sheep of Jesus Christ on the one hand with instruction, admonition, consolation, exhortation, deprecation; and on the other resisting all false doctrines and deceptions of the devil, without mixing with pure doctrine of the Scriptures their dreams or their foolish imaginings. . . . We hold that all seductive and false prophets, who abandon the purity

of the Gospel and deviate to their own inventions, ought not at all to be suffered or maintained, who are not the pastors they pretend, but rather, like ravening wolves, ought to be hunted and ejected from the people of God.

21. *Magistrates.* We hold the supremacy and dominion of kings and princes as also of other magistrates and officers, to be a holy thing and a good ordinance of God. And since in performing their office they serve God and follow a Christian vocation, whether in defending the afflicted and innocent, or in correcting and punishing the malice of the perverse, we on our part also ought to accord them honour and reverence, to render respect and subservience, to execute their commands, to bear the charges they impose on us, so far as we are able without offence to God. In sum, we ought to regard them as vicars and lieutenants of God, whom one cannot resist without resisting God himself; and their office as a sacred commission from God which has been given them so that they may rule and govern us. Hence we hold that all Christians are bound to pray God for the prosperity of the superiors and lords of the country where they live, to obey the statutes and ordinances which do not contravene the commandments of God, to promote welfare, peace and public good, endeavouring to sustain the honour of those over them and the peace of the people, without contriving or attempting anything to inspire trouble or dissension. On the other hand we declare that all those who conduct themselves unfaithfully towards their superiors, and have not a right concern for the public good of the country where they live, demonstrate thereby their infidelity towards God.

18. Calvinistic Ordinances

Ordinances for the Supervision of the Churches in the country dependent on the Seigneury of Geneva, passed February 3, 1547, and put into effect May 17, 1547, by command of their Lordships, the Syndics and Council of Geneva. Reid, *Calvin: Theological Treatises.* Used by permission.

SERMONS

1. Everyone in each house is to come on Sundays unless it be necessary to leave someone behind to take care of children or animals, under penalty of 3 sous.

2. If there be preaching any weekday, arranged with due notice, those that are able to go and have no legitimate excuse are to attend, at least one from each house, under penalty as above.

3. Those who have man or maid servants, are to bring them or have them conveyed when possible, so that they do not live like cattle without instruction.

4. Everyone is to be present at Sermon when the prayer is begun, under penalty as above, unless he absent himself for legitimate reason.

5. Everyone is to pay attention during Sermon, and there is to be no disorder or scandal.

6. No one is to leave or go out from the church until the prayer be made at the end of Sermon, under penalty as above, unless he have legitimate cause.

CATECHISM

1. Because each preacher has two parishes, Catechism is to take place each fortnight. Those who have children are to bring them, with the rest of their household who have not been to Sermon, as above.

2. The same attention, honest and regular, is to be given to Catechism as has been said for Sermon.

PENALTIES

1. Those who fail in their duty of coming are to be admonished by the Guardians, both themselves and their family.

2. If after intimation they continue to default, they are to be fined three groats, for each time. Of this one third will be applied to the Guardians; the other two thirds will be applied to the poor of the parish, and put into the funds of the Church for distribution according to need as it becomes known.

3. If anyone come after Sermon has begun, he is to be admonished, and if after this is done he does not amend, for each fault he is to be fined three sous, which will be applied as above.

4. If during Sermon anyone make any disturbance or scandal, he is to be reported

to the Consistory to be cautioned, in order that procedure be in proportion to the fault; that is, if by carelessness he is to be well told off, if it happen by intended malice or rebelliousness he is to be reported to their Lordships to be punished appropriately.

BY WHOM FINES ARE TO BE EXACTED

1. The local lord, in conjunction with the Ministers and the Guardians, is to oblige the delinquents to pay the fines they have incurred, when they will not pay of their own free will. Legitimate excuses are to be admitted, but this is to be done without any formal procedure.

2. If there be any so rebellious that, despite the above fines, they do not at all amend, they are to be reported to the Consistory with advice to the effect that their Lordships punish them according to the seriousness of the obstinacy.

3. Fathers are to be responsible for their children, and, if there be a penalty, it is to be exacted from them.

OF BAPTISM

1. Baptism is to be administered any day, provided that there be Sermon along with it. The Ministers are always to exhort the people to link it up with the Catechism.

6. If midwives usurp the office of Baptism, they are to be reproved or chastised according to the measure of fault found, since no commission is given them in this matter, under penalty of being put on bread and water for three days and fined ten sous; and all who consent to this action or conceal it will be liable to the same penalty.

OF THE SUPPER

1. No one is to be received at the Supper unless he first have made confession of his faith. That is to say, he must declare before the Minister that he desires to live according to the reformation of the gospel, and that he knows the Creed, the Lord's Prayer and the Commandments of God.

2. Those who wish to receive the Supper are to come at the beginning of the Service; those who come at the end are not to be received.

OF TIMES OF MEETING AT CHURCH

Buildings are to remain shut for the rest of the time, in order that no one outside the hours may enter for superstitious reasons. If anyone be found making any particular devotion inside or nearby, he is to be admonished: if it appear to be a superstition which he will not amend, he is to be chastised.

FAULTS CONTRAVENING THE REFORMATION BESIDES THOSE ALREADY MENTIONED
SUPERSTITIONS

1. Those found to have any paternosters or idols for adoration are to be brought before the Consistory, and, besides the punishment imposed on them there, they are to be brought before their Lordships.

2. Those who have been on pilgrimages or voyages the same.

3. Those who observe the papistical feasts or fastings are to be admonished only, unless they are obstinate in their rebellion.

4. Those who have attended mass, besides admonition, are to be brought before their Lordships.

5. In such cases, their Lordships will have the right of chastising by means of prison or otherwise, or of punishing by extraordinary fines, at their discretion.

In the case of fines, they are to apply some small portion of them to the Guardians, if the delict was notified by them.

BLASPHEMIES

1. Those who have blasphemed, swearing by the body or by the blood of our Lord, or suchlike, ought to do reverence for the first time; for the second a penalty of five sous; for the third ten sous; and for the last time put in the pillory for an hour.

2. Anyone who abjures or renounces God or his Baptism is for the first time to be put for ten days on bread and water; for the second and third time he is to be punished with some more rigorous corporal punishment, at the discretion of their Lordships.

CONTRADICTION OF THE WORD

1. If there are any who contradict the Word of God, let them be brought before

the Consistory to be admonished, or be remanded to their Lordships to receive chastisement according to the needs of the case.

2. If the contradiction or rebellion amount to scandal which demands prompter remedy, the local lord is to take a hand in the matter for the maintenance of the honour of the Ministry and the Magistracy.

DRUNKENNESS

1. There is to be no treating of one another to drinks, under penalty of three sous.

2. The taverns are to be closed during Service, under penalty that the taverner pay three sous and anyone entering them the same.

3. If anyone be found drunk, he is to pay for the first time three sous and be brought before the Consistory; the second time he must pay the sum of five sous; and the third ten sous and be put in prison.

4. There are to be no carousals, under penalty of ten sous.

SONGS AND DANCES

If anyone sing songs that are unworthy, dissolute or outrageous, or spin wildly round in the dance, or the like, he is to be imprisoned for three days, and then sent on to the Consistory.

USURY

No one is to lend at interest or for profit greater than five per cent, on pain of confiscation of the capital sum and of being required to make appropriate amends according to the needs of the case.

GAMES

No one is to play at games that are dissolute, or at games played for gold or silver or at excessive expense, on pain of five sous and loss of the sum staked.

FORNICATION

1. As to those who are caught in fornication, if it be an unmarried man with an unmarried woman, they are to be imprisoned for six days on bread and water, and pay sixty sous amends.

2. If it be adultery, one or the other being married, they are to be imprisoned for nine days on bread and water, and pay amends at the discretion of their Lordships, as the crime is much more grave.

3. Those who are promised in marriage are not to cohabit as man and wife until the marriage be celebrated in church, otherwise they will be punished as for fornication.

19. Articles Concerning Predestination

It is assumed that these uncompromising articles were written rather late in Calvin's life. Reid, *Calvin: Theological Treatises*. Used by permission.

Before the first man was created, God in his eternal counsel had determined what he willed to be done with the whole human race.

In the hidden counsel of God it was determined that Adam should fall from the unimpaired condition of his nature, and by his defection should involve all his posterity in sentence of eternal death.

Upon the same decree depends the distinction between elect and reprobate: as he adopted some for himself for salvation, he destined others for eternal ruin.

While the reprobate are the vessels of the just wrath of God, and the elect vessels of his compassion, the ground of the distinction is to be sought in the pure will of God alone, which is the supreme rule of justice.

While the elect receive the grace of adoption by faith, their election does not depend on faith but is prior in time and order.

As the beginning of faith and perseverance in it arises from the gratuitous election of God, none are truly illuminated with faith, and none granted the spirit of regeneration, except those whom God elects. But it is necessary that the reprobate remain in their blindness or be deprived of such portion of faith as is in them.

While we are elected in Christ, nevertheless that God reckons us among his own is prior in order to his making us members of Christ.

While the will of God is the supreme and primary cause of all things, and God holds the devil and the godless subject to his will, nevertheless God cannot be called the cause of sin, nor the author of evil, nor subject of any guilt.

While God is truly wrathful with sin and condemns whatever is unrighteousness in men since it displeases him, nevertheless all the deeds of men are governed not by his bare permission but by his consent and secret counsel.

While the devil and the reprobate are ministers and organs of God and promote his secret judgments, God nevertheless in an incomprehensible way operates in and through them, so that he restrains nothing of their wickedness, just because their malice is justly and rightly used to a good end, while the means are often hidden from us.

They are ignorant and malicious who say that God is the author of sin, since all things are done by his will or ordination; for they do not distinguish between the manifest wickedness of men and the secret judgments of God.

20. Calvin's Prayers

Calvin's prayers reflect his doctrines and his piety. He addresses God as "almighty," dwells on election, rejoices in God's gift in Christ, upholds the commands, and looks to eternal life. *Prayers of the Reformers,* compiled by Clyde Manschreck (Philadelphia: Muhlenberg Press, 1958). Cf. John Calvin, *Commentaries on the Prophet Jeremiah and Lamentations,* 45, trans. John Owen. Also *Commentaries on Ezekiel, Job,* etc.

Almighty God, thou dost continue this day, both morning and evening, to invite us to thyself, dost assiduously exhort us to repent, and dost testify that thou art ready to be reconciled to us, provided we flee to thy mercy. Grant that we may not close our ears and reject this thy great kindness, but that, remembering thy freely given election, the chief of all the favors thou hast been pleased to show us, we may strive so to devote ourselves to thee, that thy name may be glorified through our whole life. And should it be that we at any time turn aside from thee, may we quickly return to the right way, and become submissive to thy holy admonitions. May we thus know that we have been chosen and called by thee and desire to continue in the hope of that salvation, to which thou invitest us, which is prepared for us in heaven, through Christ, our Lord. Amen.

Almighty God, thou buildest not a temple among us of wood and stones, for the fulness of thy Godhead dwells in thine only-begotten Son, who by his power fills the whole world, and dwells in the midst of us, and even in us. Grant that we may not profane his sanctuary by our vices and sins, but so strive to consecrate ourselves to thy service, that thy name through his name may be continually glorified. May we at length be received into that eternal inheritance, where will appear to us openly, and face to face, that glory which we now see in the truth contained in thy gospel. Amen.

21. The Burning of Michael Servetus

Michael Servetus (1511-1553) trained for a position in law, but found himself vitally concerned with theology. After studying the New Testament, he reacted strongly to general religious corruption and intolerance, and was convinced that many traditional doctrines had little basis in Scripture, particularly the doctrine of the Trinity. At the age of twenty he wrote the book, *On the Errors of the Trinity,* for which he was put to death twenty-two years later. He accepted the view of three Persons in one Godhead, but pleaded that the "blasphemous and philosophical distinction of three beings in one God be rooted from the minds of men." Protestants and Catholics alike banned the book and condemned the author, forcing Servetus to live for twenty-two years in France under the assumed name of Michael Villanovanus. When his *Restoration of Christianity,* a plan to restore religion to the ways of Christ, appeared in 1553, he was soon discovered. Imprisoned by the French Inquisition, he escaped and was on his way to Naples when he was apprehended in Geneva. The following excerpts are from books by Roland H. Bainton: *Hunted Heretic, The Life and Death of Michael Servetus* (Boston: The Beacon Press, 1953) and *Concerning Heretics* (New York: Columbia University Press, 1935). From the former come the selections concerning the trial and the sentencing of Servetus; from the latter come the plea of David Joris before Servetus was condemned and the reaction of Sebastian Castellio afterward.

[David Joris, an Anabaptist leader, living in Holland under an assumed name, addressed this letter to Servetus' judges:]

Most noble, just, worthy, gracious, dear Lords, now that I, your friend and brother in the Lord Jesus Christ, have heard what has happened to the good, worthy Servetus, how that he was delivered into your hands and power by no friendliness and love but through envy and hate, as will be made manifest in the days of judgment to those whose eyes are now blinded by cunning so that they cannot understand the ground of the truth. God give them to understand. The report has gone everywhere, and even to my ears, that the learned preachers or shepherds of souls have taken counsel and written to certain cities who have resolved to pass sentence to put him to death. This news has so stirred me that I can have no peace on behalf of our religion and the holy churches far and near, which stand fast in the love and unity of Christ, until I have raised my voice as a member of the body of Christ, until I have opened my heart humbly before your Highnesses and freed my conscience. I trust that the learned, perverted, carnal, and bloodthirsty may have no weight and make no impression on you, and if they should ingratiate themselves with you as did the Scribes and Pharisees with Pilate in the case of our Lord Jesus, they will displease the King of Kings and the teacher of all, Christ, who taught that no one should be crucified or put to death for his teaching. He himself was rather crucified and put to death. Yes, not only that, but He has severely forbidden persecution. Will it not then be a great perversion, blindness, evil, and darkness to indulge in impudent disobedience through hate and envy? They must first themselves have been deranged before they could bring a life to death, damn a soul forever, and hasten it to hell. Is that a Christian procedure or a true spirit? I say eternally no, however plausible it may appear. If the preachers are not of this mind and wish to avoid the sin against the Holy Ghost, let them be wary of seizing and killing men for their good intentions and belief according to their understanding, especially when these ministers stand so badly in other people's books that they dare not go out of their own city and land. Let them remember that they are called, sent, and anointed of God to save souls, to bring men to right and truth —that is, to make alive the dead, and not to destroy, offend, and corrupt, let alone to take life. This belongs to Him alone to whom it is

II-5. Burning of Servetus. *An old print.*

given, who was crucified, who died, and who suffered. . . .

Noble, wise, and prudent Lords, consider what would happen if free rein were given to our opponents to kill heretics. How many men would be left on earth if each had this power over the other, inasmuch as each considers the other a heretic? The Jews so regard the Christians, so do the Saracens and the Turks, and the Christians reciprocate. The Papists and the Lutherans, the Zwinglians and the Anabaptists, the Calvinists and the Adiaphorists, mutually ban each other. Because of these differences of opinion should men hate and kill each other? "Whoso sheddeth man's blood, by man shall his blood be shed," as Scripture says. Let us, then, not take the sword, and if anyone is of an erroneous and evil mind and understanding let us pray for him and awaken him to love, peace, and unity. . . .

And if the aforesaid Servetus is a heretic or a sectary before God, . . . we should inflict on him no harm in any of his members, but admonish him in a friendly way and at most banish him from the city, if he will not give up his obstinacy and stop disturbing the peace by his teaching... that he may come to a better mind and no longer molest your territory. No one should go beyond this. . . .

The Lord himself will judge of soul and spirit and will separate the good from the bad. . . . He "maketh his sun to rise on the evil and the good" and wills that we should imitate Him in His long-suffering, graciousness, and mercy. He instructed the servants, who wished to anticipate the harvest as the apostles wished to call down fire from heaven, to leave the tares with the wheat. At the harvest He will send His angels who have knowledge and understanding to separate the good from the bad, the lies from the truth, the pure from the impure, for God's judgments are true and eternal and cannot fail... but great insufficiency shall be found in men when the day of light and the spirit of perfection shall appear. . . .

Those who have an evil spirit should be instructed, not put to death in the time of their ignorance and blindness similar to Paul's. That no one should assume judgment, the Lord has given us a new commandment in love that we do unto others as we would that they should do unto us. So be merciful, kind, and good, doing as it has been done to your Honors, and as the Lord wishes. "Judge not that ye be not judged." Condemn no man that ye be not condemned. Shed no blood and do no violence, my dear Lords. Understand whose disciples you are, for nothing has the Lord punished more and forgiven less than the shedding of innocent blood and idolatry. Follow no one and believe in no one above God or Christ, who is Lord in spirit and truth. . . . Although I have withheld my name, you should not give this communication less consideration.

[Servetus' examination and trial dragged on over two months. When he was not being questioned, he languished in prison, unkept and unheeded, as his letters reveal:]

I humbly beg that you [members of the Council] cut short these long delays and deliver me from prosecution. You see that Calvin is at the end of his rope, not knowing what to say and for his pleasure wishes to make me rot in prison. The lice eat me alive. My clothes are torn and I have nothing for a change, neither jacket nor shirt, but a bad one. I have addressed to you another petition which was according to God and to impede it Calvin cites Justinian. He is in a bad way to quote against me what he does not himself credit, for he does not believe what Justinian has said about the Holy Church of bishops and priests and other matters of religion and knows well that the Church was already degenerated. It is a great shame, the more so that I have been caged here for five weeks and he has not urged against me a single passage.

My lords, I have also asked you to give me a procurator or advocate as you did to my opponent, who was not in the same straits as I, who am a stranger and ignorant of the customs of the country. You permitted it to him, but not to me, and you have liberated him from prison before knowing. I petition you that my case be referred to the Council of Two Hundred with my requests, and if I may appeal there I do so ready to assume all the cost, loss and interest of the law of an eye for an eye, both against the first accuser and against Calvin, who has taken up the case himself. Done in your prisons of Geneva. September 15, 1553. Michael Servetus in his own cause.

Honored sirs, It is now three weeks that I have sought an audience and have been unable to secure one. I beg you for the love of Jesus Christ not to refuse me what you would not refuse to a Turk, who sought justice at your hands. I have some important and necessary matters to communicate to you.

As for what you commanded that something be done to keep me clean, nothing has been done and I am in a worse state than before. The cold greatly distresses me, because of my colic and rupture, causing other complaints which I should be ashamed to describe. It is great cruelty that I have not permission to speak if only to remedy my necessities. For the love of God, honored sirs, give your order whether for pity or duty.

Done in your prisons of Geneva, Oct. 10, 1553. Michael Servetus.

22. *Verdict and Sentence of Michael Servetus*

Servetus was sentenced October 26 and burned the following day at noon. The verdict and sentence read:

The sentence pronounced against Michel Servet de Villeneufve of the Kingdom of Aragon in Spain who some twenty-three or twenty-four years ago printed a book at Hagenau in Germany against the Holy Trinity containing many great blasphemies to the scandal of the said churches of Germany, the which book he freely confesses to have printed in the teeth of the remonstrances made to him by the learned and evangelical doctors of Germany. In consequence he became a fugitive from Germany. Nevertheless he continued in his errors, and, in order the more to spread the venom of his heresy, he printed secretly a book in Vienne of Dauphiny full of the said heresies and horrible, execrable blasphemies against the Holy Trinity, against the Son of God, against the baptism of infants and the foundations of the Christian religion. He confesses that in this book he called believers in the Trinity Trinitarians and atheists. He calls this Trinity a diabolical monster with three heads. He blasphemes detestably against the Son of God, saying that Jesus Christ is not the Son of God from eternity. He calls infant baptism an invention of the devil and sorcery. His execrable blasphemies are scandalous against the majesty of God, the Son of God and the Holy Spirit. This entails the murder and ruin of many souls. Moreover he wrote a letter to one of our ministers in which, along with other numerous blasphemies, he declared our holy evangelical religion to be without faith and without God and that in place of God we have a three-headed Cerberus. He confesses that because of this abominable book he was made a prisoner at Vienne and perfidiously escaped. He has been burned there in effigy together with five bales of his books. Nevertheless, having been in prison in our city, he persists maliciously in his detestable errors and calumniates true Christians and faithful followers of the immaculate Christian tradition.

Wherefore we Syndics, judges of criminal cases in this city, having witnessed the trial conducted before us at the instance of our Lieutenant against you "Michel Servet de Villeneufve" of the Kingdom of Aragon in Spain, and having seen your voluntary and repeated confessions and your books, judge that you, Servetus, have for a long time promulgated false and thoroughly heretical doctrine, despising all remonstrances and corrections and that you have with malicious and perverse obstinacy sown and divulged even in printed books opinions against God the Father, the Son and the Holy Spirit, in a word against the fundamentals of the Christian religion, and that you have tried to make a schism and trouble the Church of God by which many souls may have been ruined and lost, a thing horrible, shocking, scandalous and infectious. And you have had neither shame nor horror of setting yourself against the divine Majesty and the Holy Trinity, and so you have obstinately tried to infect the world with your stinking heretical poison. . . . For these and other reasons, desiring to purge the Church of God of such infection and cut off the rotten member, having taken counsel with our citizens and having invoked the name of God to give just judgment . . . having God and the Holy Scriptures before our eyes, speaking in the name of the Father, Son and Holy Spirit, we now in writing give final sentence and condemn you, Michel Servetus, to be bound and taken to Champel and there attached to a stake and burned with your books to ashes. And so you shall finish your days and give an example to others who would commit the like.

[Farel accompanied Servetus to the stake, commenting that Servetus asked forgiveness for his errors, ignorance and sins, but would not admit his errors and confess that Christ is the eternal Son of God.]

23. *Castellio's Reaction*

Sebastian Castellio (1515-1563), a former worker with Calvin in Geneva, reacted to the death of Servetus with a treatise on the right of conscience in religion, *Concerning Heretics, whether they are to be persecuted and how they are to be treated*, 1554. It was a collection of views from the fathers and the reformers. Below is a portion of the dedication to Duke Christoph.

Martin Bellius to Duke Christoph of Württemberg, Greeting. Most Illustrious Prince, suppose you had told your subjects that you would come to them at some uncertain time and had commanded them to make ready to go forth clad in white garments to meet you whenever you might appear. What would you do if, on your return, you discovered that they had taken no thought for the white robes but instead were disputing among themselves concerning your person? Some were saying that you were in France, others that you were in Spain; some that you would come on a horse, others in a chariot; some were asserting that you would appear with a great equipage, others that you would be unattended. Would this please you?

Suppose further that the controversy was being conducted not merely by words but by blows and swords, and that one group wounded and killed the others who did not agree with them. "He will come on a horse," one would say. "No, in a chariot," another would retort. "You lie." "You're the liar. Take that." He punches him. "And take that in the belly." The other stabs. Would you, O Prince, commend such citizens? Suppose, however, that some did their duty and followed your command to prepare the white robes, but others oppressed them on that account and put them to death. Would you not rigorously destroy such scoundrels? But what if these homicides claimed to have done all this in your name and in accord with your command, even though you had previously expressly forbidden it? Would you not consider that such outrageous conduct deserved to be punished without mercy? Now I beg you, most Illustrious Prince, be kind enough to hear why I say these things.

Christ is the Prince of this world who on His departure from the earth foretold to men that He would return some day at an uncertain hour, and He commanded them to prepare white robes for His coming, that is to say, that they should live together in a Christian manner, amicably, without controversy and contention, loving one another.

But consider now, I beg you, how well we discharge our duty....

Men are puffed up with knowledge or with a false opinion of knowledge and look down upon others. Pride is followed by cruelty and persecution so that now scarcely anyone is able to endure another who differs at all from him. Although opinions are almost as numerous as men, nevertheless there is hardly any sect which does not condemn all others and desire to reign alone. Hence arise banishments, chains, imprisonments, stakes, and gallows and this miserable rage to visit daily penalties upon those who differ from the mighty about matters hitherto unknown, for so many centuries disputed, and not yet cleared up.

If there is someone who strives to prepare the white robe, that is, to live justly and innocently, then all others with one accord cry out against him if he differ from them in anything, and they confidently pronounce him a heretic on the ground that he seeks to be justified by works. Horrible crimes of which he never dreamed are attributed to him and the common people are prejudiced by slander until they consider it a crime merely to hear him speak. Hence arises such cruel rage that some are so incensed by calumny as to be infuriated when the victim is first strangled instead of being burned alive at a slow fire.

When I consider the life and teaching of Christ who, though innocent Himself, yet always pardoned the guilty and told us to pardon until seventy times seven, I do not see how we can retain the name of Christian if we do not imitate His clemency and mercy. Even if we were innocent we ought to follow Him. How much more when we are covered with so many sins? When I examine my own life I see so many and such great sins that I do not think I could even obtain pardon from my Savior if I were thus ready to condemn others. Let each one examine himself, sound and search his conscience, and weigh his thoughts, words, and deeds. Then will he see himself as one who is not in a position to remove the mote from the eye of his brother before he has taken the beam from his own. In view of the many sins which are laid to us

100

all, the best course would be for each to look to himself, to exercise care for the correction of his life and not for the condemnation of others. This license of judgment which reigns everywhere today, and fills all with blood, constrains me, most Clement Prince, to do my best to staunch the blood, especially the blood which is so wrongfully shed—I mean the blood of those who are called heretics, which name has become today so infamous, detestable, and horrible that there is no quicker way to dispose of an enemy than to accuse him of heresy. The mere word stimulates such horror that when it is pronounced men shut their ears to the victim's defense, and furiously persecute not merely the man himself, but also all those who dare to open their mouths on his behalf; by which rage it has come to pass that many have been destroyed before their cause was really understood.

Now I say this not because I favor heretics. I hate heretics. But I speak because I see here two great dangers. And the first is that he be held for a heretic, who is not a heretic. This happened in former times, for Christ and his disciples were put to death as heretics, and there is grave reason to fear a recurrence in our century, which is not better, but rather worse. The danger is greater because Christ said, "Think not that I am come to send peace on earth; I came not to send peace, but a sword. For I am come to set a man at variance with his father, and the daughter against her mother," etc. You see how easy it is for calumniators to say of a Christian, "This man is seditious. He sets a son at variance against his father and disturbs the public peace." Great care must be exercised to distinguish those who are really seditious from Christians. Outwardly they do the same thing and are adjudged guilty of the same crime by those who do not understand. Christ was crucified among thieves.

The other danger is that he who is really a heretic be punished more severely or in a manner other than that required by Christian discipline. For these reasons I have collected in this book the opinions of many who have written on this matter, in order that a consideration of their arguments may lead to less offense for the future....

24. The Gallican Confession, 1559

This Confession was prepared under the supervision of John Calvin and represents a summary of his views in 1559. Trans. Emily O. Butler in Schaff, *The Creeds of Christendom.*

THE FRENCH SUBJECTS WHO WISH TO LIVE IN
THE PURITY OF THE GOSPEL OF
OUR LORD JESUS CHRIST

To the King

Sire, we thank God that hitherto having had no access to your Majesty to make known the rigor of the persecutions that we have suffered, and suffer daily, for wishing to live in the purity of the Gospel and in peace with our own consciences, he now permits us to see that you wish to know the worthiness of our cause, as is shown by the last Edict given at Amboise in the month of March of this present year, 1559, which it has pleased your Majesty to cause to be published. This emboldens us to speak, which we have been prevented from doing hitherto through the injustice and violence of some of your officers, incited rather by hatred of us than by love of your service. And to the end, Sire, that we may fully inform your Majesty of what concerns this cause, we humbly beseech that you will see and hear our Confession of Faith, which we present to you, hoping that it will prove a sufficient answer to the blame and opprobrium unjustly laid upon us by those who have always made a point of condemning us without having any knowledge of our cause. In the which, Sire, we can affirm that there is nothing contrary to the Word of God, or to the homage which we owe to you.

For the articles of our faith, which are all declared at some length in our Confession, all come to this: that since God has sufficiently declared his will to us through his Prophets and Apostles, and even by the mouth of his Son, our Lord Jesus Christ, we owe such respect and reverence to the Word of God as shall prevent us from adding to it any thing of our own, but shall make us con-

II-6. Church in the Desert. *Protestants worshipping by night in France.*

form entirely to the rules it prescribes. And inasmuch as the Roman Church, forsaking the use and customs of the primitive Church, has introduced new commandments and a new form of worship of God, we esteem it but reasonable to prefer the commandments of God, who is himself truth, to the commandments of men, who by their nature are inclined to deceit and vanity. And whatever our enemies may say against us, we can declare this before God and men, that we suffer for no other reason than for maintaining our Lord Jesus Christ to be our only Saviour and Redeemer, and his doctrine to be the only doctrine of life and salvation.

And this is the only reason, Sire, why the executioners' hands have been stained so often with the blood of your poor subjects, who, sparing not their lives to maintain this same Confession of Faith, have shown to all that they were moved by some other spirit than that of men, who naturally care more for their own peace and comfort than for the honor and glory of God.

And therefore, Sire, in accordance with your promises of goodness and mercy toward your poor subjects, we humbly beseech your Majesty graciously to examine the cause for which, being threatened at all times with death or exile, we thus lose the power of rendering the humble service that we owe you. May it please your Majesty, then, instead of the fire and sword which have been used hitherto, to have our Confession of Faith decided by the Word of God: giving permission and security for this. And we hope that you yourself will be the judge of our innocence, knowing that there is in us no rebellion or heresy whatsoever, but that our only endeavor is to live in peace of conscience, serving God according to his commandments, and honoring your Majesty by all obedience and submission. . . .

CONFESSION OF FAITH, MADE IN ONE ACCORD BY THE FRENCH PEOPLE, WHO DESIRE TO LIVE ACCORDING TO THE PURITY OF THE GOSPEL OF OUR LORD JESUS CHRIST, A.D. 1559

Art. I. We believe and confess that there is but one God, who is one sole and simple essence, spiritual, eternal, invisible, immutable, infinite, incomprehensible, ineffable, omnipotent; who is all-wise, all-good, all-just, and all-merciful.

II. As such this God reveals himself to men; firstly, in his works, in their creation, as well as in their preservation and control. Secondly, and more clearly, in his Word, which was in the beginning revealed through oracles, and which was afterward committed to writing in the books which we call the Holy Scriptures.

III. These Holy Scriptures are comprised in the canonical books of the Old and New Testaments. . . . [They are listed.]

IV. We know these books to be canonical, and the sure rule of our faith, not so much by the common accord and consent of the Church, as by the testimony and inward illumination of the Holy Spirit, which enables us to distinguish them from other ecclesiastical books upon which, however useful, we cannot found any articles of faith.

V. We believe that the Word contained in these books has proceeded from God, and receives its authority from him alone, and not from men. And inasmuch as it is the rule of all truth, containing all that is necessary for the service of God and for our salvation, it is not lawful for men, nor even for angels, to add to it, to take away from it, or to change it. Whence it follows that no authority, whether of antiquity, or custom, or numbers, or human wisdom, or judgments, or proclamations, or edicts, or decrees, or councils, or visions, or miracles, should be opposed to these Holy Scriptures, but, on the contrary, all things should be examined, regulated, and reformed according to them. And therefore we confess the three creeds, to wit: the Apostles', the Nicene, and the Athanasian, because they are in accordance with the Word of God.

VI, VII. [Belief in one God in three co-working persons.]

VIII. We believe that he not only created all things, but that he governs and directs them, disposing and ordaining by his sovereign will all that happens in the world; not that he is the author of evil, or that the guilt of it can be imputed to him, as his will is the sovereign and infallible rule of all right and justice; but he hath wonderful means of so making use of devils and sinners that he can turn to good the evil which they do, and of which they are guilty. And thus, confessing that the providence of God orders all things, we humbly bow before the secrets which are hidden to us, without questioning what is above our understanding; but rather making use of what is revealed to us in Holy Scripture for our peace and safety, inasmuch as God, who has all things in subjection to him, watches over us with a Father's care, so that not a hair of our heads shall fall without his will. And yet he restrains the devils and all our enemies, so that they cannot harm us without his leave.

IX. We believe that man was created pure and perfect in the image of God, and that by his own guilt he fell from the grace which he received, and is thus alienated from God, the fountain of justice and of all good, so that his nature is totally corrupt. And being blinded in mind, and depraved in heart, he has lost all integrity, and there is no good in him. And although he can still discern good and evil, we say, notwithstanding, that the light he has becomes darkness when he seeks for God, so that he can in nowise approach him by his intelligence and reason. And although he has a will that incites him to do this or that, yet it is altogether captive to sin, so that he has no other liberty to do right than that which God gives him.

X. We believe that all the posterity of Adam is in bondage to original sin, which is an hereditary evil, and not an imitation merely, as was declared by the Pelagians, whom we detest in their errors. . . .

XI. We believe, also, that this evil is truly sin, sufficient for the condemnation of the whole human race, even of little children in the mother's womb, and that God considers it as such; even after baptism it is still of the nature of sin, but the condemnation of it is abolished for the children of God, out of his mere free grace and love. And further, that it is a perversity always producing fruits of malice and of rebellion, so that the most holy men, although they resist it, are still stained with many weaknesses and imperfections while they are in this life.

XII. We believe that from this corruption and general condemnation in which all men are plunged, God, according to his eternal and immutable counsel, calls those whom he hath chosen by his goodness and mercy alone in our Lord Jesus Christ, without consideration of their works, to display in them the riches of his mercy; leaving the rest in this same corruption and condemnation to show in them his justice. For the ones are no better than the others, until God discerns them according to his immutable purpose which he has determined in Jesus Christ before the creation of the world. Neither can any man gain such a reward by his own virtue, as by nature we cannot have a single good feeling, affection, or thought, except God has first put it into our hearts.

XIII. [Jesus Christ brought salvation to men.]

XIV, XV. [Jesus Christ truly became flesh, God and man in one person, the two natures being inseparably joined.]

XVI. We believe that God, in sending his Son, intended to show his love and inestimable goodness towards us, giving him up to die to accomplish all righteousness, and raising him from the dead to secure for us the heavenly life.

XVII-XX. [By Christ's sacrifice men are reconciled to God, justified, and have access to the Father through faith.]

XXI. We believe that we are enlightened in faith by the secret power of the Holy Spirit, that it is a gratuitous and special gift which God grants to whom he will, so that the elect have no cause to glory, but are bound to be doubly thankful that they have been preferred to others. We believe also that faith is not given to the elect only to

introduce them into the right way, but also to make them continue in it to the end. For as it is God who hath begun the work, he will also perfect it.

XXII. We believe that by this faith we are regenerated in newness of life, being by nature subject to sin. Now we receive by faith grace to live holily and in the fear of God, in accepting the promise which is given to us by the Gospel, namely: that God will give us his Holy Spirit. This faith not only doth not hinder us from holy living, or turn us from the love of righteousness, but of necessity begetteth in us all good works. Moreover, although God worketh in us for our salvation, and reneweth our hearts, determining us to that which is good, yet we confess that the good works which we do proceed from his Spirit, and cannot be accounted to us for justification, neither do they entitle us to the adoption of sons, for we should always be doubting and restless in our hearts, if we did not rest upon the atonement by which Jesus Christ hath acquitted us.

XXIII. We believe that the ordinances of the law came to an end at the advent of Jesus Christ; but, although the ceremonies are no more in use, yet their substance and truth remain in the person of him in whom they are fulfilled. And, moreover, we must seek aid from the law and the prophets for the ruling of our lives, as well as for our confirmation in the promises of the Gospel.

XXIV. We believe, as Jesus Christ is our only advocate, and as he commands us to ask of the Father in his name, and as it is not lawful for us to pray except in accordance with the model God hath taught us by his Word, that all imaginations of men concerning the intercession of dead saints are an abuse and a device of Satan to lead men from the right way of worship. We reject, also, all other means by which men hope to redeem themselves before God, as derogating from the sacrifice and passion of Jesus Christ.

Finally, we consider purgatory as an illusion proceeding from the same shop, from which have also sprung monastic vows, pilgrimages, the prohibition of marriage, and of eating meat, the ceremonial observance of days, auricular confession, indulgences, and all such things by which they hope to merit forgiveness and salvation. These things we reject, not only for the false idea of merit which is attached to them, but also because they are human inventions imposing a yoke upon the conscience.

XXV-XXVII. [The Church, a company of those who follow God's Word, must have a ministry.]

XXVIII. In this belief we declare that, properly speaking, there can be no Church where the Word of God is not received, nor profession made of subjection to it, nor use of the sacraments. Therefore we condemn the papal assemblies, as the pure Word of God is banished from them, their sacraments are corrupted, or falsified, or destroyed, and all superstitions and idolatries are in them. We hold, then, that all who take part in these acts, and commune in that Church, separate and cut themselves off from the body of Christ. Nevertheless, as some trace of the Church is left in the papacy, and the virtue and substance of baptism remain, and as the efficacy of baptism does not depend upon the person who administers it, we confess that those baptized in it do not need a second baptism. But, on account of its corruptions, we cannot present children to be baptized in it without incurring pollution.

XXIX. [The Church should be governed as Christ ordained.]

XXX. We believe that all true pastors, wherever they may be, have the same authority and equal power under one head, one only sovereign and universal bishop, Jesus Christ; and that consequently no Church shall claim any authority or dominion over any other.

XXXI, XXXII. [Church officials should give evidence of their calling, and follow God's ordinances.]

XXXIII. However, we reject all human inventions, and all laws which men may introduce under the pretense of serving God, by which they wish to bind consciences; and we receive only that which conduces to concord and holds all in obedience, from the greatest to the least. In this we must follow that which the Lord Jesus Christ declared as to excommunication, which we approve and confess to be necessary with all its antecedents and consequences.

XXXIV. We believe that the sacraments are added to the Word for more ample confirmation, that they may be to us pledges and seals of the grace of God, and by this means aid and comfort our faith, because of the infirmity which is in us, and that they are outward signs through which God operates by his Spirit, so that he may not signify any thing to us in vain. Yet we hold that their substance and truth is in Jesus Christ, and that of themselves they are only smoke and shadow.

XXXV-XL. [Confession of only two sacraments, and acceptance of ordained authority.]

Bainton, Roland H., *Hunted Heretic: Servetus*. Boston: Beacon Press, 1953.

———, *The Travail of Religious Liberty*. Philadelphia: The Westminster Press, 1951.

Bender, Harold S., *Conrad Grebel*. Goshen, Ind.: The Mennonite Historical Society, 1950.

Calvin: Institutes of the Christian Religion. Good translations by John Allen (Philadelphia: Presbyterian Board of Christian Education, 1936), Henry Beveridge (Grand Rapids: Erdmans Publishing Co., 1947), John T. McNeill (Philadelphia: The Westminster Press, 1960).

Davies, Rupert E., *Problem of Authority in the Continental Reformer*. Naperville, Ill.: Allenson, 1946.

Dillenberger, John and Claude Welch, *Protestant Christianity*. New York: Charles Scribner's Sons, 1954.

Dowey, Edward A., *The Knowledge of God in Calvin's Theology*. New York: Columbia University Press, 1952.

Farner, Oskar, *Zwingli the Reformer*. New York: Philosophical Library, 1952.

Hershberger, G. F., ed., *Recovery of the Anabaptist Vision*. Scottdale, Pa.: Herald Press, 1957.

Horsch, John, *Mennonites in Europe*. Scottdale, Pa.: Herald Press, 1950.

Jackson, S. M., *Huldreich Zwingli*. New York: G. P. Putnam's Sons, 1901.

Littell, Franklin H., *The Anabaptist View of the Church*. Boston: Star King Press, 1958.

Machiavelli, Niccolò, *The Prince*. Various translations.

Mackinnon, James, *Calvin and the Reformation*. London: Longmans, Green & Co., Ltd., 1936.

McNeill, John T., *The History and Character of Calvinism*. New York: Oxford University Press, 1954.

Menno Simons, c. 1496-1561, The Complete Writings of, trans. Leonard Verduin, ed. John C. Wenger, biog. Harold S. Bender. Scottdale, Pa.: Herald Press, 1956.

Reid, Rev. J. K. S., trans., *Calvin: Theological Treatises*, Vol. XXII, *The Library of Christian Classics*. Philadelphia: The Westminster Press, 1954.

Schmidt, Albert-Marie, *John Calvin and the Calvinistic Tradition*. New York: Harper & Row, Publishers, 1960.

Wenger, John Christian, *Even Unto Death: The Heroic Witness of the Sixteenth Century Anabaptists*. Richmond, Va.: John Knox Press, 1961.

———, *Glimpses of Mennonite History and Doctrine*. Scottdale, Pa.: Herald Press, 1959.

Williams, George H., *The Radical Reformation*. Philadelphia: The Westminster Press, 1962.

Williams, George H. and Angel M. Mergal, *Spiritual and Anabaptist Writers*, Vol. XXV, *The Library of Christian Classics*. Philadelphia: The Westminster Press, 1957.

Zwingli and Bullinger, ed. G. W. Bromiley, Vol. XXIV, *The Library of Christian Classics*. Philadelphia: The Westminster Press, 1953.

Zwingli: Selected Works of, ed. S. M. Jackson. Philadelphia: University of Pennsylvania Press, 1901.

Zwingli: The Latin Works of, ed. S. M. Jackson and others. New York: G. P. Putnam's Sons, 1912, 1922, 1929.

CHRONOLOGY

Illustration opposite page 109: Descent from the Cross. *Peter Paul Rubens,*
1609. Notre Dame Cathedral, Antwerp, Belgium. Supplied by A. De Belder,
Antwerp.

III

The Roman Catholic

Counter Reformation

Revolt, not reformation, is the verdict of
Roman Catholic historians when they consider Protestantism in
the sixteenth century—an unfortunate revolt that brought
disunity to Christendom and delayed reforms already under way.
There were, of course, elements of reform that stirred within
Catholicism before, and continued after, Protestantism became
a historical reality, but whether any of them would have
terminated in anything more than the shelved report of
1537 (made by the cardinals who investigated corruption in the
church) is a matter of conjecture. The Counter Reformation,
which was not a reform movement but an attempt to
counteract the gains of the Protestants, had three main expressions:
one was found in the life and work of Ignatius Loyola and
his Jesuits, who carried to new heights the devotion and
service that were embodied in previous reform efforts; another

was in the revival of the inquisition in 1542, which used force, similar to that employed earlier in Spain, to annihilate heresy and schism; the third was in the Council of Trent, which in reaction to the claims of the Protestants restated the traditional doctrines of the church. These three developments continued into and beyond the seventeenth century, even though the rise of nationalism and other forces gradually undercut the sovereignty of church over state, from which they derived much of their strength. The Thirty Years' War (1618-1648) ended the last conflict fought mainly over religious issues, and can be called a terminal point of the Counter Reformation, but Loyola's Society of Jesus has continued as the great Roman Catholic army in missions and education, the Council of Trent is still basic to modern Catholicism, and the use of the secular arm to enforce Catholicism wherever it is politically dominant has not been officially repudiated. But circumstances have changed, and in the second half of the twentieth century many observers see signs of new attitudes in Catholicism resulting from ecumenicity within the church and militant secularism without.

Before and after Luther's break with Rome, several reform movements agitated Roman Catholicism from within, although popes like Leo X and Clement VII could hardly be called sponsors of spiritual reform, interested as they were in their own worldly ambitions, which they allowed to dictate their ineffective dealings with Protestantism. With the exception of the brief reign of Pope Adrian VI, who was pope for only one year, Leo X and Clement VII controlled the papacy from 1513 to 1534. And the politically involved papacy that put Savonarola on the stake in 1498 could hardly be called a reforming element, for it was intent on maintaining its own worldly position of power and luxury.

There were, however, elements of reform in Roman Catholicism. In Spain, Cardinal Ximenes (1436-1517), a humanist in the same tradition as Erasmus, Reuchlin, Colet, and More, but at the same time a medieval churchman, headed a flourish for reform that combined intellectual endeavors, moral rigor, and physical violence, as if in anticipation of the phases of the Counter Reformation. With medieval zeal, Ximenes loved orthodoxy and hated heresy, with monastic earnestness he sought to reform the clergy and abolish clerical abuses, and with humanistic insight he promoted education and research. Ximenes' efforts were confined largely to Spain, but even though he died just as Charles V was about to depose him, his reforms continued in the reigns of Kings Charles V and Philip II. Gold from the New World, which was beginning to fill the treasury of Spain, helped promote this revival. In large measure, Ximenes prepared the way for Ignatius Loyola. Ximenes' *Complutesian Polyglot*, an edition of the entire Bible in the original languages, appeared in 1522, and he promoted biblical studies along with the study of medicine and anatomy at the University of Alcala, which he founded. As confessor to the queen, he was politically and socially a leader in the culture of Spain. But he was, in addition, a Franciscan who had taken the vow of poverty and who continued to wear the hair shirt to indicate his kinship with the ascetics of the past. He stringently supervised monastic morality and forbade clerical concubinage; he actively preached a crusade against the Moors, and in 1507 he became the chief of the inquisition in Spain, the same institution which with Torquemade at its head had brought such horror to Spain just a few years earlier, when 10,000 people were burned and more than 100,000 imprisoned. During the ten years that Ximenes headed the Spanish inquisition, more than 2,000 people suffered death and 40,000 were imprisoned and tortured. He was a churchman employing the fruits of humanism to promote the ecclesiastical order.

In Italy, reforms originated in the Oratory of Divine Love, which was begun in 1517 in Rome. Its members, both lay and clerical, dedicated themselves to reform in their own lives and in the lives of those about them. Future cardinals Caraffa (1476-1559), Sadoleto (1477-1547), Contarini (1483-1542), and Ghiberti were among its members. They shared a zeal to live the good life, to recapture the devotion to Christ that would again make the church great. In their frequent meetings for discussion, prayer, and preaching was born the impetus for the reforms that came in Roman Catholicism in the first half of the sixteenth century, but the leaders were not agreed on the course to pursue. Contarini led one faction which was humanistic in orientation, insistent on stringent morality but latitudinarian in doctrine. Contarini sought to heal the differences between Protestants and Roman Catholics through conciliation. He could agree with the evangelical reformers on justification by faith and the need for moral reform, but he could not reject the hierarchy. At Ratisbon in 1541, Melanchthon and Contarini worked out an agreement on justification, but their basically divergent views became evident when they discussed celibacy. Melanchthon insisted on a priesthood of all believers, unfiltered through the papacy; Contarini wanted to

preserve the ancient chain of command and sacerdotalism. Neither Luther nor Pope Paul III could countenance this approach to reform through conciliation, and Contarini died a broken man.

Other currents of reform were not lacking, and many of them stemmed from the Oratory of Divine Love. The Order of the Theatines was founded in 1524 by St. Cajetan in the see of Caraffa, Theate, to encourage preaching, administer the sacraments, care for the sick, and to seek a reform of morals among the clergy. The Barnabites, established about 1530 by Zaccaria, also sought to reform morals and to serve through works of mercy. The Ursulines, started by Angela Merici in 1535, concentrated on caring for children and destitute women. The Capuchins were poor monks, a revival of the Franciscans, established by Matteo da Bascio in 1526, who

III-1. Christ Cleansing the Temple. *Panel, painted in response to a resurgence of Roman Catholic piety, by El Greco (1541–1614). National Gallery of Art, Washington, D.C., Samuel H. Kress Collection.*

were devoted to piety and service; they were blessed but also condemned by Pope Clement VII. The Sommaschi, the Fathers of the Good Death, the Brothers of Mercy, and others were dedicated to caring for the sick.

All these groups represent a ferment for reform within the church, and these elements of reform prompted Pope Paul III to appoint a committee, composed largely of members of the Oratory of Divine Love, to investigate the morals of the clergy. In March, 1537, the committee made its famous report, *Consilium de Emendenda Ecclesia*. The twenty-six sections on evils noted glaring clerical corruptions—worldly bishops, poor schools, buying of indulgences, scandals in monastic houses, bribes to pervert justice, prostitution, graft, non-residence, and so on. The report, which was too frank to be published, pointed to clerical greed for money as the source of many abuses. Pope Paul III hesitated to act, but in 1540 he did send some eighty bishops back to their resident sees. Luther used the report to substantiate his charges of widespread immorality. Vigorous reform did not reach the papacy until Caraffa was seated as Pope Paul IV, from 1555 to 1559. He led the faction within the Oratory of Divine Love that wanted to stamp out heresy by force. He advocated reform through a strong and dominating papacy, and did not hesitate to begin by combating the nepotism which his own family practiced. When he died, a medal was struck in his honor showing Christ driving the money changers from the temple.

In the very year that Contarini died, 1542, Pope Paul III, urged on by Caraffa and the Jesuits, reorganized the Holy Office of the Inquisition (6). The notorious Spanish inquisition was its immediate model, but whereas the Spanish inquisition was largely national, the new inquisition was to be universal, reaching all the way into the New World. Caraffa and five other cardinals were chosen to preside over the Holy Office, and the number was later increased to twelve. They not only directed the affairs of the inquisition, but they also decided cases and heard appeals. The effects of the resort to force were felt immediately in those areas where secular rulers supported the church.

Peter Martyr of Florence and Bernard Ochino of Siena, vicar-general of the Capuchin order, fled from Italy to become wandering refugees in Protestant lands. Both of these men had been disciples of Juan de Valdes (d. 1541), a Spaniard who settled at Naples. De Valdes sought personal peace in mystical piety based on justification by faith alone, but he did not wish to break with the established order. The inquisition condemned papal secretary Carnesecchi and sent him to the stake for his liberalism, incarcerated Cardinal Morone, and inflicted similar fates on many others, including the Spanish Archbishop Carranza of Toledo, who was condemned in 1556. The appeal to force reached its height in the Massacre of St. Bartholomew's Day in 1572 in France, which decimated the Huguenots (cf. 7), and in the Netherlands, where, Grotius estimated, a hundred thousand lost their lives under the ruthless methods of Alva and his Bloody Council.

A man dedicated to reform was Ignatius Loyola (1491-1556), a Spanish noble who spent his youth in the court of King Ferdinand. He expected to become a military leader, but a leg wound at Pampeluna in 1521 shattered this ambition, and he vowed in turmoil of spirit to become a soldier for Christ under the banner of Our Lady. In 1522, Loyola went through the experiences in a cave at Manresa that resulted in his *Spiritual Exercises*, meditations designed to make the personality completely obedient to the will of God (1). Thinking he might become a missionary to the Mohammedans, he went to Palestine, only to be sent home by the Franciscans, who considered him a hindrance to their vigil of the cross in Jerusalem. Although he was a grown man, he entered a school for boys in Barcelona, determined to acquire an education because he thought Protestant heretics could not be stopped with papal pronouncements. He soon advanced to the universities of Alcala and Salamanca, and during this period attracted so many followers, both men and women, that he was investigated three times by the inquisition, spent forty days in jail, and was forbidden to preach for a period of three years. His crime was that he dared to practice reform without

III-2. **Sufferings of the Martyrs.** *Scene by Jan Luiken from the* Dutch Martyrs' Mirror, *1685.* Mennonite Encyclopedia.

ecclesiastical authorization. But Loyola was not daunted. In 1528, at about the time that Calvin was finishing his studies there, Loyola entered the University of Paris. He gathered a small group about him to practice spiritual exercises, among them Francis Xavier, destined to become the noted missionary to the Orient, Diego Lainez, who succeeded Loyola as head of the Society of Jesus, Pierre Lefèvre, Alfonso Salmeron, Nicholas Bobadilla, and Simon Rodriguez. Convinced that they should found a society, Loyola and his companions knelt in the Parisian church of St. Mary on Montmartre, at the crypt of St. Denis, and vowed to live in poverty and celibacy, and to go to Jerusalem to labor for the church and their fellow men, or if that proved impossible, to place themselves at the disposal of the pope for whatever service he might command. In 1537, the group did hospital work in Venice and took priestly orders. Unable to continue to Jerusalem on account of war, they turned to Rome for guidance, for

Loyola had conceived the idea that they might become an army fighting the spiritual battles of the church against heretics and infidels.

Despite ecclesiastical opposition, Pope Paul III approved the Society of Jesus on September 27, 1540 (2), and Loyola served as general until his death in 1556. At first the order was limited to sixty, but it soon numbered in the thousands. Its aim was threefold: obedience, education, and missions. Obedience to the pope was absolute; for the sake of truth, the Jesuits vowed to say what appeared to be white was really black if the hierarchical church so declared. The educational system of the Jesuits was remarkable for its effectiveness. It was characterized by a dogmatic approach, rigid discipline, and strict supervision; students were never allowed to be alone, and they could not attend public functions except when a heretic was being executed. The teachers were well-trained and devoted. In the 1550's, colleges

113

were established in Rome, Vienna, Coimbra, and Munich. By 1626, the Jesuits had 15,000 members, 803 houses, 476 colleges, and 36 seminaries. By 1750, members numbered 22,000, and there were 669 colleges and 176 seminaries, besides hundreds of lesser schools. The record of the Jesuits was not less remarkable in missions, for Jesuit missionaries, beginning with the tireless efforts of Francis Xavier in the Orient (3), went all over the world, keeping pace with the geographical discoveries of the time, even suffering martyrdom among the American wilds.

Francis Xavier (1506-1552) dedicated himself to bear the cross and the sacraments to the Orient. He sailed for the Portuguese colony of Goa on the coast of India in 1541, and became the forerunner of an intrepid host. He baptized and claimed for the church hundreds of heathens many of whom could hardly comprehend what he was doing; he established schools and a missionary college, and preached throughout southern India (3). In 1549, he made his way to Japan to introduce Catholicism there, and in 1552 he died of a fever while trying to carry the cross and the sacraments to the Chinese.

In South America, especially in Peru and Paraguay, and in North America around the Great Lakes and the Mississippi River basin, the Jesuits carried on their missions. Not to be outdone, the Franciscans pushed into Mexico, Florida, and California. This missionary outreach, which preceded similar Protestant efforts by a century, became so widespread in the New World and in other countries that Pope Gregory XV in 1622 established the Congregation for the Propagation of the Faith to centralize and supervise the work from Rome. The early missionaries left an influence that is still noticeable in names, customs, architecture, and religion.

In their desire to win converts and reclaim those who had gone astray, the Jesuits developed a doctrine of probabilism, which permitted them to absolve any course of action as perfectly acceptable to Christ if any authority could be cited in support of it. They also developed a doctrine of mental reservation which permitted them to withhold part of the truth or leave a wrong impression, if the end in mind were good (cf. 13). These doctrines and the worldly success of the Jesuits caused widespread resentment. As the strong arm of the papacy, the Jesuits involved themselves in politics, controlled a great deal of wealth, operated factories, and let their colleges serve as banks of exchange. By 1773, the Jesuits had engendered so much hostility that Pope Clement XIV felt constrained to suppress the order, although that suppression was withdrawn in 1814. The Society of Jesus regained much of its influence, especially in missions and education.

The doctrinal statements of the Council of Trent (4), which because of war and the plague met intermittently from 1545 to 1563, completed the three basic expressions of the Roman Catholic Counter Reformation. Remembering the conciliar movement which erupted in the preceding century in the councils of Constance and Basel and almost wrested authority from the papacy, the popes of the sixteenth century were reluctant to summon a council to consider religious beliefs, for if a general council received the support of the secular arm, it might render the papacy inferior in power and make the popes responsible to a general body of the church. Emperor Charles V especially wanted a council, however, and political pressures finally prevailed; Pope Paul III summoned the Council of Trent.

Far from reducing papal dominance, however, the Council of Trent produced a body of doctrine that enhanced the papacy, lessened the power of national bishops, and tended to make the church even more Roman. More than half of the twenty-five public sessions were mere formalities. Protestants were invited and a few participated in some of the middle sessions, but to no effect. In reaction to the Augsburg Confession and other Protestant creeds, the Council of Trent defined Roman Catholicism on all disputed points, condemned evangelical views in a series of anathemas, and touched on reforms in discipline. There were no doctrinal concessions, not even in the carefully worded statement on justification, which remained a process of cooperation between man and God. The Council reaffirmed the

Nicene Creed, placed tradition on a par with Scripture, declared the Apocrypha a part of the canonized Bible, designated Jerome's Vulgate translation the official version of the Bible, reiterated the seven sacraments, made the mass a propitiatory sacrifice, reaffirmed transubstantiation, confirmed withholding the cup, upheld the indelible character of ordination, exalted celibacy over marriage, and sanctioned invocation of saints, masses for the dead, and the efficacy of indulgences. Another council was not deemed necessary in Roman Catholicism until the Vatican Council in 1870, which dogmatized the papal infallibility that was already inherent in the Council of Trent.

Practical reforms by the Council of Trent were negligible, but more scriptural preaching was advocated, concubinage censored, pluralities of positions restrained, and an index of prohibited books voted. This resulted in the establishment of a Congregation of the Index at Rome in 1571 to censure publications.

At the conclusion of the Council Pope Pius IV codified Roman Catholic views in the Tridentine formula of faith, which was to be recited in all parishes and used by the faithful (5). The Council of Trent, so long dreaded by the popes, actually left the papacy with more centralized power and a more efficient organization than at any time since the Great Schism. These expressions of the Counter Reformation, continued and broadened by other leaders, restored the Roman Catholic Church in the last half of the sixteenth century to much of its past vigor and moral earnestness. Spain witnessed a flowering of mystical piety in the work of St. Teresa (1515-1582), who at the age of eighteen secretly left her parental home and joined the Carmelite Monastery of the Incarnation at Avila. Though ill much of the time, she practiced intense devotions, asceticism, and self-torture, which produced periods of spiritual ecstasy in which she seemed to reach a union with God in divine love; she once even declared that Christ was physically present. She established sixteen branches of the Carmelite order for women, and fourteen for men. Forty years after her death she was canonized as the "seraphic virgin." Her auto-

biography provides a psychological insight into her own feelings and the quiescence which she advocated for prayer life—allowing the will to lie quiet while the understanding and memory are still active. One of her pupils, St. John of the Cross (1542-1591), wrote *Ascent of Mount Carmel*, in which he described the "dark night of the soul" when beset with difficulties.

Francis de Sales (1567-1622) carried this type of piety to even greater heights. He wrote *An Introduction to the Devout Life* in 1618, one of the most popular books of devotion ever published, translated into almost every European language (cf. *12*). Francis de Sales was a typical son of the Counter Reformation. He was educated by the Jesuits and entered the priesthood in 1591, where he led a life of self-denial and dedication to the church. He founded the Order of the Visitation in 1610, an order for women who vowed to do works of charity among the poor. As the Bishop of Geneva (1602-1622) he fought Calvinism, although he could not live in the cathedral city of his see. He was noted for his great preaching and kindness, but he resorted to coercive measures when persuasion failed. The bull announcing his canonization in 1665 claimed that he had converted 72,000 heretics.

Giovanni da Palestrina (1524?-1594) expressed the revitalization of Catholicism in music, for which he has been called the "Father and Prince of Church Music." The Council of Trent was considering banning music in divine worship because it was so inferior and abused until Palestrina showed how inspirational it could be. With *Missa Papae Marcelli* in 1565 he instituted pure polyphonic music and set a pattern which was officially adopted as the true form of ecclesiastical music. He rejected all embellishments which tended to obscure the liturgical texts, sought to omit all secular strains, and endeavored to excite true devotional feeling. He served as choir master of St. John's Lateran, St. Peter's, and Santa Maria Maggiore, and was named Composer to the Papal Chapel. In these positions he dominated liturgical music in Europe and rescued it from the inferiority of the mechanical conundrums of his day. He composed more

III-3. Palestrina Presenting His First Book of Masses to Pope Julius III. *Woodcut on title page, 1554. From Georg Kinsky,* A History of Music in Pictures *(New York: E. P. Dutton & Co., Inc., 1930).*

than ninety masses, five hundred motets for the church year, and numerous offertories, litanies, hymns, praises, spiritual madrigals, magnificats and lamentations. His famous *Improperia* is traditionally sung on Good Friday in the Sistine Chapel.

But the zeal of revitalized Catholicism also found expression in violence, an extension of the inquisition, especially in France and in the Netherlands. Francis I of France (1515-1547) sensed that Protestantism would be defeated on the field of battle in Germany, and lest he not be on the side of power, he instituted a policy of extermination for the Protestants in 1545 that led to the burning of twenty-two villages, the execution of three thousand people, and condemnation to the galleys or exile for hundreds of others. In 1546, a raid on the evangelical congregation at Meaux caused fourteen to die at the stake. Henry II (1547-1559) followed with an inquisition to dispel all the elements of Protestantism remaining in France, but his death

in a tournament in 1559 ended his plan and left France in political confusion. At this time Admiral Coligny, one of France's wisest statesmen, championed the Huguenots, and for a while the Protestants flourished and added thousands of converts. But in 1562 the Catholics procured the January edict which deprived the Huguenots of their places of worship and compelled them to meet in the open air outside the cities. A massacre of Huguenots at Vassy touched off a religious-civil strife that raged intermittently from 1562 to 1598. In 1572, Catherine de Medici, the queen mother, treacherously used an event that might have brought peace. Incensed over the influence of Coligny on the indecisive young King Charles IX (1560-1574), she plotted with the rival House of Guise to exterminate the Protestants when the various parties were gathered in Paris to celebrate the marriage of Henry of Navarre (a Protestant champion) to the King's sister, Margaret of Valois. This marriage created the possibility that the throne might pass in the future to a Protestant. The massacre broke out suddenly on St. Bartholomew's Day, August 24, 1572, when the bell of St. Germain L'Auxerrois tolled the signal (7). The King himself shouted "Kill, kill," and Admiral Coligny was among the first to fall; his bleeding body was flung into the street and his severed head forwarded to the Cardinal of Lorraine at Rome as a trophy. More than eight thousand Huguenots perished in Paris, and the massacre spread throughout the provinces where the most conservative estimates say 20,000 died. Henry of Navarre saved himself by accepting Catholicism. Except for Rome and Spain, Europe was shocked. Pope Gregory XIII thanked God for turning his eyes of mercy on the church; he ordered a *Te Deum*, proclaimed a jubilee, and struck a medal to commemorate the occasion. In the struggles that followed, Henry of Guise and the new King Henry III who succeeded Charles IX both met violent deaths, leaving Henry of Navarre, who had resumed his leadership of the Huguenots, to succeed to the throne. Believing that he could not be king without Catholic support, he again embraced Catholicism, and then as King Henry IV he issued

III-4. Judgment of the Reformers in the Netherlands. *Copper engraving by Franz Hogenberg.*

the Edict of Nantes in 1598, which gave freedom once more to the Huguenots (8).

In the Netherlands the policy of violence was pursued with even greater intensity against the Calvinists and Anabaptists. Charles V transferred his sovereignty to his son Philip II in 1555, and Philip vowed that he would bring political and religious unity to the Lowlands. His initial efforts, however, only caused a turn to Protestantism and created a desire for independence. To quell this development and to enforce the Council of Trent, Philip sent an army to the Netherlands under the command of the Duke of Alva, who in six years of rule, from 1567 to 1573, spread destruction and death throughout the land. He bankrupted the merchants with heavy taxes and caused many Catholic

merchants to join the Protestants. Literally thousands lost their possessions and their lives, but the Dutch would not submit; in the 1570's, William of Orange, a Calvinist, led a successful resistance that finally resulted in the compromise independence of the northern states in 1581. The southern provinces continued Catholic and became modern Belgium. The decree of toleration for Anabaptists issued by William of Orange in 1577, the first of its kind, made the Netherlands a refuge for the religiously persecuted, of which the Pilgrims later took advantage.

In France the Edict of Nantes did not last long. Under Louis XIII (1610-1643), Cardinal Richelieu, minister of state, again persecuted the Huguenots, and Louis XIV (1643-1715), prompted by the Jesuits, instituted policies of persecution that culminated in the revocation of the Edict of Nantes in 1685 (9), causing 50,000 families to seek refuge in England, Holland, and America. Only a generation earlier, the Waldenses (Vaudois), whose confession of 1655 shows that they were Calvinistic like the Huguenots of France, had suffered a wretchedly cruel persecution. The atrocities aroused the Christian world to anger. Oliver Cromwell, then Lord Protector in England, ordered a day of fasting and sorrow, started a relief fund by personally contributing £2,000, and censured the Roman Catholic sovereigns for their complacency and compliance in this human tragedy. John Milton paid tribute to the Waldensians in one of his best known sonnets (10).

Not papal supremacy but a church with nationalistic tendencies was the desire of the kings of France. Louis XIV sought a national church because of the money that he could claim from the church if he could keep the papacy from draining off various funds. This Gallican tendency, not anti-Catholic sentiment, engendered the Gallican Declaration, drawn up by Bossuet in 1682, which sought to limit the power of the papacy in favor of the French clergy and king (cf. 13). When closer cooperation became mutually advantageous to the French king and the papacy, the Gallican Declaration was quietly withdrawn in 1693.

More lasting reactions came in two other areas. As a result of the wars and persecutions in France, Hotman and Languet developed Calvinistic theories of resistance, which were to prove significant in the future of Protestantism (11). The Jesuits' attempts to destroy Port Royal brought forth the satirical *Provincial Letters* of Blaise Pascal (1623-1662), one of the most gifted men of his time, the founder of modern mathematics, inventor of the calculating machine, and a literary artist whose style greatly influenced modern French. Pascal's letters resulted from the controversy over Jansenism, which like Gallicanism had a national overtone, but which was more theologically grounded and closer to Protestantism (13). Jansen, the bishop of Ypres and a student of Augustine, wrote a book called *Augustinus,* which was published in 1640, two years after his death. The Cistercian nunnery at Port Royal incorporated Jansen's "Protestant" views, especially the idea that we have no free will and are only instruments in the hands of God, into its teaching. The Jesuits secured a condemnation of these views from Pope Urban VIII in 1642, apparently without determining whether Jansen actually taught the propositions condemned, and then secured a further condemnation in 1653 from Innocent X; students and nuns were banished from Port Royal. Blaise Pascal, who was staying at Port Royal and who had undergone a religious conversion that brought him close to the personal religion that was taught at Port Royal, produced the *Provincial Letters* in 1656 (13). He perceived the moral issue of easy religion currying favor with the world, as opposed to a sincere dedication to the claims of an all-sovereign God, and he withered the Jesuits with sharp humor. In his *Pensées,* Pascal explored insights that still inform philosophical and religious thought (cf. Ch. 6).

The Counter Reformation demonstrated the inherent strength and weakness of Catholicism. It set the stage for the entry of Catholicism into the modern era of nationalism and science; it slowed the advances of Protestantism; but it also anchored Catholicism to an ultramontane papacy based on medieval structures. Meanwhile the Counter Reformation failed to gain the secular arm in England, and there the Reformation assumed a course all its own.

1. The Jesuits: Spiritual Exercises

The Spiritual Exercises, born of Ignatius Loyola's own religious experience at Manresa, was written in its earliest form about 1521, but did not appear in print until 1548. These exercises, which directed the exercitant toward a life of complete service to God and man, served to gain dedicated recruits for the Society of Jesus. The prayer, *Anima Christi,* which Loyola recommended but which did not appear in the early editions, summarizes the tone and goal of the entire work. The exercises required four weeks and centered on sin, the early life of Christ, the passion, and the resurrection. The following excerpts are given to show the devotion and obedience that the Society cultivated. *The Spiritual Exercises of St. Ignatius of Loyola,* trans. W. H. Longridge (London: A. R. Mowbray & Co. Ltd., 1955). Used by permission.

Anima Christi:

Soul of Christ, sanctify me.
Body of Christ, save me.
Blood of Christ, inebriate me.
Water from the side of Christ, wash me.
Passion of Christ, strengthen me.
O Good Jesus, hear me.
Within thy wounds hide me.
Permit me not to be separated from thee.
From the wicked foe defend me.
At the hour of my death call me,
And bid me come to thee,
That with thy saints I may praise thee
For ever and ever. Amen.

Introductory Observations: [To aid the exercitant and the one who gives the exercises.]

1. Under the name of spiritual Exercises is understood every method of examination of conscience, of meditation, of contemplation, of vocal and mental prayer, and of other spiritual operations, as shall hereafter be declared: for as to go for a walk, to take a journey, and to run, are bodily exercises, so in like manner all methods of preparing and disposing the soul to rid itself of all inordinate affections and, after it has rid itself of them, to seek and to find the divine will in the ordering of one's life with a view to the salvation of one's soul, are called spiritual Exercises.

2. He who gives to another the method and order of meditating or contemplating ought faithfully to narrate the history of the contemplation or meditation, merely running over the points with a brief or summary exposition: because when the person who contemplates, taking the true groundwork of the history, and discoursing and reasoning for himself, finds something that makes the history a little clearer or more deeply felt (whether this happens through his own reasoning, or through the enlightenment of his understanding by divine grace), he thereby enjoys greater spiritual relish and fruit, than if he who gives the Exercises had fully explained and developed the meaning of the history: for it is not abundance of knowledge that fills and satisfies the soul, but to feel and taste the matters interiorly.

3. As in all the spiritual Exercises that follow we make use of the understanding when reasoning, and of the will when exciting affections, let us take notice that in acts of the will, when we are conversing vocally or mentally with God our Lord or with His Saints, greater reverence is required on our part than when we make use of the understanding in reasoning.

4. Although four Weeks are assigned for the following Exercises, to correspond to the four parts into which they are divided: to wit, the first, which is the consideration and contemplation of sins; the second, which is the Life of Christ our Lord until Palm Sunday inclusively; the third, the Passion of Christ our Lord; the fourth, the Resurrection and Ascension, with the addition of three methods of prayer; nevertheless this is not to be so understood, as if each Week necessarily contained seven or eight days. For since it happens that in the First Week some are slower than others in finding what they desire, namely, contrition, grief, and tears for their sins; and likewise some are more diligent than others, and more agitated or tried by divers spirits, it is necessary sometimes to shorten the Week, at other times to lengthen it, and so in all the following Weeks, seeking always the fruit proper to the subject matter. The Exercises should, however, be concluded in thirty days more or less.

5. It will greatly benefit him who receives the Exercises to enter upon them with a courageous heart and with liberality towards his Creator and Lord, offering Him all his will and liberty, in order that His Divine Majesty may make use of his person and of all he possesses according to His most holy will.

6. When he who gives the Exercises finds that the exercitant experiences no spiritual movements in his soul, such as consolations or desolations, nor is agitated by divers spirits, he ought to question him fully about the Exercises, whether he makes them at the right times, and how; and also as to the Additions, if he observes them diligently, questioning him particularly on each of these points.

7. If he who gives the Exercises sees that he who receives them is in desolation and temptation, let him not be hard or severe with him, but kind and gentle, encouraging

1.Gratias age. 2.Pete lumen. 3.Examina 4 Dole.
5.Propone.

III-5. Hand Marked with the Five Stages of Jesuit
Devotion: Thanksgiving, Petition for Light, Examination, Sorrow, and Thrust. *Engraving in one of the earliest illustrated editions of the* Exercises *of Loyola.*

and strengthening him for the future, pointing out to him the wiles of the enemy of human nature, and exhorting him to prepare and dispose himself for future consolation. . . .

FIRST WEEK: PRINCIPLE AND FOUNDATION

Man was created to praise, reverence, and serve God our Lord, and by this means to save his soul; and the other things on the face of the earth were created for man's sake, and in order to aid him in the prosecution of the end for which he was created. Whence it follows, that man ought to make use of them just so far as they help him to attain his end, and that he ought to withdraw himself from them just so far as they hinder him. It is therefore necessary that we should make ourselves indifferent to all created things, in all that is left to the liberty of our free-will, and is not forbidden; in such sort that we do not

for our part wish for health rather than sickness, for wealth rather than poverty, for honour rather than dishonour, for a long life rather than a short one, and so in all other things, desiring and choosing only that which leads us more directly to the end for which we were created.

The Particular Examination to be made daily includes three times, and an examination of oneself to be made twice.

The first time is the morning: immediately on rising, the man ought to resolve to guard himself carefully against that particular sin or defect which he desires to correct and amend.

The second time is after the midday meal, when he ought to ask of God our Lord that which he desires, viz. grace to remember how often he has fallen into that particular sin or defect, and to amend in future; after which let him make the first examination, demanding an account from his soul concerning the particular matter which he desires to correct or amend, reviewing the time elapsed, hour by hour, or period by period, beginning from the time when he rose till the moment of the present examination, and let him mark on the first line of the diagram as many points as there are times when he has fallen into that particular sin or defect; and afterwards let him resolve anew to amend himself until the second examination that he will make.

The third time is after supper, when the second examination will be made in the same way, going through the interval hour by hour from the first examination to the present one, and marking on the second line of the same diagram as many points as there are times he has again fallen into that same particular sin or defect.

The First Exercise is a meditation with the three powers of the soul upon the first, the second, and the third sin. It contains in itself, after a preparatory prayer and two preludes, three principal points and a colloquy.

The preparatory prayer is to ask God our Lord for grace that all my intentions, actions, and operations may be ordered purely to the service and praise of His divine Majesty.

The first prelude is a composition, seeing

the place. Here it is to be observed that in the contemplation or meditation of a visible object, as in contemplating Christ our Lord, Who is visible, the composition will be to see with the eye of the imagination the corporeal place where the object I wish to contemplate is found. I say the corporeal place, such as the Temple or the mountain where Jesus Christ is found, or our Lady, according to that which I desire to contemplate. In a meditation on an invisible thing, such as the present meditation on sins, the composition will be to see with the eyes of the imagination and to consider that my soul is imprisoned in this corruptible body, and my whole compound self in this vale [of misery] as in exile amongst brute beasts; I say my whole self, composed of soul and body.

The second prelude is to ask of God our Lord that which I wish and desire. The petition ought to be according to the subject-matter, i.e. if the contemplation is on the Resurrection, to ask for joy with Christ in His joy; if it be on the Passion, to beg for sorrow, tears, and fellowship with Christ in His sufferings; here it will be to ask for shame and confusion of face, seeing how many have been lost for a single mortal sin, and how many times I have deserved to be condemned eternally for my so many sins.

Before all contemplations or meditations there should always be made the preparatory prayer without change, and the two above-mentioned preludes, changing them from time to time according to the subject-matter.

The first point will be to apply the memory to the first sin, which was that of the angels; and then the understanding to the same by reasoning on it; and then the will, desiring to remember and understand the whole, in order that I may be the more ashamed and confounded, bringing into comparison with the one sin of the angels my many sins, and considering that while they have gone to hell for one sin, I have so often deserved the same punishment for my many sins. I say to apply the memory to the sin of the angels, how being created in grace, yet not willing to help themselves by means of their liberty to reverence and obey their Creator and Lord, they fell into pride, were changed from grace into malice, and cast down from heaven to hell; and then in turn to reason more in particular with the understanding, and thus to move still more the affections by means of the will.

The second point will be to do the same, i.e. to apply the three powers to the sin of Adam and Eve, bringing before the memory how for that sin they did such long penance, and how great corruption came upon the human race, so many men going towards hell. I say, to apply the memory to the second sin, that of our first parents; how, after Adam had been created in the plain of Damascus, and placed in the terrestrial Paradise, and Eve had been formed out of his rib, when they had been forbidden to eat of the tree of knowledge, yet eating of it and so sinning, they were afterwards clothed in garments made of skins, and driven out of Paradise, and lived without original righteousness, which they had lost, all their life long in toilsome labour and much penance; and then in turn to reason with the understanding more in particular, using also the will, as has been said before.

The third point will be to do in like manner in regard to the third sin, i.e. the particular sin of some one person, who for one mortal sin has gone to hell; and many others without number for fewer sins than I have committed. I say, to do the same in regard to the third particular sin, bringing before the memory the gravity and malice of sin committed by man against his Creator and Lord; then to reason with the understanding how, in sinning and acting against the infinite Goodness, such an one has justly been condemned for ever; and to conclude with acts of the will, as has been said.

Colloquy. Imagining Christ our Lord present before me on the Cross, to make a colloquy with Him, asking Him how it is that being the Creator, He has come to make Himself man, and from eternal life has come to temporal death, and in this manner to die for my sins. Again, reflecting on myself, to ask what have I done for Christ, what am I doing for Christ, what ought I to do for Christ. Then beholding Him in such a condition, and thus hanging upon the Cross, to make the reflections which may present themselves.

The colloquy is made, properly speaking, as a friend speaks to a friend, or a servant to his master, asking at one time for some grace, at another accusing oneself of some evil committed, at another making known one's affairs and seeking counsel concerning them. And then to say *Our Father*.

The Second Exercise is a meditation upon sins; it contains, after the preparatory prayer and two preludes, five points and a colloquy.

The first point is the review of the sins, that is to say, to recall to memory all the sins of my life, contemplating them from year to year, or from period to period. Three things help in this: first, to behold the place and the house where I have lived; second, to recall the intercourse I have had with others; third, the occupation in which I have been engaged.

The second, is to weigh the sins, considering the foulness and malice that each mortal sin committed has in itself, even supposing that it were not forbidden.

The third, is to consider who I am, abasing myself by comparisons: first, what am I in comparison with all men; second, what are all men in comparison with the angels and saints in heaven; third, to consider what is all creation in comparison with God—therefore, myself alone, what can I be? Fourth, to consider all my corruption and bodily foulness; fifth, to behold myself as an ulcer and abscess whence have issued so many sins and iniquities, and such vile poison.

The fourth, is to consider who God is, against Whom I have sinned, contemplating His attributes and comparing them with their contraries in myself: His wisdom with my ignorance, His omnipotence with my weakness, His justice with my iniquity, His goodness with my perversity.

The fifth, an exclamation of wonder, with great affection, running through all creatures in my mind, and thinking how they have suffered me to live, and have preserved me in life; how the angels, who are the sword of the divine justice, have borne with me and guarded me and prayed for me; how the saints have been interceding and entreating for me; and the heavens, sun, moon, stars, and elements, fruits, birds, fishes, and beasts [have ministered to me]; and the earth, how it has not opened to swallow me up, creating new hells that I might suffer in them for ever.

To end with a colloquy of mercy, reasoning and giving thanks to God our Lord, that He has given me life until now, and resolving with His grace to amend for the future.

The Third Exercise is a repetition of the first and second Exercises. [So also the Fourth.]

The Fifth Exercise is a meditation on hell; it contains, after the preparatory prayer and two preludes, five points and one colloquy. Let the preparatory prayer be the usual one. The first prelude is a composition of place, which is here to see with the eyes of the imagination the length, breadth and depth of hell.

The second, to ask for that which I desire. It will be here to ask for an interior sense of the pain which the lost suffer, in order that if through my faults I should forget the love of the eternal Lord, at least the fear of punishment may help me not to fall into sin.

The first point will be to see with the eyes of the imagination those great fires, and the souls as it were in bodies of fire.

The second, to hear with the ears the wailing, the groans, the cries, the blasphemies against Christ our Lord, and against all His saints.

The third, to smell with the sense of smell the smoke, the brimstone, the filth, and the corruption.

The fourth, to taste with the sense of taste bitter things, such as tears, sadness, and the worm of conscience.

The fifth, to feel with the sense of touch how those fires touch and burn the souls.

Making a colloquy with Christ our Lord, to bring to memory the souls that are in hell, some because they did not believe in His coming; others because, though believing, they did not act according to His commandments; making three classes: the first [those who were lost] before His coming; the second, [those who were lost] during His life in this world; the third, [those who have been lost] since that time; and herewith to give Him thanks that He has not, by putting an end to my life, permitted me to fall into any of these classes. In like manner to consider how until now He has always treated me with so great pity and mercy; ending with an *Our Father*.

Additions for the purpose of helping the exercitant to make the Exercises better, and to find more surely what he desires.

1. The first Addition is, after having gone to bed, when I wish to go to sleep, to think, for the space of a *Hail Mary*, of the hour when I ought to rise, and for what purpose, recapitulating the Exercise which I have to make.

2. The second, when I awake, not admitting other thoughts, at once to turn my mind to that which I am going to contemplate in the first Exercise at midnight, exciting myself to confusion for my many sins, setting before myself examples, e.g. as if a knight were to find himself in the presence of his king and all his court, covered with shame and confusion because he has grievously offended him from whom he has first received many gifts and favours. Likewise in the second Exercise, considering myself a great sinner, bound with chains, and about to appear before the supreme eternal Judge, taking as an example how prisoners in chains, and worthy of death, appear before their temporal judge; and with these thoughts, or with others, according to the subject-matter, to dress myself.

3. The third, one or two paces from the place in which I am about to contemplate or meditate I will stand for the space of an *Our Father*, with my mind raised on high, considering how God our Lord sees me, etc.; and make an act of reverence or humiliation.

4. The fourth, to enter upon the contemplation, at one time kneeling, at another prostrate on the ground, or lying face upwards, or seated, or standing, always intent on seeking that which I desire. Here we will make two observations: first, if kneeling I find that which I desire, I will not change to another position; and if prostrate, in like manner, etc.; secondly, in the point in which I find that which I desire, there I will rest without being anxious to proceed farther, until I have satisfied myself.

5. The fifth, after the Exercise is finished, for the space of a quarter of an hour, either sitting or walking, I will examine how it has gone with me in the contemplation or meditation; if badly, I will look for the cause whence it proceeds, and when I have discovered it I will be sorry for it, so as to amend in future; if well, I will thank God our Lord, and proceed in the same manner another time.

6. The sixth, to refuse to think of pleasant and joyful things, as of glory, the Resurrection, etc.; because any consideration of joy and delight hinders the feeling of pain, sorrow, and tears for our sins; but rather to keep before my mind that I desire to be sorry and to feel pain, remembering rather death and judgment.

7. The seventh, for the same purpose to deprive myself of all light, closing the shutters and doors while I am in my room, except to say prayers, to read, or to take food.

8. The eighth, not to laugh, nor to say anything that may provoke laughter.

9. The ninth, to restrain my eyes, except in receiving or taking leave of the person with whom I shall speak.

THE SECOND WEEK: THE KINGDOM OF CHRIST

[The exercitant contemplates the progressive stages of Jesus' life and then decides what he himself should do for the glory of God. In the third week, the exercitant contemplates the passion of Christ, and in the fourth week, the resurrection and ascension. Specific passages of Scripture in each stage are noted for visualization, as if the exercitant were actually present. At the conclusion, Loyola attaches rules—for discernment of spirits, distributing alms, and thinking with the church.]

RULES FOR THINKING WITH THE CHURCH

In order to think truly, as we ought, in the Church Militant, the following rules should be observed.

1. Laying aside all private judgment, we ought to hold our minds prepared and prompt to obey in all things the true Spouse of Christ our Lord, which is our holy Mother, the hierarchical Church.

2. We ought to praise confession to a priest, and the reception of the Most Holy

Sacrament once a year, and much better every month, and much better still every eight days, with the requisite and due conditions.

3. We ought to praise the frequent hearing of Mass, also chants, psalms, and prolonged prayers both in and out of church; likewise the hours ordained at fixed times for the whole divine office, and for prayer of every kind, and all canonical Hours.

4. We ought to praise greatly Religious Orders, virginity, and continency, and we should not praise matrimony as much as any of these.

5. We ought to praise vows of Religion, of obedience, of poverty, of chastity, and of other works of perfection and supererogation; [but we should not make vows in those things which are less perfect—business, marriage, etc.]

6. We ought to praise the relics of saints, paying veneration to the relics and praying to the saints; and to praise likewise stations, pilgrimages, indulgences, jubilees, crusades, and candles lighted in churches.

7. We ought to praise the enactments of the Church with regard to fasts and abstinences, as those of Lent, Ember days, Vigils, Fridays, and Saturdays; likewise penances, not only interior but also exterior.

8. We ought to praise the building and adornment of churches; and also images, and to venerate them according to what they represent.

9. We ought to praise in fine all the precepts of the Church, preserving a ready mind to seek reasons for defending her, and in no way impugning her.

10. We ought to be more ready to approve and praise the enactments and recommendations, and also the customs of our superiors [than to find fault with them]; because, although sometimes they may not be or may not have been praiseworthy, still to speak against them, whether in public discourse or before the common people, would give rise to murmurs and scandal, rather than edification; and thus the people would be irritated against their superiors, whether temporal or spiritual. Nevertheless, as it does harm to speak ill before the common people of superiors in their absence, so it may be useful to speak of their bad conduct to those who can apply a remedy.

11. We ought to praise theology, positive and scholastic. . . .

12. We ought to guard against making comparisons between ourselves who are now living and the blessed who have passed away, for no slight error is committed in this, for example when it is said: "This man knows more than S. Augustine; he is another S. Francis, or greater than he; he is another S. Paul in virtue and sanctity, etc."

13. To arrive at the truth in all things, we ought always to be ready to believe that what seems to us white is black, if the hierarchical Church so defines it: believing that between Christ our Lord the Bridegroom and the Church His Bride there is one and the same Spirit, Who governs and directs us for the salvation of our souls; because our holy Mother the Church is ruled and governed by the same Spirit and our Lord Who gave the ten commandments.

14. Although it is very true that no one can be saved unless he is predestined, and has faith and grace, we must be very careful in our manner of speaking and treating of these subjects.

15. We ought not habitually to speak much of predestination; but if sometimes mention should be made of it in any way, we must so speak that the common people may not fall into any error, and say, as sometimes they do, "If I am predestined to be saved or lost, the question is already determined, and whether I do good or ill there cannot be any other result"; and therewith becoming paralyzed they neglect good works conducive to their salvation, and to the spiritual profit of their souls.

16. In the same way we must take heed lest by speaking much and with great earnestness on faith, without any distinction and explanation, occasion be given to become slothful and negligent in good works, whether before faith is formed by charity or after.

17. In like manner we ought not to speak of grace at such length and so vehemently as to give rise to that poisonous teaching which takes away free-will. Accordingly, we may speak of faith and grace, so far as we

can with the help of God, for the greater praise of His divine Majesty, but not in such a way, especially in these dangerous times of ours, that works and free-will shall receive any detriment, or come to be accounted for nothing.

18. Although it is above all things praiseworthy to serve God our Lord diligently out of pure love, yet we ought greatly to praise the fear of His divine Majesty; because not only is filial fear a pious and most holy thing, but even servile fear, when a man does not attain to anything better and more useful, is of great help towards rising out of mortal sin, and, after he has risen out of it, he easily attains to filial fear, which is wholly acceptable and pleasing to God our Lord, because it is inseparable from divine love.

2. Society of Jesus Approved by Pope Paul III, 1540

Condensed papal bull approving the Jesuits. J. H. Robinson, *Readings in European History,* II (Boston: Ginn & Co., 1906). Cf. C. Mirbt, *Quellen zur Geschichte des Papsttums und des romanischen Katholizismus.*

Paul, the bishop, servant of the servants of God, for a perpetual memorial of this matter:

...Of late we have learned that our beloved sons Ignatius de Loyola, Peter Faber, James Laynez, Claude le Jay, Pasquier Brouet, Francis Xavier, Alfonzo Salmeron, Simon Rodriguez, John Codure, and Nicholas de Boabdilla, priests, masters of arts, and graduates of the University of Paris, and students of some years' standing in theology, inspired, as they piously believe, by the Holy Spirit, assembled together and, forming an association, forsook the allurements of the age to dedicate their lives to the perpetual service of our Lord Jesus Christ and of ourselves and our successors, the Roman pontiffs.

Now for many years they have labored nobly in the vineyard of the Lord, publicly preaching the word of God under a tentative license, privately exhorting the faithful to a good and blessed life and stimulating them to holy thoughts, assisting in hospitals, instructing the young and ignorant in the truths essential for the development of a Christian, and performing all these offices of charity

III-6. Ignatius Loyola. *Painting by Peter Paul Rubens.*

and acts for the consolation of souls with great approbation in whatever lands they have visited.

Then, gathering in this beautiful city and remaining within its confines in order to complete and preserve the union of their society in Christ, they have drawn up a rule of life in accordance with the principles which they have learned by experience will promote their desired ends, and in conformity with evangelical precepts and the canonical sanctions of the fathers. The tenor of the aforesaid rule is as follows:

He who desires to fight for God under the banner of the cross in our society—which we wish to distinguish by the name of Jesus—and to serve God alone and the Roman pontiff, his vicar on earth, after a solemn vow of perpetual chastity, shall set this thought before his mind, that he is a part of a society founded for the especial purpose of providing for the advancement of souls in Christian

125

life and doctrine and for the propagation of the faith through public preaching and the ministry of the word of God, spiritual exercises and deeds of charity, and in particular through the training of the young and ignorant in Christianity and through the spiritual consolation of the faithful of Christ in hearing confessions; and he shall take care to keep first God and next the purpose of this organization always before his eyes. . . .

All members shall realize, and shall recall daily, as long as they live, that this society as a whole and in every part is fighting for God under faithful obedience to one most holy lord, the pope, and to the other Roman pontiffs who succeed him. And although we are taught in the gospel and through the orthodox faith to recognize and steadfastly profess that all the faithful of Christ are subject to the Roman pontiff as their head and as the vicar of Jesus Christ, yet we have adjudged that, for the special promotion of greater humility in our society and the perfect mortification of every individual and the sacrifice of our own wills, we should each be bound by a peculiar vow, in addition to the general obligation, that whatever the present Roman pontiff, or any future one, may from time to time decree regarding the welfare of souls and the propagation of the faith, we are pledged to obey without evasion or excuse, instantly, so far as in us lies, whether he send us to the Turks or any other infidels, even to those who inhabit the regions men call the Indies; whether to heretics or schismatics, or, on the other hand, to certain of the faithful.

Wherefore those who come to us shall reflect long and deeply, before they take this burden upon their shoulders, as to whether they have among their goods enough spiritual treasure to enable them, according to the Lord's precept, to carry out their enterprise—that is, whether the Holy Spirit who impels them promises them so much grace that they may hope to support the weight of this profession with his aid; then, after they have, under God's inspiration, been enrolled in this army of Jesus Christ, day and night must they have their loins girded and themselves in readiness for the payment of their mighty obligation. Nor shall there be amongst us

any ambition or rivalry whatsoever for missions and provinces. . . . Subordinates shall, indeed, both for the sake of the wide activities of the order and also for the assiduous practice, never sufficiently to be commended, of humility, be bound always to obey the commander in every matter pertaining to the organization of the society, and shall recognize Christ as present in him, and shall do him reverence as far as is seemly. . . .

Whereas, moreover, we have found that the happier, purer, and more edifying life is that removed as far as possible from all contagion of avarice and modeled as nearly as may be upon evangelical poverty, and whereas we know that our Lord Jesus Christ will furnish the necessities of food and clothing to his servants who seek only the kingdom of God, therefore each and every member shall vow perpetual poverty, declaring that neither individually, nor even in common for the support or use of the society, will he acquire any civil right over any permanent property, rents, or incomes whatever, but that he will be content with the use only of such articles as shall be given him to meet his necessities. They may, however, maintain in universities a college or colleges with means or possessions to be applied to the needs and exigencies of the students; all control or supervision of any sort over the said colleges and students being vested in the commander and the society. . . .

The foregoing is what, by the permission of our said Lord Paul and of the apostolic see, we have been allowed to set forth as a general ideal for our profession. We have taken this step at this time in order that by this brief document we might inform the persons who are inquiring now about our way of life, and also posterity—if, by God's will, there shall be those to follow us in the path upon which (attended though it be by many grave difficulties) we have entered. We have further judged it expedient to prescribe that no one shall be received into this society until he has been long and thoroughly tried; but when he has proved himself wise in Christ as well as in doctrine, and exalted in the purity of the Christian life, then at length he shall be admitted into the army of Jesus Christ. May he deign to prosper our feeble undertaking to the glory of God the Father, to whom alone be ever praise and honor throughout the ages. Amen.

Whereas nothing may be discovered in the foregoing which is not pious or devout, in order that these associates who have made their humble application to us may be the better forwarded in their religious plan of life for feeling themselves included in the grace of the apostolic see and finding their projects meeting our approval, we do, through apostolic authority, approve, confirm, bless, and fortify with a bulwark of everlasting power the whole and every part of the aforesaid organization, and we take these associates under the protection of ourselves and this holy apostolic see.... We will also that persons who desire to profess the rules of life of this society be admitted into it and counted with the said society up to the number of sixty and no more. To no man whatsoever be it permitted to infringe or violate this statement of our approbation, benediction, and justification. If any one shall presume to attempt it, let him be assured that he incurs the wrath of Almighty God and of the blessed Peter and Paul, his apostles.

Given at St. Mark's in Rome, in the year of our Lord's incarnation 1540, September 27, in the sixth year of our pontificate.

3. St. Francis Xavier in India

Only two letters that tell about St. Xavier's first years in India have been preserved; both were written in 1543. One, from Tuticorin in the spring, is addressed to the general of the Society; one, from Cochin, December 31, is addressed to the Society at Rome. From *The Life and Letters of St. Francis Xavier*, by Henry James Coleridge (London: Burns & Oates Ltd., 1876).

TO THE REVEREND FATHER IGNATIUS,
GENERAL OF THE SOCIETY, AT ROME

May the grace and charity of Christ our Lord always help and favour us! Amen.

I wrote you a long letter from Goa about our voyage from Portugal to India. Now, because such is your wish, my best and sweetest Father, I will give you a little account of my expedition to Cape Comorin.

I set out with several native students from the Seminary at Goa, who have been under instruction, ever since their early youth, in the ceremonies of the Church, and are now in minor orders. We went through all the villages of the converts who were made Christians a few years ago. This country is too barren and poor for the Portuguese to live in, and the Christian inhabitants here have had no priests; they just know that they are Christians and nothing more. There is no one to say mass for them; no one to teach them the Creed, the Pater, the Ave Maria, and the Ten Commandments of God. So I have been incessantly occupied ever since I came here. I went diligently through the villages one after another, and baptized all the children who had not yet been baptized. In this way I have christened a multitude of children who, as the saying is, did not know their right hand from their left. Then the young boys would never let me say office, or eat, or sleep, till I had taught them some prayer. It made me understand for the first time that "of such is the Kingdom of Heaven." Their petition was too pious for me to refuse it without impiety, so I began with the profession of belief in the Father, Son, and Holy Ghost, and then taught them the Apostles' Creed, the Pater Noster, and the Ave Maria. I have found very great intelligence among them: and if they had any one to instruct them in religion, I doubt not they would turn out excellent Christians.

One day I turned out of my road into a village of heathens, where no one was willing to become Christian, though all the neighbouring villages had been converted, because they said that the lord of their territory, a heathen, had forbidden his people to do so. There was there a woman with child, who had been three days in labour with so much difficulty, that many despaired of her life. Their prayers for her were not heard, for the prayer of the wicked is an abomination in the eyes of God, because the gods of the heathen are all devils. I went, with one of my companions, to the sick woman's house, and began with confidence to call upon the Name of the Lord, forgetting that I was in a strange land. I thought of that text, "The earth is the Lord's and the fulness thereof, the compass of the world and all that dwell therein." So I began, through an interpreter, to explain to her the articles of our religion; and by the mercy of God, this woman believed what we taught her. At last I asked her whether she wished to be a Christian. She replied that she would, and gladly. Then I recited a Gospel over her—it was the first time, I suppose, that such words had been heard in those countries. I duly gave her Baptism. Not to make a long story, immediately after Baptism this good soul, who had put her hope in Christ, and believed, was delivered of her child; and I afterwards baptized her husband, his children, the infant (on the day of its birth), and all the family. The whole village was soon full of the news of the miracle which God had wrought in that house. I went to the chiefs and bade them in the Name of God to acknowledge His Son Jesus Christ, in Whom alone the salvation of all mortals is placed. They said they could not venture to leave the religion of their ancestors without the permission of their master. Then I went to the steward of this chief, who happened to be there to exact some taxes due to his lord. When he had heard me speak about religion, he declared that he thought it a good thing to be a Christian, and that he gave leave to all who like it to embrace the religion of Jesus Christ. But though he gave this good advice to others he did not practice it himself. However, the chief people of the place, with their whole households, were the first to embrace the faith, the rest followed their example, and so all, of every class and every age, received Baptism. This work done, we went straight to Tuticorin. The people there received us very kindly, and we have begun to hope that we shall reap an abundant harvest of souls in these parts.

The Governor is wonderfully fond of and kind to these converts, and not long ago gave them help against the Mussulmans who were annoying them. Most of them are fishermen living on the coast, and supporting themselves and their families by the fishery, chiefly of pearls. The Mussulmans had lately carried off the barks which they use in this fishery. When the Governor heard this, he attacked the Mussulmans with a strong squadron, defeated them with great slaughter, and took away all their ships. He gave the richer converts their own barks back again, and made the poorer presents of the Mussul-

mans' boats, thus crowning his victory by a signal act of generosity. He himself had had experience of the assistance of God in his victory, and he wished to let the Christians experience his own great kindness in their turn. The Mussulmans are quite cast down, and in a state of prostration. Not a man amongst them dares raise his eyes. Every one of their chiefs has been slain, and indeed every one else among them who seemed to be at all powerful. On account of all this the converts love the Governor as a father, and he on his side looks on them as his children. I can hardly tell you how earnestly he commended his newly planted vineyard of our Lord to my care. He has now got a grand plan in view which will be a matter for history to note as well as a great benefit to religion. He thinks of collecting all these native Christians who are now scattered at great distances from each other, of transplanting them to a certain island, and giving them a King to administer justice and look after their safety and interests. I am very sure that if the Holy Father only knew what great pains this Governor of India takes to advance religion, he would give him some mark of his approval for his very great diligence and exertions in the holy cause. So, if you think good, you might manage that the Holy Father should write to him to tell him how much he is delighted with his services. I do not mean that he should commend the converts to his care, for no one can have that matter more at heart than he has already, but rather that he should praise and thank this very religious ruler as he deserves to be praised and thanked for taking so much care of the interests of the faith, and for watching so solicitously over the flock of Christ, lest any part of it be torn to pieces and destroyed by those wolves of heathen. And I would have you write to him yourself at all events, for I know how delightful your letter will be to him. And at the same time pray God for him, you and all the Society, that He may grant him His Divine assistance, and the grace of perseverance in his good beginnings. For it is not he who has begun well, but he who shall persevere to the end, who will be saved.

As for myself, trusting in the infinite goodness of God and in your sacrifices and prayers as in those of all the Society, I hope that we shall see one another again, if not in this life, at least in that blessed life which is to come, whose joys far surpass all that we could have here. (Your child in Christ, Francis.)

TO THE SOCIETY AT ROME

May the grace and charity of Christ our Lord always help and favour us! Amen.

It is now the third year since I left Portugal. I am writing to you for the third time, having as yet received only one letter from you, dated February 1542. God is my witness what joy it caused me. I only received it two months ago—later than is usual for letters to reach India, because the vessel which brought it had passed the winter at Mozambique.

I and Francis Mancias are now living amongst the Christians of Comorin. They are very numerous, and increase largely every day. When I first came I asked them, if they knew anything about our Lord Jesus Christ? but when I came to the points of faith in detail and asked them what they thought of them, and what more they believed now than when they were Infidels, they only replied that they were Christians, but that as they are ignorant of Portuguese, they know nothing of the precepts and mysteries of our holy religion. We could not understand one another, as I spoke Castilian and they Malabar; so I picked out the most intelligent and well read of them, and then sought out with the greatest diligence men who knew both languages. We held meetings for several days, and by our joint efforts and with infinite difficulty we translated the Catechism into the Malabar tongue. This I learnt by heart, and then I began to go through all the villages of the coast, calling around me by the sound of a bell as many as I could, children and men. I assembled them twice a day and taught them the Christian doctrine: and thus, in the space of a month, the children had it well by heart. And all the time I kept telling them to go on teaching in their turn whatever they had learnt to their parents, family, and neighbours.

Every Sunday I collected them all, men and women, boys and girls, in the church.

They came with great readiness and with a great desire for instruction. Then, in the hearing of all, I began by calling on the name of the most holy Trinity, Father, Son, and Holy Ghost, and I recited aloud the Lord's Prayer, the *Hail Mary*, and the Creed in the language of the country: they all followed me in the same words, and delighted in it wonderfully. Then I repeated the Creed by myself, dwelling upon each article singly. Then I asked them as to each article, whether they believed it unhesitatingly; and all, with a loud voice and their hands crossed over their breasts, professed aloud that they truly believed it. I take care to make them repeat the Creed oftener than the other prayers; and I tell them that those who believe all that is contained therein are called Christians. After explaining the Creed I go on to the Commandments, teaching them that the Christian law is contained in those ten precepts, and that every one who observes them all faithfully is a good and true Christian and is certain of eternal salvation, and that, on the other hand, whoever neglects a single one of them is a bad Christian, and will be cast into hell unless he is truly penitent for his sin. Converts and heathen alike are astonished at all this, which shows them the holiness of the Christian law, its perfect consistency with itself, and its agreement with reason. After this I recite our principal prayers, as the *Our Father* and the *Hail Mary*, and they say them after me. Then we go back to the Creed, adding the *Our Father* and the *Hail Mary* after each article, with a short hymn; for, as soon as I have recited the first article, I sing in their language, "*Jesus, Son of the Living God, grant us the grace to believe firmly this first article of your faith: and that we may obtain this from you, we offer you this prayer taught us by yourself.*" Then we add this second invocation: "*Holy Mary, Mother of our Lord Jesus Christ, obtain for us from your most sweet Son that we may believe without hesitation this article of the Christian faith.*" We do the same after all the other eleven articles.

We teach them the Commandments in the following way. After we have sung the first, which enjoins the love of God, we pray thus: "*Jesus Christ, Son of the living God, grant us the grace to love Thee above all things"*; and then we say for this intention the Lord's Prayer. Then we all sing together, *"Holy Mary, Mother of Jesus Christ, obtain for us from your Son the grace to observe perfectly the first of His Commandments"*; and then we say the *Hail Mary*. So we go on through the other nine, changing the words of our little invocation as occasion requires. Thus I accustom them to ask for these graces with the ordinary prayers of the Church, and I tell them at the same time that if they obtain them, they will have all other things that they can wish for more abundantly than they would be able to ask for them. I make them all, and particularly those who are to be baptized, repeat the form of general confession. These last I question after each article of the Creed as it is recited, whether they believe it firmly; and after they have answered yes, I give them an instruction in their own language explaining the chief heads of the Christian religion, and the duties necessary to salvation. Last of all, I admit them thus prepared to baptism. The instruction is ended by the *Salve Regina*, begging the aid and help of our Blessed Lady.

As to the numbers who become Christians, you may understand them from this, that it often happens to me to be hardly able to use my hands from the fatigue of baptizing: often in a single day I have baptized whole villages. Sometimes I have lost my voice and strength altogether with repeating again and again the Credo and the other forms.

The fruit that is reaped by the baptism of infants, as well as by the instruction of children and others, is quite incredible. These children, I trust heartily, by the grace of God, will be much better than their fathers. They show an ardent love for the Divine law, and an extraordinary zeal for learning our holy religion and imparting it to others. Their hatred for idolatry is marvellous. They get into feuds with the heathen about it, and whenever their own parents practise it, they reproach them and come off to tell me at once. Whenever I hear of any act of idolatrous worship, I go to the place with a large band of these children, who very soon load the devil with a greater amount of insult and abuse than he has lately received of honour and worship from their parents, relations, and acquaintances. The children run at the idols, upset them, dash them down, break them to pieces, spit on them, trample on them, kick them about, and in short heap on them every possible outrage.

I had been living for nearly four months in a Christian village, occupied in translating the Catechism. A great number of natives came from all parts to entreat me to take the trouble to go to their houses and call on God by the bedsides of their sick relatives. Such numbers also of sick made their own way to us, that I had enough to do to read a Gospel over each of them. At the same time we kept on with our daily work, instructing the children, baptizing converts, translating the Catechism, answering difficulties, and burying the dead. For my part I desired to satisfy all, both the sick who came to me themselves, and those who came to beg on the part of others, lest if I did not, their confidence in, and zeal for, our holy religion should relax, and I thought it wrong not to do what I could in answer to their prayers. But the thing grew to such a pitch that it was impossible for me myself to satisfy all, and at the same time to avoid their quarrelling among themselves, every one striving to be the first to get me to his own house; so I hit on a way of serving all at once. As I could not go myself, I sent round children whom I could trust in my place. They went to the sick persons, assembled their families and neighbours, recited the Creed with them, and encouraged the sufferers to conceive a certain and well founded confidence of their restoration. Then after all this, they recited the prayers of the Church. To make my tale short, God was moved by the faith and piety of these children and of the others, and restored a great number of sick persons health both of body and soul. How good He was to them! He made the very disease of their bodies the occasion of calling them to salvation, and drew them to the Christian faith almost by force!

I have also charged these children to teach the rudiments of Christian doctrine to the ignorant in private houses, in the streets, and the crossways. As soon as I see that this has been well started in one village, I go on to another and give the same instructions and the same commission to the children, and so I go through in order the whole number of their villages. When I have done this and am going away, I leave in each place a copy of the Christian doctrine, and tell all those who know how to write to copy it out, and all the others are to learn it by heart and to recite it from memory every day. Every feast day I bid them meet in one place and sing all together the elements of the faith. For this purpose I have appointed in each of the thirty Christian villages men of intelligence and character who are to preside over these meetings, and the Governor, Don Martin Alfonso, who is so full of love for our society and of zeal for religion has been good enough at our request to allot a yearly revenue of 4000 gold *fanams* for the salary of these catechists. He has an immense friendship for ours, and desires with all his heart that some of them should be sent hither, for which he is always asking in his letters to the King. . . .

4. Canons and Decrees of the Council of Trent, 1545-1563

The Council of Trent, held in the imperial city of Trent, redefined the faith of the Roman Catholic Church over against the reformed views which emerged in the sixteenth century. Protestants were invited, but did not attend as official participants. The sessions were not continuous because of plague and threat of war. Another ecumenical council was not held until the Vatican Council, 1870. Biblical quotes from the Vulgate are in italics. Philip Schaff, *Creeds of Christendom*, II (New York: Harper & Row, Publishers, 1905).

THIRD SESSION, FEBRUARY 4, 1546

Decree Touching the Symbol of Faith

In the name of the Holy and Undivided Trinity, Father, and Son and Holy Ghost.

This sacred and holy, ecumenical, and general Synod of Trent . . . considering the magnitude of the matters to be treated of, especially of those comprised under the two heads, of the extirpating of heresies, and the reforming of manners, for the sake of which chiefly it is assembled, and recognizing with the apostles, that its *wrestling is not against flesh and blood, but against the spirits of wickedness in the high places*, exhorts, with the same apostle, all and each, above all

things, to be *strengthened in the Lord, and in the might of his power, in all things taking the shield of faith, wherewith they may be able to extinguish all the fiery darts of the most wicked one, and to take the helmet of salvation, with the sword of the Spirit, which is the word of God.* Wherefore, that this its pious solicitude may begin and proceed by the grace of God, it ordains and decrees that, before all other things, a confession of faith is to be set forth, which symbol is as follows: [Nicene Creed].

FOURTH SESSION, APRIL 8, 1546

Decree Concerning the Canonical Scriptures

The sacred and holy ecumenical and general Synod of Trent—keeping this always in view, that, errors being removed, the purity itself of the Gospel be preserved in the Church; which [Gospel], before promised through the prophets in the holy Scriptures, our Lord Jesus Christ, the Son of God, first promulgated with His own mouth, and then commanded to be preached by his Apostles to every creature, as the fountain of all, both saving truth, and moral discipline; and seeing clearly that this truth and discipline are contained in the written books, and the unwritten traditions which, received by the Apostles from the mouth of Christ himself, or from the Apostles themselves, the Holy Ghost dictating, have come down even unto us, transmitted as it were from hand to hand: [The Synod] following the examples of the orthodox fathers, received and venerated with an equal affection of piety and reverence, all the books both of the Old and of the New Testament—seeing that one God is the author of both—as also the said traditions, as well those appertaining to faith as to morals, as having been dictated, either by Christ's own word of mouth, or by the Holy Ghost, and preserved in the Catholic Church by a continuous succession.

And it has thought it meet that a list of the sacred books be inserted in this decree, lest a doubt may arise in any one's mind, which are the books that are received by this Synod. [Books of Old and New Testament are named with additions from the Apocrypha (I Esdras, Tobith, Judith, Ecclesiasticus, Baruch and I and II Maccabees).]

III-7. Council of Trent in Session, 1563. *An old woodcut.*

But if anyone receive not, as sacred and canonical, the said books entire with all their parts, as they have been used to be read in the Catholic Church, and as they are contained in the old Latin vulgate edition; and knowingly and deliberately contemn the traditions aforesaid; let him be anathema.

FIFTH SESSION, JUNE 17, 1546

Decree Concerning Original Sin

That our Catholic faith, *without which it is impossible to please God,* may, errors being purged away, continue in its own perfect and spotless integrity, ... [it] ordains, confesses, and declares these things touching the said original sin:

1. If any one does not confess that the first man, Adam, when he had transgressed the commandment of God in Paradise, immediately lost the holiness and justice wherein he had been constituted; and that

he incurred, through the offense of that prevarication, the wrath and indignation of God, and consequently death, with which God had previously threatened him, and, together with death, captivity under his power who thenceforth *had the empire of death, that is to say, the devil,* and that the entire Adam, through that offense of prevarication, was changed, in body and soul, for the worse; let him be anathema.

2. If any one asserts, that the prevarication of Adam injured himself alone, and not his posterity; and that the holiness and justice, received of God, which he lost, he lost for himself alone, and not for us also; or that he, being defiled by the sin of disobedience, has only transfused death and pains of the body into the whole human race, but not sin also, which is the death of the soul; let him be anathema.

3. If any one asserts, that this sin of

132

Adam—which in its origin is one, and being transfused into all by propagation, not by imitation, is in each one as his own—is taken away either by the powers of human nature, or by any other remedy than the merit of the *one mediator, our Lord Jesus Christ, who hath reconciled us to God in his own blood, being made unto us justice, sanctification, and redemption,* or if he denies that the said merit of Jesus Christ is applied, both to adults and to infants, by the sacrament of baptism rightly administered in the form of the Church; let him be anathema.

4. If any one denies, that infants, newly born from their mothers' wombs, even though they be sprung from baptized parents, are to be baptized; or says that they are baptized indeed *for the remission of sins,* but that they derive nothing of original sin from Adam, which has need of being expiated by the laver of regeneration for obtaining life everlasting—whence it follows as a consequence, that in them the form of baptism, *for the remission of sins,* is understood to be not true, but false—let him be anathema.

5. If anyone denies that, by the grace of our Lord Jesus Christ, which is conferred in baptism, the guilt of original sin is remitted; or even asserts that the whole of that which has the true and proper nature of sin is not taken away; but says that it is only rased, or not imputed; let him be anathema. . . .

SIXTH SESSION, JANUARY 13, 1547

Decree on Justification

I. The holy Synod declares first, that, for the correct and sound understanding of the doctrine of Justification, it is necessary that each one recognize and confess, that, whereas all men had lost their innocence in the prevarication of Adam—having become unclean, and, as the apostle says, by nature *children of wrath,* as [this Synod] has set forth in the decree on original sin—they were so far *the servants of sin,* and under the power of the devil and of death, that not the Gentiles only by the force of nature, but not even the Jews by the very letter itself of the law of Moses, were able to be liberated, or to arise, therefrom; although free-will, attenuated as it was in its powers, and bent down, was by no means extinguished in them.

II. Whence it came to pass that the heavenly Father, *the Father of mercies, and the God of all comfort,* when that blessed *fullness of the times was come, sent* unto men, Jesus Christ, *his own Son*—who had been, both before the Law, and during the time of the Law, to many of the holy fathers announced and promised—*that he might both redeem the Jews who were under the Law,* and that the *Gentiles, who followed not after justice,* might attain to justice, and that all men might receive the adoption of sons. Him God hath *proposed* as a propitiator, *through faith in his blood, for our sins, and not for our sins only, but also for those of the whole world.*

III. But, though *He died for all,* yet do not all receive the benefit of his death, but those only unto whom the merit of his passion is communicated. For as in truth men, if they were not born propagated of the seed of Adam, would not be born unjust—seeing that, by that propagation, they contract through him, when they are conceived, injustice as their own—so, if they were not born again in Christ, they never would be justified; seeing that, in that new birth, there is bestowed upon them, through'the merit of his passion, the grace whereby they are made just.

IV. By which words, a description of the Justification of the impious is indicated—as being a translation, from that state wherein man is born a child of the first Adam, to the state of grace, and of *the adoption of the sons of God,* through the second Adam, Jesus Christ, our Saviour. And this translation, since the promulgation of the Gospel, cannot be effected, without the laver of regeneration, or the desire thereof, as it is written: *unless a man be born again of water and the Holy Ghost, he cannot enter into the Kingdom of God.*

V. The Synod furthermore declares, that, in adults, the beginning of the said Justification is to be derived from the prevenient grace of God, through Jesus Christ, that is to say, from his vocation, whereby, without any merits existing on their parts, they are called; that so they, who by sins were alienated from God, may be disposed through his quickening and assisting grace, to convert themselves to their own justification, by freely assenting to and cooperating with that said grace: in such sort that, while God touches the heart of man by the illumination of the Holy Ghost, neither is man himself utterly inactive while he receives that inspiration, forasmuch as he is also able to reject it; yet is he not able, by his own free will, without the grace of God, to move himself unto justice in his sight. Whence, when it is said in the sacred writings: *Turn ye to me, and I will turn to you,* we are admonished of our liberty; and when we answer: *Convert us, O Lord, to thee, and we shall be converted,* we confess that we are prevented [anticipated] by the grace of God.

.   .   .   .   .

X. Having, therefore, been thus justified, and made the friends and *domestics of God,* advancing from *virtue to virtue,* they are *renewed,* as the Apostle says, *day by day,* that is, *by mortifying the members* of their own flesh, and *by presenting them as instruments of justice unto sanctification,* they, through the observance of the commandments of God and of the Church, faith cooperating with good works, increase in that justice which they have received through the grace of Christ, and are still further justified as it is written: *He that is just, let him be justified still;* and again, *Be not afraid to be justified even to death;* and also, *Do you see that by works a man is justified, and not by faith only.* And this increase of justification holy Church begs, when she prays, "Give unto us, O Lord, increase of faith, hope, and charity."

On Justification

Canon I. If any one saith, that man may be justified before God by his own works, whether done through the teaching of human nature, or that of the law, without the grace of God through Jesus Christ: let him be anathema.

Canon II. If any one saith that the grace of God, through Jesus Christ, is given only for this, that man may be able more easily to live justly, and to merit eternal life, as if, by free-will without grace, he were able to do both, though hardly indeed and with difficulty: let him be anathema.

Canon III. If any one saith, that without the prevenient inspiration of the Holy Ghost, and without his help, man can believe, hope, love, or be penitent as he ought, so that the grace of Justification may be bestowed upon him: let him be anathema.

Canon IV. If anyone saith, that man's free-will moved and excited by God, by assenting to God exciting and calling, nowise cooperates towards disposing and preparing itself for obtaining the grace of Justification; that it can not refuse its consent, if it would, but that, as something inanimate, it does nothing whatever and is merely passive: let him be anathema.

Canon V. If any one saith, that, since Adam's sin, the free-will of man is lost and extinguished; or, that it is a thing with only a name, yea a name without a reality, a figment, in fine, introduced into the Church by Satan: let him be anathema.

Canon VI. If any one saith, that it is not in man's power to make his ways evil, but that the works that are evil God worketh as well as those that are good, not permissively only, but properly, and of himself, in such wise that the treason of Judas is no less his own proper work than the vocation of Paul: let him be anathema.

Canon VII. If any one saith, that all works done before Justification, in whatsoever way they be done, are truly sins, or merit the hatred of God; or that the more earnestly one strives to dispose himself for grace, the more grievously he sins: let him be anathema.

Canon IX. If any one saith, that by faith alone the impious is justified, in such wise as to mean, that nothing else is required to cooperate in order to the obtaining the grace of Justification, and that it is not in any way necessary, that he be prepared and disposed by the movement of his own will: let him be anathema.

Canon XIII. If any one saith, that it is necessary for every one, for the obtaining the remission of sins, that he believe for certain, and without any wavering arising from his own infirmity and indisposition, that his sins are forgiven him: let him be anathema.

Canon XXI. If any one saith, that Christ Jesus was given of God to men, as a redeemer in whom to trust, and not also as a legislator whom to obey: let him be anathema.

Canon XXIII. If any one saith, that a man once justified can sin no more, nor lose grace, and that therefore he that falls and sins was never truly justified; or, on the other hand, that he is able during his whole life, to avoid all sins, even those that are venial—except by a special privilege from God, as the Church holds in regard of the Blessed Virgin: let him be anathema.

Canon XXIV. If any one saith, that the justice received is not preserved and also increased before God through good works; but that the said works are merely the fruits and signs of Justification obtained, but not a cause of the increase thereof: let him be anathema.

Canon XXXII. If any one saith, that the good works of one that is justified are in such manner the gifts of God, that they are not also the good merits of him that is justified; or, that the said justified, by the good works which he performs through the grace of God and the merit of Jesus Christ, whose living member he is, does not truly merit increase of grace, eternal life, and the attainment of that eternal life—if so be, however, that he depart in grace—and also an increase of glory: let him be anathema.

SEVENTH SESSION, MARCH 3, 1547

Decree on the Sacraments

For the completion of the salutary doctrine on Justification, which was promulgated with the unanimous consent of the Fathers in the last preceding Session, it hath seemed suitable to treat of the most holy Sacraments of the Church, through which all true justice either begins, or being begun is increased, or being lost is repaired.

Canon I. If any one saith, that the sacraments of the New Law were not all instituted by Jesus Christ, our Lord; or, that they are more, or less, than seven, to wit, Baptism, Confirmation, the Eucharist, Penance, Extreme Unction, Order, and Matrimony; or even that any one of these seven is not truly and properly a sacrament: let him be anathema.

Canon III. If any one saith, that these seven sacraments are in such wise equal to each other, as that one is not in any way more worthy than another: let him be anathema.

Canon IV. If any one saith, that the sacraments of the New Law are not necessary unto salvation, but superfluous; and that, without them, or without the desire thereof, men obtain of God, through faith alone, the grace of justification—though all [the sacraments] are not indeed necessary for every individual: let him be anathema.

Canon IX. If any one saith, that, in the three sacraments, to wit, Baptism, Confirmation, and Order, there is not imprinted in the soul a character, that is, a certain spiritual and indelible sign, on account of which they cannot be repeated: let him be anathema.

Canon XI. If any one saith, that, in ministers, when they effect, and confer the sacraments, there is not required the intention at least of doing what the Church does: let him be anathema.

Canon XIII. If any one saith, that the received and approved rites of the Catholic Church, wont to be used in the solemn administration of the sacraments, may be contemned, or without sin be omitted at pleasure by the ministers, or be changed, by every pastor of the churches, into other new ones: let him be anathema.

On Baptism

Canon III. If anyone saith, that in the Roman Church, which is the mother and mistress of all churches, there is not the true doctrine concerning the sacrament of baptism: let him be anathema.

Canon IV. If any one saith, that the baptism which is even given by heretics in the names of the Father, and of the Son, and of the Holy Ghost, with the intention of doing what the Church doth, is not true baptism: let him be anathema.

Canon V. If any one saith, that baptism is free, that is, not necessary unto salvation: let him be anathema.

On Confirmation

Canon I. If any one saith, that the confirmation of those who have been baptized is an idle ceremony, and not rather a true and proper sacrament; or that of old it was nothing more than a kind of catechism, whereby they who were near adolescence gave an account of their faith in the face of the church: let him be anathema.

Decree Concerning the Most Holy Sacrament of the Eucharist

In the first place, the holy Synod teaches, and openly and simply professes, that, in the august sacrament of the holy Eucharist, after the consecration of the bread and wine, our Lord Jesus Christ, true God and man, is truly, really, and substantially contained under the species of those sensible things.

IV. And because that Christ, our Redeemer, declared that which he offered under the species of bread to be truly his own body, therefore has it ever been a firm belief in the Church of God, and this holy Synod doth now declare it anew, that, by the consecration of the bread and of the wine, a conversion is made of the whole substance of the bread into the substance of the body of Christ our Lord, and of the whole substance of the wine into the substance of his blood; which conversion is, by the holy Catholic Church, suitably and properly called Transubstantiation.

On the Most Holy Sacrament of the Eucharist

Canon II. If any one saith, that in the sacred and holy sacrament of the Eucharist, the substance of the bread and wine remains conjointly with the body and blood of our Lord Jesus Christ, and denieth that wonderful and singular conversion of the whole substance of the bread into the body, and of the whole substance of the wine into the blood—the species only of the bread and wine remaining—which conversion indeed the Catholic Church most aptly calls Transubstantiation: let him be anathema.

Canon III. If any one denieth, that, in the venerable sacrament of the Eucharist, the whole Christ is contained under each species, and under every part of each species, when separated: let him be anathema.

Canon VIII. If any one saith, that Christ, given in the Eucharist, is eaten spiritually only, and not also sacramentally and really; let him be anathema.

Canon IX. If any one denieth, that all and each of Christ's faithful of both sexes are bound, when they have attained to years of discretion, to communicate every year, at least at Easter, in accordance with the holy Mother Church: let him be anathema.

On the Most Holy Sacrament of Penance

Canon I. If any one saith, that in the Catholic Church Penance is not truly and properly a sacrament, instituted by Christ our Lord for reconciling the faithful unto God, as often as they fall into sin after baptism: let him be anathema.

Canon IV. If any one denieth, that, for the entire and perfect remission of sins, there are required three acts in the penitent, which are as it were the matter of the sacrament of Penance, to wit, contrition, confession, and satisfaction, which are called the three parts of penance; or saith that there are two parts only of penance, to wit, the terrors with which the conscience is smitten upon being convinced of sin, and the faith, generated by the gospel, or by the absolution, whereby one believes that his sins are forgiven him through Christ: let him be anathema.

Canon VIII. If any one saith, that the confession of all sins, such as it is observed in the Church, is impossible, and is a human tradition to be abolished by the godly; or that all and each of the faithful of Christ, of either sex, are not obliged thereunto once a year, conformably to the constitution of the great Council of Lateran, and that, for this cause, the faithful of Christ are to be persuaded not to confess during Lent: let him be anathema.

Canon XIV. If any one saith, that the satisfactions, by which penitents redeem their sins through Jesus Christ, are not a worship of God, but traditions of men, which obscure the doctrine of grace, and the true worship of God, and the benefit itself of the death of Christ: let him be anathema.

On the Sacrament of Extreme Unction

Canon I. If any one saith, that Extreme Unction is not truly and properly a sacrament, instituted by Christ our Lord, and promulgated by the blessed Apostle James;

but is only a rite received from the Fathers, or a human figment: let him be anathema.

Canon IV. If any one saith, that the *Presbyters of the Church*, whom blessed James exhorts to be brought to anoint the sick, are not the priests who have been ordained by a bishop, but the elders in each community, and that for this cause a priest alone is not the proper minister of Extreme Unction: let him be anathema.

TWENTY-SECOND SESSION, SEPTEMBER 17, 1562

Doctrine on the Sacrifice of the Mass

II. And forasmuch as, in this divine sacrifice which is celebrated in the mass, that same Christ is contained and immolated in an unbloody manner who once offered himself in a bloody manner on the altar of the cross; the holy Synod teaches, that this sacrifice is truly propitiatory, and that by means thereof this is effected, that we obtain mercy, and find grace *in seasonable aid,* if we draw nigh unto God, contrite and penitent, with a sincere heart and upright faith, with fear and reverence. For the Lord, appeased by the oblation thereof, and granting the grace and gift of penitence, forgives even heinous crimes and sins. For the victim is one and the same, the same now offering by the ministry of priests, who then offered himself on the cross, the manner alone of offering being different. The fruits indeed of which oblation, of that bloody one to wit, are received most plentifully through this unbloody one; so far is this [latter] from derogating in any way from that [former oblation]. Wherefore, not only for the sins, punishments, satisfactions, and other necessities of the faithful who are living, but also for those who are departed in Christ, and who are not as yet fully purified, is it rightly offered, agreeably to a tradition of the apostles.

On the Sacrifice of the Mass

Canon III. If any one saith, that the sacrifice of the mass is only a sacrifice of praise and of thanksgiving; or, that it is a bare commemoration of the sacrifice consummated on the cross, but not a propitiatory sacrifice; or, that it profits him only who receives; and that it ought not to be offered for the living and the dead for sins, pains,

satisfactions, and other necessities: let him be anathema.

Canon IX. If any one saith, that the rite of the Roman Church, according to which a part of the canon and the words of consecration are pronounced in a low tone, is to be condemned; or, that the mass ought to be celebrated in the vulgar tongue only; or that water ought not to be mixed with the wine that is to be offered in the chalice, for that it is contrary to the institution of Christ: let him be anathema.

TWENTY-THIRD SESSION, JULY 15, 1563

On the Sacrament of Order

Canon V. If any one saith, that the sacred unction which the Church uses in holy ordination is not only not required, but is to be despised and is pernicious, as likewise are the other ceremonies of order: let him be anathema.

Canon VI. If any one saith, that, in the Catholic Church there is not a hierarchy by divine ordination instituted, consisting of bishops, priests, and ministers: let him be anathema.

TWENTY-FOURTH SESSION, NOVEMBER 11, 1563

On the Sacrament of Matrimony

Canon I. If any one saith, that matrimony is not truly and properly one of the seven sacraments of the evangelic law [a sacrament] instituted by Christ the Lord; but that it has been invented by men in the Church; and that it does not confer grace: let him be anathema.

Canon IV. If any one saith, that the Church could not establish impediments dissolving marriage; or, that she has erred in establishing them: let him be anathema.

Canon V. If any one saith, that on account of heresy, or irksome cohabitation, or the affected absence of one of the parties, the bond of matrimony may be dissolved: let him be anathema.

Canon VI. If any one saith, that matrimony contracted, but not consummated, is not dissolved by the solemn profession of religion by one of the parties: let him be anathema.

Canon VII. If any one saith, that the

Church has erred, in that she hath taught and doth teach, in accordance with the evangelical and apostolical doctrine, that the bond of matrimony cannot be dissolved on account of the adultery of one of the married parties; and that both, or even the innocent one who gave not occasion to the adultery, cannot contract another marriage during the lifetime of the other; and, he is guilty of adultery, who, having put away the adulteress, shall take another wife, as also she, who, having put away the adulterer, shall take another husband: let him be anathema.

Canon VIII. If any one saith, that the Church errs, in that she declares that, for many causes, a separation may take place between husband and wife, in regard of bed, or in regard of cohabitation, for a determinate or for an indeterminate period: let him be anathema.

Canon IX. If any one saith, that clerics constituted in sacred orders, or regulars, who have solemnly professed chastity, are able to contract marriage, and that being contracted it is valid, notwithstanding the ecclesiastical law, or vow; and that the contrary is nothing else than to condemn marriage; and, that all who do not feel that they have the gift of chastity, even though they have made a vow thereof, may contract marriage: let him be anathema; seeing that God refuses not that gift to those who ask for it rightly, neither does *he suffer us to be tempted above that which we are able.*

Canon X. If anyone saith, that the marriage state is to be placed above the state of virginity, or of celibacy, and that it is not better and more blessed to remain in virginity, or in celibacy, than to be united in matrimony: let him be anathema.

Canon XII. If any one saith, that matrimonial causes do not belong to ecclesiastical judges: let him be anathema.

TWENTY-FIFTH SESSION, DECEMBER 3-4, 1563

Decree Concerning Purgatory

Whereas the Catholic Church, instructed by the Holy Ghost, has, from the Sacred Writings and the ancient tradition of the Fathers, taught, in sacred Councils, and very recently in this ecumenical Synod, that there is a Purgatory, and that the souls there de-

tained are helped by the suffrages of the faithful, but principally by the acceptable sacrifice of the altar—the holy Synod enjoins on bishops that they diligently endeavor that the sound doctrine concerning Purgatory, transmitted by the holy Fathers and sacred Councils, be believed, maintained, taught, and everywhere proclaimed by the faithful of Christ.

On the Invocation, Veneration, and Relics of Saints, and on the Sacred Images

The holy Synod enjoins on all bishops and others who sustain the office and charge of teaching, that, agreeably to the usage of the Catholic and Apostolic Church, received from the primitive times of the Christian religion, and agreeably to the consent of the holy Fathers, and to the decrees of sacred Councils, they especially instruct the faithful diligently concerning the intercession and invocation of saints; the honor [paid] to relics; and the legitimate use of images: teaching them, that the saints, who reign together with Christ, offer up their own prayers to God for men; that it is good and useful suppliantly to invoke them, and to have recourse to their prayers, aid [and] help for obtaining benefits from God, through his Son, Jesus Christ our Lord, who is our alone Redeemer and Saviour; but that they think impiously who deny that the saints, who enjoy eternal happiness in heaven, are to be invocated; or who assert either that they do not pray for men; or that the invocation of them to pray for each of us even in particular is idolatry; or that it is repugnant to the Word of God, and is opposed to the honor of the *one mediator of God and men, Christ Jesus;* or that it is foolish to supplicate, vocally or mentally, those who reign in heaven.

Moreover, that the images of Christ, of the Virgin Mother of God, and of the other saints, are to be had and retained particularly in temples, and that due honor and veneration are to be given them; not that any divinity, or virtue, is believed to be in them, on account of which they are to be worshipped; or that any thing is to be asked of them; or that trust is to be reposed in images, as was of old done by the Gentiles, who placed their hope in idols; but because the honor which is shown them is referred to the prototypes which those images represent; in such wise that by the images which we kiss, and before which we uncover the head, and prostrate ourselves, we adore Christ, and we venerate the saints, whose similitude they bear: as, by the decrees of Councils, and especially of the second Synod of Nicaea, has been defined against the opponents of images.

Moreover, in the invocation of saints, the veneration of relics, and the sacred use of images, every superstition shall be removed, all filthy lucre be abolished; finally, all lasciviousness be avoided; in such wise that figures shall not be painted or adorned with a beauty exciting to lust; nor the celebration of the saints and the visitation of relics be by any perverted into revelings and drunkenness; as if festivals were celebrated to the honor of the saints by luxury and wantonness.

In fine, let so great care and diligence be used herein by bishops, as that there be nothing seen that is disorderly, or that is unbecomingly or confusedly arranged, nothing that is profane, nothing indecorous, seeing that *holiness becometh the house of God.*

Decree Concerning Indulgences

Whereas the power of conferring Indulgences was granted by Christ to the Church, and she has, even in the most ancient times, used the said power delivered unto her of God, the sacred holy Synod teaches and enjoins that the use of Indulgences, for the Christian people most salutary, and approved of by the authority of sacred Councils, is to be retained in the Church; and it condemns with anathema those who either assert that they are useless, or who deny that there is in the Church the power of granting them. In granting them, however, it desires that, in accordance with the ancient and approved custom in the Church, moderation be observed; lest, by excessive facility, ecclesiastical discipline be enervated. And being desirous that the abuses which have crept therein, and by occasion of which this honorable name of Indulgences is blasphemed by heretics, be amended and corrected, it ordains generally by this decree, that all evil gains for the obtaining thereof—whence a

most prolific cause of abuses amongst the Christian people has been derived—be wholly abolished. . . .

5. *Profession of Tridentine Faith, 1564*

This statement, issued by Pope Paul IV, summarizes in the form of a creed many of the conclusions of the Council of Trent. The views expressed at Trent could thus have more widespread profession. Schaff, *Creeds of Christendom*, II.

I, ——, with a firm faith believe and profess all and every one of the things contained in that Creed which the holy Roman Church makes use of: "I believe in one God, the Father Almighty," etc. [The Nicene Creed]

I most steadfastly admit and embrace apostolic and ecclesiastic traditions, and all other observances and constitutions of the same Church.

I also admit the holy Scriptures, according to that sense which our holy mother Church has held and does hold, to which it belongs to judge of the true sense and interpretation of the Scriptures; neither will I ever take and interpret them otherwise than according to the unanimous consent of the Fathers.

I also profess that there are truly and properly seven sacraments of the new law, instituted by Jesus Christ our Lord, and necessary for the salvation of mankind, though not all for every one, to wit: baptism, confirmation, the eucharist, penance, extreme unction, holy orders, and matrimony; and that they confer grace; and that these, baptism, confirmation, and ordination can not be reiterated without sacrilege. I also receive and admit the received and approved ceremonies of the Catholic Church, used in the solemn administration of the aforesaid sacraments.

I embrace and receive all and every one of the things which have been defined and declared in the holy Council of Trent concerning original sin and justification.

I profess, likewise, that in the mass there is offered to God a true, proper, and propitiatory sacrifice for the living and the dead; and that in the most holy sacrament of the eucharist there is truly, really and substantially, the body and blood, together with the soul and divinity of our Lord Jesus Christ; and that there is made a change of the whole essence of the bread into the body, and of the whole essence of the wine into the blood; which change the Catholic Church calls transubstantiation.

I also confess that under either kind alone Christ is received whole and entire, and a true sacrament.

I firmly hold that there is a purgatory, and that the souls therein detained are helped by the suffrages of the faithful. Likewise, that the saints reigning with Christ are to be honored and invoked, and that they offer up prayers to God for us, and that their relics are to be had in veneration.

I most firmly assert that the images of Christ, and of the perpetual Virgin the Mother of God, and also of other saints, ought to be had and retained, and that due honor and veneration are to be given them. I also affirm that the power of indulgences was left by Christ in the Church, and that the use of them is most wholesome to Christian people.

I acknowledge the holy Catholic Apostolic Roman Church for the mother and mistress of all churches; and I promise and swear true obedience to the Bishop of Rome, successor to St. Peter, Prince of the Apostles, and Vicar of Jesus Christ.

I likewise undoubtingly receive and profess all other things delivered, defined, and declared by the Sacred Canons and General Councils, particularly by the holy Council of Trent; and I condemn, reject, and anathematize all things contrary thereto, and all heresies which the Church has condemned, rejected, and anathematized.

I do, at this present, freely profess and truly hold this true Catholic faith, without which no one can be saved; and I promise most constantly to retain and confess the same entire and inviolate, with God's assistance, to the end of my life. And I will take care, as far as in me lies, that it shall be held, taught, and preached by my subjects, or by those the care of whom shall appertain to me in my office. This I promise, vow, and swear— so help me God, and these holy Gospels of God.

6. *The Establishment of the Roman Inquisition by Paul III, July 21, 1542*

A condensed translation of the Latin text in B. J. Kidd, *Documents Illustrative of the Continental Reformation*, No. 141 (Oxford, 1901). Roland H. Bainton, *The Age of the Reformation* (Princeton: D. Van Nostrand Co., Inc., 1956).

Although from the beginning of our Pontificate we have been concerned for the flourishing of the Catholic faith and the expurgation of heresy that those seduced by diabolical wiles might return to the fold and unity of the Church and that those who persist in their damnable course should be removed and their punishment might serve as an example to others, nevertheless hoping that the mercy of God, the prayers of the faithful and the preaching of the learned would cause them to recognize their errors, and come back to the Holy Catholic Church, and if any delayed they would be induced by the authority of the sacred, ecumenical and general council, which we hope speedily to convene, therefore we deferred the establishment of the Inquisition of heretical Pravity, but now, since for a variety of reasons, the council has not met and the enemy of the human race has disseminated even more heresy among the faithful and the robe of Christ is further rent, consequently, lest pending a council things grow worse, we have appointed our beloved sons, Giovanni Caraffa [and five others], Inquisitors General with jurisdiction throughout Christendom including Italy and the Roman Curia. They are to investigate by way of inquisition all and single who wander from the way of the Lord and the Catholic faith, as well as those suspected of heresy, together with their followers and abettors, public or private, direct or indirect. The guilty and the suspects are to be imprisoned and proceeded against up to the final sentence. Those adjudged guilty are to be punished in accord with canonical penalties. After the infliction of death goods may be put up for sale. The aid of the civil arm may be invoked to implement whatever measures the above named deem needful. Any who impede will incur the indignation of Almighty God and of the blessed Apostles, Peter and Paul.

7. The Massacre of St. Bartholomew, August 24, 1572

De Thou (1553-1617), who as a young man witnessed the horrors of the Massacre of St. Bartholomew, wrote a vivid account of the climax of the religious struggles in France in his *Histoire des choses arrivées de son temps* (Paris, 1659). Trans. B. Wilson, *De Thou's History of His Own Time* (London, 1730). Selections below are from De Thou, with excerpts from *Relation du massacre de la St. Barthélemy in archives curieuses,* VII, trans. James Mackinnon in *The Growth and Decline of the French Monarchy* (New York: Longmans, Green & Co., Inc., 1902). Cf. J. H. Robinson, *Readings in European History,* II (Boston: Ginn & Co., 1906).

Guise, to whom the execution of the scheme had been entrusted, sent for the leaders of the Swiss from the five Catholic cantons and some of the French colonels very early in the night and, having informed them of the King's orders, added: "The time has come to punish this rebel hated by God and man and to exterminate all his partisans: the animal is in the toils, do not let it escape. Profit by so splendid an opportunity of crushing the enemies of the Kingdom: the glory of the triumphs in past wars which have cost the faithful subjects of the King so much blood is nothing to that which you can win to-day."

After speaking thus he posted the Swiss and some of the French companies around the Louvre, with orders not to allow any of the servants of the King of Navarre or of the prince of Condé to leave it. (Likewise for Coligny's house.) He then sent for President Jean Charon . . . and ordered him to tell the Captains of the quarters to arm their companies and to go to the Town Hall although he no longer held any post but because he was known to be held in esteem by the Queen whom he had secretly served, and it was he who announced on behalf of the King that the King allowed them to take up arms, that his intention was that they should exterminate Coligny and his party, that they should take care that none of his band should escape and that no one should hide them in their homes, and that all towns should follow the example of Paris. The signal would be the sounding of the tocsin and they were to wear a white band on the left arm and a white cross on their hat and come well armed. Marcel's orders were received with joy by all—soldiers were detailed for all

III-8. St. Bartholomew's Night. *Painting by François Dubois d'Amiens (d. 1584).*

squares and crossroads but were hidden to start with in neighboring houses. Guise and Angoulême, on the other hand, forgot nothing tending to the success of their plan.

At midnight the Queen, fearing that the King might change his mind, went to his room, and was at once joined by the Dukes of Anjou, Nevers, Birague, Tavane, the Count de Rais, and Guise. The King thought she was reproaching him with cowardice and so gave the order to start, and the Queen, fearing he might change his mind, had the tocsin sounded at once.

So it was determined to exterminate all the Protestants, and the plan was approved by the Queen. They discussed for some time whether they should make an exception of the King of Navarre and the prince of Condé. All agreed that the King of Navarre should be spared by reason of the royal dignity and the new alliance. The duke of Guise, who was put in full command of the enterprise, summoned by night several captains of the Catholic Swiss mercenaries from the five little cantons, and some commanders of French companies, and told them that it was the will of the King that, according to God's will, they should take vengeance on the band of rebels while they had the beasts in the toils. Victory was easy and the booty great and to be obtained without danger. The signal to commence the massacre should be given by the bell of the palace, and the marks by which they should recognize each other in the darkness were a bit of white linen tied around the left arm and a white cross on the hat.

Meanwhile Coligny awoke and recognized from the noise that a riot was taking place. Nevertheless he remained assured of the King's good will, being persuaded thereof either by his credulity or by Teligny, his son-in-law: he believed the populace had been stirred up by the Guises, and that quiet would be restored as soon as it was seen that soldiers of the guard, under the command of Cosseins, had been detailed to protect him and guard his property.

But when he perceived that the noise increased and that someone had fired an arquebus in the courtyard of his dwelling, then at length, conjecturing what it might

be, but too late, he arose from his bed and having put on his dressing gown he said his prayers, leaning against the wall. Labonne held the key of the house, and when Cosseins commanded him, in the King's name, to open the door he obeyed at once without fear and apprehending nothing. But scarcely had Cosseins entered when Labonne, who stood in his way, was killed with a dagger thrust. The Swiss who were in the courtyard, when they saw this, fled into the house and closed the door, piling against it tables and all the furniture they could find. It was in the first scrimmage that a Swiss was killed with a ball from an arquebus fired by one of Cosseins' people. But finally the conspirators broke through the door and mounted the stairway, Cosseins, Attin, Corberan de Cordillac, Seigneur de Sarlabous, first captains of the regiment of the guards, Achilles Petrucci of Siena, all armed with cuirasses, and Besme the German, who had been brought up as a page in the house of Guise; for the duke of Guise was lodged at court, together with the great nobles and others who accompanied him.

After Coligny had said his prayers with Merlin the minister, he said, without any appearance of alarm, to those who were present (and almost all were surgeons, for few of them were of his retinue): "I see clearly that which they seek, and I am ready steadfastly to suffer that death which I have never feared and which for a long time past I have pictured to myself. I consider myself happy in feeling the approach of death and in being ready to die in God, by whose grace I hope for the life everlasting. I have no further need of human succor. Go then from this place, my friends, as quickly as you may, for fear lest you shall be involved in my misfortune, and that some day your wives shall curse me as the author of your loss. For me it is enough that God is here, to whose goodness I commend my soul, which is so soon to issue from my body." After these words they ascended to an upper room, whence they sought safety in flight here and there over the roofs.

Meanwhile the conspirators, having burst through the door of the chamber, entered, and when Besme, sword in hand, had demanded of Coligny, who stood near the door,

*Pope Gregory XIII, "Ugonotorum stranges, 1572"
(Slaughter of the Huguenots, 1572). Note the
angel upholding the cross as prostrate Protestants
are being slain.*

*Hercules (Charles IX) fighting the hydra of
heresy with fire and a club.*

*Charles IX bearing the pillars of the church,
symbolizing that Charles is to be greater than
Hercules.*

*Charles IX on his throne. The sword and palm
in his right hand symbolize victory; the sceptre
in his left symbolizes justice; the heads and
bodies on the ground with the motto, "Valor
against rebels," symbolize conquest of heretical
traitors.*

III-9. Medals Struck in Paris and Rome in Celebration of St. Bartholomew's
Massacre.

"Are you Coligny?" Coligny replied, "Yes, I am he," with fearless countenance. "But you, young man, respect these white hairs. What is it you would do? You cannot shorten by many days this life of mine." As he spoke, Besme gave him a sword thrust through the body, and having withdrawn his sword, another thrust in the mouth, by which his face was disfigured. So Coligny fell, killed with many thrusts. Others have written that Coligny in dying pronounced as though in anger these words: "Would that I might at least die at the hands of a soldier and not of a valet." But Attin, one of the murderers, has reported as I have written, and added that he never saw any one less afraid in so great a peril, nor die more steadfastly.

Then the duke of Guise inquired of Besme from the courtyard if the thing were done, and when Besme answered him that it was, the duke replied that the Chevalier d'Angoulême was unable to believe it unless he saw it; and at the same time that he made the inquiry they threw the body through the window into the courtyard, disfigured as it was with blood. When the Chevalier d'Angoulême, who could scarcely believe his eyes, had wiped away with a cloth the blood which overran the face and finally had recognized him, some say that he spurned the body with his foot. However this may be, when he left the house with his followers he said: "Cheer up, my friends! Let us do thoroughly that which we have begun. The King commands

143

it." He frequently repeated these words, and as soon as they had caused the bell of the palace clock to ring, on every side arose the cry, "To arms!" and the people ran to the house of Coligny. After his body had been treated to all sorts of insults, they threw it into a neighboring stable, and finally cut off his head, which they sent to Rome. They also shamefully mutilated him, and dragged his body through the streets to the bank of the Seine, a thing which he had formerly almost prophesied, although he did not think of anything like this.

As some children were in the act of throwing the body into the river, it was dragged out and placed upon the gibbet of Montfauçon, where it hung by the feet in chains of iron; and then they built a fire beneath, by which he was burned without being consumed; so that he was, so to speak, tortured with all the elements, since he was killed upon the earth, thrown into the water, placed upon the fire, and finally put to hang in the air. After he had served for several days as a spectacle to gratify the hate of many and arouse the just indignation of many others, who reckoned that this fury of the people would cost the King and France many a sorrowful day, François de Montmorency, who was nearly related to the dead man, and still more his friend, and who moreover had escaped the danger in time, had him taken by night from the gibbet by trusty men and carried to Chantilly, where he was buried in the chapel.

[Description of the orgy of St. Bartholomew's by a contemporary in *Relation du massacre*:]

The streets were covered with dead bodies, the rivers stained, the doors and gates of the palace bespattered with blood. Wagon loads of corpses, men, women, girls, even infants, were thrown into the Seine, while streams of blood ran in many quarters of the city.... A horse-dealer, having received a shower of blows in his house, was dragged to the river. His two children, following the murderers, attempted to rescue him, and clinging to their father, were dragged along, hacked, and thrown into the river together. Spire Niquet, a poor bookbinder, who was the support of seven children, was slowly roasted over a bonfire of the books found in his house, and then pitched, half dead, into the water.... They forced the wife of a procurator, Le Clerc, to pass before the body of her butchered husband, and then drowned her, though she was in an advanced state of pregnancy. The same fate befell the wife of Antoine Saunier, who was in the same condition.... In the Rue St. Martin, another woman, about to be delivered, had taken refuge on the roof of her house, and after being killed, was ripped up and her infant dashed against the wall. The wife of Jean de Cologne, mercer, was betrayed by her own daughter and murdered, the daughter marrying one of her mother's murderers. The Commissary Aubert thanked the miscreants who had massacred his wife. One of these wretches entered a house, and after killing husband and wife, put their two little children into a basket, and carrying it through the town emptied it into the river. One little girl was bathed in the blood of her butchered father and mother, and threatened with the same fate if she ever became a Huguenot.... The greater number were killed by blows from daggers and poignards. These were the least maltreated, for others were hacked in every part of their bodies, mutilated, mocked, outraged by low jests. Several old men had their heads knocked on the kerbstones, and were then thrown into the river. One infant was dragged through the streets with a cord, fastened round its neck, by a pack of boys from nine to ten years old. Another baby, seized by a murderer, began to play with his beard and to smile, when the diabolical barbarian, instead of being moved to compassion, plunged his dagger into its body and threw it into the water....

[De Thou assessed the consequences:]

The cause of the Protestants was ruined in most of the Provinces and they sought a refuge, some at la Rochelle, others at Montauban, at Nîmes, in le Vivarey, and in some castles of the Cevennes: many others, whom fear had forced to leave their houses, after having wandered about in different places, decided to settle outside the kingdom. The Queen of England, the Elector of the Palatinate, who was a very humane prince, the cantons of Zurich and Berne, and especially the town of Geneva, received them with open arms. But as they were in a bad way in this town because pillage and the abandoning of their property had reduced them to dire poverty, Beza and his colleagues took great care to relieve them by collections which they levied on their behalf. The two eldest sons of Coligny were saved from danger; the Count of Laval, son of Dandelot, and Louis de Coligny, widow of Teligny, retreated first of all to Geneva, whence they went to Bâle, and stayed there several months; finally they went to stay at Berne, where they were received by the Republic with as much honour as humanity. Many others, not having enough courage to put up with the inconveniences of exile, which involved also living far from their houses, their wives, and all the other ties which everyone has in his birthplace, yielded to pressure, and, adapting themselves to the times, returned to the religion of their ancestors. They drew up in Paris a formula of abjuration which those who decided to stay in their homes were obliged to take.

Although the undertakings of the King had had up to then all the success which he could desire, there were three things which made him uneasy; the first was that the King of Navarre and the prince of Condé would not renounce their religion; the second that in Poland and Switzerland, where it was of importance to us that they should have a good opinion of the King, the Massacre of Paris was ill seen; the third was lest la Rochelle should always serve as an asylum to Protestants who had enough courage to take up arms.

8. The Edict of Nantes, April 13, 1598

The ninety-two articles of this voluminous document, with its fifty-six additional articles, were designed by Henry IV "for the pacification of the troubles of his realm," and especially to reassure the Huguenots. Some of the more important provisions are given below. Robinson, *Readings in European History*, II. Cf. Dumont, *Corps diplomatique*, V.

Henry, by the grace of God King of France and of Navarre, to all to whom these presents come, greeting:

Among the infinite benefits which it has pleased God to heap upon us, the most signal and precious is his granting us the strength and ability to withstand the fearful disorders and troubles which prevailed on our advent in this kingdom. The realm was so torn by innumerable factions and sects that the most legitimate of all the parties was fewest in numbers. God has given us strength to stand out against this storm; we have finally surmounted the waves and made our port of safety—peace for our state. For which his be the glory all in all, and ours a free recognition of his grace in making use of our instrumentality in the good work. . . . We implore and await from the Divine Goodness the same protection and favor which he has ever granted to this kingdom from the beginning. . . .

We have, by this perpetual and irrevocable edict, established and proclaimed and do establish and proclaim:

I. First, that the recollection of everything done by one party or the other between March, 1585, and our accession to the crown, and during all the preceding period of troubles, remain obliterated and forgotten, as if no such things had ever happened.

III. We ordain that the Catholic Apostolic and Roman religion shall be restored and reestablished in all places and localities of this our kingdom and countries subject to our sway, where the exercise of the same has been interrupted, in order that it may be peaceably and freely exercised, without any trouble or hindrance; forbidding very expressly all persons of whatsoever estate, quality, or condition, from troubling, molesting, or disturbing ecclesiastics in the celebration of divine service, in the enjoyment or collection of tithes, fruits, or revenues of their benefices, and all other rights and dues belonging to them; and that all those who during the troubles have taken possession of churches, houses, goods or revenues, belonging to the said ecclesiastics, shall surrender to them entire possession and peaceable enjoyment of such rights, liberties, and sureties as they had before they were deprived of them.

VI. And in order to leave no occasion for troubles or differences between our subjects, we have permitted, and herewith permit, those of the said religion called Reformed to live and abide in all the cities and places of this our kingdom and countries of our sway, without being annoyed, molested, or compelled to do anything in the matter of religion contrary to their consciences ... upon condition that they comport themselves in other respects according to that which is contained in this our present edict.

VII. It is permitted to all lords, gentlemen, and other persons making profession of the said religion called Reformed, holding the right of high justice (or a certain feudal tenure), to exercise the said religion in their houses.

IX. We also permit those of the said religion to make and continue the exercise of the same in all villages and places of our dominion where it was established by them and publicly enjoyed several and divers times in the year 1597, up to the end of the month of August, notwithstanding all decrees and judgments to the contrary.

XIII. We very expressly forbid to all those of the said religion its exercise, either in respect to ministry, regulation, discipline, or the public instruction of children, or otherwise, in this our kingdom and lands of our dominion, otherwise than in the places permitted and granted by the present edict.

XIV. It is forbidden as well to perform any function of the said religion in our court or retinue, or in our lands and territories beyond the mountains, or in our city of Paris, or within five leagues of the said city.

XVIII. We also forbid all our subjects, of whatever quality and condition, from carrying off by force or persuasion, against the will of their parents, the children of the said religion, in order to cause them to be baptized or confirmed in the Catholic Apostolic and Roman Church; and the same is forbidden to those of the said religion called Reformed, upon penalty of being punished with especial severity.

XXI. Books concerning the said religion called Reformed may not be printed and publicly sold, except in cities and places where the public exercise of the said religion is permitted.

XXII. We ordain that there shall be no difference or distinction made in respect to the said religion, in receiving pupils to be instructed in universities, colleges, and schools; nor in receiving the sick and poor into hospitals, retreats, and public charities.

XXIII. Those of the said religion called Reformed shall be obliged to respect the laws of the Catholic Apostolic and Roman Church, recognized in this our kingdom, for the consummation of marriages contracted, or to be contracted, as regards the degrees of consanguinity and kinship.

9. *Revocation of the Edict of Nantes, 1685*

The Edict of Nantes in 1598 gave the Huguenots certain religious privileges and brought to France a measure of religious tolerance. When Louis XIV revoked the Edict of Nantes, turmoil resulted. Some 50,000 Huguenots left or were driven from France, many of them coming to America. This action against the Huguenots contributed greatly to the downfall of Louis XIV. Robinson, *Readings in European History*, II.

Louis, by the grace of God King of France and Navarre, to all present and to come, greeting:

King Henry the Great, our grandfather of glorious memory, being desirous that the peace which he had procured for his subjects after the grievous losses they had sustained in the course of domestic and foreign wars, should not be troubled on account of the R.P.R. [i.e. *Religion prétendue réformée*, "the religion called the Reformed"], as had happened in the reigns of the kings, his predecessors, by his edict, granted at Nantes in the month of April, 1598, regulated the procedure to be adopted with regard to those of the said religion, and the places in which they might meet for public worship, established extraordinary judges to administer justice to them, and, in fine, provided in particular articles for whatever could be thought necessary for maintaining the tranquillity of his kingdom and for diminishing mutual aversion between the members of the two religions, so as to put himself in a better position to labor, as he had resolved to do, for the reunion to the Church of those who had so lightly withdrawn from it.

.   .   .   .   .

And now we perceive, with thankful acknowledgment of God's aid, that our endeavors have attained their proposed end, inasmuch as the better and the greater part of our subjects of the said R.P.R. have embraced the Catholic faith. And since by this fact the execution of the Edict of Nantes and of all that has ever been ordained in favor of the said R.P.R. has been rendered nugatory, we have determined that we can do nothing better, in order wholly to obliterate .the memory of the troubles, the confusion, and the evils which the progress of this false religion has caused in this kingdom, and which furnished occasion for the said edict and for so many previous and subsequent edicts and declarations, than entirely to revoke the said Edict of Nantes, with the special articles granted as a sequel to it, as well as all that has since been done in favor of the said religion.

I. Be it known that for these causes and others us hereunto moving, and of our certain knowledge, full power, and royal authority, we have, by this present perpetual and irrevocable edict, suppressed and revoked, and do suppress and revoke, the edict of our said grandfather, given at Nantes in April, 1598, in its whole extent, together with the particular articles agreed upon in the month of May following, and the letters patent issued upon the same date; and also the edict given at Nîmes in July, 1629; we declare them null and void, together with all concessions, of whatever nature they may be, made by them as well as by other edicts, declarations, and orders, in favor of the said persons of the R.P.R., the which shall remain in like manner as if they had never been granted; and in consequence we desire, and it is our pleasure, that all the temples of those of the R.P.R. situated in our kingdom, countries, territories, and the lordships under our crown, shall be demolished without delay.

II. We forbid our subjects of the R.P.R. to meet any more for the exercise of the said religion in any place or private house, under any pretext whatever. . . .

IV. We enjoin all ministers of the said R.P.R., who do not choose to become converts and to embrace the Catholic, apostolic, and Roman religion, to leave our kingdom and the territories subject to us within a fortnight of the publication of our present edict,

without leave to reside therein beyond that period, or, during the said fortnight, to engage in any preaching, exhortation, or any other function, on pain of being sent to the galleys. . . .

VII. We forbid private schools for the instruction of children of the said R.P.R., and in general all things whatever which can be regarded as a concession of any kind in favor of the said religion.

VIII. As for children who may be born of persons of the said R.P.R., we desire that from henceforth they be baptized by the parish priests. We enjoin parents to send them to the churches for that purpose, under penalty of five hundred livres fine, to be increased as circumstances may demand; and thereafter the children shall be brought up in the Catholic, apostolic, and Roman religion, which we expressly enjoin the local magistrates to see done.

X. We repeat our most express prohibition to all our subjects of the said R.P.R., together with their wives and children, against leaving our kingdom, lands, and territories

III-10. Medals Honoring Louis XIV for His Revocation of the Edict of Nantes, 1685. *Victory of religion, extinction of heresy, a garland for virtue.*

subject to us, or transporting their goods and effects therefrom under penalty, as respects the men, of being sent to the galleys, and as respects the women, of imprisonment and confiscation.

XII. As for the rest, liberty is granted to the said persons of the R.P.R., pending the time when it shall please God to enlighten them as well as others, to remain in the cities and places of our kingdom, lands, and territories subject to us, and there to continue their commerce, and to enjoy their possessions, without being subjected to molestation or hindrance on account of the said R.P.R., on condition of not engaging in the exercise of the said religion, or of meeting under pretext of prayers or religious services, of whatever nature these may be, under the penalties above mentioned of imprisonment and confiscation.

10. *The Piedmont Massacre, 1655*

The persecution of the Waldenses in the Piedmont by the Duke of Savoy in 1655 brought forth a confession that was also a plea for justice. The thirty-three articles were a summary of the Gallican Confession of 1559, but the introduction and conclusion, printed below, were calls to others to understand. John Milton (1608-1674), greatest of the English Puritan poets, responded with his sonnet, *On the Late Massacre in Piedmont.* Schaff, *Creeds of Christendom.*

Having understood that our adversaries, not contented to have most cruelly persecuted us, and robbed us of all our goods and estates, have yet an intention to render us odious to the world by spreading abroad many false reports, and so not only to defame our persons, but likewise to asperse with most shameful calumnies that holy and wholesome doctrine which we profess, we feel obliged, for the better information of those whose minds may perhaps be preoccupied by sinister opinions, to make a short declaration of our faith, such as we have heretofore professed as conformable to the Word of God; and so every one may see the falsity of those their calumnies, and also how unjustly we are hated and persecuted for a doctrine so innocent.

We believe....

And for a more ample declaration of our faith we do here reiterate the same protestation which we caused to be printed in 1603, that is to say, that we do agree in sound doctrine with all the Reformed Churches of France, Great Britain, the Low Countries, Germany, Switzerland, Bohemia, Poland, Hungary, and others, as it is set forth by them in their confessions; as also in the Confession of Augsburg, as it was explained by the author, promising to persevere constantly therein with the help of God, both in life and death, and being ready to subscribe to that eternal truth of God with our own blood, even as our ancestors have done from the days of the Apostles, and especially in these latter ages.

Therefore we humbly entreat all of the Evangelical and Protestant Churches, notwithstanding our poverty and lowness, to look upon us as true members of the mystical body of Christ, suffering for his name's sake, and to continue unto us the help of their prayers to God, and all other effects of their charity, as we have heretofore abundantly experienced, for which we return them our most humble thanks, entreating the Lord with all our heart to be their rewarder, and to pour upon them the most precious blessings of grace and glory, both in this life and in that which is to come. Amen.

ADDITIONS TO THIS CONFESSION

Brief justification concerning the points or articles of faith which the doctors of Rome impute to us and to all the Reformed Churches. They accuse us of believing the following articles:

1. That God is the author of sin;
2. That God is not omnipotent;
3. That Jesus Christ fell into despair upon the cross;
4. That man, in the work of salvation, where he is moved by the Spirit of God, is no more active than a log or a stone;
5. That, according to our notion on the subject of predestination, it is of no consequence whether we do good or evil;
6. That good works are not necessary to salvation;
7. That we entirely reject confession of sins and repentance;

8. That fasting and other mortifications of the flesh must be rejected, in order to lead a dissolute life;

9. That any one may explain the Holy Scripture as he pleases, and according to the fanciful suggestions of his own mind;

10. That the Church can entirely fail and be destroyed;

11. That baptism is not necessary;

12. That in the sacrament of the eucharist we have no communion with Christ in fact, but in a figure only;

13. That obedience is not due to magistrates, kings, princes, etc.;

14. That we despise, because we do not invoke, the most holy Virgin and glorified saints; while in fact we pronounce them blessed and worthy both of praise and imitation, and hold above all the holy Virgin Mary to be "blessed amongst women."

All these articles maliciously imputed to us, far from believing or teaching them, we hold to be heretical and damnable, and we denounce from all our heart every one who would maintain them.

ON THE LATE MASSACRE IN PIEDMONT

By John Milton

Avenge, O Lord, thy slaughtered Saints, whose bones
  Lie scattered on the Alpine mountains cold;
  Even them who kept thy truth so pure of old,
  When all our fathers worshiped stocks and stones,
Forget not: in thy book record their groans
  Who were thy sheep, and in their ancient fold
  Slain by the bloody Piedmontese, that rolled
  Mother with infant down the rocks. Their moans
The vales redoubled to the hills, and they
  To heaven. Their martyred blood and ashes sow
  O'er all the Italian fields, where still doth sway
The triple Tyrant; ° that from these may grow
  A hundredfold, who having learnt thy way,
  Early may fly the Babylonian woe.† 1655

° The pope, so called from his triple-crowned tiara.
† Refers to the judgment in Rev. 18, which Milton thought would come to Babylon, the Church of Rome.

11. Hotman and Languet

In Mackinnon, *The Growth and Decline of the French Monarchy.* The author comments on and gives the following running summary of the works of two writers of the sixteenth century—François Hotman and Hubert Languet.

. . . Theological strife led to political debate, and this period is remarkably fertile in political theories, born of the contentions of the day, but not limited in their interest and their influence to these. Many of the great political doctrines of modern times are already enunciated in this political literature. Some of these are not new—the doctrine of the sovereignty of the people, for instance—some of them are, such as the doctrine of liberty of conscience, and whether old or new, they produced a tremendous ferment in the national mind, and were to become the battle-cries of much of modern political history. Religious persecution was the handmaid of political liberty, for persecution led men to question the right of the persecutor. The Protestant had begun by denying the power of the Pope; he ended by challenging the power of the king—in those countries, at least, where the civil power showed itself hostile to his creed. While he might exalt that power in Germany, England, and even in republican Geneva, as ordained of God, in France, Holland, and Scotland, he questioned its authority, exalted the sovereignty of the people, and refused allegiance to a persecuting king as a usurper and a tyrant. Conscience postulated political as well as moral liberty; resistance to moral was in reality resistance to political slavery. The one was impossible without the other. Of this there is abundant evidence in the works of men like François Hotman and Hubert Languet.

Hotman's life (1524-1590) was typical of that of the cultured Huguenot refugee. . . . It was at Geneva in 1573 that he wrote his most celebrated work—the "Franco-Gallia"— which passed through three editions in as many years, and created a sensation in learned circles, and, by means of a translation, in the wider circle of the nation. His aim is to show that the ancient Franco-Gallic monarchy was based on the sovereignty of the people, that this sovereignty was usurped by the kings of a later time, particularly by

III-11. Protestant Pastor and Huguenots Worshipping in Secret.

Louis XI, and that the disorders and sufferings of the present are due to this usurpation. His method is admirable, because it is historic. He questions history, studies the chroniclers in a professedly critical spirit, examines the origins of the monarchy in order to discover which was the ancient form of government in France, and how it became absolute. He possesses the intuition of the true historian, seeking the genesis of the present in the past. . . . These results, it is safe to say, were the political gospel of his co-religionists after the Massacre of St. Bartholomew.

The kings of ancient Gaul were not hereditary, but elective, and exercised no unlimited or arbitrary authority. They were no less subject to the people than the people were to them. The Romans deprived the Gauls of their liberty, but they did not succeed in killing the spirit of freedom. From this tyranny they were delivered by the Franks, German freemen who established the kingdom of Franco-Gallia. The Franks, like the ancient Gauls, elected their kings, who held the throne on certain conditions, and deposed them if they failed to fulfil these conditions. There was no certain rule of succession, the choice of the king depending on the will of the council of the people, though it usually elected a member of the royal family for the time being. In this council, annually convened, the supreme administrative power was lodged. Its modern representative is the States-General, and it combined, like them, the three elements of kingly, aristocratic, and popular government, in whose concert lies the harmony of the commonwealth. A most wise institution, for it is essential to liberty that the State should be governed by the authority and advice of those whose interests are so closely concerned, and who should, therefore, be careful to control the king's ministers. The council of the king tends to consult only the royal advantage; the council of the people, the advantage of the kingdom. For this purpose the council or parliament, i.e., the Estates, of the nation met once a year, and every king who ignores this custom is a violator of the law of nations (Hotman holds that all States were anciently governed by a parliamentary council) and an enemy of human society. In those ancient days the king was not surrounded with the meretricious pomp which ministers to his vanity in these degenerate times, for the king rode to the place of meeting in an ox-wagon, and only as the representative of the people, sitting on the golden throne in the midst of the assembly, was he the bearer of the royal majesty. How unlike these profane days of ours, when the king is styled your majesty, whether he sings, or dances, or trifles with his women. The authority of the council is supreme, and embraces all affairs of State–

150

the election or deposition of the king, the declaration of peace or war, legislation, the disposal of honours, commands, offices, etc. But was not Pepin created king by Pope Zacharias? No, returned Hotman. This is a lying story invented by Pope Gelasius, and repeated by the chroniclers. There are plenty of ancient testimonies to prove that Pepin was chosen by the council of the nation. This council retained its authority throughout the period of the Merovingian and Carolingian kings. It, and not the person who happens to be king, is the real source and possessor of the royal majesty or power.

Observe, he exhorts, the distinction between the king and the kingdom. The king is a single person, the kingdom is the whole body of the people, for whose sake the king is instituted. The king is accidental, the kingdom is permanent. A people may exist without a king, but a king without a people is inconceivable. Though Hugh Capet obtained the kingship by arms and craft, and encroached on the right of the council of the nation to confer honours and jurisdiction—formerly temporary—by making the title of duke, earl, etc., perpetual, the power of the council nevertheless continued under the Capetian dynasty. Witness in particular the adjudication of the kingdom in 1328 to Philip of Valois, in preference to Edward III, and many other instances of the exercise of sovereign power in the fourteenth and fifteenth centuries. The council, however, suffered in its jurisdiction and power by the establishment of the parliaments, whose privileges were gradually increased by the king in order to augment his own power, and counteract that of the Estates. With the increase of parliaments, litigation has increased, but liberty has suffered.

Hotman's book, though not strictly historic, is at least original, though it cannot be called revolutionary, since it is a passionate plea for a return to the ancient constitution of the kingdom. Yet, though conservative in form, it is intensely revolutionary in spirit, strongly reactionary against the absolutist *régime* of the Valois. It insists on the sovereignty of the people as represented by the States-General, insists on it at times in language equally dogmatic and uncompromising with that of Rousseau. It is a plea for democracy, though the democracy is that of the traditional free people of Germans amalgamated with that of ancient Gaul. Though not critically historical . . . its influence on Catholics as well as Protestants was immense. It continued to be read when the struggle that inspired it was over, and to nurture the democratic spirit of the eighteenth century, even after the more sober and scientific labours of Adrien de Valois, and especially of Fréret, had discredited many of its naive, but imaginary assertions. [Fréret read his dissertation to the Académie des Inscriptions et Belles Lettres in 1714. He was thrown into the Bastille by a suspicious government for his pains.]

While Hotman subjects the dominant absolutism to historical criticism, the author of the *"Vindiciae contra Tyrannos,"* published in 1579, undertakes to show the right and the duty of resistance to it. He adopted the pseudonym of Junius Brutus, and conjecture has identified him with Hotman, Beza, Du Plessis-Mornay, and Hubert Languet. The last mentioned is now generally credited with its authorship. Hotman had demonstrated the sovereignty of the people from French history. Languet asserts it as a right, and seeks to prove it on both religious and political grounds. In order to establish it he posits the following questions: Are subjects bound to obey a king who commands what is contrary to the law of God? If not, may they resist such a king? Thirdly, may they resist a king who oppresses the State? Finally, may they call in the aid of neighbouring princes for their deliverance from an irreligious and tyrannical sovereign? He appeals to Scripture for an answer to the first two, and in so doing, views the subject from the theological standpoint, in his relation to God and revealed religion. For the answer to the third he appeals to history and reason as well as Scripture, and views the subject from the purely political standpoint. In treating all three he uses the inductive method, reasoning by the aid of the facts of Scripture and history to general conclusions, and he claims for his doctrines the warrant of logic as well as history, sacred and profane. I am not concerned here to dispute or approve these doctrines. As in the case of Hotman, his ideas are for us the main thing, inasmuch as they are the ideas of the party he represents.

Question one: Are subjects bound to obey a king who commands what is contrary to the law of God? Our author unhesitatingly answers in the negative. Yet the question is not so superfluous as may appear, since many in these days of Christian princes, who claim unlimited power, and are deemed by their flatterers gods on earth, are led by fear and constraint to believe that they should be obeyed in all things. Sovereignty over the conscience belongs to God alone. This sovereignty princes calling themselves Christians have usurped, and deem those who refuse to recognise this usurpation rebels. In this sense Christ and the apostles were rebels, and the flatterers of kings still teach them to overlook the distinction between God and Caesar. But what saith Scripture: Scripture teaches that kings derive their authority from God, are His delegates or lieutenants, and that their power is limited by Him. He alone is absolute sovereign, and has never consented to share His absolute sovereignty with any mortal. Kings are His vassals, not the sharers of His sovereign power, and, as vassals, are invested with their jurisdiction on certain conditions. They are kings by covenant or contract, and this covenant or contract is, according to Scripture, which our author quotes incessantly, twofold; first between God and the king and the people, secondly, between the people and the king. By the first, to which he limits consideration in the meantime, the people and the king undertake to obey and serve God, and are subject to punishment in case of contravention, as when the people made a covenant with Baal, and Saul declined from his obligations to serve Him. Even pagan kings have not escaped punishment for usurping the sovereign power reserved by God to Himself. And what holds of Jewish and even of pagan kings, holds of Christian princes who command what is contrary to God's law. They are on the same footing with rebellious vassals, and if so, who is so mad as to deny that we should obey the sovereign Lord, rather than the rebellious vassal? All who refuse this obedience are rebels, as much rebels as those who join a vassal in insurrection against his overlord.

Question two: May subjects resist a king who commands what is contrary to the law of God, and if so, by whom, how, and to what extent is resistance lawful? Once more, what saith Scripture? The covenant or contract is not merely between God and the king, but between God, the king, and the people. The people was a party to the transaction, it had authority to promise and to keep promise; if not, the transaction would not have been a contract. Its participation, on the other hand, served to strengthen the contract, just as two or more warranters afford more security for the payment of a debt than one. The king and the people are bound to God for each other. *Ergo*, if the king forsake God, and the people strive not to win him from the evil of his ways, but connive at his sin, the people is guilty of his sin, and *vice versa*. Resistance is thus involved in the contract. If the king may resist the people, should the people forsake God, the people may equally resist the king, if the king forsake God. To make a contract with the people as one of the parties, and yet doom the people to bondage to the king's will is both unscriptural and illogical. There can be no contract with a slave. And God would not punish the people for the sins of the prince, if their negligence, connivance, or stupidity were not punishable according to contract. The people is the guardian of religion as well as the prince, and if the prince takes arms against the people for their adherence to their trust, the people may take arms against the prince.

But is the people not a beast with many heads and liable to many disorders? Were it not insane to give the direction of affairs to an unruly and unbridled multitude? True, but by the people our author understands the constituted representatives of the people, the magistrates, the States-General, whom it has substituted for itself to restrain encroachments on its sovereignty. For the people which establishes the king is superior to the king, and the principal persons of the kingdom may associate together as its representatives in resistance to tyranny. Nay, in the case in which the king persuades the majority to become idolaters, the minority led by the chief men—princes and magistrates—may resist the majority. Such a minority are not rebels, for there is a contract, not only between God and the king and the people, but between the king and the people. By this second contract the people promised obedience only as far as the king ruled them justly, and if the king breaks faith with them, he is the rebel. Where there is no justice there is no commonwealth, and resistance to what is unlawful is no rebellion. It does not, however, pertain to individuals to resist, for the covenant is not with individuals but with the people, and only the people, or those who represent it, are bound to observe its stipulations.

Question three: May subjects resist a prince who oppresses the State? God hath appointed kings, but it is the people who establishes them. Kings hold their sovereignty under God from the people. It is from God, but by the people and for the people that they reign. Let them not imagine that they are of higher race than other men. They are not lords of a flock of sheep or a herd of oxen. This, too, is attested by Scripture. The kingship in Israel was not hereditary, but elective. The Roman kings, too, were elected, and though the elective origin of the kingship has been obscured by hereditary succession in more modern countries, it is still apparent in the fact that the heir to the crown is not, properly speaking, king till he has taken the coronation oath at the hands of the representatives of the people, as in Spain, France, England. These are as much kings by election as is the Emperor, or the King of Bohemia. Kings, in a word, are created, not born. If the next heir is unworthy, the people may displace him by some other prince of the blood. The whole body of the people is superior to the king, for it is from the people that he derives his power. Only Roman tyrants suffered themselves to be called lords. The king is merely the pilot, not the owner of the ship of State. The people is the owner, and therefore the king is its servant, not its lord. Take away the people and where is the king? Like the Rhodesian Colossus, he falls in pieces. And not only the king, but all the officers of government derive their powers from the same source, which axioms are proved by the history of Judea, Egypt, Sparta, Rome, France, England, Scotland,

Germany, Poland. But is the legitimate power of the king less because it is limited by the people? Certainly not. Only usurpers and their flatterers will believe so. Is a man less healthful because he is surrounded by discreet physicians, who counsel him to avoid what is hurtful? Similarly they are the king's best friends who care most for the commonwealth. Remember the words of King Theopompus of Sparta. The more the people watch over the State, the better for both king and State. Unhappily what is every man's business is no man's business, and the people has neglected, with sad results to itself, its sovereign functions. Yet no usurpation can prejudice its right, or alienate liberty. Kings die, but the commonwealth is immortal. Its rights never die, and no modern king can claim more than his ancestors obtained. If he does, he is a thief, and if the peers and chief officers of the kingdom have granted more, their action is treason to the people and does not justify tyranny, or legitimate the loss of liberty. A conspiracy of the magistrates to subject the people is as indefensible as the betrayal by a perfidious advocate of the interests of his client. There is one prescription which carries it above all others, viz., that the people be maintained in the enjoyment of their property and their liberty. Liberty is the privilege of nature, and no people would ever establish a king to rob it of this privilege. Kings were established to maintain justice, defend the State, and protect its members from outrage. The kingship is not an honour but a duty, a burden which consists in protecting the poor from the rich, and the nation from foreign enemies. This is the true secret of its origin, and all kings who pursue their own ends, not the interests of the people, are tyrants. It follows from this that the king is not above the law, but merely its administrator, and subject to it like the rest. To place the king above the law is to place a premium on human passions. Law is as necessary for a king as for a people. Beware of those court marmosets who make gods of kings, and bow down to their oracles, nay, will have it that justice is nothing in itself, but only what the king ordains. They forget that the king receives the laws as well as the crown from the people. He may not even make a new law without their consent and the co-operation of the Estates. He has not the power of life and death over his subjects as a master over his slaves, he may only with the advice of sage lawyers exercise the right of pardon in certain cases.

Other axioms need only be stated to be understood, though our author dips deep in his historic lore in order to elucidate them. The property of the people does not belong to the king, nor is the king the owner of the kingdom. Such is a tyrant, not a king, and a tyrant is one who comes into possession by violence, or governs not according to law, and thus breaks the contract. The first is a tyrant without title, the second a tyrant by practice. The law of nature, the law of nations, the civil law empower all to resist a tyrant without title, who is simply a robber, and the meanest person in the commonwealth may put the robber to death. Only if he acquire the right of possession, and the people acquiesce in this right, is he to be regarded as having established a title, and the people must then submit to his rule. In the case of tyrants by practice, more circumspection is necessary. Even if a king does not conform exactly to the laws, he is not to be forthwith proclaimed a tyrant. Absolutely perfect kings do not exist, and the subjects may account themselves happy if their kings are indifferently good. But if he purposely ruin the commonwealth, if he pervert the laws, if he break contracts and proscribe his subjects, he is a tyrant and an enemy of both God and man. The more he is tolerated, the more intolerable does he become. The people through its representatives should first remonstrate and use persuasive means in order to turn him from his evil course; if persuasion fail, they ought to use force, and pursue him as a rebel against the sovereignty of the people. If a General Council may depose a Pope, who claims to be king of kings, for his sins, much more may the States-General depose a king for his tyranny. And if the majority of the States-General concur in the royal tyranny, the true patriots in its ranks are entitled to save the commonwealth in spite of them.

Question four: May subjects call in the aid of foreign sovereigns for their deliverance from the irreligion or tyranny of the prince?

Princes are ready enough to act on the principle of intervention for their political interests. Are they also entitled to intervene on religious and moral grounds? Certainly. The Church being one and universal, the protection of the Church is the duty of all Christian princes. Humanity, too, demands intervention. Virtue, as Cicero says, being the mother of mankind, enjoins every man to seek the good of the whole. Foreign princes may not, however, invade the territories of an irreligious tyrant for purposes of conquest, and by this reservation the author saves his patriotism on paper at least.

We can well understand the sensational effect of this work. It systematized the political ideas of the Huguenots with great logical power and no little lore. It was at once an apology, a defense, and an attack. Hotman had sought to attain the same end by indirect means, by a historical rather than a logical exposition of the doctrine of the sovereignty of the people. Languet shoots straight at the target. He argues, demonstrates, dogmatizes direct from reason, Scripture, and history, lays bare in the sight of king and people the fiction, the iniquity of absolute role. He has made use of the "Franco-Gallia," but he goes beyond it, beyond the history of ancient Gaul and Germany to the Jewish theocracy, and even at times beyond this to human nature, the basis of human right. His doctrine of the contract is especially noteworthy. In this respect he is the father of Locke and Rousseau. He emphasizes all through the sovereignty of the people based on this contract, and the subordination of the king to the people. With that sovereignty is bound the right of Protestantism not only to existence, but to supremacy. In this respect he is intolerant and extreme, but he is at least logical from the Protestant standpoint, and the stress of the times may be allowed to mitigate his fierce logic. He is face to face with the enemy, and if he does not demolish the enemy, the enemy will demolish him. Though democratic in principle, he is, like Hotman, not revolutionary. His book is an appeal to ancient right on grounds of reason and Scripture, and like Hotman he would reform the State by its constitutional institutions. He is not anti-monarchic and republican, for he is careful to distinguish between good and bad kings, and even hazards the assertion that a good king represents in some sort the Divine Majesty. Yet the work teems with revolutionary dogmas, and it might, in part at least, equally with the "Contract Social," have served as the handbook of the revolutionists of 1789, for it is an exposure of a vast usurpation by convention and self-interests, and a call to return to the original contract. Only, with Languet the contract is theocratic, with Rousseau the contract will be purely democratic.

12. *To A Religious, A Letter on Self-Love, 1615*

From *The Spiritual Letters of S. Francis de Sales,* trans. H. L. Sidney Lear (London, 1889).

... In reply to your letter: Self-love may be mortified, but it never dies within us; from time to time, and on sundry occasions, it puts forth fresh shoots, which prove that, though cut down, it is not rooted up. This is why we do not find the satisfaction that we ought to have in seeing others do well; we do not altogether rejoice in good works which are not to be found in ourselves, whereas we greatly admire all that is our own, and that because we love ourselves so exceedingly. But if we had a perfect charity, which causes us to be of one heart and soul with our neighbour, we should rejoice unfeignedly in whatever of his is good and perfect.

This same self-love leads us to do certain things because we choose them for ourselves, although we would not do them at another's bidding, or from mere obedience. If things are our own originating we like them, but not when they come through other people. Self is for ever seeking self, self-will and self-love; but if we were perfect in the love of God, we should prefer to obey, because in obedience there is more of God and less of self.

As to finding it easier to do disagreeable things oneself than to see them done by others, that may arise from charity, or because self-love secretly fears that other people may equal or surpass us. Sometimes we feel more at seeing others suffer than in

suffering ourselves, out of genuine kindliness; but sometimes it is because we think ourselves more enduring and more able to bear suffering, thanks to a good opinion of ourselves.... But I am sure that these are only the feelings of your natural mind; the higher, supernatural mind rejects them all. The only remedy is to disown all such thoughts, striving after obedience, and resolving to prefer it, in spite of all things, to self-pleasing; thanking God for whatever good we see in others, and asking him to increase it fourfold.

We must never be surprised to find self-love alive within ourselves; it is ever there. At times it sleeps like a crafty fox, but then suddenly it dashes out anew. We must keep a steady watch over it, and be always on the defensive, though gently and patiently. If sometimes self-love wounds us, and we are forced to unsay what we have said, to disown what it has made us do, we shall be partly cured.

13. *Pascal's Provincial Letters*

These letters satirized the Jesuits' emphasis on man's part in salvation and constituted a reaction to the vigorous attempts of the Jesuits to stamp Jansenism out of the convent at Port Royal. The controversy fed the French spirit of Gallicanism, a protest of the Church in France against increasing papal control. King Louis XIV and Pope Innocent XI both wanted the revenues of vacant French bishoprics. The French clergy supported the king, and in 1682 the Gallican Declaration, prepared by Bishop Bossuet, became operative. It declared that the king, in temporal matters, is not subject to the Pope and cannot be deposed, that the king's subjects cannot be absolved of obedience, and that the Pope's decisions are not necessarily final in matters of faith. It was condemned by Pope Alexander VIII in 1690 and retracted by the king in 1693, but the controversy flared again in the next century (cf. Ch. 6). Cf. Henry Bettenson, *Documents of the Christian Church* (New York: Oxford University Press, 1947); and W. F. Reddaway, *Select Documents of European History, 1492-1715* (New York: Henry Holt & Co., 1930). *Provincial Letters,* trans. Thomas M'Crie (Boston: Houghton Mifflin Co., 1887).

In this letter from *Provincial Letters,* dated "Paris, March 20, 1656," Pascal reports an interview concerning a new system of morals which is being established by a number of modern Jesuit writers. The Jesuit father to whom he is talking informs him that both lax and severe casuistry is sanctioned by the Jesuits in order to gain control over more people and that probability is the doctrinal basis for this double standard.

"But," said I, "how can these same superiors give their consent to maxims so contradictory?"

"That is what you have yet to learn," he replied. "Know, then, that their object is not the corruption of manners—that is not their design. But as little is it their sole aim to reform them—that would be bad policy. Their idea is briefly this: They have such a good opinion of themselves as to believe that it is useful, and in some sort essentially necessary to the good of religion, that their influence should extend everywhere, and that they should govern all consciences. And the Evangelical or severe maxims being best fitted for managing some sorts of people, they avail themselves of these when they find them favorable to their purpose. But as these maxims do not suit the views of the great bulk of the people, they waive them in the case of such persons, in order to keep on good terms with all the world. Accordingly, having to deal with persons of all classes and of all different nations, they find it necessary to have casuists assorted to match this diversity.

"On this principle, you will easily see that if they had none but the looser sort of casuists, they would defeat their main design, which is to embrace all; for those that are truly pious are fond of a stricter discipline. But as there are not many of that stamp, they do not require many severe directors to guide them. They have a few for the select few; while whole multitudes of lax casuists are provided for the multitudes that prefer laxity.

"It is in virtue of this 'obliging and accommodating, conduct,' as Father Petau calls it, that they may be said to stretch out a helping hand to all mankind. Should any person present himself before them, for example, fully resolved to make restitution of some ill-gotten gains, do not suppose that they would dissuade him from it. By no means; on the contrary, they would applaud and confirm him in such a holy resolution. But suppose another should come who wishes to be absolved without restitution, and it will be a particularly hard case indeed, if they cannot furnish him with means of evading the duty, of one kind or another, the lawfulness of which they will be ready to guarantee.

"By this policy they keep all their friends, and defend themselves against all their foes; for, when charged with extreme laxity, they have nothing more to do than produce their austere directors, with some books which they have written on the severity of the Christian code of morals; and simple people, or those who never look below the surface of things, are quite satisfied with these proofs of the falsity of the accusation.

"Thus are they prepared for all sorts of persons, and so ready are they to suit the supply to the demand, that when they happen to be in any part of the world where the doctrine of a crucified God is accounted foolishness, they suppress the offence of the cross, and preach only a glorious and not a suffering Jesus Christ. This plan they followed in the Indies and in China, where they permitted Christians to practise idolatry itself, with the aid of the following ingenious contrivance: they made their converts conceal under their clothes an image of Jesus Christ, to which they taught them to transfer mentally those adorations which they rendered ostensibly to the idol of Cachinchoam and Keum-fucum. This charge is brought against them by Gravina, a Dominican, and is fully established by the Spanish memorial presented to Philip IV, king of Spain, by the Cordeliers of the Philippine Islands, quoted by Thomas Hurtado, in his 'Martyrdom of the Faith,' page 427. To such a length did this practice go, that the Congregation *De Propaganda* were obliged expressly to forbid the Jesuits, on pain of excommunication, to permit the worship of idols on any pretext whatever, or to conceal the mystery of the cross from their catechumens; strictly enjoining them to admit none to baptism who were not thus instructed, and ordering them to expose the image of the crucifix in their churches: all of which is amply detailed in the decree of that Congregation, dated the 9th of July, 1646, and signed by Cardinal Capponi.

"Such is the manner in which they have spread themselves over the whole earth, aided by *the doctrine of probable opinions,* which is at once the source and the basis of all this licentiousness. You must get some of themselves to explain this doctrine to you. They make no secret of it, any more than of what you have already learned; with this difference only, that they conceal their carnal and worldly policy under the garb of divine and Christian prudence; as if the faith, and tradition, its ally, were not always one and the same at all times and in all places; as if it were the part of the rule to bend in conformity to the subject which it was meant to regulate; and as if souls, to be purified from their pollutions, had only to corrupt the law of the Lord, in place of 'the law of the Lord, which is clean and pure, converting the soul which lieth in sin,' and bringing it into conformity with its salutary lessons!

"Go and see some of these worthy fathers, I beseech you, and I am confident that you will soon discover, in the laxity of their moral system, the explanation of their doctrine about grace. You will then see the Christian virtues exhibited in such a strange aspect, so completely stripped of the charity which is the life and soul of them—you will see so many crimes palliated and irregularities tolerated, that you will not longer be surprised at their maintaining that 'all men have always enough of grace' to lead a pious life, in the sense in which they understand piety. Their morality being entirely Pagan, nature is quite competent to its observance. When we maintain the necessity of efficacious grace, we assign it another sort of virtue for its object. Its office is not to cure one vice by means of another; it is not merely to induce men to practise the external duties of religion: it aims at a virtue higher than that propounded by Pharisees, or the greatest sages of Heathenism. The law and reason are 'sufficient graces' for these purposes. But to disenthral the soul from the love of the world—to tear it from what it holds most dear—to make it die to itself—to lift it up and bind it wholly, only, and forever, to God—can be the work of none but an all-powerful hand. And it would be as absurd to affirm that we have the full power of achieving such objects, as it would be to allege that those virtues, devoid of the love of God, which these fathers confound with the virtues of Christianity, are beyond our power."

Such was the strain of my friend's discourse, which was delivered with much feeling; for he takes these sad disorders very much to heart. For my own part, I began to entertain a high admiration for these fathers, simply on account of the ingenuity of their policy; and following his advice, I waited on a good casuist of the Society, one of my old acquaintances, with whom I now resolved purposely to renew my former intimacy. Having my instructions how to manage them, I had no great difficulty in getting him afloat. Retaining his old attachment, he received me immediately with a profusion of kindness; and after talking over some indifferent matters, I took occasion from the present season, to learn something from him about fasting, and thus slip insensibly into the main subject. I told him, therefore, that I had difficulty in supporting the fast. He exhorted me to do violence to my inclinations; but as I continued to murmur, he took pity on me, and began to search out some ground for a dispensation. In fact he suggested a number of excuses for me, none of which happened to suit my case, till at length he bethought himself of asking me, whether I did not find it difficult to sleep without taking supper. "Yes, my good father," said I; "and for that reason I am obliged often to take a refreshment at mid-day, and supper at night."

"I am extremely happy," he replied, "to have found out a way of relieving you without sin: go in peace—you are under no obligation to fast. However, I would not have you depend on my word: step this way to the library."

On going thither with him he took up a book, exclaiming, with great rapture, "Here is the authority for you: and, by my conscience, such an authority! It is *Escobar!*"

"Who is Escobar?" I inquired.

"What! not know Escobar!" cried the monk; "the member of our Society who compiled this Moral Theology from twenty-four of our fathers, and on this founds an analogy, in his preface, between his book and 'that in the Apocalypse which was sealed with seven seals,' and states that 'Jesus presents it thus sealed to the four living creatures, Suarez,

Vasquez, Molina, and Valencia, in presence of the four-and-twenty Jesuits who represent the four-and-twenty elders."

He read me, in fact, the whole of that allegory, which he pronounced to be admirably appropriate, and which conveyed to my mind a sublime idea of the excellence of the work. At length, having sought out the passage on fasting, "Oh here it is!" he said; "treatise I, example 13, no. 67: 'If a man cannot sleep without taking supper, is he bound to fast? Answer: *By no means!*' Will that not satisfy you?"

"Not exactly," replied I; "for I might sustain the fast by taking my refreshment in the morning, and supping at night."

"Listen, then, to what follows; they have provided for all that: 'And what is to be said, if the person might make a shift with a refreshment in the morning and supping at night?'"

"That's my case exactly."

"'Answer: Still he is not obliged to fast; because no person is obliged to change the order of his meals.'"

"A most excellent reason!" I exclaimed.

"But tell me, pray," continued the monk, "do you take much wine?"

"No my dear father," I answered; "I cannot endure it."

"I merely put the question," returned he, "to apprise you that you might, without breaking the fast, take a glass or so in the morning, or whenever you felt inclined for a drop; and that is always something in the way of supporting nature. Here is the decision at the same place, no. 57: 'May one, without breaking the fast, drink wine at any hour he pleases, and even in a large quantity? Yes, he may: and a dram of hippocrass too.' I had no recollection of the hippocrass," said the monk; "I must take a note of that in my memorandum-book."

"He must be a nice man, this Escobar," observed I.

"Oh! everybody likes him," rejoined the father; "he has such delightful questions! Only observe this one in the same place, no. 38: 'If a man doubt whether he is twenty-one years old, is he obliged to fast? No. But suppose I were to be twenty-one tonight an hour after midnight, and tomorrow were the fast,

would I be obliged to fast tomorrow? No; for you were at liberty to eat as much as you pleased for an hour after midnight, not being till then fully twenty-one; and therefore having a right to break the fast day, you are not obliged to keep it.'"

"Well, that is vastly entertaining!" cried I.

"Oh," rejoined the father, "it is impossible to tear one's self away from the book: I spend whole days and nights in reading it; in fact, I do nothing else."

The worthy monk, perceiving that I was interested, was quite delighted, and went on with his quotations. "Now," said he, "for a taste of Filiutius, one of the four-and-twenty Jesuits: 'Is a man who has exhausted himself any way—by profligacy, for example—obliged to fast? By no means. But if he has exhausted himself expressly to procure a dispensation from fasting, will he be held obliged? He will not, even though he should have had that design.' There now! would you have believed that?"

"Indeed, good father, I do not believe it yet," said I. "What! is it no sin for a man not to fast when he has it in his power? And is it allowable to court occasions of committing sin, or rather, are we not bound to shun them? That would be easy enough, surely."

"Not always so," he replied; "that is just as it may happen."

"Happen, how?" cried I.

"Oh!" rejoined the monk, "so you think that if a person experience some inconvenience in avoiding the occasions of sin, he is still bound to do so? Not so thinks Father Bauny. 'Absolution,' says he, 'is not to be refused to such as continue in the proximate occasions of sin, if they are so situated that they cannot give them up without becoming the common talk of the world, or subjecting themselves to personal inconvenience.'"

"I am glad to hear it, father," I remarked; "and now that we are not obliged to avoid the occasions of sin, nothing more remains but to say that we may deliberately court them."

"Even that is occasionally permitted," added he; "the celebrated casuist Basil Ponce has said so, and Father Bauny quotes his sentiment with approbation, in his Treatise on Penance, as follows: 'We may seek an occasion of sin directly and designedly—*primo et per se*—when our own or our neighbor's spiritual or temporal advantage induces us to do so.' "

"Truly," said I, "it appears to be all a dream to me, when I hear grave divines talking in this manner! . . ."

"I can easily see," replied the good father, "that you know nothing about our doctrine of *probable opinions*. If you did, you would speak in another strain. Ah, my dear sir, I must really give you some instructions on this point; without knowing this, positively you can understand nothing at all. It is the foundation—the very A, B, C, of our whole moral philosophy. . . ."

" 'An opinion is called probable, when it is founded upon reasons of some consideration. Hence it may sometimes happen that a single *very grave doctor* may render an opinion probable.' The reason is added: 'For a man particularly given to study would not adhere to an opinion unless he was drawn to it by a good and sufficient reason.'

" 'A person may do what he considers allowable according to a probable opinion, though the contrary may be the safer one. The opinion of a single grave doctor is all that is requisite.' "

"And if an opinion be at once the less probable and the less safe, is it allowable to follow it," I asked, "even in the way of rejecting one which we believe to be more probable and safe?"

"Once more, I say yes," replied the monk. "Hear what Filiutius, that great Jesuit of Rome, says: 'It is allowable to follow the less probable opinion, even though it be the less safe one. That is the common judgment of modern authors.' Is not that quite clear?"

"Well, reverend father," said I, "you have given *us* elbow-room, at all events! Thanks to your probable opinions, we have got liberty of conscience with a witness! And are you casuists allowed the same latitude in giving your responses?"

"Oh, yes," said he, "we answer just as we please; or rather, I should say, just as it may please those who ask our advice. Here are our rules, taken from Fathers Layman, Basquez, Sanchez, and the four-and-twenty worthies, in the words of Layman: 'A doctor, on being consulted, may give an advice, not only probable according to his own opinion, but contrary to his opinion, provided this judgment happens to be more favorable or more agreeable to the person that consults him—*si forte haec favorabilior seu exoptatior sit.* Nay, I go further, and say, that there would be nothing unreasonable in his giving those who consult him a judgment held to be probable by some learned person, even though he should be satisfied in his own mind that it is absolutely false.' "

"Well, seriously, father," I said, "your doctrine is a most uncommonly comfortable one! Only think of being allowed to answer yes or no, just as you please! It is impossible to prize such a privilege too highly. I see now the advantage of the contrary opinions of your doctors. One of them always serves your turn, and the other never gives you any annoyance. If you do not find your account on the one side, you fall back on the other, and always land in perfect safety."

"That is quite true," he replied; "and accordingly, we may always say with Diana, on his finding that Father Bauny was on his side, while Father Lugo was against him: *Saepe premente deo, fert deus alter opem.*"

[In subsequent conversations, Pascal learned that the doctrines of probability and intention can be used to justify assassination, lying, broken promises, and easy devotions.]

Baird, H. M., *The History of the Rise of the Huguenots of France*. New York: Charles Scribner's Sons, 1900.

Blok, P. J., *A History of the People of the Netherlands*, 5 vols. New York: G. P. Putnam's Sons, 1912.

Brodrick, James, *Origin of the Jesuits*. New York: David McKay Co., Inc., 1940.

Church, F. C., *The Italian Reformers*. New York: Columbia University Press, 1932.

Coleridge, H. J., *Life and Letters of St. Francis Xavier*. London: Burns Oates & Washbourne, Ltd., 1876.

Cristiani, Leon, *The Revolt Against the Church*, trans. R. R. Trevett. New York: Hawthorn Books, Inc., 1962.

Dyke, Paul van, *Ignatius Loyola*. New York: Charles Scribner's Sons, 1927.

Fülöp-Miller, René, *Power and Secret of the Jesuits*. New York: George Braziller, Inc., 1960.

Geyl, P., *The Revolt of the Netherlands, 1555-1609*. London: Williams and Norgate, Ltd., 1932.

Green, V. H. H., *Renaissance and Reformation*. London: Longmans, Green & Co., Ltd., 1952.

Hulme, E. M., *The Renaissance, Protestant Revolution, and Catholic Reformation in Continental Europe*. Watkins Glen, N.Y.: Century House, Inc., 1915.

Jacobsen, Jerome V., *Educational Foundations of the Jesuits in the Sixteenth Century in New Spain*. Berkeley: University of California Press, 1938.

Janelle, P., *The Catholic Reformation*. Milwaukee: Bruce Publishing Co., 1949.

Jedin, Hubert, *History of the Council of Trent*. St. Louis: Herder & Herder, Inc., 1957.

Kidd, B. J., *Counter-Reformation*. Naperville, Ill.: Alec R. Allenson, Inc., 1933.

Latourette, K. S., *Three Centuries of Advance, 1500-1800*. New York: Harper & Row, Publishers, 1939.

Lortz, Joseph, *Die Reformation in Deutschland*, 2 vols. Freiburg, 1939.

Loyola, Ignatius, *The Spiritual Exercises*. Various editions.

Mackinnon, James, *Growth and Decline of the French Monarchy*. New York: David McKay Co., Inc., 1902.

Palestrina, Giovanni da (Recordings): *Adoramus Te*, Stokowski, United Artists; *Missa Papae Marcelli*, De Nobel, Netherlands Church Choir, Epic, and Grossmann, Vienna Pro Musica Choir, Vox; *Supplicationes* and *Stabat Mater*, Harvard-Radcliffe Choral Society, Cambridge.

Pascal, Blaise, *Penseés* and *Provincial Letters*. Various editions.

Ricci, Matthew, *Journals of Matthew Ricci, 1583-1610*. New York: Random House, Inc., 1953.

Sales, Francis de, *Introduction to the Devout Life*. Various editions.

Schroeder, H. J., *Canons and Decrees of the Council of Trent*. St. Louis: B. Herder Book Co., 1941.

Wilkins, C. A., *Spanish Protestants in the Sixteenth Century*. London, 1897.

Zoff, Otto, *The Huguenots*. New York: L. B. Fischer Publishing Co., 1942.

CHRONOLOGY

Illustration opposite page 163: **Valley of the Shadow of Death.** *Illustration in Bunyan's* Pilgrim's Progress.

IV

The Revolt in England

The key to the Reformation in England is
the struggle for royal supremacy, a doctrine which
necessitated the denial of an ultramontane papacy and engendered the
strife that gave to the Reformation in England a political aspect
that shaped events from the time of Henry VIII (1509-1547)
to the Act of Toleration in 1689. The revolt in England
in its early stages had little to do with the religious reforms that were
stirring in Germany, Switzerland, and France. Henry VIII,
who initiated the revolt, broke the power of the medieval
church in England and asserted his own supremacy in
religion and politics, but he simply took the place of
the pope; reform was incidental to his desire to control ecclesiastical
and secular affairs. And after Henry, royal supremacy
continued to be the focal point around which the various
aspects of religion revolved.

The seeds of the English revolt go back to John Wycliffe
(1328?-1384) and his Lollards, who in the fourteenth century
advocated that the church be deprived of its wealth on account of
its abuse of the stewardship of the Lord's gifts. Wycliffe

believed poverty would make the church more Christlike, and he taught that the church is centered not in the pope but in Christ, and that the church's true congregation is the company of the elect who live by the Scriptures. His views led him to translate the Bible, which the Lollards preached, and to combat transubstantiation, which he regarded as an unscriptural doctrine protecting the clergy in its privileged status. These ideas were still present in the sixteenth century, and Henry was able to capitalize on them to assert his own supremacy, for there were many Englishmen who for reasons of their own resented the wealth of the church and the ignorance and immorality of the clergy.

Ignorance of Scripture was especially widespread. In the days of the Lollards Bible reading had been made a crime, and the king's statute, *De haeretico comburendo* (1401), under which many Lollards were burned, was still in effect in the sixteenth century. Erasmus noted that the Gospel of Nicodemus was being read in Canterbury Cathedral by priests who did not know it was not part of the Bible. A growing nationalism, which reached a climax in the opposition of Englishmen to the Spanish Armada, fed the feeling that the pope had no genuine right to interfere in political affairs or to drain the country of ever enlarging revenues. Humanists, like John Colet and Sir Thomas More, sought to advance Renaissance learning and were critical of clerical immorality and ignorance. Erasmus himself taught for five years at Cambridge. Sir Thomas More produced his *Utopia* in 1516 to stir men to greater social and intellectual achievements. But the English revolt in the first half of the sixteenth century had little in common with Wittenberg and Geneva.

Kingly protest against the claims of the papacy was foremost in the revolt, and was not new. Although King John at the beginning of the thirteenth century bowed to Pope Innocent III and accepted his kingdom as a fief from the pope, subsequent Englishmen repeatedly disowned papal supremacy in temporal affairs. The *Magna Charta* in 1215 curbed not only the king's power but also that of the pope, and asserted the independence of the Church of England. Innocent III declared it null and void for all time, but it became the foundation of English law. Later English monarchs challenged the appeal from English courts to the Roman Curia, and made such appeal a crime in the reign of Richard II in the statute of *Praemunire* in 1353. Henry appealed directly to this statute. The struggle for political and religious sovereignty had deep roots in English history, and Henry VIII brought the struggle a step forward in establishing the Anglican Church with himself as head.

Henry's father, Henry VII, was the first king of the house of Tudor. Uncertain of his royal tenure, he sought to strengthen his position by marrying his eldest son Arthur to Catharine of Aragon, daughter of powerful King Ferdinand and Queen Isabella of Spain. After Arthur's early death, Henry sought to preserve his alliance by having Catharine marry his second son Henry, now heir to the throne. Pope Julius II in 1503 set aside the divine laws of kinship and granted a questionable dispensation for Henry to marry his brother's widow. This action was valid only if the ultramontane claims of the papacy were justified. When Henry VIII became king, he supported papal supremacy, for it meant validation of his marriage and his children's claims to the throne. It is not surprising that in 1521 he answered Luther's criticisms of the church with an *Assertion of the Seven Sacraments Against Luther,* which earned him the title of Defender of the Faith. For eighteen years Henry VIII acknowledged papal supremacy. But Mary was the only surviving child of the six born to him and Catharine; he had no male heir. Henry came not only to doubt that his marriage was legitimate but to feel that the judgment of God was upon him; the struggles for power between the pope, the emperor, and the Protestants caused Henry to wonder about the future. Never had a woman ruled England!

Henry resolved, therefore, to marry again, that he might hope for a son and lawful successor. Through Cardinal Wolsey, his minister, he petitioned the pope to grant a divorce. Pope Clement VII refused, for he did not want to alienate the emperor, who was Catharine's nephew. With all the force of his stubborn personality, Henry then resolved to obtain a divorce anyway. Thomas Cranmer suggested an appeal to the universities of Europe, and their favorable responses emboldened Henry to act. Irked at Cardinal Wolsey's failure to secure a divorce, Henry accused him, the papal legate in England, of breaking the law of *Praemunire* in accepting his office, and he accused the clergy of England of the same crime in accepting the pope's ambassador. Cardinal Wolsey died in 1530 before he could be tried for treason, and the intimidated clergy presented Henry with a gift of £118,000 to augment his treasury, and a statement that he was the supreme lord of the church, as far as was permitted by the law of Christ. Henry expanded this guarded statement by threatening the Convocation of the Church of England in 1532 into giving him virtual control over the church. The Convocation renounced papal allegiance, accepted the king's supremacy over ecclesiastical law, and agreed to withhold the annates, or first year's income from each benefice that traditionally went to the pope. Henry, badly in need of money, later appropriated these annates for himself. This submission of the clergy in 1532 marked a long step toward despotism in English religion (*1*). In January of 1533, Henry secretly married Anne Boleyn, and threatened to take the pope's annates, already withheld, unless Thomas Cranmer were named the Archbishop of Canterbury. When Cranmer was confirmed, he declared Henry's marriage to Catharine null and void, and the *de facto* submission of the clergy in England was complete.

Henry needed only the sanction of Parliament to finalize his position, and Parliament obliged. In answer to the bull of Pope Clement of July 11, 1533, which threatened excommunication of the king, Henry's Parliament passed a series of laws that made him supreme in the land. In late 1533 and 1534, Parliament forbade the clergy to pay annates to the pope, abolished appeals to Rome, and reiterated that any appeal to Rome would violate *Praemunire,* even though the case might be wholly ecclesiastical (*2*). Parliament also said that the pope could no longer nominate for offices, and declared that

papal dispensations should henceforth be exercised by the Archbishops of Canterbury and York (*3*). Parliament then passed the Act of Succession which declared Princess Mary, daughter of Catharine of Aragon, illegitimate, and designated Elizabeth, the infant daughter of Anne Boleyn, the heir to the throne. The Act of Treason, or Supremacy Act, followed, November 3, 1534, making it a capital crime not to accept the Act of Succession, or not to acknowledge royal supremacy (*4*). In May, 1535, a number of Carthusian monks were barbarously executed, and in the same year Bishop John Fisher and Sir Thomas More were beheaded, all for not accepting the supremacy of the king and the Act of Succession. These acts did not alter religious doctrine; they simply changed supremacy from pope to king. Parliament decreed that heretics would still be burned according to *De haeretico comburendo,* although not for speaking evil of the pope. Lutheran heretics were still hunted; no one could speak against the mass, transubstantiation, veneration of the saints, good works to achieve righteousness, and so on. Tyndale (1492-1536), because he translated and distributed Erasmus' New Testament, was widely sought, and escaped the English authorities only to be martyred by papal agents in Vilvorde, near Brussels. John Frith, his friend, returned to England and was burned in London in 1533 for denying purgatory and transubstantiation. Kingly supremacy, not reform, was Henry's basic aim; Catholics and Protestants alike suffered for not accepting supremacy.

Looking for a means to justify his actions and also to replenish his treasury, Henry commissioned Thomas Cromwell in 1534 to have the monasteries visited and examined. On the report that corruption was prevalent, Parliament in February, 1536, passed a law giving all the monasteries with incomes of less than £200 yearly to Henry. He sequestered 376 and sold them at auction to build up his treasury. Henry was supreme and his coffers full, but lavish spending soon depleted the treasury once again.

Thomas Cranmer, Archbishop of Canterbury, aided the king in these moves, as did Thomas Cromwell, the king's chief political adviser. Both shared a propensity toward the reformed religion of Luther and Zwingli, and they persuaded Henry that he should champion the Protestant cause against Emperor Charles V by heading an evangelical alliance. Conversations were held with Continental leaders, and Henry, with some reluctance, drew up the *Ten Articles* of 1536. They were Roman Catholic in tone, but they did place authority in the Scriptures, the ancient creeds, and the first four ecumenical councils, and they denied the authority of the pope over purgatory and modified the honoring of images. No alliance resulted, however, and Henry never again ventured so near the Protestants.

The political picture changed. Catharine of Aragon died in 1536, and in the same year Anne Boleyn was beheaded for adultery. Henry then married Jane Seymour, and Parliament declared Elizabeth illegitimate and made Edward, his son by Jane Seymour, who died in giving birth to him, the heir to the throne. When Catholic dissidents in Lincolnshire and Yorkshire mounted an insurrection, called the Pilgrimage of Grace, Henry ruthlessly squelched it.

Although Henry was not Protestant, Cranmer seized the opportunity to promote the evangelical faith. In 1537, he and his associates published the *Bishop's Book* and the *Thirteen Articles*, drawn largely from the Augsburg Confession. But Henry soon showed his displeasure. Thomas Cromwell persisted in telling Henry that he should cement his evangelical tendencies by marrying Anne of Cleves, sister of the wife of John Frederick of Saxony. This Henry did on January 6, 1540. Before the year was out, he had annulled the marriage, beheaded Cromwell, and was negotiating with Charles V to improve his political position. He opposed Cranmer's articles by publishing, in June, 1539, his famous *Six Articles*, known as the "Whip with Six Strings" (5). Persecution of evangelicals followed. Henry's new wife was Catharine Howard, a Roman Catholic who was beheaded in 1542 for adultery, and his last wife was Catharine Parr, who outlived him.

When Henry died in 1547 he left three heirs: Mary, who was thirty-one, Elizabeth, who was fourteen, and Edward, a boy of ten, who inherited the throne. Under Edward VI England went forward with the Reformation, despite a Roman Catholic majority in the population. The Council of Regency, appointed to advise the boy king, was dominated by the Earl of Hertford and the Duke of Somerset, who also bore the title of Lord Protector of the Realm. He and several members of the Council launched a program not only to maintain royal supremacy but also to write Protestantism into the customs and laws of the land. With this in view, a royal visitation of all the churches was ordered, and Cranmer's evangelical *Book of Homilies* was sent to all parishes for reading in the churches, along with a translation of Erasmus' *Paraphrase of the New Testament* and Cranmer's *Book of Common Prayer* (First Prayer Book of Edward VI) to be used in worship services. Parliament repealed the *Six Articles,* decreed that the laity should be given the cup in Communion, and two years later, in 1549, released priests from vows of celibacy. Relics and images were removed from churches, and Archbishop Cranmer openly discarded old rules about fasting. Within three years the royal visitation had changed the outward expression of religion in England.

Archbishop Cranmer brought men from the Continent to teach, preach, and spread reformed ideas. Martin Bucer and Paul Fagius came from Strassburg to Cambridge; Peter Martyr of Florence and Bernard Ochino of Siena came to Oxford. They trained a future generation of teachers and clergymen, and their public disputations and books carried the new ideas to the people. These Calvinists and the influence of Calvinists from Holland and France gave the reforms in England a definite Genevan stamp. Cranmer's *Forty-two Articles,* which John Knox helped write, were decidedly Calvinistic and were to give the land unity in doctrine, but they came just shortly before Edward VI died in 1553. The *Thirty-nine Articles,* adopted during Elizabeth's reign, were based directly on them.

Criticism of the Council of Regency and of Cranmer came from two sources. Bishop Gardiner of Winchester, one of the framers of Henry's *Six Articles*, strongly opposed the new trends and sought to return to the old Roman practices. And John Hooper, a former Cistercian monk who had become a noted evangelical preacher, led a group that desired more reform—the Puritans. The Puritans wanted pure biblical worship—no vestments, no oaths in the name of saints, no altars separating priests and people, and no practices that might detract from the doctrine of the priesthood of all believers. They wanted nothing to interfere with the privilege of every man to approach God directly in faith, for confession of sins and forgiveness, without any priestly mediation. Hooper's consecration as Bishop of Gloucester was delayed in 1550 because he would not swear by "God and all the saints." In his defense he wrote *Godly Confession and Protestation*, one of the earliest Puritan treatises (6). During the reign of Edward VI, both Gardiner and Hooper were imprisoned for their views. Nicolas Ridley escaped prison at this time, but he carried reform to an extreme as Bishop of London when he removed the altar, installed communion tables, and abolished all images, relics, and holy water.

Before Edward VI died in 1553, he named Lady Jane Grey, a Protestant, to succeed him, but the people responded to a show of force by Mary, the daughter of Catharine of Aragon, who easily secured the throne and beheaded the young Lady Jane. Gardiner, an implacable foe of Cranmer, became her guide, and Parliament went along with the new regime by sweeping aside the reforms of Edward, declaring Mary legitimate, abolishing the Prayer Book, and returning England to the status quo at the end of Henry's reign. Cranmer, Ridley, the popular Hugh Latimer, and others were imprisoned.

Mary was a belligerent Roman Catholic. In 1554 she married Philip II, son of Charles V of Spain, an alliance deeply resented by most Englishmen. Uprisings occurred in Cornwall, Devon, Suffolk, and Kent, but Mary proceeded with her program of returning England to Catholicism. The lands seized by Henry and sold to individual buyers presented a problem, but the pope finally relinquished his claims to them, and the Queen and Parliament prepared to welcome

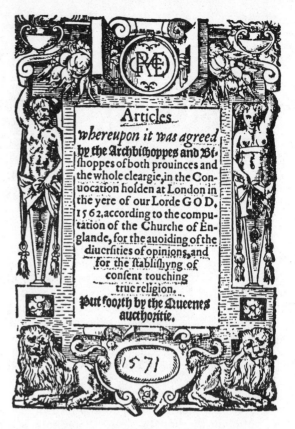

IV-1. Title Page of the Thirty-nine Articles, 1571 edition. *British Museum.*

Cardinal Legate Reginald Pole, an English noble who fled England rather than accept the royal supremacy of Henry VIII. With Mary, Philip, and Parliament kneeling before him, Cardinal Pole on St. Andrew's Day, 1554, absolved the nation of heresy. Parliament repealed all the supremacy acts and England was again Roman Catholic.

In the persecutions which immediately followed, Latimer, Ridley, Hooper, Cranmer and seventy-five others died. Later persecutions were even more fearful. Mary was without a child, and when Philip left her after one year, she felt that God's judgment had come on her for not completely eliminating Protestantism. To atone, she launched a persecution in which more than three hundred died, and she became known as Bloody Mary. She returned to the papacy the sequestered church lands still held by the crown, and property owners throughout England saw

167

IV-2. Medals Showing the Return of Catholicism to England. *The kneeling figure is Queen Mary; Pole is the Cardinal; the third figure is Emperor Charles V; next Pope Julius III; the fifth is King Philip II of Spain; and the last is Catherine of Aragon.*

their land titles in jeopardy and resented the new taxes imposed by her. When Mary died of dropsy in 1558, revolution was stirring in England.

Elizabeth's rule (1558-1603) brought a change of policy, not because she was strongly Protestant or Roman Catholic, but because she desired a peaceful, strong England, and the *via media* enforced by royal supremacy seemed to be the means of accomplishing religious tranquility. She went to mass to please Catholics, and forbade elevation of the host to please Protestants. She moved cautiously, under the guidance of Lord William Cecil, for she had to deal with an overwhelmingly Protestant Parliament, papal objection to her legitimacy, and the threat of war with France, Spain, or both. Parliament re-enacted the supremacy acts of Henry VIII, but modified her title to "Supreme Governor" of the Church of England (7), and the Prayer Book was revised to lessen offense to Catholics. But the Act of Uniformity in 1559 kept the liturgy of Edward VI, and caused Roman Catholic bishops to resign their sees (8). Undaunted, Elizabeth directed Matthew Parker, a cleric with Protestant leanings, to fill the vacancies. The validity of Parker's consecrations is still disputed in Anglo-Catholic circles; in 1896, Pope Leo XIII declared that Anglican Orders were not valid. To provide a uniform confession, Elizabeth ordered the *Forty-two Articles* revised, resulting in the *Thirty-nine Articles* which were officially adopted in 1563. The *Thirty-nine Articles* were Calvinistic, and the Prayer Book was Roman Catholic; the *via media* was the Elizabethan

Settlement, which prevailed despite strong Roman Catholic and Puritan opposition.

Elizabeth's opposition to Catholicism solidified when Catholic uprisings occurred in 1569 in Northern England, and the pope excommunicated her in 1570 (10). Plots against her life and plans to place Mary Stuart of Scotland, a Catholic, on the throne, were repeatedly discovered, and Elizabeth realized more and more that her strength lay with the Anglicans, and even with the Puritans whom she opposed. In 1570, Catholics brought about the treacherous murder of the Regent Moray in Scotland, and in 1571 Elizabeth discovered the Ridolfi Plot which involved the Duke of Alva, Philip II, the pope, and the English Duke of Norfolk in a scheme to mount a Roman Catholic insurrection to seize the throne. The Duke of Norfolk forfeited his life. In 1580, Jesuit missionaries and Catholic emissaries began spreading the doctrine that assassination to insure the future of the church was a good thing. At the seminary at Douai, newly established in 1568 by William Allen, priests were being trained to inflame the Catholics of England. Edmund Champion, a Jesuit leader in these schemes, was apprehended and executed, but Robert Parson, another Jesuit leader, escaped to France to continue to plot an uprising and the murder of Elizabeth. When the Babington conspiracy, in which Mary was personally involved, was discovered, Elizabeth and her counsellors resolved to execute the already imprisoned Queen of Scots, a resolve carried out on February 8, 1587. Catholic priests were everywhere suspect, and many were executed; Jesuits were expelled from the kingdom (*13, 15*). By 1586, circumstances had forced Elizabeth to break completely with Rome; she was sending money to aid the Huguenots in France, had dispatched troops to Holland, and was encouraging men like Sir Francis Drake to harass Spanish merchant ships. Foxe's *Book of Martyrs* was being widely read (*9*).

The Roman Catholics then abandoned dark plots and resorted to warfare. Philip II and Pope Sixtus V, who had excoriated Elizabeth, realized that the medieval dream of a united Europe under one emperor and the church could not be accomplished without crushing England. In 1588, the grand scheme was launched. The pope helped outfit a mammoth fleet of Spanish ships, the Armada, to sail against England, and the crack Spanish troops in the Netherlands under Alexander of Parma were to cross the channel. Elizabeth appealed to the nationalism of her subjects, who responded by outfitting two hundred small, swift ships with guns heavier than those of the Spanish. Under the leadership of pirating seamen like Drake, the English harassed and then defeated the Spanish fleet in battles off Plymouth and Gravelines. Only a few ships ever returned to Spain. England emerged the most powerful nation in Europe.

Protestantism experienced a renewal, but the religious question in England was by no means settled. Elizabeth insisted on royal supremacy, and when the Puritans refused to wear vestments, copes, and surplices, which suggested to them a sacerdotal separation of the clergy and laity, Elizabeth simply deprived them of their benefices. This caused the Puritans to resent royal supremacy and the episcopal government of the church which complied; they demanded a presbyterial or congregational form more in keeping with the New Testament. When Elizabeth's Court of High Commission enforced uniformity, many churches served by Puritans became vacant, and the newly appointed pastors were stoned. Inflammatory tracts appeared. Thomas Cartwright (1535?-1603), a learned scholar and teacher at Cambridge, who stood for the priesthood of all believers, the election of pastors by the people, abolition of episcopacy, and a presbyterian form

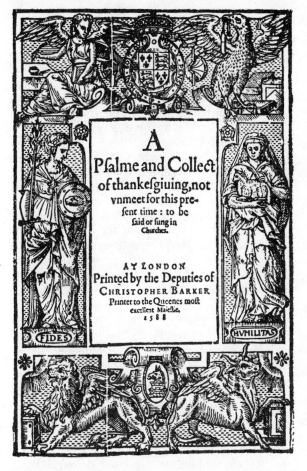

IV-3. Title Page of a Special Psalm and Collect to Celebrate the Defeat of the Armada. *British Museum.*

of government, was deprived of his professorship and sent into exile. Sympathizers John Field and Thomas Wilcox in 1572 presented *An Admonition to Parliament,* which landed them in jail. John Whitgift, later to become Archbishop of Canterbury, vigorously combatted Cartwright's views. Elizabeth temporarily placated the Puritans by appointing Edmund Grindal, a Puritan, to succeed Parker as Archbishop when he died in 1575. But Grindal would not act against the Puritan "prophesyings," gatherings in which clergymen discussed theology, and he was suspended from performance of his duties. John Whitgift succeeded Grindal as Archbishop in 1583, and rigorously implemented Elizabeth's ideas, with the result that many churches became vacant and people gathered in "conventicles," often in the open.

Conservative Puritans decided to wait for a more favorable government, and others called for separation, and formation of independent congregations. Robert Browne (1550-1633) adopted Separatist views about 1580, and with Robert Harrison formed an independent congregation in Norwich in 1581. After being imprisoned a number of times, Browne sought refuge with his congregation in Holland, where he penned his famous *Reformation Without Tarrying for Any* (*12*). John Greenwood and Henry Barrow organized Separatist meetings in London and suffered martyrdom for their efforts in 1593. The *Marprelate* pamphlets, bitterly critical of the episcopacy and vestiges of popery, circulated at this time, and Nicolas Udal, one of the supposed authors, was executed in 1593 (*14*).

In the meantime, Anglican authors began rallying to the support of Elizabeth's policy by combatting Calvinism. Thomas Bilson defended the episcopacy in his *Perpetual Government of Christ's Church*, 1593, and Richard Hooker, between 1594 and 1597, published his voluminous *Laws of Ecclesiastical Polity*, in which he defended episcopacy as scriptural and reasonable.

Despite all opposition, Elizabeth's *via media*, Anglicanism, prevailed and became firmly established during her long reign (cf. *16, 24, 25*).

When James I (1603-1625) became king, Englishmen hardly knew what to expect. He was the son of Mary, Queen of Scots, and Darnley. Mary's wretched marital affairs had led to her dethronement by Protestant and Catholic forces in Scotland in 1567. The next year she escaped to England, was imprisoned, and became the center of Catholic intrigue against Elizabeth until she was executed in 1587. James' parentage was Catholic, but his upbringing by John Knox's followers was Calvinistic (*11*). On his way from Scotland to London, in 1603, he was presented with the Millenary Petition, supposedly representing the desire of a thousand Puritans who wanted to abolish abuses in worship, eliminate the ring in marriage, and cease the use of signs of the cross, surplices, and rites of confirmation (*17*). James granted nothing, but did promise a conference. The

Roman Catholic recusants might have fared well under James, but a series of plots on the king's life were discovered, and James issued a proclamation ordering all Jesuits and seminarists to leave England. The worst threat was the Gunpowder Plot, in which Roman Catholics headed by Guy Fawkes planned to blow up Parliament and the king. The Jesuits justified this plot with the casuistry that any means could be used to promote the church. Many Catholics were arrested, some executed, and the Oath of Allegiance required them to condemn any papal excommunication which might expose rulers to violence. Another act in 1606 forbade Catholics' becoming guardians, trustees, lawyers, or doctors.

King James held his Hampton Court Conference with the Puritans in 1604. He promised a new translation of the Bible, the famous King James Version of 1611, a translation vastly superior to the Bishops' Bible of 1568, the Genevan Bible of 1557-1560, and the Roman Catholic Rheims-Douai Bible of 1582-1610. Fifty scholars from Oxford, Cambridge, and Westminster made the authorized version a superior literary and religious achievement. But James did not concede a revision of the Prayer Book, the *Thirty-nine Articles*, nor the *Catechism*. The Conference showed James' Anglican tendencies—royal supremacy and the episcopacy, "no bishop, no king." In a series of acts he enforced supremacy, the Articles, and the Prayer Book. Those Puritans who objected, perhaps as many as three hundred, lost their appointments. The *Book of Sports*, issued by James in 1618, sought to loosen the grip of the Puritans on Sunday activities by making various sports lawful. When James ordered this book read from the pulpits, the Puritan furore was so fierce that the book was withdrawn.

Two influential Separatist congregations emerged in the reign of James: one was at Gainsborough, led by John Smyth, an Anglican clergyman; the other was at Scrooby, led by William Brewster, who was joined by William Bradford and John Robinson, a former Anglican priest. Harassed by authorities, the congregation at Gainsborough moved to Amsterdam, and the one at Scrooby to Leyden. Other acts of James increased

IV-4. The Conspirators in the Guy Fawkes Plot, Early in the Reign of King James I. *A contemporary print.*

their numbers. On September 6, 1620, one hundred and one Pilgrim Fathers sailed on the *Mayflower* from Plymouth for America, which they reached two months later. Some of the original Smyth congregation returned to England to become Baptists and strong advocates of religious toleration. Some of the Leyden group returned to establish congregational churches, the first founded by Henry Jacob in Southwark in 1616.

When Charles I (1625-1649) became king, he insisted on divine right, and royal supremacy and Anglicanism became closely identified with each other. In 1628, Charles named William Laud bishop of London, and in 1633 made him Archbishop of Canterbury; from that time, Charles relied heavily on Laud. Laud believed that the Anglicans were the bearers of the purest branch of the Catholic tradition, and he became the symbol of all that the Puritans hated. John Winthrop led a group of Pilgrims to Plymouth Colony in 1630, and during the next decade, 20,000 more followed.

In 1629, King Charles dismissed Parliament and ruled alone for the next eleven years; but Laud's policies were so irksome that the Scots rebelled in 1639, and Charles was forced to summon Parliament to levy taxes

to finance the suppression of the Scots. Instead, the Presbyterian Puritans of Parliament presented Charles with a Grand Remonstrance and took control. Laud was imprisoned and executed in 1645. Civil war flared when the king tried to arrest members of Parliament for treason. To strengthen its cause, Parliament agreed to the Solemn League and Covenant of the Scotch, which abolished the episcopacy (*18*). An assembly of Presbyterian Puritans was called to sit at Westminster and advise Parliament. This was the Assembly that wrote the Confession, *Directory of Worship,* and Catechism which have become standards of Presbyterian belief. The *Short Catechism* of 1647 is regarded as one of the best expositions of Calvinism (*19*). In 1645, Parliament forbade the Prayer Book and outlawed Anglicanism; this act remained in force for fifteen years.

Oliver Cromwell (1599-1658) rose to lead the "religious" men against Romanism and prelacy. Cromwell defeated Charles and demanded religious toleration from Parliament, rather than Presbyterianism (*20*). When a Scottish army invaded, Cromwell scattered it. Many Presbyterian Puritans were dismissed from Parliament, and Charles was beheaded in 1649. Europe hailed Cromwell as the new champion of Protestantism (21, 22). As Lord Protector, in 1653 he granted religious liberty to all except Roman Catholics, Anglicans, and Antinomians.

Under Cromwell a Commission of Triers was established. This commission, with thirty-eight members, examined all ministerial candidates and dispossessed scores of Anglicans. Ornate church altars were destroyed, Christmas and other festivals forbidden, dancing prohibited, and marriage reduced to a civil rite. When Cromwell died in 1658, his son Richard was too inept to cope with the anarchy that ensued, and Presbyterians, Royalists, and part of the army united in inviting Charles' son to assume control.

Charles II (1660-1685), who was Roman Catholic, if anything, came in promising religious freedom in the Breda Declaration of 1660; but reaction to the Puritans was almost inevitable. The Act of Uniformity in 1662 re-established Anglican worship and many Puritans went to jail, among them John Bunyan (1628-1688). During his twelve years in prison Bunyan wrote *The Holy City*, 1665, and *Grace Abounding*, 1666. His *Pilgrim's Progress*, 1678, made him the most popular religious author in England. All efforts to reconcile the Puritans and Anglicans failed. A series of acts, called the Clarendon Code because they were issued under the Lord Chancellor Clarendon, weighed heavily on the Puritan nonconformists; two thousand left their parishes. The Corporation Act, 1661, required all members of corporations to swear against the Solemn League and Covenant and to practice Holy Communion according to the Anglican rite. The Conventicle Act, 1664, prohibited the assembling of more than five extra people in any household, and justices of the peace were empowered to enter and arrest without warrants. The Five Mile Act, 1665, declared ministers could not return to within five miles of their former parishes (23). The Second Conventicle Act, 1670, increased fines for attending dissenting services, and declared that the fines could be collected from anyone in the group.

Charles II sought to strengthen his position by cultivating Roman Catholicism, and in 1670 he made a secret Treaty of Dover with Louis XIV to re-establish the papacy in England. His Declaration of Indulgences in 1672 aroused the suspicion of Parliament, for it granted freedom of worship to Catholics in their homes. In 1673, Parliament enacted the Test Act, requiring ministers to swear an oath of supremacy, reject transubstantiation, and accept the Anglican rite of the Lord's Supper. This occasioned years of struggle between the Puritan elements (called Whigs), and those oriented toward King and Catholicism (called Tories). On his deathbed, Charles confessed his Catholicism.

Catholicism waged a losing struggle, however; people could not forget the Jesuit intrigues, the Armada, the Gunpowder Plot, and the plight of the Huguenots in France and the Waldenses in Italy. James II (1685-1688) succeeded his brother Charles II and frantically tried to entrench Catholicism in the churches and universities. He imported Jesuits and monks to aid him. His efforts to give the Catholics freedom of worship met the combined resistance of Puritans, Anglicans, and Parliament. Seven bishops who resisted him and went to jail became national Protestant heroes (cf. 24, 25).

To rescue the deteriorating situation, William of Orange, who had married Mary, the daughter of James, was summoned by popular demand. He landed an army on English soil in 1688 and James fled to France. William and Mary endeavored to unite the Puritans and Anglicans, but the seeds of tolerance and distrust of vested supremacy swayed Parliament to pass the Toleration Act of 1689, which granted liberty of worship to all except Roman Catholics and Unitarians, namely to those who would accept the *Thirty-nine Articles* and reject transubstantiation, the pope, and invocation of Mary.

Roman Catholics were persecuted further. An act in 1700 prohibited them from purchasing or inheriting land, and denied Catholic children an education except in their own homes. Effective relief for Roman Catholics did not come until the end of the eighteenth century, and not completely until

1829. Modified toleration prevailed, but indifference set in and reduced the church and religion in England to an innocuous state on the eve of the evangelical revival of the Wesleys and Whitefield.

During this long time of strife and persecution, England produced some of its greatest literature. Early in the period, in 1516, stands Sir Thomas More with his *Utopia,* as if to prophesy the future, and at the end stands John Dryden (1631-1700), who was religious enough to profess a faith and secular enough to change with each new regime. His *Heroic Stanzas,* 1659, eulogizes Oliver Cromwell, while his *Religio Laici,* 1682, in the reign of Charles II, celebrates the temperateness of Anglicanism. *The Hind and the Panther* during the time of James II, 1687, pictures Catholicism as a stainless, white hind, Anglicanism as a spotted, vicious panther, and the Dissenters as insignificant small beasts.

William Tyndale's translation of the New Testament was published at Cologne in 1525, and Miles Coverdale's translation of the Old Testament came in 1535; these led to the masterful King James Version in 1611, probably the most influential book in English literature. John Foxe produced his *Book of Martyrs* in 1563, a monument to years of persecution and violence over religion (9). Marking the secular interests of the period were Edmund Spenser's *Faerie Queene,* 1591, and Ben Jonson's *Every Man in His Humor,* 1598. A mixture of religious and secular allegory appeared in the works of John Donne (1573-1631). Francis Bacon with his *Novum Organum,* 1620, and *Advancement of Learning,* 1622, heralded an age of empirical science. But William Shakespeare (1564-1616) towers above all the others as the literary giant of the early period with his numerous tragedies, histories, comedies, and sonnets, in which the moral insight and mundane interests of the period seem to have been combined.

After 1642, the year when Puritan influence forced the closing of the theaters, religious concerns dominated English literature so much so that Thomas Hobbes, with his *Leviathan* in 1651, and Izaac Walton, with his *Compleat Angler,* 1653, have been characterized as eccentrics. This was the time of Jeremy Taylor (1613-67), who produced *Liberty of Prophesying* in 1646, the devotional classics, *Holy Living* and *Holy Dying,* 1650-1651, and Anglican prose at its best in his popular sermons (25). George Herbert (1593-1633) preceded the period with the most popular of Anglican poems, *The Temple,* 1633. John Milton (1608-1674) stands as the dominating figure of the later period; he probed the Bible for its two greatest themes, the Fall and the Redemption of man, and embodied them in his masterpieces, *Paradise Lost,* 1667, and *Paradise Regained,* 1671. The former is a drama of conscience, temptation, and fall—Satan and man in rebellion—in which Milton's personal reflections abound. The latter is based on Luke 4:1-3, Christ's resisting temptation after forty days of fasting and ending the reign of the devil. *Samson Agonistes* appeared in 1671, picturing a blind Samson, betrayed by Dalila, as a captive among the Philistines—a work of blind Milton in his later life, contemptuous of women, the Puritan bid for power having failed. John Bunyan (1628-1688) directly expressed the Puritan faith in *Grace Abounding,* 1666, and in *Pilgrim's Progress,* 1678. The former is concerned with the mystery of conversion, and the latter is an allegorical novel showing the progress of every Christian in his struggles, failures, and triumphs. To these Bunyan added *The Life and Death of Mr. Badman,* 1680, and *The Holy War,* 1682. George Fox (1624-1690), founder of the Quakers, belongs also to this period, although his *Journal* was more influential later (cf. Ch. 6).

Only a few of these literary achievements are included below, for they can hardly be excerpted; they must be read in their complete form.

1. The Submission of the Clergy, 1532

The following document, agreed to by the clergy of England in Convocation, May 15, 1532, marked the submission of the clergy to the demands of King Henry VIII. Henry Gee and W. J. Hardy, *Documents Illustrative of English Church History* (London: Macmillan & Co., Ltd., 1896).

We your most humble subjects, daily orators and bedesmen of your clergy of England, having our special trust and confidence in your most excellent wisdom, your princely goodness and fervent zeal to the promotion of God's honour and Christian religion, and also in your learning, far exceeding, in our judgment, the learning of all other kings and princes that we have read of, and doubting nothing but that the same shall still continue and daily increase in your majesty—

First, do offer and promise, *in verbo sacerdotii*, here unto your highness, submitting ourselves most humbly to the same, that we will never from henceforth enact, put in ure, promulge, or execute, any new canons or constitutions provincial, or any other new ordinance, provincial or synodal, in our Convocation or synod in time coming, which Convocation is, always has been, and must be, assembled only by your highness' commandment of writ, unless your highness by your royal assent shall license us to assemble our Convocation, and to make, promulge, or execute such constitutions and ordinances as shall be made in the same; and thereto give your royal assent and authority.

Secondly, that whereas divers of the constitutions, ordinances, and canons, provincial or synodal, which have been heretofore enacted, be thought to be not only much prejudicial to your prerogative royal, but also overmuch onerous to your highness' subjects, your clergy aforesaid is contented, if it may stand so with your highness' pleasure, that it be committed to the examination and judgment of your grace, and of thirty-two persons, whereof sixteen to be of the upper and nether house of the temporalty, and other sixteen of the clergy, all to be chosen and appointed by your most noble grace. So that, finally, whichsoever of the said constitutions, ordinances, or canons, provincial or synodal, shall be thought and determined by your grace and by the most part of the said thirty-two persons not to stand with God's laws and the laws of your realm, the same to be abrogated and taken away by your grace and the clergy; and such of them as shall be seen by your grace, and by the most

part of the said thirty-two persons, to stand with God's laws and the laws of your realm, to stand in full strength and power, your grace's most royal assent and authority once impetrate and fully given to the same.

2. *The Restraint of Appeals, 1533*

The Restraint of Appeals of 1533, which forbade all appeals to Rome, thus following and exceeding the Act of Praemunire of 1353, is known as the legal principle of the Reformation under Henry VIII. Repealed by Mary and reinstated by Elizabeth, the ecclesiastical principle is embodied in the document which follows, the Act Forbidding Papal Dispensations and Payment of Peter's Pence, 1534. Gee and Hardy, *Documents Illustrative of English Church History.*

Whereas by divers sundry old authentic histories and chronicles, it is manifestly declared and expressed, that this realm of England is an empire, and so hath been accepted in the world, governed by one supreme head and king, having the dignity and royal estate of the imperial crown of the same, unto whom a body politic, compact of all sorts and degrees of people divided in terms and by names of spiritualty and temporalty, be bounden and ought to bear, next to God, a natural and humble obedience: he being also institute and furnished, by the goodness and sufferance of Almighty God, with plenary, whole, and entire power, pre-eminence, authority, prerogative and jurisdiction, to render and yield justice, and final determination to all manner of folk, residents, or subjects within this his realm, in all causes, matters, debates, and contentions, happening to occur, insurge, or begin within the limits thereof, without restraint, or provocation to any foreign princes or potentates of the world; the body spiritual whereof having power, when any cause of the law divine happened to come in question, or of spiritual learning, then it was declared, interpreted, and showed by that part of the said body politic, called the spiritualty, now being usually called the English Church, which always hath been reputed, and also found of that sort, that both for knowledge, integrity, and sufficiency of number, it hath been always thought, and is also at this hour, sufficient and meet of itself, without the intermeddling of any exterior person or persons, to declare and determine all such doubts, and to administer all such offices and duties, as to their rooms spiritual doth appertain; for the due administration whereof, and to keep them from corruption and sinister affection, the king's most noble progenitors, and the antecessors of the nobles of this realm, have sufficiently endowed the said Church, both with honour and possessions; and the laws temporal, for trial of property of lands and goods, and for the conservation of the people of this realm in unity and peace, without ravin or spoil, was and yet is administered, adjudged, and executed by sundry judges and ministers of the other part of the said body politic, called the temporalty; and both their authorities and jurisdictions do conjoin together in the due administration of justice, the one to help the other:

And whereas the king, his most noble progenitors, and the Nobility and Commons of this said realm, at divers and sundry Parliaments, as well in the time of King Edward I, Edward III, Richard II, Henry IV, and other noble kings of this realm, made sundry ordinances, laws, statutes, and provisions for the entire and sure conservation of the prerogatives, liberties, and pre-eminences of the said imperial crown of this realm, and of the jurisdiction spiritual and temporal of the same, to keep it from the annoyance as well of the see of Rome, as from the authority of other foreign potentates, attempting the diminution or violation thereof, as often, and from time to time, as any such annoyance or attempt might be known or espied:

And notwithstanding the said good statutes and ordinances made in the time of the king's most noble progenitors . . . divers and sundry inconveniences and dangers, not provided for plainly by the said former acts, statutes, and ordinances, have arisen and sprung by reason of appeals sued out of this realm to the see of Rome, in causes testamentary, causes of matrimony and divorces, right of tithes, oblations and obventions, not only to the great inquietation, vexation, trouble, cost and charges of the king's highness, and many of his subjects and residents in this his realm, but also to the great delay and let to the true and speedy determination of the said causes, for so much as the parties appealing to the said Court of Rome most commonly do the same for the delay of justice:

And forasmuch as the great distance of way is so far out of this realm, so that the necessary proofs, nor the true knowledge of the cause, can neither there be so well known, nor the witnesses there so well examined, as within this realm, so that the parties grieved by means of the said appeals be most times without remedy:

In consideration whereof the king's highness, his nobles and Commons, considering the great enormities, dangers, long delays and hurts, that as well to his highness, as to his said nobles, subjects, Commons, and residents of this his realm, in the said causes testamentary, causes of matrimony and divorces, tithes, oblations and obventions, do daily ensue, does therefore by his royal assent, and by the assent of the lords spiritual and temporal, and the Commons, in this present Parliament assembled, and by authority of the same, enact, establish, and ordain, that all causes testamentary, causes of matrimony and divorces, rights of tithes, oblations and obventions (the knowledge whereof by the goodness of princes of this realm, and by the laws and customs of the same, appertaineth to the spiritual jurisdiction of this realm) already commenced, moved, depending, being, happening, or hereafter coming in contention, debate, or question within this realm, or within any the king's dominions, or marches of the same, or elsewhere, whether they concern the king our sovereign lord, his heirs and successors, or any other subjects or residents within the same, of what degree soever they be, shall be from henceforth heard, examined, discussed, clearly, finally, and definitively adjudged and determined within the king's jurisdiction and authority, and not elsewhere, in such courts spiritual and temporal of the same, as the natures, conditions, and qualities of the causes and matters aforesaid in contention, or hereafter happening in contention, shall require, without having any respect to any custom, use, or sufferance, in hindrance, let, or prejudice of the same, or to any other thing used or suffered to the contrary thereof by any other manner of person or persons in any manner of wise; any foreign inhibitions, appeals, sentences, summons, citations, suspensions, interdictions, excommunications, restraints, judgments, or any other process or impediments, of what natures, names, qualities, or conditions soever they be, from the see of Rome, or any other foreign courts or potentates of the world, or from and out of this realm, or any other the king's dominions, or marches of the same, to the see of Rome, or to any other foreign courts or potentates, to the let or impediment thereof in any wise notwithstanding. . . .

3. Act Forbidding Papal Dispensations and the Payment of Peter's Pence, 1534

Most humbly beseeching your most royal majesty, your obedient and faithful subjects, the Commons of this your present Parliament assembled, by your most dread commandment, that where your subjects of this your realm, and of other countries and dominions, being under your obeisance, by many years past have been, and yet be greatly decayed and impoverished, by such intolerable exactions of great sums of money as have been claimed and taken, and yet continually be claimed to be taken out of this your realm, and other your said countries and dominions, by the Bishop of Rome, called the pope, and

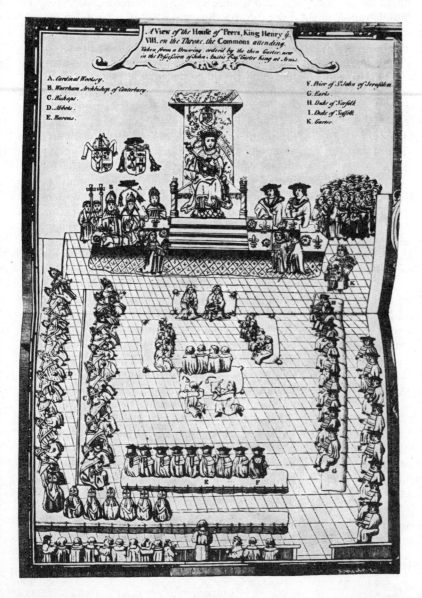

IV-5. King Henry VIII and His Parliament. *A contemporary drawing.*

the see of Rome, as well in pensions, censes, Peter-pence, procurations, fruits, suits for provisions, and expeditions of bulls for archbishoprics and bishoprics, and for delegacies, and rescripts in causes of contentions and appeals, jurisdictions legatine, and also for dispensations, licences, faculties, grants, relaxations, writs called *perinde valere*, rehabilitations, abolitions, and other infinite sorts of bulls, briefs, and instruments of sundry natures, names, and kinds, in great numbers heretofore practiced and obtained otherwise than by the laws, laudable uses, and customs of this realm should be permitted, the specialties whereof be over long, large in number, and tedious here particularly to be inserted; wherein the Bishop of Rome aforesaid has not been only to be blamed for his usurpation in the premises, but also for his abusing and beguiling your subjects, pretending and persuading to them that he has full power to dispense with all human laws, uses, and customs of all realms, in all causes which be called spiritual, which matter has been usurped and practised by him and his predecessors by many years, in great derogation of your imperial crown and authority royal, contrary to right and conscience:

For where this your grace's realm recognizing no superior under God, but only your grace, has been and is free from subjection to any man's laws, but only to such as have been devised, made, and ordained within this realm, for the wealth of the same, or to such other as, by sufferance of your grace and your progenitors, the people of this your realm have taken at their free liberty, by their own consent to be used amongst them, and have bound themselves by long use and custom to the observance of the same, not as to the observance of the laws of any foreign prince, potentate, or prelate, but as to the accustomed and ancient laws of this realm, originally established as laws of the same, by the said sufferance, consents, and custom, and none otherwise:

It stands therefore with natural equity and good reason, that in all and every such laws human made within this realm, or induced into this realm by the said sufferance, consents, and custom, your royal majesty, and your lords spiritual and temporal, and Commons, representing the whole state of your realm, in this your most High Court of Parliament, have full power and authority, not only to dispense, but also to authorize some elect person or persons to dispense with those, and all other human laws of this your realm, and with every one of them, as the quality of the persons and matter shall require; and also the said laws, and every of them, to abrogate, annul, amplify, or diminish, as it shall be seen unto your majesty, and the nobles and Commons of your realm present in your Parliament, meet and convenient for the wealth of your realm, as by divers good and wholesome Acts of Parliaments, made and established as well in your time, as in the time of your most noble progenitors, it may plainly and evidently appear:

And because that it is now in these days present seen, that the state, dignity, superiority, reputation, and authority of the said imperial crown of this realm, by the long sufferance of the said unreasonable and uncharitable usurpations and exactions practised in the times of your most noble progenitors, is much and sore decayed and diminished, and the people of this realm thereby impoverished, and so or worse be like to continue, if remedy be not therefor shortly provided:

It may therefore please your most noble majesty, for the honour of Almighty God, and for the tender love, zeal, and affection that ye bear, and always have borne to the wealth of this your realm and subjects of the same, forasmuch as your majesty is supreme head of the Church of England, as the prelates and clergy of your realm, representing the said Church, in their synods and convocations have recognized, in whom consisteth full power and authority, upon all such laws as have been made and used within this realm, to ordain and enact, by the assent of your lords spiritual and temporal, and the Commons in this your present Parliament assembled, and by authority of the same, that no person or persons of this your realm, or of any other your dominions, shall from henceforth pay any pensions, censes, portions,

177

Peter-pence or any other impositions, to the use of the said bishop, or the see of Rome, like as heretofore they have used, by usurpation of the said Bishop of Rome and his predecessors, and sufferance of your highness, and your most noble progenitors, to do; but that all such pensions, censes, portions and Peter-pence, which the said Bishop of Rome, otherwise called the pope, has heretofore taken and perceived, or caused to be taken and perceived to his use, and his chambers which he calls apostolic, by usurpation and sufferance, as is abovesaid, within this your realm, or any other your dominions, shall from henceforth clearly surcease, and never more be levied, taken, perceived, nor paid to any person or persons in any manner of wise; any constitution, use, prescription, or custom to the contrary thereof notwithstanding.

And be it further enacted by the authority aforesaid, that neither your highness, your heirs nor successors, kings of this realm, nor any your subjects of this realm, nor of any other your dominions, shall from henceforth sue to the said Bishop of Rome, called the pope, or to the see of Rome, or to any person or persons having or pretending any authority by the same, for licences, dispensations, compositions, faculties, grants, rescripts, delegacies, or any other instruments or writings, of what kind, name, nature, or quality soever they be of, for any cause or matter, for the which any licence, dispensation, composition, faculty, grant, rescript, delegacy, instrument, or other writing, heretofore has been used and accustomed to be had and obtained at the see of Rome, or by authority thereof, or of any prelate of this realm; nor for any manner of other licences, dispensations, compositions, faculties, grants, rescripts, delegacies, or any other instruments or writings that in causes of necessity may lawfully be granted without offending of the Holy Scriptures and laws of God:

But that from henceforth every such licence, dispensation, composition, faculty, grant, rescript, delegacy, instrument, and other writing afore named and mentioned, necessary for your highness, your heirs or successors, and your and their people and subjects, upon the due examinations of the causes and qualities of the persons procuring such dispensations, licences, compositions, faculties, grants, rescripts, delegacies, instruments, or other writings, shall be granted, had, and obtained, from time to time, within this your realm, and other your dominions, and not elsewhere, in manner and form following, and none otherwise; that is to say:

The Archbishop of Canterbury for the time being, and his successors, shall have power and authority, from time to time, by their discretions, to give, grant, and dispose, by an instrument under the seal of the said archbishop, unto your majesty, and to your heirs and successors, kings of this realm, as well all manner such licences, dispensations, compositions, faculties, grants, rescripts, delegacies, instruments, and all other writings, for causes not being contrary or repugnant to the Holy Scriptures and laws of God, as heretofore has been used and accustomed to be had and obtained by your highness, or any your most noble progenitors, or any of your or their subjects, at the see of Rome, or any person or persons by authority of the same; and all other licences, dispensations, faculties, compositions, grants, rescripts, delegacies, instruments, and other writings, in, for, and upon all such causes and matters as shall be convenient and necessary to be had, for the honour and surety of your highness, your heirs and successors, and the wealth and profit of this your realm; so that the said archbishop, or any of his successors, in no manner wise shall grant any dispensation, licence, rescript, or any other writing afore rehearsed, for any cause or matter repugnant to the law of Almighty God. . . .

4. The Supremacy Act, 1534

The Supremacy Act of November, 1534, made Henry VIII the supreme head of the Anglican Church, without any saving clauses. Gee and Hardy, *Documents Illustrative of English Church History.*

Albeit the king's majesty justly and rightfully is and ought to be the supreme head of the Church of England, and so is recognized by the clergy of this realm in their Convocations, yet nevertheless for corroboration and confirmation thereof, and for increase of virtue in Christ's religion within this realm of England, and to repress and extirp all errors, heresies, and other enormities and abuses heretofore used in the same; be it enacted by authority of this present Parliament, that the king our sovereign lord, his heirs and successors, kings of this realm, shall be taken, accepted, and reputed the only supreme head in earth of the Church of England called *Anglicana Ecclesia;* and shall have and enjoy, annexed and united to the imperial crown of this realm, as well the title and style thereof, as all honors, dignities, preeminences, jurisdictions, privileges, authorities, immunities, profits, and commodities to the said dignity of supreme head of the same Church belonging and appertaining; and that our said sovereign lord, his heirs and successors, kings of this realm, shall have full power and authority from time to time to visit, repress, redress, reform, order, correct, restrain, and amend all such errors, heresies, abuses, offences, contempts, and enormities, whatsoever they be, which by any manner spiritual authority or jurisdiction ought or may lawfully be reformed, repressed, ordered, redressed, corrected, restrained, or amended, most to the pleasure of Almighty God, the increase of virtue in Christ's religion, and for the conservation of the peace, unity, and tranquillity of this realm; any usage, custom, foreign law, foreign authority, prescription, or any other thing or things to the contrary hereof notwithstanding.

5. The Six Articles Act, 1539

The "Whip with Six Strings," imposed by Henry VIII, brought widespread persecution to evangelical sympathizers and also marked a return to Catholicism. Gee and Hardy, *Documents Illustrative of English Church History.*

First, that in the most blessed Sacrament of the altar, by the strength and efficacy of Christ's mighty word (it being spoken by the priest), is present really, under the form of bread and wine, the natural body and blood of our Saviour Jesus Christ, conceived of the Virgin Mary; and that after the consecration

IV-6. **King Henry VIII.** *Portrait by Holbein. Reproduced by the gracious permission of Her Majesty Queen Elizabeth II.*

there remaineth no substance of bread or wine, nor any other substance, but the substance of Christ, God and man.

Secondly, that communion in both kinds is not necessary *ad salutem,* by the law of God, to all persons; and that it is to be believed, and not doubted of, but that in the flesh, under the form of bread, is the very blood; and with the blood, under the form of wine, is the very flesh; as well apart, as though they were both together.

Thirdly, that priests after the order of priesthood received, as afore, may not marry, by the law of God.

Fourthly, that vows of chastity or widowhood, by man or woman made to God advisedly, ought to be observed by the law of God; and that it exempts them from other liberties of Christian people, which without that they might enjoy.

Fifthly, that it is meet and necessary that private masses be continued and admitted in this the king's English Church and congregation, as whereby good Christian people, ordering themselves accordingly, do receive both godly and goodly consolations and benefits; and it is agreeable also to God's law.

Sixthly, that auricular confession is expedient and necessary to be retained and continued, used and frequented in the Church of God.

6. *Bishop Hooper, 1551, A Puritan View*

John Hooper's *Godly Confession and Protestation of Faith,* 1550, is one of the earliest expressions of Puritan views. He asserts the usual beliefs according to the creeds, and elaborates on the necessity of obeying the magistrate even though he be tyrannical. He stresses Scripture as his standard and declares that he will witness to God's Word even though he forfeit his life. It is a remarkable document. However, the instructions that he sent to the clergymen in his bishopric are still more revealing of the Puritan view. The following is from Hooper's *Visitation Book,* 1551. *Later Writings of Bishop Hooper* (Cambridge: Parker Society, 1852). The *Godly Confession* may be found in the same volume.

To the glory of God the Father, the Son, and the Holy Ghost. Forasmuch as of all charges and vocations the charge of such as be appointed to the ministry and function of the church is the greatest, it is to be provided and foreseen that such as be called and appointed to such vocation and office be such as can satisfy the said office; which may be done, as St. Paul saith, two manner of ways: the one, if they be of sound doctrine, apt to teach, and to exhort after knowledge, and able to withstand and confute the evil-sayers: the other, if their life and manners be unculpable, and cannot justly be blamed; which consisteth in this: if the minister be sober, modest, keeping hospitality, honest, religious, chaste, not dissolute, angry, nor given to much wine, no fighter, no covetous man, such as governeth well his own house, and giveth an example of virtue and honesty unto others. For as the godly life and conversation of the parson or doctor doth no less avail in the reformation of other than the doctrine itself, so likewise they which hath no respect nor regard what evil, mischievous, and devilish example of life outwardly appeareth to be in them, cannot have in them any just authority to reform or correct the faults of other. For by what just means canst thou reprehend and blame any other in that fault wherein thou thyself art to be blamed? Or by what occasion canst thou praise charity, or desire to have the same in another man, when as thou thyself, despising both God and holy matrimony, dost other nourish and keep a whore or concubine at home in thy house, or else dost defile other men's beds? Neither is he anything less to be ashamed, that will persuade other to live in sobriety, he himself being drunk. Wherefore what authority shall he obtain or get unto himself and his ministry, which is daily seen and marked of his to be a common haunter of alehouses and taverns, of whores, cards, dice, and such like? Hereby shall you perceive and know how that the old priests and pastors of Christ's church did by their truth and gravity subjugate and bring under the hard-necked and stiff stubborn ethnics, and caused them to have the same in fear; insomuch that the wicked emperor Julian caused the priests of the pagans to order their lives according to the example of the other. But look, what authority and reverence that old severity and graveness of the pastors and priests did bring unto them at that time, even as much shame and contempt (or else a great deal more, as I fear,) doth the lechery, covetousness, ambition, simony, and such other corrupt means, bring unto the priests, pastors, and ministers that be now in our days, of all men. Wherefore I (being not forgetful of my office and duty towards God, my prince, and you) do desire and beseech all you, for Christ's sake, who commanded that your light should so shine before men that they, seeing and perceiving the same, might glorify the Father which is in heaven, give your diligence together with me, well-beloved brethren, so that the dignity and majesty of the order of priests and pastors, being fallen in decay, may not only be restored again, but that, first and principally, the true and pure worship of God may be restored; and that so many souls, being committed to my faith and

IV-7. The Burning of Hooper at Gloucester. *An old print.*

yours, may, by our wholesome doctrine and cleanness of conversation, be moved unto the true study of perfect charity, and called back from all error and ignorance, and finally to be reduced and brought unto the high Bishop and Pastor of souls, Jesus Christ. And to the intent ye may the more easily perform the same, I have (according to the talent and gift given me of the Lord) collected and gathered out of God's holy word a few articles, which I trust shall much profit and do ye good. And if that anything shall be now wanting or lacking, I trust (by the help of your prayers and good counsel) they shall be shortly hereafter performed. Let every one of you, therefore, take good heed to approve yourselves faithful and wise ministers of Christ; so that when I shall come to visit the parishioners committed to my cure and faith from God and the king's majesty, ye be able not only to make answer unto me in that behalf, but also unto our Lord Jesus Christ, judge both of the quick and the dead, and a

very strait revenger of his church. Thus fare you well unto the day of my coming unto you.

John Hooper, Bishop of Gloucester, all deans, parsons, prebends, vicars, curates, and other ecclesiastical ministers within the diocese of Gloucester, for unity and agreement in God's word, and the ceremonies agreeing with God's Word.

I.   First, that none of the abovenamed do teach or preach any manner of thing to be necessary for the salvation of man other than that which is contained in the book of God's holy word, called the old and new testament; and that they beware to establish and confirm any manner of doctrine concerning the old superstitious and papistical doctrine, which cannot be duly and justly approved by the authority of God's holy word.

III.   That they and every of them do diligently teach and preach, as is aforesaid, all the doctrine contained in the creed or

181

articles of our faith, commonly called and known by the name and names of the creed of the apostles, Nicen, and Athanasius; for that as those creeds are in such wise taken out of the word of God, that [they] do contain in them the sum of all christian doctrine.

IV. That they and every of them do diligently teach and preach that the church of God is the congregation of the faithful, wherein the word of God is truly preached, and the sacraments justly ministered according to the institution of Christ, and his doctrine taught unto us by his holy word: and that the church of God is not by God's word taken for the multitude or company of men, as of bishops, priests, and such other, but that it is the company of all men hearing God's word, and obeying unto the same; lest that any man should be seduced, believing himself to be bound unto any ordinary succession of bishops and priests, but only unto the word of God, and to the right use of his sacraments.

V. Albeit that the true church of Christ cannot err from the faith, for that it is the only pillar of verity; yet nevertheless, forasmuch as no man is free from sin and lies, there is nor can be any church known and apparent unto us (be it never so perfect or holy) but it may err.

VI. That the doctrine of the Anabaptists, denying the christening of infants, and affirming the rebaptizing and christening again of those which were before baptized in their infancy, as also affirming all manner of goods and chattel to be in common (saving such as are contained in the law of charity), and that all authority of magistrates should be removed from the church of God, and such other like doctrines, and their sects, are very pernicious and damnable.

VII. That they and every of them do diligently teach and preach the justification of man to come only by the faith of Jesus Christ, and not by the merit of any man's good works; albeit that good works do necessarily follow justification, the which before justification are of no value or estimation before God.

IX. That the doctrine of the schoolmen of purgatory, pardons, prayers for them that are departed out of this world, the veneration, invocation, and worshipping of saints or images, is contrary and injurious to the honour of Christ our only Mediator and Redeemer, and also against the doctrine of the first and second commandment of God, contained in the first table.

X. That in the sacrament of the body and blood of the Lord there is no transubstantiation of the bread and wine into the body and blood of Christ, or any manner of corporal or local presence of Christ in, under, or with the bread and wine, but spiritually by faith, believing the Son of God Jesus Christ to be made man, and that by his death he might satisfy for the sins of the world....

XI. That they which unworthily do come to baptism, or unto the supper of the Lord, do not receive the virtue and true effect of the same sacraments although they receive the external signs and elements of the sacraments.

XIII. That no man, although he be regenerated, but sin doth remain in him as long as he liveth; albeit in some sin doth not reign or bear any rule. Wherefore if he sin, being admonished by the Spirit of God, by his word, or some other way, he repenteth his sins, and so by faith shall obtain the remission thereof: and whereas we speak of a man, we intend not to make any difference of ages; for a child is also a man, which being conceived and born in sin, by reason thereof he is subject to the wrath of God and everlasting damnation, if his sins be not forgiven.

XIV. That, according to the doctrine of St. Paul, it is not lawful for any man to sing or say in the church in any kind of tongue other than such as the people shall be able to understand; and that it is not sufficient to speak or read in the English, or mother-tongue, but that there be due and distinct pronunciation, whereby all the people may have true knowledge.

XV. That the oblation of Christ once made on the cross is a full satisfaction for all manner of sins, be they original, actual, present, past, or to come, to all men believing in the same sacrifice; and that there is not other means, propitiation, redemption, satisfaction, or sacrifice for sin.

XVI. That it is not necessary that the ceremonies of the church should be one everywhere, and at all times used and frequented; but that they may be lawfully changed and altered, according to the diversity of time and manner of countries, so that there be nothing done or made contrary to the word of God. . . .

XVIII. Even as all vain and unadvised oaths are of Christ and his apostle St. James forbidden unto all christian men, even so it is lawful for all men, at the command of the magistrate or otherwise, in the cause of faith and charity to swear, so that (according to the mind of the prophet) it be done in judgment, justice, and verity.

XXV. That the church of God is not to be contemned for certain evil parsons annexed unto it. Although when their malice and ignorance is known, they should be put from their office; for they ought to be found blameless in all their lives and conversation, having good report and testimony of all men; and therefore to beware of all such things as may cause them to be had in contempt; as of riotous eating and drinking, of whoredom, adultery, unlawful games, dice, cards, and all other like; nor the time which they should of their bounden duty bestow in reading and studying of the holy scriptures, should be misspent in hunting, hawking, and such other vain pastimes, if they will be approved or allowed faithful ministers of Christ and his church.

XXVIII. That such doctrines doth plainly approve that the popish mass is a mere enemy against God's word and Christ's institution; and albeit it doth retain in it certain lessons of the holy scriptures, yet it is nothing better to be esteemed than the verses of the sorcerer or enchanter, that be nothing more to be esteemed [than] for certain holy words murmured and spoken in secret.

XXIX. Seeing that St. Paul doth plainly say that the forbidding of marriage is the doctrine of devils, therefore it is not to be judged that the marriage of priests, bishops, or any other ministers of the church, should be unlawful, but that the same is both holy, and agreeable with God's word.

XXXI. That the catechism be read and taught unto the children every Sunday and festival-day in the year, at one or two of the clock after dinner, and that they may be thereof duly examined one after another by order; and that all other elder people be commanded to be present at the same.

XXXIII. That a christian and brotherly admonition, correction, and punishment is lawful to be had by the word of God, and also excommunication against rebels and obstinate persons, which are not to be admitted unto any communion of the sacraments or prayers, before that they have openly reconciled themselves unto the church with public and open penance.

XXXV. That the bishop of Rome hath not (nor by God's word or of right ought to have) any manner of authority, power, or jurisdiction within this realm of England and Ireland, or any part of the same.

XXXVI. That every man ought to give place and obedience unto the civil magistrates (being lawfully authorised) in all things, so that they do command nothing that is contrary unto God and his law.

XXXVII. That it is lawful amongst christian men to exercise and use punishments and pains of death in certain offences; and also to bear weapon, and armies to go unto the wars withal, for the tuition and defense of his country, so that the same be done by the commandment of the king's majesty or by his lawful authority.

XL. That you do not read any such injunctions as extolleth and setteth forth the popish mass, candles, images, chantries, and such like.

XLI. That none of you do counterfeit the popish mass in blessing the Lord's board, washing your hands or fingers after the gospel, or receipt of the holy communion, shifting the book from one place unto another, laying down and licking of the chalice after the communion, blessing his eyes with the sudary thereof, or paten, or crossing his hands with the same, holding up his forefingers and thumbs joined together towards the temples of his head after the receiving of the sacrament, breathing on the bread or chalice, saying the "Agnus" before the communion, shewing the sacrament openly before the distribution of the same, or making any elevation thereof, ringing of the sacring-bell, or setting any light upon the Lord's board.

XLVI. That none, of you maintain the Six Articles, bead-rolls, images, relics, rubrics, primers, holy bread, palms, ashes, candles, sepulch, paschal, creeping to the cross, hallowing of the fire or altar, and other such like abuses and superstitions taken away by the king's grace's most godly proceedings.

XLVIII. That the churchwardens do not permit any buying, selling, gaming, outrageous noises, tumult, or any other idle occupying of youth, in the church, church-porch, or church-yard, during the time of common prayer, sermon or reading of the homily.

7. Elizabeth's Supremacy Act, 1559

The only limitation on Elizabeth's supreme authority was the provision that heresy be determined by Scripture, the first four councils, other councils which acted against heresy on the basis of Scripture, or by Parliament, with the assent of the clergy in Convocation. Gee and Hardy, *Documents Illustrative of English Church History.*

[The oath required:]

I, *A. B.*, do utterly testify and declare in my conscience, that the queen's highness is the only supreme governor of this realm, and of all other her highness's dominions and countries, as well in all spiritual or ecclesiastical things or causes, as temporal, and that no foreign prince, person, prelate, state or potentate, has, or ought to have, any jurisdiction, power, superiority, pre-eminence, or authority ecclesiastical or spiritual, within this realm; and therefore I do utterly renounce and forsake all foreign jurisdictions, powers, superiorities, and authorities, and do promise that from henceforth I shall bear faith and true allegiance to the queen's highness, her heirs and lawful successors, and to my power shall assist and defend all jurisdictions, pre-eminences, privileges, and authorities granted or belonging to the queen's highness, her heirs and successors, or united and annexed to the imperial crown of this realm. So help me God, and by the contents of this book.

8. Elizabeth's Act of Uniformity, 1559

Note the stringency of the penalties in this act. Gee and Hardy, *Documents Illustrative of English Church History.*

Where at the death of our late sovereign lord King Edward VI there remained one uniform order of common service and prayer, and of the administration of sacraments, rites, and ceremonies in the Church of England, which was set forth in one book, intituled: The Book of Common Prayer, and Administration of Sacraments, and other rites and ceremonies in the Church of England; authorized by Act of Parliament holden in the sixth year of our said late sovereign lord King Edward VI, intituled: An Act for the uniformity of common prayer, and administration of the sacraments; the which was repealed and taken away by Act of Parliament in the first year of the reign of our late sovereign lady Queen Mary, to the great decay of the due honour of God, and discomfort to the professors of the truth of Christ's religion:

Be it therefore enacted by the authority of this present Parliament, that the said statute of repeal, and everything therein contained, only concerning the said book, and the service, administration of sacraments, rites, and ceremonies contained or appointed in or by the said book, shall be void and of none effect, from and after the feast of the Nativity of St. John Baptist next coming; and that the said book, with the order of service, and of the administration of sacraments, rites, and ceremonies, with the alterations and additions therein added and appointed by this statute, shall stand and be, from and after the said feast of the Nativity of St. John Baptist, in full force and effect, according to the tenor and effect of this statute; anything in the aforesaid statute of repeal to the contrary notwithstanding.

And further be it enacted by the queen's highness, with the assent of the Lords [*sic*] and Commons in this present Parliament assembled, and by authority of the same, that all and singular ministers in any cathedral or parish church, or other place within this realm of England, Wales, and the marches of the same, or other the queen's dominions, shall from and after the feast of the Nativity of St. John Baptist next coming be bounden to say and use the Matins, Evensong, celebration of the Lord's Supper and administration of each of the sacraments, and all their common and open prayer, in such order and form as is mentioned in the said book, so authorized by Parliament in the said fifth and sixth years of the reign of King Edward VI, with one alteration or addition of certain lessons to be used on every Sunday in the year, and the form of the Litany altered and corrected, and two sentences only added in the delivery of the sacrament to the communicants, and none other or otherwise.

And that if any manner of parson, vicar, or other whatsoever minister, that ought or should sing or say common prayer mentioned in the said book, or minister the sacraments, from and after the feast of the Nativity of St. John Baptist next coming, refuse to use the said common prayers, or to minister the sacraments in such cathedral or parish church, or other places as he should use to minister the same, in such order and form as they be mentioned and set forth in the said book, or shall wilfully or obstinately standing in the same, use any other rite, ceremony, order, form, or manner of celebrating of the Lord's Supper, openly or privily, or Matins, Evensong, administration of the sacraments, or other open prayers, than is mentioned and set forth in the said book (open prayer in and throughout this Act, is meant that prayer which is for other to come unto, or hear, either in common churches or private chapels or oratories, commonly called the service of the Church), or shall preach, declare, or speak anything in the derogation or depraving of the said book, or anything therein contained, or of any part thereof, and shall be thereof lawfully convicted, according to the laws of this realm, by verdict of twelve men, or by his own confession, or by the notorious evidence of the fact, shall lose and forfeit to the queen's highness, her heirs and successors, for his first offence, the profit of all his spiritual benefices or promotions coming or arising in one whole year next after his conviction; and also that the person so convicted shall for the same offence suffer

imprisonment by the space of six months, without bail or mainprize.

And if any such person once convicted of any offence concerning the premises, shall after his first conviction eftsoons offend, and be thereof, in form aforesaid, lawfully convicted, that then the same person shall for his second offence suffer imprisonment by the space of one whole year, and also shall therefor be deprived, *ipso facto*, of all his spiritual promotions; and that it shall be lawful to all patrons or donors of all and singular the same spiritual promotions, or of any of them, to present or collate to the same, as though the person and persons so offending were dead.

And that if any such person or persons, after he shall be twice convicted in form aforesaid, shall offend against any of the premises the third time, and shall be thereof, in form aforesaid, lawfully convicted, that then the person so offending and convicted the third time, shall be deprived, *ipso facto*, of all his spiritual promotions, and also shall suffer imprisonment during his life.

And if the person that shall offend, and be convicted in form aforesaid, concerning any of the premises, shall not be beneficed, nor have any spiritual promotion, that then the same person so offending and convicted shall for the first offence suffer imprisonment during one whole year next after his said conviction, without bail or mainprize. And if any such person, not having any spiritual promotion, after his first conviction shall eftsoons offend in anything concerning the premises, and shall be, in form aforesaid, thereof lawfully convicted, that then the same person shall for his second offence suffer imprisonment during his life....

9. John Foxe, 1563

Acts and Monuments of the Christian Martyrs, 1563, by John Foxe, was a compilation of legal and personal accounts of martyrs from the earliest days of Christianity to the time of Foxe. In his prefaces, which were almost as sensational as the stories themselves, Foxe called on the "papists" to behold the horror of their "slaughter," crimes committed not by the secular powers but by the church because men rejected the headship of the pope. "Reform yourselves, repent your murders, cease your persecutions.

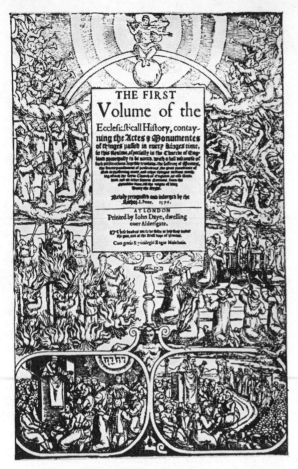

IV-8. Title Page of Foxe's *Book of Martyrs*, 1576 edition. *British Museum*.

strive not against the Lord," and receive the forgiveness of Christ. It was a sensational book, carefully and accurately compiled, that went through many editions. The selections given below concern ordinary people. One of the selections retains the old English. John Foxe, *Actes and Monuments*. Cf. S. R. Cattley edition (London: Seeley and Burnside, 1837-41).

PERSECUTION IN SUFFOLK: THREE MEN
BURNT AT BECCLES, MAY 21, 1556

After the death of these above rehearsed, were three men burnt at Beccles in Suffolk, in one fire, about the 21st of May, anno 1556, whose names are here specified: Thomas Spicer of Winston, labourer; John Denny, and Edmund Poole. This Thomas Spicer was a single man, of the age of nineteen years, and by vocation a labourer, dwelling in Winston in the county of Suffolk, and there

taken in his master's house in summer, about or anon after the rising of the sun (being in his bed) by James Ling and John Keretch of the same town, and William Davies of Debenham in the said county.

The occasion of his taking was, for that he would not go to their popish church to hear mass and receive their idol, at the commandment of sir John Tyrrel knight, of Gipping-hall in Suffolk, and certain other justices there, who sent both him and them to Eye dungeon in Suffolk, till at length they were all three together brought before Dunning, then chancellor of Norwich, and master Mings the registrar sitting at the town of Beccles, to be examined.

And there the said chancellor, persuading what he could to turn them from the truth, could by no means prevail of his purpose. Wherefore, minding in the end to give sentence on them, he burst out in tears, entreating them to remember themselves, and to turn again to the holy mother church, for that they were deceived and out of the truth, and that they should not wilfully cast away themselves, with such like words.

Now as he was thus labouring them, and seemed very loth to read the sentence (for they were the first that he condemned in that diocese), the registrar there sitting by, being weary belike of tarrying, or else perceiving the constant martyrs to be at a point, called upon the chancellor in haste to rid them out of the way, and to make an end. At the which words the chancellor read the condemnation over them with tears, and delivered them to the secular powers.

The Articles, Whereupon
They Were Condemned

The articles objected to these, and commonly to all others condemned in that diocese by Dr. Hopton, bishop of Norwich, and by Dunning his chancellor, were these:

First, It was articulate against them, that they believed not the pope of Rome to be supreme head immediately under Christ in earth of the universal catholic church.

2. Item, That they believed not holy bread and holy water, ashes, palms, and all other like ceremonies used in the church, to

be good and laudable for stirring up the people to devotion.

3. Item, That they believed not, after the words of consecration spoken by the priest, the very natural body of Christ, and no other substance of bread and wine, to be in the sacrament of the altar.

4. Item, That they believed it to be idolatry to worship Christ in the sacrament of the altar.

5. Item, That they took bread and wine in remembrance of Christ's passion.

6. Item, That they would not follow the cross in procession, nor be confessed to a priest.

7. Item, That they affirmed no mortal man to have in himself free will to do good or evil.

For this doctrine and articles, these three were condemned, and the next day following upon the same, they were all burnt together in the said town of Beccles.

THE TRIAL OF JULIANA LIVING, 1558

Examiner: Dr. Thomas Darbishire, London

DARBISHIRE: Ah, syrra! I see by your gown you be one of the Sisters.

JULIANA: I weare not my gowne for sisterhood, neither for nunnery, but to kepe me warme.

DARBISHIRE: Nunne? No, I dare say you be none. Is that man your husband?

JULIANA: Yea.

DARBISHIRE: He is a priest.

JULIANA: No, he sayth no masse.

DARBISHIRE: What then? He is a priest. How darest thou marry him?

Then he shewed me a roll of certaine names of citizens. To whom I answered, I knew none of them. Then said he: "You shal be made to know them."

Then sayd I: "Do no other but justice and righte. For the day wyl come that you shal answer for it."

DARBISHIRE: Why, woman! thinkest thou not that I have a soule?

JULIANA: Yes, I knowe you have a soule; but whether it bee to salvation or damnation, I cannot tell.

DARBISHIRE: Ho, Cluny! have her to the Lollards' Tower!

And so he tooke me, and caried me to his house, where was one Dale, a promoter, which saide to me: "Alas, good woman! wherefore be you here?"

"What is that to you?" said I.

"You be not ashamed," quoth Dale, "to tel wherefore you came hyther?"

"No," quoth I, "that I am not. For it is for Christes testament."

"Christes testament?" quoth he. "It is the Divel's testament."

"Oh Lord!" quoth I, "God forbyd that any man should speake any such woorde!"

"Wel, wel," quoth he, "you shalbe ordered wel inough. You care not for burning," quoth he. "By God's bloud! there must be some other meanes founde for you."

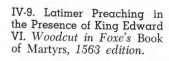

IV-9. Latimer Preaching in the Presence of King Edward VI. *Woodcut in Foxe's* Book of Martyrs, *1563 edition.*

IV-10. Ridley and Latimer Being Burned at the Stake, with Smith Preaching.
Foxe's Book of Martyrs.

"What!" quoth I, "wyl you find any worse than you have found?"

"Wel," quoth he, "you hope and you hope; but your hope shall be a slope. For though the Quene faile, she that you hope for shal never come at it. For there is my Lord Cardinal's Grace, and manye more, betwene her and it."

"Then," quoth I, "my hope is in none but in God."

Then saide Cluny, "Come wyth me."

And so went I to the Lollardes' Tower.

And on the neste daye Darbishire sent for me again, and enquired of those citizens that he enquired of me before. I aunswered, I knewe them not.

"Where were you," quoth he, "at the Communion the Sonday fortenenight before?"

And I said, "In no place."

Then the Constable of St. Bride's being there made sute to him for me. And Darbishire demaunded of him if he would be bound for me. And he answered, "Yea." And so he was bounde for my appearaunce betwyxt that and Christmas.

188

Then Darbishire said: "You be Constable, and should geve her good counsell."

"So do I," quoth hee. "For I byd her go to masse, and to say as you say. For, by the masse! if you saye the crowe is white, I wyll say so too."

[The death of Queen Mary, November 17, saved Juliana from the stake.]

10. The Papal Bull Against Elizabeth, 1570

The pope called upon France and Spain to carry out this Bull. "From that moment until the defeat of the Spanish Armada in 1588 there was war, more or less overt, between England and the Counter Reformation. On the one side was the unconquerable patriotism of Englishmen, on the other the combined forces of political ambition and religious enthusiasm," H. O. Wakeman, *History of the Church of England* (London: Rivingtons, 1899). From Henry Bettenson, *Documents of the Christian Church* (New York: Oxford University Press, 1947).

He that reigns in the highest, to whom has been given all power in heaven and earth, entrusted the government of the one Holy Catholic and Apostolic Church (outside which there is no salvation) to one man alone on the earth, namely to Peter, the chief of the Apostles, and to Peter's successor, the Roman pontiff, in fullness of power [*potestatis plenitudo*]. This one man he set up as chief over all nations and all kingdoms, to pluck up, destroy, scatter, dispose, plant and build....

3. ...resting then upon the authority of him who has willed to place us (albeit unequal to such a burden) in this supreme throne of justice, we declare the aforesaid Elizabeth a heretic and an abettor of heretics, and those that cleave to her in the aforesaid matters to have incurred the sentence of anathema, and to be cut off from the unity of Christ's body.

4. Moreover we declare her to be deprived of her pretended right to the aforesaid realm, and from all dominion, dignity and privilege whatsoever.

5. And the nobles, subjects and peoples of the said realm, and all others who have taken an oath of any kind to her we declare to be absolved forever from such oath and from all dues of dominion, fidelity, and obedience, as by the authority of these presents we do absolve them; and we deprive the said Elizabeth of her pretended right to the realm and all other things aforesaid: and we enjoin and forbid all and several the nobles, etc.... that they presume not to obey her and her admonitions, commands, and laws. All who disobey our command we involve in the same sentence of anathema.

11. The Second Scottish Confession, or The National Covenant, 1580

This Confession was an appendix to the twenty-five Calvinistic articles of the Scottish Confession of 1560. Its strongly antipapal tone marks the advance of Calvinistic views, so ably disseminated by John Knox in Scotland. This was accepted by the king, council, and court in 1580, by the nation in 1581, and again in 1590 and 1638. From Philip Schaff, *Creeds of Christendom*, III (New York: Harper & Row, Publishers, 1877). Reproduced in the old English.

We all, and every ane of us underwritten, protest, That after lang and dew examination of our awne consciences in matters of trew and false religion, we ar now throughlie resovit in the trewth be the Word and spreit

IOANNES CNOXVS, SCOTVS.
Scottorum primum te Ecclesia, CNOXe, decentem
Audyt, auspicys es tque reducta tuis.
Nam te cales tis pietas super omnia traxit.
Atque reformata Relligionis amor.   *Cum priuill.*

IV-11. John Knox of Scotland. *Copper engraving by Hendrix Hondias, Jr. (1580–1644).*

of God: and theirfoir we believe with our heartis, confesse with our mouthis, subscrive with our handis, and constantlie affirme before God and the haill warld, That this only is the trew Christian Faith and Religion, pleasing God, and bringing salvation to man, quhilk is now, be the mercie of God, revealed to the warld be the preaching of the blessed Evangell; and is received, believed, and defendit by mony and sundrie notabil kirkis and realmes, but chiefly be the Kirke of *Scotland*, the Kings Majestie and three Estatis of this Realme, as Godis eternall trewth, and only ground of our salvation; as mair particularlie is expressed in the Confession of our Faith, stablished, and publickly confirmed by sundrie Actis of Parliaments, and now of a lang tyme hath been openlie professed by the Kings Majesty, and haill body of this Realme both in brugh and land. To the quhilk Confession and forme of Religion we willingly agree in our consciences in all pointis, as unto Godis undouted trewth and veritie, groundit only upon his written word.

And theirfoir we abhorre and detest all contrare Religion and Doctrine; but chiefly all kynde of *Papistrie* in generale and particular headis, even as they ar now damned and confuted by the word of God and kirk of *Scotland*. But in special, we detest and refuse the usurped authoritie of that *Romane* Antichrist upon the scriptures of God, upon the Kirk, the civill Magistrate, and consciences of men: All his tyranous lawes made upon indifferent thingis againis our Christian libertie: His erroneous doctrine againis the sufficiencie of the written word, the perfection of the law, the office of *Christ*, and his blessed Evangell: His corrupted doctrine concerning originall sinne, our natural inhabilitie and rebellion to Godis Law, our justification by faith onlie, our unperfect sanctification and obedience to the law; the nature, number, and use of the holy sacraments: His fyve bastard sacraments; with all his ritis, ceremonies, and false doctrine, added to the ministration of the trew sacraments without the Word of God: His cruell judgement againis infants departing without the sacrament: His absolute necessitie of baptisme: His blasphemous opinion of transubstantiation, or reall presence of *Christis* body in the elements, and receiving of the same by the wicked, or bodies of men: His dispensations with solemnit aithis, perjuries, and degrees of marriage forbidden in the Word: His crueltie againis the innocent divorcit: His divilish messe: His blasphemous priesthead: His prophane sacrifice for the sinnis of the deade and the quicke: His canonization of men, calling upon angelis or sanctis depairted; worshipping of imagerie, reliques, and crocis; dedicating of kirkis, altares, dayes; vowes to creatures: His purgatory, prayers for the dead; praying or speaking in a strange language: His processions and blasphemous letany: His multitude of advocatis or mediatours with his manifold orders, and auricular confessions: His despered and uncertain Repentance: His general and doutsum Faith: His Satisfactionis of men for their sinnis: His justification by warkis, *opus operatum*, warkis of supererogation, merites, pardons, peregrinations, and stations: His holie water, baptising of bellis, conjuring of spreits, crocing, saining, anointing, conjuring, hallouing of Godis gude creatures, with the superstitious opinion joyned therewith: His warldlie monarchie and wicked hierarchie: His three solemnet vowes, with all his shavellings of sundrie sortis: His erroneous and bloodie Decreets made at *Trente*, with all the Subscryvars and approvers of that cruell and bloodie Band conjured againis the Kirk of God. And finallie, We detest all his vain allegories, ritis, signes, and traditions brought in the Kirk, without or againis the Word of God and doctrine of this trew reformed Kirk; to the quhilk we joyn our selves willinglie in Doctrine, Faith, Religion, Discipline, and use of the holy sacraments, as livelie members of the same, in *Christ* our head: Promising and swearing be the Great Name of the LORD Our God, That we sall contenow in the obedience of the Doctrine and Discipline of this Kirk, and sall defend the same according to our vocation and power, all the dayes of our lyves; under the pains conteined in the law, and danger baith of bodie and saul in the day of Godis fearfull Judgment....

12. *Reformation Without Tarrying for Any, by Robert Browne*

Robert Browne's "Reformation without Tarying for Anie" was first published at Middelburgh, Holland, in 1582, during his two-year exile there. Two other pamphlets were also published, "A Booke which Sheweth the Life and Manners of all True Christians" and "A Treatise upon the 23. of Matthewe." The sheets were sent to England and there bound and circulated. They drew a proclamation from the queen, and two men were hanged for dispersing them. Robert Browne was among the very first to set forth the principle of Congregationalism or Independency, namely, the relation of the magistrate to the church: so long as men properly conduct themselves and show respect for other men and their rights, the magistrate has nothing to do with their religion. The church he defined as a company of believers in a covenant with God to live under the government of God and Christ and to keep his laws in one holy communion. Browne did not advocate a separate clerical order. Ministers were simply brethren like the others in the congregation. Many of his ideas were reflected among the Pilgrims in New England. Some words in the following selections have been modernized in spelling. Robert Browne, *A Treatise of Reformation without Tarying for Anie.* Cf. T. G. Crippen edition (London: Congregational Union of England and Wales, 1903).

A Treatise of Reformation Without Tarrying for Any, and of the Wickedness of Those Preachers Which Will Not Reform till the Magistrate Command or Compel Them. Middelburgh, 1582.

Seeing in this book we show the state of Christians, and have labored also in good conscience to live as Christians, it is marvelled and often talked of among many, why we should be so reviled and troubled of many, and also leave our country. Forsooth (say the enemies) there is some hidden thing in them more than plainly appeareth: for they bear evil will to their Princess Queen Elizabeth and to their country, yea they forsake the church of God and condemn the same, and are condemned of all, and they also discredit and bring into contempt the preachers of the Gospel. To answer them, we say that they are the men which trouble Israel, and seek evil to the Prince, and not we. And that they forsake and condemn the Church and not we. . . . But for the magistrate, how far by their authority or without it, the Church must be builded and reformation made, and whether any open wickedness must be tolerated in the Church because of them, let this be our answer. For chiefly in this point they have wrought us great trouble, and dismayed many weaklings from embracing the truth. We say therefore, and often have taught, concerning our sovereign Queen Elizabeth, that neither the Pope nor other Popeling, is to have any authority either over her or over the Church of God, and that the Pope of Rome is Antichrist, whose kingdom ought utterly to be taken away. Again we say, that her authority is civil, and that power she hath as highest under God within her Dominions, and that over all persons and causes. By that she may put to death all that deserve it by Law, either of the Church or commonwealth, and none may resist her or the magistrates under her by force or wicked speeches, when they execute the laws. Seeing we grant and hold thus much, how do they

charge us as evil willers to the Queen? Surely, for that we hold all those preachers and teachers accursed, which will not do the duties of pastors and teachers till the magistrates do force them thereto. They say, the time is not yet come to build the Lord's House [Hag. 1], they must tarry for the magistrates and for parliaments to do it. They want the civil sword, forsooth, and the magistrates do hinder the Lord's building and kingdom and keep away his government. Are they not ashamed thus to slander the magistrate? They have run their own swords upon the wall and broken them and now would they snatch unto them the magistrates' sword. . . . Those bands and chains which is the spiritual power of the Church, they have broken from themselves and yet would they have magistrates bound with them, to begin discipline. They would make the magistrates more than gods and yet also worse than beasts. For they teach that a lawful pastor must give over his charge at their discharging and when they withhold the church government, it ought for to cease, though the church go to ruin thereby. Behold now, doth not the Lord's kingdom give place unto theirs? And do they not pull down the head Christ Jesus [Col. 1:18], to set up the hand of the magistrate? Yea and more than this, for they first proclaim the names and titles of wicked bishops and popish officers, and the Lord's name after: Seeing also the bishops must discharge the lawful preachers, and stop their mouths, though the Lord God have given them a charge for to speak, and not to keep silence. The Lord hath exalted Christ Jesus [Phil. 2] and given him a name above every name, that all things should bow and serve unto him, and yet have they exalted the power of wicked bishops above him. Behold a great and most wholesome river, and yet their puddle water is preferred before it. Except the magistrates will go into the tempest and rain and be weatherbeaten with the hail of God's wrath, they must keep under the roof of Christ's government. They must be under a pastoral charge; they must obey to the scepter of Christ, if they be Christians. How then should the pastor, which hath the oversight of the magistrate, if he be of his flock, be so overseen of the magistrate as to leave his flock, when the magistrate shall unjustly and wrongfully discharge him. Yet these preachers and teachers will not only do so, but even holding their charge and keeping with it, will not guide and reform it aright because the magistrates do forbid them forsooth. But they slander the magistrate and because they dare not charge them as forbidding them their duties, they have gotten this shift, that they do but tarry for the magistrate's authority, and then they will guide and reform as they ought. Behold, is not all this one thing, seeing they lift up the throne of the magistrates, to thrust out the kingdom of Christ? . . . Jerusalem (sayeth the Prophet) [Dan. 91] and the streets and wall thereof, shall be built even in a troublous time, and to tarry till it be built without troubles, is to look for a conquest without going to battle, and for an end and reward of our labors which would never take pains. My kingdom, sayeth Christ, is not of this world, and they would shift in both bishops and magistrates into his spiritual throne to make it of this world; yea to stay the church government on them is not only to shift but to thrust them before Christ. Yet under him in his spiritual kingdom are [I Cor. 12] first apostles, secondly prophets, thirdly teachers, etc. Also helpers and spiritual guides: But they put the magistrates first, which in a commonwealth indeed are first, and above the preachers, yet have they no ecclesiastical authority at all, but only as any other Christians, if so be they be Christians. . . . The Church is God's building and not theirs. They are but members thereof if they be Christians, and are not any way to stay the building, neither is it to tarry or wait upon them. But these wicked preachers eat up and spoil the Lord's harvest themselves, and then set open the gap, as though the magistrates broke in like wild boars and spoiled the harvest. They say, behold we have a Christian prince, and a mother in Israel: but can they be Christians, when they make them to refuse, or withstand the government of Christ in his Church, or will not be subject unto it? If they therefore refuse and withstand, how should they be tarried for? If they be with

them, there is no tarrying: and if they be against them, they are no Christians, and therefore also there can be no tarrying. . . .

He that will be saved must not tarry for this man or that: and he that puts his hand to the plow, and then looks back, is not fit for the kingdom of God [Luke 9]. Therefore woe unto you ye blind guides, which cast away all by tarrying for the magistrates. The Lord will remember this iniquity and visit this sin upon you. Ye will not have the kingdom of God, to go forward by his spirit, but by an army and strength forsooth [Zech. 4]: ye will not have it as leaven hidden in three pecks of meal, till it leaven all [Matt. 13], but at once ye will have all aloft, by civil power and authority: you are offended at the baseness and small beginnings, and because of the troubles in beginning reformation, you will do nothing. Therefore shall Christ be that rock of offense unto you, and ye shall stumble and fall, and shall be broken, and shall be snared, and shall be taken. You will be delivered from the yoke of Antichrist, to the which you do willingly give your necks by bow and by swords, and by battle, by horses and by horsemen [Hos. 2], that is, by civil power and pomp of magistrates: by their proclamations and parliaments: and the kingdom of God must come with observation [Luke 17], that men may say, Lo, the parliament or lo the bishops' decrees: but the kingdom of God should be within you. The inward obedience to the outward preaching and government of the Church, with newness of life, that is the Lord's kingdom. This ye despise. Therefore shall ye desire to see the kingdom of God, and shall not see it, and to enjoy one day of the Son of man, and ye shall not enjoy it. For ye set aloft man's authority above God's, and the preacher must hang on his sleeve for the discharge of his calling.

.   .   .   .   .

Whatsoever doth most edify, that must we choose, and avoid the contrary; and whatsoever is most expedient, that must be done, and so we must apply ourselves all unto all, that notwithstanding we hold our liberty. For if either magistrate or other would take that from us, we must not give place by yielding unto them, no, not for an hour [Gal. 2], and this liberty is the free use of our callings and gifts, as we see most agreeing to the word of God, and expedient for his glory. Therefore, the magistrate's commandment must not be a rule unto me of this and that duty, but as I see it agree with the word of God. So then it is an abuse of my gift and calling if I cease preaching for the magistrate, when it is my calling to preach, yea and woe unto me, if I preach not, for necessity is laid upon me, and if I do it unwillingly, yet the dispensation is committed unto me [I Cor. 9]. And this dispensation did not the magistrate give me, but God by consent and ratifying of the Church, and therefore as the magistrate gave it not, so can he not take it away. Indeed, if God take it away for my wickedness and evil desert, he may remove me from the Church and withhold me from preaching; but if God do it not, and his word doth approve me as most meet for that calling, I am to preach still, except I be shut up in prison, or otherwise with violence withheld from my charge. For the magistrate so using me cannot be a Christian, but forsaketh the Church; and how then should my office in the Church depend on him which is none of the Church? And the welfare of the Church must be more regarded and sought, than the welfare of whole kingdoms and countries, as it is written [Isa. 43]. . . .

They are afraid of the face of the magistrate and do flatter and curry favor with them, and they would have us also to do the like. But ye the Lord's faithful servants truss up your loins as Jeremiah [Jer. 1], which in your charges have greater authority than Jeremiah, as we proved before. Arise and speak unto them, all that I command you, sayeth the Lord. For I, behold I have made you as defended cities, and iron pillars and walls of brass, against the whole land, against the kings and against the princes, against the priests and against the people. For they shall fight against you, but they shall not prevail, for I am with you to deliver you even to the end of the world. Therefore, ye vanish in vanity, ye wicked preachers; for know ye not that they which have their full and sufficient

authority and calling are not to tarry for a further authorizing. . . .

If they be of their flocks, why should they tarry for them. Unless they will have the sheep to force the shepherd unto his duty. Indeed the magistrate may force him, but it is his shame to tarry till he be forced. Be ashamed therefore ye foolish shepherds, and lay not the burden on the magistrates, as though they should do that in building the Lord's kingdom, which the apostles and prophets could not do. . . .

.   .   .   .   .

Go to therefore, and the outward power and civil forcings, let us leave to the magistrates: to rule the commonwealth in all outward justice, belongeth to them: but let the church rule in spiritual wise, and not in worldly manner: by a lively law preached, and not by a civil law written: by holiness in inward and outward obedience, and not in straightness of the outward only. But these handsome prelates would have the mace and the scepter in their hands, and then having safety and assurance by a law on their sides, they would make a goodly reformation. . . .

13. Elizabeth's Act Against the Jesuits and Seminarists, 1585

Because of plots by the Jesuits against the life of Elizabeth, the Act Against the Jesuits was passed in 1585, expelling them from the kingdom and making the entry of any Jesuit into England an act of treason. During the rule of James I, proclamations in 1604, 1606, and 1625 expelled Roman Catholic priests for suspected subversive activity. Gee and Hardy, *Documents Illustrative of English Church History.*

Whereas divers persons called or professed Jesuits, seminary priests, and other priests, which have been, and from time to time are made in the parts beyond the seas, by or according to the order and rites of the Romish Church, have of late years come and been sent, and daily do come and are sent, into this realm of England and other the queen's majesty's dominions, of purpose (as has appeared, as well by sundry of their own examinations and confessions, as by divers other manifest means and proofs) not only to withdraw her highness's subjects from their due obedience to her majesty, but also to stir up and move sedition, rebellion, and open hostility within the same her highness's realms and dominions, to the great endangering of the safety of her most royal person, and to the utter ruin, desolation, and overthrow of the whole realm, if the same be not the sooner by some good means foreseen and prevented:

For reformation whereof be it ordained, established, and enacted by the queen's most excellent majesty, and the Lords spiritual and temporal, and the Commons, in this present Parliament assembled, and by the authority of the same Parliament, that all and every Jesuits, seminary priests, and other priests whatsoever made or ordained out of the realm of England or other her highness's dominions, or within any of her majesty's realms or dominions, by any authority, power, or jurisdiction derived, challenged, or pretended from the see of Rome, since the feast of the Nativity of St. John Baptist in the first year of her highness's reign, shall within forty days next after the end of this present session of Parliament depart out of this realm of England, and out of all other her highness's realms and dominions, if the wind, weather, and passage shall serve for the same, or else so soon after the end of the said forty days as the wind, weather, and passage shall so serve. . . .

[Entry of any Jesuit after the above stated time] shall for his offence be adjudged a traitor, and shall suffer, lose, and forfeit, as in case of high treason. . . .

[A Jesuit could stay in England by submitting to the sovereign's supremacy.]

14. Elizabeth's Act Against Puritans, 1593

Elizabeth's acts against the Puritans reached a climax in 1593. She would not tolerate protests and criticisms of the *via media* from the Puritans, Dissenters, Nonconformists, and Separatists. Gee and Hardy, *Documents Illustrative of English Church History.*

For the preventing and avoiding of such great inconveniences and perils as might happen and grow by the wicked and dangerous practices of seditious sectaries and disloyal persons; be it enacted by the Queen's most excellent majesty, and by the Lords spiritual and temporal, and the Commons, in this present Parliament assembled, and by the authority of the same, that if any person or persons above the age of sixteen years, which shall obstinately refuse to repair to some church, chapel, or usual place of common prayer, to hear divine service established by her majesty's laws and statutes in that behalf made, and shall forbear to do the same by the space of a month next after, without lawful cause, shall at any time after forty days next after the end of this session of Parliament, by printing, writing, or express words or speeches, advisedly and purposely practice or go about to move or persuade any of her majesty's subjects, or any other within her highness's realms or dominions, to deny, withstand, and impugn her majesty's power and authority in causes ecclesiastical, united, and annexed to the imperial crown of this realm; or to that end or purpose shall advisedly and maliciously move or persuade any other person whatsoever to forbear or abstain from coming to church to hear divine service, or to receive the communion according to her majesty's laws and statutes aforesaid, or to come to or be present at any unlawful assemblies, conventicles, or meetings, under colour or pretence of any exercise of religion, contrary to her majesty's said laws and statutes; or if any person or persons which shall obstinately refuse to repair to some church, chapel, or usual place of common prayer, and shall forbear by the space of a month to hear divine service, as is aforesaid, shall after the said forty days, either of him or themselves, or by the motion, persuasion, enticement, or allurement of any other, willingly join, or be present at, any such assemblies, conventicles, or meetings, under colour or pretence of any such exercise of religion, contrary to the laws and statutes of this realm, as is aforesaid; that then every such person so offending as aforesaid, and being thereof lawfully convicted, shall be committed to prison, there to remain without bail or mainprise, until they shall conform and yield themselves to come to some church, chapel, or usual place of common prayer, and hear divine service, according to her majesty's laws and statutes aforesaid, and to make such open submission and declaration of their said conformity, as hereafter in this Act is declared and appointed.

.   .   .   .   .

And furthermore be it enacted by the authority of this present Parliament, that if any person or persons that shall at any time hereafter offend against this Act, shall before he or they be so warned or required to make abjuration according to the tenor of this Act, repair to some parish church on some Sunday or other festival day, and then and there hear divine service, and at service-time, before the sermon, or reading of the gospel, make public and open submission and declaration of his and their conformity to her majesty's laws and statutes, as hereafter in this Act is declared and appointed; that then the same offender shall thereupon be clearly discharged of and from all and every the penalties and punishments inflicted or imposed by this Act for any of the offences aforesaid. The same submission to be made as hereafter follows, that is to say:

"I, *A. B.*, do humbly confess and acknowledge, that I have grievously offended God in condemning her majesty's godly and lawful government and authority, by absenting myself from church, and from hearing divine service, contrary to the godly laws and statutes of this realm, and in using and frequenting disordered and unlawful conventicles and assemblies, under pretence and colour of exercise of religion: and I am heartily sorry for the same, and do acknowledge and testify in my conscience that no other person has or ought to have any power or authority over her majesty: and I do promise and protest, without any dissimulation, or any colour or means of any dispensation, that from henceforth I will from time to time obey and perform her majesty's laws and statutes, in repairing to the church and hearing divine service, and do my uttermost endeavour to maintain and defend the same."

15. Elizabeth's Act Against Recusants, 1593

The act in 1593 against the Recusants, those who wanted Roman Catholicism re-established, marked the height of Elizabeth's antipapal legislation. Gee and Hardy, *Documents Illustrative of English Church History.*

IV-12. Queen Elizabeth. *Portrait by Zucchero, 1575.*

For the better discovering and avoiding of all such traitorous and most dangerous conspiracies and attempts as are daily devised and practiced against our most gracious sovereign lady the queen's majesty and the happy estate of this commonweal, by sundry wicked and seditious persons, who, terming themselves Catholics, and being indeed spies and intelligencers, not only for her majesty's foreign enemies, but also for rebellious and traitorous subjects born within her highness's realms and dominions, and hiding their most detestable and devilish purposes under a false pretext of religion and conscience, do secretly wander and shift from place to place within this realm, to corrupt and seduce her majesty's subjects, and to stir them to sedition and rebellion:

Be it ordained and enacted by our sovereign lady the queen's majesty, and the Lords spiritual and temporal, and the Commons, in this present Parliament assembled, and by the authority of the same, that every person above the age of sixteen years, born within any of the queen's majesty's realms and dominions, or made denizen, being a popish recusant, and before the end of this session of Parliament, convicted for not repairing to some church, chapel, or usual place of common prayer, to hear divine service there, but forbearing the same, contrary to the tenor of the laws and statutes heretofore made and provided in that behalf, and having any certain place of dwelling and abode within this realm, shall within forty days next after the end of this session of Parliament (if they be within this realm, and not restrained or stayed either by imprisonment, or by her majesty's commandment, or by order and direction of some six or more of the privy council, or by such sickness or infirmity of body, as they shall not be able to travel without imminent danger of life, and in such cases of absence out of this realm, restraint, or stay, then within twenty days next after they shall return into the realm, and be enlarged of such imprisonment or restraint, and shall be able to travel) repair to their place of dwelling where they usually heretofore made their common abode, and shall not, any time after, pass or remove about five miles from thence. . . . Every person and persons that shall offend against the tenor and intent of this act in anything before mentioned, shall lose and forfeit all his and their goods and chattels, and shall also forfeit to the queen's majesty all the lands, tenements, and hereditaments, and all the rents and annuities of every such person so doing or offending, during the life of the offender.

And furthermore be it enacted by the authority of this present Parliament, that if any person, or persons, that shall at any time hereafter offend against this Act, shall before he or they shall be thereof convicted come to some parish church on some Sunday or other festival day, and then and there hear divine service, and at service-time, before the sermon, or reading of the gospel, make public and open submission and declaration of his and their conformity to her majesty's laws and statutes, as hereafter in this Act is declared and appointed; that then the same

offender shall thereupon be clearly discharged of and from all and every pains and forfeitures inflicted or imposed by this Act for any of the said offenses in this Act contained: the same submission to be made as hereafter follows, that is to say:

"I, *A. B.*, do humbly confess and acknowledge, that I have grievously offended God in condemning her majesty's godly and lawful government and authority, by absenting myself from church, and from hearing divine service, contrary to the godly laws and statutes of this realm: and I am heartily sorry for the same, and do acknowledge and testify in my conscience, that the bishop or see of Rome has not, nor ought to have, any power or authority over her majesty, or within any her majesty's realms or dominions: and I do promise and protest, without any dissimulation, or any colour or means of any dispensation, that from henceforth I will from time to time obey and perform her majesty's laws and statutes, in repairing to the church, and hearing divine service, and do my uttermost endeavour to maintain and defend the same."

And that every minister or curate of every parish, where such submission and declaration of confirmity shall hereafter be made by any such offender as aforesaid, shall presently enter the same into a book to be kept in every parish for that purpose, and within ten days then next following shall certify the same in writing to the bishop of the same diocese. . . .

16. The Lambeth Articles, 1595

Because Elizabeth had not called the meeting and was not personally inclined toward Calvinism, which she considered too austere, she objected to and would not approve the articles which came from the Lambeth conference in 1595. Inasmuch as Archbishops Whitgift and Hutton of Canterbury and York did approve these articles, her stand is an interesting revelation of how she would interpret the *via media*. Thomas Fuller, *Church History of Britain* (Oxford University Press, 1845), V, 220.

1. God from eternity hath predestined certain men unto life; certain men he hath reprobated.
2. The moving or efficient cause of predestination unto life is not the foresight of

faith, or of perseverance, or of good works, or of any thing that is in the person predestinated, but only the good will and pleasure of God.

3. There is predetermined a certain number of the predestinate, which can neither be augmented nor diminished.

4. Those who are not predestinated to salvation shall be necessarily damned for their sins.

5. A true, living, and justifying faith, and the Spirit of God justifying [sanctifying], is not extinguished, falleth not away; it vanisheth not away in the elect, either finally or totally.

6. A man truly faithful, that is, such a one who is endued with a justifying faith, is certain, with the full assurance of faith, of the remission of his sins and of his everlasting salvation by Christ.

7. Saving grace is not given, is not granted, is not communicated to all men, by which they may be saved if they will.

8. No man can come unto Christ unless it shall be given unto him and unless the Father shall draw him; and all men are not drawn by the Father, that they may come to the Son.

9. It is not in the will or power of every one to be saved.

17. The Millenary Petition, 1603

This petition, supposedly representing a thousand Puritans, was presented to James I on his way to London. He granted a conference the following year, authorized a new version of the Scriptures, and made a few concessions, but he insisted on conformity to the Prayer Book, which was only slightly changed. Gee and Hardy, *Documents Illustrative of English Church History.* Cf. Fuller, *Church History of Britain.*

Most gracious and dread sovereign,— Seeing it has pleased the Divine majesty, to the great comfort of all good Christians, to advance your highness, according to your just title, to the peaceable government of this Church and Commonwealth of England, we, the ministers of the gospel in this land, neither as factious men affecting a popular parity in the Church, nor as schismatics aiming at the dissolution of the State ecclesiastical, but as the faithful servants of Christ and

loyal subjects to your majesty, desiring and longing for the redress of divers abuses of the Church, could do no less in our obedience to God, service to your majesty, love to His Church, than acquaint your princely majesty with our particular griefs; for as your princely pen writeth, "the king, as a good physician, must first know what peccant humours his patient naturally is most subject unto, before he can begin his cure"; and although divers of us that sue for reformation have formerly, in respect of the times, subscribed to the book—some upon protestation, some upon exposition given them, some with condition rather than the Church should have been deprived of their labour and ministry—yet now we, to the number of more than a thousand of your majesty's subjects and ministers, all groaning as under a common burden of human rites and ceremonies, do with one joint consent humble ourselves at your majesty's feet, to be eased and relieved in this behalf. Our humble suit, then, unto your majesty is that these offences following, some may be removed, some amended, some qualified:

1. In the Church service: that the cross in baptism, interrogatories ministered to infants, confirmation, as superfluous, may be taken away; baptism not to be ministered by women, and so explained; the cap and surplice not urged; that examination may go before the communion; that it be ministered with a sermon; that divers terms of priests, and absolution, and some other used, with the ring in marriage, and other such like in the book, may be corrected; the longsomeness of service abridged, Church songs and music moderated to better edification; that the Lord's Day be not profaned; the rest upon holy days not so strictly urged; that there may be a uniformity of doctrine prescribed; no popish opinion to be any more taught or defended; no ministers charged to teach their people to bow at the name of Jesus; that the canonical Scriptures only be read in the Church.

2. Concerning Church ministers: that none hereafter be admitted into the ministry but able and sufficient men, and those to preach diligently and especially upon the

197

Lord's day; that such as be already entered and cannot preach, may either be removed, and some charitable course taken with them for their relief, or else be forced, according to the value of their livings, to maintain preachers; that non-residency be not permitted; that King Edward's statute for the lawfulness of ministers' marriages be revived; that ministers be not urged to subscribe, but according to the law, to the Articles of Religion, and the king's supremacy only.

3. For Church livings and maintenance: that bishops leave their commendams, some holding parsonages, some prebends, some vicarages, with their bishoprics; that double-beneficed men be not suffered to hold some two, some three benefices with cure, and some two, three, or four dignities besides; that impropriations annexed to bishoprics and colleges be demised only to the preachers' incumbents, for the old rent; that the impropriations of laymen's fees be charged, with a sixth or seventh part of their worth, to the maintenance of the preaching minister.

4. For Church discipline: that the discipline and excommunication may be administered according to Christ's own institution, or, at the least, that enormities may be redressed, as namely, that excommunication come not forth under the name of lay persons, chancellors, officials, etc.; that men be not excommunicated for trifles and twelve-penny matters; that none be excommunicated without consent of his pastor; that the officers be not suffered to extort unreasonable fees; that none having jurisdiction or registers' places, put out the same to farm; that divers popish canons (as for restraint of marriage at certain times) be reversed; that the longsomeness of suits in ecclesiastical courts (which hang sometimes two, three, four, five, six, or seven years) may be restrained; that the oath *Ex Officio*, whereby men are forced to accuse themselves, be more sparingly used; that licenses for marriages without banns asked, be more cautiously granted:

These, with such other abuses yet remaining and practised in the Church of England, we are able to show not to be agreeable to the Scriptures, if it shall please your highness

further to hear us, or more at large by writing to be informed, or by conference among the learned to be resolved. . . .

18. The Solemn League and Covenant, 1643

Resenting and revolting against the attempt to force the English Prayer Book on them, the Scots in 1638-39 drew up and signed a national covenant that was strongly Calvinistic. The Solemn League and Covenant of 1643 was based on the Scotch covenant. In exchange for military aid from the Scotch, the Westminster Assembly and Parliament approved the 1643 covenant, and in 1644 it was imposed on all Englishmen over eighteen years of age. Gee and Hardy, *Documents Illustrative of English Church History.*

A solemn league and covenant for reformation and defence of religion, the honour and happiness of the king, and the peace and safety of the three kingdoms of England, Scotland, and Ireland.

We noblemen, barons, knights, gentlemen, citizens, burgesses, ministers of the gospel, and commons of all sorts in the kingdoms of England, Scotland, and Ireland, by the providence of God living under one king, and being of one reformed religion; having before our eyes the glory of God, and the advancement of the kingdom of our Lord and Saviour Jesus Christ, the honour and happiness of the king's majesty and his posterity, and the true public liberty, safety, and peace of the kingdoms, wherein every one's private condition is included; and calling to mind the treacherous and bloody plots, conspiracies, attempts, and practices of the enemies of God against the true religion and professors thereof in all places, especially in these three kingdoms, ever since the reformation of religion, and how much their rage, power, and presumption are of late, and at this time increased and exercised, whereof the deplorable estate of the Church and kingdom of Ireland, the distressed estate of the Church and kingdom of England, and the dangerous estate of the Church and kingdom of Scotland, are present and public testimonies: we have (now at last), after other means of supplication, remonstrance, protestations, and sufferings, for the preservation of ourselves and our religion from utter ruin and destruction, according to the commendable practice of these kingdoms in former times, and the example of God's people in other nations, after mature deliberation, resolved and determined to enter into a mutual and solemn league and covenant, wherein we all subscribe, and each one of us for himself, with our hands lifted up to the most high God, do swear:

I. That we shall sincerely, really, and constantly, through the grace of God, endeavour in our several places and callings, the preservation of the reformed religion in the Church of Scotland, in doctrine, worship, discipline, and government, against our common enemies; the reformation of religion in the kingdoms of England and Ireland, in doctrine, worship, discipline, and government, according to the word of God and the example of the best reformed Churches; and we shall endeavour to bring the Churches of God in the three kingdoms to the nearest conjunction and uniformity in religion, confession of faith, form of Church government, directory for worship and catechizing, that we, and our posterity after us, may, as brethren, live in faith and love, and the Lord may delight to dwell in the midst of us.

II. That we shall in like manner, without respect of persons, endeavour the extirpation of popery, prelacy (that is, Church government by archbishops, bishops, their chancellors and commissaries, deans and chapters, archdeacons, and all other ecclesiastical officers depending on that hierarchy), superstition, heresy, schism, profaneness, and whatsoever shall be found to be contrary to sound doctrine and the power of godliness, lest we partake in other men's sins, and thereby be in danger to receive of their plagues; and that the Lord may be one, and His name one in the three kingdoms.

III. We shall, with the same sincerity, reality, and constancy, in our several vocations, endeavour with our estates and lives mutually to preserve the rights and privileges of the Parliaments, and the liberties of the kingdoms, and to preserve and defend the king's majesty's person and authority, in the preservation and defence of the true religion and liberties of the kingdoms, that the world may bear witness with our con-

sciences of our loyalty, and that we have no thoughts or intentions to diminish his majesty's just power and greatness.

IV. We shall also with all faithfulness endeavour the discovery of all such as have been or shall be incendiaries, malignants, or evil instruments, by hindering the reformation of religion, dividing the king from his people, or one of the kingdoms from another, or making any faction or parties amongst the people, contrary to the league and covenant, that they may be brought to public trial and receive codign punishment, as the degree of their offences shall require or deserve, or the supreme judicatories of both kingdoms respectively, or others having power from them for that effect, shall judge convenient.

V. And whereas the happiness of a blessed peace between these kingdoms, denied in former times to our progenitors, is by the good providence of God granted unto us, and hath been lately concluded and settled by both Parliaments: we shall each one of us, according to our places and interest, endeavour that they may remain conjoined in a firm peace and union to all posterity, and that justice may be done upon the wilful opposers thereof, in manner expressed in the precedent articles.

VI. We shall also, according to our places and callings, in this common cause of religion, liberty, and peace of the kingdom, assist and defend all those that enter into this league and covenant, in the maintaining and pursuing thereof; and shall not suffer ourselves, directly or indirectly, by whatsoever combination, persuasion, or terror, to be divided and withdrawn from this blessed union and conjunction, whether to make defection to the contrary part, or give ourselves to a detestable indifferency or neutrality in this cause, which so much concerneth the glory of God, the good of the kingdoms, and the honour of the king; but shall all the days of our lives zealously and constantly continue therein, against all opposition, and promote the same according to our power, against all lets and impediments whatsoever; and what we are not able ourselves to suppress or overcome we shall reveal and make known, that it may be timely prevented or removed: all which we shall do as in the sight of God.

And because these kingdoms are guilty of many sins and provocations against God and His Son Jesus Christ, as is too manifest by our present distresses and dangers, the fruits thereof: we profess and declare, before God and the world, our unfeigned desire to be humbled for our sins, and for the sins of these kingdoms; especially that we have not as we ought valued the inestimable benefit of the gospel; that we have not laboured for the purity and power thereof; and that we have not endeavoured to receive Christ in our hearts, nor to walk worthy of Him in our lives, which are the causes of other sins and transgressions so much abounding amongst us, and our true and unfeigned purpose, desire, and endeavour, for ourselves and all others under our power and charge, both in public and in private, in all duties we owe to God and man, to amend our lives, and each one to go before another in the example of a real reformation, that the Lord may turn away His wrath and heavy indignation, and establish these Churches and kingdoms in truth and peace. And this covenant we make in the presence of Almighty God, the Searcher of all hearts, with a true intention to perform the same, as we shall answer at that great day when the secrets of all hearts shall be disclosed; most humbly beseeching the Lord to strengthen us by His Holy Spirit for this end, and to bless our desires and proceedings with such success as may be a deliverance and safety to His people, and encouragement to the Christian Churches, groaning under or in danger of the yoke of antichristian tyranny, to join in the same or like association and covenant, to the glory of God, the enlargement of the kingdom of Jesus Christ, and the peace and tranquillity of Christian kingdoms and commonwealths.

19. Westminster Shorter Catechism, 1647

Prepared by the Westminster Assembly in 1647 and adopted by the Church of Scotland in 1648, and by almost all of the Calvinistic Presbyterian and Congregational Churches, this Catechism is probably the most influential in the English language. It is regarded as one of the best expositions of Calvinism, and for three centuries has basically informed millions of Protestants. Schaff, *Creeds of Christendom*, III.

Question 1. What is the chief aim of man?

Answer. Man's chief end is to glorify God and to enjoy him forever.

Ques. 2. What rule hath God given to direct us how we may glorify and enjoy him?

Ans. The Word of God, which is contained in the Scriptures of the Old and New Testaments, is the only rule to direct us how we may glorify and enjoy him.

Ques. 3. What do the Scriptures principally teach?

Ans. The Scriptures principally teach what man is to believe concerning God, and what duty God requires of man.

Ques. 4. What is GOD?

Ans. God is a Spirit, infinite, eternal, and unchangeable, in his being, wisdom, power, holiness, justice, goodness, and truth.

Ques. 5. Are there more Gods than one?

Ans. There is but one only, the living and true God.

Ques. 6. How many persons are there in the Godhead?

Ans. There are three persons in the Godhead: the Father, the Son, and the Holy Ghost; and these three are one God, the same in substance, equal in power and glory.

Ques. 7. What are the decrees of God?

Ans. The decrees of God are his eternal purpose according to the counsel of his will, whereby, for his own glory, he hath fore-ordained whatsoever comes to pass.

Ques. 8. How doth God execute his decrees?

Ans. God executeth his decrees in the works of creation and providence.

Ques. 9. What is the work of creation?

Ans. The work of creation is God's making all things of nothing, by the word of his power, in the space of six days, and all very good.

Ques. 10. How did God create man?

Ans. God created man, male and female, after his own image, in knowledge, righteousness, and holiness, with dominion over the creatures.

Ques. 11. What are God's works of providence?

Ans. God's works of providence are his

most holy, wise, and powerful preserving and governing all his creatures, and all their actions.

Ques. 12. What special act of providence did God exercise towards man, in the estate wherein he was created?

Ans. When God had created man, he entered into a covenant of life with him, upon condition of perfect obedience; forbidding him to eat of the tree of knowledge of good and evil, upon pain of death.

Ques. 13. Did our first parents continue in the estate wherein they were created?

Ans. Our first parents, being left to the freedom of their own will, fell from the estate wherein they were created, by sinning against God.

Ques. 14. What is sin?

Ans. Sin is any want of conformity unto, or transgression of, the law of God.

Ques. 15. What was the sin whereby our first parents fell from the estate wherein they were created?

Ans. The sin whereby our first parents fell from the estate wherein they were created, was their eating the forbidden fruit.

Ques. 16. Did all mankind fall in Adam's first transgression?

Ans. The covenant being made with Adam, not only for himself, but for his posterity, all mankind descending from him by ordinary generation, sinned in him, and fell with him, in his first transgression.

Ques. 17. Into what estate did the fall bring mankind?

Ans. The fall brought mankind into an estate of sin and misery.

Ques. 18. Wherein consists the sinfulness of that estate whereinto man fell?

Ans. The sinfulness of that estate whereinto man fell, consists in the guilt of Adam's first sin, the want of original righteousness, and the corruption of his whole nature, which is commonly called original sin; together with all actual transgressions which proceed from it.

Ques. 19. What is the misery of that estate whereinto man fell?

Ans. All mankind by their fall lost communion with God, and are under his wrath and curse, and so made liable to all the miseries in this life, to death itself, and to the pains of hell forever.

Ques. 20. Did God leave all mankind to perish in the estate of sin and misery?

Ans. God, having out of his mere good pleasure, from all eternity, elected some to everlasting life, did enter into a covenant of grace, to deliver them out of the estate of sin and misery, and to bring them into an estate of salvation by a Redeemer.

Ques. 21. Who is the Redeemer of God's elect?

Ans. The only Redeemer of God's elect is the Lord Jesus Christ, who being the eternal Son of God became man, and so was, and continueth to be, God and man, in two distinct natures, and one person forever.

Ques. 22. How did Christ, being the Son of God, become man?

Ans. Christ, the Son of God, became man, by taking to himself a true body, and a reasonable soul, being conceived by the power of the Holy Ghost, in the womb of the Virgin Mary, and born of her, yet without sin.

Ques. 23. What offices doth Christ execute as our Redeemer?

Ans. Christ, as our Redeemer, executeth the offices of a Prophet, of a Priest, and of a King, both in his estate of humiliation and exaltation.

Ques. 24. How doth Christ execute the office of a Prophet?

Ans. Christ executeth the office of a Prophet, in revealing to us by his Word and Spirit, the will of God for our salvation.

Ques. 25. How doth Christ execute the office of a Priest?

Ans. Christ executeth the office of a Priest, in his once offering up of himself a sacrifice to satisfy divine justice, and reconcile us to God, and in making continual intercession for us.

Ques. 26. How doth Christ execute the office of a King?

Ans. Christ executeth the office of a King, in subduing us to himself, in ruling and defending us, and in restraining and conquering all his and our enemies.

Ques. 27. Wherein did Christ's humiliation consist?

Ans. Christ's humiliation consisted in his being born, and that in a low condition, made under the law, undergoing the miseries of this life, the wrath of God, and the cursed death of the cross; in being buried, and continuing under the power of death for a time.

Ques. 28. Wherein consisteth Christ's exaltation?

Ans. Christ's exaltation consisteth in his rising again from the dead on the third day, in ascending up into heaven, in sitting at the right hand of God the Father, and in coming to judge the world at the last day.

Ques. 29. How are we made partakers of the redemption purchased by Christ?

Ans. We are made partakers of the redemption purchased by Christ, by the effectual application of it to us by his Holy Spirit.

Ques. 30. How doth the Spirit apply to us the redemption purchased by Christ?

Ans. The Spirit applieth to us the redemption purchased by Christ, by working faith in us, and thereby uniting us to Christ in our effectual calling.

Ques. 31. What is effectual calling?

Ans. Effectual calling is the work of God's Spirit, whereby, convincing us of our sin and misery, enlightening our minds in the knowledge of Christ, and renewing our wills, he doth persuade and enable us to embrace Jesus Christ, freely offered to us in the gospel.

Ques. 32. What benefits do they that are effectually called partake of in this life?

Ans. They that are effectually called do in this life partake of justification, adoption, sanctification, and the several benefits which, in this life, do either accompany or flow from them.

Ques. 33. What is justification?

Ans. Justification is an act of God's free grace, wherein he pardoneth all our sins, and accepteth us as righteous in his sight, only for the righteousness of Christ imputed to us, and received by faith alone.

Ques. 34. What is adoption?

Ans. Adoption is an act of God's free grace, whereby we are received into the number, and have a right to all the privileges, of the sons of God.

Ques. 35. What is sanctification?

Ans. Sanctification is the work of God's free grace, whereby we are renewed in the whole man after the image of God, and are enabled more and more to die unto sin, and live unto righteousness.

Ques. 36. What are the benefits which in this life do accompany or flow from justification, adoption, and sanctification?

Ans. The benefits which in this life do accompany or flow from justification, adoption, and sanctification, are, assurance of God's love, peace of conscience, joy in the Holy Ghost, increase of grace, and perseverance therein to the end.

Ques. 37. What benefits do believers receive from Christ at death?

Ans. The souls of believers are, at their death, made perfect in holiness, and do immediately pass into glory; and their bodies, being still united to Christ, do rest in their graves till the resurrection.

Ques. 38. What benefits do believers receive from Christ at the resurrection?

Ans. At the resurrection, believers being raised up in glory, shall be openly acknowledged and acquitted in the day of judgment, and made perfectly blessed in the full enjoying of God to all eternity.

Ques. 39. What is the duty which God requireth of man?

Ans. The duty which God requireth of man is obedience to his revealed will.

Ques. 40. What did God at first reveal to man for the rule of his obedience?

Ans. The rule which God at first revealed to man, for his obedience, was the moral law.

Ques. 41. Wherein is the moral law summarily comprehended?

Ans. The moral law is summarily comprehended in the ten commandments.

Ques. 42. What is the sum of the ten commandments?

Ans. The sum of the ten commandments is, to love the Lord our God with all our heart, with all our soul, with all our strength, and with all our mind; and our neighbor as ourselves.

Ques. 43. What is the preface to the ten commandments?

Ans. The preface to the ten commandments is in these words: "I am the Lord thy

202

God, which brought thee out of the land of Egypt, out of the house of bondage."

Ques. 44. What doth the preface to the ten commandments teach us?

Ans. The preface to the ten commandments teacheth us, that because God is the Lord, and our God and Redeemer, therefore we are bound to keep all his commandments.

Ques. 45. Which is the first commandment?

Ans. The first commandment is, Thou shalt have no other gods before me.

Ques. 46. What is required in the first commandment?

Ans. The first commandment requireth us to know and acknowledge God, to be the only true God, and our God; and to worship and glorify him accordingly.

Ques. 58. What is required in the fourth commandment?

Ans. The fourth commandment requireth the keeping holy to God such set times as he hath appointed in his Word; expressly one whole day in seven, to be a holy Sabbath to himself.

Ques. 59. Which day of the seven hath God appointed to be the weekly Sabbath?

Ans. From the beginning of the world to the resurrection of Christ, God appointed the seventh day of the week to be the weekly Sabbath; and the first day of the week, ever since, to continue to the end of the world, which is the Christian Sabbath.

Ques. 60. How is the Sabbath to be sanctified?

Ans. The Sabbath is to be sanctified by a holy resting all that day, even from such worldly employments and recreations as are lawful on other days; and spending the whole time in the public and private exercises of God's worship, except so much as is to be taken up in the works of necessity and mercy.

Ques. 61. What is forbidden in the fourth commandment?

Ans. The fourth commandment forbiddeth the omission, or careless performance, of the duties required, and the profaning the day by idleness, or doing that which is in itself sinful, or by unnecessary thoughts, words, or works about our worldly employments and recreations.

Ques. 87. What is repentance unto life?

Ans. Repentance unto life is a saving grace, whereby a sinner, out of a true sense of his sin, and apprehension of the mercy of God in Christ, doth, with grief and hatred of his sin, turn from it unto God, with full purpose of, and endeavor after, new obedience.

Ques. 88. What are the outward and ordinary means whereby Christ communicateth to us the benefits of redemption?

Ans. The outward and ordinary means whereby Christ communicateth to us the benefits of redemption, are his ordinances, especially the word, sacraments, and prayer; all which are made effectual to the elect for salvation.

Ques. 89. How is the word made effectual to salvation?

Ans. The Spirit of God maketh the reading, but especially the preaching of the word, an effectual means of convincing the converting sinners, and of building them up in holiness and comfort through faith unto salvation.

Ques. 90. How is the Word to be read and heard, that it may become effectual to salvation?

Ans. That the Word may become effectual to salvation, we must attend thereunto with diligence, preparation, and prayer; receive it with faith and love, lay it up in our hearts, and practice it in our lives.

Ques. 91. How do the sacraments become effectual means of salvation?

Ans. The sacraments become effectual means of salvation, not from any virtue in them, or in him that doth administer them, but only by the blessing of Christ, and the working of his Spirit in them that by faith receive them.

Ques. 92. What is a sacrament?

Ans. A sacrament is a holy ordinance instituted by Christ; wherein, by sensible signs, Christ and the benefits of the new covenant are represented, sealed, and applied to believers.

Ques. 93. Which are the sacraments of the New Testament?

Ans. The sacraments of the New Testament are Baptism and the Lord's Supper.

20. Selections from the Agreement of the People, 1649

The Solemn League and Covenant brought a Presbyterian system to England. The episcopacy was abolished, and in 1645 the *Directory* replaced the Prayer Book. This imposed Calvinism was resented by many people, and in 1648 the Grand Army under Cromwell issued a remonstrance against forcing religion into one mould. At the close of the Civil War in 1649, with Cromwell in power, the people entered into an agreement that granted liberty in religion to all but papists and prelatists. Gee and Hardy, *Documents Illustrative of English Church History*.

An Agreement of the People of England, and the Places Therewith Incorporated, for a Secure and Present Peace, upon Grounds of Common Right, Freedom and Safety.

9. Concerning religion, we agree as followeth: (1) It is intended that the Christian religion be held forth and recommended as the public profession in this nation, which we desire may, by the grace of God, be reformed to the greatest purity in doctrine, worship, and discipline, according to the word of God; the instructing the people thereunto in a public way, so it be not compulsive; as also the maintaining of able teachers for that end, and for the confutation or discovering of heresy, error, and whatsoever is contrary to sound doctrine, is allowed to be provided for by our representatives; the maintenance of which teachers may be out of public treasury, and we desire, not by tithes: provided that popery or prelacy be not held forth as the public way or profession in this nation. (2) That, to the public profession so held forth, none be compelled by penalties or otherwise; but only may be endeavoured to be won by sound doctrine, and the example of a good conversation. (3) That such as profess faith in God by Jesus Christ, however differing in judgment from the doctrine, worship, or discipline publicly held forth as aforesaid, shall not be restrained from, but shall be protected in, the profession of their faith and exercise of religion, according to their consciences, in any place except such as shall be set apart for the public worship; where we provide not for them, unless they have leave so as they abuse not this liberty to the civil injury of others, or to actual disturbance of the public peace on their parts. Nevertheless it is not intended to be hereby provided that this liberty shall necessarily extend to popery or prelacy. (4) That all laws, ordinances, statutes, and clauses in any law, statute, or ordinance to the contrary of the liberty herein provided for, in the two particulars next preceding concerning religion, be, and are hereby, repealed and made void.

21. John Milton

John Milton (1608-1674) looms as the literary genius of Puritanism. By 1652 he was completely blind, yet in 1667 he published *Paradise Lost,* and in 1671, *Samson Agonistes* and *Paradise Regained. Paradise Lost* centers on the Fall of man, and *Paradise Regained* on man's Redemption. His writings are deeply introspective and biblical, unsurpassed as studies in Puritanism. *Paradise Lost* and *Paradise Regained* should be read in their entirety. As a Puritan independent, Milton wanted full freedom of conscience and worship. The lines below were an appeal to Cromwell to save England from an enforced Presbyterian system that would eliminate the episcopacy.

TO THE LORD GENERAL CROMWELL ON THE
PROPOSALS OF CERTAIN MINISTERS AT
THE COMMITTEE FOR PROPAGATION
OF THE GOSPEL [1652]

Cromwell, our chief of men, who through a cloud
  Not of war only, but detractions rude,
  Guided by faith and matchless fortitude,
    To peace and truth thy glorious way has ploughed.
And on the neck of crownèd Fortune proud
  Hast reared God's trophies, and his work pursued,
  While Darwen stream, with blood of Scots imbrued,
  And Dunbar field, resounds thy praises loud,
And Worcester's laureate wreath: yet much remains
  To conquer still; Peace hath her victories
  No less renowned than War: new foes arise,
  Threatening to bind our souls with secular chains.
    Help us to save free conscience from the paw
    Of hireling wolves, whose Gospel is their maw.

22. In the Time of Cromwell

The following documents give a glimpse of the religious turbulence of Cromwell's time. The first is from T. Carlyle, *Letters and Speeches of Oliver Cromwell*, I (London, 1904); the second, S. Gardiner, *The Constitutional Documents of the Puritan Revolution*, 1628-1660 (London, 1889); and the third, Earl of Clarendon, *History of the Rebellion and Civil Wars in England* (Oxford, 1843).

CROMWELL DESCRIBES THE TAKING OF TREDAH, 1648

... being in the heat of action, I forbade them to spare any that were in arms in the town, and, I think, that night they put to the sword about 2,000 men, divers of the officers and soldiers being fled over the Bridge into the other part of the town, where about one hundred of them possessed St. Peter's church-steeple, some the west gate, and others a strong round tower next the gate called St. Sunday's. These being summoned to yield to mercy, refused, whereupon I ordered the steeple of St. Peter's Church to be fired, where one of them was heard to say in the midst of the flames: "God damn me, God confound me; I burn, I burn."

The next day, the other two towers were summoned, in one of which was about six or seven score; but they refused to yield themselves, and we knowing that hunger must compel them, set only good guards to secure them from running away until their stomachs were come down. From one of the said towers, notwithstanding their condition, they killed and wounded some of our men. When they submitted, their officers were knocked on the head, and every tenth man of the soldiers killed, and the rest shipped for the Barbadoes. The soldiers in the other tower were ... shipped likewise for the Barbadoes.

I am persuaded that this is a righteous judgment of God upon these barbarous wretches, who have imbrued their hands in so much innocent blood; and that it will tend to prevent the effusion of blood for the future, which are the satisfactory grounds to such actions, which otherwise cannot but work remorse and regret. . . .

And now give me leave to say how it comes to pass that this work is wrought. It was set upon some of our hearts, that a great thing should be done, not by power or might, but by the Spirit of God. And is it not so clear? That which caused your men to storm so courageously, it was the Spirit of God, who gave your men courage, and took it away again; and gave the enemy courage, and took it away again; and gave your men courage again, and therewith this happy success. And therefore it is good that God alone have all the glory.

It is remarkable that these people, at the first, set up the mass in some places of the town that had been monasteries; but afterwards grew so insolent that, the last Lord's day before the storm, the Protestants were thrust out of the great Church called St. Peter's, and they had public mass there: and in this very place near one thousand of them were put to the sword, fleeing thither for safety. I believe all their friars were knocked on the head promiscuously but two; and one of which was Father Peter Taaff [brother to the Lord Taaff], whom the soldiers took, the next day, and made an end of; the other was taken in the round tower, under the repute of lieutenant, and when he understood that the officers in that tower had no quarter, he confessed he was a friar; but that did not save him.

I do not think we lost one hundred men upon the place, though many be wounded.

WARRANT FOR BEHEADING OF CHARLES I

At the High Court of Justice for the trying and judging of Charles Stuart, King of England, January 29, Anno Domini 1649.

Whereas Charles Stuart, King of England, is and standeth convicted, attainted, and condemned of high treason, and other high crimes; and sentence upon Saturday last was pronounced against him by this Court, to be put to death by the severing of his head from his body; of which sentence, execution yet remaineth to be done; these are therefore to will and require you to see the said sentence executed in the open street before Whitehall, upon the morrow, being the thirtieth day of this instant month of January, be-

The Common wealth ruleing with a standing Army

The Fruits of a Common wealth.

IV-13. Cartoon Picturing the Military Rule of the Commonwealth During the Time of Cromwell.

tween the hours of ten in the morning and five in the afternoon of the same day, with full effect. And for so doing this shall be your sufficient warrant. And these are to require all officers, soldiers, and others, the good people of this nation of England, to be assisting unto you in this service.

To Col. Francis Hacker, Col. Huncks, and Lieut.-Col. Phayre, and to every of them.

Given under our hands and seals:

John Bradshaw
Thomas Grey
Oliver Cromwell
etc. [47 other names].

BEHEADING OF CHARLES I

This unparalleled murder and parricide was committed ... in the forty and ninth year of his age, and when he had such excellent health, and so great vigour of body, that when his murderers caused him to be opened, (which they did, and were some of them present at it with great curiosity,) they confessed and declared, "that no man had ever all his vital parts so perfect and unhurt: and that he seemed to be of so admirable a composition and constitution, that he would probably have lived as long as nature could subsist." His body ... was exposed for many days to the public view, that all men might

know that he was not alive. And he was then embalmed, and put into a coffin, and so carried to St. James's; where he likewise remained several days. [At Windsor, the form of the Common Prayer Book being vetoed by the governor of the castle,] the King's body was laid without any words, or other ceremonies than the tears and sighs of the few beholders....

The kings and princes of Christendom ... made haste and sent over that they might get shares in the spoils of a murdered monarch. Cardinal Mazarin ... had long adored the conduct of Cromwell ... purchased the rich bed, hangings and carpets, which furnished his palace at Paris. [The Spanish Ambassador] who had always a great malignity towards the King, bought as many pictures and other precious goods ... as, being sent in ships to the Corunna in Spain, were carried from thence to Madrid upon eighteen mules. Christina, queen of Sweden, purchased the choice of all the medals, and jewels, and some pictures of a great price, and received Cromwell's ambassador with great joy and pomp, and made an alliance with them. The archduke Leopold, who was governor of Flanders, disbursed a great sum of money for many of the best pictures.... In this manner did the neighbour princes join to assist Cromwell . . . to extinguish monarchy in this renowned Kingdom.

23. *The Five Mile Act, 1665*

An Act for Restraining Nonconformists from Inhabiting in Corporations. Peter Bayne, ed., *Documents Relating to the Settlement of the Church of England by the Act of Uniformity of 1662* (London: W. Kent Co., 1862).

Whereas divers parsons, vicars, curates, lecturers, and other persons in holy orders, have not declared their unfeigned assent and consent to the use of all things contained and prescribed in the Book of Common Prayer, and administration of the sacraments, and other rites and ceremonies of the church, according to the use of the church of England, or have not subscribed the declaration or acknowledgment contained in a certain Act of Parliament made in the fourteenth year of his majesty's reign, and entitled, an Act for the Uniformity of Public Prayers and Administration of Sacraments, and other Rites and Ceremonies, and for the Establishing the form of Making, Ordaining, and Consecrating of Bishops, Priests, and Deacons in the Church of England, according to the said Act, or any other subsequent Act. And whereas they or some of them, and divers other person and persons not ordained according to the form of the church of England, and as have since the Act of Oblivion taken upon them to preach in unlawful assemblies, conventicles, or meetings, under colour or pretence of exercise of religion, contrary to the laws and statutes of this kingdom, have settled themselves in divers corporations in England, sometimes three or more of them in a place, thereby taking an opportunity to distil the poisonous principles of schism and rebellion into the hearts of his majesty's subjects, to the great danger of the church and kingdom:

II.   Be it therefore enacted by the king's most excellent majesty, by and with the advice and consent of the lords spiritual and temporal, and the Commons in this present parliament assembled, and by the authority of the same, that the said parsons, vicars, curates, lecturers, and other persons in holy orders, or pretended holy orders, or pretending to holy orders, and all stipendiaries, and other persons who have been possessed of any ecclesiastical or spiritual promotion, and every of them, who have not declared their unfeigned assent and consent, as aforesaid, and subscribed the declaration aforesaid, and shall not take and subscribe the oath following:

"I *A. B.*, do swear, that it is not lawful upon any pretence whatsoever, to take arms against the king; and that I do abhor that traitorous position of taking arms by his authority against his person, or against those that are commissioned by him, in pursuance of such commissions; and that I will not at any time endeavour any alteration of government, either in church or state."

III.   And all such person and persons as shall take upon them to preach in any unlawful assembly, conventicle, or meeting, under colour or pretence of any exercise of religion, contrary to the laws and statutes of this kingdom; shall not at any time from and after the four and twentieth day of March, which shall be in this present year of our Lord God one thousand six hundred sixty-and-five, unless only in passing upon the road, come or be within five miles of any city or town corporate, or borough that send burgesses to the parliament, within his majesty's kingdom of England, principality of Wales, or of the town of Berwick-upon-Tweed; or within five miles of any parish, town or place, wherein he or they have since the Act of Oblivion been parson, vicar, curate, stipendiary, or lecturer, or taken upon them to preach in any unlawful assembly, conventicle, or meeting, under colour or pretence of any exercise of religion, contrary to the laws and statutes of this kingdom; before he or they have taken and subscribed the oath aforesaid, before the justices of the peace at their quarter sessions to be holden for the county, riding, or division, next unto the said corporation, city, or borough, parish, place, or town in open court, (which said oath the said justices are hereby empowered there to administer); upon forfeiture for every such offence the sum of forty pounds of lawful English money; the one third part thereof to his majesty and his successors; the other third part to the use of the poor of the parish where the offence shall be committed; and the other third part thereof to such person or persons as shall or will sue for the same by action of debt, plaint, bill, or information in any court of record at Westminster, or before any justices of assize, Oyer and Terminer, or gaol delivery . . . or before any justices of peace in their quarter sessions, wherein no essoin, protection, or wager of law shall be allowed. . . .

24. John Cosin: Anglicanism and Catholicism

John Cosin (1594-1672) wrote a letter to the Countess of Peterborough in 1660 that has become well-known for its statement of the differences and agreements between Anglicanism and Catholicism. *Works of John Cosin*, Vol. 4, Library of Anglo-Catholic Theology (Oxford: John Henry Parker, 1861).

The Differences, in the Chief Points of Religion, between the Roman Catholics and us of the Church of England; together with the Agreements, which we for our parts profess, and are ready to embrace, if they for theirs were as ready to accord with us in the same.

The Differences

We that profess the Catholic Faith and Religion in the Church of England do not agree with the Roman Catholics in anything whereunto they now endeavour to convert us. But we totally differ from them (as they do from the ancient Catholic Church) in these points:

1. That the Church of Rome is the Mother and Mistress of all other Churches in the world.

2. That the Pope of Rome is the vicar-general of Christ, or that he hath an universal jurisdiction over all Christians that shall be saved.

3. That either the Synod of Trent was a General Council or that all the canons thereof are to be received as matters of Catholic Faith under pain of damnation.

4. That Christ hath instituted seven true and proper Sacraments in the New Testament, neither more nor less, all conferring grace and all necessary to salvation.

5. That the priests offer up our Saviour in the Mass, as a real, proper, and propitiatory sacrifice for the quick and the dead, and that whosoever believes it not is eternally damned.

6. That, in the Sacrament of the Eucharist, the whole substance of bread is converted into the substance of Christ's Body, and the whole substance of wine into His Blood, so truly and properly, as that after consecration there is neither any bread nor wine remaining there; which they call Transubstantiation, and impose upon all persons under pain of damnation to be believed.

7. That the communion under one kind is sufficient and lawful (notwithstanding the institution of Christ under both), and that whosoever believes or holds otherwise is damned.

8. That there is a purgatory after this life, wherein the souls of the dead are punished, and from whence they are fetched out by the prayers and offerings of the living; and that there is no salvation possibly to be had by any that will not believe as much.

9. That all the old saints departed, and all those dead men and women whom the Pope hath of late canonized for saints or shall hereafter do, whosoever they be, are and ought to be invocated by the religious prayers and devotions of all persons; and that they who do not believe this as an article of their Catholic Faith cannot be saved.

10. That the relics of all these true or reputed saints ought to be religiously worshipped; and that whosoever holdeth the contrary is damned.

11. That the images of Christ and the blessed Virgin and of the other saints ought not only to be had and retained, but likewise to be honoured and worshipped, according to the use and practices of the Roman Church; and that this is to be believed as of necessity to salvation.

12. That the power and use of indulgences, as they are now practised in the Church of Rome, both for the living and the dead, is to be received and held of all, under pain of eternal perdition.

13. That all the ceremonies used by the Roman Church in the administration of the

Sacraments (such as are spittle and salt at Baptism, the five crosses upon the Altar and Sacrament of the Eucharist, the holding of that Sacrament over the Priest's head to be adored, the exposing of it in their churches to be worshipped by the people, and circumgestation and carrying of it abroad in procession upon their Corpus Christi Day, and to their sick for the same, the oil and chrism in confirmation, the anointing of the ears, the eyes, and noses, the hands, the reins, of those that are ready to die, the giving of an empty chalice and paten to them that are to be ordained Priests, and many others of this nature now in use with them) are of necessity to salvation to be approved and admitted by all other churches.

14. That all the ecclesiastical observations and constitutions of the same Church (such as are their laws of forbidding all Priests to marry, and appointing several orders of monks, friars, and nuns, in the Church, the service of God in an unknown tongue, the saying of a number of Ave Marias by tale upon their chaplets, the sprinkling of themselves and the dead bodies with holy water as operative and effectual to the remission of venial sins, the distinctions of meats to be held for true fasting, the religious consecration and incensing of images, the baptizing of bells, the dedicating of divers holidays for the Immaculate Conception and the Bodily Assumption of the blessed Virgin, and for Corpus Christi or transubstantiation of the Sacrament, the making of the Apocryphal books to be as canonical as any of the rest of the holy and undoubted Scriptures, the keeping of those Scriptures from the free use and reading of the people, the approving of their own Latin translation only, and divers other matters of the like nature) are to be approved, held, and believed, as needful to salvation; and that whoever approves them not is out of the Catholic Church, and must be damned.

All which, in their several respects, we hold, some to be pernicious, some unnecessary, many false, and many fond, and none of them to be imposed upon any church, or any Christian, as the Roman Catholics do upon all Christians and all churches whatsoever, for matters needful to be approved for eternal salvation.

Our Agreements

If the Roman Catholics would make the essence of their Church (as we do ours) to consist in these following points, we are at accord with them in the reception and believing of:

1. All the two and twenty canonical books of the Old Testament, and the twenty-seven of the New, as the only foundation and perfect rule of our faith.

2. All the apostolical and ancient Creeds, especially those which are commonly called the Apostles' Creed, the Nicene Creed, and the Creed of St. Athanasius; all which are clearly deduced out of the Scriptures.

3. All the decrees of faith and doctrine set forth, as well in the first four General Councils, as in all other Councils, which those first four approved and confirmed, and in the fifth and sixth General Councils besides (than which we find no more to be General), and in all the following Councils that be thereunto agreeable, and in all the anathemas and condemnations given out by those Councils against heretics, for the defence of the Catholic Faith.

4. The unanimous and general consent of the ancient Catholic Fathers and the universal Church of Christ in the interpretation of the Holy Scriptures, and the collection of all necessary matters of Faith from them during the first six hundred years, and downwards to our own days.

5. In acknowledgment of the Bishop of Rome, if he would rule and be ruled by the ancient canons of the Church, to be the Patriarch of the West, by right of ecclesiastical and imperial constitution, in such places where the kings and governors of those places had received him, and found it behooveful for them to make use of his jurisdiction, without any necessary dependence upon him by divine right.

6. In the reception and use of the two blessed Sacraments of our Saviour; in the confirmation of those persons that are to be strengthened in their Christian Faith, by prayer and imposition of hands, according

to the examples of the holy Apostles and ancient Bishops of the Catholic Church; in the public and solemn benediction of persons that are to be joined together in Holy Matrimony; in public or private absolution of penitent sinners; in the consecrating of Bishops, and the ordaining of Priests and Deacons, for the service of God in His Church by a lawful succession; and in visiting the sick, by praying for them, and administering the blessed Sacrament to them, together with a final absolution of them from their repented sins.

7. In commemorating at the Eucharist the Sacrifice of Christ's Body and Blood once truly offered for us.

8. In acknowledging His sacramental, spiritual, true, and real Presence there to the souls of all them that come faithfully and devoutly to receive Him according to His own institution in that Holy Sacrament.

9. In giving thanks to God for them that are departed out of this life in the true Faith of Christ's Catholic Church; and in praying to God, that they may have a joyful resurrection, and a perfect consummation of bliss, both in their bodies and souls, in His eternal kingdom of glory.

10. In the historical and moderate use of painted and true stories, either for memory or ornament, where there is no danger to have them abused or worshipped with religious honour.

11. In the use of indulgences, or abating the rigour of the canons imposed upon offenders, according to their repentance, and their want of ability to undergo them.

12. In the administration of the two Sacraments, and other rites of the Church, with ceremonies of decency and order, according to the precept of the Apostle, and the free practice of the ancient Christians.

13. In observing such Holy days and times of fasting as were in use in the first ages of the Church, or afterwards received upon just grounds, by public or lawful authority.

14. Finally, in the reception of all ecclesiastical constitutions and canons made for the ordering of our Church; or others which are not repugnant either to the Word of God, or the power of kings, or the laws established by right authority in any nation.

25. Jeremy Taylor

Jeremy Taylor (1613-1667) was one of the most popular Anglican writers of the seventeenth century. He lived through the enforced Anglican establishment and then the Presbyterian control of religion, and like Milton in his *Areopagitica*, desired to see no more intolerance. Taylor's *Liberty of Prophesying* is a plea for freedom of conscience. *The Whole Works of Jeremy Taylor*, 10 vols., ed. Reginald Heber (London: Longmans, Green & Co., 1850-54).

THE LIBERTY OF PROPHESYING

I have chosen a subject in which, if my own reason does not abuse me, I needed no other books or aids than what a man carries with him on horseback, I mean the common principles of Christianity, and those ἀξιώματα [axioms] which men use in the transactions of the ordinary occurrences of civil society: and upon the strength of them, and some other collateral assistances, I have run through it *utcunque;* and the sum of the following discourses is nothing but the sense of these words of Scripture, that since "we know in part, and prophesy in part, and that now we see through a glass darkly," we would not despise or contemn persons not so knowing as ourselves, but "him that is weak in the faith we should receive, but not to doubtful disputations"; therefore, certainly to charity, and not to vexations, not to those which are the idle effects of impertinent wranglings. And provided they keep close to the foundation, which is faith and obedience, let them build upon this foundation matter more or less precious, yet if the foundation be entire, they shall be saved with or without loss. And since we profess ourselves servants of so meek a Master, and disciples of so charitable an institute, "Let us walk worthy of the vocation wherewith we are called, with all lowliness and meekness, with long-suffering, forbearing one another in love"; for this is the best endeavoring to keep the unity of the Spirit, when it is fast tied in the bond of peace. And although it be a duty of Christianity that "we all speak the same thing, that there be no divisions among us, but that we be perfectly joined together in the same mind and in the same judgment," yet this unity is to be estimated according to the unity of faith, in things necessary, in matters of creed, and articles fundamental: for as for other things, it is more to be wished than to be hoped for. There are some "doubtful disputations," and in such "the scribe, the wise, the disputer of this world," are, most commonly, very far from certainty, and many times, from truth. There are diversity of persuasions in matters adiaphorous, as meats, drinks, and holy days, etc., and both parties, the affirmative and the negative, affirm and deny with innocence enough; for the observer, and he that observes not, intend both to God; and God is our common Master, and we all fellow-servants, and not the judge of each other in matters of conscience or doubtful disputation; and every man that "hath faith, must have it to himself before God," but no man must, in such matters, either "judge his brother or set him at naught"; but "let us follow after the things which make for peace, and things wherewith one may edify another." And the way to do that is not by knowledge, but by charity, for "Knowledge puffeth up, but charity edifieth." And since there is not in every man the same knowledge, but the consciences of some are weak"; as "my liberty must not be judged of another man's weak conscience," so must not I please myself so much in my right opinion but I must also take order that his "weak conscience be not offended or despised"; for no man must "seek his own, but every man another's wealth." And although we must contend earnestly for the faith, yet "above all things, we must put on charity, which is the bond of perfectness." And, therefore, this contention must be with arms fit for the Christian warfare, "the sword of the Spirit and the shield of faith, and preparation of the Gospel of peace, instead of shoes, and a helmet of salvation." But not with other arms; for a churchman must not be πληκτικὸς, a "striker"; for "the weapons of our warfare are not carnal, but spiritual," and the persons that use them ought to be "gentle, and easy to be entreated"; and we "must give an ac-

count of our faith to them that ask us, with meekness and humility, for so is the will of God, that with well-doing ye may put to silence the ignorance of foolish men." These, and thousands more to the same purpose, are the doctrines of Christianity, whose sense and intendment I have prosecuted in the following discourse, being very much displeased that so many opinions and new doctrines are commenced among us; but more troubled that every man that hath an opinion thinks his own and other men's salvation is concerned in its maintenance; but most of all, that men should be persecuted and afflicted for disagreeing in such opinions, which they cannot, with sufficient grounds, obtrude upon others necessarily, because they cannot propound them infallibly, and because they have no warrant from Scripture so to do. For if I shall tie other men to believe my opinion, because I think I have a place of Scripture which seems to warrant it to my understanding, why may not he serve up another dish to me in the same dress, and exact the same task of me to believe the contradictory? And then, since all the heretics in the world have offered to prove their articles by the same means by which true believers propound theirs, it is necessary that some separation either of doctrine or of persons be clearly made, and that all pretences may not be admitted, nor any just allegations be rejected; and yet, that in some other questions, whether they be truly or falsely pretended, if not evidently or demonstratively, there may be considerations had to the persons of men, and to the laws of charity, more than to the triumphing in any opinion or doctrine not simply necessary. Now because some doctrines are clearly not necessary, and some are absolutely necessary, why may not the first separation be made upon this difference, and articles necessary be only urged as necessary, and the rest left to men indifferently, as they were by the Scripture indeterminately? And it were well if men would as much consider themselves as the doctrines, and think that they may as well be deceived by their own weakness as persuaded by the arguments of a doctrine which other men, as wise, call inevident. For it is a hard case that we should think all Papists and Anabaptists and sacramentaries to be fools and wicked persons; certainly among all these sects there are very many wise men and good men, as well as erring. And although some zeals are so hot, and their eyes so inflamed with their ardors, that they do not think their adversaries look like other men; yet certainly we find by the results of their discourses and the transactions of their affairs of civil society, that they are men that speak and make syllogisms, and use reason, and read Scripture; and although they do no more understand all of it than we do, yet they endeavor to understand as much as concerns them, even all that they can, even all that concerns repentance from dead works, and faith in our Lord Jesus Christ. And, therefore, methinks this also should be another consideration distinguishing the persons: for, if the persons be Christians in their lives, and Christians in their profession, if they acknowledge the eternal Son of God for their Master and their Lord, and live in all relations as becomes persons making such professions, why then should I hate such persons whom God loves, and who love God, who are partakers of Christ, and Christ hath a title to them, who dwell in Christ and Christ in them, because their understandings have not been brought up like mine, have not had the same masters, they have not met with the same books, nor the same company, or have not the same interest, or are not so wise, or else are wiser; that is, for some reason or other, which I neither do understand nor ought to blame,— have not the same opinions that I have, and do not determine their school-questions to the sense of my sect or interest? . . .

And first, I answer that whatsoever is against the foundation of faith, or contrary to good life and the laws of obedience, or destructive to human society and the public and just interests of bodies politic, is out of the limits of my question, and does not pretend to compliance or toleration: so that I allow no indifferency nor any countenance to those religions whose principles destroy government, nor to those religions (if there be any such) that teach ill life; nor do I think

that anything will now excuse from belief of a fundamental article except stupidity or sottishness, and natural inability. This alone is sufficient answer to this vanity, but I have much more to say.

Secondly, the intendment of my discourse is that permissions should be in questions speculative, indeterminable, curious, and unnecessary; and that men would not make more necessities than God made, which indeed are not many. The fault I find, and seek to remedy, is that men are so dogmatical and resolute in their opinions, and impatient of others disagreeing, in those things wherein is no sufficient means of union and determination; but that men should let opinions and problems keep their own forms, and not be obtruded as axioms, nor questions in the vast collection of the system of divinity be adopted into the family of faith. And, I think, I have reason to desire this.

Thirdly, it is hard to say that he who would not have men put to death, or punished corporally, for such things for which no human authority is sufficient, either for cognizance or determination, or competent for infliction, that he persuades to an indifferency when he refers to another judicatory which is competent, sufficient, infallible, just, and highly severe. No man or company of men can judge or punish our thoughts or secret purposes, whilst they so remain. And yet it will be unequal to say that he who owns this doctrine, preaches it lawful for men to think or purpose what they will. And so it is in matters of doubtful disputation, such as are the distinguishing articles of most of the sects of Christendom; so it is in matters intellectual which are not cognizable by a secular power: in matters spiritual, which are to be discerned by spiritual authority, which cannot make corporal inflictions; and in questions indeterminate, which are doubtfully propounded, or obscurely, and, therefore, may be *in utramque partem* disputed or believed. For God alone must be judge of these matters, who alone is master of our souls, and hath a dominion over human understanding; and he that says this does not say that indifferency is persuaded, because God alone is judge of erring persons.

Fourthly, no part of this discourse teaches or encourages variety of sects and contradiction in opinions, but supposes them already in being: and, therefore, since there are, and ever were, and ever will be, variety of opinions, because there is variety of human understandings and uncertainty in things, no man should be too forward in determining all questions, nor so forward in prescribing to others, nor invade that liberty which God hath left to us entire, by propounding many things obscurely, and by exempting our souls and understandings from all power externally compulsory. So that the restraint is laid upon men's tyranny, but no license given to men's opinions; they are not considered in any of the conclusions, but in the premises only, as an argument to exhort to charity. So that if I persuade a license of discrediting anything which God hath commanded us to believe, and allow a liberty where God hath not allowed it, let it be shown, and let the objection press as hard as it can: but to say that men are too forward in condemning, where God hath declared no sentence, nor prescribed any rule, is to dissuade from tyranny, not to encourage licentiousness; is to take away a license of judging, not to give a license of dogmatizing what every one please, or as may best serve his turn. And for the other part of the objection:

Fifthly, this discourse is so far from giving leave to men to profess anything, though they believe the contrary, that it takes order that no man shall be put to it: for I earnestly contend that another man's opinion shall be no rule to mine, and that my opinion shall be no snare and prejudice to myself; that men use one another so charitably and so gently that no error or violence tempt men to hypocrisy; this very thing being one of the arguments I use to persuade permissions, lest compulsion introduce hypocrisy, and make sincerity troublesome and unsafe.

Sixthly, if men would not call all opinions by the name of religion, and superstructures by the name of fundamental articles, and all fancies by the glorious appellative of faith, this objection would have no pretence or footing: so that it is the disease of the men, not any cause that is ministered by such precepts of charity, that makes them perpetually clamorous. And it would be hard to say that such physicians are incurious of their patients, and neglectful of their health, who speak against the unreasonableness of such empirics, that would cut off a man's head if they see but a wart upon his cheek or a dimple upon his chin, or any lines in his face to distinguish him from another man: the case is altogether the same, and we may as well decree a wart to be mortal, as a various opinion *in re alioqui non necessaria* to be capital and damnable. . . .

Bunyan, John, *Grace Abounding, Pilgrim's Progress*. Various editions.

Butterworth, C. C., *English Primers*. Philadelphia: University of Pennsylvania Press, 1953.

Clark, H. W., *History of English Non-Conformity*, 2 vols. London: Chapman and Hall, Ltd., 1911-13.

Cragg, G. P., *Puritanism in the Period of the Great Persecution, 1660-1688*. Cambridge, Eng.: Cambridge University Press, 1957.

D'Aubigne, M., *History of the Reformation in England*, 2 vols. Ft. Washington, Pa.: Christian Literature Crusade, 1961.

Dawley, P. M., *John Whitgift and the English Reformation*. New York: Charles Scribner's Sons, 1954.

Dickens, A. G., *Thomas Cromwell and the English Reformation*. New York: The Macmillan Company, 1960.

Dort, J. L. C., *The Old Religion, English Reformation*. London: SPCK, 1956.

Dugmore, C. W., *The Mass and the English Reformers*. London: Macmillan & Co., Ltd., 1958.

Foxe, John, *Book of Martyrs*. Various editions.

French, Allen, *Charles I and the Puritan Upheaval*. Boston: Houghton Mifflin Company, 1955.

George, Charles and Katharine, *Protestant Mind of the English Reformation, 1570-1640*. Princeton: Princeton University Press, 1961.

Haller, William, *Rise of Puritanism*. New York: Columbia University Press, 1938.

Hopf, C., *Martin Bucer and the English Reformation*. New York: The Macmillan Company, 1947.

Hutchinson, F. E., *Cranmer and the English Reformation*. New York: The Macmillan Company, 1951.

Jordan, W. K., *Development of Religious Toleration in England*, 4 vols. Cambridge: Harvard University Press, 1941.

Milton, John, *Paradise Lost, Paradise Regained, Samson Agonistes*. Various editions.

Parker, T. M., *The English Reformation to 1558*. New York: Oxford University Press, 1952.

Patterson, M. W., *A History of the Church of England*. New York: David McKay Co., Inc., 1909.

Pollard, A. F., *Thomas Cranmer*. London: Longmans, Green & Co., Ltd., 1904.

———, *Wolsey*. London: Longmans, Green & Co., Ltd., 1929.

Powicke, F. M., *Reformation in England*. New York: Oxford University Press, 1941.

Read, Conyers, *Social and Political Forces in the English Reformation*. Princeton: D. Van Nostrand Co., Inc., 1953.

Renwick, A. M., *Story of the Scottish Reformation*. Grand Rapids, Mich.: Wm. B. Eerdmans Publishing Co., 1960.

Smith, L. B., *Tudor Prelates and Politics, 1536-1558*. Princeton: Princeton University Press, 1953.

Sykes, Norman, *From Sheldon to Secker, 1660-1768*. Cambridge, Eng.: Cambridge University Press, 1959.

Taylor, Jeremy, *Holy Living, Holy Dying, Sermons*, from The Whole *Works* of Jeremy Taylor, 10 vols., ed. by Reginald Heber. London: Longmans, Green & Co., Ltd., 1850-54.

Trevelyan, G. M., *English Social History, Chaucer to Queen Victoria*. New York: David McKay Co., Inc., 1942.

White, H. C., *Social Criticism in Popular Religious Literature in the Sixteenth Century*. New York: The Macmillan Company, 1944.

1516	More's Utopia		1603	Millenary Petition
1525	Tyndale's New Testament		1605	Gunpowder Plot
1530	Death of Wolsey		1608–1674	John Milton
1531	Praemunire resurrected		1611	King James Version, Bible
1532	Submission of clergy		1620	Pilgrims land in Massachusetts
1533	Cranmer made Archbishop		1640	Long Parliament assumes control
1533	Restraint of Appeals		1643	Solemn League and Covenant
1534	Supremacy Act		1645	Presbyterian Directory replaces Prayer Book
1535	Coverdale's Old Testament		1647–1648	Westminster Assembly, Confession, Catechism
1536	The Ten Articles		1649	Charles I beheaded
1539	The Six Articles		1665	Five Mile Act
1540	Fall of Cromwell		1667	Milton's Paradise Lost
1549	First Prayer Book		1678	Bunyan's Pilgrim's Progress
1552	Second Prayer Book		1689	Toleration Act, William and Mary
1554	Cardinal Pole absolves England			
1555	Cranmer, Ridley, Latimer martyred			
1559	Act of Uniformity			**RULERS**
1563	Thirty-nine Articles			
1563	Foxe's Book of Martyrs			*England*
1564–1616	William Shakespeare		1509–1547	Henry VIII
1570	Elizabeth excommunicated by Pius V		1547–1553	Edward VI
1572	Bartholomew Day massacre, Paris		1553–1558	Mary
1585	Jesuits expelled from England		1558–1603	Elizabeth I
1587	Mary, Queen of Scots, executed		1603–1625	James I
1588	Defeat of Spanish Armada		1625–1649	Charles I
1593	Acts against Puritans and Catholics Barrow and Greenwood, Puritan Separatists, martyred		1649–1658	Cromwell, Protector
			1660–1685	Charles II
			1685–1688	James II
			1689–1702	William III and Mary

Illustration opposite page 217: Two Freemasons Contemplating a Globe. *Porcelain (Meissen ware) by Johann Kändler, 1744. Collection Irwin Untermyer, New York.*

V

The Age of Reason

The scientific-rationalistic spirit that
altered the expression of religion in the life of modern man
noticeably began in the seventeenth century, reached a
climax in the German enlightenment, and
reverberated in the nineteenth century in waves of modernism.
The Peace of Westphalia (1648) ended the last war in
which religion was the dominant cause, not that religion did not figure
in warfare after 1648; but in Western civilization, religion
simply ceased to be the central cause of national
conflicts. Westphalia marked the end of an old age and
the beginning of a new era, an era that looked to a new authority,
the authority of human reason. Reason displaced the church as
man's spiritual symbol, and man confidently believed that
human reason could unravel the secrets of man's origin,
nature, and destiny. The ineffectiveness of *Zelo Domus Dei,*
the bull of Pope Innocent X, which condemned the
treaty of Westphalia as "null and void, and accursed, and without
influence for the past, present or future" was a prophetic
symbol of the lack of ecclesiastical authority in the age of reason.

The papacy could still interdict and depose, but its fulminations were regarded with indifference and disdain. Protestant sermonic injunctions echoed from empty pews as institutional religion fell to a low social ebb, for men's lives were organized around other centers—the reason of every man.

The first phase of the age of reason began in the late seventeenth century in England, in men like Sir Isaac Newton, John Locke, and John Toland, and in the next century in men like David Hume. The second phase occurred on the Continent, in Germany and France, in the eighteenth century, dominated by men like Voltaire, Lessing, Kant, and Paine. The age reached its philosophical zenith in Immanuel Kant, its most direct religious embodiment in the free-thinking of Deism and Unitarianism, its destructive political expression in the French Revolution, and its polemical climax in Thomas Paine. The effects of the period continued into the nineteenth century, for modernism represented an attempt to come to terms with the repercussions of the age of reason. To it can be traced the liberal-fundamentalist division in Protestantism, and to it can be traced the ultramontane reaction of modern Catholicism, which expressed itself in the claims of infallibility.

Reliance on man's rational ability was not new in Christianity; it reached all the way back to the early days, when Greek philosophy made its impact on the Christian tradition. It can be found in many individual thinkers along the historical path of Christianity, and it attained considerable vogue in the humanism of the Renaissance in men like Erasmus, Reuchlin, and More. The Protestant Reformation introduced the right of individual conscience. At Worms in 1521, Luther appealed both to right reason and to Scripture, thus giving historical precedence to the use of reason in testing faith and in interpreting Scripture. But the Reformation in general tended toward the establishment of authoritative, confessional creeds, often coercively enforced, and the Bible was generally held to be as sacrosanct in Protestantism as the pope was in Catholicism. After the Peace of Augsburg, 1555, Lutheranism settled for the confining scholasticism of the Formula of Concord, 1577, and Calvinism and the Reformed branches settled for the orthodoxy of the Synod of Dort and the Heidelberg Catechism. In Germany, Switzer-

V-1. An Eighteenth Century Coffee House, Favorite Gathering Place for Discussion. *A contemporary drawing.*

land, and England, different forms of Protestant orthodoxy prevailed, established not by reason but by the secular arm of power. Not even the persecuted Anabaptists wholly escaped these tendencies.

When reason asserted itself as an authority in the seventeenth century, men followed it as if utopia were within their grasp, for the age of reason came after a period of acrimonious persecution and religious strife, and the relative tolerance that marked the eighteenth century was like an inalienable right which man had at last obtained. Men were weary of fanatical orthodoxy, whether Roman Catholic or Protestant, of witchburning, heretic hunting, inquisitorial racks, and wholesale slaughter. Alexander Pope caught much of the feeling of the time when he wrote, "For modes of faith let graceless zealots fight" (6).

Man's investigations of nature led him to believe that the world is a grand mechanism controlled by constant laws which man can know and manipulate. The dramatic triumphs of science in the discoveries of Copernicus, Kepler, and Galileo received mathematical demonstration in Sir Isaac Newton's *Principia*, published in 1687, in which he showed that gravitation is the key to the motions of heavenly bodies. And in his principles of reasoning, Newton (1642-1727) reduced the scientific method to a convincing, logical basis for further investigation (2). Newton's ideas became common knowledge. A translation of his Latin treatise was popularized and widely circulated under the title, "Newtonianism for Ladies." His ideas led men to regard the universe as a realm in which the laws of cause and effect, rather than the actions of arbitrary divinity, prevail. In the four principles of reasoning, Newton laid down the steps for discovering the unchangeable laws of the universe. Armed with Newton's rules, men increasingly questioned old forms of authority, called for tolerance, and glorified reason. Tangible scientific achievements increased man's confidence in reason as a universal guide in every field. Why should the so-called revelations of the keepers of religion be any more sacred or reliable than the discoveries of the divinely-given, universal reason of mankind? Men became more interested in the God of Nature than in the God of Scripture, and natural reason as the discoverer of that God of Nature acted as the regulative force in the affairs of man, resulting in a generalized ethical theism, a tolerant broadening of religious forms, a scepticism with regard to supernatural claims, and a confidence in human ability to solve all mysteries. Free will was extolled, predestination and depravity decried. Former distrust of man's reason and human culture, as seen in the traditional emphasis on original sin, gave way to dependence on reason and the glorification of man's culture as the flower of that reliance. The Bible and institutional ecclesiasticism seemed anachronistic (5).

When reason appeared as the tester of authority, it seemed to threaten government and the scriptural foundation of religion; but tolerance and trust in reason prevailed, despite the revocation of the Edict of Nantes in 1685 by Louis XIV, despite the blood baths that Spain initiated in trying to reestablish church and empire as in medieval days, despite the expulsion of 15,000 Protestants from Salzburg, and despite the widespread efforts of the Society of Jesus. The old age had passed.

Reaction, however, did come from other quarters, induced by the arrogant claims of rationalism itself. In England, competent thinkers like Butler, Berkeley, and Hume showed that reliance on reason leads to scepticism and self-destruction. In Germany and later in England, the pietists and evangelicals effectively demonstrated that fervent, emotional religion still had power to change men's lives, and that arid intellectualism is not a final solution. In the French Revolution, men witnessed and recoiled from the destructive anarchy of rampant reason without authority. Immanuel Kant shattered the traditional aspects of theology, limited religion to the laws of reason, and branded many Christian rites and ceremonies as pseudo-services to God with questionable social effects.

Philosophy combined with science to give the immediate background for the spirit of the age. René Descartes (1596-1650), a Catholic, who was born in France but spent most of his life in the Netherlands, wrote *Discourse on Method* in 1637, *First Philosophy* in 1641, and *Principia* in 1644. Only that which is clear and certain is really knowledge, he said, and if man is to find a sure foundation for his knowledge, he must doubt everything until he finds that basis or point of departure which cannot be doubted. Descartes believed he had found such a basis in his own thinking existence; "I think, therefore I am." From this basis, step by step, "with mathematical clarity," he proved the existence of God, in whom being and thought are united, and sought to show that matter, which has its source in God, has been given both extension and mechanical motion by God. However, it was not the details of his philosophy that were to be so momentous for religion, but his twin assertions: *All conceptions must be doubted until adequately demonstrated, and adequate proof must have the certainty of mathematics.* A clearer standard for the age of reason could hardly have been devised. Matched with the call of Sir Francis Bacon (1561-1626) to observe nature, the dramatic discoveries of science, and the scientific method of Newton's rules of reasoning, the age of reason had a formidable sounding board for its voice of confidence.

William Chillingworth (1602-1644), an apostate from the Church of England who later renounced Rome and returned to the Anglican fold, is sometimes called the father of the rationalists in religion. In 1638 he published a book, *The Religion of Protestants, A Safe Way of Salvation*, in which he contended that free inquiry was the great principle of Protestantism, and that it was a safe way of salvation because, despite human error, it would if honestly followed lead to a participation in God's promises (*1*). "For my part," wrote Chillingworth, "I am certain that God hath given us our reason to discern between truth and falsehood, and he that makes not this use of it but believes things he knows not why, I say, it is by chance that he believes the truth and not by choice; and that I cannot but fear, that God will not ac-

cept this sacrifice of fools." Neither Geneva, Canterbury, nor Rome liked this view, but Chillingworth's book attracted much attention and by 1742 had gone through seven editions.

The interest of Lord Herbert of Cherbury (1583-1648) in other religions tended to undercut the claim of Christianity to be the one, true, revealed religion, for he called attention to many similarities in all religions. He developed some of the principles of Deism and fathered the science of comparative religion. In *De Veritate*, 1624, he maintained that the five essential parts of religion could be deduced from a comparison of various religions, namely, that God exists, that He should be worshipped, that virtue and piety are bound to worship, that men should repent of their sins, and that a future life of rewards and punishments awaits man. When Lord Herbert lay dying, Archbishop Usher refused to give him communion.

John Locke (1632-1704) greatly influenced the trend to rationalism. In his *Essay Concerning Human Understanding* in 1690, he maintained that we are not born with innate ideas, that instead the mind at birth is like a piece of white paper on which sensations write their impressions. These are combined by the mind through reflection into simple and complex ideas. Knowledge, therefore, is to be judged by reason based on experience. He sought to demonstrate the existence of God from cause and effect, and to show that morality is demonstrable, for he believed that religion, although it might be above reason or beyond experience, could not be contradictory to reason. In his *Reasonableness of Christianity*, 1695 (*3*), Locke sought to show that the excellence of Christianity is in its reasonableness, that even the miracles do not attest anything unreasonable. He believed that the ethical injunctions of the Bible are in accord with the dictates of reason, but he would not dispense with the corroboration of revelation; he was content to show that it did not really contradict reason and experience. He accepted Christ as Messiah and King, and he denounced John Toland for trying to make the revealed elements of Scripture superfluous. When he died, Locke was in full communion with the Church of England. These views, his pleas for toleration, and his ideas on politics profoundly affected the eighteenth century.

When John Toland (1670-1722) published *Christianity Not Mysterious* in 1696, he aroused much controversy (4). His book prompted the writing of more than 115 answers and was burned by the common hangman in Dublin on order of the House of Commons of Ireland. One member wanted the book burned in front of the House, that he might have the pleasure of treading on its ashes. So much was said about Toland from the pulpits that an Irish peer in Dublin justified his not attending church on the ground that it was John Toland and not Jesus Christ who was discussed there. Toland refused to accept any belief without proof. He lauded the Scriptures as reasonable and simple, and accused professional religionists of having obscured the clear and simple teachings of Jesus, especially with regard to the Eucharist and Baptism.

Anthony Collins's *Discourse of Freethinking,* Woolston's *Six Discourses on the Miracles,* and Thomas Chubb's *Remarks on the Scriptures* stirred the controversy to a boiling point. In 1730, Matthew Tindal (1657-1733) wrote *Christianity as Old as Creation,* in which he argued that natural religion is all that man needs, and that this can be apprehended by reason. What is valuable in revelation is also in natural religion, and so what is valuable in Christianity is as old as creation. Whatever does not conform to reason is either superfluous, superstitious, or worthless. Miracles do not add anything to what reason discovers, and are an insult to the perfectly ordered, mechanical laws which the divine Creator has set going. These arguments and attacks on revealed Christianity circulated freely among the Deists.

William Law (1686-1761) answered Tindal in a book entitled *The Case of Reason,* 1732, in which he declared that far from finding truth in religion, reason "is the cause of all the disorders of our passions, the corruptions of our hearts" (7). He placed God beyond the power of reason to comprehend, and made divine goodness arbitrary. His de-

votional works added to his effectiveness in this controversy (cf. Ch. 6).

The arguments over Deism as such seem to have quieted with the publication of Joseph Butler's (1692-1752) *Analogy of Religion* in 1736 (8). Butler was a Presbyterian by descent, but he entered the Church of England at an early age. Two years after the publication he was named bishop of Bristol, and later of Durham. He admitted the Deist position that God exists, that nature is uniform in its course, and that man's knowledge has limitations; then he developed his theory of probability. Since the same objections can be raised against the course of nature as against revelation, it is probable that both have the same author. This theory of probability became his answer to the Deists. Since conduct now influences happiness, it is probable that conduct will also influence the future. Revelation is probable, rather than improbable or impossible, and it becomes a historical question so far as its attestation is concerned. The book was an immensely popular answer to Deism, and for many years was required reading in universities, both in England and America.

Lasting criticism of both the Deists and their opponents came from David Hume (1711-1776), the most influential British philosopher of his century. His *Treatise of Human Nature* in 1739 did not receive much attention, but *Philosophical Essays* in 1748 and the *Natural History of Religion* in 1757 revealed him as one of the great thinkers of the time. He maintained that all our knowledge comes from experience, and that we receive it in isolated impressions and ideas. There are no causal connections between things and events; our minds are simply by habit accustomed to inferring such connections because they are observed in association. By subverting causality, Hume ruled out any argument for God based thereon, and by denying a permanent "I" behind experience, he left no philosophical basis for immortality. In his "Essay on Miracles" in 1748, Hume applied his philosophical ideas and alleged the impossibility of producing enough testimony to justify belief in miracles (9). Since our knowledge comes from experience, and experience testifies to the uniformity of nature, one must weigh this against the probability of human error or deceit in alleging a miracle. That human fallibility has led to the report of a miracle is thus more likely than that the uniform course of nature has been interrupted. To base doctrine on a miracle, granted that one occurred, would require the further proof that the miracle occurred in order to establish the doctrine. Hume's criticism was telling. In 1776, his *Dialogue on Natural Religion* attacked the argument from the standpoint of design, which was widely used by the Deists to assert the existence of the God of Nature. Hume left scepticism in his wake, and after him Deism tended to wane in England.

On the Continent, however, especially in France and Germany, Deism asserted itself with renewed vigor. Its greatest proponent in France was undoubtedly Voltaire (1694-1778), one of the sharpest minds of the century. He had become acquainted with many of the tenets of Deism when on a three-year sojourn in England between 1726 and 1729. He boasted that it might have taken twelve men to establish Christianity, but it would take only one to destroy it. He believed in a God and in a simple, ethical religion based on nature, but he repudiated Christianity as an unreasonable fraud. He hated tyranny and hypocrisy in any form, and lost no opportunity to pillory them with ridicule, whether he found them in the church, the forum, or the public square. His attacks on the church, the Bible, and the creeds were devastating (10). Associated with him in the debunking of revealed religion were the French encyclopedists, who between 1751 and 1765 published the thirty-five volumes of the *Dictionnaire universel et raisonné de connaissances humaines*. Their views tended more and more toward atheism and disrespect for all authority. Although Voltaire had been brought up by the Jesuits, he saw in the Roman Church only a pattern of priestly exploitation, superstition, intolerance, and persecution. In Voltaire, rationalism advanced beyond cautious probing and questioning to bitter belligerency.

When Tindal's *Christianity as Old as Crea-* tion was translated and published in Germany in 1741, it was an immediate sensation. Christian Wolff (1679-1754) continued the arguments of deistic rationalism by maintaining that religious truths can be mathematically demonstrated. In 1723 he was ordered to leave the pietistic stronghold of Halle or be hanged. Herman S. Reimarus (1694-1768), in *Wolfenbüttel Fragments*, argued that true natural religion teaches the existence of God, a primitive morality, and immortality, all within the scope of man's reason, and that the great miracle and revelation is our world. Wolff and Reimarus made the Bible and inspired revelation superfluous. Gotthold E. Lessing (1729-1781), in a tract called *The Education of the Human Race*, 1780, theorized that the race is going through three successive stages, just as do individual men, and that God gave guideposts for each stage: The Old Testament promises of reward and punishment for the stage of childhood, the New Testament ideals of self-surrender and eternality for the stage of youth, and the dutiful demands of reason without hope of reward or fear of punishment for the stage of manhood. He thus placed reason above Scripture; reason is for mature men, the Bible for children and youth.

Immanuel Kant (1724-1804) brought the enlightened age of reason to a climax and pushed the entire discussion to a new phase. His pietistic background would not permit him to discard Christianity as outworn, and his philosophical insight would not allow him to rest in the scepticism of Hume. In the preface to the *Critique of Pure Reason*, 1781, he declared he would set forth the limits of reason in order to make way for faith. Kant argued that our knowledge of the external world of nature is the result of sensations that come to us through our mind's forms of space and time and the twelve categories. These forms and categories are the mechanism of the mind. We have no direct knowledge of the outside world; we have only the sensations that have been organized by our minds. Such contact with outside things constitutes experience, but we never know any actual entity. Consequently, our knowledge of nature is no more absolute than our intimations of divine things, which because they are of a different nature seem vague and unverifiable in comparison. This tended to undercut the foundations of the naturalists in religion, and to open the way for idealism based on the categorical imperative of the practical reason of man. Anything beyond space and time is outside the realm of the senses and cannot be a subject of pure reason. Religion is beyond pure reason. But man uses reason practically with regard to morality, as well as purely with regard to knowledge. In the *Critique of Practical Reason,* 1788, Kant maintained that man's practical reason convinces him of his moral personality, freedom, and immortality, although, as in the realm of knowledge, he never realizes these absolutely in this life. Man's sense of moral necessity he termed the categorical imperative or moral law, which is present in all men: "so act in all things as if the maxim of your action by your will were to become a universal law of nature" (*11*). From this Kant developed all ethics. He maintained that infinite progress is demanded by the moral law, and that the immortality of man is a necessary assumption for this fulfillment. God must exist as a guarantee of the moral law, and freedom is derived from God and moral law (*12*). In *Religion Within the Limits of Reason Alone,* 1793, Kant considered religion as a theistic ethic in which evil and the categorical imperative vie for the obedience of man.

Kant rescued revealed religion from the mire into which it was being trampled by rationalistic Deists, but in doing so he deprived Scripture and the church of any distinctive place, and virtually reduced religion to the moral imperative and those necessary laws and laudable practices which can be deduced from it. His idealism found expression in Hegel, Schleiermacher, Ritschl, Harnack, and many others; his scepticism was recast in another mould by Schopenhauer, Nietzsche, and Marx.

Thomas Paine (1737-1809), an English Quaker, was prominently associated with the American Revolution through his *Common Sense* in 1776, which placed the issue of political freedom squarely before the American people, and with the French Revolution through his *Rights of Man* in 1791. More than any other person in his age, he vigorously presented Deism in a popular garb. He penned the *Rights of Man* in reply to Edmund Burke's reactionary *Reflections on the French Revolution,* which was a defense of hereditary succession in government, and then he fled England to escape being jailed for his efforts. In France, he promoted democratic processes but was imprisoned for objecting to the execution of Louis XVI. On the way to prison he gave the first part of *The Age of Reason* to a friend who had it published in England, in 1794 (*13*). The publisher was fined £1,500 and sentenced to three years in jail. Paine ended his career in New Rochelle, New York, where ironically he was denied the right to vote.

Reactions to the deistic-rationalistic movement came from the giants of the romantic movement—Jean Jacques Rousseau (1712-1778) in France, and Johann Wolfgang von Goethe (1749-1832) and Johann Christoph Friedrich von Schiller (1759-1805) in Germany.

However, it was the Evangelical Movement (cf. Ch. 6) that most effectively combatted rationalism and revived the fervor of warm-hearted Christianity. To it belong Spener, Zinzendorf, Wesley, Whitefield, Watts, Bach, Handel, Goldsmith, and Gray, to mention only a few.

The selections which follow are intended to give an introduction to the main lines of thought in the age of reason. The philosophical aspects, especially those of Kant, should be studied in their entirety.

1. *William Chillingworth, 1638*

In his spirited defense of Protestantism, William Chillingworth maintains that Roman Catholicism in its claims to infallibility has led men astray, and that Protestantism, with its authority grounded in Scripture and reason, is a safer way of salvation. He refutes the charges that Protestants are heretical and schismatic, and argues that it is not a sin for Protestants to remain separated from the Roman Church. The following excerpts are only a small part of this very large book, but they indicate the attitude of Protestants concerning the place of reason and Scripture in their religion. Chillingworth is replying to statements made by the author of a book called *Charity Maintained,* by Catholics. William Chillingworth, *The Religion of Protestants: A Safe Way of Salvation,* with excerpts from *Charity Maintained,* by Edward Knott [Matthew Wilson] (London: Bohn Library, 1854).

CHARITY MAINTAINED

II. We acknowledge Holy Scripture to be a most perfect rule, for as much as writing can be a rule: we only deny that it excludes either Divine tradition, though it be unwritten, or an external judge, to keep, to propose, to interpret it in a true, orthodox, and catholic sense. . . . That Scripture alone cannot be judge in controversies of faith, we gather very clearly from the quality of a writing in general; from the nature of holy writ in particular, which must be believed as true and infallible; from the editions and translations of it; from the difficulty to understand it without hazard of error; from the inconveniences that must follow upon the ascribing of sole judicature to it; and, finally, from the confessions of our adversaries. And, on the other side, all these difficulties ceasing, and all other qualities requisite to a judge concurring in the visible church of Christ our Lord, we must conclude, that she it is to whom, in doubts concerning faith and religion, all Christians ought to have recourse. . . .

CHILLINGWORTH ANSWERS

II. In your second paragraph, you sum up those arguments wherewith you intend to prove that "Scripture alone cannot be judge in controversies": wherein I profess unto you beforehand, that you will fight without an adversary. For though Protestants, being warranted by some of the fathers, have called Scripture *the judge of controversy,* and you, in saying here that "Scripture *alone* cannot be judge," imply that it may be called in some sense a judge, though not alone; yet to speak properly (as men should speak when they write of controversies in religion), the Scripture is not a judge of controversies, but a rule only, and the only rule, for Christians to judge them by. Every man is to judge for himself with the judgment of discretion, and to choose either

his religion first, and then his church, as we say; or, as you, his church first, and then his religion. But, by the consent of both sides, every man is to judge and choose; and the rule whereby he is to guide his choice, if he be a natural man, is reason; if he be already a Christian, Scripture; which we say is a rule to judge controversies by. Yet not all simply, but all the controversies of Christians, of those that are already agreed upon this first principle, that the Scripture is the word of God. But that there is any man, or any company of men, appointed to be judge for all men, that we deny; and that, I believe, you will never prove. The very truth is, we say no more in this matter than evidence of truth hath made you confess in plain terms in the beginning of this chapter; viz. "that Scripture is a perfect rule of faith, for as much as a writing can be a rule." So that all your reasons, whereby you labor to dethrone the Scripture from this office of judging, we might let pass as impertinent to the conclusion which we maintain, and you have already granted; yet out of courtesy we will consider them.

Your first is this: "A judge must be a person fit to end controversies; but the Scripture is not a person, nor fit to end controversies, no more than the law would be without the judges; therefore, though it may be a rule, it cannot be a judge." Which conclusion I have already granted: only my request is, that you will permit Scripture to have the properties of a rule, that is, to be fit to direct every one that will make the best use of it, to that end for which it was ordained; and that is as much as we need desire. For as if I were to go a journey, and had a guide which could not err, I needed not to know my way; so, on the other side, if I know my way, or have a plain rule to know it by, I shall need no guide. Grant therefore Scripture to be such a rule, and it will quickly take away all necessity of having an infallible guide. . . .

[You say] you must not use your own reason nor your judgment, but refer all to the church, and believe her to be conformable to antiquity, though they have no reason for it; nay, though they have evident reason to the contrary. For my part, I am certain that God hath given us our reason to discern between truth and falsehood, and he that makes not this use of it, but believes things he knows not why, I say, it is by chance that he believes the truth, and not by choice; and that I cannot but fear that God will not accept this *sacrifice of fools.*

VI. Know then, sir, that when I say the religion of Protestants is in prudence to be preferred before yours, as, on the one side, I do not understand by your religion, the doctrine of Bellarmine or Baronius, or any other private man amongst you; nor the doctrine of the Sorbonne, or of the Jesuits, or of the Dominicans, or of any other particular company among you, but that wherein you all agree, or profess to agree, "The doctrine of the council of Trent": so accordingly on the other side, by the "religion of Protestants," I do not understand the doctrine of Luther, or Calvin, or Melanchthon; nor the confession of Augusta, or Geneva, nor the Catechism of Heidelberg, nor the Articles of the Church of England, no, nor the harmony of Protestant confessions; but that wherein they all agree, and which they all subscribe with a greater harmony, as a perfect rule of their faith and actions; that is, the *Bible.* The *Bible,* I say, the *Bible* only, is the religion of Protestants! Whatsoever else they believe besides it, and the plain, irrefragable, indubitable consequences of it, well may they hold it as a matter of opinion; but as matter of faith and religion, neither can they with coherence to their own grounds believe it themselves, nor require the belief of it of others, without most high and most schismatical presumption. I for my part, after a long and (as I verily believe and hope) impartial search of "The true way to eternal happiness," do profess plainly that I cannot find any rest for the sole of my foot but upon this rock only. I see plainly and with mine own eyes, that there are popes against popes, councils against councils, some fathers against others, the same fathers against themselves, a consent of fathers of one age against the consent of fathers of another age, the church of one age against the church of another age. Traditive interpretations of Scripture are pretended; but there are few or none to be found: no tradition, but only of Scripture, can derive itself from the fountain, but may be plainly proved either to have been brought in, in such an age after Christ, or that in such an age it was not in. In a word, there is no sufficient certainty but of Scripture only for any considering man to build upon. This therefore, and this only, I have reason to believe: this I will profess, according to this I will live, and for this, if there be occasion, I will not only willingly, but even gladly, lose my life, though I should be sorry that Christians should take it from me. Propose me anything out of this book, and require whether I believe it or no, and seem it never so incomprehensible to human reason, I will subscribe it with hand and heart, as knowing no demonstration can be stronger than this; God hath said so, therefore it is true. In other things I will take no man's liberty of judgment from him, neither shall any man take mine from me. I will think no man the worse man, nor the worse Christian, I will love no man the less, for differing in opinion from me. And what measure I mete to others, I expect from them again. I am fully assured that God does not, and therefore that men ought not, to require any more of any man than this, to believe the Scripture to be God's word, to endeavour to find the true sense of it, and to live according to it.

.   .   .   .   .

Following your church, I must hold many things not only above reason, but against it, if anything be against; whereas, following the Scripture, I shall believe many mysteries, but no impossibilities; many things above reason, but nothing against it; many things which, had they not been revealed, reason could never have discovered, but nothing which by true reason may be confuted; many things, which reason cannot comprehend how they can be, but nothing which reason can comprehend that it cannot be. Nay, I shall believe nothing which reason will not convince that I ought to believe it; for reason will convince any man, unless he be of a perverse mind, that the Scripture is the word of God: and then no reason can be greater than this; God says so, therefore it is true.

Following your church, I must hold many things, which to any man's judgment, that will give himself the liberty of judgment, will seem much more plainly contradicted by Scripture, than the infallibility of your church appears to be confirmed by it; and consequently, must be so foolish as to believe your church exempted from error upon less evidence, rather than subject to the common condition of mankind upon greater evidence. Now, if I take the Scripture only for my guide, I shall not need to do anything so unreasonable. . . .

2. Newton's Four Rules of Reasoning

These rules, assuming that every effect has a cause, helped open the way for a scientific understanding of phenomena, and also for a deistic, mechanical view of a universe which God created and set in motion to run by certain fixed laws. The result was a trend in religion that was critical of supernatural elements, revelations, miracles, and so on, as shown in subsequent selections. *Sir Isaac Newton's Mathematical Principles,* revised translation by Florian Cajori (Berkeley: University of California Press, 1934).

Rule I. *We are to admit no more causes of natural things than such as are both true and sufficient to explain their appearances.* To this purpose the philosophers say that Nature does nothing in vain, and more is in vain when less will serve; for Nature is pleased with simplicity, and affects not the pomp of superfluous causes.

Rule II. *Therefore to the same natural effects we must, as far as possible, assign the same causes.* As to respiration in a man and in a beast . . . the light of our culinary fire and of the sun; the reflection of light in the earth, and in the planets.

Rule III. *The qualities of bodies . . . which are found to belong to all bodies within the reach of our experiments, are to be esteemed the universal qualities of all bodies whatsoever. . . .* If it universally appears, by experiments and astronomical observations, that all bodies about the earth gravitate towards the earth; that the moon likewise gravitates towards the earth; that,

on the other hand, our sea gravitates towards the moon; and all the planets one towards the other; and the comets in like manner towards the sun; we must, in consequence of this rule, universally allow that all bodies whatsoever are endowed with a principle of mutual gravitation. . . .

Rule IV. *In experimental philosophy we are to look upon propositions collected by general induction from phenomena as accurately or very nearly true, notwithstanding any contrary hypotheses that may be imagined, till such time as other phenomena occur, by which they may be made more accurate, or liable to exceptions.* This rule must follow, that the argument of induction may not be evaded by hypotheses.

3. John Locke, 1695

"By examining the life and teachings of Jesus and his Apostles' preaching, step by step, all through the history of the four Evangelists, and the acts of the Apostles," Locke sought to show the simple reasonableness of Christianity in what it demands one to believe and do. The following excerpts indicate the nature of his conclusions. He acknowledged reason, and at the same time remained orthodox. *The Works of John Locke* (London: C. & J. Rivington, 1824). Cf. Locke, *The Reasonableness of Christianity* (Boston: T. B. Wait & Co., 1811).

. . . [Paul] tells the Athenians, that they and the rest of the world (who were given up to superstition,) were given what light was in the works of creation and providence to lead them to the true God, yet few of them found him. He was every where near them; yet they were but like people groping and feeling for something in the dark, and did not see him with a full clear daylight; "But thought the godhead like to gold and silver and stone, graven by art and man's device." [Acts 17:22-29]

In this state of darkness and error in reference to the true God, our Saviour found the world. But the clear revelation he brought with him, dissipated this darkness; and made the one, invisible, true God known to the world: And that, with such evidence and energy, that polytheism and idolatry have no where been able to withstand it; but wherever the preaching of the truth and the light of the gospel have come, those mists have been dispelled. And, in effect, we see, that since our Saviour's time, the belief of *One God* has prevailed and spread itself over the face of the earth. For even to the light that the Messiah brought into the world with him, we must ascribe the owning and profession of one God, which the Mahometan religion hath derived and borrowed from it. So that, in this sense, it is certainly and manifestly true of our Saviour, what St. John says of him: "For this purpose the Son of God was manifested; that he might destroy the works of the devil." [I John 3:8] This light the world needed, and this light it received from him; namely, that there is but one God; and he, eternal, invisible; not like to any visible objects, nor to be represented by them.

Next to the knowledge of one God, maker of all things; a clear knowledge of their duty was wanting to mankind.... We see how unsuccessful in this, the attempts of philosophers were, before our Saviour's time. How short their several systems came of the perfection of a true and complete morality, is indeed very visible. And if, since that time, the christian philosophers have much outdone them; yet we may observe that the first knowledge of the truths they have added, are owing to revelation; though as soon as they are heard and considered, they are found to be agreeable to reason, and such as can by no means be contradicted. Every one may observe a great many truths which he receives at first from others, and readily assents to, as consonant to reason; which he would have found it hard, and perhaps beyond his strength, to have discovered himself. Experience shews that the knowledge of morality, by mere natural light (how agreeable soever it be to it,) makes but a slow progress and little advance in the world. And the reason of it is not hard to be found in men's necessities, passions, vices, and mistaken interests; which turn their thoughts another way. And the designing leaders, as well as the following herd, find it not to their purpose to employ much of their meditations this way. Or, whatever else was the cause, it is plain in fact, that human reason when unassisted, failed men in its great and proper business of morality. It never,

from unquestionable principles, by clear deductions, made out an entire body of the law of nature. And he that shall collect all the moral rules of the philosophers, and compare them with those contained in the New Testament, will find them to come short of the morality delivered by our Saviour, and taught by his apostles: (a college made up for the most part, of ignorant, but inspired fishermen)....

Such a law of morality, Jesus Christ hath given us in the New Testament, but it was by the latter of these ways, by revelation. We have from him a full and sufficient rule for our direction; and conformable to that of reason. But the truth and obligation of its precepts have their force, and are put past doubt to us, by the evidence of his mission. He was sent by God; his miracles shew it; and the authority of God in his precepts cannot be questioned. Here morality has a sure standard, which revelation vouches, and reason cannot gainsay nor question; but which both together witness to come from God the great law-maker....

Be the cause [of reason's failure to establish morality] what it will, our Saviour found mankind under a corruption of manners and principles, which ages after ages had prevailed, and which, it must be confessed, was not in a way or tendency to be mended. The rules of morality were, in different countries and sects, different. And natural reason no where had cured, nor was likely to cure, the defects and errors in them. Those just measures of right and wrong, which necessity had any where introduced, and which the civil laws prescribed, or philosophy recommended, stood not on their true foundations. They were looked on as bonds of society, and conveniences of common life, and laudable practices: But where was it that their obligation was thoroughly known and allowed, and where were they received as precepts of a law, the highest law, the law of nature? That could not be, with out a clear knowledge and acknowledgment of the lawmaker, and of the great rewards and punishments [provided] for those that would or would not obey him. But the religion of the heathens (as was before observed) little concerned itself in their morals. The priests that delivered the oracles of heaven, and pretended to speak from the god, spoke little of virtue and a good life. And on the other side, the philosophers who spoke from reason, made not much mention of the Deity, in their ethics. [Their writings on morality] depended on reason and her oracles, which contain nothing but truth, yet some parts of that truth lie too deep for our natural powers easily to reach and make plain and visible to mankind, without some light from above to direct. . . .

God, out of the infiniteness of his mercy, has dealt with man as a compassionate and tender father. He gave him reason; and with it a law, that could not be otherwise than what reason should dictate; unless we should think, that a reasonable creature, should have an unreasonable law. But considering the frailty of man, (apt to run into corruption and misery,) he promised a deliverer, whom in his good time he sent; and then declared to all mankind, that whoever would believe him to be the Saviour promised, and take him now raised from the dead and constituted the lord and judge of all men, to be their king and ruler, should be saved.

This is a plain intelligible proposition; and the all-merciful God seems herein to have consulted the poor of this world, and the bulk of mankind. These are articles that the laboring and illiterate man may comprehend. . . .

. . . That the poor had the gospel preached to them, Christ makes a [sign] as well as the business, of his mission. [Matt. 11:5] And if the poor had the gospel preached to them, it was, without doubt, such a gospel as the poor could understand, plain and intelligible.

4. John Toland, 1696

John Toland, *Christianity Not Mysterious* (London: Sam Buckley, 1696).

Christianity Not Mysterious: Or, A Treatise Shewing, That There Is Nothing in the Gospel Contrary to Reason, Nor Above It: And That No Christian Doctrine Can Be Properly Call'd A Mystery.

[From the Preface] I hope to make it appear, that the Use of Reason is not so dangerous in Religion as it is commonly represented, and that too by such as mightily extol it, when it seems to favour 'em, yet vouchsafe it not a hearing when it makes against them, but oppose its own Authority to itself. . . . I hold nothing as an Article of my Religion, but what the highest Evidence forc'd me to embrace. . . . Since Religion is calculated for reasonable Creatures, 'tis Conviction and not Authority that should bear Weight with them. . . . Truth is always and everywhere the same; and an unintelligible or absurd Proposition is to be never the more respected for being ancient or strange, for being originally written in Latin, Greek, or Hebrew. . . . The true Religion must necessarily be reasonable and intelligible. . . .

[From the Essay] There is nothing that Men make a greater Noise about, in our Time especially, than what they generally profess least of all to understand . . . I mean the Mysteries of the Christian Religion. . . . Some say the Mysteries of the Gospel are to be understood only in the Sense of the Ancient Fathers. . . . Others tell us we must be of the Mind of some particular Doctors, pronounc'd Orthodox by the Authority of the Church. . . . Some give a decisive Voice in the Unravelling of Mysteries, and the Interpretation of Scripture, to a General Council; and others to one Man whom they hold to be the head of the Church Universal upon Earth, and the infallible Judge of all Controversies. . . . But they come nearest the thing who affirm, that we are to keep what the Scriptures determine about these Matters: and there is nothing more true, if rightly understood. . . . Some will have us always believe what the literal Sense imports, with little or no Consideration for Reason, which they reject as not fit to be employ'd about the reveal'd Part of Religion. Others assert, that we may use Reason as the Instrument, but not the Rule of our Belief. The first contend, some Mysteries may be, or at least seem to be contrary to Reason, and yet be receiv'd by Faith. The second, that no Mystery is contrary to Reason, but that all are above it. Both of 'em from different Principles agree, that several Doctrines of the New Testament belong no farther to the Enquiries of Reason than to prove 'em divinely reveal'd, and that they are properly Mysteries still.

On the contrary, we hold that Reason is the only Foundation of all Certitude; and that nothing reveal'd whether as to its Manner or Existence, is more exempted from its Disquisitions, than the ordinary Phenomena of Nature. Wherefore, we likewise maintain, that there is nothing in the Gospel contrary to Reason, nor above it; and that no Christian Doctrine can be properly call'd a Mystery. . . .

Every one experiences in himself a Power or Faculty of forming various Ideas or Perceptions of Things: Of affirming or denying, according as he sees them to agree or disagree: And so of loving and desiring what seems good unto him; and of hating and avoiding what he thinks evil. The right Use of all these Faculties is what we call Common Sense, or Reason in general. But the bare Act of receiving Ideas into the Mind . . . is not strictly Reason, because the Soul herein is purely passive. When a proper Object is conveniently presented to the Eye, Ear, or any other sense rightly dispos'd, it necessarily makes those Impressions which the Mind at the same time cannot refuse to lodge. (Not the object, but an idea lodges in the mind) and I have not only an Idea of the Picture that is before me, but likewise know, I perceive, and affirm that I see it, I consider it, it pleases me, I wish it were mine. And thus I form or rather after this manner I have first form'd, the Ideas of Knowing, Perceiving, Affirming, Denying, Considering, Willing, Desiring, and the Ideas of all the other operations of the Mind, which are thus occasion'd by the Antecedent Impressions of sensible Objects.

By the word Idea . . . I understand the immediate Object of the Mind when it thinks, or any Thought that the Mind imploys about anything. But these simple and distinct Ideas be not what we call strictly Reason, yet they are the sole Matter and Foundation of all our Reasoning: For the Mind does compare them together, compound, enlarge, contract, or separate them. . . . So all our Knowledge is, in effect, nothing else but the Perception of the Agreement or Disagreement of our Ideas in a greater or lesser Number, whereinsoever

this Agreement or Disagreement may consist. . . . This Method of Knowledge is properly call'd Reason or Demonstration, That Faculty of the Soul which discovers the Certainty of any thing dubious or obscure, by comparing it with something evidently known. . . . What is evidently repugnant to clear and distinct Ideas, or to our common Notions, is contrary to Reason; so I prove that the Doctrines of the Gospel, if it be the Word, cannot be so.

The first thing I shall insist upon is, that if any Doctrine of the New Testament be contrary to Reason, we have no manner of Idea of it. To say for instance, that a Ball is white and black at once, is to say just nothing; for these Colours are so incompatible in the same subject, as to exclude all Possibility of a real positive Idea or Conception. So to say, as the Papists, that Children dying before Baptism are damn'd without Pain, signifies nothing at all: For if they be intelligent Creatures in the other World, to be eternally excluded from God's Presence, and the Society of the Blessed, must prove ineffable Torment to them: But if they think they have no Understanding, then they are not capable of Damnation in their Sense; and so they should not say they are in Limbo-Dungeon, but that either they had no Souls, or were annihilated; which would be reasonable enough, and easily conceiv'd. Now if we have no Ideas of a thing, it is certainly but lost Labour for us to trouble our selves about it: For what I don't conceive, can no more give me right Notions of God, or influence my Actions, than a Prayer deliver'd in an unknown Tongue can excite my Devotion.

The next thing I shall remark is, That those, who stick [choke] not to say they could believe a downright Contradiction to Reason, did they find it contain'd to the Scripture, do justify all Absurdities whatsoever; and, by opposing one Light to another, undeniably make God the Author of all Incertitude. The very Supposition that Reason might authorize one thing, and the Spirit of God another, throws us into inevitable Scepticism; for we shall be at a perpetual Uncertainty which to obey: Nay, we can never be sure which is which. . . .

The natural Result of what has been said is, That to believe the Divinity of Scripture, or the Sense of any Passsage thereof, without rational Proofs, and an evident Consistency, is a blameable Credulity, and a temerarious Opinion, ordinarily grounded upon an ignorant and wilful Disposition, but more generally maintain'd out of a gainful Prospect. For we frequently embrace certain Doctrines not from any convincing Evidence in them, but because they serve our Designs better than the Truth; and because other Contradictions we are not willing to quit, are better defended by their means. . . .

I [have] said that Revelation was not a necessitating Motive of Assent, but a Means of Information. We should not confound the Way whereby we come to the knowledge of a thing, with the Grounds we have to believe it. A man may inform me concerning a thousand Matters I never heard of before, and of which I should not as much as think if I were not told; yet I believe nothing purely upon his word without Evidence in the things themselves. Not the bare Authority of him that speaks, but the clear Conception I form of what he says, is the Ground of my Persuasion.

If the sincerest Person on Earth should assure me he saw a Cane without two ends, I neither should nor could believe him; because this Relation plainly contradicts the Idea of a Cane. But if he told me he saw a Staff that, being by chance laid in the Earth, did after some time put forth Sprigs and Branches, I could easily rely upon his Veracity; because this no way contradicts the Idea of a Staff, nor transcends Possibility. I say Possibility; for Omnipotency itself can do no more. . . . We heartily believe God can do all things: But that mere Nothing should be the Object of his Power, the very Omnipotency alleg'd will not permit us to conceive. And that every Contradiction, which is a Synonym for Impossibility, is pure nothing, we have already sufficiently demonstrated. . . . When we say then, that nothing is impossible with God, or that he can do all things, we mean whatever is possible in itself, however far above the Power of Creatures to effect.

Thus God is pleas'd to reveal to us in Scripture several wonderful Matters of Fact, as the Creation of the World, the last Judgment, and many other important Truths, which no Man left to himself could ever imagine, no more than any of my fellow-Creatures can be sure of my private Thoughts. . . . Secret things belong unto the Lord; [but] those things which are reveal'd, belong unto us and to our Children. Yet, as we discours'd before, we do not receive them only because they are reveal'd: For besides the infallible Testimony of the Revelation from all requisite Circumstances, we must see in its Subject the indisputable Characters of Divine Wisdom and Sound Reason; which are the only Marks we have to distinguish the Oracles and Will of God, from the Impostures and Traditions of Men.

Whoever reveals any thing, that is, whoever tells us something we did not know before, his Words must be intelligible, and the Matter possible. This Rule holds good, let God or Man be the Revealer. If we count that Person a Fool who requires our Assent to what is manifestly incredible, how dare we blasphemously attribute to the most perfect Being, what is an acknowledg'd Defect in one of our selves? As for unintelligible Relations, we can no more believe them from the Revelation of God, than from that of Man; for the conceiv'd Ideas of things are the only Subjects of Believing, Denying, Approving, and every other Act of the Understanding: Therefore all Matters reveal'd by God or Man, must be equally intelligible and possible; so far both Revelations agree. But in this they differ, that tho the Revelation of Man should be thus qualifi'd, yet he may impose upon me as to the Truth of a thing; whereas what God is pleas'd to discover to me is not only clear to my Reason, (without which his Revelation could make me no wiser) but likewise it is always true. A Man, for Example, acquaints me that he has found a Treasure: This is plain and possible, but he may easily deceive me. God assures me, that he has form'd Man of Earth: This is not only possible to God, and to me very intelligible; but the thing is also most certain, God not being capable to deceive me, as Man is. In how many places are we exhorted to beware of false Prophets and Teachers, Seducers and Deceivers? We are not only to prove or try all things, and to hold fast that which is best, but also to try the Spirits whether they be of God. But how shall we try? how shall we discern? Not as the Horse and Mule which have no Understanding, but as circumspect and wise Men, judging what is said. . . .

The New Testament (if it be indeed Divine) must consequently agree with Natural Reason, and our own ordinary Ideas. The Apostles commend themselves to every Man's Conscience, that is, they appeal to every Man's Reason, in the Sight of God. Peter exhorts Christians to be ready always to give an Answer to every one that asks them a Reason of their Hope. Now to what purpose serv'd all these Appeals, if no Regard was to be had to Men's Understandings? if the Doctrines of Christ were incomprehensible, contradictory; or were we oblig'd to believe reveal'd Nonsense?

There is nothing Mysterious or above Reason in the Gospel [no matter how veiled or obscured some things may be in the ceremonies and rituals of men] . . . and I affirm that nothing can be said to be a Mystery, because we have not an adequate Idea of it, or a distinct View of all its Properties at once; for then every thing would be a Mystery. . . . I understand nothing better than this Table upon which I am now writing: I conceive it divisible into Parts beyond all Imagination; but shall I say it is above my Reason because I cannot count these Parts, nor distinctly perceive their Quantity and Figures? No Christian Doctrine, no more than any ordinary Piece of Nature, can be reputed a Mystery, because we have not an adequate or compleat Idea of whatever belongs to it. What is reveal'd in Religion, as it is most useful and necessary, so it must and may be as easily comprehended, and found as consistent with our common Notions, as what we know of Wood or Stone, of Air or Water. . . .

.   .   .   .   .

Now since by Revelation Men are not endu'd with any new Faculties, it follows

that God should lose his end in speaking to them, if what he said did not agree with their common Notions. . . . No matter of Fact can be known without Revelation [either divine or human], but what is once reveal'd we must as well understand as any other Matter in the World, Revelation being only of use to inform us whilst the Evidence of its Subject persuades us. Reason is not less from God than Revelation. . . .

No Miracle is contrary to Reason, for the Action must be intelligible, and we learn from Scripture and Reason that no Miracle is ever wrought without some special and important End, which is either appointed by those for whom the Miracle is made, or intended and declar'd by him that works it.

[Toland concludes his discussion by asserting that so-called Mysteries were introduced into Christianity by self-interested professionals who endeavored to secure their own desires by obscuring the simple, reasonable things of Christianity in a maze of ceremonies, customs, and exalted claims of special insight. In particular, this happened to Baptism and the Supper.]

I acknowledge no Orthodoxy but the Truth; and, I'm sure, where-ever the Truth is, there must be also the Church, of God I mean, and not any Human Faction or Policy.

5. Jonathan Swift, 1708

The Reverend Jonathan Swift (1667-1745) was an eccentric but loyal churchman, and a bitter enemy of that general "religion of nature" known as Deism. Advocates of Deism presupposed that the world was a giant machine, set in motion by the Creator and left to function according to natural laws. They also presupposed man's ability to find the common, rational elements in all religions, which then could be sublimated into a faith free of the supernatural revelations in Christianity. In the *Argument Against Abolishing Christianity,* selections from which follow, Swift has produced a masterpiece of comic irony. He supposes that the "witty, intellectual free-thinkers" have proposed the abolition of Christianity, and he proceeds to argue against this radical step. His satire is not only a defense of Christianity, but also an indictment of smug hypocrisies found not only among the free-thinking Deists but also among the "nominal Christians." Swift is better known as the author of *Gulliver's Travels*, 1726, and as an opponent of Alexander Pope's "Whatever is. is right." Swift believed that man's primordial selfishness would assert itself except for constant,

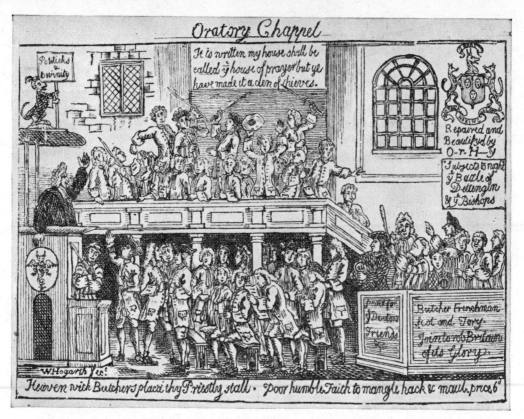

V-2. Oratory Chappel. *Drawing satirizing English church services in the eighteenth century, by William Hogarth. British Museum.*

rigorous self-control and the grace of God. His struggle against poverty and bad health left him with a contempt for petty humanity. Jonathan Swift, *An Argument to Prove That the Abolishing of Christianity in England May, as Things Now Stand, Be Attended with Some Inconveniences, and Perhaps Not Produce Those Many Good Effects Proposed Thereby* (London: T. Atkins, 1717). Cf. *The Prose Works of Jonathan Swift* (London: G. Bell & Sons, 1900-1914).

... it may perhaps be neither safe nor prudent to argue against the abolishing of Christianity, at a juncture when all parties appear so unanimously determined upon the point, as we cannot but allow from their actions, their discourses, and their writings. However, I know not how, whether from the affectation of singularity, or the perverseness of human nature, but so it unhappily falls out, that I cannot be entirely of this opinion. Nay, though I were sure an order were issued for my immediate prosecution by an attorney-general, I should still confess that,

in the present posture of our affairs at home or abroad, I do not yet see the absolute necessity of extirpating the Christian religion from among us. ...

However, since the undertakers propose such wonderful advantages to the nation by this project, and advance many plausible objections against the system of Christianity, I shall briefly consider the strength of both, fairly allow them their greatest weight, and offer such answers as I think most reasonable. After which I will beg leave to show what inconveniences may possibly happen by such an innovation, in the present posture of our affairs.

First, one great advantage proposed by the abolishing of Christianity is, that it would very much enlarge and establish liberty of conscience, that great bulwark of our nation, and of the Protestant religion; which is still too much limited by priestcraft, notwithstanding all the good intentions of the legislature, as we have lately found by a severe instance. For it is confidently reported that two young gentlemen of real hopes, bright wit, and profound judgment, who, upon a thorough examination of causes and effects, and by the force of natural abilities, without the least tincture of learning, having made a discovery that there was no God, and generously communicating their thoughts for the good of the public, were some time ago, by an unparalleled severity, and upon I know not what obsolete law, broke for blasphemy. And as it has been wisely observed, if persecution once begins, no man alive knows how far it may reach or where it will end.

In answer to all which, with deference to wiser judgments, I think this rather shows the necessity of a nominal religion among us. Great wits love to be free with the highest objects; and if they cannot be allowed a God to revile or renounce, they will speak evil of dignities, abuse the government, and reflect upon the ministry; which I am sure few will deny to be of much more pernicious consequence....

.   .   .   .   .

It is further objected against the gospel system, that it obliges men to the belief of things too difficult for free-thinkers, and such who have shaken off the prejudices that usually cling to a confined education. To which I answer, that men should be cautious how they raise objections which reflect upon the wisdom of the nation. Is not everybody freely allowed to believe whatever he pleases, and to publish his belief to the world whenever he thinks fit, especially if it serves to strengthen the party which is in the right? Would any indifferent foreigner, who should read the trumpery lately written by Asgil, Tindal, Toland, Coward, and forty more, imagine the gospel to be our rule of faith, and confirmed by parliaments? Does any man either believe, or say he believes, or desire to have it thought that he says he believes, one syllable of the matter? And is any man worse received upon that score, or does he find his want of nominal faith a disadvantage to him in the pursuit of any civil or military employment? What if there be an old dor-

mant statute or two against him, are they not now obsolete to a degree, that Empson and Dudley themselves, if they were now alive, would find it impossible to put them in execution?

It is likewise urged that there are, by computation, in this kingdom, above ten thousand parsons, whose revenues, added to those of my lords the bishops, would suffice to maintain at least two hundred young gentlemen of wit and pleasure, and free-thinking, enemies to priestcraft, narrow principles, pedantry, and prejudices, who might be an ornament to the court and town: and then again, so great a number of able divines might be a recruit to our fleet and armies. This, indeed, appears to be a consideration of some weight; but then, on the other side, several things deserve to be considered likewise: as first, whether it may not be thought necessary that in certain tracts of country, like what we call parishes, there shall be one man at least of abilities to read and write. Then it seems a wrong computation, that the revenues of the church throughout this island would be large enough to maintain two hundred young gentlemen, or even half that number, after the present refined way of living; that is, to allow each of them such a rent as, in the modern form of speech, would make them easy. But still there is in this project a greater mischief behind; and we ought to beware of the woman's folly, who killed the hen that every morning laid her a golden egg. For, pray, what would become of the race of men in the next age, if we had nothing to trust to beside the scrofulous, consumptive productions furnished by our men of wit and pleasure, when, having squandered away their vigor, health and estates, they are forced, by some disagreeable marriage, to piece up their broken fortunes, and entail rottenness and politeness on their posterity? Now, here are ten thousand persons reduced, by the wise regulations of Henry VIII, to the necessity of a low diet and moderate exercise, who are the only great restorers of our breed, without which the nation would, in an age or two become one great hospital.

Another advantage proposed by the abolishing Christianity, is the clear gain of one day in seven, which is now entirely lost, and consequently the kingdom one-seventh less considerable in trade, business, and pleasure; besides the loss to the public of so many stately structures, now in the hands of the clergy, which might be converted into playhouses, market-houses, exchanges, common dormitories, and other public edifices.

I hope I shall be forgiven a hard word, if I call this a perfect *cavil*. I readily own there has been an old custom, time out of mind, for some people to assemble in the churches every Sunday, and that shops are still frequently shut, in order, as it is conceived, to preserve the memory of that ancient practice; but how this can prove a hindrance to business or pleasure is hard to imagine. What if the men of pleasure are forced, one day in the week, to game at home instead of the chocolate-houses? are not the taverns and coffee-houses open? can there be a more convenient season for taking a dose of physic? are fewer claps got upon Sundays than other days? is not that the chief day for traders to sum up the accounts of the week, and for lawyers to prepare their briefs? But I would fain know how it can be pretended that the churches are misapplied? where are the more appointments and rendezvouses of gallantry? where more care to appear in the foremost box, with greater advantage of dress? where more meetings for business? where more bargains driven of all sorts? and where so many conveniences or incitements to sleep? . . .

It is again objected, as a very absurd, ridiculous custom, that a set of men should be suffered, much less employed and hired, to bawl one day in seven against the lawfulness of those methods most in use, toward the pursuit of greatness, riches, and pleasure, which are the constant practice of all men alive on the other six. But this objection is, I think a little unworthy of so refined an age as ours. Let us argue this matter calmly: I appeal to the breast of any polite free-thinker, whether, in the pursuit of gratifying a predominant passion, he has not always felt a wonderful incitement, by reflecting it was a thing forbidden; and therefore we see, in order to cultivate this taste, the wisdom of

the nation has taken special care that the ladies should be furnished with prohibited silks, and the men with prohibited wine. And indeed it were to be wished that some other prohibitions were promoted, in order to improve the pleasure of the town; which for want of such expedients begin already, as I am told, to flag and grow languid, giving way daily to cruel inroads from the spleen. . . .

.   .   .   .   .

And to urge another argument of a parallel nature: if Christianity were once abolished, how could the free-thinkers, the strong reasoners, the men of profound learning, be able to find another subject, so calculated in all points, whereon to display their abilities? What wonderful productions of wit should we be deprived of from those whose genius, by continual practice, has been wholly turned upon raillery and invectives against religion, and would therefore never be able to shine or distinguish themselves upon any other subject? We are daily complaining of the great decline of wit among us, and would we take away the greatest, perhaps the only topic we have left? Who would ever have suspected Asgil for a wit, or Toland for a philosopher, if the inexhaustible stock of Christianity had not been at hand to provide them with materials? What other subject, through all art or nature, could have produced Tindal for a profound author, or furnished him with readers? It is the wise choice of the subject that alone adorns and distinguishes the writer. For had a hundred such pens as these been employed on the side of religion, they would have immediately sunk into silence and oblivion. . . .

.   .   .   .   .

[Swift also suggests that since Toland was once a Roman Catholic, the abolishing of Christianity may be a subtle attempt to introduce popery.]

And therefore, if, notwithstanding all I have said, it still be thought necessary to have a bill brought in for repealing Christianity, I would humbly offer an amendment, that instead of the word Christianity, may be put religion in general, which, I conceive, will much better answer all the good ends proposed by the projectors of it. For, as long as we leave in being a God and his providence, with all the necessary consequences which curious and inquisitive men will be apt to draw from such premises, we do not strike at the root of the evil, though we should ever so effectually annihilate the present scheme of the gospel: for of what use is freedom of thought, if it will not produce freedom of action? which is the sole end, how remote soever in appearance, of all objections against Christianity.... I think nothing can be more manifest than that the quarrel is not against any particular points of hard digestion in the Christian system, but against religion in general; which, by laying restraints on human nature, is supposed the great enemy to the freedom of thought and action.

.   .   .   .   .

To conclude: whatever some may think of the great advantages to trade by the favorite scheme, I do very much apprehend that in six months time after the act is passed for the extirpation of the gospel, the Bank and East India stock may fall at least one percent. And since that is fifty times more than ever the wisdom of our age thought fit to venture for the preservation of Christianity, there is no reason we should be at so great a loss, merely for the sake of destroying it.

6. Alexander Pope, 1733

In 1733, Alexander Pope (1688-1744) wrote his *Essay on Man, Epistle I*. In addition to mirroring the view of English Deists, he also reflects Leibniz's philosophy, which conceived this world to be the best of all possible worlds. He depicts the grand order of nature, man's place in it, and identifies rectitude with whatever is. The following two verses are typical. *The Works of Alexander Pope* (London: J. Johnson, 1906).

IX.   What if the foot, ordained the dust to tread,
Or hand to toil, aspired to be the head?
What if the head, the eye, or ear repined
To serve mere engines to the ruling mind?
Just as absurd for any part to claim
To be another in this general frame;
Just as absurd to mourn the tasks or pains
The great directing Mind of All ordains.

V-3. Alexander Pope. *A contemporary sketch.*

All are but parts of one stupendous Whole,
Whose body Nature is, and God the soul;
That changed thro' all, and yet in all the same,
Great in the earth as in th' ethereal frame,
Warms in the sun, refreshes in the breeze,
Glows in the stars, and blossoms in the trees;
Lives thro' all life, extends thro' all extent,
Spreads undivided, operates unspent;
Breathes in our soul, informs our mortal part,
As full, as perfect, in a hair as heart;
As full, as perfect, in vile man that mourns,
As the rapt Seraph that adores and burns.
To him no high, no low, no great, no small;
He fills, he bounds, connects, and equals all!
X.   Cease, then, nor Order imperfection name;
Our proper bliss depends on what we blame.
Know thy own point: this kind, this due degree
Of blindness, weakness, Heaven bestows on thee.
Submit: in this or any other sphere,
Secure to be as blessed as thou canst bear;

Safe in the hand of one disposing Power,
Or in the natal or the mortal hour.
All Nature is but Art unknown to thee;
All Chance, Direction, which thou canst not see;
All Discord, Harmony not understood;
All partial Evil, universal Good:
And spite of Pride, in erring Reason's spite,
One truth is clear, *Whatever is, is right.*

7. *William Law, 1732*

The Case of Reason, or Natural Religion, Fairly and Fully Stated In answer to a book, entitled, Christianity as Old as the Creation, by William Law (London: Innys and J. Richardson, 1732).

SHEWING THE STATE OF THE CONTROVERSY

The Infidelity which is now openly declared for, pretends to support itself upon the *sufficiency, excellency,* and *absolute perfection* of Reason, or Natural Religion.

The author with whom I am here engaged, makes no attempt to disprove or invalidate that *historical evidence* on which Christianity is founded; but by arguments drawn from the nature of God, and natural Religion, pretends to prove, that no Religion can come from God, which teaches anything more than that, which is fully manifest to all mankind by the mere light of nature.

His chief principles may be reduced to these following propositions.

1. That human reason, or natural light, is the *only means* of knowing all that God requires of us.

2. That reason, or natural light, is so full, sufficient, plain, and certain a rule or guide in all religious duties, that no external divine revelation can add anything to it, or require us to believe or practise anything, that was not as fully known before. A revelation, if ever made, can only differ from natural religion, in the manner of its being communicated. It can only declare those very *same* things *externally,* which were before equally declared by the *internal* light of nature.

3. That this must be the case of natural and revealed religion, unless God be an arbitrary Being. For if God be not an arbitrary Being, but acts according to the reason and nature of things; then he can require nothing of us by revelation, but what is already re-

quired by the nature and reason of things. And therefore, as he expresses it, *reason and revelation must exactly answer one another like two tallies.*

4. That whatever is at any time admitted as matter of religion, that is not manifest from the reason of the thing, and plainly required by the light of nature, is gross superstition.

5. That it is inconsistent with the divine perfections, to suppose, that God can by an external revelation give any religious light or knowledge, at *any time* to *any people,* which was not equally given at *all* times, and to *all* people.

This is the state of the controversy. As to the railing accusations, and scurrilous language, which this author pours out, at all adventures, upon the Christian Clergy, I shall wholly pass them over; my intention being only to appeal to the reason of the Reader, and to add nothing to it, but the safe, unerring light of divine Revelation.

CHAPTER I

Enquiring, whether there be anything in the nature and condition of man, to oblige him to think, that he is not to admit of any doctrines or institutions, as revealed from God, but such as his own Reason can prove to be necessary from the nature of things.

I begin with enquiring what there is to *oblige* a man to hold this opinion, because if there is not some strong and plain proof arising from the *nature* and *condition* of man, to *oblige* him thus to abide by the sole light of his own Reason; it may be so far from being a duty, which he owes to God, that it may be reckoned amongst his most criminal presumptions. And the pleading for this authority of his own Reason, may have the guilt of pleading for his greatest vanity. And if, as this Writer observes, *spiritual pride be the worst sort of pride,* a confident reliance upon our own Reason, as having a right to determine all matters between God and man, if it should prove to be a *groundless pretension,* bids fair to be reckoned the highest instance of the *worst* kind of the worst of sins.

Every other instance of vanity, every degree of personal pride, and self-esteem, may be a pardonable weakness in comparison of this. For how small is that pride which only makes us prefer our own personal beauty or merit to that of our fellow creatures, when compared with a self-confiding Reason, which is too haughty to adore anything in the divine counsels, which it cannot fully comprehend; or to submit to any directions from God, but such as its own wisdom could prescribe? Thus much is certain, that there can be no *medium* in this matter. The claiming this authority to our Reason, must either be a very great duty, or amongst the greatest of sins.

If it be a *sin* to admit of any *secrets* in divine providence, if it be a *crime* to ascribe wisdom and goodness to God in things we cannot comprehend. If it be a *baseness* and *meanness* of spirit to believe that God can teach us *better*, or *more* than we can teach ourselves. If it be a *shameful apostasy* from the dignity of our nature, to be humble in the hands of God, to submit to any *mysterious providence* over us, to comply with any other methods of *homage* and *adoration* of him, than such as we could of ourselves contrive and justify; then it is certainly a great duty to assert and maintain this authority of our own Reason.

On the other hand; If the profoundest humility towards *God*, be the highest instance of piety. If everything within us and without us, if everything we know of God, everything we know of ourselves preaches up humility to us, as the foundation of every virtue, as the life and soul of all holiness. If *sin* had its beginning from *pride*, and *hell* be the effect of it, if *devils* are what they are through spiritual pride and self-conceit, then we have great reason to believe, that the claiming this authority to our Reason, in opposition to the revealed wisdom of God, is not a frailty of *flesh* and *blood*, but that same spiritual pride which turned Angels into *apostate* Spirits.

Since therefore this appealing to our own Reason, as the absolutely *perfect measure and rule* of all that ought to pass between God and man, has an *appearance* of a pride of the *worst* kind, and such as unites us both in temper and conduct with the fallen spirits

of the kingdom of darkness, it highly concerns every pleader on that side, to consider what grounds he proceeds upon, and to ask himself, what there is in the *state* and *condition* of human nature, to oblige him to think that nothing can be *divine* or *holy*, or *necessary*, in religion, but what *human* Reason dictates? . . .

The Writers against Revelation appeal to the *Reason* and *Nature* of things, as infallibly discovering everything that a Revelation from God can teach us.

Thus our Author; *If the relations between things, and the fitness resulting from thence, be not the sole Rule of God's actions, must not God be an arbitrary Being? But if God only commands what the nature of things shew to be fit, it is scarce possible that men should mistake their duty; since a mind that is attentive can as easily distinguish fit from unfit, as the Eye can beauty from deformity.*

It is granted, that there is a fitness and unfitness of actions founded in the nature of things, and resulting from the relations that persons and things bear to one another. It is also granted, that the reasonableness of most of the duties of children to their parents, of parents to their children, and of men to men, is very apparent, from the relations they bear to one another; and that several of the duties which we owe to God, plainly appear to us, as soon as we acknowledge the relation that is between God and us.

But then, all this granted, this *whole argument* proves directly the contrary to that which this Author intended to prove by it.

I here therefore join with this Author: I readily grant, that the Nature, Reason and Relations of things and persons, and the fitness of actions resulting from thence, is the *sole rule* of God's actions. And I appeal to this one common and confessed principle, as a sufficient proof that a man cannot thus abide by the *sole Light* of his own Reason, without contradicting the nature and reason of things, and denying this to be the *sole Rule* of God's actions.

For if the *fitness* of actions is founded in the *nature* of things and persons, and this fitness be the *sole Rule* of God's actions, it is certain that the Rule by which he acts, must in many instances be *entirely* inconceivable by us, so as not to be known *at all*, and in no instances *fully* known, or *perfectly* comprehended.

For if God is to act according to a *fitness founded* in the *nature* of things, and nothing can be fit for him to do, but what has its fitness founded in his own *divinely perfect* and *incomprehensible* nature, must he not necessarily act by a Rule *above* all human comprehension? This argument supposes that he cannot do what is *fit* for him to do, unless what he does has its fitness founded in his own *Nature;* but if he must govern his actions by his own nature, he must act by a *Rule* that is just as *incomprehensible* to us as his own nature.

And we can be no farther *competent judges* of the *fitness* of the conduct of God, than we are competent judges of the divine nature; and can no more tell what is, or is not *infinitely wise* in God, than we can raise ourselves to a *state* of infinite wisdom.

So that if the *fitness* of actions is founded in the *particular nature* of things and persons, and the fitness of God's actions must arise from that which is *particular* to his nature, then we have from this argument, the *utmost certainty* that the *Rule* or *Reasons* of God's actions must in many cases be entirely inconceivable by us, and in no cases perfectly and fully apprehended; and for this very reason, because he is not an *arbitrary being*, that acts by *mere will*, but is governed in everything he does, by the reason and nature of things. For if he is not arbitrary, but acts according to the nature of things, then he must act according to his *own nature*. But his own nature must be the *reason, rule* and *measure* of his actions; if they are only fit and reasonable because they are according to this *Rule and Reason*, then it necessarily follows, that the fitness of many of God's actions must be incomprehensible to us, *merely* for this reason, because they have their *proper fitness;* such a fitness as is founded in the divine nature.

How mistaken therefore is this Author, when he argues after this manner. *If God requires things of us, whose fitness our Reason cannot prove from the nature of things,*

must he not be an arbitrary being? For how can that prove God to be an arbitrary agent, which is the necessary consequence of his not being arbitrary?

For supposing God to be an *arbitrary Being*, there would then be a bare possibility of our comprehending the fitness of everything he required of us. For as he might act by *mere will,* so he might choose to act according to our nature, and suitable to our comprehensions, and not according to his own nature, and infinite perfections.

But supposing God not to be an *arbitrary Being*, but to act constantly, as the perfections of his own nature make it *fit* and *reasonable* for him to act, then there is an utter impossibility of our comprehending the reasonableness and fitness of many of his actions.

For instance; look at the *reason* of things, and the *fitness* of actions, and tell me how they moved God to create mankind in the state and condition they are in. Nothing is more above the reason of men, than to explain the reasonableness and infinite wisdom of God's providence in creating man of such a *form* and *condition*, to go through *such* a state of things as human life has shewn itself to be. No revealed mysteries can more exceed the Comprehension of man, than the state of human life itself.

Shew me according to what *fitness*, founded in the *nature* of things, God's infinite wisdom was determined to form you in such a manner, bring you into such a world, and suffer and preserve *such a state* of things, as human life is, and then you may have some pretence to believe no revealed doctrines, but such as your own reason can deduce from the nature of things and the fitness of actions.

But whilst your own *form*, whilst *Creation* and *Providence* are depths which you cannot thus look into, 'tis strangely absurd to pretend, that God cannot reveal anything to you as a matter of religion, except your own reason can shew its foundation in the nature and reason of things.

.   .   .   .   .

Again: The origin of *sin* and *evil,* or how it entered into the world consistently with the infinite wisdom of God, is a mystery of *natural religion,* which reason cannot unfold. For who can shew from the *reason* and *nature* of things, that it was *fit* and *reasonable,* for the providence of God to suffer sin and evil to enter, and continue in the world as they have? Here therefore the man of natural religion must drop his method of reasoning from the nature and fitness of things, and that in an article of the highest concern to the moral world, and be as mere a believer, as he that believes the most incomprehensible mystery of revealed religion.

Now as there have been in the several ages of the world, some *impatient, restless* and *presuming* spirits, who because they could not in these points explain the justice of God's providence, have taken refuge in horrid *Atheism,* so they made just the same *sober use* of their reason, as our *modern unbelievers,* who because they cannot comprehend, as they would, the *fitness* and *necessity* of certain Christian doctrines, resign themselves up to an hardened *infidelity.* For it is just as wise and reasonable to allow of no mysteries in *Revelation,* as to allow of no mysteries or secrets in *Creation* and *Providence.*

And whenever this writer, or any other, shall think it a proper time, to attack *natural* religion with as much freedom, as he has now fallen upon *revealed,* he need not enter upon any *new* hypothesis or *different* way of reasoning. For the same turn of thought, the same manner of cavilling may soon find materials in the natural state of man, for as large a bill of complaints against natural religion, and the mysteries of providence, as is here brought against revealed doctrines.

To proceed: If the *fitness of actions is founded in the nature and relations of beings,* then nothing can be fit for God to do, but so far as it is fit for the *Governor of all created beings,* whether on earth, or in any other part of the universe; and he cannot act fitly towards mankind, but by acting as is fit for the Governor of all beings.

Now what is fit for the *Governor of all created* nature to do in this or that particular part of his creation, is as much above our reason to *tell,* as it is above our power to

govern all beings. And how mankind ought to be governed, with relation to the whole creation, of which they are so small a part, is a matter equally above our knowledge, because we know not how they are a part of the whole, or what relation they bear to any other part, or how their state affects the whole, or any other part, than we know what beings the whole consists of.

Now there is nothing that we know with more certainty than that God is Governor of the *whole,* and that mankind are a *part* of the whole; and that the uniformity and harmony of divine providence must arise from his infinitely wise government of the *whole;* and therefore we have the utmost certainty, that we are *vastly incompetent* judges of the fitness or unfitness of any methods, that God uses in the government of so small a part of the universe, as mankind are.

.   .   .   .   .

And if some people, by a *long* and *strict* attention to *Reason, clear* ideas, the *fitness* and *unfitness* of things, have at last arrived at a demonstrative certainty, that all these sentiments of piety and devotion are mere *bigotry, superstition,* and *enthusiasm;* I shall only now observe, that *youthful extravagance, passion,* and *debauchery,* by their own *natural tendency,* without the assistance of any other guide, seldom fail of making the same discovery. And though it is not reckoned any reflection upon *great wits,* when they hit upon the same thought, yet it may seem some disparagement of that *reason* and *philosophy,* which teaches *old men* to think and judge the same of religion, that *passion* and *extravagance* teaches the young....

Ask Reason, what *effect* sin has upon the soul, and it can tell you no more, than if you had asked, what effect the *omnipresence* of God has upon the soul.

Ask Reason, and the nature of things, what is, or ought to be, the *true nature* of an atonement for sin, how far it is like *paying a debt, reconciling a difference,* or *healing a wound,* or how far it is different from them? and it can tell you no more, than if you had asked, what is the *true degree* of power that *preserves* us in existence, how far it is *like* that

239

which at first created us, and how far it is *different* from it.

All these enquiries are, by the nature of things, made impossible to us, so long as we have no light but from our own natural capacities, and we cannot take upon us to be *knowing*, and *philosophers*, in these matters, but by deserting our Reason, and giving ourselves up to vision and imagination.

And we have as much authority from the reason and nature of things, to appeal to *hunger* and *thirst*, and *sensual pleasure*, to tell us *how* our souls shall live in the beatific presence of God, as to appeal to our *reason* and *logic*, to demonstrate how sin is to be *atoned*, or the soul *altered, prepared*, and *purified*, for future happiness.

For God has no more given us our Reason to *settle* the nature of an atonement for sin; or to find out what can, or cannot, take away its guilt, than he has given us *senses* and *appetites* to state the nature, or discover the ingredients, of future happiness.

And he who rejects the *atonement* for sins made by the Son of God, as *needless*, because he cannot prove it to be *necessary*, is as extravagant, as he that should deny that God created him by his *only Son*, because he did not *remember* it. For our memory is as proper a faculty to tell us, whether God at first created us, and all things, by his only Son, as our *Reason* is to tell us, whether we ought to be restored to God, with, or without the mediation of Jesus Christ.

When therefore this writer says, *Can anything be more evident, than that if doing evil be the only cause of God's displeasure, that the ceasing to do evil, must take away that displeasure?* [This is:]

Just as if he had said, if conversing with a *leper* has been the only cause of a man's getting a *leprosy*, must not departing from him, be the removal of the *leprosy*? For if anyone, guessing at the *guilt* of sin, and its *effects* on the soul, should compare it to a *leprosy* in the body, he can no more say, that he has reached its *real, internal* evil, than he, that comparing the happiness of heaven to a crown of glory, can be said to have described its real happiness.

This *writer* has no occasion to appeal to

reason, and the nature of things, if he can be thus certain about things, whose nature is not only obscure, but *impossible* to be known. For it is as impossible for him to know the *guilt* and *effects* of sin, as to know the shape of an Angel. It is as impossible to know by the mere light of reason what God's *displeasure* at sin is, what *contrariety* to, or *separation* from sinners it implies, or how it obliges God to deal with them; as to know what the internal essence of God is. Our author therefore has here found the utmost degree of evidence, where it was *impossible* for him to have the *smallest degree* of knowledge.

For though it is very evident, that in the case of sin, Reason can prescribe nothing but repentance; yet it is equally evident, that Reason cannot say, nothing more is required, to destroy the effects of sin, and to put the sinner in the *same state*, as if it had never been committed.

If a man, having *murdered* twenty of his fellow creatures, should afterward be sorry for it, and wish that he had a power to bring them to life again, or to create others in their stead, would this be an *evident* proof, that he was no *murderer*, and that he had never killed one man in his life? Will his ceasing to kill, and wishing he had a power to create others in their stead, be a *proof*, that he is just in the *same state* with God, as if he had never murdered a man in his life? But, unless this can be said, unless a man's repentance sufficiently proves that he *never* was a sinner, it cannot be evident, that repentance is sufficient to put a man in the *same state*, as if he never had sinned.

He therefore that says, *If sin be the only cause of God's displeasure, must not ceasing from sin take away his displeasure?* has just as much sense and reason on his side, as if he had said, if a man's *murdering* of himself is the cause of God's displeasure, must not his restoring himself to life again, take away God's displeasure?

For there is as much foundation in reason, and the nature of things, to affirm, that the soul of a *self-murderer* must have a sufficient power to undo the effects of murder, and put him in his former state; as to affirm, that *every sinner* must have a sufficient natural power of undoing all the effects of sin, and putting himself in the same state as if he had never sinned.

This objection, therefore, against any *super-natural* means of atoning for sin, taken from the *sufficiency* of our own repentance, is as *clear* and *philosophical*, as that *knowledge* that is without *any ideas;* and as justly to be relied upon, as that *conclusion* which has no *premises....*

.   .   .   .   .

The truth of the matter is this; reason is in God and man, as power is in God and man. And as the divine power has some degree of likeness to human power, yet with an *infinite* difference from it; so that perfection which we call *reason* in God, has some degree of likeness to reason as it is in man, yet is *infinitely* and beyond all conception different from it.

Nor can anyone shew, that we enjoy reason in a *higher degree* in respect of God, than we enjoy power; or that the *manner*, or *light* of our reason, bears any greater likeness to the light and knowledge of God, than the *manner* and *extent* of our power bears to the omnipotence of God.

And as our enjoyment of power is so limited, so imperfect, so superficial, as to be scarce sufficient to tell us, what power is, much less what omnipotence is; so our share of reason is so small, and we enjoy it in so imperfect a manner, that we can scarce think or talk intelligibly of it, or so much as define our own faculties of reasoning.

[The remaining titles of chapters are:]

Chapter II, shewing, from the state and relation between God and man, that human reason cannot possibly be a competent judge of the fitness and reasonableness of God's proceedings with mankind, either as to the time, or matter, or manner, of any external revelation.

Chapter III, shewing how far human reason is enabled to judge of the reasonableness, truth, and certainty of divine revelation.

Chapter IV, of the state and nature of reason, as it is in man; and how its perfection in matters of religion is to be known.

Chapter V, shewing that all the mutability of our tempers, the disorders of our passions, the corruption of our hearts, all the reveries of the imagination, all the contradictions and absurdities that are to be found in human life, and human opinions, are strictly and precisely the mutability, disorders, corruption, and absurdities of human reason.

8. *Joseph Butler, 1736*

Joseph Butler, *The Analogy of Religion, Natural and Revealed, to the Constitution and Course of Nature. Works of Joseph Butler* (New York: Robert Carter & Brothers, 1860).

Probable evidence is essentially distinguished from demonstrative by this, that it admits of degrees; and of all variety of them, from the highest moral certainty, to the very lowest presumption. We cannot indeed say a thing is probably true upon one very slight presumption for it; because, as there may be probabilities on both sides of a question, there may be some against it; and though there be not, yet a slight presumption does not beget that degree of conviction, which is implied in saying a thing is probably true. But that the slightest possible presumption is of the nature of a probability, appears from hence; that such low presumption often repeated, will amount even to moral certainty. Thus a man's having observed the ebb and flow of the tide to-day, affords some sort of presumption, though the lowest imaginable, that it may happen again to-morrow: but the observation of this event for so many days, and months, and ages together, as it has been observed by mankind, gives us a full assurance that it will....

Probable evidence, in its very nature, affords but an imperfect kind of information; and is to be considered as relative only to beings of limited capacities. For nothing which is the possible object of knowledge, whether past, present, or future, can be probable to an infinite Intelligence; since it cannot but be discerned absolutely as it is in itself, certainly true, or certainly false. But to us, probability is the very guide of life.

From these things it follows, that in questions of difficulty, or such as are thought so, where more satisfactory evidence cannot be had, or is not seen; if the result of examination be, that there appears upon the whole, any the lowest presumption on one side, and none on the other, or a greater presumption on one side, though in the lowest degree greater; this determines the question, even in matters of speculation; and in matters of practice, will lay us under an absolute and formal obligation, in point of prudence and of interest, to act upon that presumption or low probability, though it be so low as to leave the mind in very great doubt which is the truth. . . .

.　　.　　.　　.　　.

Strange difficulties have been raised by some concerning personal identity, or the sameness of living agents, implied in the notion of our existing now and hereafter, or in any two successive moments. . . . But without regard to any of them here, let us consider what the analogy of nature and the several changes which we have undergone, and those which we know we may undergo without being destroyed, suggest, as to the effect which death may, or may not, have upon us; and whether it be not from thence probable, that we may survive this change, and exist in a future state of life and perception.

I.　From our being born into the present world in the helpless imperfect state of infancy, and having arrived from thence to mature age, we find it to be a general law of nature in our own species, that the same creatures, the same individuals, should exist in degrees of life and perception, with capacities of action, of enjoyment and suffering, in one period of their being, greatly different from those appointed them in another period of it. And in other creatures the same law holds. For the difference of their capacities and states of life at their birth (to go no higher) and in maturity; the change of worms into flies, and the vast enlargement of their locomotive powers by such change: and birds and insects bursting the shell of their habitation, and by this means entering into a new world, furnished with new accom-

modations for them, and finding a new sphere of action assigned them; these are instances of this general law of nature. Thus all the various and wonderful transformations of animals are to be taken into consideration here. But the states of life in which we ourselves existed formerly in the womb and in our infancy, are almost as different from our present in mature age, as it is possible to conceive any two states or degrees of life can be. Therefore that we are to exist hereafter, in a state as different (suppose) from our present, as this is from our former, is but according to the analogy of nature; according to a natural order or appointment of the very same kind, with what we have already experienced.

II.　We know we are endued with capacities of action, of happiness and misery: for we are conscious of acting, of enjoying pleasure and suffering pain. Now that we have these powers and capacities before death, is a presumption that we shall retain them through and after death; indeed a probability of it abundantly sufficient to act upon, unless there be some positive reason to think that death is the destruction of those living powers: because there is in every case a probability, that all things will continue as we experience they are, in all respects, except those in which we have some reason to think they will be altered. This is that *kind* of presumption or probability from analogy, expressed in the very word *continuance,* which seems our only natural reason for believing the course of the world will continue to-morrow, as it has done so far as our experience or knowledge of history can carry us back. Nay it seems our only reason for believing, that any one substance now existing will continue to exist a moment longer; the self-existent substance only excepted. Thus if men were assured that the unknown event, death, was not the destruction of our faculties of perception and of action, there would be no apprehension, that any other power or event, unconnected with this of death, would destroy these faculties just at the instant of each creature's death; and therefore no doubt but that they would remain after it; which shows the high probability that our living powers will continue after death, unless there be some ground to think that death is their destruction. For, if it would be in a manner certain that we should survive death, provided it were certain that death would not be our destruction, it must be highly probable we shall survive it, if there be no ground to think death will be our destruction.

Now, though I think it must be acknowledged, that prior to the natural and moral proofs of a future life commonly insisted upon, there would arise a general confused suspicion, that in the great shock and alteration which we shall undergo by death, we, i.e. our living powers, might be wholly destroyed; yet even prior to those proofs, there is really no particular distinct ground or reason for this apprehension at all, so far as I can find. If there be, it must arise either from *the reason of the thing*, or from *the analogy of nature*.

But we cannot argue from *the reason of the thing*, that death is the destruction of living agents, because we know not at all what death is in itself; but only some of its effects, such as the dissolution of flesh, skin, and bones. And these effects do in no wise appear to imply the destruction of a living agent. And besides, as we are greatly in the dark, upon what the exercise of our living powers depends, so we are wholly ignorant what the powers themselves depend upon; the powers themselves as distinguished, not only from their actual exercise, but also from the present capacity of exercising them; and as opposed to their destruction: for sleep, or however a swoon, shows us, not only that these powers exist when they are not exercised, as the passive power of motion does in inanimate matter; but shows also that they exist, when there is no present capacity of exercising them: or that the capacities of exercising them for the present, as well as the actual exercise of them, may be suspended, and yet the powers themselves remain undestroyed. Since then we know not at all upon what the existence of our living powers depends, this shows further, there can no probability be collected from the reason of the thing, that death will be their

destruction: because their existence may depend upon somewhat in no degree affected by death; upon somewhat quite out of the reach of this king of terrors. So that there is nothing more certain, than that *the reason of the thing* shows us no connexion between death and the destruction of living agents. Nor can we find any thing throughout the whole *analogy of nature,* to afford us even the slightest presumption, that animals ever lose their living powers; much less if it were possible, that they lose them by death; for we have no faculties wherewith to trace any beyond or through it, so as to see what becomes of them. This event removes them from our view. It destroys the *sensible* proof, which we had before their death, of their being possessed of living powers, but does not appear to afford the least reason to believe that they are, then, or by that event, deprived of them.

And our knowing, that they were possessed of these powers, up to the very period to which we have faculties capable of tracing them, is itself a probability of their retaining them beyond it. And this is confirmed, and a sensible credibility is given to it, by observing the very great and astonishing changes which we have experienced; so great, that our existence in another state of life, of perception and of action, will be but according to a method of providential conduct, the like to which has been already exercised even with regard to ourselves; according to a course of nature, the like to which we have already gone through....

That which makes the question concerning a future life to be of so great importance to us, is our capacity of happiness and misery. And that which makes the consideration of it to be of so great importance to us, is the supposition of our happiness and misery hereafter depending upon our actions here. Without this, indeed, curiosity could not but sometimes bring a subject, in which we may be so highly interested, to our thoughts; especially upon the mortality of others, or the near prospect of our own. But reasonable men would not take any further thought about hereafter, than what should happen thus occasionally to rise in their minds, if it were certain that our future interest no way depended upon our present behaviour; whereas, on the contrary, if there be ground, either from analogy or any thing else, to think it does; then there is reason also for the most active thought and solicitude, to secure that interest; to behave so as that we may escape that misery, and obtain that happiness, in another life, which we not only suppose ourselves capable of, but which we apprehend also is put in our own power. And whether there be ground for this last apprehension, certainly would deserve to be most seriously considered, were there no other proof of a future life and interest, than that presumptive one, which the foregoing observations amount to.

Now in the present state, all which we enjoy, and a great part of what we suffer, *is put in our own power*. For pleasure and pain are the consequences of our actions; and we are endued by the Author of our nature with capacities of foreseeing these consequences. We find by experience he does not so much as preserve our lives, exclusively of our own care and attention, to provide ourselves with, and to make use of that sustenance, by which he has appointed our lives shall be preserved; and without which, he has appointed, they shall not be preserved at all. And in general we foresee, that the external things, which are the objects of our various passions, can neither be obtained nor enjoyed, without exerting ourselves in such and such manners: but by thus exerting ourselves, we obtain and enjoy these objects, in which our natural good consists; or by this means God gives us the possession and enjoyment of them. I know not, that we have any one kind or degree of enjoyment, but by the means of our own actions. And by prudence and care, we may, for the most part, pass our days in tolerable ease and quiet: or, on the contrary, we may, by rashness, ungoverned passion, wilfulness, or even by negligence, make ourselves as miserable as ever we please. And many do please to make themselves extremely miserable, i.e. to do what they know beforehand will render them so. They follow those ways, the fruit of which they know, by instruction, example, experi-

ence, will be disgrace, and poverty, and sickness, and untimely death. This every one observes to be the general course of things; though it is to be allowed, we cannot find by experience, that all our sufferings are owing to our own follies.

.   .   .   .   .

Now from this general observation, obvious to every one, that God has given us to understand, he has appointed satisfaction and delight to be the consequence of our acting in one manner, and pain and uneasiness of our acting in another, and of our not acting at all; and that we find the consequences, which we were beforehand informed of, uniformly to follow; we may learn, that we are at present actually under his government in the strictest and most proper sense.... An Author of nature being supposed, it is not so much a deduction of reason, as a matter of experience, that we are thus under his government.... There is no possibility of answering or evading the general thing here intended, without denying all final causes. For final causes being admitted, the pleasure and pains now mentioned must be admitted too as instances of them. And if they are; if God annexes delight to some actions, and uneasiness to others, with an apparent design to induce us to act so and so: then he not only dispenses happiness and misery, but also rewards and punishes actions.... And thus the whole analogy of Nature, the whole present course of things, most fully shows, that there is nothing incredible in the general doctrine of religion, that God will reward and punish men for their actions hereafter: nothing incredible, I mean, arising out of the notion of rewarding and punishing. For the whole course of nature is a present instance of his exercising that government over us, which implies in it rewarding and punishing....

9. David Hume, 1748

In a long footnote, Hume defines a miracle as "a transgression of a law of nature by a particular volition of the Deity, or by the interposition of some invisible agent. A miracle may either be discoverable by men or not." David

Hume, "Of Miracles," from *An Enquiry Concerning the Human Understanding* (Oxford: The Clarendon Press, 1877, 1894).

...We may observe, that there is no species of reasoning more common, more useful, and even necessary to human life, than that which is derived from the testimony of men, and the reports of eye-witnesses and spectators. This species of reasoning, perhaps, one may deny to be founded on the relation of cause and effect. I shall not dispute about a word. It will be sufficient to observe that our assurance in any argument of this kind is derived from no other principle than our observation of the veracity of human testimony, and of the usual conformity of facts to the reports of witnesses. It being a general maxim, that no objects have any discoverable connexion together, and that all the inferences, which we can draw from one to another, are founded merely on our experience of their constant and regular conjunction; it is evident, that we ought not to make an exception to this maxim in favour of human testimony, whose connexion with any event seems, in itself, as little necessary as any other. Were not the memory tenacious to a certain degree; had not men commonly an inclination to truth and a principle of probity; were they not sensible to shame, when detected in a falsehood: were not these, I say, discovered by *experience* to be qualities, inherent in human nature, we should never repose the least confidence in human testimony. A man delirious, or noted for falsehood and villainy, has no manner of authority with us.

And as the evidence, derived from witnesses and human testimony, is founded on past experience, so it varies with the experience, and is regarded either as a *proof* or a *probability,* according as the conjunction between any particular kind of report and any kind of object has been found to be constant or variable. There are a number of circumstances to be taken into consideration in all judgements of this kind; and the ultimate standard, by which we determine all disputes, that may arise concerning them, is always derived from experience and observation....

V-4. Portrait of David Hume.

A Miracle is a violation of the laws of nature; and as a firm and unalterable experience has established these laws, the proof against a miracle, from the very nature of the fact, is as entire as any argument from experience can possibly be imagined. Why is it more than probable, that all men must die; that lead cannot, of itself, remain suspended in the air; that fire consumes wood, and is extinguished by water; unless it be, that these events are found agreeable to the laws of nature, and there is required a violation of these laws, or in other words, a miracle to prevent them? Nothing is esteemed a miracle, if it ever happen in the common course of nature. It is no miracle that a man, seemingly in good health, should die on a sudden: because such a kind of death, though more unusual than any other, has yet been frequently observed to happen. But it is a miracle, that a dead man should come to life; because that has never been observed in any age or country. There must, therefore, be a uniform experience against every miraculous event, otherwise the event would not merit that appellation. And as a uniform experience amounts to a proof, there is here a direct and full *proof,* from the nature of the fact, against the existence of any miracle; nor can such a proof be destroyed, or the miracle rendered credible, but by an opposite proof, which is superior.

The plain consequence is (and it is a general maxim worthy of our attention), that no testimony is sufficient to establish a miracle, unless the testimony be of such a kind, that its falsehood would be more miraculous, than the fact, which it endeavors to establish; and even in that case there is a mutual destruction of arguments, and the superior only gives us an assurance suitable to that degree of force, which remains, after deducting the inferior. When anyone tells me, that he saw a dead man restored to life, I immediately consider with myself, whether it be more probable, that this person should either deceive or be deceived, or that the fact, which he relates, should really have happened. I weigh the one miracle against the other; and according to the superiority, which I discover, I pronounce my decision, and always reject the greater miracle. If the falsehood of his testimony would be more miraculous, than the event which he relates; then, and not till then, can he pretend to command my belief or opinion.

In the foregoing reasoning we have supposed, that the testimony, upon which a miracle is founded, may possibly amount to an entire proof, and that the falsehood of that testimony would be a real prodigy: but it is easy to shew, that we have been a great deal too liberal in our concession, and that there never was a miraculous event established on so full an evidence.

For *first,* there is not to be found, in all history, any miracle attested by a sufficient number of men, of such unquestioned good sense, education, and learning, as to secure us against all delusion in themselves; of such undoubted integrity, as to place them beyond all suspicion of any design to deceive others; of such credit and reputation in the eyes of mankind, as to have a great deal to lose in case of their being detected in any falsehood; and at the same time, attesting facts performed in such a public manner and in so celebrated a part of the world, as to render the detection unavoidable: all which circumstances are requisite to give us a full assurance in the testimony of men.

Secondly. We may observe in human nature a principle which, if strictly examined, will be found to diminish extremely the assurance, which we might, from human testimony, have in any kind of prodigy. The maxim by which we commonly conduct ourselves in our reasonings is, that the objects, of which we have no experience, resemble those, of which we have; that what we have found to be most usual is always most probable; and that where there is an opposition of arguments, we ought to give the preference to such as are founded on the greatest number of past observations. But though, in proceeding by this rule, we readily reject any fact which is unusual and incredible in an ordinary degree; yet in advancing farther, the mind observes not always the same rule; but when anything is affirmed utterly absurd and miraculous, it rather the more readily admits of such a fact, upon account of that very circumstance, which ought to destroy all its authority. The passion of *surprise* and *wonder,* arising from miracles, being an agreeable emotion, gives a sensible tendency towards the belief of those events, from which it is derived. And this goes so far, that even those who cannot enjoy this pleasure immediately, nor can believe those miraculous events, of which they are informed, yet love to partake of the satisfaction at second-hand or by rebound, and place a pride and delight in exciting the admiration of others.

.　.　.　.　.

Thirdly. It forms a strong presumption against all supernatural and miraculous relations, that they are observed chiefly to abound among ignorant and barbarous nations; or if a civilized people has ever given admission to any of them, that people will be found to have received them from ignorant and barbarous ancestors, who transmitted them with that inviolable sanction and authority, which always attend received opinions. . . .

It is strange, a judicious reader is apt to say, upon the perusal of these wonderful historians, *that such prodigious events never happen in our days.* But it is nothing strange, I hope, that men should lie in all ages. . . .

.   .   .   .   .

Upon the whole, then, it appears, that no testimony for any kind of miracle has ever amounted to a probability, much less to a proof; and that, even supposing it amounted to a proof, it would be opposed by another proof; derived from the very nature of the fact, which it would endeavour to establish. It is experience only, which gives authority to human testimony; and it is the same experience which assures us of the laws of nature. When, therefore, these two kinds of experience are contrary, we have nothing to do but subtract the one from the other, and embrace an opinion, either on one side or the other, with that assurance which arises from the remainder. But according to the principle here explained, this subtraction, with regard to all popular religions, amounts to an entire annihilation; and therefore we may establish it as a maxim, that no human testimony can have such force as to prove a miracle, and make it a just foundation for any such system of religion.

.   .   .   .   .

But suppose, that all the historians who treat of England, should agree, that, on the first of January, 1600, Queen Elizabeth died; that both before and after her death she was seen by her physicians and the whole court, as is usual with persons of her rank; that her successor was acknowledged and proclaimed by the parliament; and that, after being interred a month, she again appeared, resumed the throne, and governed England for three years: I must confess that I should be surprised at the concurrence of so many odd circumstances, but should not have the least inclination to believe so miraculous an event. I should not doubt of her pretended death, and of those other public circumstances that

followed it: I should only assert it to have been pretended, and that it neither was, nor possibly could be real. You would in vain object to me the difficulty, and almost impossibility of deceiving the world in an affair of such consequence; the wisdom and solid judgement of that renowned queen; with the little or no advantage which she could reap from so poor an artifice: all this might astonish me; but I would still reply, that the knavery and folly of men are such common phenomena, that I should rather believe the most extraordinary events to arise from their concurrence, than admit of so signal a violation of the laws of nature. . . .

.   .   .   .   .

10. *Voltaire, 1764*

François-Marie Arouet de Voltaire (1694-1778) epitomized the deistic, free-thinking, revolutionary spirit of France in the eighteenth century. Although he was educated in a Jesuit school, he despised established religion. Before he was thirty, he had been imprisoned in the Bastille twice, once by mistake and once because of his scathing satire. His caustic pen created many enemies for him, but his popular essays, plays, poems, and philosophical works virtually molded the rebellious spirit of France. Among his many books are *Mahomet*, 1741; *Candide*, 1759; *Tancrede*, 1760; and *Dictionnaire Philosophique*, 1764, from which the following two selections were taken. *The Works of Voltaire* (New York: E. R. Dumont, 1903).

GOD

In the reign of Arcadius, Logomachos, a theologue of Constantinople, went into Scythia and stopped at the foot of Mount Caucasus in the fruitful plains of Zephirim, on the borders of Colchis. The good old man Dondindac was in his great hall between his large sheepfold and his extensive barn; he was on his knees with his wife, his five sons and five daughters, his kinsmen and servants; and all were singing the praises of God, after a light repast. "What are you doing, idolater?" said Logomachos to him. "I am not an idolater," said Dondindac. "You must be an idolater," said Logomachos, "for you are not a Greek. Come, tell me what you were singing in your barbarous Scythian jargon?" "All tongues are alike to the ears of God," answered the Scythian; "we were singing His praises." "Very extraordinary!" returned the theologue; "a Scythian family praying to God without having been instructed by us!" He soon entered into conversation with the Scythian Dondindac; for the theologue knew a little Scythian, and the other a little Greek. This conversation has been found in a manuscript preserved in the library of Constantinople.

LOGOMACHOS: Let us see if you know your catechism. Why do you pray to God?

DONDINDAC: Because it is just to adore the Supreme Being, from whom we have everything.

LOGOMACHOS: Very fair for a barbarian. And what do you ask of him?

DONDINDAC: I thank Him for the blessings I enjoy, and even for the trials which He sends me; but I am careful to ask nothing of Him; for He knows our wants better than we do; besides, I should be afraid of asking for fair weather while my neighbor was asking for rain.

LOGOMACHOS: Ah! I thought he would say some nonsense or other. Let us begin farther back. Barbarian, who told you that there is a God?

DONDINDAC: All nature tells me.

LOGOMACHOS: That is not enough. What idea have you of God?

DONDINDAC: The idea of my Creator; my Master, who will reward me if I do good, and punish me if I do evil.

LOGOMACHOS: Trifles! trash! Let us come to some essentials. Is God *infinite secundrum quid,* or according to essence?

DONDINDAC: I don't understand you.

LOGOMACHOS: Brute beast! Is God in one place, or in every place?

DONDINDAC: I know not . . . just as you please.

LOGOMACHOS: Ignoramus! . . . Can He cause that which has not been to have been, or that a stick shall not have two ends? Does He see the future as future, or as present? How does He draw being from nothing, and how reduce being to nothing?

DONDINDAC: I have never examined these things.

LOGOMACHOS: What a stupid fellow! Well, I must come nearer to your level. . . . Tell me, friend, do you think that matter can be eternal?

DONDINDAC: What matters it to me whether it exists from all eternity or not? I do not exist from all eternity. God must still be my Master. He has given me the nature of justice; it is my duty to follow it: I seek not to be a philosopher; I wish to be a man.

LOGOMACHOS: One has a great deal of trouble with these blockheads. Let us proceed step by step. What is God?

DONDINDAC: My sovereign, my judge, my father.

LOGOMACHOS: That is not what I ask. What is His nature?

DONDINDAC: To be mighty and good.

LOGOMACHOS: But is He corporeal or spiritual?

DONDINDAC: How should I know that?

LOGOMACHOS: What; do you not know what a spirit is?

DONDINDAC: Not in the least. Of what service would that knowledge be to me? Should I be more just? Should I be a better husband, a better father, a better master, or a better citizen?

LOGOMACHOS: You must absolutely be taught what a spirit is. It is—it is—it is—I will say what another time.

DONDINDAC: I much fear that you will tell me rather what it is not than what it is. Permit me, in turn, to ask you one question. Some time ago, I saw one of your temples: why do you paint God with a long beard?

LOGOMACHOS: That is a very difficult question, and requires preliminary instruction.

DONDINDAC: Before I receive your instruction, I must relate to you a thing which one day happened to me. I had just built a closet at the end of my garden, when I heard a mole arguing thus with an ant: "Here is a fine fabric," said the mole; "it must have been a very powerful mole that performed this work." "You jest," returned the ant; "the architect of this edifice is an ant of mighty genius." From that time I resolved never to dispute.

THEIST

The theist is a man firmly persuaded of the existence of a Supreme Being equally good and powerful, who has formed all extended,

Populus me sibilat, at mihi plaudo —

Ite Domi — Horat: sht: 1. L: 1.

Were all oblig'd to practise what they teach
Some warm sleek Clerks would still more seldom preach.
Stall-fed TARTUFF reclining in his Seat,
High heap'd his Board, himself brimfull of Meat,
Yawning, with Pain thus sleepy Silence broke.
And to his meagre Curates Sagely spoke,,
My loving Brethren; we should rest content
With the small Pittance gracious Heav'n has sent.

'Tis better much to want, than much abound;
Hunger and Thirst hereafter will be crown'd.
If ne're Prunella, which will hang together,
Like the good Baptist, girt about with Leather;;
And Bread and Water; we should ne'er complaine.
Here, John, give me a — Bumper of Champagne.

Seasonable Reproof.

V-5. Tartuff's Banquet. *Satire on hypocritical preachments about poverty, by William Hogarth. British Museum.*

vegetating, sentient, and reflecting existences; who perpetuates their species, who punishes crimes without cruelty, and rewards virtuous actions with kindness.

The theist does not know how God punishes, how He rewards, how He pardons; for he is not presumptuous enough to flatter himself that he understands how God acts; but he knows that God does act, and He is just. The difficulties opposed to a providence do not stagger him in his faith, because they are only great difficulties, not proofs; he submits himself to that providence, although he only perceives some of its effects and some ap-

pearances; and judging of the things he does not see from those he does see, he thinks that this providence pervades all places and all ages.

United in this principle with the rest of the universe, he does not join any of the sects, who all contradict themselves; his religion is the most ancient and the most extended; for the simple adoration of a God has preceded all the systems in the world. He speaks a language which all nations understand, while they are unable to understand each other's. He has brethren from Pekin to Cayenne, and he reckons all the wise his brothers. He be-

249

lieves that religion consists neither in the opinions of incomprehensible metaphysics, nor in vain decorations, but in adoration and justice. To do good—that is his worship; to submit oneself to God—that is his doctrine. The Mahometan cries out to him: "Take care of yourself, if you do not make the pilgrimage to Mecca." "Woe be to thee," says a Franciscan, "if thou dost not make a journey to our Lady of Loretto." He laughs at Loretto and Mecca; but he succors the indigent and defends the oppressed.

11. Immanuel Kant, Imperatives, 1788

The selections for the categorical imperative and the postulates of the moral law are taken from "Kant's Moral Philosophy" in *The Critique of Practical Reason and Other Works on Ethics*, trans. T. K. Abbott (New York: Longmans, Green & Co., Ltd., 1879).

All *imperatives* command either *hypothetically* or *categorically*. The former represent the practical necessity of a possible action as means to something else that is willed (or at least which one might possibly will). The categorical imperative would be that which represented an action as necessary of itself without reference to another end, i.e., objectively necessary.

Since every practical law represents a possible action as good, and on this account, for a subject who is practically determinable by reason, necessary, all imperatives are formulae determining an action which is necessary according to the principle of a will good in some respects. If now the action is good only as a means *to something else*, then the imperative is *hypothetical;* if it is conceived as good *in itself* and consequently as being necessarily the principle of a will which of itself conforms to reason, then it is *categorical.*

Thus the imperative declares what action possible by me would be good, and presents the practical rule in relation to a will which does not forthwith perform an action simply because it is good, whether because the subject does not always know that it is good, or because, even if it know this, yet its maxims might be opposed to the objective principles of practical reason.

Accordingly the hypothetical imperative only says that the action is good for some purpose, *possible* or *actual.* In the first case it is a Problematical, in the second an Assertorial practical principle. The categorical imperative which declares an action to be objectively necessary in itself without reference to any purpose, i.e., without any other end, is valid as an Apodictic (practical) principle.

Whatever is possible only by the power of some rational being may also be conceived as a possible purpose of some will; and therefore the principles of action as regards the means necessary to attain some possible purpose are in fact infinitely numerous. All sciences have a practical part, consisting of problems expressing that some end is possible for us, and of imperatives directing how it may be attained. These may, therefore, be called in general imperatives of Skill. Here there is no question whether the end is rational and good, but only what one must do in order to attain it. The precepts for the physician to make his patient thoroughly healthy, and for a poisoner to ensure certain death, are of equal value in this respect, that each serves to effect its purpose perfectly. Since in early youth it cannot be known what ends are likely to occur to us in the course of life, parents seek to have their children taught a *great many things*, and provide for their *skill* in the use of means for all sorts of arbitrary ends, of none of which can they determine whether it may not perhaps hereafter be an object to their pupil, but which it is at all events *possible* that he might aim at; and this anxiety is so great that they commonly neglect to form and correct their judgment on the value of the things which may be chosen as ends.

There is *one* end, however, which may be assumed to be actually such to all rational beings (so far as imperatives apply to them, viz., as dependent beings), and, therefore, one purpose which they not merely *may* have but which we may with certainty assume that they all actually *have* by a natural necessity, and this is *happiness.* The hypothetical imperative which expresses the practical necessity of an action as means to the advancement of happiness is Assertorial.

We are not to present it as necessary for an uncertain and merely possible purpose, but for a purpose which we may presuppose with certainty and *a priori* in every man, because it belongs to his being. Now skill in the choice of means to his own greatest well-being may be called *prudence,** in the narrowest sense. And thus the imperative which refers to the choice of means to one's own happiness, i.e., the precept of prudence, is still always *hypothetical;* the action is not commanded absolutely, but only as means to another purpose.

Finally, there is an imperative which commands a certain conduct immediately, without having as its condition any other purpose to be attained by it. This imperative is Categorical. It concerns not the matter of the action, or its intended result, but its form and the principle of which it is itself a result; and what is essentially good in it consists in the mental disposition, let the consequence be what it may. This imperative may be called that of Morality. . . .

There is but one categorical imperative, namely this: *Act only on that maxim whereby thou canst at the same time will that it should become a universal law.*

Now if all imperatives of duty can be deduced from this one imperative as from their principle, then, although it should remain undecided whether what is called duty is not merely a vain notion, yet at least we shall be able to show what we understand by it and what this notion means.

Since the universality of the law according to which effects are produced constitutes what is properly called *nature* in the most general sense (as to form), that is the existence of things so far as it is determined by general laws, the imperative of duty may be expressed thus: *Act as if the maxim of thy*

action were to become by thy will a Universal Law of Nature. . . .

Now I say: man and generally any rational being *exists* as an end in himself, *not merely as a means* to be arbitrarily used by this or that will, but in all his actions, whether they concern himself or other rational beings, must be always regarded at the same time as an end. All objects of the inclinations have only a conditional worth, for if the inclinations and the wants founded on them did not exist, then their object would be without value. But the inclinations themselves being sources of want, are so far from having an absolute worth for which they should be desired, that on the contrary it must be the universal wish of every rational being to be wholly free from them. Thus the worth of any object which is *to be acquired* by our action is always conditional. Beings whose existence depends not on our will but on nature's, have nevertheless, if they are irrational beings, only a relative value as means, and are therefore called *things;* rational beings, on the contrary, are called persons, because their very nature points them out as ends in themselves, that is as something which must not be used merely as means, and so far therefore restricts freedom of action (and is an object of respect). These, therefore, are not merely subjective ends whose existence has a worth *for us* as an effect of our action, but objective ends, that is things whose existence is an end in itself; an end moreover for which no other can be substituted, which they should subserve *merely* as a means, for otherwise nothing whatever would possess *absolute worth;* but if all worth were conditioned and therefore contingent, then there would be no supreme practical principle of reason whatever.

If then there is a supreme practical principle or, in respect of the human will a categorical imperative, it must be one which, being drawn from the conception of that which is necessarily an end for every one because it is *an end in itself*, constitutes an *objective* principle of will, and can therefore serve as a universal practical law. The foundation of this principle is: *rational nature exists as an end in itself*. Man necessarily con-

---

* The word prudence is taken in two senses: in the one it may bear the name of knowledge of the world, in the other that of private prudence. The former is a man's ability to influence others so as to use them for his own purposes. The latter is the sagacity to combine all these purposes for his own lasting benefit. This latter is properly that to which the value even of the former is reduced, and when a man is prudent in the former sense, but not in the latter, we might better say of him that he is clever and cunning, but, on the whole, imprudent.

ceives his own existence as being so; so far then this is a *subjective* principle of human actions. But every other rational being regards its existence similarly, just on the same rational principle that holds for me: so that it is at the same time an objective principle, from which as a supreme practical law all laws of the will must be capable of being deduced. Accordingly the practical imperative will be as follows: *So act as to treat humanity, whether in thine own person or in that of any other, in every case as an end withal, never as means only.*

This principle, that humanity and generally every rational nature is *an end in itself* (which is the supreme limiting condition of every man's freedom of action), is not borrowed from experience, firstly, because it is universal, applying as it does to all rational beings whatever, and experience is not capable of determining anything about them; secondly, because it does not present humanity as an end to men (subjectively), that is as an object which men do of themselves actually adopt as an end; but as an objective end, which must as a law constitute the supreme limiting condition of all our subjective ends, let them be what we will; it must therefore spring from pure reason. In fact the objective principle of all practical legislation lies (according to the first principle) in *the rule* and its form of universality which makes it capable of being a law (say, e.g., a law of nature); but the subjective principle is in the end; now by the second principle the subject of all ends is each rational being, inasmuch as it is an end in itself. Hence follows the third practical principle of the will, which is the ultimate condition of its harmony with universal practical reason, *viz.*: the idea of *the will of every rational being as a universally legislative will.*

On this principle all maxims are rejected which are inconsistent with the will being itself universal legislator. Thus the will is not subject simply to the law, but so subject that it must be regarded *as itself giving the law,* and on this ground only, subject to the law (of which it can regard itself as the author).

In the previous imperatives, namely, that based on the conception of the conformity of actions to general laws, as in a *physical system of nature,* and that based on the universal *prerogative* of rational beings as *ends* in themselves—these imperatives just because they were conceived as categorical, excluded from any share in their authority all admixture of any interest as a spring of action; they were however only *assumed* to be categorical, because such an assumption was necessary to explain the conception of duty. But we could not prove independently that there are practical propositions which command categorically, nor can it be proved in this section; one thing however could be done, namely, to indicate in the imperative itself by some determinate expression, that in the case of volition from duty all interest is renounced, which is the specific criterion of categorical as distinguished from hypothetical imperatives. This is done in the present (third) formula of the principle, namely in the idea of the will of every rational being as a *universally legislating will.*

12. Immanuel Kant, Postulates

The Immortality of the Soul as a Postulate of Pure Practical Reason.—The realization of the *summum bonum* in the world is the necessary object of a will determinable by the moral law. But in this will the *perfect accordance* of the mind with the moral law is the supreme condition of the *summum bonum.* This then must be possible, as well as its object, since it is contained in the command to promote the latter. Now the perfect accordance of the will with the moral law is holiness, a perfection of which no rational being of the sensible world is capable at any moment of his existence. Since, nevertheless, it is required as practically necessary, it can only be found in a *progress in infinitum* towards that perfect accordance, and on the principles of pure practical reason it is necessary to assume such a practical progress as the real object of our will.

Now, this endless progress is only possible on the supposition of an *endless* duration of the *existence* and personality of the same rational being (which is called the immortality of the soul). The *summum bonum,* then, practically is only possible on the supposition of the immortality of the soul; consequently this immortality, being inseparably connected with the moral law, is a Postulate of pure practical reason (by which I mean a *theoretical* proposition, not demonstrable as such, but which is an inseparable result of an unconditional *a priori practical* law).

This principle of the moral destination of our nature, namely, that it is only in an endless progress that we can attain perfect accordance with the moral law, is of the greatest use, not merely for the present purpose of supplementing the impotence of speculative reason, but also with respect to religion. In default of it, either the moral law is quite degraded from its *holiness,* being made out to be *indulgent,* and conformable to our convenience, or else men strain their notions of their vocation and their expectation to an unattainable goal, hoping to acquire complete holiness of will, and so they lose themselves in fanatical *theosophic* dreams, which wholly contradict self-knowledge. In both cases the unceasing *effort* to obey punctually and thoroughly a strict and inflexible command of reason, which yet is not ideal but real, is only hindered. For a rational but finite being, the only thing possible is an endless progress from the lower to higher degrees of moral perfection. The *Infinite* Being, to whom the condition of time is nothing, sees in this to us endless succession a whole of accordance with the moral law; and the holiness which his command inexorably requires, in order to be true to his justice in the share which He assigns to each in the *summum bonum,* is to be found in a single intellectual intuition of the whole existence of rational beings. All that can be expected of the creature in respect of the hope of this participation would be the consciousness of his tried character, by which from the progress he has hitherto made from the worse to the morally better, and the immutability of purpose which has thus become known to him, he may hope for a further unbroken continuance of the same, however long his existence may last, even beyond this

life,* and thus he may hope, not indeed here, nor at any imaginable point of his future existence, but only in the endlessness of his duration (which God alone can survey) to be perfectly adequate to his will (without indulgence or excuse, which do not harmonize with justice).

The Existence of God as a Postulate of Pure Practical Reason.—In the foregoing analysis the moral law led to a practical problem which is prescribed by pure reason alone, without the aid of any sensible motives, namely, that of the necessary completeness of the first and principal element of the *summum bonum, viz.* Morality; and as this can be perfectly solved only in eternity, to the postulate of *immortality.* The same law must also lead us to affirm the possibility of the second element of the *summum bonum, viz.* Happiness proportioned to that morality, and this on grounds as disinterested as before, and solely from impartial reason; that is, it must lead to the supposition of the existence of a cause adequate to this effect; in other words, it must postulate the *existence of God,* as the necessary condition of the possibility of the *summum bonum* (an object of the will which is necessarily connected with the moral legislation of pure reason). We proceed to exhibit this connection in a convincing manner.

---

* It seems, nevertheless, impossible for a creature to have the conviction of his unwavering firmness of mind in the progress towards goodness. On this account the Christian religion makes it come only from the same Spirit that works sanctification, that is, this firm purpose, and with it the consciousness of steadfastness in the moral progress. But naturally one who is conscious that he has persevered through a long portion of his life up to the end in the progress to the better, and this from genuine moral motives, may well have the comforting hope, though not the certainty, that even in an existence prolonged beyond this life he will continue steadfast in these principles; and although he is never justified here in his own eyes, nor can ever hope to be so in the increased perfection of his nature, to which he looks forward, together with an increase of duties, nevertheless in this progress which, though it is directed to a goal infinitely remote, yet is in God's sight regarded as equivalent to possession, he may have a prospect of a *blessed* future; for this is the word that reason employs to designate perfect *well-being* independent of all contingent causes of the world, and which, like *holiness,* is an idea that can be contained only in an endless progress and its totality, and consequently is never fully attained by a creature.

253

Happiness is the condition of a rational being in the world with whom *everything goes according to his wish and will;* it rests, therefore, on the harmony of physical nature with his whole end, and likewise with the essential determining principle of his will. Now the moral law as a law of freedom commands by determining principles, which ought to be quite independent of nature and of its harmony with our faculty of desire (as springs). But the acting rational being in the world is not the cause of the world and of nature itself. There is not the least ground, therefore, in the moral law for a necessary connection between morality and proportionate happiness in a being that belongs to the world as part of it, and therefore dependent on it, and which for that reason cannot by his will be a cause of this nature, nor by his own power make it thoroughly harmonize, as far as his happiness is concerned, with his practical principles. Nevertheless, in the practical problem of pure reason, *i.e.,* the necessary pursuit of the *summum bonum,* such a connection is postulated as necessary: we ought to endeavor to promote the *summum bonum,* which, therefore, must be possible. Accordingly, the existence of a cause of all nature, distinct from nature itself and containing the principle of this connection, namely, of the exact harmony of happiness with morality, is also *postulated.* Now this supreme cause must contain the principle of the harmony of nature, not merely with a law of the will of rational beings, but with the conception of this law, in so far as they make it the *supreme determining principle of the will,* and consequently not merely with the form of morals, but with their morality as their motive, that is, with their moral character. Therefore, the *summum bonum* is possible in the world only on the supposition of a supreme Being having a causality corresponding to moral character. Now a being that is capable of acting on the conception of laws is an *intelligence* (a rational being), and the causality of such a being according to this conception of laws is his *will;* therefore, the supreme cause of nature, which must be presupposed as a condition of the *summum bonum,* is a being which is the cause of nature by *intelligence* and *will,* consequently its author, that is God. It follows that the postulate of the possibility of the *highest derived good* (the best world) is likewise the postulate of the reality of a *highest original good,* that is to say, of the existence of God. Now it was seen to be a duty for us to promote the *summum bonum;* consequently it is not merely allowable, but it is a necessity connected with duty as a requisite, that we should presuppose the possibility of this *summum bonum,* and as this is possible only on condition of the existence of God, it inseparably connects the supposition of this with duty; that is, it is morally necessary to assume the existence of God.

Of the Postulates of Pure Practical Reason in General.—They all proceed from the principle of morality, which is not a postulate but a law, by which reason determines the will directly, which will, because it is so determined as a pure will, requires these necessary conditions of obedience to its precept. These postulates are not theoretical dogmas, but suppositions practically necessary; while then they do [not] extend our speculative knowledge, they give objective reality to the ideas of speculative reason in general (by means of their reference to what is practical), and give it a right to concepts, the possibility even of which it could not otherwise venture to affirm.

These postulates are those *of immortality, freedom* positively considered (as the causality of a being so far as he belongs to the intelligible world), and the *existence of God.* The *first* results from the practically necessary condition of a duration adequate to the complete fulfilment of the moral law; the *second* from the necessary supposition of independence of the sensible world, and of the faculty of determining one's will according to the law of an intelligible world, that is, of freedom; the *third* from the necessary condition of the existence of the *summum bonum* in which an intelligible world, by the supposition of the supreme independent good, that is, the existence of God.

Thus the fact that respect for the moral law necessarily makes the *summum bonum* an object of our endeavors, and the supposition thence resulting of its objective reality, lead through the postulates of practical reason to conceptions which speculative reason might indeed present as problems, but could never solve. Thus it leads— 1. To that one in the solution of which the latter could do nothing but commit paralogisms (namely, that of immortality), because it could not lay hold of the character of permanence, by which to complete the psychological conception of an ultimate subject necessarily ascribed to the soul in self-consciousness, so as to make it the real conception of a substance, a character which practical reason furnishes by the postulate of a duration required for accordance with the moral law in the *summum bonum*, which is the whole end of practical reason. 2. It leads to that of which speculative reason contained nothing but *antinomy*, the solution of which it could only found on a notion problematically conceivable indeed, but whose objective reality it could not prove or determine, namely, the *cosmological* idea of an intelligible world and the consciousness of our existence in it, by means of the postulate of freedom (the reality of which it lays down by virtue of the moral law), and with it likewise the law of an intelligible world, to which speculative reason could only point, but could not define its conception. 3. What speculative reason was able to think, but was obliged to leave undetermined as a mere transcendental *ideal*, viz. the *theological* conception of the first Being, to this it gives significance (in a practical view, that is, as condition of the possibility of the object of a will determined by that law), namely, as the supreme principle of the *summum bonum* in an intelligible world, by means of moral legislation in it invested with sovereign power.

Is our knowledge, however, actually extended in this way by pure practical reason, and is that *immanent* in practical reason which for the speculative was only *transcendent?* Certainly, but *only in a practical point of view.* For we do not thereby take knowledge of the nature of our souls, nor of the intelligible world, nor of the Supreme Being, with respect to what they are in themselves, but we have merely combined the concep-

tions of them in the *practical* concept of the *summum bonum* as the object of our will, and this altogether *a priori*, but only by means of the moral law, and merely in reference to it, in respect of the object which it commands. But how freedom is possible, and how we are to conceive this kind of causality theoretically and positively, is not thereby discovered; but only that there is such a causality is postulated by the moral law and in its behoof. It is the same with the remaining ideas, the possibility of which no human intelligence will ever fathom, but the truth of which, on the other hand, no sophistry will ever wrest from the conviction even of the commonest man.

[In *Religion Within the Limits of Reason Alone,* Kant declared: "Whatever over and above good life-conduct, man fancies that he can do to become well pleasing to God is mere religious illusion and pseudo-service of God." This provided the basis for a critical evaluation and rejection of rites and actions for which man claimed supernatural benefits beyond the knowable world of reason. Cf. *Religion Within the Limits of Reason Alone,* trans. Theodore M. Greene and Hoyt H. Hudson (Chicago: Open Court Publishing Company, 1934).]

13. Thomas Paine

Paine was a Deist, not an atheist. He founded the first Theistic Society in Paris, and was a foe of tyranny, fraud, and privilege. The following selections from Chapters 1, 7, 9, 10, and 18 of *The Age of Reason* reflect his popular brand of Deism. Thomas Paine, *The Age of Reason* (New York: G. P. Putnam's Sons, 1896). Cf. *The Age of Reason* (London: D. I. Eaton, 1796).

THE AUTHOR'S PROFESSION OF FAITH

I believe in one God, and no more; and I hope for happiness beyond this life.

I believe the equality of man, and I believe that religious duties consist in doing justice, loving mercy, and endeavouring to make our fellow-creatures happy.

But, lest it should be supposed that I believe many other things in addition to these,

I shall, in the progress of this work, declare the things I do not believe, and my reasons for not believing them.

I do not believe in the creed professed by the Jewish church, by the Roman church, by the Greek church, by the Turkish church, by the Protestant church, nor by any church that I know of. My own mind is my own church.

All national institutions of churches, whether Jewish, Christian, or Turkish, appear to me no other than human inventions set up to terrify and enslave mankind, and monopolize power and profit.

I do not mean by this declaration to condemn those who believe otherwise; they have the same right to their belief as I have to mine. But it is necessary to the happiness of man that he be mentally faithful to himself. Infidelity does not consist in believing, or in disbelieving; it consists in professing to believe what he does not believe.

It is impossible to calculate the moral mischief, if I may so express it, that mental lying has produced in society. When a man has so far corrupted and prostituted the chastity of his mind, as to subscribe his professional belief to things he does not believe, he has prepared himself for the commission of every other crime. He takes up the trade of a priest for the sake of gain, and, in order to qualify himself for that trade, he begins with a perjury. Can we conceive anything more destructive to morality than this?

Soon after I had published the pamphlet *Common Sense*, in America, I saw the exceeding probability that a revolution in the system of government would be followed by a revolution in the system of religion. The adulterous connection of church and state, wherever it had taken place, whether Jewish, Christian, or Turkish, had so effectually prohibited, by pains and penalties, every discussion upon established creeds, and upon first principles of religion, that until the system of government should be changed, those subjects could not be brought fairly and openly before the world; but that whenever this should be done, a revolution in the system of religion would follow. Human inventions and priest-craft would be detected; and man would return to the pure, unmixed, and un adulterated belief of one God, and no more.

Every national church or religion has established itself by pretending some special mission from God, communicated to certain individuals. The Jews have their Moses; the Christians their Jesus Christ, their apostles and saints; and the Turks their Mahomet; as if the way to God was not open to every man alike.

Each of those churches shows certain books, which they call *revelation,* or the Word of God. The Jews say that their Word of God was given by God to Moses face to face; the Christians say that their Word of God came by divine inspiration; and the Turks say that their Word of God (the Koran) was brought by an angel from heaven. Each of those churches accuses the other of unbelief; and, for my own part, I disbelieve them all.

As it is necessary to affix right ideas to words, I will, before I proceed further into the subject, offer some observations on the word *revelation*. Revelation, when applied to religion, means something communicated *immediately* from God to man.

No one will deny or dispute the power of the Almighty to make such a communication if he pleases. But admitting, for the sake of a case, that something has been revealed to a certain person, and not revealed to any other person, it is revelation to that person only. When he tells it to a second person, a second to a third, a third to a fourth, and so on, it ceases to be a revelation to all those persons. It is revelation to the first person only, and *hearsay* to every other, and, consequently, they are not obliged to believe it.

It is a contradiction in terms and ideas to call anything a revelation that comes to us at second hand, either verbally or in writing. Revelation is necessarily limited to the first communication. After this, it is only an account of something which that person says was a revelation made to him; and though he may find himself obliged to believe it, it cannot be incumbent on me to believe it in the same manner, for it was not a revelation to *me,* and I have only his word for it that it was made to *him....*

Revelation is a communication of something, which the person, to whom that thing is revealed, did not know before. For if I have done a thing, or seen it done, it needs no revelation to tell me I have done it, or seen it, nor to enable me to tell it, or to write it.

Revelation, therefore, cannot be applied to anything done upon earth of which man is himself the actor or the witness; and consequently all the historical and anecdotal part of the Bible, which is almost the whole of it, is not within the meaning and compass of the word revelation, and, therefore, is not the word of God. . . .

IN WHAT THE TRUE REVELATION CONSISTS

But some perhaps will say—Are we to have no word of God—no revelation? I answer yes. There is a word of God; there is a revelation.

The Word of God is the Creation We Behold: And it is in *this word*, which no human invention can counterfeit or alter, that God speaketh universally to man.

Human language is local and changeable, and is therefore incapable of being used as the means of unchangeable and universal information. The idea that God sent Jesus Christ to publish, as they say, the glad tidings to all nations, from one end of the earth unto the other, is consistent only with the ignorance of those who know nothing of the extent of the world, and who believed, as those world-saviours believed, and continued to believe for several centuries, (and that in contradiction to the discoveries of philosophers and the experience of navigators,) that the earth was flat like a trencher; and that a man might walk to the end of it.

But how was Jesus Christ to make anything known to all nations? He could speak but one language, which was Hebrew; and there are in the world several hundred languages. Scarcely any two nations speak the same language, or understand each other; and as to translations, every man who knows anything of languages, knows that it is impossible to translate from one language into another, not only without losing a great part of the original, but frequently of mistaking

the sense; and besides all this, the art of printing was wholly unknown at the time Christ lived.

It is always necessary that the means that are to accomplish any end be equal to the accomplishment of that end, or the end cannot be accomplished. It is in this that the difference between finite and infinite power and wisdom discovers itself. Man frequently fails in accomplishing his end, from a natural inability of the power to the purpose; and frequently from the want of wisdom to apply power properly. But it is impossible for infinite power and wisdom to fail as man faileth. The means it useth are always equal to the end: but human language, more especially as there is not an universal language, is incapable of being used as an universal means of unchangeable and uniform information; and therefore it is not the means that God useth in manifesting himself universally to man.

It is only in the *Creation* that all our ideas and conceptions of a *word of God* can unite. The Creation speaketh an universal language, independently of human speech or human language, multiplied and various as they be. It is an ever existing original, which every man can read. It cannot be forged; it cannot be counterfeited; it cannot be lost; it cannot be altered; it cannot be suppressed. It does not depend upon the will of man whether it shall be published or not; it publishes itself from one end of the earth to the other. It preaches to all nations and to all worlds; and this *word of God* reveals to man all that is necessary for man to know of God.

Do we want to contemplate his power? We see it in the immensity of the creation. Do we want to contemplate his wisdom? We see it in the unchangeable order by which the incomprehensible Whole is governed. Do we want to contemplate his munificence? We see it in the abundance with which he fills the earth. Do we want to contemplate his mercy? We see it in his not withholding that abundance even from the unthankful. In fine, do we want to know what God is? Search not the book called the scripture, which any human hand might make, but the scripture called the Creation.

V-6. Adam and Eve. *Etching depicting the fall of man, by Rembrandt van Rijn, 1638. Courtesy of The Museum of Fine Arts, Boston.*

The only idea man can affix to the name of God, is that of a *first cause*, the cause of all things. And, incomprehensibly difficult as it is for a man to conceive what a first cause is, he arrives at the belief of it, from the tenfold greater difficulty of disbelieving it. It is difficult beyond description to conceive that space can have no end; but it is more difficult to conceive an end. It is difficult beyond the power of man to conceive an eternal duration of what we call time; but it is more impossible to conceive a time when there shall be no time.

In like manner of reasoning, everything we behold carries in itself the internal evidence that it did not make itself. Every man is an evidence to himself that he did not make himself; neither could his father make himself, nor his grandfather, nor any of his race;

neither could any tree, plant, or animal make itself; and it is the conviction arising from this evidence, that carries us on, as it were, by necessity, to the belief of a first cause eternally existing, of a nature totally different to any material existence we know of, and by the power of which all things exist; and this first cause, man calls God.

It is only by the exercise of reason, that man can discover God. Take away that reason, and he would be incapable of understanding anything; and in this case it would be just as consistent to read even the book called the Bible to a horse as to a man. How then is it that those people pretend to reject reason? . . .

OF THE MEANS EMPLOYED IN ALL TIME,
AND ALMOST UNIVERSALLY, TO
DECEIVE THE PEOPLES

Having thus shewn the irreconcilable inconsistencies between the real word of God existing in the universe, and that which is called *the word of God*, as shewn to us in a printed book that any man might make, I proceed to speak of the three principal means that have been employed in all ages, and perhaps in all countries, to impose upon mankind.

Those three means are Mystery, Miracle, and Prophecy. The first two are incompatible with true religion, and the third ought always to be suspected.

With respect to Mystery, every thing we behold is, in one sense, a mystery to us. Our own existence is a mystery: the whole vegetable world is a mystery. We cannot account how it is that an acorn, when put into the ground, is made to develop itself and become an oak. We know not how it is that the seed we sow unfolds and multiplies itself, and returns to us such an abundant interest for so small a capital.

The fact however, as distinct from the operating cause, is not a mystery, because we see it; and we know also the means we are to use, which is no other than putting the seed in the ground. We know, therefore, as much as is necessary for us to know; and that part of the operation that we do not know, and which if we did, we could not perform, the Creator takes upon himself and performs it for us. We are, therefore, better off than if we had been let into the secret, and left to do it for ourselves.

But though every created thing is, in this sense, a mystery, the word mystery cannot be applied to *moral truth*, any more than obscurity can be applied to light. The God in whom we believe is a God of moral truth, and not a God of mystery or obscurity. Mystery is the antagonist of truth. It is a fog of human invention that obscures truth, and represents it in distortion. Truth never envelops *itself* in mystery; and the mystery in which it is at any time enveloped, is the work of its antagonist, and never of itself.

Religion, therefore, being the belief of a God, and the practice of moral truth, cannot have connection with mystery. The belief of a God, so far from having any thing of mystery in it, is of all beliefs the most easy, because it arises to us, as is before observed, out of necessity. And the practice of moral truth, or, in other words, a practical imitation of the moral goodness of God, is no other than our acting towards each other as he acts benignly towards all. We cannot *serve* God in the manner we serve those who cannot do without such service; and, therefore, the only idea we can have of serving God, is that of contributing to the happiness of the living creation that God has made. This cannot be done by retiring ourselves from the society of the world, and spending a recluse life in selfish devotion.

The very nature and design of religion, if I may so express it, prove even to demonstration that it must be free from every thing of mystery, and unincumbered with every thing that is mysterious. Religion, considered as a duty, is incumbent upon every living soul alike, and, therefore, must be on a level to the understanding and comprehension of all. Man does not learn religion as he learns the secrets and mysteries of a trade. He learns the theory of religion by reflection. It arises out of the action of his own mind upon the things which he sees, or upon what he may happen to hear or to read, and the practice joins itself thereto.

When men, whether from policy or pious fraud, set up systems of religion incompatible with the word or works of God in the creation, and not only above but repugnant to human comprehension, they were under necessity of inventing or adopting a word that should serve as a bar to all questions, inquiries and speculations. The word *mystery* answered this purpose, and thus it has happened that religion, which is in itself without mystery, has been corrupted into a fog of mysteries.

As *mystery* answered all general purposes, *miracle* followed as an occasional auxiliary. The former served to bewilder the mind, the latter to puzzle the senses. The one was the lingo, the other the legerdemain.

But before going further into this subject, it will be proper to inquire what is to be understood by a miracle.

In the same sense that every thing may be said to be a mystery, so also may it be said that every thing is a miracle, and that no one thing is a greater miracle than another. The elephant, though larger, is not a greater miracle than a mite: nor a mountain a greater miracle than an atom. To an almighty power it is no more difficult to make the one than the other, and no more difficult to make a million of worlds than to make one. Every thing, therefore, is a miracle, in one sense; whilst in the other sense, there is no such thing as a miracle. It is a miracle when compared to our power, and to our comprehension. It is not a miracle compared to the power that performs it. But as nothing in this description conveys the idea that is affixed to the word miracle, it is necessary to carry the inquiry further.

Mankind have conceived to themselves certain laws, by which what they call nature is supposed to act; and that a miracle is something contrary to the operation and effect of those laws. But unless we know the whole extent of those laws, and of what are commonly called the powers of nature, we are not able to judge whether any thing that may appear to us wonderful or miraculous, be within, or be beyond, or be contrary to, her natural power of acting. . . .

As Mystery and Miracle took charge of the past and the present, Prophecy took charge of the future, and rounded the tenses of *faith*. It was not sufficient to know what had been done, but what would be done. The supposed prophet was the supposed historian of times to come; and if he happened, in shooting with a long bow of a thousand years, to strike within a thousand miles of a mark, the ingenuity of posterity could make it point-blank; and if he happened to be directly wrong, it was only to suppose, as in the case of Jonah and Nineveh, that God had repented himself and changed his mind. What a fool do fabulous systems make of man! . . .

If by a prophet we are to suppose a man to whom the Almighty communicated some event that would take place in future, either there were such men, or there were not. If there were, it is consistent to believe that the event so communicated would be told in terms that could be understood, and not related in such a loose and obscure manner as to be out of the comprehension of those that heard it, and so equivocal as to fit almost any circumstance that might happen afterwards. It is conceiving very irreverently of the Almighty, to suppose he would deal in this jesting manner with mankind; yet all the things called prophecies in the book called the Bible come under this description.

But it is with Prophecy as it is with Miracle. It could not answer the purpose even if it were real. Those to whom a prophecy should be told could not tell whether the man prophesied or lied, or whether it had been revealed to him, or whether he conceived it; and if the thing that he prophesied, or pretended to prophesy, should happen, or some thing like it, among the multitude of things that are daily happening, nobody could again know whether he foreknew it, or guessed at it, or whether it was accidental. A prophet, therefore, is a character useless and unnecessary; and the safe side of the case is to guard against being imposed upon, by not giving credit to such relations.

Upon the whole, Mystery, Miracle, and Prophecy, are appendages that belong to fabulous and not to true religion. They are the means by which so many *Lo heres!* and *Lo theres!* have been spread about the world, and religion been made into a trade. The success of one impostor gave encouragement to another, and the quieting salvo of doing some good by keeping up a *pious fraud* protected them from remorse.

SUGGESTED READINGS

Becker, Carl, *Heavenly City of the Eighteenth Century Philosophers*. New Haven: Yale University Press, 1932.

Bredvold, L. J., *Brave New World of Enlightenment*. Ann Arbor: University of Michigan Press, 1961.

Cassirer, E., *Philosophy of the Enlightenment*. Boston: Beacon Press, 1955.

Cragg, G. R., *From Puritanism to the Age of Reason*. Cambridge, Eng.: Cambridge University Press, 1950.

Creed, J. M. and J. S. Boys Smith, *Religious Thought in the Eighteenth Century*. New York: Cambridge University Press, 1934.

Crocker, L. G., *Age of Crisis: Man and World in Eighteenth Century French Thought*. Baltimore: The Johns Hopkins Press, 1959.

Dillenberger, J. and C. Welch, *Protestant Christianity Interpreted Through Its Development*. New York: Charles Scribner's Sons, 1954.

Drummond, A. L., *German Protestantism Since Luther*. London: The Epworth Press, Publishers, 1951.

English Philosophers, Locke, Berkeley, Hume. New York: P. F. Collier, Inc., 1910.

French and English Philosophers, Descartes, Rousseau, Voltaire, Hobbes. New York: P. F. Collier, Inc., 1910.

French Thought in the Eighteenth Century, Rousseau, Voltaire, Diderot. New York: David McKay Co., Inc., 1953.

Hazard, Paul, *The European Mind*, 1680-1714. London: Hollis & Carter, Ltd., Publishers, 1953.

Hume, David, *Works*. Various editions and selections.

Kant, Immanuel, *Critique of Pure Reason, Critique of Practical Reason, Religion Within the Limits of Reason Alone*. Various editions and selections.

Lecky, W. E. H., *History of the Rise and Influence of the Spirit of Rationalism in Europe*. New York: George Braziller, Inc., 1866.

Manuel, Frank E., *Eighteenth Century Confronts the Gods*. Cambridge: Harvard University Press, 1959.

McGiffert, A. C., *Protestant Thought Before Kant*. New York: Charles Scribner's Sons, 1911.

Nicholson, H. G., *Age of Reason, Eighteenth Century*. New York: Doubleday & Company, Inc., 1961.

Paine, Thomas, *Age of Reason, Rights of Man*. Various editions.

Palmer, R. R., *Catholics and Unbelievers in the Eighteenth Century*. Princeton: Princeton University Press, 1939.

Sampson, R. V., *Progress in the Age of Reason*. Cambridge: Harvard University Press, 1957.

Santillana, G. and Edgar Zilsel, *Development of Rationalism and Empiricism*. Chicago: University of Chicago Press, 1941.

Stephen, Leslie, *History of English Thought in the Eighteenth Century*, 2 vols. New York: G. P. Putnam's Sons, 1876.

Sykes, Norman, *Church and State in England in the Eighteenth Century*. Cambridge, Eng.: Cambridge University Press, 1934.

Torrey, N. L., *Spirit of Voltaire*. New York: Columbia University Press, 1938.

Voltaire, François, *Works*. Various editions and selections.

CHRONOLOGY

1577	Formula of Concord	1751–1765	*35 volumes of French encyclopedia*
1618	*Synod of Dort*	1759	*Jesuits expelled from Portugal*
1624	*Herbert*, De Veritate	1767	*Jesuits expelled from Spain and France*
1637	*Descartes*, Discourse on Method		
1638	*Chillingworth*, Religion of Protestants	1773	*Jesuits dissolved*
1648	*Peace of Westphalia*	1776	*Declaration of Independence*
1656	*Pascal*, Provincial Letters		*Paine*, Common Sense
1685	*Revocation of Edict of Nantes*		*Joseph II, Austria, religious liberty*
1687	*Newton*, Principia		*Hume*, Dialogue on Natural Religion
1690	*Locke*, Essay Concerning Human Understanding		*Gibbon*, Decline and Fall of the Roman Empire
1695	*Locke*, Reasonableness of Christianity	1780	*Lessing*, Education of the Human Race
1696	*Toland*, Christianity Not Mysterious	1781	*Kant*, Critique of Pure Reason
1730	*Tindal*, Christianity as Old as Creation	1788	*Kant*, Critique of Practical Reason
1732	*Law*, Case of Reason	1789	*Fall of the Bastille*
1736	*Butler*, Analogy of Religion	1791	*Paine*, Rights of Man
1748	*Hume*, Philosophical Essays	1793	*Kant*, Religion Within Limits of Reason Alone
		1794	*Paine*, Age of Reason

Illustration opposite page 263: **Christ Crucified Between Two Thieves.** *A reflection of seventeenth century piety. Line drawing by Peter Paul Rubens.*

VI

The Rise of

Evangelical Pietism

Evangelical pietism was a reaction to a complex
of social forces that marked a transition in Western civilization from
religion to secularism. From 1650 to 1800, a society emerged in
which religion was but one of many interests. Evangelical pietism,
in protest to this development, reasserted the power of Christianity
to change the lives of men, rescued the church from the slump into
which it had fallen, and stayed the march of rampant secularism,
but it did not reverse this transition, which had taken place almost
imperceptibly. The Thirty Years' War marked the change, and
in the wake of that struggle pietism in a vigorous evangelical form
emerged; the Thirty Years' War was the last of Europe's great
struggles over religion, and by the time it ceased the Roman Catholic
and Lutheran opponents, ironically, had largely forgotten the
symbolical issues for which they were fighting. Lawless armies
plundered and devastated northern Europe, and ten million of

Germany's sixteen million people were killed. Whole cities were destroyed, and almost none were left unscathed; orphaned children roamed the woods in packs, like wild animals. Religious and intellectual life were stagnated. The religious issues were so much forgotten that the voluminous treaty, which terminated the war in 1648, paid relatively little attention to religion.

The Peace of Augsburg, 1555, had established a truce between Lutherans and Roman Catholics which lasted for more than fifty years, even though it was an uneasy truce, for it was officially regarded by Roman Catholics as a temporary expedient. In 1608, the militant Jesuits in Germany pressed a demand for restitution of ecclesiastical property. They claimed that the Peace of Augsburg was a temporary concession of toleration designed to last only until the conclusion of the Council of Trent, and that the emperor had no authority to make peace without the consent of the pope. Protestants and Catholics both formed "defensive" alliances, and hostilities began in May of 1618, when the Protestants of Bohemia threw from a high window in Prague the two Roman Catholic regents who were trying to negotiate terms. For two years the Protestants dominated the situation, but in the fall of 1620 an imperial army under Baron Tilly subdued the Protestant forces near Prague. This triumph was followed by a confiscation of Protestant property, largely to the benefit of the Jesuits, and Roman Catholicism was stringently enforced in Bohemia, Moravia, and Austria. Albrecht von Wallenstein was among those who were enriched through this confiscation. Wallenstein, as much for political as for religious reasons, then led a victorious army through Germany, until by 1629 the Catholics controlled the Palatinate, Hanover, Brunswick, Silesia, Holstein, Schleswig, Pomerania, and Mecklenburg. An edict of restitution ordered the restoration of all Roman Catholic property confiscated since 1552 and the expulsion of all Protestants from Catholic territories. But Wallenstein proved so ruthless in his enforcement that, in 1630, even the Catholic princes petitioned the Emperor Ferdinand of Austria for his dismissal; his army had

burned and plundered so widely that people were reduced to eating leaves and grass to sustain themselves. In some cases, they even resorted to cannibalism.

In 1630, the Protestant situation improved when Gustavus Adolphus of Sweden landed on German soil, ostensibly to help the Protestants but also to insure his own country's borders. Although Adolphus was slain in 1632, he checked Catholicism in the northern areas of Germany. Wallenstein was pressed into active service again to counteract the successes of Adolphus, but his own soldiers murdered him in 1634. Neither side could subdue the other, and the war dragged on. By the time of the Peace of Westphalia, October 27, 1648, the various factions had virtually lost sight of the underlying religious issues. The weary opponents more or less agreed to let matters stand as they were stalemated in 1648, and to let the people keep their religion whenever a new prince of a different faith came into power. Pope Innocent X denounced the treaty as "null and void, invalid, iniquitous, unjust, condemned, rejected, frivolous, without force or effect, not to be observed even when ratified by an oath." But it brought to an end the last great religious war in Europe, and the ineffectiveness of the pope's denunciation indicated that henceforth religion would be secondary to national loyalty and other interests.

Other developments pointed in the same direction. The religious struggle in England resulted in the Toleration Act in 1689, which pointed to national sovereignty rather than religion as supreme. The age of reason, culminating in Kant, questioned the authority and privilege of ecclesiastical institutions. Gallicanism asserted itself in France, and although Louis XIV revoked the Edict of Nantes in 1685 to satisfy the papacy, national secular interests proved more dominant than religion. Even in Italy, in the church itself, secular interests emerged. This was especially true in the baroque styles in sculpture, architecture, and music, which embodied and spread a secular spirit throughout Europe and even into Russia.

Baroque was the style of splendor, pro-

VI-1. Etching in *Les Misères et malheures de la guerre. Military judgment was quick and cruel in the Thirty Years' War. Jacques Callot (1594–1635).*

moted by the Jesuits in Europe as the symbol of the triumphant, militant church. But it was not confined to churches; it was employed for palaces and courts as well. Rome was the center of the baroque style. Colored marble, lavish decorations, intricate designs, extra embellishments, dramatic eloquence, and style as an end in itself marked baroque architecture. Francesco Borromini, who committed suicide in 1667, and Giovanni Bernini (1598-1680) were its two great Italian masters. Borromini dared to defy past conventions and achieved the imposing effects found in such churches as St. Agnese in Piazza Narona and La Sapienza in Rome. Bernini, who was also a painter, built on the old forms, but sought to bring architecture, sculpture and art into synthetic harmony, so as to dignify the splendor of his creations. He was a court favorite at Rome and was patronized by Maffeo Barberini, who afterwards became Pope Urban VIII and for whom Bernini designed a palace. On every hand his sensuous creations are to be seen in Rome, from his early sculpture of Apollo and Daphne to the great colonnade at St. Peter's. Bernini became the most famous architect in all Europe.

Baroque reached its climax in the lavish palaces of kings who ruled by divine right, such as those of Louis XIV at Versailles and at Paris (the Louvre). These epitomize the secular splendor of the era. Bernini was invited to France to present plans for building the Louvre; his fame preceded him and his journey was a triumphal march. He was lionized and richly rewarded, but his plans were rejected, for Louis XIV believed his own architects could produce more imposing, lavish, ornamental creations. In Spain, baroque was promoted to extremes in fantastic ornamentation by José Churriguera (d. 1725); in the Netherlands, Peter Paul Rubens (1577-1640) with his color, technical skill, and sensuous nudes brought baroque to its greatest magnificence in painting; and Germany and Austria replaced the ruins of the Thirty Years' War with castles, marble halls, residences, abbeys, and churches after the baroque designs of Fischer von Erlach, Balthasar Neumann, and Prandtauer. Elaborate altars, cupolas, frescoes, stucco designs, painted ceilings, and organ cases received special attention. Heidelberg, Karlsruhe, Mannheim, Würzburg, Ansbach, Vienna, and Melk showed the baroque trends which reached such spectacular splendor in the Zwinger of Dresden and the Belvedere of Vienna. But for all its drama and theatrical effect, baroque was a religious façade; its exuberance

265

VI-2. Louis XIV. *Bronze,
showing the flowing lines
of Baroque sculpture, by
Giovanni Lorenzo Bernini.
National Gallery of Art,
Washington, D.C.,
Samuel H. Kress Collection.*

suggested worldly gaiety and involvement rather than the glory of God and discipline, the enjoyment of man rather than service and worship. Rococo extended baroque themes with utter freedom and imagination, but with more grace and charm, less imposing dignity, more ornamentation, and less discipline. By 1800, however, neoclassical styles had begun to curtail the excesses of baroque and rococo. Secularism also marked the transitional period and continued into the nineteenth and twentieth centuries.

Sir Christopher Wren (1631-1723) was part of this neoclassical movement. He was the son of a clergyman and was educated at Oxford. His work reflected the desires and aims of the Church of England, but also exemplified the spirit of his time. St. Paul's Cathedral, begun in 1675, opened in 1697

and completed in 1710, stands as his masterpiece; a special import tax on coal provided more than half the funds. The great London fire of 1666 provided Wren with his opportunity and his limitation. After the fire he was called upon to rebuild more than fifty churches. Old property lines prevented the lavish settings so common to baroque, scarcity of funds curtailed the elaborate ornamentation, and the spirit of Protestanism eliminated the excessive statuary and spectacularity of churches in southern Europe. In his spires and towers, all different, Wren showed his imagination and ingenuity. His creations reflect restrained baroque, and are not without a secular strain more easily seen in Buckingham House, Sheldonian Theater, and Ashmolean Museum. Nicholas Hawksmoor and James Gibbs followed the lines begun by

266

Wren; Sir John Vanbrugh tended more to the sensational baroque. The master of the lesser arts of wood carving and marble and metal decorating was Grinling Gibbons.

In the seventeenth century, opera opened exciting possibilities for the secular spirit of the time, and the baroque style of opera invaded church music. The mass was subjected to dramatic treatment—Pergolesi's *Stabat Mater* is not essentially different from the music of his comic opera. George Frederick Handel (1685-1759), German by birth, English by adoption, shows the influence of opera on religious compositions. His masterpieces *Israel in Egypt,* 1738, and *The Messiah,* 1741, use the oratorio with operatic effect. He was master of the orchestra, and his arias border on the rococo in their embellishments. For all his religious interests, Handel's music resounds with secular tones and triumphs.

By the time of Franz Joseph Haydn (1732-1809) and Wolfgang Amadeus Mozart (1756-1791), musicians were no longer dependent on the clerical patronage for their livelihood. Even though religious interests are still strong in Haydn's *Creation* and Mozart's *Requiem Mass,* their sacred composition and masses are something apart; they found elaborate secular expression in the orchestra and operatic forms. Mozart and Haydn, when compared to Palestrina, reflect the change and the increasing secular spirit.

The patterns of ecclesiastical culture did not break easily nor did they completely disappear, but by the end of the eighteenth century men knew that their affairs were not geared to religious institutions. National interests had displaced the overarching control of the church, and standards derived from nature and reason had displaced revelation and doctrine. Yet during this period, the greatest of all church musicians, Johann Sebastian Bach (1685-1750), expressed his musical genius, and during this period evangelical piety expressed its profound faith, vigor, and warmth, to affect the religious developments of the next two centuries and offset the impact of the secular spirit of the time.

Bach was the culmination in music of the Lutheran tradition. Bach came from a long line of musicians; he knew the works of Pa-lestrina, heard the organist Buxtehude at Lübeck, and mastered the organ and pianoforte; he felt the religious depth of evangelical faith, distrusted the secular ornateness of the Italian style, and used his genius to compose and perform music as an act of worship. During the Reformation, Luther introduced hymns to help evangelical congregations to participate in the worship, and Lutheran chorales not only expressed personal joy and gratitude but were part of the Lutheran educational media. Chorales were thus deeply ingrained in the tradition of the Lutherans, and Bach found in the themes and tunes of that tradition an inexhaustible source of inspiration for his cantatas, preludes, oratorios, fugues, symphonias, and arias. A sense of faith and spiritual integrity pervade his creations. In all his dramatic intensity, skill, and harmonic beauty, he did not sacrifice the inward commitment and introspection of religious devotion. His magnificent *Mass in B Minor* follows and intensifies each portion of the Lutheran liturgy, so that his music heightens the worship and praise. His Passions on St. John and St. Matthew draw the worshipper into the historical realism of the biblical narratives. Perhaps no one with as much consummate skill has embodied a tradition in music as completely as Bach did the intense devotion of the Lutheran faith.

Others also tapped the springs of evangelical faith, springs that had been all but buried in the sociological changes of the seventeenth and eighteenth centuries. The Protestant emphasis on right doctrine produced scholastic creeds, narrowed the life of the church to strict confession, and engendered persecution, fanaticism, and destruction. The continuing Catholic and Lutheran struggle for uniform culture in the church and state in the seventeenth century erupted in the Thirty Years' War. In the midst of these vast sociological changes, evangelical pietism asserted its convictions. It was a reaction to orthodox formalism and creeds; it knew no national boundaries; it found personal fulfillment in an experience of the spiritual presence in simple Christian living. Its dominant characteristics were a Bible-centered faith, a keen sense of human guilt and the forgiveness possible through Christ, personal conversion, practical holiness, a warm concern for the common needs of people, and an emotional outpouring of feelings and aspirations in hymns which have become known and loved throughout Christendom.

Philip Jakob Spener (1635-1705) was one of its earliest representatives. Born thirteen years before the end of the Thirty Years' War, he knew the demoralizing effects of that struggle and longed for a renaissance of moral earnestness in Germany. Despairing of reform through the formalized Lutheran state church, Spener began organizing small groups that met in his home for Bible reading, prayer, and discussion. These groups of Christians seeking to deepen their spiritual lives came to be known as *collegia pietatis*. In 1675, Spener published his *Pia Desideria*, in which he summoned pastors to speak the Word of God to the common man, capable and pious laymen to act as preachers, and all Christians to show love, piety, and moderation. He called attention to governmental domination, an unworthy clergy, and a laity given to drunkenness and licentiousness. He urged that small groups seriously study the Bible, give themselves to prayer, and practice Christian living (*1*). He left his pastorate in Frankfurt in 1686 to become court preacher at Dresden, but soon encountered opposition from the established clergy and the universities of Leipzig and Wittenberg. In 1691 he accepted an invitation to Berlin, where he spent the remaining years of his life. Devotees of orthodoxy attacked him from every side. In 1695, the theological faculty of Wittenberg charged him with 264 errors, for they recognized in him a threat to the authority of their confessional standards. Spener not only urged a direct study of the Bible, he also declared a right feeling in the heart was more important than pure doctrine.

August Hermann Francke (1663-1727), who began a pietistic study group in Leipzig in 1689, was Spener's most famous disciple. Opposition caused him to leave the university of Leipzig, as well as a post at Erfurt, but when Francke became a member of the faculty at the newly-established University of Halle, he built pietism into the curriculum and for three decades dominated this school, which trained, graduated, and placed more than two hundred ministers each year in the church in Germany. Francke's social work set a pattern that was widely imitated. An interest in the plight of poor children led him to establish his famous Orphan House at Halle in 1698. A box in his own home brought the first contributions for his work, but it became too small for the offerings which came from all over Germany, England, and other parts of Europe. *The Marvellous Footsteps of Divine Providence*, published in London in 1707, told the story of his receiving answers to prayers for money. Donations poured in, enabling him to care for thousands of destitute people and establish a pauper school, a Bible institute, a Latin school, and subsidiary facilities (*2*). Literally thousands of children received instruction under his supervision, many became missionaries, others clergymen, and some helped establish Lutheranism in the American colonies. When Frederick IV (1699-1730) of Denmark sought Protestant missionaries for India, he found them only among Francke's students—Bartholomäus Ziegenbalg and Heinrich Plutchau. The most noted of the sixty missionaries who went out from Halle in the eighteenth century was Christian Friedrich Schwartz (1726-1798), who labored for forty-eight years in India.

As a result of Spener's and Francke's work, the Protestant church of Germany again possessed zealous ministers and laymen. The Bible was studied, devotional sincerity increased, social service spread, and ministers and laymen were stirred to new seriousness. But pietism neglected intellectual pursuits, despite its connection with the university, and it tended to reduce religion to a narrow mold. By the middle of the eighteenth century, Halle pietism in Germany had reached its zenith.

But evangelical pietism found further vigorous expression in the renewal of the Church of the Unitas Fratrum, the Moravians, under the leadership of Count Zinzendorf. About 1722 German-speaking Protestants from Moravia began seeking refuge in Saxony, and

Count Zinzendorf allowed them to establish a village on his estate at Herrnhut. By 1727 he had become their spiritual leader, with a dream that the Moravians might become the *collegia pietatis* within the Lutheran Church, a committed, zealous group of soldiers for Christ, ready to carry the Gospel anywhere in the world. Children were reared and trained apart from parental supervision, like the children at the Halle Orphan House, and in some ways the Moravian settlement at Herrnhut resembled a monastery. But opposition from orthodox Lutherans caused the Moravians increasingly to go their separate way and become a new church. Feeling a call to missionize distant lands, the Moravians sent missionaries to the West Indies in 1732 and to Greenland in 1733; two years later Spangenberg led a party to Georgia. In 1741, Count Zinzendorf came to America and gave the name Bethlehem to the Moravian settlement in Pennsylvania. Other missionaries went to Guiana, Egypt, South Africa, and Labrador. No other Protestant group practiced missions more wholeheartedly than the Moravians in the eighteenth century. Their evangelical piety found expression in Christ-mysticism, hymns, and liturgy, and their lives were geared to Christ's Sermon on the Mount.

The Moravians at Herrnhut directly affected the Wesleyan movement in England, for it was Spangenberg who confronted John Wesley in Savannah, Georgia, with the question of assurance of salvation, which Wesley did not have. And when Wesley returned to England, it was Peter Böhler, a leading Moravian, who convinced him "of the want of that faith whereby alone we are saved." In his diary, Wesley confessed that he went to America to convert others but was not himself converted to God. He lacked an inward assurance of forgiveness and reconciliation, but within a short time the Aldersgate experience came, on May 24, 1738, when he felt his heart strangely warmed (4).

The tie between John Wesley and the Moravians at Herrnhut was very direct, but Wesley came to distrust a group of Moravian "still men" who would do nothing, not even read the Bible or take communion while

VI-3. Contemporary Satire on the Open-Air Preaching of George Whitefield (1714–1770). *Inspired by Satan, Whitefield stands with Lady Huntingdon at his side and an ass bowing in admiration.*

waiting for mystical assurance of absolute salvation (9). The tie with William Law, whose *Serious Call* and *Treatise on Perfection* he closely studied, was equally direct (3). Wesley took many of his precepts from Law and the Moravians, but he rejected the mystical element in both. He stressed justifying faith as the one thing necessary to salvation, inward assurance as the sign of reconciliation of sinful man to God, and good works as the fruits of earnest Christian living (5, 7). Calvinism was also strong in his background, for from his Oxford days he was close to George Whitefield (1714-1770), whose field preaching stirred thousands both in England and in Colonial America, where his astonishing eloquence vitalized the Great Awakening, about 1740. But Wesley broke with Whitefield in 1741 because he could not abide Whitefield's adherence to Calvinistic predestination; Wesley believed salvation was possible for all (6).

John Wesley, whose life spanned the eighteenth century, 1703-1791, was the great exponent of English evangelical pietism. The son of Samuel Wesley, a clergyman in the Church of England, and Susana Wesley, who instilled strict rules of conduct in the hearts of her eighteen children, he was educated at Christ Church, Oxford, and became a Fellow of Lincoln College in 1726. While at Oxford he became the leader of a group of young men who lived strictly by rule, studied the Bible, fasted on Wednesdays and Fridays, took communion once a week, visited prisoners, helped the sick, and reproved and assisted each other through mutual confession and criticism. Included in the group were Charles Wesley and George Whitefield, and their ways earned for them various nicknames—Sacramentarians, the Holy Club, and the Methodists.

After being ordained, John served with his father, but he felt no satisfaction in his work. In 1735, shortly after the death of his father, John, accompanied by Charles and two companions, sailed for Georgia. He went under the auspices of the Society for the Propagation of the Gospel to minister to the colonists and missionize the Indians, but really, as he wrote to his mother, he went to save his own soul. As a strict Anglican, he alienated many of his parishioners, never got started among the Indians, became entangled in a disappointing love affair, and finally, in a mood of depression, he sailed back to England.

After the Aldersgate experience, Wesley was encouraged by George Whitefield to take up open-air preaching; this marked the beginning of an astounding career in evangelical preaching. During the next fifty years he traveled over 250,000 miles, mostly on horseback, and delivered over 40,000 sermons. He made numerous trips to Ireland, Scotland, Wales, Germany, and Holland. When he died, the Methodist Society in England numbered 80,000 members with 1,300 local and itinerant preachers. Members in America numbered 60,000 with almost two hundred preachers. Denied the use of pulpits in London and other places, Wesley preached wherever there were people and called the world his parish. Good organiza-

tion, a system of lay preachers, warm fellowship, personal conversion, fervent preaching, and hymn-singing made the Wesleyan evangelization of England a potent force in the lives of the people, credited with saving England from the disruptions of a French Revolution (5, 6).

The Wesleys never intended a separation from the Church of England, but the Methodists moved inevitably in that direction, especially since many of the lay preachers had been Dissenters. Under necessity and the conviction that he as a presbyter had as much right to ordain as to celebrate the Lord's Supper, John Wesley in 1784 laid his hands on Thomas Coke, setting him apart as a Superintendent of the Methodists in America (8). There Coke and Francis Asbury soon took the office of bishop. The formal separation from the Anglicans came in England in 1795 and in Ireland in 1870. Since then Methodism has become one of the world's largest Protestant bodies.

The convictions of the Methodists were fervently expressed in their hymns. They drew freely on the creations of Isaac Watts (1674-1748), a Congregational pastor in London who directed Protestant singing away from doleful metrical Psalms, and they produced many hymns of their own. John Wesley composed a few and translated many hymns of the German evangelicals, and Charles Wesley (1707-1788), for his numerous hymns, is acknowledged as the genius of English hymnody. Associated with John from the beginning, Charles experienced conversion just three days before John, and he labored in Bristol and London with marked success; but his major legacy is hundreds of hymns, still loved and sung throughout Protestantism. They express the thought and feeling of evangelical pietism with a warmth characteristic of the Wesleyan movement (10).

One of the most popular of all the evangelical tomes (400 pages) was that of William Wilberforce (1758-1833), published in 1797 under the title *Practical View of the Prevailing Religious System of Professed Christians in the Higher and Middle Classes in this Country Contrasted with Real Chris-*

tianity. Like William Law, he called for serious, holy living. He was "converted" to the evangelical movement in 1784, and as a wealthy, popular member of Parliament he wielded great influence. In 1787, he began fighting slavery; he won the abolition of slave trade in the British dominions in 1807 and of slavery itself in 1833. Wilberforce gave up card-playing, denied himself luxuries, distributed a fourth of his wealth to the destitute, and became a student of the Bible. He was typical of men in places of leadership directly affected by the evangelical piety of the Methodists.

But evangelical pietism was by no means confined to the awakenings in Spener and Wesley. The desire for a more personal religion, a living presence within, motivated many others. George Fox (1624-1691), founder of the Quakers, in his protest against formal religiosity and open licentiousness, was a living example of evangelical pietism (*12*), and Robert Barclay in 1675 clearly enunciated the convictions of the Quakers in his *Apology* (*13*). Blaise Pascal (1623-1662), whose writings were widely circulated after his death, deeply probed the meaning of religion for his day (*11*). Paul Gerhardt (1607-1676) gave voice to his devotion in some of Christendom's greatest hymns. Miguel de Molinos (1627-1696), a Spanish priest who became noted in Rome as a spiritual director, published *The Spiritual Guide* in 1675, and while it was more mystical than evangelical, it sought to bypass the externals of ecclesiasticism—images, rites, sacraments, rules, and even vocal prayer—to bring the individual into a truly Christian life of immediate fellowship with God, into a state of contemplation in which the soul in passive receptivity of celestial bliss "desires nothing, not even its own salvation, and fears nothing, not even hell." This was similar to Moravian quietism. The Jesuits suspected his unorthodoxy, and in 1687 Molinos was sentenced to life imprisonment for having written sixty-eight "heretical, suspicious, erroneous, scandalous, blasphemous, and offensive" propositions. Madame de Guyon, who claimed that a divine Penman directed her hand when she wrote, furthered the movement in France with her *Short and Easy Method of Prayer* in 1685. The pope condemned Madame de Guyon for her views, and she too spent her last days in prison.

Evangelical pietism was a powerful reaction to formal orthodoxy and secularism. It expressed a personal concern and warmth that seemed to have been lost in Christianity. It revived Bible reading and study, it brought men to their knees in dedication, it stirred a social concern for the underprivileged, it rejuvenated preaching and missions, and it bequeathed its fervor in stirring hymns. The future, however, did not lie entirely with evangelical piety. It continued as a powerful force, but rationalism emerged stronger than ever in the nineteenth century, and ultramontane orthodoxy reasserted itself in Roman Catholicism.

1. *Philip Jacob Spener*

In writing on the spiritual priesthood of every Christian, Spener tried to impress on believers in his day the far-reaching implications of Luther's priesthood of all believers. He published *Pia Desideria* in 1675, and two years later brought out a separate tractate on spiritual priesthood. The first of the selections which follow is from *Pia Desideria* (Devout Wishes), and the second is from the tractate of 1677. From *The Spiritual Priesthood*, by Philip Spener, trans. A. G. Voigt (Philadelphia: The Fortress Press Society, 1917).

PIA DESIDERIA

Every careful reader of Luther's writings will have observed with what earnestness the sainted man stressed spiritual priesthood, by which not only ministers, but also all Christians have been made priests through their Redeemer, anointed with the Holy Spirit, and consecrated to spiritual priestly functions. For Peter does not speak only of ministers, when he says, "But ye are an elect race, a royal priesthood, a holy nation, a people for God's only possession, that ye may show forth the excellences of Him who called you out of darkness into His marvelous light" (I Peter 2:9). If anyone desires to learn and read our teacher's opinion more fully on this matter, and on what the priestly offices are, let him read his book to the Bohemians, "How Ministers of the Church are to be Elected and Installed." There he will see a fine proof that all spiritual offices belong to all Christians without distinction, although their regular and public administration is committed to the ordained ministers. However, in a case of necessity they may also be performed by others, and especially those offices, which are not of a public character, shall always be exercised at home and in common life by all.

Indeed it has been one of the chief artifices of the hateful devil that under the papacy he brought it about that all these spiritual offices were turned over to the clergy alone, who for this reason also haughtily appropriated to themselves alone the name of spiritual, which is really common to all Christians. Other Christians were excluded from these spiritual offices, as if it were not proper for them earnestly to study the Word of the Lord, much less to instruct, admonish, reprove and comfort others, and to do privately what the ministers of the Church have to do publicly, as though these were matters attached to their office alone. Hereby, on the one hand, the so-called laymen were made indolent in things which ought justly also to concern them, from which resulted frightful ignorance and thereby wild life; on the other hand, the so-called spirituals were able to do what they pleased, because nobody was permitted to look into their cards or make the least remonstrance. This arrogated monopoly of the spiritual estate, together with the debarring of the laity from the Scriptures, was one of the chief means under the papacy by which papal Rome established, and where it still holds sway, maintains its power over poor Christians. Hence no severer blow could have been given to it than when Luther showed, on the contrary, that all Christians have been called to spiritual offices, and are not only authorized, but, if they wish to be real Christians, are in duty bound to fulfill them; although they are not called to the public administration of them, for which, in view of the equal right of all, appointment by the congregation is required. Accordingly the Christian is obligated not only to offer prayer, thanks, good works, alms, etc., for himself and what pertains to him, but also to study the Word of the Lord earnestly and to teach, reprove, exhort, convert and edify others, especially those of his own house, as grace is given to him, to observe their life, to pray for all, and as much as possible to have a care for their salvation. If people were shown this, everyone would give more heed to himself and become active in those things which pertain to his own and his neighbor's edification. On the contrary, when this doctrine is not made known and is not impressed, all manner of security and indolence results. Then everyone will think that this does not concern him, and will imagine that just as he is called to his office, business, trade and such like, to which the minister is not called, so likewise the minister alone is called to spiritual functions, occupations with the divine Word, prayer, reading, teaching, exhortation, comforting, reproof, etc., and that it is not the business of others to concern themselves about these matters. Indeed, he thinks he would encroach upon the office of the minister, if he in any way engaged in them; much less would he dare to take note of the minister himself and fraternally admonish him, when he is negligent, or to try to be of assistance to him in all these matters.

For this reason it is worth considering, not only how this subject, which since Luther's time has almost ceased to be agitated any more, might be made better known to the people, but also how it might be brought again into better practice. To this end the previous recommendation, namely, to introduce some exercise for the reading and understanding of the Scriptures, would also contribute not a little. For my part, I am quite confident that if in every congregation only a few could be led to do these two things, to make diligent use of the divine Word and to exercise their priestly functions, especially in fraternal admonition and correction, much would be gained. Then others would be gradually won, and finally the entire Church would be noticeably improved.

THE SPIRITUAL PRIESTHOOD BRIEFLY DESCRIBED ACCORDING TO THE WORD OF GOD IN SEVENTY QUESTIONS AND ANSWERS

1. What is the spiritual priesthood?
It is the right which our Saviour Jesus Christ

has purchased for all men, and for which He anoints all believers with His Holy Spirit, in virtue of which they may and shall bring sacrifices acceptable to God, pray for themselves and others, and severally edify themselves and their neighbors. . . .

10. Who then are such spiritual priests? All Christians without distinction, I Peter 2:9, old and young, male and female, bond and free, Gal. 3:28.

11. Does not the name priests belong only to ministers?
No. Ministers, according to their office, are not properly priests, nor are they so called anywhere in the New Testament, but they are ministers of Christ, stewards of the mysteries of God, bishops, elders, ministers of the Gospel, ministers of the Word. The name priest is a general name for all Christians and applies to ministers not otherwise than to other Christians, I Cor. 4:1, 3:5; I Tim. 3:1-2, 5:17; Eph. 3:7; Acts 26:16; Luke 1:2.

12. But are not ministers alone the spiritual?
No. This character also belongs to all Christians, Rom. 8:5, 9.

13. What are the offices of a spiritual priest?
They are manifold. But we can divide them into three chief offices: (1) The office of sacrifice; (2) That of praying and blessing; and (3) That of the divine Word. The first two are always called priestly offices; the last is also called a prophetic office.

14. But what must spiritual priests sacrifice?
First of all themselves with all that they are, so that they may no longer desire to serve themselves, but Him who has bought and redeemed them, Rom. 6:13, 14:7-8; I Cor. 6:20; II Cor. 5:15; Ps. 4:5, 110:3; I Peter 3:18. Therefore, just as in the Old Testament the sacrifices were separated from other animals, so they must also separate themselves from the world and its uncleanness, Ex. 12:3-6; Rom. 12:2; II Cor. 6:14-18; James 1:27. For this reason they are called the chosen generation, Lev. 20:26; I Peter 2:9.

15. How in particular must we offer our bodies and their members to God?
By not using our bodies for sins, but alone for the glory and service of God, Rom. 12:1, 6:13, cf. questions 14; accordingly by keeping them in subjection, I Cor. 9:27; and by suppressing evil desires which work evil through our members, what the Scriptures call cutting off our members, Matt. 5:29-30, 18:8-9, 19:12.

16. How shall we offer our souls to God?
By letting them as well as our bodies be holy temples and abodes of God, I Cor. 3:16-17; by bringing our reason into captivity to the obedience of Christ, II Cor. 10:5; by surrendering our wills to the divine will in true submission and obedience, I Sam. 15:22; Matt. 6:10, 26:39; Heb. 10:5-7; and by making an acceptable sacrifice of our spirits and souls in true repentance, Ps. 51:16-17.

26. Are then all Christians preachers and are they to exercise the preaching office?
No; to exercise the office publicly in the congregation before all and over all requires a special call. Hence if anyone were to arrogate this to himself as a power over others, or were to encroach upon the office of the ministry, he would commit sin, Rom. 10:15; Heb. 5:4. For this reason some are teachers and others hearers, I Cor. 12:28-30, whose respective duties towards each other are treated in the Table of Duties in the Catechism.

27. But how shall they occupy themselves with the Word of God?
They shall use it for themselves and among or with others.

28. How shall they use the Word of God for themselves?
Not only shall they hear it, when it is preached and proclaimed in the congregation, but they shall also diligently read it and have it read to them.

29. Is it proper for all Christians diligently to read the Scriptures?
Yes; since they are the letter of the heavenly Father to all His children, no child of God can be excluded from them, but all have both the right and command to read them, John 5:38.

30. But would it not be better simply to believe their preachers and what they hear from them?
No; for they also are to search the Scriptures, so that they may test the teaching of their preacher, in order that their faith may not be

founded upon the reputation and faith of a man, but upon divine truth, Acts 17:11.

32. But are not many things in the Scriptures obscure and too high for the uneducated?

The Scriptures in themselves are not obscure, for they are light and not darkness, Ps. 119:105; II Peter 1:19. However, there are many things in them too high not only for the uneducated, but also for the learned, which, on account of our darkened eyes, appear obscure to us, I Cor. 13:9-10.

33. Would it not be better for this reason if the uneducated did not read them?

No. The learned are not deterred from searching more and more in them, although they must confess that in many places they often miss the meaning. Just as little can uneducated pious souls be prohibited from the Word, in which they can seek and find the corroboration of their faith.

37. How shall they conduct themselves when they read the Scriptures, that they may be assured of the truth?

(1) They should not take the Scriptures into their hands without sincere prayer for the grace of the Holy Spirit, nor without the purpose to admit into their hearts His working and power, and they should not stop with the mere knowledge, but should obediently apply what they have learned to God's glory. (2) They should not let their reason be master, but should give close attention to the words of the Holy Spirit, how they are framed, compare them with what precedes and follows, consider their meaning, and believe that every word is recorded by the Holy Spirit designedly as it is, and also compare the portion read with other passages of Scripture. (3) They should read all with application to themselves, how far it concerns them and may be serviceable for their edification. (4) They should lay hold of that first which is altogether clear and build their faith upon that, and also immediately seek to order their life according to the duty perceived. (5) They should pass over what at first they cannot understand at once and what they find too difficult and high, and commit it to God until after repeated reading and prayer, when they have been faithful to God in the truth

previously perceived, gradually they attain more light even in the passages not understood before. (6) They should always humbly receive, keep and practice whatever God has granted them to know, and be content with His grace. (7) They should speak about the Scriptures to godly ministers and other Christians, and obtain their advice where they cannot get on themselves, and when by God's grace they are shown the true meaning of a passage, they should receive it in humility and the fear of God. . . .

40. Would it not be better to leave the more careful searching of the Scriptures to ministers, and for the rest to abide by simplicity?

All Christians are obligated to this simplicity, not to desire to search out what God has not revealed, and also not to make their reason master in matters of faith. But if by simplicity is meant that they who are not ministers shall not seek nor exert themselves to grow in knowledge, this is against God's will and is disgraceful ignorance, indolence and ingratitude towards the rich divine revelation. Here we ought to seek not to be simple, but wise and understanding, and to have by reason of use senses exercised to discern good and evil, Heb. 5:14; Rom. 16:19; I Cor. 14:20; Eph. 1:15-19, 4:14; Col. 1:9-12, 28. . . .

52. But how shall believing Christians use the divine Word among their fellow-men?

The Scriptures have been given for teaching, for reproof, for correction, for discipline in righteousness, II Tim. 3:16, and also for comfort, Rom. 15:4. Accordingly believing Christians are to use the Scriptures to all these intents and to teach, convert from error, admonish, reprove and comfort, as the Scriptures themselves everywhere indicate.

53. Is this proper for all Christians?

Yes, according to the gifts bestowed by God upon each one; but with the restriction that this is not to be done publicly before the whole congregation, but privately as occasion offers and without hindrance to the public office of the regular ministry.

60. But do women also share in these priestly offices?

Assuredly; for here is neither Jew nor Greek,

bond nor free, male nor female, but all are one in Christ Jesus, Gal. 3:28. In Christ, therefore, the difference between man and woman, in regard to what is spiritual, is abolished. Since God dignifies believing women also with His spiritual gifts, Joel 2:28-29; Acts 21:9; I Cor. 11:5, the exercise of them in proper order cannot be forbidden. The apostles themselves make mention of those godly women, who worked together with them and edified their fellow-men; and far from censuring them for this, they accorded them love and praise for it, Acts 18:26; Rom. 16:1-2, 12; Phil. 4:2-3; Titus 2:3-5.

61. But are women not forbidden to teach?

Yes; namely, in the public congregation. But that it is permitted to them outside of the public congregation, is clear from the passages and apostolic examples cited, I Cor. 14:34 sq.; I Tim. 2:11-12.

62. In what way are Christians to exercise these offices?

As God and love present the occasion to them. They must not forcibly obtrude themselves upon anyone, but deal only with those who are willing to accept such help in love.

63. May a number also meet together for such a purpose?

They may mutually edify each other when occasion brings them together. In the same way it cannot be wrong if several good friends sometimes meet by appointment to go over a sermon together and recall what they heard, to read in the Scriptures, and to confer in the fear of the Lord how they may put into practice what they read. Only the gatherings should not be large so as not to have the appearance of a separation and a public assembly. Nor should they, by reason of them, neglect the public worship or contemn it, or disdain the ordained ministers. They should also otherwise keep within their bounds, not omit their necessary work and not neglect their calling against the will of employers or parents, be willing to render an account of their doings, and avoid every form of evil.

64. Shall anyone set himself up as a teacher or allow others to appoint him as such?

No; for this priesthood is common to all, and according to it each must be just as willing to learn from others as to teach in divine order.

2. August Hermann Francke, 1716

The two selections which follow are from *Three Practical Discourses*, by August Hermann Francke (London: Joseph Downing, 1716).

OF THE LOVE OF GOD TOWARDS MEN

Yes, God loved the people. That God loves people, Moses affirms in his blessings, Deut. 33:3. And our Savior Jesus Christ has expressed it in this manner: "God so loved the world that he gave his only begotten

VI-4. Moravian Ceremonial Prostration Before the Lord.

Son," John 3:16. This is the love which St. Paul calls "philanthropy," or "the love of God towards men," Tit. 3:4. [Francke refers to the "great Majesty of God, his unutterable Glory, his infinite Might and Power, his unlimited Bliss and Happiness, standing in no need of Help and Support"; he draws a picture of man groaning under the sentence of death, filled with sin, depraved in his desires, and sinking in ruin; and then continues to describe the disproportionate relationship.]

Do but observe particularly, that there is not only nothing lovely to be found in man, the object of God's love; but on the contrary, he is full of everything which may render him odious to the Lord, and bring upon him his just hatred and indignation. And that none should think himself free from so foul and universal a stain, or value himself upon any prerogative whatsoever, the Apostle represents both Jews and heathens in the most black and detestable colors, and declares them both guilty of the most vile and abominable crimes; as plainly appears from the three first chapters of his Epistle to the Romans, to which may be added Psalm 5 and Ezekiel 16 to give us a just sense of the fall of man, and of the horrid corruption of his nature. Yet even while he is in this deplorable state, the love of God begins its work, and calls upon man to return and be saved.

Consider therefore, again and again, that the divine Lover is moved to love, not by any worth or dignity which he perceives in him whom he loves, but entirely and purely by the motive of his own inconceivable love and compassion.

. . . . .

Observe that this divine love does not require of man any merit by works at all, but only a profound acknowledgment of his extreme want and unworthiness, attended with unfeigned grief and repentance for his former wicked and profligate life, whereby he has deprived himself for so long of the enjoyment of this pure and heavenly love. The consequence will be, that, after he has once regained a sense of so invaluable a love, he will then, with the greater care and concern, watch over it, lest by unbelief, or disobedience, he lose again the only comfort of his life. He will suffer, that it may act in him freely, and without opposition. He will be ready to receive it, whenever it offers itself, to quicken his dead heart, to enflame his cold heart, to melt his icy heart, to cleanse more and more his profane and worldly heart, to diffuse itself in and about it, to display therein its wonderful glory and beauty, and to deliver it at last from all its sin and misery.

. . . . .

First then, cast an eye upon yourself, and consider how you have hitherto valued the love of God, what price you have set upon it: Whether you have regarded it as your greatest and most valuable treasure; or whether you have made light of it, as of a thing that cannot give any great satisfaction.

Consider further the place you afforded it in your heart when it presented itself to you and endeavored to gain admittance into the choicest faculties of your soul.

Consider whether you have suffered it freely to operate, and to effect its divine work in you; whether it has transformed you into its own nature, and happily united you to itself.

And lastly, I would have you consider, what the present disposition of your soul is, in relation to this love: Whether your sentiments, thoughts, affections, and intentions, discourses and actions; in a word, whether your outward and inward conduct and manner of life convinces you that this love has a real influence upon you, and that it continues to gain ground in you every day, so that you may hope that the God of love will also finish his work in his time, and carry it to a happy conclusion at last.

But, alas! if you find no such thing as the love of God in your souls, but rather what is contrary to it, I mean the love of sin and vanity; I then beseech you to return and suffer yourselves to be found and embraced by the love of God: For it seeks you as a tender mother seeks her lost child, and waits patiently, that you may receive the comfort it is willing to bestow upon you.

Secondly, you ought well to weigh the nature of that love which you bear to your neighbor, and your deportment towards him. Consider whether the purity of the love of God towards you has wrought you into a pure and disinterested love towards your neighbor, and whether the compassionate tenderness of the divine love has had so happy an effect upon you as to clothe you with bowels of mercy towards your neighbor, with kindness and humbleness of mind, with meekness and long-suffering, and other virtues which accompany that love, which is the bond of perfection, Col. 3:12. For truly, the good will and love of God towards us ought to be the constant model and foundation of that love and affection we ought to bestow on our neighbor, as the Apostle plainly sets forth, Tit. 3:1 compared with verse 4.

Thirdly and lastly, you ought to consider that God himself is love, and that consequently love is the nearest way to unite you to him who is love in a most universal and essential manner. If you are not able to reach into the bottom of this sea of love, suffer then, that a drop of a living faith may fall into this vast ocean, and believe what as yet you cannot see. This sea of love will never be drawn dry, and this ocean will never be fathomed by the narrow dimensions of our understanding: Therefore, let your faith sink into that love which passeth knowledge; and let it sink freely, without fear and anxiety. If you lose yourselves in the depth of this love, you shall certainly find yourselves again and live eternally where it will be displayed in its sublimest perfection and luster.

TWENTY-FOUR MOTIVES TO A FAITHFUL DISCHARGE OF THE DUTY OF BOUNTY TO THE POOR

Mark 8:1 ff. To encourage us to a faithful performance of the duty of bounty or charity to the poor, the following motives may prove very strong and engaging:

I. The first motive to Christian bounty and charity is the "unspeakable and incomprehensible love and mercy of God towards mankind." This love is explained to us by our Lord, John 3:16, telling us, that God loved the World. And in what manner did he love it? "That he gave his only begotten Son." To what end? "That all who believe in him, might not perish, but have everlasting life."

The same love of God towards men is plainly set forth by the Apostle, Eph. 2:4 and Rom. 8:32. . . . God delivered his own only begotten Son to the most infamous death of the cross and thereby redeemed us from eternal death and damnation. There is no doubt that whoever ponders this love, whoever lets it revolve again and again in his mind, will be excited thereby to bestow a like love on his poor and indigent neighbor. This divine love, seriously weighed and laid to heart, will stir up in him these and like considerations: "Has this infinitely great God been so merciful unto me, as not to spare his only begotten Son, but to give him up freely for me? Then, why should I be so stingy, as to spare my worldly estate and income, while I see so many miserable objects about me, who stand in need of my help and assistance? Nay, if I should bestow all that I have on the poor, what an inconsiderable proportion would it bear to that love, which the Lord has conferred on me?" . . .

XI. The description of the last judgment, as it is exhibited, Matt. 25, is another powerful monitor to relieve the poor in their straits and indigencies.

Want of love and charity is the blackest, nay, the only crime alledged against those that shall receive their doom in that Day; particularly if this uncharitable temper be shown to the poor and indigent members of Christ. Who can be so hard and refractory, as not to be melted into tenderness towards the poor members of Christ, when he ponders with himself this moving invitation which then will drop from the Lord's mouth: "Come ye blessed of my Father, inherit the Kingdom prepared for you from the foundation of the world: For I was an hungered, and ye gave me meat; I was thirsty, and ye gave me drink; I was a stranger, and ye took me in; naked, and ye clothed me; I was sick, and ye visited me; I was in prison, and ye came unto me." And who can read that dreadful sentence, pronounced against the unmerciful, and not forever abhor a cruel and unmerciful temper? "Depart from me ye cursed into everlasting fire, prepared for the devil and his angels; for I was an hungered, etc." Whoever does but seriously muse on this final sentence, the good and the bad are to receive in that Day, will thereby find himself rid from those frivolous shifts and evasions wherewith a covetous niggard will put off a poor man applying to him for relief. People are apt to say: "There are too many, one cannot give to all. Why, if I should happen to want hereafter, who will then give unto me? I have a large family of my own, and can spare but little for the poor." Another says: "God knows where these hard and troublesome times may end at last. 'Tis but fit a man should make some provision against old age, and the difficulties attending it.'"

Such, and the like excuses, are frequently heard from those, who call themselves Christians, but are at the same time too intent upon the uncertain riches of this world, though they will never prove a sufficient guard against the day of trouble and common calamities.

They should rather argue with themselves in this manner: If so unmerciful a judgment shall be given against those who have practised no mercy here, how shall I lift up my head in so dreadful a day? And how can I expect mercy from the Judge, when I have been so hard and unmerciful to my brother? 'Tis true, I cannot pretend to deserve any mercy by any charitable deeds, let them be never so liberally scattered among the poor and needy, for whatever I do is duty, and no merit. But since the Lord, in his infinite mercy, has declared to regard the least charity done to my brother, as if it was done to himself, and to annex a most sure and exceeding great reward to it, let it be henceforth far from me to harbor any uncharitable temper within me, or to express any roughness towards the poor, in my daily life and conversation with them.

XXI. The uncertainty of our days, and shortness of life, ought to be a prevailing inducement to remember the poor, and to relieve their wants betimes.

Let us consider again and again that dreadful word, Luke 12:20: "Thou fool, this night thy soul shall be required of thee: then whose shall those things be which thou hast provided?" Such a consideration will in a manner shame us out of our covetousness and teach us the prudence recommended by the Lord, Luke 16:9: "Make to yourselves friends of the mammon of unrighteousness, that when ye fail, they may receive you into everlasting habitations."

May the eternal and uncreated love, that love which has so wonderfully manifested itself in Christ Jesus, our Lord, plant all these graces in your hearts, and water them constantly by the healing influence of his Spirit!

3. William Law, 1728

William Law (1686-1761) was educated at Cambridge, became a fellow of Emmanuel College, and was ordained to the ministry in 1711; because he refused to take an oath supporting the accession of George I, however, he forfeited his academic position, and as a Nonjuror lived the final twenty years of his life in retirement. A bitter opponent of Deism, he denied that reason could speak authoritatively for religion. In 1732 he wrote *A Case of Reason*, which was an answer to Tindal's *Christianity As Old As Creation*. He asserted that reason not only has no final power in religion but, on the contrary, is the source of all the disorders in man's heart, for it pretends to comprehend that which by its very nature is beyond comprehension (cf. Ch. 5). An indirect but more positive answer to Deism was *A Serious Call to a Devout and Holy Life*, 1728. Dr. Johnson, John Wesley, George Whitefield, and a host of others were directly influenced by it. Later Protestants sought to order their lives by its precepts. *A Serious Call* and *Pilgrim's Progress* rank as the two most influential religious books in the English language. Law called upon Christians to take their religion seriously: if Christianity is true, then all our lives, everything we do, not just part of our affairs, should be devoted to following Christ. With the art of a master, he applied this principle to every walk of life, to man's pursuit of happiness and virtue, to public and private actions, to education, to prayer, and so on. The following selections are from Chs. 1 and 2 of *A Serious Call to a Devout and Holy Life* (Boston: Larkin, Greenough, Stebbins, 1808), in which Law discusses the nature of devotion and our failure to practice it.

CONCERNING THE NATURE AND EXTENT

OF CHRISTIAN DEVOTION

Devotion is neither private nor public prayer; but prayers, whether private or public, are particular parts or instances of devotion. Devotion signifies a life given, or devoted, to God.

VI-5. Gin Lane. *A depiction of intemperance in the eighteenth century. Drawing by William Hogarth. British Museum.*

He, therefore, is the devout man, who lives no longer to his own will, or the way and spirit of the world, but to the sole will of God; who considers God in everything, who serves God in everything, who makes all the parts of his common life parts of piety, by doing everything in the Name of God, and under such rules as are conformable to His glory.

We readily acknowledge, that God alone is to be the rule and measure of our prayers; that in them we are to look wholly unto Him, and act wholly for Him; that we are only to pray in such a manner, for such things, and such ends, as are suitable to His glory.

Now let any one but find out the reason why he is to be thus strictly pious in his prayers, and he will find the same as strong a reason to be as strictly pious in all the other parts of his life. For there is not the least shadow of a reason why we should make God the rule and measure of our prayers; why we should then look wholly unto Him, and pray according to His will; but what equally proves it necessary for us to look wholly unto God, and make Him the rule and measure of all the other actions of our life. For any ways of life, any employment of our talents, whether of our parts, our time, or money, that is not strictly according to the will of God, that is not for such ends as are suitable to His glory, are as great absurdities and failings, as prayers that are not according to the will of God. For there is no other reason why our prayers should be according to the will of God, why they should have nothing in them but what is wise, and holy,

279

and heavenly; there is no other reason for this, but that our lives may be of the same nature, full of the same wisdom, holiness, and heavenly tempers, that we may live unto God in the same spirit that we pray unto Him. Were it not our strict duty to live by reason, to devote all the actions of our lives to God, were it not absolutely necessary to walk before Him in wisdom and holiness and all heavenly conversation, doing everything in His Name, and for His glory, there would be no excellency or wisdom in the most heavenly prayers. Nay, such prayers would be absurdities; they would be like prayers for wings, when it was not part of our duty to fly.

As sure, therefore, as there is any wisdom in praying for the Spirit of God, so sure is it, that we are to make that Spirit the rule of all our actions; as sure as it is our duty to look wholly unto God in our prayers, so sure is it that it is our duty to live wholly unto God in our lives. But we can no more be said to live unto God, unless we live unto Him in all the ordinary actions of our life, unless He be the rule and measure of all our ways, than we can be said to pray unto God, unless our prayers look wholly unto Him. So that unreasonable and absurd ways of life, whether in labour or diversion, whether they consume our time, or our money, are like unreasonable and absurd prayers, and are as truly an offence unto God.

It is for want of knowing, or at least considering this, that we see such a mixture of ridicule in the lives of many people. You see them strict as to some times and places of devotion, but when the service of the Church is over, they are but like those that seldom or never come there. In their way of life, their manner of spending their time and money, in their cares and fears, in their pleasures and indulgences, in their labour and diversions, they are like the rest of the world. This makes the loose part of the world generally make a jest of those that are devout, because they see their devotion goes no farther than their prayers, and that when they are over, they live no more unto God, till the time of prayer returns again; but live by the same humour and fancy, and in as full an enjoyment of all the follies of life as other people. This is the reason why they are the jest and scorn of careless and worldly people; not because they are really devoted to God, but because they appear to have no other devotion but that of occasional prayers.

Julius is very fearful of missing prayers; all the parish supposes Julius to be sick, if he is not at Church. But if you were to ask him why he spends the rest of his time by humour or chance? why he is a companion of the silliest people in their most silly pleasures? why he is ready for every impertinent entertainment and diversion? . . . If you ask him why he never puts his conversation, his time, and fortune, under the rules of religion, Julius has no more to say for himself than the most disorderly person. For the whole tenor of Scripture lies as directly against such a life, as against debauchery and intemperance: he that lives such a course of idleness and folly, lives no more according to the religion of Jesus Christ, than he that lives in gluttony and intemperance.

If a man was to tell Julius that there was no occasion for so much constancy at prayers, and that he might, without any harm to himself, neglect the service of the Church, as the generality of people do, Julius would think such a one to be no Christian, and that he ought to avoid his company. But if a person only tells him, that he may live as the generality of the world does, that he may enjoy himself as others do, that he may spend his time and money as people of fashion do, that he may conform to the follies and frailties of the generality, and gratify his tempers and passions as most people do, Julius never suspects that man to want a Christian spirit, or that he is doing the devil's work. And if Julius was to read all the New Testament from the beginning to the end, he would find his course of life condemned in every page of it.

And indeed there cannot anything be imaged more absurd in itself, than wise, and sublime, and heavenly prayers, added to a life of vanity and folly, where neither labour nor diversions, neither time nor money, are under the direction of the wisdom and heavenly tempers of our prayers. . . .

The short of the matter is this; either reason and religion prescribe rules and ends to all the ordinary actions of our life, or they do not: if they do, then it is as necessary to govern all our actions by those rules, as it is necessary to worship God. . . .

It is very observable, that there is not one command in all the Gospel for public worship; and perhaps it is a duty that is least insisted upon in Scripture of any other. The frequent attendance at it is never so much as mentioned in all the New Testament. Whereas that religion or devotion which is to govern the ordinary actions of our life is to be found in almost every verse of Scripture. Our blessed Saviour and His Apostles are wholly taken up in doctrines that relate to common life. They call us to renounce the world, and differ in every temper and way of life, from the spirit and the way of the world: to renounce all its goods, to fear none of its evils, to reject its joys, and have no value for its happiness: to be as new-born babes, that are born into a new state of things: to live as pilgrims in spiritual watching, in holy fear, and heavenly aspiring after another life: to take up our daily cross, to deny ourselves, to profess the blessedness of mourning, to seek the blessedness of poverty of spirit: to forsake the pride and vanity of riches, to take no thought for the morrow, to live in the profoundest state of humility, to rejoice in worldly sufferings: to reject the lust of the flesh, the lust of the eyes, and the pride of life: to bear injuries, to forgive and bless our enemies, and to love mankind as God loveth them: to give up our whole hearts and affections to God, and strive to enter through the strait gate into a life of eternal glory.

This is the common devotion which our blessed Saviour taught, in order to make it the common life of all Christians. Is it not therefore exceeding strange, that people should place so much piety in the attendance upon public worship, concerning which there is not one precept of our Lord's to be found, and yet neglect these common duties of our ordinary life, which are commanded in every page of the Gospel? I call these duties the devotion of our common life, because if they are to be practised, they must be made parts of our common life; they can have no place anywhere else.

If contempt of the world and heavenly affection is a necessary temper of Christians, it is necessary that this temper appear in the whole course of their lives, in their manner of using the world, because it can have no place anywhere else. If self-denial be a condition of salvation, all that would be saved must make it a part of their ordinary life. If humility be a Christian duty, then the common life of a Christian is to be a constant course of humility in all its kinds. If poverty of spirit be necessary, it must be the spirit and temper of every day of our lives. If we are to relieve the naked, the sick, the prisoner, it must be the common charity of our lives, as far as we can render ourselves able to perform it. If we are to love our enemies, we must make our common life a visible exercise and demonstration of that love. If content and thankfulness, if the patient bearing of evil be duties to God, they are the duties of every day, and in every circumstance of our life. If we are to be wise and holy as the newborn sons of God, we can no otherwise be so, but by renouncing every thing that is foolish and vain in every part of our common life. If we are to be in Christ new creatures, we must show that we are so, by having new ways of living in the world. If we are to follow Christ, it must be in our common way of spending every day.

Thus it is in all the virtues and holy tempers of Christianity; they are not ours unless they be the virtues and tempers of our ordinary life. So that Christianity is so far from leaving us to live in the common ways of life, conforming to the folly of customs, and gratifying the passions and tempers which the spirit of the world delights in, it is so far from indulging us in any of these things, that all its virtues which it makes necessary to salvation are only so many ways of living above, and contrary to, the world in all the common actions of our life. If our common life is not a common course of humility, self-denial, renunciation of the world, poverty of spirit, and heavenly affection, we do not live the lives of Christians.

But yet though it is thus plain that this

and this alone is Christianity, a uniform, open, and visible practice of all these virtues, yet it is as plain that there is little or nothing of this to be found, even among the better sort of people. You see them often at church, and pleased with fine preachers; but look into their lives, and you see them just the same sort of people as others are that make no pretenses to devotion. The difference that you find betwixt them is only the difference of their natural tempers. They have the same taste of the world, the same worldly cares, and fears, and joys; they have the same turn of mind, equally vain in their desires. You see the same fondness for state and equipage, the same pride and vanity of dress, the same self-love and indulgence, the same foolish friendships and groundless hatreds, the same levity of mind and trifling spirit, the same fondness for diversions, the same idle dispositions and vain ways of spending their time in visiting and conversation, as the rest of the world, that make no pretenses to devotion.

I do not mean this comparison betwixt people seemingly good, and profest rakes, but betwixt people of sober lives. Let us take an instance in two modest women: let it be supposed that one of them is careful of times of devotion, and observes them through a sense of duty, and that the other has no hearty concern about it, but is at church seldom or often, just as it happens. Now it is a very easy thing to see this difference betwixt these persons. But when you have seen this, can you find any farther difference betwixt them: Can you find that their common life is of a different kind? Are not the tempers and customs, and manners of the one of the same kind as of the other? Do they live as if they belonged to different worlds, had different views in their heads, and different rules and measures of all their actions? Have they not the same goods and evils? Are they not pleased and displeased in the same manner, and for the same things? Do they not live in the same course of life? Does one seem to be of this world, looking at the things that are temporal, and the other to be of another world, looking wholly at the things that are eternal? ... Does the one follow public diversions, and trifle away her time in idle visits and corrupt conversation, and does the other study all the arts of improving her time, living in prayer and watching, and such good works as may make all her time turn to her advantage and be placed to her account at the last day? Is the one careless of expense, and glad to be able to adorn herself with every costly ornament of dress, and does the other consider her fortune as a talent given by God, which is to be improved religiously, and no more to be spent in vain and needless ornaments than it is to be buried in the earth?

Where must you look, to find one person of religion differing in this manner from another that has none? And yet if they do not differ in these things which are here related, can it with any sense be said, the one is a good Christian and the other not? ...

AN INQUIRY INTO THE REASON, WHY THE GENERALITY OF CHRISTIANS FALL SO FAR SHORT OF THE HOLINESS AND DEVOTION OF CHRISTIANITY

It may now be reasonably inquired, how it comes to pass, that the lives even of the better sort of people are thus strangely contrary to the principles of Christianity?

But before I give a direct answer to this, I desire it may also be inquired, how it comes to pass that swearing is so common a vice among Christians? ... Do but now find the reason why the generality of men live in this notorious vice, and then you will have found the reason why the generality even of the better sort of people live so contrary to Christianity.

Now the reason of common swearing is this; it is because men have not so much as the intention to please God in all their actions. For let a man but have so much piety as to intend to please God in all the actions of his life, as the happiest and best thing in the world, and then he will never swear more. It will be as impossible for him to swear, whilst he feels this intention within himself, as it is impossible for a man that intends to please his prince, to go up and abuse him to his face.

It seems but a small and necessary part of

piety to have such a sincere intention as this; and he has no reason to look upon himself as a disciple of Christ who is not thus far advanced in piety. And yet it is purely for want of this degree of piety, that you see such a mixture of sin and folly in the lives even of the better sort of people. . . .

Let a clergyman be but thus pious, and he will converse as if he had been brought up by an Apostle; he will no more think and talk of noble preferment, than of noble eating, or a glorious chariot. He will no more complain of the frowns of the world, or a small cure, or the want of a patron, than he will complain of the want of a laced coat, or a running horse. Let him but intend to please God in all his actions, as the happiest and best thing in the world, and then he will know, that there is nothing noble in a clergyman, but a burning zeal for the salvation of souls; nor anything poor in his profession, but idleness and a worldly spirit.

Again, let a tradesman but have this intention, and it will make him a saint in his shop; his every-day business will be a course of wise and reasonable actions, made holy to God, by being done in obedience to His will and pleasure. He will buy and sell, and labour and travel, because by so doing he can do some good to himself and others. But then, as nothing can please God but what is wise, and reasonable, and holy, so he will neither buy nor sell, nor labour in any other manner, nor to any other end, but such as may be shown to be wise, and reasonable, and holy. He will therefore consider, not what arts, or methods, or application, will soonest make him richer and greater than his brethren, or remove him from a shop to a life of state and pleasure; but he will consider what arts, what methods, what application, can make worldly business most acceptable to God, and make a life of trade a life of holiness, devotion, and piety. This will be the temper and spirit of every tradesman; he cannot stop short of these degrees of piety, whenever it is his intention to please God in all his actions, as the best and happiest thing in the world. And on the other hand, whoever is not of this spirit and temper in his trade and profession, and does not carry it on

only so far as is best subservient to a wise, and holy, and heavenly life, it is certain that he has not this intention; and yet without it, who can be shown to be a follower of Jesus Christ?

.   .   .   .   .

This doctrine does not suppose that we have no need of divine grace, or that it is in our own power to make ourselves perfect. It only supposes that, through the want of a sincere intention of pleasing God in all our actions, we fall into such irregularities of life as by the ordinary means of grace we should have power to avoid. And that we have not that perfection, which our present state of grace makes us capable of, because we do not so much as intend to have it. It only teaches us that the reason why you see no real mortification or self-denial, no eminent charity, no profound humility, no heavenly affection, no true contempt of the world, no Christian meekness, no sincere zeal, no eminent piety in the common lives of Christians, is this—because they do not so much as intend to be exact and exemplary in these virtues.

WE CAN PLEASE GOD IN NO STATE OR EMPLOYMENT OF LIFE, BUT BY INTENDING AND DEVOTING IT ALL TO HIS HONOR AND GLORY

Having stated the general nature of devotion, I shall now show how we are to devote our labor and employment, our time and fortunes, unto God.

As a good Christian should consider every place as holy, because God is there, so he should look upon every part of his life as a matter of holiness, because it is to be offered unto God.

The profession of a clergyman is a holy profession, because it is a ministration in holy things, an attendance at the altar. But worldly business is to be made holy unto the Lord by being done as a service to him, and in conformity to his divine will. For as all men, and all things in the world, as truly belong unto God as any places, things, or persons that are devoted to divine service, so all things are to be used, and all persons are

to act in their several states and employments, for the glory of God. . . . As all men
have the same relation to God, as all men
have their powers and faculties from God,
so all men are obliged to act for God, with all
their powers and faculties. As all things are
God's, so all things are to be used and regarded as the things of God. For men to
abuse things on earth, and live to themselves,
is the same rebellion against God as for
angels to abuse things in heaven; because
God is just the same Lord of all on earth
as he is the Lord of all in heaven.

Things may, and must, differ in their use,
but yet they are all to be used according
to the will of God. Men may, and must, differ
in their employments, but yet they must
all act for the same ends, as dutiful servants
of God, in the right and pious performances
of several callings.

.   .   .   .   .

The husbandman that tilleth the ground is
employed in an honest business that is necessary in life and very capable of being made
an acceptable service unto God. But if he
labors and toils, not to serve any reasonable
ends of life, but in order to have his plow
made of silver, and to have his horses har-
nessed in gold, the honesty of his employment is lost as to him, and his labor becomes
his folly.

.   .   .   .   .

No Christian is to enter any farther into
business, nor for any other ends, than such
as he can in singleness of heart offer unto
God as a reasonable service. For the Son of
God has redeemed us for this only end, that
we should, by a life of reason and piety, live
to the glory of God; this is the only rule and
measure for every order and state of life.
Without this rule, the most lawful employment becomes a sinful state of life. Take
this away from the life of a clergyman, and
his holy profession serves only to expose him
to a greater damnation. Take away this from
tradesmen, and shops are but so many houses
of greediness and filthy lucre.

If therefore we desire to live unto God, it
is necessary to bring our whole life under

this law, to make his glory the sole rule and
measure of our acting in every employment
of life. For there is no other true devotion,
but this of living devoted to God in the common business of our lives.

4. John Wesley's Journal, May 24, 1738

The Works of the Reverend John Wesley, A.M.,
ed. John Emory (New York: Methodist Episcopal Church, 1831).

What occurred on *Wednesday*, 24, I think
best to relate at large, after premising what
may make it the better understood. Let him
that cannot receive it, ask of the Father of
lights, that he would give more light to him
and me.

1. I believe, till I was about ten years
old I had not sinned away that "washing of
the Holy Ghost" which was given me in baptism; having been strictly educated and carefully taught, that I could only be saved "by
universal obedience, by keeping all the commandments of God"; in the meaning of which
I was diligently instructed. And those instructions, so far as they respected outward
duties and sins, I gladly received, and often
thought of. But all that was said to me of inward obedience, or holiness, I neither understood nor remembered. So that I was indeed
as ignorant of the true meaning of the Law,
as I was of the Gospel of Christ.

2. The next six or seven years were spent
at school; where outward restraints being
removed, I was much more negligent than
before, even of outward duties, and almost
continually guilty of outward sins, which I
knew to be such, though they were not
scandalous in the eye of the world. However,
I still read the Scriptures, and said my
prayers, morning and evening. And what I
now hoped to be saved by, was, (1) Not
being so bad as other people. (2) Having
still a kindness for religion. And (3) Reading
the Bible, going to church, and saying my
prayers.

3. Being removed to the University for
five years, I still said my prayers both in
public and in private, and read, with the
Scriptures, several other books of religion,
especially comments on the New Testament.
Yet I had not all this while so much as a

notion of inward holiness; nay, went on habitually and, for the most part, very contentedly, in some or other known sin: indeed, with some intermission and short struggles, especially before and after the holy communion, which I was obliged to receive thrice a year. I cannot well tell what I hoped to be saved by now, when I was continually sinning against that little light I had; unless by those transient fits of what many divines taught me to call repentance.

4. When I was about twenty-two, my father pressed me to enter into holy orders. At the same time, the providence of God directing me to Kempis's "Christian Pattern," I began to see, that true religion was seated in the heart, and that God's Law extended to all our thoughts as well as words and actions. I was, however, very angry at Kempis for being too strict; though I read him only in Dean Stanhope's translation. Yet I had frequently much sensible comfort in reading him, such as I was an utter stranger to before: and meeting likewise with a religious friend, which I never had till now, I began to alter the whole form of my conversation, and to set in earnest upon a new life. I set apart an hour or two a day for religious retirement. I communicated every week. I watched against all sin, whether in word or deed. I began to aim at, and pray for, inward holiness. So that now, "doing so much, and living so good a life," I doubted not but I was a good Christian.

5. Removing soon after to another college, I executed a resolution which I was before convinced was of the utmost importance,—shaking off at once all my trifling acquaintance. I began to see more and more the value of time. I applied myself closer to study. I watched more carefully against actual sins; I advised others to be religious, according to that scheme of religion by which I modelled my own life. But meeting now with Mr. Law's "Christian Perfection" and "Serious Call," although I was much offended at many parts of both, yet they convinced me more than ever of the exceeding height and breadth and depth of the Law of God. The light flowed in so mightily upon my soul, that every thing appeared in a new view. I cried

VI-6. John Wesley. *Portrait by George Romney (1734–1802), English portrait painter.*

to God for help, and resolved not to prolong the time of obeying him as I had never done before. And by my continued endeavour to keep his whole Law, inward and outward, to the utmost of my power, I was persuaded that I should be accepted of him, and that I was even then in a state of salvation.

6. In 1730 I began visiting the prisons; assisting the poor and sick in town; and doing what other good I could, by my presence, or my little fortune, to the bodies and souls of all men. To this end I abridged myself of all superfluities, and many that are called necessaries of life. I soon became a by-word for so doing, and I rejoiced that my name was cast out as evil. The next spring I began observing the Wednesday and Friday fasts, commonly observed in the ancient Church, tasting no food till three in the afternoon. And now I knew not how to go any further. I diligently strove against all sin. I omitted no sort of self denial which I thought lawful: I carefully used, both in public and in

VI-7. Wesley Preaching at Newgate Prison. *Sketch by John Jackson in* Wesley and His Friends at Oxford.

private, all the means of grace at all opportunities. I omitted no occasion of doing good: I for that reason suffered evil. And all this I knew to be nothing, unless as it was directed toward inward holiness. Accordingly this, the image of God, was what I aimed at in all, by doing his will, not my own. Yet when, after continuing some years in this course, I apprehended myself to be near death, I could not find that all this gave me any comfort, or any assurance of acceptance with God. At this I was then not a little surprised; not imagining I had been all this time building on the sand, nor considering that "other foundation can no man lay, than that which is laid" by God, "even Christ Jesus."

7. Soon after, a contemplative man convinced me still more than I was convinced before, that outward works are nothing, being alone; and in several conversations instructed me, how to pursue inward holiness, or a union of the soul with God. But even of his instructions (though I then received them as the words of God) I cannot but now observe, (1) That he spoke so incautiously against trusting in outward works, that he discouraged me from doing them at all. (2) That he recommended (as it were, to supply what was wanting in them) *mental prayer*, and the like exercises, as the most effectual means of purifying the soul, and uniting it with God. Now these were, in truth, as much my own works as visiting the sick or clothing the naked; and the union with God thus pursued, was as really my own righteousness, as any I had before pursued under another name.

8. In this refined way of trusting to my own works and my own righteousness, (so zealously inculcated by the mystic writers,)

286

I dragged on heavily, finding no comfort or help therein, till the time of my leaving England. On shipboard, however, I was again active in outward works; where it pleased God of his free mercy to give me twenty-six of the Moravian brethren for companions, who endeavoured to show me "a more excellent way." But I understood it not at first. I was too learned and too wise. So that it seemed foolishness unto me. And I continued preaching, and following after, and trusting in, that righteousness whereby no flesh can be justified.

9. All the time I was at Savannah I was thus beating the air. Being ignorant of the righteousness of Christ, which, by a living faith in him, bringeth salvation "to every one that believeth," I sought to establish my own righteousness; and so laboured in the fire all my days. I was now properly "under the Law"; I knew that "the Law" of God was "spiritual; I consented to it, that it was good." Yea, "I delighted in it, after the inner man." Yet was I "carnal, sold under sin." Every day was I constrained to cry out, "What I do, I allow not: for what I would, I do not; but what I hate that I do. To will is" indeed "present with me; but how to perform that which is good, I find not. For the good which I would, I do not; but the evil which I would not, that I do. I find a law, that when I would do good, evil is present with me": Even "the law in my members, warring against the law of my mind," and still "bringing me into captivity to the law of sin."

10. In this vile, abject state of bondage to sin, I was indeed fighting continually, but not conquering. Before, I had willingly served sin; now it was unwillingly; but still I served it. I fell, and rose, and fell again....

11. In my return to England, January, 1738, being in imminent danger of death, and very uneasy on that account, I was strongly convinced that the cause of that uneasiness was unbelief; and that the gaining a true, living faith, was the "one thing needful" for me. But still I fixed not this faith on its right object: I meant only faith in God not faith in or through Christ. Again, I knew not that I was wholly void of this faith; but only thought, I had not enough of it. So that

when Peter Bohler, whom God prepared for me as soon as I came to London, affirmed of true faith in Christ, (which is but one,) that it had those two fruits inseparably attending it, "Dominion over sin, and constant peace from a sense of forgiveness," I was quite amazed, and looked upon it as a new Gospel. If this was so, it was clear I had not faith. But I was not willing to be convinced of this. Therefore, I disputed with all my might, and laboured to prove that faith might be where these were not; especially where the sense of forgiveness was not: for, all the Scriptures relating to this, I had been long since taught to construe away; and to call all Presbyterians who spoke otherwise. Besides, I well saw, no one could, in the nature of things, have such a sense of forgiveness, and not *feel* it. But I felt it not. If then there was no faith without this, all my pretensions to faith dropped at once.

12. When I met Peter Bohler again, he consented to put the dispute upon the issue which I desired, namely, Scripture and experience. I first consulted the Scripture. But when I set aside the glosses of men, and simply considered the words of God, comparing them together, endeavouring to illustrate the obscure by the plainer passages; I found they all made against me, and was forced to retreat to my last hold, "that experience would never agree with the *literal interpretation* of those scriptures. Nor could I therefore allow it to be true, till I found some living witnesses of it." He replied, he could show me such at any time; if I desired it, the next day. Accordingly, the next day he came again with three others, all of whom testified, of their own personal experience, that a true living faith in Christ is inseparable from a sense of pardon for all past, and freedom from all present, sins. They added with one mouth, that this faith was the gift, the free gift of God; and that he would surely bestow it upon every soul who earnestly and perseveringly sought it. I was now throughly convinced; and by the grace of God I resolved to seek it unto the end: (1) By absolutely renouncing all dependence, in whole or in part, upon *my own* works or righteousness; on which I had really grounded

my hope of salvation, though I knew it not, from my youth up. (2) By adding to the constant use of all the other means of grace, continual prayer for these very things, justifying, saving faith, a full reliance on the blood of Christ shed for *me;* a trust in him, as *my* Christ, as *my* sole justification, sanctification, and redemption.

13. I continued thus to seek it, (though with strange indifference, dulness, and coldness, and unusually frequent relapses into sin,) till Wednesday, May 24. I think it was about five this morning, that I opened my Testament on those words: "There are given unto us exceeding great and precious promises, even that ye should be partakers of the Divine nature," II Pet. 1:4. Just as I went out, I opened it again on those words, "Thou art not far from the Kingdom of God." In the afternoon I was asked to go to St. Paul's. The anthem was, "Out of the deep have I called unto thee, O Lord: Lord, hear my voice. O let thine ears consider well the voice of my complaint. If thou, Lord, wilt be extreme to mark what is done amiss, O Lord, who may abide it? For there is mercy with thee; therefore shalt thou be feared. O Israel, trust in the Lord: for with the Lord there is mercy, and with him is plenteous redemption. And he shall redeem Israel from all his sins."

14. In the evening I went very unwillingly to a society in Aldersgate Street, where one was reading Luther's preface to the Epistle to the Romans. About a quarter before nine, while he was describing the change which God works in the heart through faith in Christ, I felt my heart strangely warmed. I felt I did trust in Christ, Christ alone for salvation: and an assurance was given me, that he had taken away *my* sins, even *mine,* and saved *me* from the law of sin and death.

5. Rules for the Methodist Societies

Anyone who had a "desire to flee from the wrath to come, to be saved from their sins" was eligible to join Wesley's Society. Wesley boasted that the Methodists "do not impose, in order to their admission, any opinions whatsoever. Let them hold particular or general redemption, absolute or conditional decrees: let them be Churchmen, or Dissenters, Presbyterians or In-dependents, it is no obstacle. Let them choose one mode of baptism or another, it is no bar to their admission. The Presbyterian may be a Presbyterian still; the Independent and Anabaptist use his own mode of worship. So may the Quaker; and none will contend with him about it. They think and let think." However, Wesley did insist that those who continued in the Society observe certain rules, which were adopted for his societies in 1743 and are still printed in the Methodist *Discipline. Doctrines and Disciplines of the Methodist Church* (New York: The Methodist Publishing House, 1940-1960).

It is therefore expected of all who continue therein, that they should continue to evidence their desire of salvation,

First; By doing no harm: by avoiding evil in every kind; especially that which is most generally practiced. Such as: the taking the name of God in vain; the profaning the day of the Lord, either by doing ordinary work thereon, or by buying or selling; drunkenness, buying or selling spirituous liquors, or drinking them (unless in cases of extreme necessity); fighting, quarrelling, brawling; going to law; returning evil for evil or railing for railing; the using many words in buying or selling; the buying or selling uncustomed goods; the giving or taking things on usury, that is, unlawful interest; uncharitable or unprofitable conversation, particularly speaking evil of magistrates or ministers; doing to others as we would not they should do unto us; doing what we know is not for the glory of God: as the putting on of gold, or costly apparel; the taking such diversions as cannot be used in the name of the Lord Jesus; the singing those songs, or reading those books, which do not tend to the knowledge or love of God; softness, and needless self-indulgence; laying up treasures upon earth; borrowing without a probability of paying; or taking up goods without a probability of paying for them.

It is expected of all who continue in these societies that they should continue to evidence their desire for salvation,

Secondly, By doing good; by being, in every kind, merciful after their power; as they have opportunity, doing good of every possible sort, and as far as possible, to all men:

To their bodies, of the ability which God

VI-8. Sketch of the First Methodist Conference, June 25, 1744, London.

giveth, by giving food to the hungry, by clothing the naked, by visiting or helping them that are sick, or in prison:

To their souls, by instructing, reproving, or exhorting all we have any intercourse with; trampling underfoot that enthusiastic doctrine of devils, that "we are not to do good unless our heart is free to it."

By doing good, especially, to them that are of the household of faith, or groaning so to be; employing them preferably to others, buying one of another, helping each other in business; and that so much the more because the world will love its own, and them only.

By all possible diligence and frugality, that the gospel be not blamed.

By running with patience the race that is set before them; denying themselves and taking up their cross daily; submitting to bear the reproach of Christ, to be as the filth and offscouring of the world; and looking that men should say all manner of evil of them falsely, for the Lord's sake.

It is expected of all who desire to continue in these societies that they should continue to evidence their desire of salvation,

Thirdly, By attending upon all the ordinances of God; such are: the public worship of God; the ministry of the word, either read or expounded; the supper of the Lord; family and private prayer; searching the Scriptures; and fasting, or abstinence.

6. *John Wesley, 1740*

Wesley's sermon "Free Grace," preached at Bristol, 1740. *The Works of the Reverend John Wesley, A.M.,* ed. Emory.

"He that spared not his own Son, but delivered him up for us all, how shall he not with him also freely give us all things?" Rom. 8:32.

1. How freely does God love the world! While we were yet sinners, "Christ died for the ungodly." While we were "dead in sin," God "spared not his own Son, but delivered him up for us all." And how freely with him does he "give us all things!" Verily, *Free Grace* is all in all!

2. The grace or love of God, whence cometh our salvation, is *free in all,* and *free for all.*

3. First: It is free *in all* to whom it is given. It does not depend on any power or merit in man; no, not in any degree, neither in whole, nor in part. It does not in any wise depend either on the good works or righteousness of the receiver; not on any thing he

VI-9. John Wesley Preaching at Bolton Cross.

has done, or any thing he is. It does not depend on his endeavours. It does not depend on his good tempers, or good desires, or good purposes and intentions; for all these flow from the free grace of God; they are the streams only, not the fountain. They are the fruits of free grace, and not the root. They are not the cause, but the effects of it. Whatsoever good is in man, or is done by man, God is the author and doer of it. Thus is his grace free in all; that is, no way depending on any power or merit in man, but on God alone, who freely gave us his own Son, and "with him freely giveth us all things."

4. But is it free *for all*, as well as *in all?* To this some have answered, "No: it is free only for those whom God hath ordained to life; and they are but a little flock. The greater part of mankind God hath ordained to death;

and it is not free for them. Them God hateth; and therefore, before they were born, decreed they shoud die eternally. And this he absolutely decreed; because so was his good pleasure; because it was his sovereign will. Accordingly they are born for this, to be destroyed body and soul in hell. And they grow up under the irrevocable curse of God, without any possibility of redemption; for what grace God gives, he gives only for this, to increase, not prevent, their damnation."

5. This is that decree of predestination. But methinks I hear one say, "This is not the predestination which I hold: I hold only, the election of grace. What I believe is no more than this: that God, before the foundation of the world, did elect a certain number of men to be justified, sanctified, and glorified. Now all these will be saved, and none else: for the rest of mankind God leaves to themselves; so they follow the imaginations of their own hearts, which are only evil continually, and, waxing worse and worse, are at length justly punished with everlasting destruction."

6. Is this all the predestination which you hold? Consider: perhaps this is not all. Do not you believe, God ordained them to this very thing? If so, you believe the whole decree; you hold predestination in the full sense, which has been above described. But it may be, you think you do not. Do not you then believe, God hardens the hearts of them that perish? Do you not believe, he (literally) hardened Pharaoh's heart, and that for this end he raised him up, or created him? Why this amounts to just the same thing. If you believe Pharaoh, or any one man upon earth, was created for this end, to be damned, you hold all that has been said of predestination. And there is no need you should add, that God seconds his decree, which is supposed unchangeable and irresistible, by hardening the hearts of those vessels of wrath, whom that decree had before fitted for destruction.

7. Well; but it may be you do not believe even this: you do not hold any decree of reprobation: you do not think God decrees any man to be damned, nor hardens, irresistibly fits him for damnation: you only say, "God eternally decreed, that all being dead

in sin, he would say to some of the dry bones, Live, and to others he would not; that, consequently, these should be made alive, and those abide in death,—these should glorify God by their salvation, and those by their destruction."

8. Is not this what you mean by the election of grace? If it be, I would ask one or two questions: Are any who are not thus elected, saved? Or, were any, from the foundation of the world? Is it possible any man should be saved, unless he be thus elected? If you say, No; you are but where you were: you are not got one hair's breadth farther: you still believe, that in consequence of an unchangeable, irresistible decree of God, the greater part of mankind abide in death, without any possibility of redemption; inasmuch as none can save them but God, and he will not save them. You believe he hath absolutely decreed not to save them; and what is this, but decreeing to damn them? It is, in effect, neither more nor less: it comes to the same thing: for if you are dead, and altogether unable to make yourself alive; then, if God has absolutely decreed he will make only others alive, and not you, he hath absolutely decreed your everlasting death; you are absolutely consigned to damnation. So then, though you use softer words than some, you mean the self same thing; and God's decree concerning the election of grace, according to your own account of it, amounts to neither more nor less than what others call, "God's decree of reprobation."

9. Call it therefore by whatever name you please, election, preterition, predestination, or reprobation, it comes in the end to the same thing. The sense of all is plainly this: by virtue of an eternal, unchangeable, irresistible decree of God, one part of mankind are infallibly saved, and the rest infallibly damned; it being impossible that any of the former should be damned, or that any of the latter should be saved.

10. But if this be so, then is all preaching vain. It is needless to them that are elected; for they, whether with preaching or without, will infallibly be saved. Therefore the end of preaching, to save souls, is void with regard to them. And it is useless to them that are not elected, for they cannot possibly be saved. They, whether with preaching or without, will infallibly be damned. The end of preaching is therefore void with regard to them likewise; so that in either case, our preaching is vain, as your hearing is also vain.

11. This, then, is a plain proof that the doctrine of predestination is not a doctrine of God, because it makes void the ordinance of God: and God is not divided against himself. A second is, that it directly tends to destroy that holiness, which is the end of all the ordinances of God. I do not say, none who hold it are holy; (for God is of tender mercy to those who are unavoidably entangled in errors of any kind;) but that the doctrine itself,—That every man is either elected or not elected from eternity, and that the one must inevitably be saved, and the other inevitably damned,—has a manifest tendency to destroy holiness in general. For it wholly takes away those first motives to follow after it, so frequently proposed in Scripture, the hope of future reward and fear of punishment, the hope of heaven and fear of hell. That these shall go away into everlasting punishment, and those into life eternal, is no motive to him to struggle for life, who believes his lot is cast already: it is not reasonable for him so to do, if he thinks he is unalterably adjudged either to life or death. You will say, "But he knows not whether it is life or death." What then?—this helps not the matter: for if a sick man knows that he must unavoidably die, or unavoidably recover, though he knows not which, it is unreasonable for him to take any physic at all. He might justly say, (and so I have heard some speak, both in bodily sickness and in spiritual,) "If I am ordained to life, I shall live; if to death, I shall die: so I need not trouble myself about it." So directly does this doctrine tend to shut the very gate of holiness in general, to hinder unholy men from ever approaching thereto, or striving to enter in thereat.

13. Thirdly, This doctrine tends to destroy the comfort of religion, the happiness of Christianity. This is evident as to all those who believe themselves to be reprobated; or who only suspect or fear it. All the great and

precious promises are lost to them; they afford them no ray of comfort: for they are not the elect of God; therefore they have neither lot nor portion in them. This is an effectual bar to their finding any comfort or happiness, even in that religion whose ways are designed to be "ways of pleasantness, and all her paths peace."

14. And as to you who believe yourselves the elect of God, what is your happiness? I hope not a notion; a speculative belief; a bare opinion of any kind; but a feeling possession of God in your heart, wrought in you by the Holy Ghost, or the witness of God's Spirit with your spirit that you are a child of God. This, otherwise termed "the full assurance of faith," is the true ground of a Christian's happiness. And it does indeed imply a full assurance that all your past sins are forgiven, and that you are *now* a child of God. But it does not necessarily imply a full assurance of our future perseverance. I do not say this is never joined to it, but that it is not necessarily implied therein; for many have the one, who have not the other.

15. Now this witness of the Spirit, experience shows to be much obstructed by this doctrine; and not only in those who, believing themselves reprobated, by this belief thrust it far from them, but even in them that have tasted of that good gift, who yet have soon lost it again, and fallen back into doubts, and fears, and darkness,—horrible darkness, that might be felt! And I appeal to any of you who hold this doctrine, to say, between God and your own hearts, whether you have not often a return of doubts and fears concerning your election or perseverance? If you ask, who has not? I answer, very few of those that hold this doctrine,—but many, very many of those that hold it not, in all parts of the earth, many of those who know and feel they are in Christ to day, and "take no thought for the morrow," who "abide in him" by faith from hour to hour, or rather from moment to moment,—many of these have enjoyed the uninterrupted witness of his Spirit, the continual light of his countenance, from the moment wherein they first believed, for many months or years, to this day.

16. That assurance of faith, which these enjoy, excludes all doubt and fear. It excludes all kinds of doubt and fear concerning their future perseverance; though it is not properly, as was said before, an assurance of what is future, but only of what *now* is. And this needs not for its support a speculative belief that whoever is once ordained to life must live; for it is wrought, from hour to hour, by the mighty power of God, "by the Holy Ghost which is given unto them." And therefore that doctrine is not of God, because it tends to obstruct, if not destroy, this great work of the Holy Ghost, whence flows the chief comfort of religion, the happiness of Christianity.

17. Again: how uncomfortable a thought is this, that thousands and millions of men, without any preceding offence or fault of theirs, were unchangeably doomed to everlasting burnings! How peculiarly uncomfortable must it be to those who have put on Christ! To those who, being filled with bowels of mercy, tenderness, and compassion, could even "wish themselves accursed for their brethren's sake!"

18. Fourthly: This uncomfortable doctrine directly tends to destroy our zeal for good works. . . .

19. But, fifthly, This doctrine not only tends to destroy Christian holiness, happiness, and good works, but hath also a direct and manifest tendency to overthrow the whole Christian revelation. The point which the wisest of the modern unbelievers most industriously labour to prove, is that the Christian revelation is not necessary. They well know, could they once show this, the conclusion would be too plain to be denied, "If it be not necessary, it is not true." Now this fundamental point you give up. For supposing that eternal, unchangeable decree, one part of mankind must be saved though the Christian revelation were not in being, and the other part of mankind must be damned, notwithstanding that revelation. And what would an infidel desire more? You allow him all he asks. In making the gospel thus unnecessary to all sorts of men, you give up the whole Christian cause. "Oh tell it not in Gath! Publish it not in the streets

of Askelon! lest the daughters of the uncircumcised rejoice"; lest the sons of unbelief triumph!

20. And as this doctrine manifestly and directly tends to overthrow the whole Christian revelation, so it does the same thing, by plain consequence, in making that revelation contradict itself. For it is grounded on such an interpretation of some texts (more or fewer it matters not) as flatly contradicts all the other texts, and indeed the whole scope and tenor of Scripture. For instance: the assertors of this doctrine interpret that text of Scripture, "Jacob have I loved, but Esau have I hated," as implying, that God in a literal sense hated Esau, and all the reprobated, from eternity. Now what can possibly be a more flat contradiction than this, not only to the whole scope and tenor of Scripture, but also to all those particular texts which expressly declare, "God is love"? . . .

21. And, "the same Lord over all is rich in mercy to all that call upon him," Rom. 10:12: But you say, no; he is such only to those for whom Christ died. And those are not all, but only a few, whom God hath chosen out of the world; for he died not for all, but only for those who were "chosen in him before the foundation of the world," Eph. 1:4. Flatly contrary to your interpretation of these Scriptures, also is the whole tenor of the New Testament; as are in particular those texts;— "Destroy not him with thy meat, for whom Christ died," Rom. 14:15; (a clear proof that Christ died, not only for those that are saved, but also for them that perish;) he is "The Saviour of the world," John 4:42; he is "The Lamb of God that taketh away the sins of the world," John 1:29; "He is the propitiation, not for our sins only, but also for the sins of the whole world," I John 2:2; "He (the living God) is the Saviour of all men," I Tim. 4:10; "He gave himself a ransom for all," I Tim. 2:6; "He tasted death for every man," Heb. 2:9.

22. If you ask, why then are not all men saved? The whole law and the testimony answer, first, not because of any decree of God; not because it is his pleasure they should die; for, "as I live, saith the Lord God, I have no pleasure in the death of him that dieth," Ez. 18:32. Whatever be the cause of their perishing, it cannot be his will if the oracles of God are true; for they declare, "He is not willing that any should perish but that all should come to repentance," II Pet. 3:9; "He willeth that all men should be saved." And they, secondly, declare what is the cause why all men are not saved, namely, that they will not be saved: so our Lord expressly; "Ye will not come unto me that you may have life," John 5:40. "The power of the Lord is present to heal" them, but they will not be healed. "They reject the counsel," the merciful counsel of God "against themselves," as did their stiff necked forefathers. And therefore are they without excuse because God would save them, but they will not be saved: this is the condemnation, "How often would I have gathered you together, and ye would not," Matt. 23:37. . . .

7. Repentance of Believers

Wesley urged on his followers a doctrine of perfection or sanctification, which for him meant a growth in grace exhibited in the life of the justified Christian. That Wesley did not conceive this "pressing on towards the prize of the high calling of God in Christ Jesus" in a Pelagian sense, as if one were increasing his merit before God, is illustrated by his emphasis on the continual necessity of faith and repentance. The following is from a sermon, "Repentance of Believers," preached at Londonderry, April 24, 1767. *The Works of the Reverend John Wesley, A.M.*, ed. Emory.

Thus it is, that in the children of God, repentance and faith exactly answer each other.

VI-10. A Typical Methodist Love Feast Ticket.

By repentance, we feel the sin remaining in our hearts, and cleaving to our words and actions: by faith we receive the power of God in Christ, purifying our hearts, and cleansing our hands. By repentance we are still sensible that we deserve punishment for all our tempers, and words, and actions: by faith we are conscious, that our Advocate with the Father is continually pleading for us, and thereby continually turning aside all condemnation and punishment from us. By repentance we have an abiding conviction that there is no help in us: by faith we receive not only mercy, "but grace to help in" *every* "time of need." Repentance disclaims the very possibility of any other help: faith accepts all the help we stand in need of, from him that hath all power in heaven and earth. Repentance says, "Without him I can do nothing": Faith says, "I can do all things through Christ strengthening me." Through him I can not only overcome, but expel, all the enemies of my soul. Through him I can "love the Lord my God with all my heart, mind, soul, and strength": yea, and "walk in holiness and righteousness before him all the days of my life."

From what has been said, we may easily learn the mischievousness of that opinion, that we are *wholly* sanctified when we are justified; that our hearts are then cleansed from all sin. It is true, we are then delivered, as was observed before, from the dominion of outward sin; and at the same time, the power of inward sin is so broken that we need no longer follow, or be led by it: but it is by no means true, that inward sin is then totally destroyed; that the root of pride, self will, anger, love of the world, is then taken out of the heart; or that the carnal mind, and the heart bent to backsliding, are entirely extirpated. And to suppose the contrary, is not, as some may think, an innocent, harmless mistake. No: it does immense harm; it entirely blocks up the way to any farther change: for it is manifest, "They that are whole do not need a physician, but they that are sick." If, therefore, we think we are quite made whole already, there is no room to seek any farther healing. On this supposition it is absurd to expect a farther deliverance from

sin, whether gradual or instantaneous.

On the contrary, a deep conviction that we are not yet whole; that our hearts are not fully purified; that there is yet in us a "carnal mind," which is still in its nature "enmity against God"; that a whole body of sin remains in our heart, weakened indeed, but not destroyed; shows, beyond all possibility of doubt, the absolute necessity of a farther change. We allow, that at the very moment of justification, we are *born again:* in that instant we experience that inward change, from "darkness into marvellous light"; from the image of the brute and the devil, into the image of God; from the earthly, sensual, devilish mind, to the mind which was in Christ Jesus. But are we then *entirely* changed? Are we *wholly* transformed into the image of him that created us? Far from it: we still retain a depth of sin: and it is the consciousness of this, which constrains us to groan for a full deliverance, to him that is mighty to save....

8. Dr. Coke's Letter of Ordination

John Wesley did not intend to originate a separate church, but historical circumstances dictated otherwise. Although he was a loyal Anglican, Wesley came to believe that Christ did not ordain a threefold ministry of bishops, elders, and deacons; he believed that bishops are simply elders set aside for the administration of the church. He also rejected the idea that valid ordination depends on a succession of ordained bishops extending back to Christ's laying of his hands on the Apostles. Accordingly, when the Bishop of London, who was in charge of the churches in the colonies, refused to ordain one of Wesley's preachers for America, he decided to ordain preachers himself. Dr. Thomas Coke, like Wesley an ordained presbyter in the Church of England, consented to accept ordination at Wesley's hands as superintendent of the work in America. In 1784 Wesley, assisted by James Creighton, a presbyter, ordained Richard Whatcoat and Thomas Vasey as deacons and elders, and then ordained Thomas Coke as superintendent. Charles Wesley expressed his disgust in doggerel:

> So easily are bishops made
> By man's or woman's whim!
> Wesley his hands on Coke hath laid,
> But who laid hands on him?

At the Baltimore conference, December 24, 1784, the Methodist Episcopal Church was organized. Coke was named superintendent along with Francis Asbury, who was ordained deacon, elder, and superintendent in three successive days. To Dr. Coke Wesley gave his famous

"Letter of Ordination," as well as an abridgment of the English liturgy and of the Thirty-nine Articles of the Church of England, which with one addition became the Articles of Religion of the new Methodist Church. Afterwards Wesley ordained men for Scotland, Newfoundland, Antigua, Nova Scotia, West Indies, and even for England.

To all to whom these presents shall come, John Wesley, late Fellow of Lincoln College in Oxford, Presbyter of the Church of England, sendeth greeting.

Whereas many of the people in the Southern provinces of North America, who desire to continue under my care, and still adhere to the doctrine and discipline of the Church of England, are greatly distressed for want of ministers to administer the sacraments of baptism and the Lord's Supper, according to the usage of the said church; and whereas there does not appear to be any other way of supplying them with ministers.

Know all men, that I, John Wesley, think myself to be providentially called, at this time to set apart some persons for the work of the ministry in America. And, therefore, under the protection of Almighty God, and with a single eye to his glory, I have this day set apart as a Superintendent, by the imposition of my hands and prayer (being assisted by other ordained ministers), Thomas Coke, doctor of civil law, a presbyter of the Church of England, and a man whom I judge to be well qualified for that great work. And I do hereby recommend him to all whom it may concern, as a fit person to preside over the flock of Christ. In testimony whereof, I have hereunto set my hand and seal, this second day of September, in the year of our Lord one thousand seven hundred and eighty-four. (*John Wesley.*)

9. *Wesley and the Moravians*

An extract from "A Short View of the Difference Between the Moravian Brethren and the Rev. Mr. John and Charles Wesley," *The Works of the Reverend John Wesley, A.M.*, ed. Emory.

TO THE READER

As those who are under the direction of Count Zinzendorf (vulgarly called Moravian Brethren) are the most plausible, and therefore far the most dangerous, of all the Antinomians now in England, I first endeavour to guard such as are simple of heart against being taken by those cunning hunters.

The difference between the Moravian doctrine and ours (in this respect) lies here:—
They believe and teach,—
"1. Christ has done all that was necessary for the salvation of all mankind."
This is ambiguous. Christ has not done all which was necessary for the absolute salvation of all mankind. For notwithstanding all that Christ has done, he that believeth not shall be damned. But he has done all which was necessary for the conditional salvation of all mankind; that is, if they believe; for through his merits all that believe to the end, with the faith that worketh by love, shall be saved.
"2. We are to do nothing as necessary to salvation, but simply to believe in him."
If we allow the Count's definition of faith, namely, "the historical knowledge of this truth, that Christ has been a man and suffered death for us," (*Sixteen Discourses,* p. 57), then is this proposition directly subversive of the whole revelation of Jesus Christ.
"3. There is but one duty now, but one command, viz. to believe in Christ."
Almost every page in the New Testament proves the falsehood of this assertion.
"4. Christ has taken away all other commands and duties, having wholly abolished the law."
How absolutely contrary is this to his own solemn declaration!—
"Think not that I am come to destroy the law or the Prophets. I am not come to destroy but to fulfil. One jot or one tittle shall in no wise pass from the law, till heaven and earth pass."
"Therefore a believer is free from the law." That he is "free from the curse of the law," we know; and that he is "free from the law," or power, "of sin and death": but where is it written that he is free from the law of God?
"He is not obliged thereby to do or omit any thing, it being inconsistent with his liberty to do any thing as commanded."
So your liberty is a liberty to disobey God;

whereas ours is a liberty to obey him in all things: so grossly, while we "establish the law," do you "make void the law through faith!"

"5. We are sanctified wholly the moment we are justified, and are neither more nor less holy to the day of our death; entire sanctification and entire justification being in one and the same instant."

Just the contrary appears both from the tenor of God's word, and the experience of his children.

"6. A believer is never sanctified or holy in himself, but in Christ only. He has no holiness in himself at all; all his holiness being imputed, not inherent."

Scripture holiness is the image of God; the mind which was in Christ; the love of God and man; lowliness, gentleness, temperance, patience, chastity. And do you coolly affirm, that this is only imputed to a believer, and that he has none at all of this holiness in him? Is temperance imputed only to him that is a drunkard still; or chastity, to her that goes on in whoredom? Nay, but a believer is really chaste and temperate. And if so, he is thus far holy in himself.

Does a believer love God, or does he not? If he does, he has the love of God in him. Is he lowly, or meek, or patient at all? If he is, he has these tempers in himself; and if he has them not in himself, he is not lowly, or meek, or patient. You cannot therefore deny, that every believer has holiness in, though not from, himself; else you deny, that he is holy at all; and if so, he cannot see the Lord.

And indeed, if holiness in general be the mind which was in Christ, what can any one possibly mean by, "A believer is not holy in himself, but in Christ only? that the mind which was in Christ is in a believer also; but it is in Him,—not in himself, but in Christ!" What a heap of palpable self-contradiction, what senseless jargon, is this!

"7. If a man regards prayer, or searching the Scriptures, or communicating, as matter of duty; if he judges himself obliged to do these things, or is troubled when he does them not, he is in bondage, he has no faith at all, but is seeking salvation by the works of the law."

Thus obedience with you is a proof of unbelief, and disobedience a proof of faith! What is it, to put darkness for light, and light for darknesss, if this is not?

10. Evangelical Hymns

What the Methodists believed they put into their hymns. Many collections of hymns followed after the popular early collection of 1737. In 1780, the Methodist Societies first used a large hymn book entitled *A Collection of Hymns for the Use of the People Called Methodists.* Its 539 hymns were almost "creeds in verse," for every aspect of the evangelical movement found fervent expression. In the preface John Wesley characterized the hymnal as "A little body of experimental and practical divinity; no doggerel, no botches, nothing put in to patch up the rhyme, no feeble expletives . . . no words without meaning . . . large enough to contain all the most important truths of our most holy religion, whether speculative or practical; yea, to illustrate them all, and to prove them by Scripture and reason." John not only claimed that the hymnal was a "distinct and full account of scriptural Christianity," but that it contained "clear direction for making your calling and election sure, for perfecting holiness in the fear of God."

The hymns afforded opportunity for expression of personal convictions and feelings such as had not been experienced in England for many years. Anglicanism was still tied to metrical psalms, despite the efforts of Isaac Watts. The Nonconformists had lost much of their vigor after winning toleration. Even the Quakers tended to lose their enthusiasm. The impact of rationalism with its doubt about traditional Christian claims was widely evident, but the evangelical hymns infused new fervor into many flagging hearts.

Most of the Methodist hymns were composed by Charles Wesley. In addition to the ones given below, Charles composed such favorites as "Thou hidden source of calm repose," "Come, thou almighty King," "Christ, the Lord is risen today," "Depth of mercy, can there be," "Hark, the herald angels sing," "Love, divine, all loves excelling," and "Soldiers of Christ arise." John Wesley translated as many as thirty hymns from Paul Gerhardt, Gerhard Tersteegen, A. G. Spangenberg, Ernst Lange, and others. Credited to John as original compositions are "How happy is the pilgrim's lot," "O Sun of righteousness arise," "We lift our hearts to thee," and paraphrases of the Lord's Prayer.

Other evangelical hymns were composed by Isaac Watts, often called the father of English hymnody, who wrote such favorites as "Jesus shall reign where'er the sun," "Before Jehovah's awful throne," and "From all that dwell below the skies." Other popular hymn writers were Philip Doddridge (1702-1751), John Newton (1725-1807), William Cowper (1731-1800), and Augustus M. Toplady (1740-1778), authors respectively of "O happy day," "Amazing grace! How sweet the sound," "There is a fountain filled with blood," and "Rock of ages, cleft for me."

COME, SINNERS, TO THE GOSPEL FEAST

Charles Wesley

Come sinners, to the gospel feast;
Let every soul be Jesus' guest:
Ye need not one be left behind,
For God hath bidden all mankind.

Sent by my Lord, on you I call;
The invitation is to all:
Come all the world! come, sinner, thou!
All things in Christ are ready now.

Come, all ye souls by sin oppressed,
Ye restless wanderers after rest;
Ye poor, and maimed, and halt, and blind,
In Christ a hearty welcome find.

My message as from God receive;
Ye all may come to Christ and live:
O let his love your hearts constrain
Nor suffer him to die in vain.

See him set forth before your eyes,
That precious, bleeding sacrifice:
His offered benefits embrace,
And freely now be saved by grace.

O LOVE DIVINE, WHAT HAST THOU DONE!

Charles Wesley

O love divine, what hast thou done!
    The incarnate God hath died for me!
The Father's co-eternal Son,
    Bore all my sins upon the tree!
The Son of God for me hath died:
My Lord, my Love, is crucified.

Behold him, all ye that pass by,—
    The bleeding Prince of life and peace!
Come, sinners, see your Saviour die,
    And say, was ever grief like his?
Come, feel with me his blood applied
My Lord, my Love, is crucified:

Is crucified for me and you,
    To bring us rebels back to God:
Believe, believe the record true,
    Ye all are bought with Jesus' blood:
Pardon for all flows from his side:
My Lord, my Love, is crucified.

Then let us sit beneath his cross,
    And gladly catch the healing stream;
All things for him account but loss,
    And give up all our hearts to him:
Of nothing think or speak beside,—
My Lord, my Love, is crucified.

WHEN I SURVEY THE WONDROUS CROSS

Isaac Watts

When I survey the wondrous cross
    On which the Prince of glory died,
My richest gain I count but loss,
    And pour contempt on all my pride.

Forbid it, Lord, that I should boast,
    Save in the death of Christ, my God;
All the vain things that charm me most,
    I sacrifice them to his blood.

See, from his head, his hands, his feet,
    Sorrow and love flow mingled down:
Did e'er such love and sorrow meet,
    Or thorns compose so rich a crown?

Were the whole realm of nature mine,
    That were a present far too small;
Love so amazing, so divine,
    Demands my soul, my life, my all.

O GOD, OUR HELP IN AGES PAST

Isaac Watts

O God, our help in ages past,
    Our hope for years to come,
Our shelter from the stormy blast,
    And our eternal home!

Under the shadow of thy throne
    Still may we dwell secure;
Sufficient is thine arm alone,
    And our defense is sure.

Before the hills in order stood,
    Or earth received her frame,
From everlasting thou art God,
    To endless years the same.

A thousand ages, in thy sight,
    Are like an evening gone;
Short as the watch that ends the night,
    Before the rising sun.

The busy tribes of flesh and blood,
  With all their cares and fears,
Are carried downward by the flood,
  And lost in following years.

Time, like an ever-rolling stream,
  Bears all its sons away;
They fly, forgotten, as a dream
  Dies at the opening day.

O God, our help in ages past,
  Our hope for years to come;
Be thou our guide while life shall last,
  And our perpetual home!

ALAS! AND DID MY SAVIOUR BLEED?

Isaac Watts

Alas! And did my Saviour bleed?
  And did my sovereign die?
Would he devote that sacred head
  For such a worm as I?

Was it for crimes that I have done,
  He groaned upon the tree?
Amazing pity! grace unknown!
  And love beyond degree!

Well might the sun in darkness hide,
  And shut his glories in,
When Christ, the mighty Maker, died,
  For man the creature's sin.

Thus might I hide my blushing face
  While his dear cross appears;
Dissolve my heart in thankfulness,
  And melt mine eyes to tears.

But drops of grief can ne'er repay
  The debt of love I owe:
Here, Lord, I give myself away,—
  'Tis all that I can do.

11. Blaise Pascal

Blaise Pascal (1623-1662) was one of the keenest scientists of his age, seeking by means of scientific truth to probe the secrets of man's nature and destiny. In 1654, he had a remarkable religious experience of conversion, and thereafter sought to find a Christian solution to the problem of existence. He lived at Port Royal, a Jansenist stronghold, but never joined a religious order. When the Jesuits attacked Arnauld, a Jansenist leader, Pascal defended him in the famous satires known as *The Provincial Letters*, 1656. (Cf. Ch. 3.) Eight years after Pascal's death, a collection called *Pensées* (*Thoughts*) appeared. They were brief observations, sometimes only a sentence or a few words, often on mere scraps of paper. They were Pascal's thoughts about man's nature and his relation to his environment, his neighbors, and his God. They show Pascal's penetrating insight, his deep convictions, and his passionate piety. *Thoughts*, trans. W. F. Trotter (New York: P. F. Collier and Son, 1910). The remaining selections are from *The Thoughts, Letters, and Opuscles of Blaise Pascal*, trans. O. W. Wight (New York: Houghton Mifflin Company, 1887).

OF THE MEANS OF BELIEF

We know truth, not only by the reason, but also by the heart, and it is in this last way that we know first principles; and reason, which has no part in it, tries in vain to impugn them. The sceptics, who have only this for their object, labour to no purpose. We know that we do not dream, and however impossible it is for us to prove it by reason, this inability demonstrates only the weakness of our reason, but not, as they affirm, the uncertainty of all our knowledge. For the knowledge of first principles, as space, time, motion, number, is as sure as any of those which we get from reasoning. And reason must trust these intuitions of the heart, and must base on them every argument. (We have intuitive knowledge of the tri-dimensional nature of space, and of the infinity of number, and reason then shows that there are no two square numbers one of which is double of the other. Principles are intuited, propositions are inferred, all with certainty, though in different ways.) And it is as useless and absurd for reason to demand from the heart proofs of her first principles, before admitting them, as it would be for the heart to demand from reason an intuition of all demonstrated propositions before accepting them.

This inability ought, then, to serve only to humble reason, which would judge all, but not to impugn our certainty, as if only reason were capable of instructing us. Would to God, on the contrary, that we had never need of it, and that we knew everything by instinct and intuition! But nature has refused us this boon. On the contrary, she has given us but very little knowledge of this kind; and all the rest can be acquired only by reasoning.

Therefore, those to whom God has imparted religion by intuition are very fortunate, and justly convinced. But to those who do not have it, we can give it only by reasoning, waiting for God to give them spiritual insight, without which faith is only human, and useless for salvation.

THE HUMAN ME

... The nature of self-love and of this human *Me* is to love only self and to consider only self. But what will man do? He knows not how to prevent this object that he loves from being full of defects and miseries: he wishes to be great, and he sees himself small; he wishes to be happy, and sees himself miserable; he wishes to be perfect, and sees himself full of imperfections; he wishes to be the object of the love and esteem of men, and he sees that his defects merit only their aversion and contempt. This embarrassment wherein he finds himself produces in him the most unjust and most criminal passion that it is possible to imagine; for he conceives a mortal hatred of that truth which reproves him, and convinces him of his defects. He desires to annihilate it, and, not being able to destroy it in itself, he destroys it, as far as he can, in his own conscience and that of others: that is, he does his utmost to conceal his defects, both from others and himself, and cannot bear that they should be shown to him, or that they should be seen.

It is doubtless an evil to be full of defects; but it is a still greater evil to be full of them and to be unwilling to acknowledge them, since this is adding to them the farther evil of voluntary illusion. We are unwilling that others should deceive us; we do not regard it as just that they should wish to be esteemed by us more than they deserve: it is equally unjust then that we should deceive them, and that we should wish them to esteem us more than we deserve.

Thus, when they manifest only the imperfections and vices that we have in fact, it is evident that they do us no wrong, since they are not the cause of them; and that they do us a good, since they aid us in delivering ourselves from an evil, which is ignorance of these imperfections. We ought not to be displeased that they know them, and that they despise us, it being just both that they should know us for what we are, and that they should despise us, if we are despicable.

Such are the sentiments that would spring from a heart full of equity and justice. What ought we to say then of ours, seeing in it a wholly contrary disposition? For is it not true that we hate the truth and those who tell it to us, and that we love to have men deceive themselves in our favor, and that we wish to be esteemed by them as other than what we are in reality?

And here is a proof of it that horrifies me. The Catholic religion does not oblige us to discover our sins indifferently to everybody; it allows us to remain concealed to all other men; but it excepts one alone, to whom it commands us to discover the bottom of our hearts, and to show ourselves as we are. To none in the world but this man does the Church order us to reveal ourselves, and she binds him to inviolable secrecy, whereby this knowledge becomes in him as though it were not. Can any thing be imagined more charitable and more mild? And nevertheless the corruption of man is such, that he still finds severity in this law; and it is one of the principal reasons that has made a great part of Europe revolt against the Church.

How unjust and unreasonable is the heart of man, to be displeased with the obligation to do in regard to one man what it would be just, in some sort, he should do in regard to all men! For is it just that we should deceive them?

There are different degrees in this aversion to the truth; but it may be said that it is in all to a certain extent, since it is inseparable from self-love. It is this wretched delicacy that obliges those who are under the necessity of reproving others, to use so many circumlocutions and palliating expressions in order to avoid shocking them. It is necessary that they should diminish our defects, that they should seem to excuse them, that they should mix with them praises, and protestations of affection and esteem. Even then this medicine does not fail to be bitter to self-love. It takes as little as it can, and always with disgust, and often even with a secret spite against those by whom it is administered.

Hence it happens that, if any one has an interest in being esteemed by us, he shrinks from rendering us an office that he knows to be disagreeable to us; he treats us as we wish to be treated: we hate the truth and he conceals it from us; we wish to be flattered and he flatters us; we love to be deceived and he deceives us.

The reason why each degree of good fortune that elevates us in the world removes us farther from truth, is that men are the more apprehensive of wounding those whose affection is more useful and whose aversion is more dangerous. A prince shall be the talk of all Europe, and he alone know nothing of it. I do not wonder at it: to speak the truth is useful to him to whom it is spoken, but disadvantageous to those who speak it, because they make themselves hated. Now, those who live with princes love their own interest more than that of the prince whom they serve; and thus they do not care to secure him an advantage at their own expense.

This evil is doubtless greater and more common in the highest fortunes; but the lowest are not exempt from it, because there is always some interest in making ourselves esteemed of men. Thus human life is but a perpetual illusion; men do nothing but mutually deceive and flatter each other. No one speaks of us in our presence as he speaks of us in our absence. The union that exists among men is founded upon this mutual deception; and few friendships would subsist if each one knew what his friend says of him when he is absent, although he then speaks of him sincerely and without passion.

Man is therefore only dissimulation, only falsehood and hypocrisy, both in himself and in regard to others. He does not wish that the truth should be told him, he avoids telling it to others; and all these dispositions, so far removed from justice and reason, have a natural root in his heart. . . .

. . . Greatness of Man.—We have such a grand idea of the soul of man, that we cannot endure to be despised by it, or even not to be esteemed by it; and the whole felicity of men consists in this esteem.

The greatest baseness of man is his seeking for glory: but even this is the greatest indication of his excellence; for, whatever possession he may have on earth, whatever health and essential comfort he may have, he is not satisfied without the esteem of men. He esteems the reason of man so great, that whatever advantage he may have on earth, if he is not also advantageously situated in the reason of man, he is not content. This is the most beautiful situation in the world; nothing can turn him aside from this desire, and it is the most ineffaceable quality of man's heart.

And those who most despise men, and place them on a level with the brutes, still wish to be admired and believed by them, and contradict themselves by their own sentiment; their nature, which is stronger than all, more forcibly convincing them of man's greatness than reason convinces them of his baseness.

Man is but a reed, the weakest in nature, but he is a thinking reed. It is not necessary that the entire universe arm itself to crush him. A breath of air, a drop of water, suffices to kill him. But were the universe to crush him, man would still be more noble than that which kills him, because he knows that he dies; and the universe knows nothing of the advantage it has over him.

Our whole dignity consists, then, in thought. Our elevation must be derived from this, not from space and duration, which we cannot fill. Let us endeavor, then, to think well, this is the principle of ethics.

It is dangerous to make man see too clearly how nearly equal he is to the brutes, without showing him his greatness. It is also dangerous to make him see too clearly his greatness without his baseness. It is still more dangerous to leave him in ignorance of both. But it is very advantageous to represent to him both.

Contrarieties. After having shown the baseness and the greatness of man:—Let man now rightly estimate himself. Let him love himself, for he has in him a nature capable of good; but let him not love for this reason what is base therein. Let him despise himself, since this capacity is void; but let him not, on this account, despise the natural capacity itself. Let him hate himself, let him love himself: he has in himself the capacity of knowing truth, and of being happy; but he has no truth, either constant or satisfying.

I would therefore bring man to desire to find truth, to be ready, and free from passions, to follow it wherever he shall find it, knowing how much his knowledge is obscured by the passions; I would indeed that he hated in himself the concupiscence that determines him of itself, in order that it could not blind him in making his choice, and arrest him when he has chosen.

I equally blame those who determine to praise man, those who determine to blame him, and those who determine to divert him; and I can approve only those who seek in sorrow.

The stoics say: Enter into yourselves; there you will find your repose: and this is not true. Others say: Go out of yourselves; seek happiness in diverting yourselves: and this is not true. Diseases come: happiness is neither out of us, nor in us; it is in God, both out of, and in us. . . .

THE QUEST FOR RELIGIOUS CERTAINTY

. . . Let them at least learn what the religion is which they oppose before they oppose it. If this religion boasted of having a clear vision of God, and of possessing him directly, and without a veil, it would be indeed opposing it to declare that we see nothing in the world which discovers it with such evidence. But since religion says, on the contrary, that men are in darkness, and far from God, that he has hidden himself from their knowledge, that the very name which he gives himself in the Scriptures is, *Deus absconditus;* and, in fine, as religion equally labors to establish these two things, that God has established perceptible signs in the Church, in order to make himself known to those who seek him sincerely, and that, nevertheless, he has so far concealed these signs that he will be found only by those who seek him with all their heart, what advantage do the opponents of religion gain when, professedly neglecting to search after the truth, they cry out that nothing discovers it to them, since the very obscurity in which they are, and which they bring as an objection to the Church, does but establish one of the things which she maintains, without affecting the other, and, far from ruining, confirms her doctrine?

The opponents of religion, in order to combat it, should be able to affirm that they have used their utmost endeavors in seeking it everywhere, and even in what the Church proposes for instruction, but without any satisfaction. If they could say this, they would indeed combat one of her pretensions. But I hope to show here that no rational person can affirm this; and I even venture to assert that no person ever did. We know very well how those act who are in this spirit. They think that they have made great efforts to instruct themselves, when they have spent a few hours in reading some book of Scripture, and have put a few questions to some ecclesiastic on the truths of the faith. After that, they boast of having made fruitless searches in books, and among men. But in truth, I cannot help saying to them, what I have often said, that this negligence is insufferable. The question is not about the petty interest of some stranger, that it should be dealt with in such a manner; it is about ourselves, and our all.

The immortality of the soul is a thing which is of so much importance to us, which touches us so deeply, that we must have lost all feeling, if we are indifferent about knowing whether it is true or not. All our actions and thoughts must take such different directions, according as we have or have not the hope of eternal blessings, that it is impossible to take one step with sense and judgment, except in regulating it by keeping this point ever in view as our ultimate object.

Thus, our first interest and our first duty is to enlighten ourselves on this subject, upon which all our conduct depends. And therefore it is that, among those who are not convinced of its truth, I make an extreme difference between those who use every endeavor to instruct themselves in regard to it, and those who live without troubling themselves about it, and without thinking of it.

I can feel only compassion for those who sincerely mourn in this doubt, who regard it as the last of misfortunes, and who, sparing no effort to free themselves from it, make this investigation their chief and most serious occupation.

But those who pass their lives without thinking of this ultimate end of existence, and who, for the sole reason that they cannot find in themselves the lights which persuade them, neglect to seek them elsewhere, and to examine fundamentally whether this opinion is one of those which the people receive through credulous simplicity, or one of those which, although obsure in themselves, have nevertheless a solid and impregnable basis, I regard in a wholly different manner.

This negligence, in an affair wherein the question is concerning themselves, their eternity, and their all, irritates me much more than it excites my pity; it astonishes and overwhelms me: it is for me something monstrous. I do not say this through the pious zeal of a spiritual devotion. I mean, on the contrary, that one ought to have this sentiment by a principle of human interest and by an interest of self-love: it is only necessary for this to see what is seen by the least enlightened.

It is not necessary to have a very elevated soul in order to comprehend that there is here no true and solid enjoyment; that all our pleasures are but vanity; that our ills are infinite; and that, in fine, death which threatens us every instant must, in a few years, infallibly reduce us to the horrible necessity of eternal annihilation or misery.

There is nothing more real, more terrible, than this. We may put as brave a face on it as we will, this is the end that awaits the fairest worldly life. Let one reflect upon this, and then let him say whether it is not unquestionable that there is no good in this life but the hope of another life; that we are happy only in proportion as we attain this

hope; and that as there remain no misfortunes for those who have a full assurance of eternity, so there is no happinesss for those who, in regard to it, have no light.

It is then, assuredly, a great evil to be in doubt concerning immortality; but it is at least an indispensable duty to seek, when we are in this doubt; and, therefore, he who doubts and neglects inquiry, is at once very unhappy and very perverse. But if he is calm and contented in his doubt, if he avows it, if he boasts of it, if he is even in such a state as to make it the subject of delight and vanity, I have no terms to characterize so extravagant a being.

Where can men get these sentiments? What subject of delight is found in expecting nothing but irremediable miseries? What subject of vanity is it to behold ourselves in the midst of impenetrable darkness? And how can it happen that a rational man reasons in this way?

"I know not who has put me in the world, nor what the world is, nor what I am myself. I am in terrible ignorance of all things. I know not what my body is, what my senses are, what my soul is, and that very part of me which thinks what I am saying, which reflects upon every thing and upon itself, and knows itself no more than the rest. I view these awful spaces of the universe that surround me, and I find myself fixed to a corner of this vast extent, without knowing wherefore, I have been placed here rather than elsewhere, why this brief period of time that has been given me to live has been assigned to me now rather than at some other moment of the whole eternity that has preceded me, and of that which is to follow. I see nothing but infinities on every side, which enclose me like an atom, and like a shadow that appears but a moment and returns no more. All that I know is that I must soon die; but what I am most ignorant of, is the very death which I am unable to avoid.

"As I know not whence I came, so I know not whither I go; and I know only that in leaving this world I fall forever either into nothingness or into the hands of an angry God, without knowing which of these two conditions is to be my eternal lot. Such is my state—full of misery, weakness, obscurity. And from all this I conclude, that I ought to pass all the days of my life without thinking of what is to happen to me hereafter. Perhaps I might find some enlightenment in my doubts; but I am unwilling to take the trouble, or go a single step in search of it; and, treating with contempt those who give themselves up to such labor, I will go without forethought and without fear to try the great event, and will passively approach death, in uncertainty of the eternity of my future condition."

Who would desire to have for a friend a man who discourses in this manner? Who would select such a one for the confidant of his affairs? Who would have recourse to such a one in his afflictions? And, in fine, for what use of life could such a man be destined?

In truth it is the glory of religion to have for its enemies men so irrational; and their opposition is so little dangerous to religion, that it tends on the contrary to the establishment of her principal truths. For the Christian faith goes mainly to the establishment of these two things: The corruption of nature, and the redemption of Jesus Christ. Now if these persons do not serve to show the truth of redemption by the sanctity of their lives, they at least admirably serve to show the corruption of nature by sentiments so unnatural.

Nothing is so important to man as his condition; nothing is to him so fearful as eternity. It is, therefore, something wholly unnatural to find men indifferent to the loss of their being, and to the peril of an eternity of miseries. They are quite different in regard to all other things. They fear the merest trifles, anticipate them, feel them when they come; and that man who passes so many days and nights in rage and despair on account of the loss of an office, or some imaginary offence to his honor, is the very one who knows, without uneasiness or emotion, that he must lose everything by death. It is something monstrous to see in the same heart, and at the same time, such sensibility for the least things, and such strange insensibility for the greatest things. It is an incomprehensible delusion, and a supernatural su-

pineness, that indicates an omnipotent force as its cause.

There must be a strange revulsion in the nature of man, to make him glory in that state wherein it seems incredible that a single person should be found. Yet experience shows me so great a number of such, that this would be astonishing, if we knew not that most of those who are thus involved, counterfeit, and are not such in reality. They are people who have heard that fine worldly manners consist in thus acting the abandoned. This is what they call throwing off the yoke, and what they try to imitate. But it would not be difficult to make them understand how much they deceive themselves in thus seeking esteem. This is not the means of acquiring it, I would say, even among persons of the world, who have a sound judgment of things, and know that the only way of gaining esteem is to show themselves honest, faithful, judicious, and capable of usefully serving their friends, because men naturally love only what can be useful to them. Now, what advantage is it to us to hear a man say that he has thrown off the yoke, that he does not believe there is a God, who takes cognizance of his actions; that he regards himself as the sole master of his conduct, and that he expects to render an account of it to none but himself? Does he think thereby to induce us to have henceforth more confidence in him, and to expect from him consolation, counsel, and aid in the various needs of life? Does he think to afford us satisfaction, by telling us that he regards the human soul only as a breath or a vapor, and that too, in a proud and self-sufficient tone? Is this, then, a thing to be gayly said? Is it not a thing to be said with sadness, on the contrary, as of all things the saddest?

12. The Quakers: George Fox

From the *Journal of George Fox*. Everyman's Library Edition. Reprinted by permission of E. P. Dutton & Co., Inc. and J. M. Dent & Sons, Ltd.

[1624-1644] That all may know the dealings of the Lord with me, and the various exercises, trials, and troubles through which

He led me, in order to prepare and fit me for the work unto which He had appointed me, and may thereby be drawn to admire and glorify His infinite wisdom and goodness, I think fit (before I proceed to set forth my public travels in the service of Truth) briefly to mention how it was with me in my youth, and how the work of the Lord was begun and gradually carried on in me, even from my childhood.

I was born in the month called July, 1624, at Drayton-in-the-Clay, in Leicestershire. My father's name was Christopher Fox: he was by profession a weaver, an honest man; and there was a seed of God in him. The neighbours called him Righteous Christer. My mother was an upright woman; her maiden name was Mary Lago, of the family of the Lagos, and of the stock of the martyrs.

In my very young years I had a gravity and stayedness of mind and spirit, not usual in children; insomuch, that when I saw old men carry themselves lightly and wantonly towards each other, I had a dislike thereof raised in my heart, and said within myself, "If ever I come to be a man surely I shall not do so, nor be so wanton."

When I came to eleven years of age, I knew pureness and righteousness; for while a child I was taught how to walk to be kept pure. The Lord taught me to be faithful in all things, and to act faithfully two ways, viz., inwardly to God, and outwardly to man; and to keep to Yea and Nay in all things. For the Lord shewed me, that though the people of the world have mouths full of deceit, and changeable words, yet I was to keep to Yea and Nay in all things; and that my words should be few and savoury, seasoned with grace; and that I might not eat and drink to make myself wanton, but for health, using the creatures in their service, as servants in their places, to the glory of Him that created them; they being in their covenant, and I being brought up into the covenant, as sanctified by the Word which was in the beginning, by which all things are upheld; wherein is unity with the creation.

But people being strangers to the covenant of life with God, they eat and drink to make themselves wanton with the creatures, devouring them upon their own lusts, and living in all filthiness, loving foul ways, and devouring the creation; and all this in the world, in the pollutions thereof, without God: therefor I was to shun all such.

Afterwards, as I grew up, my relations thought to make me a priest; but others persuaded to the contrary: whereupon I was put to a man, a shoemaker by trade, and who dealt in wool, and used grazing, and sold cattle; and a great deal went through my hands. While I was with him, he was blessed; but after I left him he broke, and came to nothing. I never wronged man or woman in all that time; for the Lord's power was with me, and over me to preserve me. While I was in that service, I used in my dealings the word *Verily*, and it was a common saying among people that knew me, "If George say *Verily*, there is no altering him." When boys and rude people would laugh at me, I let them alone, and went my way; but people had

VI-11. **A Quaker Synod, 1696.** *From Arnold Lloyd,* Quaker Social History, 1669–1738 *(New York: David McKay Co., Inc., 1950). (Courtesy Trinity College, Cambridge.)*

generally a love to me for my innocency and honesty.

When I came towards nineteen years of age, being upon business at a fair, one of my cousins, whose name was Bradford, a professor, and having another professor with him, came to me and asked me to drink part of a jug of beer with them, and I, being thirsty, went in with them; for I loved any that had a sense of good, or that sought after the Lord. When we had drunk a glass apiece they began to drink healths, calling for more, and agreeing together that he that would not drink should pay all. I was grieved that any who made profession of religion should do so. They grieved me very much, having never had such a thing put to me before, by any sort of people; wherefore I rose up to be gone, and putting my hand into my pocket, laid a groat on the table before them, and said, "If it be so, I'll leave you." So I went away; and when I had done what business I had to do, I returned home, but did not go to bed that night, nor could not sleep, but sometimes walked up and down, and sometimes prayed and cried to the Lord, who said unto me, "Thou seest how young people go together into vanity, and old people into the earth; thou must forsake all, both young and old, and keep out of all, and be as a stranger unto all."

Then at the command of God, on the ninth day of the seventh month, 1643, I left my relations and brake off all familiarity or fellowship with old or young. I passed to Lutterworth, where I stayed some time; and thence to Northampton, where also I made some stay; then to Newport Pagnell, whence, after I had stayed a while, I went to Barnet, in the fourth month, called June, in 1644. As I thus traveled through the countries, professors took notice and sought to be acquainted with me; but I was afraid of them, for I was sensible they did not possess what they professed.

Now during the time that I was at Barnet, a strong temptation to despair came upon me.... I went to many a priest to look for comfort, but found no comfort from them.

From Barnet I went to London, where I took lodging, and was under great misery and trouble there; for I looked upon the great professors of the city of London, and I saw all was dark and under the chain of darkness. I had an uncle there, one Pickering, a Baptist (and they were tender then), yet I could not impart my mind to him, or join with them; for I saw all, young and old, where they were. Some tender people would have had me stay, but I was fearful, and returned homewards into Leicestershire again, having a regard upon my mind unto my parents and relations, lest I should grieve them; who, I understood, were troubled at my absence.

When I was come down into Leicestershire, my relations would have had me marry, but I told them I was but a lad, and I must get wisdom. Others would have had me into the Auxiliary Band among the soldiery, but I refused; and I was grieved that they proffered such things to me, being a tender youth. Then I went to Coventry, where I took a chamber for a while at a professor's house, till people began to be acquainted with me; for there were many tender people in that town. . . .

[1647] Now after I had received that opening from the Lord that to be bred at Oxford or Cambridge was not sufficient to fit a man to be a minister of Christ, I regarded the priests less, and looked more after the Dissenting people. Among them I saw there was some tenderness; and many of them came afterwards to be convinced, for they had some openings. But as I had forsaken the priests, so I left the Separate preachers also, and those called the most experienced people; for I saw there was none among them all that could speak to my condition. And when all my hopes in them and in all men were gone, so that I had nothing outwardly to help me, nor could I tell what to do; then, oh! then I heard a voice which said, "There is one, even Christ Jesus, that can speak to thy condition": and when I heard it, my heart did leap for joy. Then the Lord did let me see why there was none upon the earth that could speak to my condition, namely, that I might give Him all the glory; for all are concluded under sin, and shut up in unbelief, as I had been, that Jesus Christ might have the pre-eminence, who enlightens, and gives grace and faith and power. . . .

[1649] On a certain time, as I was walking in the fields, the Lord said unto me, "Thy name is written in the Lamb's book of life which was before the foundation of the world"; and, as the Lord spake it, I believed, and saw it in the new birth. Then, some time after, the Lord commanded me to go abroad into the world, which was like a briery, thorny wilderness; and when I came, in the Lord's mighty power, with the word of life into the world, the world swelled, and made a noise like the great raging waves of the sea. Priests and professors, magistrates and people, were all like a sea when I came to proclaim the day of the Lord amongst them, and to preach repentance to them.

I was sent to turn people from darkness to light, that they might receive Christ Jesus: for, to as many as should receive Him in His light, I saw that He would give power to become the sons of God; which I had obtained by receiving Christ. I was to direct people to the Spirit that gave forth the Scriptures, by which they might be led into all Truth, and so up to Christ and God, as they had been who gave them forth. I was to turn them to the grace of God, and to the truth in the heart, which came by Jesus; that by this grace they might be taught, which would bring them salvation, that their hearts might be established by it, and their words might be seasoned, and all might come to know their salvation nigh. I saw that Christ died for all men, and was a propitiation for all, and enlightened all men and women with His divine and saving light; and that none could be a true believer but who believed in it. I saw that the grace of God, which bringeth salvation, had appeared to all men, and that the manifestation of the Spirit of God was given to every man to profit withal. These things I did not see by the help of man, nor by the letter, though they are written in the letter, but I saw them in the light of the Lord Jesus Christ, and by His immediate spirit and power, as did the holy men of God by whom the Holy Scriptures were written. Yet I had no slight esteem of the Holy Scrip-

tures, but they were very precious to me, for I was in that Spirit by which they were given forth: and what the Lord opened in me I afterwards found was agreeable to them. I could speak much of these things, and many volumes might be written, but all would prove too short to set forth the infinite love, wisdom, and power of God, in preparing, fitting and furnishing me for the service He had appointed me to; letting me see the depths of Satan on the one hand, and opening to me, on the other hand, the divine mysteries of His own everlasting kingdom. . . .

[1649] Now while I was at Mansfield-Woodhouse, I was moved to go to the steeple-house there on a First-day, out of the meeting in Mansfield, and declare the truth to the priest and people; but the people fell upon me in great rage, struck me down and almost stifled and smothered me; and I was cruelly beaten and bruised by them with their hands, Bibles and sticks. Then they haled me out, though I was hardly able to stand, and put me into the stocks, where I sate some hours; and they brought dog-whips and horse-whips, threatening to whip me, and as I sate in the stocks they threw stones at me. After some time they had me before the magistrate, at a knight's house, where were many great persons; who, seeing how evilly I had been used, after much threatening set me at liberty. But the rude people stoned me out of the town, and threatened me with pistols, for preaching the word of life to them. I was scarce able to move or stand, by reason of the ill-usage I had received; yet with considerable effort I got about a mile from the town, and then I met with some people who gave me something to comfort me, because I was inwardly bruised; but the Lord's power went through me and healed me. That day some people were convinced of the Lord's truth, and turned to His teaching, at which I rejoiced. . . .

[1656] Now the Assize being over, and we settled in prison upon such a commitment, that we were not likely to be soon released, we brake off from giving the jailer seven shillings a week each for our horses, and seven for ourselves; and sent our horses out into the country. Upon which he grew very wicked and devilish; and put us down into Doomsdale, a nasty, stinking place where they used to put witches and murderers, after they were condemned to die. The place was so noisome, that it was said few went in ever came out again alive. There was no house of office in it; and the excrements of the prisoners that from time to time had been put there, had not been carried out (as we were told) for many years. So that it was all like mire, and in some places to the top of the shoes in water and piss; and he would not let us cleanse it, nor suffer us to have beds or straw to lie on. At night some friendly people of the town brought us a candle and a little straw, and we burnt a little of our straw to take away the stink. The thieves lay over our heads, and the head jailer in a room by them, over us also. Now it seems the smoke went up into the jailer's room, which put him into such a rage that he took the pots of excrements of the thieves, and poured them through a hole upon our heads in Doomsdale; whereby we were so bespattered that we could not touch ourselves or one another. And the stink increased upon us, so that what with that, and what with smoke, we had nearly been choked and smothered. We had the stink under our feet before, but now we had it on our heads and backs also; and he, having quenched our straw with the filth he poured down, had made a great smother in the place. Moreover he railed at us most hideously, calling us "hatchet-faced dogs," and such strange names as we had never heard in our lives. In this manner were we fain to stand all night, for we could not sit down, the place was so full of filthy excrements. A great while he kept us after this manner before he could let us cleanse it, or suffer us to have any victuals brought in but what we had through the grate. Once a lass brought us a little meat, and he arrested her for breaking his house, and sued her in the town Court for breaking the prison. Much trouble he put the young woman to, whereby others were so discouraged that we had much to do to get water or drink or victuals. Near this time we sent for a young woman, Anne

Downer, from London (that could write, and take things well in short-hand), to get and dress our meat for us, which she was very willing to do, it being also upon her spirit to come to us in the love of God; and she was very serviceable to us.

The head jailer, we were informed, had been a thief, and was branded in the hand and in the shoulder; his wife, too, had been branded in the hand for some wickedness.

By this time the General Quarter Sessions drew nigh; and the jailer still carrying himself basely and wickedly towards us, we drew up our sufferings and sent it to the Sessions at Bodmin; upon reading of which the justices gave order that Doomsdale door should be opened and that we should have liberty to cleanse it, and to buy our meat in the town. . . .

[1657] We passed from Manchester, having many previous meetings in several places, till we came over the Sands to Swarthmoor, where Friends were glad to see me. I stayed there two First-days, visiting Friends in their meetings thereaways. They rejoiced with me in the goodness of the Lord, who by His eternal power had carried me through and over many difficulties and dangers in His service: to Him to be the praise for ever!

And in the old Parliament's days, many people that used to wear ribands, and lace, and costly apparel, and followed junketing and feasting with priests and professors, came to leave it off when they came to be convinced of God's eternal truth, and to walk and serve God in the spirit as the Apostle did. They left off their curious apparel and ribands and lace, and their sporting and feasting with priests and professors, and would not go to wakes or plays or shows, as they formerly had used to do, and would not wear gold or silver or lace or ribands, nor make them.

Then the priests and professors raged exceedingly against us and printed books against us; and said that our religion lay in not wearing fine clothes, and lace, and ribands, and in not eating good cheer.

We told them that when they went to their sports, and games, and plays, and the like, they had better serve God than spend their time so vainly. And that costly apparel, with the lace that we formerly had hung upon our backs that kept us not warm, with that we could maintain a company of poor people that had no clothes.

And so our religion lay not in meats, nor drinks, nor clothes, nor Thee nor Thou, nor putting off hats nor making curtseys (at which they were greatly offended because we Thee'd and Thou'd them and could not put off our hats nor bow to them), and therefore they said our religion lay in such things. But our answer was, "Nay; for though the spirit of God led into that which was comely and decent, and from chambering and wantonness, and from sporting and pastimes and feasting as in the day of slaughter, and from wearing costly apparel, as the Apostle commands, and from the world's honour, fashions and customs—our religion lies in that which brings to visit the poor, and fatherless, and widows, and keeps from the spots of the world (which religion is pure and undefiled before God). This is our religion which we own, which the apostles were in above 1600 years since; and we do deny all vain religions got up since, which are not only spotted with the world, but plead for a body of sin and death to the grave; and their widows and fatherless lie begging up and down the streets and countries."

13. The Quakers: Robert Barclay

In 1675 Robert Barclay, an educated disciple of George Fox, drew up fifteen propositions to explain and vindicate the principles and doctrines of the people called Quakers. They form the headings of the fifteen chapters of his *Apology for the True Christian Divinity* (Philadelphia: Friend's Bookstore, n.d.). Cf. *Apology* . . . (New York: S. Wood & Sons, 1826). A prefatory letter was addressed to King Charles II of England.

THE FIRST PROPOSITION: CONCERNING THE
TRUE FOUNDATION OF KNOWLEDGE

Seeing the height of all happiness is placed in the true knowledge of God, ("This is life eternal, to know thee the only true God, and Jesus Christ whom thou hast sent,") the true and right understanding of this foundation and ground of knowledge, is that which is most necessary to be known and believed in the first place.

THE SECOND PROPOSITION: CONCERNING
IMMEDIATE REVELATION

Seeing "no man knoweth the Father but the Son, and he to whom the Son revealeth him"; and seeing the revelation of the Son is in and by the Spirit; therefore the testimony of the Spirit is that alone by which the true knowledge of God hath been, is, and can be only revealed; who as, by the moving of his own Spirit, he converted the chaos of this world into that wonderful order wherein it was in the beginning, and created man a living soul, to rule and govern it, so by the revelation of the same Spirit he hath manifested himself all along unto the sons of men, both patriarchs, prophets, and apostles; which revelations of God by the Spirit, whether by outward voices and appearances, dreams, or inward objective manifestations in the heart, were of old the formal object of their faith, and remain yet so to be; since the object of the saints' faith is the same in all ages, though set forth under divers administrations. Moreover, these divine inward revelations, which we make absolutely necessary for the building up of true faith, neither do nor can ever contradict the outward testimony of the scriptures, or right and sound reason. Yet from hence it will not follow, that these divine revelations are to be subjected to the examination, either of the outward testimony of the scriptures, or of the natural reason of man, as to a more noble or certain rule or touchstone: for this divine revelation and inward illumination, is that which is evident and clear of itself, forcing, by its own evidence and clearness, the well-disposed understanding to assent, irresistibly moving the same thereunto. . . .

THE THIRD PROPOSITION: CONCERNING
THE SCRIPTURES

From these revelations of the Spirit of God to the saints, have proceeded the scriptures of truth, which contain, (1) A faithful historical account of the actings of God's people in divers ages, with many singular and remarkable providences attending them.

(2) A prophetical account of several things, whereof some are already past, and some yet to come. (3) A full and ample account of all the chief principles of the doctrine of Christ, held forth in divers precious declarations, exhortations, and sentences, which, by the moving of God's spirit, were at several times, and upon sundry occasions, spoken and written unto some churches and their pastors: nevertheless, because they are only a declaration of the fountain, and not the fountain itself, therefore they are not to be esteemed the principal ground of all truth and knowledge, nor yet the adequate primary rule of faith and manners. Nevertheless, as that which giveth a true and faithful testimony of the first foundation, they are and may be esteemed a secondary rule, subordinate to the Spirit, from which they have all their excellency and certainty; for as by the inward testimony of the Spirit we do alone truly know them, so they testify, that the Spirit is that guide by which the saints are led into all truth: therefore, according to the scriptures, the Spirit is the first and principal leader....

THE FOURTH PROPOSITION: CONCERNING THE CONDITION OF MAN IN THE FALL

All Adam's posterity, or mankind, both Jews and Gentiles, as to the first Adam, or earthly man, is fallen, degenerated, and dead, deprived of the sensation of feeling of this inward testimony or seed of God, and is subject unto the power, nature, and seed of the serpent.... Man, therefore, as he is in this state, can know nothing aright; yea, his thoughts and conceptions concerning God and things spiritual, until he be disjoined from this evil seed, and united to the divine light, are unprofitable both to himself and others: hence are rejected the Socinian and Pelagian errors, in exalting a natural light; as also of the Papists, and most Protestants, who affirm, That man, without the true grace of God, may be a true minister of the gospel. Nevertheless, this seed is not imputed to infants, until by transgression they actually join themselves therewith; for they are by nature the children of wrath, who walk according to the power of the prince of the air.

THE FIFTH AND SIXTH PROPOSITIONS: CONCERNING THE UNIVERSAL REDEMPTION BY CHRIST, AND ALSO THE SAVING AND SPIRITUAL LIGHT, WHEREWITH EVERY MAN IS ENLIGHTENED

. . . .

THE SEVENTH PROPOSITION: CONCERNING JUSTIFICATION.

As many as resist not this light, but receive the same, in them is produced an holy, pure, and spiritual birth, bringing forth holiness, righteousness, purity, and all those other blessed fruits which are acceptable to God; by which holy birth, to wit, Jesus Christ, formed within us, and working his works in us—as we are sanctified, so we are justified in the sight of God.... Therefore it is not by our works wrought in our will, nor yet by good works, considered as of themselves, but by Christ, who is both the gift and the giver, and the cause producing the effects in us; who, as he hath reconciled us while we were enemies, doth also in his wisdom save us, and justify us after this manner....

THE EIGHTH PROPOSITION: CONCERNING PERFECTION

In whom his holy and pure birth is fully brought forth the body of death and sin comes to be crucified and removed, and their hearts united and subjected unto the truth, so as not to obey any suggestion or temptation of the evil one, but to be free from actual sinning, and transgressing of the law of God, and in that respect perfect. Yet doth this perfection still admit of a growth; and there remaineth a possibility of sinning, where the mind doth not most diligently and watchfully attend unto the Lord.

THE NINTH PROPOSITION: CONCERNING PERSEVERANCE, AND THE POSSIBILITY OF FALLING FROM GRACE

. . . .

THE TENTH PROPOSITION: CONCERNING THE MINISTRY

As by this gift, or light of God, all true knowledge in things spiritual is received and revealed; so by the same, as it is manifested and received in the heart, by the strength and power thereof, every true minister of the gospel is ordained, prepared and supplied in the work of the ministry: and by the leading, moving, and drawing hereof, ought every evangelist and Christian pastor to be led and ordered in his labour and work of the gospel, both as to the place where, as to the persons to whom, and as to the times when he is to minister. Moreover, those who have this authority may and ought to preach the gospel, though without human commission or literature; as on the other hand, those who want the authority of this divine gift, however learned or authorized by the commissions of men and churches, are to be esteemed but as deceivers, and not true ministers of the gospel. Also, who have received this holy and unspotted gift, "as they have freely received, so are they freely to give," without hire or bargaining, far less to use it as a trade to get money by it: yet if God hath called any from their employments, or trades, by which they acquire their livelihood, it may be lawful for such, according to the liberty which they feel given them in the Lord, to receive such temporals—to wit, what may be needful to them for meat and clothing— as are freely given them by those to whom they have communicated spirituals.

THE ELEVENTH PROPOSITION:
CONCERNING WORSHIP

All true and acceptable worship of God is offered in the inward and immediate moving and drawing of his own Spirit, which is neither limited to places, times, or persons; for though we be to worship him always, in that we are to fear before him, yet as to the outward signification thereof in prayers, praises, or preachings, we ought not to do it where and when we will, but where and when we are moved thereunto by the secret inspirations of his Spirit in our hearts, which God heareth and accepteth of, and is never wanting to move us thereunto, when need is, of which he himself is the alone proper judge. All other worship then, both praises,

prayers and preachings, which man sets about in his own will, and at his own appointment, which he can both begin and end at his pleasure, do or leave undone, as himself sees meet, whether they be a prescribed form, as a liturgy, or prayers conceived extemporarily, by the natural strength and faculty of the mind, they are all but superstitions, will-worship, and abominable idolatry in the sight of God; which are to be denied, rejected, and separated from, in this day of his spiritual arising. . . .

THE TWELFTH PROPOSITION:
CONCERNING BAPTISM

As there is one Lord and one faith, so there is "one baptism; which is not the putting away the filth of the flesh, but the answer of a good conscience before God, by the resurrection of Jesus Christ." And this baptism is a pure and spiritual thing, to wit, the baptism of the spirit and fire, by which we are buried with him, that being washed and purged from our sins, we may "walk in newness of life"; of which the baptism of John was a figure, which was commanded for a time, and not to continue for ever. As to the baptism of infants, it is a mere human tradition, for which neither precept nor practice is to be found in all the scripture.

THE THIRTEENTH PROPOSITION: CONCERNING
THE COMMUNION, OR PARTICIPATION OF
THE BODY AND BLOOD OF CHRIST

The communion of the body and blood of Christ is inward and spiritual, which is the participation of his flesh and blood, by which the inward man is daily nourished in the hearts of those in whom Christ dwells; of which things and breaking of bread by Christ with his disciples was a figure, which they even used in the church for a time, who had received the substance, for the cause of the weak; even as "abstaining from things strangled, and from blood"; the washing one another's feet, and the anointing of the sick with oil; all which are commanded with no less authority and solemnity than the former; yet seeing they are but the shadows of better things, they cease in such as have obtained the substance.

THE FOURTEENTH PROPOSITION: CONCERNING THE POWER OF THE CIVIL MAGISTRATE, IN MATTERS PURELY RELIGIOUS, AND PERTAINING TO THE CONSCIENCE

Since God hath assumed to himself the power and dominion of the conscience, who alone can rightly instruct and govern it, therefore it is not lawful for any whatsoever, by virtue of any authority or principality they bear in the government of this world, to force the consciences of others; and therefore all killing, banishing, fining, imprisoning, and other such things, which men are afflicted with, for the alone exercise of their conscience, or difference in worship or opinion, proceedeth from the spirit of Cain, the murderer, and is contrary to the truth; provided always, that no man, under the pretence of conscience, prejudice his neighbour in his life or estate; or do anything destructive to, or inconsistent with human society; in which case the law is for the transgressor, and justice to be administered upon all, without respect of persons.

THE FIFTEENTH PROPOSITION: CONCERNING SALUTATIONS AND RECREATIONS, &C.

Seeing the chief end of all religion is to redeem man from the spirit and vain conversation of this world, and to lead into inward communion with God, before whom, if we fear always, we are accounted happy; therefore all the vain customs and habits thereof, both in word and deed, are to be rejected and forsaken by those who come to this fear; such as the taking off the hat to a man, the bowings and cringings of the body, and such other salutations of that kind, with all the foolish and superstitious formalities attending them; all which man has invented in his degenerate state, to feed his pride in the vain pomp and glory of this world; as also the unprofitable plays, frivolous recreations, sportings and gamings, which are invented to pass away the precious time, and divert the mind from the witness of God in the heart.

SUGGESTED READINGS

Addison, W. G., *Renewed Church of the United Brethren,* 1722-1930. London: SPCK, 1932.

Anderson, W. K., ed., *Methodism.* Nashville: Methodist Publishing House, 1947.

Brailsford, Mabel R., *A Tale of Two Brothers: John and Charles Wesley.* New York: Oxford University Press, Inc., 1954.

Braithwaite, W. C., *Beginnings of Quakerism.* New York: Cambridge University Press, 1912.

———, *Second Period of Quakerism.* New York: Cambridge University Press, 1961.

Bready, J. W., *England: Before and After Wesley, the Evangelical Revival and Social Reform.* New York: Harper & Row, Publishers, 1938.

Brinton, Howard, *Friends for Three Hundred Years.* New York: Harper & Row, Publishers, 1952.

Brown, Ford K., *Fathers of the Victorians.* New York: Cambridge University Press, 1961.

Caillet, Emile, *Pascal.* New York: Harper & Row, Publishers, 1961.

Cannon, William R., *The Theology of John Wesley.* Nashville: Abingdon Press, 1946.

Carter, Henry, *The Methodist Heritage.* Nashville: Abingdon Press, 1951.

Cell, George C., *The Rediscovery of John Wesley.* New York: Holt, Rinehart & Winston, Inc., 1935.

Davies, Horton, *The English Free Churches.* London: Oxford University Press, 1952.

Deschner, John, *Wesley's Christology.* Dallas: Southern Methodist University Press, 1960.

Edwards, M., *John Wesley and the 18th Century.* Nashville: Abingdon Press, 1933.

Elliott-Binns, L. E., *The Early Evangelicals: A Religious and Social Study.* London: Lutterworth Press, 1953.

Flew, R. Newton, *The Idea of Perfection in Christian Theology*. London: Oxford University Press, 1934.

Green, J. Brazier, *John Wesley and William Law*. London: The Epworth Press, 1945.

Knox, R. A., *Enthusiasm*. London: Oxford University Press, 1950.

Langton, Edward, *History of the Moravian Church*. London: George Allen & Unwin, 1956.

Lee, Umphrey, *John Wesley and Modern Religion*. Nashville: Abingdon Press, 1936.

Legg, J. W., *English Church Life, 1660-1833*. London: Longmans, Green & Company, Ltd., 1914.

Lindström, Harald, *Wesley and Sanctification*. Stockholm: Nya Bokförlags Aktiebolaget, 1946.

MacArthur, Kathlene W., *The Economic Ethics of John Wesley*. Nashville: Abingdon Press, 1936.

Moorman, J. R. H., *A History of the Church in England*. London: Adam and Charles Black, Ltd., 1953.

Nagler, A. W., *Pietism and Methodism*. Nashville: Smith and Lamar, 1918.

Noble, Vernon, *The Man in Leather Breeches*. New York: Philosophical Library, 1953.

Piette, Maximin, *John Wesley in the Evolution of Protestantism*. New York: Sheed & Ward, 1937.

Rattenbury, J. E., *Wesley's Legacy to the World*. Nashville: Abingdon Press, 1928.

————, *Eucharistic Hymns of John and Charles Wesley*. Naperville, Ill.: Alec R. Allenson, Inc., 1948.

————, *Evangelical Doctrines of Charles Wesley's Hymns*. Naperville, Ill.: Alec R. Allenson, Inc., 1954.

Simon, John S., *John Wesley and the Methodist Societies*. London: Epworth Press, 1921.

————, *John Wesley and the Advance of Methodism*. London: The Epworth Press, 1925.

————, *John Wesley, the Last Phase*. London: The Epworth Press, 1934.

————, *John Wesley, The Master Builder*. London: The Epworth Press, 1934.

Sykes, N., *Church and State in England in the XVIIIth Century*. Cambridge, England: Cambridge University Press, 1934.

Telford, John, *Methodist Hymnbook*, 6th ed. London: Epworth Press, 1952.

Towlson, Clifford W., *Moravian and Methodist*. Naperville, Ill.: Alec R. Allenson, Inc., 1957.

Wesley, John, *Works*. Various editions.

Wilberforce, William, *A Practical View of the Prevailing Religious System*. London: Student Christian Movement Press, Ltd., 1958.

Williams, Colin, *John Wesley and Theology Today*. Nashville: Abingdon Press, 1960.

Recordings:

Bach, J. S., *Mass in B*, Marshall, Epic Records; Robert Shaw Chorale, RCA Victor Records. (Many Chorales, Fugues, Concertos, Sonatas, Preludes, etc.)

Handel, G., *Israel in Egypt*, Christiansen, Bumbry, Blackburn, Utah Symphony, Utah University Choruses, Westminster Recording Corp., Morison, Sinclair, Lewis, Sargent, Huddersfield Choral Society, Liverpool Philharmonic, Angel Records.

————, *Messiah*, Addison, Sydney, Lloyd, Gramm, Stine, Boston Handel & Haydn Society, Kapp Records; RCA Vyvyan, Sinclair, Vickers, Tozzi, Beecham, Royal Philharmonic and Chorus, Victor Records.

Haydn, Franz Joseph, *Creation*, Grummer, Traxel, Frick, Berlin Symphony, Electra Records; Seefried, St. Hedwig's Choir, Berlin Philharmonic, Decca Records, Inc.

Mozart, W., *Requiem*, Jurinac, West, Loeffler, Guthrie, Vienna Academy Chorus, Westminster Recording Corp., Seefried, Tourel, Simoneau, New York Philharmonic, Columbia Records.

Pergolesi, G., *Stabat Mater*, Sailer, Muench, Mainz Chorus and Orchestra, Vox Recordings.

CHRONOLOGY

1555	Peace of Augsburg	1727	Death of August Francke
1607–1676	Paul Gerhardt, hymns	1728	Law's Serious Call
1618–1648	Thirty Years' War, Peace of Westphalia	1735–1737	Wesleys in America
		1737	Early Methodist hymnal
1630	Invasion, Gustavus Adolphus	1738	Handel's Israel in Egypt
1632	Death of Adolphus	1738	Wesley's Aldersgate Experience
1634	Death of Wallenstein	1740	Great Awakening in America
1640	Death of Rubens	1741	Handel's Messiah
1643	Fox begins his wanderings	1743	Rules for Methodist Societies
1656	Pascal's Provincial Letters	1748	Death of Isaac Watts
1670	Pascal's Pensées published	1750	Death of J. S. Bach
1675	Spener's Pia Desideria Barclay's Apology Molinos' Spiritual Guide	1750–1798	Christian F. Schwartz in India
		1758–1833	William Wilberforce
1680	Death of Giovanni Bernini	1761	Death of William Law
1685	Edict of Nantes revoked	1776	American Declaration of Independence
1689	English Act of Toleration		
1698	Francke's Orphan House, Halle	1780	Methodist large hymn book
1703	Birth of John Wesley	1784	Coke "ordained" bishop
1705	Death of Philip Spener	1784	Methodist Twenty-five Articles
1707	Francke's Marvellous Footsteps	1788	Death of Charles Wesley
1710	St. Paul's Cathedral completed	1789	French Revolution
1722	Moravians at Herrnhut	1791	Death of John Wesley

Illustration opposite page 315: The Book of Job: Then the Lord Answered Job Out of the Whirlwind. *Engraving by William Blake, poet and painter, author of* "Tiger, tiger burning bright." *A romantic reaction to rationalism. National Gallery of Art, Washington, D.C., Rosenwald Collection.*

Who is this that darkeneth counsel by words without knowledge

Then the Lord answered Job out of the Whirlwind

Who maketh the Clouds his Chariot & walketh on the Wings of the Wind   the Drops of the Dew

Hath the Rain   a Father & who hath begotten

WBlake invent & sculp

VII

Modernism and New Forms

The French Revolution constitutes one of
the great crises in modern Christianity. With it, the already
tottering old regime came to a dramatic, sudden end,
and the forces of free thought and liberalism that marked the
nineteenth century became dominant. Many quarters hailed the
Revolution as a political victory in the extension of the universal rights
of man, for it was a revolt against institutional corruption,
inefficiency, oppression, and privilege. It was the outburst
of a new individualism which was rooted in Gallicanism,
the rationalistic understanding of man's worth, and the
principles of Marsiglio of Padua and William of Occam, who startled
the fourteenth century with the theory that power comes from
the people, who simply delegate it to those who govern
and who can rightfully deprive the rulers of it if it is misused.
The Revolution was dedicated to the ideal that every man
is entitled to liberty, equality, and fraternity.
Back of it were the probes of philosophers like Hume and Kant,
who were skeptical of the assertions that men have knowledge
of divine or ultimate realities; the caustic pens of Voltaire and

the French *philosophes*, who lashed out at hypocrisy and injustice in the institutions of men; and the emotional writings of men like Rousseau and Jefferson, who wanted to restore life to its natural simplicity (*1*).

But the French Revolution seemed to others to be the end of law and order, especially when its violence became widespread. Conservative Roman Catholicism and Protestantism both recoiled from the French Revolution with a sense of horror and a feeling that something drastic had occurred. Both felt its challenge. Roman Catholicism refused to assimilate the new trends, and Protestantism tended to compromise with them. Despite the dramatic shattering of many old forms, the Roman Catholics reasserted their ultramontane claims. They took defensive measures against a liberalism that seemed to them to question and disdain the authoritative claims of the church. The reconstitution in 1814 of the Society of Jesus and the pronouncement of the *Syllabus of Errors* in 1864, the dogma of infallibility of the pope in 1870, and the encyclicals of Pope Leo XIII were expressions of Roman Catholic defensive reaction. (Cf. Ch. 8.) Protestantism tended to cling to traditional forms, but cautiously explored new ways and adopted new ideas from the theologies of men like Schleiermacher, who brought psychological insights into religion, and of men like Strauss and Renan, who brought higher criticism to bear on the Bible. In attempting to come to terms with the new trends, Protestantism drifted farther away from the orthodoxies of the Reformation and acquired a liberalistic spirit that expressed itself in the social gospel. (Cf. Ch. 9.)

The French Revolution was complex in its origins, but the corruption and fiscal desperation of the French state under Louis XVI were its immediate causes. The French national debt in 1789 had soared to four and a half billion *livres*, a debt comparable to that of the United States after World War II, and Louis XVI was hard pressed to find a way out of his fiscal morass. When the King convoked the Estates-General in 1789, it was the first time it had been done in almost two hundred years. Many Frenchmen who had deep grievances against the entrenched aristocracy of a privileged royalty and clergy began to imagine that a new form of representative government similar to the American experiment might be inaugurated. They looked for far-reaching changes. But the King's original aim was to use the Estates-General only to enact measures that would stabilize the fiscal condition of the country and curb the abuses of economic and political privilege exercised by a parasitic nobility in the church and state. The bourgeoisie of the Third Estate—the bankers, industrialists, business men, and professionals—provided the strength of the first phase of the Revolution and gave it stability; but the second phrase erupted into a reign of terror and a *culte decadaire,* secular culture based on a ten-day week in order to offset the influence of Christianity.

On June 20, 1789, many members of the Estates-General took the famous Tennis Court Oath, in which they swore that they would not disband until France had a new constitution that would establish the government on a firm foundation. They proclaimed themselves the National Assembly, and by June 27 the King and the estates of the clergy and nobles acquiesced. But open revolt was already in the air. On July 14, the Bastille, symbol of authoritarian oppression, fell before the onslaught of a Parisian mob. Although the Bastille's fall became a rallying cry for the revolutionary forces of France, only a few criminals, two of whom were mental cases, were found behind its walls. The breach of the Bastille signalled rioting and disorder, which the new National Assembly sought to quell in a series of revolutionary decrees. Meeting on the night of August 4-5, 1789, the Assembly abolished feudal dues, and on August 27 published the *Declaration of the Rights of Man and Citizen* (*2, 3*). A feeling prevailed that the old ways were yielding to new, which were unleashing fearful forces that could not easily be controlled. The National Assembly had wrested power from the nobility and the clergy, violence had occurred in Paris and the provinces, and neighboring countries had mustered military forces to protect their interests.

On November 2, 1789, the National Assembly, which had already deprived the church of its papal annates, seized the property of the church in France, about one-fifth of the total property of the country, and used it as security for the issuance of assignats. In return, the Assembly announced that henceforth all salaries of local clergymen would be paid from the funds of the state. Because the wealth of the church had previously been unevenly distributed, many of the lower clergy, whose Gallican loyalties were already strong, supported the Assembly's nationalization and sale of clerical lands. *Te Deums* rang from many churches in celebration of the revolutionary progress. On February 13, 1790, the Assembly suspended all monastic vows, retroactive three months. The clergy had become functionaries of the state.

That appeals were not made to Pope Pius VI shows how strongly France was entrenched in Gallicanism. On March 29, 1790, the Pope did condemn the liberalism and democracy that were implied in the course of the Revolution, for these principles ran counter to those of the church. He reacted against the ideas that law is derived from the people, that all citizens have a right to legislative representation, that non-Roman Catholic religions should have rights in a state, and that non-Catholics should have an equal right to hold public office. The Pope's protest was not publicized, however, and the Revolution gained momentum.

On July 12, 1790, the Assembly enacted into law the *Civil Constitution of the Clergy*, which was an idealistic attempt to bring the clergy into line with the reforms of the state (4). The *Constitution* disestablished Roman Catholicism, pruned the number of dioceses from 139 to 83 to conform with the boundaries of the civil departments, dissolved papal investiture, discontinued monasteries, set a scale for clerical salaries, decreased the number of clergymen, and regulated the election of pastors and the naming of the metropolitan bishops. The principles of election and a committee for control of bishops were Gallican ideals readily acceptable to the lower clergy, who were already receiving more salary than formerly and to whom the way for advancement would be opened. Opposition was negligible; the committee which drew up the civil constitution was chaired by a bishop!

Opposition did not materialize until October 30, 1790, when one French cardinal and twenty-nine bishops issued a manifesto decrying the altering of the ways of the church by civil powers. In angry reaction, the Assembly passed a law requiring that all clerics take an oath to obey the law and the constitution. But this ran counter to the deep loyalties of Catholics to the church as the representative of God on earth, to whom they should be obedient rather than to men; only a little more than half the clergy complied. This Gallican crisis developed largely without reference to the Pope, who did not speak decisively until April 13, 1791, when he told the clergy not to sign the oath and reprimanded such bishops as Talleyrand and Lomenie de Brienne for having done so. He annulled the elections and consecrations that had taken place in accordance with the civil constitution and pronounced the document schismatical and heretical. Signers were given forty days to retract.

This papal action led to a divided church in France, some clergymen, the jurors, supporting the French civil constitution, and some, the non-jurors, supporting the papacy. The laity was also divided, and occasional violence flared into civil war. The King, who agreed to the constitution because he saw no other real alternative, now prepared for flight. He and his Queen, Marie Antoinette, disguised as a Russian lady and her valet, fled Paris on June 21, 1791. At Varennes, about one hundred fifty miles from Paris, they were recognized and detained for return to Paris, where they were imprisoned in the Tuileries. Reports circulated that if France were attacked, the King would be decapitated and the Queen would be tied to a horse's tail and dragged through the streets of Paris. Royalists and papalists, now identified as counter-revolutionaries, suffered increased persecution. The Assembly, to appease foreign political critics, moved to guarantee freedom of worship in August, 1791, but this meant little to the non-jurors, for local churches were closed except for officially sanctioned services.

When France was pressed by outside military foes in 1792, the King was formally deposed and a newly organized National Convention declared France a Republic. To secure internal unity, priests were required to take an oath to maintain liberty and equality. Those who refused were given fifteen days to emigrate. Many of these *émigrés* were abused, robbed, and lynched, but some 40,000 managed to leave France. Others suffered in the September massacres, which claimed the lives of two thousand antirevolutionary sympathizers and left France in the hands of its most extreme revolutionists.

Although the National Convention sought to establish a Republic of Virtue, charges that the Revolution was utterly atheistic and lawless prompted external alliances against France, and massive fear gripped the country. By 387 to 334, the Convention voted to execute the King; Louis XVI was beheaded January 21, 1793 (5). His execution served as a warning that none, regardless of position, could defy the Convention. The La Vendée revolt in the spring of 1793 brought sentences of exile to Guiana and decrees of death to many Frenchmen. By June of 1793, literally thousands went to the guillotine, bringing to a bloody climax the Reign of Terror.

Ironically, the revolutionaries promoted Worship of Reason during this period, so that outside critics would not think France was without virtue. They equated the Worship of Reason with patriotism, and Christianity was emasculated. The National Convention, on May 7, 1794, passed a decree establishing worship of a Supreme Being (6). "My Country" oaths were required on Bastille Day, libations were poured out to statues of nature, political heroes replaced saints, and churches were turned into "temples of reason." Goddesses of Reason appeared in Notre Dame, and in more than 2,000 village churches. The state forbade clergymen and nuns to teach in the public schools and discontinued the payment of clerical salaries. The inauguration of a ten-day week abolished Sundays and saints' days. The *culte decadaire* reached its climax when Robespierre celebrated Reason's Festival of the Supreme Being on June 8, 1794. Representations of Vice, Folly, and Atheism were burned and a Statue of Wisdom raised, with an inscription declaring that "the French people recognize the existence of the Supreme Being and the immortality of the soul." Bishop Gobel and eleven priests donned red caps in the Convention and discarded their crosses and rings.

When Robespierre's program of reason and virtue failed to bring the desired results in foreign negotiations, the Thermidorian revolt ensued and cost Robespierre his head on the guillotine. Two days later, on July 30, 1794, his supporting commune, about sixty persons, were guillotined in less than an hour and a half. The Thermidorian reaction continued the nationalistic cult of reason, but it also opened the way for a religious revival late in 1795 when Abbé Gregoire, a member of the Convention, spoke up for liberty of worship. During the period of the Directory, 1795 to 1799, Gregoire managed a Gallican compromise of the constitution, so that by 1797 Catholic parish churches were again crowded. Even Protestants were allowed to worship publicly.

This was the religious situation that Napoleon Bonaparte (1769-1821) inherited when he worked his *coup d'état* in 1799. Military genius that he was, Napoleon took charge of the tottering French armies, stabilized the fronts in the Netherlands, along the Rhine, and in Switzerland. He then invaded Italy with the intention of securing indemnity from the Pope and a retraction of all anti-Revolution bulls and encyclicals. When Pope Pius VI sought Austrian aid, Napoleon marched on Rome itself. Radicals in Rome rioted, and the Pope was forced to abdicate. He died in exile at Valence in that same year. His obituary in the French registry was terse: "Citizen John Braschi. Trade: pontiff." Some cardinals assisted in the *Te Deum* in St. Peter's which marked the deposition of Pius VI.

Unlike the early French extremists, Napoleon saw the utility of the papacy in his schemes for empire, and in 1801 he sought a reconciliation with the papacy, saying that only the one true church could lay a firm foundation for government. As emperor he would need the respectability of a Roman Catholic sanction, and a reconciliation with the papacy would undercut any moves toward royal restoration in France. By the Concordat of 1801, Napoleon resumed the paying of clerical salaries, stabilized the finances of the French church, and guaranteed freedom of worship; but at the same time he required an oath of loyalty and the right to nominate new bishops. Pope Pius VII subscribed to these terms, believing that only Napoleon was powerful enough to sway Europe's future (7).

To the surprise of the Pope, when the Concordat was proclaimed it was accompanied by a series of Organic Articles declaring that Napoleon could act as he saw fit for the advancement of France. The Articles provided that Gallican principles be taught, that governmental approval be sought for all church meetings and papal pronouncements, and that appeals be made from the church to civil powers. The Pope was unable to protest effectively; he even journeyed to Paris and assisted in the crowning of Napoleon as emperor in 1804. But Napoleon, remembering Charlemagne, placed the crown on his own head.

When Pope Pius VII refused to play the role of Napoleon's lackey, in 1809 the Emperor seized the papal states and confined Pius to prison in France. Even though Pope Pius seemed to have no influence, he excommunicated Napoleon. For five years the Pope languished in prison, but when Napoleon's empire crumbled in 1815, the papacy emerged with greater moral prestige than at any time since the sixteenth century. The reconstitution of the Jesuits in 1814 marked the return of Catholicism to ultramontane principles. Although liberal Gallican principles flared briefly in France in the 1830's, successive encyclicals marked the rejection of rationalistic liberalism in its many forms and set the stage for modern Roman Catholic conservativism. (Cf. Ch. 8.)

The violent disintegration of the old regime left Europe in turmoil, but the French Revolution for all its complexity was the crucible from which modern religion emerged. A shocked Europe awakened to the necessity of facing ideas and forces that were to shape Western civilization.

Rationalism dominated the eighteenth century. Its manifestations, especially in the French Revolution, prompted a variety of reactions, one of which was an upsurge of romanticism. In contrast to rationalism, the romantic movement was characterized by an emphasis on the emotions of man, a desire for the simplicity of idealized nature, a longing for the beauty and tranquility of the past, and a renewed interest in man's universal feeling for the supernatural (8, 9).

VII-1. Tampoco. *A depiction of the horrors of the Napoleonic wars. Etching and aquatint from* The Disasters of War *by Francisco Goya, 1810. National Gallery of Art, Washington, D.C., Rosenwald Collection.*

Jean Jacques Rousseau (1712-1778) was one of romanticism's early representatives. In 1749, in his first serious essay, which won him a literary prize, he argued that man's achievements in the sciences have tended to retard human development. His two best-known works, published in 1762, were *Emile*, on education, and *The Social Contract*, on man's social organization. In the latter, he maintained that men originally were equal and good, and that social environment subsequently rendered them unequal and bad. He called on men to return to the happy "state of nature" through a strict enforcement of the social compact, that is, by keeping the laws which are an expression of the general will, so that all men may have a maximum of protection and freedom. Unlike most of his rationalist contemporaries in France, Rousseau gave much attention to man's emotional promptings. This linked him to the romantic movement, while his thoughts on popular sovereignty endeared him to the French revolutionists (1).

In England, a towering romanticist was William Wordsworth (1770-1850). Rousseau directly influenced his interest in nature, and the French Revolution deepened his sympa-

VII-2. The Thinker. *A symbol of rational man displacing Christ and brooding over the possible meaninglessness of life. Sculpture by Auguste Rodin (1840–1917), Rodin Museum, Philadelphia Museum of Art, Philadelphia, Pennsylvania.*

thy with the poor and unjustly oppressed. In all his poetry, Wordsworth sought to find harmony and to bring beauty out of the chaos of life. The simple, familiar things of nature and human life furnished him with inspiration, for he felt that the artificialities of society had obscured the unspoiled goodness of man (8). The novels of Sir Walter Scott (1771-1832) were popular, in part at least, because Scott introduced the pageantry and color of the medieval world to an age tired of orthodoxy and critical rationalism.

In Germany, romanticism found expression, especially in its early period, in the literary works of Johann Wolfgang von Goethe (1749-1832) and Johann Christoph Friedrich von Schiller (1759-1805). But the greatest expression of religious romanticism came from Friedrich Schleiermacher (1768-1834), often called the father of modern theology. A hospital chaplain in Berlin when he wrote his *Speeches* in 1799, he later became professor of theology at the newly established University of Berlin, a post which he held from 1810 to the time of his death. In *On Religion: Speeches to Its Cultured Despisers*, 1799, he boldly proclaimed religion as one of mankind's noblest intellectual pursuits, and in his principal theological work, *The Christian Faith*, 1821-22, he developed a system of dogmatics based on a feeling of Absolute Dependence (9).

Immanuel Kant (1724-1804) had left uncertain the position of religion. In the *Critique of Pure Reason*, 1781, Kant limited knowledge to phenomena or appearances. If man cannot know things-in-themselves, i.e. ultimate reality, a rational theology which deals with ultimates is impossible. However, in his *Critique of the Practical Reason*, 1788, Kant recognized a categorical, unconditional moral obligation in man which makes sense only in relation to the postulates of God, freedom, and immortality. In his work, *Religion Within the Limits of Reason Alone*, 1793, Kant showed the practical consequences of his insights. (Cf. Ch. 5.) Kant discussed morality, without which human life becomes chaos, as a recognition and acceptance of the sense of ought which is common to mankind. However, moral consciousness, as developed by Kant, did not necessarily vindicate religious consciousness, and, indeed it left many religious practices suspect as expressions of vested interests.

Schleiermacher brought to this critical analysis of morality a deep sense of Moravian piety and romantic idealism which pictured man as a mirror of the universe. He discarded the notion that Christianity is a system of fixed dogmas, divinely revealed, and looked to himself for the springs of religion. There he found a sense of absolute dependence, revealed to him by his creaturely existence in time. He felt an utter dependence on something beyond himself, something which is the very ground of all creation. The consciousness of this dependence is man's immediate consciousness of God. This feeling, this intuited contact with reality, Schleiermacher averred, is the spring of all religions, and the goal of all religion is to unite man with God, the Absolute on which he depends. This inward consciousness of God manifests itself in actions, which are its ceremonies, and in doctrines, which are its convictions; but the emotions of the religious self-consciousness are antecedent to the development of ceremonies and doctrines. For Schleiermacher, Christianity was superior to other religions because Christ was fully God-conscious; he brought together the temporal and the eternal. In him, the God-consciousness was so powerful and perfect that God could be said to dwell in him. Christ redeems men by imparting to them the strength and vitality of his own consciousness of God, which men are to seek for themselves. The religious life requires men to live individually and corporately in accordance with the consciousness of the Absolute which is immanent in the world, throughout all, and it has myriad expressions. To sin is to allow something other than this God-consciousness to become the mainspring of one's life; self-centeredness breaks the harmony of man's relation to the family, the community, the state, the world, and the Absolute. The church is the institutionalized, corporate fellowship, animated by the Holy Spirit, for the preservation of the feeling of God-consciousness. Dogmas are never absolute; they are temporary expressions of the feeling of absolute dependence, and may be altered to conform with one's feeling (9). Both the orthodox and the rationalists thought Schleiermacher was too extreme, but he influenced all of modern theology.

Samuel Taylor Coleridge (1772-1834) was Schleiermacher's counterpart in England. Religious romanticism echoed in Coleridge's *Rhyme of the Ancient Mariner,* in the God who "made and loveth all." In his *Aids to Reflection,* 1825, he found that the proofs of Christianity are internal and moral, rooted in a religious consciousness. He insisted that reason by an inward sense intuits realities beyond the natural realm of cause and effect, and that the existence of God is presupposed in the conscience of mankind.

Schleiermacher's contemporary, G. W. F. Hegel (1770-1831), stressed an entirely different aspect of Kant. He discarded the position that things-in-themselves are unknowable and declared that in back of all reality is the Absolute Spirit, which is manifesting itself in this world in a grandiose scheme of thesis, antithesis, and synthesis. Reality, therefore, is open to man's intellect; he has only to see the rhythm of this rational process, which is in all aspects of life, in order to comprehend the Absolute Spirit or Idea in its latest manifestation. All philosophy, history, and nature are but manifestations in time of the Absolute Spirit coming to self-consciousness. As no manifestation is adequate to express the Absolute Spirit, every thesis gives rise to an antithesis, and the reconciliation of the two in a synthesis, which becomes another thesis in a process in which all differentiations will finally be reconciled. This Absolute Spirit comes to its highest expression in man, in philosophy; religion is a figurative expression of it for those who do not understand philosophy. Hegel exalted Christianity as the one absolutely true religion because its figurative expressions coincided with his philosophical notions. He saw in the Trinity of Father, Son, and Holy Spirit an example of thesis (the abstract idea, Father), antithesis (the Son incarnate), and synthesis (return of the Absolute to itself, Holy Spirit). Hegel believed that he had

321

found the key to all truth. His impact on religion was felt not so much in content as in method, for he felt that his pattern of thought could be applied to everything—science, literature, history, art, and so on.

Disciples were not long in applying Hegel's method. F. C. Baur (1792-1860) inaugurated a new era of biblical criticism by applying it to the Bible. In Peter's picturing of Jesus as the normal fulfillment of the Messianic expectations of the Jews, Baur found the thesis. In Paul's depiction of Jesus as divine he found the antithesis. And in the early creeds he found a synthesis of the conflict between these Petrine and Pauline concepts of early Christianity. Armed with this theory, Baur redated many biblical writings. He declared that Matthew was the oldest Gospel because of its Judaizing tones; he dated Mark late because it seemed to obscure the early conflict. He accepted only Romans, Galatians, and Corinthians as genuine early Pauline epistles, because only in them did he find strong anti-Judaizing tendencies.

Elements of both Hegel and Schleiermacher found expression in D. F. Strauss (1808-1874), who applied the tools of rationalistic criticism to the sources of the life of Jesus and concluded that Jesus was simply a man, around whom the expectations of a Messiah crystallized and produced the myth of Christ. These views he embodied in his *Life of Jesus*, 1835. Even more widely read than this was Ernest Renan's *Life of Jesus*, 1863. He united critical skepticism and romantic imagination so as to divest Jesus of divinity and to present him as a human being with all the ordinary emotions of a man (10).

Albert Ritschl (1822-1889) carried the rationalistic process and romanticism further by asserting that we may never know a thing-in-itself, but we do know the value of something. We may not know the exact nature of a pencil, but we know its value. In the same way, said Ritschl, we may not know the exact historical or metaphysical nature of Christ, but we are conscious of the value of Christ in our lives, not only as individuals but as a community, the church. Thus Ritschl introduced value judgments as a basic element in religion, and explored the ramifications of

this in his monumental theological work, *The Christian Doctrine of Justification and Reconciliation*, 1870-1874.

Many Christians feared that religion had been betrayed and that critical rationalism was too confidently leading people too far afield.

Other men reacted to the trends by drifting back to the orthodox certainties expressed in Roman Catholicism. Typical of the return to orthodoxy was the revival of religious fervor in the Oxford Movement. As early as 1827 John Keble (1792-1866), who became Professor of Poetry at Oxford, wrote *The Christian Year*, a series of poems based on the Collects, Epistles, and Gospels of the English church. Some of Keble's poems are sung as hymns today: "Sun of my soul, Thou Saviour dear," "New every morning is the love," "Blest are the pure in heart," and so forth. These poems were immensely popular, although they predated the Oxford Movement by six years.

As a result of the French Revolution many institutions felt threatened, particularly the Church of England, where the rising industrial classes and liberals in religion were demanding a voice in government. A sign of the times was that London University, founded in the 1820's and chartered in 1836, required no religious tests. The established church bitterly fought the Reform Bill of 1832, which sought to break the political hold of the Church of England. Roman Catholics who had fled to England as a result of the French Revolution supported orthodoxy, but wanted recognition for themselves. The Anglican Church was entrenched but was manifestly lacking in spiritual vigor and the highest morals, as *The Extraordinary Black Book* with its propagandized scandals disclosed in 1831.

The leaders of the Oxford Movement felt that the Church of England was being disfranchised and that religion would cease to be central in English life. In his sermon on National Apostasy, July 14, 1833, John Keble accused the nation of infringing on apostolic rights and thus disavowing the sovereignty of God. Salvation, he declared, is possible only through the sacraments administered through bishops in the apostolic succession. To the Oxford group, apostolic succession and the dignity of the Prayer Book were primary, and their writings revolved around these. In 1833 John Henry Newman (1801-1890), who had been on a trip to Italy during which time he wrote "Lead, kindly Light, amid the encircling gloom," began writing *Tracts for the Times,* soon to create a sensation by their defense of orthodox religious views. The state did not create the church, he declared, and the state had no right to destroy it. Edward B. Pusey (1800-1882) also became active in 1833, and was so powerful a voice that the movement is sometimes called "Puseyism" as a mark of disdain. The group's defense of apostolic succession drew it closer and closer to the historic tenets of Roman Catholicism. Newman expounded the conservative way of the Church of England as the *Via Media* between Roman Catholicism and Protestantism. His arguments drifted more and more toward Catholicism

VII-3. Dr. Pusey Preaching. *A contemporary sketch. British Museum.*

(*11*). His *Tract XC* in 1841 tried to show that Anglicanism and Roman Catholicism were basically in agreement and that the *Thirty-nine Articles* of Anglicanism opposed only the corruptions in Romanism (*12*). *Tract XC* brought forth charges of Jesuitism, Roman Catholic infiltration, and betrayal, and the movement lost much of its force. Pusey was suspended from preaching at the University in 1843. W. G. Ward in 1844 wrote his *Ideal of a Christian Church*, in which he defended his right to hold Roman Catholic doctrine and still be an Anglican; for this his university degrees were taken from him. Newman joined the Roman Catholic Church on October 9, 1845, along with several hundred other Englishmen. *Apologia Pro Vita Sua*, 1864, is his long defense of the move. As the controversies continued, the number of secessionists to Rome grew. In 1851 Archbishop Manning, who had been a tract writer, made the decision to join Rome. For his ultramontane support he was made Archbishop of Westminster in 1865 and cardinal ten years later. Newman, who was not ultramontane, did not become a cardinal until 1879.

The Oxford Movement opposed latitudinarianism and state dominance of the church. It appealed to tradition as a source of doctrine, looked upon the early councils as authoritative, emphasized apostolic succession, and stressed sacramental grace. No other movement served more to vitalize English church life in the mid-nineteenth century.

Religious music was not one of the dominant aspects of the period during and following the French Revolution. The musical giant of the time was Ludwig van Beethoven (1770-1827), but he was not especially interested in church music, even though he wrote some masses. He brought instrumental music to its culmination. The period did not produce a Charles Wesley or an Isaac Watts, although some well-known hymns reflect facets of the times, such as, "Thou whose almighty hand" by John Marriott (1780-1825), "Silent Night" by Joseph Mohr (1792-1848), "Holy, holy, holy" and "Brightest and best of the Sons of the morning" by Reginald Heber (1783-1826), "Angels from the realms of glory" and "Prayer is the soul's sincere desire" by James Montgomery (1771-1854), and others.

The French Revolution brought rationalism to its political climax, disintegrated the old regime, and ushered in the nineteenth century with its complexities of reaction and new forms, its intermingling of liberalism, orthodoxy, and romanticism. The restoration of the Jesuits in 1814 marked the orthodox reaction to radical change, and the 1817 decree of Frederick William II of Germany, uniting the Lutheran and Calvinistic churches as the United Evangelical Church, a decree supported by Schleiermacher, marked a broader expression of Protestantism which de-emphasized dogmantic creeds. These two responses to the complicated factors of the French Revolution are the subjects of the two following chapters.

1. Voltaire, Rousseau, and Jefferson

François-Marie Arouet de Voltaire was one of the firebrands that ignited the French Revolution. When he died in 1778, the Bishop of Paris refused him Christian burial. May 30, 1791, the revolutionary French National Assembly ordered his remains brought to Paris and interred with a hero's honors. His popular acclaim by the revolutionaries is shown in the accounts of his funeral, the first from the diary of Lord Palmerston (1885) and the other from J. G. Milligen's *Recollections of Republican France* (1848). From Louis L. Snyder and Richard B. Morris, *They Saw it Happen* (Harrisburg, Pa.: The Stackpole Co., 1951).

Jean Jacques Rousseau was not a revolutionary, but his *Social Contract*, exploring the idea that individuals unite in society for self-preservation, and that society is to protect each person and allow him as much freedom as possible, provided a backdrop for the changes that came to France. His description of "civil religion" in the closing chapters of *The Social Contract* seems to presage the French Revolution. James H. Robinson, *Readings in European History*, II (Boston: Ginn & Company, 1906).

Thomas Jefferson (1743-1826), author of America's Declaration of Independence, influenced the French Revolution with his political and religious ideas. He was the author of the "Statute of Virginia for Religious Freedom," adopted in 1786, and his deistic views of religion helped establish reason as a popular authority. His Deism is well expressed in a letter to his nephew, Peter Carr, in 1787. *The Statutes at Large; Being a Collection of All the Laws of Virginia,* ed. William W. Hening (Richmond: George Cochran, 1823); also Andrienne Koch and William Peden, eds., *Life and Selected Writings of Thomas Jefferson* (New York: Modern Library, Inc., 1944).

I. This afternoon the procession of Voltaire took place though the weather was very unfavorable as it was found inconvenient to defer it. It was very long, but a great part of it consisted of very shabby, ill-dressed people whose appearance was made worse by the mud and dirt they had collected. Great quantities of National Guards attended; but in disorder and without arms, except such as were on duty. Deputations of different orders of people and among others the Academy.

A figure of Voltaire, very like him, in a gown was carried first sitting in an elbow chair, and afterwards came the coffin on a very fine triumphal car drawn by twelve beautiful grey horses four abreast. The coffin was covered and over it a waxen figure was laid on a bed. After having made a great circuit round the town they came to the house of the Marquis de Villette, who is married to Voltaire's niece and where he died. There the figures stopped, a kind of hymn was sung, Madame Villette and her child came down, mounted the car and embraced the figure and then with several other ladies followed it on foot during the remainder of the procession, to the new Church of St. Geneviève where it is to be deposited.

II. My father took me, on the preceding evening, to the place of the Bastille, where the remains of this illustrious writer were placed on a pedestal raised on the ruins of the very prison in which he had once been confined. The following day, the procession that accompanied his sarcophagus to the Pantheon, was as numerous as the mass of mourners who followed the mortal remains of Mirabeau. The whole was got up in theatrical style. All the actors and actresses, singers and dancers, of the different theatres, were grouped round a statue of the philosopher, in the various costumes of his *dramatis personae.* Zaire was walking next to Mohammed, Julius Caesar arm-in-arm with Oedipus, and Brutus with the widow of Malabar; while another group represented Calas and his family. One of the most singular objects in the procession was a portable press, which worked off various hand-bills, as the *cortège* proceeded, which were scattered amongst the people. [The rehabilitation of the Huguenot, Jean Calas, a victim of religious prejudice, was considered to be one of Voltaire's greatest strokes against intolerance.]

ROUSSEAU ON CIVIL RELIGION

Christianity is a purely spiritual religion, occupied solely with heavenly things; the country of a Christian is not of this world. He does his duty, it is true, but he does it with a profound indifference as to the good or ill success of his efforts. Provided he has nothing to reproach himself with, it matters little to him whether things go well or ill here below. If the state is flourishing, he scarcely dares enjoy the public felicity; he fears to become proud of the glory of his country. If the state degenerates, he blesses the hand of God which lies heavy upon his people. . . .

Should the depository of this [political] power abuse it, he regards this abuse as the rod with which God punishes his children. People would have scruples about driving out the usurper: it would be necessary to disturb the public repose, to use violence, to shed blood; all this accords ill with the gentleness of a Christian, and, after all, what matters it whether one is a slave or free in this vale of misery? The essential thing is to go to paradise, and resignation is but one more means to accomplish it.

Should some foreign war supervene, the citizens march to combat without difficulty. None among them think of flying; they do their duty but without passion for victory; they know better how to die than to win. Whether they are victors or vanquished, what matters it? Does not Providence know better than they what they need? . . .

But I am in error in speaking of a Christian republic; each of these words excludes the other. Christianity preaches only servitude and dependence. Its spirit is too favorable to tyranny not to be taken advantage of by it. Christians are made to be slaves: they know it and do not care; this short life has too little value in their eyes. . . .

There is, however, a profession of faith purely civil, of which it is the sovereign's [i.e., the people's] duty to decide upon the articles, not precisely as dogmas of religion, but as sentiments of sociality without which it is impossible to be a good citizen or a faithful subject. Without being able to oblige any one to believe them, the sovereign can banish from the state whoever does not believe them; the sovereign should banish him, not as impious, but as unsocial, as incapable of loving law and justice sincerely, and of sacrificing at need his life to his duty. If any one, having publicly acknowledged these dogmas, conducts himself as if he did not acknowledge them, he should be punished with death; he has committed the greatest of crimes,—he has lied before the law.

The dogmas of civil religion should be simple, few in number, announced with precision, without explanation or commentary. The existence of a powerful, intelligent, benevolent, prescient, and provident Divinity, the life to come, the happiness of the just, the punishment of the wicked, the sacredness of the social contract and the law,—these are the positive dogmas.

As to the negative dogmas, I limit them to one,—intolerance: it enters into the religions which we have excluded. Those who make a distinction between civil intolerance and theological intolerance deceive themselves, to my mind. These two intolerances are inseparable. It is impossible to live in peace with people whom one believes to be damned; to love them is to hate God, who punishes them; they must be redeemed or else tortured. Wherever theological intolerance is admitted, it must have some civil effects; and as soon as it has them the sovereign is no more a sovereign, even in temporal matters. From that time priests are the true masters; kings are but their officers.

JEFFERSON'S DEISM

Your reason is now mature enough to examine this object [religion]. In the first place, divest yourself of all bias in favor of novelty and singularity of opinion. Indulge them in any other subject rather than that of religion. It is too important, and the consequences of error may be too serious. On the other hand, shake off all the fears and servile prejudices, under which weak minds are servilely crouched. Fix reason firmly in her seat, and call to her tribunal every fact, every opinion. Question with boldness even the existence of a God; because, if there be one, he must more approve of the homage of reason, than that of blindfolded fear. You will naturally examine first, the religion of your own country. Read the Bible, then, as you would read Livy or Tacitus. The facts which are within the ordinary course of nature, you will believe on the authority of the writer, as you do those of the same kind in Livy and Tacitus. The testimony of the writer weighs in their favor, in one scale, and their not being against the laws of nature, does not weigh against them. But those facts in the Bible which contradict the laws of nature, must be examined with more care, and under a variety of faces. Here you must recur to the pretensions of the writer to inspiration from God. Examine upon what evidence his pretensions are founded, and whether that evidence is so strong, as that its falsehood would be more improbable than a change in the laws of nature, in the case he relates. For example, in the book of Joshua, we are told, the sun stood still several hours. Were we to read that fact in Livy or Tacitus, we should class it with their showers of blood, speaking of statues, beasts, etc. But it is said, that the writer of that book was inspired. Examine, therefore, candidly, what evidence there is of his having been inspired. The pretension is entitled to your inquiry, because millions believe it. On the other hand, you are astronomer enough to know how contrary it is to the law of nature that a body revolving on its axis, as the earth does, should have stopped, should not, by that sudden stoppage, have prostrated animals, trees, buildings, and should after a certain time have resumed its revolution, and that without a second general prostration. Is this arrest of the earth's motion, or the evidence which affirms it, most within the law of probabilities? You will next read the New Testament. It is the history of a personage called Jesus. Keep in your eye the opposite pretensions: 1) of those who say he was begotten by God, born of a virgin, suspended and re-

versed the laws of nature at will, and ascended bodily into heaven; and 2) of those who say he was a man of illegitimate birth, of a benevolent heart, enthusiastic mind, who set out with pretensions to divinity, ended in believing them, and was punished capitally for sedition, by being gibbeted, according to the Roman law, which punished the first commission of that offence by whipping, and the second by exile, or death in furea....

Do not be frightened from this inquiry by any fear of its consequences. If it ends in a belief that there is no God, you will find incitements to virtue in the comfort and pleasantness you feel in its exercise, and the love of others which it will procure you. If you find reason to believe there is a God, a consciousness that you are acting under his eye, and that he approves you, will be a vast additional incitement; if that there be a future state, the hope of a happy existence in that increases the appetite to deserve it; if that Jesus was also a God, you will be comforted by a belief of his aid and love. In fine, I repeat, you must lay aside all prejudice on both sides, and neither believe nor reject anything, because any other persons, or description of persons, have rejected or believed it. Your own reason is the only oracle given you by heaven, and you are answerable, not for the rightness, but uprightness of the decision....

2. The Feudal System

The fall of the Bastille signaled riots and pillaging throughout France. The Assembly sought to pacify the aroused peasants by abolishing many ancient abuses, and on the night of August 4 and 5, 1789, decreed an end to the feudal system. When enacted into law August 11, the revolutionary fervor was tempered by providing for certain redemptions, compensations, and obligations. Robinson, *Readings in European History*.

DECREE ABOLISHING THE FEUDAL SYSTEM, AUGUST 11, 1789

1. The National Assembly hereby completely abolishes the feudal system. It decrees that, among the existing rights and dues, both feudal and *censuel*, all those originating in or representing real or personal

serfdom shall be abolished without indemnification. All other dues are declared redeemable, the terms and mode of redemption to be fixed by the National Assembly. Those of the said dues which are not extinguished by this decree shall continue to be collected until indemnification shall take place.

2. The exclusive right to maintain pigeon houses and dovecotes is abolished. The pigeons shall be confined during the seasons fixed by the community. During such periods they shall be looked upon as game, and every one shall have the right to kill them upon his own land.

3. The exclusive right to hunt and to maintain uninclosed warrens is likewise abolished, and every landowner shall have the right to kill, or to have destroyed on his own land, all kinds of game, observing, however, such police regulations as may be established with a view to the safety of the public.

All hunting *capitaineries*, including the royal forests, and all hunting rights under whatever denomination, are likewise abolished. Provision shall be made, however, in a manner compatible with the regard due to property and liberty, for maintaining the personal pleasures of the king.

The President of the Assembly shall be commissioned to ask of the king the recall of those sent to the galleys or exiled, simply for violations of the hunting regulations, as well as for the release of those at present imprisoned for offenses of this kind, and the dismissal of such cases as are now pending.

5. Tithes of every description, as well as the dues which have been substituted for them, under whatever denomination they are known or collected (even when compounded for), possessed by secular or regular congregations, by holders of benefices, members of corporations (including the Order of Malta and other religious and military orders), as well as those devoted to the maintenance of churches, those impropriated to lay persons, and those substituted for *portion congrue*, are abolished, on condition, however, that some other method be devised to provide for the expenses of divine worship, the support of the officiating clergy, for the assistance of

the poor, for repairs and rebuilding of churches and parsonages, and for the maintenance of all institutions, seminaries, schools, academies, asylums, and organizations to which the present funds are devoted. Until such provision shall be made and the former possessors shall enter upon the enjoyment of an income on the new system, the National Assembly decrees that the said tithes shall continue to be collected according to law and in the customary manner.

Other tithes, of whatever nature they may be, shall be redeemable in such manner as the Assembly shall determine. Until this matter is adjusted, the National Assembly decrees that these, too, shall continue to be collected.

9. Pecuniary privileges, personal or real, in the payment of taxes are abolished forever. Taxes shall be collected from all the citizens, and from all property, in the same manner and in the same form. Plans shall be considered by which the taxes shall be paid proportionally by all, even for the last six months of the current year.

11. All citizens, without distinction of birth, are eligible to any office or dignity, whether ecclesiastical, civil, or military; and no profession shall imply any derogation.

12. Hereafter no remittances shall be made for annates or for any other purpose to the court of Rome, the vice legation at Avignon, or to the nunciature at Lucerne. The clergy of the diocese shall apply to their bishops in regard to the filling of benefices and dispensations, the which shall be granted *gratis* without regard to reservations, expectancies, and papal months, all the churches of France enjoying the same freedom.

3. *Declaration of the Rights of Man and of the Citizen, August 27, 1789*

On August 27, 1789, the Assembly enacted its Declaration of the Rights of Man, a document which became the Revolution's gospel. It was aimed at entrenched abuses, but note its inadequacy on right of assembly and religious liberty. Robinson, *Readings in European History.*

The representatives of the French people, organized as a National Assembly, believing that the ignorance, neglect, or contempt of the rights of man are the sole cause of public calamities and of the corruption of governments, have determined to set forth in a solemn declaration the natural, inalienable, and sacred rights of man, in order that this declaration, being constantly before all the members of the social body, shall remind them continually of their rights and duties; in order that the acts of the legislative power, as well as those of the executive power, may be compared at any moment with the objects and purposes of all political institutions and may thus be more respected; and, lastly, in order that the grievances of the citizens, based hereafter upon simple and incontestable principles, shall tend to the maintenance of the constitution and redound to the happiness of all. Therefore the National Assembly recognizes and proclaims, in the presence and under the auspices of the Supreme Being, the following rights of man and of the citizen:

1. Men are born and remain free and equal in rights. Social distinctions may be founded only upon the general good.

2. The aim of all political association is the preservation of the natural and imprescriptible rights of man. These rights are liberty, property, security, and resistance to oppression.

3. The principle of all sovereignty resides essentially in the nation. No body nor individual may exercise any authority which does not proceed directly from the nation.

4. Liberty consists in the freedom to do everything which injures no one else; hence the exercise of the natural rights of each man has no limits except those which assure to the other members of the society the enjoyment of the same rights. These limits can only be determined by law.

5. Law can only prohibit such actions as are hurtful to society. Nothing may be prevented which is not forbidden by law, and no one may be forced to do anything not provided for by law.

6. Law is the expression of the general will. Every citizen has a right to participate personally, or through his representative, in its formation. It must be the same for all, whether it protects or punishes. All citizens, being equal in the eyes of the law, are equally eligible to all dignities and to all public positions and occupations, according to their abilities, and without distinction except that of their virtues and talents.

7. No person shall be accused, arrested, or imprisoned except in the cases and according to the forms prescribed by law. Any one soliciting, transmitting, executing, or causing to be executed, any arbitrary order, shall be punished. But any citizen summoned or arrested in virtue of the law shall submit without delay, as resistance constitutes an offense.

8. The law shall provide for such punishments only as are strictly and obviously necessary, and no one shall suffer punishment except it be legally inflicted in virtue of a law passed and promulgated before the commission of the offense.

9. As all persons are held innocent until they shall have been declared guilty, if arrest shall be deemed indispensable, all harshness not essential to the securing of the prisoner's person shall be severely repressed by law.

10. No one shall be disquieted on account of his opinions, including his religious views, provided their manifestation does not disturb the public order established by law.

11. The free communication of ideas and opinions is one of the most precious of the rights of man. Every citizen may, accordingly, speak, write, and print with freedom, but shall be responsible for such abuses of this freedom as shall be defined by law.

12. The security of the rights of man and of the citizen requires public military forces. These forces are, therefore, established for the good of all and not for the personal advantage of those to whom they shall be intrusted.

13. A common contribution is essential for the maintenance of the public forces and for the cost of administration. This should be equitably distributed among all the citizens in proportion to their means.

14. All the citizens have a right to decide, either personally or by their representatives, as to the necessity of the public contribution; to grant this freely; to know to what uses it is put; and to fix the proportion, the mode of assessment and of collection and the duration of the taxes.

15. Society has the right to require of every public agent an account of his administration.

16. A society in which the observance of the law is not assured, nor the separation of power defined, has no constitution at all.

17. Since property is an inviolable and sacred right, no one shall be deprived thereof except where public necessity, legally determined, shall clearly demand it, and then only on condition that the owner shall have been previously and equitably indemnified.

4. The Civil Constitution of the Clergy, July 12, 1790

The Civil Constitution represented the assumption of control of the church by the National Assembly, but it also produced a division in the loyalty of the clergy which was to last throughout the Revolution. The Assembly assumed that it had every right to take this action and made no overtures to the papacy. In accordance with Gallican tradition, the Assembly reorganized the episcopal structure, provided for elections, and set a new salary scale—in effect disfranchised the papacy. The most important articles are given below. John Hall Stewart, *A Documentary Survey of the French Revolution* (New York: The Macmillan Company, 1951). Reprinted with permission of the publisher.

The National Assembly, having heard the report of its Ecclesiastical Committee, has decreed and does decree the following as constitutional articles.

TITLE I: OF ECCESIASTICAL OFFICES

1. Each and every department shall constitute a single diocese, and each and every diocese shall have the same extent and limits as the department.

2. The episcopal sees of the eighty-three departments of the kingdom shall be established as follows: . . .

All bishoprics in the eighty-three departments of the kingdom which are not included by name in the present article are and shall forever remain suppressed.

The kingdom shall be divided into ten metropolitan districts, the seats of which shall be Rouen, Rheims, Besançon, Rennes, Paris, Bourges, Bordeaux, Toulouse, Aix, and Lyons. The metropolitan sees shall have the following denominations. . . .

4. No church or parish of France, and no French citizen, may, under any circumstances or on any pretext whatsoever, acknowledge the authority of an ordinary bishop or archbishop whose see is established under the name of a foreign power, or that of its delegates residing in France or elsewhere; without prejudice, however, to the unity of faith and communion, which shall be maintained with the Visible Head of the Universal Church as hereinafter provided.

6. A new organization and division of all parishes of the kingdom shall be undertaken immediately, upon the advice of the diocesan bishop and the district administrations; the number and extent thereof shall be determined according to rules to be established.

8. The episcopal parish shall have no other immediate pastor than the bishop. All priests established therein shall be his vicars, and shall perform the duties thereof.

9. There shall be sixteen vicars of the cathedral church in cities of more than 10,000 inhabitants, but only twelve where the population is fewer than 10,000 inhabitants.

15. In all cities and towns of not more than 6,000 inhabitants there shall be only one parish; other parishes shall be suppressed and united with the principal church.

16. In cities of more than 6,000 inhabitants every parish may include a greater number of parishioners, and as many parishes shall be preserved or established as the needs of the people and the localities require.

20. All titles and offices, other than those mentioned in the present constitution, dignities, canonries, prebends, half prebends, chapels, chaplaincies, in both cathedral and collegiate churches, and all regular and secular chapters of either sex, abbeys and priories, regular or *in commendam,* of either sex, and all other benefices and *prestimonies* in general, of whatever kind and under whatever denomination, are abolished and suppressed dating from the day of publication of the present decree, and similar ones may never be established.

TITLE II: OF APPOINTMENT TO BENEFICES

1. Dating from the day of publication of the present decree, appointments to bishoprics and cures are to be made by election only.

2. All elections shall be by ballot and absolute majority of votes.

6. The election of the bishop may take place or be initiated only on a Sunday, in the principal church of the chief town of the department, following the parochial mass, at which all electors are required to be present.

7. To be eligible for a bishopric, one must have performed for at least fifteen years the duties of ecclesiastical ministry in the diocese, in the capacity of *curé*, officiating minister or vicar, or as superior or directing vicar of the seminary.

16. Not later than a month subsequent to his election, the bishop-elect shall present himself in person to his metropolitan bishop; and if elected to the metropolitan see, to the oldest bishop of the *arrondissement,* with the *procès-verbal* of the election and proclamation, and shall request him to grant canonical confirmation.

17. The metropolitan or the senior bishop shall have the right to examine the bishop-elect, in the presence of his council, concerning his doctrine and morals. If he considers him qualified, he shall give him canonical institution; if he believes it his duty to refuse, the reasons for such refusal shall be given in writing, signed by the metropolitan bishop and his council, reserving to the interested parties the right to appeal by writ of error as provided hereinafter.

18. The bishop from whom confirmation is requested may not exact of the bishop-elect any oath other than profession of the Catholic, Apostolic, and Roman religion.

19. The new bishop may not apply to the Pope for confirmation, but shall write to him as the Visible Head of the Universal Church, in testimony of the unity of faith and communion which he is to maintain therewith.

21. Before the ceremony of consecration begins, the bishop-elect shall take a solemn oath, in the presence of the municipal officials, the people, and the clergy, to watch with care over the faithful of the diocese entrusted to him, to be faithful to the nation, to the law, and to the King, and to maintain with all his power the Constitution decreed by the National Assembly and accepted by the King.

TITLE III: OF SALARIES OF MINISTERS OF RELIGION

1. Ministers of religion, performing the primary and most important functions of society, and obliged to reside continuously in the place of service to which the confidence of the people has called them, shall be maintained by the nation.

2. All bishops, *curés*, and officiating ministers in annexes and chapels of ease shall be furnished with suitable dwellings, on condition, however, that they make all repairs for which tenants are liable, without intending for the present to introduce anything new with regard to parishes where the priest now receives money instead of a dwelling, and reserving to the department cognizance of demands made by parishes and *curés;* moreover, salaries shall be assigned to all as indicated hereinafter.

TITLE IV: OF THE LAW OF RESIDENCE

1. The law of residence shall be strictly observed, and all who are invested with an ecclesiastical office or function shall be subject thereto without distinction or exception.

2. No bishop may absent himself from his diocese for more than fifteen consecutive days during any year, except in case of real necessity and with the consent of the directory of the department in which his see is located.

3. Likewise, *curés* and vicars may not absent themselves from the place of their duties beyond the term established above, except for serious reasons; and even in such cases the *curés* shall be required to obtain the consent of both their bishop and their district directory, the vicars that of their *curés*.

6. Bishops, *curés*, and vicars may be present at the primary and electoral assemblies as active citizens. They may be appointed electors, deputies of the legislatures, elected members of the general council of the commune and of the district and departmental administrative councils; but their functions are declared incompatible with those of mayor and other municipal officials, and of members of the district and departmental

directories; and if elected thereto they shall be required to make their choice.

5. *The Guillotine and Its Victims*

The guillotine became the dreaded machine of the French Revolution. Dr. Guillotin, a member of the Assembly, proposed its use on December 1, 1789, as a quick and painless method of execution. A German named Schmidt contracted to build eighty-three of the machines, one for each of the departments of France, at a cost of 824 francs each. First tried on three corpses, April 18, 1792, it proved so efficient that it was used to decapitate literally hundreds in the weeks that followed. During the Reign of Terror, 1793-94, 2,500 were executed in Paris alone, and 10,000 in other parts of France. The following are eyewitness accounts which describe the work of the guillotine and the execution of Louis XVI. The first is from Snyder and Morris, *They Saw It Happen*. The second is taken from *The Times*, London, January 26, 1793.

ACCOUNT OF ARCHIBALD H. ROWAN

Never can I forget the mournful appearance of the funereal processions to the place of execution. The march was opened by a detachment of mounted gendarmes—the carts followed. They were the same carts as those that are used in Paris for carrying wood; four boards were placed across them for seats, and on each board sat two, and sometimes three victims. Their hands were tied behind their backs, and the constant jolting of the carts made them nod their heads up and down, to the great amusement of the spectators. On the front of the cart stood Samson, the executioner, or one of his sons or assistants. Gendarmes on foot marched by the side. Then followed a hackney-coach, in which was the *Rapporteur* and his clerk, whose duty it was to witness the execution, and then return to Fouquier-Tinville, the *Accusateur Public,* to report the execution to what they called the law.

The process of execution was also a sad and heart-rending spectacle. In the middle of the Place de la Révolution was erected a guillotine, in front of a colossal statue of Liberty, represented seated on a rock, a Phrygian cap on her head, a spear in her hand, and the other reposing in a shield.

On one side of the scaffold were drawn out a sufficient number of carts, with large baskets painted red, to receive the heads and bodies of the victims. Those bearing the condemned moved on slowly to the foot of the guillotine; the culprits were led out in turn, and, if necessary, supported by two of the executioner's valets, but their assistance was rarely required.

Most of these unfortunates ascended the scaffold with a determined step—many of them looked up firmly on the menacing instrument of death, beholding for the last time the rays of the glorious sun, beaming on the polished axe. I have seen some young men actually dance a few steps before they went up to be strapped to the perpendicular plane, which was then tilted to a horizontal plane in a moment, and ran on the grooves until the neck was secured and closed in by a moving board, when the head passed through what was called, in derision, *la lunette républicaine* (the republican toilet-seat). The weighty knife was then dropped with a heavy fall; and with incredible dexterity and rapidity, two executioners tossed the body into the basket, while another threw the head after it.

THE EXECUTION OF LOUIS XVI

By an express which arrived yesterday morning from Messrs. Fester & Co. at Dover, we learn the following particulars of the King's execution:

At six o'clock on Monday morning, the King went to take a farewell of the Queen and royal family. After staying with them some time, and taking a very affectionate farewell of them, the King descended from the Tower to the Temple, and entered the Mayor's carriage, with his confessor and two members of the Municipality, and passed slowly along the boulevards which led from the Temple to the place of execution. All women were prevented from appearing in the streets, and all persons from being seen in their windows. A strong guard cleared the procession.

The greatest tranquillity prevailed in every street through which the procession passed. At about half past nine the procession arrived at the place of execution, which was the Place de Louis XV between the pedestal which formerly supported the statue of his grandfather and the promenade of the

Elysian Fields. Louis mounted the scaffold with composure, and that modest intrepidity peculiar to oppressed innocence, the trumpets sounding and drums beating during the whole time. He made a sign of wishing to harangue the multitude, when the drums ceased, and Louis spoke these few words: "I die innocent; I pardon my enemies, I only sanctioned upon compulsion the Civil Constitution of the Clergy." He was proceeding, but the beat of the drums drowned his voice. His executioners then laid hold of him, and, an instant later, his head was separated from his body. This was about a quarter past ten o'clock.

After the execution the people threw their hats up in the air, and cried out *Vive la Nation!* Some of them endeavored to seize the body, but it was removed by a strong guard to the Temple, and the lifeless remains of the King were exempted from those outrages which his Majesty had experienced during his life.

The King was attended on the scaffold by an Irish priest as his confessor, not choosing to be accompanied by one who had taken the National oath. He was dressed in a brown great coat, white waist coat and black breeches, and his hair was powdered.

M. de Malsherbes announced to Louis the final sentence of death. "Ah," exclaimed the monarch, "I shall then at length be delivered from cruel suspense."

Since the decree of death was issued, a general consternation has prevailed through Paris—the Sans Culottes are the only persons to rejoice. The honest citizens, immured within their habitations, could not express their heartfelt grief and mourned in private with their families the murder of their much-loved sovereign.

The last requests of the unfortunate Louis breathe the soul of magnanimity, and a mind enlightened with the finest of human virtues. He appears not to be that man which the enemies reported. His heart was sound, his head was clear, and he would have reigned in glory, had he but possessed those faults which his assassins laid to his charge. His mind possessed the suggestions of wisdom; and even in his last moments, when the spirit of life was winged for another world,

his lips gave utterance to them, and he spoke with firmness and resignation.

Thus has ended the life of Louis XVI, after a period of four years' detention; during which he experienced from his subjects every species of ignominy and cruelty which a people could inflict upon the most sanguinary tyrant.

Long in the habit of supporting the virtues of this unhappy victim of savage Republicanism; and, steady in persevering to declare, that his highest ambition was the happiness of his people, we hold ourselves justified, from the universal indignation which has marked this last act of cruelty exercised against him, to pay our sorrowing tribute to his memory, and join with the millions in Europe, in supplicating the wrath of Heaven, and the vengeance of mankind, to extend to his unnatural murderers the most exemplary punishment.

6. Decree Establishing the Worship of the Supreme Being, May 7, 1794

To implement the "civic religion" implied in Rousseau's idea that the state should be responsible for the spiritual life of its citizens, the Convention enacted a decree establishing worship of the Supreme Being. The decree extended the already widespread cult of reason and nationalism, and was a conscious attempt to displace traditional Catholicism. In the following month, Robespierre celebrated the famous Festival of the Supreme Being. Stewart, *A Documentary Survey of the French Revolution.*

1. The French people recognize the existence of the Supreme Being and the immortality of the soul.

2. They recognize that the worship worthy of the Supreme Being is the observance of the duties of man.

3. They place in the forefront of such duties detestation of bad faith and tyranny, punishment of tyrants and traitors, succoring of unfortunates, respect of weak persons, defence of the oppressed, doing to others all the good that one can, and being just towards everyone.

4. Festivals shall be instituted to remind man of the concept of the Divinity and of the dignity of his being.

5. They shall take their names from the glorious events of our Revolution, or from

the virtues most dear and most useful to man, or from the greatest benefits of nature.

6. The French Republic shall celebrate annually the festivals of 14 July, 1789, 10 August, 1792, 21 January, 1793, and 31 May, 1793.

7. On the days of *decade* it shall celebrate the following festivals:

To the Supreme Being and to nature; to the human race; to the French people; to the benefactors of humanity; to the martyrs of liberty; to liberty and equality; to the Republic; to the liberty of the world; to the love of the *Patrie;* to the hatred of tyrants and traitors; to truth; to justice; to modesty; to glory and immortality; to friendship; to frugality; to courage; to good faith; to heroism; to disinterestedness; to stoicism; to love; to conjugal love; to paternal love; to maternal tenderness; to filial piety; to infancy; to youth; to manhood; to old age; to misfortune; to agriculture; to industry; to our forefathers; to our posterity; to happiness.

8. The Committees of Public Safety and Public Instruction are responsible for presenting a plan of organization for said festivals.

9. The National Convention summons all talents worthy of serving the cause of humanity to the honor of concurring in their establishment by hymns and civic songs, and by every means which may contribute to their embellishment and utility.

10. The Committee of Public Safety shall designate the works which seem to it the most suitable to realize these objectives, and shall compensate their authors.

11. Liberty of worship is maintained, in conformity with the decree of 18 Frimaire.

12. Every assembly which is aristocratic and contrary to public order shall be repressed.

13. In case of disturbances occasioned or motivated by any worship whatsoever, those who instigate them by fanatical preaching or counter-revolutionary insinuations, or those who provoke them by unjust and gratuitous violence, likewise shall be punished according to the rigor of the law.

14. A special report shall be made concerning the arrangements of detail relative to the present decree.

15. A festival in honor of the Supreme Being shall be celebrated on 20 Prairial next.

David is charged with presenting a plan therefor to the National Convention.

7. Concordat Between Pope Pius VII and Napoleon, July 15, 1801

Sensing the value of the Pope for his political ambitions, Napoleon resolved in 1800, while still a French consul, to end the tensions that had resulted from the enforcement of the Civil Constitution of 1790. He would recognize the Roman Catholic Church as "dominant" in France and assume the payment of all clerical salaries if the Pope would make all bishops resign and let the state name new ones. After negotiations in Paris, the Concordat of July 15, 1801, was signed. The Pope thought Napoleon was to be the great leader of Europe, and he approved the Concordat, even though Catholicism was recognized only as the religion of the majority. The Organic Articles, proclaimed by Napoleon in April, 1802, stripped the Pope of real power and position and led to the disputes that resulted in Napoleon's seizing the papal states in 1809. The Articles stressed that the state, by necessity, had to approve papal announcements, religious ceremonies, and so on. From *Church and State Through the Centuries,* by Sidney Z. Ehler and John B. Morrall (London: Burns, Oates & Washburne, Ltd., 1954). Reprinted with permission of the Newman Press. Originally in *Raccolta di Concordati tra la Santa Sede e le autorita civili* (Vatican, 1919).

[After noting the authorized signers, the document continues:]

The Government of the Republic recognizes that the Catholic, Apostolic and Roman religion is the religion of the vast majority of French citizens.

His Holiness, for his part, recognizes that this same religion has received and is receiving at the present time the greatest benefit and prestige from the establishment of Catholic worship in France and from the individual professions of it which are made by the Consuls of the French Republic.

As a result, after this mutual recognition, they have, for the good of religion and the maintenance of internal peace, agreed on the following:

Art. 1. The Catholic, Apostolic, and Roman religion shall be freely practised in France; its worship shall be public, in conformity with police regulations which the Government shall judge to be necessary for public tranquillity.

Art. 2. The Holy See, in conjunction with

the Government, shall make a new delimitation of the French dioceses.

Art. 3.   His Holiness shall declare to the titular holders of French bishoprics that he expects with firm confidence the utmost sacrifice from them, even if it be that of their Sees, for the sake of peace and unity. After this exhortation, if they refuse this sacrifice prescribed by the good of the Church (a refusal which, however, His Holiness does not expect), the appointment of new nominees to the government of the bishoprics, according to their new delimitation, shall be proceeded with in the following manner.

Art. 4.   The First Consul of the Republic shall, within three months following the publication of a Bull of His Holiness, nominate to archbishoprics and bishoprics according to the new delimitation. His Holiness shall confer canonical institution according to the forms established in regard to France before the change of government.

Art. 5.   Nominations to bishoprics which shall fall vacant in the future shall also be made by the First Consul and canonical institution shall be given by the Holy See in conformity with the preceding Article.

Art. 6.   The bishops, before commencing their duties, shall take personally between the hands of the First Consul the oath of fidelity which was in use before the change of government, expressed in the following terms: "I swear and promise to God on the Holy Gospels to observe obedience and fidelity to the Government established by the Constitution of the French Republic. I also promise not to have any knowledge, not to take part in any scheme, not to associate in any conspiracy, whether internal or external, which may be inimical to public tranquillity and, if in my diocese or elsewhere, I learn that something prejudicial to the State is contemplated, I will make it known to the Government."

Art. 7.   Ecclesiastics of subordinate rank shall take the same oath between the hands of civil authorities, designated by the Government.

Art. 8.   The following form of prayer shall be recited at the end of Divine worship in all Catholic churches in France: "O Lord, save the Republic. O Lord, save the Consuls."

Art. 9.   The bishops shall make a new delimitation of the parishes of their dioceses; this shall not come into effect without the consent of the Government.

Art. 10.   The bishops shall nominate parish priests. Their choice shall not fall on any except persons approved by the Government.

Art. 11.   The bishops will be able to have a Chapter in their Cathedral, and a seminary for their diocese, but the Government does not guarantee to subsidize them.

Art. 12.   All metropolitan churches, cathedrals, parish churches and others not alienated which are necessary for worship, shall be put at the disposal of the bishops.

Art. 13.   His Holiness, for the sake of peace and the happy restoration of the Catholic religion, declares that neither himself nor his successors will disturb in any way those who have acquired alienated Church property and that in consequence the ownership of such property, and the rights and revenues attached to it, shall remain unchallenged in their possession or in that of their heirs.

Art. 14.   The Government will guarantee a suitable settlement for bishops and parish priests whose dioceses and livings shall be affected by the new delimitation.

Art. 15.   The Government will also take measures to ensure that French Catholics can, if they desire, make bequests in favour of churches.

Art. 16.   His Holiness recognizes to the First Consul of the French Republic the same rights and prerogatives which the former Government enjoyed in relation to the Holy See.

Art. 17.   It is agreed between the contracting parties that in the event that any of the successors of the present First Consul shall not be a Catholic, the rights and prerogatives mentioned in the previous Article and the nomination to bishoprics shall be arranged in collaboration with him by a new convention.

The ratifications shall be exchanged at Paris within fourteen days.

Drawn up at Paris on Messidor 26 of the year IX of the French Republic (July 15, 1801).

(*Signatures.*)

8. William Wordsworth: Romantic Reaction

In the poetry of William Wordsworth (1770-1850), romantic tones of interest in nature and protests against artificiality are unmistakable. In nature, Wordsworth beholds God; in familiar things, he sees an inner harmony and beauty. In human society, he sees the sham and chaos of what man has done to man. The following selections are typical. *The Complete Poetical Works of William Wordsworth* (Boston: Houghton Mifflin Company, 1903).

LINES WRITTEN IN EARLY SPRING (1798)

I heard a thousand blended notes
While in a grove I sate reclined,
In that sweet mood when pleasant thoughts
Bring sad thoughts to the mind.

To her fair works did Nature link
The human soul that through me ran;
And much it grieved my heart to think
What Man has made of Man.

Through primrose tufts, in that sweet bower,
The periwinkle trailed its wreaths;
And 'tis my faith that every flower
Enjoys the air it breathes.

The birds around me hopped and played,
Their thoughts I cannot measure,—
But the least motion which they made,
It seemed a thrill of pleasure.

The budding twigs spread out their fan
To catch the breezy air;
And I must think, do all I can,
That there was pleasure there.

If this belief from heaven be sent,
If such be Nature's holy plan,
Have I not reason to lament
What Man has made of Man?

FROM LINES, COMPOSED A FEW MILES
ABOVE TINTERN ABBEY, JULY 13, 1798

       . . . For I have learned
To look on nature, not as in the hour
Of thoughtless youth; but hearing oftentimes
The still, sad music of humanity,
Nor harsh nor grating, though of ample power
To chasten and subdue. And I have felt
A presence that disturbs me with the joy
Of elevated thoughts; a sense sublime
Of something far more deeply interfused,
Whose dwelling is the light of setting suns,
And the round ocean and the living air,
And the blue sky, and in the mind of man:

A motion and a spirit, that impels
All thinking things, all objects of all thought,
And rolls through all things. . . .

9. Friedrich Schleiermacher

On Religion: Speeches to its Cultured Despisers, 1799, by Friedrich Schleiermacher (1768-1834), was a vindication of religion before those who had relegated it to an inferior status, as if it were something outmoded and unfit for the intellectual consideration of the cultured. Schleiermacher wanted to show that religion is a basic ingredient in the life of man, worthy of his highest thought, an ingredient that only the dilettante would ignore. Religion in Germany had not suffered the outward setback that it had in France, but religious life had reached a low ebb, and morality moved on a level of superficial, enlightened self-interest. Schleiermacher's *Speeches* were like a series of electric shocks; they presaged but did not expound a system of doctrine. That came later in *The Christian Faith* (1821-1822), the nineteenth century's most distinctive Protestant theology. The selections are from the *Speeches*, trans. John Oman (London: Routledge & Kegan Paul, Ltd., 1893).

ON RELIGION: SPEECHES TO ITS
CULTURED DESPISERS, 1799

Defence

It may be an unexpected and even a marvellous undertaking, that any one should still venture to demand from the very class that have raised themselves above the vulgar, and are saturated with the wisdom of the centuries, attention for a subject so entirely neglected by them. And I confess that I am aware of nothing that promises any easy success, whether it be in winning for my efforts your approval, or in the more difficult and more desirable task of instilling into you my thought and inspiring you for my subject. From of old faith has not been every man's affair. At all times but few have discerned religion itself, while millions, in various ways, have been satisfied to juggle with its trappings. Now especially the life of cultivated people is far from anything that might have even resemblance to religion. Just as little, I know, do you worship the Deity in sacred retirement, as you visit the forsaken temples. In your ornamented dwellings, the only sacred things to be met with are the sage maxims of our wise men, and the splendid compositions of our poets. Suavity and sociability, art and science have so fully taken possession of your minds, that no room remains for the eternal and holy Being that lies beyond the world. I know how well you have succeeded in making your earthly life so rich and varied, that you no longer stand in need of an eternity. Having made a universe for yourselves, you are above the need of thinking of the Universe that made you. You are agreed, I know, that nothing new, nothing convincing can any more be said on this matter, which on every side by sages and seers, and I might add by scoffers and priests, has been abundantly discussed. To priests, least of all, are you inclined to listen. They have long been outcasts for you, and are declared unworthy of your trust, because they like best to lodge in the battered ruins of their sanctuary and cannot, even there, live without disfiguring and destroying it still more. All this I know, and yet, divinely swayed by an irresistible necessity within me, I feel myself compelled to speak, and cannot take back my invitation that you and none else should listen to me.

Might I ask one question? On every subject, however small and unimportant, you would most willingly be taught by those who have devoted to it their lives and their powers. In your desire for knowledge, you do not avoid the cottages of the peasant or the workshops of the humble artizans. How then does it come about that, in matters of religion alone, you hold every thing the more dubious when it comes from those who are experts, not only according to their own profession, but by recognition from the state, and from the people? Or can you perhaps, strangely enough, show that they are not more experienced, but maintain and cry up anything rather than religion? Scarcely, my good sirs! Not setting much store on a judgment so baseless I confess, as is right, that I also am a member of this order. I venture, though I run the risk, if you do not give me an attentive hearing, of being reckoned among the great crowd from which you admit so few exceptions. . . .

You know how the Deity, by an immutable law, has compelled Himself to divide His great work even to infinity. Each definite thing can only be made up by melting together two opposite activities. Each of His eternal thoughts can only be actualized in

two hostile yet twin forms, one of which cannot exist except by means of the other. The whole corporeal world, insight into which is the highest aim of your researches, appears to the best instructed and most contemplative among you, simply a never-ending play of opposing forces. Each life is merely the uninterrupted manifestation of a perpetually renewed gain and loss, as each thing has its determinate existence by uniting and holding fast in a special way the opposing forces of Nature. Wherefore the spirit also, in so far as it manifests itself in a finite life, must be subject to the same law. The human soul, as is shown both by its passing actions and its inward characteristics, has its existence chiefly in two opposing impulses. Following the one impulse, it strives to establish itself as an individual. For increase, no less than sustenance, it draws what surrounds it to itself, weaving it into its life, and absorbing it into its own being. The other impulse, again, is the dread fear to stand alone over against the Whole, the longing to surrender oneself and be absorbed in a greater, to be taken hold of and determined. All you feel and do that bears on your separate existence, all you are accustomed to call enjoyment or possession works for the first object. The other is wrought for when you are not directed towards the individual life, but seek and retain for yourselves what is the same in all and for all the same existence, that in which, therefore, you acknowledge in your thinking and acting, law and order, necessity and connection, right and fitness. Just as no material thing can exist by only one of the forces of corporeal nature, every soul shares in the two original tendencies of spiritual nature. At the extremes one impulse may preponderate almost to the exclusion of the other, but the perfection of the living world consists in this, that between these opposite ends all combinations are actually present in humanity.

And not only so, but a common band of consciousness embraces them all, so that though the man cannot be other than he is, he knows every other person as clearly as himself, and comprehends perfectly every single manifestation of humanity. Persons, however, at the extremes of this great series, are furthest removed from such a knowledge of the whole. The endeavour to appropriate, too little influenced by the opposite endeavour, takes the form of insatiable sensuality that is mindful only of its individual life, and endeavours only in an earthly way to incorporate into it more and more material and to keep itself active and strong. Swinging eternally between desire and enjoyment, such persons never get beyond consciousness of the individual, and being ever busy with mere self-regarding concerns, they are neither able to feel nor know the common, the whole being and nature of humanity. To persons, on the other hand, too forcibly seized by the opposite impulse, who, from defective power of grasp, are incapable of acquiring any characteristic, definite culture, the true life of the world must just as much remain hidden. It is not granted them to penetrate with plastic mind and to fashion something of their own, but their activity dissipates itself in a futile game with empty notions. They never make a living study of anything, but devote their whole zeal to abstract precepts that degrade everything to means, and leave nothing to be an end. They consume themselves in mistaken hate against everything that comes before them with prosperous force. How are these extremes to be brought together, and the long series be made into a closed ring, the symbol of eternity and completeness?

Persons in whom both tendencies are toned down to an unattractive equilibrium are not rare, but, in truth, they stand lower than either. For this frequent phenomenon which so many value highly, we are not indebted to a living union of both impulses, but both are distorted and smoothed away to a dull mediocrity in which no excess appears, because all fresh life is wanting. This is the position to which a false discretion seeks to bring the younger generation.... Elements so separated or so reduced to equilibrium would disclose little even to men of deep insight, and, for a common eye that has no power of insight to give life to the scattered bones, a world so peopled would be only a mock mirror that neither reflects their own forms nor allows them to see behind it. Wherefore the Deity at all times sends

some here and there, who in a fruitful manner are imbued with both impulses, either as a direct gift from above, or as the result of a severe and complete self-training. They are equipped with wonderful gifts, their way is made even by an almighty indwelling word. They are interpreters of the Deity and His works, and reconcilers of things that otherwise would be eternally divided. I mean, in particular, those who unite those opposing activities, by imprinting in their lives a characteristic form upon just that common nature of spirit, the shadow of which only appears to most in empty notions, as an image upon mist....

The Nature of Religion

In order to make quite clear to you what is the original and characteristic possession of religion, it resigns at once, all claims on anything that belongs either to science or morality. Whether it has been borrowed or bestowed it is now returned. What then does your science of being, your natural science, all your theoretical philosophy, in so far as it has to do with the actual world, have for its aim? To know things, I suppose, as they really are; to show the peculiar relations by which each is what it is; to determine for each its place in the Whole, and to distinguish it rightly from all else; to present the whole real world in its mutually conditioned necessity; and to exhibit the oneness of all phenomena with their eternal laws. This is truly beautiful and excellent, and I am not disposed to depreciate. Rather, if this description of mine, so slightly sketched, does not suffice, I will grant the highest and most exhaustive you are able to give....

It is true that religion is essentially contemplative. You would never call anyone pious who went about in impervious stupidity, whose sense is not open for the life of the world. But this contemplation is not turned, as your knowledge of nature is, to the existence of a finite thing, combined with and opposed to another finite thing. It has not even, like your knowledge of God—if for once I might use an old expression—to do with the nature of the first cause, in itself and in its relation to every other cause and operation. The contemplation of the pious is the immediate consciousness of the universal existence of all finite things, in and through the Infinite, and of all temporal things in and through the Eternal. Religion is to seek this and find it in all that lives and moves, in all growth and change, in all doing and suffering. It is to have life and to know life in immediate feeling, only as such an existence in the Infinite and Eternal. Where this is found religion is satisfied, where it hides itself there is for her unrest and anguish, extremity and death. Wherefore it is a life in the infinite nature of the Whole, in the One and in the All, in God, having and possessing all things in God, and God in all. Yet religion is not knowledge and science, either of the world or of God. Without being knowledge, it recognizes knowledge and science. In itself it is an affection, a revelation of the Infinite in the finite, God being seen in it and it in God....

What can man accomplish that is worth speaking of, either in life or in art, that does not arise in his own self from the influence of this sense for the Infinite? Without it, how can anyone wish to comprehend the world scientifically, or if, in some distinct talent, the knowledge is thrust upon him, how should he wish to exercise it? What is all science, if not the existence of things in you, in your reason? what is all art and culture if not your existence in the things to which you give measure, form and order? And how can both come to life in you except in so far as there lives immediately in you the eternal unity of Reason and Nature, the universal existence of all finite things in the Infinite?

Wherefore, you will find every truly learned man devout and pious. Where you see science without religion, be sure it is transferred, learned up from another. It is sickly, if indeed it is not that empty appearance which serves necessity and is no knowledge at all. And what else do you take this deduction and weaving together of ideas to be, which neither live nor correspond to any living thing? Or in ethics, what else is this wretched uniformity that thinks it can grasp the highest human life in a single dead formula? The former arises because there is no fundamental feeling of that living nature which everywhere presents variety and in-

dividuality, and the latter because the sense fails to give infinity to the finite by determining its nature and boundaries only from the Infinite. Hence the dominion of the mere notion; hence the mechanical erections of your systems instead of an organic structure; hence the vain juggling with analytical formulas, in which, whether categorical or hypothetical, life will not be fettered. Science is not your calling, if you despise religion and fear to surrender yourself to reverence and aspiration for the primordial. Either science must become as low as your life, or it must be separated and stand alone, a division that precludes success. If man is not one with the Eternal in the unity of intuition and feeling which is immediate, he remains, in the unity of consciousness which is derived, for ever apart....

The sum total of religion is to feel that, in its highest unity, all that moves us in feeling is one; to feel that aught single and particular is only possible by means of this unity; to feel, that is to say, that our being and living is a being and living in and through God. But it is not necessary that the Deity should be presented as also one distinct object. To many this view is necessary, and to all it is welcome, yet it is always hazardous and fruitful in difficulties. It is not easy to avoid the appearance of making Him susceptible of suffering like other objects. It is only one way of characterizing God, and, from the difficulties of it, common speech will probably never rid itself. But to treat this objective conception of God just as if it were a perception, as if apart from His operation upon us through the world the existence of God before the world, and outside of the world, though for the world, were either by or in religion exhibited as science is, so far as religion is concerned, vain mythology. What is only a help for presentation is treated as a reality. It is a misunderstanding very easily made, but it is quite outside the peculiar territory of religion....

The whole religious life consists of two elements, that man surrender himself to the Universe and allow himself to be influenced by the side of it that is turned towards him is one part, and that he transplant this contact which is one definite feeling, within, and take it up into the inner unity of his life and being, is the other. The religious life is nothing else than the constant renewal of this proceeding. When, therefore, anyone is stirred, in a definite way, by the World, is it his piety that straightway sets him to such working and acting as bear the traces of commotion and disturb the pure connection of the moral life? Impossible. On the contrary, his piety invites him to enjoy what he has won, to absorb it, to combine it, to strip it of what is temporal and individual, that it may no more dwell in him as commotion but be quiet, pure and eternal. From this inner unity, action springs of its own accord, as a natural branch of life. As we agreed, activity is a reaction of feeling, but the sum of activity should only be a reaction of the sum of feeling, and single actions should depend on something quite different from momentary feeling. Only when each action is in its own connection and in its proper place, and not when, dependently and slavishly, it corresponds to one emotion, does it exhibit, in a free and characteristic way, the whole inner unity of the spirit. . . .

If then this, that I trust I have indicated clearly enough for you all, is really the nature of religion, I have already answered the questions, Whence do those dogmas and doctrines come that many consider the essence of religion? Where do they properly belong? And how do they stand related to what is essential in religion? They are all the result of that contemplation of feeling, of that reflection and comparison, of which we have already spoken. The conceptions that underlie these propositions are, like your conceptions from experience, nothing but general expressions for definite feelings. They are not necessary for religion itself, scarcely even for communicating religion, but reflection requires and creates them. Miracle, inspiration, revelation, supernatural intimations, much piety can be had without the need of any one of these conceptions. But when feeling is made the subject of reflection and comparison, they are absolutely unavoidable. In this sense all these conceptions do certainly belong to the sphere of religion, and indeed belong without condition or the smallest limit to their application.

The strife about what event is properly a miracle, and wherein its character properly consists, how much revelation there may be and how far and for what reasons man may properly believe in it, and the manifest endeavour to deny and set aside as much as can be done with decency and consideration, in the foolish notion that philosophy and reason are served thereby, is one of the childish operations of the metaphysicians and moralists in religion. They confuse all points of view and bring religion into discredit, as if it trespassed on the universal validity of scientific and physical conclusions. Pray do not be misled, to the detriment of religion, by their sophistical disputations, nor even by their hypocritical mystery about what they would only too willingly publish. Religion, however loudly it may demand back all those well abused conceptions, leaves your physics untouched, and please God, also your psychology.

What is a miracle? What we call miracle is everywhere else called sign, indication. Our name, which means a wonder, refers purely to the mental condition of the observer. It is only in so far appropriate that a sign, especially when it is nothing besides, must be fitted to call attention to itself and to the power in it that gives it significance. Every finite thing, however, is a sign of the Infinite, and so these various expressions declare the immediate relation of a phenomenon to the Infinite and the Whole. But does that involve that every event should not have quite as immediate a relation to the finite and to nature? Miracle is simply the religious name for event. Every event, even the most natural and usual, becomes a miracle, as soon as the religious view of it can be the dominant. To me all is miracle. In your sense the inexplicable and strange alone is miracle, in mine it is no miracle. The more religious you are, the more miracle would you see everywhere. All disputing about single events, as to whether or not they are to be called miraculous, gives me a painful impression of the poverty and wretchedness of the religious sense of the combatants. One party shows it by protesting everywhere against miracle, whereby they manifest their wish not to see anything of immediate relationship to the In-

339

finite and to the Deity. The other party displays the same poverty by laying stress on this and that. A phenomenon for them must be marvellous before they will regard it as a miracle, whereby they simply announce that they are bad observers.

What is revelation? Every original and new communication of the Universe to man is a revelation, as, for example, every such moment of conscious insight as I have just referred to. Every intuition and every original feeling proceeds from revelation. As revelation lies beyond consciousness, demonstration is not possible, yet we are not merely to assume it generally, but each one knows best himself what is repeated and learned elsewhere, and what is original and new. If nothing original has yet been generated in you, when it does come it will be a revelation for you also, and I counsel you to weigh it well....

You see that all these ideas, in so far as religion requires, or can adopt ideas, are the first and the most essential. They indicate in the most characteristic manner a man's consciousness of his religion, because they indicate just what necessarily and universally must be in it. The man who does not see miracles of his own from the standpoint from which he contemplates the world, the man in whose heart no revelation of his own arises, when his soul longs to draw in the beauty of the world, and to be permeated by its spirit; the man who does not, in supreme moments, feel, with the most lively assurance, that a divine spirit urges him, and that he speaks and acts from holy inspiration, has no religion. The religious man must, at least, be conscious of his feelings as the immediate product of the Universe; for less would mean nothing. He must recognize something individual in them, something that cannot be imitated, something that guarantees the purity of their origin from his own heart. To be assured of this possession is the true belief....

I have tried, as best I could, therefore, to show you what religion really is. Have you found anything therein unworthy of you, nay, of the highest human culture? Must you not rather long all the more for that universal union with the world which is only possible through feeling, the more you are separated and isolated by definite culture and individuality? Have you not often felt this holy longing, as something unknown? Become conscious of the call of your deepest nature and follow it, I conjure you. Banish the false shame of a century which should not determine you but should be made and determined by you. Return to what lies so near to you, yes, even to you, the violent separation from which you cannot fail to destroy the most beautiful part of your nature....

This then is my view of these subjects. The usual conception of God as one single being outside of the world and behind the world is not the beginning and the end of religion. It is only one manner of expressing God, seldom entirely pure and always inadequate. Such an idea may be formed from mixed motives, from the need for such a being to console and help, and such a God may be believed in without piety, at least in my sense, and I think in the true and right sense. If, however, this idea is formed, not arbitrarily, but somehow by the necessity of a man's way of thinking, if he needs it for the security of his piety, the imperfections of his idea will not cumber him nor contaminate his piety. Yet the true nature of religion is neither this idea nor any other, but immediate consciousness of the Deity as He is found in ourselves and in the world. Similarly the goal and the character of the religious life is not the immortality desired and believed in by many—or what their craving to be too wise about it would suggest—pretended to be believed in by many. It is not the immortality that is outside of time, behind it, or rather after it, and which still is in time. It is the immortality which we can now have in this temporal life; it is the problem in the solution of which we are for ever to be engaged. In the midst of finitude to be one with the Infinite and in every moment to be eternal is the immortality of religion.

Association in Religion

If there is religion at all, it must be social, for that is the nature of man, and it is quite peculiarly the nature of religion. You must confess that when an individual has produced and wrought out something in his own mind, it is morbid and in the highest degree unnatural to wish to reserve it to himself. He should express it in the indispensable fellowship and mutual dependence of action. And there is also a spiritual nature which he has in common with the rest of his species which demands that he express and communicate all that is in him. The more violently he is moved and the more deeply he is impressed, the stronger that social impulse works. And this is true even if we regard it only as the endeavour to find the feeling in others, and so to be sure that nothing has been encountered that is not human.

You see that this is not a case of endeavouring to make others like ourselves, nor of believing that what is in one man is indispensable for all. It is only the endeavour to become conscious of and to exhibit the true relation of our own life to the common nature of man. . . .

The Religions

Why have I assumed that religion can only be given fully in a great multitude of forms of the utmost definiteness? Only on grounds that naturally follow from what has been said of the nature of religion. The whole of religion is nothing but the sum of all relations of man to God, apprehended in all the possible ways in which any man can be immediately conscious in his life. In this sense there is but one religion, for it would be but a poverty-stricken and halting life, if all these relations did not exist wherever religion ought to be. Yet all men will not by any means apprehend them in the same way, but quite differently. Now this difference alone is felt and alone can be exhibited while the reduction of all difference is only thought. . . .

As nothing is more irreligious than to demand general uniformity in mankind, so nothing is more unchristian than to seek uniformity in religion. In all ways the Deity is to be contemplated and worshipped. Varied types of religion are possible, both in proximity and in combination, and if it is necessary that every type be actualized at one time or another, it is to be desired that, at all times, there should be a dim sense of many religions. The great moments must be few in which all things agree to ensure to one among them a wide-extended and enduring life, in which the same view is developed unanimously and irresistibly in a great body, and many persons are deeply affected by the same impression of the divine. Yet what may not be looked for from a time that is so manifestly the border land between two different orders of things? If only the intense crisis were past, such a moment might arrive. Even now a prophetic soul, such as the fiery spirits of our time have, turning its thoughts to creative genius, might perhaps indicate the point that is to be for the future generations the centre for their fellowship with the Deity. But however it be, and however long such a moment may still linger, new developments of religion, whether under Christianity or alongside of it, must come and that soon, even though for a long time they are only discernible in isolated and fleeting manifestations. Out of nothing a new creation always comes forth, and in all living men in whom the intellectual life has power and fulness, religion is almost nothing. From some one of the countless occasions it will be developed in many and take new shape in new ground. Were but the time of caution and timidity past! Religion hates loneliness, and in youth especially, which for all things is the time of love, it wastes away in a consuming longing. When it is developed in you, when you are conscious of the first traces of its life, enter at once into the one indivisible fellowship of the saints, which embraces all religions and in which alone any can prosper. Do you think that because the saints are scattered and far apart, you must speak to unsanctified ears? You ask what language is secret enough—is it speech, writing, deed, or quiet copying of the Spirit? All ways, I answer, and you see that I have not shunned the loudest. In them all sacred things remain secret and hidden from the profane. They may gnaw at the shell as they are able, but to worship the God that is in you, do you not refuse us.

10. Ernest Renan, 1863

Renan's *The Life of Jesus* drew heavily on Strauss's *Life of Jesus*, 1835, but Renan's work was more sensational and was not bound so closely to the Hegelian thesis. The selections below are from the introduction and the chapter on the death of Jesus. Renan consistently omitted all miracles and any details that would not conform to his conception of the living, human Jesus. *The Life of Jesus*, trans. C. E. Wilbour (London: Trübner & Co., 1864).

That the Gospels are in part legendary, is evident, since they are full of miracles and of the supernatural; but legends have not all the same value. No one doubts the principal features of the life of Francis d'Assisi, although we meet the supernatural at every step. No one, on the other hand, accords credit to the "Life of Apollonius of Tyana," because it was written long after the time of the hero, and purely as a romance. At what time, by what hands, under what circumstances, have the Gospels been compiled? This is the primary question upon which depends the opinion to be formed of their credibility.

Each of the four Gospels bears at its head the name of a personage, known either in the apostolic history, or in the Gospel history itself. These four personages are not strictly given us as the authors. The formulæ "according to Matthew," "according to Mark," "according to Luke," "according to John," do not imply that, in the most ancient opinion, these recitals were written from beginning to end by Matthew, Mark, Luke, and John; they merely signify that these were the traditions proceeding from each of these apostles, and claiming their authority. It is clear that, if these titles are exact, the Gospels, without ceasing to be in part legendary, are of great value, since they enable us to go back to the half century which followed the death of Jesus, and in two instances, even to the eye-witnesses of his actions.

Firstly, as to Luke, doubt is scarcely possible. The Gospel of Luke is a regular composition, founded on anterior documents. It is the work of a man who selects, prunes, and combines. The author of this Gospel is certainly the same as that of the Acts of the Apostles [Luke 1:1-4; Acts 1:1]. Now, the author of the Acts is a companion of St. Paul, a title which applies to Luke exactly. I know that more than one objection may be raised against this reasoning; but one thing, at least, is beyond doubt, namely, that the author of

the third Gospel and of the Acts, was a man of the second apostolic generation, and that is sufficient for our object. The date of this Gospel can moreover be determined with much precision by considerations drawn from the book itself. The 21st chapter of Luke, inseparable from the rest of the work, was certainly written after the siege of Jerusalem, and but a short time after. We are here then upon solid ground; for we are concerned with a work written entirely by the same hand, and of the most perfect unity.

The Gospels of Matthew and Mark have not nearly the same stamp of individuality. They are impersonal compositions, in which the author totally disappears. A proper name written at the head of works of this kind does not amount to much. But if the Gospel of Luke is dated, those of Matthew and Mark are dated also; for it is certain that the third Gospel is posterior to the first two; and exhibits the character of a much more advanced compilation. We have, besides, on this point, an excellent testimony from a writer of the first half of the second century—namely, Papias, bishop of Hierapolis, a grave man, a man of traditions, who was all his life seeking to collect whatever could be known of the person of Jesus. After having declared that on such matters he preferred oral tradition to books, Papias mentions two writings on the acts and words of Christ: first, a writing of Mark, the interpreter of the apostle Peter, written briefly, incomplete, and not arranged in chronological order, including narratives and discourses, composed from the information and recollections of the apostle Peter; second, a collection of sentences (*Logia*) written in Hebrew by Matthew, "and which each one has translated as he could." It is certain that these two descriptions answer pretty well to the general physiognomy of the two books now called "Gospel according to Matthew," "Gospel according to Mark";—the first characterised by its long discourses; the second, above all, by anecdote,—much more exact than the first upon small facts, brief even to dryness, containing few discourses, and indifferently composed. That these two works, such as we now read them, are absolutely similar to those read by Papias, cannot be sustained:

firstly, because the writings of Matthew were to Papias solely discourses in Hebrew, of which there were in circulation very varying translations; and, secondly, because the writings of Mark and Matthew were to him profoundly distinct, written without any knowledge of each other, and, as it seems, in different languages. Now, in the present state of the texts, the "Gospel according to Matthew" and the "Gospel according to Mark" present parallel parts so long and so perfectly identical, that it must be supposed, either that the final compiler of the first had the second under his eyes, or *vice versa,* or that both copied from the same prototype. That which appears the most likely, is, that we have not the entirely original compilations of either Matthew or Mark; but that our first two Gospels are versions in which the attempt is made to fill up the gaps of the one text by the other. Every one wished, in fact, to possess a complete copy. He who had in his copy only discourses, wished to have narratives, and *vice versa.* It is thus that "the Gospel according to Matthew" is found to have included almost all the anecdotes of Mark, and that "the Gospel according to Mark" now contains numerous features which come from the *Logia* of Matthew. Every one, besides, drew largely on the Gospel tradition then current. This tradition was so far from having been exhausted by the Gospels, that the Acts of the Apostles and the most ancient Fathers quote many words of Jesus which appear authentic, and are not found in the Gospels we possess.

It matters little for our present object to push this delicate analysis further, and to endeavour to reconstruct in some manner, on the one hand, the original *Logia* of Matthew, and on the other, the primitive narrative such as it left the pen of Mark. The *Logia* are doubtless represented by the great discourses of Jesus which fill a considerable part of the first Gospel. These discourses form, in fact, when detached from the rest, a sufficiently complete whole. As to the narratives of the first and second Gospels, they seem to have for basis a common document, of which the text reappears sometimes in the one and sometimes in the other, and of which the second Gospel, such as we read it to-day,

is but a slightly modified reproduction. In other words, the scheme of the Life of Jesus, in the synoptics, rests upon two original documents—first, the discourses of Jesus collected by Matthew; second, the collection of anecdotes and personal reminiscences which Mark wrote from the recollections of Peter. We may say that we have these two documents still, mixed with accounts from another source, in the two first Gospels, which bear, not without reason, the name of the "Gospel *according* to Matthew" and of the "Gospel *according* to Mark."

What is indubitable, in any case, is, that very early the discourses of Jesus were written in the Aramean language, and very early also his remarkable actions were recorded. These were not texts defined and fixed dogmatically. Besides the Gospels which have come to us, there were a number of others professing to represent the tradition of eye-witnesses. Little importance was attached to these writings, and the preservers, such as Papias, greatly preferred oral tradition. As men still believed that the world was nearly at an end, they cared little to compose books for the future; it was sufficient merely to preserve in their hearts a lively image of him whom they hoped soon to see again in the clouds. Hence the little authority which the Gospel texts enjoyed during one hundred and fifty years. There was no scruple in inserting additions, in variously combining them, and in completing some by others. The poor man who has but one book wishes that it may contain all that is dear to his heart. These little books were lent, each one transcribed in the margin of his copy the words, and the parables he found elsewhere, which touched him. The most beautiful thing in the world has thus proceeded from an obscure and purely popular elaboration. No compilation was of absolute value. Justin, who often appeals to that which he calls "The Memoirs of the Apostles," had under his notice Gospel documents in a state very different from that in which we possess them. At all events, he never cares to quote them textually. The Gospel quotations in the pseudo-Clementinian writings, of Ebionite origin, present the same character. The Spirit was everything; the letter was nothing. It was when tradition became weakened, in the second half of the second century, that the texts bearing the names of the apostles took a decisive authority and obtained the force of law.

Who does not see the value of documents thus composed of the tender remembrances, and simple narratives, of the first two Christian generations, still full of the strong impression which the illustrious Founder had produced, and which seemed long to survive him?

So far we have only spoken of the three Gospels named the synoptics. There remains a fourth, that which bears the name of John. Concerning this one, doubts have a much better foundation, and the question is further from solution. Papias—who was connected with the school of John, and who, if not one of his auditors, as Irenaeus thinks, associated with his immediate disciples, among others, Aristion, and the one called *Presbyteros Joannes*—says not a word of a "Life of Jesus" written by John, although he had zealously collected the oral narratives of both Aristion and *Presbyteros Joannes*. If any such mention had been found in his work, Eusebius, who points out everything therein that can contribute to the literary history of the apostolic age, would doubtless have mentioned it.

The intrinsic difficulties drawn from the perusal of the fourth Gospel itself are not less strong. For myself, I dare not be sure that the fourth Gospel has been entirely written by the pen of a Galilean fisherman.

Firstly, no one doubts that, towards the year 150, the fourth Gospel did exist, and was attributed to John. Explicit texts from St. Justin, from Athenogoras, from Tation, from Theophilus of Antioch, from Irenaeus, shew that thenceforth this Gospel mixed in every controversy, and served as corner-stone for the development of the faith. Irenaeus is explicit; now, Irenaeus came from the school of John, and between him and the apostle there was only Polycarp. The part played by this Gospel in Gnosticism, and especially in the system of Valentinus, in Montanism, and in the quarrel of the Quartodecimans, is not less decisive. The school of John was the most influential one during the second century; and it is only by regarding the origin of the Gospel as coincident with the rise of the the school, that the existence of the latter can be understood at all. Let us add that the first epistle attributed to St. John is certainly by the same author as the fourth Gospel; now, this epistle is recognised as from John by Polycarp, Papias, and Irenaeus.

But it is, above all, the perusal of the work itself which is calculated to give this impression. The author always speaks as an eye-witness; he wishes to pass for the apostle John. If, then, this work is not really by the apostle, we must admit a fraud of which the author convicts himself. Now, although the ideas of the time respecting literary honesty differed essentially from ours, there is no example in the apostolic world of a falsehood of this kind. Besides, not only does the author wish to pass for the apostle John, but we see clearly that he writes in the interest of this apostle. On each page he betrays the desire to fortify his authority, to shew that he has been the favourite of Jesus; that in all the solemn circumstances (at the Lord's supper, at Calvary, at the tomb) he held the first place. We are tempted to believe that John in his old age, having read the Gospel narratives, on the one hand, remarked their various inaccuracies, on the other, was hurt at seeing that there was not accorded to him a sufficiently high place in the history of Christ; that then he commenced to dictate a number of things which he knew better than the rest, with the intention of shewing that in many instances, in which only Peter was spoken of, he had figured with him and even before him. Already during the life of Jesus, these trifling sentiments of jealousy had been manifested between the sons of Zebedee and the other disciples. After the death of James, his brother, John remained sole inheritor of the intimate remembrances of which these two apostles, by the common consent, were the depositaries. Hence his perpetual desire to recall that he is the last surviving eye-witness, and the pleasure which he takes in relating circumstances which he alone could know. Hence, too, so many minute details which seem like the commentaries of an annotator—"it was the sixth hour"; "it was night"; "the servant's name was Malchus"; "they had made a fire of coals, for it was cold"; "the coat was without seam." Hence, lastly, the disorder of the compilation, the irregularity of the narration, the disjointedness of the first chapters, all so many inexplicable features on the supposition that his Gospel was but a theological thesis, without historic value, and which, on the contrary, are perfectly intelligible, if, in conformity with tradition, we see in them the remembrances of an old man, sometimes of remarkable freshness, sometimes having undergone strange modifications.

A primary distinction, indeed, ought to be made in the Gospel of John. On the one side, this Gospel presents us with a rough draft of the life of Jesus, which differs considerably from that of the synoptics. On the other, it puts into the mouth of Jesus discourses of which the tone, the style, the treatment, and the doctrines, have nothing in common with the *Logia* given us by the synoptics. In this second respect, the difference is such that we must make choice in a decisive manner. If Jesus spoke as Matthew represents, he could not have spoken as John relates. Between these two authorities no critic has ever hesitated, or can ever hesitate. Far removed from the simple, disinterested, impersonal tone of the synoptics, the Gospel of John shews incessantly the pre-occupation of the apologist,—the mental reservation of the sectarian, the desire to prove a thesis, and to convince adversaries. It was not by pretentious tirades, heavy, badly written, and appealing little to the moral sense, that Jesus founded his divine work. If even Papias had not taught us that Matthew wrote the sayings of Jesus in their original tongue, the natural, ineffable truth, the charm beyond comparison of the discourses in the synoptics, their profoundly Hebraistic idiom, the analogies which they present with the sayings of the Jewish doctors of the period, their perfect harmony with the natural phenomena of Galilee,—all these characteristics, compared with the obscure Gnosticism, with the distorted metaphysics, which fill the discourses of John, would speak loudly enough. This by no means implies that there are not in the discourses of John some

admirable gleams, some traits which truly come from Jesus. But the mystic tone of these discourses does not correspond at all to the character of the eloquence of Jesus, such as we picture it according to the synoptics. A new spirit has breathed; Gnosticism has already commenced; the Galilean era of the kingdom of God is finished; the hope of the near advent of Christ is more distant; we enter on the barrenness of metaphysics, into the darkness of abstract dogma. The spirit of Jesus is not there, and, if the son of Zebedee has truly traced these pages, he had certainly, in writing them, quite forgotten the Lake of Gennesareth, and the charming discourses which he had heard upon its shores.

.   .   .   .   .

On the whole, we may say that the synoptical compilation has passed through three stages: First, the original documentary state, primary compilations which no longer exist; second, the state of simple mixture, in which the original documents are amalgamated without any effort at composition, without there appearing any personal bias of the authors, (the existing Gospels of Matthew and Mark;) third, the state of combination or of intentional and deliberate compiling, in which we are sensible of an attempt to reconcile the different versions, (Gospel of Luke). The Gospel of John, as we have said, forms a composition of another order, and is entirely distinct.

It is not, then, in the name of this or that philosophy, but in the name of universal experience, that we banish miracle from history. We do not say, "Miracles are impossible." We say, "Up to this time a miracle has never been proved." If to-morrow a thaumaturgus present himself with credentials sufficiently important to be discussed, and announce himself as able, say, to raise the dead; what would be done? A commission, composed of physiologists, physicists, chemists, persons accustomed to historical criticism, would be named. This commission would choose a corpse, would assure itself that the death was real, would select the room in which the experiment should be made, would arrange the whole system of precautions, so as to leave no chance of doubt. If under such conditions, the resurrection were effected, a probability almost equal to certainty would be established. As, however, it ought to be possible always to repeat an experiment,—to do over again which has been done once; and as, in the order of miracle, there can be no question of ease or difficulty, the thaumaturgus would be invited to reproduce his marvellous act under other circumstances, upon other corpses, in another place. If the miracle succeeded each time, two things would be proved: first, that supernatural events happen in the world; second, that the power of producing them belongs, or is delegated to, certain persons. But who does not see that no miracle ever took place under these conditions? but that always hitherto the thaumaturgus has chosen the subject of the experiment, chosen the spot, chosen the public; that, besides, the people themselves—most commonly in consequence of the invincible want to see something divine in great events and great men—create the marvellous legends afterwards? Until a new order of things prevails, we shall maintain then, this principle of historical criticism—that a supernatural account cannot be admitted as such, that it always implies credulity or imposture, that the duty of the historian is to explain it, and seek to ascertain what share of truth, or of error, it may conceal.

.　　.　　.　　.　　.

In histories such as this, the great test that we have got the truth is, to have succeeded in combining the texts in such a manner that they shall constitute a logical, probable narrative, harmonious throughout. The secret laws of life, of the progression of organic products, of the melting of minute distinctions, ought to be consulted at each moment; for what is required to be reproduced, is not the material circumstance, which it is impossible to verify, but the very soul of history; what must be sought is not the petty certainty about trifles, it is the correctness of the general sentiment, the truthfulness of the colouring. Each trait which departs from the rules of classic narration ought to warn us to be careful; for the fact which has to be related, has been living, natural, and harmoni-

ous. If we do not succeed in rendering it such by the recital, it is surely because we have not succeeded in seeing it aright.

This idea of a living organism we have not hesitated to take as our guide in the general arrangement of the narrative.

If the love of a subject can help one to understand it, it will also, I hope, be recognised that I have not been wanting in this condition. To write the history of a religion, it is necessary, firstly, to have believed it (otherwise we should not be able to understand how it has charmed and satisfied the human conscience); in the second place, to believe it no longer in an absolute manner, for absolute faith is incompatible with sincere history. But love is possible without faith. To abstain from attaching one's self to any of the forms which captivate the adoration of men, is not to deprive ourselves of the enjoyment of that which is good and beautiful in them. No transitory appearance exhausts the Divinity; God was revealed before Jesus—God will reveal Himself after him. Profoundly unequal, and so much the more Divine, as they are grander and more spontaneous, the manifestations of God hidden in the depths of the human conscience are all of the same order. Jesus cannot belong solely to those who call themselves his disciples. He is the common honour of all who share a common humanity. His glory does not consist in being relegated out of history; we render him a truer worship in shewing that all history is incomprehensible without him.

JESUS IN THE TOMB

It was about three o'clock in the afternoon, according to our manner of reckoning, when Jesus expired. A Jewish law forbade a corpse suspended on the cross to be left beyond the evening of the day of the execution. It is not probable that in the executions performed by the Romans this rule was observed; but as the next day was the Sabbath, and a Sabbath of peculiar solemnity, the Jews expressed to the Roman authorities their desire that this holy day should not be profaned by such a spectacle. Their request was granted; orders were given to hasten the death of the three condemned ones, and to remove them from the cross. The soldiers executed this order by applying to the two thieves a second punishment much more speedy than that of the cross, the *crurifragium*, or breaking of the legs, the usual punishment of slaves and of prisoners of war. As to Jesus, they found him dead, and did not think it necessary to break his legs. But one of them, to remove all doubt as to the real death of the third victim, and to complete it, if any breath remained in him, pierced his side with a spear. They thought they saw water and blood flow, which was regarded as a sign of the cessation of life.

John, who professes to have seen it, insists strongly on this circumstance. It is evident, in fact, that doubts arose as to the reality of the death of Jesus. A few hours of suspension on the cross appeared to persons accustomed to see crucifixions entirely insufficient to lead to such a result. They cited many instances of persons crucified, who, removed in time, had been brought to life again by powerful remedies. Origen afterwards thought it needful to invoke miracle in order to explain so sudden an end. The same astonishment is found in the narrative of Mark. To speak truly, the best guarantee that the historian possesses upon a point of this nature is the suspicious hatred of the enemies of Jesus. It is doubtful whether the Jews were at that time preoccupied with the fear that Jesus might pass for resuscitated; but, in any case, they must have made sure that he was really dead. Whatever, at certain periods, may have been the neglect of the ancients in all that belonged to legal proof and the strict conduct of affairs, we cannot but believe that those interested here had taken some precautions in this respect.

According to the Roman custom, the corpse of Jesus ought to have remained suspended in order to become the prey of birds. According to the Jewish law, it would have been removed in the evening, and deposited in the place of infamy set apart for the burial of those who were executed. If Jesus had had for disciples only his poor Galileans, timid and without influence, the latter course would have been adopted. But we have seen that, in spite of his small success at Jerusalem, Jesus had gained the sympathy of some important persons who expected the kingdom of God, and who, without confessing themselves his disciples, were strongly attached to him. One of these persons, Joseph, of the small town of Arimathea, (*Ha-rama-thaim*,) went in the evening to ask the body from the procurator. Joseph was a rich and honourable man, a member of the Sanhedrin. The Roman law, at this period, commanded, moreover, that the body of the person executed should be delivered to those who claimed it. Pilate, who was ignorant of the circumstance of the *crurifragium*, was astonished that Jesus was so soon dead, and summoned the centurion who had superintended the execution, in order to know how that was. Pilate, after having received the assurances of the centurion, granted to Joseph the object of his request. The body probably had already been removed from the cross. They delivered it to Joseph, that he might do with it as he pleased.

Another secret friend, Nicodemus, whom we have already seen employing his influence more than once in favour of Jesus, came forward at this moment. He arrived bearing an ample provision of the materials necessary for embalming. Joseph and Nicodemus interred Jesus according to the Jewish custom— that is to say, they wrapped him in a sheet with myrrh and aloes. The Galilean women were present, and no doubt accompanied the scene with piercing cries and tears.

It was late, and all this was done in great haste. The place had not yet been chosen where the body would be finally deposited. The carrying of the body, moreover, might have been delayed to a late hour, and have involved a violation of the Sabbath—now the disciples still conscientiously observed the prescriptions of the Jewish law. A temporary interment was determined upon. There was at hand, in the garden, a tomb recently dug out in the rock, which had never been used. It belonged, probably, to one of the believers. The funeral caves, when they were destined for a single body, were composed of a small room, at the bottom of which the place for the body was marked by a trough or couch let into the wall, and surmounted by an arch. As these caves were dug out of the sides of sloping rocks, they were entered by the floor; the door was shut by a stone very difficult to move. Jesus was deposited in the cave, and the stone was rolled to the door, as it was intended to return in order to give him a more complete burial. But the next day being a solemn Sabbath, the labour was postponed till the day following.

The women retired after having carefully noticed how the body was laid. They employed the hours of the evening which remained to them in making new preparations for the embalming. On the Saturday all rested.

On the Sunday morning, the women, Mary Magdalen the first, came very early to the tomb. The stone was displaced from the opening, and the body was no longer in the place where they had laid it. At the same time, the strangest rumours were spread in the Christian community. The cry, "He is risen!" quickly spread amongst the disciples. Love caused it to find ready credence everywhere. What had taken place? In treating of the history of the apostles we shall have to examine this point and to make inquiry into the origin of the legends relative to the resurrection. For the historian, the life of Jesus finishes with his last sigh. But such was the impression he had left in the hearts of his disciples and of a few devoted women, that during some weeks more it was as if he were living and consoling them. Had his body been taken away, or did enthusiasm, always credulous, create afterwards the group of narratives by which it was sought to establish faith in the resurrection? In the absence of opposing documents this can never be ascertained. Let us say, however, that the strong imagination of Mary Magdalen played an important part in this circumstance. Divine power of Love! Sacred moments in which the passion of one possessed gave to the world a resuscitated God!

11. John Henry Newman and the Oxford Movement, 1833-45

John Henry Newman wrote on the nature of Roman and Protestant errors in 1837, at the height of the Oxford Movement. One can glimpse in his essay those tendencies in thought which drew him closer to Rome and caused many critics of Oxford Reformers to hurl charges of papalism. *Tract XC* in 1841, just four years before Newman defected to Rome, averred that the *Thirty-nine Articles* of the Anglican communion were in all major aspects in agreement with basic Roman views. *Tract XC* is a long essay, full of quotations from contemporaries and predecessors of Newman. Only a few portions are quoted to give the tenor of this controversial work. Both are from *Via Media of the Anglican Church*, by John Henry Cardinal Newman (London: Longmans, Green & Co., 1888).

THE NATURE AND GROUND OF ROMAN AND PROTESTANT ERRORS

All Protestant sects of the present day may be said to agree with us and differ from Roman Catholics, in considering the Bible as the only standard of appeal in doctrinal inquiries. They differ indeed from each other as well as from us in the matter of their belief; but they one and all accept the written word of God as the supreme and sole arbiter of their differences. This makes their contest with each other and us more simple; I do not say shorter,—on the contrary, they have been engaged in it almost three hundred years, (as many of them, that is, as are so ancient,) and there are no symptoms of its ending— but it makes it less laborious. It narrows the ground of it; it levels it to the intelligence of all ranks of men; it gives the multitude a right to take part in it; it encourages all men, learned and unlearned, religious and irreligious, to have an opinion in it, and to turn controversialists. The Bible is a small book; any one may possess it; and every one, unless he be very humble, will think he is able to understand it. And therefore, I say, controversy is easier among Protestants, because any one whatever can controvert; easier, but not shorter; because though all sects agree together as to the standard of faith, viz. the Bible, yet no two agree as to the interpreter of the Bible, but each person makes himself the interpreter, so that what seemed at first a means of peace, turns out to be a chief occasion or cause of discord.

It is a great point to come to issue with an opponent; that is, to discover some position which oneself affirms and the other denies, and on which the decision of the controversy will turn. It is like two armies meeting, and settling their quarrel in a pitched battle, instead of wandering to and fro, each by itself, and inflicting injury and gaining advantages where no one resists it. Now the Bible is this common ground among Protestants, and seems to have been originally assumed in no small degree from a notion of its simplicity in argument. But, if such a notion was entertained in any quarter, it has been disappointed by this difficulty,—the Bible is not so written as to force its meaning upon the reader; no two Protestant sects can agree together whose interpretation of the Bible is to be received; and under such circumstances each naturally prefers his own;—his own "interpretation," his own "doctrine," his own "tongue," his own "revelation." Accordingly, acute men among them see that the very elementary notion which they have adopted, of the Bible without note or comment being the sole authoritative judge in controversies of faith, is a self-destructive principle, and practically involves the conclusion, that dispute is altogether hopeless and useless, and even absurd. After whatever misgivings or reluctance, they seem to allow, or to be in the way to allow, that truth is but matter of opinion; that that is truth to each which each thinks to be truth, provided he sincerely and really thinks it; that the divinity of the Bible itself is the only thing that need be believed, and that its meaning varies with the individuals who receive it; that it has no one meaning to be ascertained as a matter of fact, but that it may mean anything because it may be made to mean so many things; and hence that our wisdom and our duty lie in discarding all notions of the importance of any particular set of opinions, any doctrines, or any creed, each man having a right to his own, and in living together peaceably with men of all persuasions, whatever our private judgments and leanings may be.

2. I do not say that these conclusions need to follow by logical necessity from the principle from which I have deduced them; but that practically they will follow in the long run, and actually have followed where there were no counteracting causes in operation. Nor do I allow that they will follow at all in our own case, though we agree with Protestant sects in making Scripture the document of ultimate appeal in matters of faith. For though we consider Scripture as satisfactory, we do not consider it our sole infor-

VII-4. Drawing for Isaac Williams' *The Altar*, London, 1847. *Note the emphasis on sacramental devotion.*

mant in divine truths. We have another source of information in reserve, as I shall presently show. We agree with the sectaries around us so far as this, to be ready to take their ground, which Roman Catholics cannot and will not do, to believe that our creed can be proved entirely, and to be willing to prove it solely from the Bible; but we take this ground only in controversy, not in teaching our own people or in our private studies. We are willing to argue with Protestants from "texts"; they may feel the force of these or not, we may convince them or not, but if such conviction is a necessary criterion of good argument, then sound reasoning is to be found on no side, or else there would soon cease to be any controversy at all. It is enough that by means of their weapon we are able to convince and convert others, though not them; for this proves its cogency in our use of it. We have joined issue with them, and done all that can be done, though with them we have not succeeded. The case

349

is not as if we were searching after some unknown and abstruse ground of proof which we were told they had, but were uncertain about, and could not ascertain or circumscribe. We know their greatest strength, and we discover it to be weakness. They have no argument behind to fall back upon: we have examined and decided against their cause.

And they themselves, as I have observed, have decided against it too; their adoption of the latitudinarian notion that one creed is as good as another, is an evidence of it. . . .

3. Protestant denominations, I have said, however they may differ from each other in important points, so far agree, that one and all profess to appeal to Scripture, whether they be called Independents, or Baptists, or Unitarians, or Presbyterians, or Wesleyans, or by any other title. But the case is different as regards Roman Catholics: they do not appeal to Scripture unconditionally; they are not willing to stand or fall by mere arguments from Scripture; and therefore, if we take Scripture as our ground of proof in our controversies with them, we have not yet joined issue with them. Not that they reject Scripture, it would be very unjust to say so; they would shrink from doing so, or being thought to do so; and perhaps they adhere to Scripture as closely as some of those Protestant bodies who profess to be guided by nothing else; but, though they admit Scripture to be the word of God, they conceive that it is not the whole word of God, they openly avow that they regulate their faith by something else besides Scripture, by the existing Traditions of the Church. They maintain that the system of doctrine which they hold came to them from the Apostles as truly and certainly as the apostolic writings; so that, even if those writings had been lost, the world would still have had the blessings of a Revelation. Now, they must be clearly understood, if they are to be soundly refuted. We hear it said, that they go by tradition, and we fancy in consequence that there are a certain definite number of statements ready framed and compiled, which they profess to have received from the Apostles. . . . By tradition they mean the whole system of faith and ordinances which they have received from the generation before them, and that

generation again from the generation before itself. And in this sense undoubtedly we all go by tradition in matters of this world. Where is the corporation, society, or fraternity of any kind, but has certain received rules and understood practices which are nowhere put down in writing? How often do we hear it said, that this or that person has "acted unusually," that so and so "was never done before," that it is "against rule," and the like; and then perhaps, to avoid the inconvenience of such irregularity in the future, what was before a tacit engagement, is turned into a formal and explicit order or principle. The absence of a regulation must be felt before it is supplied; and the virtual transgression of it goes before its adoption. At this very time a great part of the law of the land is administered under the sanction of such a tradition; it is not contained in any formal or authoritative code, it depends on custom or precedent. There is no explicit written law, for instance, simply declaring murder to be a capital offence; unless indeed we have recourse to the divine command in the ninth chapter of the book of Genesis. Murderers are hanged by custom. Such as this is the tradition of the church; tradition is uniform custom. When the Romanists say they adhere to Tradition, they mean that they believe and act as Christians have always believed and acted; they go by the custom, as judges and juries do. And then they go on to allege that there is this important difference between their custom and all other customs in the world; that the tradition of the law, at least in its details, though it has lasted for centuries upon centuries, anyhow had a beginning in human appointments; whereas theirs, though it has a beginning too, yet, when traced back, has none short of the Apostles of Christ, and is in consequence of divine not of human authority,—is true and intrinsically binding as well as expedient.

4. If we ask, why it is that these professed traditions were not reduced to writing, it is answered, that the Christian doctrine, as it has proceeded from the mouth of the Apostles, is too varied and too minute in its details to allow of it. No one you fall in with on the highway, can tell you all his mind at once; much less could the Apostles,

possessed as they were of great and supernatural truths, and busied in the propagation of the church, digest in one Epistle or Treatise a systematic view of the Revelation made to them. And so much at all events we may grant, that they did not do so; there being confessedly little of system or completeness in any portion of the New Testament.

If again it be objected that, upon the notion of an unwritten transmission of doctrine, there is nothing to show that the faith of today was the faith of yesterday, nothing to connect this age and the Apostolic, the theologians of Rome maintain, on the contrary, that over and above the corroborative though indirect testimony of ecclesiastical writers, no error could have arisen in the church without its being protested against and put down on its first appearance; that from all parts of the church a cry would have been raised against the novelty, and a declaration put forth, as we know in fact was the practice of the early church, denouncing it. And thus they would account for the indeterminateness on the one hand, yet on the other the accuracy and availableness of their existing tradition or unwritten creed. It is latent, but it lives. It is silent, like the rapids of a river, before the rocks intercept it. It is the church's unconscious habit of opinion and sentiment; which she reflects upon, masters, and expresses, according to the emergency. We see then the mistake of asking for a complete collection of the Roman Traditions; as well we might ask for a full catalogue of a man's tastes and thoughts on a given subject. Tradition in its fulness is necessarily unwritten; it is the mode in which a society has felt or acted during a certain period, and it cannot be circumscribed any more than a man's countenance and manner can be conveyed to strangers in any set of propositions.

Such are the traditions to which the Roman Catholics appeal, whether viewed as latent in the church's teaching, or as passing into writing and being fixed in the decrees of the Councils or amid the works of the ancient Fathers.

5. Now how do we of the English church meet these statements? or, rather, how do Roman Catholics prove them? For it will be observed, that what has been said hitherto, does not prove that their traditions are such as they aver them to be, but merely that their theory is consistent with itself. And as a beautiful theory it must, as a whole, ever remain. To a certain point indeed it is tenable: but this is a very different thing from admitting that it is so as regards those very tenets for which Roman theologians would adduce it. They have to show, not merely that there was such a living and operative tradition, and that it has lasted to this day, but that their own characteristic doctrines are parts of it. Here then we see how, under such condition of controversy, we ought to meet their pretensions. Shall we refuse to consider the subject of tradition at all, saying that the Bible contains the whole of Divine Revelation, and that the doctrines professedly conveyed by tradition are only so far apostolic as they are contained in Scripture? This will be saying what is true, but it will be assuming the point in dispute; it will in no sense be meeting our opponents. We shall only involve ourselves in great difficulties by so doing. For, let us consider a moment; we are sure to be asked, and shall have to answer, a difficult question; so we had better consider it beforehand. I mean, how do we know that Scripture comes from God: It cannot be denied that we of this age receive it upon general tradition; we receive through tradition both the Bible itself, and the doctrine that it is divinely inspired. That doctrine is one of those pious and comfortable truths "which we have heard and known, and such as our fathers have told us," "which God commanded our forefathers to teach their children, that their posterity might know it, and the children which were yet unborn; to the intent that when they came up, they might show their children the same." The great multitude of Protestants believe in the divinity of Scripture precisely on the ground on which the Roman Catholics take their stand in behalf of their own system of doctrine, viz. because they have been taught it. To deride tradition therefore as something irrational or untrustworthy in itself, is to weaken the foundation of our own faith in Scripture, and is very cruel towards the great multitude of unedu-

cated persons, who believe in Scripture because they are told to believe in it. If, however, it be said that pious Protestants have "the witness in themselves," as a sure test to their own hearts of the truth of Scripture, the fact is undeniable; and a sufficient and consoling proof is it to them that the teaching of Scripture is true; but it does not prove that the very book we call the Bible was written, and all of it written, by inspiration; nor does it allow us to dispense with the external evidence of tradition assuring us that it is so.

6. But if, again, it be said that the New Testament is received as divine, not upon the present traditionary belief of Christians, but only the evidence of antiquity this, too, even were it true,—for surely the multitude of Christians know nothing about antiquity at all,—yet this is exactly what the Romanists maintain of their unwritten doctrines also. They argue that their present creed has been the universal belief of all preceding ages, and is recorded in the writings still extant of those ages. Suppose, I say, we take this ground in behalf of the divinity of Holy Scripture, viz. that it is attested by all the writers and other authorities of primitive times: doubtless we are right in doing so; it is the very argument by which we actually do prove the divinity of the sacred Canon; but it is also the very argument which Roman Catholics put forward for their peculiar tenets; viz. that while received on existing tradition, they are also proved by the unanimous consent of the first ages of Christianity. If then we would leave ourselves room for proving that Scripture is inspired, we must not reject the notion and principle of the argument from Tradition and from Antiquity as something in itself absurd and unworthy of Almighty wisdom. In other words, to refuse to listen to these informants because we have a written word, is a self-destructive course, inasmuch as that written word itself is proved to be such mainly by these very informants which, as if to do honour to it, we reject. This is to overthrow our premises by means of our conclusion. That which ascertains for us the divinity of Scripture, may convey to us other Articles of Faith also, unless Scripture has expressly determined this in the negative.

7. But the sacred volume itself, as well as the doctrine of its inspiration, comes to us by traditional conveyance. The Protestant of the day asks his Roman antagonist, "*How* do you know your unwritten word comes from the apostles, received as it is through so many unknown hands through so many ages? A book is something definite and trustworthy; what is written remains. We have the apostles' writings before us; but we have nothing to guarantee to us the fidelity of those successive informants who stand between the apostles and the unwritten doctrines you ascribe to them." But the other surely may answer by the counter inquiry, *how* the Anglican on his part knows that what he considers to be their writings are really such, and really the same as the fathers possessed and witness to be theirs: "You have a printed book," he may argue; "the apostles did not write that; it was printed from another book, and that again from another, and so on. After going back a long way, you will trace it to a manuscript in the dark ages, written by you know not whom, copied from some other manuscript you know not what or when, and there the trace is lost. You profess, indeed, that it runs up to the very autograph of the apostles; but with your rigorous notions of proof, it would be more to your purpose to produce that autograph than to give merely probable reasons for the fidelity of the copy. Till you do this, you are resting on a series of unknown links as well as we; you are trusting a mere tradition of men. It is quite as possible for human hands to have tampered with the written as with the unwritten word; or at least if corruption of the latter is somewhat the more probable of the two, the difference of the cases is one of degree, and not any essential distinction." Now whatever explanations the Protestant in question makes in behalf of the preservation of the written word, will be found applicable to the unwritten. For instance, he may argue, and irresistibly, that manuscripts of various, and some of very early times, are still extant, and that these belong to different places and are derived from sources distinct from each other; and that they all agree together. If the text of the New Testament has been tampered with,

this must have happened before all these families of copies were made; which is to throw back the fraud upon times so early as to be a guarantee for believing it to have been impracticable. Or he may argue that it was the acknowledged duty of the church to keep and guard the Scriptures, and that in matter of fact her various branches were very careful to do so; that in consequence it is quite incredible that the authentic text should be lost, considering it had so many trustees, as they may be called, and that an altered copy or a forgery should be substituted. Or again, he may allege that the early fathers are frequent in quoting the New Testament in their own works; and that these quotations accord substantially with the copy of it which we at present possess. But it must be confessed that they are applicable in their nature to traditionary teaching also. . . .

8. How then are we to meet the Romanists, seeing we cannot join issue with them, or cut short the controversy, by a mere appeal to Scripture? We must meet them, and may do so fearlessly, on the ground of antiquity, to which they betake themselves. We accepted the Protestant's challenge, in arguing from mere Scripture in our defence; we must not and need not shrink from the invitation of our Roman opponent, when he would appeal to the witness of antiquity. Truth alone is consistent with itself; we are willing to take either the test of antiquity or of Scripture. As we accord to the Protestant sectary, that Scripture is the inspired treasury of the whole faith, but maintain that his doctrines are not in Scripture, so when the controversialist of Rome appeals to antiquity as our great teacher, we accept his appeal, but we deny that his special doctrines are to be found in antiquity. So far then is clear; we do not deny the force of tradition; we do not deny the soundness of the argument from antiquity any more than they are in the Bible; and we maintain that his professed tradition is not really such, that it is a tradition of men, that it is not continuous, that it stops short of the apostles, that the history of its introduction is known. On both accounts then his doctrines are innovations; because they run counter to the doctrine of antiquity, and because they rest upon what is historically an upstart tradition.

This view is intelligible and clear, but it leads to this conclusion. The Bible indeed is a small book, but the writings of antiquity are voluminous; and to read them is the work of a life. It is plain then that the controversy with Rome is not an easy one, not open to every one to take up. And this is the case for another reason also. A private Christian may put what meaning he pleases on many parts of the Scripture, and no one can hinder him. If interfered with, he can promptly answer that it is his opinion, and may appeal to his right of private judgment. But he cannot so deal with antiquity. History is a record of facts; and "facts," according to the proverb, "are stubborn things." Ingenious men may misrepresent them, or suppress them for a while; but in the end they will be duly ascertained and appreciated. The writings of the fathers are far too ample to allow of a disputant resting in one or two obscure or ambiguous passages in them and permanently turning such to his own account, which he may do in the case of Scripture. For two reasons, then, controversy with Romanists is laborious; because it takes us to ancient church history, and because it does not allow scope to the offhand or capricious decisions of private judgment.

However, it must be observed, for the same reasons, though more laborious, it is a surer controversy. We are more likely to come to an end; it does not turn upon opinions, but on facts.

9. This may be regarded from somewhat a different point of view. You know that three centuries ago took place a great schism in the West, which thenceforth was divided into two large bodies, the Roman communion on one hand, the Protestant on the other. On the latter side it is usual to reckon our own church, though it is really on neither; from it after a time certain portions split off, and severally set up a religion and communion for themselves. Now supposing we had to dispute with these separated portions, the Presbyterians, Baptists, Independents, or other Protestants, on the subject of their separation, they would at once avow the fact, but they would deny that it was a sin. The elementary controversy between us and them

353

would be one of doctrine and principle; viz. whether separation was or was not a sin. It is far otherwise as regards the Roman Catholics; they as well as ourselves allow, or rather maintain, the criminality of schism, and that a very great sin was committed at the Reformation, whether by the one party or by the other, or by both. The only question is, which party committed it; they lay it at our door, we retort it, and justly, upon them. Thus we join issue with them on a question of fact; a question which cannot be settled without a sufficient stock of learning on the part of the disputants. So again the Calvinistic controversy is in great measure dependent on abstract reasoning and philosophical discussion; whereas no one can determine by *a priori* arguments whether or not the Papacy be a persecuting power.

On the whole, then, it appears from what has been said, that our controversies with the Protestants are easy to handle, but interminable, being disputes about opinions. But those with Rome are arduous, but instructive, as relating rather to matters of fact.

10. These last remarks throw some light on the difference of internal character between Protestant and Roman teaching, as well as of argumentative basis. Our controversy with Rome, I have said, turns more upon facts than upon first principles; with Protestant sectaries it is more about principles than about facts. This general contrast between the two religions, which I would not seem to extend, for the sake of an antithesis, beyond what the sober truth warrants, is paralleled in the common remark of our most learned controversialists, that Romanism *holds the foundation,* or *is the truth overlaid with corruptions.* This is saying the same thing in other words. They discern in it the great outlines of primitive Christianity, but they find them touched, if nothing worse, touched and tainted by error, and so made dangerous to the multitude,—dangerous except to men of spiritual minds, who can undo the evil, arresting the tendencies of the system by their own purity, and restoring it to the sweetness and freshness of its original state. The very force of the word *corruption* implies that this is the peculiarity of Romanism. All error indeed of whatever kind may

be called a corruption of truth; still we properly apply the term to such kinds of error as are not denials but perversions, distortions, or excesses of it. Such is the relations of Romanism towards true Catholicity. It is the misdirection and abuse, not the absence of right principle. To take a familiar illustration; rashness and cowardice are both faults, and both unlike true courage; but cowardice implies the absence of the principle of courage, whereas rashness is but the extravagance of the principle. Again, prodigality and avarice are both vices, and unlike true and wise liberality; but avarice differs from it in principle, prodigality in matters of detail, in the time, place, person, manner of giving, and the like. On the other hand, prodigality may accidentally be the more dangerous extreme, as being the more subtle vice, the more popular, the more likely to attract noble minds, the more like a virtue. This is somewhat like the position of Romanism, Protestantism, and Catholic Truth, relatively to each other. Romanism may be considered as an unnatural and misshapen development of the truth; not the less dangerous because it retains traces of its genuine features, and usurps its name, as vice borrows the name of virtue, as pride is often called self-respect, or cowardice or worldly wisdom goes by the name of prudence, or rashness by that of courage. On the other hand, no one would ever call a miser liberal; and so no one would call a mere Protestant a Catholic, except an altogether new sense was put on the word to suit a purpose. Rome retains the principle of true Catholicism perverted; popular Protestantism is wanting in the principle. Lastly, virtue lies in a mean, is a point, almost invisible to the world, hard to find, acknowledged but by the few; and so Christian truth in these latter ages, when the world has broken up the church, has been but a stranger upon earth, and has been hidden and superseded by counterfeits.

11. The same view of Romanism is implied when we call our ecclesiastical changes in the sixteenth century a Reformation. A building has not been reformed or repaired, when it has been pulled down and built up again; but the word is used when it has been

left substantially what it was before, only amended or restored in detail. In like manner, we Anglo-Catholics do not profess a different religion from that of Rome, we profess their faith *all but* their corruptions.

Again, this same character of Romanism as a perversion, not a contradition of Christian truth, is confessed as often as members of our church in controversy with it contend, as they may rightly do, that it must be judged, not by the formal decrees of the Council of Trent, as its advocates wish, but by its practical working and its existing state in the countries which profess it. Romanists would fain confine us in controversy to the consideration of the bare and acknowledged principles of their church; we consider this to be an unfair restriction; why? because we conceive that Romanism is far more faulty in its details than in its formal principles, and that Councils, to which its adherents would send us, have more to do with its abstract system than with its practical working, that the abstract system contains for the most part tendencies to evil, which the actual working brings out, thus supplying illustrations of that evil which is really though latently contained in principles capable in themselves of an honest interpretation. Thus, for instance, the decree concerning Purgatory might be charitably made almost to conform to the doctrine of St. Austin or St. Chrysostom, were it not for the comment on it afforded by the popular belief as existing in those countries which hold it, and by the opinions of the Roman Schools.

12. It is something to the purpose also to observe, that this peculiar character of Roman teaching, as being substantial Trust corrupted, has tended to strengthen the popular notion, that it, or the Church of Rome, or the Pope or Bishop of Rome, is the Antichrist foretold in Scripture. That there is in Romanism something very unchristian, I fully admit, or rather maintain; but I will observe here that this strange two-fold aspect of the Roman system seems in matter of fact to have been in part a cause of that fearful title attaching to it,—and in this way. When Protestants have come to look at it closely, they have found truth and error united in so subtle a combination (as is the case with all

corruptions, as with sullied snow, or fruit over-ripe, or metal alloyed), they have found truth so impregnated with error, and error so sheltered by truth,—so much too adducible in defence of the system, which, from want of learning or other cause, they could not refute without refuting their own faith and practice at the same time,—so much in it of high and noble principle, or salutary usage, which they had lost, and, as losing, were, in that respect, in an inferior state,—that for this very reason it is so difficult to refute, so subtle and crafty, so seductive,—properties which are tokens of the hateful and fearful deceiver who is to come. Of course I do not mean to say that this perplexing aspect of the Roman Church has originally brought upon it the stigma under consideration; but that it has served to induce people indolently to acquiesce in it without examination.

In these remarks on the relation which Romanism bears to Catholic truth, I have appealed to the common opinion of the world; which is altogether confirmed when we come actually to compare together the doctrinal articles of our own and of the Roman faith. In both systems the same Creeds are acknowledged. Besides other points in common, we both hold, that certain doctrines are necessary to be believed for salvation; we both believe in the doctrines of the Trinity, Incarnation, and Atonement; in original sin; in the necessity of regeneration; in the supernatural grace of the Sacraments; in the apostolical succession; in the obligation of faith and obedience, and in the eternity of future punishment.

13. In conclusion I would observe, that in what I have been saying of the principles and doctrines of Romanism, I have mainly regarded it, not as an existing political sect among us, but in itself, in its abstract system, and in a state of quiescence. Viewed indeed in action, and as realized in its present partisans, it is but one out of the many denominations which are the disgrace of our age and country. In temper and conduct it does but resemble that unruly Protestantism which lies on our other side, and it submits without reluctance to be allied and to act with that Protestantism for the overthrow of a purer religion. But herein is the differ-

ence of the one extreme from the other; the political Romanist of the day becomes such in spite of his fundamental principles, the political Protestant in accordance with his. The best Dissenter is he who is least of a Dissenter; the best Roman Catholic is he who comes nearest to be a Catholic.... I have here considered the religion of Rome in its abstract professions for two reasons. First, I would willingly believe, that in spite of the violence and rancour of its public supporters, there are many individuals in its communion of gentle, affectionate, and deeply religious minds; and such a belief is justified when we find that the necessary difference between us and them is not one of essential principle, that it is the difference of superstition, and not of unbelief, from religion. Next, I have insisted upon it, by way of showing what must be the nature of their Reformation, if in God's merciful counsels a Reformation awaits them. It will be far more a reform of their popular usages and opinions, and ecclesiastical policy, that is, a destruction of what is commonly called Popery, than of their abstract principles and maxims.

On the other hand, let it not be supposed, because I have spoken without sympathy of popular Protestantism in the abstract, that this is all the abstract, that this is all one with being harsh towards individuals professing it; far from it. The worse their creed, the more sympathy is due to their persons; chiefly to those, for they most demand and will most patiently suffer it, who least concur in their own doctrine, and are held so by it in an unwilling captivity. Would that they would be taught that their peculiar form of religion, whatever it is, never can satisfy their souls, and does not admit of reform, but must come to nought! Would that they could be persuaded to transfer their misplaced and most unrequired affection from the systems of men to the One Holy Spouse of Christ, the Church Catholic, which in this country manifests herself in the Church, commonly so called, as her representative! Nor need we despair that, as regards many of them, this wish may yet be fulfilled.

12. Remarks on Certain Passages in the Thirty-nine Articles, Tract 90, London, 1841

Newman, *Via Media of the Anglican Church.*

It is often urged, and sometimes felt and granted, that there are in the Articles propositions or terms inconsistent with the Catholic faith.... The following Tract is drawn up with the view of showing how groundless the objection is.... That there are real difficulties to a Catholic Christian in the Ecclesiastical position of our church at this day, no one can deny; but the statements of the Articles are not in the number; and it may be right at the present moment to insist upon this. If in any quarter it is supposed that persons who profess to be disciples of the early church will silently concur with those of very opposite sentiments in furthering a relaxation of subscriptions, which, it is imagined, are galling to both parties, though for different reasons, and that they will do this against the wish of the great body of the church, the writer of the following pages would raise one voice, at least, in protest against any such anticipation... Religious changes, to be beneficial, should be the act of the whole body; they are worth little if they are the mere act of a majority. No good can come of any change which is not heartfelt, a development of feelings springing up freely and calmly within the bosom of the whole body itself....

VII-5. John Henry Newman. *Early sketch by Richard Doyle.*

The present writer, for one, will be no party to the ordinary political methods by which professed reforms are carried or compassed in this day. We can do nothing well till we act "with one accord"; we can have no accord in action till we agree together in heart; we cannot agree without a supernatural influence; we cannot have a supernatural influence unless we pray for it; we cannot pray acceptably without repentance and confession. Our church's strength would be irresistible, humanly speaking, were it but at unity with itself: if it remains divided, part against part, we shall see the energy which was meant to subdue the world preying upon itself, according to our Saviour's express assurance that such a house "cannot stand." Till we feel this, till we seek one another as brethren, not lightly throwing aside our private opinions, which we seem to feel we have received from above, from an ill-regulated, untrue desire of unity, but returning to each other in heart, and coming together to God to do for us what we cannot do for ourselves, no change can be for the better. Till we, her children, are stirred up to this religious course, let the Church, our Mother, sit still; let her children be content to be in bondage; let us work in chains; let us submit to our imperfections as a punishment; let us go on teaching with the stammering lips of ambiguous formularies, and inconsistent precedents, and principles but partially developed. We are not better than our fathers; let us bear to be what Hammond was, or Andrewes, or Hooker; let us not faint under that body of death, which they bore about in patience; nor shrink from the penalty of sins, which they inherited from the age before them.

But these remarks are beyond our present scope, which is merely to show that, while our Prayer Book is acknowledged on all hands to be of Catholic origin, our Articles also, the offspring of an uncatholic age, are, through God's good providence, to say the least, not uncatholic, and may be subscribed by those who aim at being catholic in heart and doctrine. . . .

[The articles considered are Nos. 6 and 20, 11, 12 and 13, 19, 21, 22, 25, 28, 31, 32, 35 and 37.]

1. HOLY SCRIPTURE AND THE AUTHORITY OF THE CHURCH

. . . Not a word is said, . . . in favour of there being no external rule or method to fix the interpretation of Scripture by, or, as it is commonly expressed, of Scripture being the sole rule of faith; nor of the private judgment of the individual being the ultimate standard of interpretation. . . .

6. PURGATORY, PARDONS, IMAGES, RELICS, INVOCATION OF SAINTS

Now the first remark that occurs on perusing this Article is, that the doctrine objected to is "the *Romish* doctrine." For instance, no one would suppose that the *Calvinistic* doctrine concerning purgatory, pardons, and image-worship, is spoken against. Not every doctrine on these matters is a fond thing, but the *Romish* doctrine. Accordingly, the *Primitive* doctrine is not condemned in it, unless, indeed, the Primitive doctrine be the Romish, which must not be supposed. Now there *was* a primitive doctrine on all these points,—how far Catholic or universal, is a further question,—but still so widely received and so respectably supported, that it may well be entertained as a matter of opinion by a theologian now; this, then, whatever be its merits, is not condemned by this Article.

This is clear without proof on the face of the matter, at least as regards pardons. Of course, the Article never meant to make light of *every* doctrine about pardons, but a certain doctrine, the Romish doctrine, as indeed the plural form itself shows. . . .

If, then, in the judgment of the Homilies, not all doctrine concerning veneration of relics is condemned in the Article before us, but a certain toleration of them is compatible with its wording; neither is all doctrine concerning purgatory, pardons, images and saints, condemned by the Article, but only "the Romish."

And further by "the Romish doctrine," is not meant the Tridentine doctrine, because this Article was drawn up before the decree of the Council of Trent. What is opposed is the *received doctrine* of that day, and unhappily of this day too, or the doctrine of the *Roman Catholic schools.* . . .

None of these doctrines does the Article condemn; any of them may be held by the Anglo-Catholic as a matter of private belief; not that they are here advocated, one or other, but they are adduced as an illustration of what the Article does *not* mean, and to vindicate our Christian liberty in a matter where the church has not confined it. . . .

7. THE SACRAMENTS

This Article does not deny the five rites in question to be sacraments, but to be sacraments in *the sense* in which Baptism and the Lord's Supper are sacraments; "sacraments *of the Gospel*," sacraments *with an outward sign ordained* of God.

9. MASSES

Nothing can show more clearly than this passage that the Articles are not written against the creed of the Roman Church, but against actual existing errors in it, whether taken into its system or not. Here the sacrifice of the *Mass* is not spoken of. . . .

On the whole, then, it is conceived that the Article before us neither speaks against the Mass in itself, nor against its being an offering for the quick and the dead for the remission of sin; but against its being viewed, on the one hand, as independent of or distinct from the Sacrifice on the Cross, which is blasphemy, and, on the other, its being directed to the emolument of those to whom it pertains to celebrate it, which is imposture in addition.

CONCLUSION

It may be objected that the tenor of the above explanation is anti-Protestant, whereas it is notorious that the Articles were drawn up by Protestants, and intended for the establishment of Protestantism; accordingly, that it is an evasion of their meaning to give them any other than a Protestant drift, possible as it may be to do so grammatically, or in each separate part.

But the answer is simple:

1. In the first place, it is a *duty* which we owe both to the Catholic Church and to our own, to take our reformed confessions in the most Catholic sense they will admit; we have no duties towards their framers. Nor do we receive the Articles from their original framers, but from several successive Convocations after their time; in the last instance, from that of 1662.

2. In giving the Articles a Catholic interpretation, we bring them into harmony with the Book of Common Prayer, an object of the most serious moment for those who have given their assent to both formularies.

3. Whatever be the authority of the Declaration prefixed to the Articles, so far as it has any weight at all, it sanctions the mode of interpreting them above given. For its enjoining the "literal and grammatical sense," relieves us from the necessity of making the known opinions of their framers, a comment upon their text; and its forbidding any person to "affix any *new* sense to any Article," was promulgated at a time when the leading men of our church were especially noted for those Catholic views which have been here advocated. . . .

5. Further: the Articles are evidently framed on the principle of leaving open large questions, on which the controversy hinges. They state broadly extreme truths, and are silent about their adjustment. . . .

7. Lastly, their framers constructed them in such a way as best to comprehend those who did not go so far in Protestantism as themselves. Anglo-Catholics then are but the successors and representatives of those moderate reformers; and their case has been directly anticipated in the wording of the Articles. It follows that they are not perverting, they are using them for an express purpose for which, among others, their authors framed them.

The Protestant Confession was drawn up with the purpose of including Catholics; and Catholics now will not be excluded. What was an economy in the Reformers, is a protection to us. What would have been a perplexity to us then, is a perplexity to Protestants now. We could not then have found fault with their words; they cannot now repudiate our meaning.

Oxford. The Feast of the Conversion of St. Paul. 1841.

Aulard, F. O., *Christianity and the French Revolution*. London: Ernest Benn, Ltd., 1927.

Becker, Carl L., *The Heavenly City of the Eighteenth Century Philosophers*. New Haven: Yale University Press, 1932.

Brandt, Richard B., *The Philosophy of Schleiermacher*. New York: Harper & Row, Publishers, 1941.

Bremond, Henri, *The Mystery of Newman*, trans. H. C. Corrance. London: Williams and Norgate, Ltd., 1907.

Brilioth, Y. T., *The Anglican Revival*. London: Longmans, Green & Company, Ltd., 1925.

Brinton, C. C., *A Decade of Revolution, 1789-1799*. New York: Harper & Row, Publishers, 1934.

Church, R. W., *The Oxford Movement, 1833-45*. London: Macmillan & Co., Ltd., 1891.

Culler, A. D., *The Imperial Intellect: Newman's Educational Ideal*. New Haven: Yale University Press, 1955.

Edghill, E. A., *Faith and Fact: A Study of Ritschlianism*. London: Macmillan & Co., Ltd., 1910.

Elton, Godfrey, *The Revolutionary Idea in France, 1780-1871*. New York: David McKay Co., Inc., 1923, 1931, and other editions.

Geffcken, F. H., *Church and State*. London: Longmans, Green & Company, Ltd., 1877.

Gooch, George P., *The French Revolution*. New York: The Macmillan Company, 1920.

Gottschalk, Louis R., *The Era of the French Revolution, 1715-1815*. Boston: Houghton Mifflin Company, 1929.

Hales, E. E. Y., *The Catholic Church in the Modern World*. London: Eyre & Spottiswoode, Ltd., 1958.

——, *Revolution and Papacy, 1769-1846*. London: Eyre & Spottiswoode, Ltd., 1960.

Hall, T. C., *The Social Meaning of Modern Religious Movements in England*. New York: Charles Scribner's Sons, 1900.

Higham, Florence, *Frederick Denison Maurice*. London: Student Christian Movement Press, 1947.

Hook, Sidney, *From Hegel to Marx*. New York: Reynal & Company, Inc., 1936.

Knox, E. A., *The Tractarian Movement, 1833-1845*. New York: G. P. Putnam's Sons, 1933.

Mackintosh, Hugh R., *Types of Modern Theology: Schleiermacher to Barth*. London: James Nisbet & Co., Ltd., 1937.

Marcuse, Herbert, *Reason and Revolution: Hegel and the Rise of Social Theory*. New York: Humanities Press, 1954.

Mathieson, W. L., *English Church Reform, 1815-40*. London: Longmans, Green & Company, Ltd., 1923.

Newman, John Henry, *Apologia Pro Vita Sua*. Various editions.

——, *Living Thoughts of Cardinal Newman*, ed. by Henry Tristram. New York: David McKay Co., Inc., 1953.

——, *Prose and Poetry*, ed. by Geoffrey Tillotson. Cambridge: Harvard University Press, 1957.

Nichols, J. H., *History of Christianity, 1650-1950*. New York: The Ronald Press Company, 1956.

Osborn, Andrew R., *Schleiermacher and Religious Education*. London: Oxford University Press, 1934.

Overton, J. H., *The English Church in the Nineteenth Century, 1800-33*. London: Longmans, Green & Company, Ltd., 1894.

Pfleiderer, O., *Development of Theology in Germany Since Kant*, 3rd Edition. London: Sonnenschein, 1909.

Phillips, C. S., *The Church in France, 1789-1848*. London: Mowbray, 1929.

Rose, John H., *The Revolutionary and Napoleonic Era, 1789-1815*. Cambridge: Cambridge University Press, 1935.

Rousseau, J. J., *Emile*, ed. by W. H. Boyd. New York: Teachers College, 1962.

Rousseau, J. J., *Political Writings*, trans. F. M. Watkins. New York: Thomas Nelson & Sons, 1953.

Schleiermacher, F., *Soliloquies*, trans. Horace L. Friess. Chicago: Open Court Publishing Co., 1926.

Sloane, William M., *The French Revolution and Religious Reform*. New York: Charles Scribner's Sons, 1901.

Stewart, John Hall, *A Documentary Survey of the French Revolution.* New York: The Macmillan Company, 1951.

Storr, V. F., *The Development of English Theology in the Nineteenth Century, 1800-1860.* London: Longmans, Green & Company, Ltd., 1913.

Thompson, James M., *The French Revolution.* Oxford: B. H. Blackwell, Ltd., 1944.

Vidler, Alec R., *The Church in an Age of Revolution.* Baltimore: Penguin Books, Inc., 1961.

Webb, C. C. J., *Religious Thought in the Oxford Movement.* London: SPCK, 1928.

White, James F., *The Cambridge Movement: The Ecclesiologists and the Gothic Revival.* Cambridge: Cambridge University Press, 1962.

CHRONOLOGY

1724–1804	*Immanuel Kant*
1743–1826	*Thomas Jefferson*
1749–1832	*Johann Wolfgang von Goethe*
1751–1780	*Diderot's Encyclopedia*
1759–1805	*Christoph Friedrich von Schiller*
1762	*Rousseau's Emile, Social Contract*
1768–1834	*Friedrich Schleiermacher*
1770–1831	*G. W. F. Hegel*
1770–1850	*William Wordsworth*
1771–1832	*Sir Walter Scott*
1772–1834	*Samuel Taylor Coleridge*
1775	*Paine's Age of Reason*
1776	*July 4, American Declaration of Independence*
1778	*Death of Rousseau and Voltaire*
1781	*Kant's Critique of Pure Reason*
1788	*Kant's Critique of Practical Reason*
1789	*January 24, Convocation of Estates-General in Paris*
	June 20, Tennis Court Oath
	June 27, National Constituent Assembly (to September 30, 1791)
	July 14, Fall of Bastille
	August 4–5, Abolition of Feudal System
	August 27, Declaration of Rights of Man and Citizen
	November 2, Confiscation of Church property

1790	*February 13, Decree prohibiting monastic vows*
	July 12, Civil Constitution of the Clergy
	November 27, Decree requiring clerical oath
1791	*Paine's Rights of Man*
	Death of John Wesley
	April 13, Papal Bull Charitas
	June 21–25, Flight of French royal family
1792–1860	*F. C. Baur*
1792	*September 19–22, French National Convention organized and Republic declared*
1643–1715	*Louis XIV, King of France*
1715–1754	*Louis XV, King of France*
1754–1793	*Louis XVI, King of France*
1793	*January 21, King Louis XVI beheaded*
	April 6, Committee on Public Safety
	June 3 to July 28, 1794, Reign of Terror
	Nov. 10, Worship of Reason inaugurated
	Burke's Reflections on the French Revolution
	Kant's Religion Within the Limits of Reason Alone
1793–1795	*Louis XVII, nominal king of France*
1794	*May 7, Decree establishing worship of Supreme Being*
	June 8, Festival of Supreme Being

Illustration opposite page 363: **Christ after the Resurrection.** *By Erwin F. Frey. Ferdinand Howald Collection, Columbus Gallery of Fine Arts.*

VIII

Roman Catholic

Reaction to Modernism

In the eighteenth century, the tide against
Roman Catholicism mounted to unusual heights. Criticism
came not only from the rationalistic, liberal spirit that
poured from the pens of men like Voltaire and the *philosophes*,
Hume and Kant, but also from the rising monarchies who were
seeking to establish their own sovereignty. The waves of criticism
washed heavily against the militantly ultramontane
Society of Jesus. In 1713, the Jesuits won what appeared to be
a signal victory; the famous bull *Unigenitus* outlawed Jansenism
by condemning more than a hundred propositions in Quesnel's
devotional book *Moral Reflections on the New Testament*,
published twenty-five years earlier. *Unigenitus* climaxed years of effort
by the Jesuits to smash their old rivals from Port Royal. But
Jansenism had penetrated deeply into the heart of the
French, and, though many of its tenets had been forgotten, it had

become identified with the Gallican spirit of the people. When the Jesuits pressed their advantage through their questionable doctrines of probabilism and expediency in order to advance papal domination, their very success caused reaction. The Jesuits' attempt to use *Unigenitus* against all those who did not agree with them, even to the point of denying extreme unction to any who rejected the bull, created a popular wave of disgust and protest. Under the continual press of persecution, Jansenism lost much of its distinctively religious force and developed extreme apocalyptic notions and miraculous claims, but it gained strength as a rallying point for French dissidents. The unrest was so obvious that the French Parliament decreed that the Jesuits were no longer to advocate the *Unigenitus* as a rule of faith, and in 1757 it forbade mentioning the bull in public.

The Jesuit Order had proved an effective weapon in the Counter Reformation, but there arose in the eighteenth and nineteenth centuries a rationalistic and nationalistic spirit that had little in common with ultramontane papal policies. Country after country sensed the threat of increasing Jesuit power, and monarchies which were advocating their own sovereignty felt constrained to take direct action against the Jesuits. In 1764, the celebrated LaValette lawsuit resulted in a confiscation of Jesuit property and a decree by King Louis XVI banning the existence of the Society in France. Similar reaction occurred in other lands. In 1759, the Society was forced out of Portugal, accused of trying to usurp royal prerogatives and even to assassinate the king. In 1767 the Order, suspected of disloyalty and intrigue against the king of Spain, was suddenly dissolved in all Spanish lands. In the same year the Jesuits were expelled from Naples.

Similar antipapal sentiments developed in other lands. In Germany, Nicholas von Hontheim (1701-1790) published a book in 1763 on the conditions of the church and the legitimate powers of the pope; he appealed for reform by conciliar action. His book was so influential that "Febronianism," derived from his pseudonym Justinus Febro-

nius, became a symbol for antipapalism in Germany. In Austria, antipapalism, known as "Josephism," developed under Emperor Joseph II (1765-1790), one of the most enlightened despots of the time. He advocated toleration of other faiths, which became a partial reality in 1781, and demanded that the Jesuits cease taking orders from their foreign generals. By regulating the seminaries and forcing reforms in monasteries and education, he transferred ecclesiastical training from the church to the state. Josephism collapsed with the death of Joseph in 1790, but his actions were expressive of the feelings of the times.

When Clement XIV (1769-1774) became pope, the Bourbon rulers insisted that he suppress the Jesuits. Fearing the establishment, particularly in France, of national churches which would have only a nominal relationship to the papacy, he resolved to suppress the Society of Jesus. On July 21, 1773, Clement dissolved the Order in his bull *Dominus ac Redemptor Noster*. Rationalism and the Catholic monarchies had triumphed. Ultramontanism had reached a new low. In 1797, Napoleon invaded the Eternal City and forced Pope Pius VI (1775-1799) into exile. His successor, Pope Pius VII (1800-1823), entered into the Concordat of 1801, which reduced the papacy to a pawn in the plans of Napoleon. The final papal rebuff, and also the turning point, came in 1809 when Napoleon invaded the papal states and imprisoned the pope. Because of the moral integrity of Pope Pius VII, who refused to play the role of Napoleon's chaplain and lackey, the papacy emerged from the war-torn years of the French Revolution and the Napoleonic era as one of Europe's strongest institutions. On being released from prison in France, one of the first acts of Pope Pius VII was the restoration of the Society of Jesus, August 7, 1814.

The revival of the Jesuits was more than a symbol; it marked a return to the ultramontane principles that had carried the church to pre-eminence before the ascendancy of rationalism and nationalism. The destruction, confusion, insecurity, and uncertainty that accompanied the French Revolution and Napoleon's military conquests indicated what could be expected from a disavowal of ecclesiastical authority. Consequently, the papacy recoiled, and with only a few hesitant exceptions, resolutely set a course diametrically opposed to the secularizing, democratic forces in Western Europe. In a series of monumental bulls and encyclicals, the Roman Catholic Church sought to curtail all change; in opposition to all liberalizing trends, the papacy asserted that it and it alone had the divine right to control and to guide all aspects of culture. This was the basic reaction of the church, but the church was no longer supreme in Western culture. The Civil Constitution of France and the Concordat of 1801 proved to be the harbingers of the future.

Pius VII died in 1823 and his successor, Leo XII, was relatively insignificant. But ultramontanism took a big step forward in the brief pontificate of Pius VIII (1829-1830), and was wielded as a spiritual and political weapon by successive popes throughout the nineteenth century. To combat the effectiveness of various tract societies that were distributing Scriptures, Pope Pius VIII issued his encyclical *Traditi humilitati*, May 21, 1829, in which he condemned latitudinarian indifferentism in religion and reaffirmed the church's stand against unauthorized, heretical translations of the Bible. Scripture and tradition, properly interpreted by the clergy, constitute authority, he declared; and he excoriated those who, claiming the help of the Holy Spirit, dared to interpret Scripture on their own. To strengthen Catholicism on the local level, particularly in Germany, Pius objected strenuously to marriages of Catholics to non-Catholics. In his encyclical *Litteris alto*, March 25, 1830, he branded such marriages "grave crimes" and declared that the "Church has a horror of these unions, which present so many deformities and spiritual dangers." He called such marriages direct sins against canon and divine law. To show that Catholicism was not accepting the principle of national sovereignty, and that the church could not tolerate interference with its program, Pius asserted just before his death that the church, the Spouse of Christ, is by divine institution free from all human power.

Liberalism had not lost its vigor, however, and there was a strong tendency in some areas for Roman Catholicism to compromise with the changed climate of thought. Liberals, both Protestant and Catholic, brought about the Catholic Emancipation Act of Great Britain and Ireland in 1829, and Catholic liberals as well as others insisted on provisions guaranteeing freedom of religion in the Belgian Constitution in 1831, although Roman Catholicism retained important privileges as a semiestablished religion. The Belgian Constitution was one of the few attempts of a Catholic majority to come to terms with democratic liberalism. But the papacy feared that liberalism would undercut authority and foster anarchy, and other liberal developments met stern papal resistance, the most celebrated instance being that of Lamennais in France.

For a time, liberal Catholics appeared to have a chance to influence the election of a pope in 1831, but ultramontane zealots, the *Zelanti*, finally secured the election of Gregory XVI (1831-1846), who opposed building railroads and making other modern improvements in the papal states. But he is particularly remembered for condemning attempts to reconcile Catholicism with modern political ideas and for alienating the liberal element in France that centered around Abbé de Lamennais (1782-1854). Lamennais was actually ultramontane in sympathy, but he was also aware of the liberal forces that were changing society, and felt that the papacy, in alignment with the monarchies, was making a grave mistake. When his efforts to reconcile Catholicism and liberalism failed, Lamennais left the church and finally died a Deist.

Impatient for action Lamennais and his cohorts, Montalembert and Lacordaire, began publishing a daily journal, *L'Avenir*, which severely criticized the Gallican bishops and the monarchy of France. *L'Avenir*, during its brief life from October, 1830, to November, 1831, advocated universal suffrage, self-determination for the Poles and Belgians, and freedom of worship, press, assembly, education, and speech. Lamennais made liberty his watchword, for he believed that the church was too involved in the government of France, and that only by being free could she do her distinctive work and be herself. But Lamennais' criticism of the Gallican bishops and the church's ties with the monarchy was politically inexpedient. When he appealed to the pope for support, he was rebuffed. When he journeyed to Rome to support his case, he was snubbed by Pope Gregory, who had no intention of supporting a liberalism that would acknowledge Catholicism merely as a party in a state. In *Mirari vos*, 1832, Pope Gregory condemned the position of Lamennais and insisted on submission to constituted authority. By implication he linked Lamennais with "unbridled license," "contempt for the Church," "an ever-approaching revolutionary-abyss of bottomless miseries," and a filthy sewer full of "heretical vomit."

Lamennais submitted, but he was stunned, and soon felt that he had to work outside the church for his ideals. His anonymous, but soon discovered *Paroles d'un Croyant*, 1834, was a fierce denunciation of tyranny and an appeal for democratic socialism. He referred to Gregory as an old man who speaks of justice while holding a poisoned cup in one hand and caressing a harlot with the other. The sensational *Paroles* was translated into several languages, and on June 25, 1834, the encyclical *Singulari vos* appeared in which Lamennais himself was condemned. Lamennais' popularity dwindled during the final decades of his life; he separated himself from the church, was sent to prison for one year, became disillusioned with the violence of the revolutionaries in 1848, and died in 1854 almost forgotten.

If Pius IX (1846-1878) had plans to encourage liberalism when he took office, they were soon shattered in the wave of liberal and national revolutions that swept over Europe in 1848, the year in which Marx and Engels published the *Communist Manifesto*. The revolutions of 1848 witnessed the *coup d'état* of Louis Napoleon and the Second Empire in France, an intensification of the struggle to unify Italy, and the beginning of the process which deprived the pope of his temporal territories. For a time, Pope Pius IX seemed to foster reform in the Italian states. He granted a more liberal constitution in 1848, and his popularity was such that he might even have been selected to head an Italian federation. But when the revolutionaries expelled him from Rome in 1848 and established a Republic of Rome, February 9, 1849, he turned against all forms of liberal government and soon said that Roman Catholic liberals were no better than traitors to their church.

In 1850, French troops reinstated Pius in the Vatican, and after that he pursued a policy of a reactionary character. In his own words, he vowed to make war on "modernism." His mouthpiece was the fanatically ultramontane journalist, Louis Veuillot, whose journal, the *Univers*, advocated extreme authoritarianism and set the stage for Pius' most important encyclicals. But Pius' pronouncements could not stem the grass-roots drive for a united Italy, and even the papal states rebelled and joined the struggle. Napoleon III came to the aid of the pope in 1859, but foreign troops were no match for the inspired followers of Garibaldi, who told his men that the day would come when the "blindfolded masses shall understand that the priest is an impostor and tyrannies a monstrous anachronism. How glorious were thy Thousand, O Italy, fighting against the plumed and gilded agents of despotism and driving them before them like sheep! glorious in their motley array, just as they came from their offices and workshops at the trumpet call of duty, in the student's coat and hat or the modest garb of the mason, carpenter, or smith. . . ." Victor Emmanuel, King of Sardinia, declared that his conscience would not allow him to support the temporal claims of the church. The first meeting of the Italian Parliament, February 18, 1861, proclaimed Emmanuel King of Italy. This act the papacy protested, saying that a Catholic had betrayed his church, broken every law, and had usurped a title to cover his iniquitous acts against the Apostolic See. Pius vowed never to recognize the title.

When Austria was defeated in 1866, Venice joined the new Italian Kingdom; Rome was incorporated when French troops left it to fight in the Franco-Prussian War in 1870. A plebiscite proved that the incorporation move had popular support, and Rome became Italy's new capital. But what to do about the "Roman question" and the pope's territorial claims? Because the pope refused to negotiate, on May 13, 1871, the Kingdom of Italy passed the unilateral Law of Guarantees, which delineated the status of the papacy. Privileges and immunities equal to those bestowed upon the King of Italy were accorded the pope, and financial endowments were made to insure papal security in view of the loss of papal patrimony. Freedom to publish and to communicate with the Italian clergy and laity and with the rest of the world were guaranteed. The Law of Guarantees embodied Cavour's and Montalembert's ideas of "a free church in a free state," but this was no ideal for the papacy. Although the papacy lived by the law for the next fifty years, the pope decried the status that those of his own flock had reduced him to by their unwarranted seizure of the church's divine prerogatives. Pius referred to himself as the "prisoner of the Vatican." Sympathy mounted for the "imprisoned" pope, and Peter's Pence was revived to fill the Vatican coffers again. To strengthen its negotiating stance and in the hope of crippling the new kingdom, the papacy imposed a *non expedit* which forbade faithful Roman Catholics to participate in Italian politics. This situation prevailed until 1929, when Mussolini's Fascist government abrogated the Law of Guarantees and negotiated an agreement with the papacy known as the Lateran Treaty, which acknowledged the Vatican City as a state.

Pius IX had difficulties in other areas. *Kulturkampf,* "the struggle for civilization," developed in Germany. The Kingdom of Prussia, constituted in 1701, was oriented toward Protestantism, despite a large Catholic population. When Prussia rose to power and defeated the Catholic countries of France and Austria in 1866 and 1870, a powerful new nation with a Protestant ruler had come upon the European scene. The German Empire was proclaimed at Versailles in January,

VIII-1. Symbol of the Church on the Apse, Lateran Basilica, Rome. *Water from the Holy Spirit (the dove) flows through Christ (the Cross) into the Church (the rock), from which rivers of salvation flow to quench the thirst of the faithful. Angels guard Paradise beneath the rock. From Carl van Treeck and Aloysius Croft,* Symbols of the Church *(Milwaukee: The Bruce Publishing Company, 1936).*

1871, and its political mentor, Bismarck, inaugurated a policy of *Kulturkampf* with the intention of making the state supreme in all cultural affairs. Opposition came from the Catholic Center Party, which was organized on a confessional basis and limited to Catholics, but Bismarck pushed ahead. In 1872, the state assumed control of schools of religion and the training of priests, debarred the Society of Jesus from the territory of the German Reich, and placed various monastic orders under police supervision. Kulturminister Falk instituted state examinations in history, philosophy, and literature, in an effort to liberalize the church's clergy. Despite heavy objection from Catholic bishops and priests, the May laws of 1873 and 1875 gave the state more control over education and marriage, made appointments to vacant bishoprics subject to the state, banned monastic orders, curtailed the Catholic press, permitted confiscation of some church property, and instituted punishment for recalcitrant priests. The pope objected, but Bismarck vowed that he would not go to Canossa in the spirit or in the flesh. However, the Catholic Center Party created popular reaction to Bismarck's radical *Kulturkampf*, so that the antireligious measures had to be relaxed in the 1880's. By 1886, the seminaries again had control of ecclesiastical education, and appointments were again being made by the episcopacy. Bismarck deemed it expedient to come to political terms with the papacy and his Catholic constituency in order to counteract the rising threat of the "red international."

Pius was more successful in Ecuador, where in 1862 the papacy signed a concordat that realized the aims of the ultramontanists. The President of Ecuador was a devout Catholic who rose to power in a revolution against liberal, anti-clerical forces. The concordat officially recognized Catholicism as the only legal faith, forbade toleration of other religions, gave the church complete control of education, and, in general, made the church dominant in the life of Ecuador.

This was the background against which Pius IX, pope from 1846 to 1878, proclaimed his encyclicals and engineered the dogma of papal infallibility. On December 8, 1854, Pius IX, on his own authority, issued the dogma of the Immaculate Conception of the Blessed Virgin, a dogma long desired by Marialotrists, but hardly favored by the liberals (1). In 1864, just one year after Renan's modernistic *Life of Jesus* appeared, Pius declared war on all forms of modernism in his encyclical, the *Syllabus of Errors*. Stating various propositions as errors, Pius condemned rationalism, freemasonry, indifferentism, socialism, communism, separation of church and state, liberty of religion, and even the idea that the Roman Church should attempt to reconcile herself to the premises of progress and modern democratic liberalism (2). The sweeping character of the *Syllabus* astounded many Catholics, who hastened to explain and soften its most extreme ideas. French Bishop Dupanloup explained that the pope was addressing himself to an ideal (the thesis) rather than to an actual circumstance (the hypothesis), but Pius was in fact reacting in particular to Italian liberalism and his loss of temporal power.

Pius had even larger schemes. In 1867, he announced that a Vatican Council would be summoned shortly, the first ecumenical council since the Council of Trent, 1545-1563. No one knew just what to expect; an air of mystery surrounded the event. Speculation that infallibility or the assumption of Mary would be on the agenda prompted debates in Catholicism. Liberal laymen at Coblenz asked that there be no return to the Middle Ages, that the clergy be trained in keeping with the times, and that the Index be curtailed. Others asked assurances that nothing be done contrary to Scripture, and that freedom be safeguarded. When the delegates, most of whom were ultramontane, assembled in the Vatican in March, 1870, procedures were adopted which insured papal control. Silence was enjoined as to the proceedings, and all motions had to be approved by the pope. Prolonged debates on clerical beards and the breviary wore down the opponents of ultramontanism. When the vote on infallibility was finally taken on July 18, only 535 of more than 1,000 who were eligible voted. More than a hundred bishops withdrew rather than ballot. Of those remaining, 533 voted yes, two voted no. The dogma of infallibility made future councils unnecessary; the pope could speak finally on anything relating to faith and morals (3).

Ironically, in the same year that infallibility was proclaimed, the French troops were withdrawn from Rome to be used in the Franco-Prussian War, and Italian armies seized the city of Rome and incorporated it into the Kingdom of Italy, bringing the temporal power of the pope to an end. In Germany, a group of dissident Catholics rejected the Vatican decrees and organized the "Old Catholic Church," which took episcopal ordination from the Jansenist Church in Amsterdam and formally organized itself in 1873 at a congress in Constance. Among its leaders were the historian Döllinger and Herzog, who became a bishop in Switzerland. Prussia, Bavaria, Austria, Baden, Hesse, and Switzerland officially recognized the new church.

Ultramontane claims reached a climax under Pius IX, but it was Leo XIII who won worldwide respect for ultramontane principles. Leo XIII (1878-1903) was already sixty-eight years old when his pontificate began, but he recognized what his predecessors refused to accept: Liberalism had come to stay; sovereign nationalities were entrenched. Roman Catholicism would have to reinterpret its principles, so that Catholics could live in democratic states as both loyal citizens and faithful Catholics.

Leo had been born in the papal states, had studied with the Jesuits at the Roman College, had taken a doctorate in canon law at Sapienza, and was ordained to the priesthood at the age of twenty-seven. After a variety of offices, from the head of police in Benevento to the bishop of Perugia, he became one of the greatest of popes. He issued eighty-six encyclicals, most of which laid down guidelines for Roman Catholics living in a society that did not acknowledge the supremacy of the church. His task was not easy. When he became pope, anti-clericalism was strong in France; *Kulturkampf* had triumphed in Germany; nationalism had made Italians hostile to the Vatican; and the spirit of scientific rationalism and socialism was rapidly gaining recognition. Charles Darwin published his *Origin of Species* in 1859, and Karl Marx proclaimed his *Communist Manifesto* at the international congress of socialists in London in 1848.

The Leonine Corpus refers to the twelve major encyclicals on social subjects which Leo proclaimed. His first one was *Aeterni Patris*, August 4, 1879, insisting that the philosophy of Thomas Aquinas be taught in the schools; his greatest was *Rerum Novarum*, May 15, 1891, on the condition of the working classes, which pointed the way for Roman Catholic attitudes toward the problems of social industrialization.

Portions of three of Leo's encyclicals are given in the following documents. They should be read carefully. *Immortale Dei*, November 1, 1885, deals with the Christian Constitution of States and answers the question of whether a Catholic can be a good citizen in a secular state (4). Prior to the publishing of this encyclical, France had grown increasingly anticlerical, and tension had grown between French Gallicans and ultramontanes. Leo maintained that all authority comes from God, and that the state ought publicly to acknowledge Catholicism as the only true religion. But he noted the necessity of church and state working together, despite fundamental differences, and declared that Catholics could tolerate religious error in a state "for the sake of securing some great good or of hindering some great evil." He did not retreat from the claim that the church is superior to the state in civil matters. He approved democracy but not popular sovereignty, and he condemned separation of church and state, for the church ought ideally to control the state.

Libertas Praestantissimum, June 20, 1888, delineated human liberty in a context of natural law, divine authority, and social responsibility. Liberty must be subject to law, otherwise it becomes a license for the destruction of social order (5).

Rerum Novarum, without sacrificing any of the traditional claims of the church to a superior place in society, urged a bettering of the social conditions of the working class for the good of society as a whole (6).

Leo's masterful statements won wide respect for the papacy, but they did not turn the tide of events. In 1901, just one hundred years after the concordat between Napoleon and Pius VII, France passed its Law of Associations, which stringently curtailed the remnants of ultramontanism in France. The Law of Associations proclaimed complete liberty of conscience, disavowed any established church, and made all religious groups—Protestant, Catholic, or Jewish—dependent on local associations of laymen, which in effect dissolved Catholicism in France into a multitude of autonomous local congregations. The Law of Separation, December 9, 1905, officially established separation of church and state in France, and jeopardized the property claims of Roman Catholicism in France by not according the church legal recognition.

When Pius X became pope in 1903, this explosive political situation greeted him. In 1904, he protested a public snubbing that he had received at the hands of the French president, and France retaliated by withdrawing its ambassador from the Vatican and seizing some church properties in France. Then came the Law of Separation, to which Pius sternly objected in 1906 in a letter to the bishops of France (7).

In the meantime, another modernist development had begun to threaten the ultramontane position. Historical and higher criticism, the scientific concept of evolution, and rationalistic ideas caused many scholars in the Roman Catholic fold to advocate a reinterpretation of the Catholic attitude toward the Bible. Prominent among these were Alfred Loisy and Louis Duchesne in France, George Tyrrell in England, Hermann Schell and Baron von Hügel in Germany, and Senator Fogazzaro in Italy. They raised questions about church history, the inspiration and inerrancy of the Bible, the Mosaic authorship of the Pentateuch, and the reliability of scientific conclusions based on Genesis. The ultramontanists were disturbed, and Duchesne and Loisy were both dismissed from their professorships in Paris. As early as 1893 Leo XIII issued his *Providentissimus Deus,* in which he upheld biblical inerrancy and the finality of the church as a teacher, guide, and interpreter of Scripture.

Nevertheless, higher criticism continued to develop. Baron von Hügel read a paper in 1897 propounding multiple sources for the Hexateuch, Hermann Schell in 1899 raised questions about the eternity of hell-fire, and others expressed biblical opinions that seemed contrary to established doctrine. In 1899, Leo lashed out at these liberal scholars in his paternal reprimand of "Americanism" in a letter to Cardinal Gibbons of Baltimore,

in another letter to the bishops of France, and in a reassertion of the philosophical basis which he set forth in *Aeterni Patris.* To control the biblical dissidents, Leo established a Biblical Commission in 1902. In 1903, this Commission put five of Loisy's books on the Index and later issued rulings against the findings of higher criticism on the authorship, dates, and values of biblical writings.

When Pius X became pope, he first attended to the problem of the separation of church and state in France and then turned on the Catholic modernists. In *Lamentabili Sane,* July 3, 1907, Pius condemned modernism in sixty-five propositions, fifty of which were drawn from Loisy's writings (8). Many of the "errors" were caricatures of the position of the liberals, but the intent of Pius was clear; he was against higher criticism, immanentism, socialism, and other modernisms. Within a few weeks, Pius published his much longer *Pascendi gregis,* to combat a supposed schismatic group within the church that was intent on setting up its own system of belief. Tyrrell, who had been dismissed from the Society of Jesus in 1906, strongly protested and predicted that many would leave the church rather than submit. Loisy and a few others did leave, but the modernist trend subsided after the death of Tyrrell in 1909. However, to eliminate all remnants of modernism, in 1910 Pius insisted on an oath against modernism by all professors of philosophy and theology in all Catholic seminaries (9). Those who refused were to be deposed and considered as teachers no longer. This was extended to laymen and clerics at universities in 1931.

After World War I, the papacy suffered restrictions from the rise of totalitarianism, which to many seemed to be an echo of the principles of the French Revolution. At first the papacy cooperated with the totalitarians. Benito Mussolini imposed his Fascism on Italy in the 1920's, and Pope Pius XI (1922-1939) concluded the Lateran Treaty with the Fascists in 1929, establishing the Vatican City as a state. In June of 1931, Pius XI denounced Mussolini for breaking his treaty and for curtailing Catholic Action in Italy; *Non abbiamo bisogno* said that a true Catholic could not be a Fascist.

When Adolph Hitler with his National Socialist Workers' Party seized power in 1933, Pius XI concluded a concordat with him on July 20, 1933. The concordat dissolved the Catholic Center Party in Germany, but gave the church a number of concessions. However, like Napoleon earlier, Hitler was using the church, and in the succeeding years the Third Reich did not hesitate to deprive the Catholic Church of its schools and other conceded prerogatives. The sterilization and racist laws of Hitler in 1933 and the years following showed that the Nazis were not oriented toward the Christian Church. Catholic Reich Chancellor von Papen was removed from office in June of 1934. These events prompted the encyclical, *Mit brennender Sorge*, March 14, 1937, in which the pope denounced Nazism as a way of life alien to Catholicism.

But the pope's sharpest condemnation of totalitarianism came in *Divini Redemptoris*, March 19, 1937 (*10*). The immediate causes of *Divini Redemptoris* were the war in Spain in 1936 and the Communist International disturbances in Mexico, plus the fact that Russian Communism had resolutely tried to eradicate religion as an opiate of the people. The first encyclical to mention communism was *Qui pluribus*, 1846, which labeled communism an "execrable doctrine" contrary to natural law and individual rights. In July of 1949, Pope Pius XII excommunicated communists in general, and declared that Roman Catholics could not join or favor communist parties, publish or distribute their literature, or even read their propaganda. Those who courted communism would be excluded from the sacraments, excommunicated, and apostasized.

There is considerable evidence that the ultramontane stand is beginning to be modified in the twentieth century, but the import of this trend cannot as yet be clearly assessed. An encyclical such as *Divino afflante Spiritu* in 1943, which encouraged historical criticism in biblical studies, was followed by the dogma of the Assumption of Mary in 1950 (*11*), which, contrary to the trends of modern scholarship and the absence of such a doctrine in Scripture, declared that Mary bodily arose to heaven. What is abundantly

VIII-2. The Immaculate Conception. *A painting deifying the Madonna as a result of the recognition of the doctrine of immaculate conception in 1615. Painting by Bartolome Esteban Murillo. Murrillo Workshop. Courtesy of the Detroit Institute of Arts. Louvre, Paris.*

clear, however, is that Catholicism, for political as well as spiritual reasons, reacted to the French Revolution and its tendencies by launching a program that has stood solidly against those facets of modernism and national sovereignties which threatened the claims of an ultramontane papacy.

1. The Decree of Pope Pius IX on the Immaculate Conception of the Blessed Virgin Mary, December 8, 1854

Philip Schaff, *The Creeds of Christendom*, II (New York: Harper & Row, Publishers, 1877).

Since we have never ceased in humility and fasting to offer up our prayers and those of the Church to God the Father through his Son, that he might deign to direct and confirm our mind by the power of the Holy

Ghost, after imploring the protection of the whole celestial court, and after invoking on our knees the Holy Ghost the Paraclete, under his inspiration *we pronounce, declare, and define,* unto the glory of the Holy and Indivisible Trinity, the honor and ornament of the holy Virgin the Mother of God, for the exaltation of the Catholic faith and the increase of the Christian religion, by the authority of our Lord Jesus Christ and the blessed Apostles Peter and Paul, and in our own authority, that the *doctrine which holds the Blessed Virgin Mary to have been, from the first instant of her conception, by a singular grace and privilege of almighty God, in view of the merits of Jesus Christ the Saviour of Mankind, preserved free from all stain of original sin, was revealed by God, and is, therefore, to be firmly and constantly believed by all the faithful.* Therefore, if some should presume to think in their hearts otherwise than we have defined (which God forbid), they shall know and thoroughly understand that they are by their own judgment condemned, have made shipwreck concerning the faith, and fallen away from the unity of the Church; and, moreover, that they, by this very act, subject themselves to the penalties ordained by law, if, by work or writing, or any other external means, they dare to signify what they think in their hearts.

2. The Papal Syllabus of Errors, Pius IX, 1864

Schaff, *The Creeds of Christendom,* II.

The Syllabus of the principal errors of our time, which are stigmatized in the Consistorial Allocutions, Encyclicals, and other Apostolical letters of our Most Holy Lord, Pope Pius IX.

I. PANTHEISM, NATURALISM, AND ABSOLUTE RATIONALISM

1.   There exists no supreme, most wise, and most provident divine being distinct from the universe, and God is none other than nature, and is therefore subject to change. In effect, God is produced in man and in the world, and all things are God, and have the very substance of God. God is therefore one and the same thing with the world, and thence spirit is the same thing with matter, necessity with liberty, true with false, good with evil, justice with injustice.

2.   All action of God upon man and the world is to be denied.

3.   Human reason, without any regard to God, is the sole arbiter of truth and falsehood, of good and evil; it is its own law to itself, and suffices by its natural force to secure the welfare of men and or nations.

4.   All the truths of religion are derived from the native strength of human reason; whence reason is the master rule by which man can and ought to arrive at the knowledge of all truths of every kind.

5.   Divine revelation is imperfect, and, therefore, subject to a continual and indefinite progress, which corresponds with the progress of human reason.

III.   INDIFFERENTISM, LATITUDINARIANISM

15.   Every man is free to embrace and profess the religion he shall believe true, guided by the light of reason.

16.   Men may in any religion find the way of eternal salvation, and obtain eternal salvation.

17.   We may entertain at least a well-founded hope for the eternal salvation of all those who are in no manner in the true Church of Christ.

18.   Protestantism is nothing more than another form of the same true Christian religion, in which it is possible to be equally pleasing to God as in the Catholic Church.

IV.   SOCIALISM, COMMUNISM, SECRET SOCIETIES, BIBLICAL SOCIETIES, CLERICO-LIBERAL SOCIETIES

Pests of this description are frequently rebuked in the severest terms in the Encyclicals. . . . [Five encyclicals noted.]

V.   ERRORS CONCERNING THE CHURCH AND HER RIGHTS

19.   The Church is not a true, and perfect, and entirely free society, nor does she enjoy peculiar and perpetual rights conferred upon her by her Divine Founder, but it appertains to the civil power to define what are the rights and limits with which the Church may exercise authority.

20. The ecclesiastical power must not exercise its authority without the permission and assent of the civil government.

21. The Church has not the power of defining dogmatically that the religion of the Catholic Church is the only true religion.

24. The Church has not the power of availing herself of force, or any direct or indirect temporal power.

27. The ministers of the Church, and the Roman Pontiff, ought to be absolutely excluded from all charge and dominion over temporal affairs.

30. Ecclesiastical courts for temporal causes, of the clergy, whether civil or criminal, ought by all means to be abolished, either without the concurrence and against the protest of the Holy See.

35. There would be no obstacle to the sentence of a general council, or the act of all the universal peoples, transferring the pontifical sovereignty from the Bishop and City of Rome to some other bishopric and some other city.

37. National churches can be established, after being withdrawn and plainly separated from the authority of the Roman Pontiff.

38. Roman Pontiffs have, by their too arbitrary conduct, contributed to the division of the Church into eastern and western.

VI. ERRORS ABOUT CIVIL SOCIETY, CONSIDERED BOTH IN ITSELF AND IN ITS RELATION TO THE CHURCH

39. The commonwealth is the origin and source of all rights, and possesses rights which are not circumscribed by any limits.

40. The teaching of the Catholic Church is opposed to the well-being and interests of society.

42. In the case of conflicting laws between the two powers, the civil law ought to prevail.

47. The best theory of civil society requires that popular schools open to the children of all classes, and, generally, all public institutes intended for instruction in letters and philosophy, and for conducting the education of the young, should be freed from all ecclesiastical authority, government, and interference, and should be fully subject to the civil and political power, in confirmity with the will of rulers and the prevalent opinions of the age.

48. This system of instructing youth, which consists in separating it from the Catholic faith and from the power of the Church, and in teaching exclusively, or at least primarily, the knowledge of natural things and the earthly ends of social life alone, may be approved by Catholics.

55. The Church ought to be separated from the State, and the State from the Church.

VII. ERRORS CONCERNING NATURAL AND CHRISTIAN ETHICS

56. Moral laws do not stand in need of the divine sanction, and there is no necessity that human laws should be conformable to the law of nature, and receive their sanction from God.

57. Knowledge of philosophical things and morals, and also civil laws, may and must depart from divine and ecclesiastical authority.

60. Authority is nothing else but the result of numerical superiority and material force.

64. The violation of a solemn oath, even every wicked and flagitious action repugnant to the eternal law, is not only not blamable, but quite lawful, and worthy of the highest praise, when done for the love of country.

VIII. THE ERRORS CONCERNING CHRISTIAN MARRIAGE

65. It can not be by any means tolerated, to maintain that Christ has raised marriage to the dignity of a sacrament.

67. By the law of nature, the marriage tie is not indissoluble, and in many cases divorce, properly so called, may be pronounced by the civil authority.

68. The Church has not the power of laying down what are diriment impediments to marriage. The civil authority does possess such a power, and can do away with existing impediments to marriage.

73. A merely civil contract may, among Christians, constitute a true marriage; and it is false, either that the marriage contract between Christians is always a sacrament, or

that the contract is null if the sacrament be excluded.

74. Matrimonial causes and espousals belong by their very nature to civil jurisdiction.

IX. ERRORS REGARDING THE CIVIL POWER OF THE SOVEREIGN PONTIFF

75. The children of the Christian and Catholic Church are not agreed upon the compatibility of the temporal with the spiritual power.

76. The abolition of the temporal power, of which the Apostolic See is possessed, would contribute in the greatest degree to the liberty and prosperity of the Church.

X. ERRORS HAVING REFERENCE TO MODERN LIBERALISM

77. In the present day, it is no longer expedient that the Catholic religion shall be held as the only religion of the State, to the exclusion of all other modes of worship.

78. Whence it has been wisely provided by law, in some countries called Catholic, that persons coming to reside therein shall enjoy the public exercise of their own worship.

79. Moreover, it is false that the civil liberty of every mode of worship, and the full power given to all of overtly and publicly manifesting their opinions and their ideas, of all kinds whatsoever, conduce more easily to corrupt the morals and minds of the people, and to the propagation of the pest of indifferentism.

80. The Roman Pontiff can and ought to reconcile himself to, and agree with, progress, liberalism, and civilization as lately introduced.

3. *The Dogmatic Decrees of the Vatican Council, Pius IX, 1870*

Schaff, *The Creeds of Christendom*, II.

On the Power and Nature of the Primacy of the Roman Pontiff.

Wherefore, resting on plain testimonies of the Sacred Writings, and adhering to the plain and express decrees both of our predecessors, the Roman Pontiffs, and of the General Councils, we renew the definition of the oecumenical Council of Florence, in virtue of which all the faithful of Christ must believe that the holy Apostolic See and the Roman Pontiff possesses the primacy over the whole world, and that the Roman Pontiff is the successor of blessed Peter, Prince of the Apostles, and is the true vicar of Christ, and head of the whole Church, and father and teacher of all Christians; and that full power was given to him in blessed Peter to rule, feed, and govern the universal Church by Jesus Christ our Lord; as is also contained in the acts of the General Councils and in the sacred Canons.

Hence we teach and declare that by the appointment of our Lord the Roman Church possesses a superiority of ordinary power over all other churches, and that this power of jurisdiction of the Roman Pontiff, which is truly episcopal, is immediate; to which all, of whatever rite and dignity, both individually and collectively, are bound, by their

VIII-3. Symbols of the Passion of Christ, Grouped Around the Five Sacred Wounds of Christ. *Metal design by Peter Seel, Salzburg, c. 1670. From Carl van Treeck and Aloysius Croft,* Symbols of the Church *(Milwaukee: The Bruce Publishing Company, 1936).*

duty of hierarchical subordination and true obedience, to submit not only in matters which belong to faith and morals, but also in those that appertain to the discipline and government of the Church throughout the world, so that the Church of Christ may be one flock under one supreme pastor through preservation of unity both of communion and of profession of the same faith with the Roman Pontiff. This is the teaching of Catholic truth, from which no one can deviate without loss of faith and of salvation.

.   .   .   .   .

Therefore faithfully adhering to the tradition received from the beginning of the Christian faith, for the glory of God our Saviour, the exaltation of the Catholic religion, and the salvation of Christian people, the sacred Council approving, we teach and define that it is a dogma divinely revealed: that the Roman Pontiff, when he speaks *ex cathedra,* that is, when in discharge of the office of pastor and doctor of all Christians, by virtue of his supreme Apostolic authority, he defines a doctrine regarding faith or morals to be held by the universal Church, by the divine assistance promised to him in blessed Peter, is possessed of that infallibility with which the divine Redeemer willed that his Church should be endowed for defining doctrine regarding faith or morals; and that therefore such definitions of the Roman Pontiff are irreformable of themselves, and not from the consent of the Church.

But if any one—which may God avert—presume to contradict this our definition: let him be anathema.

4. The Christian Constitution of States

Leo XIII, Encyclical Letter *Immortale Dei,* November 1, 1885. From *The Great Encyclical Letters of Pope Leo XIII,* Rev. John J. Wynne, S.J., ed. (New York: Benziger Brothers, 1903).

The Catholic Church, that imperishable handiwork of our all-merciful God, has for her immediate and natural purpose the saving of souls and securing our happiness in heaven. Yet in regard to things temporal she is the source of benefits as manifold and great as if the chief end of her existence were to ensure the prospering of our earthly life. And in truth, wherever the Church has set her foot, she has straightway changed the face of things, and has attempered the moral tone of the people with a new civilization, and with virtues before unknown. All nations which have yielded to her sway have become eminent for their culture, their sense of justice, and the glory of their high deeds.

... Many, indeed are they who have tried to work out a plan of civil society based on doctrines other than those approved by the Catholic Church. Nay, in these latter days a novel scheme of law has begun here and there to gain increase and influence, the outcome, as it is maintained, of an age arrived at full stature, and the result of liberty in evolution. But no better mode has been devised for the building up and ruling the State than that which is the necessary growth of the teachings of the Gospel. We deem it, therefore, of the highest moment, and a strict duty of Our Apostolic office, to contrast with the lessons taught by Christ the novel theories now advanced touching the State. By this means We cherish hope that the bright shining of the truth may scatter the mists of error and doubt, so that one and all may see clearly the imperious law of life which they are bound to follow and obey.

It is not difficult to determine what would be the form and character of the State were it governed according to the principles of Christian philosophy. Man's natural instinct moves him to live in civil society, for he cannot, if dwelling apart, provide himself with the necessary requirements of life, nor procure the means of developing his mental and moral faculties. Hence, it is divinely ordained that he should lead his life—be it family, social, or civil—with his fellow-men, amongst whom alone his several wants can be adequately supplied. But as no society can hold together unless some one be over all, directing all to strive earnestly for the common good, every civilized community must have a ruling authority, and this authority, no less than society itself, has its source in nature, and has consequently, God for its author. Hence it follows that all public power must proceed from God. For God alone is the true and supreme Lord of the world. Everything, without exception, must be subject to Him, and must serve Him, so that whosoever holds the right to govern, holds it from one sole and single source, namely, God, the Sovereign Ruler of all.

The right to rule is not necessarily, however, bound up with any special mode of government. It may take this or that form, provided only that it be of a nature to insure the general welfare. But whatever be the nature of the government, rulers must ever bear in mind that God is the paramount ruler of the world, and must set Him before themselves as their exemplar and law in the administration of the State. . . .

.   .   .   .   .

As a consequence, the State, constituted as it is, is clearly bound to act up to the manifold and weighty duties linking it to God, by the public profession of religion. Nature and reason, which command every individual devoutly to worship God in holiness, because we belong to Him and must return to Him since from Him we came, bind also the civil community by a like law. . . . Since no one is allowed to be remiss in the service due to God, and since the chief duty of all men is to cling to religion in both its teaching and practice—not such religion as they may have a preference for, but the religion which God enjoins, and which certain and most clear marks show to be the only one true religion— it is a public crime to act as though there were no God. So, too, is it a sin in the State not to have care for religion, as a something beyond its scope, or as of no practical benefit; or out of many forms of religion to adopt that one which chimes in with the fancy; for we are bound absolutely to worship God in that way which He has shown to be His will. All who rule, therefore, should hold in honor the holy name of God, and one of their chief duties must be to favor religion, to protect it, to shield it under the credit and sanction of the laws, and neither to organize nor enact any measure that may compromise its safety. This is the bounden duty of rulers to the people over whom they rule. For one and all are we destined by our birth and adoption to enjoy, when this frail and fleeting life is ended, a supreme and final good in heaven, and to the attainment of this every endeavor should be directed. Since, then, upon this depends the full and perfect happiness of mankind, the securing of this end should be of all imaginable interests the most urgent. . . .

Now, it cannot be difficult to find out which is the true religion, if only it be sought with an earnest and unbiased mind; for proofs are abundant and striking. We have, for example, the fulfilment of prophecies; miracles in great number; the rapid spread of the faith in the midst of enemies and in the face of overwhelming obstacles; the witness of the martyrs, and the like. From all these it is evident that the only true religion is the one established by Jesus Christ Himself, and which He committed to His Church to protect and to propagate. For the only-begotten Son of God established on earth a society which is called the Church, and to it He handed over the exalted and divine office which He had received from His Father, to be continued through the ages to come. . . . And He has willed that one should be head of all, and the chief and unerring teacher of the truth, to whom He has given the keys of the kingdom of heaven.

This society is made up of men, just as civil society is, and yet is supernatural and spiritual, on account of the end for which it was founded, and of the means by which it aims at attaining that end. Hence it is distinguished and differs from civil society, and what is of highest moment, it is a society chartered as of right divine, perfect in its nature and in its title, to possess in itself and by itself, through the will and loving kindness of its Founder, all needful provision for its maintenance and action. And just as the end at which the Church aims is by far the noblest of ends, so is its authority the most exalted of all authority, nor can it be looked upon as inferior to the civil power, or in any manner dependent upon it.

.   .   .   .   .

[But in modern times disruptive principles have developed.]

Among these principles the main one lays down that as all men are alike by race and nature, so in like manner are all equal in the control of their life; that each one is so far his own master as to be in no sense under the rule of any other individual; that each is free to think on every subject just as he may choose, and to do whatever he may like to do; that no man has any right to rule over other men. In a society grounded upon such maxims, all government is nothing more nor less than the will of the people, and the people, being under the power of itself alone, is alone its own ruler. It does choose nevertheless some to whose charge it may commit itself, but in such wise that it makes over to them not the right so much as the business of governing, to be exercised, however, in its name.

The authority of God is passed over in silence, just as if there were no God; or as if He cared nothing for human society; or as if men, whether in their individual capacity or bound together in social relations, owed nothing to God; or as if there could be a government of which the whole origin and power and authority did not reside in God Himself. Thus, as is evident, a State becomes nothing but a multitude, which is its own master and ruler. And since the populace is declared to contain within itself the spring-head of all rights and of all power, it follows that the State does not consider itself bound by any kind of duty towards God. Moreover, it believes that it is not obliged to make public profession of any religion; or to inquire which of the very many religions is the only one true; or to prefer one religion to all the rest; or to show to any form of religion special favor; but, on the contrary, is bound to grant equal rights to every creed, so that public order may not be disturbed by any particular form of religious belief.

And it is part of this theory that all questions that concern religion are to be referred to private judgment; that everyone is to be free to follow whatever religion he prefers, or none at all if he disapprove of all. From this the following consequences logically flow: that the judgment of each one's conscience is independent of all law; that the most unrestrained opinions may be openly expressed as to the practice or omission of divine worship; and that everyone has unbounded license to think whatever he chooses and to publish abroad whatever he thinks.

When the management of public business is in harmony with doctrines of such a kind, the Catholic religion is allowed a standing in civil society equal only, or inferior, to societies alien from it; no regard is paid to the laws of the Church, and she who, by the order and commission of Jesus Christ, has the duty to teach all nations, finds herself forbidden to take any part in the instruction of the people. . . . Accordingly, it has become the practice and determination under this condition of public polity (now so much admired by many) either to forbid the action of the Church altogether, or to keep her in check and bondage to the State. Public enactments are in great measure framed with this design. The drawing up of laws, the administration of State affairs, the godless education of youth, the spoilation and suppression of religious orders, the overthrow of the temporal power of the Roman Pontiff, all alike aim at this one end—to paralyze the action of Christian institutions, to cramp to the utmost the freedom of the Catholic Church, and to curtail her every single prerogative.

.   .   .   .   .   .

To hold therefore that there is no difference in matters of religion between forms that are unlike each other, and even contrary to each other, most clearly leads in the end to the rejection of all religion in both theory and practice. And this is the same thing as atheism, however it may differ from it in name. Men who really believe in the existence of God must, in order to be consistent with themselves and to avoid absurd conclusions, understand that differing modes of divine worship involving dissimilarity and conflict even on most important points, cannot all be equally probable, equally good, and equally acceptable to God.

So, too, the liberty of thinking, and of publishing, whatsoever each one likes, without any hindrance, is not in itself an advantage over which society can wisely rejoice. On the contrary, it is the fountain-head and origin of many evils. Liberty is a power perfecting man, and hence should have truth and goodness for its object. But the character of goodness and truth cannot be changed at option. These remain ever one and the same, and are no less unchangeable than Nature herself. . . .

To wish the Church to be subject to the civil power in the exercise of her duty is a great folly and a sheer injustice. Whenever this is the case, order is disturbed, for things natural are put above things supernatural; the many benefits which the Church, if free to act, would confer on society are either prevented or at least lessened in number; and a way is prepared for enmities and contentions between the two powers, with how evil result to both the issue of events has taught us only too frequently.

Doctrines such as these, which cannot be approved by human reason, and most seriously affect the whole civil order, Our predecessors the Roman Pontiffs have never allowed to pass uncondemned. Thus Gregory XVI in his Encyclical Letter *Mirari vos,* August 15, 1832, inveighed with weighty words against the sophisms, which even at his time were being publicly inculcated—namely, that no preference should be shown for any particular form of worship; that it is right for individuals to form their own personal judgments about religion; that each man's conscience is his sole and all-sufficing guide; and that it is lawful for every man to publish his own views, whatever they may be, and even to conspire against the State. On the question of the separation of Church and State the same Pontiff writes as follows: "Nor can we hope for happier results either for religion or for the civil government from the wishes of those who desire that the Church be separated from the State, and the concord between the secular and ecclesiastical authority be dissolved." . . . From the pronouncements of the Popes it is evident . . . that it is not lawful for the State, any more than for the individual, either to disregard all religious duties or to hold in equal favor different kinds of religion; that the unrestrained freedom of thinking and of openly making known one's thoughts is not inherent in the rights of citizens, and is by no means to be reckoned worthy of favor and support. . . .

This then is the teaching of the Catholic Church concerning the constitution and government of the State. By the words and decrees just cited, if judged dispassionately, no one of the several forms of government is in itself condemned, inasmuch as none of them contain anything contrary to Catholic doctrine, and all of them are capable, if wisely and justly managed, to insure the welfare of the State. Neither is it blameworthy in itself, in any manner, for the people to have a share, greater or less, in the government: for at certain times, and under certain laws, such participation may not only be of benefit to the citizens, but may even be of obligation. Nor is there any reason why any one should accuse the Church of being wanting in gentleness of action or largeness of view, or of being opposed to real and lawful liberty. The Church, indeed, deems it unlawful to place the various forms of divine worship on the same footing as the true religion, but does not, on that account, condemn those rulers who, for the sake of securing some great good or of hindering some great evil, allow patiently custom or usage to be a kind of sanction for each kind of religion having its place in the State. And in fact the Church is wont to take earnest heed that no one shall be forced to embrace the Catholic faith against his will, for, as St. Augustine wisely reminds us, "Man cannot believe otherwise than of his own free will."

In the same way the Church cannot approve of that liberty which begets contempt of the most sacred laws of God, and casts off the obedience to lawful authority, for this is not liberty so much as license. . . .

.   .   .   .   .

Especially with reference to the so-called "Liberties" which are so greatly coveted in these days, all must stand by the judgment of the Apostolic See, and have the same mind. Let no man be deceived by the outward appearance of the *liberties,* but let each one reflect whence these have had their origin, and by what efforts they are everywhere upheld and promoted. . . .

.   .   .   .   .

. . . It is the duty of all Catholics worthy of the name and wishful to be known as most loving children of the Church, to reject without swerving whatever is inconsistent with so fair a title; to make use of popular institutions, so far as can honestly be done, for the advancement of truth and righteousness; to strive that liberty of action shall not transgress the bounds marked out by nature and the law of God; to endeavor to bring back all civil society to the pattern and form of Christianity which We have described. It is barely possible to lay down any fixed method by which such purposes are to be attained, because the means adopted must suit places and times widely differing from one another. Nevertheless, above all things, unity of aim must be preserved, and similarity must be sought after in all plans of action. Both these objects will be carried into effect without fail if all will follow the guidance of the Apostolic See as their rule of life and obey the bishops whom the Holy Ghost has placed to rule the Church of God....

5. Human Liberty

Leo XIII, Encyclical Letter *Libertas Praestantissimum,* June 20, 1888. From Wynne, *The Great Encyclical Letters of Pope Leo XIII.*

Liberty, the highest of natural endowments, being the portion only of intellectual or rational natures, confers on man this dignity—that he is *in the hand of his counsel* and has power over his actions. But the manner in which such dignity is exercised is of the greatest moment, inasmuch as on the use that is made of liberty the highest good and the greatest evil alike depend. Man, indeed, is free to obey his reason, to seek moral good, and to strive unswervingly after his last end. Yet he is free also to turn aside to all other things, and, in pursuing the empty semblance of good, to disturb rightful order and to fall headlong into the destruction which he has voluntarily chosen. The Redeemer of mankind, Jesus Christ, having restored and exalted the original dignity of nature, vouchsafed special assistance to the will of man; and by the gifts of His grace here, and the promise of heavenly bliss hereafter, He raised it to a nobler state. In like manner, this great gift of nature has ever been, and always will be, deservingly cherished by the Catholic Church, for to her alone has been committed the charge of handing down to all ages the benefits purchased for us by Jesus Christ. Yet there are many who imagine that the Church is hos-

tile to human liberty. Having a false and absurd notion as to what liberty is, either they pervert the very idea of freedom, or they extend it at their pleasure to many things in respect of which man cannot rightly be regarded as free....

.　　.　　.　　.　　.

Liberty ... belongs only to those who have the gift of reason or intelligence. Considered as to its nature, it is the faculty of choosing means fitted for the end proposed, for he is master of his actions who can choose one thing out of many. Now, since everything chosen as a means is viewed as good or useful, and since good, as such, is the proper object of our desire, it follows that freedom of choice is a property of the will, or, rather, is identical with the will in so far as it has in its action the faculty of choice. But the will cannot proceed to act until it is enlightened by the knowledge possessed by the intellect....

.　　.　　.　　.　　.

Such, then, being the condition of human liberty, it necessarily stands in need of light and strength to direct its actions to good and to restrain them from evil. Without this, the freedom of our will would be our ruin. First of all there must be *law;* that is, a fixed rule of teaching what is to be done and what is to be left undone....

Foremost in this office comes the *natural law,* which is written and engraved in the mind of every man; and this is nothing but our reason, commanding us to do right and forbidding sin. Nevertheless all prescriptions of human reason can have force of law only inasmuch as they are the voice and interpreters of some higher power on which our reason and liberty necessarily depend. For, since the force of law consists in the imposing of obligations and the granting of rights, authority is the one and only foundation of all law—the power, that is, of fixing duties and defining rights, as also of assigning the necessary sanctions of reward and chastisement to each and all of its commands. But all this, clearly, cannot be found in man, if, as his own supreme legislator, he is to be the rule of his own actions. It follows therefore that the law of nature is the same thing as the *eternal law*, implanted in rational creatures, and inclining them to their right action and end; and can be nothing else but the eternal reason of God, the Creator and Ruler of all the world. To this rule of action and restraint of evil God has vouchsafed to give special and most suitable aids for strengthening and ordering the human will. The first and most excellent of these is the power of his divine *grace*, whereby the mind can be enlightened and the will wholesomely invigorated and moved to the constant pursuit of moral good, so that the use of our inborn liberty becomes at once less difficult and less dangerous. Not that the divine assistance hinders in any way the free movement of our will; just the contrary, for grace works inwardly in man and in harmony with his natural inclinations, since it flows from the very Creator of his mind and will, by whom all things are moved in conformity with their nature.

What has been said of the liberty of individuals is no less applicable to them when considered as bound together in civil society. For, what reason and the natural law do for individuals, that *human law*, promulgated for their good, does for the citizens of States. Of the laws enacted by men, some are concerned with what is good or bad by its very nature; and they command men to follow after what is right and to shun what is wrong, adding at the same time a suitable sanction. But such laws by no means derive their origin from civil society; because just as civil society did not create human nature, so neither can it be said to be the author of the good which befits human nature, or of the evil which is contrary to it. Laws come before men live together in society, and have their origin in the natural, and consequently in the eternal, law....

From this it is manifest that the eternal law of God is the sole standard and rule of human liberty, not only in each individual man, but also in the community and civil society which men constitute when united. Therefore, the true liberty of human society does not consist in every man doing what he pleases, for this would simply end in turmoil and confusion, and bring on the overthrow of the State; but rather in this, that

through the injunctions of the civil law all may more easily conform to the prescriptions of the eternal law....

.   .   .   .   .

These precepts of the truest and highest teaching, made known to us by the light of reason itself, the Church, instructed by the example and doctrine of her divine Author, has ever propagated and asserted; for she has ever made them the measure of her office and of her teaching to the Christian nations. Thus the powerful influence of the Church has ever been manifested in the custody and protection of the civil and political liberty of the people....

The highest duty is to respect authority, and obediently to submit to just law; and by this the members of a community are effectually protected from the wrongdoing of evil men. Lawful power is from God, *and whosoever resisteth authority resisteth the ordinance of God;* wherefore obedience is greatly ennobled when subjected to an authority which is the most just and supreme of all. But where the power to command is wanting, or where a law is enacted contrary to reason, or to the eternal law, or to some ordinance of God, obedience is unlawful, lest, while obeying man, we become disobedient to God. Thus, an effectual barrier being opposed to tyranny, the authority in the State will not have all its own way, but the interests and rights of all will be safeguarded—the rights of individuals, of domestic society, and of all the members of the commonwealth; all being free to live according to law and right reason; and in this, as We have shown, true liberty really consists.

If when men discuss the question of liberty they were careful to grasp its true and legitimate meaning, such as reason and reasoning have just explained, they would never venture to affix such a calumny on the Church as to assert that she is the foe to individual and public liberty. But many there are who follow in the footsteps of Lucifer, and adopt as their own his rebellious cry, "I will not serve"; and consequently substitute for true liberty what is sheer and most foolish license. Such, for instance, are the men belonging to that widely spread and powerful organization, who, usurping the name of liberty, style themselves *Liberals*.

What *naturalists* or *rationalists* aim at in philosophy, that the supporters of *liberalism*, carrying out the principles laid down by naturalism, are attempting in the domain of morality and politics. The fundamental doctrine of rationalism is the supremacy of the human reason, which, refusing due submission to the divine and eternal reason, proclaims its own independence and constitutes itself the supreme principle and source and judge of truth. Hence, these followers of liberalism deny the existence of any divine authority to which obedience is due, and proclaim that every man is the law to himself; from which arises that ethical system which they style *independent morality*, and which, under the guise of liberty, exonerates man from any obedience to the commands of God, and substitutes a boundless license....

.   .   .   .   .

To make this more evident, the growth of liberty ascribed to our age must be considered apart in its various details. And, first, let us examine that liberty in individuals which is so opposed to the virtue of religion, namely, the *liberty of worship*, as it is called. This is based on the principle that every man is free to profess as he may choose any religion or none.

But, assuredly, of all the duties which man has to fulfill, that, without doubt, is the chiefest and holiest which commands him to worship God with devotion and piety. This follows of necessity from the truth that we are ever in the power of God, are ever guided by His will and providence, and, having come forth from Him, must return to Him. Add to which no true virtue can exist without religion, for moral virtue is concerned with those things which lead to God as man's supreme and ultimate good; and therefore religion, which (as St. Thomas says) "performs those actions which are directly and immediately ordained for the divine honor," rules and tempers all virtues. And if it be asked which of the many conflicting religions it is necessary to adopt, reason and the natural law unhesitatingly tell us to practise that one which God enjoins, and which men

can easily recognize by certain exterior notes, whereby divine Providence has willed that it should be distinguished, because, in a matter of such moment, the most terrible loss would be the consequence of error. Wherefore, when a liberty such as We have described is offered to man, the power is given him to pervert or abandon with impunity the most sacred of duties, and to exchange the unchangeable good for evil; which, as We have said is no liberty, but its degradation, and the abject submission of the soul to sin.

This kind of liberty, if considered in relation to the State, clearly implies that there is no reason why the State should offer any homage to God, or should desire any public recognition of Him; that no one form of worship is to be preferred to another, but that all stand on an equal footing, no account being taken of the religion of the people, even if they profess the Catholic faith. But, to justify this, it must needs be taken as true that the State has no duties toward God, or that such duties, if they exist, can be abandoned with impunity, both of which assertions are manifestly false.... Justice therefore forbids, and reason itself forbids, the State to be godless; or to adopt a line of action which would end in godlessness—namely, to treat the various religions (as they call them) alike, and to bestow upon them promiscuously equal rights and privileges. Since, then, the profession of one religion is necessary in the State, that religion must be professed which alone is true, and which can be recognized without difficulty, especially in Catholic States, because the marks of truth are, as it were, engraven upon it. This religion, therefore, the rulers of the State must preserve and protect, if they would provide—as they should do—with prudence and usefulness for the good of the community....

.   .   .   .   .

We must now consider briefly *liberty of speech,* and liberty of the press. It is hardly necessary to say that there can be no such right as this, if it be not used in moderation, and if it pass beyond the bounds and end of all true liberty. For right is a moral power which—as We have before said and must again and again repeat—it is absurd to suppose that nature has accorded indifferently to truth and falsehood, to justice and injustice. Men have a right freely and prudently to propagate throughout the State what things soever are true and honorable, so that as many as possible may possess them; but lying opinions, than which no mental plague is greater, and vices which corrupt the heart and moral life, should be diligently repressed by public authority, lest they insidiously work the ruin of the State. . . .

A like judgment must be passed upon what is called *liberty of teaching*. There can be no doubt that truth alone should imbue the minds of men. . . .

.   .   .   .   .

Another liberty is widely advocated, namely, *liberty of conscience*. If by this is meant that everyone may, as he chooses, worship God or not, it is sufficiently refuted by the arguments already adduced. . . .

Yet, with the discernment of a true mother, the Church weighs the great burden of human weakness, and well knows the course down which the minds and actions of men are in this our age being borne. For this reason, while not conceding any right to anything save what is true and honest, she does not forbid public authority to tolerate what is at variance with truth and justice, for the sake of avoiding some greater evil, or of obtaining or preserving some greater good.

But, to judge aright, we must acknowledge that, the more a State is driven to tolerate evil, the further is it from perfection; and that the tolerance of evil which is dictated by political prudence should be strictly confined to the limits which its justifying cause, the public welfare, requires. Wherefore, if such tolerance would be injurious to the public welfare, and entail greater evils on the State, it would not be lawful; for in such case the motive of good is wanting. And although in the extraordinary condition of these times the Church usually acquiesces in certain modern liberties, not because she prefers them in themselves, but because she judges it expedient to permit them, she would in happier times exercise her own liberty; and, by persuasion, exhortation, and entreaty would endeavor, as she is bound, to fulfill

the duty assigned to her by God of providing for the eternal salvation of mankind. One thing, however, remains always true—that the liberty which is claimed for all to do all things is not, as We have often said, of itself desirable, inasmuch as it is contrary to reason that error and truth should have equal rights. . . .

6. The Condition of the Working Classes

Leo XIII, Encyclical Letter *Rerum Novarum*, May 15, 1891. From Wynne, *The Great Encyclical Letters of Pope Leo XIII.*

That the spirit of revolutionary change, which has long been disturbing the nations of the world, should have passed beyond the sphere of politics and made its influence felt in the cognate sphere of practical economics is not surprising. The elements of the conflict now raging are unmistakable in the vast expansion of industrial pursuits and the marvellous discoveries of science; in the changed relations between masters and workmen; in the enormous fortunes of some few individuals, and the utter poverty of the masses; in the increased self-reliance and closer mutual combination of the working classes; as also, finally, in the prevailing moral degeneracy. The momentous gravity of the state of things now obtaining fills every mind with painful apprehension; wise men are discussing it; practical men are proposing schemes; popular meetings, legislatures, and rulers of nations are all busied with it—and actually there is no question which has taken a deeper hold on the public mind.

Therefore, Venerable Brethren, as on former occasions when it seemed opportune to refute false teaching, We have addressed you in the interests of the Church and of the commonweal, and have issued Letters bearing on "Political Power," "Human Liberty," "The Christian Constitution of the State," and like matters, so have We thought it expedient now to speak on *the condition of the working classes*. It is a subject on which We have already touched more than once, incidentally. But in the present Letter, the responsibility of the Apostolic office urges us to treat the question of set purpose and in detail, in order that no misapprehension may exist as to the principles which truth and justice dictate for its settlement. The discussion is not easy, nor is it void of danger. It is no easy matter to define the relative rights and mutual duties of the rich and of the poor, of capital and of labor. And the danger lies in this, that crafty agitators are intent on making use of these differences of opinion to pervert men's judgments and to stir up the people to revolt.

But all agree, and there can be no question whatever, that some remedy must be found, and found quickly, for the misery and wretchedness pressing so heavily and unjustly at this moment on the vast majority of the working classes.

For the ancient workingmen's guilds were abolished in the last century, and no other organization took their place. Public institutions and the very laws have set aside the ancient religion. Hence by degrees it has come to pass that workingmen have been surrendered, all isolated and helpless, to the hard-heartedness of employers and the greed of unchecked competition. The mischief has been increased by rapacious usury, which, although more than once condemned by the Church, is nevertheless, under a different guise, but with the like injustice, still practised by covetous and grasping men. To this must be added the custom of working by contract, and the concentration of so many branches of trade in the hands of a few individuals; so that a small number of very rich men have been able to lay upon the teeming masses of the laboring poor a yoke little better than that of slavery itself.

To remedy these wrongs the Socialists, working on the poor man's envy of the rich, are striving to do away with private property, and contend that individual possessions should become the common property of all, to be administered by the State or by municipal bodies. They hold that by thus transferring property from private individuals to the community, the present mischievous state of things will be set to rights, inasmuch as each citizen will then get his fair share of whatever there is to enjoy. But their contentions are so clearly powerless to end the controversy that were they carried into effect the workingman himself would be among the first to suffer. They are, moreover, emphat-ically unjust, because they would rob the lawful possessor, bring State action into a sphere not within its competence, and create utter confusion in the community.

It is surely undeniable that, when a man engages in remunerative labor, the impelling reason and motive of his work is to obtain property, and thereafter to hold it as his very own. If one man hires out to another his strength or skill, he does so for the purpose of receiving in return what is necessary for sustenance and education; he therefore expressly intends to acquire a right full and real, not only to the remuneration, but also to the disposal of such remuneration, just as he pleases. Thus, if he lives sparingly, saves money, and, for greater security, invests his savings in land, the land, in such case is only his wages under another form; and consequently, a workingman's little estate thus purchased should be as completely at his full disposal as are the wages he received for his labor. But it is precisely in such power of disposal that ownership obtains, whether the property consist of land or chattels. Socialists, therefore, by endeavoring to transfer the possessions of individuals to the community at large, strike at the interests of every wage-earner, since they would deprive him of the liberty of disposing of his wages, and thereby of all hope and possibility of increasing his stock and of bettering his condition in life.

What is of far greater moment, however, is the fact that the remedy they propose is manifestly against justice. For every man has by nature the right to possess property as his own. This is one of the chief points of distinction between man and the animal creation, for the brute has no power of self-direction, but is governed by two main instincts, which keep his powers on the alert, impel him to develop them in a fitting manner, and stimulate and determine him to action without any power of choice. One of these instincts is self-preservation, the other the propagation of the species. But both can attain their purpose by means of things which lie within range; beyond their verge the brute creation cannot go, for they are moved to action by their senses only, and in the special direction which these suggest. But with man it is wholly different. He possesses, on the one hand, the full perfection of the animal being, and hence enjoys, at least as much as the rest of the animal kind, the fruition of things material. But animal nature, however perfect, is far from representing the human being in its completeness, and is in truth but humanity's humble handmaid, made to serve and to obey. It is the mind, or reason, which is the predominant element in us who are human creatures; it is this which renders a human being human, and distinguishes him essentially and generically from the brute. And on this very account—that man alone among the animal creation is endowed with reason—it must be within his right to possess things not merely for temporary and momentary use, as other living things do, but to have and to hold them in stable and permanent possession; he must have not only things that perish in the use of them, but those also which, though they have been reduced into use, remain his own for further use.

.   .   .   .   .

The rights here spoken of, belonging to each individual man, are seen in much stronger light when considered in relation to man's social and domestic obligations. In choosing a state of life, it is indisputable that all are at full liberty to follow the counsel of Jesus Christ as to observing virginity, or to bind themselves by the marriage tie. No human law can abolish the natural and original right of marriage, nor in any way limit the chief and principal purpose of marriage, ordained by God's authority from the beginning. *Increase and multiply.* Hence we have the family; the "society" of man's house—a society to every kind of State or nation, invested with rights and duties of its own, totally independent of the civil community.

The right of property, therefore, which has been proved to belong naturally to individual persons, must in like wise belong to a man in his capacity of head of a family; nay, such person must possess this right so much the more clearly in proportion as his position multiplies his duties. For it is a most sacred law of nature that a father should provide food and all necessaries for those whom he has begotten; and, similarly, nature dictates that a man's children, who carry on, so to speak, and continue his own personality, should be by him provided with all that is needful to enable them to keep themselves honorably from want and misery amid the uncertainties of this mortal life. Now in no other way can a father effect this except by the ownership of lucrative property, which he can transmit to his children by inheritance. A family, no less than a State, is, as we have said, a true society, governed by a power within its sphere, that is to say, by the father. Provided, therefore, the limits which are prescribed by the very purposes for which it exists be not transgressed, the family has at least equal rights with the State in the choice and pursuit of the things needful to its preservation and its just liberty.

.   .   .   .   .

The contention, then, that the civil government should at its option intrude into and exercise intimate control over the family and the household, is a great and pernicious error. True, if a family finds itself in exceeding distress, utterly deprived of the counsel of friends, and without any prospect of extricating itself, it is right that extreme necessity be met by public aid, since each family is a part of the commonwealth. In like manner, if within the precincts of the household there occur grave disturbances of mutual rights, public authority should intervene to force each party to yield to the other its proper due; for this is not to deprive citizens of their rights, but justly and properly to safeguard and strengthen them. But the rulers of the State must go no further: here nature bids them stop. Paternal authority can be neither abolished nor absorbed by the State; for it has the same source as human life itself. "The child belongs to the father," and is, as it were the continuation of the father's personality; and, speaking strictly, the child takes its place in civil society, not of its own right, but in its quality as member of the family in which it is born. And for the very reason that "the child belongs to the father," it is, as St. Thomas of Aquin says, "before it attains the use of free-will, under power and charge of its parents." The Socialists, therefore, in setting aside the parent and setting up a State supervision, act *against natural justice,* and break into pieces the stability of all family life.

.   .   .   .   .

Hence it is clear that the main tenet of Socialism, community of goods, must be utterly rejected, since it only injures those whom it would seem meant to benefit, is directly contrary to the natural rights of mankind, and would introduce confusion and disorder into the commonweal. The first and most fundamental principle, therefore, if one would undertake to alleviate the condition of the masses, must be the inviolability of private property. This being established, we proceed to show where the remedy sought for must be found.

We approach the subject with confidence, and in the exercise of the rights which manifestly appertain to us, for no practical solution of this question will be found apart from the intervention of Religion and of the Church. It is We who are the chief guardian of Religion and the chief dispenser of what pertains to the Church, and We must not by silence neglect the duty incumbent on Us. Doubtless this most serious question demands the attention and the efforts of others besides ourselves—to wit, of the rulers of States, of employers of labor, of the wealthy, aye, of the working classes themselves, for whom We are pleading. But We affirm without hesitation that all the striving of men will be vain if they leave out the Church. . . .

Let it, then, be taken as granted, in the first place, that the condition of things human must be endured, for it is impossible to reduce civil society to one dead level. Socialists may in that intent do their utmost, but all striving against nature is in vain. There naturally exist among mankind manifold differences of the most important kind; people differ in capacity, skill, health, strength; and unequal fortune is a necessary result of unequal condition. Such inequality is far from being disadvantageous either to individuals or to the community. Social and public life can only be maintained by means of various kinds of capacity for business and the playing of many parts; and each man, as a rule, chooses the part which suits his own

peculiar domestic condition. As regards bodily labor, even had man never fallen from *the state of innocence,* he would not have remained wholly unoccupied; but that which would then have been his free choice and his delight became afterwards compulsory, and the painful expiation for his disobedience. *Cursed be the earth in thy work; in thy labor thou shalt eat of it all the days of thy life.* In like manner, the other pains and hardships of life will have no end or cessation on earth; for the consequences of sin are bitter and hard to bear, and they must accompany man so long as life lasts. To suffer and to endure, therefore, is the lot of humanity; let them strive as they may, no strength and no artifice will ever succeed in banishing from human life the ills and troubles which beset it. . . .

The great mistake made in regard to the matter now under consideration is to take up with the notion that class is naturally hostile to class, and that the wealthy and the workingmen are intended by nature to live in mutual conflict. So irrational and so false is this view, that the direct contrary is the truth. Just as the symmetry of the human frame is the resultant of the disposition of the bodily members, so in a State is it ordained by nature that these two classes should dwell in harmony and agreement, and should, as it were, groove into one another, so as to maintain the balance of the body politic. Each needs the other: Capital cannot do without Labor, nor Labor without Capital. Mutual agreement results in pleasantness of life and the beauty of good order; while perpetual conflict necessarily produces confusion and savage barbarity. Now, in preventing such strife as this, and in uprooting it, the efficacy of Christian institutions is marvellous and manifold. First of all, there is no intermediary more powerful than Religion (whereof the Church is the interpreter and guardian) in drawing the rich, and the poor bread-winners, together, by reminding each class of its duties to the other, and especially of the obligations of justice. Thus Religion teaches the laboring man and the artisan to carry out honestly and fairly all equitable agreements freely entered into; never to injure the property, nor to outrage the person, of an employer; never to resort to violence in defending their own cause, nor to engage in riot or disorder; and to have nothing to do with men of evil principles, who work upon the people with artful promises, and excite foolish hopes which usually end in useless regrets, followed by insolvency. Religion teaches the wealthy owner and the employer that their work-people are not to be accounted their bondsmen; that in every man they must respect his dignity and worth as a man and as a Christian; that labor is not a thing to be ashamed of, if we lend ear to right reason and to Christian philosophy, but is an honorable calling, enabling a man to sustain his life in a way upright and creditable; and that it is shameful and inhuman to treat men like chattels to make money by, or to look upon them merely as so much muscle or physical power. Again, therefore, the Church teaches that, as Religion and things spiritual and mental are among the workingman's main concerns, the employer is bound to see that the worker has time for his religious duties; that he be not exposed to corrupting influences and dangerous occasions; and that he be not led away to neglect his home and family, or to squander his earnings. Furthermore, the employer must never tax his work-people beyond their strength, or employ them in work unsuited to their sex or age. His great and principal duty is to give every one a fair wage. Doubtless, before deciding whether wages are adequate, many things have to be considered; but wealthy owners and all masters of labor should be mindful of this—that to exercise pressure upon the indigent and the destitute for the sake of gain, and to gather one's profit out of the need of another, is condemned by all laws, human and divine. To defraud any one of wages that are his due is a crime which cries to the avenging anger of Heaven. . . .

.   .   .   .   .   .

But the Church, with Jesus Christ as her Master and Guide, aims higher still. She lays down precepts yet more perfect, and tries to bind class to class in friendliness and good feeling. The things of earth cannot be understood or valued aright without taking into consideration the life to come, the life that will know no death. Exclude the idea of futurity, and forthwith the very notion of what is good and right would perish; nay, the whole scheme of the universe would become a dark and unfathomable mystery. The great truth which we learn from Nature herself is also the grand Christian dogma on which Religion rests as on its foundation—that when we have given up this present life, then shall we really begin to live. God has not created us for the perishable and transitory things of earth, but for things heavenly and everlasting; He has given us this world as a place of exile, and not as our abiding-place. As for riches and the other things which men call good and desirable, whether we have them in abundance, or lack them altogether—so far as eternal happiness is concerned—it matters little; the only important thing is to use them aright. Jesus Christ, when He redeemed us with *plentiful redemption,* took not away the pains and sorrows which in such large proportion are woven together in the web of our mortal life. He transformed them into motives of virtue and occasions of merit: and no man can hope for eternal reward unless he follow in the blood-stained footprints of his Saviour. *If we suffer with Him, we shall also reign with Him.* Christ's labors and sufferings, accepted of His own free-will, have marvellously sweetened all suffering and all labor. And not only by His example, but by His grace and by the hope held forth of everlasting recompense, has He made pain and grief more easy to endure; *for that which is at present momentary and light of our tribulation, worketh for us above measure exceedingly an eternal weight of glory.*

Therefore those whom fortune favors are warned that freedom from sorrow and abundance of earthly riches are no warrant for the bliss that shall never end, but rather are obstacles; that the rich should tremble at the threatenings of Jesus Christ—threatenings so unwonted in the mouth of Our Lord—and that a most strict account must be given to the Supreme Judge for all we possess. The chief and most excellent rule for the right use of money is one which the heathen philosophers hinted at, but which the Church has traced out clearly, and has not only made known to men's minds, but has impressed upon their lives. It rests on the principle that it is one thing to have a right to the possession of money, and another to have a right to use money as one wills. Private ownership, as we have seen, is the natural right of man; and to exercise that right, especially as members of society, is not only lawful, but absolutely necessary. "It is lawful," says St. Thomas of Aquin, "for a man to hold private property; and it is also necessary for the carrying on of human existence." . . . Whoever has received from the divine bounty a large share of temporal blessings, whether they be external and corporeal, or gifts of the mind, has received them for the purpose of using them for the perfecting of his own nature, and, at the same time, that he may employ them, as the steward of God's providence, for the benefit of others. "He that hath a talent," says St. Gregory the Great, "Let him see that he hide it not; he that hath abundance, let him quicken himself to mercy and generosity; he that hath art and skill, let him do his best to share the use and the utility thereof with his neighbor."

As for those who possess not the gifts of fortune, they are taught by the Church that in God's sight poverty is no disgrace, and that there is nothing to be ashamed of in seeking one's bread by labor. . . .

But, if Christian precepts prevail, the respective classes will not only be united in the bonds of friendship, but also in those of brotherly love. For they will understand and feel that all men are children of the same common Father, who is God; that all have alike the same last end, which is God Himself, who alone can make either men or angels absolutely and perfectly happy; that each and all are redeemed and made sons of God, by Jesus Christ, *the first-born among many brethren;* that the blessings of nature and the gifts of grace belong to the whole human race in common, and that from none except the unworthy is withheld the inheritance of the kingdom of heaven. *If sons, heirs also; heirs indeed of God, and co-heirs of Christ.*

Such is the scheme of duties and of rights which is shown forth to the world by the Gospel. Would it not seem that, were society penetrated with ideas like these, strife must quickly cease?

But the Church, not content with pointing out the remedy, also applies it. . . .

.   .   .   .

There is another and deeper consideration which must not be lost sight of. As regards the State, the interests of all, whether high or low, are equal. The poor are members of the national community equally with the rich; they are real component living members which constitute through the family, the living body; and it need hardly be said that they are in every State very largely in the majority. It would be irrational to neglect one portion of the citizens and favor another, and, therefore, the public administration must duly and solicitously provide for the welfare and the comfort of the working classes; otherwise, that law of justice will be violated which ordains that each man shall have his due. . . .

But although all citizens, without exception, can and ought to contribute to that common good in which individuals share so advantageously to themselves, yet it should not be supposed that all can contribute in the like way and to the same extent. No matter what changes may occur in forms of government, there will ever be differences and inequalities of condition in the State. Society cannot exist or be conceived of without them. Some there must be who devote themselves to the work of the commonwealth, who make the laws or administer justice, or whose advice and authority govern the nation in times of peace, and defend it in war. Such men clearly occupy the foremost place in the State, and should be held in highest estimation, for their work concerns most nearly and effectively the general interests of the community. Those who labor at a trade or calling do not promote the general welfare in such measure as this; but they benefit the nation, if less directly, in a most important manner. Still we have insisted that, since the end of society is to make men better, the chief good that society can possess is virtue. Nevertheless, in all well-constituted States it is in no wise a small matter to provide those bodily and external commodities, "the use of which is necessary to virtuous action." And in order to provide such material well-being, the labor of the poor—the exercise of their skill, and the employment of their strength, in the culture of the land, and in the workshops of trade—is of great account and quite indispensable. Indeed, their cooperation is in this respect so important that it may be truly said that it is only by the labor of working men that States grow rich. . . .

.   .   .   .   .

Whenever the general interest or any particular class suffers, or is threatened with harm, which can in no other way be met or prevented, the public authority must step in to deal with it. Now, it interests the public, as well as the individual, that peace and good order should be maintained; that family life should be carried on in accordance with God's laws and those of nature; that religion should be reverenced and obeyed; that a high standard of morality should prevail both in public and private life; that the sanctity of justice should be respected and that no one should injure another with impunity; that the members of the commonwealth should grow up to man's estate strong and robust, and capable, if need be, of guarding and defending their country. If, by a strike of workers or concerted interruption of work, there should be imminent danger of disturbance to the public peace; or if circumstances were such as that among the laboring population the ties of family life were relaxed; if religion were found to suffer through the workers not having time and opportunity afforded them to practice its duties; if in workshops and factories there were danger to morals through the mixing of the sexes or from other harmful occasions of evil; or if employers laid burdens upon their workmen which were unjust, or degraded them with conditions repugnant to their dignity as human beings; finally, if health were endangered by excessive labor, or by work unsuited to sex or age—in such cases, there can be no question but that, within certain limits, it would be right to invoke the aid and authority of the law. The limits must be determined by the nature of the occasion which calls for the law's interference—the principle being that the law must not undertake more, nor proceed further, than is required for the remedy of the evil or the removal of the mischief.

Rights must be religiously respected wherever they exist; and it is the duty of the public authority to prevent and to punish injury, and to protect everyone in the possession of his own. Still, when there is question of defending the rights of individuals, the poor and helpless have a claim to especial consideration. The richer class have many ways of shielding themselves, and stand less in need of help from the State; whereas those who are badly off have no resources of their own to fall back upon, and must chiefly depend upon the assistance of the State. And it is for this reason that wage-earners, who are undoubtedly among the weak and needy, should be specially cared for and protected by the government.

.   .   .   .   .

If we turn now to things external and corporeal, the first concern of all is to save the poor workers from the cruelty of greedy speculators, who use human beings as mere instruments of money-making. It is neither just nor human so to grind men down with excessive labor as to stupefy their minds and wear out their bodies. Man's powers, like his general nature, are limited, and beyond these limits he cannot go. His strength is developed and increased by use and exercise, but only on condition of due intermission and proper rest. Daily labor, therefore, should be so regulated as not to be protracted over longer hours than strength admits. How many and how long the intervals of rest should be must depend on the nature of the work, on circumstances of time and place, and on the health and strength of the workmen. Those who work in mines and quarries, and extract coal, stone, and metals from the bowels of the earth, should have shorter hours in proportion as their labor is more severe and trying to health. Then, again, the season of the year should be taken into account; for not infrequently a kind of labor is easy at one time which at another is intolerable or exceedingly difficult. Finally, work which is quite suitable for a strong man cannot reasonably be required from a woman or a child. And, in regard to children, great care should be taken not to place them in workshops and factories until their bodies and minds are sufficiently developed. For just as very rough weather destroys the buds of spring, so does too early an experience of life's hard toil blight the young promise of a child's faculties, and render any true education impossible. Women, again, are not suited for certain occupations; a woman is by nature fitted for home work, and it is that which is best adapted at once to preserve her modesty and to promote the good bringing up of children and the well-being of the family. As a general principle it may be laid down that a workman ought to have leisure and rest proportionate to the wear and tear of his strength; for waste of strength must be repaired by cessation from hard work.

.   .   .   .   .

Let it be then taken for granted that workman and employer should, as a rule, make free agreements, and in particular should agree freely as to the wages; nevertheless, there underlies a dictate of natural justice more imperious and ancient than any bargain between man and man, namely, that remuneration ought to be sufficient to support a frugal and well-behaved wage-earner. If through necessity or fear of a worse evil the workman accept harder conditions because an employer or contractor will afford him no better, he is made the victim of force and injustice. . . .

Those Catholics are worthy of all praise—and they are not a few—who, understanding what the times require, have striven, by various undertakings and endeavors, to better the condition of the working class without any sacrifice of principle being involved. They have taken up the cause of the workingman, and have spared no efforts to better the condition both of families and individuals; to infuse a spirit of equity into the mutual relations of employers and employed; to keep before the eyes of both classes the precepts of duty and the laws of the Gospel—that Gospel which by inculcating self-restraint, keeps men within the bounds of moderation, and tends to establish harmony among the divergent interests, and the vari-

ous classes which compose the State. It is with such ends in view that we see men of eminence meeting together for discussion, for the promotion of concerted action, and for practical work. Others, again, strive to unite workingmen of various grades into associations, help them with their advice and means, and enable them to obtain fitting and profitable employment. The bishops, on their part, bestow their ready good-will and support; and with their approval and guidance many members of the clergy, both secular and regular, labor assiduously in behalf of the spiritual and mental interests of the members of such associations. And there are not wanting Catholics blessed with affluence, who have, as it were, cast in their lot with the wage-earners, and who have spent large sums in founding and widely spreading benefit and insurance societies, by means of which the workingman may without difficulty acquire, through his labor, not only many present advantages but also the certainty of honorable support in days to come. How greatly such manifold and earnest activity has benefited the community at large is too well known to require Us to dwell upon it. We find therein grounds for most cheering hope in the future, provided always that the associations We have described continue to grow and spread, and are well and wisely administered. Let the State watch over these societies of citizens banded together for the exercise of their rights; but let it not thrust itself into their peculiar concerns and their organization; for things move and live by the spirit inspiring them, and may be killed by the rough grasp of a hand from without.

In order, then, that an association may be carried on with unity of purpose and harmony of action, its organization and government should be firm and wise. All such societies, being free to exist, have the further right to adopt such rules and organizations as may best conduce to the attainment of their respective objects. . . .

. . . Let our associations, then, look first and before all things to God; let religious instruction have therein the foremost place, each one being carefully taught what is his duty to God, what he has to believe, what to hope for, and how he is to work out his salvation; and let all be warned and strengthened with special care against wrong principles and false teaching. ...

7. Pius X's Denunciation of the French Law of Separation, February, 1906

The Concordat of 1801 served as a contract between France and the papacy throughout the nineteenth century, but the Third Republic was not satisfied and passed measure after measure designed to decentralize the power of the papacy in France. Some monastic orders were curtailed, church properties were seized, and education was placed under the state. In December, 1905, the French parliament passed a law separating the church and state in France and abrogating the Concordat. On February 11, 1906, in a letter to all bishops in France, Pope Pius X strongly denounced the separation. A condensation of his letter, which shows the papal view of the modern state, follows. James H. Robinson and Charles A. Beard, *Readings in Modern European History,* II (Boston: Ginn and Co., 1909).

Venerable Brethren, beloved sons, salutation and apostolic benediction:

Our soul is full of tender solicitude and our heart is wrung with anguish as our thoughts dwell upon you. And how, indeed, could it be otherwise on the morrow of the promulgation of the law which, in breaking violently the ancient ties by which your nation was united to the Apostolic See, places the Catholic Church in France in a situation unworthy of her and forever lamentable. This event is unquestionably of the gravest character, for it is as fatal to civil society as to religion. Nevertheless it cannot be a matter of surprise to any one who has given any attention to the religious policy pursued in France in these later years. To you, venerable brethren, it will come neither as an innovation nor a surprise, witnesses as you have been of the numerous and powerful blows unnecessarily inflicted on religion by the public authority.

You have seen the sanctity and inviolability of Christian marriage attacked by certain legislative provisions; the schools and hospitals put under the control of the laity; pupils torn from their studies and from ecclesiastical discipline and forced into military schools; the religious congregations dispersed and plundered and their members commonly reduced to the last stages of destitution. Other legal measures have followed, all of which you know: the abrogation of the law ordering public prayers at the opening of each parliamentary session and of the courts; the suppression of the signs of mourning on Good Friday, traditional on board of the ships; the elimination from the judiciary oath of all that gave to it religious character; the banishment from the courts, schools, army, navy, and finally from all public establishments, of every act or emblem which could recall religion in any way. These measures and others still, which little by little separated Church and State, were only the landmarks placed with the view of arriving at a complete and official separation; their promoters themselves did not hesitate to acknowledge it proudly and often.

The Apostolic See, on the contrary, has spared no pains in warding off so great a calamity. On the one hand, it has never tired of warning those who were at the head of French affairs, and has implored them repeatedly to consider well the enormity of the evils which their separatist policy would inevitably bring; on the other hand, it has multiplied striking evidences of its condescending affection toward France. It had the right to hope, therefore, in consideration of the obligations of gratitude, that it might be able to restrain these politicians from their wayward course and induce them at last to renounce their projects.

But attentions, good offices, efforts, as much on the part of our predecessor as on our own part, have all been without avail. The violence of the enemies of religion has ended in their carrying into execution plans which were for a long time merely aspirations,—plans opposed to your rights as a Catholic nation and contrary to all which the wise desire. Accordingly, in an hour so grave for the Church, we, conscious of our apostolic duty, have considered it an obligation to lift our voice and open our soul to you, venerable brethren, and to your clergy and your people,—you whom we have always surrounded with a protecting solicitude and whom we properly love at this moment more tenderly than ever.

That it is necessary to separate Church and State is a thesis absolutely false,—a most pernicious error. Based in fact upon the principle that the State ought not to recognize any religious faith, it is, to begin with, deeply insulting to God; for the creator of man is also the founder of human societies, and he maintains them as he does us. We owe him, therefore, not only private worship, but also a public and social worship in his praise.

Moreover, this thesis is clearly the negation of the supernatural order. It limits the action of the State to the sole pursuit of prosperity during this life, which is only the secondary reason for political societies; and it does not recognize in any manner the highest object of the State, namely, eternal bliss offered to man at the close of this present life, so short in duration, but regards it as foreign to the concerns of State. This thesis reverses the order very wisely established by God in the world, the order which requires a harmonious concord between the two societies.

The Roman Pontiffs have not ceased, according to circumstances and times, to refute and condemn the doctrine of the separation of Church and State....

And if in separating itself from the Church, any Christian State commits an act eminently baleful and censurable, how much is such action to be deplored in the case of France above all nations! France, we say, which during the course of centuries has been the object of such great and peculiar favor on the part of the Holy See; France whose fortune and glory have always been intimately united with the practice of Christian virtues and respect for religion! The same Pontiff, Leo XIII, had good reason for saying: "France should never forget that her providential destiny has united her to the Holy See with bonds too close and too ancient for her ever to wish to break them. From this union, indeed, have come forth her true greatness and her purest glory.... To disturb this traditional union would be to take from the nation itself a part of its moral strength and high mission in the world."

The bonds that consecrate this union ought, moreover, to be doubly inviolable on account of the sworn faith which treaties exact. The Concordat agreed upon by the sovereign Pontiff and the French government, like all similar treaties that States conclude between themselves, was a bilateral contract which was binding on both sides. The Roman Pontiff, on the one part, the head of the French nation on the other, agreed then solemnly, both for themselves and for their successors, to maintain inviolable the compact they had signed. The French government has not hesitated to ignore, with reference to the Holy See, the ordinary considerations and the courtesy with which even the smallest States do not dispense in dealing with each other. And its agents who were, moreover, the representatives of a Catholic nation, have not feared to treat with brutal disrespect the dignity and power of the Pontiff, supreme head of the Church, for whom they should have shown a respect superior to that which all political powers inspire,—all the more because this Pontiff labors for the eternal good of souls.

If we now examine the law itself which has just been promulgated we shall find a fresh reason to complain still more loudly. Since the State, breaking the bonds of the Concordat, separates itself from the Church, it was due the latter naturally to let it enjoy its independence and rights in peace and in the liberty ostensibly conceded to it. Now nothing has been further from the facts: we note in the law several exceptional measures which are odiously restrictive and place the Church under the dominion of the civil power. It has indeed been a source of bitter sorrow to us to see the State thus invade the exclusive province of the ecclesiastical power; and we grieve the more, since, forgetful of equity and justice, it has thus placed the Church in France in a critical situation, subversive of its most sacred rights.

The provisions of the new law are, in effect, contrary to the constitution on which the Church was founded by Jesus Christ. The Scriptures teach us and the traditions of the fathers confirm it, that the Church is the mystic body of Christ, a body ruled by pastors and teachers,—hence a body of men in the midst of whom are found those leaders who have full power to govern, teach, and judge. [Here the Pope enumerates his objections to the associations of laymen in whose hands the Law of Separation placed the administration of the various local churches.]

The law suppressing the appropriations for public worship frees the State from the obligation of providing for the expenses of religious worship, but it at the same time repudiates an engagement contracted in a diplomatic agreement, and seriously violates the principles of justice. On that point there can indeed be no possible doubt, and historical documents themselves bear witness to the fact in the clearest fashion. If the French government assumed in the Concordat the burden of assuring to the members of the clergy a salary which would enable them to provide in a suitable fashion for themselves and religious worship, it did not make this as a gratuitous concession; it pledged itself to do this by way of indemnification, partial at least, to the Church whose property the State had appropriated during the Revolution. On the other hand also, when the Roman Pontiff in the same Concordat and for the sake of peace engaged in his own name and that of his successors not to disturb the holders of property which had been thus taken from the Church, it is certain that he only made that promise on one condition: that is, that the French government should agree for all time adequately to pay the clergy and provide for the expenses of divine worship.

.   .   .   .   .

Accordingly we, remembering our Apostolic charge and bound to defend against every attack and to maintain in their absolute integrity the inviolable and sacred rights of the Church, by virtue of the supreme authority which God has conferred upon us, we, for the reasons given above, reject and condemn the law passed in France for the separation of the Church and State, as profoundly insulting to God whom it officially denies by making it a principle that the Republic recognizes no religion. We reject and condemn it as violating natural law, the law of nations, and the public faith due to treaties, as contrary to the divine constitution of the Church, to its fundamental rights, and to its liberty, as overturning justice and

trampling under foot the property rights which the Church has acquired by manifold titles and especially by virtue of the Concordat. We reject and condemn it as grievously offensive to the dignity of this Apostolic See, to our person, to the episcopacy, to the clergy, and to all the French Catholics. . . .

8. *Pius X*

From *Lamentabili Sane*, July 3, 1907, translated in *All Things in Christ*, by Vincent A. Yzermans (Westminster, Md.: The Newman Press, 1954).

SYLLABUS CONDEMNING THE ERRORS OF THE MODERNISTS

With truly lamentable results, our age, casting aside all restraint in its search for the ultimate causes of things, frequently pursues novelties so ardently that it rejects the legacy of the human race. Thus it falls into very serious errors, which are even more serious when they concern sacred authority, the interpretation of Sacred Scripture, and the principal mysteries of Faith. The fact that many Catholic writers also go beyond the limits determined by the Fathers and the Church herself is extremely regrettable. In the name of higher knowledge and historical research (they say), they are looking for that progress of dogmas which is, in reality, nothing but the corruption of dogmas.

These errors are being daily spread among the faithful. Lest they captivate the faithfuls' minds and corrupt the purity of their faith, His Holiness, Pius X, by Divine Providence, Pope, has decided that the chief errors should be noted and condemned by the Office of this Holy Roman and Universal Inquisition.

.   .   .   .   .

1. The ecclesiastical law which prescribes that books concerning the Divine Scriptures are subject to previous examination does not apply to critical scholars and students of scientific exegesis of the Old and New Testament.

2. The Church's interpretation of the Sacred Books is by no means to be rejected;

nevertheless, it is subject to the more accurate judgment and correction of the exegetes.

3. From the ecclesiastical judgments and censures passed against free and more scientific exegesis, one can conclude that the Faith the Church proposes contradicts history and that Catholic teaching cannot really be reconciled with the true origins of the Christian religion.

5. Since the deposit of Faith contains only revealed truths, the Church has no right to pass judgment on the assertions of the human sciences.

7. In proscribing errors, the Church cannot demand any internal assent from the faithful by which the judgments she issues are to be embraced.

8. They are free from all blame who treat lightly the condemnations passed by the Sacred Congregation of the Index or by the Roman Congregations.

9. They display excessive simplicity or ignorance who believe that God is really the author of the Sacred Scriptures.

11. Divine inspiration does not extend to all of Sacred Scriptures so that it renders its parts, each and every one, free from every error.

12. If he wishes to apply himself usefully to Biblical studies, the exegete must first put aside all preconceived opinions about the supernatural origin of Sacred Scripture and interpret it the same as any other merely human document.

14. In many narrations the Evangelists recorded, not so much things that are true, as things which, even though false, they judged to be more profitable for their readers.

15. Until the time the canon was defined and constituted, the Gospels were increased by additions and corrections. Therefore there remained in them only a faint and uncertain trace of the doctrine of Christ.

16. The narrations of John are not properly history, but a mystical contemplation of the Gospel. The discourses contained in his Gospel are theological meditations, lacking historical truth concerning the mystery of salvation.

17. The fourth Gospel exaggerated miracles not only in order that the extraordinary might stand out but also in order that it might become more suitable for showing forth the work and glory of the Word Incarnate.

19. Heterodox exegetes have expressed the true sense of the Scriptures more faithfully than Catholic exegetes.

20. Revelation could be nothing else than the consciousness man acquired of his relation to God.

23. Opposition may, and actually does, exist between the facts narrated in Sacred Scripture and the Church's dogmas which rest on them. Thus the critic may reject as false, facts the Church holds as most certain.

24. The exegete who constructs premises from which it follows that dogmas are historically false or doubtful is not to be re-

VIII-4. Jesus Curing the Sick. *Fresco by Brigitte West, Church of the Sacred Heart, Denmark.*

proved as long as he does not directly deny the dogmas themselves.

25. The assent of faith ultimately rests on a mass of probabilities.

26. The dogmas of the Faith are to be held only according to their practical sense; that is to say, as preceptive norms of conduct and not as norms of believing.

27. The divinity of Jesus Christ is not proved from the Gospels. It is a dogma which the Christian conscience has derived from the notion of the Messias.

28. While He was exercising His ministry, Jesus did not speak with the object of teaching He was Messias, nor did His miracles tend to prove it.

29. It is permissible to grant that the Christ of history is far inferior to the Christ Who is the object of faith.

31. The doctrine concerning Christ taught by Paul, John, and the Councils of Nicaea, Ephesus and Chalcedon is not that which Jesus taught but that which the Christian conscience conceived concerning Jesus.

32. It is impossible to reconcile the natural sense of the Gospel texts with the sense taught by our theologians concerning the conscience and the infallible knowledge of Jesus Christ.

33. Everyone who is not led by preconceived opinions can readily see that either

Jesus professed an error concerning the immediate Messianic coming or the greater part of His doctrine as contained in the Gospels is destitute of authenticity.

34. The critics can ascribe to Christ a knowledge without limits only on a hypothesis which cannot be historically conceived and which is repugnant to the moral sense. That hypothesis is that Christ as man possessed the knowledge of God and yet was unwilling to communicate the knowledge of a great many things to His disciples and posterity.

35. Christ did not always possess the consciousness of His Messianic dignity.

36. The Resurrection of the Saviour is not properly a fact of the historical order. It is a fact of merely the supernatural order (neither demonstrated nor demonstrable) which the Christian conscience gradually derived from other facts.

37. In the beginning, faith in the Resurrection of Christ was not so much in the fact itself of the Resurrection as in the immortal life of Christ with God.

39. The opinions concerning the origin of the Sacraments which the Fathers of Trent held and which certainly influenced their dogmatic canons are very different from those which now rightly exist among historians who examine Christianity.

41. The Sacraments are intended merely to recall to man's mind the ever-beneficent presence of the Creator.

43. The practice of administering Baptism to infants was a disciplinary evolution, which became one of the causes why the Sacrament was divided into two, namely, Baptism and Penance.

44. There is nothing to prove that the rite of the Sacrament of Confirmation was employed by the Apostles. The formal distinction of the two Sacraments of Baptism and Confirmation does not pertain to the history of primitive Christianity.

45. Not everything which Paul narrates concerning the institution of the Eucharist (I Cor. 11:23-25) is to be taken historically.

47. The words of the Lord, "Receive the Holy Spirit; whose sins you shall forgive, they are forgiven them; and whose sins you shall retain, they are retained" (John 20:

VIII-5. Incense of a New Church. *By Charles Demuth. Ferdinand Howald Collection, Columbus Gallery of Fine Arts.*

22-23), in no way refer to the Sacrament of Penance, in spite of what it pleased the Fathers of Trent to say.

49. When the Christian supper gradually assumed the nature of a liturgical action those who customarily presided over the supper acquired the sacerdotal character.

50. The elders who fulfilled the office of watching over the gatherings of the faithful were instituted by the Apostles as priests or bishops to provide for the necessary ordering of the increasing communities and not properly for the perpetuation of the Apostolic mission and power.

51. It is impossible that Matrimony could have become a Sacrament of the new law until later in the Church since it was necessary that a full theological explication of the doctrine of grace and the Sacraments should first take place before Matrimony should be held as a Sacrament.

52. It was far from the mind of Christ to found a Church as a society which would continue on earth for a long course of centuries. On the contrary, in the mind of Christ the kingdom of heaven together with the end of the world was about to come immediately.

53. The organic constitution of the Church is not immutable. Like human society, Christian society is subject to a perpetual evolution.

54. Dogmas, Sacraments and hierarchy, both their notion and reality, are only interpretations and evolutions of the Christian intelligence which have increased and perfected by an external series of additions the little germ latent in the Gospel.

55. Simon Peter never even suspected that Christ entrusted the primacy in the Church to him.

56. The Roman Church became the head of all the churches, not through the ordinance of Divine Providence, but merely through political conditions.

57. The Church has shown that she is hostile to the progress of the natural and theological sciences.

58. Truth is no more immutable than man himself, since it evolved with him, in him, and through him.

62. The chief articles of the Apostles' Creed did not have the same sense for the Christians of the first ages as they have for the Christians of our time.

63. The Church shows that she is incapable of effectively maintaining evangelical ethics since she obstinately clings to immutable doctrines which cannot be reconciled with modern progress.

64. Scientific progress demands that the concepts of Christian doctrine concerning God, creation, revelation, the Person of the Incarnate Word, and Redemption be readjusted.

65. Modern Catholicism can be reconciled with true science only if it is transformed into a non-dogmatic Christianity; that is to say, into a broad and liberal Protestantism.

9. *Pius X's Oath Against Modernism, 1910*

This was Pius X's encyclical, *Sacrorum Antistitum*, September 1, 1910. This oath was reaffirmed by the Holy Office, March 22, 1918, as obligatory for Roman Catholic priests and teachers. Schaff, *The Creeds of Christendom*, II.

I firmly embrace and accept all and singly those articles which have been defined, set forth and declared by the Church's inerrant teaching-authority and especially those heads of doctrines which directly conflict with the errors of this age. And, (1), I confess that God, the beginning and end of all things, can with certainty be known and proved to be by the natural light of reason from those things which are made, that is by the visible works of creation, even as a cause may be certainly proved from its effects. (2) I accept and acknowledge the external arguments of revelation, that is the divine facts especially miracles and prophecy, and I also accept the most sure proofs of the divine origin of the Christian religion and hold that they are pre-eminently adapted to the intelligence of all ages and men and, in particular, of this age. (3) And with firm faith, I equally believe that the Church, the guardian and teacher of the revealed Word, was directly founded by the real and historical Christ himself, as he dwelt with us, and that she was built upon Peter, the prince of the Apostolic hierarchy and his successors forever. (4) I sincerely receive the teaching of the faith as it has been handed down to us from the Apostles and orthodox Fathers and handed down in the same sense and meaning; and furthermore, I utterly reject the heretical fiction—*commentum*—of the evolution of dogmas according to which they change from one meaning to another and a meaning contradictory to that meaning which the Church before had given; and equally do I condemn that entire error according to which philosophical discovery suffices, although the divine deposit was given to Christ's bride and given to be faithfully guarded by her, or according to which it [the teaching] is little by little transformed in meaning by the creations of the human consciousness and man's effort and brought to perfection in the future by an indefinite progression. (5) I most surely hold and sincerely declare that faith is not a blind realization of religion drawn out of the darkness of the subconscience, morally enlightened by the influence of the heart and the inflexions of the will, but that it is an honest assent by the intellect, given to truth accepted through hearing of the ear by the which we believe as true those things which have been revealed and confirmed by a personal God, our Creator and Lord, and on the basis of the authority of God, who in the highest sense is trustworthy.

Likewise,—and this is equally important—I submit myself reverently and with my whole mind to all the condemnations, declarations and commands contained in the encyclical *pascendi* and the decree *lamentabli* especially in regard to that which they call the history of dogmas—*historiam dogmatum*. I also reprobate the error of those who assert that the faith offered by the Church may by any possibility conflict with history; and the error that it is not possible to harmonize, in the sense in which they are now understood, the Catholic dogmas with the origins of the Christian religion which are the more trustworthy.—I condemn and reject the opinions of those who say that the more learned Christians may represent at one and the same time two persons, the one a believer the other a historian, as if it were possible to hold on as an historian to things which are contradictory to the faith of the believer or lay down premises according to which it follows that dogmas are either false or dubious, just so they be not openly set aside.—Equally, do I reprobate that principle of judging the holy Scriptures and interpreting them, which, in defiance of the Church's tradition, the analogy of faith and the rules of the Apostolic See, suits itself to the comments of rationalists and, scarcely less lawlessly than rashly, accepts textual criticism as the one only and supreme rule.—Further, I reject the theory of those who hold that the teacher in the department of historic theology as well as the writer on its subjects must place opinion above the principle of the supernatural origin of Catholic tradition and the promise of divine aid in the preservation of all truth and, further, that the writings of the individual Fathers must be explained by the principles of science alone apart from any sacred authority and by the same free judgment that any profane document is studied or investigated.—Finally, I profess myself most averse to the error of the Modernists who hold that in sacred tradition there is not a divine element; or—what is far worse,—who reason in a pantheistic sense, so that nothing is left but the bare and naked historic occurrence like unto other occurrences of history which are left to men to carry on in subsequent periods by their industry, shrewdness and genius the teaching—*scholam*—begun by Christ and his Apostles. And I do most firmly hold to the faith of the Fathers and will continue so to do to the last breath of life, the faith concerning the unfailing charism of the truth which now inheres, has inhered and will always continue to inhere in the episcopal succession from the Apostles; that nothing is to be regarded as better or more opportune which the culture of this age or that age can suggest and that nothing is at any time to be otherwise believed or otherwise understood as the absolute and immutable truth preached from the beginning by the Apostles.

To all these things I promise to hold faithfully, sincerely, and wholly and I promise to keep them inviolably, never departing from them in teaching or by any words or writings. Thus I promise and swear, so help me God and these holy Gospels of God.

10. *Pius XI on Atheistic Communism, 1937*

Pius XI, *Divini Redemptoris*, from *Five Great Encyclicals*, trans. Rev. Gerald C. Treacy, S.J. (New York: The Paulist Press, 1939). Reprinted with permission of The Paulist Press.

The promise of a redeemer brightens the first page of the history of mankind, and the confident hope aroused by this promise softened the keen regret for a paradise which had been lost. It was this hope that accompanied the human race on its weary journey, until in the fullness of time the expected Saviour came to begin a new universal civilization, the Christian civilization, far superior even to that which up to this time had been laboriously achieved by certain more privileged nations.

2. Nevertheless, the struggle between good and evil remained in the world as a sad legacy of the original fall. Nor has the ancient tempter ever ceased to deceive mankind with false promises. It is on this account that one convulsion following upon another has marked the passage of the centuries, down to the revolution of our own days. This modern revolution, it may be said, has actually broken out or threatens everywhere, and it exceeds in amplitude and violence anything yet experienced in the preceding persecutions launched against the Church. Entire peoples find themselves in danger of falling back into a barbarism worse than that which oppressed the greater part of the world at the coming of the Redeemer.

3. This all too imminent danger, Venerable Brethren, as you have already surmised, is Bolshevistic and Atheistic Communism, which aims at upsetting the social order and at undermining the very foundations of Christian civilization.

8. The Communism of today, more emphatically than similar movements in the past, conceals in itself a false messianic idea. A pseudo-ideal of justice, of equality and fraternity in labor impregnates all its doctrine and activity with a deceptive mysticism, which communicates a zealous and contagious enthusiasm to the multitudes entrapped by delusive promises. This is especially true in an age like ours, when unusual misery has resulted from the unequal distribution of the goods of this world. This pseudo-ideal is even boastfully advanced as if it were responsible for a certain economic progress. As a matter of fact, when such progress is at all real, its true causes are quite different, as for instance the intensification of industrialism in countries which were formerly almost without it, the exploitation of immense natural resources, and the use of the most brutal methods to insure the achievement of gigantic projects with a minimum of expense.

9. The doctrine of modern Communism, which is often concealed under the most seductive trappings, is in substance based on the principles of dialectical and historical materialism previously advocated by Marx, of which the theoreticians of Bolshevism claim to possess the only genuine interpretation. According to this doctrine there is in the world only one reality, matter, the blind forces of which evolve into plant, animal and man. Even human society is nothing but a phenomenon and form of matter, evolving in the same way. By a law of inexorable necessity and through a perpetual conflict of forces, matter moves toward the final synthesis of a classless society. In such a doctrine, as is evident, there is no room for the idea of God; there is no difference between matter and spirit, between soul and body; there is neither survival of the soul after death nor any hope in a future life. Insisting on the dialectical aspect of their materialism, the Communists claim that the conflict which carries the world towards its final synthesis can be accelerated by man. Hence they endeavor to sharpen the antagonisms which arise between the various classes of society. Thus the class-struggle with its consequent violent hate and destruction takes on the aspect of a crusade for the progress of humanity. On the other hand, all other forces whatever, as long as they resist such systematic violence, must be annihilated as hostile to the human race.

10. Communism moreover, strips man of his liberty, robs human personality of all its dignity, and removes all the moral restraints that check the eruptions of blind impulse. There is no recognition of any right of the individual in his relations to the collectivity;

no natural right is accorded to human personality, which is a mere cogwheel in the Communist system. In man's relations with other individuals, besides, Communists hold the principle of absolute equality, rejecting all hierarchy and divinely-constituted authority, including the authority of parents. What men call authority and subordination is derived from the community as its first and only font. Nor is the individual granted any property rights over material goods or the means of production, for inasmuch as these are the source of further wealth, their possession would give one man power over another. Precisely on this score, all forms of private property must be eradicated, for they are at the origin of all economic enslavement.

11. Refusing to human life any sacred or spiritual character, such a doctrine logically makes of marriage and the family a purely artificial and civil institution, the outcome of a specific economic system. There exists no matrimonial bond of a juridico-moral nature that is not subject to the whim of the individual or of the collectivity. Naturally, therefore, the notion of an indissoluble marriage-tie is scouted. Communism is particularly characterized by the rejection of any link that binds woman to the family and the home, and her emancipation is proclaimed as a basic principle. She is withdrawn from the family and the care of her children, to be thrust instead into public life and collective production under the same conditions as man. The care of home and children then devolves upon the collectivity. Finally, the right of education is denied to parents, for it is conceived as the exclusive prerogative of the community, in whose name and by whose mandate alone parents may exercise this right.

15. How is it possible that such a system, long since rejected scientifically and now proved erroneous by experience, how is it, We ask, that such a system could spread so rapidly in all parts of the world? The explanation lies in the fact that too few have been able to grasp the nature of Communism. The majority instead succumb to its deception, skillfully concealed by the most extravagant promises. By pretending to desire only the betterment of the condition of the working-classes, by urging the removal of the very real abuses chargeable to the liberalistic economic order, and by demanding a more equitable distribution of this world's goods (objects entirely and undoubtedly legitimate), the Communist takes advantage of the present world-wide economic crisis to draw into the sphere of his influence even those sections of the populace which on principle reject all forms of materialism and terrorism. And as every error contains its element of truth, the partial truths to which We have referred are astutely presented according to the needs of time and place, to conceal, when convenient, the repulsive crudity and inhumanity of Communistic principles and tactics. Thus the Communist ideal wins over many of the better-minded members of the community. These in turn become the apostles of the movement among the younger intelligentsia who are still too immature to recognize the intrinsic errors of the system. The preachers of Communism are also proficient in exploiting racial antagonism and political divisions and oppositions. They take advantage of the lack of orientation characteristic of modern agnostic science in order to burrow into the universities where they bolster up the principles of their doctrine with pseudo-scientific arguments.

21. Nor can it be said that these atrocities are a transitory phenomenon, the usual accompaniment of all great revolutions, the isolated excesses common to every war. No, they are the natural fruit of a system which lacks all inner restraint. Some restraint is necessary for man considered either as an individual or in society. Even the barbaric peoples had this inner check in the natural law written by God in the heart of every man. And where this natural law was held in higher esteem, ancient nations rose to a grandeur that still fascinates—more than it should!—certain superficial students of human history. But tear the very idea of God from the hearts of men, and they are necessarily urged by their passions to the most atrocious barbarity.

22. This, unfortunately, is what we now behold. For the first time in history we are witnessing a struggle, cold-blooded in pur-

pose and mapped out to the least detail, between man and "all that is called God." Communism is by its nature anti-religious. It considers religion as "the opiate of the people" because the principles of religion which speak of a life beyond the grave dissuade the proletariat from the dream of a Soviet paradise which is of this world.

23. But the law of nature and its Author cannot be flouted with impunity. Communism has not been able, and will not be able, to achieve its objectives even in the merely economic sphere. It is true that in Russia it has been a contributing factor in rousing men and materials from the inertia of centuries, and in obtaining by all manner of means, often without scruple, some measure of material success. Nevertheless We know from reliable and even very recent testimony that not even there, in spite of slavery imposed on millions of men, has Communism reached its promised goal. After all, even the sphere of economics needs some morality, some moral sense of responsibility, which can find no place in a system so thoroughly materialistic as Communism. Terrorism is the only possible substitute, and it is terrorism that reigns today in Russia, where former comrades in revolution are exterminating each other. Terrorism, having failed despite all to stem the tide of moral corruption, cannot even prevent the dissolution of society itself.

24. In making these observations it is no part of Our intention to condemn *en masse* the peoples of the Soviet Union. For them We cherish the warmest paternal affection. We are well aware that not a few of them groan beneath the yoke imposed on them by men who in very large part are strangers to the real interests of the country. We recognize that many others were deceived by fallacious hopes. We blame only the system, with its authors and abettors who considered Russia the best-prepared field for experimenting with a plan elaborated decades ago, and who from there continue to spread it from one end of the world to the other.

25. We have exposed the errors and the violent, deceptive tactics of Bolshevistic and Atheistic Communism. It is now time, Venerable Brethren, to contrast with it the true notion, already familiar to you, of the "*civitas humana*" or human society, as taught by reason and Revelation through the mouth of the Church, "*Magistra gentium*."

26. Above all other reality there exists one supreme Being: God, the omnipotent Creator of all things, the all-wise and just Judge of all men. This supreme reality, God, is the absolute condemnation of the impudent falsehoods of Communism. In truth, it is not because men believe in God that He exists; rather because He exists do all men whose eyes are not deliberately closed to the truth believe in Him and pray to Him.

27. In the Encyclical on Christian Education We explained the fundamental doctrine concerning man as it may be gathered from reason and Faith. Man has a spiritual and immortal soul. He is a person, marvelously endowed by his Creator with gifts of body and mind. He is a true "microcosm," as the ancients said, a world in miniature, with a value far surpassing that of the vast inanimate cosmos. God alone is his last end, in this life and the next. By sanctifying grace he is raised to the dignity of a son of God, and incorporated into the Kingdom of God in the Mystical Body of Christ. In consequence he has been endowed by God with many and varied prerogatives: the right to life, to bodily integrity, to the necessary means of existence; the right to tend toward his ultimate goal in the path marked out for him by God; the right of association and the right to possess and use property.

30. Man cannot be exempted from his divinely-imposed obligations toward civil society, and the representatives of authority have the right to coerce him when he refuses without reason to do his duty. Society, on the other hand, cannot defraud man of his God-granted rights, the most important of which We have indicated above. Nor can society systematically void these rights by making their use impossible. It is therefore according to the dictates of reason that ultimately all material things should be ordained to man as a person, that through his mediation they may find their way to the Creator. In this wise we can apply to man, the human person, the words of the Apostle of the Gentiles, who writes to the Corinthians on the

Christian economy of salvation: "All things are yours, and you are Christ's and Christ is God's." While Communism impoverishes human personality by inverting the terms of the relation of man to society, to what lofty heights is man not elevated by reason and Revelation!

33. In view of this organized common effort towards peaceful living, Catholic doctrine vindicates to the State the dignity and authority of a vigilant and provident defender of those divine and human rights on which the Sacred Scriptures and the Fathers of the Church insist so often. It is not true that all have equal rights in civil society. It is not true that there exists no lawful social hierarchy. Let it suffice to refer to the Encyclicals of Leo XIII already cited, especially to that on State powers and to the other on the Christian Constitution of States. In these documents the Catholic will find the principles of reason and the Faith clearly explained, and these principles will enable him to defend himself against the errors and perils of a Communistic conception of the State. The enslavement of man despoiled of his rights, the denial of the transcendental origin of the State and its authority, the horrible abuse of public power in the service of a collectivistic terrorism, are the very contrary of all that corresponds with natural ethics and the will of the Creator. Both man and civil society derive their origin from the Creator, who has mutually ordained them one to the other. Hence neither can be exempted from their correlative obligations, nor deny or diminish each other's rights. The Creator Himself has regulated this mutual relationship in its fundamental lines, and it is by an unjust usurpation that Communism arrogates to itself the right to enforce, in place of the divine law based on the immutable principles of truth and charity, a partisan political program which derives from the arbitrary human will and is replete with hate.

36. But the enemies of the Church, though forced to acknowledge the wisdom of her doctrine, accuse her of having failed to act in conformity with her principles, and from this conclude to the necessity of seeking other solutions. The utter falseness and injustice of this accusation is shown by the whole history of Christianity. To refer only to a single typical trait, it was Christianity that first affirmed the real and universal brotherhood of all men of whatever race and condition. This doctrine she proclaimed by a method, and with an amplitude and conviction, unknown to preceding centuries; and with it she potently contributed to the abolition of slavery. Not bloody revolution, but the inner force of her teaching made the proud Roman matron see in her slave a sister in Christ. It is Christianity that adores the Son of God, made Man for love of man, and become not only the "Son of a Carpenter" but Himself a "Carpenter." It was Christianity that raised manual labor to its true dignity, whereas it had hitherto been so despised that even the moderate Cicero did not hesitate to sum up the general opinion of his time in words of which any modern sociologist would be ashamed: "All artisans are engaged in sordid trades, for there can be nothing ennobling about a workshop."

37. Faithful to these principles, the Church has given new life to human society. Under her influence arose prodigious charitable organizations, great guilds of artisans and workingmen of every type. These guilds, ridiculed as "medieval" by the liberalism of the last century, are today claiming the admiration of our contemporaries in many countries who are endeavoring to revive them in some modern form. And when other systems hindered her work and raised obstacles to the salutary influence of the Church, she was never done warning them of their error. We need but recall with what constant firmness and energy Our Predecessor, Leo XIII, vindicated for the workingman the right to organize, which the dominant liberalism of the more powerful States relentlessly denied him. Even today the authority of this Church doctrine is greater than it seems; for the influence of ideas in the realm of facts, though invisible and not easily measured, is surely of predominant importance.

38. It may be said in all truth that the Church, like Christ, goes through the centuries doing good to all. There would be today neither Socialism nor Communism if

the rulers of the nations had not scorned the teachings and maternal warnings of the Church. On the bases of liberalism and laicism they wished to build other social edifices which, powerful and imposing as they seemed at first, all too soon revealed the weakness of their foundations, and today are crumbling one after another before our eyes, as everything must crumble that is not grounded on the one corner stone which is Christ Jesus.

40. What then must be done, what remedies must be employed to defend Christ and Christian civilization from this pernicious enemy? As a father in the midst of his family, We should like to speak quite intimately of those duties which the great struggle of our day imposes on all the children of the Church; and We would address Our paternal admonition even to those sons who have strayed far from her.

41. As in all the stormy periods of the history of the Church, the fundamental remedy today lies in a sincere renewal of private and public life according to the principles of the Gospel by all those who belong to the Fold of Christ, that they may be in truth the salt of the earth to preserve human society from total corruption.

44. And here We wish, Venerable Brethren, to insist more particularly on two teachings of our Lord which have special bearing on the present condition of the human race: detachment from earthly goods and the precept of charity. "Blessed are the poor in spirit" were the first words that fell from the lips of the Divine Master in His sermon on the mount. This lesson is more than ever necessary in these days of materialism athirst for the goods and pleasures of this earth. All Christians, rich or poor, must keep their eye fixed on heaven, remembering that "we have not here a lasting city, but we seek one that is to come." The rich should not place their happiness in things of earth nor spend their best efforts in the acquisition of them. Rather, considering themselves only as stewards of their earthly goods, let them be mindful of the account they must render of them to their Lord and Master, and value them as precious means that God has put into their hands for doing good; let them not fail, be-

sides, to distribute of their abundance to the poor, according to the evangelical precept. Otherwise there shall be verified of them and their riches the harsh condemnation of St. James the Apostle: "Go to now, ye rich men; weep and howl in your miseries which shall come upon you. Your riches are corrupted, and your garments are moth-eaten; your gold and silver is cankered; and the rust of them shall be for a testimony against you and shall eat your flesh like fire. You have stored up to yourselves wrath against the last days. . . ."

45. But the poor, too, in their turn, while engaged, according to the laws of charity and justice in acquiring the necessities of life and also in bettering their condition, should always remain "poor in spirit," and hold spiritual goods in higher esteem than earthly property and pleasures. Let them remember that the world will never be able to rid itself of misery, sorrow and tribulation, which are the portion even of those who seem most prosperous. Patience, therefore, is the need of all, that Christian patience which comforts the heart with the divine assurance of eternal happiness. "Be patient, therefore, brethren," We repeat with St. James "until the coming of the Lord. Behold the husbandman waiteth for the precious fruit of the earth, patiently bearing until he receives the early and the later rain. Be you therefore also patient and strengthen your hearts, for the coming of the Lord is at hand." Only thus will be fulfilled the consoling promise of the Lord: "Blessed are the poor!" These words are no vain consolation, a promise as empty as those of the Communists. They are the words of life, pregnant with a sovereign reality. They are fully verified here on earth, as well as in eternity. Indeed, how many of the poor, in anticipation of the Kingdom of Heaven already proclaimed their own: "for yours is the Kingdom of Heaven," find in these words a happiness which so many of the wealthy, uneasy with their riches and ever thirsting for more, look for in vain!

46. Still more important as a remedy for the evil we are considering, or certainly more directly calculated to cure it, is the precept of charity. We have in mind that Christian charity, "patient and kind," which avoids all semblance of demeaning paternalism, and

all ostentation; that charity which from the very beginning of Christianity won to Christ the poorest of the poor, the slaves. And We are grateful to all those members of charitable associations, from the conferences of St. Vincent de Paul to the recent great relief organizations, which are perseveringly practicing the spiritual and corporal works of mercy. The more the workingmen and the poor realize what the spirit of love animated by the virtue of Christ is doing for them, the more readily will they abandon the false persuasion that Christianity has lost its efficacy and that the Church stands on the side of the exploiters of their labor.

50. Therefore We turn again in a special way to you, Christian employers and industrialists, whose problem is often so difficult for the reason that you are saddled with the heavy heritage of an unjust economic régime whose ruinous influence has been felt through many generations. We bid you be mindful of your responsibility. It is unfortunately true that the manner of acting in certain Catholic circles has done much to shake the faith of the working-classes in the religion of Jesus Christ. These groups have refused to understand that Christian charity demands the recognition of certain rights due to the workingman, which the Church has explicitly acknowledged. What is to be thought of the action of those Catholic employers who in one place succeeded in preventing the reading of Our Encyclical *Quadragesimo Anno*, in their local churches? Or of those Catholic industrialists who even to this day have shown themselves hostile to a labor movement that We Ourselves recommended? Is it not deplorable that the right of private property defended by the Church should so often have been used as a weapon to defraud the workingman of his just salary and his social rights?

51. In reality, besides commutative justice, there is also social justice with its own set of obligations, from which neither employers nor workingmen can escape. Now it is of the very essence of social justice to demand from each individual all that is necessary for the common good. But just as in the living organism it is impossible to provide for the good of the whole unless each single part and each individual member is given what it needs for the exercise of its proper functions, so it is impossible to care for the social organism and the good of society as a unit unless each single part and each individual member—that is to say, each individual man in the dignity of his human personality—is supplied with all that is necessary for the exercise of his social functions. If social justice be satisfied, the result will be an intense activity in economic life as a whole, pursued in tranquillity and order. This activity will be proof of the health of the social body, just as the health of the human body is recognized in the undisturbed regularity and perfect efficiency of the whole organism.

54. If, therefore, We consider the whole structure of economic life, as We have already pointed out in Our Encyclical *Quadragesimo Anno*, the reign of mutual collaboration between justice and charity in social-economic relations can only be achieved by a body of professional and inter-professional organizations, built on solidly Christian foundations, working together to effect, under forms adapted to different places and circumstances, what has been called the Corporation.

57. On this point We have already insisted in Our Allocution of May 12th of last year, but We believe it to be a duty of special urgency, Venerable Brethren, to call your attention to it once again. In the beginning Communism showed itself for what it was in all its perversity; but very soon it realized that it was thus alienating the people. It has therefore changed its tactics, and strives to entice the multitudes by trickery of various forms, hiding its real designs behind ideas that in themselves are good and attractive. Thus, aware of the universal desire for peace, the leaders of Communism pretend to be the most zealous promoters and propagandists in the movement for world amity. Yet at the same time they stir up a class-warfare which causes rivers of blood to flow, and, realizing that their system offers no internal guarantee of peace, they have recourse to unlimited armaments. Under various names which do not suggest Communism, they establish organizations and periodicals with the sole purpose of carrying their ideas into quarters

otherwise inaccessible. They try perfidiously to worm their way even into professedly Catholic and religious organizations. Again, without receding an inch from their subversive principles, they invite Catholics to collaborate with them in the realm of so-called humanitarianism and charity; and at times even make proposals that are in perfect harmony with the Christian spirit and the doctrine of the Church. Elsewhere they carry their hypocrisy so far as to encourage the belief that Communism, in countries where faith and culture are more strongly entrenched, will assume another and much milder form. It will not interfere with the practice of religion. It will respect liberty of conscience. There are some even who refer to certain changes recently introduced into Soviet legislation as a proof that Communism is about to abandon its program of war against God.

58. See to it, Venerable Brethren, that the Faithful do not allow themselves to be deceived! Communism is intrinsically wrong, and no one who would save Christian civilization may collaborate with it in any undertaking whatsoever. Those who permit themselves to be deceived into lending their aid towards the triumph of Communism in their own country, will be the first to fall victims of their error. And the greater the antiquity and grandeur of the Christian civilization in the regions where Communism successfully penetrates, so much more devastating will be the hatred displayed by the Godless.

64. After this appeal to the clergy, We extend Our paternal invitation to Our beloved sons among the laity who are doing battle in the ranks of Catholic Action. On another occasion We have called this movement so dear to Our heart "a particularly providential assistance" in the work of the Church during these troublous times. Catholic Action is in effect a *social* apostolate also, inasmuch as its object is to spread the Kingdom of Jesus Christ not only among individuals, but also in families and in society. It must, therefore, make it a chief aim to train its members with special care and to prepare them to fight the battles of the Lord. This task of formation, now more urgent and indispensable than ever, which must always

precede direct action in the field, will assuredly be served by study circles, conferences, lecture courses and the various other activities undertaken with a view to making known the Christian solution of the social problem.

65. The militant leaders of Catholic Action, thus properly prepared and armed, will be the first and immediate apostles of their fellow workmen. They will be an invaluable aid to the priest in carrying the torch of truth, and in relieving grave spiritual and material suffering, in many sectors where inveterate anticlerical prejudice or deplorable religious indifference has proved a constant obstacle to the pastoral activity of God's ministers. In this way they will collaborate, under the direction of especially qualified priests, in that work of spiritual aid to the laboring classes on which We set so much store, because it is the means best calculated to save these, Our beloved children, from the snares of Communism.

66. In addition to this individual apostolate which, however useful and efficacious, often goes unheralded, Catholic Action must organize propaganda on a large scale to disseminate knowledge of the fundamental principles on which, according to the Pontifical documents, a Christian Social Order must build.

69. Even where the State, because of changed social and economic conditions, has felt obliged to intervene directly in order to aid and regulate such organizations by special legislative enactments, supposing always the necessary respect for liberty and private initiative, Catholic Action may not urge the circumstance as an excuse for abandoning the field. Its members should contribute prudently and intelligently to the study of the problems of the hour in the light of Catholic doctrine. They should loyally and generously participate in the formation of the new institutions, bringing to them the Christian spirit which is the basic principle of order wherever men work together in fraternal harmony.

73. Such is the positive task, embracing at once theory and practice, which the Church undertakes in virtue of the mission, confided to her by Christ, of constructing a

Christian society, and, in our own times, of resisting unto victory the attacks of Communism. It is the duty of the Christian State to concur actively in this spiritual enterprise of the Church, aiding her with the means at its command, which although they be external devices, have none the less for their prime object the good of souls.

74. This means that all diligence should be exercised by States to prevent within their territories the ravages of an anti-God campaign which shakes society to its very foundations. For there can be no authority on earth unless the authority of the Divine Majesty be recognized; no oath will bind which is not sworn in the Name of the Living God. We repeat what We have said with frequent insistence in the past, especially in Our Encyclical *Caritate Christi:* "How can any contact be maintained, and what value can any treaty have, in which every guarantee of conscience is lacking? And how can there be talk of guarantees of conscience when all faith in God and all fear of God have vanished? Take away this basis, and with it all moral law falls, and there is no remedy left to stop the gradual but inevitable destruction of peoples, families, the State, civilization itself."

75. It must likewise be the special care of the State to create those material conditions of life without which an orderly society cannot exist. The State must take every measure necessary to supply employment, particularly for the heads of families and for the young. To achieve this end demanded by the pressing needs of the common welfare, the wealthy classes must be induced to assume those burdens without which human society cannot be saved nor they themselves remain secure. However, measures taken by the State with this end in view ought to be of such a nature that they will really affect those who actually possess more than their share of capital resources, and who continue to accumulate them to the grievous detriment of others.

76. The State itself, mindful of its responsibility before God and society, should be a model of prudence and sobriety in the administration of the commonwealth. Today more than ever the acute world crisis demands that those who dispose of immense funds, built up on the sweat and toil of millions, keep constantly and singly in mind the common good. State functionaries and all employees are obliged in conscience to perform their duties faithfully and unselfishly, imitating the brilliant example of distinguished men of the past and of our own day, who with unremitting labor sacrificed their all for the good of their country. In international trade-relations let all means be sedulously employed for the removal of those artificial barriers to economic life which are the effects of distrust and hatred. All must remember that the peoples of the earth form but one family in God.

77. At the same time the State must allow the Church full liberty to fulfill her divine and spiritual mission, and this in itself will be an effectual contribution to the rescue of nations from the dread torment of the present hour. Everywhere today there is an anxious appeal to moral and spiritual forces; and rightly so, for the evil we must combat is at its origin primarily an evil of the spiritual order. From this polluted source the monstrous emanations of the Communistic system flow with satanic logic. Now, the Catholic Church is undoubtedly pre-eminent among the moral and religious forces of today. Therefore the very good of humanity demands that her work be allowed to proceed unhindered.

78. Those who act otherwise, and at the same time fondly pretend to attain their objective with purely political or economic means, are in the grip of a dangerous error. When religion is banished from the school, from education and from public life, when the representatives of Christianity and its sacred rites are held up to ridicule, are we not really fostering the materialism which is the fertile soil of Communism? Neither force, however well-organized it be, nor earthly ideals however lofty or noble, can control a movement whose roots lie in the excessive esteem for the goods of this world.

11. Assumption of Mary, 1950

Munificentissimus Deus, by Pope Pius XII, defined the dogma of faith that Mary, God's Virgin Mother, was assumed body and soul into heavenly glory. Trans. Dominic J. Unger, *Mary All-Glorious* (Paterson, N.J.: St. Anthony Guild Press, 1956).

1. All-bountiful is God, and all-powerful. The designs of His providence consist in wisdom and love. According to the hidden purpose of His mind, then, He assuages the sorrows of peoples and individuals with an interspersion of joys, so that by different ways and in different modes all things may work together unto good for those who love Him (cf. Rom. 8:28).

2. Our pontificate, just like the present age itself, is burdened with ever so many cares, anxieties and troubles because of very grave calamities and because of the straying of many from truth and virtue. And yet it is a great solace for Us to see that, while Catholic faith is manifested publicly and actively, piety toward God's Virgin Mother is gaining daily in vigor and fervor, and almost everywhere this is a token of a better and holier life. The result is that while the Blessed Virgin is most lovingly fulfilling her duties as mother on behalf of those who were redeemed by Christ's blood, her children's minds and hearts are being earnestly aroused to a more diligent contemplation of her privileges.

3. God, in truth, from all eternity regards Mary with a most favorable and singular affection. So "when the fullness of time came" (Gal. 4:4), He executed the designs of His providence in such wise that the privileges and prerogatives which He bestowed on her with supreme liberality would be resplendent in perfect harmony. Now, although the Church has always acknowledged this supreme liberality and perfect harmony of graces and has explored them daily more and more through the course of the centuries, it is in our own age, nevertheless, that the well-known privilege of the bodily Assumption into Heaven of Mary, God's Virgin Mother, has surely shone forth with a brighter light.

4. This privilege has shone indeed with new splendor since Our predecessor of immortal memory, Pius IX, solemnly ratified the dogma of the Immaculate Conception of the loving Mother of God. For these two privileges are most closely related. Christ, to

VIII-6. The Divine Eagle and the Immaculate Virgin. *A seventeenth century symbol of the Virgin Mary. From E. D. O'Connor, ed.* The Dogma of the Immaculate Conception *(South Bend: University of Notre Dame Press, 1958).*

be sure, by His own death overcame sin and death; and one who, through Baptism, is reborn supernaturally has conquered sin and death through the same Christ. Still, according to the general law, God does not will to grant to the just the full effect of the victory over death until the end of time has come. And so it is that the bodies of even the just disintegrate after death, and only on the last day will they at length be united, each with its own glorified soul.

5. From this general law, nevertheless, God willed that the Blessed Virgin Mary should be exempt. Because of an altogether singular privilege she conquered sin by her Immaculate Conception, and consequently she was not liable to the well-known law of remaining in the corruption of the grave, nor was she bound to await the end of time for the redemption of her body.

405

6. When, then, it was solemnly ratified that Mary, God's Virgin Mother, was from the beginning immune from the hereditary stain, the minds of the faithful were spurred on by a more ardent hope that the dogma of the Virgin Mary's bodily Assumption into Heaven would at the earliest opportunity be defined by the Church's supreme teaching office.

10. For this reason We sent up earnest prayers to God that He might grant to Our mind the light of the Holy Spirit in making a decision in this most important matter....

11. Since, however this matter was of such great moment and importance, We deemed it opportune to request Our venerable brethren in the episcopacy directly and officially that each should make his mind known to Us in an express statement. With this in view, We sent them, on May 1, 1946, Our letter *Deiparae Virginis Mariae*, which contained these words: "Do you, Venerable Brethren, in your eminent wisdom and prudence, judge that the most Blessed Virgin's bodily Assumption can be proposed and defined as a dogma of faith; and do you, together with your clergy and people, desire that this be done?"

12. Now those whom "the Holy Spirit has placed...as bishops, to rule the Church of God" (Acts 20:28) almost unanimously gave an affirmative answer to both questions.... Thus, from the universal consent of the Church's ordinary teaching office one obtains a certain and solid argument for proving that the Blessed Virgin Mary's bodily Assumption into Heaven—which, as far as the heavenly "glorification" itself of the virginal body of God's loving Mother is concerned, no faculty of man's mind could know by its natural powers—is a truth which was revealed by God and which must therefore be firmly and faithfully believed by all the children of the Church. For, as the same Vatican Council asserts, "All those things must be believed by divine and Catholic faith which are contained in the written or traditional word of God and are proposed by the Church, either by a solemn decree, or by the ordinary and universal teaching office, to be believed as divinely revealed."

13. Various testimonies, signs and traces of this common belief of the Church are dis-

cernible from remote times down through the course of the centuries; and with the progression of time this same faith has displayed itself with a brighter light.

[References and testimonies from the faithful, custom, Marian Rosary, liturgy, church fathers, etc., follow.]

26. Often one meets theologians and sacred orators who, following in the footsteps of the holy Fathers, allowed themselves a certain liberty in adducing events and statements borrowed from the Sacred Scriptures, in order to illustrate their faith in the Assumption. Thus, to recall only a few of the passages more frequently employed for this purpose, there are those who quote the Psalmist's words: "Arise, O Lord, into Thy resting place: Thou and the ark which Thou hast sanctified" (Ps. 131:8). And the Ark of the Covenant, built of incorruptible wood and set in the temple of God, they regard as an image of the Virgin Mary's most pure body, preserved immune from all corruption of the grave and elevated to such great glory in Heaven. Similarly, in treating this subject, they describe her as the Queen triumphantly entering the royal palace of Heaven and enthroned at the right hand of the Divine Redeemer (Ps. 44:10, 14-16). Likewise, they introduce the spouse of the Canticles, "that goeth up by the desert, as a pillar of smoke of aromatical spices, of myrrh and frankincense" (Cant. 3:6; cf 4:8, 6:9), that she may be adorned with a crown. These, of course, are presented by them as images of that heavenly Queen and heavenly Bride who, together with the Divine Bridegroom, has been taken up to the palace of Heaven.

27. The Scholastic Doctors, moreover, saw the Assumption of God's Virgin Mother signified, not only in various figures of the Old Testament, but also in that renowned "Woman clothed with the sun," whom the Apostle John contemplated on the island of Patmos (Apoc. 12:1 *sq.*). Again, among the passages of the New Testament, they considered with special care these words: "Hail, full of grace, the Lord is with thee; blessed art thou among women" (Luke 1:28), because they viewed the mystery of the Assumption as the complement of that most complete grace bestowed on the Blessed

Virgin and as a singular blessing opposed to the curse of Eve.

[Testimonies cited in St. Anthony of Padua, St. Albert the Great, St. Thomas Aquinas, St. Bonaventure, St. Francis de Sales, and others.]

38. All these arguments and considerations of the Holy Fathers and the theologians are based on the Sacred Scriptures as their ultimate foundation. Indeed, these Scriptures place before our very eyes God's loving Mother as most closely united to her Divine Son and always sharing His lot. For this reason, it seems nearly impossible to view her who conceived Christ, gave Him birth, nursed Him with her milk, held Him in her arms and clasped Him to her breast, as being separated from Him in body, even though not in soul, after this earthly life. Since our Redeemer is Mary's Son, being most perfectly observant of the divine law He could not but honor, not only His eternal Father, but also His most beloved Mother. Now, since He was able to adorn her with the great honor of preserving her, unimpaired, from the corruption of the grave, we must believe that He really did so.

44. Wherefore, after having again and again poured forth suppliant prayers to God and having invoked the light of the Spirit of Truth, so now, to the glory of Almighty God, who has lavished His special benevolence on the Virgin Mary, to the honor of her Son, the immortal King of the ages and the Conqueror of sin and death, for an increase of glory for His revered Mother, and for the joy and delight of the entire Church, by the authority of Our Lord Jesus Christ, of the blessed Apostles Peter and Paul, and Our own authority, We proclaim, declare, and define that it is a divinely revealed dogma, that God's Immaculate Mother, the Ever-Virgin Mary, when the course of her earthly life was finished, was assumed body and soul into heavenly glory.

45. Hence, if anyone—which God forbid—should willfully dare either to deny or to call into doubt what We have defined, let him know that he has completely forsaken the divine and Catholic Faith.

SUGGESTED READINGS

Binchy, D. A., *Church and State in Fascist Italy.* London: Oxford University Press, 1941.

Blanshard, Paul, *American Freedom and Catholic Power.* Boston: Beacon Press, 1949.

———, *Freedom and Catholic Power in Spain and Portugal.* Boston: Beacon Press, 1962.

———, *The Irish and Catholic Power.* Boston: Beacon Press, 1953.

Bury, J. B., *History of the Papacy in the Nineteenth Century.* London: Macmillan & Co., Ltd., 1930.

Butler, E. C., *The Vatican Council,* 2 vols. New York: Longmans, Green & Co., Inc., 1930.

Cadoux, C. J., *Roman Catholicism and Freedom.* London: Independent Press, Ltd., 1936.

Chadwick, Owen, *From Bossuet to Newman.* Cambridge: Cambridge University Press, 1957.

Collins, R. W., *Catholicism and the Second French Republic.* New York: Columbia University Press, 1923.

Eckhardt, C. C., *The Papacy and World Affairs.* Chicago: University of Chicago Press, 1937.

Ehler, Sidney Z., *Twenty Centuries of Church and State.* Westminster, Md.: The Newman Press, 1957.

Garrison, W. E., *Catholicism and the American Mind.* Chicago: Willett, Clark & Company, 1928.

Geffcken, F. H., *Church and State,* 2 vols. London: Longmans, Green & Co., Ltd., 1877.

Gilson, E., *Church Speaks to the Modern World, Leo XIII.* New York: Doubleday & Co., Inc., 1954.

Greene, E. B., *Religion and the State.* New York: New York University Press, 1941.

Guérard, A. L., *French Prophets of Yesterday.* London: T. F. Unwin, 1913.

Gwynn, D. R., *The Catholic Reaction in France.* New York: The Macmillan Co., 1924.

Hales, E. E. Y., *Revolution and Papacy, 1769-1846.* New York: Doubleday & Co., Inc., 1960.

Halperin, S. W., *Italy and the Vatican at War, 1870-1878.* Chicago: University of Chicago Press, 1939.

Hudson, Winthrop S., *Understanding Roman Catholicism: A Guide to Papal Teachings for Protestants.* Philadelphia: The Westminster Press, 1959.

Hughes, Philip, *A Popular History of the Catholic Church*. New York: The Macmillan Co., 1957.

Kittler, Glenn D., *Papal Princes: History of the Sacred College of Cardinals*. New York: Funk & Wagnalls Co., 1960.

Laski, H. J., *Authority and the Modern State*. New Haven: Yale University Press, 1919.

Lenski, Gerhard, *The Religious Factor: A Sociological Study of Religion's Impact on Politics, Economics, and Family Life*. New York: Doubleday & Co., Inc., 1961.

Manhattan, Avro, *The Vatican in World Politics*. New York: Gaer Associates, 1949.

Moehlman, C. H., *The Catholic-Protestant Mind*. New York: Harper & Row, Publishers, 1929.

Moss, C. B., *The Old Catholic Movement*. London: S.P.C.K., 1948.

Murray, J. C., S.J., *We Hold These Truths: Catholic Reflections on the American Proposition*. New York: Sheed & Ward, 1960.

Nielsen, F. K., *History of the Papacy in the XIXth Century*. London: John Murray Publishers, Ltd., 1906.

O'Dea, Thomas, *American Catholic Dilemma*. New York: Sheed & Ward, 1958.

Paris, Edmund, *The Vatican Against Europe*, trans. A. Robson. London: Macmillan & Co., Ltd., 1959.

Pelikan, Jaroslav, *Riddle of Roman Catholicism*. New York: Abingdon Press, 1959.

Phillips, C. S., *The Church in France, 1789-1848*. Milwaukee: Morehouse-Barlow Co., Inc., 1929.

———, *The Church in France, 1848-1907*. New York: The Macmillan Co., 1936.

Pichon, Charles, *The Vatican and Its Role in World Affairs*. New York: E. P. Dutton & Co., 1950.

Ryan, John A. and F. Boland, *Catholic Principles of Politics*. New York: The Macmillan Co., 1958.

Salmon, G., *The Infallibility of the Church*. London: John Murray Publishers, Ltd., 1923.

Soderini, E., *Leo XIII, Italy and France*. London: Burns Oates & Washbourne, Ltd., 1959.

Stokes, A. P., *Church and State in the United States*, 3 vols. New York: Harper & Row, Publishers, 1950.

Stuber, Stanley, *Primer on Roman Catholicism for Protestants*. New York: Association Press, 1953.

Sugrue, Thomas, *A Catholic Speaks His Mind*. New York: Harper & Row, Publishers, 1951.

Thompson, R. W., *The Papacy and the Civil Power*. New York: Harper & Row, Publishers, 1876.

Tyrrell, George, *Christianity at the Cross-roads*. London: Longmans, Green, & Co., 1909.

———, *Lex Credenti*. London: Longmans, Green & Co., 1906.

Vidler, A. R., *The Modernist Movement in the Roman Church*. Cambridge: Cambridge University Press, 1934.

———, *Prophecy and Papacy*. New York: Charles Scribner's Sons, 1954.

Weigel, Gustave, S.J., *Faith and Understanding in America*. New York: The Macmillan Co., 1959.

Yzermans, V. A., *All Things in Christ: Encyclicals of Pius X*. Westminster, Md.: The Newman Press, 1954.

CHRONOLOGY

[See chapters 7 and 9 for other related events.]

1713	Unigenitus, against Jansenism
1759	Portugal outlaws Jesuits
1763	Febronianism in Germany
1764	France expels Jesuits
1765–1790	Josephism in Austria
1767	Spain and Naples ban Jesuits
1773	Dominus ac Redemptor Noster, dissolution of Jesuit Order
1781	Toleration act in Austria
1782–1854	Abbé de Lamennais
1797	Napoleon forces Pius VI out of Rome
1801	Concordat, Napoleon and Pius VII
1809	Napoleon invades papal states, imprisons Pius VII
1814	Pius VII returns to Rome. Restoration of Jesuits
	May, Napoleon banished to Elba
1815	Vienna Congress reshapes Europe
	March, Napoleon lands in France
	June 18, Battle of Waterloo
	July, Louis XVIII reenters Paris
1818	Lamennais' Indifference in Matters of Religion
1821	Death of Napoleon
1823	Monroe Doctrine
1824	Death of Louis XVIII. Accession of Charles X in France
1829	Catholic Emancipation Act of Great Britain and Ireland
	Pius VIII, Traditi humilitati, against heretical biblical translations
1830	Overthrow of Charles X in France. Accession of Louis Philippe

1830	Pius VIII, Litteris alto, objection to mixed marriages	1888	Leo XIII, Libertas, human liberty
	Revolutions in France, Belgium, Poland	1891	Leo XIII, Rerum Novarum, working classes
1830–1831	L'Avenir, Lamennais' journal	1893	Leo XIII, Providentissimus, biblical inerrance and inspiration
1831	Belgian Constitution	1901	French Law of Associations
1832	Reform Bill, wider representation in English parliament	1902	Leo XIII, Biblical Commission established
	Gregory XVI, Mirari vos, against Lamennais' liberalism	1905	French separation of church and state
1834	Lamennais' Paroles d'un Croyant	1906	Pius X, reaction to French liberal laws
	Gregory XVI, Singulari vos, against Lamennais		Tyrrell dismissed from Jesuit Order
1845	Newman joins Roman Catholicism	1907	Pius X, Lamentabili sane, against modernism
1848	Overthrow of Louis Philippe. Louis Napoleon becomes President of French Republic		Pius X, Pascendi gregis, against modernism
	Communist Manifesto, Marx and Engels	1910	Pius X, anti-modernist oath
	Wave of liberal and national revolutions in Europe	1929	Lateran Treaty, papacy and Mussolini
	Pius IX expelled from Rome		Wall Street Stock Market Crash
1849	Republic of Rome proclaimed	1931	Pius XI, Quadragesimo anno, reassertion of Rerum novarum
1850	Pius IX restored to Vatican by French troops		Pius XI, Non abbiamo bisogno, denunciation of Fascism
1850–1906	Hermann Schell, German modernist	1933	Nazis seize power in Germany
1851	December 2, Coup d'état in France by Louis Napoleon		Pius XI, concordat with Nazis
1852	Second empire established under Napoleon III	1937	Pius XI, Mit brennender Sorge, against Nazism
1853	Commodore Perry goes to Japan		Pius XI, Divini Redemptoris, against Communist totalitarianism
1854	Pius IX, Immaculate Conception of Mary	1943	Pius XII, Divino afflante Spiritu, encourages higher criticism
1857–1940	Alfred Loisy, French modernist	1949	Pius XII, general excommunication of Communists
1859	Darwin's Origin of Species		
1861	Victor Emmanuel named King of Italy	1950	Pius XII, Assumption of Mary
1861–1865	American Civil War	1954	Pius X canonized, first in modern times
1861–1909	George Tyrrell		
1862	Ultramontane concordat with Ecuador		**POPES**
1864	Pius IX, Syllabus of Errors	1769–1774	Clement XIV
1870	Napoleon III overthrown. Third Republic established	1775–1799	Pius VI
	Vatican Council, infallibility of pope	1800–1823	Pius VII
	Franco-Prussian war begins	1823–1829	Leo XII
	Rome taken into Kingdom of Italy	1829–1830	Pius VIII
1871	Italian Law of Guarantees	1831–1846	Gregory XVI
	German Empire proclaimed	1846–1878	Pius IX
1872–1875	Bismarck's Kulturkampf, anti-Catholic laws	1878–1903	Leo XIII
1879	Leo XIII, Aeterni Patris, Christian philosophy	1903–1914	Pius X
		1914–1922	Benedict XV
1885	Leo XIII, Immortale Dei, concept of state	1922–1939	Pius XI
		1939–1958	Pius XII
		1958–1963	John XXIII
		1963–	Paul VI

Illustration opposite page 411: Christ and the Blind Man. By P. O. Hodgell. Courtesy of P. O. Hodgell and of motive, where it first appeared.

18

Liberal Trends

and the Social Gospel

The French Revolution and the forces
that produced it created in Roman Catholicism in the nineteenth
century a reassertion of ultramontane principles and a
repeated rejection of aspects of modernism which seemed to be related
to the French political upheaval (cf. Ch. 8). Despite adverse
criticism, Catholicism upheld revealed religion in
opposition to increasing humanistic rationalism. Such a
development was possible because of papal authoritarianism
and a hierarchy through which singleness of belief could be imposed,
even though individuals within the system occasionally
rebelled. Protestantism, on the other hand, had no centralized
authority. Faced with the dynamic new forces of the
nineteenth century, Protestantism resisted, compromised, and
adjusted in a variety of ways. At the beginning of the nineteenth
century, conservative reaction prevailed in Protestant churches;

but, after the initial shock of the Revolution, Protestant reform surged forward, and the evangelical spirit as well as liberal trends found powerful expression. At the end of the century a social gospel, quite unwilling to accept social abuses and inequities as providential, had arisen, biblical inspiration and inerrancy were no longer sacrosanct, and adjustments between scientific, historical research and traditional orthodoxy had been achieved. But new patterns did not always predominate; old forms persisted with the new.

As in Roman Catholicism, the immediate Protestant reaction to the French Revolution, particularly in England, was a retreat to the old status quo. The Oxford Movement demonstrated the inherent power and appeal of the high-church tradition, and men like William Wordsworth recoiled from the "inhumanity of man to man" and the destruction which they saw in the French political upheaval. But the reaction only delayed the impact of the humanitarian and liberal forces that had awakened, for in addition to the political events in France, the Industrial Revolution with its widespread use of mechanical inventions wrought social changes in the nineteenth century that demanded attention. Power looms replaced the hand looms of the cottage weavers and became the nuclei for factories that drew men to urban centers. Exploitation of the new city populations through low wages and long working hours for women and children as well as men produced slum subsistence in many of the industrial centers. The old political forms offered little relief, and people clamored for changes in the governments which favored the wealthy with privileges. The revolutions that swept over Europe in 1830 and 1848 indicated deep unrest.

Evangelical Protestantism proved sensitive to the need for change and combined with other elements to produce reform. England was the center of much of the religious turmoil of the nineteenth century, and English Methodism, carrying on the Wesleyan evangelical impetus, proved to be one of the strongest forces for reform. Despite splinterings—the Methodist New Connection in 1797, the Primitive Methodists in 1810, and the Bible Methodists in 1815—Methodism gathered strength, and from 1860 to 1880 it quadrupled in membership; its influence was felt throughout English society. The Methodists were not alone. The evangelical spirit developed in other nonconformist groups. Phenomenal increases in membership were registered by the Baptists. The voice of liberal Unitarianism became strong. In 1772, Theophilus Lindsey (1723-1808), along with 250 other clergymen, petitioned Parliament for relief from subscription to the Thirty-nine Articles, saying they preferred to subscribe to the Bible. When their petition was denied, Lindsey withdrew from the established church, and in 1774 set up the first Unitarian Church in London. By 1813, a law had been passed which relieved the Unitarians from the taint of crime for denying the Trinity. Congregational circles also displayed a willingness to accept individual conscience. The Declaration of Faith of the Congregational Union of England and Wales in 1833 was decidedly orthodox, expressing belief in original sin, the Trinity, the divine-human Christ, salvation by divine faith, inspired Scriptures, final judgment, and so forth; nevertheless, the preliminary statement sounded a new note. The framers of the Declaration said that their statements were not intended to be "a standard to which assent should be required," and that they "reserved to everyone the most perfect liberty of conscience." They specifically objected to "the imposition of any human standard, whether of faith or discipline." These groups combined with others to loosen the grip of the established Church of England, and to foster greater freedom of religious expression. Lord Byron, English poet of revolt who expressed the weariness of man in bondage to institutions, might well have been a symbol of these times.

In 1828, the Test and Corporation Acts were repealed, and in the following year the Roman Catholic Emancipation gave the Catholics the right to hold seats in the House of Commons, as well as other public offices. The Reform Bill of 1832 broadened the base of representation in Parliament to include more members of the middle class. Four years later, marriages were permitted in nonconformists' places of worship, but not until

1868 were nonconformists freed from taxes for the established church, and not until 1880 were dissenters allowed burials in church-yards by ministers using the rituals of the dissenters. Through the efforts of men like Wilberforce, slave trading was curtailed in the colonies at the turn of the century and abolished throughout the English dominions in 1833-1834. Lord Ashley championed a ten-hour working day, better care for the insane, and public health programs.

The Anglicans were reluctant to foster changes that affected their prerogatives, and laxity in the established church often produced rebellious evangelical expression. John Nelson Darby (1800-1882), a clergyman of the Anglican Church in Ireland, reacted to the staid Anglicans by organizing the Plymouth Brethren, so-called because of their place of worship. He rejected the formal ministry, asserted that all Christians are priests, and disavowed creeds in favor of the active guidance of the Holy Spirit. The new group, organized about 1830, spread to Switzerland, France, Germany, Canada, and the United States, and founded famous orphan houses in Bristol, which they boasted were supported by prayer. The new social consciousness was finally felt in the Church of England, however, particularly in the second half of the century. The Christian Socialist Movement, 1848-1854, had as its spiritual leader the Anglican clergyman and Cambridge professor, J. F. D. Maurice (1805-1872), who was one of the period's most influential theologians. He was a friend of the workingman, and in 1854 founded the Working Men's College. Also active in the Christian Socialist Movement were a layman, J. M. Ludlow (1821-1911), who had been educated in France and who was keenly aware of the social disturbances of the 1848 revolutions, and Charles Kingsley (1819-1875), a prolific writer and novelist, rector of Eversley. These men believed that the established church was not making the Gospel sufficiently relevant to the social conditions of men. They resented the idea that poverty is the result of the wrath of God, and they believed that society had a responsibility to the people whose lives were being distorted and abused by increasing indus-trialization. They rejected strict Calvinistic predestination, eternal punishment in hell, and the other-worldliness that tended to devalue life on earth. No man is cursed; all can and should recognize their sonship; none will be lost. They published *Politics for the People* and initiated early cooperative associations for tailors and other tradesmen. Although their organized efforts did not extend beyond 1854, they prompted later legislation and provided the background for the larger efforts of men like William Booth and Walter Rauschenbusch.

In 1877, other English high churchmen felt the need of organization for social reform and founded the influential Guild of St. Matthew, headed by liberal-minded Steward Duckworth Headlam. In 1889, the Christian Social Union was founded, which organized study groups on a large scale, investigated working conditions in factories, and blacklisted workshops which did not meet its standards.

In Germany, Johann Heinrich Wichern (1808-1881) championed the social application of Christianity. His evangelical piety prompted him in 1833 to establish a home for underprivileged boys, and he extended his work in Sunday Schools, city missions, lodging houses for the destitute, and agencies for seamen, prisoners, the unemployed, and so forth. His work was continued by Chancellor Bismarck, Adolf Stoecker, and Friedrich Naumann, but their work was complicated by the rise of Marxist socialism, the desire of men like Bismarck to keep the church out of politics, and an entrenched traditional Lutheranism that tended to be pessimistic and quietistic about prevailing social conditions. In Switzerland Leonhard Ragaz, a Protestant liberal, and Herman Kutter, a converted priest, sought to promote the Kingdom through cooperatives, folk schools, settlements, and pacifism.

Evangelical social concern found many expressions, but probably none of these was as international and as enduring as the work of William Booth (1829-1912), founder of the Salvation Army. He had been associated with the Methodist New Connection, but he withdrew in order to be unhampered in his street preaching and his mission to London's "submerged tenth," whom he tried to net "at the sewers." In 1864, his work in the East End of London met with phenomenal success. By 1875, he had established thirty-two London stations to carry on evangelism and social services. By 1878 his organization, because of its discipline and chain of command, had acquired the name Salvation Army, and within ten years Booth had established one thousand British corps. Patrols were dispatched to other nations in the 1880's, and the Army's rescue work met with great success in Scotland, Wales, Ireland, the United States, Australia, Canada, Sweden, India, New Zealand, South Africa, Ceylon, Japan, China, and most of Continental Europe, including Russia.

1890 marked the appearance of Booth's book, *In Darkest England and the Way Out,* which graphically depicted a social darkness in England as foreboding as the darkness of the Africa of Stanley and Livingstone, who were being discussed at the time. After picturing the need, Booth outlined the measures which he thought would bring relief: rescue missions, shelter stations, food centers, city and farm colonies, and a preaching of the Gospel. His work was very practical, for the immediate need was great. In a picture chart accompanying his publication, he depicted a sea of unbelief, deceit, murder, adultery, theft, drunkenness, and so on, from the raging midst of which men were crying for help. Booth's statistics, which he insisted were reliable, would hardly bear out the usual image of Victorian society. He noted that in London in one year, 2,157 people had been found dead, 2,297 had committed suicide, 30,000 were living in prostitution, 160,000 were convicted of drunkenness, and more than 900,000 were classed as paupers. Evangelical in fervor and dramatic in presentation, *In Darkest England and the Way Out* aroused thousands to an awareness of human suffering (1).

Vigorous evangelical revivalism received much attention during this period through the preaching of men like Finney, Moody, and Drummond. Charles G. Finney (1792-1875), sometimes called the first professional revivalist, stirred American evangelicals, particularly the Presbyterians, and also won re-nown as Professor of Theology and later as President at Oberlin. He had trained for a career in law, but his early education had included Latin, Hebrew, and Greek, and in 1821 he felt an invasion of the Holy Spirit, "like a wave of electricity going through and through me." He was licensed to preach in 1824 and held revivals not only in America but also in England, until age caused him to stop in 1860. He concentrated on man's consciousness of sin, and urged repentance and immediate surrender. He departed from Calvinistic narrowness by insisting on the ability of the sinner to repent, even though a radical change of heart had to come through the Holy Spirit. His *Lectures on Revivals,* 1835, showed how to promote revivals, and his *Lectures on Systematic Theology,* 1846-1848, furnished revivalism with a theology.

Finney's Methodist contemporary, Peter Cartwright (1785-1872), won thousands of converts on the frontiers in Kentucky and Illinois. He published his *Autobiography* in 1856 and his reminiscences, *Fifty Years a Presiding Elder,* in 1872. This early revivalism reached its height in the 1850's. ·

After Cartwright and Finney, between the Civil War and World War I, the spirit of Dwight L. Moody (1837-1899), a layman, dominated American evangelism. Moody's revivals swept over the nation, virtually creating a second great awakening. In the face of rationalistic and scientific trends which were disparaging biblical authority, Moody called for massive Bible Conferences and prayer meetings. His stirring messages brought thousands in America and England to the altar in repentance. His tabernacle meetings crossed denominational lines, and he became an important figure in the drive toward cooperative world missions. He founded Northfield School for Girls, Mount Herman School for Boys, and Moody Bible Institute for laymen interested in religion.

Henry Drummond (1851-1897), an English scientist, was part of this revival movement; he typified Christian commitment to individualistic evangelism toward the end of the nineteenth century and indicated how the evangelical spirit of piety, in its disparagement of intellectual speculation and its emphasis on action, formed a bridge to the social gospel. Drummond was born in Stirling, Scotland, and was educated at the University of Edinburgh and Tübingen University, in Germany. Interested in science as well as religion, he pondered the problem of reconciliation between the two, and in 1877 became a lecturer and later a professor of science at the Free Church College in Glasgow. In 1883, he wrote his popular *Natural Laws in the Spiritual World,* which went through thirty-five editions in England and America, not counting additional editions in French, Dutch, German, and Norwegian. In 1889, at Dwight L. Moody's college at Oxford, he delivered one of the most famous lectures ever made, *The Greatest Thing in the World.* Popular demand forced its printing, and hundreds of thousands of copies sold almost immediately. It caught the imagination of an era of individualistic evangelical commitment, and has become a classic (2).

The man who most effectively tapped this giant reservoir of Christian concern and channeled it to larger social areas was Walter Rauschenbusch (1861-1918), whose name has become synonymous with the social gospel. Born in Rochester, N. Y., just seven years after his father had migrated from revolution-torn Germany, and educated in both America and Germany, Rauschenbusch fused in his person the characteristics of the old and the new world. He was pietistic on the one hand and passionately social-minded on the other. In 1907, Rauschenbusch published his epoch-making book, *Christianity and the Social Crisis,* giving voice to a Christian social conscience that had become all but obscured in an individualistic, capitalistic society (5). From 1860 to 1890, America's population increased from thirty-one to seventy-six million, largely because of migration. The effects of rampant, laissez faire exploitation of this population mass became painfully evident in the larger cities. Rauschenbusch was not content to rescue human wrecks in the wake of depersonalized economic aggrandizement; his ministry among the destitute in Hell's Kitchen in New York City brought home to him the one-sidedness, even hypocrisy, of a Christianity that evangelized

IX-1. The Sawdust Trail. *A drawing inspired by mass evangelism in America. By George Bellows (1882–1925). Courtesy of the Print Department, Boston Public Library.*

for the soul of an individual without doing anything substantially to change his social plight. He lamented the effects of economic principalities and political powers, and like the Hebrew prophets of old, cried out for the poor, the orphans, and the widows. As the minister of the Second German Baptist Church in Hell's Kitchen, 1886-1897, he came slowly to realize the oppressive ills of the economic exploitation of immigrants, the poor, and the laboring classes. He lashed out at economic and social injustice with everything at his command, tirelessly preaching, writing, and campaigning. In 1889 he became editor of *For the Right,* a paper dedicated to alleviating the physical and spiritual burdens of the laboring man (3). Rauschenbusch advocated more equitable taxation, socialization of railroads, and public ownership of utilities such as water and electricity. He campaigned for museums, parks, playgrounds, and libraries, proposed elimination

415

of child labor, and called for better, safer working conditions and social security insurance. This was at a time when men like Andrew Carnegie, John D. Rockefeller, and G. F. Baer were saying that wealth was their providential blessing, and when preachers like Henry Ward Beecher and Horace Bushnell were saying that poverty is the result of vice.

In 1892, Rauschenbusch helped organize the Brotherhood of the Kingdom, hoping to spur attempts to relate Christianity to the social as well as the individual needs of man (4). But Rauschenbusch did not feel that external improvements were enough; he felt that personal, spiritual regeneration was essential. "Material improvements are important, but social reformers must not forget to look deeper than that," he said. As Professor of Church History at Rochester Theological Seminary, he found time to write the many books which made him the voice of the social gospel, and of a new era of Christian conscience. These include *Prayers of the Social Awakening*, 1909, from which some excerpts are given (6), *Christianizing the Social Order*, 1912, *The Social Principles of Jesus*, 1916, and *A Theology for the Social Gospel*, 1917, in which he gave the evangelical-social movement a much needed theological grounding.

Concomitant with the work of Rauschenbusch was that of Washington Gladden (1836-1918), who made more moderate proposals for unions, cooperatives, profit sharing, and the nationalization of railroads, utilities, and so forth. The labors of Methodist Harry F. Ward helped to establish the social gospel in the aims and goals of the Federal Council of Churches in 1908, and later, in a fuller form, in the social creed in 1912 (7). In Germany in 1912, Ernst Troeltsch (1865-1923) published his monumental *Social Teaching of the Christian Churches*.

Many of the proposals of the ministers of the social gospel received fulfillment in legislative reforms under Theodore Roosevelt, Woodrow Wilson, and Franklin Roosevelt, but its grass-roots achievement was to make the church aware of the scope of its social responsibilities. Unfortunately, however, many Christians remained unmoved, continuing an exclusive emphasis on individual piety and old-time religion. Rauschenbusch confessed that he often felt alone, and the outbreak of World War I shook his confidence in the notion of progressive social improvement.

Other powerful forces contributed to the complex movements of the nineteenth century and directly affected Christian developments. Auguste Xavier Comte (1798-1857) emerged from the revolutionary situation in France to advocate a new religion of humanity, which he said should replace orthodox religion if man were to establish a sound social doctrine (8). In his discourses on positivism, in 1844, 1848, and 1852-1854, he depicted three stages of cultural development through which all human knowledge passes if it expands properly—the theological, the metaphysical, and the positive. The first stage culminates with God, the second with nature, and the third with universal law. Comte examined science, religion, and the experience of the individual to substantiate his claims. He wanted men to accept universal social laws by which they would be governed, laws which would displace obligations to a supernatural deity.

Comte was aided by and strongly influenced John Stuart Mill (1806-1873), English advocate of utilitarianism and democratic liberalism. Mill was precocious enough to learn Greek at three, write history at twelve, and organize a "Utilitarian Society" at sixteen. His *Principles of Political Economy*, 1848, became a textbook, and his other books, *On Liberty*, 1859, *Utilitarianism*, 1863, and *Three Essays on Religion*, 1873, all advocated utilitarian programs in order to realize a democratic society. To alleviate the exploitation of human beings and the evils inherent in private property and laissez faire, he championed mass education, trade unions, profit sharing, cooperatives, universal suffrage, and broader representation in government. His "religion of humanity" emphasized that religion is designed to give reality to our ideals, and that we must concentrate on what our earthly life may be in order to make religion useful. He believed that an emphasis on the relief of human needs was more altruistic and useful than an

416

individualistic striving for heavenly immortality, and more harmonious with modern knowledge than the worship of nature or a supernatural deity. Both Mill and Comte felt that the old authorities had outlived their usefulness.

One of the most far-reaching trends of the century was that which received dramatic presentation in Charles Darwin's (1809-1882) *Origin of Species* in 1859, and in his *Descent of Man* in 1871. His theory of evolution seemed not only to destroy biblical inspiration, but also any claim of man to moral uniqueness (9). How could the Bible be true if men, animals, worms, and plants all evolved over thousands of years from a common, low form? Sir Charles Lyell had already shown by a study of rock formations that creation could hardly have taken place in six days; but this finding was controverted by the argument that a "day" of creation did not necessarily mean twenty-four hours, and that God may have created the puzzling rock layers to test man's faith. Darwin, however, produced startling evidence that higher animals and man had evolved from a low form of life during centuries of struggles to survive, and churchmen felt that Genesis had been attacked and that the Fall had received a mortal blow. Many denounced Darwin's theory as a brutalizing philosophy that would never be proved, others felt that God's Holy Spirit was at work in the world, revealing fresh truth that could not penetrate the walls of orthodox idolatry, and still others saw evolution simply as a part of God's providence that could be reconciled with the Bible.

In England, *Essays and Reviews*, 1860, to which seven noted men contributed, was one of the first serious attempts to interpret Christianity in conformity with the new scientific researches. Two of the writers, H. B. Wilson and Rowland Williams, were hailed into court and charged with denying biblical inspiration and the reality of hell. Although they were acquitted by a higher court, their case and the theories advanced in *Essays and Reviews* stirred England to a reappraisal of orthodox views. Was it possible that evolution had permanently undermined and discredited such time-honored beliefs as biblical

inspiration and inerrancy? Eleven thousand clergymen of the established Church in England, Wales, and Ireland felt constrained to reaffirm their belief in inspiration and eternal punishment, and 137,000 laymen signed petitions supporting them. Christendom was gravely concerned, and the trial of Bishop John William Colenso in 1862 for his views on the Pentateuch created spirited controversies. In 1874 John Fiske published *Cosmic Philosophy*, an elaborate attempt to reconcile religion with science and philosophy and to give religion a respectable epistemology. Many in Christendom were further disturbed when men like Brooke Foss Westcott (1825-1901), Joseph Barber Lightfoot (1828-1889), and Fenton John A. Hort (1828-1892) in England and Julius Wellhausen (1844-1918) in Germany brought historical criticism and some of the implications of science to bear on the Old Testament, and indicated that centuries of orthodox interpretation would have to be realigned or the truth of historical research ignored. Wellhausen's influential *History of Israel*, in which he applied the results of historical scholarship to Old Testament writings to show that they were products of their times and, as such, quite human, was published in 1878.

In 1889 a group of English scholars, headed by Charles Gore (1853-1932), frankly faced the problem of the new knowledge and what it might mean for the future of religion. For twelve years, the group pondered the problems of historical criticism and scientific research as they affected the whole of Christian faith, and gave their views in *Lux Mundi*. In the preface to this work, Gore explained that they were committed Christians trying to explain their faith: "We have written with the conviction that the epoch in which we live is one of profound transformation, intellectual and social, abounding in new needs, new points of view, new questions; and certain therefore to involve great changes in the outlying departments of theology, where it is linked to other sciences, and to necessitate some general restatement of its claim and meaning." The authors expressed a belief in the reasonableness of the Bible, accepted some elements as nonhistorical, and explained incongruities in revelation in terms of progressive evolution. *Lux Mundi* went through ten editions in one year; despite its bulk and scholarly tone, ministers and laymen eagerly read it through. Gore, who greatly influenced Anglican theology with the development of his views in the next four decades, received much attention for his essay on inspiration (*11*). *Lux Mundi* symbolized the scholarly reconciliation of science and religion.

A symbol of the popular reconciliation was William Herbert Carruth's widely quoted poem, *Each in His Own Tongue*, 1909.

A firemist and a planet,
    A crystal and a cell,
A jellyfish and a saurian,
    And caves where the cave men dwell;
Then a sense of law and beauty,
    And a face turned from the clod—
Some call it Evolution,
    And others call it God.

By 1900, liberal theologians had adapted and were building new concepts of religion on the new scientific orientation. William James' lecture before the philosophical club of Yale and Brown in 1896 was at once a defense, an adaptation, and a superseding of the orthodox orientation to religion (*10*). Nevertheless, many churchmen persisted in the rejection of evolution, even after it had become widely accepted. The consequences of the theory of evolution for theology were at the heart of the bitter struggles between liberalism and fundamentalism in the twentieth century. Although William Jennings Bryan's noted Scopes trial defense of orthodoxy did not come until 1925, it symbolized the persistent rejection of evolution by many Christians who felt that sacred Scripture and ethics had been gravely threatened.

One of the by-products of the turmoil of the nineteenth century was Christian Science, in which Mary Baker Eddy, its founder, mingled Hinduistic concepts, New England transcendentalism, and Christian Scripture with her own religious thought and experience. Mrs. Eddy (1821-1910) had her healing experience in 1866, and produced *Science and Health with a Key to the Scriptures* in 1875 (*12*). "God is all-in-all; God is Spirit.

We live and move and have our being in God; we, therefore, are Spirit. Matter is an illusion. Since man is Spirit and body is illusion, there can be no illness." "Evil, sin, sickness and death are the results of error and illusion." As human ills center in the mind, Mrs. Eddy employed mental means to eradicate them, and hundreds have testified to the success of her methods. Though often ridiculed and discredited, the phenomenon of Christian Science persists with strength in American culture.

The nineteenth century began with a reaction to the French Revolution, but Christianity gradually awakened to the needs of a society undergoing profound social change. By the end of the century, evangelical Christianity reasserted itself in programs like those of William Booth and Walter Rauschenbusch, although individualistic evangelism also continued in mass revivals. Darwin's theory of evolution shook Christianity to its foundations and prompted a reappraisal of traditional interpretation. Attempts to reconcile Christianity with scientific and historical research developed into twentieth-century liberalism, and liberalism in conflict with orthodoxy and biblical fundamentalism gave rise to neo-orthodoxy.

In the field of music, the nineteenth century did not produce a Palestrina or a Bach. Mendelssohn's *Elijah* and *St. Paul*, Schubert's masses, Verdi's *Requiem Mass*, Brahms' *German Mass*, and the music of Caesar Franck and Charles Gounod were outstanding expressions of religious themes, but Christian motifs were not dominant in the century. The works of Chopin, Tchaikovsky, Schumann, Wagner, Liszt, and Richard Strauss expressed the secular trends of the age.

Nor was religion a dominant concern of the literary artists of the period; the nineteenth century did not produce a Milton or a Bunyan. But the variegated face of religion in its individual and social concern did shine in the writings of Christina Rossetti, Francis Thompson, Robert Browning, Leo Tolstoy, and Feodor Dostoevski. Byron, Carlyle, Tennyson, and Ibsen also were sensitive to the religious overtones of the changing social scene, even though their religious attitudes were more varied in expression. Thomas Hardy and Theodore Dreiser reflected the effects of science in their depictions of man under the control of blind forces, Friedrich Nietzsche spewed his superman scorn on religion, and Walt Whitman celebrated the emancipation of man. Religion, however, was not central to nineteenth-century literature, which seemed to be "wandering between two worlds, one dead, the other powerless to be born." Religious culture belonged to the past, and open secularism to the future.

1. William Booth, 1890

In the first eighty-five pages of his book, Booth describes the "darkness"; in the remaining two hundred pages, he describes his scheme of "deliverance." A large chart accompanying the book pictures a sea of sin from which uniformed Salvation Army soldiers are rescuing men and women and directing them to the City and Farm Colonies, and to the Colony Across the Sea. In the colonies they could have food, shelter, and clothing, be trained for a trade, and receive a stake for a new way of life. For immediate needs there were cheap food depots, homes for children, household salvage brigades, homes for inebriates, and so on. Graphic figures on prostitution, suicides, paupers, hungry children, and insane asylums indicated the magnitude of the need. In the preface, Booth tells of how he had longed when still a child to help the poor, and how at last he saw his way clear to do so. "My only hope for the permanent deliverance of mankind from misery, either in this world or in the next, is the regeneration or remaking of the individual by the power of the Holy Ghost through Jesus Christ. But in providing for the relief of temporal misery, I reckon that I am only making it easy where it is now difficult, and possible where it is now all but impossible, for men and women to find their way to the Cross of our Lord Jesus Christ." The following excerpts indicate the darkness and the deliverance. William Booth, *In Darkest England and the Way Out* (London, 1890).

THE DARKNESS

It is a terrible picture, and one that has engraved itself deep on the heart of civilisation. But while brooding over the awful presentation of life as it exists in the vast African forest, it seemed to me only too vivid a picture of many parts of our own land. As there is a darkest Africa is there not also a darkest England? Civilisation, which can breed its own barbarians, does it not also breed its own pygmies? May we not find a parallel at our own doors, and discover within a stone's throw of our cathedrals and palaces similar horrors to those which Stanley has found existing in the great Equatorial forest?

The Equatorial forest traversed by Stanley resembles that Darkest England of which I have to speak, alike in its vast extent—both stretch, in Stanley's phrase, "as far as from Plymouth to Peterhead"; its monotonous darkness, its malaria and its gloom, its dwarfish de-humanized inhabitants, the slavery to which they are subjected, their privations and their misery. That which sickens the stoutest heart, and causes many of our bravest and best to fold their hands in despair, is the apparent impossibility of doing more than merely to peck at the outside of the endless tangle of monotonous undergrowth; to let light into it, to make a road clear through it, that shall not be immediately choked up by the ooze of the morass and the luxuriant parasitical growth of the forest—who dare hope for that? At present, alas, it would seem as though no one dares even to hope! It is the great Slough of Despond in our time.

And what a slough it is no man can gauge who has not waded therein, as some of us have done, up to the very neck for long years. Talk about Dante's Hell, and all the horrors and cruelties of the torture-chamber of the lost! The man who walks with open eyes and with bleeding heart through the shambles of our civilisation needs no such fantastic images of the poet to teach him horror. Often and often, when I have seen the young and the poor and the helpless go down before my eyes into the morass, trampled underfoot by beasts of prey in human shape that haunt these regions, it seemed as if God were no longer in His world, but that in His stead reigned a fiend, merciless as Hell, ruthless as the grave. Hard it is, no doubt, to read in Stanley's pages of the slave-traders coldly arranging for the surprise of a village, the capture of the inhabitants, the massacre of those who resist, and the violation of all the women; but the stony streets of London, if they could but speak, would tell of tragedies as awful, of ruin as complete, of ravishments as horrible, as if we were in Central Africa; only the ghastly devastation is covered, corpselike, with the artificialities and hypocrisies of modern civilisation.

· · · · · ·

Darkest England, like Darkest Africa, reeks from malaria. The foul and fetid breath of our slums is almost as poisonous as that of the African swamp. Fever is almost as chronic there as on the Equator. Every year thousands of children are killed off by what is called defects of our sanitary system. They are in reality starved and poisoned, and all that can be said is that, in many cases, it is better for them they were taken away from the trouble to come.

...A population sodden with drink, steeped in vice, eaten up by every social and physical malady, these are the denizens of Darkest England amidst whom my life has been spent, and to whose rescue I would now summon all that is best in the manhood and womanhood of our land.

THE DELIVERANCE

To the Rescue!—The City Colony

The first section of my Scheme is the establishment of a Receiving House for the Destitute in every great centre of population. We start, let us remember, from the individual, the ragged, hungry, penniless man who confronts us with despairing demands for food, shelter, and work. Now, I have had some two or three years' experience in dealing with this class. I believe, at the present moment, the Salvation Army supplies more food and shelter to the destitute than any other organisation in London, and it is the experience and encouragement which I have gained in the working of these Food and Shelter Depots which has largely encouraged me to propound this scheme.

Section I—Food and Shelter for Every Man

As I rode through Canada and the United States some three years ago, I was greatly impressed with the superabundance of food which I saw at every turn. Oh, how I longed that the poor starving people, and the hungry children of the East of London and of other centres of our destitute populations, should come into the midst of this abundance, but as it appeared impossible for me to take them to it, I secretly resolved that I would endeavour to bring some of it to them. I am thankful to say that I have already been able to do so on a small scale, and hope to accomplish it ere long on a much vaster one.

With this view, the first Cheap Food Depot was opened in the East of London

FOOD SOLD IN DEPOTS AND SHELTERS
DURING 1889

Article	Weight	Measure	Remarks
Soup		116,400 gals.	
Bread	192½ tons	106,964 4 lb. loaves	
Tea	2½ tons	46,980 gals.	
Coffee	15 cwt.	13,949 gals.	
Cocoa	6 tons	29,229 gals.	
Sugar	25 tons		300 bags
Potatoes	140 tons		2,800 bags
Flour	18 tons		180 sacks
Peaflour	28½ tons		288 sacks
Oatmeal	3½ tons		36 sacks
Rice	12 tons		120 sacks
Beans	12 tons		240 sacks
Onions and parsnips	12 tons		240 sacks
Jam	9 tons		2,880 jars
Marmalade	6 tons		1,920 jars
Meat	15 tons		
Milk		14,300 qts.	

420

two and a half years ago. This has been followed by others, and we have now three establishments: others are being arranged for.

Since the commencement in 1888, we have supplied over three and a half million meals.

Some idea can be formed of the extent to which these Food and Shelter Depots have already struck their roots into the strata of society which it is proposed to benefit, by the following figures, which give the quantities of food sold during the year at our Food Depots.

This includes returns from three Food Depots and five Shelters. I propose to multiply their number, to develop their usefulness, and to make them the threshold of the whole Scheme. Those who have already visited our Depots will understand exactly what this means. The majority, however, of the readers of these pages have not done so, and for them it is necessary to explain what they are.

At each of our Depots, which can be seen by anybody that cares to take the trouble to visit them, there are two departments, one dealing with food, the other with shelter. Of these both are worked together and minister to the same individuals. Many come for food who do not come for shelter, although most of those who come for shelter also come for food, which is sold on terms to cover, as nearly as possible, the cost price and working expenses of the establishment. In this our Food Depots differ from the ordinary soup kitchens. There is no gratuitous distribution of victuals. The following is our Price List [1d. equals approximately 1 cent]:

WHAT IS SOLD AT THE FOOD DEPOTS

For a Child

Soup	per basin	¼d.
Soup	with bread	½d.
Coffee or cocoa	per cup	¼d.
Coffee or cocoa	with bread and jam	½d.

For Adults

Soup	per basin	½d.
Soup	with bread	1d.
Soup in own jugs (per quart)		1d.
Potatoes		½d.
Cabbage		½d.
Haricot beans		½d.

Boiled jam pudding		½d.
Boiled plum pudding	each	1d.
Rice pudding		½d.
Baked plum pudding		½d.
Baked jam roll		½d.
Meat pudding and potatoes		3d.
Corned beef and potatoes		2d.
Corned mutton and potatoes		2d.
Coffee, per cup, ½d.; per mug		1d.
Cocoa, per cup, ½d.; per mug		1d.
Tea, per cup, ½d; per mug		1d.
Bread and butter, jam, or marmalade,		
	per slice	½d.

A certain discretionary power is vested in the Officers in charge of the Depot, and they can in very urgent cases give relief, but the rule is the food is to be paid for, and the financial results show that working expenses are just about covered.

These Cheap Food Depots I have no doubt have been and are of great service to numbers of hungry starving men, women and children, at the prices just named, which must be within the reach of all, except the absolutely penniless; but it is the Shelter that I regard as the most useful feature in this part of our undertaking, for if anything is to be done to get hold of those who use the Depot, some more favourable opportunity must be afforded than is offered by the mere coming into the food store to get, perhaps, only a basin of soup. This part of the Scheme I propose to extend very considerably.

Suppose that you are a casual in the streets of London, homeless, friendless, weary with looking for work all day and finding none. Night comes on. Where are you to go? You have perhaps only a few coppers, or it may be, a few shillings, left of the rapidly dwindling store of your little capital. You shrink from sleeping in the open air; you equally shrink from going to the fourpenny Doss-house where, in the midst of strange and ribald company, you may be robbed of the remnant of the money still in your possession. While at a loss as to what to do, someone who sees you suggests that you should go to our Shelter. You cannot, of course, go to the Casual Ward of the Workhouse as long as you have any money in your possession. You come along to one of our Shelters. On entering you pay fourpence, and are free of the establishment for the night. You can come in early or late. The company begins to assemble about five o'clock in the afternoon. In the women's Shelter you find that many come much earlier and sit sewing, reading or chatting in the sparsely furnished but well warmed room from the early hours of the afternoon until bedtime.

You come in, and you get a large pot of coffee, tea, or cocoa, and a hunk of bread. You can go into the wash-house, where you can have a wash with plenty of warm water, and soap and towels free. Then after having washed and eaten you can make yourself comfortable. You can write letters to your friends, if you have any friends to write to, or you can read, or you can sit quietly and do nothing. At eight o'clock the Shelter is tolerably full, and then begins what we consider to be the indispensable feature of the whole concern. Two or three hundred men in the men's Shelter, or as many women in the women's Shelter, are collected together, most of them strange to each other, in a large room. They are all wretchedly poor—what are you to do with them? This is what we do with them.

We hold a rousing Salvation meeting. The Officer in charge of the Depot, assisted by detachments from the Training Homes, conducts a jovial free-and-easy social evening. The girls have their banjos and their tambourines, and for a couple of hours you have as lively a meeting as you will find in London. There is prayer, short and to the point; there are addresses, some delivered by the leaders of the meeting, but the most of them the testimonies of those who have been saved at previous meetings, and who, rising in their seats, tell their companions their experiences. Strange experiences they often are of those who have been down in the very bottomless depths of sin and vice and misery, but who have found at last firm footing on which to stand, and who are, as they say in all sincerity, "as happy as the day is long." There is a joviality and a genuine good feeling at some of these meetings which is refreshing to the soul. There are all sorts and conditions of men; casuals, gaol birds, out-of-works, who have come there for the first time, and who find men who last week or

last month were even as they themselves are now—still poor but rejoicing in a sense of brotherhood and a consciousness of their being no longer outcasts and forlorn in this wide world. There are men who have at last seen revive before them a hope of escaping from that dreadful vortex, into which their sins and misfortunes had drawn them, and being restored to those comforts that they had feared so long were gone for ever; nay, of rising to live a true and Godly life. These tell their mates how this has come about, and urge all who hear them to try for themselves and see whether it is not a good and happy thing to be soundly saved. In the intervals of testimony—and these testimonies, as every one will bear me witness who has ever attended any of our meetings, are not long, sanctimonious lackadaisical speeches, but simple confessions of individual experience—there are bursts of hearty melody. The conductor of the meeting will start up a verse or two of a hymn illustrative of the experiences mentioned by the last speaker, or one of the girls from the Training Home will sing a solo, accompanying herself on her instrument, while all join in a rattling and rollicking chorus.

There is no compulsion upon anyone of our dossers to take part in this meeting; they do not need to come in until it is over; but as a simple matter of fact they do come in. Any night between eight and ten o'clock you will find these people sitting there, listening to the exhortations and taking part in the singing, many of them, no doubt, unsympathetic enough, but nevertheless preferring to be present with the music and the warmth, mildly stirred, if only by curiosity, as the various testimonies are delivered.

Sometimes these testimonies are enough to rouse the most cynical of observers. . . .

.   .   .   .   .

The meeting over, the singing girls go back to the Training Home, and the men prepare for bed. Our sleeping arrangements are somewhat primitive; we do not provide feather beds, and when you go into our dormitories, you will be surprised to find the floor covered by what look like an endless array of packing cases. These are our beds, and each of them forms a cubicle. There is a mattress laid on the floor, and over the mattress a leather apron, which is all the bedclothes that we find it possible to provide. The men undress, each by the side of his packing box, and go to sleep under their leather covering. The dormitory is warmed with hot water pipes to a temperature of 60 degrees, and there has never been any complaint of lack of warmth on the part of those who use the Shelter. The leather can be kept perfectly clean, and the mattresses, covered with American cloth, are carefully inspected every day, so that no stray specimen of vermin may be left in the place. The men turn in about ten o'clock and sleep until six. We have never any disturbances of any kind in the Shelters. We have provided accommodation now for several thousand of the most helplessly broken-down men in London, criminals many of them, mendicants, tramps, those who are among the filth and offscouring of all things; but such is the influence that is established by the meeting and the moral ascendancy of our officers themselves, that we have never had a fight on the premises, and very seldom do we ever hear an oath or an obscene word. Sometimes there has been trouble outside the Shelter, when men insisted upon coming in drunk or were otherwise violent; but once let them come to the Shelter, and get into the swing of the concern, and we have no trouble with them. In the morning they get up and have their breakfast and, after a short service, go off their various ways.

2. Henry Drummond, 1889

"The Greatest Thing in the World," from *Addresses,* by Henry Drummond (Philadelphia: Altemus, 1891).

Every one has asked himself the great question of antiquity as of the modern world: What is the *summum bonum*—the supreme good? You have life before you. Once only you can live it. What is the noblest object of desire, the supreme gift to covet?

We have been accustomed to be told that the greatest thing in the religious world is Faith. That great word has been the keynote for centuries of the popular religion; and we

have easily learned to look upon it as the greatest thing in the world. Well, we are wrong. If we have been told that, we may miss the mark. I have taken you, in the chapter which I have just read (I Cor. 13) to Christianity at its source; and there we have seen, "The greatest of these is love." It is not an oversight. Paul was speaking of faith just a moment before. He says, "If I have all faith, so that I can remove mountains, and have not love, I am nothing." So far from forgetting he deliberately contrasts them, "Now abideth Faith, Hope, Love," and without a moment's hesitation the decision falls, "The greatest of these is Love."

. . . . .

It is the rule for fulfilling all rules, the new commandment for keeping all the old commandments, Christ's one secret of the Christian life.

Now Paul had learned that; and in this noble eulogy he has given us the most wonderful and original account extant of the *summum bonum.* We may divide it into three parts. In the beginning of the short chapter, we have Love *contrasted;* in the heart of it, we have Love *analyzed;* toward the end, we have Love *defended* as the supreme gift.

Paul begins by contrasting Love with other things that men in those days thought much of. I shall not attempt to go over those things in detail. Their inferiority is already obvious.

He contrasts it with eloquence.... He contrasts it with prophecy. He contrasts it with mysteries. He contrasts it with faith. He contrasts it with charity....

. . . . .

After contrasting Love with these things, Paul, in three verses, very short, gives us an amazing analysis of what this supreme thing is. I ask you to look at it. It is a compound thing, he tells us. It is like light. As you have seen a man of science take a beam of light and pass it through a crystal prism, as you have seen it come out on the other side of the prism broken up into its component colors—red, and blue, and yellow, and violet, and orange, and all the colors of the rainbow

—so Paul passes this thing, Love, through the magnificent prism of his inspired intellect, and it comes out on the other side broken up into its elements. And in these few words we have what one might call the Spectrum of Love, and the analysis of Love. . . .

The Spectrum of Love has nine ingredients: Patience—"Love suffereth long"; Kindness—"And is kind"; Generosity—"Love envieth not"; Humility—"Love vaunteth not itself, is not puffed up"; Courtesy—"Doth not behave itself unseemly"; Unselfishness—"Seeketh not her own"; Good Temper—"Is not easily provoked"; Guilelessness—"Thinketh no evil"; Sincerity—"Rejoiceth not in iniquity, but rejoiceth in the truth."

Patience; kindness; generosity; humility; courtesy; unselfishness; good temper; guilelessness; sincerity—these make up the supreme gift, the stature of the perfect man. You will observe that all are in relation to men, in relation to life, in relation to the known today and the near tomorrow, and not to the unknown eternity. We hear much of love to God; Christ spoke much of love to man. We make a great deal of peace with heaven; Christ made much of peace on earth. Religion is not a strange or added thing, but the inspiration of the secular life, the breathing of an eternal spirit through this temporal world. The supreme thing, in short, is not a thing at all, but the giving of a further finish to the multitudinous words and acts which make up the sum of every common day.

There is no time to do more than make a passing note upon each of these ingredients. . . .

. . . . .

The fifth ingredient is a somewhat strange one to find in this *summum bonum: Courtesy*. This is Love in society, Love in relation to etiquette. "Love doth not behave itself unseemly." Politeness has been defined as love in trifles. Courtesy is said to be love in little things. And the one secret of politeness is to love. Love *cannot* behave itself unseemly. You can put the most untutored persons into the highest society, and if they have a reservoir of Love in their heart, they will not behave themselves unseemly. They simply cannot do it. Carlyle said of Robert Burns that there was no truer gentleman in Europe than the ploughman-poet. It was because he loved everything—the mouse, and the daisy, and all the things, great and small, that God had made. So with this simple passport he could mingle with any society, and enter courts and palaces from his little cottage on the banks of the Ayr. You know the meaning of the word "gentleman." It means a gentle man—a man who does things gently with love. And that is the whole art and mystery of it. The gentle man cannot in the nature of things do an ungentle, an ungentlemanly thing. The ungentle soul, the inconsiderate, unsympathetic nature cannot do anything else. "Love doth not behave itself unseemly."

Unselfishness. "Love seeketh not her own." Observe: Seeketh not even that which is her own. In Britain the Englishman is devoted, and rightly, to his rights. But there come times when a man may exercise even the higher right of giving up his rights. Yet Paul does not summon us to give up our rights. Love strikes much deeper. It would have us not seek them at all, ignore them, eliminate the personal element altogether from our calculations. It is not hard to give up our rights. They are often external. The difficult thing is to give up ourselves. The more difficult thing still is not to seek things for ourselves at all. . . . The most obvious lesson in Christ's teaching is that there is no happiness in having and getting anything, but only in giving. I repeat, *there is no happiness in having or in getting, but only in giving.* And half the world is on the wrong scent in pursuit of happiness. They think it consists in having and getting, and in being served by others. It consists in giving, and in serving others. He that would be great among you, said Christ, let him serve. He that would be happy, let him remember that there is but one way—it is more blessed, it is more happy, to give than to receive. The next ingredient is a very remarkable one: *Good Temper.* "Love is not easily provoked." Nothing could be more striking than to find this here. We are inclined to look upon bad temper as a very harmless weakness. We speak of it as a mere infirmity of nature, a family failing, a matter of temperament, not a thing to take into very serious account in estimating a man's character. And yet here, right in the heart of this analysis of love, it finds a place; and the Bible again and again returns to condemn it as one of the most destructive elements in human nature.

The peculiarity of ill temper is that it is the vice of the virtuous. It is often the one blot on an otherwise noble character. You know men who are all but perfect, and women who would be entirely perfect, but for an easily ruffled, quick-tempered, or "touchy" disposition. This compatibility of ill temper with high moral character is one of the strangest and saddest problems of ethics. The truth is there are two great classes of sins—sins of the *Body*, and sins of the *Disposition*. The Prodigal Son may be taken as a type of the first, the Elder Brother of the second. Now, society has no doubt whatever as to which of these is the worse. Its brand falls, without a challenge, upon the Prodigal. But are we right? We have no balance to weigh one another's sins, and coarser and finer are but human words; but faults in the higher nature may be less venial than those in the lower, and to the eye of Him who is Love, a sin against Love may seem a hundred times more base. No form of vice, not worldliness, not greed of gold, not drunkenness itself, does more to un-Christianize society than evil temper. For embittering life, for breaking up communities, for destroying the most sacred relationships, for devastating homes, for withering up men and women, for taking the bloom of childhood, in short, for sheer gratuitous misery-producing power, this influence stands alone. . . . Judge if such sins of the disposition are not worse to live in, and for others to live with, than sins of the body. Did Christ indeed not answer the question Himself when He said, "I say unto you, that the publicans and the harlots go into the Kingdom of Heaven before you." There is really no place in Heaven for a disposition like this. A man with such a mood could only make Heaven miserable for all the people in it. Except, therefore, such a man be born again, he cannot, he simply *cannot,* enter the Kingdom of Heaven. For it is perfectly certain—and you will not misunder-

stand me—that to enter Heaven a man must take it with him.

You will see then why Temper is significant. It is not in what it is alone, but in what it reveals. This is why I take the liberty now of speaking of it with such unusual plainness. It is a test for love, a symptom, a revelation of an unloving nature at bottom. It is the intermittent fever which bespeaks unintermittent disease within; the occasional bubble escaping to the surface which betrays some rottenness underneath; a sample of the most hidden products of the soul dropped involuntarily when off one's guard; in a word, the lightning form of a hundred hideous and un-Christian sins. For a want of patience, a want of courtesy, a want of unselfishness, are all instantaneously symbolized in one flash of Temper.

Hence it is not enough to deal with the Temper. We must go to the source, and change the inmost nature, and the angry humors will die away of themselves. Souls are made sweet not by taking the acid fluids out, but by putting something in—a great Love, a new Spirit, the Spirit of Christ. Christ, the Spirit of Christ, interpenetrating ours, sweetens, purifies, transforms all. This only can eradicate what is wrong, work a chemical change, renovate and regenerate, and rehabilitate the inner man. Will-power does not change men. Time does not change men. Christ does. Therefore "Let that mind be in you which was also in Christ Jesus." Some of us have not much time to lose. Remember, once more, that this is a matter of life or death. I cannot help speaking urgently, for myself, for yourselves. "Whoso shall offend one of these little ones, which believe in me, it were better for him that a millstone were hanged about his neck, and that he were drowned in the depth of the sea." That is to say, it is the deliberate verdict of the Lord Jesus that it is better not to live than not to love. *It is better not to live than not to love.*

. . . . .

So much for the analysis of Love. Now the business of our lives is to have these things fitted into our characters. . . . What makes a man a good artist, a good sculptor, a good musician? Practice. What makes a man a good linguist, a good stenographer? Practice. What makes a man a good man? Practice. Nothing else. There is nothing capricious about religion. We do not get the soul in different ways, under different laws, from those in which we get the body and the mind. If a man does not exercise his arm he develops no biceps muscle; and if a man does not exercise his soul, he acquires no muscle in his soul, no strength of character, no vigor of moral fibre, nor beauty of spiritual growth. Love is not a thing of enthusiastic emotion. It is a rich, strong, manly, vigorous expression of the whole round Christian character— the Christlike nature in its fullest development. And the constituents of this great character are only to be built up by ceaseless practice.

.   .   .   .   .

If you turn to the Revised Version of the First Epistle of John you will find these words: "We love because He first loved us." "We love," not "We love *Him*." That is the way the old version has it, and it is quite wrong. "*We love*—because He first loved us." Look at that word "because." It is the *cause* of which I have spoken. "*Because* he first loved us," the effect follows that we love, we love Him, we love all men. We cannot help it. Because He loved us, we love, we love everybody. Our heart is slowly changed. Contemplate the love of Christ, and you will love. Stand before that mirror, reflect Christ's character, and you will be changed into the same image from tenderness to tenderness. There is no other way. You cannot love to order. You can only look at the lovely object, and fall in love with it, and grow into likeness to it. And so look at this Perfect Character, this Perfect Life. Look at the great Sacrifice as He laid down Himself, all through life, and upon the Cross of Calvary; and you must love Him. And loving Him, you must become like Him. Love begets love. It is a process of induction. Put a piece of iron in the presence of an electrified body, and that piece of iron for a time becomes electrified. It is changed into a temporary magnet in the mere presence of a perma-

nent magnet, and as long as you leave the two side by side, they are both magnets alike. Remain side by side with Him who loved us, and gave Himself for us, and you too will become a permanent magnet, a permanently attractive force; and like Him you will draw all men unto you, like Him you will be drawn unto all men. That is the inevitable effect of Love. Any man who fulfils that cause must have that effect produced in him. Try to give up the idea that religion comes to us by chance, or by mystery, or by caprice. It comes to us by natural law, or by supernatural law, for all law is Divine. . . .

Now I have a closing sentence or two to add about Paul's reason for singling out love as the supreme possession. It is a very remarkable reason. In a single word it is this: *it lasts*. "Love," urges Paul, "never faileth." Then he begins again one of his marvellous lists of the great things of the day, and exposes them one by one. He runs over the things that men thought were going to last, and shows that they are all fleeting, temporary, passing away.

"Whether there be prophecies, they shall fail." . . .

. . . "Whether there be tongues, they shall cease." . . .

Then Paul goes farther, and with even greater boldness adds, "Whether there be knowledge, it shall vanish away." The wisdom of the ancients, where is it? It is wholly gone. A schoolboy today knows more than Sir Isaac Newton knew. His knowledge has vanished away. You put yesterday's newspaper in the fire. Its knowledge has vanished away. You buy the old editions of the great encyclopedias for a few pence. Their knowledge has vanished away. Look how the coach has been superseded by the use of steam. Look how electricity has superseded that, and swept a hundred almost new inventions into oblivion. One of the greatest living authorities, Sir William Thompson, said the other day, "The steam engine is passing away." "Whether there be knowledge, it shall vanish away." At every workshop you will see, in the back yard, a heap of old iron, a few wheels, a few levers, a few cranks, broken and eaten with rust. Twenty years ago that was the pride of the city. Men flocked in from the country to see the great invention; now it is superseded, its day is done. And all the boasted science and philosophy of this day will soon be old. But yesterday, in the University of Edinburgh, the greatest figure in the faculty was Sir James Simpson, the discoverer of chloroform. The other day his successor and nephew, Professor Simpson, was asked by the librarian of the University to go to the library and pick out the books on his subject that were no longer needed. And his reply to the librarian was this: "Take every textbook that is more than ten years old, and put it down in the cellar." Sir James Simpson was a great authority only a few years ago: men came from all parts of the earth to consult him; and almost the whole teaching of that time is consigned by the science of today to oblivion. And in every branch of science it is the same. "Now we know in part. We see through a glass darkly."

Can you tell me anything that is going to last? . . .

.   .   .   .   .

To love abundantly is to live abundantly, and to love forever is to live forever. Hence, eternal life is inextricably bound up with love. We want to live forever for the same reason that we want to live tomorrow. Why do you want to live tomorrow? It is because there is someone who loves you, and whom you want to see tomorrow, and be with, and love back. There is no other reason why we should live on than that we love and are beloved. It is when a man has no one to love him that he commits suicide. So long as he has friends, those who love him and whom he loves, he will live, because to live is to love. Be it but the love of a dog, it will keep him in life; but let that go and he has no contact with life, no reason to live. He dies by his own hand. Eternal life also is to know God, and God is love. This is Christ's own definition. Ponder it. "This is life eternal, that they might know Thee the only true God, and Jesus Christ whom Thou hast sent." Love must be eternal. It is what God is. On the last analysis, then, love is life. Love never faileth, and life never faileth, so long

as there is love. That is the philosophy of what Paul is showing us; the reason why in the nature of things Love should be the supreme thing—because it is going to last; because in the nature of things it is an Eternal Life. It is a thing that we are living now, not that we get when we die; that we shall have a poor chance of getting when we die unless we are living now. No worse fate can befall a man in this world than to live and grow old alone, unloving and unloved. To be lost is to live in an unregenerate condition, loveless and unloved; and to be saved is to love; and he that dwelleth in love dwelleth already in God. For God is Love.

Now I have all but finished. How many of you will join me in reading this chapter once a week for the next three months? A man did that once and it changed his whole life. Will you do it? It is for the greatest thing in the world. You might begin by reading it every day, especially the verses which describe the perfect character. "Love suffereth long, and is kind; love envieth not; love vaunteth not itself." Get these ingredients into your life. Then everything that you do is eternal. It is worth doing. It is worth giving time to. No man can become a saint in his sleep; and to fulfil the condition required demands a certain amount of prayer and meditation and time, just as improvement in any direction, bodily or mental, requires preparation and care. Address yourselves to that one thing; at any cost have this transcendent character exchanged for yours. You will find as you look back upon your life that the moments that stand out, the moments when you have really lived, are the moments when you have done things in a spirit of love. As memory scans the past, above and beyond all the transitory pleasures of life, there leap forward those supreme hours when you have been enabled to do unnoticed kindnesses to those round about you, things too trifling to speak about, but which you feel have entered into your eternal life. I have seen almost all the beautiful things God has made; I have enjoyed almost every pleasure that He has planned for man; and yet as I look back I see standing out above all the life that has gone four or five short experiences when the love of God reflected itself in some poor imitation, some small act of love of mine, and these seem to be the things which alone of all one's life abide. Everything else in all our lives is transitory. Every other good is visionary. But the acts of love which no man knows about, or can ever know about—they never fail.

In the Book of Matthew, where the Judgment Day is depicted for us in the imagery of One seated upon a throne and dividing the sheep from the goats, the test of a man then is not, "How have I believed?" but "How have I loved?" The test of religion, the final test of religion, is not religiousness, but Love; not what I have done, not what I have believed, not what I have achieved, but how I have discharged the common charities of life. Sins of commission in that awful indictment are not even referred to. By what we have not done, *by sins of omission*, we are judged. It could not be otherwise. For the withholding of love is the negation of the spirit of Christ, the proof that we never knew Him, that for us He lived in vain. It means that He suggested nothing in all our thoughts, that He inspired nothing in all our lives, that we were not once near enough to Him to be seized with the spell of His compassion for the world. It means that—

I lived for myself, I thought for myself,
For myself, and none beside—
Just as if Jesus had never lived,
As if he had never died.

It is the Son of *Man* before whom the nations of the world shall be gathered. It is in the presence of *Humanity* that we shall be charged. And the spectacle itself, the mere sight of it, will silently judge each one. Those will be there whom we have met and helped; or there, the unpitied multitude whom we neglected or despised. No other Witness need to be summoned. No other charge than lovelessness shall be preferred. Be not deceived. The words which all of us shall one day hear sound not of theology but of life, not of churches and saints but of the hungry and the poor, not of creeds and doctrines but of shelter and clothing, not of Bibles and prayerbooks but of cups of cold water in the name of Christ. . . .

3. *Walter Rauschenbusch and the Social Gospel*

In 1889, Walter Rauschenbusch and three friends, Elizabeth Post, J. E. Raymond, and Leighton Williams, founded *For the Right*, a monthly journal for the working people. The first issue appeared in November, 1889, and the final one in March, 1891. It was extremely controversial, lashing out at social abuse and corruption in their many forms. The following excerpts, expressive of Rauschenbusch's social views, are culled from its pages. Cf. Dores Robinson Sharpe, *Walter Rauschenbusch*, Chap. 6 (New York: The Macmillan Co., 1942).

FOR THE RIGHT

This paper is published in the interests of the working people of New York City. It proposes to discuss, from the standpoint of Christian socialism, such questions as engage their attention and affect their life. The paper is not the organ of any party or association whatever. Nor has it any new theories to propound. Its aim is to reflect in its pages the needs, the aspirations, the longings of the tens of thousands of wage-earners who are sighing for better things; and to point out, if possible, not only the wrongs that men suffer, but the methods by which these wrongs may be removed. The editors freely give their time and labor to this undertaking, animated solely by the hope that their efforts may aid the advancement of that kingdom in which wrong shall have no place, but Right shall reign for evermore. The friends of social reform are invited to write for the columns of this paper and wage earners are especially requested to do so. . . .

Purpose

We desire to make this paper a "people's paper": one that shall express their best sentiments, their highest thoughts, their truest aspirations, and their sincerest opinions on all matters of a practical, social, literary, or religious significance. We want to make it the organ of the wage earners, in which their ideas may be freely and plainly made known. Our columns will always be opened to them, and we cordially and earnestly invite their cooperation in making the paper a success. We promise to meet them kindly and frankly with our own views. But the editors of this little journal do not intend to assume the position of teachers or preachers in any sense.

They are in hearty sympathy with all who depend upon their own exertions for a livelihood, and especially with all those who are toiling for subsistence under discouraging circumstances; and any word that they may utter which may bring cheer or hope to comfortless or discouraged souls, will be earnestly spoken. Special attention will be given to economic questions, and to the discussion of social problems. We heartily invite questions of any kind, for which we shall open a question box. And we shall also indicate a course of good reading, and bring to the notice of our readers the best popular books of the day. (Nov. 1889)

No, friend, we have not undertaken to reform Society. Far be it from us to attempt what greater men have failed to do. But we do aim to point out the wrongs that men suffer, and the methods by which these wrongs may be righted; to say a word now and then to the toiler along the highway of life that will make life seem brighter, and the world better; to put our hands under the burdens that men bear, and let the love of our hearts go out towards them, and prove to them that there is a spirit in the world which is not of the devil. (Dec. 1889)

Principles

To apply the ethical principles of Jesus Christ so that our industrial relationships may be humanized, our economic system be moralized, justice pervade legislation, and the State grown into a true commonwealth—we band together as Christian Socialists.

1. As Christians we believe that the words and example of Jesus Christ have a direct bearing upon our social problems.

2. As students of political economy we believe that the disorders of our present system point on towards a higher order, that such a higher social order will be characterized by better forms of association, by more perfectly moralized industrial relationships, by a more equably ordered legislation, and by a more rational and humanized economic system.

In Socialism ... we recognize an aspiration after this higher social order and an attempt to prefigure it in economic forms. ... As such an aspiration Socialism is distinctly a moral protest against existing disorders. ... As a body, we see no need now of committing ourselves to Socialism in the sense of any specific system of economic doctrine. ... We are concerned with principle, not with methods. ... The natural movement of society seems to us to be towards some sort of co-operative commonwealth [favorite expression]. ... We believe that whatever better social order is coming in on the earth will come as an evolution. We are evolutionists, not revolutionists. ... We would do our little towards developing competition into cooperation, towards basing private property on a solid commonwealth and throning Justice as the law of the land. ... In this sense we are Socialists, Socialists in the spirit rather than the letter. ... We follow the methods by which Jesus Christ applied His principles. It is after His pattern that we would be Christian Socialists.

3. We propose to call upon the clergy to preach the gospel of wealth until the money-making power shall be held by society to its true responsibility as a social function, and the force of public opinion shall exact of it the discharge of this trust, not in charity but in justice ... to call upon the churches to enlist their members in a study of social problems and in works of social reform, as part of their religion ... to aid in educating society by meetings, literature, etc., by works of mediation between classes ... to work for special measures of reform, industrial education, shorter hours of labor, improved conditions of labor and laborers' homes, the identification of the interests of the employee and employer, more equitable taxation, control or ownership by the city and state of natural monopolies, the reassertion of the underlying right of the commonwealth over the land in the interests of the people at large. (April 1890)

Good Men and Good Government

One of the peculiarities which distinguish "For the Right" from many other papers akin to it, is that it stands for a combination of personal regeneration and social reform. Most of the social reformers claim that if only poverty and the fear of poverty could be abolished, men would cease to be grasping, selfish, overbearing and sensual. We do not see it so. We acknowledge that evil surroundings tempt to evil actions and strengthen evil character and we go as far as any in the earnestness of our protest against any social institution which makes null the prayer: "Lead us not into temptation." But we can conceive of a state of society in which plenty would reign, but where universal opulence would only breed universal pride and wantonness. Mankind rolling in material wealth, with no moral earnestness and spiritual elevation, would only be something worse than swine champing in a full trough or maggots burrowing in a carcass. We believe that every individual soul ought voluntarily to subject itself to the law of God and obey it because it loves it. Only if the number of such God-conquered souls is great and increasing in any nation, will the progress of that nation in material wealth be of real benefit to the people! This is the point on which we differ from many with whom we are at one in the plans for social reform.

On the other hand, we differ from many Christian men and women in our insistence on good institutions. They believe that if only men are personally converted, wrong and injustice will gradually disappear from the construction of society. It does not appear so to us. Revivals in the South were not directly followed by a general freeing of the slaves. Revivals in the North do not ease the pressure of competition in a community or stop speculation in land. Special work and hard work has to be done in pointing out a social wrong and thinking out its remedy, before the righteous purposes of a community can be brought to bear on it. This is essentially a function of those who profess to know and love God's will, and we raise the charge of negligence and sloth against the church of God in suffering injustice to be incorporated in the very construction of society! (Sept. 1890)

4. The Brotherhood of the Kingdom

In 1892, Walter Rauschenbusch and a few friends formed The Brotherhood of the Kingdom to bring together some Baptist ministers "for the better understanding of the idea of the Kingdom of God." Later the membership was enlarged. In the following selection, Rauschenbusch records its origin and purpose. Dores R. Sharpe, *Walter Rauschenbusch* (New York: The Macmillan Co., 1942).

The Brotherhood has taken shape very gradually, naturally, and, as we believe, under the guidance of God. It began in the friendship of a number of us who had been drawn together by kinship of spirit and similarity of convictions. As we exchanged our thoughts about this Kingdom of our Master, our views grew more definite and more united. We saw the Church of Christ divided by selfishness; every denomination intent on its own progress, often at the expense of the progress of the Kingdom; churches and pastors absorbed in their own affairs and jealous of one another; external forms of church worship and polity magnified and the spirit neglected; the people estranged from the church and the church indifferent to the movements of the people; aberrations from creeds severely censured, and aberrations from the Christian spirit tolerated.

As we contemplated these blemishes of the body of Christ, and sorrowed over them in common with all earnest lovers of the church of Jesus, it grew clear to us that many of these evils have their root in the wrongful abandonment and the perversion of the great aim of Christ: the Kingdom of God. As the idea of the Kingdom is the key to the teachings and work of Christ, so its abandonment or misconstruction is the key to the blasé or one-sided conceptions of Christianity and our halting realization of it. Because the Kingdom of God has been dropped as the primary and complete aim of Christianity, and personal salvation has been substituted for it, therefore men seek to save their own souls and are selfishly indifferent to the evangelization of the world. Because the individualistic conception of personal salvation has pushed out of sight the collective idea of a Kingdom of God on earth, Christian men seek for the salvation of individuals and are comparatively indifferent to the spread of the spirit of Christ in the political, industrial, social, scientific, and artistic life of humanity, and have left these as the undisturbed possessions of the spirit of the world. Because the Kingdom of God has been understood as a state to be inherited in a future life rather than as something to be realized here and now, therefore Christians have been contented with a low plane of life here and have postponed holiness to the future. Because the Kingdom of God has been confounded with the Church, therefore the church has been regarded as an end instead of a means, and men have thought they were building up the Kingdom when they were only cementing a strong church organization.

As these thoughts took shape through observation and the study of Scripture and church history, and grew hot through prayer, and as we felt in our personal efforts the magnitude of the task of removing these evils, we determined to strike hands in the name of Christ, and by union to multiply our opportunities, increase our wisdom, and keep steadfast our courage. So we formed ourselves into a "Brotherhood of the Kingdom," in order to re-establish this idea in the thought of the church and to assist in its practical realization in the world.

We desire to see the Kingdom of God once more the great object of Christian preaching; the inspiration of Christian hymnology; the foundation of systematic theology; the enduring motive of evangelistic and missionary work; the religious inspiration of social work and the social outcome of a religious inspiration; the object to which a Christian man surrenders his life, and in that surrender saves it to eternal life; the common object in which all religious bodies find their unity; the great synthesis in which the regeneration of the Spirit, the enlightenment of the intellect, the development of the body, the reform of political life, the sanctification of industrial life, and all that concerns the redemption of humanity shall be embraced.

To this task, God helping us, we desire to dedicate our lives. We invite others, ministers and laymen, to join us in it. We are not a proselyting body. We care little for numbers. We care much for the spirit. . . . We hope to carry the thoughts and spirit of the King whose bond servants we are, and hasten with all our strength the time when the kingdoms of the earth shall be the Kingdom of Christ. . . .

5. *Christianity and the Social Crisis*

Walter Rauschenbusch's *Christianity and the Social Crisis* (New York: The Macmillan Co., 1907) aroused a relatively complacent America to the claims of the social gospel. He appealed to the social consciousness of the Hebrew prophets, depicted the social aims of Jesus, discussed the early Christian community, theorized on why the church never undertook social reconstruction, and outlined the meaning of the present crisis and what to do about it. The following excerpts indicate to some extent the spirit of Rauschenbusch. By permission of Lisa Rauschenbusch.

Western civilization is passing through a social revolution unparalleled in history for scope and power. Its coming was inevitable. The religious, political, and intellectual revolutions of the past five centuries, which together created the modern world, necessarily had to culminate in an economic and social revolution such as is now upon us.

By universal consent, this social crisis is the overshadowing problem of our generation. The industrial and commercial life of the advanced nations are in the throes of it. In politics all issues and methods are undergoing upheaval and re-alignment as the social movement advances. In the world of thought all the young and serious minds are absorbed in the solution of the social problems. Even literature and art point like compass-needles to this magnetic pole of all our thought.

The social revolution has been slow in reaching our country. We have been exempt, not because we had solved the problems, but because we had not yet confronted them. We have now arrived, and all the characteristic conditions of American life will henceforth combine to make the social struggle here more intense than anywhere else. The vastness and the free sweep of our concentrated wealth on the one side, the independence, intelligence, moral vigor, and political power of the common people on the other side, promise a long-drawn grapple of contesting forces which may well make the heart of every American patriot sink within him.

It is realized by friend and foe that religion can play, and must play, a momentous part in this irrepressible conflict.

The Church, the organized expression of the religious life of the past, is one of the most potent institutions and forces in Western civilization. Its favor and moral influence are wooed by all parties. It cannot help throwing its immense weight on one side or the other. If it tries not to act, it thereby acts; and in any case its choice will be decisive for its own future.

Apart from the organized Church, the religious spirit is a factor of incalculable power in the making of history. In the idealistic spirits that lead and in the masses that follow, the religious spirit always intensifies thought, enlarges hope, unfetters daring, evokes the willingness to sacrifice, and gives coherence in the fight. Under the warm breath of religious faith, all social institutions become plastic. The religious spirit removes mountains and tramples on impossibilities. Unless the economic and intellectual factors are strongly reenforced by religious enthusiasm, the whole social movement may prove abortive, and the New Era may die before it comes to birth.

It follows that the relation between Christianity and the social crisis is one of the most pressing questions for all intelligent men who realize the power of religion, and most of all for the religious leaders of the people who give direction to the forces of religion.

The question has, in fact, been discussed frequently and earnestly, but it is plain to any thoughtful observer that the common mind of the Christian Church in America has not begun to arrive at any solid convictions or any permanent basis of action. The conscience of Christendom is halting and groping, perplexed by contradicting voices, still poorly informed on essential questions, justly reluctant to part with the treasured maxims of the past, and yet conscious of the imperious call of the future. . . .

The life and thought of the Old Testament prophets are more to us than classical illustrations and sidelights. They are an integral part of the thought-life of Christianity. From the beginning the Christian Church appropriated the Bible of Israel as its own book and thereby made the history of Israel part of the history of Christendom. That history lives in the heart of the Christian nations with a very real spiritual force. The average American knows more about David than about King Arthur, and more about the exodus from Egypt than about the emigrations of the Puritans. Throughout the Christian centuries the historical material embodied in the Old Testament has been regarded as not merely instructive, but as authoritative. The social ideas drawn from it have been powerful factors in all attempts of Christianity to influence social and political life. In so far as men have attempted to use the Old Testament as a code of model laws and institutions and have applied these to modern conditions, regardless of the historical connections, these attempts have left a trail of blunder and disaster. In so far as they have caught the spirit that burned in the hearts of the prophets and breathed in gentle humanity through the Mosaic Law, the influence of the Old Testament has been one of the great permanent forces making for democracy and social justice. However our views of the Bible may change, every religious man will continue to recognize that to the elect minds of the Jewish people God gave so vivid a consciousness of the divine will that, in its main tendencies at least, their life and thought carries a permanent authority for all who wish to know the higher right of God. Their writings are like channel-buoys anchored by God, and we shall do well to heed them now that the roar of an angry surf is in our ears.

We shall confine this brief study of the Old Testament to the prophets, because they are the beating heart of the Old Testament. Modern study has shown that they were the real makers of the unique religious life of Israel. If all that proceeded from them, directly or indirectly, were eliminated from the Old Testament, there would be little left to appeal to the moral and religious judgment of the modern world. Moreover, a comprehension of the essential purpose and spirit of the prophets is necessary for a comprehension of the purpose and spirit of Jesus and of genuine Christianity. In Jesus and the primitive Church the prophetic spirit rose from the dead. To the ceremonial aspects of Jewish religion Jesus was either indifferent or hostile; the thought of the prophets was the spiritual food that he assimilated in his own process of growth. With them he linked his points of view, the convictions which he regarded as axiomatic. Their spirit was to him what the soil and climate of a country are to its flora. The real meaning of his life and the real direction of his purposes can be understood only in that historical connection.

Thus a study of the prophets is not only an interesting part in the history of social movements but it is indispensable for any full comprehension of the social influence exerted by historical Christianity, and for any true comprehension of the mind of Jesus Christ....

The fundamental conviction of the prophets, which distinguished them from the ordinary religious life of their day, was the conviction that God demands righteousness and demands nothing but righteousness....

The prophets insisted on a right life as the true worship of God. Morality to them was not merely a prerequisite of effective ceremonial worship. They brushed sacrificial ritual aside altogether as trifling compared with righteousness, nay, as a harmful substitute and a hindrance for ethical religion. "I desire goodness and not sacrifice," said Hosea, and Jesus was fond of quoting the words. The Book of Isaiah begins with a description of the disasters which had overtaken the nation, and then in impassioned words the prophet spurns the means taken to appease Jehovah's anger. He said the herds of beasts trampling his temple-court, the burning fat, the reek of blood, the clouds of incense, were a weariness and an abomination to the God whom they were meant to please. Their festivals and solemn meetings, their prayers and prostrations, were iniquity from which he averted his face. What he wanted was a right life and the righting of social wrongs: "Your hands are full of blood. Wash you! Make you clean! Put away the evil of your doings from before mine eyes! Cease to do evil! Learn to do right! Seek justice! Relieve the oppressed! Secure justice for the orphaned and plead for the widow!"

Perhaps the simplest and most beautiful expression of that reformatory conception of true religion is contained in the words of Micah: "Wherewith shall I come before Jehovah, and bow myself before the high God? Shall I come before him with burnt-offerings, with calves a year old? Will Jehovah be pleased with thousands of rams, or with ten thousands of rivers of oil? Shall I give my firstborn for my transgression, the fruit of my body for the sin of my soul? He hath shewed thee, O man, what is good; and what doth Jehovah require of thee, but to do justly, and to love kindness, and to walk humbly with thy God?"

Amos and Jeremiah even tried to cut away the foundation of antiquity on which the sacrificial system rested, by denying that God had commanded sacrifices at all when he constituted the nation after the exodus from Egypt. Obedience was all that he required.

This insistence on religious morality as the only thing God cares about is of fundamental importance for the question before us. The social problems are moral problems on a large scale. Religion is a tremendous generator of self-sacrificing action. Under its impulse men have burned up the animals they laboriously raised; they have sacrificed their first-born whom they loved and prized; they have tapped their own veins and died with a shout of triumph. But this unparalleled force has been largely diverted to ceremonial actions which wasted property and labor, and were either useless to social health or injurious to it. In so far as men believed that the traditional ceremonial was what God wanted of them, they would be indifferent to the reformation of social ethics. If the hydraulic force of religion could be turned toward conduct, there is nothing which it could not accomplish....

.   .   .   .   .

Here then we have a succession of men perhaps unique in religious history for their moral heroism and spiritual insight. They were the moving spirits in the religious progress of their nation; the creators, directly or indirectly, of its law, its historical and poetical literature, and its piety; the men to whose personality and teaching Jesus felt most kinship; the men who still kindle modern religious enthusiasm. Most of us believe that their insight was divinely given and that the course they steered was set for them by the Captain of history.

We have seen that these men were almost indifferent, if not contemptuous, about the ceremonial side of customary religion, but turned with passionate enthusiasm to moral righteousness as the true domain of religion. Where would their interest lie if they lived to-day?

We have seen that their religious concern was not restricted to private religion and morality, but dealt preeminently with the social and political life of their nation. Would they limit its range to-day?

We have seen that their sympathy was wholly and passionately with the poor and oppressed. If they lived to-day, would they place the chief blame for poverty on the poor and give their admiration to the strong?

We have seen that they gradually rose above the kindred prophets of other nations through their moral interest in national affairs, and that their spiritual progress and education were intimately connected with their open-eyed comprehension of the larger questions of contemporary history. Is it likely that the same attitude of mind which enlarged and purified the religion of the Hebrew leaders would deteriorate and endanger the religion of Christian leaders?

We have seen that the religious concern in politics ceased only when politics ceased; that religious individualism was a triumph of faith under abnormal conditions and not a normal type of religious life; and that the enforced withdrawal of religion from the wider life was one cause for the later narrowness of Judaism. Does this warrant the assumption that religion is most normal when it is most the affair of the individual?

We have seen that the sane political programme and the wise historical insight of the great prophets turned into apocalyptic dreams and bookish calculations when the nation lost its political self-government and training. How wise is it for the Christian leaders of a democratic nation to take their interpretation of God's purposes in history and their theories about the coming of the kingdom of God from the feeblest and most decadent age of Hebrew thought?

We have seen that the true prophets opposed the complacent optimism of the people and of their popular spokesmen, and gave warning of disaster as long as it was coming. If they lived among the present symptoms of social and moral decay, would they sing a lullaby or sound the reveille?

No true prophet will copy a prophet. Their garb, their mannerisms of language, the vehemence of their style, belong to their age and not to ours. But if we believe in their divine mission and in the divine origin of the religion in which they were the chief factors, we cannot repudiate what was fundamental in their lives. If any one holds that religion is essentially ritual and sacramental; or that it is purely personal; or that God is on the side of the rich; or that social interest is likely to lead preachers astray; he must prove his case with his eye on the Hebrew prophets, and the burden of proof is with him. . . .

. . . .

As with the Old Testament prophets, the fundamental sympathies of Jesus were with the poor and oppressed. In the glad opening days of his preaching in Galilee, when he wanted to unfold his programme, he turned to the passage of Isaiah where the prophet proclaimed good tidings to the poor, release to the captives, liberty to the bruised, and the acceptable year of the Lord for all. Now, said Jesus, that is to be fulfilled. To John in prison he offered as proof that the Messiah had really come, that the helpless were receiving help, and the poor were listening to glad news. The Church has used the miracles of Jesus for theological purposes as evidences of his divine mission. According to the Synoptic gospels, Jesus himself flatly refused to furnish them for such a purpose to the contemporary theologians. His healing power was for social help, for the alleviation of human suffering. It was at the service of any wretched leper, but not of the doubting scribes. To get the setting of his life we must remember the vast poverty and misery of Oriental countries. It threatened to ingulf him entirely and to turn him into a travelling medical dispensary.

It is often possible nowadays to detect the social studies and sympathies of a public speaker by an unpurposed phrase or allusion which shows where his mind had been dwelling. This is constantly true of Jesus. If he had not known how much a strayed sheep or a lost coin meant to the poor, he would not have told the anecdotes about their joy in recovering them. If he had not appreciated the heroic generosity of the poor, he would not have breathed more quickly when he saw the widow dropping her two mites in the temple treasury. He knew how large a share the lawyers get in settling an estate and how little is left for the widow. He knew how bitterly hard it is for the poor to set the judicial machinery of organized society in motion in their favor; hence he used the illustration of the widow and the judge. He knew the golden rule of "society": dine those by whom you want to be dined. Those who most need a dinner are never asked to have a dinner. He suggested to his hosts a reversal of this policy, and he loved to think of the Messianic salvation as an actual reversal on a grand scale, in which the regular guests would be left out in the cold, while the halt and blind were gathered from the highways and hedges to enjoy the fat things. . . .

There was a revolutionary consciousness in Jesus; not, of course, in the common use of the word "revolutionary," which connects it with violence and bloodshed. But Jesus knew that he had come to kindle a fire on earth. . . .

.   .   .   .   .

The Church has never been able to get entirely away from the revolutionary spirit of Jesus. It is an essential doctrine of Christianity that the world is fundamentally good and practically bad, for it was made by God, but is now controlled by sin. If a man wants to be a Christian, he must stand over against things as they are and condemn them in the name of that higher conception of life which Jesus revealed. If a man is satisfied with things as they are, he belongs to the other side. For many centuries the Church felt so deeply that the Christian conception of life and the actual social life are incompatible, that any one who wanted to live the genuine Christian life, had to leave the world and live in a monastic community. Protestantism has abandoned the monastic life and settled down to live in the world. If that implies that it accepts the present condition

as good and final, it means a silencing of its Christian protest and its surrender to "the world." There is another alternative. Ascetic Christianity called the world evil and left it. Humanity is waiting for a revolutionary Christianity which will call the world evil and change it. We do not want "to blow all our existing institutions to atoms," but we do want to remould every one of them. A tank of gasolene can blow a car sky-high in a single explosion, or push it to the top of a hill in a perpetual succession of little explosions. We need a combination between the faith of Jesus in the need and the possibility of the kingdom of God, and the modern comprehension of the organic development of human society.

.   .   .   .   .

In the preceding chapters we have studied the origins of Christianity. It rested historically on the religion of the Hebrew prophets, and the great aim of the prophets was to constitute the social and political life of their nation in accordance with the will of God. The fundamental purpose of Jesus was the establishment of the kingdom of God, which involved a thorough regeneration and reconstitution of social life. Primitive Christianity cherished an ardent hope of a radically new era, and within its limits sought to realize a social life on a new moral basis.

Thus Christianity as an historical movement was launched with all the purpose and hope, all the impetus and power, of a great revolutionary movement, pledged to change the world-as-it-is into the world-as-it-ought-to-be.

.   .   .   .   .

As we have seen, the industrial and commercial life to-day is dominated by principles antagonistic to the fundamental principles of Christianity, and it is so difficult to live a Christian life in the midst of it that few men even try. If production could be organized on a basis of cooperative fraternity; if distribution could at least approximately be determined by justice; if all men could be conscious that their labor contributed to the welfare of all and that their personal well-being was dependent on the prosperity of the

Commonwealth; if predatory business and parasitic wealth ceased and all men lived only by their labor; if the luxury of unearned wealth no longer made us all feverish with covetousness and a simpler life became the fashion; if our time and strength were not used up either in getting a bare living or in amassing unusable wealth and we had more leisure for the higher pursuits of the mind and the soul—then there might be a chance to live such a life of gentleness and brotherly kindness and tranquillity of heart as Jesus desired for men. It may be that the cooperative Commonwealth would give us the first chance in history to live a really Christian life without retiring from the world, and would make the Sermon on the Mount a philosophy of life feasible for all who care to try.

This is the stake of the Church in the social crisis. If society continues to disintegrate and decay, the Church will be carried down with it. If the Church can rally such moral forces that injustice will be overcome and fresh red blood will course in a sounder social organism, it will itself rise to higher liberty and life. Doing the will of God it will have new visions of God. With a new message will come a new authority. If the salt lose its saltness, it will be trodden under foot. If the Church fulfils its prophetic functions, it may bear the prophet's reproach for a time, but it will have the prophet's vindication thereafter.

The conviction has always been embedded in the heart of the Church that "the world"—society as it is—is evil and some time is to make way for a true human society in which the spirit of Jesus Christ shall rule. For fifteen hundred years those who desired to live a truly Christian life withdrew from the evil world to live a life apart. But the principle of such an ascetic departure from the world is dead in modern life. There are only two other possibilities. The Church must either condemn the world and seek to change it, or tolerate the world and conform to it. In the latter case it surrenders its holiness and its mission. The other possibility has never yet been tried with full faith on a large scale. All the leadings of God in contemporary history and all the promptings of Christ's spirit

in our hearts urge us to make the trial. On this choice is staked the future of the Church.

6. Rauschenbusch's Social Prayers

Rauschenbusch's prayers express his deep concern for a Christianity socially aware of the needs of the common man. He desired religious hymns that would strike "the triumphant chords of social hope," and church liturgies that would "enrich and purify man's social thoughts and feelings." He hoped that his prayers would make men more conscious of the relationship between the social conditions of man and the Gospel message. His prayers were immensely popular, many of them being first printed in the secular journals of the time. *Prayers of the Social Awakening,* by Walter Rauschenbusch (Boston: Pilgrim Press, 1925).

GRACE BEFORE MEAT

Our Father, thou art the final source of all our comforts and to thee we render thanks for this food. But we also remember in gratitude the many men and women whose labor was necessary to produce it, and who gathered it from the land and afar from the sea for our sustenance. Grant that they too may enjoy the fruit of their labor without want, and may be bound up with us in a fellowship of thankful hearts.

O God, we thank thee for the abundance of our blessings, but we pray that our plenty may not involve want for others. Do thou satisfy the desire of every child of thine. Grant that the strength which we shall draw from this food may be put forth again for the common good, and that our life may return to humanity a full equivalent in useful work for the nourishment which we receive from the common store.

FOR THE COOPERATIVE COMMONWEALTH

O God, we praise thee for the dream of the golden city of peace and righteousness which has ever haunted the prophets of humanity, and we rejoice with joy unspeakable that at last the people have conquered the freedom and knowledge and power which may avail to turn into reality the vision that so long has beckoned in vain.

Speed now the day when the plains and the hills and the wealth thereof shall be the people's own, and thy freemen shall not live as tenants of men on the earth which thou hast given to all; when no babe shall be born without its equal birthright in the riches and knowledge wrought out by the labor of the ages; and when the mighty engines of industry shall throb with a gladder music because the men who ply these great tools shall be their owners and masters.

Bring to an end, O Lord, the inhumanity of the present, in which all men are ridden by the pale fear of want while the nation of which they are citizens sits throned amid the wealth of their making; when the manhood in some is cowed by helplessness, while the soul of others is surfeited and sick with power which no frail son of the dust should wield.

O God, save us, for our nation is at strife with its own soul and is sinning against the light which thou aforetime hast kindled in it. Thou hast called our people to freedom, but we are withholding from men their share in the common heritage without which freedom becomes a hollow name. Thy Christ has kindled in us the passion for brotherhood, but the social life we have built, denies and slays brotherhood.

We pray thee to revive in us the hardy spirit of our forefathers that we may establish and complete their work, building on the basis of their democracy the firm edifice of a cooperative commonwealth, in which both government and industry shall be of the people, by the people, and for the people. May we, who now live, see the oncoming of the great day of God, when all men shall stand side by side in equal worth and real freedom, all toiling and all reaping, masters of nature but brothers of men, exultant in the tide of the common life, and jubilant in the adoration of Thee, the source of their blessings and the Father of all.

7. *The Federal Council of Churches, 1908*

The Federal Council of the Churches of Christ in America, holding its first meeting in Philadelphia in 1908, adopted a social creed that was confined largely to the field of industrial relations. In 1912, at its quadrennial meeting in Chicago, the Council adopted a more comprehensive declaration of principles known as "The Social Creed of the Churches." It expressed the social faith of thirty-one Protestant denominations, representing seventeen million members. The spirit of the liberal social gospel is clearly evident. Harry F. Ward, *The Social Creed of the Churches* (New York: Abingdon Press, 1914).

The Federal Council of the Churches of Christ in America stands:

For equal rights and complete justice for all men in all stations of life.

For the protection of the family, by the single standard of purity, uniform divorce laws, proper regulations of marriage, and proper housing.

For the fullest possible development for every child, especially by the provision of proper education and recreation.

For the abolition of child-labor.

For such regulation of the conditions of toil for women as shall safeguard the physical and moral health of the community.

For the abatement and prevention of poverty.

For the protection of the individual and society from the social, economic, and moral waste of the liquor traffic.

For the conservation of health.

For the protection of the worker from dangerous machinery, occupational disease, injuries, and mortality.

For the right of all men to the opportunity for self-maintenance, for safeguarding this right against encroachments of every kind, and for the protection of workers from the hardships of enforced unemployment.

For suitable provision for the old age of the workers, and for those incapacitated by injury.

For the right of employees and employers alike to organize and for adequate means of conciliation and arbitration in industrial disputes.

For a release from employment one day in seven.

For the gradual and reasonable reduction of the hours of labor to the lowest practicable point, and for that degree of leisure for all which is a condition of the highest human life.

For a living wage as a minimum in every industry, and for the highest wage that each industry can afford.

For a new emphasis on the application of Christian principles to the acquisition and use of property, and for the most equitable

437

division of the product of industry that can ultimately be devised. . . .

8. *Comte on the Religion of Humanity*

Auguste Xavier Comte, *A General View of Positivism*, trans. J. H. Bridges (London: Trübner and Co., 1865).

. . . All the points, then, in which the morality of Positive science excels the morality of revealed religion are summed up in the substitution of Love of Humanity for Love of God. It is a principle as adverse to metaphysics as to theology, since it excludes all personal considerations, and places happiness, whether for the individual or for society, in constant exercise of kindly feeling. To love Humanity may be truly said to constitute the whole duty of Man; provided it be clearly understood what such love really implies, and what are the conditions required for maintaining it. The victory of Social Feeling over our innate Self-love is rendered possible only by a slow and difficult training of the heart, in which the intellect must cooperate. The most important part of this training consists in the mutual love of Man and Woman, with all other family affections which precede and follow it. But every aspect of morality, even the personal virtues, are included in love of Humanity. It furnishes the best measure of their relative importance, and the surest method for laying down incontestable rules of conduct. And thus we find the principles of systematic morality to be identical with those of spontaneous morality, a result which renders Positive doctrine equally accessible to all.

Science, therefore, Poetry, and Morality, will alike be regenerated by the new religion, and will ultimately form one harmonious whole, on which the destinies of Man will henceforth rest. With women, to whom the first germs of spiritual power are due, this consecration of the rational and imaginative faculties to the source of feeling has always existed spontaneously. But to realise it in social life it must be brought forward in a systematic form as part of a general doctrine. This is what the medieval system attempted upon the basis of Monotheism. A moral power arose composed of the two elements essential to such a power, the sympathetic influence of women in the family, the systematic influence of the priesthood on public life. As a preliminary attempt the Catholic system was most beneficial; but it could not last, because the synthesis on which it rested was imperfect and unstable. The Catholic doctrine and worship addressed themselves exclusively to our emotional nature, and even from the moral point of view their principles were uncertain and arbitrary. The field of intellect, whether in art or science, as well as that of practical life, would have

IX-2. Prayer Meeting No. 2. *Lithograph satirizing "old-time religion," by George Bellows. National Gallery of Art, Washington, D.C. Rosenwald Collection.*

been left almost untouched but for the personal character of the priests. But with the loss of their political independence, which had been always in danger from the military tendencies of the time, the priesthood rapidly degenerated. The system was in fact premature; and even before the industrial era of modern times had set in, the esthetic and metaphysical growth of the times had already gone too far for its feeble power of control; and it then became as hostile to progress as it had formerly been favourable to it. Moral qualities without intellectual superiority are not enough for a true spiritual power; they will not enable it to modify to any appreciable extent the strong preponderance of material considerations. Consequently it is the primary condition of social reorganization to put an end to the state of utter revolt which the intellect maintains against the heart; a state which has existed ever since the close of the Middle Ages, and the source of which may be traced as far back as the Greek Metaphysicians. Positivism has at last overcome the immense difficulties of this task. Its solution consists in the foundation of social science on the basis of the preliminary sciences, so that at last there is unity of method in our conceptions. Our active faculties have always been guided by the Positive spirit: and by its extension to the sphere of Feeling, a complete synthesis, alike spontaneous and systematic in its nature, is constructed; and every part of our nature is brought under the regenerating influence of the worship of Humanity. Thus a new spiritual power will arise, complete and homogeneous in structure; coherent and at the same time progressive; and better calculated than Catholicism to engage the support of women which is so necessary to its efficient action on society.

Were it not for the material necessities of human life, nothing further would be required for its guidance than a spiritual power such as is here described. We should have in that case no need for any laborious exertion; and universal benevolence would be looked upon as the sovereign good, and would become the direct object of all our efforts. All that would be necessary would be to call our reasoning powers, and still more,

our imagination into play, in order to keep this object constantly in view. Purely fictitious as such an hypothesis may be, it is yet an ideal limit, to which our actual life should be more and more nearly approximated. As a Utopia, it is a fit subject for the poet: and in his hands it will supply the new religion with resources far superior to any that Christianity derived from vague and unreal pictures of future bliss. In it we may carry out a more perfect social classification, in which men may be ranked by moral and intellectual merit, irrespectively of wealth or position. For the only standard by which in such a state men could be tried would be their capacity to love and to please Humanity.

Such a standard will of course never be practically accepted, and indeed the classification in question would be impossible to effect: yet it should always be present to our minds; and should be contrasted dispassionately with the actual arrangements of social rank, with which power, even where accidentally acquired, has more to do than wealth. The priests of Humanity with the assistance of women will avail themselves largely of this contrast in modifying the existing order. Positivist education will fully explain its moral validity, and in our religious services appeal will frequently be made to it. Although an ideal abstraction, yet being based on reality, except so far as the necessities of daily life are concerned, it will be far more efficacious than the vague and uncertain classification founded on the theological doctrine of a future state. When society learns to admit no other Providence than its own, it will go so far in adopting this ideal classification as to produce a strong effect on the classes who are the best aware of its impracticability. But those who press this contrast must be careful always to respect the natural laws which regulate the distribution of wealth and rank. They have a definite social function, and that function is not to be destroyed, but to be improved and regulated. In order, therefore, to reconcile these conditions, we must limit our ideal classification to individuals, leaving the actual subordination of office and position unaffected. Well-marked personal superiority is not very common, and society would be wasting its powers in useless and interminable controversy if it undertook to give each function to its best organ, thus dispossessing the former functionary without taking into account the conditions of practical experience. Even in the spiritual hierarchy, where it is easier to judge of merit, such a course would be utterly subversive of discipline. But there would be no political danger, and morally there would be great advantage, in pointing out all remarkable cases which illustrate the difference between the order of rank and the order of merit. Respect may be shown to the noblest without compromising the authority of the strongest. St. Bernard was esteemed more highly than any of the Popes of his time; yet he remained in the humble position of an abbot, and never failed to show the most perfect deference for the higher functionaries of the Church. A still more striking example was furnished by St. Paul in recognizing the official superiority of St. Peter, of whose moral and mental inferiority to himself he must have been well aware. All organized corporations, civil or military, can show instances on a less important scale where the abstract order of merit has been adopted consistently with the concrete order of rank. Where this is the case the two may be contrasted without any subversive consequences. The contrast will be morally beneficial to all classes, at the same time that it proves the imperfection to which so complicated an organism as human society must be ever liable.

Thus the religion of Humanity creates an intellectual and moral power, which, could human life be freed from the pressure of material wants, would suffice for its guidance. Imperfect as our nature assuredly is, yet social sympathy has an intrinsic charm which would make it paramount, but for the imperious necessities by which the instincts of self-preservation are stimulated. So urgent are they, that the greater part of life is necessarily occupied with actions of a self-regarding kind, before which Reason, Imagination, and even Feeling, have to give way. Consequently this moral power, which seems so well adapted for the direction of society, must only attempt to act as a modifying influence. Its sympathetic element, in other words, women, accept this necessity without difficulty; for true affection always takes the right course of action, as soon as it is clearly indicated. But the intellect is far more unwilling to take a subordinate position. Its rash ambition is far more unsettling to the world than the ambition of rank and wealth, against which it so often inveighs. It is the hardest of social problems to regulate the exercise of the intellectual powers, while securing them their due measure of influence; the object being that theoretical power should be able really to modify, and yet should never be permitted to govern. For the nations of antiquity this problem was insoluble; with them the intellect was always either a tyrant or a slave. The solution was attempted in the Middle Ages; but without success, owing to the military and theological character of the times. Positivism relies for solving it on the reality which is one of its principal features, and on the fact that Society has now entered on its industrial phase. Based on accurate inquiry into the past and future destinies of man, its aim is so to regenerate our political action, as to transform it ultimately into a practical worship of Humanity; Morality being the worship rendered by the affections, Science and Poetry that rendered by the intellect. Such is the principal mission of the Occidental priesthood, a mission in which women and the working classes will actively co-operate.

The most important object of this regenerated polity will be the substitution of Duties for Rights; thus subordinating personal to social considerations. The word *Right* should be excluded from political language, as the word *Cause* from the language of philosophy. Both are theological and metaphysical conceptions; and the former is as immoral and subversive as the latter is unmeaning and sophistical. Both are alike incompatible with the final state; and their value during the revolutionary period of modern history has simply consisted in their solvent action upon previous systems. Rights, in the strict sense of the word, are possible only so long as power is considered as emanating from a superhuman will. Rights, under all theological systems, were divine; but in their opposition to theocracy, the metaphysicians of the last five centuries introduced what they called the rights of Man; a conception, the value of which consisted simply in its destructive effects. Whenever it has been taken as the basis of a constructive policy, its anti-social character, and its tendency to strengthen individualism have always been apparent. In the Positive state, where no supernatural claims are admissible, the idea of *Right* will entirely disappear. Every one has duties, duties toward all; but Rights in the ordinary sense can be claimed by none. Whatever security the individual may require is found in the general acknowledgement of reciprocal obligations; and this gives a moral equivalent for rights as hitherto claimed, without the serious political dangers which they involved. In other words, no one has in any case any Right but that of doing his Duty. The adoption of this principle is the one way of realising the grand ideal of the Middle Ages, the subordination of Politics to Morals. In those times, however, the vast bearings of the question were but very imperfectly apprehended; its solution is incompatible with every form of theology, and is only to be found in Positivism.

The solution consists in regarding our political and social action as the service of Humanity. Its object should be to assist by conscious effort all functions, whether relating to Order or to Progress, which Humanity has hitherto performed spontaneously. This is the ultimate object of Positive religion. Without it all other aspects of that religion would be inadequate, and would soon cease to have any value. True affection does not stop short at desire for good; it strains every effort to attain it. The elevation of soul arising from the act of contemplating and adoring Humanity is not the sole object of religious worship. Above and beyond this there is the motive of becoming better able to serve Humanity; unceasing action on our part being necessary for her preservation and development. This indeed is the most distinctive feature of Positive religion. The Supreme Being of former times had really little need of human services. The consequence was, that with all theological believers, and with monotheists especially, devotion always tends to degenerate into quietism. The danger could only be obviated when the priesthood had sufficient wisdom to take advantage of the vagueness of these theories, and to draw from them motives for practical exertion. Nothing could be done in this direction unless the priesthood retained their social independence. As soon as this was taken from them by the usurpation of the temporal power, the more sincere amongst Catholics lapsed into the quietistic spirit which for a long time had been kept in check. In Positivism, on the contrary, the doctrine itself, irrespective of the character of its teachers, is a direct and continuous incentive to exertion of every kind. The reason for this is to be found in the relative and dependent nature of our Supreme Being, of whom her own worshippers form a part.

In this, which is the essential service of Humanity, and which infuses a religious spirit into every act of life, the feature most prominent is cooperation of effort; cooperation on so vast a scale that less complicated organisms have nothing to compare with it. The consensus of the social organism extends to Time as well as Space. Hence the two distinct aspects of social sympathy: the feeling of Solidarity, or union with the Present; and of Continuity, or union with the Past. Careful investigation of any social phenomenon, whether relating to Order or to Progress, always proves convergence, direct or indirect, of all contemporaries and of all former generations, within certain geographical and chronological limits; and those limits recede as the development of Humanity advances. In our thoughts and feelings such convergence is unquestionable; and it should be still more evident in our actions, the efficacy of which depends on cooperation to a still greater degree. Here we feel how false as well as immoral is the notion of *Right*, a word which, as commonly used, implies absolute individuality. The only principle on which Politics can be subordinated to Morals is, that individuals should be regarded, not as so many distinct beings, but as organs of one Supreme Being. Indeed, in all settled states of society, the individual has always been considered as a public functionary, filling more or less efficiently a definite post, whether formally appointed to it or not. So fundamental a principle has ever been recognised instinctively up to the period of revolutionary transition, which is now at length coming to an end; a period in which the obstructive and corrupt character of organized society roused a spirit of anarchy which, though at first favourable to progress, has now become an obstacle to it. Positivism, however, will place this principle beyond reach of attack, by giving a systematic demonstration of it, based on the sum of our scientific knowledge.

And this demonstration will be the intellectual basis on which the moral authority of the new priesthood will rest. What they have to do is to show the dependence of each important question, as it arises, upon social cooperation, and by this means to indicate the right path of duty. For this purpose all their scientific knowledge and esthetic power will be needed, otherwise social feeling could never be developed sufficiently to produce any strong effect upon conduct. It would never, that is, go further than the feeling of mere solidarity with the Present, which is only its incipient and rudimentary form. We see this unfortunate narrowness of view too often in the best socialists, who, leaving the Present without roots in the Past, would carry us headlong towards a Future, of which they have no definite conception. In all social phenomena, and especially in those of modern times, the participation of our predecessors is greater than that of our contemporaries. This truth is especially apparent in industrial undertakings, for which the combination of efforts required is so vast. It is our filiation with the Past, even more than our connection with the Present, which teaches us that the only real life is the collective life of the race; that individual life has no existence except as an abstraction. Continuity is the feature which distinguishes our race from all others. Many of the lower races are able to form a union among their living members; but it was reserved for Man to conceive and realize cooperation of successive generations, the source to which the gradual growth of civilization is to be traced. Social sympathy is a barren and imperfect feeling, and indeed it is a cause of disturbance, so long as it extends no further than the present time. It is a disregard for historical Continuity which induces that mistaken antipathy to all forms of inheritance which is now so common. Scientific study of history would soon convince those of our socialist writers who are sincere of their radical error in this respect. If they were more familiar with the collective inheritance of society, the value of which no one can seriously dispute, they would feel less objection to inheritance in its application to individuals or families. Practical experience, moreover, bringing them into contact with the facts of the case, will gradually show them that without the sense of continuity with the Past they cannot really understand their solidarity with the Present. For, in the first place, each individual in the course of his growth passes spontaneously through phases corresponding in a great measure to those of our historical development; and therefore, without some knowledge of the history of society, he cannot understand the history of his own life. Again, each of these successive phases may be found amongst the less advanced nations who do not as yet share in the general progress of Humanity; so that we cannot properly sympathize with these nations, if we ignore the successive stages of development in Western Europe. The nobler socialists and communists, those especially who belong to the working classes, will soon be alive to the error and danger of these inconsistencies, and will supply this deficiency in their education, which at present vitiates their efforts. With women, the purest and most spontaneous element of the moderating power, the priests of Humanity will find it less difficult to introduce the broad principles of historical science. They are more inclined than any other class to recognise our continuity with the Past, being themselves its original source. . . .

9. Charles Darwin, 1859

Charles Darwin (1809-1882) was a famed naturalist who established the theory of Natural Selection. The *Origin of Species*, which promulgated the theory, appeared in 1859. It revolutionized the sciences of Botany and Zoology and universalized the doctrine of Organic Evolution. He was not the very first to conceive the idea that all species of plants or animals are derived from a single original ancestor, but he did secure for the idea general acceptance through his conception of Natural Selection. Admitting that his abstract is necessarily imperfect, Darwin nevertheless presents a wealth of fascinating data and theories concerning domestic and natural variation, transformation of a simple organ into a highly developed organ, the development of instinct, the infertility of species and the fertility of varieties when intercrossed, the imperfection of the geological record, geographical distribution, and embryonic similarities of organic beings. Below are excerpts from Darwin's introduction and recapitulation. Charles Darwin, *Origin of Species* (London: J. Murray, 1859).

When on board H.M.S. *Beagle*, as naturalist, I was much struck with certain facts in the distribution of the inhabitants of South America, and in the geological relations of the present to the past inhabitants of that continent. These facts seemed to me to throw some light on the origin of species—that mystery of mysteries, as it has been called by one of our greatest philosophers. On my return home, it occurred to me, in 1837, that something might perhaps be made out on this question by patiently accumulating and reflecting on all sorts of facts which could possibly have any bearing on it. After five years' work I allowed myself to speculate on the subject, and drew up some short notes; these I enlarged in 1844 into a sketch of the conclusions, which then seemed to me probable: from that period to the present day I have steadily pursued the same object. I hope that I may be excused for entering on these personal details, as I give them to show that I have not been hasty in coming to a decision. . . .

.   .   .   .   .

As this whole volume is one long argument, it may be convenient to the reader to have the leading facts and inferences briefly recapitulated.

That many and serious objections may be advanced against the theory of descent with modification through natural selection, I do not deny. I have endeavoured to give to them their full force. Nothing at first can appear more difficult to believe than that the more complex organs and instincts should have been perfected, not by means superior to, though analogous with, human reason, but by the accumulation of innumerable slight variations, each good for the individual possessor. Nevertheless, this difficulty, though appearing to our imagination insuperably great, cannot be considered real if we admit the following propositions, namely,—that gradations in the perfection of any organ or instinct which we may consider, either do now exist or could have existed, each good of its kind,—that all organs and instincts are, in ever so slight a degree, variable,—and, lastly, that there is a struggle for existence leading to the preservation of each profitable deviation of structure or instinct. The truth of these propositions cannot, I think, be disputed.

It is, no doubt, extremely difficult even to conjecture by what gradations many structures have been perfected, more especially amongst broken and failing groups of organic beings; but we see so many strange gradations in nature, that we ought to be extremely cautious in saying that any organ or instinct, or any whole being, could not have arrived at its present state by many graduated steps. There are, it must be admitted, cases of special difficulty on the theory of natural selection; and one of the most curious of these is the existence of two or three defined castes of workers or sterile females in the same community of ants; but I have attempted to show how this difficulty can be mastered.

With respect to the almost universal sterility of species when first crossed, which forms so remarkable a contrast with the almost universal fertility of varieties when crossed, I must refer the reader to the recapitulation of the facts given at the end of the eighth chapter, which seem to me conclusively to show that this sterility is . . . incidental on constitutional differences in the reproductive systems of the intercrossed species. . . . The vigour and fertility of all organic beings are increased by slight changes in their conditions of life, and the offspring of slightly modified forms or varieties acquire from being crossed increased vigour and fertility. So that, on the one hand, considerable changes in the conditions of life and crosses between greatly modified forms, lessen fertility; and on the other hand, lesser changes in the conditions of life and crosses between less modified forms, increase fertility. . . .

443

As on the theory of natural selection an interminable number of intermediate forms must have existed, linking together all the species in each group by gradations as fine as our present varieties, it may be asked, Why do we not see these linking forms all around us? Why are not all organic beings blended together in an inextricable chaos? With respect to existing forms, we should remember that we have no right to expect (excepting in rare cases) to discover *directly* connecting links between them, but only between each and some extinct and supplanted form. Even on a wide area, which has during a long period remained continuous, and of which the climate and other conditions of life change insensibly in going from a district occupied by one species into another district occupied by a closely allied species, we have no just right to expect often to find intermediate varieties in the intermediate zone. For we have reason to believe that only a few species are undergoing change at any one period; and all changes are slowly effected. I have also shown that the intermediate varieties which will at first probably exist in the intermediate zones, will be liable to be supplanted by the allied forms on either hand; and the latter, from existing in greater numbers, will generally be modified and improved at a quicker rate than the intermediate varieties, which exist in lesser numbers; so that the intermediate varieties will, in the long run, be supplanted and exterminated.

On this doctrine of the extermination of an infinitude of connecting links, between the living and extinct inhabitants of the world, and at each successive period between the extinct and still older species, why is not every geological formation charged with such links? Why does not every collection of fossil remains afford plain evidence of the gradation and mutation of the forms of life? . . .

I can answer these questions and grave objections only on the supposition that the geological record is far more imperfect than most geologists believe. It cannot be objected that there has not been time sufficient for any amount of organic change; for the lapse of time has been so great as to be utterly inappreciable by the human intellect. The num-

ber of specimens in all our museums is absolutely as nothing compared with the countless generations of countless species which certainly have existed. We should not be able to recognise a species as the parent of any one or more species if we were to examine them ever so closely, unless we likewise possessed many of the intermediate links between their past or parent and present states; and these many links we could hardly ever expect to discover, owing to the imperfection of the geological record. . . . As long as most of the links between any two species are unknown, if any one link or intermediate variety be discovered, it will simply be classed as another and distinct species. Only a small portion of the world has been geologically explored. Only organic beings of certain classes can be preserved in a fossil condition, at least in any great number. Widely ranging species vary most, and varieties are often at first local,—both causes rendering the discovery of intermediate links less likely. Local varieties will not spread into other and distant regions until they are considerably modified and improved; and when they do spread, if discovered in a geological formation, they will appear as if suddenly created there, and will be simply classed as new species. Most formations have been intermittent in their accumulation; and their duration, I am inclined to believe, has been shorter than the average duration of specific forms. Successive formations are separated from each other by enormous blank intervals of time; for fossiliferous formations, thick enough to resist future degradation, can be accumulated only where much sediment is deposited on the subsiding bed of the sea. During the alternate periods of elevation and of stationary level the record will be blank. During these latter periods there will probably be more variability in the forms of life; during periods of subsidence, more extinction. . . .

[Man] adapts animals and plants for his own benefit or pleasure. He may do this methodically, or he may do it unconsciously by preserving the individuals most useful to him at the time, without any thought of altering the breed. It is certain that he can largely influence the character of a breed by selecting, in each successive generation, individual differences so slight as to be quite inappreciable by an uneducated eye. This process of selection has been the great agency in the production of the most distinct and useful domestic breeds. . . .

There is no obvious reason why the principles which have acted so efficiently under domestication should not have acted under nature. In the preservation of favoured individuals and races, during the constantly-recurrent Struggle for Existence, we see the most powerful and ever-acting means of selection. The struggle for existence inevitably follows from the high geometrical ratio of increase which is common to all organic beings. This high rate of increase is proved by calculation,—by the rapid increase of many animals and plants during a succession of peculiar seasons, or when naturalised in a new country. More individuals are born than can possibly survive. A grain in the balance will determine which individual shall live and which shall die,—which variety or species shall increase in number, and which shall decrease, or finally become extinct. . . . The slightest advantage in one being, at any age or during any season, over those with which it comes into competition, or better adaptation in however slight a degree to the surrounding physical conditions, will turn the balance. . . .

Why, if man can by patience select variations most useful to himself, should nature fail in selecting variations useful, under changing conditions of life, to her living products? What limit can be put to this power, acting during long ages and rigidly scrutinizing the whole constitution, structure, and habits of each creature,—favouring the good and rejecting the bad? I can see no limit to this power, in slowly and beautifully adapting each form to the most complex relations of life. The theory of natural selection, even if we looked no further than this, seems to me to be in itself probable. . . .

As each species tends by its geometrical ration of reproduction to increase inordinately in number; and as the modified descendants of each species will be enabled to increase by so much the more as they become diversified in habits and structure, so

as to be enabled to seize on many and widely different places in the economy of nature, there will be a constant tendency in natural selection to preserve the most divergent offspring of any one species. Hence during a long-continued course of modification, the slight differences, characteristic of varieties of the same species, tend to be augmented into the greater differences characteristic of species of the same genus. New and improved varieties will inevitably supplant and exterminate the older, less improved and intermediate varieties; and thus species are rendered to a large extent defined and distinct objects. Dominant species belonging to the larger groups tend to give birth to new and dominant forms; so that each large group tends to become still larger, and at the same time more divergent in character. But as all groups cannot thus succeed in increasing in size, for the world would not hold them, the more dominant groups beat the less dominant. This tendency in the large groups to go on increasing in size and diverging in character, together with the almost inevitable contingency of much extinction, explains the arrangement of all the forms of life, in groups subordinate to groups, all within a few great classes, which we now see everywhere around us, and which has prevailed throughout all time. This grand fact of the grouping of all organic beings seems to me utterly inexplicable on the theory of creation. . . .

.   .   .   .   .

The real affinities of all organic beings are due to inheritance or community of descent. The natural system [of classification] is a genealogical arrangement, in which we have to discover the lines of descent by the most permanent characters, however slight their vital importance may be.

The framework of bones being the same in the hand of a man, wing of a bat, fin of the porpoise, and leg of the horse,—the same number of vertebrae forming the neck of the giraffe and of the elephant,—and innumerable other such facts, at once explain themselves on the theory of descent with slow and slight successive modifications. The similarity of pattern in the wing and leg of a bat, though used for such different purpose,—in the jaws and legs of a crab,—in the petals, stamens, and pistils of a flower, is likewise intelligible on the view of the gradual modification of parts or organs, which were alike in the early progenitor of each class. On the principle of successive variations not always supervening at an early age, and being inherited at a corresponding not early period of life, we can clearly see why the embryos of mammals, birds, reptiles, and fishes should be so closely alike, and should be so unlike the adult forms. We may cease marvelling at the embryo of an air-breathing mammal or bird having branchial slits and arteries running in loops, like those in a fish which has to breathe the air dissolved in water, by the aid of well-developed branchiae.

Disuse, aided sometimes by natural selection, will often tend to reduce an organ, when it has become useless by changed habits or under changed conditions of life; and we can clearly understand on this view the meaning of rudimentary organs....

I see no good reason why the views given in this volume should shock the religious feelings of any one. A celebrated author and divine has written to me that "he has gradually learnt to see that it is just as noble a conception of the Deity to believe that He created a few original forms capable of self-development into other and needful forms, as to believe that He required a fresh act of creation to supply the voids caused by the action of His laws."

.   .   .   .   .

It may be asked how far I extend the doctrine of modification of species. The question is difficult to answer, because the more distinct the forms are which we may consider, by so much the arguments fall away in force. But some arguments of the greatest weight extend very far. All the members of whole classes can be connected together by chains of affinities, and all can be classified on the same principle, in groups subordinate to groups. Fossil remains sometimes tend to fill up very wide intervals between existing orders. Organs in a rudimentary condition plainly show that an early progenitor had the organ in a fully developed state; and this in some instances necessarily implies an enormous amount of modification in the descendants. Throughout whole classes various structures are formed on the same pattern, and at an embryonic age the species closely resemble each other. Therefore I cannot doubt that the theory of descent with modification embraces all the members of the same class. I believe that animals have descended from at most only four or five progenitors, and plants from an equal or lesser number.

Analogy would lead me one step further, namely, to the belief that all animals and plants have descended from some one prototype. But analogy may be a deceitful guide. Nevertheless all living things have much in common, in their chemical composition, their germinal vesicles, their cellular structure, and their laws of growth and reproduction. We see this even in so trifling a circumstance as that the same poison often similarly affects plants and animals; or that the poison secreted by the gall-fly produces monstrous growths on the wild rose or oak-tree. Therefore I should infer from analogy that probably all the organic beings which have ever lived on this earth have descended from some one primordial form, into which life was first breathed by the Creator....

.   .   .   .   .

It is interesting to contemplate an entangled bank, clothed with many plants of many kinds, with birds singing on the bushes, with various insects flitting about, and with worms crawling through the damp earth, and to reflect that these elaborately constructed forms, so different from each other, and dependent on each other in so complex a manner, have all been produced by laws acting around us. These laws, taken in the largest sense, being Growth with Reproduction; Inheritance, which is almost implied by reproduction; Variability, from the indirect and the direct action of the external conditions of life, and from use and disuse; a Ratio of Increase so high as to lead to a Struggle for Life, and as a consequence to Natural Selection, entailing Divergence of Character and the Extinction of less-improved forms. Thus, from the war of nature, from famine and death, the most exalted object which we are capable of conceiving, namely, the production of the higher animals, directly follows. There is grandeur in this view of life, with its several powers, having been originally breathed by the Creator into a few forms or into one; and that, whilst this planet has gone cycling on according to the fixed law of gravity, from so simple a beginning endless forms most beautiful and most wonderful have been, and are being, evolved.

10. William James

William James first read his address to the Philosophical Clubs of Yale and Brown Universities in 1896. He described it as "an essay in justification *of* faith, a defense of our right to adopt a believing attitude in religious matters, in spite of the fact that our merely logical intellect may not have been coerced." As examples of the type of thought to which he objects, James quotes Huxley: "My only consolation lies in the reflection that, however bad our posterity may become, so far as they hold by the plain rule of not pretending to believe what they have no reason to believe, because it may be to their advantage so to pretend, they will not have reached the lowest depth of immorality." James also quotes "that delicious *enfant terrible* Clifford": "It is wrong always, everywhere, and for every one, to believe anything upon insufficient evidence." James asserts that our belief in truth itself is because we want to have a truth and want to believe that our studies put us in a better position towards it, "and on this line we agree to fight out our thinking lives." This is not logic, says James, but one volition against another. "The thesis I defend is, briefly stated, this: Our passional nature not only lawfully may, but must, decide an option between propositions, whenever it is a genuine option that cannot by its nature be decided on intellectual grounds; for to say, under such circumstances, 'Do not decide, but leave the question open,' is itself a passional decision—just like deciding yes or no,—and is attended with the same risk of losing the truth." This selection is from the latter part of the essay, "The Will to Believe." William James, *The Will to Believe and Other Essays in Popular Philosophy* (New York: Longmans, Green & Co., Inc., 1896).

VII. One more point, small but important, and our preliminaries are done. There are two ways of looking at our duty in the matter of opinion,—ways entirely different, and yet ways about whose difference the theory of knowledge seems hitherto to have shown very little concern. *We must know the truth;* and *we must avoid error.* These are our first and great commandments as would be knowers; but they are not two ways

of stating an identical commandment, they are two separable laws. Although it may indeed happen that when we believe the truth A, we escape as an incidental consequence from believing the falsehood B, it hardly ever happens that by merely disbelieving B we necessarily believe A. We may in escaping B fall into believing other falsehoods, C or D, just as bad as B; or we may escape B by not believing anything at all, not even A.

Believe truth! Shun error! These, we see, are two materially different laws; and by choosing between them we may end by coloring differently our whole intellectual life. We may regard the chase for truth as paramount, and the avoidance of error as secondary; or we may, on the other hand, treat the avoidance of error as more imperative, and let truth take its chance. Clifford, in the instructive passage which I have quoted, exhorts us to the latter course. Believe nothing, he tells us, keep your mind in suspense forever, rather than by closing it on insufficient evidence incur the awful risk of believing lies. You, on the other hand, may think that the risk of being in error is a very small matter when compared with the blessings of real knowledge, and be ready to be duped many times in your investigation rather than postpone indefinitely the chance of guessing true. I myself find it impossible to go with Clifford. We must remember that these feelings of our duty about either truth or error are in any case only expressions of our passional life. Biologically considered, our minds are as ready to grind out falsehood as veracity, and he who says, "Better go without belief forever than believe a lie!" merely shows his own preponderant private horror of becoming a dupe. He may be critical of many of his desires and fears, but this fear he slavishly obeys. He cannot imagine any one questioning its binding force. For my own part, I have also a horror of being duped; but I can believe that worse things than being duped may happen to a man in this world: so Clifford's exhortation has to my ears a thoroughly fantastic sound. It is like a general informing his soldiers that it is better to keep out of battle forever than to risk a single wound. Not so are victories either over enemies or over nature gained. Our errors are surely not such awfully solemn things. In a world where we are so certain to incur them in spite of all our caution, a certain lightness of heart seems healthier than this excessive nervousness on their behalf. At any rate, it seems the fittest thing for the empiricist philosopher.

VIII. And now, after all this introduction, let us go straight at our question. I have said, and now repeat it, that not only as a matter of fact do we find our passional nature influencing us in our opinions, but that there are some options between opinions in which this influence must be regarded both as an inevitable and as a lawful determinant of our choice.

I fear here that some of you my hearers will begin to scent danger, and lend an inhospitable ear. Two first steps of passion you have indeed had to admit as necessary,—we must think so as to avoid dupery, and we must think so as to gain truth; but the surest path to those ideal consummations, you will probably consider, is from now onwards to take no further passional step.

Well, of course, I agree as far as the facts will allow. Whenever the option between losing truth and gaining it is not momentous, we can throw the chance of *gaining truth* away, and at any rate save ourselves from any chance of *believing falsehood*, by not making up our minds at all till objective evidence has come. In scientific questions, this is almost always the case; and even in human affairs in general, the need of acting is seldom so urgent that a false belief to act on is better than no belief at all. Law courts, indeed, have to decide on the best evidence attainable for the moment, because a judge's duty is to make law as well as to ascertain it, and (as a learned judge once said to me) few cases are worth spending much time over: the great thing is to have them decided on *any* acceptable principle, and got out of the way. But in our dealings with objective nature we obviously are recorders, not makers, of the truth; and decisions for the mere sake of deciding promptly and getting on to the next business would be wholly out of place. Throughout the breadth of physical nature facts are what they are quite independently of us, and seldom is there any

such hurry about them that the risks of being duped by believing a premature theory need be faced. The questions here are always trivial options, the hypotheses are hardly living (at any rate not living for us spectators), the choice between believing truth or falsehood is seldom forced. The attitude of sceptical balance is therefore the absolutely wise one if we would escape mistakes. What difference, indeed, does it make to most of us whether we have or have not a theory of the Roentgen rays, whether we believe or not in mind-stuff, or have a conviction about the causality of conscious states? It makes no difference. Such options are not forced on us. On every account it is better not to make them, but still keep weighing reasons *pro et contra* with an indifferent hand.

... On the other hand, if you want an absolute duffer in an investigation, you must, after all, take the man who has no interest whatever in its results: he is the warranted incapable, the positive fool. The most useful investigator, because the most sensitive observer, is always he whose eager interest in one side of the question is balanced by an equally keen nervousness lest he become deceived. Science has organized this nervousness into a regular *technique,* her so-called method of verification; and she has fallen so deeply in love with the method that one may even say she has ceased to care for truth by itself at all. It is only truth as technically verified that interests her....

The question next arises: Are there not somewhere forced options in our speculative questions, and can we (as men who may be interested at least as much in positively gaining truth as in merely escaping dupery) always wait with impunity till the coercive evidence shall have arrived? It seems *a priori* improbable that the truth should be so nicely adjusted to our needs and powers as that. In the great boarding-house of nature, the cakes and butter and the syrup seldom come out so even and leave the plates so clean. Indeed, we should view them with scientific suspicion if they did.

IX. *Moral questions* immediately present themselves as questions whose solution cannot wait for sensible proof. A moral question is a question not of what sensibly exists, but of what is good, or would be good if it did exist. Science can tell us what exists; but to compare the *worths*, both of what exists and of what does not exist, we must consult not science, but what Pascal calls our heart. Science herself consults her heart when she lays it down that the infinite ascertainment of fact and correction of false belief are the supreme goods for man. Challenge the statement, and science can only repeat it oracularly, or else prove it by showing that such ascertainment and correction bring man all sorts of other goods which man's heart in turn declares. The question of having moral beliefs at all or not having them is decided by our will. Are our moral preferences true or false, or are they only odd biological phenomena, making things good or bad for *us*, but in themselves indifferent? How can your pure intellect decide? If your heart does not *want* a world of moral reality, your head will assuredly never make you believe in one. Mephistophelian scepticism, indeed, will satisfy the head's play-instincts much better than any rigorous idealism can. Some men (even at the student age) are so naturally cool-hearted that the moralistic hypothesis never has for them any pungent life, and in their supercilious presence the hot young moralist always feels strangely ill at ease. The appearance of knowingness is on their side, of *naïveté* and gullibility on his. Yet, in the inarticulate heart of him, he clings to it that he is not a dupe, and that there is a realm in which (as Emerson says) all their wit and intellectual superiority is no better than the cunning of a fox. Moral scepticism can no more be refuted or proved by logic than intellectual scepticism can. When we stick to it that there *is* truth (be it of either kind), we do so with our whole nature, and resolve to stand or fall by the results. The sceptic with his whole nature adopts the doubting attitude; but which of us is the wiser, Omniscience only knows.

Turn now from these wide questions of good to a certain class of questions of fact, questions concerning personal relations, states of mind between one man and another. *Do you like me or not?*—for example. Whether you do or not depends, in countless instances, on whether I meet you half-way, am willing to assume that you must like me, and show you trust and expectation. The previous faith on my part in your liking's existence is in such cases what makes your liking come. But if I stand aloof, and refuse to budge an inch until I have objective evidence, until you shall have done something apt, as the absolutists say, *ad extorquendum assensum meum,* ten to one your liking never comes. How many women's hearts are vanquished by the mere sanguine insistence of some man that they *must* love him! He will not consent to the hypothesis that they cannot. The desire for a certain kind of truth here brings about that special truth's existence; and so it is in innumerable cases of other sorts. Who gains promotions, boons, appointments, but the man in whose life they are seen to play the part of live hypotheses, who discounts them, sacrifices other things for their sake before they have come, and takes risks for them in advance? His faith acts on the powers above him as a claim, and creates its own verification.

A social organism of any sort whatever, large or small, is what it is because each member proceeds to his own duty with a trust that the other members will simultaneously do theirs. Wherever a desired result is achieved by the co-operation of many independent persons, its existence as a fact is a pure consequence of the precursive faith in one another of those immediately concerned. A government, an army, a commercial system, a ship, a college, an athletic team, all exist on this condition, without which not only is nothing achieved, but nothing is even attempted. . . . There are, then, cases where a fact cannot come at all unless a preliminary faith exists in its coming. *And where faith in a fact can help create the fact,* that would be an insane logic which should say that faith running ahead of scientific evidence is the "lowest kind of immorality" into which a thinking being can fall. Yet such is the logic by which our scientific absolutists pretend to regulate our lives!

X. In truths dependent on our personal action, then, faith based on desire is certainly a lawful and possibly an indispensable thing.

But now, it will be said, these are all childish human cases, and have nothing to do with great cosmical matters, like the question of religious faith. Let us then pass on to that. Religions differ so much in their accidents that in discussing the religious question we must make it very generic and broad. What then do we now mean by the religious hypothesis? Science says things are; morality says some things are better than other things; and religion says essentially two things.

First, she says that the best things are the more eternal things, the overlapping things, the things in the universe that throw the last stone, so to speak, and say the final word. "Perfection is eternal,"—this phrase of Charles Secrétan seems a good way of putting this first affirmation of religion, an affirmation which obviously cannot yet be verified scientifically at all.

The second affirmation of religion is that we are better off even now if we believe her first affirmation to be true.

Now, let us consider what the logical elements of this situation are *in case the religious hypothesis in both its branches be really true.* (Of course, we must admit that possibility at the outset. If we are to discuss the question at all, it must involve a living option. If for any of you religion be a hypothesis that cannot, by any living possibility be true, then you need go no further. I speak to the "saving remnant" alone.) So proceeding, we see, first, that religion offers itself as a *momentous* option. We are supposed to gain, even now, by our belief, and to lose by our non-belief, a certain vital good. Secondly, religion is a *forced* option, so far as that good goes. We cannot escape the issue by remaining sceptical and waiting for more light, because, although we do avoid error in that way *if religion be untrue*, we lose the good, *if it be true*, just as certainly as if we positively chose to disbelieve. It is as if a man should hesitate indefinitely to ask a certain woman to marry him because he was not perfectly sure that she would prove an angel after he brought her home. Would he not cut himself off from that particular angel-possibility as decisively as if he went and married some one else? Scepticism, then, is not avoidance of option; it is option of a certain particular kind of risk. *Better risk loss of truth than chance of error,*—that is your faith-vetoer's exact position. He is actively playing his stake as much as the believer is; he is backing the field against the religious hypothesis, just as the believer is backing the religious hypothesis against the field. To preach scepticism to us as a duty until "sufficient evidence" for religion be found, is tantamount therefore to telling us, when in presence of the religious hypothesis, that to yield to our fear of its being error is wiser and better than to yield to our hope that it may be true. It is not intellect against all passions, then; it is only intellect with one passion laying down its law. And by what, forsooth, is the supreme wisdom of this passion warranted? Dupery for dupery, what proof is there that dupery through hope is so much worse than dupery through fear? I, for one, can see no proof; and I simply refuse obedience to the scientist's command to imitate his kind of option, in a case where my own stake is important enough to give me the right to choose my own form of risk. . . .

. . . Now, to most of us religion comes in a still further way that makes a veto on our active faith even more illogical. The more perfect and more eternal aspect of the universe is represented in our religions as having personal form. The universe is no longer a mere *It* to us, but a *Thou*, if we are religious; and any relation that may be possible from person to person might be possible here. For instance, although in one sense we are passive portions of the universe, in another we show a curious autonomy, as if we were small active centres on our own account. We feel, too, as if the appeal of religion to us were made to our own active good-will, as if evidence might be forever withheld from us unless we met the hypothesis half-way. To take a trivial illustration: just as a man who in a company of gentlemen made no advances, asked a warrant for every concession, and believed no one's word without proof, would cut himself off by such churlishness from all the social rewards that a more trusting spirit would earn,—so here, one who should shut himself up in snarling logicality and try to make the gods extort his recognition willy-nilly, or not get it at all, might cut himself off forever from his only opportunity of making the gods' acquaintance. This feeling, forced on us we know not whence, that by obstinately believing that there are gods (although not to do so would be so easy both for our logic and our life) we are doing the universe the deepest service we can, seems part of the living essence of the religious hypothesis. If the hypothesis *were* true in all its parts, including this one, then pure intellectualism, with its veto on our making willing advances, would be an absurdity; and some participation of our sympathetic nature would be logically required. I, therefore, for one, cannot see my way to accepting the agnostic rules for truth-seeking, or wilfully agree to keep my willing nature out of the game. I cannot do so for this plain reason, that *a rule of thinking which would absolutely prevent me from acknowledging certain kinds of truth if those kinds of truth were really there, would be an irrational rule.* That for me is the long and short of the formal logic of the situation, no matter what the kinds of truth might materially be.

. . . When I look at the religious question as it really puts itself to concrete men, and when I think of all the possibilities which both practically and theoretically it involves, then this command that we shall put a stopper on our heart, instincts, and courage, and *wait*—acting of course meanwhile more or less as if religion were *not* true—till doomsday, or till such time as our intellect and senses working together may have raked evidence enough,—this command, I say, seems to me the queerest idol ever manufactured in the philosophic cave. . . . Indeed we *may* wait if we will,—I hope you do not think that I am denying that,—but if we do so, we do so at our peril as much as if we believed. In either case we *act,* taking our life in our hands. No one of us ought to issue vetoes to the other, nor should we bandy words of abuse. We ought on the contrary, delicately and profoundly to respect one another's mental freedom: then only shall we bring about the intellectual republic; then only shall we have that spirit of inner tolerance without which all our outer tolerance is soulless, and which is empiricism's glory; then only shall

we live and let live, in speculative as well as in practical things.

I began by a reference to Fitz James Stephen; let me end by a quotation from him. "What do you think of yourself? . . . If a man chooses to turn his back altogether on God and the future, no one can prevent him; no one can show beyond reasonable doubt that he is mistaken. If a man thinks otherwise and acts as he thinks, I do not see that any one can prove that *he* is mistaken. Each must act as he thinks best; and if he is wrong, so much the worse for him. We stand on a mountain pass in the midst of whirling snow and blinding mist, through which we get glimpses now and then of paths which may be deceptive. If we stand still we shall be frozen to death. If we take the wrong road we shall be dashed to pieces. We do not certainly know whether there is any right one. What must we do? 'Be strong and of a good courage.' Act for the best, hope for the best, and take what comes. . . . If death ends all, we cannot meet death better" [*Liberty, Equality, Fraternity,* 2nd ed. London, 1874].

11. Charles Gore

"The Holy Spirit and Inspiration," by Charles Gore, was one of the most significant essays in *Lux Mundi,* a volume of essays attempting to reconcile Christian doctrines with the results of historical and scientific research. Gore first dealt with the Holy Spirit as the giver of life in nature, in man, and in the church, and then he examined the work of the Holy Spirit in relation to the controversial subject of biblical inspiration. In the preface, he defined development of theology as the process "in which the Church, standing firm in her old truths, enters into the apprehension of the new social and intellectual movements of each age." His essay exemplifies this statement. *Lux Mundi,* 3rd ed., ed. Charles Gore (London: John Murray, 1890).

5. But here certain important questions arise. (a) The revelation of God was made in a historical process. Its record is in large part the record of a national life: it is historical. Now the inspiration of the recorder lies, as we have seen, primarily in this, that he sees the hand of God in the history and interprets His purpose. Further, we must add, his sense of the working of God in history, increases his realization of the importance of historical fact. Thus there is a

profound air of historical truthfulness pervading the Old Testament record from Abraham downward. The weaknesses, the sins, of Israel's heroes are not spared. Their sin and its punishment is always before us. There is no flattering of national pride, no giving the reins to boastfulness. In all this the Old Testament appears to be in marked contrast, as to contemporary Assyrian monuments, so also to a good deal of much later ecclesiastical history. But does the inspiration of the recorder guarantee the exact historical truth of what he records? And in matter of fact can the record, with due regard to legitimate historical criticism, be pronounced true? Now, to the latter of these two questions (and they are quite distinct questions), we may reply that there is nothing to prevent our believing, as our faith certainly strongly disposes us to believe, that the record from Abraham downward is in substance in the strict sense historical. . . . Internal evidence again certainly commends to our acceptance the history of the patriarchs, of the Egyptian bondage, of the great redemption, of the wanderings, as well as of the later period as to which there would be less dispute. In a word we are, we believe, not wrong in anticipating that the Church will continue to believe and to teach that the Old Testament from Abraham downwards is really historical, and that there will be nothing to make such belief and teaching unreasonable or wilful. But within the limits of what is substantially historical, there is still room for an admixture of what, though marked by spiritual purpose, is yet not strictly historical—for instance, for a feature which characterizes all early history, the attribution to first founders of what is really the remoter result of their institutions. Now historical criticism assures us that this process has been largely at work in the Pentateuch. By an analysis, for instance, the force of which is very great, it distinguishes distinct stages in the growth of the law of worship: at least an early stage such as is represented in "the Book of the Covenant," a second stage in the Book of Deuteronomy, a last stage in "the Priestly Code." What we may suppose to have happened is that Moses himself established a certain germ of ceremonial enactment in connection with the ark and its sacred tent, and with the "ten words"; and that this developed always as "the law of Moses," the whole result being constantly attributed, probably unconsciously and certainly not from any intention to deceive, to the original founder. This view would certainly imply that the recorders of Israel's history were subject to the ordinary laws in the estimate of evidence, that their inspiration did not consist in a miraculous communication to them of facts as they originally happened: but if we believe that the law, as it grew, really did represent the Divine intention for the Jews, gradually worked out upon the basis of a Mosaic institution, there is nothing materially untruthful, though there is something uncritical, in attributing the whole legislation to Moses acting under the Divine command. It would be only of a piece with the attribution of the collection of Psalms to David and of Proverbs to Solomon. Nor does the supposition that the law was of gradual growth interfere in any way with the symbolical and typical value of its various ordinances.

Once again, the same school of criticism would assure us that the Books of Chronicles represent a later and less historical version of Israel's history than that given in Samuel and Kings: they represent, according to this view, the version of that history which had become current in the priestly schools. What we are asked to admit is not conscious perversion, but unconscious idealizing of history, the reading back into past records of a ritual development which was really later. Now inspiration excludes conscious deception or pious fraud, but it appears to be quite consistent with this sort of idealizing; always supposing that the result read back into the earlier history does represent the real purpose of God and only anticipates its realization.

Here then is one great question. Inspiration certainly means the illumination of the judgment of the recorder. "By the contact of the Holy Spirit," says Origen, "they became clearer in their mental perceptions, and their souls were filled with a brighter light." But have we any reason to believe that it means, over and above this, the miraculous communication of facts not otherwise to be known, a miraculous communication such as would make the recorder independent of the ordinary processes of historical tradition? Certainly neither St. Luke's preface to his Gospel, nor the evidence of any inspired record, justifies us in this assumption. Nor would it appear that spiritual illumination, even in the highest degree has any tendency to lift men out of the natural conditions of knowledge which belong to their time. Certainly in the similar case of exegesis, it would appear that St. Paul is left to the method of his time, though he uses it with inspired insight into the function and meaning of law and of prophecy as a whole. Thus, without pronouncing an opinion, where we have no right to do so, on the critical questions at present under discussion, we may maintain with considerable assurance that there is nothing in the doctrine of inspiration to prevent our recognising a considerable idealizing element in the Old Testament history. The reason is of course obvious enough why what can be admitted in the Old Testament, could not without results disastrous to the Christian Creed, be admitted in the New. It is because the Old Testament is the record of how God produced a need, or anticipation, or ideal, while the New Testament records how in fact He satisfied it. The absolute coincidence of idea and fact is vital in the realization, not in the preparation for it. It is equally obvious, too, that where fact is of supreme importance, as in the New Testament, the evidence has none of the ambiguity or remoteness which belongs to much of the record of the preparation.

But once again; we find all sorts of literature in the inspired volume: men can be inspired to think and to write for God under all the forms of natural genius. Now one form of genius is the dramatic: its essence is to make characters, real or imaginary, the vehicles for an ideal presentation. It presents embodied ideas. Now the Song of Solomon is of the nature of a drama. The Book of Job, although it works on an historical basis, is, it can hardly be denied, mainly dramatic. The Book of Wisdom, which with us is among the books of the Bible, though in the second rank outside the canon, and which is inside the canon of the Roman Church, professes to be written by Solomon, but is certainly written not by him, but in his person by another author. We may then conceive the same to be true of Ecclesiastes, and of Deuteronomy; i.e. we may suppose Deuteronomy to be a republication of the law "in the spirit and power" of Moses put dramatically into his mouth. Criticism goes further, and asks us to regard Jonah and Daniel, among the prophetic books, as dramatic compositions worked up on a basis of history. The discussion of these books has often been approached from a point of view from which the miraculous is necessarily unhistorical. With such a point of view we are not concerned. The possibility and reality of miracles has to be vindicated first of all in the field of the New Testament; and one who admits them there, cannot reasonably exclude their possibility in the earlier history. The question must be treated simply on literary and evidential grounds. But we would contend that if criticism should shew these books to be probably dramatic, that would be no hindrance to their performing "an important canonical function," or to their being inspired. Dramatic composition has played an immense part in training the human mind. It is as far removed as possible from a violation of truth, though in an uncritical age its results may very soon pass for history. . . .

Once again: an enlarged study of comparative history has led to our perceiving that the various sorts of mental or literary activity develop in their different lines out of an earlier condition in which they lie fused and undifferentiated. This we can vaguely call the mythical stage of mental evolution. A myth is not a falsehood; it is a product of mental activity, as instructive and rich as any later product, but its characteristic is that it is not yet distinguished into history, and poetry, and philosophy. It is all of these in the germ, as dream and imagination, and thought and experience, are fused in the mental furniture of a child's mind. "These myths or current stories," says Grote writing of Greek history, "the spontaneous and earliest growth of the Greek mind, constituted at the same time the entire intellectual stock of the age to which they belonged. They are the common root of all those different ramifications into which the mental activity of the Greeks subsequently diverged; containing as it were the preface and germ of the positive history and philosophy, the dogmatic theology and the professed romance, which we shall hereafter trace, each in its separate development." Now has the Jewish history such earlier stage: does it pass back out of history into myth? In particular, are not its earlier narratives, before the call of Abraham, of the nature of myth, in which we cannot distinguish the historical germ, though we do not at all deny that it exists? The inspiration of these narratives is as conspicuous as that of any part of Scripture, but is there anything to prevent our regarding these great inspirations about the origin of all things,—the nature of sin, the judgment of God on sin, and the alienation among men which follows their alienation from God,— as conveyed to us in that form of myth or allegorical picture, which is the earliest mode in which the mind of man apprehended truth?

6. The present writer, believing that the modern development of historical criticism is reaching results as sure, where it is fairly used, as scientific inquiry, and feeling therefore that the warning which the name of Galileo must ever bring before the memory of churchmen, is not unneeded now, believes also that the Church is in no way restrained from admitting the modifications just hinted at, in what has latterly been the current idea of inspiration.

The Church is not restrained, in the first place, by having committed herself to any dogmatic definitions of the meaning of inspiration. It is remarkable indeed that Origen's almost reckless mysticism, and his accompanying repudiation of the historical character of large parts of the narrative of the Old Testament, and some parts of the New, though it did not gain acceptance, and indeed had no right to it (for it had no sound basis), on the other hand never roused the Church to contrary definitions. Nor is it only Origen who disputed the historical character of parts of the narrative of Holy Scripture. Clement before him in Alexandria, and

the mediaeval Anselm in the West, treat the seven days' creation as allegory and not history.... In a different line, Chrysostom, of the literal school of interpreters, explains quite in the tone of a modern apologist, how the discrepancies in detail between the different Gospels, assure us of the independence of the witnesses, and do not touch the facts of importance, in which all agree.

The Church is not tied then by any existing definitions. We cannot make any exact claim upon any one's belief in regard to inspiration, simply because we have no authoritative definition to bring to bear upon him. Those of us who believe most in the inspiration of the Church, will see a Divine Providence in this absence of dogma, because we shall perceive that only now is the state of knowledge such as admits of the question being legitimately raised.

Nor does it seem that the use which our Lord made of the Old Testament is an argument against the proposed concessions. Our Lord, in His use of the Old Testament, does indeed endorse with the utmost emphasis the Jewish view of their own history. He does thus imply, on the one hand, the real inspiration of their canon in its completeness, and, on the other hand, that He Himself was the goal of that inspired leading and the standard of that inspiration. "Your father Abraham rejoiced to see My day": "I am not come to destroy, but to fulfil." This, and it is the important matter for all that concerns our spiritual education, is not in dispute. What is questioned is that our Lord's words foreclose certain critical positions as to the character of Old Testament literature. For example, does His use of Jonah's resurrection, as a *type* of His own, depend in any real degree upon whether it is historical fact or allegory? It is of the essence of a type to *suggest* an idea, as of the antitype to *realize* it. The narrative of Jonah suggested certainly the idea of resurrection after three days, of triumph over death, and by suggesting this gave our Lord what His discourse required. Once more, our Lord uses the time before the flood to illustrate the carelessness of men before His own coming. He is using the flood here as a typical judgment, as elsewhere He uses other contemporary visitations for a like purpose. In referring to the flood He certainly suggests that He is treating it as typical, for He introduces circumstances—"eating and drinking, marrying and giving in marriage"—which have no counterpart in the original narrative. Nothing in His use of it depends on its being more than a typical instance. Once more, He argues with the Pharisees on the assumption of the Davidic authorship of Psalm 110. But the point of His argument is directed to convincing the Pharisees that they did not understand their own teaching, that they were not true to their own premises. It is surely pressing His words unduly to represent them as positive teaching on a literary point, just as it would be pressing His conclusion unduly to make Him maintain that the relation of sonship to David was inconsistent with lordship over him: or, as in another place, it is monstrous to urge that "Why callest thou Me good? there is none good but God" is a general repudiation of the claim to goodness. To argue "ad hominem," to reason with men on their premises, was, in fact, a part of our Lord's method. ... The Incarnation was a self-emptying of God to reveal Himself under conditions of human nature and from the human point of view. We are able to draw a distinction between what He revealed and what He used. He revealed God, His mind, His character, His claim, within certain limits His Threefold Being: He revealed man, his sinfulness, his need, his capacity: He revealed His purpose of redemption, and founded His Church as a home in which man was to be through all the ages reconciled to God in knowledge and love. All this He revealed, but through, and under conditions of, a true human nature. Thus He *used* human nature, its relation to God, its conditions of experience, its growth in knowledge, its limitation of knowledge. He feels as we men ought to feel: he sees as we ought to see. We can thus distinguish more or less between the Divine truth which He revals, and the human nature which He uses. Now when He speaks of the "sun rising" He is using ordinary human knowledge. He shews no signs at all of transcending the science of His age. Equally He shews no signs of transcending the history of His age. He does not reveal His eternity by statements as to what had happened in the past, or was to happen in the future, outside the ken of existing history. His true Godhead is shewn in His attitude towards men and things about Him, in His moral and spiritual claims, in His expressed relation to God, not in any miraculous exemptions of Himself from the conditions of natural knowledge in its own proper province. Thus the utterances of Christ about the Old Testament do not seem to be nearly definite or clear enough to allow of our supposing that in this case He is departing from the general method of the Incarnation, by bringing to bear the unveiled omniscience of the Godhead, to anticipate or foreclose a development of natural knowledge....

12. Mary Baker Eddy and Christian Science

Excerpts from Mary Baker Eddy's *Retrospection and Introspection* (Boston, 1891) and *Science and Health with a Key to the Scriptures* (Boston, 1906).

THE GREAT DISCOVERY

It was in Massachusetts, in February, 1866, and after the death of the magnetic doctor, Mr. P. P. Quimby, whom spiritualists would associate therewith, but who was in no wise connected with this event, that I discovered the Science of divine metaphysical healing which I afterwards named Christian Science. The discovery came to pass in this way. During twenty years prior to my discovery I had been trying to trace all physical effects to a mental cause; and in the latter part of 1866 I gained the scientific certainty that all causation was Mind, and every effect a mental phenomenon.

My immediate recovery from the effects of an injury caused by an accident, an injury that neither medicine nor surgery could reach, was the falling apple that led me to the discovery how to be well myself, and how to make others so.

Even to the homoeopathic physician who attended me, and rejoiced in my recovery, I could not then explain the *modus* of my relief. I could only assure him that the divine Spirit had wrought the miracle—a miracle which later I found to be in perfect scientific accord with divine law.

I then withdrew from society about three years,—to ponder my mission, to search the Scriptures, to find the Science of Mind that should take the things of God and show them to the creature, and reveal the great curative Principle,—Deity.

The Bible was my textbook. It answered my questions as to how I was healed; but the Scriptures had to me a new meaning, a new tongue. Their spiritual signification appeared; and I apprehended for the first time, in their spiritual meaning, Jesus' teaching and demonstration, and the Principle and rule of spiritual Science and metaphysical healing,—in a word, Christian Science.

I named it *Christian*, because it is compassionate, helpful, and spiritual. God I called *immortal Mind*. That which sins, suffers, and dies, I named *mortal mind*. The physical senses, or sensuous nature, I called *error* and *shadow*. Soul I denominated *substance*, because Soul alone is truly substantial. God I characterized as individual entity, but His corporeality I denied. The real I claimed as eternal; and its antipodes, or the temporal, I described as unreal. Spirit I called the *reality*; and matter, the *unreality*.

I knew the human conception of God to be that He was a physically personal being, like unto man; and that the five physical senses are so many witnesses to the physical personality of mind and the real existence of matter; but I learned that these material senses testify falsely, that matter neither sees, hears, nor feels Spirit, and is therefore inadequate to form any proper conception of the infinite Mind. "If I bear witness of myself, my witness is not true." (John 5:31.)

I beheld with ineffable awe our great Master's purpose in not questioning those he healed as to their disease or its symptoms, and his marvellous skill in demanding neither obedience to hygienic laws, nor prescribing drugs to support the divine power which heals. Adoringly I discerned the Principle of his holy heroism and Christian example on the cross, when he refused to drink the "vinegar and gall," a preparation of poppy, or aconite, to allay the tortures of crucifixion.

Our great Way-shower, steadfast to the end in his obedience to God's laws, demonstrated for all time and peoples the supremacy of good over evil, and the superiority of Spirit over matter.

The miracles recorded in the Bible, which had before seemed to me supernatural, grew divinely natural and apprehensible; though uninspired interpreters ignorantly pronounce Christ's healing miraculous, instead of seeing therein the operation of the divine law.

Jesus of Nazareth was a natural and divine Scientist. He was so before the material world saw him. He who antedated Abraham, and gave the world a new date in the Christian era, was a Christian Scientist, who needed no discovery of the Science of being in order to rebuke the evidence. To one "born of the flesh," however, divine Science must be a discovery. Woman must give it birth. It must be begotten of spirituality, since none but the pure in heart can see God,—the Principle of all things pure; and none but the poor in spirit could first state this Principle, could know yet more of the nothingness of matter and the allness of Spirit, could utilize Truth, and absolutely reduce the demonstration of being, in Science, to the apprehension of the age.

I wrote also, at this period, comments on the Scriptures, setting forth their spiritual interpretation, the Science of the Bible, and so laid the foundation of my work called Science and Health, published in 1875.

If these notes and comments, which have never been read by any one but myself, were published, it would show that after my discovery of the absolute Science of Mind-healing, like all great truths, this spiritual Science developed itself to me until Science and Health was written. These early comments are valuable to me as waymarks of progress, which I would not have effaced.

.   .   .   .   .

The starting-point of divine Science is that God, Spirit, is All-in-all, and that there is no other might nor Mind,—that God is Love, and therefore He is divine Principle.

To grasp the reality and order of being in its Science, you must begin by reckoning God as the divine Principle of all that really is. Spirit, Life, Truth, Love, combine as one,—and are the Scriptural names for God. All substance, intelligence, wisdom, being, immortality, cause, and effect belong to God. These are His attributes, the eternal manifestations of the infinite divine Principle, Love. No wisdom is wise but His wisdom; no truth is true, no love is lovely, no life is Life but the divine; no good is, but the good God bestows.

Divine metaphysics, as revealed to spiritual understanding, shows clearly that all is Mind, and that Mind is God, omnipotence, omnipresence, omniscience,—that is, all power, all presence, all Science. Hence all is in reality the manifestation of Mind.

Our material human theories are destitute of Science. The true understanding of God is spiritual. It robs the grave of victory. It destroys the false evidence that misleads thought and points to other gods, or other so-called powers, such as matter, disease, sin, and death, superior or contrary to the one Spirit.

Truth, spiritually discerned, is scientifically understood. It casts out error and heals the sick.

.   .   .   .   .

When apparently near the confines of mortal existence, standing already within the shadow of the death-valley, I learned these truths in divine Science: that all real being is in God, the divine Mind, and that Life, Truth, and Love are all-powerful and ever-present; that the opposite of Truth,—called error, sin, sickness, disease, death,—is the false testimony of false material sense, of mind in matter; that this false sense evolves, in belief, a subjective state of mortal mind which this same so-called mind names *matter*, thereby shutting out the true sense of Spirit.

My discovery, that erring, mortal, misnamed *mind* produces all the organism and action of the mortal body, set my thoughts to work in new channels, and led up to my demonstration of the proposition that Mind is All and matter is naught as the leading factor in Mind-science.

Christian Science reveals incontrovertibly that Mind is All-in-all, that the only realities are the divine Mind and idea. This great fact is not, however, seen to be supported by sensible evidence, until its divine Principle is demonstrated by healing the sick and thus proved absolute and divine. This proof once seen, no other conclusion can be reached.

.   .   .   .   .

The three great verities of Spirit, omnipotence, omnipresence, omniscience,—Spirit possessing all power, filling all space, constituting all Science,—contradict forever the belief that matter can be actual. These eternal verities reveal primeval existence as the radiant reality of God's creation, in which all that He has made is pronounced by His wisdom good.

Thus it was that I beheld, as never before, the awful unreality called evil. The equipollence of God brought to light another glorious proposition,—man's perfectibility and the establishment of the kingdom of heaven on earth.

In the following these leadings of scientific revelation, the Bible was my only textbook. The Scriptures were illumined; reason and revelation were reconciled, and afterwards the truth of Christian Science was demonstrated. No human pen nor tongue taught me the Science contained in this book, *Science and Health;* and neither tongue nor pen can overthrow it. This book may be distorted by shallow criticism or by careless or malicious students, and its ideas may be temporarily abused and misrepresented; but the Science and truth therein will forever remain to be discerned and demonstrated.

.   .   .   .   .

Question.—Is there no sin?

Answer.—All reality is in God and His creation, harmonious and eternal. That which He creates is good, and He makes all that is made. Therefore the only reality of sin, sickness, or death is the awful fact that unrealities seem real to human, erring belief, until God strips off their disguise. They are not true, because they are not of God. We learn in Christian Science that all inharmony of mortal mind or body is illusion, possessing neither reality nor identity though seeming to be real and identical.

The Science of Mind disposes of all evil. Truth, God, is not the father of error. Sin,

457

sickness, and death are to be classified as effects of error. Christ came to destroy the belief of sin. The God-principle is omnipresent and omnipotent. God is everywhere, and nothing apart from Him is present or has power. Christ is the ideal Truth, that comes to heal sickness and sin through Christian Science, and attributes all power to God. Jesus is the name of the man who, more than all other men, has presented Christ, the true idea of God, healing the sick and the sinning and destroying the power of death. Jesus is the human man, and Christ is the divine idea; hence the duality of Jesus the Christ. . . .

SUGGESTED READINGS

Barzun, Jacques, *Darwin, Marx, Wagner.* Boston: Little, Brown & Co., 1941.

Begbie, Harold, *The Life of General William Booth.* New York: The Macmillan Co., 1920.

Binyon, Gilbert C., *The Christian Socialist Movement in England.* London: S.P.C.K., 1931.

Briggs, C. A., *General Introduction to the Study of Holy Scripture.* New York: Charles Scribner's Sons, 1900.

Brilioth, Y. T., *The Anglican Revival.* New York: Longmans, Green & Co., 1925.

Campbell, James M., *What Christian Science Means and What We Can Learn From It.* Nashville: Abingdon Press, 1920.

Carpenter, S. C., *Church and People, 1789-1889.* London: S.P.C.K., 1933.

Clark, H. W., *History of English Nonconformity.* London: Chapman & Hall, Ltd., 1913.

Curtis, R. K., *They Called Him Mister Moody.* New York: Doubleday & Company, Inc., 1962.

Dakin, E. F., *Mrs. Eddy.* New York: Charles Scribner's Sons, 1929.

Darwin, Charles, *Charles Darwin's Autobiography.* New York: Henry Schuman, Inc., Publishers, 1950.

———, *Descent of Man.* New York: Appleton-Century-Crofts, Inc., 1871.

Elliott-Binns, L. E., *Essays and Reviews.* London: 1860, 1861.

———, *Religion in the Victorian Era.* London: Lutterworth Press, 1936.

Fiske, John, *Outlines of Cosmic Philosophy.* Boston: Houghton Mifflin Company, 1874.

———, *Through Nature to God.* Boston: Houghton Mifflin Company, 1899.

Fosdick, Harry Emerson, *Modern Use of the Bible.* New York: The Macmillan Co., 1925.

Gladden, Washington, *Christianity and Socialism.* Cincinnati: Jennings & Graham, 1905.

———, *Social Salvation.* Boston: Houghton Mifflin Company, 1902.

Glover, W. B., *Evangelical Nonconformists and Higher Criticism in the Nineteenth Century.* London: Independent Press, Ltd., 1954.

Grant, R. M., *The Bible in the Church: A Short History of Interpretation.* New York: The Macmillan Co., 1948.

Gunkel, Hermann, *What Remains of the Old Testament.* New York: The Macmillan Co., 1928.

Hall, T. C., *The Social Meaning of Modern Religious Movements in England.* New York: Charles Scribner's Sons, 1900.

Hopkins, Charles H., *The Rise of the Social Gospel in American Protestantism, 1865-1915.* New Haven: Yale University Press, 1940.

Irvine, William, *Apes, Angels, and Victorians.* New York: McGraw-Hill Book Co., Inc., 1955.

John, DeWitt, *The Christian Science Way of Life.* Englewood Cliffs, N.J.: Prentice-Hall, Inc., 1962.

Lotz, Philip, *Founders of Christian Movements.* New York: Association Press, 1941.

Mathieson, W. L., *English Church Reform, 1815-40.* London: Longmans, Green & Co., 1923.

Milmine, Georgine, *Life of Mary Baker Eddy.* London: Hodder & Stoughton, 1909.

Peel, Robert, *Christian Science.* New York: Holt, Rinehart & Winston, Inc., 1958.

Rauschenbusch, Walter, *A Theology for the Social Gospel.* New York: The Macmillan Company, 1917.

———, *Christianizing the Social Order.* New York: The Macmillan Company, 1912.

———, *Prayers of the Social Awakening.* Boston: Pilgrim Press, 1909.

Raven, C. E., *Christian Socialism, 1848-54.* London: Macmillan & Co., Ltd., 1920.

Sharpe, Dores R., *Walter Rauschenbusch.* New York: The Macmillan Co., 1942.

Sheldon, H. C., *Unbelief in the Nineteenth Century.* New York: Eaton & Mains, 1907.

Storr, V. F., *Development of English Theology in the XIXth Century.* London: Longmans, Green & Co., 1913.

Taylor, E. R., *Methodism and Politics, 1791-1851.* Cambridge: Cambridge University Press, 1935.

Troeltsch, Ernest, *Social Teaching of the Christian Churches*, trans. O. Wyon. New York: Harper & Row, Publishers, 1960.

Ward, Charles H., *Charles Darwin: The Man and His Warfare*. Chicago: The Bobbs-Merrill Company, 1927.

Ward, Harry F., *The New Social Order*. New York: The Macmillan Co., 1919.

——, *Our Economic Morality and the Ethic of Jesus*. New York: The Macmillan Co., 1929.

Wearmouth, R. F., *Methodism and the Working Class Movements of England, 1800-1850*. London: The Epworth Press, Publishers, 1937.

White, Andrew D., *A History of the Warfare of Science and Theology in Christendom*. New York: Appleton-Century-Crofts, Inc., 1922.

Willey, B., *Nineteenth Century Studies*. London: Chatto & Windus, Ltd., 1949.

CHRONOLOGY

[Cf. Chapters 7, 8, and 10 for related events]

1772	Petition of Unitarians against 39 articles
1774	First Unitarian Church, London
1785–1872	Peter Cartwright
1788–1824	George Gordon Byron
1792–1875	Charles G. Finney
1798–1857	August Xavier Comte
1805–1872	J. F. D. Maurice
1806–1873	John Stuart Mill
1809–1882	Charles Darwin
1813	Denial of Trinity no longer criminal
1821–1910	Mary Baker Eddy
1828	Test and Corporation Acts repealed
1829–1912	William Booth
1830	Revolutions in France, Belgium, Poland
	Plymouth Brethren
1832	British Reform Bill
1833	Declaration of Faith, Congregational Union of England and Wales
	Wichern's social work, home for boys, Germany
1833–1834	Slavery abolished in British dominions
1835	Finney, Lectures on Revivals
1836	Marriages permitted in nonconformist churches, England
1836–1918	Washington Gladden
1837–1899	Dwight L. Moody
1840–1860	Frontier revivals in America
1844–1854	Comte's lectures and writings on positivism
1846	Finney, Lectures on Systematic Theology
1848	Revolutions throughout Europe
	Marx, Communist Manifesto
1848–1854	Christian Socialist Movement
1854	Working Men's College, Maurice
1856	Cartwright, Autobiography
1859	Darwin, Origin of Species
1860	Essays and Reviews
1861–1865	American Civil War
1861–1918	Walter Rauschenbusch
1863	Mill, Utilitarianism
1865–1923	Ernest Troeltsch
1868	Nonconformists relieved of taxes for Church of England
1872	Cartwright, Fifty Years a Presiding Elder
1873	Mill, Three Essays on Religion
1875	Eddy, Science and Health with a Key to the Scriptures
1877	Guild of St. Matthew, England
1878	Salvation Army
	Wellhausen, History of Israel
1880	Dissenters allowed burials in churchyards in England
1883	Drummond, Natural Laws in the Spiritual World
1889	Christian Social Union, England
	Drummond, The Greatest Thing in the World
	Gore, Lux Mundi
1889–1891	Rauschenbusch, For the Right
1890	Booth, In Darkest England and the Way Out
1892	Rauschenbusch, Brotherhood of the Kingdom
1896	James, Will to Believe
1907	Rauschenbusch, Christianity and the Social Crisis
1909	Rauschenbusch, Prayers of the Social Awakening
1912	Social Creed, Federal Council of Churches (also 1908)
	Troeltsch, Social Teaching of the Christian Churches
	Rauschenbusch, Christianizing the Social Order
1914–1918	First World War
1916	Rauschenbusch, Social Principles of Jesus
1917	Rauschenbusch, A Theology for the Social Gospel

Illustration opposite page 461: **St. Michael.** *Sculpture on the east façade of Coventry Cathedral, by Jacob Epstein. The Germans bombed England's Coventry Cathedral in 1940. On the ruins of the 500-year-old church penitent German Christians after the war helped build a new cathedral along modern lines. Photograph courtesy of Thompson, Coventry.*

8

Missions and Ecumenicity

$\mathbb{M}$issions and ecumenicity are two
interrelated movements; ecumenicity grew out of the missionary
movement in the nineteenth century, and the two merged in
the World Council of Churches at New Delhi in 1961.
Missionaries recognized the validity of the New Testament
injunction to preach the Gospel to all the world, and the leaders of
ecumenicity recognized the need for a cooperating
Christianized world. In the twentieth century, the notion of a
Christian Occident taking the Gospel to a non-Christian Orient is
passé; local Christians in what were once foreign missionary
fields are now struggling with problems common to all
Christians who would evangelize in a secularized culture and seek
a common unity in one faith and one Lord. The addition of
"younger" churches to the World Council of Churches
has been indicative of this trend. Ecumenicity stands as a symbol
of the success of the missionaries who carried the Gospel
"From Greenland's icy mountains," to "India's coral strand."
One year after Columbus discovered America, Pope Alexander VI
issued a bull called *Inter Cetera,* which divided trading privileges

and missionary responsibilities in the New World between Spain and Portugal. Through the monastic orders, particularly the newly formed Society of Jesus, the papacy sent its missionaries out along with the forces of explorers and colonizers, and for a century before the Protestants, the Catholics planted their chapels, schools, and monasteries in the New World, Africa, and the Orient. Xavier (cf. Ch. 3) exemplified the dedication and perseverance of early Catholic missionaries.

Protestantism did not fully develop its missionary consciousness until the beginning of the nineteenth century. That Luther and Calvin in the sixteenth century did not stress missions is a well-established fact. Latourette has said that this was due to the struggle to establish Protestantism, the drain of the wars of religion, a belief in eschatology, the absence of a centralized machinery to promote missions, indifference on the part of rulers, and the lack of contact between the Protestants and foreign lands. But it was also due to a rejection of monasticism, which was the sixteenth century's means of missionizing, and to the feeling that God in his sovereignty would take care of the heathen. As late as 1651, the theological faculty at Wittenberg insisted that the Gospel had in theory been carried into the world and that those who were still languishing in heathenism were obviously under the judgment of God. In 1664, Baron von Weltz proposed that Lutherans organize a missionary society to carry the Gospel to other lands, and he himself died as a missionary in Dutch Guiana; but there was little response in Germany. Other proposals among Protestants met with disappointing indifference. With the rise of the eighteenth century Enlightenment, Europe became more world conscious, but not necessarily more evangelical; the belief was common that there is nothing in Christian revelation that cannot be discovered in nature or in the reason of man.

The Protestant consciousness of missions did not noticeably develop until the rise of evangelical pietism in Lutheranism under the leadership of Philip J. Spener (d. 1705) and A. H. Francke (d. 1727). At the University of Halle, Francke interested his students in spreading the Gospel to other lands, and the Danish-Halle Mission came into existence in 1705. In the following year, Ziegenbalg and Plütschau sailed for India as the first Lutheran missionaries to the land where Xavier had gone in 1542.

The Moravians at Herrnhut, guided by Count Nicholas von Zinzendorf (d. 1760), continued the work of Spener and Francke. In 1732, Leonard Dober and David Nitschmann went to the West Indies. In the next year, Christian David went to Greenland. The Moravian zeal for missions prompted whole families to traverse the seas to foreign lands and support themselves in mission work. The intrepid Moravians penetrated into North America, Labrador, Southern Asia, Africa, the Caribbean Islands, and remote parts of Europe.

The Lutheran pietists directly influenced John Wesley and the evangelical awakening in England. Wesley's rejection of the Calvinistic doctrines of election and predestination, his rejection of the mystical, quietistic strain that developed in Moravianism, and his emphasis on the gift of salvation, offered to all men through Christ if men would but respond, opened the way for world-wide evangelization. Protestant evangelicals at last felt an obligation to give men in remote lands that opportunity to respond.

Some evangelical missionary work had already started. John Eliot (1604-1690), a Puritan pastor, undertook to evangelize the Indians of New England. In 1663, he completed his translation of the Moheecan Bible. With remarkable zeal and acumen he organized whole Indian villages in accordance with Exodus 18:23 ff. and trained twenty-four Indian preachers. Others became interested. The work of David Brainerd (1718-1747) among the American Indians was brief, for he died at the age of thirty, but Jonathan Edwards' biography of him (1749) directly affected the outlook of William Carey and other early missionaries to the Orient. To carry on missionary work in the colonies, the Society for Propagation of the Gospel in New England (1649), the Society for Promoting Christian Knowledge (1699), and the Society for the Propagation of the Gospel in Foreign Parts (1701) were founded. One of the most important results of the Puritans' attempts to missionize the Indians was the growing realization that the elect in every land must be given the opportunity openly to glorify God.

Important as these early missionary endeavors were, they did not create inspiration and enthusiasm as great or as general as that which came from the work of William Carey (1761-1834), a British cobbler, who had taught himself Latin, Greek, Hebrew, Dutch, and French. After his conversion experience in 1779, Carey turned from Anglicanism to the Baptist Church and began preaching in Baptist gatherings. In 1792 at Leicester, with a subsidy of £10 from a friend, he published his small but influential book, *An Enquiry into the Obligation of Christians to Use Means for the Conversion of the Heathen* (1). Carey's grasp of history, the Bible, ethnology, and geography, and his evangelical fervor aroused a lethargic England to the need to follow the command to go into all the world. On May 31, 1792, at Nottingham, Carey preached a sermon based on Isaiah 54:2-3, in which he exhorted his hearers to "expect great things from God" and "attempt great things for God." The ministers to whom he preached were profoundly moved, and by October of that same year, they founded at Kettering the Particular Baptist Society for the Propagation of the Gospel amongst the Heathen. The society chose William Carey and John Thomas to promote mission work in India, and on June 13, 1793, after considerable difficulty raising funds and securing passage, Carey, with his large family, sailed for India. By the end of the year he reached the Bay of Bengal. Lack of funds and illness brought him to the verge of starvation and despair, but he became self-supporting through his work in the indigo factory at Malda, and later as a teacher. After a short while he gained great facility in the language, and within five years he had translated the New Testament into Bengali and had preached in hundreds of villages in the native tongue. But difficulties often seemed overwhelming; for twelve years he nursed his insane wife and wondered about the future of his children in an alien land. Excerpts from his letters indicate some of his tribulations and triumphs (2). In 1801, Carey settled at Serampore, where with the aid of four new missionaries he finally printed the New Testament in Bengali. When Fort William College opened at Calcutta he was appointed professor of Oriental languages, a position which he held for thirty years. By 1809 he had printed the entire Bible in Bengali, and parts of it in twenty-six other languages and dialects. In addition to his work as a missionary and teacher, he produced grammars and dictionaries in Sanskrit, Marathi, Punjabi and Telugu, and made valuable contributions to botany through his study of flora.

The letters that Carey sent back to England were widely publicized, and inspired Christians in Europe and America to undertake missionary programs.

In July, 1794, Dr. Ryland of Bristol received a letter from Carey which directly inspired an article by David Bogue that appeared in the *Evangelical Magazine*, September, 1794, under the title, "To the Evangelical Dissenters who Practice Infant Baptism." The article led to the formation of the London Missionary Society, 1795, one of the first and most influential interdenominational organizations for the promotion of foreign missions. But Mr. Bogue's appeal was not the only factor. Clergymen and laymen were earnestly asking, "What is the duty of Christians to spread the Gospel?" As early as June, 1793, shortly after Carey sailed for India, a group of ministers at Warwickshire resolved, "That it is the duty of all Christians to employ every means in their power to spread the knowledge of the Gospel both at home and abroad; that we unite in a determination to promote this great design in our respective connexions; that we will immediately recommend to our friends the formation of a fund for the above purpose; that the first Monday of every month, at seven o'clock in the evening, be a season fixed on for united prayer to God, for the success of every attempt by all denominations of Christians for the spread of the Gospel." This resolution along with Bogue's appeal figured prominently in instigating action. At Baker's Coffee House, Change Alley, Cornhill, on November 4, 1794, a number of ministers discussed the possibility of a new missionary society.

463

Other ministers were invited to the next meeting on February 17, 1795, in London, where thirty-four ministers expressed a desire "to exert ourselves for promoting the great work of introducing the Gospel and its ordinances to heathen and other unenlightened countries, and unite together, purposing to use our best endeavours, that we may bring forward the formation of an extensive and regularly organized society, to consist of evangelical ministers and lay brethren of all denominations, the object of which society shall be to concert and pursue the most effectual measures for accomplishing this important and glorious design."

After a third meeting, September, 1795, with more than two hundred ministers assembled at Old Spa Fields Chapel, the London Missionary Society was formally organized. Its plan was simple, and it was to be supported through annual subscriptions. Most of the men involved in founding the Society were also involved in establishing the Religious Tract Society, 1799, and the Bible Society, 1804. Probably no other society has done as much to promote missions as the London Missionary Society. Its efforts have reached round the world: Tahiti, Polynesia, West Indies, North America, Africa, Madagascar, India, China, Amoy, North China, and other areas. Literally hundreds of missionaries have gone out under its auspices. Numbered among its famous missionaries are Alexander Duff, Robert Moffat, John Eyre, Henry Nott, David Livingston, and Robert Morrison.

Dr. Carey and the London Missionary Society are but two representatives of the vast number of individuals and groups that carried Christianity and its Scriptures to every country of the globe in the nineteenth century. Other societies quickly followed, one of the most remarkable of which was the American Board of Commissioners of Foreign Missions, organized in 1810 for the specific purpose of sending an inspired group of young men and their wives as Congregational missionaries to Southeast Asia. In 1808, the nucleus of this group under Samuel J. Mills held their famous haystack prayer meeting at Williams College. In the same year Adoniram Judson (1788-1850) experienced his call to the ministry, and in 1809 he vowed to carry the Gospel to the Golden Shores of Burma. Judson and part of the group from Williams College met as students at Andover Theological Seminary, and in February, 1812, Judson and Samuel Newell sailed with their brides from Salem on the *Caravan,* and Luther Rice, Samuel Notts, and Gordon Hall sailed from Philadelphia on the *Harmony.* Their final commissioning prompted a veritable revival throughout New England. Five months later the young missionaries reached Calcutta. Judson, after a study of baptism in the New Testament, became convinced that immersion was the only way, and was baptized by Carey in Calcutta. The American Baptists formed the American Baptist Missionary Union in 1814 to support him in the field. After incredible hardships, not the least of which was no communication from America for two and a half years, Judson became skilled in Burmese, and in 1816 began distributing literature to the Burmese. Not until 1819 did he hold his first worship and preaching service, and not until 1834 did he complete the Bible in Burmese, which, along with his many converts, stands as his monument; he was a living inspiration to the hundreds who followed his pioneering.

In 1817, the United Foreign Missionary Society was organized, and in 1826 it merged with the American Board, bringing together some of the cooperative efforts of the Congregational, Presbyterian, Baptist, and Reformed Churches. The Netherlands' Missionary Society was founded in 1798, the Church Missionary Society in 1799, the British and Foreign Bible Society, 1804, the Basel Evangelical Missionary Society, 1815, American Bible Society, 1816, the Wesleyan Methodist Missionary Society, 1817-18, American Methodist and Episcopalian boards of missions, 1821, the Danish Missionary Society, 1821, the Rhenish Missionary Society, 1828, and the Leipzig Evangelical Lutheran Mission, 1836. And still others continued to arise.

By 1825 the great missionary movement had expanded into the islands of the Pacific, and was moving forward in the Orient and Africa. Stations were established, schools started, and Scriptures translated wherever the early pioneers went. Appropriately,

Heber's famous hymn became the rallying hymn of the expansion (3).

The missionaries quickly saw the evils of Christian denominations competing with one another. Why should Christians remain doctrinally and practically divided? Should Christians who are the one body of Christ be sundered and opposed to one another? Their field discussions led to the calling of world conferences in New York and London in 1854. A series of meetings followed, the eighth of which was the World Missionary Conference at Edinburgh in 1910 (7). That meeting, furthered by the *Lambeth Appeal* in 1920 (8), gave rise to the three major prongs of ecumenical endeavor—the International Missionary Council, 1921, the Universal Christian Conference on Life and Work, at Stockholm in 1925, and the World Conference on Faith and Order, at Lausanne in 1927—culminating finally in the World Council of Churches in 1948 (*14, 15*) and its significant enlargement to include the IMC in 1961 (*16*).

Other powerful appeals for federation came from quarters not directly concerned with missions. One such quarter was the Evangelical Alliance of 1846 (*4*). Samuel S. Schmucker (1799-1873), a Lutheran professor of theology at the Theological Seminary at Gettysburg, published his *Fraternal Appeal to the American Churches*, 1838. In 1845, he issued his *Overture for Christian Union* and a composite *United Protestant Confession,* which was drawn from the credal statements of various churches and indicates a commonly accepted core of belief among Protestants in 1845. The *Appeal* and *Overture* aroused much discussion and might well have led to an ecumenical group in America, but in 1846 evangelicals from America and representatives from around the world were called to meet in London to organize the Evangelical Alliance. Professor Schmucker and other American evangelicals abandoned their own plans in order to form an American branch of the Evangelical Alliance, only to be delayed in their efforts by disputes concerning the admission of slaveholders. Not until 1867 did the American branch become active.

Although the Evangelical Alliance was composed only of interested individuals and had no official connections with organized churches, it was a sounding board for many opinions, and gave its members a vision of what could be done. Eight hundred Christian leaders from the United States, Canada, and Continental Europe hailed the organization of the Evangelical Alliance as the beginning of the "millennium." The Alliance defended religious liberty wherever it was threatened and became a powerful advocate of missions. Its journal, *Evangelical Christendom,* was the Ecumenical Press Service of its day, and its world-wide annual week of prayer enlisted the participation of 50,000 churches. Its international conferences stimulated a sense of unity. But its very organization prevented further ecumenical development.

The formation of national federations and church unions marked another step in ecumenical growth. Josiah Strong (1847-1916), succeeding Philip Schaff, Irenaeus Prime, and William E. Dodge, was one of the last of the notable secretaries of the American branch of the Alliance. In 1898, Josiah Strong resigned to take a more active part in the formation of the Federal Council of Churches of Christ in America. This group, promoted by Elias B. Sanford (1843-1932), sought a federated union not of individuals but of churches, an advisory group rather than an organic union, "with no authority to draw up a common creed or form of government or of worship or in any way to limit the full autonomy of the Christian bodies adhering to it." It was formally organized in 1908 and embraced thirty-one of the major American denominations (5). Forty-two years later it represented 144,000 local congregations and a total membership of 32,000,000. In 1950, the Federal Council merged with a number of other interdenominational agencies in the United States to form the National Council of the Churches of Christ in the United States of America, which, though not a superchurch, speaks as the conscience of Protestantism on issues embracing almost every branch of Christian living. The National Council represented an enlargement of the Federal Council in order to incorporate and consolidate various agencies and tasks with which it was already concerned; its aims remain virtually the same. Organizations similar to the Federal Council formed in France in 1905, in Switzerland, 1920, Germany, 1922, New Zealand, 1941, Great Britain, 1942, Canada, 1944, and Australia, 1946.

The ecumenical consciousness early in the nineteenth century also stimulated the uniting of many groups with similar historical backgrounds and geographical affinities. Among these were the United Presbyterian Church and the Free Church of Scotland, which joined in 1900 as the United Free Church of Scotland. In the United States, the United Lutheran Church was formed in 1918, and the American Lutheran Church in 1930, although these two unions did not embrace the majority of Lutherans. The Methodists completed their organic union as The Methodist Church in 1939. In Canada, despite bitter discussions, the Methodists, Congregationalists, and Presbyterians joined in the United Church of Canada in 1925, although a little more than a third of the Presbyterians remained outside the union. In 1908, the South India United Church brought together Presbyterian and Congregational missions, paving the way for the formation in 1947 of the Church of South India.

Still another influence contributing to the ecumenical drives of the nineteenth century was the organization of the energies of youth, a movement which recruited most of the leaders for ecumenicity in the twentieth century. George Williams (1821-1905) founded the Young Men's Christian Association in London in 1844, and it spread throughout the world. The World's Alliance of the YMCA was organized in 1855, and in the same year the Young Women's Christian Association, which in 1894 expanded into the World's YWCA. The Y cut across denominational lines to lead youth everywhere in the realization of Christian ideals of living.

John R. Mott (1865-1955), known as the architect of the ecumenical movement, was the organizing genius who tapped the wellsprings of youth for ecumenical service. Mott was a Methodist layman, but he was made a canon in the Anglican Church and honored with the degree of doctor by the Russian Orthodox Church. In 1946, he received the Nobel Peace Prize for distinguished humanitarian service. Around the world his name became synonymous with ecumenical cooperation and service. Mott joined the YMCA at Cornell, and on his graduation in 1888 he became the national secretary of the Intercollegiate Young Men's Christian Association of the United States of America and Canada. In this capacity, and later as international secretary, he visited campuses throughout the United States and Canada, everywhere being impressed by the possibilities inherent in the college situation. His success in organization and recruitment soon led him to take over the floundering Student Volunteer Movement for Foreign Missions, an organization with which he was already acquainted, having been among those students at Dwight L. Moody's 1886 conference at Mount Hermon, Northfield, Massachusetts, when the SVM began. There, two hundred students had pledged themselves to promote foreign missions, forming the nucleus of the Student Volunteer Movement, which under Mott's leadership a few years later caught the imagination of hundreds of college students around the world. Their watchword was "the evangelization of the world in our generation" (6). Volunteers came from Britain, the Netherlands, Germany, Scandinavia, Switzerland, and other countries in Europe, all vowing, "It is my purpose, if God permit, to become a foreign missionary." Mott agreed to supervise the Volunteers on a trial basis for only one year, but he continued for thirty-two years, from 1888 to 1920. Three-fourths of the missionaries from North America have come from the Volunteers, a total of some 20,000 recruits!

In 1891, at the YMCA conference in Amsterdam, John R. Mott instituted plans for an international student Christian fellowship, and with Dr. Karl Fries of Sweden, he founded the World's Student Christian Federation at Vadstena in 1895. Without requiring the sacrifice of individual convictions, the WSCF promoted international cooperation. Its objects were "to unite student Christian movements throughout the world, to gather information regarding the religious conditions of students in all lands, to deepen the spiritual life of students, and to enlist students in extending the Kingdom of Christ." Its motto was: "That they all may be one." Mott's success brought him invitations to organize youth in India, Ceylon, Japan, Australia, New Zealand, Hong Kong, China, and Hawaii. In 1907, the first world meeting of the WSCF was held in Tokyo. No one worked harder to bring about the epochal World Missionary Conference at Edinburgh in 1910, and no one more fully deserved to be its chairman than John R. Mott. His widely read books include *The Evangelization of the World in this Generation,* 1900, *The Pastor and Modern Missions,* 1904, and *The Future Leadership of the Church,* 1908.

Galen M. Fisher, Mott's biographer, cites testimonies from the many ecumenical leaders whom Mott recruited, trained, or influenced: J. H. Oldham, Dr. W. A. Visser't Hooft, Dr. T. Z. Koo, Miss Ruth Rouse, Canon Anson Phelps Stokes, Dr. Hendrik Kraemer, Dr. Samuel M. Zwemer, Professor Kenneth S. Latourette, Bishop G. Bromley Oxnam, Dr. S. M. Cavert, Dr. Roswell F. Barnes, Archbishop William Temple, Bishop Stephen Neill, Dr. John A. Mackay, and many others, all of whom have had prominent roles in ecumenicity.

Basically, the ecumenical movement in the twentieth century grew out of the missionary enterprise. The many discussions in the late nineteenth century culminated in the World Missionary Conference at Edinburgh in 1910, from which came the inspiration of the ecumenical movement (7). Almost all of the later leaders in ecumenicity participated in the Edinburgh meeting; among its ushers were William Temple, John McLeod Campbell, John Baillie, Kenneth Kirk, and Sir Walter Moberly. Advance detailed study for the meeting was directed by J. H. Oldham. Participants came from those societies actually engaged in missions among non-Christian peoples. While most of the topics for discussion pertained to missions, three reflected ecumenical emphasis: carrying the Gospel to all the non-Christian world, the church and the mission field, and cooperation and promotion of unity among churches.

The immediate development from the Edinburgh Conference was the Continuation Committee, of which Mott was chairman. In 1921, this committee became the International Missionary Council, Mott serving as its director until 1942. The IMC sought to coordinate the work of various interdenominational missionary organizations, and especially to promote the development of national leaders (*11*). Mott, operating through the IMC, organized the National Missionary Councils of India, China, and Japan, and promoted missions in the Congo, the Near East, and the Pacific. The 1928 IMC world conference in Jerusalem included racism and secularism in its discussions, and the Tambaram meeting in 1938 used Hendrik Kraemer's book, *The Christian Message in a Non-Christian World,* as a basis of discussion. Prominent among its leaders, besides Mott and Oldham, were A. L. Warnshuis, William Paton, and William Temple. At New Delhi in 1961, the IMC united with the World Council of Churches.

The famous *Lambeth Appeal* of the Episcopalians in 1920 created much discussion on the underlying doctrines and practicality of the ecumenical endeavor (*8*). Ordination, the Lord's Supper, and episcopal versus congregational organization proved to be major obstacles (*8, 9, 10, 13*). Nevertheless, the major bodies of Christendom shelved their differences to form the Universal Christian Conference on Life and Work at Stockholm in 1925. Nathan Söderblom (1866-1931), a Swedish Lutheran pastor and scholar who became the Archbishop of Uppsala, led the Life and Work conference into a study of the social ills of the world and how they might be alleviated.

Two years later the Faith and Order World Conference was held at Lausanne, Switzerland (*12, 13*). Charles H. Brent (1862-1929), an American Episcopal missionary bishop, inspired the conference to study the doctrinal differences separating the various communions. They frankly faced their differences on the ministry and the sacraments.

These two groups, Life and Work and Faith and Order, soon realized that their efforts could not be disjoined. In separate meetings at Oxford and Edinburgh in 1937, they voted to form a World Council of Churches, "a fellowship of churches which accept our Lord Jesus Christ as God and

Savior." A provisional structure for union was adopted at Utrecht in 1938, but actual union did not come until after World War II. The World Council of Churches finally became a reality at Amsterdam in 1948, when one hundred forty-four church groups from forty-four countries completed the organization (*14, 15*). In recognition of the work of John R. Mott, then retired, the delegates named him honorary chairman of the first meeting.

At the meeting of the World Council in New Delhi, the theme was "Jesus Christ the Light of the World." The 600,000 copies of the preliminary study booklet on Unity, Witness, and Service were printed in thirty-three languages. Important among the actions of this meeting were the appeal to all governments and peoples and the admission of Eastern Orthodox churches (*16*). The WCC is not a superchurch, but rather an organization for counsel, exchange of opinion, study, and promotion of common projects. It cannot legislate for individual member churches. It recognizes that the Church of Christ is one, but it is not based on any one concept of the church; the member churches believe that membership in the Church of Christ is more inclusive than membership in a single church, and that the varied communions can enlighten one another.

Although the WCC embraces almost two hundred member churches, including such diverse bodies as the Presbyterian Church of Australia, the Mar Thoma Syrian Church of Malabar, the Salvation Army, and the Seventh Day Baptist General Conference, still it does not include all the church groups; noticeably absent are the Southern Baptists of America, the Missouri Synod of Lutherans, and some Presbyterian groups. Fundamentalism has caused many churches to hold themselves aloof, and some have organized active opposition. Carl McIntyre, deposed from the ministry in the Presbyterian Church in the United States of America, organized his own Presbyterian Church in America, from which he seceded to form the Bible Presbyterian Church. He formed the International Council of Christian Churches and the related body known as the American Council of Churches. The former actively opposes the WCC, which McIntyre has referred to as "the Woman of

Babylon." The later has combatted the Federal and National Council of Churches of Christ in America. McIntyre has called the Revised Standard Version of the Bible "the work of Satan and his agents." More moderate, but still representative of the evangelicals who feel that the Bible is not emphasized sufficiently in the WCC, is the World Evangelical Fellowship. When the Evangelical Alliance was dissolved in 1944, there evolved the National Association of Evangelicals, "a voluntary association of Bible-believing Christians from various denominations, who wish to bear positive and united witness to the Christian faith once delivered as it is revealed in the New Testament." In Holland in 1951, the American National Association of Evangelicals joined with the British Evangelical Alliance to form the World Evangelical Fellowship, representing evangelical interests (*17*).

The Roman Catholic Church has persistently held that there can be no council of churches because there is only one church, "the Holy, Catholic, Apostolic Roman Church." The papacy has insisted that unity means a return of all Christian groups to Roman Catholic order and rule. Rome has refused to participate in ecumenical gatherings on the grounds that its truth must not be compromised with untruth. This position was forcefully stated in *Mortalium Animos* in 1928 (*18*). In 1949, *Ecclesia Catholica* reiterated this stand, although some observers have felt that the absolute stand of Roman Catholicism had softened slightly (*19*). In 1950, *Humani Generis* warned against compromise with aspects of modernism. Nevertheless, there has been cooperation in chaplaincy work in hospitals, prisons, and the armed forces. In 1960, Pope John XXIII created a new Secretariat for Promoting Christian Unity, and official observers went to New Delhi. In 1962, Pope John convened an ecumenical council at the Vatican to which Protestants were officially invited. A succession of Protestant notables have since been received by the Pope, including the Archbishop of Canterbury and Queen Elizabeth II, religious dialogue is being pursued by Catholics and Protestants in Germany, and prayer groups for unity have been organized by both. Pope Paul VI rescheduled the Vatican Council II in 1963, amid increasing indications of basic changes in the ecumenical stance of Roman Catholicism.

The WCC has been criticized for being too loose in its organization and too vague in its doctrinal commitment, while others have claimed that it is a superchurch, taking pride in its size. Meanwhile, the leaders of the ecumenical movement recognize that many problems remain yet to be solved before there can be true unity, and they do not presume to know the form of "true unity." They persevere, and pray that unity will come in "a renewal of holiness and truth" as each member of the World Council of Churches truly seeks that "deeper unity in witness and service in the name of Jesus Christ, the light of the world."

1. William Carey, 1792

In the opening section, Dr. Carey argues that the commission, "Go into all the world, and preach the gospel to every creature," is still binding on us. "It was not restricted to the apostles any more than Christ's other commandments, and no new commandment is needed, as Christ has promised to be with us to the end of the world. His command has not been repealed, like the commands of the ceremonial law; nor can we plead that there are no objects upon which to exercise his command: nor can we appeal to a counter-revelation. . . ." William Carey, *An Enquiry into the Obligation of Christians to Use Means for the Conversion of the Heathen* (Leicester: Ann Ireland, 1792).

Neither can we alledge a natural impossibility in the case. It has been said that we ought not to force our way, but to wait for the openings, and leadings of Providence; but it might with equal propriety be answered in this case, neither ought we to neglect embracing those openings in providence which daily present themselves to us. What openings of providence do we wait for? We can neither expect to be transported into the heathen world without ordinary means, nor to be endowed with the gift of tongues, &c. when we arrive there. These would not be providential interpositions, but miraculous ones. Where a command exists nothing can be necessary to render it binding but a removal of those obstacles which render obedience impossible, and these are removed already. Natural impossibility can never be

pleaded so long as facts exist to prove the contrary. Have not the popish missionaries surmounted all those difficulties which we have generally thought to be insuperable? Have not the missionaries of the *Unitas Fratrum,* or Moravian Brethren, encountered the scorching heat of Abyssinia, and the frozen climes of Greenland, and Labrador, their difficult languages, and savage manners? Or have not English traders, for the sake of gain, surmounted all those things which have generally been counted insurmountable obstacles in the way of preaching the gospel? Witness the trade to Persia, the East-Indies, China, and Greenland, yea even the accursed Slave-Trade on the coasts of Africa. Men can insinuate themselves into the favour of the most barbarous clans, and uncultivated tribes, for the sake of gain; and how different soever the circumstances of trading and preaching are, yet this will prove the possibility of ministers being introduced there; and if this is but thought a sufficient reason to make the experiment, my point is gained. . . .

It has been objected that there are multitudes in our own nation, and within our immediate spheres of action, who are as ignorant as the South-Sea savages, and that therefore we have work enough at home, without going into other countries. That there are thousands in our own land as far from God as possible, I readily grant, and that this ought to excite us to ten-fold diligence in our work, and in attempts to spread divine knowledge amongst them is a certain fact; but that it ought to supersede all attempts to spread the gospel in foreign parts seems to want proof. Our own countrymen have the means of grace, and may attend on the word preached if they chuse it. They have the means of knowing the truth, and faithful ministers are placed in almost every part of the land, whose spheres of action might be much extended if their congregations were but more hearty and active in the cause: but with them the case is widely different, who have no Bible, no written language, (which many of them have not), no ministers, no good civil government, nor any of those advantages which we have. Pity therefore, humanity, and much more Christianity, call loudly for every possible exertion to introduce the gospel amongst them. . . .

[Dr. Carey reviews the undertakings for the conversion of the heathen. Beginning with Pentecost, he surveys the book of Acts, shows the spread of the Gospel, mentions the labors of early Christians such as Justin Martyr, and depicts the spread of the Gospel throughout most of the Roman empire and adjacent lands. He continues:]

Soon after this the kingdom of Christ was further extended among the Scythian Nomades, beyond the Danube, and about the year 430, a people called the Burgundians, received the gospel. Four years after that Palladius was sent to preach in Scotland, and the next year Patrick was sent from Scotland to preach to the Irish, who before his time were totally uncivilized, and, some say, cannibals; he, however, was useful, and laid the foundations of several churches in Ireland. Presently after this, truth spread further among the Saracens, and in 522, Zathus, king of the Colchians encouraged it, and many of that nation were converted to Christianity. About this time also the work was extended in Ireland, by Finian, and in Scotland by Constantine and Columba; the latter of whom preached also to the Picts, and Brudaeus, their king, with several others, were converted. About 541, Adad, the king of Ethiopia, was converted by the preaching of Mansionarius; the Heruh beyond the Danube, were now made obedient to the faith, and the Abasgi, near the Caucasian Mountains.

But now popery, especially the compulsive part of it, was risen to such an height, that the usual method of propagating the gospel, or rather what was so called, was to conquer pagan nations by force of arms, and then oblige them to submit to Christianity, after which bishopricks were erected, and persons then sent to instruct the people. I shall just mention some of those who are said to have laboured thus.

In 596, Austin, the monk, Melitus, Justus, Paulinus, and Ruffinian, laboured in England, and in their way were very successful. Paulinus, who appears to have been one of the best of them, had great success in Northumberland; Birinnius preached to the West Saxons, and Felix to the East Angles. In 589, Amandus Gallus laboured in Ghent, Chelenus in Artois, and Gallus and Columbanus in Suabia. In 648, Egidius Gallus in Flanders, and the two Evaldi, in Westphalia. In 684, Willified, in the Isle of Wight. In 688, Chilianus, in upper Franconia. In 698, Boniface, or Winifred, among the Thuringians, near Erford, in Saxony, and Willibroad in West-Friesland. Charlemagne conquered Hungary in the year 800, and obliged the inhabitants to profess Christianity, when Modestus likewise preached to the Venedi, at the source of the Save and Drave. In 833, Anigarius preached in Denmark, Gaudibert in Sweden, and about 861, Methodius and Cyril, in Bohemia.

About the year 500, the Scythians over-ran Bulgaria, and Christianity was extirpated; but about 870 they were re-converted. Poland began to be brought over about the same time, and afterwards, about 960 or 990, the work was further extended amongst the Poles and Prussians. The work was begun in Norway in 960, and in Muscovy in 989, the Swedes propagated Christianity in Finland, in 1168, Lithuania became Christian in 1386, and Samogitia in 1439. The Spaniards forced popery upon the inhabitants of South-America, and the Portuguese in Asia. The Jesuits were sent into China in 1552. Xavier, whom they call the apostle of the Indians, laboured in the East-Indies and Japan, from 1541 to 1552, and several missions of Capuchins were sent to Africa in the seventeenth century. But blind zeal, gross superstition, and infamous cruelties, so marked the appearances of religion all this time, that the professors of Christianity needed conversion, as much as the heathen world. A few pious people had fled from the general corruption, and lived obscurely in the vallies of Piedmont and Savoy, who were like the seed of the church. Some of them were now and then necessitated to travel into other parts, where they faithfully testified against the corruptions of the times. About 1369, Wickliffe began to preach the faith in England, and his preaching and writings were the means of the conversion of great numbers, many of whom became excellent preachers; and a work was begun which afterwards spread in England, Hungary, Bohemia, Germany, Switzerland, and many other places. John Huss and Jerom of Prague, preached boldly and successfully in Bohemia, and the adjacent parts. In the following century Luther, Calvin, Melancton, Bucer, Martyr, and many others, stood up against all the rest of the world; they preached, and prayed, and wrote; and nations agreed one after another to cast off the yoke of popery, and to embrace the doctrine of the gospel.

In England, episcopal tyranny succeeded to popish cruelty, which, in the year 1620, obliged many pious people to leave their native land and settle in America; these were followed by others in 1629, who laid the foundations of several gospel churches, which have increased amazingly since that time, and the Redeemer has fixed his throne in that country, where but a little time ago, Satan had universal dominion.

In 1632, Mr. Elliot, of New-England, a very pious and zealous minister, began to preach to the Indians, among whom he had great success; several churches of Indians were planted, and some preachers and schoolmasters raised up amongst them; since which time others have laboured amongst them with some good encouragement. About the year 1743, Mr. David Brainerd was sent a missionary to some more Indians, where he preached, and prayed, and after some time an extraordinary work of conversion was wrought, and wonderful success attended his ministry. And at this present time, Mr. Kirkland and Mr. Sergeant are employed in the same good work, and God has considerably blessed their labours.

In 1706, the king of Denmark sent a Mr. Ziegenbalg, and some others, to Tranquebar, on the Coromandel coast in the East-Indies, who were useful to the natives, so that many of the heathens were turned to the Lord. The Dutch East-India Company likewise having extended their commerce, built the city of Batavia, and a church was opened there; and the Lord's Supper was administered for the first time, on the 3d of January, 1621, by their minister James Hulzibos; from hence some ministers were sent to Amboyna, who were very successful. A seminary of learning was erected at Leyden, in which ministers and as-

sistants were educated, under the renowned *Walaeus,* and some years a great number were sent to the East, at the Company's expense, so that in a little time many thousands at Formosa, Malabar, Ternate, Jaffanapatnam, in the town of Columba, at Amboyna, Java, Banda, Macassar, and Malabar, embraced the religion of our Lord Jesus Christ. The work was delayed in some places, but they now have churches in Ceylon, Sumatra, Java, Amboyna, and some other of the spice islands, and at the Cape of Good Hope, in Africa.

But none of the moderns have equalled the Moravian Brethren in this good work; they have sent missions to Greenland, Labrador, and several of the West-Indian Islands, which have been blessed for good. They have likewise sent to Abyssinia, in Africa, but what success they have had I cannot tell.

The late Mr. Wesley lately made an effort in the West-Indies, and some of their ministers are now labouring amongst the Caribbs and Negroes, and I have seen pleasing accounts of their success. . . .

[In section three, Dr. Carey presents tables showing the area, population, and religions of countries in Europe, Asia, Africa, and America. He estimates the world's population at 731,000,000: 420,000,000 pagans, 130,000,000 Mohammedans, 100,000,000 Catholics, 44,000,000 Protestants, 30,000,000 Greek Orthodox, and 7,000,000 Jews. He then considers "the practicability of something being done, more than what is done, for the conversion of the heathen." Neither distance, danger, difficulty, nor language should deter us, nor even their barbarous ways:]

Secondly, As to their uncivilized, and barbarous way of living, this can be no objection to any, except those whose love of ease renders them unwilling to expose themselves to inconveniencies for the good of others.

It was no objection to the apostles and their successors, who went among the barbarous *Germans* and *Gauls,* and still more barbarous *Britons!* They did not wait for the ancient inhabitants of these countries to be civilized, before they could be christianized, but went simply with the doctrine of the cross; and *Tertullian* could boast that "those parts of Britain which were proof against the

Roman armies, were conquered by the gospel of Christ.". . . It was no objection to an *Elliot*, or a *Brainerd*, in later times. They went forth, and encountered every difficulty of the kind, and found that a cordial reception of the gospel produced those happy effects which the longest intercourse with Europeans, without it could never accomplish. It *is* no objection to commercial men. It only requires that we should have as much love to the souls of our fellow-creatures, and fellow sinners, as they have for the profits arising from a few otter-skins, and all these difficulties would be easily surmounted.

After all, the uncivilized state of the heathen, instead of affording an objection *against* preaching the gospel to them, ought to furnish an argument *for* it. Can we as men, or as Christians, hear that a great part of our fellow creatures, whose souls are as immortal as ours, and who are as capable as ourselves, of adorning the gospel, and contributing by their preaching, writings, or practices to the glory of our Redeemer's name, and the good of his church, are inveloped in ignorance and barbarism? Can we hear that they are without the gospel, without government, without laws, and without arts, and sciences; and not exert ourselves to introduce amongst them the sentiments of men, and of Christians? Would not the spread of the gospel be the most effectual means of their civilization? Would not that make them useful members of society? We know that such effects did in a measure follow the afore-mentioned efforts of Elliot, Brainerd, and others amongst the American Indians; and if similar attempts were made in other parts of the world, and succeeded with a divine blessing (which we have every reason to think they would) might we not expect to see able Divines, or read well-conducted treatises in defence of the truth, even amongst those who at present seem to be scarcely human? . . .

DUTY AND MEANS TO PROMOTE THIS WORK

If the prophecies concerning the increase of Christ's kingdom be true, and if what has been advanced, concerning the commission given by him to his disciples being obligatory on us, be just, it must be inferred that all Christians ought heartily to concur with God in promoting his glorious designs, for *he that is joined to the Lord is one Spirit.*

One of the first, the most important of those duties which are incumbent upon us, is *fervent and united prayer.* However the influence of the Holy Spirit may be set at nought, and run down by many, it will be found upon trial, that all means which we can use, without it, will be ineffectual. If a temple is raised for God in the heathen world, it will not be *by might, nor by power,* nor by the authority of the magistrate, or the eloquence of the orator; but by my Spirit, saith the Lord of Hosts. We must therefore be in real earnest in supplicating his blessing upon our labours. . . .

We must not be contented however with praying, without *exerting ourselves in the use of means* for the obtaining of those things we pray for. Were *the children of light,* but *as wise in their generation as the children of this world,* they would stretch every nerve to gain so glorious a prize, nor ever imagine that it was to be obtained in any other way. . . .

If congregations were to open subscriptions of *one penny,* or more per week, according to their circumstances, and deposit it as a fund for the propagation of the gospel, much might be raised in this way. By such simple means they might soon have it in their power to introduce the preaching of the gospel into most of the villages in England; where, though men are placed whose business it should be to give light to those who sit in darkness, it is well known that they have it not. Where there was no person to open his house for the reception of the gospel, some other building might be procured for a small sum, and even then something considerable might be spared for the baptist, or other committees, for propagating the gospel amongst the heathen.

Many persons have of late left off the use of *West-India sugar,* on account of the iniquitous manner in which it is obtained. Those families who have done so, and have not substituted any thing else in its place, have not only cleansed their hands of blood, but have made a saving to their families, some of sixpence, and some of a shilling a week. If this, or a part of this were appropriated to the uses before-mentioned, it would abundantly suffice. We have only to keep the end in view, and have our hearts thoroughly engaged in the pursuit of it, and means will not be very difficult....

Surely it is worth while to lay ourselves out with all our might, in promoting the cause, and kingdom of Christ.

2. Carey in India

Excerpts from a *Memoir of William Carey, D.D.*, by Eustace Carey (Hartford: Canfield and Robins, 1837).

[When William Carey approached India from the Bay of Bengal, October 17, 1793, he wrote to the Society for the Propagation of the Gospel amongst the Heathen:]

... I have a growing satisfaction in having undertaken this work, and a growing desire for its success; though I feel so much barrenness, and so little lively continual sense of divine things upon my mind, that I almost despair of ever being of any use. But in general I feel a pleasure in the thought that Christ has promised to be with his ministers until the end of the world, and that as our day is, so shall our strength be.... I hope the society will go on and increase, and that the multitudes of heathen in the world may hear the glorious words of truth. Africa is but a little way from England; Madagascar but a little way further; South America, and all the numerous and large islands in the Indian and Chinese seas, I hope will not be passed over. A large field opens on every side, and millions of perishing heathens, tormented in this life by idolatry, superstition, and ignorance, exposed to eternal miseries in the world to come, are pleading; yea, all their miseries plead as soon as they are known, with every heart that loves God, and with all the churches of the living God. Oh, that many laborers may be thrust out into the vineyard of our Lord Jesus Christ, and that the Gentiles may come to the knowledge of the truth as it is in Him!...

(Journal, May 26, 1794.) This day kept Sabbath at Chundareea; had a pleasant day. In the morning and afternoon addressed my family, and in the evening began my work of publishing the word of God to the heathen. Though imperfect in the knowledge of the language, yet, with the help of Mounshi, I conversed with two Brahmuns in the presence of about two hundred people, about the things of God. I had been to see a temple, in which were the images of Dukkinroy, the god of the woods, riding on a tiger; Sheetulla, goddess of the small-pox, without a head, riding on a horse without a head; Punchanon, with large ears; and Colloroy, riding on a horse. In another apartment was Seeb, which was only a smooth post of wood, with two or three mouldings in it, like the base of a Tuscan pillar. I therefore discoursed with them upon the vanity of idols, the folly and wickedness of idolatry, the nature and attributes of God, and the way of salvation by Christ. One Brahmun was quite confounded, and a number of people were all at once crying out to him, "Why do you not answer him? Why do you not answer him?" He replied, "I have no words." Just at this time a very learned Brahmun came up, who was desired to talk with me; which he did, and so acceded to what I said, that he at last said, images had been used of late years, but not from the beginning. I inquired what I must do to be saved; he said I must repeat the name of God a great many times. I replied, would you, if your son had offended you, be so pleased with him as to forgive him if he were to repeat the word "father" a thousand times? This might please children or fools, but God is wise. He told me that I must get faith; I asked what faith was, to which he gave me no intelligible reply, but said I must obey God. I answered, what are his commands? What is his will? They said God was a great light, and as no one could see him, he became incarnate, under the threefold character of Brhumma, Bishno, and Seeb, and that either of them must be worshipped in order to live. I told them of the sure word of the gospel, and the way of life by Christ; and, night coming on, left them. I cannot tell what effect it may have, as I may never see them again....

(To the Baptist Missionary Society, August 5, 1794, after having taken over the management of the indigo-factory at Malda.) ... Here, then, is the principal seat of the mission; and if any lose caste for the gospel, we have good and profitable employment for them. Mr. Udney allows us each two hundred rupees per month, with commission for all the indigo we make, and promises next year to present us each with a fourth share of our respective works. In consequence of which I now inform the society, that I can subsist without any further assistance from them; and at the same time sincerely thank them for the exertions they have made, and hope that what was intended to supply my wants, may be appropriated to some other mission. At the same time it will be my glory and joy to stand in the same near relation to the society as if I needed supplies from them, and to maintain the same correspondence with them. The only favor that I beg is, that I may have the pleasure of seeing the new publications that come out in our connexion, and the books that I wrote for before, viz., a polyglot Bible, Arabic Testament, Malay Gospel, and Botanical Magazine.

(Letter, August 9, 1794.) As for the dangers and difficulties of the country, we think very little about them. Some diseases are very common here; as dysentery, which generally arises from the coldness of the night air, after the heat of the day. With this disorder my wife and eldest son have been afflicted for eight months: my wife is nearly well, but my son very ill now. Fevers are frequent in the rains, or rather agues; perhaps arising from the number of rice-fields which are full of water. But the country agrees better with my health than England did: I never was better in my life.

We have no fear of beasts, though there are many buffaloes, hogs and tigers in our neighborhood. Tigers seldom attack men, but commit dreadful devastation among cattle; except those of the Sunderbunds, a very large forest near the sea, where there are no cattle; there they seize men. Serpents are numerous; and some so mortal that the patient never survives two hours, and often dies in five minutes; but they give us no concern, or very little. Crocodiles no man minds: I have one in a pond about ten yards from my door, yet sleep with the door open every night. . . . The language is very copious, and I think

beautiful. I begin to converse in it a little; but my third son, about five years old, speaks it fluently. Indeed, there are two distinct languages spoken all over the country, viz., the Bengali, spoken by the Brahmuns and higher Hindus; and the Hindostani, spoken by the Mussulmans and lower Hindus, which is a mixture of Bengali and Persian. I intend to send you soon a copy of Genesis, Matthew, Mark, and James, in Bengali; with a small vocabulary and grammar of the language, in manuscript, of my own composing, to which you will afford a place on one of the shelves in your library. . . .

(Journal, September 1–October 1, 1794.) During this time I have had a heavy and long affliction, having been taken with a violent fever. One of the paroxysms continued for twenty-six hours without intermission, when, providentially, Mr. Udney came to visit us, not knowing that I was ill, and brought a bottle of bark with him. This was a great providence, as I was growing worse every day; but the use of this medicine, by the blessing of God, recovered me. In about two days I relapsed, and the fever was attended with a violent vomiting and a dysentery; and even now I am very ill, Mr. Thomas says, with some of the very worst symptoms. On the last of these days it pleased God to remove, by death, my youngest child but one; a fine engaging boy of rather more than five years of age. He had been seized with a fever, and was recovering; but relapsed, and a violent dysentery carried him off. On the same day we were obliged to bury him, which was an exceedingly difficult thing. I could induce no person to make a coffin, though two carpenters are constantly employed by us at the works. Four Mussulmans, to keep each other in countenance, dug a grave; but, though we had between two and three hundred laborers employed, no man would carry him to the grave. We sent seven or eight miles to get a person to do that office; and I concluded that I and my wife would do it ourselves, when at last a servant, kept for the purpose of cleaning, and a boy who had lost caste, were prevailed upon to carry the corpse, and secure the grave from jackals. This was not owing to any disrespect in the natives towards us, but only to the cursed caste. The Hindus burn their dead, or throw them into the rivers to be devoured by birds and fishes. The Mussulmans inhume their dead; but this is only done by their nearest relations; and so much do they abhor every thing belonging to a corpse, that the bamboos on which they carry their dead to the water or the grave, are never touched or burnt, but stand in the place and rot; and if they only tread upon a grave, they are polluted, and never fail to wash after it.

(Journal, February 22, 1795.) . . . But a missionary finds far greater hindrance to his work from the metaphysical and idolatrous use of language, than simply from the paucity of words. The former has restricted all the terms applicable to intellectual and spiritual subjects to mere abstractions and subtle speculation. And to disengage them from their long philosophical application, and appropriate them to a simple, popular, and religious use, is a work of time and labor. By the Hindu system, the Supreme Essence is itself merely an abstraction, an ideal existence, without positive attributes, natural or moral, a mere figment of the imagination. And yet this mere metaphysical abstraction, this essential "nihil," is the primordial of all mind, and of all spiritual existence in the universe; besides it, indeed, there is no mind, no spirit, no mover, no cause, no final end. It pervades every thing, it contains every thing, nay, it is itself every thing, and every thing is it, whether on earth, or in the lowest hell, or in the highest heaven. And, again, since there is strictly but one doer of all things, all spontaneous agency and all accountability are annihilated; and all distinction in morals is lost, and only tolerated in discourse as a vulgar absurdity. The contact and union of mind with matter, animal or otherwise sensitive, throughout the universe, with all its agencies and susceptibilities of pleasure and pain, yea, and with all we understand by virtue and vice, and their retributions through the horrors and all but interminable mazes of metempsychosis or transmigration of souls; all are illusion in the estimation of an oriental philosopher and religious devotee, whose ultimate and only proper good is in the loss of their identical existence and final absorption. Hence, with them, all things are involved in a circle which nothing can dissolve, and from which no power on earth can move them.

(Letter, November 16, 1796.) Translating the Bible. I have, through the good hand of my God upon me, now nearly translated all the New Testament. I have begun the seventh chapter of Revelations, and all the other is translated except the Acts of the Apostles, which I left to Mr. T. He has not, however, touched it scarcely; the gospel by Luke is all he has done in translating since he came into the country. I have a pundit, who has, with me, examined and corrected all the Epistles, to the second of Peter; we go through a chapter every day. The natives, who can read and write, understand it perfectly; and as it is corrected by a learned native, the style and syntax cannot be very bad. I intend to go through it again, and, as critically as I can, compare it with the Greek Testament; but wish to have a Greek Concordance sent by the very next conveyance. I expect the New Testament will be complete before you receive this, except a very few words, which may want altering on a third and fourth revisal. . . .

(Letter, December 29, 1800.) Yesterday was a day of great joy. I had the happiness to desecrate the Gunga, by baptizing the first Hindu, viz., Krishnu, and my son Felix; some circumstances turned up to delay the baptism of Gokul, and the two women. . . . We intended to have baptized at nine in the morning; but, on account of the tide, were obliged to defer it till nearly one o'clock, and it was administered just after the English preaching. The governor and a good number of Europeans were present. . . . Thus, you see, God is making way for us, and giving success to the word of his grace! We have toiled long, and have met with many discouragements; but at last the Lord has appeared to us. May we have the true spirit of nurses, to train them up in the words of faith and sound doctrine! I have no fear of any one, however, in this respect, but myself. I feel much concerned that they may act worthy of their vocation, and also, that they may be able to teach others. I think it becomes us to make the most of every one whom the Lord gives us. . . .

(Letter, Serampore, November 1801.) Hitherto the Lord has helped me. I have lived to see the Bible translated into Bengali, and the whole New Testament printed. The first volume of the Old Testament will also soon appear. I have lived to see two of my sons converted, and one of them join the church of Christ. I have lived to baptize five native Hindus, and to see a sixth baptized; and to see them walk worthy of the vocation for twelve months since they first made a profession of faith in our Lord Jesus Christ. I have lived to see the temporal concerns of the mission in a state far beyond my expectation, so that we have now two good houses contiguous to each other, with two thousand pounds; a flourishing school; the favor of both the Danish and English governments; and, in short, the mission almost in a state of ability to maintain itself. Having seen all this, I sometimes am almost ready to say, "Lord, now lettest thou thy servant depart in peace, according to thy word; for mine eyes have seen thy salvation." . . .

(Letter, Calcutta, December 31, 1805.) This year God has increased us with thirty persons added by baptism; twenty-seven of them natives, and three Europeans. Several of our native brethren have gifts for preaching the gospel, and are much more useful in this work than we are. I hope a few more are inquiring the way to Zion, with their faces thitherward. O that the Lord may greatly increase their number, and carry on his cause till all India, and the whole world, are obedient to the faith!

We are now engaged in translating and printing the Bible in seven languages, and expect to begin it in six more in a little time.

(Letter, October 24, 1810.) About a month ago, I received a letter from my son Felix, of which the following extract will give you pleasure. "The present viceroy is uncommonly kind to strangers of every description, but more especially to us. He has been once to see us, and wishes us to call on him as often as we can find it convenient. . . . The other day I went to him in behalf of a poor sufferer who was crucified, and condemned to die in that situation. After I had pleaded for about half an hour, he granted my request, though he had denied several other

people, among whom was the Ceylon priest. I took the poor man down, after he had been nailed up for more than six hours, brought him home, and dressed his wounds, and now he is nearly cured. This man will now, by law, belong to me as long as he lives, and I hope, may not only be a useful servant, but become a real Christian." [Commenting on this, Dr. Carey said later, "I abhor slavery, and shall this week write to him to give the man his liberty, if it be possible."] In a letter to William, Felix says that he was going to see some patients, and saw the poor man on the cross. He immediately went the nearest way to the viceroy's house. . . . The entering was attended with danger, where the will of the governor was law; and, had he been in an ill humor, might have occasioned the loss of his head. He however ventured, presented his petition, and, according to the Burman custom, insisted on its being granted before he left the place. The viceroy refused several times, but at last said he would grant it, if he received promise never to intercede for another. This Felix refused. He then made him promise to go up to Ava with him, when he shall have occasion to go thither. To this he assented, when the order for the poor man's release was given, [and with the order he] went to the cross. When he arrived there, not one of the officers who attended would read it without a reward. After remonstrating and threatening for a considerable time, he was obliged to offer them a piéce of cloth; then the man was immediately taken down, and had just strength left to express his thanks. I understand that the punishment of crucifixion is not performed on separate crosses, elevated to a considerable height, after the manner of the Romans, but several posts are set up, which are connected by rails near the top, to which the hands are nailed, and by a rail at the bottom, to which the feet are nailed in a horizontal manner. The crucifixion of this man took place about the 10th of August. He was nailed up about three in the afternoon, and took down between nine and ten at night. Brother Chater says, he believes Felix was the only person in the place who could have succeeded, and that it gained him much renown among the Burmans. . . .

3. A Hymn for Missions

One of the most popular of all missionary hymns was "From Greenland's icy mountains," written by Reverend Reginald Heber for a worship service at Wrexham Church, Wales, on Whitsunday, 1819. The sermon for the occasion was in behalf of the Society for the Propagation of the Gospel.

THE CRY OF THE HEATHEN

From Greenland's icy mountains,
  From India's coral strand;
Where Afric's sunny fountains
  Roll down their golden sand;
From many an ancient river
  From many a palmy plain,
They call us to deliver
  Their land from error's chain.

What though the spicy breezes
  Blow soft o'er Ceylon's isle;
Though every prospect pleases,
  And only man is vile:
In vain with lavish kindness
  The gifts of God are strown;
The heathen in his blindness
  Bows down to wood and stone.

Shall we, whose souls are lighted
  With wisdom from on high,
Shall we to men benighted
  The lamp of life deny?
Salvation!—O Salvation!
  The joyful sound proclaim,
Till earth's remotest nation
  Has learn'd Messiah's name.

Waft, waft, ye winds, his story,
  And you, ye waters, roll,
Till, like a sea of glory,
  It spreads from pole to pole:
Till o'er our ransom'd nature
  The Lamb for sinners slain,
Redeemer, King, Creator,
  In bliss returns to reign.

4. The Evangelical Alliance, 1846

The restrained statement upon which the Evangelical Alliance was established, London, 1846. From *Christian Unity in Practice and Prophecy*, by Charles S. MacFarland (New York: The Macmillan Co., 1933).

The members of this Conference are deeply convinced of the desirableness of forming a confederation, on the basis of great Evangelical principles held in common by them, which may afford opportunity to members of the Church of Christ of cultivating brotherly love, enjoying Christian intercourse, and promoting such other objects as they may hereafter agree to prosecute together; and they hereby proceed to form such a confederation, under the name of "The Evangelical Alliance." ...

The parties composing the Alliance shall be such persons only as hold and maintain what are usually understood to be evangelical views, namely:

1. The Divine inspiration, authority, and sufficiency of the Holy Scriptures;
2. The right and duty of private judgment in the interpretation of the Holy Scriptures;
3. The unity of the Godhead, and the Trinity of persons therein;
4. The utter depravity of human nature in consequence of the fall;
5. The incarnation of the Son of God, his work of atonement for the sins of mankind, and his mediatorial intercession and reign;
6. The justification of the sinner by faith alone;
7. The work of the Holy Spirit in the conversion and sanctification of the sinner;
8. The immortality of the soul, the resurrection of the body, the judgment of the world by our Lord Jesus Christ, with the eternal blessedness of the righteous, and the eternal punishment of the wicked;
9. The divine institution of the Christian ministry, and the obligation and perpetuity of the ordinances of Baptism and the Lord's Supper.

... This brief summary is not to be regarded, in any formal or Ecclesiastical sense, as a Creed or Confession, nor the adoption of it as involving an assumption of the right authoritatively to define the limits of Christian Brotherhood; but simply as an indication of the class of persons whom it is desirable to embrace within the Alliance: The selection of certain tenets, with the omission of others, is not to be held as implying that the former constitute the whole body of important Truth, or that the latter are unimportant.

5. The Federal Council of Churches

The preamble and plan of federation for the Federal Council of the Churches of Christ in America, Philadelphia, December, 1908, and the wartime message, 1917. McFarland, *Christian Unity in Practice and Prophecy.*

PREAMBLE

Whereas, in the providence of God, the time has come when it seems fitting more fully to manifest the essential oneness of the Christian Churches of America in Jesus Christ as their Divine Lord and Saviour, and to promote the spirit of fellowship, service, and cooperation among them, the delegates to the Interchurch Conference on Federation, assembled in New York City, do hereby recommend the following Plan of Federation to the Christian bodies represented in this Conference for their approval.

PLAN OF FEDERATION

For the prosecution of work that can be better done in union than in separation a Council is hereby established whose name shall be the Federal Council of the Churches of Christ in America. The object of this Federal Council shall be:

I. To express the fellowship and catholic unity of the Christian Church.

II. To bring the Christian bodies of America into united service for Christ and the world.

III. To encourage devotional fellowship and mutual counsel concerning the spiritual life and religious activities of the churches.

IV. To secure a larger combined influence for the churches of Christ in all matters affecting the moral and social condition of the people, so as to promote the application of the law of Christ in every relation of human life.

V. To assist in the organization of local branches of the Federal Council to promote its aims in their communities.

This Federal Council shall have no authority over the constituent bodies adhering to it; but its province shall be limited to the expression of its counsel and the recommending of a course of action in matters of common interest to the churches, local councils, and individual Christians.

It has no authority to draw up a common creed or form of government or of worship, or in any way to limit the full autonomy of the Christian bodies adhering to it.

IN TIME OF WAR: OUR SPIRIT AND PURPOSE

After long patience, and with a solemn sense of responsibility, the government of the United States has been forced to recognize that a state of war exists between this country and Germany, and the President has called upon all the people for their loyal support and their wholehearted allegiance. As American citizens, members of Christian Churches gathered in Federal Council, we are here to pledge both support and allegiance in unstinted measure.

We are Christians as well as citizens. Upon us therefore rests a double responsibility. We owe it to our country to maintain intact and to transmit unimpaired to our descendants our heritage of freedom and democracy. Above and beyond this, we must be loyal to our divine Lord, who gave His life that the world might be redeemed, and whose loving purpose embraces every man and every nation.

As citizens of a peace-loving nation, we abhor war. We have long striven to secure the judicial settlement of all international disputes. But since, in spite of every effort, war has come, we are grateful that the ends to which we are committed are such as we can approve. To vindicate the principles of righteousness and the inviolability of faith as between nation and nation; to safeguard the right of all the peoples, great and small alike, to live their life in freedom and peace; to resist and overcome the forces that would prevent the union of the nations in a commonwealth of free peoples conscious of unity in the pursuit of ideal ends—these are aims for which every one of us may lay down his all, even life itself.

We enter the war without haste or passion, not for private or national gain, with no hatred or bitterness against those with whom we contend.

No man can foresee the issue of the struggle. It will call for all the strength and heroism of which the nation is capable. What now is the mission of the church in this hour of crisis and danger? It is to bring all that is done or planned in the nation's name to the test of the mind of Christ.

That mind upon one point we do not all interpret alike. With sincere conviction some of us believe that it is forbidden the disciple of Christ to engage in war under any circumstances. Most of us believe that the love of all men which Christ enjoins demands that we defend with all the power given us the sacred rights of humanity. But we are all at one in loyalty to our country, and in steadfast and whole-hearted devotion to her service.

As members of the church of Christ, the hour lays upon us special duties:

To purge our own hearts clean of arrogance and selfishness;

To steady and inspire the nation;

To keep ever before the eyes of ourselves and of our allies the ends for which we fight;

To hold our own nation true to its professed aims of justice, liberty, and brotherhood;

To testify to our fellow-Christians in every land, most of all to those from whom for the time we are estranged, our consciousness of unbroken unity in Christ;

To unite in the fellowship of service multitudes who love their enemies and are ready to join with them in rebuilding the waste places as soon as peace shall come;

To be diligent in works of relief and mercy, not forgetting those ministries to the spirit to which, as Christians, we are specially committed;

To keep alive the spirit of prayer, that in these times of strain and sorrow men may be sustained by the consciousness of the presence and power of God;

To hearten those who go to the front, and to comfort their loved ones at home;

To care for the welfare of our young men in the army and navy, that they may be fortified in character and made strong to resist temptation;

To be vigilant against every attempt to arouse the spirit of vengeance and unjust suspicion toward those of foreign birth or sympathies;

To protect the rights of conscience against every attempt to invade them;

To maintain our Christian institutions and activities unimpaired, the observance of the Lord's Day and the study of the Holy Scriptures, that the soul of our nation may be nourished and renewed through the worship and service of Almighty God;

To guard the gains of education, and of social progress and economic freedom, won at so great a cost, and to make full use of the occasion to set them still further forward, even by and through the war;

To keep the open mind and the forward look, that the lessons learned in war may not be forgotten when comes that just and sacred peace for which we pray;

Above all, to call men everywhere to new obedience to the will of our Father God, who in Christ has given Himself in supreme self-sacrifice for the redemption of the world, and who invites us to share with Him His ministry of reconciliation.

To such service we would summon our fellow-Christians of every name. In this spirit we would dedicate ourselves and all that we have to the nation's cause. With this hope we would join hands with all men of goodwill of every land and race, to rebuild on this war-ridden and desolated earth the commonwealth of mankind, and to make of the kingdoms of the world the Kingdom of the Christ.

6. The Watchcry of the Student Volunteer Movement

An Article by John R. Mott in *The Student Volunteer*, Great Britain, February, 1895. Reprinted in *Addresses and Papers of John R. Mott*, I (New York: Association Press, 1946).

1. The Meaning of the Watchcry. "The Evangelization of the World in This Generation" is the watchcry of the Student Volunteer Movement for Foreign Missions. It is emphatically a watchcry, not a prophecy. It states what the Movement will unswervingly and prayerfully strive to accomplish.

What is meant by "the evangelization of the world"? (1) Positively: It means for us to give every person in the world an opportunity to know Jesus Christ as a personal Saviour. (2) Negatively: It does not mean the conversion of the world, for the acceptance of Christ rests with the hearer, and not with the speaker. It does not mean the Christianization or the civilization of the world—important as both of these are. Nor must it be construed to mean an imperfect preaching of the gospel. Moreover, it must not be interpreted as in any way detracting from the real importance of any phase of missionary work which is being used by the Spirit. The Movement stands pre-eminently for the emphasis of the belief that by a great enlargement of the agencies employed by the missionary societies today, the gospel can and should be brought within the reach of every creature within the generation.

What is the meaning of "this generation"? As far as the activities and direct influence of the individual volunteer are concerned it means within his own lifetime. As far as the activities and direct influence of the Volunteer Movement as a whole at any given time are concerned, it means within a period commonly known as a generation from that time. It is of constant application to successive generations as long as the world remains unevangelized. Each generation of Christians must obviously evangelize its own generation of the unevangelized inhabitants of the world if they are to be evangelized at all.

2. Necessity of Evangelizing the World in This Generation. The Scriptures clearly teach that if men are to be saved they must be saved through Christ. Over half the inhabitants of the earth have never heard the gospel. Shall hundreds of millions go out of the world in this generation without having an opportunity to hear of Christ? If we know from experience that Christ is necessary for us, have we a right to assume that others do not need Him?

3. The Duty of Evangelizing the World in This Generation. It is a duty because it is a necessity. More than this, it is a duty because Christ has commanded it. It is impossible to interpret in any other way the last commission of Christ as given in Matthew, Mark, Luke and Acts. It is also impossible to explain in any other way the interpretation which the Apostles unmistakably gave the commission. Christ's command has acquired tremendous momentum in eighteen centuries of invention, of opening the doors of nations, and of Christian organization.

4. The Possibility of Evangelizing the World in This Generation. What ought to be done, can be done. Christ never commands an impossible thing. Furthermore, it should never be forgotten that this is God's enterprise. In carrying it on we are absolutely sure of the constant presence and help of Him with whom resides all power in heaven and on earth. "Behold, I am the Lord, the God of all flesh: is there anything too hard for Me?" It will greatly strengthen a man's faith in the possibility of evangelizing the world in this generation, to consider thoughtfully and prayerfully the following examples of what has been done in the realm of Christian enterprise: what Christ accomplished in three years of preaching; what Paul accomplished as an evangelist and an organizer; the devotion of the Moravian Church to foreign missions (note the proportion of its members sent to the foreign field, and also the average amount of money given by each member to foreign missions); the achievements of the Gossner Missionary Society in one generation; the work carried on under the leadership of Pastor Harms; the labor of the English Wesleyans in the Fiji Islands; and the work of the American missionaries in the Hawaiian Islands. The record of the Apostolic Church should be read with this point of possibility in mind. In contrast, recall the extent and resources of the Church today; her membership, her wealth, her organizations, her accumulated experience, and the wonderful facilities at her disposal. The power and influence of the native church must also be taken into consideration. Above all, the church today can avail herself of that which made possible the mighty works of the early Christians, "the Holy Ghost, whom God hath given to them that obey him."

5. Favorable Opinions Concerning Speedy and World-wide Evangelization. Among many opinions which might be quoted only three are given.

At the General Conference of Protestant Missionaries of China held at Shanghai in 1877, attended by 126 missionaries, the report of the Committee on Appeal to the Churches, containing the following burning words, was adopted: "Ought we not to make an effort to save China in this generation? Is God's power limited? Is the efficacy of prayer limited? This grand achievement is in the hands of the Church. ... We want China emancipated from the thraldom of sin in this generation. It is possible. Our Lord has said, 'According to your faith be it unto you.' The Church of God can do it, if she be only faithful to her great commission."

Again, at the conference held at Shanghai in 1890, attended by 427 regular missionaries, the following resolution, entitled "Of the Supreme Importance of Evangelistic Work," was adopted: "Resolved: That, while we regard the educational and literary branches of our work as indispensable and likely to yield large fruits in the future, we nevertheless urge that in view of its paramount importance, the evangelistic work be pushed forward with increased vigor and earnestness, in order, if possible, to save the present generation."

From the appeal "To the Secretaries of the Missionary Societies in Europe, America, Australasia, and Asia," sent by the Third Decennial Missionary Conference held at Bombay, 1892-1893, attended by over 600 missionaries, we quote the following: "In the name of Christ and of these unevangelized masses for whom He dies, we appeal to you to send more laborers at once.... Face to face with 284,000,000 in this land, for whom in this generation you as well as we are responsible, we ask, Will you not speedily double the present number of laborers? The manifestation of Christ is greatest to those who keep His Commandments, and this is His Commandment: 'Go ye into all the world and preach the Gospel to every creature.'"

6. Conditions Essential to the Realization of the Watchcry. A thorough, honest, personal consideration of the claims of the enterprise of world-wide evangelization on the part of the Christian students of this generation; clear and settled convictions on the subject on the part of the volunteers themselves; volunteers thoroughly equipped, above all filled with the Holy Spirit, before they go forth to their fields of labor; giving commensurate with the project on the part of all Christians; a Church obedient to Christ's prayer command: "Pray ye therefore the Lord of the harvest, that He send forth laborers into His harvest."

7. Advantages of the Watchcry. Although the experience of the Student Volunteer Movement in the use of this watchcry has been comparatively limited, the results which have attended its use have abundantly justified its adoption. It is true that it has been misunderstood and misinterpreted by men both in and outside the Movement; but by no means as much as has been the case with the volunteer declaration. The watchcry is gaining in favor year by year. It is a power in the lives of a hundred students today where it was in the life of one at the inception of the Movement. It puts the whole missionary enterprise in a more attractive form to many men in our colleges. It holds out a very definite end to be accomplished. It lends additional intensity to all one's missionary activity. It affords a new and powerful incentive. It gives the impetus to an individual which comes from realizing that he is a part of a mighty movement. It appeals to the heroic, the enterprising, and the self-sacrificing in a man's nature. Invariably it drives a man more to prayer, and leads him to rely more fully upon the Spirit of God.

7. *World Missionary Conference, 1910*

The World Missionary Conference in Edinburgh, 1910, stirred its delegates with a sense of spiritual unity and common need for greater co-operation. Discussion of the resolution to have a Continuation Committee showed that great cooperation had already been achieved, especially in China, and that strong desire existed to continue unified efforts in order to be more effective. The two following speeches, which were received with great enthusiasm, bring this out. The succeeding short excerpts indicate the reaction of the delegates to various phases of the discussion. When the vote on the resolution for a Continuation Committee was taken, there was not a single negative voice. The Continuation Committee eventually evolved into the International Missionary Council, and it strongly influenced the formation of the Life and Work and the Faith and Order ecumenical movements. For this reason, Edinburgh, 1910, is often referred to as the key conference in the ecumenical movement. *World Missionary Conference, 1910, Co-operation and the Promotion of Unity,* Vol. VIII (New York: Fleming H. Revell Co., 1910).

Rev. O. L. Kilborn, M.D. (Methodist Church of Canada, Chengtu, West China): As to the practical possibilities of comity and unity I speak, of course, from the point of view of missionaries on the field. I should say, first of all, that what we aim at first ought to be that which seems for the time being to be practical or practicable. We will meet with difficulties certainly in these aims, but I would submit that almost everything or anything that is worth having has been obtained by conquering difficulties, and that we should not consider so much the difficulties as the final aim as to what ought to be, and work definitely for that end. I would suggest that we missionaries in the field should be willing to be used for the principle of comity and co-operation. We must be prepared for difficulties here, sometimes for rebuffs, for delays, and for obstacles which seem to those at the home base to be insuperable, but with perseverance in prayer and work on the field I believe that in a great many cases, if not in all, these can be overcome. I would like to submit something of what has been actually accomplished in the way of comity and co-operation in West China as an illustration of the practical possibilities. I have ten of them. In the first place we have an Advisory Board in West China—the three provinces in Western China. At an estimate there are eighty millions of people there. We have nine organisations that work in West China. We have an Advisory Board of missionaries that is composed of representatives from these nine organisations. These meet annually and they consult together with reference to anything and everything which affects the interests of any two or more than two Boards or Missions. In the second place we have in West China a division of the field; we have no overlapping there. West China is mapped out amongst these nine different organisations. In the third place we have a large measure of union in educational work; we have a Christian educational union. We have a common course of study, common examinations; we have a board of examiners made up of missionaries from all these Missions scattered all over the country. Examinations are held annually, and certificates are issued to successful candidates from the schools in all the Missions. We have an Inspector of schools for the whole of this union. In the fourth place we have a Union University comprising normal college,

arts college, theological college, and medical college. Some of these colleges are in immediate prospect of erection. Some have already begun work. The union university is formed by the co-operation or federation of four Missions. In the fifth place—just as an instance of something that happened this year a few months ago—one of the Missions at work in Shantung with a large hospital found itself unable to supply a doctor for that hospital. By friendly arrangement doctors from two other Missions have been supplied and are carrying on the work during the year, 1910, in the hospital of that third Mission. In the sixth place we have a mission press which is controlled and financed by one Mission, but which is definitely understood to be doing work for all the other branches. In the seventh place we have a Christian magazine—not a Methodist magazine, or a Presbyterian magazine, but a Christian magazine, which circulates freely amongst the Missions of all these nine different organisations. In the eighth place we have a hymn book, and in the ninth place we have free interchange of ideas amongst all these organisations. Lastly, we have a Standing Committee on Church Union, whose aim is definitely expressed as one Christian Church for Western China.

Mr. Chang Ching-Yi (London Missionary Society, China): I count as one of the most gracious blessings that God has bestowed upon the Church in China in recent years the spirit of unity. Something has already been done in the way of Christian federation, and the result is at once practical and remarkable. It is a great blessing for the Church in China to-day, and it will be a much greater blessing for the Church in the days to come. As a representative of the Chinese Church I speak entirely from the Chinese standpoint. We may, and we may not, all agree, but I feel it my duty to present before you the mind of the Chinese Church as frankly as possible. The Christian federation movement occupies a chief place in the hearts of our leading Christian men in China, and they welcome every effort that is made towards that end. This is notably in the provinces of Szechwan, Honan, Shantung, and Chihli. In educational work, evangelistic work, and so on, the Churches joined hand in hand, and the result of this is most encouraging. Since the Chinese Christians have enjoyed the sweetness of such a unity, they long for more, and look for yet greater things. They are watching with keen eyes, and listening with attentive ears what this Conference will show and say to them concerning this all-important question. I am sure they will not be disappointed. Speaking plainly we hope to see, in the near future, a united Christian Church without any denominational distinctions. This may seem somewhat peculiar to some of you, but, friends, do not forget to view us from *our* standpoint, and if you fail to do that, the Chinese will remain always as a mysterious people to you!

In dealing with such a great problem one is naturally led to consider the following points: (1) Why do we want such a union? (2) Is it possible? (3) Is it desirable? (4) Is it timely? (5) Is it an ideal to be aimed at? (6) Will such a union be lasting? (7) How is such a union to be accomplished?

To these questions I will try to answer very briefly.

1. Such a union is needed for these reasons: (a) Things that really help the growing movement of the self-support and self-government of the Church of China are welcomed. A united effort both spiritual and physical is absolutely necessary. (b) Speaking generally, denominationalism has never interested the Chinese mind. He finds no delight in it, but sometimes he suffers for it! (c) Owing to the powerful force of heathenism from without, and the feebleness of the Church from within, the Christians are compelled to unite in building up a defence of the Church.

2. From the Chinese standpoint there is nothing impossible about such a union. Such difficulties as may be experienced will be due to our Western friends and not ourselves. These difficulties are possibilities only, and must not be allowed to overshadow the advantages of the union I speak of.

3. In China, and for the Chinese, such a union is certainly desirable. China, with all her imperfections, is a country that loves unity both in national and family life.

4. There is no time more important than the present. These days are days of founda-

tions from both political and religious standpoints. The future China will largely depend upon what is done at the present time. This is a time of unspeakable responsibilities, and we have to be most careful of what we now do.

5. This is the partial ideal Church. The Church of Christ is universal, not only irrespective of denominations, but also irrespective of nationalities—"All one in Christ Jesus." The world is, to use a Chinese expression, one family, and China is a member of that family.

6. Will such a united Church in China remain unbroken for ever is a question I can only answer by saying "I do not know." But what it will do itself is one thing, and what we press it to do is another. We can only deal with what is to hand to-day, and the unknown future will settle its own affairs!

7. I would, if you will allow me, make one suggestion, and that is, that this Conference will recommend that the Continuation Committee, when appointed, make careful investigation, and will consult all the Chinese pastors and Christian leaders, and obtain from them a free and frank expression of their opinion as to the needs of such a united effort, and the best methods to bring it about. For after all it is not your particular denomination, nor even is it your particular Mission that you are working for, but the establishment of the Church of Christ in China that you have in view.

It is the earnest hope of your present speaker, humble as he is, that this Conference will not allow the present opportunity to pass away without taking some definite action. In conclusion, let us go, with our Divine Master, up on the top of the Mount of Olives, and there we will obtain a wider, broader, and larger view of the needs of the Church and the world.

Discussion Comments

Dr. Julius Richter: Studying the history of Christian Missions in different fields I have often had the impression of a great busy municipal site or newly started township where it is hoped that a very big city shall be built up. But there is no underlying plan, everybody builds where he chooses, according to his own ideas, often without regard of his neighbour and of the future development of the city. So the different missionary organisations are building more or less according to their own ideas, everyone trying to incorporate as much of its own peculiarities as possible. Would it not be advisable in such case that by friendly consultation the new settlers should institute some sort of central organisation with, however, restricted powers to bring harmony into the scattered endeavours, to concentrate effort on needy points. These days have brought us again in view of the great mission fields, of the great, overwhelming tasks lying before us, of the pressing obligations, and on the other hand they have given us a strong impression of the comparative weakness of our own forces and of our isolated position. How useful and helpful would some sort of central organisation be.

Rev. J. Campbell Gibson (Presbyterian Church, England): While I rejoice equally in co-operation I do not believe that the minds of Christian men can ultimately rest in less than that highest level of all, the unity of the Church of God, of which we have robbed ourselves too long, and which it may cause ourselves weary years to restore. But it will be restored by our Lord Himself if we seek it in humility, with infinite patience and with an endless consideration for the difficulties of our brethren.

Rev. R. W. Thompson (London Missionary Society): My impulse in speaking just now is that I want to sing a doxology. I have come to a point in my religious experience in this Conference which five years ago I think I should not have dreamt of.... I long for the time when we shall see another Conference and when the men of the Greek Church and the Roman Church shall talk things over with us in the service of Christ. The kingdom will not come until every branch of the Church can unite together in some common effort of service for the Lord.

Rt. Rev. Bishop of Southwark: Unity when it comes must be something richer, grander, more comprehensive than anything which we can see at present. It is something into which and up to which we must grow, something of which and for which we must become worthy. We need to have sufficient faith in God, to believe that He can bring us to something higher and more Christlike than anything to which at present we see a way.

Continuation Committee

The Resolution proposed by the Commission was as follows:—

I.   That a Continuation Committee of the World Missionary Conference be appointed, international and representative in character, to carry out, on the lines of the Conference itself, which are interdenominational and do not involve the idea of organic and ecclesiastical union, the following duties:—

1.   To maintain in prominence the idea of the World Missionary Conference as a means of co-ordinating missionary work, of laying sound lines for future development, and of generating and claiming by corporate action fresh stores of spiritual force for the evangelisation of the world.

2.   To finish any further investigations, or any formulation of the results of investigations, which may remain after the World Missionary Conference is over, and may be referred to it.

3.   To consider when a further World Missionary Conference is desirable and to make the initial preparations.

4.   To devise plans for maintaining the intercourse which the World Missionary Conference has stimulated between different bodies of workers, *e.g.* by literature or by a system of correspondence and mutual report, or the like.

5.   To place its services at the disposal of the Home Boards in any steps which they may be led to take (in accordance with the recommendation of more than one Commission) towards closer mutual counsel and practical co-operation.

6.   To confer with the Societies and Boards as to the best method of working towards the formation of such a permanent International Missionary Committee as is suggested by the Commissions of the Conference and by various missionary bodies apart from the Conference.

7.   And to take such steps as may seem desirable to carry out, by the formation of Special Committees or otherwise, any prac-

tical suggestions made in the Reports of the Commissions.

8. *The Lambeth Conference, 1920*

Documents on Christian Unity, 1920-30, No. 1, ed. by G. K. A. Bell (London: Oxford University Press, 1955).

1. AN APPEAL TO ALL CHRISTIAN PEOPLE

From the Bishops Assembled In The Lambeth Conference of 1920

We, Archbishops, Bishops Metropolitan, and other Bishops of the Holy Catholic Church in full communion with the Church of England, in Conference assembled, realizing the responsibility which rests upon us at this time and sensible of the sympathy and the prayers of many, both within and without our own Communion, make this appeal to all Christian people.

We acknowledge all those who believe in our Lord Jesus Christ, and have been baptized into the name of the Holy Trinity, as sharing with us membership in the universal Church of Christ which is His Body. We believe that the Holy Spirit has called us in a very solemn and special manner to associate ourselves in penitence and prayer with all those who deplore the divisions of Christian people, and are inspired by the vision and hope of a visible unity of the whole Church.

I. We believe that God wills fellowship. By God's own act this fellowship was made in and through Jesus Christ, and its life is in His Spirit. We believe that it is God's purpose to manifest this fellowship, so far as this world is concerned, in an outward, visible, and united society, holding one faith, having its own recognized officers, using God-given means of grace, and inspiring all its members to the world-wide service of the Kingdom of God. This is what we mean by the Catholic Church.

II. This united fellowship is not visible in the world today. On the one hand there are other ancient episcopal Communions in East and West, to whom ours is bound by many ties of common faith and tradition. On the other hand there are the great non-episcopal Communions, standing for rich elements of truth, liberty and life which might otherwise have been obscured or neglected. With them we are closely linked by many affinities, racial, historical and spiritual. We cherish the earnest hope that all these Communions, and our own, may be led by the Spirit into the unity of the Faith and of the knowledge of the Son of God. But in fact we are all organized in different groups, each one keeping to itself gifts that rightly belong to the whole fellowship, and tending to live its own life apart from the rest.

III. The causes of division lie deep in the past, and are by no means simple or wholly blameworthy. Yet none can doubt that self-will, ambition, and lack of charity among Christians have been principal factors in the mingled process, and that these, together with blindness to the sin of disunion, are still mainly responsible for the breaches of Christendom. We acknowledge this condition of broken fellowship to be contrary to God's will, and we desire frankly to confess our share in the guilt of thus crippling the Body of Christ and hindering the activity of His Spirit.

IV. The times call us to a new outlook and new measures. The Faith cannot be adequately apprehended and the battle of the Kingdom cannot be worthily fought while the body is divided, and is thus unable to grow up into the fullness of the life of Christ. The time has come, we believe, for all the separated groups of Christians to agree in forgetting the things which are behind and reaching out towards the goal of a reunited Catholic Church. The removal of the barriers which have arisen between them will only be brought about by a new comradeship of those whose faces are definitely set this way.

The vision which rises before us is that of a Church, genuinely Catholic, loyal to all Truth, and gathering into its fellowship all "who profess and call themselves Christians," within whose visible unity all the treasures of faith and order, bequeathed as a heritage by the past to the present, shall be possessed in common, and made serviceable to the whole Body of Christ. Within this unity Christian Communions now separated from one another would retain much that has long been distinctive in their methods of worship and service. It is through a rich diversity of

485

life and devotion that the unity of the whole fellowship will be fulfilled.

V. This means an adventure of goodwill and still more of faith, for nothing less is required than a new discovery of the creative resources of God. To this adventure we are convinced that God is now calling all the members of His Church.

VI. We believe that the visible unity of the Church will be found to involve the whole-hearted acceptance of:—

The Holy Scriptures, as the record of God's revelation of Himself to man, and as being the rule and ultimate standard of faith; and the Creed commonly called Nicene, as the sufficient statement of the Christian faith, and either it or the Apostles' Creed as the Baptismal confession of belief:

The divinely instituted sacraments of Baptism and the Holy Communion, as expressing for all the corporate life of the whole fellowship in and with Christ:

A ministry acknowledged by every part of the Church as possessing not only the inward call of the Spirit, but also the commission of Christ and the authority of the whole body.

VII. May we not reasonably claim that the Episcopate is the one means of providing such a ministry? It is not that we call in question for a moment the spiritual reality of the ministries of those Communions which do not possess the Episcopate. On the contrary, we thankfully acknowledge that these ministries have been manifestly blessed and owned by the Holy Spirit as effective means of grace. But we submit that considerations alike of history and of present experience justify the claim which we make on behalf of the Episcopate. Moreover, we would urge that it is now and will prove to be in the future the best instrument for maintaining the unity and continuity of the Church. But we greatly desire that the office of a Bishop should be everywhere exercised in a representative and constitutional manner, and more truly express all that ought to be involved for the life of the Christian Family in the title of Father-in-God. Nay more, we eagerly look forward to the day when through its acceptance in a united Church we may all share in that grace which is pledged to the members of the whole body

in the apostolic rite of the laying-on of hands, and in the joy and fellowship of a Eucharist in which as one Family we may together, without any doubtfulness of mind, offer to the one Lord our worship and service.

VIII. We believe that for all the truly equitable approach to union is by the way of mutual deference to one another's consciences. To this end, we who send forth this appeal would say that if the authorities of other Communions should so desire, we are persuaded that, terms of union having been otherwise satisfactorily adjusted, Bishops and clergy of our Communion would willingly accept from these authorities a form of commission or recognition which would commend our ministry to their congregations, as having its place in the one family life. It is not in our power to know how far this suggestion may be acceptable to those to whom we offer it. We can only say that we offer it in all sincerity as a token of our longing that all ministries of grace, theirs and ours, shall be available for the service of our Lord in a united Church.

It is our hope that the same motive would lead ministers who have not received it to accept a commission through episcopal ordination, as obtaining for them a ministry throughout the whole fellowship.

In so acting no one of us could possibly be taken to repudiate his past ministry. God forbid that any man should repudiate a past experience rich in spiritual blessings for himself and others. Nor would any of us be dishonouring the Holy Spirit of God, whose call led us all to our several ministries, and whose power enabled us to perform them. We shall be publicly and formally seeking additional recognition of a new call to wider service in a reunited Church, and imploring for ourselves God's grace and strength to fulfil the same.

IX. The spiritual leadership of the Catholic Church in days to come, for which the world is manifestly waiting, depends upon the readiness with which each group is prepared to make sacrifices for the sake of a common fellowship, a common ministry, and a common service to the world.

We place this ideal first and foremost before ourselves and our own people. We call upon them to make the effort to meet the demands of a new age with a new outlook. To all other Christian people whom our words may reach we make the same appeal. We do not ask that any one Communion should consent to be absorbed in another. We do ask that all should unite in a new and great endeavour to recover and to manifest to the world the unity of the Body of Christ for which He prayed.

2. RESOLUTIONS ON THE REUNION OF CHRISTENDOM

10. The Conference recommends to the authorities of the Churches of the Anglican Communion that they should, in such ways and at such times as they think best, formally invite the authorities of other Churches within their areas to confer with them concerning the possibility of taking definite steps to co-operate in a common endeavour, on the lines set forth in the above Appeal, to restore the unity of the Church of Christ. . . .

12. The Conference approves the following statements. . . .

(A) *In view of prospects and projects of reunion*— (i) A Bishop is justified in giving occasional authorization to ministers, not episcopally ordained, who in his judgement are working towards an ideal of union such as is described in our Appeal, to preach in churches within his Diocese, and to clergy of the Diocese to preach in the churches of such ministers: (ii) The Bishops of the Anglican Communion will not question the action of any Bishop who, in the few years between the initiation and the completion of a definite scheme of union, shall countenance the irregularity of admitting to Communion the Baptized but unconfirmed Communicants of the non-episcopal congregations concerned in the scheme. . . .

(B) *Believing, however, that certain lines of action might imperil both the attainment of its ideal and the unity of its own communion, the Conference declares that*—(i) It cannot approve of general schemes of intercommunion or exchange of pulpits: (ii) In accordance with the principle of Church order set forth in the Preface to the Ordinal attached to the Book of Common Prayer, it cannot approve the celebration in Anglican

churches of the Holy Communion for members of the Anglican Church by ministers who have not been episcopally ordained; and that it should be regarded as the general rule of the Church that Anglican communicants should receive Holy Communion only at the hands of ministers of their own Church, or of Churches in communion therewith. . . .

9. Consideration of the Lambeth Appeal

Report of the Joint Conference of Representatives of the Federal Council of the Evangelical Free Churches of England and the Church of England, May 1922. *Documents on Christian Unity, 1920-30*, No. 44, *ed.* G. K. A. Bell (London: Oxford University Press, 1955).

I. ON THE NATURE OF THE CHURCH

1. The foundation of the Church rests not upon the will or consent or beliefs of men, whether as individuals or as societies, but upon the creative Will of God.

2. The Church is the Body of Christ, and its constitutive principle is Christ Himself, living in His members through His Spirit.

3. As there is but one Christ, and one Life in Him, so there is and can be but one Church.

4. This one Church consists of all those who have been, or are being, redeemed by and in Christ, whether in this world or in the world beyond our sight, but it has its

X-1. The Ecclesiastical East Wall of Coventry Cathedral. *Photograph courtesy of Thompson, Coventry.*

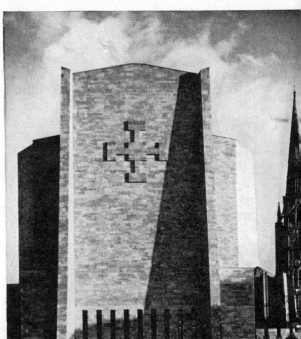

expression in this world in a visible form. Yet the Church, as invisible and as visible, is, by virtue of its one life in Christ, one.

5. This visible Church was instituted by Christ as a fellowship of men united with Him, and in Him with one another, to be His witness and His instrument in the spread of His Kingdom on earth.

6. As a visible Church it must possess certain visible recognizable marks whereby it can be seen and known by men. These have been since the days of the Apostles at least the following: (a) The Profession of faith in God as revealed and incarnate in Christ; (b) the observance of the two Sacraments ordained by Christ Himself; (c) an ideal of the Christian life protected by a common discipline; (d) a ministry, representative of the Church, for the preaching of the Word, the administration of the Sacraments, and the maintenance of the unity and continuity of the Church's witness and work. (See II, 1.)

7. Baptism is by the ordinance of Christ and of His Apostles the outward and visible sign of admission into membership of the Church.

8. The Church visible on earth ought to express and manifest to the world by its own visible unity the one Life in Christ of the one Body.

9. The true relation of the Church and local Churches is that which is described in the New Testament—namely, that the Churches are the local representatives of the One Church. The actual situation brought about in the course of history in which there are different and even rival denominational Churches independent of each other and existing together in the same locality, whatever justification arising out of historical circumstances may be claimed for these temporary separations, cannot be regarded as in accordance with the Purpose of Christ, and every endeavour ought to be made to restore the true position as set forth in the New Testament.

10. The marks which ought to characterize the Church visible on earth are possessed by these existing separate Churches and societies of Christian people in very varying degrees of completeness or defect. Hence,

even though they be parts of the visible Church, they cannot be considered as all alike giving equally adequate expression to the Lord's Mind and Purpose. Some, indeed, may be so defective that they cannot rightly be judged to be parts of that Church. But such judgements, though made in trust that they are in accordance with the Divine Mind, must be regarded as limited to the sphere of the visible Church as an ordered society here on earth. It would be presumption to claim that they have a like validity in the sphere of the whole Church as the One Body of the redeemed in Christ, for within that sphere judgement can only be given by the All-Knowing Mind and Sovereign Mercy of God.

II. THE MINISTRY

1. A ministry of the Word and Sacrament is a Divine ordinance for the Church, and has been since the days of the Apostles an integral part of its organized life.

2. It is a ministry within the Church exercising representatively, in the Name and by the authority of the Lord Who is the Head of the Church, the powers and functions which are inherent in the Church.

3. It is a ministry of the Church, and not merely of any part thereof.

4. No man can take this ministry upon himself. It must be conferred by the Church, acting through those who have authority given to them in the Church to confer it. There must be not only an inward call of the Spirit, but also an outward and visible call and commission by the Church.

5. It is in accordance with Apostolic practice and the ancient custom of the Church that this commission should be given through Ordination, with prayer and the laying on of hands by those who have authority given to them to ordain.

6. We believe that in Ordination, together with this commission to minister, Divine Grace is given through the Holy Spirit in response to prayer and faith for the fulfilment of the charge so committed.

7. Within the many Christian Communions into which in the course of history Christendom has been divided, various forms of ministry have grown up according to the circumstances of these several Communions

and their beliefs as to the Mind of Christ and the guidance of the New Testament. These various ministries of Word and Sacrament have been, in God's providence, manifestly and abundantly used by the Holy Spirit in His work of "enlightening the world, converting sinners, and perfecting saints." But the differences which have arisen with regard to the authority and functions of these various forms of ministry have been and are the occasion of manifold doubts, questions, and misunderstandings. For the allaying of doubts and scruples in the future, and for the more perfect realization of the truth that the ministry is a ministry of the Church, and not merely of any part thereof, means should be provided for the United Church which we desire, whereby its ministry may be acknowledged by every part thereof as possessing the authority of the whole body.

8. In view of the fact that the Episcopate was from early times and for many centuries accepted, and by the greater part of Christendom is still accepted, as the means whereby this authority of the whole body is given, we agree that it ought to be accepted as such for the United Church of the future.

9. Similarly, in view of the place which the Council of Presbyters and the Congregation of the faithful had in the constitution of the early Church, and the preservation of these elements of presbyteral and congregational order in large sections of Christendom, we agree that they should be maintained with a representative and constitutional Episcopate as permanent elements in the order and life of the United Church.

10. The acceptance of Episcopal Ordination for the future would not imply the acceptance of any particular theory as to its origin or character, or the disowning of past ministries of Word and Sacrament otherwise received, which have, together with those received by Episcopal Ordination, been used and blessed by the Spirit of God.

III. THE PLACE OF THE CREED
IN A UNITED CHURCH

1. In a united Church there must be unity of Faith, which implies both the subjective element of personal adhesion and an objective standard of truth.

2. The supreme standard of truth is the revelation of God contained in the Scriptures of the Old and New Testaments as summed up in Jesus Christ.

3. As the Church in its corporate capacity confesses Christ before men, there should be in the United Church a formal statement of its corporate faith in Christ as an expression of what is intellectually implied by its confession of Him.

4. The Creed commonly called Nicene should be accepted by the United Church as the sufficient statement of this corporate faith. The manner and occasions in which the Creed is to be used should be determined by the United Church.

5. With regard to a confession of faith at Baptism, the United Church would be justified in using the Creed which has been for centuries the Baptismal Creed of the Western Church, commonly called the Apostles' Creed. Its use at Baptism would imply recognition of the corporate faith of the Church therein expressed as the guide and inspiration of the Christian life.

6. The use of the Creeds liturgically in the public worship of the Church should be regarded as an expression of corporate faith and allegiance; and the United Church should be prepared to recognize diversities of use in this as in other liturgical customs.

7. When assent to the Creeds is required by the United Church, such assent should not be understood to imply the acceptance of them as a complete expression of the Christian Faith, or as excluding reasonable liberty of interpretation. It should be understood to imply the acceptance of them as agreeable to the Word of God contained in the Holy Scriptures, as affirming essential elements in the Christian Faith, and as preserving that Faith in the form in which it has been handed down through many centuries in the history of the Christian Church.

8. While we thus recognize the rightful place of the Creeds in the United Church, we also recognize most fully and thankfully the continued Presence and Teaching of the Living Spirit in His Body, and emphasize the duty of the Church to keep its mind free and ready to receive from Him in each day and

generation ever-renewed guidance in the apprehension and expression of the truth.

10. Baptist View of Organic Union

Baptist View of Organic Union, Northern Baptist Convention, Denver, May, 1919. McFarland, *Christian Unity in Practice and Prophecy.*

Whereas, the Northern Baptist Convention has been invited to send delegates to a council looking toward organic union of the Protestant denominations, it is

Resolved, That the Northern Baptist Convention, while maintaining fraternal relations with evangelical denominations in extending the influence of the Gospel of Jesus Christ, does not believe that organic union with other denominations is possible. It therefore declines to send delegates to the proposed council.

In declining this invitation, however, Christian courtesy demands that the Northern Baptist Convention should state its position as to organic union with other Christian denominations. This we make not with any desire to pose as judge of our Christian brethren, but in the interest of mutual understanding.

The Baptist denomination is a collection of independent democratic churches. Not one of these churches recognizes any ecclesiastical authority superior to itself. They are grouped in associations, state conventions, and a national Convention, but none of these groups has any control over a local church beyond that which lies in common faith, practice, and service. The denomination, in so far as it has unity, is a federation of independent democracies. In the nature of the case, therefore, anything like organic union of Baptist Churches with other denominations is impossible. There is no centralized body that could deliver Baptist Churches to any merger or corporate unity. If Baptist Churches do not have organic unity among themselves, they obviously cannot have organic unity with other denominations. By the very nature of our organization, we are stopped from seeking organic union with other denominations.

This situation does not arise from any desire on our part as Baptists to withhold ourselves from fellowship with other Christian bodies in the pursuance of Christian work. Nor does it arise from any desire to impose upon them our own convictions. We grant to others all rights that we claim for ourselves. But the liberty of conscience and the independence of the churches which characterize our position are involved in our fundamental conception as to the nature of the Church and of its relation to the religious life.

We believe in the complete competency of the individual to come directly into saving relationship with God. We hold that a church is a local community of those who have consciously committed themselves to Jesus Christ. The only Church Universal is, in our belief, spiritual fellowship of individual souls with God. We do not believe in any form of sacerdotalism or sacramentalism among Christians, who are all equally priests of the Most High. We reject ecclesiastical orders and hold that all believers are on a spiritual equality. With us ordination is only a formal recognition on the part of some local church that one of its members is judged worthy to serve as a pastor. The fact that such appointment is generally recognized in all our churches is simply a testimony to denominational good faith.

We cannot modify these convictions for the sake of establishing a corporate unity with other denominations. Any compromise at this point would be an abandonment of structural beliefs.

We heartily believe in the necessity of a combined impact of Christian forces upon the evil of the world. Such impact, however, does not depend for its efficiency upon organic union of the churches. We are convinced that our fundamental conception of the Church, the nature of our organization, the democracy which is the very basis of our denominational life, make any organic union with groups of Christians holding opposite views unwise and impossible.

11. Resolution of the International Missionary Council

Resolution of the International Missionary Council at Oxford on Missionary Cooperation in View

The International Missionary Council has given attention to the anxiety which is felt in many quarters about the possibility of missionary cooperation in face of doctrinal differences and thinks it opportune to review the cooperation which has actually been undertaken under its auspices or those of the national and other councils which it correlates and other similar cooperative action, and to set out afresh the principles which have emerged from these experiences.

The International Missionary Council has never sought nor is it its function to work out a body of doctrinal opinions of its own. The only doctrinal opinions in the Council are those which the various members bring with them into it from the churches and missionary boards to which they belong. It is no part of the duty of the Council to discuss the merits of those opinions, still less to determine doctrinal questions.

But it has never been found in practice that in consequence of this the Council is left with nothing but an uncertain mass of conflicting opinions. The Council is conscious of a great measure of agreement which centers in a common obligation and a common loyalty. We are conscious of a common obligation to proclaim the Gospel of Christ in all the world, and this sense of obligation is made rich and deep because of our knowledge of the havoc wrought by sin and of the efficacy of the salvation offered by Christ. We are bound together further by a common loyalty to Jesus Himself, and this loyalty is deep and fruitful because we rejoice to share the confessions of St. Peter, "Thou art the Christ, the Son of the Living God," and of St. Thomas, "My Lord and My God." The secret of our cooperation is the presence with us of Jesus Christ, Human Friend and Divine Helper. From this common obligation and this common loyalty flow many other points of agreement, and our differences in doctrine, great though in some instances they are, have not hindered us from profitable cooperation in counsel. When we have gathered together, we have experienced a growing unity among ourselves in which we recognize the influence of the Holy Spirit. At these meetings we have come to a common mind on many matters and been able to frame recommendations and statements. These have never had the character of command or direction, and it has always rested with the churches or missions to give them, if they would, authority by adopting them or carrying them into action.

Cooperation in work is more likely to be embarrassed by doctrinal differences than cooperation in Council. Yet there is a wide range of matters such as negotiations with governments, the securing of religious liberty, the combating of the evils arising from the sale of narcotic drugs, collection and survey of facts, investigation of educational method, etc., which are not affected by doctrinal differences. A still more imposing list might be drawn up of types of work in which impediments from doctrinal differences might have been anticipated, but experience in many lands has shown that most valuable cooperation is possible between many churches and missions. Such are the translation of the Holy Scriptures, the production and dissemination of Christian literature, the conduct of schools and colleges and medical institutions, and provision for the training of missionaries. Every piece of cooperation in work which this Council or, as we believe, any council connected with it encourages or guides is confined to those churches or missions which freely and willingly take part in it. It would be entirely out of harmony with the spirit of this movement to press for such cooperation in work as would be felt to compromise doctrinal principles or to strain consciences.

12. Faith and Order

As the individual disciple is known by his fruits, so the unity of the disciples is shown by their fellowship in the service of the Master. Report V declares that, "pending the solution of the questions of faith and order in which agreements have not yet been reached, it is possible for us, not simply as individuals but as churches, to unite in the activities of brotherly service which Christ has committed to His disciples"; but there is difference as to the exact form this cooperation should take.

In his Encyclical Letter of 1920, the Ecumenical Patriarch proposed "that a league or council of the churches should be formed for practical purposes." It has been suggested that such a council might be evolved from already existing organizations, such as the Continuation Committee on Life and Work, consisting of representatives officially appointed by almost all the Christian communions, and other organizations of similar nature. Some of us believe that such a council if formed should include, as its two branches, questions of life and work and of faith and order. Others believe that, for the present, it would be wiser for the movements represented by Stockholm and Lausanne to develop in independence, each following its own way; but there is general agreement that ultimately life, work, faith and order are expressions of an existing spiritual unity, and that each requires the other for its complete fruition. "We therefore commend to our Churches the consideration of the steps which may be immediately practicable to bring our existing unity in service to more effective expression" (Report V).

As material for such consideration, the following suggestions which it was impossible adequately to discuss at Lausanne are passed on to the churches:

1. In preparation for closer fellowship, each communion should seek more intimate knowledge of the faith and life, worship and order of the others. Differences which are the outgrowth of complicated historical developments, may preserve some aspect of truth or of life which is of value to the church as a whole, or they may sometimes prove to be less important than they are supposed to be. As the different communions come to know one another better they will grow in understanding and in appreciation of one another.

2. It has not been possible for the Conference to consider with the care which it deserves the relation of the existing churches to one another or the place which each or any of them may hold in the undivided church. We commend to the churches the suggestions which have been made on this subject in the addresses delivered at the Conference. In the meantime, we welcome the movement already under way for the union of bodies of similar doctrine, polity and worship, and trust that it may continue with ever greater success.

3. Pending the complete, organic union of the different churches, we note with satisfaction a number of movements for practical cooperation along social, evangelistic and other lines. Experience shows that it has been possible for widely separate bodies to cooperate in such movements with mutual profit and without surrender of principle. (See the appended "Notes to Section IV," Note A.) There is abundant evidence that when communions undertake together the divine task of bringing the love of Christ to those who do not know Him, they become closer to one another. Especially we commend to the churches the consideration of what steps can be taken to eliminate needless overlapping and competition in the local community; that in ways consistent with the genius of the several communions, our existing unity in Christ may be manifest to the world. (See the appended "Notes to Section IV," Note B.)

We note with gratitude to God the recent increase of effective cooperation in the mission field. The purpose of all missionary work is to carry the eternal Gospel to the ends of the earth, so that it may meet the spiritual needs of every nation and bring all men to the Savior. Here more than anywhere else unity is essential. We note with sympathy the degree of union which has already been attained in many countries and the plans which are proposed for further union. We commend these plans to the churches for their careful consideration.

The demand which comes from the

492

churches of the Mission field is that the churches at home should grant them greater freedom of action, and that their hopes of unity should not be frustrated by the long-continued acquiescence in disunion at home which makes it difficult to recognize how fatal disunion is to the new indigenous churches.

[The following note was added to this report:]

A. There are some who believe that co-operation should take the form of federation, either local, national, or international; others oppose federation, fearing that it may become a substitute for complete organic union. In the interest of clarity of thought it is important to remember that the word "federation" is used in at least three different senses. It may denote either (1) A substitute for organic union, (2) A step on the road to organic union, (3) A form of organic union.

In discussing federation it is important to make clear in which of these different senses the word is used.

B. It is suggested that in the case of communions of similar doctrine and polity, the desired expression of unity may often be secured by the method of denominational comity. In the case of those communions which are separated by fundamental differences of view, the problem is more difficult and will require special consideration.

13. "A Step Forward in Church Relations"

Extract from a sermon preached before the University of Cambridge by the Archbishop of Canterbury, Dr. Fisher, November 3, 1946. *Documents on Christian Unity, 1948-57*, Fourth Series, No. 236, ed. G. K. A. Bell (London: Oxford University Press, 1958).

There is a suggestion which I should like in all humility to make to my brethren of other denominations. We do not desire a federation: that does not restore the circulation. As I have suggested, the road is not yet open, we are not yet ready for organic or constitutional union. But there can be a process of assimilation, of growing alike. What we need is that while the folds remain distinct, there should be a movement towards a free and unfettered exchange of life in worship and sacrament between them as

there is already of prayer and thought and Christian fellowship—in short, that they should grow towards the full communion with one another, which already in their separation they have with Christ.

The Church of England is in full communion with the Old Catholics on the Continent: and its relations with the Orthodox Churches on the one hand and with the Churches of Sweden and Finland on the other approach, if they do not yet reach, full communion. My longing is, not yet that we should be *united* with other Churches in this country, but that we should grow to *full communion* with them. As I have said and as negotiations have shown, no insuperable barrier to that remains until we come to questions of the ministry and government of the Church. Full communion between Churches means not that they are identical in all ways, but that there is no barrier to exchange of their ministers and ministries. Every Church's ministry is effective as a means by which the life of Christ reaches His people. Every Church's ministry is defective because it is prevented from operating in all the folds of His flock. For full communion between Churches there is needed a ministry mutually acknowledged by all as possessing not only the inward call of the Spirit but also the authority which each Church in conscience requires.

At the Lausanne Conference of Churches in 1927, it was said that in view of the place which the Episcopate, the Council of Presbyters, and the Congregation of the Faithful respectively had in the constitution of the early Church, in view of the fact that these three elements are each today and have been for centuries accepted by great Communions in Christendom, and that they are each believed by many to be essential to the good order of the Church, "We recognise that these several elements must all . . . have an appropriate place in the order of life of a reunited Church." Every constitutional scheme has proceeded on those lines. The non-episcopal Churches have accepted the principle that episcopacy must exist along with the other elements in a reunited Church. For reasons obvious enough in Church History, they fear what may be made of episcopacy. But they accept the fact of it. If they do so for a reunited Church, why not also and earlier for the process of assimilation, as a step towards full communion? It may be said that in a reunited Church they could guard themselves in the constitution against abuses of episcopacy. But they could do so far more effectively by taking it into their own system. The Church of England has not yet found the finally satisfying use of episcopacy in practice: nor certainly has the Church of Rome. If non-episcopal Churches agree that it must come into the picture, could not they take it and try it out on their own ground first?

It is not of course quite as simple as all that. There are requirements and functions which Catholic tradition attaches to the office of a Bishop in the Church of God, which, if our aim is assimilation and full communion, must be safeguarded. Negotiators in the past have been able to agree upon them, and could with hope enquire into them further, if our non-episcopal brethren were able to contemplate the step I suggest. As it seems to me, it is an easier step for them to contemplate than those involved in a union of Churches: and if achieved, it would immensely carry us forward towards full communion, without the fearful complexities and upheavals of a constitutional union. In such a giving and receiving of episcopacy, there would be a mutual removal of a barrier between the folds. Nor would any fresh barriers be raised, such as may be by a constitutional scheme. For no previous existing affiliations would be impaired. The Church of England can be in communion with the Church of Sweden which in its turn is in communion with the Church of Norway, although as yet the Church of England is not in communion with the Church of Norway. That may be illogical, but it is the way of Christian life and love. William Temple used to quote Fr. Kelly as saying that we must not regard the Churches as we regard a row of separate boxes, but as rays of coloured lights shading into one another.

ESSENTIAL PRINCIPLES

In putting forward this suggestion, I am presupposing that between the Churches which concerned themselves with it there would be found to be agreement upon the essential principles of the Church, the Scriptures, the Creeds, the Sacraments and of the Ministry itself as "a gift of God through Christ to His Church, essential to its being and well being, perpetually authorized and made effective through Christ and His Spirit" (Lausanne, Report 5): and I believe that presupposition to be reasonable. Differences of interpretation are not such as to forbid communion and indeed are to be found within each body. If then non-episcopal Churches could thus take episcopacy into their systems I hope that that step would not stand alone. I should hope that in preparation for it, along the lines of recent Canadian proposals, each communion, episcopal and non-episcopal, would contribute the whole of its separate ministry to so many of the ministers of the other as were willing to receive it. By that means there would be assimilation at work from the start at the presbyteral level as well as at the episcopal level.

It is because I fear a stalemate, that I venture to put this suggestion forward for examination. I love the Church of England, as the Presbyterian and the Methodist love their Churches. It is, I think, not possible yet nor desirable that any Church should merge its identity in a newly constituted union. What I desire is that I should be able freely to enter their Churches and they mine in the Sacraments of the Lord and in the full fellowship of worship, that His life may freely circulate between us. Cannot we grow to full communion with each other before we start to write a constitution? Have we the wisdom, the humility, the love and the spirit of Christ sufficient for such venture as I have suggested? If there were agreement on it, I would thankfully receive at the hands of others their commission in their accustomed form and in the same way confer our own; that is the mutual exchange of love and enrichment to which Lambeth, 1920, called us.

To some of you here my theme must have seemed remote from your own interests and needs. It is not really so: for it concerns the life of Christ in His Church, and therefore reaches down to everyone to whom the Church would minister that life. Let me at least recall you to the point at which I began. Look through and beyond the Churches, to the Lord, the Door, the Shepherd. He knows you. He calls you by name. The thieves are all round us, stealing our spiritual values, killing and destroying what was made for God and eternal life. The Christian soul stoops humbly to the lowly Door and enters and safely goes in and out, finding his pasture, and lives. Christ comes to us that we may live and grow in life beyond our seeing into His eternal Kingdom.

14. The World Council of Churches

The first section consists of The Constitution of the World Council of Churches, as adopted by the First Assembly of Amsterdam, 1948, and amended at Evanston, 1954. Bell, *Documents on Christian Unity, 1948-57,* Fourth Series, No. 276. The second selection comprises the World Council's Amsterdam Message. *Man's Disorder and God's Design: The Amsterdam Assembly Series,* IV (New York: Harper & Row, Publishers, 1949).

THE CONSTITUTION OF THE WORLD COUNCIL OF CHURCHES

I. Basis

The World Council of Churches is a fellowship of churches which accept our Lord Jesus Christ as God and Saviour. It is constituted for the discharge of the functions set out below.

II. Membership

Those churches shall be eligible for membership in the World Council of Churches which express their agreement with the basis upon which the Council is founded and satisfy such criteria as the Assembly or the Central Committee may prescribe. Election to membership shall be by a two-thirds vote of the member churches represented at the Assembly, each member church having one vote. Any application for membership between meetings of the Assembly may be considered by the Central Committee; if the application is supported by a two-thirds majority of the members of the Committee present and voting, this action shall be communicated to the churches that are members of the World Council of Churches, and unless objection is received from more than one-third of the member churches within six months the applicant shall be declared elected.

III. Functions

The functions of the World Council shall be: (i) To carry on the work of the two world movements for Faith and Order and for Life and Work. (ii) To facilitate common action by the churches. (iii) To promote cooperation in study. (iv) To promote the growth of ecumenical consciousness in the members of all churches. (v) To establish relations with denominational federations of world-wide scope and with other ecumenical movements. (vi) To call world conferences on specific subjects as occasion may require, such conferences being empowered to publish their own findings. (vii) To support the churches in their task of evangelism.

X-2. The World Council of Churches, 1948. *Scene at opening service of Amsterdam Assembly in Nieuwe Kerk. In the pulpit is Dr. K. H. E. Gravemeyer of the Dutch Reformed Church. Others, left to right: Archbishop Germanos, the Rev. D. T. Niles, Dr. John R. Mott, the Archbishop of Canterbury, pastor Marc Boegner, and Archbishop Eidem of Sweden. Photograph courtesy of the World Council of Churches.*

IV. Authority

The World Council shall offer counsel and provide opportunity of united action in matters of common interest.

It may take action on behalf of constituent churches in such matters as one or more of them may commit to it.

It shall have authority to call regional and world conferences on specific subjects as occasion may require.

The World Council shall not legislate for the churches; nor shall it act for them in any manner except as indicated above or as may hereafter be specified by the constituent churches.

V. Organization

The World Council shall discharge its functions through the following bodies: (i) An Assembly which shall be the principal authority in the Council, and shall ordinarily meet every five years. . . . Seats in the Assembly shall be allocated to the member churches by the Central Committee, due regard being given to such factors as numerical size, adequate confessional representation and adequate geographical distribution. . . . The members of the Assembly shall be both clerical and lay persons—men and women. In order to secure that approximately one-third of the Assembly shall consist of lay persons, the Central Committee, in allocating to the member churches their places in the Assembly, shall strongly urge each church, if possible, to observe this provision. (ii) A Central Committee which shall be a Committee of the Assembly and which shall consist of the President or Presidents of the World Council, together with not more than ninety members chosen by the Assembly from among persons whom the churches have appointed as members of the Assembly. . . .

The Central Committee shall have the following powers: (a) It shall, between meetings of the Assembly, carry out the Assembly's instructions and exercise its functions, except that of amending the Constitution, or modifying the allocation of its own members; (b) It shall be the finance committee of the Assembly formulating its budget and securing its financial support; (c) It shall name and elect its own Officers from among its members and appoint its own secretarial staff; (d) The Central Committee shall meet normally once every calendar year, and shall have power to appoint its own Executive Committee. *Quorum:* No business, except what is required for carrying forward the current activities of the Council, shall be transacted in either the Assembly or the Central Committee unless one-half of the total membership is present.

VI. Appointment of Commissions

The World Council shall discharge part of its functions by the appointment of Commissions. . . .

There shall be a Faith and Order Commission of which the following shall be the functions: (i) To proclaim the essential oneness of the Church of Christ and to keep prominently before the World Council and the churches the obligation to manifest that unity and its urgency for the work of evangelism; (ii) to study questions of faith, order and worship with the relevant social, cultural, political, racial and other factors in their bearing on the unity of the churches; (iii) to study the theological implications of the existence of the ecumenical movement; (iv) to study matters in the present relationships of the churches to one another which cause difficulties and need theological clarification; (v) to provide information concerning actual steps taken by the churches towards reunion.

The Commission shall discharge these functions in accordance with a constitution approved by the Central Committee. . . .

AMSTERDAM MESSAGE, 1948

The World Council of Churches, meeting at Amsterdam, sends this message of greeting to all who are in Christ, and to all who are willing to hear.

We bless God our Father, and our Lord Jesus Christ, who gathers together in one the children of God that are scattered abroad. He has brought us here together at Amsterdam. We are one in acknowledging Him as our God and Saviour. We are divided from one another not only in matters of faith, order and tradition, but also by pride of nation, class and race. But Christ has made us His own, and He is not divided. In seeking Him we find one another Here at Amsterdam we have committed ourselves afresh to Him, and have covenanted with one another in constituting this World Council of Churches. We intend to stay together. We call upon Christian congregations everywhere to endorse and fulfill this covenant in their relations one with another. In thankfulness we commit the future to Him.

When we look to Christ, we see the world as it is—His world, to which He came and for which He died. It is filled both with great hopes and also with disillusionment and despair. Some nations are rejoicing in new freedom and power, some are bitter because freedom is denied them, some are paralysed by division, and everywhere there is an undertone of fear. There are millions who are hungry, millions who have no home, no country and no hope. Over all mankind hangs the peril of total war. We have to accept God's judgment upon us for our share in the world's guilt. Often we have tried to serve God and mammon, put other loyalties before loyalty to Christ, confused the Gospel with our own economic or national or racial interests, and feared war more than we have hated it. As we have talked with each other here, we have begun to understand how our separation has prevented us from receiving correction from one another in Christ. And because we have lacked this correction, the world has often heard from us not the Word of God but the words of men.

But there is a word of God for our world. It is that the world is in the hands of the living God, Whose will for it is wholly good; that in Christ Jesus, His incarnate Word, Who lived and died and rose from the dead, God has broken the power of evil once for all, and opened for everyone the gate into freedom and joy in the Holy Spirit; that the final judgment on all human history and on every human deed is the judgment of the merciful Christ; and that the end of history will be the triumph of His Kingdom, where alone we shall understand how much God has loved the world. This is God's unchanging Word to the world. Millions of our fellowmen have never heard it. As we are met here from many lands, we pray God to stir up His whole Church to make this Gospel known to the whole world, and to call on all men to believe in Christ, to live in His love and hope for His coming.

Our coming together to form a World Council will be vain unless Christians and Christian congregations everywhere commit themselves to the Lord of the Church in a new effort to seek together, where they live, to be His witnesses and servants among their neighbors. We have to remind ourselves and all men that God has put down the mighty from their seats and exalted the humble and meek. We have to learn afresh together to speak boldly in Christ's name both to those in power and to the people, to oppose terror, cruelty and race discrimination, to stand by the outcast, the prisoner and the refugee. We have to make of the Church in every place a voice for those who have no voice, and a home where every man will be at home We have to learn afresh together what is the duty of the Christian man or woman in industry, in agriculture, in politics, in the professions and in the home. We have to ask God to teach us together to say "No" and to say "Yes" in truth. "No," to all that flouts the love of Christ, to every system, every programme and every person that treats any man as though he were an irresponsible thing or a means of profit, to the defenders of injustice in the name of order, to those who sow the seeds of war or urge war as inevitable; "Yes," to all that conforms to the love of Christ, to all who seek for justice, to the peacemakers, to all who hope, fight and suffer for the cause of man, to all who—even without knowing it—look for new heavens and a new earth wherein dwelleth righteousness.

It is not in man's power to banish sin and death from the earth, to create the unity of the Holy Catholic Church, to conquer the hosts of Satan. But it is within the power of God. He has given us at Easter the certainty that His purpose will be accomplished. But, by our acts of obedience and faith, we can on earth set up signs which point to the coming victory. Till the day of that victory our lives are hid with Christ in God, and no earthly disillusion or distress or power of hell can separate us from Him. As those who wait in confidence and joy for their deliverance, let us give ourselves to those tasks which lie in our hands, and so set up signs that men may see.

Now unto Him that is able to do exceeding abundantly above all that we ask or think, according to the power that worketh in us, unto Him be glory in the Church by Christ Jesus, throughout all ages, world without end.

15. The World Council of Churches, Amsterdam, 1948

The Report on International Disorders says, "We are one in proclaiming to mankind," that "War is contrary to the will of God: Peace requires an attack on the cause of conflict between the powers: The nations of the world must acknowledge the rule of law: The observance of Human Rights and Fundamental Freedoms should be encouraged by domestic and international action: The churches and all Christian people have obligations in the face of international disorder." The report resolved to aid refugees, to seek an international bill of human rights, and to promote religious liberty throughout the world. Its resolution on religious liberty follows. *Man's Disorder and God's Design: The Amsterdam Assembly Series.*

REPORT ON INTERNATIONAL DISORDER:
RELIGIOUS LIBERTY

Be it resolved that the World Council of Churches adopt the following *Declaration on Religious Liberty* and urge the application of its provisions through domestic and international action.

A Declaration on Religious Liberty

An essential element in a good international order is freedom of religion. This is an implication of the Christian faith and of the world-wide nature of Christianity. Christians, therefore, view the question of religious freedom as an international problem. They are concerned that religious freedom be everywhere secured. In pleading for this freedom, they do not ask for any privilege to be granted to Christians that is denied to others. While the liberty with which Christ has set men free can neither be given nor destroyed by any government, Christians, because of that inner freedom, are both jealous for its

outward expression and solicitous that all men should have freedom in religious life. The nature and destiny of man by virtue of his creation, redemption and calling, and man's activities in family, state and culture establish limits beyond which the government cannot with impunity go. The rights which Christian discipleship demands are such as are good for all men, and no nation has ever suffered by reason of granting such liberties. Accordingly:

The rights of religious freedom herein declared shall be recognised and observed for all persons without distinction as to race, colour, sex, language or religion, and without imposition of disabilities by virtue of legal provisions or administrative acts.

I. *Every person has the right to determine his own faith and creed.* The right to determine faith and creed involves both the process whereby a person adheres to a belief and the process whereby he changes his belief. It includes the right to receive instruction and education.

This right becomes meaningful when man has the opportunity of access to information. Religious, social and political institutions have the obligation to permit the mature individual to relate himself to sources of information in such a way as to allow personal religious decision and belief.

The right to determine one's belief is limited by the right of parents to decide sources of information to which their children shall have access. In the process of reaching decisions, everyone ought to take into account his higher self-interests and the implications of his beliefs for the well-being of his fellow men.

II. *Every person has the right to express his religious beliefs in worship, teaching and practice, and to proclaim the implications of his beliefs for relationships in a social or political community.* The right of religious expression includes freedom of worship both public and private; freedom to place information at the disposal of others by processes of teaching, preaching and persuasion; and freedom to pursue such activities as are dictated by conscience. It also includes freedom to express implications of belief for society and its government.

This right requires freedom from arbitrary limitation of religious expression in all means of communication, including speech, press, radio, motion pictures and art. Social and political institutions should grant immunity from discrimination and from legal disability on grounds of expressed religious conviction, at least to the point where recognised community interests are adversely affected.

Freedom of religious expression is limited by the rights of parents to determine the religious point of view to which their children shall be exposed. It is further subject to such limitations, prescribed by law, as are necessary to protect order and welfare, morals and the rights and freedom of others. Each person must recognise the right of others to express their beliefs and must have respect for authority at all times, even when conscience forces him to take issue with the people who are in authority or with the position they advocate.

III. *Every person has the right to associate with others and to organise with them for religious purposes.* This right includes freedom to form religious organisations, to seek membership in religious organisations, and to sever relationship with religious organisations.

It requires that the rights of association and organisation guaranteed by a community to its members include the right of forming associations for religious purposes.

It is subject to the same limits imposed on all associations by non-discriminatory laws.

IV. *Every religious organisation, formed or maintained by action in accordance with the right of individual persons, has the right to determine its policies and practices for the accomplishment of its chosen purposes.* The rights which are claimed for the individual in his exercise of religious liberty become the rights of the religious organisation, including the right to determine its faith and creed; to engage in religious worship, both public and private; to teach, educate, preach and persuade; to express implications of belief for society and government. To these will be added certain corporate rights which derive from the rights of individual persons, such as the right: to determine the form of organisation, its government and conditions of mem-

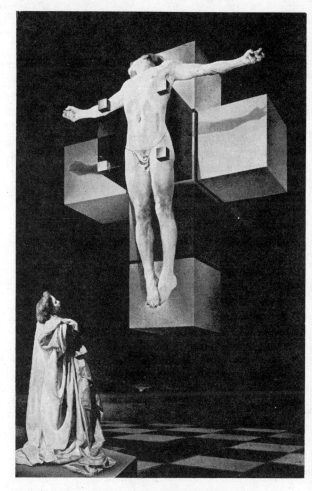

X-3. Crucifixion by Salvador Dali (1904–   ). *Symbolizes the universalization of the cross. The Metropolitan Museum of Art, gift of the Chester Dale Collection, 1955.*

bership; to select and train its own officers, leaders and workers; to publish and circulate religious literature; to carry on service and missionary activities at home and abroad; to hold property and to collect funds; to cooperate and to unite with other religious bodies at home and in other lands, including freedom to invite or to send personnel beyond national frontiers and to give or to receive financial assistance; to use such facilities, open to all citizens or associations, as will make possible the accomplishment of religious ends.

In order that these rights may be realised in social experience, the state must grant to religious organisations and their members

499

the same rights which it grants to other organisations, including the right of self-government, of public meeting, of speech, of press and publication, of holding property, of collecting funds, of travel, of ingress and egress, and generally of administering their own affairs.

The community has the right to require obedience to non-discriminatory laws passed in the interest of public order and well-being. In the exercise of its rights, a religious organisation must respect the rights of other religious organisations and must safeguard the corporate and individual rights of the entire community.

16. *World Council of Churches, New Delhi, 1961*

Excerpts from *New Delhi Speaks*, Reports of the World Council of Churches, ed. W. A. Visser't Hooft (New York: Association Press, 1962).

APPEAL TO ALL GOVERNMENTS AND PEOPLES

The Third Assembly of the World Council of Churches, at which are gathered Christians from all parts of the world, addresses this appeal to the government and people of every nation.

Today, war itself is a common enemy. War is an offence to the nature of man. The future

X-4. The Chapel at Massachusetts Institute of Technology. *An example of universality and nondenominationalism in modern religious architecture.*

of many generations and the heritage of ages past hang in the balance. They are now easy to destroy, since the actions or miscalculations of a few can bring about a holocaust. They are harder to safeguard and advance, for that requires the dedicated action of all. Let there be restraint and self-denial in the things which make for war, patience and persistence in seeking to resolve the things which divide, and boldness and courage in grasping the things which make for peace.

To turn back from the road towards war into the paths of peace, all must renounce the threat of force. This calls for an end to the war of nerves, to pressures on small countries, to the rattling of bombs. It is not possible to follow at the same time policies of menace and of mutual disarmament.

To halt the race in arms is imperative. Complete and general disarmament is the accepted goal, and concrete steps must be taken to reach it. Meanwhile, the search for a decisive first step, such as the verified cessation of nuclear tests, should be pressed forward despite all obstacles and setbacks.

To substitute reason for force and undergird the will to disarm, institutions of peace and orderly methods to effect change and to settle disputes are essential. This imposes a duty to strengthen the United Nations within the framework and spirit of the Charter. All countries share this duty, whether aligned with the major power blocs or independent of them. The non-aligned can contribute through their impartiality; with others they can be champions of the principles of the Charter.

To build peace with justice, barriers of mutual distrust must be attacked at every level. Mutual confidence is the most precious resource in the world today: none should be wasted, more must be found. The fundamentals of an open society are essential that contacts may freely develop, person to person and people to people. Barriers to communication must go, not least where they divide peoples, churches, even families. Freedom of human contact, information, and cultural exchange is essential for the building of peace.

To enhance mutual trust, nations should be willing to run reasonable risks for peace.

X-5. Presidents of the World Council of Churches, elected at the Third Assembly. *Left to right: Sir Francis Ibiam of Nigeria; Dr. Martin Niemoller of Germany; Archbishop Iakovos of North and South America; Dr. Ramsey, Archbishop of Canterbury; Dr. David Moses of India; and Mr. Charles Parlin of the U.S.A. Photograph courtesy of the World Council of Churches.*

For example, an equitable basis for disarmament involves, on the one hand, an acceptance of risks in an inspection and control which cannot be foolproof and, on the other, the danger that inspection may exceed its stated duties. Those who would break through the vicious circle of suspicion must dare to pioneer.

There is a great opportunity for constructive action in the struggle for world development. To share the benefits of civilization with the whole of humanity is a noble and attainable objective. To press the war against poverty, disease, exploitation, and ignorance calls for greater sacrifice and for a far greater commitment of scientific, educational, and material resources than hitherto. In this common task, let the peoples find a positive program for peace, a moral equivalent for war.

A creative strategy for peace with justice requires universal recognition of the claims of humanity—of all people, whatever their status, race, sex, or creed. Lest man's new powers be used to degrade his human freedom and dignity, governments must remember that they are the servants of their citizens and respect the worth of each individual human being. The supreme achievement for a government is to enhance the dignity of man, and free him for the creative exercise of his higher powers.

In making this appeal to all governments and peoples, we are constrained by obedience to Jesus Christ, the Lord of history, who demands righteousness and mercy and is a light unto the nations and the hearts of men. For the achievement of peace with justice, we pledge our unremitting efforts and call upon the churches for their support in action and in prayer. (December 5, 1961.)

17. Statement of Beliefs, the World Evangelical Fellowship, 1951

The Fellowship believes in:

1. The Holy Scriptures as originally given by God, divinely inspired, infallible, entirely trustworthy; and the supreme authority in all matters of faith and conduct.

2. One God, eternally existent in three persons, Father, Son, and Holy Spirit.

3. Our Lord Jesus Christ, God manifest in the flesh, His virgin birth, His sinless human life, His divine miracles, His vicarious and atoning death, His bodily resurrection, His ascension, His mediatorial work, and His personal return in power and glory.

4. The salvation of lost and sinful man through the shed blood of the Lord Jesus Christ by faith apart from works, and regeneration by the Holy Spirit.

5. The Holy Spirit by whose indwelling the believer is enabled to live a holy life, to witness and work for the Lord Jesus Christ.

6. The unity in the Spirit of all true believers, the Church, the Body of Christ.

7. The resurrection of both the saved and the lost; they that are saved unto the resurrection of life, and they that are lost unto the resurrection of damnation.

18. Pope Pius XI, 1928

Encyclical Letter (*Mortalium Animos*) on Fostering True Religious Union of Our Most Holy Lord Pius XI, by Divine Providence Pope (January 6, 1928). Bell, ed., *Documents on Christian Unity, 1920-30*, No. 113. By permission of Catholic Truth Society, London.

Venerable Brethren, Health and Apostolic Benediction.

[After referring to efforts to bring "unbelievers of every kind as well as Christians" into fraternal agreement, the encyclical continues:]

... Now, such efforts can meet with no kind of approval among Catholics. They presuppose the erroneous view that all religions are more or less good and praiseworthy, inasmuch as all give expression, under various forms, to that innate sense which leads men to God and to the obedient acknowledgement of His rule. Those who hold such a view are not only in error; they distort the true idea of religion, and thus reject it, falling gradually into naturalism and atheism. To favour this opinion, therefore, and to encourage such undertakings is tantamount to abandoning the religion revealed by God.

Nevertheless, when there is a question of fostering unity among Christians, it is easy for many to be misled by the apparent excellence of the object to be achieved. Is it not right, they ask, is it not the obvious duty of all who invoke the name of Christ to refrain from mutual reproaches and at last to be united in charity? Dare any one say that he loves Christ, and yet not strive with all his might to accomplish the desire of Him Who asked His Father that His disciples might be "one" (John 17:21)? ... The energy with which this scheme is being promoted has won for it many adherents, and even many Catholics are attracted by it, since it holds out the hope of a union apparently consonant with the wishes of Holy Mother Church, whose chief desire it is to recall her erring children and to bring them back to her bosom. In reality, however, these fair and alluring words cloak a most grave error, subversive of the foundations of the Catholic faith.

Conscious, therefore, of Our Apostolic office, which warns Us not to allow the flock of Christ to be led astray by harmful fallacies, We invoke your zeal, Venerable Brethren, to avert this evil. ...

This being so, it is clear that the Apostolic See can by no means take part in these assemblies, nor is it in any way lawful for Catholics to give to such enterprises their encouragement or support. If they did so, they would be giving countenance to a false Christianity quite alien to the one Church of Christ. ...

Furthermore, it is never lawful to employ in connection with articles of faith the distinction invented by some between "fundamental" and "non-fundamental" articles, the former to be accepted by all, the latter being left to the free acceptance of the faithful. The supernatural virtue of faith has as its formal motive the authority of God revealing, and this allows of no such distinction. All true followers of Christ, therefore, will believe the dogma of the Immaculate Conception of the Mother of God with the same faith as they believe the mystery of the august Trinity, the infallibility of the Roman Pontiff in the sense defined by the Oecumenical Vatican Council with the same faith as they believe the Incarnation of our Lord. That these truths have been solemnly sanctioned and defined by the Church at various times, some of them even quite recently, makes no difference to their certainty, nor to our obligation of believing them. Has not God revealed them all? . . .

There is but one way in which the unity of Christians may be fostered, and that is by furthering the return to the one true Church of Christ of those who are separated from it; for from that one true Church they have in the past fallen away. . . .

Furthermore, in this one Church of Christ no man can be or remain who does not accept, recognize, and obey the authority and supremacy of Peter and his legitimate successors. . . .

Let our separated children, therefore, draw nigh to the Apostolic See, set up in the City which Peter and Paul, Princes of the Apostles, consecrated by their blood; to the See which is "the root and womb whence issues the Church of God" (Cypr. *Ep. 48 ad Cornelium*, 3); and let them come, not with any intention or hope that "the Church of the living God, the pillar and ground of the truth" (I Tim. 3:15) will cast aside the integrity of the faith and tolerate their errors, but to submit themselves to its teaching and government. . . .

To this all-important end We implore, and We desire that others should implore, the intercession of the Blessed Virgin Mary, Mother of divine grace, Help of Christians, victorious over all heresies, that she may entreat for Us the speedy coming of that longed-for day, when all men shall hear the voice of her divine Son, and shall be "careful to keep the unity of the Spirit in the bond of peace" (Eph. 4:3).

You, Venerable Brethren, know how dear to Our heart is this desire, and We wish that our children also should know, not only those belonging to the Catholic fold, but also those separated from Us. If these will humbly beg light from heaven, there is no doubt but that they will recognize the one true Church of Jesus Christ, and entering therein, will at last be united with Us in perfect charity. In the hope of this fulfilment, and as a pledge of our fatherly goodwill, We impart most lovingly to you, Venerable Brethren, and to your clergy and people, the Apostolic Benediction. (*Pius PP. XI.*)

19. *Instruction to Local Ordinaries on the Ecumenical Movement*

Instruction to local ordinaries on the ecumenical movement, issued by the Supreme Sacred Congregation of the Holy Office (*Ecclesia Catholica*), Rome, December 20, 1949. Bell, ed., *Documents on Christian Unity, 1948-57*, Fourth Series, No. 227. By permission of *The Tablet*, London.

The Catholic Church takes no part in "Ecumenical" conferences or meetings. But, as may be seen from many papal documents, she has never ceased, nor ever will, from following with deepest interest and furthering with fervent prayers every attempt to attain that end which Christ our Lord had so much at heart, namely, that all who believe in him "may be made perfect in one." Indeed, with the true love of a mother she embraces all those who return to her as to Christ's one, true Church. . . .

The present time has witnesssed in different parts of the world a growing desire among many persons outside the church for the reunion of all who believe in Christ. . . .

Yet is it clear from experience that so far certain attempts of various individuals or groups to bring about this reconciliation of dissident Christians with the Catholic Church have not always been founded upon sound principles, even though inspired by the best of intentions. Even where the principles are sound, special dangers are always present. For this reason this Supreme Sacred Congregation, whose care it is to watch over and preserve intact the deposit of faith, considers it opportune to issue a reminder of the following points and to enjoin their observance:

I. Bishops, whom "the Holy Ghost has placed to rule the Church of God," ought to make a special object of their care and attention this work of "reunion" which is a particular charge and duty of the Church. They must not only use great diligence in keeping all this under effective supervision, but give it prudent encouragement and direction with the two-fold purpose of assisting those who are in search of truth and the true Church, and of shielding the faithful from the dangers which so easily accompany the progress of this movement. In the first place they must fully acquaint themselves with the past and present activities of the movement in their own dioceses. For this purpose they shall appoint suitable priests to make a special study of the movement and everything connected with it. These studies shall be along the lines laid down by the Holy See and in accordance with papal teaching (e.g. in the Encyclical letters *Satis cognitum, Mortalium animos* and *Mystici Corporis Christi*), and the priest shall duly report back to the Bishop from time to time.

II. As to the method to be followed in this work, the Bishops themselves will prescribe what is or is not to be done, and they will see to it that all obey. They should be on their guard against those who under false pretexts stress the points on which we agree rather than those on which we disagree. Such an approach may give rise to a dangerous indifferentism, especially amongst those who are not so well versed in theology or the practice of their religion. They must be on their guard, too, against the so-called spirit of "irenicism" which, looking in vain for a progressive assimilation of the various creeds, subjects the tenets of Catholicism, whether dogmas or truths connected with dogma, to a process of comparative study, whittling them down and bringing them into line with non-Catholic teaching. In this way the purity of Catholic doctrine is jeopardized and its original and true meaning obscured.

Certain dangerous modes of expression also must be avoided inasmuch as they give rise to false opinions and misleading hopes which can never be fulfilled: saying, for example, that what the Popes have written in their Encyclical letters about the return of our separated brethren to the Church, about the Mystical Body, or about the constitution of the Church, is not to be taken too seriously, for after all not everything is *de fide;*

worse still, saying that in the realm of dogma not even the Catholic Church yet possesses the fulness of Christ, but can be perfected from other sources. The Bishops will pay special attention to the manner in which the story of the Reformation is presented and will make a firm stand against any exaggeration of shortcomings on the Catholic side coupled with a glossing over of the Reformers' errors. They will guard against the undue focusing of attention on side issues so that the real point, a falling away from the Catholic faith, is obscured and barely perceived. Finally they will take care lest, rather than good, harm may be done to the cause by the excessive and overzealous activity of misguided enthusiasts. Catholic teaching is therefore to be set forth and explained whole and entire and none of its truths must be passed over in silence or cloaked in ambiguity; for example, the truths concerning the nature and means of salvation, the constitution of the Church, the Roman Pontiff's primacy of jurisdiction and the certainty that true reunion can only come about by the return of dissidents to the one, true Church of Christ. Non-Catholics may certainly be told that, should they return to the Church, such good as the grace of God has already wrought in their souls will not be lost, but will be completed and brought to perfection. But they must not be given the impression that by their return they are contributing to the Church something essential which formerly she lacked. All this must be stated clearly and openly since they are seeking the truth and real union will never be found outside that truth.

III. Mixed gatherings and conferences of Catholics and non-Catholics such as have been initiated in the past few years for the purpose of fostering "reunion" call for exceptional vigilance and control on the part of Ordinaries. Even though they provide a welcome opportunity for spreading knowledge of the Faith among non-Catholics, who for the most part are more or less ignorant of Catholic teaching, there is a real danger that the Catholic participants may become tainted with indifferentism. Where there is hope of good resulting the Ordinary will see that such meetings are properly conducted and will appoint priests best qualified for this work to put forward a suitable exposition and defence of Catholic doctrine. The faithful, however, may not attend these meetings without first obtaining special permission from the ecclesiastical authorities and this will only be granted to those who are known to be well instructed and firmly grounded in the Faith. Where on the other hand there is no such hope of good resulting or where special dangers arise from the particular circumstances, the faithful must prudently be prevented from attending and the meetings themselves be either suspended as soon as possible or gradually brought to a close. Experience shows that as a rule little good results from larger gatherings of this character, and that they are in fact a source of danger only to be permitted after most careful investigation.

SUGGESTED READINGS

Allen, W. O. B. and Edmund McClurd, *Two Hundred Years: The History of the Society for Promoting Christian Knowledge, 1698-1898.* London: SPCK, 1898.

Anderson, Courtney, *To the Golden Shore: Life of Adoniram Judson.* Boston: Little, Brown & Co., 1956.

Bates, M. Searle, *Religious Liberty: An Inquiry.* New York: International Missionary Council, 1945.

Bell, G. K. A., *Documents on Christian Unity, 1920-1924.* London: Oxford University Press, 1924. Second Series, 1930.

————, *Documents on Christian Unity, 1930-1948.* London: Oxford University Press, 1948.

————, *The Kingship of Christ.* Baltimore: Penguin Books, Inc., 1954.

Brown, A. J., *One Hunderd Years: A History of the Foreign Missionary Work of the Presbyterian Church in the U.S.A.* New York: Fleming H. Revell Co., 1937.

Brown, W. A., *Toward a United Church.* New York: Charles Scribner's Sons, 1946.

Carey, S. Pearce, *William Carey, D.D.* New York: Doubleday & Company, Inc., 1923.

Documents of the World Council of Churches. Amsterdam: First Assembly of the World Council of Churches, 1948.

Douglas, H. P., *A Decade of Objective Progress in Church Unity, 1927-1936.* New York: Harper & Row, Publishers, 1937.

Fisher, Galen M., *John R. Mott: Architect of Cooperation and Unity.* New York: Association Press, 1952.

Gairdner, W. H. T., *Echoes from Edinburgh, 1910.* New York: Fleming H. Revell Co., 1910.

Goodall, Norman, *The Ecumenical Movement.* London: Oxford University Press, 1961.

————, *One Man's Testimony.* London: Independent Press, 1949.

Hocking, William E., *Re-thinking Missions.* New York: Harper & Row, Publishers, 1932.

Hogg, William R., *Ecumenical Foundations.* New York: Harper & Row, Publishers, 1952.

Hooft, W. A. Visser't, *New Delhi Speaks.* New York: Association Press, 1962.

Horton, W. M., *Toward a Reborn Church.* New York: Harper & Row, Publishers, 1949.

Hutchison, J. A., *We Are Not Divided: A Critical and Historical Study of the Federal Council of Churches of Christ in America.* New York: Round Table Press, Inc., 1941.

Kraemer, Hendrik, *The Christian Message in a Non-Christian World.* New York: Harper & Row, Publishers, 1938.

Latourette, Kenneth S., *A History of Missions in China.* New York: The Macmillan Co., 1929.

————, *A History of the Expansion of Christianity,* 7 vols. New York: Harper & Row, Publishers, 1937-1945.

Lovett, Richard, *History of the London Missionary Society, 1795-1895,* 2 vols. London: Henry Frowde, 1899.

Macfarland, C. S., *Steps Toward the World Council: Life and Work.* New York: Fleming H. Revell Co., 1938.

Man's Disorder and God's Design: Amsterdam Assembly Series, 4 vols. New York: Harper & Row, Publishers, 1949.

Mathews, Basil, *John R. Mott, World Citizen.* New York: Harper & Row, Publishers, 1934.

Moody, William R., *The Life of Dwight L. Moody*. New York: Fleming H. Revell, 1900.

Mott, John R., *Addresses and Papers of John R. Mott*, 6 vols. New York: Association Press, 1946.

——, *Evangelization of the World in This Generation*. New York: Student Volunteer Movement for Foreign Missions, 1900.

——, *The Decisive Hour of Christian Missions*. New York: SVMFM, 1910.

Neill, S., *Toward Church Union, 1937-1952*. London: Faith and Order Commission, 1952.

Outler, A. C., *The Christian Tradition and the Unity We Seek*. New York: Oxford University Press, 1958.

Ranson, C. W., *The Christian Minister in India, His Vocation and Training*. London: Lutterworth Press, 1945.

Rouse, Ruth, *The World's Student Christian Federation*. London: SCM Press, Ltd., 1948.

Rouse, Ruth and S. Neill, *History of the Ecumenical Movement, 1517-1948*. Philadelphia: The Westminster Press, 1954.

Silcox, C. E., *Church Union in Canada*. New York: Institute of Social and Religious Research, 1933.

Stuber, Stanley I., *How We Got Our Denominations*. New York: Association Press, 1948.

Temple, William, *The Church Looks Forward*. New York: The Macmillan Co., 1944.

Warburton, S. R., *Eastward! Story of Adoniram Judson*. New York: Round Table Press, 1937.

Warneck, Gustav, *Outline of a History of Protestant Missions from the Reformation to the Present Time*. Edinburgh: Oliphant, Anderson & Ferrier, 1901.

Zabriskie, Alexander C., *Bishop Brent, Crusader for Christian Unity*. Philadelphia: The Westminster Press, 1948.

CHRONOLOGY

1493	Inter Cetera
1540	Society of Jesus
1542	Xavier, India
1604–1690	John Eliot, apostle to American Indians
1649	Society for the Propagation of the Gospel in New England
1663	Eliot, Moheecan Bible
1664	Baron von Weltz, Lutheran missions
1699	Society for Promoting Christian Knowledge
1701	Society for Propagation of the Gospel in Foreign Parts
1705	Danish-Halle Mission
1718–1747	David Brainerd, missionary to the American Indians
1732	Moravians, Leonard Dober and David Nitschmann, West Indies
1733	Moravians, Christian David, Greenland
1749	Jonathan Edwards' biography of Brainerd

1761–1834	William Carey, first modern missionary, India
1788–1850	Adoniram Judson, Burma
1792	Carey, An Enquiry Carey, "Expect great things. . . ." Particular Baptist Society for Propagation of the Gospel
1793	William Carey, India
1794	Mr. Bogue's Article
1795	London Missionary Society
1798	Netherlands' Missionary Society
1799–1873	Samuel S. Schmucker
1799	Religious Tract Society Church Missionary Society
1801	Carey, New Testament in Bengali
1804	British and Foreign Bible Society
1808	Haystack meeting, Williams College
1809	Carey, entire Bible in Bengali
1812	Judson, Newell, Rice, Notts, Hall sail for Burma and India
1816	American Bible Society

1819	Heber's Hymn, "From Greenland's icy mountains"	1928	Mortalium Animos
1821–1905	George Williams, founder of YMCA	1928	IMC, Jerusalem
1834	Judson, entire Bible in Burmese	1930	American Lutheran Church
1838	Schmucker, Appeal	1937	Faith and Order, Edinburgh Life and Work, Oxford
1844	YMCA	1938	Provisional Committee, World Council of Churches, Utrecht
1845	Schmucker, Overture		
1846	Evangelical Alliance	1938	IMC, Madras Kraemer, Christian Message in a Non-Christian World
1855	World's Alliance YMCA		
1862–1929	George H. Brent		
1865–1955	John R. Mott	1939	The Methodist Church, united
1866–1931	Nathan Söderblom	1944	Evangelical Alliance, American branch, dissolved
1867	Evangelical Alliance, American branch		
		1947	IMC, Whitby
1886	Student Volunteer Movement	1948	World Council of Churches established, Amsterdam
1888–1920	Mott, director of SVM		
1894	World's YWCA	1949	Ecclesia Catholica IMC and WCC, Eastern Asia Christian Conference, Bangkok
1895	World Student Christian Federation		
1900	United Free Church of Scotland Mott, Evangelization of the World in this Generation	1950	Humani Generis Federal Council becomes National Council of Churches of Christ in U.S.A.
1908	Federal Council of Churches of Christ in America		
1910	World Missionary Conference, Edinburgh	1951	World Evangelical Fellowship established
1918	United Lutheran Church	1952	IMC, Willingen
1920	Lambeth Appeal	1954	WCC, Evanston
1921	International Missionary Council organized	1957–1958	IMC, Ghana
		1960	Roman Catholic, Secretariat for Promoting Christian Unity
1921–1942	Mott, chairman, IMC		
1925	Life and Work Conference, Stockholm	1961	World Council of Churches, New Delhi IMC and WCC unite
1925	United Church of Canada		
1927	Faith and Order Conference, Lausanne	1962	Roman Catholic, Ecumenical Council, Vatican

Illustration opposite page 509: Modern Migration of the Spirit. *Christ striking down the cross, a symbol falsely associated with a materialistic age. Mural by José Orozco, 1932–1934, Baker Library, Dartmouth College.*

XI

Theological Trends and

Totalitarianism

𝔫o period can be fully documented; this is
abundantly evident in any attempt to depict the twentieth century.
The documents in this chapter center around liberalism and
totalitarianism, not because they are more important than other
things in this century, but because they are foci in relation to which
major events can be evaluated.

The continuing movement toward theological liberalism
dominated the first three decades of the twentieth century. It was
centered in the United States, where a heritage of frontier freedom
and individualism gave it voice, but it was by no means limited
to America, for the scientific rationalism at its base was not
geographically confined. The ecumenical outreach was part of the
liberal movement; the Roman Catholic pronouncements of Pope Pius X
against modernism were a reaction to it. Scientific evolution
undergirded its idea of progress, and a feeling of optimism about

the future and the possibilities of man pervaded its "on-going" activity. Schleiermacher, Ritschl, and Harnack supplied it with a theology geared to culture, and the evangelical revivals of the late nineteenth century gave it the impetus of personal piety and social concern.

Expressive of the liberal movement was *In His Steps*, a phenomenally popular novel written by Charles M. Sheldon, and read, chapter by chapter to his Sunday evening congregation in the Central Congregational Church of Topeka, Kansas, before it was published in 1898. Every chapter began with a biblical quotation, and at the top of every other page was, "What would Jesus do?"—the question that was applied to a series of life situations by the hero, the Reverend Henry Maxwell. Maxwell's climactic sermon ended with stirring words, "Each individual Christian, business man, citizen, needs to follow in His steps along the path of personal sacrifice for Him.... The call of this dying century, and of the new one soon to be, is a call for a new discipleship, a new following of Jesus, more like the early, simple, apostolic Christianity when the disciples left all and literally followed the Master.... Are we ready to reconsider our definition of a Christian? What is it to be a Christian? It is to imitate Jesus. It is to do as He would do. It is to walk in His steps." Afterward, Reverend Maxwell had a vision in which Christ and a choir of angels beckoned him and his age to welcome the dawn of the regeneration of Christendom!

Equally expressive of liberalism later was Earl Marlatt's hymn, *Are Ye Able?*

> "Are ye able," said the Master,
> "To be crucified with me?—"
> "Yea," the sturdy dreamers answered,
> "To the death we follow Thee."

In the refrain came the affirmation, "Lord, we are able.... Remold and make us like Thee divine." Liberalism breathed a spirit of optimistic improvement and dreamed of a utopian society in which evolution with man's assistance would take society beyond brutality and sin.

By 1900, the educated ministry had made its peace with the disturbing elements of rationalism, historical research, and scientific observation. Evolution was combined with providence to give further impetus to progress; scientific evolution was but God's way of developing his creatures. Sin came to be regarded as the vestige of some brute primitive time that could be evolutionized away through social betterment and more education. Henry Ward Beecher accepted evolution in the 1880's, and Lyman Abbot, his successor, wrote his *Theology of an Evolutionist* in 1897. *Lux Mundi* showed how educated clergymen in England realigned their traditional beliefs with the new discoveries (cf. Ch. 8). Everywhere in Protestantism there seemed to be a resurgence of Pelagian Arminianism, universalism, and a belief in the perfectibility of man. By contrast, Calvinism, with its gloomy assessment of sinfully depraved man and its doctrines of election and predestination, was thrust into the background. Ancient dogmas and credal formulations were regarded as shackles that Christianity had to discard to be free. In 1936, Henry P. Van Dusen spoke of liberal theology as a child of the late nineteenth century outlook and of the evangelical experience, and he listed its five fundamental presuppositions: (1) devotion to truth; (2) deference to science and the scientific method; (3) tentativeness, if not agnosticism, as to the possibility of metaphysical certainty; (4) emphasis upon the principle of continuity between revelation and natural religion, between Christianity and other religions, between Christ and other men—a principle which received its impetus from the concept of evolution and man's confidence in progress; and (5) a spirit of confidence in human reason, respect for personality, and dispassionate tolerance.

The First World War did not quench the progressive spirit and optimistic outlook of liberalism, even though some men recoiled from the sinfulness which they beheld in the struggle. Walter Rauschenbusch was so shocked at this sinfulness that he wore a black armband to symbolize the backward step that man had taken. A pastor in Europe, Karl Barth, pondered Paul's words about the sinfulness of man, and in his epochal *Epistle to the Romans*, 1919, he proclaimed a God "totally other" than man's cultural deity. Between 1918 and 1922, a scholar named Oswald Spengler wrote his pessimistic *Decline of the West*. But confidence in man's goodness, perfectibility, and knowledge continued. The war was regarded as a necessary crusade to wipe out the last great obstacles to the establishment of the brotherhood of man in the parliament of nations. Liberalism joined hands with science to usher in the new era, the Bible was adjusted to fit evolution, and limitless progress was confidently expected in the future.

Harry Emerson Fosdick, a Baptist and one of America's most popular preachers, symbolized the liberal development in Protestantism. His Cole lectures in 1922 at Vanderbilt were entitled *Christianity and Progress*. He noted that the War had cast doubt on the "rash, unmitigated enthusiasm about the earth's future," and he branded confidence in a "universal, mechanical, irresistible movement toward perfection" as nothing less than idolatrous superstition. Fosdick lamented "automatic levitation" and a "soft gospel of inevitable progress," but he was ready to accept progress through a conquest of ignorance, sin, inefficiency, apathy, and carelessness. "We are committed to the hope of making progress, and the central problem which Christianity faces in adjusting her thought and practice to the modern age is the problem of coming to intelligent terms with this dominant idea." Fosdick upheld Christ as "the light that can illuminate the way to a kingdom of righteousness on earth." In *Adventurous Religion,* 1926, Fosdick's essay "I Believe in Man" closed with the affirmation that "the root of Christianity is reverence for personality and faith that God must care for the spiritual values of his universe." "What Christian Liberals Are Driving At" in the same collection indicates the spirit and content of liberalism (*1*).

Conservative fundamentalists rejected the ideas of liberalism. The conservative views may be seen as the basis on which the Evangelical Alliance organized in 1846, and as the principles of the World Evangelical Fellowship, 1951 (cf. Ch. 10). The fundamentalist views were more adamantly biblical and anti-scientific than those of liberalism.

Controversy focused on the Genesis account of creation and the Virgin Birth, for the fundamentalists felt that to destroy these was to destroy the inspiration of the Word, the morally high place of man, and the creative sovereignty of God. At a Bible Conference at Niagara Falls, New York, in 1895, the fundamentalists, who felt threatened by science, adopted Five Fundamentals which they declared were essential to Christianity and which they were prepared to defend. These included Scriptural inerrancy, the divinity of Jesus Christ, Christ's substitutionary atonement on the cross, and the physical Resurrection and imminent Return of Jesus. This was followed by a twelve-volume work called *The Fundamentals* (1909-1915), millions of copies of which were distributed in churches, youth centers, and businesses. In many churches, ministers who did not subscribe

XI-1. The Old-Time Religion. *Caricature by William T. Ellis,* Billy Sunday, the Man and His Message *(Philadelphia: Universal Book and Bible House, 1914).*

to the Five Fundamentals were summarily dismissed. Fosdick was directly affected, and, although controversy over the Five Fundamentals was not the only factor, he was forced to leave First Presbyterian Church, New York City; he accepted the pulpit at Riverside Church, where he became the country's leading Protestant minister. No cleavage in Protestantism engendered more agitation than the split along fundamental-liberal lines.

The overt climax of the fundamentalist-liberal struggle came during the sensational trial of J. T. Scopes, who defied the Tennessee state law that forbade the teaching of the theory of evolution in public schools (cf. Ch. 9). *The New York Times* featured the controversy by inviting a scientist and a theologian to write parallel articles. Vernon Kellogg, zoologist, gave a spirited statement of evolution as a process for explaining things as they are now. J. Gresham Machen, Princeton Theological Seminary professor and leader of the conservatives, formulated the fundamentalist view of the Bible as the Word of God (2). Neither attacked the other. Machen's 400-page, scholarly defense of the Virgin Birth, published in 1932, has become a classic statement of that doctrine.

Following the Depression, and with the gathering of the clouds of World War II, liberalism tended to fade and a new theology called Neo-orthodoxy came to the fore. In a volume of essays in honor of William Adams Brown, in 1936, Henry P. Van Dusen commented on the rise and fall of "The Liberal Movement in Theology." He paid tribute to its enduring qualities, but noted that the World War, the Great Depression, and the attack of the fundamentalists had abruptly halted its progress. "Clearly, recoil from liberalism is the most important feature of the present situation in theology." In the preceding year, Harry Emerson Fosdick wrote an article for the *Christian Century* entitled "Beyond Modernism." As early as March, 1929, Reinhold Niebuhr, writing for *The World Tomorrow,* answered "Would Jesus Be a Modernist Today"? in the negative. This was a prelude to his devastating analyses of liberalism in *Moral Man and Immoral Society* and *Reflections on the End of an Era.* But liberalism was not finished, even though it was being displaced from the center of the theological circle. In 1939, Robert L. Calhoun, Professor of Historical Theology at Yale University, spoke of himself as "A Liberal Bandaged but Unbowed" in an article in the *Christian Century.* He told how he had lost his passion for rational theology and had become disillusioned about simple pacifism and naïve economics, how he had acquired a greater respect for God's judgmental action in history and shifted from a philosophic to a theological orientation in his understanding of man and God. He now saw new depths of meaning in revelation, the creeds, the Bible, and the tradition of the church. He was unbowed in his insistence on the constant need for objective criticism and for the search for rational meaning. Though they are no longer at the dynamic center of theology, liberalism and fundamentalism are still vital forces in religion.

Although Unitarianism was linked with the liberal movement, it emerged more from the rationalistic drives of the eighteenth century than from social evangelism. Theophilus Lindsey seceded from the Church of England in 1773 and in 1774 opened Essex Chapel in London as the first Unitarian Church. A similar move was made in America in 1785, when King's Chapel, Boston, became the first Unitarian center in America, under the leadership of James Freeman. Gradually, Unitarianism moved from a biblical to a rational orientation, from opposition to the dogma of the Trinity to an acceptance of reason as the arbiter of truth. J. Martineau (1805-1900) of England and Theodore Parker (1810-1860), W. E. Channing (1780-1842), and Ralph Waldo Emerson (1803-1882) of America were only a few of the free-thinkers who institutionalized rationalistic liberalism in the Unitarian tradition. Channing's famous Baltimore sermon at the ordination of Reverend Jared Sparks in 1819 pointed the way. Commenting on the Unitarian principles of interpreting the Bible, he declared that "the Bible is a book written for men, in the language of men, and its meaning is to be sought in the same manner as that of other books. . . . We feel it our bounden duty to exercise our reason upon it perpetually; to compare, to infer; to look beyond the letter to the spirit, to seek in the nature of the subject, and the aim of the writer, his true meaning. . . . We believe that God never contradicts, in revelation, what he teaches in his works and providence." Christ, distinct from God even as we are, is God's gift "to guide us to perfection." Unitarianism is no longer as consciously dependent on the Scriptures as when W. E. Channing was its spokesman, but it insists on the divine dignity of human nature. *The Ten Elements of Unitarianism* by Robert Raible, a Unitarian minister in Dallas, Texas, is a twentieth century expression of rationalistic liberalism (3).

More extreme than Unitarianism, but related both to it and to Christian liberalism, is the *Humanist Manifesto,* 1933, formulated by a group of secular liberals who felt that Christianity was passé, that, as Walter Lippmann had observed earlier, the churches could only be heplful to the needy, inferior, and the aged (4). The institutional strength of Unitarianism and of humanism in various ethical societies is hardly a measure of the influence of these views, which became widespread among the unchurched.

John Dewey's *A Common Faith,* 1934, which explains "god" and "the religious" in terms of an ever-enlarging ideal, projected out of the experiences of man until it becomes the harmonizing principle for everything, is an expression of this humanistic orientation. Dewey's religious and philosophical ideas powerfully affected educational ideals, which basically influence society. Other writers were more belligerent in their attitude toward Christianity. Frederick Nietzsche, Sigmund Freud, and a host of other authors poured scorn on the shallowness of liberal, optimistic Christianity, which could not quite fathom the depth of sin in God's noblest creature nor acknowledge the corruption of its own institutions. Theodore Dreiser, Aldous Huxley, D. H. Lawrence, Sinclair Lewis, Bertrand Russell and H. G. Wells joined the parade of those who were saying or implying that Christianity was obsolete. Secular and scientific ideas had been unleashed in the world that made Christianity seem naïve.

During the liberalistic period, American Christianity was largely unaware of the new theologians in Europe, for it rested heavily on a theology of culture derived from Albrecht Ritschl's value judgments as developed in *The Christian Doctrine of Justification and Reconciliation,* 1870-1874, Adolf Harnack's *History of Dogma,* 1886-1889, and his very liberal *What Is Christianity?* in 1901; it read Leo Tolstoy's religious essays, Julius Wellhausen's critical studies of Israel, Ernest Troeltsch's *Social Teaching of the Christian Churches,* and John Dewey's massive output on philosophy, ethics, and education. Europe was producing a rising group of dynamic writers who were challenging almost all the axioms of liberalism, theologians who were close to the fundamentalists in their biblical seriousness, but not in their epistemological grounding. Among these were Karl Barth, Emil Brunner, Paul Tillich, and Anders Nygren. Dostoevski (1821-1881), Pascal (1623-1662), and Kierkegaard (1813-1855) experienced a revival, for a new generation recognized their existential seriousness and probing of human nature. In America, men were just coming to know Reinhold Niebuhr, whose *Nature and Destiny of Man* appeared in 1941-1943. In Roman Catholicism, men like Étienne Gilson, Jacques Maritain, G. K. Chesterton, Karl Adam, Martin C. D'Arcy, Karl Rahner, and Hans Küng, to mention only a few, were seeking new dimensions in Neo-Thomism and exploring the relation of Catholicism to modern culture.

Still another strange voice was being heard, the voice of nihilism, the voice of men who could see nothing beyond this life, beyond the abyss of death, who spoke of an encounter with nothingness and utter dissolution at death. The nihilists expressed despair in their episodes of violence, sexual aberrations, and protests against normal mores. Their theme was eat, drink, and be merry, get what you can today, for tomorrow you will be dead. Soul was regarded as sentimental froth, and God was discounted as an outworn shibboleth that was no better than an opiate. Jean-Paul Sartre, Tennessee Wiliams, Albert Camus, Ernest Hemingway, William Faulkner, and Franz Kafka were its mentors, and a host of lesser writers followed. Existentialists in picturing death, sin, and

XI-2. Guernica. *Painted in 1937,* Guernica *depicts the horrors of the German bombing of the town in that year. Mural, oil on canvas, 11 feet 6 inches x 25 feet 8 inches by Pablo Picasso. Extended loan to the Museum of Modern Art, New York City, from the artist, M. Picasso.*

corruption, but not nihilists, for they spoke of Being beyond the forms of man, were Martin Buber, Nicholas Berdyaev, and Miguel Unamuno. C. S. Lewis and T. S. Eliot, affected by these new voices, explored new dimensions for expressing orthodoxy.

In the second quarter of the twentieth century, pessimism about man and his goodness became a dominant note; men began to speak of the post-Christian era. In *The Complete Book of Twentieth Century Music,* 1952, by David Ewen, religion and Christianity are not even mentioned in the index, nor is there any indication of either in the list of trends, movements, and tendencies in the twentieth century. This does not mean that there was no religious music, but it does indicate that popular interest was in other things. A sense of confusion seemed to prevail.

Men had abandoned religious authoritarianism, but individualized rationalism and science had not brought utopia, and men were not free. National sovereignties and world-embracing ideologies, which held their own self-interests as supreme, emerged as centers of power. These interests assumed openly anti-Christian forms in Communism, Fascism, and Nazism, although they were not

limited to these forms; Machiavelli's spirit was abroad in other groups, which acted as if their own ends were all-important. Against these centers of power, the struggle for liberty, for individual man to enjoy his innate dignity and his right to life and happiness, has become one of the dominant aspects of the twentieth century. This is by no means the entire picture, but it lies at the heart of the struggle of modern man to live in peace and to pursue happiness. Organized Christianity and Judaism have experienced the blunt edge of these claims to omnipotency, for they have asserted, however weakly, allegiance to a transcendent Sovereignty. The vigor with which these power centers have moved against religion indicates the depth with which the Christian-Judaic tradition has penetrated Western culture.

The remaining documents illustrate but a few facets of a complex struggle continually re-enacted, for man seems destined forever to break the commandments to love God and neighbor, and to assert himself or his group as the center of existence. If Adam's sin was self-assertion against God, it is still current.

Germany has exemplified this drive for power. Following the defeat of Germany in

World War I, on July 31, 1919, the Weimar Constitution was adopted and prevailed precariously until Hitler established the Third Reich. As early as February 25, 1920, at Munich, the National Socialist German Workers' Party proclaimed the official program of the Third Reich, as written by Hitler's colleague, Gottfried Feder. This program demanded the union of all Germans, colonies for the nourishment of the nation, the nationalization of business, profit-sharing, free education, and "liberty for all religious denominations in the State *so far as they are not a danger to it and do not militate against the morality and moral sense of the German race*" [Italics added]. It provided citizenship only for those with German blood; Jews were excluded.

In the struggle to assert itself, the Nazi party adopted the Horst Wessel Song, a song honoring a Nazi youth martyr; thousands marched to its celebration of the Brown Batallions, the Storm Troopers, the Swastika, and its promise of Hitler's victory over slavery, the Red Front, and Reactionaries. In 1932, Christians, intent on supporting Hitler, issued the Platform of the German Christians, which called for a church with the marks of Aryan nationalism (5, 7). After the burning of the Reichstag, February 27, 1933, Hitler received dictatorial powers for four years by a vote of 441 to 94, and in a series of acts the Nazis launched their program, a program already declared in the party platform of 1920 and in the party's 800-page bible, Hitler's hate-filled *Mein Kampf*, which by 1936 had sold two million copies. When President Paul von Hindenburg died on August 2, 1934, Hitler became both president and chancellor, receiving even more power. In the Civil Service Act of April 7, 1933, the Nazis dismissed from service all those officials who were non-Aryan or who had "false" political motives. Four days later, non-Aryans were officially defined as those who were descended from non-Aryan, particularly Jewish, parents or grandparents. In June of the same year, Dr. Paul Goebbels was named head of the ministry of Public Enlightenment and Propaganda. It was at this time that all political parties in Germany either dissolved or were abolished, for on July 14, 1933, the

Nazi Party ruled that it was the only legal political group in Germany. Opposition seemed to collapse. On that same day, the Nazi law to protect the future Aryan race was issued; it provided for sterilization of such undesirables as alcoholics and the feebleminded, and was extended in the Nürnberg laws of 1935 specifically to cover Jews (6).

The strong Catholic Center Party was displaced by a concordat between Pope Pius XI and the German Nazis, July 20, 1933. After the dismissal of Roman Catholic Vice-Chancellor von Papen from the Reich government in June, 1934, the papal concordat with Hitler amounted to little, but it was not until 1937 that Pius XI issued *Mit brennender Sorge,* which lamented Hitler's breach of promise and the annoyances of the church by the Reich government. In October of that crucial year, 1933, German bishops celebrated the 450th anniversary of Luther's birth and declared: "We German Protestant Christians accept the saving of our nation by our Leader Adolf Hitler as a gift from God's hand," and in January of the following year, even after Karl Barth protested, these same bishops placed themselves completely under the guidance of the state and pledged "unlimited fealty to the Third Reich and its Leader" (cf. Franklin Littell, *The German Phoenix,* New York: Doubleday & Company, Inc., 1960).

At Barmen, May 31, 1934, a group of Christians protested. One hundred and forty delegates from nineteen territorial churches representing evangelical Protestantism in Germany issued a six-point confession diametrically opposed to identifying the Christian message with national-racial politics (8). The statement was drawn up by Karl Barth and Hans Asmuszen, and while it did not represent even a majority of the Christians in Germany, it served as the rallying point for the heroic resistance of the Confessing Church, whose intellectual leader was Karl Barth. Hundreds of men like Martin Niemoeller, former U-boat captain, went to prison; others like Dietrich Bonhoeffer died in concentration camps, along with the 6,000,000 Jews who died at Dahlem, Dachau, and Buchenwald. The Confessing Church knew that it was dealing with a demonic principality, but the full extent of the demonic character of Nazi totalitarianism did not come to light until after the war had officially ended, May 8, 1945, when the horrors of the concentration camps were revealed (10).

On October 19, 1945, in the presence of representatives of the provisional World Council of Churches, at a time when Nazi war criminals were denying their guilt at the Nürnberg trials, the surviving leaders of the Confessing Church, the Evangelical Church in Germany, made their famous Stuttgart Declaration (9). Despite years of resistance to Nazism, they confessed their sin and asked for forgiveness in one of the most remarkable documents in church history. As Franklin Littell, translator of this document, has observed, it opened the way not only for the reconciliation of German Christians with Christians throughout the world, but became the basis for the remarkable recovery and strength of the Protestant church in post-war Germany under leaders like Bishop Otto Dibelius, whose Marienkirche is in East Berlin, Bishop Hanns Lilje of Hanover, and "Father" Lokies, head of the Gossner Mission in Berlin.

Another contest of men against totalitarian national sovereignty came with the rise of Communism to power. Orthodoxy in Russia, badly in need of reform, was already setting its house in order under the provisionary government that had displaced the old Tsar monarchy. The Sobor elected by lot a new patriarch, Metropolitan Tikhon of Moscow, and enthroned him with elaborate ceremony on November 21, 1917. Had the Bolshevik revolution not taken place in 1917, the Orthodox Church of Russia might have reformed itself. But the Russian people were warweary, and the promise of withdrawal from the war and agrarian reform swept the Bolsheviks into power. In the anarchy that followed, a small disciplined group gained control, a group intent on destroying Christianity, which to them was not only an opiate of the people but a beachhead from which the monarchists might attempt to regain power. The Civil War from 1918 to 1920, intensified by foreign intervention, gave to the Bolsheviks the sanctity of nationalism, and the bitter famine of 1921-1922, when five million people died despite gifts of food from America, gave them an opportunity for reform and entrenchment.

In 1918, the Bolsheviks launched a determined program designed to extirpate Christianity. Church property was confiscated without compensation, bank credits were seized, civil rights were denied to the clergy, state clerical salaries were discontinued, and educational facilities were taken away. By 1922, Christians were forbidden to teach their own children any religion. Lenin rewrote Article 13 of the Russian Constitution, guaranteeing "freedom of religion and of anti-religious propaganda" to all citizens. Thousands of church leaders were arrested. By 1923, more than a hundred bishops and priests had been martyred. Tikhon was languishing in prison, his church split between those accepting and those not accepting the government's policies. When he died in 1925, the government would not allow a new election. Atheist groups issued satirical literature, caricaturing sacred Christian emblems and events; Christmas trees disappeared. The Militant Atheists' League in 1925 sought to identify religion with disloyalty, superstition, and exploitation. Food cards were denied pastors, a six-day week, eliminating Sunday, was instituted; and more than a thousand churches were closed or used as centers of antireligious propaganda.

With the rise of Hitler in 1933, Russia saw the need of foreign allies, and a noticeable period of relaxation developed, only to be followed by another purge in 1937-1938. Further relaxation followed during the exigencies brought on by World War II. In 1943, the Council of the Orthodox hierarchy was allowed to meet; it elected Patriarch Sergius as "Patriarch of Moscow and all Russia." When he died, in 1945, Alexius was elected to succeed him. The church was again permitted to own property, monasteries opened, and church bells rang out.

State expedience brought the church some relief, but Russia did not mitigate in principle her opposition to religion, as the situation in Russian-dominated Czechoslovakia and other occupied countries shows. In 1948, the Czech churches were deprived of the right to have schools and their lands were seized. Laws in 1949 directly interfered with the Roman Catholic Church and required clergymen to pledge loyalty to the state; Roman Catholics vainly protested. All records of the churches became governmental property, clergymen were made state employees, and the church in effect was completely governed by the state. When the government brought pressure on the bishops to support the state's policies, Pope Pius XII issued a general condemnation of all Communists, July 1, 1949, saying that Catholics were not to join, favor, or in any way aid Communist parties, not even by reading their literature, on pain of exclusion from the sacraments. The petition of the Roman Catholic bishops, October 21, 1949, asking the government to cease its anti-church policy, met with no success. Priests who opposed the new church legislation were accused of subversion and hundreds were arrested. On April 5, 1950, nine high-ranking Roman Catholics were found guilty of trying to overthrow the government and received sentences of from nine years to life imprisonment. The Vatican was accused of commanding the men to act contrary to the government and of inviting American intervention for the restoration of imperialistic capitalism. In reprisal, the government confiscated more property and turned church buildings into housing units. In December of 1950, Bishops Zela, Buzalka, and Gojdic were sentenced to life in prison for espionage. The documents which follow indicate the extent to which the Communist church policy in Czechoslovakia took over religion in an attempt to make it serve the purposes of the sovereign state. The same type of story could be repeated for other Communist-dominated countries (11). In this connection one should note carefully the universal declaration of the rights of man, issued by the United Nations (12), as well as the proclamation by the Baptists (14).

That the Roman Catholic Church itself was not entirely free from totalitarian aspirations similar to those in Communist- and Nazi-dominated countries is indicated by the treatment of Protestants in Spain when Roman Catholicism won legal favor through its support of Franco. Nor did it matter that Franco was supported also by Nazis and Fascists, for expediency dominated the situation and allowed Roman Catholicism to win concessions. Such a stir was raised about this development that *Information Service*, news organ of the Federal Council of Churches of Christ in America, published a summary of the boiling situation in 1950 (13). Protestants in Spain still cannot have chapels that look like chapels, public funerals, or legal protection from fanatics who would destroy their Bibles and other church property.

Group and national aggrandizement is not limited to totalitarian countries. In the 1950's, the investigating committees of Senator Joseph R. McCarthy, Senator W. S. Jenner, and Representative H. H. Velde used tactics for rooting out Communism and un-American activities that many believed were more destructive of democracy and individual rights than any reputed subversion. In July, 1953, Dr. J. B. Matthews, chief of McCarthy's investigating staff, published an article in *American Mercury* in which he said that seven thousand Protestant clergymen provided the bulwark of Communist strength in America. Three senators resigned from the committee in protest, and Bishop G. Bromley Oxnam of the Methodist Church demanded and received a hearing. Oxnam fought back, finally telling his story in *I Protest*, 1954. Many groups and individuals complained; the Presbyterian Church issued one of the most forthright objections that came from the churches (15). Fear of McCarthyism made many Americans realize that total vigilance is the price of liberty.

Racial intolerance, in its many guises, is part of this total picture. In America, its most persistent and virulent form is the entrenched denial to Negroes of their full privileges as citizens—economic, political, and social. Totalitarian regimes throughout the world have justified their actions or nullified American protests of maltreatment of minorities by pointing to the treatment of Negroes in America. In 1920, the Federal Council of Churches issued one of the first stands on integration, and many church groups and individuals have been active in the struggle for Negro rights. The extent to which churches continue to remain segregated, however, is an indication of the church's affinity with the culture that denies basic rights. The National Association for the Advancement of Colored People, founded in 1910 and directed from 1916 to 1930 by James Weldon Johnson, has been the main protector of Negro rights. In 1954 it won a significant Supreme Court decision. On May 17, Chief Justice Earl Warren delivered the unanimous opinion of the court that racial segregation in public schools is not constitutional. It displaced the old "separate but equal" decision of Plessy v. Ferguson in 1896, and marked a new era in the struggle for individual liberties.

The story is incomplete, and only a portion of it can be conveyed in documents and writings. Many other documents could have been selected, but these have been chosen in the hope of imparting a feel for the periods covered and indicating the way to further reading and wider understanding. History does not provide answers for the present, but it does provide a perspective from which to view it. In that perspective man may find new light and resources for the future.

1. Harry Emerson Fosdick, 1926

In "What Christian Liberals Are Driving At," an essay in *Adventurous Religion* (New York: Harper & Row, Publishers, 1926), Harry Emerson Fosdick emphasized the liberal's ability to change with the march of scientific knowledge, a positive attitude toward life, man's part in establishing the Kingdom of God, a modernized version of Christianity, and a subordination of creeds to contemporary tasks. Later, under the impact of world events and neo-orthodoxy, Fosdick modified his trust in human knowledge, man's goodness, and the ability of man to establish the Kingdom. He saw more relevance of the creeds to contemporary tasks.

The subject is difficult to write about because religious liberalism is so often vague and nebulous. Misty in outline, constantly in process of alteration, liberalism bewilders many to-day who would like to understand it. The public barometers indicate that a change in the religious weather is coming on; the newspapers are full of theological controversies; such names as fundamentalist, liberal, modernist, are freely applied; but just what it is all about is often difficult for a plain man to find out.

Certainly, I cannot claim the right to speak for all Christian liberals. There are too many different sorts of them, from swashbuckling radicals, believing not much of anything, to men of well-stabilized convictions who are tolerant of differences and open-minded to new truth. But there is a large and growing group in our churches for whom I shall try to speak.

Let me propose at the start three tests by which the kind of liberal whom I shall endeavor to represent can be recognized. First, he has come into his new attitudes and ways of thinking, not simply as a matter of intellectual adventure, but through the deepening of his spiritual life. He is a liberal because he is more religious, not because he is less. His growing soul, cramped in old restraints, has struck out for air to breathe.

Some of us began our religious life under the domination of ideas about the Bible, God, Christ, heaven, and hell, that were current half a century ago. Then our minds grew up to be citizens of the twentieth century. Our experience with prayer, forgiveness, faith, and spiritual renewal deepened and enlarged. We had to dispense with a smaller mental formulation and get a larger one to save our souls. They would have smothered if they could not have broken through into freer air.

.   .   .   .   .

Most of them [the liberals] have surrendered smaller ideas and gotten larger ones to give their souls room. The new wine would not stay in the old wine-skins. Like Beethoven, discontented with prevalent musical forms and seeking new ones because he had more music in him than the old forms were adequate to convey, so they have been pushed out into their liberalism by the expansive power of their developing religious life. At any rate, I am sure that no other kind of progressiveness in religion has an abiding contribution to make to Christianity.

A second test of this liberal whom I am trying to represent is emphasis on positive convictions rather than on negative denials. Some liberals make negations their chief stock in trade. Whenever they have a chance they produce a long list of things which they no longer can believe.

How many things, for example, they disbelieve about prayer. They roll under their tongues a story from Pittsburgh: a fire broke out; a woman saw it sweeping up the block in her direction; she prayed; the wind changed; the fire burned down the other way and destroyed some other people's houses instead of hers. They do not believe that prayer has any such effect. In this world of impartial law, they do not think that God so plays favorites and, like a celestial charity organization society, doles out small gifts upon request to improvident applicants. Neither do I.

But when I observe an attitude toward prayer which mainly concerns itself with ideas discredited and disbelieved, I am impatient. What *do* we believe about prayer? "He who rises from his knees a better man, his prayer is answered." Do we know what that means? In the too great rush of our turbulent life, do we know the secret of praying which enables us to get a new grip on ourselves, to see a new perspective around our work, to let the healing influence of the Spirit restore our souls? . . . What we do not believe about prayer probably gets us nowhere; what we do positively believe may get us a long way.

In every aspect of religion this principle holds true. We cannot live upon negations and denials. Life is too complex, too hazardous, too full of mystery; sorrows go too deep; temptations assail too furiously; and the future is too uncertain. We live only on the basis of our convictions, and from religious teachers in particular we need above all else to hear what positively they do believe. . . .

One more test of the effective Christian liberal remains: he is sacrificially in earnest about establishing God's will in the earth. Some liberalism does not move in that realm at all. It is an intellectual excursion without moral consecration. It is a set of up-to-date opinions in theology which can be held and defended as a smart pose. There are dilettanti in religion, as elsewhere, who are very modern but not very much in earnest. The necessary business of reforming Christianity, however, to which liberalism has set itself, is too serious for any dilettante attitude to effect. Christianity certainly does need to be reformed. Some, indeed, still think of it as a finished system, its doctrines all defined, its rubrics all elaborated, its duties all laid down —a completed system needing nothing but to be accepted. I do not see how they do it. The Gospel came, an ideal message, into an unideal world and, as in Shakespeare's figure, like the dyer's hand it has been subdued to the stuff it worked in.

Of course Christianity needs to be reformed. Nearly one-third the population of the globe is nominally Christian. What if they were really Christian? . . . There is no cause on earth for which one who cares about the future of mankind could better pray and work than for the reformation of Christianity, and it is this that the liberals are driving at. But it can be achieved by no mere holding of up-to-date opinions. It is going to take spiritual insight, sacrificial patience, constructive statesmanship to recover the essential principles of Jesus, make them dominant in the church and in the world. The progressive in religion may well test himself at this point. Every day in every way he may be getting liberaler and liberaler; but that will not matter much if, with his new opinions, he is not being made into a more devoted, efficient, constructive builder of a Christian civilization.

These, I think, are the three tests of effective Christian liberalism: it springs from the expansion and deepening of the spiritual life; it dwells in the great centers of affirmation, not of denial; and it issues in constructive statesmanship for the Kingdom.

The representatives of such liberalism are multiplying in the churches. The uproar of the last few years associated with fundamentalism has been caused in part by the clear and true perception of the reactionaries that the liberals are gaining and that, if not stopped now, they will soon be in control. What the liberals are driving at, therefore, is an important matter, not only to the churches, but also to the public in general. Let me try to group their major aims and motives under two heads.

For one thing, liberals undoubtedly wish to modernize Christianity's expression of its faith. The Protestant Reformation was a valiant stroke for liberty, but it occurred before the most characteristic ideas of our modern age had arrived. The Augsburg Confession is a memorable document, but the Lutherans who framed it did not even know that they were living on a moving planet, and Martin Luther himself called Copernicus a new astrologer. The Westminster Confession is a notable achievement in the development of Christian thought, but it was written forty years before Newton published his work on the law of gravitation. Protestantism, that is, was formulated in prescientific days. Not one of its historic statements of faith takes into account any of the masterful ideas which constitute the framework of modern thinking—the inductive method, the new astronomy, natural law, evolution. All these have come since Protestantism arrived. Protestantism stiffened into its classic forms under the intellectual influences long antedating our modern world, and the chaos and turmoil in Christian thought to-day are the consequences. They spring directly from the impossible endeavor of large sections of the church to continue the presentation of the Gospel in forms of thought that are no longer real and cogent to well-instructed minds....

Perilous heresy to welcome modern ways of thinking in religion? The shoe is on the other foot. Our children are going to schools and colleges where scientific methods of thinking are taken for granted, where they underlie all studies and are involved in all results; and the most ruinous blow that can be struck against the faith of our youth is to make them choose between scientific thinking and the Gospel.

...As one deals with young men and women religiously upset, one must often blame their unsettlement not so much upon the colleges as upon Christian churches and Sunday schools—upon religious agencies which taught these young people in the beginning that the Christian Gospel is indissolubly associated with the prescientific view of the world in the Scriptures or the creeds; that the Gospel of the Lord Jesus is dependent upon fiat creation or the historic credibility of old miracle narratives; that the God of the Gospel, like the God of the early Hebrew documents, is a magnified man who could walk in the garden in the cool of the day or come down from the sky to confound men's speech lest they should build a tower high enough to reach his home.

It is a tragic error thus to set up in the minds of young children an artificial adhesion between the Gospel and a literal interpretation of Scripture and creed, so that, when education inevitably opens a child's mind, the whole unnatural combination of liberalism and spiritual faith collapses, and Christ is banished from a soul because he has been associated with opinions that are bound in the end to prove untenable....

.   .   .   .   .

Many popular pictures of liberalism, therefore, are sheer caricatures. Liberalism is not primarily a set of opinions; it is a spirit of free inquiry which wishes to face the new facts, accept whatever is true, and state the abiding principles of Christian faith in cogent and contemporary terms....

.   .   .   .   .

The second liberal aim is to put first things first in religion, to subordinate the details of ritual, creed, and church to the major objects of Christianity—the creation of personal character and social righteousness. At the very center of liberalism, as I understand it, is the conviction that nothing fundamentally matters in religion except those things which create private and public goodness. The reason why most of our theological controversies are idle beating of the air is that whichever side wins makes no difference to character. In historic and contemporary Christianity three elements have been continually used as competitors of character in the interest of Christians. They have repeatedly usurped the place which private and public righteousness ought to occupy as the one supreme matter with which Christianity is concerned and for which it works. These three elements are ritual, doctrine, and church.

This does not mean that ritual is unnecessary or unimportant in religion. We have ritual in courtesy when the hand is extended or the hat lifted; in love when the endearing name is used or the kiss bestowed.... Of course, religion always has had its ceremonies and always will. Ritual is a kind of shorthand by which we say things that we do not take time to put into words or could not if we would.... Nevertheless, a peril lurks in all ritualism—the supposition, namely, that the Lord God of this infinite universe cares anything about our meticulous performance of a ceremony, if it does not issue in private and public righteousness.

Nor does the liberal Christian belittle doctrine. The ordered and intelligible statement of the convictions which undergird Christian living is important. A man's creed, if real and vital, is his conviction about the nature and meaning of his life, of the world in which it is lived, and of the God who rules it. That certainly is basic and controlling.... So always a real creed, a controlling vision of what this earth is and what life means, which occupies the imagination and affects the life, is enormously important.... Only, there is an omnipresent danger in emphasis on doctrine. Doctrine in time is petrified into dogma. It is officially formulated. Then there is an ecclesiastical type of mind ready to use it, no longer as an inspiring elucidation of the convictions by which men really live, but as a mold into which men's thinking must be exactly run. Doctrine is then authoritative, a definition laid down in times past of the way in which men must always think. And men often pride themselves on this repetition of their fathers' thoughts, as though the God and Father of Jesus cared anything for that, except as it represents real convictions vitally issuing in private and public righteousness.

Furthermore, the liberal certainly does not undervalue the church....

Nevertheless, the pathos of Christian history lies in the way the church has so often misrepresented and obstructed vital Christianity. Our multiplied and meaningless denominations are doing that to-day. In one of our American communities a congregation called itself The Church of God. They could not agree among themselves and, having split asunder, the split called itself, The True Church of God. They in turn divided and the new division called itself The Only True Church of God. The tragedy of that picturesque situation, too typical of our modern Protestantism to be pleasant, is that none of these divisions has any imaginable relationship with the one supreme business of

religion: the creation of private and public righteousness.

This sort of thing is bad enough in America. It is a matter for tears in the missionary field.... As one of the missionary secretaries exclaimed, "Think of seeing an American Dutch Reformed Chinese!"

A liberal, therefore, in his emphasis is utterly careless of sectarian distinctions. He is by conviction and ideal an interdenominationalist. He deplores our divided Protestantism as a sin against God and against man. He sees that our denominational peculiarities for the most part are caused by historic reasons only, have no contemporary excuse for existence, and have no contribution to make to righteousness. He is convinced that nothing matters in any church except those few vital and transforming faiths and principles of the Gospel, common to all churches, which do create personal character and social progress.

.   .   .   .   .

Such, I take it, are the two chief aims of Christian liberals: to think the great faiths of the Gospel through in contemporary terms, and to harness the great dynamics of the Gospel to contemporary tasks. If that be heresy the orthodox will have to make the most of it. For like a member of the Westminster Assembly long ago, we are praying, "O God, we beseech Thee to guide us aright, for we are very determined."

2. J. Gresham Machen

Shortly before the Scopes' trial at Dayton, Tennessee, J. Gresham Machen, Assistant Professor of New Testament Literature and Exegesis at Princeton Theological Seminary, was asked to elucidate the stand of fundamentalists on reading the Bible as the Word of God, and Vernon Kellogg, zoologist, was asked to write on the changes accepted since Darwin's time. Machen's article, "What Fundamentalism Stands For Now," is here given as an exposition of fundamentalism. Copyright by *The New York Times*, June 21, 1925. Reprinted by permission.

The term fundamentalism is distasteful to the present writer and to many persons who hold views similar to his. It seems to suggest some strange new sect; whereas in point of fact we are conscious simply of maintaining the historic Christian faith and of moving in the great central current of Christian life.

That does not mean that we desire to be out of touch with our own time, or that we live in a static world without variety and without zest. On the contrary, there is nothing more varied and more interesting than the effect of the Christian religion upon different races and different ages; there is no more absorbing story than that of the relations between Christianity and its changing environment.

But what we do mean is that despite changes in the environment, there is something in Christianity which from the very beginning has remained the same.

·　　·　　·　　·　　·

The body of truth upon which the Christian religion is based may be divided into three parts. There is, first, the doctrine of God (or theology proper); second, the doctrine of man; and, third, the doctrine of the Christian relationship between God and man. These three divisions may now be considered briefly in turn.

The basis of the Christian view of God— by no means all of it, but the basis of it—is simply theism: the belief, namely, that the universe was created, and is now upheld by a personal Being upon whom it is dependent but who is not dependent upon it. This view is opposed to all forms of the prevalent pantheism, which either makes "God" merely a collective name for the world process itself, or else regards Him as related to the world process as the soul of man is related to his body.

Pantheism vs. Theism: All forms of pantheism differ from theism in denying the transcendence of God, the separateness of God from the world. But the transcendence of God—what the Bible calls the "holiness" of God—is at the very root of the Christian religion. God is, indeed, according to the Christian view, immanent in the world; but He is also personally distinct from the world and from the finite creatures that He has made.

The Christian doctrine of man is partly involved in the Christian doctrine of God; theism, with its distinction between God and

the world, humbles man as creature under the almighty hand of God, while the current pantheism exalts man because his life is regarded as being a part of all the God there is.

But another difference of opinion is more important still; it appears in divergent views of moral evil. According to historic Christianity, all mankind are under the just condemnation of God, and are utterly helpless because of the guilt and power of sin. According to another very widespread type of belief, human resources are sufficient for human needs, and self-development, especially the development of the religious nature, is the Christian ideal. This type of belief is optimistic about human nature as it is at present constituted, while historic Christianity regards all mankind as being in itself hopelessly lost.

Many preachers seek to arouse man's confidence in himself. "I believe in Man" is one of the cardinal articles of their creed. But the preacher of historic Christianity tries first of all to destroy man's confidence in himself and to arouse in his soul the dreadful consciousness of sin.

God enveloped in a terrible righteousness, man an offender against His law and under His just wrath—these are the two great presuppositions of the historic Christian gospel. But on the basis of these terrible presuppositions, the Christian preacher comes with a message of hope. The hope is found, not at all in any attenuation of the facts about God and man, not at all in any effort to take lightly the course of God's law, but simply and solely in an account of what God Himself has done.

We deserved eternal death, but the Son of God, who was Himself God, came into this world for our redemption, took upon Himself the just punishment of our sins, died in our stead on the cross, and finally completed His redeeming work by rising from the tomb in a glorious resurrection. There and there alone is found the Christian gospel; the piece of "good news" upon which all our hope is based.

That gospel, as indeed the term "news" implies, is an account, not of something that always was true, but of something that happened; Christianity is based not merely on ethical principles or on eternal truths of religion, but also on historical facts.

The Supernatural: The redeeming facts upon which the Christian hope is based were things done by the Lord Jesus Christ, and those facts involve the entrance into the course of this world of the creative power of God; in other words, they involve the supernatural.

Acceptance of the supernatural does not, as is often supposed, destroy the basis of science; it does not introduce an element of arbitrariness which would make impossible any exhibition of regular sequences in nature. On the contrary, a miracle, according to the Christian view, is not an arbitrary or purposeless event, but proceeds from the very source of all the order that there is in the world, namely, from the will of God.

God is the author of nature, and we Christians are willing to trust Him not to destroy that orderly system in which it is His will that we should live. Indeed, the believer in the supernatural is in some respects kinder to the scientist than the scientist ventures to be to himself; for in order to maintain the distinctness of the supernatural from the natural we are obliged to hold that there is a real order of nature—not a mere observed set of sequences, but a really existent order. Only, that order of nature, though really existent, is not self-existent; it was created by the fiat of God's will, and He has never abandoned His freedom in the presence of His world.

We are not saying that while miracles were accomplished by God ordinary events are not accomplished by Him, but only that in the case of ordinary events He uses means, or "second causes," while in the case of miracles He puts forth His creative power. A miracle, then, is an event wrought by the immediate, as distinguished from the mediate power of God; it is not a work of providence, but is akin to the work of creation.

The Resurrection: The outstanding miracle narrated in the New Testament is the emergence of the body of Jesus from the tomb. Upon that miracle the Christian Church was founded, and the evidence for it is of a singularly varied and cumulative

kind. But that event is not isolated; it is connected with a consistent representation of Jesus in the New Testament as a supernatural person—not the fairest flower of humanity, the finest thing the world has to show, not divine only because divinity courses through all things, not God only because He was the highest development of man, but the eternal Son of God who came voluntarily into the world for our redemption.

Jesus as Saviour: Acceptance of this New Testament account of Jesus involves a certain attitude toward Him which is widely different from the attitude assumed by many persons of the Church today. Jesus, we hold, was not only a teacher and example (though He was all that), but He was, and is, our Saviour and Lord. He was not the first Christian, the initiator of a new type of religious life, but stood in a far more fundamental and far more intimate relationship to Christianity than that, because He was the one who made Christianity possible by His redeeming work. At no point does our attitude appear in more characteristic fashion than just here. Many persons hold up their hands in amazement at our assertion that Jesus was not a Christian, while we regard it as the very height of blasphemy to say that He was a Christian. "Christianity" to us is a way of getting rid of sin; and, therefore, to say that Jesus was a Christian would be to deny His perfect holiness.

"But," it is said, "do you mean to tell us that if a man lives a life like the life of Jesus but rejects the doctrine of the redeeming work of Christ in His death and resurrection, he is not a Christian?" The question is often asked, but the answer is very simple. Of course, if a man really lives a life like the life of Jesus, all is well; such a man is indeed not a Christian, but he is something better than a Christian—he is a being who has never lost his high estate of sonship with God. . . .

. . . The Jesus of all the Gospels presented Himself not merely as teacher but also as Lord and as Redeemer.

This redeeming work of Christ, which is at the center of the Bible, is applied to the individual soul, according to our view, by the Holy Spirit; we find no permanent hope for society in the mere "principles of Jesus" or the like, but we find it in the new birth of individual souls. Important indeed are the social applications of Christianity, but, as Francis Shunk Downs has well observed, there can be no Christianity to apply unless there are Christian men. And men are made Christian by the Spirit of God.

The way of salvation: But the means which the Spirit of God uses in making men Christian is faith, and faith is the response of the human soul to the gospel message. A man becomes convicted of sin; he sees himself as God sees him; he is in despair. And then the Lord Jesus is offered to him in the gospel—in the good news that the guilt of sin has been blotted out by the wonderful sacrifice which God Himself provided, in His mysterious love for sinners, on Calvary. The acceptance of that message is faith, faith in the Lord Jesus Christ. Through faith a man becomes a child of God, and then follows a new life, with a victorious battle against sin.

Such is the way of salvation as it is set forth in the Bible and in historic Christianity. It seems to those who have followed it to be the most blessed thing in all the world. Who can measure the peace and joy that have been found at the foot of the cross? But to others the message seems strange and full of offense.

The offense comes—and has come ever since the very first days of the Christian Church—from the inveterate insistence and exclusiveness of the Christian message. What causes offense is not that we present this way of salvation, but that we present it as the only way. The world, according to our view, is lost in sin; the gospel provides the only way of escape; and the blackest guilt into which any Christian can fall is to deceive dying souls into thinking that some other way will answer as well.

.   .   .   .   .

3. 10 Elements of the Unitarian Religion

The Reverend Robert Raible, Unitarian minister in Dallas, Texas, published these principles of Unitarianism in 1945. Used by permission of the author.

1.   Salvation. Other religions are primarily interested in Salvation, in some future life. "There is life after death," they say, "which may be very unpleasant. If you want your next life to be filled with bliss, you must believe what we teach. Believe, join us, and you will be saved." Believe what? "Believe," says the evangelical Christian, "that Jesus Christ died for your sins. You are a sinner. But your sins can be wiped out if you believe that Christ's death was an atoning sacrifice to God, capable of saving you and all sinners."

Their emphasis is on Salvation-in-a-future-life, and the Unitarian simply is not interested. Unitarians vary concerning their belief in immortality, but all Unitarians who do believe in it, are universalists. That is, they say that all achieve it, or none do. But Salvation in the future is not the central core of the Unitarian religion, as it is in all the other religions. The primary concern of Unitarians is life on earth: improving it, perfecting it, more nearly achieving the potentialities and satisfactions which all men are capable of realizing but which most men miss.

.   .   .   .   .

2.   Authority. Another distinction lies in the fact that the Authority for religious truth is quite different for the Unitarian. The key to any religion is the Authority which it accepts. What is true? What is right? How should a man behave? If a man die, does he live again? Why must men suffer? Why is injustice so rife in the world? Each religion has its answers for these and similar questions. Where did the answers come from? They came from the Authority which that religion accepts.

.   .   .   .   .

. . . For the answers to all his questions the Unitarian looks: within himself! Buddha and Confucius, Amos and Christ, and the prophets and seers of all the ages, may have answers which are significant and germane. But the final test which the Unitarian applies to all those answers is: do they contravene his Reason, his Common Sense and his Experience; do they do violence to his Conscience, to his Inner Light, to the voice of the Divine which speaks within his soul? No matter how age-old the teaching may be, nor how august and respected the teacher, no answer has validity for a Unitarian until it has obtained the sanction of his ultimate Authority, which he finds within himself.

That is why a Unitarian minister can never tell his congregation what is right, or how its members should behave. All that he can do is to say: "This is what seems right to me."...

3. Simplicity. Another distinction is that the Unitarian religion is a simple faith with none of the speculations and theological profundities about one God being three Gods and still remaining one God....

4. Creeds. A similar distinction lies in the fact that the other religions are characterized by Creeds which all their members must accept.... The Unitarian has no set creed which everyone in the church must accept.

5. Democracy. The Unitarian church is the expression of the democratic position and principle, as applied to religion. It is a free faith for free men....

6. Sociological. Essentially, Unitarians are mystics. They look at Man and see ... a child of the Eternal, capable of unrealized potentialities.

Each one is a person (usually thwarted, often handicapped, frequently blind to his own worth) whose soul contains a spark of the Divine, ready to be fanned into a flame of supernal brightness. The perfectibility of man is a basic tenet, found in nearly every Unitarian's statement of faith. Consequently, Unitarians serve in the active leadership of many of the movements looking toward improving the living conditions of men.

7. Psychological. In the field of mental hygiene, this same belief-in-man, has conditioned the Unitarian attitude toward life. Other religions teach that man is a sinner, in danger of being damned. The result is cravenness, fear, a feeling of guilt, a desire to appease. Man is taught to propitiate the power which has him enthralled. Any psychiatrist can explain the thwarting effects on human personality of such beliefs.

The Unitarian listened with disgust to such medieval nonsense. "Shades of the Dark Ages," he says, "that anyone should believe such myths in this century. Man is a son of God, and it is not yet given him what he shall be."...

8. Suffering. In the area of tragedy and suffering, no Unitarian ever wrings his hands and asks: "Why did this happen to me?" He understands natural law and recognizes its desirability. He expects to be hurt if he puts his finger in a buzz saw. He tries to educate himself and others not to act foolishly; not to drive too fast; not to play with an unloaded gun. But he never expects a capricious God to set aside natural law to protect him from the consequences of his own foolishness.

He realizes that sometimes through pure chance and no fault of his own, he is forced to suffer from the exigencies of life. A dread disease may cause the death of some member of his family or of someone whom he loves. After the first poignant pangs of grief are past, however, he does not remain despondent, railing against his fate. Instead he turns to co-operate with the efforts that are being made to rid the world of that disease, so that in the future others shall not have to suffer from it, as he has done. Smallpox is only one of several diseases which man by his own efforts has virtually wiped out in this country....

9. Immortality, God, Jesus, The Bible. Unitarians vary in the details of their faith. Many believe in a future life, but some do not. Most of them believe in God, but a few do not, even when they are allowed to define God in their own way. Some turn much more than others, to the Bible as their first source of inspiration. All find inspiration in the teachings of Christ. To all of them, Jesus was divine, as all men are divine. But very few Unitarians consider him a deity.

10. Fellowship. Perhaps more than any other one characteristic, is the emphasis which Unitarians put upon fellowship. The legend on the seal of Kentucky: "United we stand, divided we fall" could well be the motto of the Unitarian church. They draw strength from each other and they share

strength with each other. Whether they are in need of personal solace or whether they are embarking on a joint humanitarian enterprise, they realize that their only chance of fruition is through mutually helping each other. . . .

4. "The Humanist Manifesto"

The Humanist Manifesto was drawn up by a group of humanists meeting in Chicago, 1932-1933. *The Humanist*, XIII, 2 (March–April, 1953). Reprinted by permission of The American Humanist Association, Yellow Springs, Ohio.

The time has come for widespread recognition of the radical changes in religious beliefs throughout the modern world. The time is past for mere revision of traditional attitudes. Science and economic change have disrupted the old beliefs. Religions the world over are under the necessity of coming to terms with new conditions created by a vastly increased knowledge and experience. In every field of human activity, the vital movement is now in the direction of a candid and explicit humanism. In order that religious humanism may be better understood we, the undersigned, desire to make certain affirmations which we believe the facts of our contemporary life demonstrate.

There is great danger of a final, and we believe fatal, identification of the word "religion" with doctrines and methods which have lost their significance and which are powerless to solve the problems of human living in the Twentieth Century. Religions have always been means for realizing the highest values of life. Their end has been accomplished through the interpretation of the total environing situation (theology or world view), the sense of values resulting therefrom (goal or ideal), and the technique (cult), established for realizing a satisfactory life. A change in any of these factors results in alteration of the outward forms of religion. This fact explains the changefulness of religions through the centuries. But through all changes religion itself remains constant in its quest for abiding values, an inseparable feature of human life.

Today man's larger understanding of the universe, his scientific achievements, and his deeper appreciation of brotherhood, have created a situation which requires a new statement of the means and purposes of religion. Such a vital, fearless, and frank religion capable of furnishing adequate social goals and personal satisfactions may appear to many people as a complete break with the past. While this age does owe a vast debt to the traditional religions, it is none the less obvious that any religion that can hope to be a synthesizing and dynamic force for today must be shaped for the needs of this age. To establish such a religion is a major necessity of the present. It is a responsibility which rests upon this generation. We therefore affirm the following:

First: Religious humanists regard the universe as self-existing and not created.

Second: Humanism believes that man is a part of nature and that he has emerged as the result of a continuous process.

Third: Holding an organic view of life, humanists find that the traditional dualism of mind and body must be rejected.

Fourth: Humanism recognizes that man's religious culture and civilization, as clearly depicted by anthropology and history, are the product of a gradual development due to his interaction with his natural environment and with his social heritage. The individual born into a particular culture is largely molded by that culture.

Fifth: Humanism asserts that the nature of the universe depicted by modern science makes unacceptable any supernatural or cosmic guarantees of human values. Obviously humanism does not deny the possibility of realities as yet undiscovered, but it does insist that the way to determine the existence and value of any and all realities is by means of intelligent inquiry and by the assessment of their relations to human needs. Religion must formulate its hopes and plans in the light of the scientific spirit and method.

Sixth: We are convinced that the time has passed for theism, deism, modernism, and the several varieties of "new thought."

Seventh: Religion consists of those actions, purposes, and experiences which are humanly significant. Nothing human is alien to the religious. It includes labor, art, science, philosophy, love, friendship, recreation—all that is in its degree expressive of intelligently satisfying human living. The distinction between the sacred and the secular can no longer be maintained.

Eighth: Religious Humanism considers the complete realization of human personality to be the end of man's life and seeks its development and fulfillment in the here and now. This is the explanation of the humanist's social passion.

Ninth: In the place of the old attitudes involved in worship and prayer the humanist finds his religious emotions expressed in a heightened sense of personal life and in a co-operative effort to promote social well-being.

Tenth: It follows that there will be no uniquely religious emotions and attitudes of the kind hitherto associated with belief in the supernatural.

Eleventh: Man will learn to face the crisis of life in terms of his knowledge of their naturalness and probability. Reasonable and manly attitudes will be fostered by education and supported by custom. We assume that humanism will take the path of social and mental hygiene and discourage sentimental and unreal hopes and wishful thinking.

Twelfth: Believing that religion must work increasingly for joy in living, religious humanists aim to foster the creative in man and to encourage achievements that add to the satisfactions of life.

Thirteenth: Religious humanism maintains that all associations and institutions exist for the fulfillment of human life. The intelligent evaluation, transformation, control and direction of such associations and institutions with a view to the enhancement of human life is the purpose and program of humanism. Certainly religious institutions, their ritualistic forms, ecclesiastical methods, and communal activities must be reconstituted as rapidly as experience allows, in order to function effectively in the modern world.

Fourteenth: The humanists are firmly convinced that existing acquisitive and profit-motivated society has shown itself to be inadequate and that a radical change in methods, controls, and motives must be instituted. A socialized and co-operative economic order must be established to the end that the equitable distribution of the means of life be possible. The goal of humanism is a free and universal society in which people voluntarily and intelligently cooperate for the common good. Humanists demand a shared life in a shared world.

Fifteenth and last: We assert that humanism will: (a) affirm life rather than deny it; (b) seek to elicit the possibilities of life, not flee from it; and (c) endeavor to establish the conditions of a satisfactory life for all, not merely for a few. By this positive morale and intention humanism will be guided, and from this perspective and alignment the techniques and efforts of humanism will flow.

So stand the theses of religious humanism. Though we consider the religious forms and ideas of our fathers no longer adequate, the quest for the good life is still the central task for mankind. Man is at last becoming aware that he alone is responsible for the realization of the world of his dreams, that he has within himself the power for its achievement. He must set intelligence and will to the task.

(Signed) J. A. C. Fagginger Auer, E. Burdette Backus, Harry Elmer Barnes, L. M. Birkhead, Raymond B. Bragg, Edwin Arthur Burtt, Ernest Caldecott, A. J. Carlson, John Dewey, Albert C. Dieffenbach, John H. Dietrich, Bernard Fantus, William Floyd, F. H. Hankins, A. Eustace Haydon, Llewellyn Jones, Robert Morss Lovett, Harold P. Marley, R. Lester Mondale, Charles Francis Potter, John Herman Randall, Jr., Curtis W. Reese, Oliver L. Reiser, Roy Wood Sellars, Clinton Lee Scott, Maynard Shipley, W. Frank Swift, V. T. Thayer, Eldred C. Vanderlaan, Joseph Walker, Jacob J. Weinstein, Frank S. C. Wicks, David Rhys Williams, Edwin H. Wilson.

Note [appended to Manifesto]: The Manifesto is a product of many minds. It was designed to represent a developing point of view, not a new creed. The individuals whose signatures appear, would, had they been writing individual statements, have stated the propositions in differing terms. The importance of the document is that more than thirty men have come to general agreement on matters of final concern and that these men are undoubtedly representative of a large number who are forging a new philosophy out of the materials of the modern world. It is obvious that many others might have been asked to sign the Manifesto had not the lack of time and the shortage of clerical assistance limited our ability to communicate with them.

5. A Goebbels Propaganda Pamphlet, 1930

Adapted from Joseph Goebbels, *Die verfluchten Hakenkreuzler* (Munich, 1930), trans. in *Documents of German History*, ed. Louis L. Snyder, (New Brunswick, N.J.: Rutgers University Press, 1958).

WHY ARE WE NATIONALISTS?

We are *Nationalists* because we see in the *Nation* the only possibility for the protection and the furtherance of our existence.

The *Nation* is the organic bond of a people for the protection and defense of their lives. He is nationally minded who understands this *in Word and in Deed*.

Today, in *Germany*, *Nationalism* has degenerated into *Bourgeois Patriotism*, and its power exhausts itself in tilting at windmills. It says *Germany* and means *Monarchy*. It proclaims *Freedom* and means *Black-White-Red*.

Young nationalism has its unconditional demands. *Belief in the Nation* is a matter of all the people, not for individuals of rank, a class, or an industrial clique. The eternal must be separated from the contemporary. The maintenance of a rotten industrial system has nothing to do with nationalism. I can love Germany and hate capitalism; not only *can* I do it, I also *must* do it. The germ of the rebirth of our people *lies only in the destruction of the system of plundering the healthy power of the people*.

We are Nationalists because We, as Germans, love Germany. And because we love Germany, we demand the protection of its national spirit and we battle against its destroyers.

WHY ARE WE SOCIALISTS?

We are *Socialists* because we see in *Socialism* the only possibility for maintaining our racial existence and through it the reconquest of our political freedom and the rebirth of the German state. *Socialism* has its peculiar form first of all through its comradeship in arms with the forward-driving energy of a newly awakened nationalism. Without nationalism it is nothing, a phantom, a theory, a vision of air, a book. With it, it is everything, *the Future, Freedom, Fatherland!*

It was a sin of the liberal bourgeoisie to overlook *the State-building Power of Socialism*. It was the sin of *Marxism* to degrade *Socialism* to a system of *Money and Stomach*.

We are *Socialists* because for us *the Social Question is a Matter of Necessity and Justice* and even beyond that *a Matter for the Very Existence of our People*.

Socialism is possible only in a State which is Free Inside and Outside.

Down with Political Bourgeois Sentiment: for Real Nationalism!

Down with Marxism: for True Socialism!

Up with the Stamp of the First German National Socialist State!

At the Front the National Socialist German Workers Party! . . .

WHY DO WE OPPOSE THE JEWS?

We are *Enemies of the Jews*, because we are fighters for the freedom of the German people. *The Jew is the Cause and the Beneficiary of our Misery*. He has used the social difficulties of the broad masses of our people to deepen the unholy split between Right and Left among our people. He has made two halves of Germany. He is the real cause for our loss of the Great War.

The Jew has no interest in the solution of Germany's fateful problems; he *cannot* have any. *For He Lives on the Fact That There Has Been No Solution*. If we would make the German people a unified community and give them freedom before the world, then the Jew can have no place among us. He has the best trumps in his hands when a people lives in inner and outer slavery. *The Jew is Responsible for our Misery and He Lives On It*.

That is the reason why we, *as Nationalists* and *as Socialists*, oppose the Jew. *He Has Corrupted our Race, Fouled our Morals, Undermined our Customs, and Broken our Power*.

The Jew is the Plastic Demon of the Decline of Mankind. The Jew is Uncreative. He produces nothing. *He Only Handles*

Products. As long as he struggles against the state, *He is a Revolutionary;* ·as soon as he has power, he preaches *Quiet and Order,* so that he can consume his plunder at his convenience.

Anti-Semitism is Unchristian. That means, then, that he is a Christian who looks on while the Jew sets straps around our necks. *To be a Christian means: Love Thy Neighbor as Thyself! My Neighbor is One Who is Tied to Me by his Blood. If I love Him, Then I Must Hate His Enemies. He who Thinks German Must Despise the Jews.* The one thing makes the other necessary.

We are Enemies of the Jews Because We Belong to the German People. The Jew is our Greatest Misfortune. It is not true that we eat a Jew every morning at breakfast. It is true, however, that he *Slowly but Surely Robs Us of Everything We Own.*

That Will Stop, as Surely as We are Germans.

6. Nürnberg Law for the Protection of German Blood and German Honor, September 15, 1935

Reichsgesetzblatt, Vol. I, No. 100 (September 15, 1935). Trans. in *Documents and Readings in the History of Europe Since 1918,* by Walter Consuelo Langsam (Philadelphia: J. B. Lippincott Co., 1939).

Imbued with the knowledge that the purity of German blood is the prerequisite for the continuance of the German nation and animated with the unbending will to ensure the German nation for all the future, the Reichstag unanimously resolved upon this law, which is herewith proclaimed:

I. 1. Marriages between Jews and citizens of German or kindred blood are prohibited.

2. Annulment proceedings can be brought only by the Public Prosecutor.

II. Extramarital relations between Jews and citizens of German or kindred blood are prohibited.

III. Jews may not employ in their households female citizens of German or kindred blood who are under 45 years of age.

IV. 1. Jews are forbidden to hoist the Reich and national flag and to display the Reich colors.

2. They may, on the other hand, display the Jewish colors. The exercise of this right is under state protection.

V. 1. Whoever acts contrary to the prohibition of Article 1 is liable to penal servitude.

2. The man who acts contrary to the prohibition of Article 2 is punishable by jail or penitentiary sentence.

3. Whoever acts contrary to the provisions of Articles 3 and 4 is punishable with a jail sentence up to one year and a money fine or with either of these penalties.

7. The Platform of the German Christians, 1932

The Platform of the German Christians, 1932, accepted Nazi Aryanism and would have made the church a part of the state. Karl Barth and others saw a different role for the church, and at Barmen, 1934, made the famous declaration of the Confessing Church. After the war, at Stuttgart, the surviving leaders of the Confessing Church, despite their resistance to Hitler, made their startling confession of guilt. From *The German Phoenix,* by Franklin Hamlin Littell. Copyright © 1960 by Franklin Hamlin Littell. Reprinted by permission of Doubleday & Company, Inc. Originally in Arnold Dannenmann, *Die Geschichte der Glaubensbewegung Deutsche Christen* (Dresden: Günther Verlag, 1933), and in *Kirchliches Jahrbuch, 1933-44, 1945-48,* ed. Joachim Beckmann. (Gütersloh: C. Bertelsmann Verlag, 1950).

1. These directives are to point out to all believing Germans the ways and the goals by which they can attain a new order in the church. These directives are not intended to constitute a creed nor to replace one; neither are they intended to disturb the confessional foundations of the Evangelical Church. They state a way of life.

2. We are fighting for the union of the 29 churches embraced by the "German Evangelical Church Federation" in one evangelical National Church, and we march to the call and goal:

> Nach aussen eins und geistgewaltig,
> Um Christus und sein Wort geschart,
> Nach innen reich und vielgestaltig,
> Ein jeder Christ nach Ruf und Art!
> [from *Geibel*]

3. The voting list "German Christian" will be no ecclesiastical party in the usual sense. It appeals to all Christians of German

type. The age of parliamentarianism is past, also in the church. Ecclesiastical parties have no spiritual claim to represent the church folk, and they obstruct the high purpose to become *one* church. We want a living People's Church [Volkskirche] which is the expression of all the religious powers of our nation [Volk].

4. We take our stand on the platform of positive Christianity [des positiven Christentums]. We affirm an affirmative style of Christian faith, as appropriate to the German spirit of Luther and heroic piety.

5. We want to bring to the fore in our church the reawakened German feeling for life and to make our church life of positive value for life. In the fateful battle for German freedom and future, the church has shown itself too weak in its leadership. The church has not yet marshalled for decisive battle against the God-hating Marxism and the foreign-spirited Center Party (Zentrum), but instead reached an agreement with the political parties which represent these forces. We want our church to fight in the forefront in the decisive struggle for the existence or extinction of our nation. She dare not stand aside or indeed shy away from the fighters for freedom.

6. We demand a change in the legal constitution [political paragraph] and open battle against Marxism, hostile to religion and to the nation, and against its socialist-Christian fellow-travelers of all degrees. We miss in this legal constitution the trusting dependence upon God and the mission of the church. The way into the Kingdom of God leads through battle, cross and sacrifice, not through false peace.

7. We see in race, national character and nation orders of life given and entrusted to us by God, to maintain which is a law of God for us. Therefore racial mixing is to be opposed. On the basis of its experience the German *foreign missions* have for a long time called to the German nation: "Keep yourself racially pure," and tells us that faith in Christ doesn't disturb race but rather deepens and sanctifies it.

8. We see in home missions [Inner Mission], properly understood, a living Christianity of action [Tat-Christentum] which,

according to our understanding, roots not in mere pity but in obedience to God's will and in gratitude for Christ's death on the cross. Mere pity is "charity" and becomes arrogance, coupled with bad conscience, and weakens a nation. We know something of Christian duty and love toward the helpless, but we demand also the protection of the nation from the incapable and inferior. [The Inner Mission] ... must moreover keep its distance from economic adventures and must not become a mere shopkeeper.

9. In the mission to the Jews we see a grave danger to our national character. It is the entryway for foreign blood into our national body. It has no traditional justification side by side with foreign missions. We deny the validity of the mission to the Jews in Germany, as long as the Jews have the rights of citizenship and thereby there exists the danger of racial deterioration and bastardization. The Holy Scriptures also say something about the divine wrath and self-betraying love. Marriage between Germans and Jews is especially to be forbidden.

10. We want an Evangelical Church which roots in the national character, and we repudiate the spirit of a Christian cosmopolitanism. We want to overcome the corrupt developments which have sprung from this spirit—such as pacifism, internationalism, Freemasonry, etc.—through faith in the national mission given us by God. Membership of an Evangelical minister in a lodge of Free Masons is not to be allowed.

These ten points of the "German Christians" are a call to rally, and they constitute in great outline the direction of the future Evangelical National Church [Reichskirche], which by the maintaining of confessional peace will develop the powers of our Reformation faith into the finest of the German nation.

(signed) Hossenfelder, clergyman

8. The Barmen Declaration, May, 1934
Littell, *The German Phoenix.*

According to the introductory words of its constitution of 11 July 1933, the German Evangelical Church is a federal union of confessional churches which grew out of the

Reformation, of equal rights and parallel existence. The theological premise of the association of these churches is given in Article 1 and Article 2, paragraph 1 of the constitution of the German Evangelical Church, recognized by the national government on 14 July 1933:

Article 1. The impregnable foundation of the German Evangelical Church is the Gospel of Jesus Christ, as it is revealed in Holy Scripture and came again to the light in the creeds of the Reformation. In this way the authorities, which the church needs for her mission, are defined and limited.

Article 2, Paragraph 1. The German Evangelical Church consists of churches [territorial churches].

We, assembled representatives of Lutheran, Reformed and United churches, independent synods, *Kirchentage* and local church groups, hereby declare that we stand together on the foundation of the German Evangelical Church as a federal union of German confessional churches. We are held together by confession of the one Lord of the one, holy, universal and apostolic church.

We declare, before the public view of all the Evangelical Churches of Germany, that the unity of this confession and thereby also the unity of the German Evangelical Church is severely threatened. In this year of the existence of the German Evangelical Church it is endangered by the more and more clearly evident style of teaching and action of the ruling ecclesiastical party of the German Christians and the church government which they run. This threat comes from the fact that the theological premise in which the German Evangelical Church is united is constantly and basically contradicted and rendered invalid, both by the leaders and spokesmen of the German Christians and also by the church government, by means of strange propositions. If they obtain, the church—according to all the creeds which are authoritative among us—ceases to be the church. If they obtain, moreover, the German Evangelical Church will become impossible as a federal union of confessional churches.

Together we may and must, as members of Lutheran, Reformed and United churches, speak today to this situation. Precisely because we want to be and remain true to our various confessions of faith, we may not keep silent, for we believe that in a time of common need and trial [Anfechtung] a common word has been placed in our mouth. We commit to God what this may mean for the relationship of the confessional churches with each other.

In view of the destructive errors of the German Christians and the present national church government, we pledge ourselves to the following evangelical truths:

1. "I am the way and the truth and the life: no man cometh unto the Father, but by me." (John 14:6.)

"Verily, verily, I say unto you, He that entereth not by the door into the sheepfold, but climbeth up some other way, the same is a thief and a robber. . . . I am the door; by me if any man enter in, he shall be saved." (John 10:1, 9.)

Jesus Christ, as he is testified to us in the Holy Scripture, is the one Word of God, whom we are to hear, whom we are to trust and obey in life and in death.

We repudiate the false teaching that the church can and must recognize yet other happenings and powers, images and truths as divine revelation alongside this one Word of God, as a source of her preaching.

2. "But of him are ye in Christ Jesus, who of God is made unto us wisdom, and righteousness, and sanctification, and redemption." (I Cor. 1:30.)

Just as Jesus Christ is the pledge of the forgiveness of all our sins, just so—and with the same earnestness—is he also God's mighty claim on our whole life; in him we encounter a joyous liberation from the godless claims of this world to free and thankful service to his creatures.

We repudiate the false teaching that there are areas of our life in which we belong not to Jesus Christ but another lord, areas in which we do not need justification and sanctification through him.

3. "But speaking the truth in love, may grow up into him in all things, which is the head, even Christ: from whom the whole body [is] fitly joined together and compacted. . . ." (Eph. 4:15-16.)

The Christian church is the community of

brethren, in which Jesus Christ presently works in the word and sacraments through the Holy Spirit. With her faith as well as her obedience, with her message as well as her ordinances, she has to witness in the midst of the world of sin as the church of forgiven sinners that she is his alone, that she lives and wishes to live only by his comfort and his counsel in expectation of his appearance.

We repudiate the false teaching that the church can turn over the form of her message and ordinances at will or according to some dominant ideological and political convictions.

4. "Ye know that the princes of the Gentiles exercise domination over them, and they that are great exercise authority upon them. But it shall not be so among you: but whosoever will be great among you, let him be your minister." (Matt. 20:25-26.)

The various offices in the church establish no rule of one over the other but the exercise of the service entrusted and commanded to the whole congregation.

We repudiate the false teaching that the church can and may, apart from this ministry, set up special leaders [Führer] equipped with powers to rule.

5. "Fear God, honor the king!" (I Peter 2:17.)

The Bible tells us that according to divine arrangement the state has the responsibility to provide for justice and peace in the yet unredeemed world, in which the church also stands, according to the measure of human insight and human possibility, by the threat and use of force.

The church recognizes with thanks and reverence toward God the benevolence of this, his provision. She reminds men of God's Kingdom, God's commandment and righteousness, and thereby the responsibility of rulers and ruled. She trusts and obeys the power of the word, through which God maintains all things.

We repudiate the false teaching that the state can and should expand beyond its special responsibility to become the single and total order of human life, and also thereby fulfill the commission of the church.

We repudiate the false teaching that the church can and should expand beyond its special responsibility to take on the characteristics, functions and dignities of the state, and thereby become itself an organ of the state.

6. "Lo, I am with you alway, even unto the end of the world." (Matt. 28:20.) "The word of God is not bound." (II Tim. 2:9.)

The commission of the church, in which her freedom is founded, consists in this: in place of Christ and thus in the service of his own word and work, to extend through word and sacrament the message of the free grace of God to all people.

We repudiate the false teaching that the church, in human self-esteem, can put the word and work of the Lord in the service of some wishes, purposes and plans or other, chosen according to desire.

The confessing synod of the German Evangelical Church declares that she sees in the acknowledgment of these truths and in the repudiation of these errors the not-to-be-circumvented theological foundation of the German Evangelical Church as a federal union of confessional churches. [The synod] calls upon all who can join in its declaration to be aware of these theological lessons in their ecclesiastical decisions. It begs all concerned to turn again in the unity of faith, of love, and of hope. *Verbum Dei manet in aeternum.*

9. Stuttgart Declaration of Guilt, October, 1945

Littell, *The German Phoenix.*

The Council of the Evangelical Church in Germany, at its session on October 18-19, 1945, in Stuttgart, welcomes the representatives of the World Council of Churches.

We are all the more thankful for this visit in that we are not only conscious of oneness with our nation in a great community of suffering, but also in a solidarity of guilt. With great pain we say: Unending suffering has been brought by us to many peoples and countries. That which we have often witnessed to our congregations we now proclaim in the name of the whole church: We have in fact fought for long years in the name of Jesus Christ against the spirit which found its terrible expression in National Socialist government by force; but we accuse ourselves that we didn't witness more courageously, pray more faithfully, believe more joyously, love more ardently.

Now a new beginning is to be made in our churches. Founded on the Holy Scripture, with all earnestness directed to the sole Lord of the church, they are going about it to purge themselves of influences foreign to the faith and to put themselves in order. Our hope is in the God of grace and mercy, that He will use our church as his tool and give it authority, to proclaim His Word and to create obedience to His Will among ourselves and in our whole nation.

That in this new beginning we may know ourselves to be warmly tied to the other churches of the ecumenical fellowship fills us with deep rejoicing.

We hope in God that through the joint service of the churches the spirit of violence and revenge, that begins again today to become powerful, may be controlled, and the spirit of peace and love come to command, [the spirit] in which alone tortured humanity can find healing.

So we pray in a time when the whole world needs a new beginning: *Veni creator spiritus!* (signed Bishop Wurm, Bishop Meiser, Bishop Dibelius, Superintendent Hahn, Pastor Asmussen, Pastor Niemöller, *Landesoberkirchenrat* Lilje, Pastor Niesel, Dr. Heinemann, Superintendent Held. Stuttgart, 19 October 1945.)

10. *"Gazing into the Pit"*

An Editorial which appeared in the *Christian Century,* May 9, 1945, when the horrors of the Nazi concentration camps were revealed.

The horrors disclosed by the capture of the Nazi concentration camps at Buchenwald, Belsen, Limburg and a dozen other places constitute one of those awful acts upon which a paper such as this feels under obligation to comment, but concerning which it is almost impossible to write. What can be said that will not seem like tossing little words up against a giant mountain of ineradicable evil? What human emotion can measure to such bestiality except a searing anger which calls on heaven to witness that retri-

bution shall be swift and terrible and pitiless? How can men (and, it is alleged, women) who have been capable of such deeds be thought of or dealt with save as vicious brutes who must be exterminated both to do justice and in mercy to the future of the race?

We have found it hard to believe that the reports from the Nazi concentration camps could be true. Almost desperately we have tried to think that they must be wildly exaggerated. Perhaps they were products of the fevered brains of prisoners who were out for revenge. Or perhaps they were just more atrocity-mongering, like the cadaver factory story of the last war. But such puny barricades cannot stand up against the terrible facts. The evidence is too conclusive. It will be a long, long time before our eyes will cease to see those pictures of naked corpses piled like firewood or of those mounds of carrion flesh and bones. It will be a long, long time before we can forget what scores of honorable, competent observers tell us they have seen with their own eyes. The thing is well-nigh incredible. But it happened.

What does it mean? That the Germans are beyond the pale of humanity? That they are capable of a fiendish cruelty which sets them apart from all the rest of us? No, not that. For one thing, we read that a large portion of the victims in these concentration camps were Germans. We do not believe that the sort of Germans who were subjected to this torture under any conceivable circumstances would themselves have become torturers. For another thing, we have reason to know that mass cruelty in its most revolting forms has not been confined to Germany. We have seen photographs that missionaries smuggled out of raped Nanking. We have read the affidavits of men who escaped from the Baltic states and eastern Holland. We know what horrors writers like David Dallin and William Henry Chamberlain believe would be revealed if the prison camps in the Soviet Arctic were opened to the world's inspection. We know, too, the frightful things that have happened in this country when lynching mobs ran wild—things so horrible that they can only be told in whipers.

No, the horror of the Nazi concentration camps is the horror of humanity itself when it has surrendered to its capacity for evil. When we look at the pictures from Buchenwald we are looking, to be sure, at the rightful malignity of nazism, this perversion of all values which in its final extremity is actually intent, as Hitler himself has said, on reducing all European life to "ruin, rats, and epidemics." But in the Nazis and beyond them we are looking into the very pit of hell which men disclose yawning within themselves when they reject the authority of moral law, when they deny the sacredness of human personality, when they turn from the worship of the one true God to the worship of their own wills, their own states, their own lust for power.

Buchenwald and the other memorials of Nazi infamy reveal the depths to which humanity can sink, and has sunk, in these frightful years. They reveal the awful fate which may engulf all civilizations unless these devils of our pride and of our ruthlessness and of the cult of force are exorcised. And they reveal that the salvation of man, the attainment of peace, the healing of the

nations is at the last a religious problem. The diplomats may mark out what boundary lines they please, the victorious armies may set up what zones of occupation they will, but if man continues this self-worship, the pit yawns for us all.

The foul stench of the concentration camps should burden the Christian conscience until Christian men cannot rest. The conventional ministry of past years is no ministry for these days when mankind totters on the brink of damnation. The puny plans which denominations have been making are so inadequate to this crisis that they are nearly irrelevant. Unless there is a great upsurge of testimony to the power of the Christian gospel to save men from the sin which is destroying them and their institutions, all the reconstitution of church paraphernalia now being planned will be so much building on sand. In this crisis the gospel cannot be preached dispassionately, tentatively or listlessly—not and save civilization from the pit. A time has come when the Christian must proclaim his gospel "like a dying man to dying men."

For we are dying men—dying, all of us and our institutions and our civilization, in the sins which have reached their appalling climax in the torture chambers of Europe's prison camps. Only faith in the God and Father of Jesus Christ, the God who sent his Son to reveal a common and all-inclusive brotherhood, can save us. Our contempt for the sacredness of life, our worship at the shrine of our own power, has gone so far that it has taken these horrors to shock us into awareness of the tragic fate toward which we are stumbling.

In God's providence, has not the World Council of Churches become a living hope for such a time as this? So far, progress toward the formation of the World Council has been cautious, following familiar patterns, a matter of negotiations and treaties among sovereign denominations. The goal has seemed largely to be the attainment of an organization. Is not the agony of mankind a call to the World Council to forget everything but the proclamation of the Christian evangel?

Should it not be the business of the World Council now to gather from all lands Chris-

XI-3. Conversation among the Ruins. *By Giorgio de Chirico. National Gallery of Art, Washington, D.C., Chester Dale Collection.*

tians who will go everywhere, pointing to the encroachments of human depravity which have been laid bare, proclaiming to men and nations, "Except ye repent, ye shall all likewise perish"? Let the Council gather for this common task Niemöller and the Christian leaders with him who have withstood the Nazi scourge, as many of them as may emerge from imprisonment; let it gather every Christian in the world who sees the peril and knows the means of escape, and let it send them forth with such an evangel as has not stormed this sin-stricken world since the days of the first apostles. Buchenwald and other concentration camps spell doom. But it is not simply the doom of the Nazis; it is the doom of man unless he can be brought to worship at the feet of the living God.

11. Church and State in Czechoslovakia

Some of the principal laws affecting church and state in Communist-dominated Czechoslovakia, 1949-1950. Trans. Dr. Jindrich Nosek in *Church and State Behind the Iron Curtain*, ed. Vladimir Gsovski (New York: Frederick A. Praeger, 1955). Text of the bishops' pastoral letter is from *The New York Times*, June 27, 1949. Copyright by *The New York Times*. Reprinted by permission.

LAWS ON CHURCH AND STATE IN
CZECHOSLOVAKIA

A. *Law of October 14, 1949, Establishing the Government Bureau for Church Affairs.*

The National Assembly of the Czechoslovak Republic has passed the following Law:

Sec. 1—A Government Bureau for Church Affairs shall be established as the central governmental body; a minister assigned by the President of the Republic shall direct it.

Sec. 2—The purpose of the Bureau for Church Affairs shall be to see to it that Church life develops in accordance with the Constitution and the principles of the people's democratic order and thus secure to everybody the right of freedom of religion based upon the principles of religious tolerance and equal rights for all denominations as guaranteed by the Constitution.

Sec. 3—The jurisdiction in all matters of Church and religion which until now has been exercised by other departments shall

pass to the Government Bureau for Church Affairs.

Sec. 4—The minister directing the Government Bureau for Church Affairs shall exercise his jurisdiction in Slovakia as a rule through the Slovak Bureau for Church Affairs, which shall be directed by a commissioner assigned by the Cabinet.

Sec. 5—Detailed provisions on the jurisdiction and organization of the Government Bureau for Church Affairs and the Slovak Bureau for Church Affairs and on procedure shall be established by a decree of the Cabinet.

Sec. 6—This law shall take effect on the day of promulgation; it shall be carried out by all members of the Cabinet.

B. *Cabinet Decree of October 25, 1949, on the Jurisdiction and Organization of the Government Bureau for Church Affairs.*

On the basis of Sec. 5 of the Law of October 14, 1949, establishing the Government Bureau for Church Affairs, the Cabinet of the Czechoslovak Republic decrees as follows:

Sec. 1—As the central government body the Government Bureau for Church Affairs shall exercise all jurisdiction in matters of Church and religion, and in particular the jurisdiction exercised until now by other Government departments.

Sec. 2—The jurisdiction of the Government Bureau for Church Affairs shall embrace the following matters:

a. Issuance of general rules and direction and supervision in all matters of Church and religion;

b. Administrative matters of the Churches, religious associations and their branches, communities, institutions, foundations, Church buildings, prebends, funds, monastic orders and monasteries, as well as their economic and financial matters (legal transactions relating to property, matters involving public construction, administration of Church funds and foundations, and the like);

c. Protection of religious monuments;

d. Matters involving the budget, credit, and planning in the ecclesiastical and religious sphere, without prejudice to the jurisdiction of the Government Planning Bureau;

e. Personnel matters and emoluments of

clergymen, teachers, and employees of the theological schools of universities, (other) theological schools and seminaries, as well as of teachers of religion;

f. Regulation of the teaching of religion, approval of syllabuses, textbooks, equipment and devices, and general supervision, in agreement with the Ministry of Education, Science, and Art, over the teaching of religion and over denominational educational institutions of any kind;

g. Expert evaluation of the ecclesiastical press and publications;

h. Issuance of an official gazette for clergymen and issuance of information bulletins and publications;

i. Matters involving religious associations and organizations, without prejudice to the jurisdiction of the Ministry of the Interior;

j. Matters involving charitable activities of the Churches and religious associations;

k. Taking care of the development of religious life in accordance with the Constitution;

l. Keeping informed on the development of the international relations of the Churches and religions.

Sec. 3—(1) The work of the Government Bureau for Church Affairs shall be performed in a Section for Religious Affairs, Personnel Section, Information Section, and an Economic and Administrative Section....

C. *Law of October 14, 1949, to Provide Economic Security for Churches and Religious Associations through the Government.*

The National Assembly of the Czechoslovak Republic has passed the following law:

Emoluments of Clergymen

Sec. 1—According to the provisions of the present Law stated below, the Government shall grant emoluments to the clergymen of Churches and religious associations who with the consent of the Government either perform strictly religious functions, or are employed in Church administration or in establishments for the training of clergymen. The Government Bureau for Church Affairs may, exceptionally in agreement with the Ministry of Finance, also grant emoluments to clergymen who are engaged in other activities.

Sec. 5—Governmental consent may be granted only to ministers of religion who are Czechoslovak citizens, are politically reliable, are irreproachable, and who otherwise meet the general requirements for employment with the Government. The Government Bureau for Church Affairs may waive the requirement of citizenship in cases deserving special consideration.

Sec. 7—Activities and Appointment of Clergymen. (1) Only those persons may carry on the activities of a minister of religion (preacher and the like) in a Church or religious association who have obtained the consent of the Government therefor and have taken an oath.

Sec. 10—Property. (1) The government shall supervise the property of the Churches and religious associations.

D. *Cabinet Decree of October 18, 1949, to Provide Economic Security to the Roman Catholic Church through the Government.*

On the basis of the Law of October 14, 1949, to Provide Economic Security to Churches and Religious Associations through the Government, the Cabinet of the Czechoslovak Republic decrees as follows:

Sec. 1—(1) Clergymen are employees of the Church.

Sec. 7—(1) Only clergymen who are Czechoslovak citizens, are politically reliable, are irreproachable, and who otherwise meet the general requirements for employment with the Government may be appointed to the posts established with the consent of the Government and may receive the emoluments provided by this decree.

Sec. 19—(1) A pledge of loyalty to the Czechoslovak Republic shall be a prerequisite for engaging in ecclesiastical activities.

(2) The pledge reads: I promise on my honor and conscience to be faithful to the Czechoslovak Republic and to its People's democratic order, and I will not undertake anything contrary to its interests, security, and integrity. As a citizen of a people's democratic State I shall perform conscientiously the duties of my office and I will do everything within my ability to support efforts at (social) reconstruction for the welfare of the people....

Sec. 20—(1) The Provincial People's Committee shall keep a record on every clergy-man, which shall include personal data pertinent for his service status, for the granting and determining of emoluments, and for the claims of social benefits.

Sec. 29—The patronage of Roman Catholic Churches, prebends, and other Church establishments exercised until now by public funds, foundations, communities, counties, provinces, and other entities of public law, as well as the patronage connected with the ownership of property ... shall pass over to the Government....

E. *Proclamation No. 320 of the Government Bureau for Church Affairs of May 12, 1950, concerning the Functions of the General Internal Affairs Divisions of the Provincial People's Committees in Church and Religious Matters and the Establishment of Church Sections.*

The Government Bureau for Church Affairs, in agreement with the Ministry of the Interior and other interested central agencies, provides, as follows:

Functions of the Division on Church and Religious Affairs.

.   .   .   .   .

It (the Division) shall inspect all activities of Churches and religious associations, their agents, branches and institutions.

It shall cooperate in Church and religious matters with the representatives of the agencies of Churches and religious associations.

It shall keep records of and supervise the activities of monasteries and their members; it shall provisionally approve the creation of new houses for religious orders, of social orders and congregations which already have been established in the Czechoslovak Republic.

It shall approve provisionally the creation of new parishes, congregations, communities etc., and of changes of their boundaries.

It shall confirm representatives of Churches and religious associations and their branches.

It shall receive the pledge of loyalty of clergymen.

It shall install newly appointed Roman Catholic clergymen.

It shall approve performance of ecclesiastical activities by the auxiliary clergymen and clergymen.

It shall approve the designation [election, appointment] of auxiliary clergymen and clergymen to positions established with Government approval.

It shall handle cases of removal of auxiliary clergymen and clergymen who have become ineligible for assignment to posts established with approval of the Government and of the ecclesiastical authorities.

It shall assure orderly performance of religious functions, Church administration, and the education of clergymen to fill a vacancy whenever the post of an auxiliary clergyman or of a clergyman of Class I or II becomes open.

It shall decide appeals in Church and religious matters, especially concerning the use of one Church's facilities by another Church, the use of cemeteries, burials, and interdenominational matters....

TEXT OF CZECH BISHOPS' PASTORAL LETTER
ON STATE-CHURCH FIGHT

Dear Faithful: In these overwhelmingly serious times of our religious and national life we turn to you with this letter of the right-teaching church.

Love for the nation and for the people of Czechoslovakia leads us to speak in these decisive days, in which we have become witnesses to attacks on the unity and leadership of the Catholic Church here. To know where the truth and right and your place in the church and nation are, hear the voice of your pastors who, being conscious of responsibility before God and the conscience of the whole world, after deliberate consideration cannot remain quiet.

We have all been witnesses lately to a widely based action, the aim of which is to force the Czechoslovak Bishops to come to an agreement with the state. As is our public, we also are of the opinion that relations between church and state are discordant and painful. This situation is surely unnatural, for both societies would complement each other and the present situation does not contribute to general public peace nor the internal peace of the faithful....

.   .   .   .   .

To these humanitarian and commonly recognized rights of man belong not only the freedom of privately held religious convictions and the freedom to execute religious rites, but also the free realization of the principles of this faith as the norm of life of individuals and society—and this without fear of losing personal freedom, civic equality and the endangering of the rights of existence.

For the realization and ensuring of this religious freedom for Catholics it is the church's conception, by the ordinance of God, that these further conditions are necessary prerequisites: The recognition of the authority of the Holy Father as the highest visible head of the church and recognition for the authority of his Bishops.

The non-recognition of this fundamental principle means that the Catholic Church as Christ wanted it is not recognized and that every action taken apart and against the will of the Bishops, connected with the Roman Pope, disturbs the church's basic structure, disrupts its unity and necessarily leads to its destruction.

Further basic conditions for the recognition of the rights and freedom of the church, stemming from natural law, are:

1. Respect for the sovereign right of parents over the education of their children. That means education in school and outside school.

2. Recognition of the family as a sacred tie, and the rights and duties stemming from this.

3. The right of the faithful to free assembly in congregations and organizations.

Freedom for Faith to Exist

To these belong also the conditions of free religious life, which otherwise would be unattainable for the Communist or the individual. These conditions include the necessary number of church schools, educational and social and charitable institutions, cultural and philanthropic institutions, sufficient facilities for printing periodicals and books and free unlimited access to all possibilities of social and cultural life.

Finally, financial means and material security for these institutions and establishments are also necessary as without them it would not be possible for the church successfully to develop this activity for the welfare of our people and to save church buildings from deterioration and destruction.

All this we once had to the necessary extent and all this we have been deprived of lately.

.   .   .   .   .

It (the Church) stands here today—robbed, deprived of the majority of its freedoms and rights, dishonored, soiled, persecuted secretly and openly.

Only observe how the church is faring in Czechoslovakia at the present time. A concerted campaign is waged against it on the radio and in public proclamations, especially against the Holy Father and the Bishops, who are its God-ordained heads. The sacred character of the family and the sovereign rights of parents to the education of their children are willfully undermined.

All the ecclesiastical press, with a few completely insignificant exceptions, has been stopped. Even the official gazettes of the Bishops, which informed priests also of important state directives, have been stopped. Instead, the Ministry of Education, Science and Art has published the so-called Gazette of the Catholic Clergy, which has no church endorsement and is edited against the will of the hierarchy. Although this so-called gazette is intended for Catholic priests, it is directed by non-Catholics in an anti-church spirit and attempts to govern directly by state organs affairs that are wholly ecclesiastical and thereby attempts to exclude the Bishops from practicing their rights.

Every Catholic book that is to be published—even prayer books—is subjected to preliminary state censorship.

State plenipotentiaries are planted in Catholic publishing houses. An interdiction of assembly and schooling of Catholics outside churches was edited under the threat of prosecution.

Even the fate of church buildings, as was demonstrated by the forced inventory of ritual objects and sacred vessels, is, it seems, insecure.

The church is deprived of the last remnants of its property. Not even the minimum laid down by the law is respected.

Church schools practically no longer exist and the fate of the few remaining is painfully insecure, which causes suffering to pupils and parents. Pressure was even brought to bear upon the parents to take their children out of church schools, and this under a direct threat of consequences.

Teachers of religion are tested ideologically and are given directives on how to teach religion in the materialistic spirit.

All religious education of youth in societies, eucharistic circles, etc., was in many places forbidden under punitive threats and is consistently made impossible by the fact that the state has taken a monopoly on materialist schools and extracurricular education, so that education in the Christian spirit is made impossible and considered as practically illegal.

In this respect, we have come so far that even in theological schools lectures of so-called social science were instituted whose aim it is to bring it about that even theological students should be educated in the materialistic ideology.

An inventory of all church property, even church collections, was ordered, quite illegally. With direct inspection, such inventories were carried out in many cases. They were anti-constitutional searches.

Consistent attempts are made to deprive church buildings of their religious missions, especially by the taking over of monasteries and institutions for the education of clerical and monastic youth.

Especially in Slovakia some monastic houses were forcibly cleared out and the priests taken away in trucks.

The Ministry of Interior gave instructions to the regional command of the state security [police] on how to deal with the church and its members.

In some places even the practicing of religious rites has already been forbidden. In many places religious processions were made impossible or were misused for irreligious purposes.

The conference of Bishops in Dolni Smokovec, which was to have taken a stand on the demands of the Government, was broken up when listening devices were discovered in the conference room. The Ministry of Interior was asked to make an inquiry but up to now no satisfactory answer has been forthcoming.

The latest conference of Bishops in Prague was disturbed by security organs.

At the same time the Prague consistory was occupied by state officers and the Archbishop's residence put under secret police surveillance, so that the freedom of the chairman of the Bishops' conference was totally restricted. These restrictions represent extreme breaches of constitutional freedoms and many of the still-existent laws.

On the whole it can be said that outside the church any religious activity is impossible and many fear to visit churches lest they be accused of reaction and fear the loss of their means of existence.

.   .   .   .   .

After all, the whole affair of an agreement between church and state would actually have been a rather simple matter if it had not been for the fact that the state first harmed the church and deprived it of the majority of its rights.

All this organized calling for an agreement would have been quite superfluous if Government personages, on their own initiative, had not interfered before the start of negotiations in church freedoms and rights and formed, by this one-sided action, a painful situation in which the church was deprived beforehand of that which was supposed to have been the subject of the agreement.

So in reality the church was deprived of all possibilities of successful negotiations and given this choice: submission to dictatorship or persecution.

.   .   .   .   .

We declare that we were always loyal to the republic. We have stressed this many times and it can be deduced from the oath we undertook when we assumed office. A loyal attitude toward the republic is therefore, a matter of course for us and we are sure to remain faithful to our oath. Therefore we have always demanded from our clergy that they refrain from any political activitity, especially from any illegal and anti-state activity.

But we cannot remain quiet when the rights of the Holy Church are violated and when political power is being misused against it.

Most painful is the fact that we have no way of defending ourselves against these gross and untrue attacks. All manner of attempts are being made to force us out of our pastoral offices and the conduct of the church is being taken over by unbelieving persons, persons who have broken away from the church and those who have no right, no competence and no church missions.

.   .   .   .   .

In this spirit the Czechoslovak dignitaries at the Bishops' conference of June 7, 1949, in Olomouc, laid down the basic conditions on which agreement would be possible and which should be accepted and guaranteed by the Government beforehand. These conditions are:

1. The Christian world viewpoint [philosophy] will be recognized and respected in public life and education, in word and deed.

2. The Government recognizes the spiritual authority of the Roman Pope as the supreme head of the church in matters religious and ecclesiastical, which, according to valid authority, does not touch the sovereignty of the state but is a natural consequence of recognized basic human rights, and especially the freedom of religion.

3. Before the beginning of negotiations, all measures restricting and threatening religious freedom of Catholics in the Czechoslovak Republic, especially the religious freedom and education of youth, be repealed.

In addition to this: a. The Gazette of the Catholic Clergy, published by the Ministry of Education, Arts and Sciences, will be published immediately, and that the publishing of all official dignitaries' gazettes will be permitted.

b. The decree of the Ministry of Education, Arts and Sciences of May 23, 1949, about vacant church offices and accompanying stipends, as well as the decree of the Ministry of Interior of May 5, 1949, restricting the freedom of assembly and congrega-

tion, and also the decree for regional and district command of the state security police on the procedure against the Catholic Church, must be revoked. (signed, Josef Beran, Archbishop of Prague, Josef Charles, Archbishop of Olomouc, Jan, Bishop of Spisska Nova Ves, Josef, Titular Bishop of Thagora, Apostolic Administrator in Kosice, Paul, Bishop of Presov, Maurice, Bishop of Hradec Kralove, Andrew, Bishop of Banska Bystrica, Charles, Bishop of Brno, Josef, Bishop of Ceske Budejovice, Stefan, Bishop of Litomerice, Edvard, Titular Bishop of Velicia, Apostolic Administrator of Nitra, Frantisek Onderek, Apostolic Administrator of the Czech portion of Wroclaw Archdiocese, Ambrosius Lazik, Apostolic Administrator of Trnava, Robert Pobozny, Capitular Vicar of Roznava. Prague, June 15, 1949.)

This pastoral letter is to be read in all parish churches and chapels at public services on Sunday, June 26, 1949. Let the reverend priests not be intimidated from reading this letter by any threats in these so difficult and decisive times. They are bound by their consciences to inform their faithful of the real state of affairs. Willful and intentional neglect of this duty will be prosecuted with ecclesiastical punishment.

12. Universal Declaration of Human Rights

The United Nations General Assembly at Paris, December 10, 1948, formally adopted the Declaration of Human Rights. None voted against it; eight abstained. Article 18 is significant for religion, but note that God is not referred to as Creator or Divine Origin. The world's churches were active in pressuring the United Nations for a definition of man's rights and freedoms, and freedom of religion becomes a part of other human freedoms. In the committee debates, Moslems objected to mentioning freedom to change one's belief, and the USSR wanted religion to conform to the laws of the state. As enacted, the declaration becomes a standard definition of human rights. Text from *Information Service*, January 8, 1949, news service of the Federal Council of the Churches of Christ in America.

PREAMBLE

Whereas recognition of the inherent dignity and of the equal and inalienable rights of all members of the human family is the foundation of freedom, justice and peace in the world,

Whereas disregard and contempt for human rights have resulted in barbarous acts which have outraged the conscience of mankind, and the advent of a world in which human beings shall enjoy freedom of speech and belief and freedom from fear and want has been proclaimed as the highest aspiration of the common people,

Whereas it is essential, if man is not to be compelled to have recourse, as a last resort, to rebellion against tyranny and oppression, that human rights should be protected by the rule of law,

Whereas it is essential to promote the development of friendly relations between nations,

Whereas the peoples of the United Nations have in the Charter reaffirmed their faith in fundamental human rights, in the dignity and worth of the human person and in the equal rights of men and women and have determined to promote social progress and better standards of life in larger freedom,

Whereas member states have pledged themselves to achieve, in cooperation with the United Nations, the promotion of universal respect for and observance of human rights and fundamental freedoms,

Whereas a common understanding of these rights and freedoms is of the greatest importance for the full realization of this pledge,

Now, therefore, *The General Assembly*, Proclaims this Universal Declarations of Human Rights as a common standard of achievement for all peoples and all nations, to the end that every individual and every organ of society, keeping this Declaration constantly in mind, shall strive by teaching and education to promote respect for these rights and freedoms and by progressive measures, national and international, to secure their universal and effective recognition and observance, both among the peoples of member states themselves and among the peoples of territories under their jurisdiction.

Article 1—All human beings are born free and equal in dignity and rights. They are endowed with reason and conscience and should act towards one another in a spirit of brotherhood.

Article 2—Everyone is entitled to all the rights and freedoms set forth in this Declaration, without distinction of any kind, such as race, color, sex, language, religion, political or other opinion, national or social origin, property, birth or other status.

Furthermore no distinction shall be made on the basis of political, jurisdictional or international status of the country or the territory to which a person belongs whether it be an independent, trust or non-self-governing territory or under any other limitation of sovereignty.

Article 3—Everyone has the right to life, liberty, and the security of person.

Article 4—No one shall be held in slavery or servitude; slavery and the slave trade shall be prohibited in all their forms.

Article 5—No one shall be subjected to torture or to cruel, inhuman or degrading treatment or punishment.

Article 6—Everyone has the right to recognition everywhere as a person before the law.

Article 7—All are equal before the law and are entitled without any discrimination to equal protection of the law. All are entitled to equal protection against any discrimination in violation of this Declaration and against any incitement to such discrimination.

Article 8—Everyone has the right to an effective remedy by the competent national tribunals for acts violating the fundamental rights granted him by the constitution or by law.

Article 9—No one shall be subjected to arbitrary arrest, detention or exile.

Article 10—Everyone is entitled to full equality to a fair and public hearing by an independent and impartial tribunal, in the determination of his rights and obligations and of any criminal charge against him.

Article 11-1. Everyone charged with a penal offence has the right to be presumed innocent until proved guilty according to law in a public trial at which he has had all the guarantees necessary for his defence.

2. No one shall be held guilty of any penal offence on account of any act of omission which did not constitute a penal offence, under national or international law, at the time when it was committed. Nor shall a heavier penalty be imposed than the one that

was applicable at the time the penal offence was committed.

Article 12—No one shall be subjected to arbitrary interference with his privacy, family, home or correspondence, nor to attacks upon his honor and reputation. Everyone has the right to the protection of the law against such interference or attacks.

Article 13-1. Everyone has the right to freedom of movement and residence within the borders of each state.

2. Everyone has the right to leave any country, including his own, and to return to his country.

Article 14-1. Everyone has the right to seek and to enjoy in other countries asylum from persecution.

2. This right may not be invoked in the case of prosecutions genuinely arising from non-political crimes or from acts contrary to the purposes and principles of the United Nations.

Article 15-1. Everyone has the right to a nationality.

2. No one shall be arbitrarily deprived of his nationality nor denied the right to change his nationality.

Article 16-1. Men and women of full age, without any limitation due to race, nationality or religion, have the right to marry and to found a family. They are entitled to equal rights as to marriage, during marriage and at its dissolution.

2. Marriage shall be entered into only with the free and full consent of the intending spouses.

3. The family is the natural and fundamental group unit of society and is entitled to protection by society and the state.

Article 17-1. Everyone has the right to own property alone as well as in association with others.

2. No one shall be arbitrarily deprived of his property.

Article 18—Everyone has the right to freedom of thought, conscience and religion; this right includes freedom to change his religion or belief, and freedom, either alone or in community with others and in public or private, to manifest his religion or belief in teaching, practice, worship and observance.

Article 19—Everyone has the right to freedom of opinion and expression; this right includes freedom to hold opinions without interference and to seek, receive and impart information and ideas through any media and regardless of frontiers.

Article 20-1. Everyone has the right to freedom of peaceful assembly and association.

2. No one may be compelled to belong to an association.

Article 21-1. Everyone has the right to take part in the government of his country, directly or through freely chosen representatives.

2. Everyone has the right to equal access to public service in his country.

3. The will of the people shall be the basis of the authority of government; this will be by universal and equal suffrage and shall be held by secret vote or by equivalent free voting procedures.

Article 22—Everyone, as a member of society, has the right to social security and is entitled to realization, through national effort and international cooperation and in accordance with the organization and resources of each state, of the economic, social and cultural rights indispensable for his dignity and the free development of his personality.

Article 23-1. Everyone has the right to work, to free choice of employment, to just and favorable conditions of work and to protection against unemployment.

2. Everyone, without any discrimination, has the right to equal pay for equal work.

3. Everyone who works has the right to just and favorable remuneration insuring for himself and his family an existence worthy of human dignity and supplemented, if necessary, by other means of social protection.

4. Everyone has the right to form and to join trade unions for the protection of his interests.

Article 24—Everyone has the right to rest and leisure, including reasonable limitation of working hours and periodic holidays with pay.

Article 25-1. Everyone has the right to a standard of living adequate for the health and well-being of himself and of his family, including food, clothing, housing and medical care and necessary social services, and the right to security in the event of unemployment, sickness, disability, widowhood, old age or other lack of livelihood in circumstances beyond his control.

2. Motherhood and childhood are entitled to special care and assistance. All children, whether born in or out of wedlock, shall enjoy the same social protection.

Article 26-1. Everyone has the right to education. Education shall be free, at least in the elementary and fundamental stages. Elementary education shall be compulsory. Technical and professional education shall be generally available and higher education shall be equally accessible to all on the basis of merit.

2. Education shall be directed to the full development of the human personality and to the strengthening of respect for human rights and fundamental freedoms. It shall promote understanding, tolerance and friendship among all nations, racial or religious groups, and shall further activities of the United Nations for the maintenance of peace.

3. Parents have a prior right to choose the kind of education that shall be given to their children.

Article 27-1. Everyone has the right freely to participate in the cultural life of the community, to enjoy the arts and to share in scientific advancement and its benefits.

2. Everyone has the right to the protection of the moral and material interests resulting from any scientific, literary or production of which he is the author.

Article 28—Everyone is entitled to a social and international order in which the rights and freedoms set forth in this Declaration can be fully realized.

Article 29-1. Everyone has duties to the community in which alone the free and full development of his personality is possible.

2. In the exercise of his rights and freedoms, everyone shall be subject only to such limitations as are determined by law solely for the purpose of securing due recognition and respect for the rights and freedoms of others and of meeting the just requirements of morality, public order and the general welfare in a democratic society.

3. These rights and freedoms may in no case be exercised contrary to the purposes and principles of the United Nations.

Article 30—Nothing in this Declaration may be interpreted as implying for any state, group or person any right to engage in any activity or to perform any act aimed at the destruction of any of the rights and freedoms set forth herein.

13. *Religious Liberty in Spain*

In 1949, the religious situation in Spain attracted the attention of many Protestants who felt that it was a denial of religious freedom and human rights. The following report was an attempt to elucidate the various facts in the matter. *Information Service,* news service of the Federal Council of the Churches of Christ in America, October 29, 1949.

RELIGIOUS LIBERTY IN SPAIN TODAY

Few problems concern Protestants so much as the state of religious liberty in Spain. Many Catholics share this concern. We attempt here a dispassionate review of the evidence.

The population of Spain is, of course, overwhelmingly Roman Catholic, at least nominally. There are no very adequate figures on the number of Spanish Protestants; twenty to thirty thousand, divided among several sects, is the figure most often given. Spain has been a Catholic state during most of its history in spite of "violent vicissitudes," from time to time, as Dr. M. Searle Bates has said.

Under the Spanish Republic church and state were separated and religious liberty decreed. Protestants and independent Spaniards welcomed it eagerly. During the long-drawn-out Civil War Roman Catholic churches were burned and thousands of priests, nuns and laity were killed in the area controlled by the Popular Front. Much of the bitterness today may be due to the hatreds developed on both sides of the struggle during that period. When Franco came to power in 1939 after the Civil War (1936-1939) the Law of Religious Confessions and Congregations (of the Spanish Republic) was abrogated. Protestant schools were closed, though they had been permitted under the monarchy. The accord with the Holy See reaffirmed four articles of the Concordat of 1851, declaring that Catholicism is the sole religion of the country. No rights were recognized for other religions.[1]

In July, 1945, the *Fuero de los Españoles*, usually known as the "Spanish Charter," relaxed some of the restrictions. Article VI declares, "The profession and practice of the Catholic religion, which is that of the Spanish State, shall enjoy official protection. None shall be molested for their religious beliefs or the private practice of their worship. No other ceremonies or external demonstrations than those of the Catholic religion shall be permitted." [2]

This was, of course, ambiguous. Permission to open Protestant chapels was to be secured from the civil governor of the province, according to the interpretation of the Charter issued November 12, 1945. Some of the most restrictive measures were eased for a time. The degree depended, in part at least, it seems, on the attitude of the provincial governors in different sections of the country. Naturally, the Protestants attempted to take advantage of the new freedom. Since 1947, following bitter formal statements by various members of the Spanish hierarchy against Protestant activities, the laws have been interpreted much more harshly.

During the current year two well-known foreign correspondents visited Spain and wrote articles for their newspapers on the situation of the Spanish Protestants: Homer Bigart in the New York *Herald Tribune* for February 23, and Joseph G. Harrison, chief of the Mediterranean Bureau of the *Christian Science Monitor*, in that newspaper for July 8. Within the last two or three years several well-known American clergymen have visited Spain, as well as a Swedish journalist, Björn Hallström.[3] The different accounts agree in essentials. There are also other documents, mainly directly from Spain, which must remain confidential.

The case for the Spanish government and the Roman Catholic Church in Spain is stated by Rev. F. Cavalli, S.J., in *The Position of the Protestants in Spain*, cited above. This is translated from the Italian *La Civiltá Catolica* XCIX (1948), and has apparently been widely circulated in this country. Dr. Richard Pattee made considerable use of this article in preparing *Protestant Question in Spain*, a mimeographed document dated March 4, 1949, with a by-line: "Editors: The following is the complete text of a study prepared by Dr. Richard Pattee, consultant in international affairs, NCWC [National Catholic Welfare Conference]."

Protestant Worship

Enrique Pla y Deniel, Archbishop of Toledo and Primate of Spain, told Homer Bigart in an interview reported in the New York *Herald Tribune* for January 20, 1949, but not widely noted, that Protestants and Jews are free to worship in private. The guarantee in the *Fuero de los Españoles* was undertaken, he explained, as "a sort of friendly action toward foreigners living in Spain." The reason for forbidding public worship is "because of the danger that some political minorities would take advantage of these ceremonies to disseminate their propaganda." (This is, of course, essentially the Communist argument for the repression of the Catholic Church in Hungary and Czechoslovakia.)

In 1944, Dr. M. Searle Bates found that 20 out of 200 Spanish churches seemed to be open.[4] Estimates of the number open today vary. The government states that there are 160 licensed chapels. A responsible confidential source insists that this includes as new institutions some that were reopened after the promulgation of the Spanish Charter.

Homer Bigart summed up the situation in his article already cited, saying that the chapel the Spanish Protestant attends "must not display any exterior evidence that it is a place of worship. It cannot advertise its existence—not even with a bulletin board. It cannot be listed in the public directories." Mr. Bigart quotes a Spanish Protestant minister, Rev. Carlos Aranjos: "In Madrid we can't complain," he said. "It's the national capital, and the government is anxious not to

[1] Bates, M. Searle, *Religious Liberty: An Inquiry*, pp. 18, 20.
[2] *The Position of the Protestants in Spain*. By F. Cavalli, S.J. Madrid, O.I.E. (Oficina Informativa Española), Av. José Antonio, 27, 30, 2, p. 4.
[3] His account appeared originally in the *Svenska Morgonbladet* (Stockholm) in 1947 and has since been published in England under the title *Secret Journey to Spain*. London, Lutterworth Press, 1948.
[4] *Op. cit.*, p. 20.

offend foreigners. But in the provinces it is quite different. Eight or ten chapels have been forced to close."

A very few exceptions to the rule that these chapels may not "look like churches" do not alter the situation as a whole. This is recognized by Manuel Maestro, press attaché of the Spanish Embassy, in a letter to the *Christian Science Monitor*, October 1, 1949. He adds: ". . . I do not know the reason for this measure. It has been alleged that it is to avoid confusion among simple folk who might take them to be Catholic places of worship. This does not appear to be a valid motive."

Foreign Minister Bevin of Great Britain said in the British House of Commons on April 27, in reply to an inquiry, that he had been trying "for more than a year" to secure the reopening of seven British chapels in Spain. He explained that they had been closed since January 1, 1947, "by order of the Spanish authorities." Mr. Bevin said that the British Embassy in Madrid had "appealed to the Spanish Foreign Ministry twice last year—on January 21 and December 31—and this year on March 24 in an effort to have the seven chapels reopened." [5]

In 1947 and early 1948 a number of Protestant chapels were raided and wrecked in different parts of the country. Mr. Bigart cites attacks on Protestant chapels in Madrid and Barcelona and the stoning of other buildings. In Valencia an architect who was working on a new chapel had to quit the job after receiving threatening letters. In the summer of 1948, eighteen Protestants were arrested near Valladolid on "charges of holding clandestine prayer meeting." They were imprisoned and fined 1,000 to 2,000 pesetas, which the writer comments is "equivalent to two months' pay for the average Spanish worker." A chapel in Valencia, it is reliably reported, was raided for the second time in April, 1949. In most cases the raiders were content to destroy furniture and scribble comments on the walls, such as *"Viva la Virgen!"* (Long live the Virgin!). On several occasions, however, there was physical violence.

The Requetes seem to have been respon-

[5] New York *Herald Tribune,* April 28, 1949.

sible for the raids. Emmet J. Hughes describes them as traditionally monarchist and "the archreactionary element" in his *Report from Spain.*[6] Fr. Cavalli argues that the Roman Catholic Church cannot be held responsible "without its being shown that it was the Church who ordered them." He admits that some Catholic papers (Spanish and foreign) protested vigorously against them. In some cities the chapels were given police protection after the raids. In others, it seems, they were closed by the authorities.

About the time of the raids leaflets were distributed in the streets of some cities. Excerpts from these have been published in translation by *Ecumenical Press Service* (Geneva) for November 28, 1947, and by Dr. George W. Sadler of the Southern Baptist Foreign Mission Board in *The Commission*, February, 1948. Both of them quote the pastoral letter of Cardinal Segura of Seville of September 20, 1947: "There is no doubt that we can cite the witness of thousands of martyrs who gave their blood to defend their faith in order to lend support to our request aimed at suppressing these centers of false religion in Spain. Undoubtedly those who have generously sacrificed their lives have done so in order to defend the Catholic faith. They speak to us and say, with the Apostle Paul: Keep that which is committed to thy trust." The leaflet quoted by E.P.S. went on to say: "All those in authority should ruthlessly extirpate this particularly serious evil. All Spanish Catholics have the duty—and we promise to fulfill it—not to consent to the development of Protestant activity in our national territory. . . ."

The leaflet quoted by Dr. Sadler, which was distributed in Barcelona, ended, "Long Live Christ the King! Long Live Catholic Unity!" Translations of other leaflets have been made available to this Department. They all demanded action by the government.

Another document in this connection is "Moral Orientations" by Rev. Antonio Peinador, C.M.F.[7] Fr. Peinador answers the ques-

[6] New York, Henry Holt and Company, 1947, p. 171, note.
[7] *Iris de la Paz*, vol. LXV, January 1, 1948, no. 2, p. 212.

tion whether it is "lawful" to enter Protestant chapels "with the sole idea of ... destroying furniture and other goods?" He said that it was "with the sole idea of hindering them and preventing them in this way from making proselytes.... It is necessary to distinguish between furniture and other property which has an heretical significance such as Protestant Bibles, prayer books ... tables, chairs, garments, or utensils employed in their sacrilegious rites...; [and] those things which have no other purpose ... than the personal use of those people." It is not wrong to prevent the use of articles in the first category, he said, "even by destroying them when this would be the only effective way to accomplish it.... It is the duty of charity to prevent the danger ... to simple-minded persons even by violence when the probability is that it can prevent the evil that these instruments of error can cause.... With regard to the second class, it would be a real injustice to destroy them.... These false doctors do not lose the right to existence because they are sowers of evil; they have the right to property without which life would be impossible or difficult...." (Translation ours.)

A Protestant residing in Spain stated in a recent letter that he had attended service at a new little church in one of the smaller cities in Spain, where he was afraid that "the presence of a foreigner in this little city this week will attract attention." Since permission to hold services cannot be secured "they must be clandestine, and therefore only those people who are well-known and can be trusted not to report what is being done can be invited." (From a confidential source.)

Another well-informed but confidential source indicates that only one new chapel (in Madrid) has been licensed to open in the last two years.

Protestant Translations of the Bible

In 1940 the stock of the British Bible Society in Madrid was confiscated. Publication, distribution and importation of Protestant translations of the Bible are forbidden. (Spain seems to be the only Catholic country in Europe to go so far in its restrictions.) For a time after the promulgation of the Charter less attention was paid to these and other activities. But, taking account of increased clandestine activities, it is clear that only a very small number of Bibles were distributed from 1945 to 1947 in comparison with the hundreds of thousands circulated under the monarchy. While it is not possible to know whether or not the different figures are comparable, the most favorable figures that we have seen indicate that during the period of greatest laxity the actual distribution of the Bible was possibly four or five per cent of what it was in the later years of the monarchy. Since 1947 there has been a sharp curtailment of even that activity. The data seem to indicate the failure of government efforts to check completely the distribution of Protestant translations of the Bible, rather than any degree of freedom for Protestants.

The reason for the government's position is thus stated by Fr. Cavalli: "... When freely annotated and interpreted, and presented as the sole basis of Divine Revelation, the Bible becomes the main instrument in the Protestant campaign and onslaught against the Catholic Church." There is a new Catholic Spanish translation of the Bible, and the Roman Catholic Church has been holding Bible Weeks and Bible Days in different parts of the country.

Protestant Marriages

Under the Spanish Republic only civil marriage was valid, though it might be followed by a religious ceremony. In 1938 the religious ceremony was made obligatory for Roman Catholics but a civil ceremony was permitted for non-Catholics and mixed marriages. The Order of March 10, 1941, interpreted Article 42 of the Civil Code. This, according to Mr. Cavalli, "substantially repeats" the provisions of Canon Law, "which exact the Catholic form of marriage for those who, having been baptized in the Catholic Church or belonged to it, have afterwards left it.... In this matter, then, the state does no more than follow the legislation of the Church, which continues to regard as her subjects any persons who have belonged to her, even if only for a short time." In some parts of Spain the civil ceremony, followed by a Protestant one, is possible "after long and laborious process." But "much depends on the attitude of local officials." If judges accept the interpretation given by Fr. Cavalli, then civil marriage is possible only when both parties have documents to prove that they are not Catholic or present a notarized statement that they were not baptized in the Roman Catholic Church. Rev. Carlos Aranjos of Madrid explained to Mr. Bigart: "This is a particular hardship to our workers, who, since they are not legally considered married, are thus denied wage supplements for their wives and children." (New York *Herald Tribune*, February 23, 1949.)

Protestant Schools

The Elementary Education Act of July 17, 1945, permits non-Catholic schools for foreigners only. But, as Fr. Cavalli explains, other provisions of this Act "are certainly strictly binding on all pupils of Spanish nationality and permit no other training but a Catholic one." He adds that "it is known that the school books and teachers are selected in conformity with the demands of Catholicism; and, for instance, special forms of devotion to the Virgin Mary are practiced in them." A Protestant observer reports: "In some parts of the country, no child is allowed to attend the state elementary school without a baptismal certificate from the priest, so that it is impossible to give" Protestant children elementary education. The writer also states that "one or two schools" have been reopened (in spite of the law) and that Sunday schools have been "restarted in many places." [8]

The page on which this statement appears is the authority cited by both Fr. Cavalli and Dr. Pattee for the statement that "there are Protestant schools in Spain." Since the latter adds the words: "among the very tiny communities to afford religious instruction to children of this persuasion who frequent the state schools," he must be referring to the Sunday schools.

Some Catholics in this country do not approve of making Protestant children take Catholic religious instruction. *Catholic Intercontinental Press* (edited by Anna M. Brady,

[8] *Christianity Today*. Edited by Henry Smith Leiper. New York, Morehouse-Gorham Co., 1947, p. 90.

New York) for May 7, 1949, comments that this is "not in line with the teaching of the Catholic Church that the parent has the right to determine the religious instruction of the child."

Other Problems

Most cemeteries in Spain are controlled by the Catholic Church. Protestants, of course, cannot be buried in them. Larger communities have a "second cemetery" for non-Catholics. Where there are none, Protestants often have to bury their dead in the fields. Fr. Cavalli says: "Naturally Protestants . . . must not in Spain turn a funeral into a form of proselytism. . . ." This indicates that Protestant funeral processions may not be in any way religious processions.

Spanish Protestants also complain that government positions, including teaching, are closed to them, that Protestant soldiers suffer serious penalties if they do not attend Mass, that officers' rank is denied to them, and that university students also suffer from discrimination. At some of these points considerable evidence is available. These charges are, however, as categorically denied by spokesmen for the regime. Obviously the accusations against Protestants might be stated as "insubordination" or "unsuitable for the duty," or something of that sort. Fr. Cavalli notes that for "the very few" Protestants that "might possibly be found today" in the army "special cases can be resolved . . . by goodwill on the part of the commanding officer and prudent conduct by the man himself."

The Attitude of the Church

Fr. Cavalli summarizes the attitude of the Roman Catholic Church in Spain: ". . . In a country like Spain, having a tiny minority of dissidents, the Church regards as excessive the *de jure* toleration accorded by the 1876 Constitution and confirmed, although with a restrictive definition, in the Charter. Of the government of a nation where there is absolute religious uniformity, she cannot but ask for the truth to be favoured and for the spread of error to be checked by legitimate means." Since the Roman Catholic Church is convinced that she is "the sole true Church" she will demand that other religions "shall

547

be prevented...from spreading false doctrines." Therefore "in a state where the majority is Catholic, the Church will demand that error shall not be accorded legal existence, and that if minorities of different religions exist, the latter shall have only a *de facto* existence, without the possibility of divulgation of their beliefs."

A very important aspect of the question is, as Fr. Cavalli puts it, "the indisputable uniformity of faith" as "a bond of national unity." Also "the Spanish people has the right to have its religious feelings respected, and to regard itself as insulted when [it] finds itself set on the same level as a savage tribe to be evangelized." Along the same line is the statement by Pablo G. Lopez, S.J., in *Rason y Fé* (Madrid).[9] He insists that "Spaniards discontented for *religious reasons* have no right to enjoy more ample religious freedom than they do enjoy. For one reason, they are non-Catholics, and therefore in error; and error, even when in good faith, has strictly speaking no right to show itself or be professed. For another reason, the religious ideal of a tiny erring minority ought not to be respected in its public manifestations, when these gravely injure the Catholicism of the immense majority of the nation, and can be prevented without danger to peace."

Another statement is an editorial in *El Correo Catalán* for May 25, 1949, cited by Joseph G. Harrison in the *Christian Science Monitor* for July 8, 1949. "We do not hesitate to affirm that we should prefer to see 10,000,000 Communists in Spain to 1,000,000 Protestants. The worst that could happen to our country would be a religious split.... For that reason, if religious tolerance is possible and even advisable in some countries, the present tolerance here is possible only because, practically speaking, there exists no division on religious affairs." (We do not know to what extent this publication speaks officially for the Roman Catholic Church.)

In 1948 the Spanish hierarchy issued "a joint statement addressed to all Spanish Catholics and intended as a warning against the proselytizing activities of non-Catholics. The document was signed by Enrique Cardinal Play Deniel, Primate of Spain, on behalf of all the Spanish archbishops and bishops."[10] This statement, which is more moderate in tone than some of the earlier ones, is described and summarized in O.I.E. (Oficina Informativa Española) No. 27, July, 1948: "Speaking of the Spaniards' Charter, it says that this may not be construed as a law for the toleration of different worships...for it clearly states that what is tolerated is private worship, not proselytism and the public propagation of religions other than Catholicism." (*sic.*) O.I.E. quotes "the review *Ecclesia*" as saying in a "leading article": "The Spaniards' Charter may not be invoked as a legal defence for the opening of chapels, the publication of reviews, the distribution of Bibles, and similar propaganda activities. These are quite illegal in Spain, and any remissness of the authorities in checking them would be also a breach of the spirit and letter of our fundamental law and of the agreement concluded with the Holy See. While no-one shall be molested for his religious beliefs, this is not to say that he shall be permitted to make propaganda for them. And while the private practice of his worship is not impeded, he is not thereby entitled to practise it publicly."

Catholic Criticisms of the Spanish Regime

Not all Catholics accept the position outlined in the foregoing article. Rev. John Courtney Murray, S.J., sets forth his own convictions and those of some European Catholic scholars in *Theological Studies* for September, 1949. He quotes Fr. Jacques Leclercq of the University of Louvain[11] as saying that there is "a certain alteration in the perspectives in which the problem is viewed." Fr. Murray comments that "Nazism and Communism have proclaimed a doctrine of intolerance based on a dogmatic concept of the common good that allows no contradiction. At the same time the Franco victory in Spain has resulted in the reaffirmation by Spanish Catholics of the old thesis, 'thus formulating [according to Father Leclercq] a sort of agreement in principle with the

---

[9] Vol. 134, 1946, p. 166. Cited by Murray, John Courtney. *Theological Studies*, September, 1949, p. 427.

[10] *Religious News Service*, June 22, 1948.
[11] "État chrétien et liberté de l'Église," *Vie intellectuelle*.

Communists.'" And Fr. Leclercq "has the impression" that "the Church will never bless a Catholic country which would apply in the service of the faith a policy parallel to that which the Soviets practice in favor of their conceptions."

Another scholar quoted by Fr. Murray is Rev. Max Pribilla, S.J., who wrote in *Stimmen der Zeit* [12] that "It is true that in certain countries and regions the Catholic religion was preserved or restored by the methods of the Inquisition; but in the course of doing this there was exerted a coercion on conscience whose injurious consequences are discernible to the present day." Fr. Pribilla adds: "What happens in one country finds echo in all the countries of the earth. Consequently, the Church cannot demand freedom for herself in one state, as a human right, and deny it in another state, according as Catholics are in a minority or a majority.... The man in error has undoubtedly the right to be persuaded of his error by objective arguments, instead of being hampered in his personal freedom.... The Christian churches and communities should renounce the use of force and of external pressure (in whatever form) in their mutual rivalries; they should decide spiritual matters with spiritual weapons. This means that freedom in the practice of religion is not to be demanded for oneself alone; it is also to be guaranteed to others."

Fr. Murray states the issue, which he insists is doctrinal: "Is the Spanish constitutional concept of 'religion of the state' permanently and unalterably part of the Catholic thesis, obligatory from the nature of Church and state in any 'Catholic society'? (Were I to give an answer, it would, of course, be no.)" In Spanish discussions of the subject, "Side by side with the constant assertion that Protestants are a negligible minority there stands the likewise constant assertion that they are a serious danger to the public welfare—religious and national unity. The two assertions are not reconcilable—save perhaps in the concrete. What perhaps reconciles them is the concrete fact of the weakness in religious and national unity. In this situation

[12] Vol. CXLIV, April. 1949, pp. 27-40.

religious freedom, as an institution, would be a menace, and very largely a political menace, since it would afford a focus for political protest. The only remedy therefore is recourse to the methods of governmental constraint, in which ... the Spaniard has great trust." Fr. Murray questions "whether this abstract theory of religious and civil intolerance, projected from such a concrete basis, is actually Catholic 'thesis.'"

As we go to press, *Ecumenical Press Service* (Geneva) for October 19 reports: "Members of the Synod of the Evangelical Church in Spain, meeting at Madrid from September 21 to 26, have issued a declaration stating their loyalty to their country and their desire to be of service to it."

14. Baptist World Alliance on Religious Liberty, 1960

Traditionally, the Baptists have been staunch defenders of liberty and the separation of church and state. In 1960, they adopted the following spirited statement on religious freedom. Tenth Baptist World Congress, Rio de Janeiro, Brazil, June 30, 1960. By permission of Baptist World Alliance.

The Meaning of Religious Liberty

The fellowship of Christians coming from many lands, and speaking various languages, deepens our sense of the greatness of God's mercy toward us. In gratitude for all that He has done we renew our covenant with Him who is the Lord of Lords and King of Kings.

We are glad that our fellowship is that of voluntary believers, for true Christian faith, hope, and love cannot be imposed upon men.

God created men in His own image that they might have fellowship with Him, and gave them dominion over lesser forms of creation. We are privileged to declare to the world that the grace of God's forgiving love is freely available in Christ through the simple act of personal faith. This faith permeates human life with the presence and the love of God in the person of Jesus Christ.

The Baptist Concern

Our Baptist commitment to religious liberty arises out of God's revelation of Himself and of His way of dealing with men. It comes also out of our understanding of the nature of man and his role in the universe, of true religion as personal and voluntary, and of the Christian church as a fellowship of believers.

Some hold that religious liberty is merely a practical adjustment of religious differences. This conception is inadequate. So also is the type of tolerance which is based on a skeptical view of all religions or which regards them as of less importance than other values in society.

Man's relationship to God is God-given. It is not subject to human legislation or administration. It lies beyond the scope of state authority.

Whenever religious beliefs and practices are prescribed by law or otherwise imposed, men are called upon to conform regardless of personal conviction. Submission to such a demand undermines both true religion and true character. Furthermore, wherever a state places obstacles in the way of religious faith and practice it hinders the development and expression of human personality.

Religious liberty is anchored in fundamental human rights which nations are not free to transgress without incurring great loss to themselves and to their people. Accordingly, nations which wish to be in harmony with the divine will of our sovereign God must safeguard these rights by means of their instruments of government and their judicial codes and procedures.

The Contemporary Challenge to Religious Liberty

These fundamental spiritual insights must be applied anew by every generation as the institutions of social and political life continually change. With the development of mass media for communication, the opportunities for centralized control of knowledge and propaganda have increased. New international tensions have placed new strains on the bonds of fellowship of those who claim Christ as Lord.

Nationalism sometimes brings prejudice against religions regarded as foreign. Materialistic philosophies and their ideologies attempt to claim the highest loyalties and thereby to make themselves substitutes for religion. As the functions of modern states are extended in a welfare direction the tendencies to underwrite and to control church activities also increase. All such developments call for alertness on the part of the churches and their leaders, lest the churches come to rely upon the support of the state and gradually become subject to its control.

The modern world, therefore, presents a new challenge to Christians everywhere to hold high their banner, "Loyalty to Christ." In the exercise of this loyalty Christ's place must not be pre-empted by social, political, or religious institutions. For the furtherance of true freedom under God, we urge that prayerful study be given to the meaning of the free conscience and to the importance of free churches.

Personal Freedom

The Christian conscience is enlightened and guided by awareness of dependence upon a creative and loving God, by response to redemption in Christ, and by the constant ministry of the Holy Spirit. The Bible is our recognized guide for faith and life.

Christian revelation confronts us with a God who does not coerce people to respond to His love. Christ consistently rejected all forms of force in His ministy to the spiritual needs of people. We desire to emulate our Lord in the refusal to use such coercion, giving ourselves zealously to the Christian life and witness in full reliance upon the holy Spirit.

We uphold the freedom of all to worship; to determine their own beliefs, joining a church of their own choice; and to change such allegiance without hindrance. Parents and guardians of children must be free to nurture their faith and to choose spiritual instruction for them. People should be free to express their faith and their convictions, associating themselves with others for corporate religious objectives, with freedom of movement and travel, with freedom to use their own homes for religious purposes, with due regard for public order, and with freedom to construct buildings for worship and teaching. Support of religious activities and institutions should be by voluntary stewardship, whether time, energy, or money is involved. People should be permitted freedom to make judgments on moral and public issues, having free access to pertinent information.

The Freedom of Churches

No Christian person can live adequately in spiritual isolation. The Christian life has always called for a community experience with fellow believers. Just as individuals must be free in matters of religion, so also must churches and other spiritual fellowships.

This means that such corporate bodies must have freedom to plan and order their public worship, to formulate their own doctrines, and to determine their own policy. They must be free to set standards and qualifications for membership and for leadership, and to plan and provide the religious instruction judged necessary. They should have the maximum freedom to express their corporate witness in acts of charity and service, in missionary outreach, and in the use of publication and other mass media, all at their own expense. They should be independent in their formulation of moral positions, as should all other groups and peoples, and they should be able freely to express the meaning of their insights for the various institutions of society.

Since the character of churches is different from that of governments, they shoud be separately organized. While sharing the time of the people, the terrain of the community, the interests of the participants, and the events which make up history, each should respect the sphere of the other. This calls for a difference of methods and for separation of the administrations, sources of revenue, and programs. Churches and church-sponsored institutions should care for their own expenses and should not look to the state for subsidies.

The Welfare of the Nations

It is becoming increasingly clear that no nation can rightly claim to be Christian merely on the basis of a Christian tradition and culture. The presence of real Christianity depends upon the active, personal faith of the people. We regret, however, that some nations still continue to declare some particular religion or philosophy as part of their public policy.

Our Baptist concern for the nations continues to express itself in evangelism, missions, and education. We claim religious freedom for ourselves, and we gladly use our influence to win it for others. Our deep desire is that all men may freely worship the true living God in spirit and in truth, recognizing that He has provided redemption for all men in Christ. Christian discipleship leads to sacrificial, dependable, and loyal citizenship.

Good government is essential for the welfare of people, and it has divine approval. Accordingly, to the full extent permitted by the claims of Christ, we commend patriotic living to our fellow believers. It is in well ordered social life that the rights and freedoms of men can be protected so as to permit the fulfillment of divine purposes in their lives. We pledge our prayers for those in positions of national and international responsibility, for we believe that "where the Spirit of the Lord is, there is liberty."

Manifesto on Religious Liberty

We believe: 1. That God created man in His own image and endowed him with freedom to respond to His redemptive love;

2. That man is responsible to God for his religious belief and practice;

3. That religious faith and participation must be voluntary in order to be real.

We rejoice: 1. That God gives grace to endure oppression and to use freedom;

2. That friends of religious liberty are found in all Christian communions;

3. That recent legislation in several countries is favorable to religious liberty.

We earnestly desire: 1. That all forms of discrimination against religious minorities shall cease;

2. That all religious bodies shall make an unequivocal commitment to full religious liberty for all people;

3. That all nations shall guarantee the right of all citizens to believe, to worship, to teach, to evangelize, to change their religious affiliation, and to serve their God as their conscience dictates.

We solemnly covenant: 1. To study and

proclaim the freedom men have in Jesus Christ, the Lord;

2. To show Christian understanding and love towards those whose beliefs and practices are different from our own;

3. To pray and use our influence for the preservation and extension of religious liberty for all men.

15. A Letter to Presbyterians

A Letter to Presbyterians Concerning the Present Situation in Our Country and In the World. Unanimously adopted by the General Council of the General Assembly of the Presbyterian Church in the United States of America. October 21, 1953.

Dear Fellow Presbyterians:

.   .   .   .   .

Things are happening in our national life and in the international sphere which should give us deep concern. Serious thought needs to be given to the menace of Communism in the world of today and to the undoubted aim on the part of its leaders to subvert the thought and life of the United States. Everlasting vigilance is also needed, and appropriate precautions should be constantly taken, to forestall the insidious intervention of a foreign power in the internal affairs of our country. In this connection Congressional committees, which are an important expression of democracy in action, have rendered some valuable services to the nation.

At the same time the citizens of this country, and those in particular who are Protestant Christians, have reason to take a grave view of the situation which is being created by the almost exclusive concentration of the American mind upon the problem of the threat of Communism.

Under the plea that the structure of American society is in imminent peril of being shattered by a satanic conspiracy, dangerous developments are taking place in our national life. Favored by an atmosphere of intense disquiet and suspicion, a subtle but potent assault upon basic human rights is now in progress. Some Congressional inquiries have revealed a distinct tendency to become inquisitions. These inquisitions, which find their historic pattern in medieval Spain and in the tribunals of modern totalitarian states, begin to constitute a threat to freedom of thought in this country. Treason and dissent are being confused. The shrine of conscience and private judgment, which God alone has a right to enter, is being invaded. Un-American attitudes toward ideas and books are becoming current. Attacks are being made upon citizens of integrity and social passion which are utterly alien to our democratic tradition. They are particularly alien to the Protestant religious tradition which has been a main source of the freedoms which the people of the United States enjoy.

There is something still more serious. A great many people, within and without our government, approach the problem of Communism in a purely negative way. Communism, which is at bottom a secular religious faith of great vitality, is thus being dealt with as an exclusively police problem. As a result of this there is growing up over against Communism a fanatical negativism. Totally devoid of a constructive program of action, this negativism is in danger of leading the American mind into a spiritual vacuum. Our national house, cleansed of one demon, would invite by its very emptiness, the entrance of seven others. In the case of a national crisis this emptiness could, in the high sounding name of security, be occupied with ease by a Fascist tyranny.

We suggest, therefore, that all Presbyterians give earnest consideration to the following three basic principles and their implications for our thought and life.

I. The Christian Church has a prophetic function to fulfill in every society and in every age.

Whatever concerns man and his welfare is a concern of the Church and its ministers. Religion has to do with life and its wholeness. While being patriotically loyal to the country within whose bounds it lives and works, the Church does not derive its authority from the nation but from Jesus Christ. Its supreme and ultimate allegiance is to Christ, its sole Head, and to His Kingdom, and not to any nation or race, to any class or culture. It is, therefore, under obligation to consider the life of man in the light of God's purpose in Christ for the world. While it is not the role of the Christian church to present blueprints for the organization of society and the conduct of government, the Church owes it to its own members and to men in general, to draw attention to violations of those spiritual bases of human relationship which have been established by God. It has the obligation also to proclaim those principles, and to instill that spirit, which are essential for social health, and which form the indispensable foundation of sound and stable policies in the affairs of state.

II. The majesty of truth must be preserved at all times and at all costs.

Loyalty to truth is the common basis of true religion and true culture. Despite the lofty idealism of many of our national leaders, truth is being subtly and silently dethroned by prominent public figures from the position it has occupied hitherto in our American tradition. The state of strife known as "cold war," in which our own and other nations, as well as groups within nations, are now engaged, is producing startling phenomena and sinister personalities. In this form of warfare, falsehood is frequently preferred to fact if it can be shown to have greater propaganda value. In the interests of propaganda, truth is deliberately distorted or remains unspoken. The demagogue, who lives by propaganda, is coming into his own on a national scale. According to the new philosophy, if what is true "gives aid and comfort" to our enemies, it must be suppressed. Truth is thus a captive in the land of the free. At the same time, and for the same reason, great words like "love," "peace," "justice," and "mercy," and the ideas which underlie them, are becoming suspect.

Communism, as we know to our sorrow, is committed on principle to a philosophy of lying; democracy, in fighting Communism, is in danger of succumbing, through fear and in the name of expediency, to the self-same philosophy. It is being assumed, in effect, that, in view of the magnitude of the issues at stake, the end justifies the means. Whatever the outcome of such a war, the moral consequences will be terrifying. People will become accustomed to going through life with no regard for rules or sanctities.

A painful illustration of this development is that men and women should be publicly condemned upon the uncorroborated word of former Communists. Many of these witnesses have done no more, as we know, than transfer their allegiance from one authoritarian system to another. Nothing is easier for people, as contemporary history has shown, than to make the transition from one totalitarianism to another, carrying their basic attitudes along with them. As a matter of fact, the lands that have suffered most from Communism, or that are most menaced by it today, Russia and Italy, for example, are lands which have been traditionally authoritarian in their political or their religious life. And yet the ex-Communists to whose word Congressional committees apparently give unqualified credence are in very many instances people whose basic philosophy authorizes them now, as in the past, to believe that a lie in a good cause is thoroughly justified.

III. God's sovereign rule is the controlling factor in history.

We speak of "This nation under God." Nothing is more needed today than to explore afresh and to apply to all the problems of thought and life in our generation, what it means to take God seriously in national life. There is an order of God. Even in these days of flux and nihilism, of relativism and expediency, God reigns. The American-born poet, T. S. Eliot, has written these prophetic words:

> Those who put their faith in worldly order
> Not controlled by the order of God,
> In confident ignorance, but arrest disorder,
> Make it fast, breed fatal disease,
> Degrade what they exalt.

Any attempt to impose upon society, or the course of history, a purely man-made order, however lofty the aims, can have no more than temporary success. Social disorder and false political philosophies cannot be adequately met by police measures, but only by a sincere attempt to organize society in accordance with the everlasting principles of God's moral government of the world. It is, therefore, of paramount importance that individuals, groups and nations should adjust themselves to the order of God. God's character and God's way with man provide the pattern for man's way with his fellow man.

That we have the obligation to make our nation as secure as possible, no one can dispute. But there is no absolute security in human affairs, nor is security the ultimate human obligation. A still greater obligation, as well as a more strategic procedure, is to make sure that what we mean by security, and the methods we employ to achieve it, are in accordance with the will of God. Otherwise, any human attempt to establish a form of world order which does no more than exalt the interest of a class, a culture, a race, or a nation, above God and the interests of the whole human family, is foredoomed to disaster. . . .

Let us frankly recognize that many of the revolutionary forces of our time are in great part the judgment of God upon human selfishness and complacency, and upon man's forgetfulness of man. That does not make these forces right; it does, however, compel us to consider how their driving power can be channeled into forms of creative thought and work. History, moreover, makes it abundantly clear that wherever a religion, a political system or a social order, does not interest itself in the common people, violent revolt eventually takes place.

On the other hand, just because God rules in the affairs of men, Communism as a solution of the human problem is foredoomed to failure. No political order can prevail which deliberately leaves God out of account. Despite its pretention to be striving after "liberation," Communism enslaves in the name of freedom. It does not know that evil cannot be eradicated from human life by simply changing a social structure. Man, moreover, has deep spiritual longings which Communism cannot satisfy. The Communistic order will eventually be shattered upon the bedrock of human nature, that is, upon the basic sins, and the abysmal needs, of man and society. For that reason Communism has an approaching rendezvous with God and the moral order.

Nevertheless, Communists, Communist nations and Communist-ruled peoples, should be our concern. In hating a system let us not allow ourselves to hate individuals or whole nations. History and experience teach us that persons and peoples do change. Let us ever be on the lookout for the evidence of change in the Communist world, for the effects of disillusionment, and for the presence of a God-implanted hunger. Such disillusionment and hunger can be met only by a sympathetic approach and a disposition to listen and confer.

There is clear evidence that a post-Communist mood is actually being created in many parts of Europe and Asia. Let us seek to deepen that mood. Let us explore afresh the meaning of mercy and forgiveness and recognize that both can have social and political significance when they are sincerely and opportunely applied.

Let us always be ready to meet around a conference table with the rulers of Communist countries. There should be, therefore, no reluctance to employ the conference method to the full in the settling of disputes with our country's enemies. Let us beware of the cynical attitude which prevails in certain official circles to regard as a forlorn hope any negotiated solution of the major issues which divide mankind.

In human conflicts there can be no substitute for negotiation. Direct personal conference has been God's way with man from the beginning. "Come, now, and let us reason together," was the word of God to Israel through the Prophet Isaiah. We must take the risk, and even the initiative, of seeking face-to-face encounter with our enemies. We should meet them officially, whatever their ignominious record, and regardless of the suffering they may have caused us. We too have reasons for penitence and stand in need of forgiveness. In any case, talk, unhurried talk, talk which does not rule out in advance the possibility of success, talk which takes place in private, and not before reporters or microphones or television, is the only kind of approach which can lead to sanity and fruitful understanding. Let the process of conference be private, but let its conclusions, its complete conclusions, be made public.

In this connection such an organization as the United Nations is in harmony with the principles of God's moral government. American Presbyterians should remember with pride that it is the successor of a former organization which was the creation of a great American who was also a great Presbyterian. While the United Nations organization is very far from perfection and it functions today under great handicaps, it is yet the natural and best available agent for international cooperation and the settlement of disputes among nations. It is imperative, that it be given the utmost support. It stands between us and war.

While we take all wise precautions for defense, both within and outside our borders, the present situation demands spiritual calm, historical perspective, religious faith, and an adventurous spirit. Loyalty to great principles of truth and justice has made our nation great; such loyalty alone can keep it great and ensure its destiny.

SUGGESTED READINGS

Anderson, P. B., *People, Church and State in Modern Russia*. New York: The Macmillan Co., 1944.

Baillie, John, *What Is Christian Civilization*. New York: Charles Scribner's Sons, 1945.

Barth, Karl, *The Church and the Political Problem of Our Day*. New York: Charles Scribner's Sons, 1939.

——, *The Epistle to the Romans*. London: Oxford University Press, 1933.

Bates, M. S., *Religious Liberty*. New York: International Missionary Council, 1945.

Bonhoeffer, Dietrich, *The Cost of Discipleship*. London: SCM Press, 1948.

Braybrooke, Neville, ed., *T. S. Eliot: A Symposium*. New York: Farrar, Straus & Company, 1958.

Butterfield, Herbert, *International Conflict in the Twentieth Century: A Christian View*. New York: Harper & Row, Publishers, 1960.

Cassirer, Ernst, *The Myth of the State*, New Haven: Yale University Press, 1946.

Cauthen, Kenneth, *Impact of American Religious Liberalism*. New York: Harper & Row, Publishers, 1962.

Cavert, S. and H. P. Van Dusen, *The Church Through Half a Century*. New York: Charles Scribner's Sons, 1936.

Curtiss, J. S., *Church and State in Russia, 1900-17*. New York: Columbia University Press, 1940.

——, *The Russian Church and the Soviet State*. Boston: Little, Brown, & Co., 1953.

Fagley, R. M., *The Population Explosion and Christian Responsibility*. New York: Oxford University Press, 1960.

Fey, H. and M. Frakes, *Christian Century Reader*. New York: Association Press, 1962.

Fosdick, Harry E., *Adventurous Religion*. New York: Harper & Row, Publishers, 1926.

——, *Christianity and Progress*. New York: Fleming H. Revell Co., 1922.

Frey, A., *Cross and Swastika*. London: SCM Press, 1938.

Gillispie, C. C., *Genesis and Geology*. New York: Harper & Row, Publishers, 1959.

Greene, T. M., *Liberalism, Its Theory and Practice*. Austin: University of Texas Press, 1957.

Gsovski, Vladimir, *Church and State Behind the Iron Curtain*. New York: Frederick A. Praeger, Inc., 1955.

Hayward, J. F., *Existentialism and Religious Liberalism*. Boston: Beacon Press, 1962.

Howard, G. P., *Religious Liberty in South America?* Philadelphia: The Westminster Press, 1944.

Hughley, J. N., *Trends in Protestant Social Idealism*. New York: Kings Crown Press, 1948.

Kierkegaard, Sören, *Journals*. London: Oxford University Press, 1948.

——, *Sickness Unto Death*. Princeton: Princeton University Press, 1942.

Lack, David, *Evolutionary Theory and Christian Belief*. London: Methuen & Co., Ltd., 1957.

Littell, Franklin H., *The German Phoenix*. New York: Doubleday & Company, Inc., 1960.

Lowrie, Walter, *A Short Life of Kierkegaard*. London: Oxford University Press, 1943.

Machen, J. Gresham, *The Virgin Birth of Christ*. New York: Harper & Row, Publishers, 1932.

Means, P. B., *Things That Are Caesar's*. New York: Roundtable Press, 1935.

Micklem, N., *National Socialism and the Roman Catholic Church*. London: Oxford University Press, 1939.

Miller, Alexander, *The Christian Significance of Karl Marx*. New York: The Macmillan Co., 1947.

Morrison, C. C., *The Social Gospel and the Christian Cultus*. New York: Harper & Row, Publishers, 1933.

Mozley, J. K., *Some Tendencies in British Theology*. London: S.P.C.K., 1951.

Niebuhr, Reinhold, *Beyond Tragedy*. New York: Charles Scribner's Sons, 1938.

———, *Does Civilization Need Christianity?* New York: The Macmillan Co., 1927.

———, *Moral Man and Immoral Society*. New York: Charles Scribner's Sons, 1933.

———, *Nature and Destiny of Man*. New York: Charles Scribner's Sons, 1941-1943.

———, *Reflections on the End of an Era*. New York: Charles Scribner's Sons, 1934.

Niemoeller, Martin, *From U-Boat to Pulpit*. Chicago: Willett, Clark & Company, 1937.

Parke, D. B., *Epic of Unitarianism*. Boston: Starr King Press, 1957.

Pelikan, Jaroslav, *The Riddle of Roman Catholicism*. Nashville: Abingdon Press, 1959.

Schneider, H. W., *Religion in Twentieth Century America*. Cambridge: Harvard University Press, 1952.

Schweitzer, Albert, *The Quest of the Historical Jesus*. London: A. & C. Black, 1910.

Shuster, G. N., *Religion Behind the Iron Curtain*. New York: The Macmillan Co., 1954.

Solberg, R. W., *God and Caesar in East Germany*. New York: The Macmillan Co., 1961.

Spinka, Matthew, *The Church in Soviet Russia*. New York: Oxford University Press, 1956.

Streeter, H., *Foundations: Christian Beliefs in Terms of Modern Thought*. London: The Macmillan Co., 1913.

Tillich, Paul, *The Religious Situation*. New York: Holt, Rinehart & Winston, Inc., 1932.

Timasheff, N. S., *Religion in Soviet Russia, 1917-42*. New York: Sheed & Ward, 1942.

White, A. D., *History of the Warfare of Science with Theology*. New York: Appleton-Century-Crofts, Inc., 1896.

Williams, D. D., *Interpreting Theology, 1918-52*. London: S.C.M. Press, 1953.

Zernov, N., *The Church of Eastern Christians*. New York: The Macmillan Co., 1942.

———, *Eastern Christendom*. London: George Weidenfeld & Nicholson, Ltd., 1961.

CHRONOLOGY

[For related events see Chapters 8, 9, and 10]

1870-1874 *Ritschl, Christian Doctrine of Justification and Reconciliation*

1886-1889 *Harnack, History of Dogma*

1895 *Bible Conference, Niagara Falls, N. Y., Five Fundamentals*

1897 *Abbott, Theology of an Evolutionist*

1898 *Sheldon, In His Steps*

1901 *Harnack, What Is Christianity?*

1909-1915 *The Fundamentals*

1910 *National Association for Advancement of Colored People*

1912 *Troeltsch, Social Teaching of the Christian Churches*

1914-1918 *First World War*

1917 *Bolshevik revolution*

1918-1922 *Spengler, Decline of the West*

1918-1925 *Bolsheviks proceed against religion*

1919 *Barth, Epistle to the Romans*

1920 *Nazi platform*

1921-1922 *Great famine in Russia*

1925 *Scopes' trial, Tennessee*

1929 *Lateran Treaty, papacy and Mussolini Depression, stock market crash*

1932 *Platform of the German Christians Machen, The Virgin Birth of Christ*

1933 *Niebuhr, Moral Man and Immoral Society*

1933 *Humanist Manifesto February 27, burning of Reichstag, Nazis gain control in Germany Concordat of papacy and Nazis*

1933-1935 *Nazi laws against the Jews*

1934 *Dewey, A Common Faith Barmen Declaration, Confessing Church*

1935 *Nürnberg laws, Germany*

1937-1938 *Russian purges of religion*

1936-1939 *Spanish Civil War*

1939 *Great Britain and France declare war on Germany*

1941-1943 *Niebuhr, Nature and Destiny of Man*

1941 *December 7-11, United States enters Second World War*

1945 *May 8, end of Second World War, Europe June 26, United Nations organized August 5, explosion of atomic bomb August 14, Japan surrenders Stuttgart Confession of guilt*

1945-1950 *Troubles in Spain, religious liberty*

1948 *World Council of Churches*

1948 *Universal Declaration of Human Rights*

1948-1950 *Religion suppressed in Czechoslovakia*

CHART OF MISSIONS AND ECUMENICITY

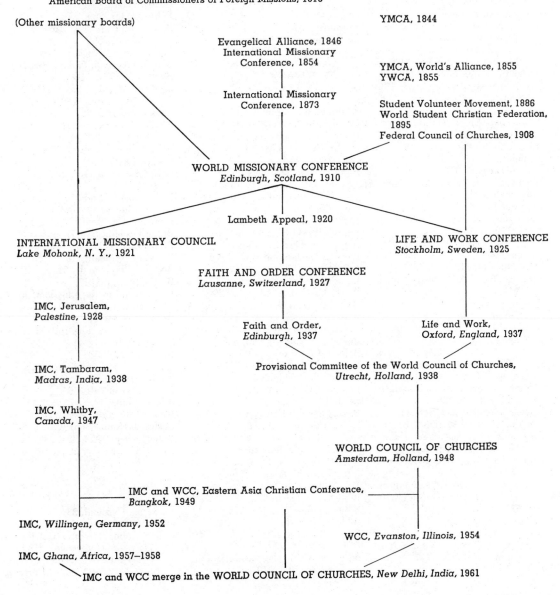

Society for Propagation of the Gospel in Foreign Parts, 1701
Danish-Halle Mission, 1705
Moravian Missions, 1732
Particular Baptist Society for the Propagation of the Gospel, 1792
William Carey, first modern missionary, 1793
London Missionary Society, 1795
American Board of Commissioners of Foreign Missions, 1810

(Other missionary boards)

YMCA, 1844

Evangelical Alliance, 1846
International Missionary
Conference, 1854

YMCA, World's Alliance, 1855
YWCA, 1855

International Missionary
Conference, 1873

Student Volunteer Movement, 1886
World Student Christian Federation,
1895
Federal Council of Churches, 1908

WORLD MISSIONARY CONFERENCE
Edinburgh, Scotland, 1910

Lambeth Appeal, 1920

INTERNATIONAL MISSIONARY COUNCIL
Lake Mohonk, N. Y., 1921

LIFE AND WORK CONFERENCE
Stockholm, Sweden, 1925

FAITH AND ORDER CONFERENCE
Lausanne, Switzerland, 1927

IMC, Jerusalem,
Palestine, 1928

Faith and Order,
Edinburgh, 1937

Life and Work,
Oxford, England, 1937

IMC, Tambaram,
Madras, India, 1938

Provisional Committee of the World Council of Churches,
Utrecht, Holland, 1938

IMC, Whitby,
Canada, 1947

WORLD COUNCIL OF CHURCHES
Amsterdam, Holland, 1948

IMC and WCC, Eastern Asia Christian Conference,
Bangkok, 1949

IMC, Willingen, Germany, 1952

WCC, Evanston, Illinois, 1954

IMC, Ghana, Africa, 1957–1958

IMC and WCC merge in the WORLD COUNCIL OF CHURCHES, New Delhi, India, 1961

557

Index

Hooker, Richard, 170
Hooper, John, 167, 180–84 (*illus.,* 181)
Hort, Fenton J. A., 417
Hotman, François, 118, 149–51
Hubmaier, Balthasar, 60, 61, 76 (*illus.,* 77); *Concerning Heretics,* 77–79; Eighteen Propositions, 76–77
Hügel, Baron von, 370
Huguenots, 101–5, 116, 117, 118, 145–48, 169
Humanist Manifesto, 513. 526–28
Humanists, French, 62
Human Rights, Declaration, United Nations, 540–43
Hume, David, 219, 221, 222, 244–47, 315, 363 (*illus.,* 245)
Hut, Hans, 60
Huter, Jacob, 61, 85–87
Hutten, Ulrich von, 3, 12
Huxley, Aldous, 513
Hymns (*see also* Music), 50–51, 296–98, 323–24, 477, 510

Ibsen, Henrik, 418
Ideal of a Christian Church, Ward, 323
Images, 58, 59, 138–39, 357
Immaculate Conception (*see also* Virgin Mary), 368, 371–72 (*illus.,* Murillo Workshop, 371)
Immortale Dei, 369
Incense of a New Church, Charles Demuth, *illus.,* 394
In Darkest England and the Way Out, Booth, 414, 419–23
Indulgences, 5, 9, 14–18, 22, 104, 139, 357 (*illus.,* 15, 18)
Industrial Revolution, 412
Infallibility (*see also* Ultramontanism), 368, 374–75
In His Steps, Sheldon, 510
In Praise of Folly, Erasmus, 2, 8–12 (*illus. for,* Holbein, 10)
Inquisition, 8, 110, 112, 140
Institutes, Calvin, 62, 87–90
Inter Cetera, 461
Interims, Augsburg and *Leipzig,* 8
International Missionary Conference, 481
International Missionary Council, 465, 467, 490–91
Invocation (*see* Prayer)

Jacob, Henry, 171
James: I, England, 170; II, 172
James, William, 418, 447–51
Jansenism (*see also* Pascal), 118, 155, 298, 363, 364

Jefferson, Thomas (*see also* Deism), 316, 324, 325–26
Jenner, W. S., 517
Jesuits (*see also* Loyola), 109, 112, 113–14, 117, 118–27 (*illus.,* 120), 155–59, 168, 170, 193–94, 219, 264, 265, 271, 316, 323, 324, 363, 367, 462; approved, 125–27; dissolved and restored, 364
Jesus Curing the Sick, Brigitte West, *illus.,* 393
Job, Book of, William Blake, *illus. for,* 314
John, the Steadfast, 7
John of the Cross, St., 115
Johnson, James Welden, 518
Jonson, Ben, 173
Joseph II, Josephism, Austria, 364
Journal, Fox, 173, 303–8
Judgment of the Reformers in the Netherlands, Franz Hogenberg, *illus.,* 117
Judson, Adoniram, 464
Justification by faith (*see also* Faith, Freedom), 42, 202, 284–88; Trent, 133–35

Kafka, Franz, 513
Kant, Immanuel, 218, 219, 222, 223, 250–55, 264, 315, 320–21, 363
Kappel, 59
Keble, John, 322
Kepler, Johannes, 219
Kierkegaard, Sören, 513
Kingsley, Charles, 413
Knox, John, 166, 170, 189 (*illus.,* Hendrix Hondias, Jr., 189)
Kraemer, Hendrik, 467
Kulturkampf, 367–68
Küng, Hans, 513
Kutter, Herman, 413

Lainez, Diego, 113
Lambeth Appeal, 465, 467, 485–87, 487–90
Lambeth Articles, 196–97
Lambeth Conference, 485–87, 487–90
Lamennais, Abbé de, 365–66
Lamentabili Sane, 370, 392–95
Lange, Ernst, 296
Languet, Hubert, 118, 149, 151–55
Lateran Treaty, 367, 370
Latimer, Hugh, 167 (*illus.,* 187, 188)
Laud, William, 171

LaValette lawsuit, 364
L'Avenir, 365
Law, William, 221, 236–41, 269, 271, 278–84
Law of Associations, France, 369
Law of Guarantees, Italy, 367
Law of Separation, France, 370, 390–92
Lawrence, D. H., 513
Lefèvre: d'Etaples, 62; Pierre, 113
Leipzig Debate, 5, 23
Lessing, Gotthold E., 218, 222
Lewis: C. S., 514; Sinclair, 513
Liberalism (*see also* Historical Criticism, Modernism, Rationalism), 509–14, 518–21, 526–28
Libertas Praestantissimum, 369, 379–82
Liberty (*see also* Church and State, Freedom, Totalitarianism), 379–82; Baptists, 549–52; Presbyterians, 552–55; Spain, 543–49
Liberty of Prophesying, Taylor, 210–13
Life of Jesus: Renan, 322, 341–48, 368; Strauss, 322, 341
Lightfoot, Joseph Barber, 417
Lilje, Hanns, 516
Lindsey, Theophilus, 412, 512
Liszt, Franz, 418
Litteris alto, 365
Livingston, David, 464
Locke, John, 218, 220, 226–28
Loci Communes, Melanchthon, 6
Loisy, Alfred, 370
Lollards, 163, 164
London Missionary Society, 463–64
London University, 322
Lord's Supper (*see also* Sacraments), 6, 7, 44, 47, 59, 72, 92, 94, 180, 467; Quakers, 310–11; Trent, 136
Louis: XIII, France, 117; XIV, 117, 118, 146, 155, 172, 219, 264, 265, 266 (*illus.,* 147; Bernini, 266); XVI, 316, 317, 318, 331–32, 364
Loyola, Ignatius (*see also* Jesuits), 109, 110, 112, 113, 118–27 (*illus.,* Rubens, 125)
Ludlow, J. M., 413
Luther, Martin, 2, 3, 4, 5, 6, 7, 8, 14, 22, 34, 50–51, 59, 61, 462 (*illus.,* 29; 32; Cranach, 42); Christian freedom, 22–29; home life, 51–52; hymns, 50–51; *Ninety-five Theses,* 14–18; peasants, 35–40; Worms, 29–33
Lutheranism, 263, 267
Lux Mundi, Gore, 417–18, 451–55, 510

Pole, Cardinal Reginald, 167
Pope, Alexander, 219, 235–36 (*illus.*, 235)
Popes: Adrian VI, 110; Alexander VI, 2, 461; VIII, 155; Clement VII, 110, 112, 164; XIV, 114, 364; Gregory XIII, 116 (*illus.*, 143); XV, 114; XVI, 365; Innocent III, 118, 164; VIII, 2, 15; X, 217, 264; XI, 155; John XXIII, 468; Julius II, 2; Leo X, 2, 6, 22, 23, 24, 110; XII, 364; XIII, 168, 316, 369–70, 375–92; Paul III, 112, 113, 114, 125–27, 140; IV, 112, 139–40; VI, 469; Pius IV, 115; VI, 317, 318–19, 364; VII, 319, 333, 364, 365, 369; VIII, 365; IX, 366–69, 371–75; X, 370, 390–97, 509; XI, 370, 371, 397–404, 502–3, 515; XII, 371, 404–7, 517; Sixtus V, 169; Urban VIII, 118, 265
Positivism, Comte, 416, 438–42
Praemunire, 164, 165
Prayer, 52–53, 91–92, 96, 268, 436–37
Prayer Meeting No. 2, George Bellows, *illus.*, 442
Prayers of the Social Awakening, Rauschenbusch, 436–37
Predestination (*see also* Calvin, Sovereignty), 63, 89–90, 95–96, 289–93
Presbyterianism (*see also* Calvin, *Gallican Confession*, Huguenots, Knox), 171–73, 200–203, 210
Priesthood of believers, 19–22, 272–75
Probabilism, 114, 156–59
Providentissimus Deus, 370
Purgatory, 138, 357
Puritans, 167, 169, 170, 171, 172, 173, 180–84, 194–95, 197–98
Pusey, Edward B., 323 (*illus.*, 323)

Quakers, 173, 303–11 (*illus.*, 304)
Qui pluribus, 371

Ragaz, Leonhard, 413
Rahner, Karl, 513
Raible, Robert, 513, 524–26
Rationalism (*see also* Historical Criticism, Liberalism, Modernism), 217–60, 319, 320, 321, 322, 372

Rauschenbusch, Walter, 413, 415–16, 418, 428–37, 510
Reason, Age of, 217–60
Reasonableness of Christianity, Locke, 220, 221, 226–28
Reformation: England, 163–214; extended, 57–105; Lutheran, 1–53
Reformation without Tarrying for Any, Browne, 170, 190–93
Reform Bill, 322, 412
Reimarus, Herman S., 222
Reinhard, Anna, 58
Relics (*see also* Images, Indulgences, Saints, invocation), 3, 5, 357
Religion of humanity, 416, 438–42
Religion of Protestants, Chillingworth, 220, 223–26
Religious Tract Society, 464
Renan, Ernst, 316, 322, 341–48, 368
Rerum Novarum, 369, 382–90
Restraint of Appeals, 174–76
Reuchlin, Johann, 2, 12, 110, 218
Revivalism (*see also* Fundamentalism), 411, 414–15, 423–28
Rice, Luther, 464
Ridley, Nicolas, 167 (*illus.*, 188)
Ridolfi Plot, 168
Ritschl, Albrecht, 223, 322, 510, 513
Robinson, John, 170
Romanticism, 319–22
Rousseau, Jean Jacques, 223, 316, 320, 324, 325
Rubens, Peter Paul, 265
Rubianus, Crotius, 3, 12
Rules of Reasoning, Newton, 226
Russell, Bertrand, 513

Sacraments (*see also* Baptism, Lord's Supper, Marriage), 42–44, 72, 105–6, 135–38, 203, 358
Sadoleto, Cardinal, 110
St. Bartholomew's Day, 112, 116, 141–45 (*illus.*, 141, 143)
Saints, invocation (*see also* Images, Indulgences, Relics), 47, 138–39, 357
Sales, Francis de, 115, 155
Salvation Army, 413, 414, 419–23
Sanford, Elias B., 465
Sartre, Jean-Paul, 513
Sattler, Michael, 61, 79–85
Savonarola, Girolamo, 3 (*illus.*, 2, 3)
Sawdust Trail, The, George Bellows, *illus.*, 415
Schaff, Philip, 465

Schell, Hermann, 370
Schiller, Johann Christoph, 223, 320
Schleiermacher, Friedrich, 223, 320, 321, 322, 335–41, 510
Schmucker, Samuel S., 465
Schleitheim Confession, 61, 79–82
Schmuman, Robert, 418
Schubert, Franz, 418
Schumann, Robert, 418
Schwabach Articles, 7
Schwartz, Christian Friedrich, 268
Scopes, J. T., 418, 512, 521–24
Scott, Sir Walter, 320
Scottish Confession, 189–90
Scripture (*see also* Authority, Bible, Historical Criticism), 58, 61, 88–89, 90, 91, 103, 131, 164, 166, 180, 218, 223–26, 308–9, 341–48, 348–56, 357
Separatists (*see* Puritans)
Serious Call, Law, 269, 278–84
Servetus, Michael, 62–63, 96–99 (*illus.*, 97)
Shakespeare, William, 173
Sheldon, C. M., 510
Simons, Menno, 61
Sin (*see* Original Sin)
Singulari vos, 366
Six Articles, 166, 167, 179–80
Sixty-seven Articles, Zwingli, 58, 67–70
Smyth, John, 170
Social Creed, Federal Council of Churches, 437–38
Social Gospel, 411–12, 413–16, 419–23, 428–37, 437–38
Societies for Propagation of the Gospel, 270, 462
Society for Promoting Christian Knowledge, 462
Society of Jesus (*see* Jesuits)
Söderblom, Nathan, 467
Solemn League and Covenant, 171, 172, 198–200
Sommaschi, 112
Sovereignty (*see also* Calvin, Predestination), 71, 88–89
Spangenberg, A. G., 269, 296
Speier, Diet of, 7, 40–41
Spener, Philip Jakob, 223–268, 271–75, 462
Spengler, Oswald, 511
Spenser, Edmund, 173
Spiritual Exercises, Loyola, 112, 118–25
Stoecker, Adolf, 413
Strauss: D. F., 316, 322, 341; Richard, 418
Strong, Josiah, 465
Student Volunteer Movement, 466, 479–81
Stuttgart Declaration, 516, 532–33
Sunday, Billy, *illus.*, 511